The Humanities
Culture, Continuity & Change

SECOND EDITION

Henry M. Sayre
OREGON STATE UNIVERSITY

VOLUME II

1600 TO THE PRESENT

Prentice Hall

Boston   Columbus   Indianapolis   New York   San Francisco   Upper Saddle River
Amsterdam   Cape Town   Dubai   London   Madrid   Milan   Munich   Paris   Montréal   Toronto
Delhi   Mexico City   São Paulo   Sydney   Hong Kong   Seoul   Singapore   Taipei   Tokyo

For Bud Therien, art publisher and editor par excellence, and a good friend.

Editorial Director: Craig Campanella
Editor in Chief: Sarah Touborg
Acquisitions Editor: Billy Grieco
Assistant Editor: David Nitti
Editor-in-Chief, Development: Rochelle Diogenes
Development Editor: Margaret Manos
Media Director: Brian Hyland
Senior Media Editor: David Alick
Media Project Manager: Rich Barnes
Vice President of Marketing: Brandy Dawson
Executive Marketing Manager: Kate Stewart Mitchell
Senior Managing Editor: Ann Marie McCarthy
Associate Managing Editor: Melissa Feimer
Senior Project Manager: Barbara Marttine Cappuccio
Project Manager: Marlene Gassler
Senior Manufacturing Manager: Mary Fisher

Senior Operations Specialist: Brian Mackey
Senior Art Director: Pat Smythe
Interior Design: PreMediaGlobal
Cover Designer: Pat Smythe
Manager, Visual Research: Beth Brenzel
Photo Research: Francelle Carapetyan / Image Research Editorial Services
Pearson Imaging Center: Corin Skidds, Robert Uibelhoer
Full-Service Project Management: PreMediaGlobal
Composition: PreMediaGlobal
Printer/Binder: Courier / Kendallville
Cover Printer: Phoenix Color, Corp.
Cover Image: Vincent van Gogh (1853–90), *Portrait of Patience Escalier*. 1888. Oil on canvas. Private Collection/Photo ©Lefevre Fine Art, Ltd., London/ The Bridgeman Art Library.

Credits and acknowledgments borrowed from other sources and reproduced, with permission, in this textbook appear on appropriate page within text and beginning on page Credits-1.

Library of Congress Cataloging-in-Publication Data
Sayre, Henry M.
    The humanities: culture, continuity & change / Henry M. Sayre.—2nd ed.
    p. cm.
    Includes bibliographical references and index.
ISBN-13: 978-0-205-78215-4 (alk. paper)
ISBN-10: 0-205-78215-9 (alk. paper)
  1. Civilization—History—Textbooks. 2. Humanities—History—Textbooks. I. Title.
CB69.S29 2010
909—dc22
                    2010043097

10 9 8 7 6 5 4

Volume II
ISBN-10: 0-205-01335-X
ISBN-13: 978-0-205-01335-7

Examination Copy
ISBN-10: 0-205-01260-4
ISBN-13: 978-0-205-01260-2

Volume I à la carte
ISBN-10: 0-205-02170-0
ISBN-13: 978-0-205-02170-3

Prentice Hall
is an imprint of

www.pearsonhighered.com

SERIES CONTENTS

CONTENTS

26 The Rights of Man
REVOLUTION AND THE NEOCLASSICAL STYLE 837

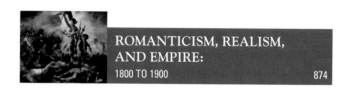

BOOK FIVE

ROMANTICISM, REALISM, AND EMPIRE:
1800 TO 1900   874

27 The Romantic World View
THE SELF IN NATURE AND THE NATURE OF SELF 877

28 Industry and the Working Class
A NEW REALISM   921

Global Confrontation and Civil War

In Pursuit of Modernity

MODERNISM AND THE GLOBALIZATION OF CULTURES: 1900 TO THE PRESENT   1114

34 The Era of Invention
PARIS AND THE MODERN WORLD   1117

Pablo Picasso's Paris: At the Heart of the Modern   1119

35 The Great War and Its Impact
A LOST GENERATION AND A NEW IMAGINATION   1143

Trench Warfare and the Literary Imagination   1145

Escape from Despair: Dada in the Capitals   1148

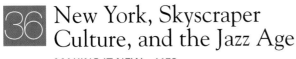

36 New York, Skyscraper Culture, and the Jazz Age
MAKING IT NEW   1173

Without Boundaries
MULTIPLE MEANINGS IN A POSTMODERN WORLD   1313

SEE CONTEXT AND MAKE CONNECTIONS . . .

DEAR READER,

You might be asking yourself, why should I be interested in the Humanities? Why do I care about ancient Egypt, medieval France, or the Qing Dynasty of China?

I asked myself the same question when I was a sophomore in college. I was required to take a year long survey of the Humanities, and I soon realized that I was beginning an extraordinary journey. That course taught me where it was that I stood in the world, and why and how I had come to find myself there. My goal in this book is to help you take the same journey of discovery. Exploring the humanities will help you develop your abilities to look, listen, and read closely; and to analyze, connect, and question. In the end, this will help you navigate your world and come to a better understanding of your place in it.

What we see reflected in different cultures is something of ourselves, the objects of beauty and delight, the weapons and wars, the melodies and harmonies, the sometimes troubling but always penetrating thought from which we spring. To explore the humanities is to explore ourselves, to understand how and why we have changed over time, even as we have, in so many ways, remained the same.

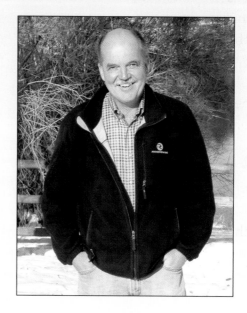

I've come to think of this second edition in something of the same terms. What I've tried to do is explore new paths of inquiry even as I've tried to keep the book recognizably the same. My model, I think, has been Bob Dylan. Over the years, I've heard the man perform more times than I can really recall, and I just saw him again in concert this past summer. He has been performing "Highway 61" and "Just Like a Woman" for nearly fifty years, but here they were again, in new arrangements that were totally fresh—recognizably the same, but reenergized and new. That should be the goal of any new edition of a book, I think, and I hope I've succeeded in that here.

ABOUT THE AUTHOR

Henry M. Sayre is Distinguished Professor of Art History at Oregon State University–Cascades Campus in Bend, Oregon. He earned his Ph.D. in American Literature from the University of Washington. He is producer and creator of the 10-part television series, *A World of Art: Works in Progress*, aired on PBS in the Fall of 1997; and author of seven books, including *A World of Art, The Visual Text of William Carlos Williams, The Object of Performance: The American Avant-Garde since 1970*; and an art history book for children, *Cave Paintings to Picasso.*

The Humanities: Culture, Continuity & Change helps students see context and make connections across the humanities by tying together the entire cultural experience through a narrative story-telling approach. Written around Henry Sayre's belief that students learn best by remembering stories rather than memorizing facts, it captures the voices that have shaped and influenced human thinking and creativity throughout our history.

With a stronger focus on engaging students in the critical thinking process, this new edition encourages students to deepen their understanding of how cultures influence one another, how ideas are exchanged and evolve over time, and how this collective process has led us to where we stand today. With several new features, this second edition helps students to understand context and make connections across time, place, and culture.

To prepare the second edition, we partnered with our current users to hear what was successful and what needed to be improved. The feedback we received through focus groups, online surveys, and reviews helped shape and inform this new edition. For instance, to help students make stronger global connections, the organization of the text and the Table of Contents have been modified. As an example, reflections of this key goal can be seen in Chapters 6 and 7, which are now aligned to show parallels more easily in the developments of urban culture and imperial authority between Rome, China, and India.

Through this dialogue, we also learned how humanities courses are constantly evolving. We learned that more courses are being taught online and that instructors are exploring new ways to help their students engage with course material. We developed MyArtsLab with these needs in mind. With powerful online learning tools integrated into the book, the online and textbook experience is more seamless than ever before. In addition, there are wonderful interactive resources that you, as the instructor, can bring directly into your classroom.

All of these changes can be seen through the new, expanded, or improved features shown here.

NEW
THINKING AHEAD

These questions open each chapter and represent its major sections, leading students to think critically and focus on important issues.

NEW
THINKING BACK

These end-of-chapter reviews follow up on the **Thinking Ahead** questions, helping students further engage with the material they've just read and stimulate thought and discussion.

NEW
CLOSER LOOK

Previously called "Focus" in the first edition, these highly visual features offer an in-depth look at a particular work from one of the disciplines of the humanities. The annotated discussions give students a personal tour of the work–with informative captions and labels–to help students understand its meaning. A new critical thinking question, *Something to Think About*, prompts students to make connections and further apply this detailed knowledge of the work.

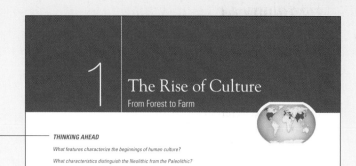

1 The Rise of Culture
From Forest to Farm

THINKING AHEAD

What features characterize the beginnings of human culture?

What characteristics distinguish the Neolithic from the Paleolithic?

What is a megalith?

How can we understand the role of myth in prehistoric culture?

THINKING BACK

What features characterize the beginnings of human culture?

The widespread use of stone tools and weapons by Homo sapiens, the hominid species that evolved around 120,000 to 100,000 years ago, gives rise to the name of the earliest era of human development, the Paleolithic era. Carvers fashioned stone figures, both in the round and in relief. In cave paintings, such as those discovered at Chauvet Cave, the artists' great skill in rendering animals helps us to understand that the ability to represent the world with naturalistic fidelity is an inherent human skill, unrelated to cultural sophistication. Culture can be defined as a way of living—religious, social, and/or political—formed by a group of people and passed on from one generation to the next. What can the earliest art tell us about the first human cultures? What questions remain a mystery?

What characteristics distinguish the Neolithic from the Paleolithic?

As the ice that covered the Northern Hemisphere slowly melted, people began cultivating edible grasses and domesticating animals. Gradually, farming supplanted hunting as the primary means of sustaining life, especially in the great river valleys where water was abundant. The rise of agriculture is the chief characteristic of the Neolithic age. Along with agriculture, permanent villages such as Skara Brae begin to appear. What does the appearance of fire-baked pottery tell us about life in Neolithic culture?

What is a megalith?

During the fifth millennium BCE, Neolithic peoples began constructing monumental stone architecture, or megaliths, in France and England. Upright, single stone posts called menhirs were placed in the ground, either individually or in groups, as at Carnac in Brittany. Elementary post-and-lintel construction was employed to create dolmens, two posts roofed with a capstone. The most famous of the third type of monumental construction, the circular cromlech, is Stonehenge, in England. What does the enormous amount of human labor required for the construction of these megaliths suggest about the societies that built them?

How can we understand the role of myth in prehistoric culture?

Neolithic culture in the Americas lasted well into the second millennium CE. Much of our understanding of the role of myth in prehistoric cultures derives from the traditions of contemporary Native American tribes that still survive in tribes such as the Hopi and Zuni, who are the direct descendents of the Anasazi. Their legends, such as the Zuni emergence tale, encapsulate the fundamental religious principles of the culture. Such stories, and the ritual practices that accompany them, reflect the general beliefs of most Neolithic peoples. Can you describe some of these beliefs? What role do sacred sites, such as those at Ise in Japan, or Cahokia in the Mississippi Valley, play?

PRACTICE MORE Get flashcards for images and terms and review chapter material with quizzes at www.myartslab.com

CLOSER LOOK
The Design and Making of Stonehenge

How the Neolithic peoples of Britain constructed Stonehenge is uncertain. Scholars believe that the giant stones of the Sarsen Circle, which weigh up to 50 tons, were transported from the Marlborough Downs, roughly 20 miles to the north, by rolling them on logs. Most of the way, the going is relatively easy, but at the steepest part of the route, at Redhorn Hill, modern work studies estimate that it would have taken at least 600 men to push the stones up the hill. A relatively sophisticated understanding of basic physics—the operation of levers and pulleys—was needed to lift the stones, and their lintels, into place.

Recently, archeologists at Stonehenge have uncovered a second cromlech-like circle at Durrington Wells, about 2 miles north of the stone megalith, consisting of a circular ditch surrounding a ring of postholes out of which very large timber posts would have risen. The circle was the center of a village consisting of as many as 300 houses. The site is comparable in scale to Stonehenge itself. These discoveries—together with the ability to carbon-date human remains found at Stonehenge with increased accuracy—suggest that Stonehenge was itself a burial grounds. Archeologist Mike Parker-Pearson of the University of Sheffield speculates that villagers would have transported their dead down an avenue leading to the River Avon, then journeyed downstream, in a ritual symbolizing the passage to the afterlife, finally arriving at an avenue leading up to Stonehenge from the river. "Stonehenge wasn't set in isolation," Parker-Pearson says, "but was actually one half of this monument complex. We are looking at a pairing-one in timber to represent the transience of life, the other in stone marking the eternity of the ancestral dead."

Something to Think About . . .

The circle is a geometric form that appears in the earliest manifestations of art and architecture. Can you speculate on its appeal?

The Heel Stone
On Midsummer's Eve, it casts a shadow directly into the circle. The stone stands 16 feet high and weighs 35 tons. It was brought from a quarry 23 miles away.

The Avenue
The shadow cast by the Heel Stone on Midsummer's Eve would extend directly down this ceremonial approach.

The Slaughter Stone
It was once believed that humans were sacrificed on this stone, which now lies flat on the ground, but it was originally part of a great portal.

The Sarsen Circle
Erected about 1500 BCE, the circle is capped by lintel stones held in place by mortise-and-tenon joints, similar to those used by woodworkers. The end of the post is narrowed and slotted into a hole in the lintel.

The sarsen stone is raised with a long lever. Logs are placed under the stone, and then it is rolled into place.

One by one, layers of timber are placed under the lever, both raising the stone and dropping it into the prepared pit.

As many as 200 men pull the stone upright on ropes as timbers support it from behind.

The pit around the stone is filled with stones and chalks to pack it into place.

The lintel is raised on successive layers of a timber platform.

Once the platform reaches the top of the posts, the lintel is levered onto the posts.

Finally, the platform is removed, and the trilithon is complete.

The Outer Bank
This ditch, 330 feet in diameter, is the oldest construction at the site, originally exposing the white limestone beneath the surface soil to form a giant circle.

Five Massive Trilithons
Inside the outer circle stood a horseshoe of trilithons, two on each side and three at the closed end at the southwest. Only one of the largest trilithons still stands. It rises 22 feet above ground, with 8 feet more below ground level. The stone weighs about 50 tons.

The Altar Stone
One of the most distinct stones at Stonehenge, the so-called altar stone is a 16-foot block of smoothed green sandstone located near the center of the complex.

The Bluestone Circle
This circle of 80 smaller slabs was built in about 2000 BCE from stone quarried in South Wales.

SEE MORE For a Closer Look at Stonehenge, go to www.myartslab.com

CONTINUITY & CHANGE ESSAYS

These full-page essays at the end of each chapter illustrate the influence of one cultural period upon another and show cultural changes over time.

CONTINUITY & CHANGE ICONS

These in-text references provide a window into the past. The eye-catching icons enable students to refer to material in other chapters that is relevant to the topic at hand.

CONTINUITY & CHANGE

The Pyramids of Menkaure, **p. 74**

CONTEXT

These boxes summarize important background information in an easy-to-read format.

MATERIALS AND TECHNIQUES

These features explain and illustrate the methods artists and architects use to produce their work.

CONTINUITY & CHANGE

Representing the Power of the Animal World

The two images shown here in some sense bracket the six volumes of *The Humanities*. The first (Fig. 1.24), from the Chauvet Cave, is one of the earliest known drawings of a horse. The second (Fig. 1.25), a drawing by contemporary American painter Susan Rothenberg (b. 1945), also represents a horse, though in many ways less realistically than the cave drawing. The body of Rothenberg's horse seems to have disappeared and, eyeless, as if blinded, it leans forward, its mouth open, choking or gagging or gasping for air.

In his catalog essay for a 1993 retrospective exhibition of Rothenberg's painting, Michael Auping, chief curator at the Albright-Knox Museum in Buffalo, New York, described Rothenberg's kind of drawing: "Relatively spontaneous, the drawings are Rothenberg's psychic energy made imminent . . . . [They] uncover realms of the psyche that are perhaps not yet fully explicable." The same could be said of the cave drawing executed by a nameless hunter-gatherer more than 20,000 years ago. That artist's work must have seemed just as strange as Rothenberg's, lit by flickering firelight in the dark recesses of the cave, its body disappearing, too, into the darkness that surrounded it.

It seems certain that in some measure both drawings were the expression of a psychic need on the part of the artist—whether derived from the energy of the hunt or of nature itself—to fix upon a surface an image of the power and vulnerability of the animal world. That drive, which we will see in the art of the Bronze Age of the Middle East in the next chapter—for instance, in the haunting image of a dying lion in the palace complex of an Assyrian king at Nineveh—remains constant from the beginnings of art to the present day. It is the compulsion to express the inexpressible, to visualize the mind as well as the world. ∎

Fig. 1.24 **Horse. Detail from Chauvet Cave, Vallon-Pont-d'Arc, Ardèche gorge, France (Fig. 1.1). ca. 30,000 BCE.** Note the realistic shading that defines the volume of the horse's head. It is a realism that artists throughout history have sometimes sought to achieve, and sometimes ignored, in their efforts to express for the forces that drive them.

Fig. 1.25 **Susan Rothenberg. Untitled. 1976.** Acrylic, flashe, and pencil on paper, 20″ × 20″. Collection Walker Art Center, Minneapolis. Art Center Acquisition Fund, 1979 © 2008 Susan Rothenberg/Artist's Rights Society (ARS), NY. Part of the eeriness of this image comes from Rothenberg's use of flashe, a French vinyl-based color that is clear and so creates a misty, ghostlike surface.

Materials & Techniques

Methods of Carving

Carving is the act of cutting or incising stone, bone, wood, or another material into a desired form. Surviving artifacts of the Paleolithic era were carved from stone or bone. The artist probably held a sharp instrument, such as a stone knife or a chisel, in one hand and drove it into the stone or bone with another stone held in the other hand to remove excess material and realize the figure. Finer details could be scratched into the material with a pointed stone instrument. Artists can carve into any material softer than the instrument they are using. Harder varieties of stone can cut into softer stone as well as bone. The work was probably painstakingly slow.

There are basically two types of sculpture: sculpture in the round and relief sculpture. **Sculpture in the round** is fully three-dimensional; it occupies 360 degrees of space. The Willendorf statuette (see Fig. 1.3) was carved from stone and is an example of sculpture in the round. **Relief sculpture** is carved out of a flat background surface; it has a distinct front and no back. Not all relief sculptures are

alike. In *high relief* sculpture, the figure extends more than 180 degrees from the background surface. *Woman Holding an Animal Horn,* found at Laussel, in the Dordogne region of France, is carved in high relief and is one of the earliest relief sculptures known. This sculpture was originally part of a great stone block that stood in front of a Paleolithic rock shelter. In *low* or *bas relief,* the figure extends less than 180 degrees from the surface. In *sunken relief,* the image is carved, or incised, into the surface, so that the image recedes below it. When a light falls on relief sculptures at an angle, the relief casts a shadow. The higher the relief, the larger the shadows and the greater the sense of the figure's three-dimensionality.

Woman Holding an Animal Horn, Laussel (Dordogne), France. ca. 30,000–15,000 BCE. Limestone, height 17 3/8″. Musée des Antiquités Nationales, St. Germain-en-Laye, France.

EXPLORE MORE To see a studio video about carving, go to **www.myartslab.com**

PRIMARY SOURCES

Each chapter of *The Humanities* includes Primary Source Readings in two formats. Brief readings from important works are included within the body of the text. Longer readings located at the end of each chapter allow for a more in-depth study of particular works. The organization offers great flexibility in teaching the course.

(for example, "the land shattered like a pot").

Perhaps most important, the epic illuminates the development of a nation or race. It is a national poem, describing a people's common heritage and celebrating its cultural identity. It is hardly surprising, then, that Ashurbanipal preserved the *Epic of Gilgamesh.* Just as Sargon II depicted himself at the gates of Khorsabad in the traditional horned crown of Akkad and the beard of Sumer, containing within himself all Mesopotamian history, the *Epic of Gilgamesh* preserves the historical lineage of all Mesopotamian kings—Sumerian, Akkadian, Assyrian, and Babylonian. The tale embodies their own heroic grandeur, and thus the grandeur of their peoples.

The poem opens with a narrator guiding a visitor (the reader) around Uruk. The narrator explains that the epic was written by Gilgamesh himself and was deposited in the city's walls, where visitors can read it for themselves. Then the narrator introduces Gilgamesh as an epic hero, two parts god and one part human. The style of the following list of his deeds is the same as in hymns to the gods (**Reading 2.3a**):

READING 2.3a

from the *Epic of Gilgamesh,* Tablet I
(ca. 1200 BCE)

Supreme over other kings, lordly in appearance,
he is the hero, born of Uruk, the goring wild bull.
He walks out in front, the leader,
and walks at the rear, trusted by his companions.
Mighty net, protector of his people,
raging floodwave who destroys even walls of stone! . . .
It was he who opened the mountain passes,
who dug wells on the flank of the mountain.

READINGS

READING 2.3

from the *Epic of Gilgamesh,* Tablet I (ca. 1200 BCE) (translated by Maureen Gallery Kovacs)
The Epic of Gilgamesh describes the exploits of the Sumerian ruler Gilgamesh and his friend Enkidu. The following passage, from the first of the epic's 12 tablets, recounts how Enkidu, the primal man raised beyond the reach of civilization and fully at home with animals, loses his animal powers, and with them his innocence, when a trapper, tired of Enkidu freeing animals from his traps, arranges for a harlot from Uruk to seduce him. The story resonates in interesting ways with the biblical tale of Adam and Eve and their loss of innocence in the Garden of Eden.

TABLET I

THE HARLOT

The trapper went, bringing the harlot, Shamhat, with him,
they set off on the journey, making direct way.
On the third day they arrived at the appointed place,
and the trapper and the harlot sat down at their posts(?).
A first day and a second they sat opposite the watering hole.
The animals arrived and drank at the watering hole,
the wild beasts arrived and slaked their thirst with water.
Then he, Enkidu, offspring of the mountains,
who eats grasses with the gazelles,
came to drink at the watering hole with the animals,
with the wild beasts he slaked his thirst with water.
Then Shamhat saw him—a primitive,
a savage fellow from the depths of the wilderness!
"That is he, Shamhat! Release your clenched arms,
expose your sex so he can take in your voluptuousness.

Shamhat unclutched her bosom, exposed her sex, and he
took in her voluptuousness.
She was not restrained, but took his energy.
She spread out her robe and he lay upon her,
she performed for the primitive the task of womankind.
His lust groaned over her;
for six days and seven nights Enkidu stayed aroused,
and had intercourse with the harlot
until he was sated with her charms.
But when he turned his attention to his animals,
the gazelles saw Enkidu and darted off,
the wild animals distanced themselves from his body.
Enkidu . . . his utterly depleted (?) body,
his knees that wanted to go off with his animals went rigid;
Enkidu was diminished, his running was not as before.
But then he drew himself up, for his understanding had
broadened.

MORE CONNECTIONS TO MyArtsLab

The text is keyed to the dynamic resources on MyArtsLab, allowing instructors and students online access to additional information, music, videos, and interactive features.

The **'SEE MORE'** icon correlates to the Closer Look features in the text, directing students to MyArtsLab to view interactive **Closer Look** tours online. These features enable students to zoom in to see detail they could not otherwise see on the printed page or even in person. **'SEE MORE'** icons also indicate when students can view works of architecture in full 360-degree panoramas.

No trace of the city's famous Hanging Gardens survives, once considered among the Seven Wonders of the World, and only the base and parts of the lower stairs of the Marduk ziggurat still remain. But in the fifth century BCE, the Greek historian Herodotus [he-ROD-uh-tus] (ca. 484–430/420 BCE) described the ziggurat as follows:

There was a tower of solid masonry, a furlong in length and breadth, on which was raised a second tower, and on that a third, and so on up to eight. The ascent to the top is on the outside, by a path which winds round all the towers. . . . On the topmost tower, there is a spacious temple, and inside the temple stands a couch of unusual size, richly adorned with a golden table by its side. . . . They also declare that the god comes down in person into this chamber, and sleeps on the couch, but I do not believe it.

Although the ziggurat has disappeared, we can glean some sense of the city's magnificence from the Ishtar Gate (Fig. 2.18), named after the Babylonian goddess of fertility.

Fig. 2.18 **Ishtar Gate (restored), from Babylon. ca. 575 BCE.** Glazed brick. Staatliche Museen, Berlin. The dark blue bricks are glazed—that is, covered with a film of glass—and they would have shown brilliantly in the sun.

SEE MORE To view a Closer Look feature about the Ishtar Gate, go to www.myartslab.com

CHAPTER 2 *Mesopotamia* **55**

Fig. 9.13 **Great Mosque of Córdoba. Begun 785, extensions 852, 950, 961–76, and 987.** The caliphs of Spain intended their mosque to rival those in Jerusalem, Damascus, and Iraq. The forestlike expanse of the interior is a result of these aspirations. Even though only 80 of the original 1,200 columns survive, the space appears infinite, like some giant hall of mirrors.

LEARN MORE View an architectural simulation of Islamic arches at www.myartslab.com

by the Umayyads in Toledo [toh-LEH-doh] soon was responsible for spreading the nearly forgotten texts throughout the West. Muslim mathematicians in Spain invented algebra and introduced the concept of zero to the West, and soon their Arabic numerals replaced the unwieldy Roman system. By the time of Abd ar-Rahman III (r. 912–61), Córdoba was renowned for its medicine, science, literature, and commercial wealth, and it became the most important center of learning in Europe. The elegance of Abd ar-Rahman III's court was unmatched, and his tolerance and benevolence extended to all, as Muslim students from across the Mediterranean found their way to the mosque-affiliated madrasa that he founded—the

earliest example of an institution of higher learning in the Western world.

Outside of Córdoba, Abd ar-Rahman III built a huge palace complex, Madinat al-Zahra, to honor his wife. (Its extensive remains are still being excavated.) Its staff included 13,750 male servants along with another 3,500 pages, slaves, and eunuchs. Its roof required the support of 4,300 columns, and elaborate gardens surrounded the site. As many as 1,200 loaves of bread were required daily just to feed the fish in the garden ponds.

The decorative arts of the era are equally impressive. A famous example is a **pyxis**, a small, cylindrical box with a lid, made for Prince al-Mughira, Abd ar-Rahman III's

CHAPTER 9 *The Rise and Spread of Islam* **301**

The **'HEAR MORE'** icons indicate where musical performances can be listened to in streaming audio on www.myartslab.com. Online audio also includes **'Voices'**– vivid first-person accounts of the experiences of ordinary people during the period covered in the chapter.

The **'LEARN MORE'** icons lead students online for additional primary source readings or to watch architectural simulations.

The **'EXPLORE MORE'** icons direct students to videos of artists at work in their studios, allowing them to see and understand a wide variety of materials and techniques used by artists throughout time.

Designed to save instructors time and to improve students' results, MyArtsLab, is keyed specifically to the chapters of Sayre's *The Humanities*, second edition. In addition, MyArts-Lab's many features will encourage students to experience and interact with works of art. Here are some of those key features:

• A complete **Pearson eText** of the book, enriched with multimedia, including: a unique human-scale figure by all works of fine art, an audio version of the text, primary source documents, video demonstrations, and much more. Students can highlight, make notes, and bookmark pages.

• 360-degree **Architectural Panoramas** for major monuments in the book help students understand buildings from the inside and out.

• **Closer Look Tours** These interactive walk-throughs offer an in-depth look at key works of art, enabling students to zoom in to see detail they could not otherwise see on the printed page or even in person. Enhanced with expert audio, they help students understand the meaning and message behind the work of art.

• Robust **Quizzing** and **Grading Functionality** is included in MyArtsLab. Students receive immediate feedback from the assessment questions that populate the instructor's gradebook. The gradebook reports give an in-depth look at the progress of individual students or the class as a whole.

• MyArtsLab is your one stop for instructor material. Instructors can access the Instructor's Manual, Test Item File, PowerPoint images, and the Pearson MyTest assessment-generation program.

MyArtsLab with eText is available for no additional cost when packaged with *The Humanities*, second edition. The program may also be used as a stand-alone item, which costs less than a used text.

To register for your MyArtsLab account, contact your local Pearson representative or visit the instructor registration page located on the homepage of www.myartslab.com.

FLEXIBLE FORMATS

CourseSmart eTextbooks offer the same content as the printed text in a convenient online format—with highlighting, online search, and printing capabilities. With a CourseSmart eText, student can search the text, make notes online, print out reading assignments that incorporate lecture notes, and bookmark important passages for later review. *Students save 60% over the list price of the traditional book. www.coursesmart.com.*

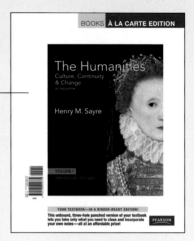

Books à la Carte editions feature the exact same text in a convenient, three-hole-punched, loose-leaf version at a discounted price— allowing students to take only what they need to class. Books à la Carte editions are available both with and without access to MyArtsLab. *Students save 35% over the net price of the traditional book.*

Custom Publishing Opportunities

The Humanities is available in a custom version specifically tailored to meet your needs. You may select the content that you would like to include or add your own original material. See you local publisher's representative for further information. **www.pearsoncustom.com**

INSTRUCTOR RESOURCES

Classroom Response System (CRS) In-Class Questions

Get instant, class-wide responses to beautifully illustrated chapter-specific questions during a lecture to gauge students' comprehension—and keep them engaged. Available for download under the "For Instructors" tab within your MyArtsLab account–**www.myartslab.com.**

Instructor's Manual and Test Item File

This is an invaluable professional resource and reference for new and experienced faculty. Each chapter contains the following sections: Chapter Overview, Chapter Objectives, Key Terms, Lecture and Discussion Topics, Resources, and Writing Assignments and Projects. The test bank includes multiple-choice, true/false, short-answer, and essay questions. Available for download from the instructor support section at **www.myartslab.com.**

ClassPrep

Instructors who adopt Sayre's *The Humanities* will receive access to ClassPrep, an online site designed to make lecture preparation simpler and less time-consuming. The site includes the images from the text in both high-resolution JPGs, and ready-made PowerPoint slides for your lectures. ClassPrep can be accessed through your MyArtsLab instructor account.

MyTest

This flexible, online test-generating software includes all questions found in the printed Test Item File. Instructors can quickly and easily create customized tests with MyTest. **www.pearsonmytest.com**

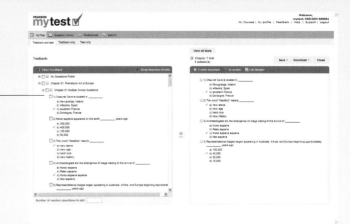

ADDITIONAL PACKAGING OPTIONS

Penguin Custom Editions: The Western World lets you choose from an archive of more than 1,800 readings excerpted from the Penguin Classics™, the most comprehensive paperback library of Western history, literature, culture, and philosophy available. You'll have the freedom to craft a reader for your humanities course that matches your teaching approach exactly! Using our online book-building system, you get to select the readings you need, in the sequence you want, at the price you want your students to pay. **www.pearsoncustom.com** keyword: penguin

 Titles from the renowned Penguin Classics series can be bundles with *The Humanities* for a nominal charge. Please contact your Pearson Arts and Sciences sales representative for details.

 The Prentice Hall Atlas of World History, second edition includes over 100 full-color maps in world history, drawn by Dorling Kindersley, one of the world's most respected cartographic publishers. Copies of the Atlas can be bundled with *The Humanities* for a nominal charge. Please contact your Pearson Arts and Sciences sales representative for details.

 Connections: Key Themes in World History. Series Editor Alfred J. Andrea. Concise and tightly focused, the titles in the popular Connections Series are designed to place the latest research on selected topics of global significance, such as disease, trade, slavery, exploration, and modernization, into an accessible format for students. Available for a 50% discount when bundled with *The Humanities*. For more information, please visit **www.pearsonhighered.com.**

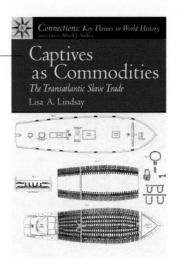

THE HUMANITIES: *CULTURE, CONTINUITY & CHANGE*

is the result of an extensive development process involving the contributions of over one hundred instructors and their students. We are grateful to all who participated in shaping the content, clarity, and design of this text. Manuscript reviewers and focus group participants include:

ALABAMA
Cynthia Kristan-Graham, Auburn University

CALIFORNIA
Collette Chattopadhyay, Saddleback College
Laurel Corona, San Diego City College
Cynthia D. Gobatie, Riverside Community College
John Hoskins, San Diego Mesa College
Gwenyth Mapes, Grossmont College
Bradley Nystrom, California State University-Sacramento
Joseph Pak, Saddleback College
John Provost, Monterey Peninsula College
Chad Redwing, Modesto Junior College
Stephanie Robinson, San Diego City College
Alice Taylor, West Los Angeles College
Denise Waszkowski, San Diego Mesa College

COLORADO
Renee Bragg, Arapahoe Community College
Marilyn Smith, Red Rocks Community College

CONNECTICUT
Abdellatif Hissouf, Central Connecticut State University

FLORIDA
Wesley Borucki, Palm Beach Atlantic University
Amber Brock, Tallahassee Community College
Connie Dearmin, Brevard Community College
Kimberly Felos, St. Petersburg College
Katherine Harrell, South Florida Community College
Ira Holmes, College of Central Florida
Dale Hoover, Edison State College
Theresa James, South Florida Community College
Jane Jones, State College of Florida, Manatee-Sarasota
Jennifer Keefe, Valencia Community College
Mansoor Khan, Brevard Community College
Connie LaMarca-Frankel, Pasco-Hernando Community College
Sandi Landis, St. Johns River Community College-Orange Park
Joe Loccisano, State College of Florida
David Luther, Edison College
James Meier, Central Florida Community College
Brandon Montgomery, State College of Florida
Pamela Wood Payne, Palm Beach Atlantic University
Gary Poe, Palm Beach Atlantic University
Frederick Smith, Florida Gateway College
Kate Myers de Vega, Palm Beach Atlantic University
Bill Waters, Pensacola State College

GEORGIA
Leslie Harrelson, Dalton State College
Lawrence Hetrick, Georgia Perimeter College
Priscilla Hollingsworth, Augusta State University
Kelley Mahoney, Dalton State College
Andrea Scott Morgan, Georgia Perimeter College

IDAHO
Jennifer Black, Boise State University
Rick Davis, Brigham Young University-Idaho
Derek Jensen, Brigham Young University-Idaho

ILLINOIS
Thomas Christensen, University of Chicago
Timothy J. Clifford, College of DuPage
Leslie Huntress Hopkins, College of Lake County
Judy Kaplow, Harper College
Terry McIntyre, Harper College
Victoria Neubeck O'Connor, Moraine Valley Community College
Sharon Quarcini, Moraine Valley Community College
Paul Van Heuklom, Lincoln Land Community College

INDIANA
Josephina Kiteou, University of Southern Indiana

KENTUCKY
Jonathan Austad, Eastern Kentucky University
Beth Cahaney, Elizabethtown Community and Technical College
Jeremy Killian, University of Louisville
Lynda Mercer, University of Louisville
Sara Northerner, University of Louisville
Elijah Pritchett, University of Louisville

MASSACHUSETTS
Peter R. Kalb, Brandeis University

MICHIGAN
Martha Petry, Jackson Community College
Robert Quist, Ferris State University

MINNESOTA
Mary Johnston, Minnesota State University

NEBRASKA
Michael Hoff, University of Nebraska

NEVADA
Chris Bauer, Sierra College

NEW JERSEY
Jay Braverman, Montclair State University
Sara E. Gil-Ramos, New Jersey City University

NEW MEXICO
Sarah Egelman, Central New Mexico Community College

NEW YORK
Eva Diaz, Pratt Institute
Mary Guzzy, Corning Community College
Thelma Ithier Sterling, Hostos Community College
Elizabeth C. Mansfield, New York University
Clemente Marconi, New York University

NORTH CAROLINA
Melodie Galloway, University of North Carolina at Asheville
Jeanne McGlinn, University of North Carolina at Asheville

Sophie Mills, University of North Carolina at Asheville
Constance Schrader, University of North Carolina at Asheville
Ronald Sousa, University of North Carolina at Asheville
Samer Traboulsi, University of North Carolina at Asheville

NORTH DAKOTA
Robert Kibler, Minot State University

OHIO
Darlene Alberts, Columbus State Community College
Tim Davis, Columbus State Community College
Michael Mangus, The Ohio State University at Newark
Keith Pepperell, Columbus State Community College
Patrice Ross, Columbus State Community College

OKLAHOMA
Amanda H. Blackman, Tulsa Community College-Northeast Campus
Diane Boze, Northeastern State University
Jacklan J. Renee Cox, Rogers State University
Jim Ford, Rogers State University
Diana Lurz, Rogers State University
James W. Mock, University of Central Oklahoma
Gregory Thompson, Rogers State University

PENNSYLVANIA
Elizabeth Pilliod, Rutgers University-Camden
Douglas B. Rosentrater, Bucks County Community College
Debra Thomas, Harrisburg Area Community College

RHODE ISLAND
Mallica Kumbera Landrus, Rhode Island School of Design

TEXAS
Mindi Bailey, Collin County Community College
Peggy Brown, Collin County Community College
Marsha Lindsay, Lone Star College-North Harris
Aditi Samarth, Richland College
Lee Ann Westman, University of Texas at El Paso

UTAH
Matthew Ancell, Brigham Young University
Terre Burton, Dixie College
Nate Kramer, Brigham Young University
Joseph D. Parry, Brigham Young University

VIRGINIA
Margaret Browning, Hampton University
Carey Freeman, Hampton University
John Long, Roanoke College
Anne Pierce, Hampton University
Jennifer Rosti, Roanoke College

No project of this scope could ever come into being without the hard work and perseverance of many more people than its author. In fact, this author has been humbled by a team at Pearson Prentice Hall that never wavered in their confidence in my ability to finish this enormous undertaking (or if they did, they had the good sense not to let me know); never hesitated to cajole, prod, and massage me to complete the project in something close to on time; and always gave me the freedom to explore new approaches to the materials at hand. At the down-and-dirty level, I am especially grateful to fact-checker, Julia Moore; to Mary Ellen Wilson for the pronunciation guides; for the more specialized pronunciations offered by David Atwill (Chinese and Japanese), Jonathan Reynolds (African), Nayla Muntasser (Greek and Latin), and Mark Watson (Native American); to Margaret Gorenstein for tracking down the readings; to Laurel Corona for her extraordinary help with Africa; to Arnold Bradford for help with critical thinking questions; and to Francelle Carapetyan for her remarkable photo research. The maps and some of the line art are the work of cartographer and artist, Peter Bull, with Precision Graphic drafting a large portion of the line art for the book. I find both in every way extraordinary.

In fact, I couldn't be more pleased with the look of the book, which is the work of Pat Smythe, senior art director. Cory Skidds, senior imaging specialist, worked on image compositing and color accuracy of the artwork. The production of the book was coordinated by Melissa Feimer, associate managing editor, Barbara Cappuccio, senior production project manager, and Marlene Gassler, production project manager, who oversaw with good humor and patience the day-to-day, hour-to-hour crises that arose. Brian Mackey, production-planning and operations specialist, ensured that this project progressed smoothly through its production route. And I want to thank Lindsay Bethoney and the staff at PreMedia Global for working so hard to make the book turn out the way I envisioned it.

The marketing and editorial teams at Prentice Hall are beyond compare. On the marketing side, Brandy Dawson, vice president of marketing, and Kate Mitchell, executive marketing manager, helped us all to understand just what students want and need. On the editorial side, my thanks to Yolanda de Rooy, president of the Social Sciences and the Arts division; to Sarah Touborg, editor-in-chief; Billy Grieco, editor; Bud Therien, special projects manager; David Nitti, assistant editor; and Theresa Graziano, editorial assistant. The combined human hours that this group has put into this project are staggering. This book was Bud's idea in the first place; Billy and Sarah have supported me every step of the way in making it as good, or even better, than I envisioned; and Yolanda's over-arching vision is responsible for helping to make Pearson such an extraordinarily good publisher to write for.

Deserving of special mention is my development team, Rochelle Diogenes, editor-in-chief of development; and Margaret Manos, development editor. Margaret has been an especially valuable partner, helping me literally to "re-vision" this revision and bringing clarity and common sense to those moments where they were lost.

Finally, I want to thank, with all my love, my beautiful wife, Sandy Brooke, who has supported this project in every way. She has continued to teach, paint, and write, while urging me on, listening to my struggles, humoring me when I didn't deserve it, and being a far better wife than I was a husband. In some ways, enduring what she did in the first edition must have been tougher in the second, since she knew what was coming from the outset. She was, is, and will continue to be, I trust, the source of my strength.

BOOK FOUR

Excess, Inquiry, and Restraint

1600 TO 1800

Detail of Jean-Antoine Watteau, ***The Embarkation from Cythera.*** **ca. 1718–19.** Oil on canvas, 50$^{1}/_{4}$″ × 76$^{1}/_{8}$″ (See Fig. 25.3). Staatliche Museen, Schloss Charlottenburg, Berlin.

For more than 200 years, from the late sixteenth century until the dawn of the nineteenth, the entrenched traditions of culture were challenged as never before. Not just in the West, but around the world, no era had been entangled in such a complex web of competing values. Indeed, it began with a civil war and ended with two revolutions. England, in the last half of the sixteenth century, was embroiled in conflict between Catholic and Protestant factions that led to civil war, the execution of a king, and abolition of monarchical authority. Two hundred years later, in the late eighteenth century, the American colonies would rebel against British control, and the French people against their king.

The question of political power—who possessed the right to rule—dominated the age. In the centuries before, the papacy had exercised authority over all people. Now, the rulers of Europe emphatically asserted their divine right to rule with unquestioned authority over their own dominions. In contrast, the thinkers of the age increasingly came to believe that human beings were by their very nature free, equal, and independent, and that they were not required to surrender their own sovereignty to any ruler. In essence, these thinkers developed a secularized version of the contest between Catholicism and Protestantism that had defined the sixteenth century after the Reformation. Protestant churches had freed themselves from what they believed to be a tyrannical and extravagant papacy. In fact, many people found strong similarities between the extravagances of the European monarchies and the extravagance of Rome. Now, many believed, individuals should free themselves from the tyrannical and profligate rule of any government to which they did not freely choose to submit.

At the beginning of the era, the Counter-Reformation was in full swing, and the Church, out to win back the hearts and minds of all whom the Reformation had drawn away, appealed not just to the intellect, but to the full range of human emotion and feeling. In Rome, it constructed theatrical, even monumental, spaces—not just churches, but avenues, fountains, and plazas—richly decorated in an exuberant style that we have come to call "the Baroque." This dramatic and emotional style found expression in painting and music as well, and artistic virtuosity became the hallmark of this new Baroque style.

The courts of Europe readily adapted the Baroque to their own ends. In France, Louis XIII never missed an opportunity to use art and architecture to impress his grandeur and power upon the French people (and the other courts of Europe). In the arts, the stylistic tensions of the French court were most fully expressed. The rational clarity and moral uprightness of the classical contrasted with the emotional drama and flamboyant sensuality of the Baroque. In music, for example, we find both the clarity of the classical symphony and the spectacle of Baroque opera.

At the same time, scientific and philosophical investigation—the invention, for instance, of new tools of observation like the telescope and microscope—helped to sustain a newfound trust in the power of the rational mind to understand the world. When Isaac Newton demonstrated in 1687, to the satisfaction of just about everyone, that the universe was an intelligible system, well-ordered in its operations and guiding principles, it seemed possible that the operations of human society—the production and consumption of manufactured goods, the social organization of families and towns, the operations of national governments, to say nothing of its arts—might be governed by analogous universal laws. The pursuit of these laws is the defining characteristic of the eighteenth century, the period we have come to call the Enlightenment.

Thus, the age developed into a contest between those who sought to establish a new social order forged by individual freedom and responsibility, and those whose taste favored a decorative and erotic excess—primarily the French court. But even the high-minded champions of freedom found themselves caught up in morally complex dilemmas. Americans championed liberty, but they also defended the institution of slavery. The French would overthrow their dissolute monarch, only to see their society descend into chaos, requiring, in the end, a return to imperial rule. And, when the Europeans encountered other cultures—in the South Pacific, China, India, and, most devastatingly, in the American West—they tended to impose their own values on cultures that were, in many ways, not even remotely like their own. But if the balance of power fell heavily to the West, increasingly the dynamics of global encounter resulted in the exchange of ideas and values.

1625
Artemisia Gentileschi, *Judith and Maidservant with Head of Holofernes*

1609–10
Galileo Galilei observes moon's craters

1632–48
Taj Mahal

1643–1715
Louis XIV, the "Sun King," reigns

1645–52
Bernini, *The Ecstasy of Saint Teresa*

1662–64
Johannes Vermeer, *Lady at the Virginal with a Gentleman*

1666
Fire of London

1687
Isaac Newton, *Principia Mathematica*

1719
Daniel Defoe, *Robinson Crusoe*

1721
Johann Sebastian Bach, *Brandenburg concertos*

1751
William Hogarth, *Gin Lane*

1756–91
Wolfgang Amadeus Mozart

1767
Jean-Honorè Fragonard, *The Swing*

1769
Sidney Parkinson, *Portrait of a Maori*

1770
Captain Cook encounters aboriginal cultures in Australia

1776
James Watt improves steam engine; Declaration of Independence; Adam Smith, *Wealth of Nations*

1778
John Singleton Copley, *Watson and the Shark*

1781
Immanuel Kant, *Critique of Pure Reason*

1789
Fall of the Bastille in Paris; Olaudah Equiano's autobiography describes slave living conditions

1791
Pierre Charles L'Enfant, *Plan for Washington, D.C.*

1792
Mary Wollstonecraft, *Vindication of the Rights of Women*

1799–1812
Napoleon rules France

LEARN MORE Explore an interactive timeline on **www.myartslab.com**

21

The Baroque in Italy
The Church and Its Appeal

THINKING AHEAD

What is the Baroque?

How does the Baroque style manifest itself in painting?

How is the Baroque style manifest in music, particularly in Venice?

As the seventeenth century began, the Catholic Church was struggling to win back those who had been drawn away by the Protestant Reformation. To wage its campaign, the Church took what can best be described as a sensual turn, an appeal not just to the intellect but to the range of human emotion and feeling. This appeal was embodied in an increasingly ornate and grandiose form of expression that came to be known as the Baroque [bah-ROAK] style. Its focal point was the Vatican City, in Rome (Fig. **21.1** and Map **21.1**). The oval colonnade defining the square is considered one of greatest works of Gianlorenzo Bernini [jahn- lor-EN-zo bair-NEE-nee] (1598–1680), and it fully captures the grandeur and drama of the Baroque style.

Bernini's curved porticoes, composed of 284 huge Doric columns placed in rows of four, create a vast open space—nearly 800 feet across—designed specifically for its dramatic effect. Bernini considered the colonnade enclosing the square to symbolize "the motherly arms of the Church" embracing its flock. Here, as crowds gathered to receive the blessing of the pope, the architecture dramatized the blessing itself.

Attention to the way viewers would emotionally experience a work of art is a defining characteristic of the Baroque, a term many believe takes its name from the Portuguese *barroco* [bah-roh-koh], literally a large, irregularly shaped pearl. It was originally used in a derogatory way to imply a style so heavily ornate and strange that it verges on bad taste. The rise of the Baroque is the subject of this chapter. We look at it first as it developed in Rome, and at the Vatican in particular, as a conscious style of art and architecture dedicated to furthering the aims of the Counter-Reformation, then in Venice, which in the seventeenth century was the center of musical activity in Europe.

Just as in the sixteenth century Pope Julius II (papacy 1503–1513) had attempted to revitalize Rome as the center of the Christian world by constructing a new Saint Peter's Basilica, so at the beginning of the seventeenth century Pope Paul V (papacy 1605–1621) began his own monumental changes to Saint Peter's, which

◀ **Fig. 21.1 Vatican Square as seen from Michelangelo's dome, looking east toward the Tiber.** The long, straight street leading to the Tiber is the Via della Conciliazione, cut by the Fascist dictator Benito Mussolini in the 1930s. Previously, visitors to the Vatican wandered through twisting medieval streets until suddenly they found themselves in the vast, open expanse of the Vatican Square.

SEE MORE View an architectural panorama of the Vatican Square at **www.myartslab.com**

HEAR MORE Listen to an audio file of your chapter at **www.myartslab.com**

Fig. 21.2 Carlo Maderno, facade of Saint Peter's Basilica, Vatican, Rome. 1607–15. Originally the end bays of the facade had bell towers, but because Saint Peter's stood on marshy ground, with underground springs, the towers cracked, and they had to be demolished.

represented the seat of Roman Catholicism. He commissioned the leading architect of his day, Carlo Maderno [mah-DAIR-noh] (1556–1629), to design a new facade for the building (Fig. **21.2**). The columns on the facade "step out" in three progressively projecting planes: At each corner, two flat, rectangular, engaged columns surround the arched side entrances; inside these, two more sets of fully rounded columns step forward from the wall and flank the rectangular side doors of the portico; and finally four majestic columns, two on each side, support the projecting triangular pediment above the main entrance. Maderno also transformed Michelangelo's central Greek-cross plan into a basilican Latin-cross design, extending the length of the nave to just over 636 feet in order to accommodate the large congregations that gathered to celebrate the elaborate ritual of the new Counter-Reformation liturgy (Fig. **21.3**). The visual impact of this facade, extending across the front of the church to the entire width of Michelangelo's original Greek-cross plan, was carefully conceived to leave viewers in a state of awe. As one writer described the effect in 1652, "Anyone contemplating the new church's majesty and grandeur has to admit . . . that its beauty must be the work of angels or its immensity the work of giants. Because its magnificent

Michelangelo, Plan for New
Saint Peter's. 1546–64

Maderno, Plan of Saint
Peter's Basilica. 1607–12

Fig. 21.3 Left: Michelangelo, plan for New Saint Peter's. 1546–1564. Right: Carlo Maderno, plan of Saint Peter's Basilica. 1607–1612. Maderno's plan was motivated by Pope Paul V's belief that Saint Peter's should occupy the footprint of the original wooden basilica that had stood in the spot until Pope Julius II tore it down in 1506.

Map 21.1 Vatican City. ca. 1600. From Vatican City, the pope exercised authority over Rome and the Papal States, most of which were in Central Italy.

proportions are such that . . . neither the Greeks, the Egyptians nor the Jews, nor even the mighty Romans ever produced a building as excellent and vast as this one." It was, in short, an embodiment—and an announcement—of the Church's own triumph over the Protestant threat.

BAROQUE STYLE AND THE COUNTER-REFORMATION

As early as the 1540s, the Catholic Church had begun a program of reform and renewal designed to mitigate the appeal of Protestantism that came to be known as the Counter-Reformation (see Chapter 20). The building and decoration programs that developed in response to this religious program gradually evolved into the style known as Baroque. During the Renaissance, composition had tended to be frontal, creating a visual space that moved away from the viewer in parallel planes, following the rules of scientific perspective. This produced a sense of calm and balance or symmetry. In the Baroque period, elements usually are placed on a diagonal and seem to swirl and flow into one another, producing a sense of action, excitement, and sensuality. Dramatic contrasts of light and dark often serve to create theatrical effects designed to move viewers and draw them into the emotional orbit of the composition.

A profound, sometimes brutally direct, naturalism prevails, as well as a taste for increasingly elaborate and decorative effects, testifying to the Baroque artist's technical skill and mastery of the media used.

In Rome, the patronage of the papal court at the Vatican was most responsible for creating the Baroque style. Pope Sixtus V (papacy 1585–1590) inaugurated the renewal of the city. He cut long, straight avenues through it, linking the major pilgrimage churches to one another, and ordered a **piazza** [pee-AHT-sah]—a space surrounded by buildings—to be opened in front of each church, decorating many of them with Egyptian obelisks salvaged from Roman times. In his brief reign, Sixtus also began to renovate the Vatican, completing the dome of Saint Peter's Basilica, building numerous palaces throughout the city, and successfully reopening one of the city's ancient aqueducts to stabilize the water supply. Over the course of the next century, subsequent popes followed his example with building and art programs of their own.

Sculpture and Architecture: Bernini and His Followers

The new interior space of Saint Peter's Basilica inspired the same feelings of vastness and grandeur as did Carlo Maderno's new facade. The crossing, under Michelangelo's dome, was immense, and its enormity dwarfed the main

Fig. 21.4 Gianlorenzo Bernini, baldachino at crossing of Saint Peter's Basilica, Vatican, Rome. 1624–33. Gilt bronze, height approx. 100ʹ. So grand is the space, and so well does Bernini's baldachino fit in it, that the viewer can scarcely recognize that the structure is the height of the tallest apartment buildings in seventeenth-century Rome.

altar. When Urban VIII (papacy 1623–1644) became pope, he commissioned the young Bernini to design a cast bronze **baldachino** [bahl-da-KEE-noh], or canopy, to help define the altar space (Fig. **21.4**). Part architecture, part sculpture, Bernini's baldachino consists of four twisted columns decorated with spiraling grooves and bronze vines. This undulating, spiraling, decorative effect symbolized the union of the Old and New Testaments, the vine of the Eucharist [YOO-kuh-rist] climbing the columns of the Temple of Solomon. Elements that combine both the Ionic and Corinthian orders top the columns. Figures of angels and putti stand along the entablature, which is decorated with tasseled panels of bronze that imitate cloth. Above the entablature, the baldachino rises crownlike to an orb, symbolizing the universe, and is topped by a cross, symbolizing the reign of Christ. In its immense size, its realization of an architectural plan in sculptural terms, and its synthesis of a wide variety of symbolic elements in a single form, the baldachino is uniquely Baroque in spirit.

The Cornaro Chapel Probably no image sums up the Baroque movement better than Bernini's sculptural program for the Cornaro [kor-NAH-roh] Chapel. Located in Carlo Maderno's Church of Santa Maria della Vittoria in Rome (Fig. **21.5**), it was a commission from the Cornaro family and executed by Bernini in the middle of the century, at about the same time he was working on the colonnade for Saint Peter's Square. Bernini's theme is a pivotal moment in the life of Teresa of Ávila [AH-vih-la] (1515–1582), a Spanish nun, eventually made a saint, who at the age of 40 began to experience mystical religious visions (see Chapter 20). She was by no means the first woman to experience such visions—Hildegard of Bingen had recorded similar visions in her *Scivias* in the twelfth century (see Chapter 10). However, Teresa's own *converso* background—her father was a Jew who had converted to Catholicism—adds another dimension to her faith. Teresa was steeped in the mystical tradition of the Jewish Kabbalah [kuh-BAH-luh], the brand of mystical Jewish thought that seeks to attain the perfection of Heaven while still living in this world by transcending the boundaries of time and space. Bernini illustrates the vision she describes in the following passage (**Reading 21.1**):

READING 21.1

from Teresa of Ávila,"Visions," Chapter 29 of *The Life of Teresa of Ávila* (before 1567)

It pleased the Lord that I should sometimes see the following vision. I would see beside me, on my left hand, an angel in bodily form. . . . He was not tall, but short, and very beautiful, his face so aflame that he appeared to be one of the highest types of angel who seem to be all afire. They must be those who are called cherubim; they do not tell me their names but I am well aware that there is a great difference between certain angels and others, and between these and others still, of a kind that I could not possibly explain. In his hands I saw a long golden spear and at the end of the iron tip I seemed to see a point of fire. With this he seemed to pierce my heart several times so that it penetrated to my entrails. When he drew it out, I thought he was drawing them out with it and he left me completely afire with a great love for God. The pain was so sharp that it made me utter several moans; and so excessive was the sweetness caused me by this intense pain that one

Bernini's program is far more elaborate than just its sculptural centerpiece. The angel and Teresa are positioned beneath a marble canopy from which gilded rays of light radiate, following the path of the real light entering the chapel from the glazed yellow panes of a window hidden from view behind the canopy pediment. Painted angels, sculpted in stucco relief, descend across the ceiling, bathed in a similarly yellow light that appears to emanate from the dove of Christ at the top center of the composition. On each side of the chapel, life-size marble re-creations of the Cornaro family lean out of what appear to be theater boxes into the chapel proper, as if witnessing the vision of Saint Teresa for themselves. Indeed, Bernini's chapel is nothing less than high drama, the stage space of not merely religious vision, but visionary spectacle. Here is an art designed to appeal to the feelings and emotions of its viewers and draw them emotionally into the theatrical space of the work.

Fig. 21.5 Anonymous, Cornaro Chapel. ca. 1654. Oil on canvas, 5'6¼" × 3'¼" Staatliches Museum, Schwerin, Germany. This seventeenth-century painting reproduces the relatively shallow and narrow space of the actual chapel and reveals the Cornaro family portraits at each side of the space.

can never wish to lose it, nor will one's soul be content with anything less than God. It is not bodily pain, but spiritual, though the body has a share in it—indeed, a great share. So sweet are the colloquies of love which pass between the soul and God that if anyone thinks I am lying I beseech God, in His goodness, to give him the same experience.

Bernini recognized in Teresa's words a thinly veiled description of sexual orgasm. And he recognized as well that the sexuality that Protestantism and the Catholic Counter-Reformation had deemed inappropriate to religious art, but which had survived in Mannerism, had found, in Saint Teresa's vision, a properly religious context, uniting the physical and the spiritual. Thus, the sculptural centerpiece of his chapel decoration is Teresa's implicitly erotic swoon, the angel standing over her, having just withdrawn his penetrating arrow from her "entrails," as Teresa throws her head back in ecstasy (Fig. 21.6).

Fig. 21.6 Gianlorenzo Bernini, *The Ecstasy of Saint Teresa,* Cornaro Chapel, Santa Maria della Vittoria, Rome. 1645–52. Marble, height of group, 11' × 6".

LEARN MORE Gain insight from a primary source document on Gian Lorenzo Bernini at **www.myartslab.com**

Fig. 21.7 Gianorenzo Bernini, *David*, 1623. Marble, height 5′ 7″. Galleria Borghese, Rome. Bernini carved this work when he was 25 years old, but he was already carving sculptures of remarkable quality by age 8.

Bernini's *David* The Cornaro Chapel program suggests that the Baroque style is fundamentally theatrical in character, and the space it creates is theatrical space. It also demonstrates how central action was to Baroque representation. Bernini's *David* (Fig. 21.7), commissioned by a nephew of Pope Paul V, appears to be an intentional contrast to Michelangelo's sculpture of the same subject (see Fig. 14.30). Michelangelo's hero is at rest, in a moment of calm anticipation before confronting Goliath. In contrast, Bernini's sculpture captures the young hero in the midst of action. David's body twists in an elaborate spiral, creating dramatic contrasts of light and shadow. His teeth are clenched, and his muscles strain as he prepares to launch the fatal rock. So real is his intensity that viewers tend to avoid standing directly in front of the sculpture, moving to

one side or the other in order, apparently, to avoid being caught in the path of David's shot.

In part, David's action defines Bernini's Baroque style. Whereas Michelangelo's *David* seems to contemplate his own prowess, his mind turned inward, Bernini's David turns outward, into the viewer's space as if Goliath were a presence, although unseen, in the sculpture. In other words, the sculpture is not self-contained, and its active relationship with the space surrounding it—often referred to as its **invisible complement**—is an important feature of Baroque art. (The light source in his Cornaro Chapel *Saint Teresa* is another invisible complement.)

Bernini's Fountains Bernini is responsible for a series of figurative fountains that changed the face of Rome. One of the most celebrated is the *Four Rivers Fountain* in the Piazza Navona [nah-VOH-nuh] (Fig. **21.8**). Bernini designed the fountain for Pope Innocent X, who commissioned it in 1648 to celebrate his diversion of the water from one of Rome's oldest sources of drinking water, the Acqua Vergine [ak-wuh ver-ghin-ee] aqueduct, to the square in front of the Palazzo Pamphili [PAHM-fee-lee], his principal family residence. Rising above the fountain is an Egyptian obelisk that had lain in pieces in the Circus Maxentius [mak-SEN-shus] until restored and re-erected for use here. The sculptor intended the obelisk to represent the triumph of the Roman Catholic Church over the rivers of the world, represented by the four large figures lying on the stones below—the Danube for Europe, the Nile for Africa, the Ganges for Asia, and the Plata for the Americas.

Bernini's fountain was executed by a large group of coworkers under his supervision. In fact, it became commonplace during the Baroque era for leading artists to employ numbers of skilled artists in their studios. This allowed an artist of great stature to turn out massive quantities of work without any apparent loss in quality. Bernini and other Baroque artists like him were admired not so much for the actual finished work, but for the originality of their concepts or designs.

In fact, Bernini spent much of his time writing plays and designing stage sets for them. Only one of his theatrical works survives, a farcical comedy, but we have descriptions of others that suggest his complete dedication to involving the audience in the theatrical event. In a play entitled *Inundation of the Tiber*, he constructed an elaborate set of dikes and dams that seemed to give way as the flooding Tiber advanced from the back of the stage toward the audience. "When the water broke through the last dike," Bernini's biographer tells us, "it flowed forward with such a rush and spread so much terror among the spectators that there was no one, not even among the most knowledgeable, who did not quickly get up to leave in the fear of an actual flood. Then, suddenly, with the opening of a sluice gate, all the water was drained away.

The Society of Jesus

As Bernini conceived it, the Baroque was a compromise between Mannerist exuberance and religious propriety. He fully supported the edicts of the Council of Trent (see Chapter 20) and the teachings of the Society of Jesus founded by the Spanish nobleman Ignatius [ig-NAY-shuhs] of Loyola [loy-OH-luh] (1491–1556). From their headquarters at the

Fig. 21.8 Gianlorenzo Bernini, *Four Rivers Fountain*, Rome. 1648–51. Each major figure was sculpted by a different artist in Bernini's workshop: the Nile, representing Africa, by Jacopo Antonio Fancelli; the Danube, representing Europe, by Antonio Raggi; the Ganges, representing Asia, by Claude Poussin; and the Plata, representing the Americas, by Francesco Baratta.

Fig. 21.9 Giacomo della Porta, facade of Il Gesù, Rome. ca. 1575–84. The church originally appeared much plainer—the sculptures are sixteenth-century additions.

Church of Il Gesù [eel jay-ZOO] in Rome (Fig. **21.9**), the Jesuits, as they were known, led the Counter-Reformation and, as we will see later in the chapter, the influence of the Catholic Church worldwide. All agreed that the purpose of religious art was to teach and inspire the faithful, that it should always be intelligible and realistic, and that it should be an emotional stimulus to piety.

Originally, Michelangelo had agreed, in 1554, to produce drawings and a model for the Church, and although no trace of these survives, the facade, finally designed by Giacomo della Porta (ca. 1533–1602), reflects a certain Michelangelo flair, especially in the swirled volute scrolls flanking the second level, reminiscent of the stairway of the Laurentian Library in Florence (see Fig. 15.17). Likewise, della Porta's use of double pilasters (and, surrounding the portal, a double pilaster and column) is reminiscent of both the double pilasters in Michelangelo's original design for St. Peter's and the double columns surrounding the stairway of the Laurentian Library. Such doubling lends the facade a sense of massive sturdiness—a kind of architectural self-confidence—and a sculptural presence, a three-dimensional play of surfaces in contrast to the two-dimensional effects of the typical Renaissance facade (see *Materials & Techniques*, page 685).

The forcefulness and muscularity of della Porta's design is consistent with Jesuit doctrine. In his *Spiritual Exercises*, published in 1548, Loyola had called on Jesuits to develop all of their senses. By engaging the body, he believed, one might begin to perfect the soul—an idea that surely influenced the

many and richly diverse elements of the Baroque style. For instance, in the Fifth Exercise, a meditation on the meaning of Hell, Loyola invokes all five senses (**Reading 21.2a**):

READING 21.2a

from Ignatius Loyola, *Spiritual Exercises*, Fifth Exercise (1548)

FIRST POINT: This will be to see in imagination the vast fires, and the souls enclosed, as it were, in bodies of fire.
SECOND POINT: To hear the wailing, the howling, cries, and blasphemies against Christ our Lord and against His saints.
THIRD POINT: With the sense of smell to perceive the smoke, the sulphur, the filth, and corruption.
FOURTH POINT: To taste the bitterness of tears, sadness, and remorse of conscience.
FIFTH POINT: With the sense of touch to feel the flames which envelop and burn the souls.

Such a call to the senses would manifest itself in an increasingly elaborate church decoration, epitomized, perhaps best, by a ceiling fresco painted by Andrea Pozzo [POH-tzoh] (1642–1709) for the church of Sant'Ignazio in Rome depicting *The Apotheosis of Saint Ignatius* [sahntig-NAH-tzee-oh] (see *Closer Look*, pages 686–687). But despite this call to sensual experience, Loyola was a strict traditionalist, as is demonstrated by his set of rules for those who comprise what is known as the Church Militant—that is, the living members of the Church who are struggling against sin so that they may one day join those who comprise the Church Triumphant, those who are in heaven (**Reading 21.2b**):

READING 21.2b

from Ignatius Loyola, *Spiritual Exercises*, Rules (1548)

TO HAVE THE TRUE SENTIMENT WHICH WE OUGHT TO HAVE IN THE CHURCH MILITANT
Let the following Rules be observed.
First Rule. All judgment laid aside, we ought to have our mind ready and prompt to obey, in all, the true Spouse of Christ our Lord, which is our holy Mother the Church Hierarchical.
Second Rule. To praise confession to a Priest, and the reception of the most Holy Sacrament of the Altar once in the year, and much more each month, and much better from week to week, with the conditions required and due.
Third Rule. To praise the hearing of Mass often, likewise hymns, psalms, and long prayers, in the church and out of it; likewise the hours set at the time fixed for each Divine Office and for all prayer and all Canonical Hours.

Materials & Techniques

The Facade from Renaissance to Baroque

Typically the facade of a building carries architectural embellishment that announces its style. One of the most influential facades in Renaissance architecture is Leon Battista Alberti's for Santa Maria Novella in Florence. Limited only by the existing portal, doors, and rose window, Alberti designed the facade independently of the structure behind it. He composed it of three squares, two flanking the portal at the bottom and a third set centrally above them. A mezzanine, or low intermediate story, separates them, at once seemingly supported by four large engaged Corinthian columns and serving as the base of the top square. The pediment at the top actually floats free of the structure behind it. Perhaps Alberti's most innovative and influential additions are the two scrolled **volutes** [vuh-LOOTS], or counter-curves. They hide the clerestory structure of the church behind, masking the difference in height of the nave and the much lower side-aisle roofs.

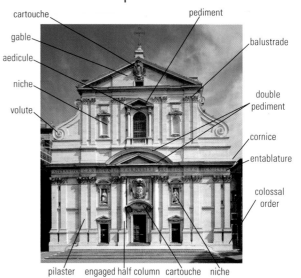

Giacomo della Porta, facade of Il Gesù, Rome. ca. 1575–1584.

Giacomo della Porta's facade for the church of Il Gesù in Rome, constructed more than 100 years later, is still recognizably indebted to Alberti's church, retaining the classic proportions of Renaissance architecture: The height of the structure equals the width. However, it has many more architectural features, and is considered by many the first architectural manifestation of the Baroque. Notice that the architect adds dimensionality to the facade by a projecting entablature and supporting pairs of engaged **pilasters** [pih-LASS-turz] (rectangular columns) that move forward in steps. These culminate in engaged circular columns on each side of the portal. A double pediment, one traditional and triangular, the other curved, crowns the portal itself. Together with the framing column, the double pediment draws attention to the portal, the effect of which is repeated in miniature in the **aedicule** [e-DIK-yool] (composed of an entablature and pediment supported by columns or pilasters) above.

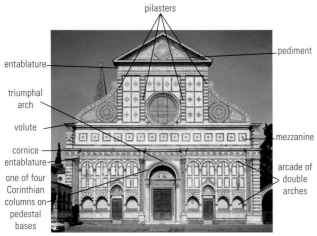

Leon Battista Alberti, facade of Santa Maria Novella, Florence. 1458–70. Dagli Orti/Picture Desk, Inc./Klobal Collection.

Fourth Rule. To praise much Religious Orders, virginity and continence, and not so much marriage as any of these.

Fifth Rule. To praise vows of Religion, of obedience, of poverty, of chastity and of other perfections of supererogation. And it is to be noted that as the vow is about the things which approach to Evangelical perfection, a vow ought not to be made in the things which withdraw from it, such as to be a merchant, or to be married, etc.

Sixth Rule. To praise relics of the Saints, giving veneration to them and praying to the Saints; and to praise Stations, pilgrimages, Indulgences, pardons, Cruzadas, and candles lighted in the churches.

Seventh Rule. To praise Constitutions about fasts and abstinence, as of Lent, Ember Days, Vigils, Friday and Saturday; likewise penances, not only interior, but also exterior.

Eighth Rule. To praise the ornaments and the buildings of churches; likewise images, and to venerate them according to what they represent.

Ninth Rule. Finally, to praise all precepts of the Church, keeping the mind prompt to find reasons in their defence and in no manner against them. . . .

Thirteenth Rule. To be right in everything, we ought always to hold that the white which I see, is black, if the Hierarchical Church so decides it. . . .

By the middle of the seventeenth century, one of the techniques most widely used by Baroque painters was foreshortening, a technique in which perspective is modified in order to decrease the distortion that results when a figure or object extends backward from the picture plane at an angle approaching the perpendicular (for instance, a hand extended out to the viewer will look larger, and the arm shorter, as they actually are). With this technique, artists could break down the barrier between the painting's space and that of the viewer, thus enveloping the viewer in the painting's space, an effect favored for painting the ceilings of Baroque churches and palaces. To create this illusion, the artist would paint representations of architectural elements—such as vaults or arches or niches—and then fill the remaining space with foreshortened figures that seem to fly out of the top of the building into the heavens above. One of the most dramatic instances was painted by a Jesuit lay brother, Fra Andrea Pozzo, for the Church of Sant'Ignazio. Its subject is the *Triumph of Saint Ignatius of Loyola.*

It is difficult for a visitor to Sant'Ignazio to tell that the space above the nave is a barrel vault. Pozzo painted it over with a rising architecture that seems to extend the interior walls an extra story and then explode into the open sky above. A white marble square in the pavement below indicates to the viewer just where to stand to appreciate the perspective properly. On each side of the space overhead are allegorical figures representing the four continents. Inscriptions on each end of the ceiling read, in Latin, "I am come to send fire on the earth," Christ's words to Luke (Luke 12:49), and Ignatius's last words to Francis Xavier as he set out on his mission to Asia, "Go and set the world aflame." Both passages are plays between Ignatius's name and the Latin word for fire, *ignis*, but both also refer to the Jesuit belief in the power of the gospel to transform the world.

Something to Think About . . .

Although Pozzo creates a highly dramatic space by means of foreshortening, how does the painting also impart a sense of physical—and hence moral—order?

America sits on a cougar, spear in hand, and wearing a feathered headdress.

Saint Ignatius follows Christ into heaven, beams of light emanating from his chest to the four corners of the globe.

Europe, sitting on a stallion, holds a sceptre in one hand, while her other rests on an orb, signifying her domination of the world.

Africa sits atop a crocodile and holds an elephant tusk in her hand.

Saint Francis Xavier, co-founder of the Jesuits, who in 1541 left Portugal for India, Indonesia, Japan, and China, where he died in 1552. He was the model for all subsequent Jesuit missionary zeal.

Asia rides a camel, while the small putti to the left offers her a blue-and-white porcelain bowl, presumably from China.

Fra Andrea Pozzo, *Triumph of Saint Ignatius of Loyola.* 1691–94. Ceiling fresco, approx. 56′ × 115′. Sant'Ignazio, Rome.

Loyola's rules are a clear response to the attacks and positions taken up by the Protestant Reformation. They are a call for a discipline that many in the Church seemed to have forgotten, but, perhaps above all, they ask—particularly in Rule 13—for unquestioning submission to Church doctrine, something the Reformation, from the Catholic point of view, had forsaken altogether. Thus, on the one hand, Loyola encouraged the sensual ornamentation of the Church even as he called for an austere intellectual discipline.

San Carlo alle Quattro Fontane Thus it was the grandiose, the elaborate, the ornate—all used to involve the audience in a dramatic action—that came to characterize the Baroque style of the Counter-Reformation. Yet another characteristic is *surprise*. Perhaps the most stunning demonstration of this principle is the Church of San Carlo alle Quattro Fontane (Saint Charles at the Four Fountains) (Fig. **21.10**), the work of Bernini's pupil Francesco Borromini [bor-roh-MEE-nee] (1599–1667). In undertaking this church, Borromini was challenged by a narrow piece of property, its corner cut off for one of the four fountains from which the church takes its name. The nave is a long, oval space—unique in church design—with curved walls and chapels that create an uncanny feeling of movement, as if the walls are breathing in and out (Fig. **21.11**). The dome seems to float above the space. Borromini achieved this effect by inserting windows, partially hidden, at the base of the dome. Light coming through illuminates coffers of alternating hexagons, octagons, and crosses growing smaller as they approach the apex so that they appear visually to ascend to a much greater height than they actually do (Fig. **21.12**).

The church facade is equally bold (see Fig. 21.10). In Baroque church architecture, the facade would increasingly leave the Renaissance traditions of architecture behind, replacing the clarity and balance of someone like Alberti with increasingly elaborate ornamentation (see *Materials & Techniques*, page 685). San Carlo's facade is distinguished

Fig. 21.11 Francesco Borromini, plan of San Carlo alle Quattro Fontane, Rome. 1638.

Fig. 21.10 Francesco Borromini, facade of San Carlo alle Quattro Fontane, Rome. 1665–67. Borromini's innovative church had little impact on Italian architecture, but across the rest of Europe, it freed architecture from the rigors of Renaissance symmetry and balance.

Fig. 21.12 Francesco Borromini, dome of San Carlo alle Quattro Fontane. 1638–41. At the top of the dome is a golden dove. A symbol of the Holy Spirit, it seems about to fly out to the roof to the heavens above.

by colossal columns and concave niches, oval windows on the first floor and square ones above, all topped by a decorative railing, or **balustrade** [BAL-uh-strade], that peaks over a giant **cartouche** [car-TOOCH] (oval frame) supported by angels who seem to hover free of the wall. One four-sided and pointed tower sits oddly at the corner above the fountain; another tower, five-sided, rounded, and slightly taller, stands over the middle of the structure. The balance and symmetry that dominated Church architecture since the early Renaissance are banished. In their stead is a new sense of the building as a living thing, as an opportunity for innovation and freedom. So liberating, in fact, was the design of San Carlo Quattro Fontane that Church fathers answered requests for its plan from all over Europe.

THE DRAMA OF PAINTING: CARAVAGGIO AND THE CARAVAGGISTI

One of the characteristics of San Carlo alle Quattro Fontane is the play of light and dark that its irregular walls and geometries create. Ever since the Middle Ages, when Abbot Suger [soo-ZHAY] of Saint-Denis [san duh-NEE], Paris, had insisted on the power of light to heighten spiritual feeling in the congregation, particularly through the use of stained glass, light had played an important role in church architecture (see Chapter 12). Bernini used it to great effect in his *Ecstasy of Saint Theresa* (see Fig. 21.6), and Baroque painters, seeking to intensify the viewer's experience of their paintings, sought to manipulate light and dark to great advantage as well. The acknowledged master of light and dark, and perhaps the most influential painter of his day, was Michelangelo Merisi, known as Caravaggio [kah-rah-VAH-gee-oh] (1571–1610), after the town in northern Italy where he was born. His work inspired many followers, who were called the Caravaggisti [kah-rah-vah-GEE-stee].

Master of Light and Dark: Caravaggio

Caravaggio arrived in Rome in about 1593 and began a career of revolutionary painting and public scandal. His first major commission in Rome was *The Calling of Saint Matthew* (Fig. **21.13**), arranged for by his influential patron Cardinal del Monte and painted about 1599 to 1600 for the Contarelli [con-tah-RAY-lee] Chapel in the Church of San Luigi dei Francesi [sahn LWEE-gee day frahn-CHAY-zee], the church of the French community (dei Francesi) in Rome. The most dramatic element in this work is light.

Fig. 21.13 Caravaggio, *The Calling of Saint Matthew*. ca. 1599–1600. Oil on canvas, 11′ 1″ × 11′ 5″. Contarelli Chapel, San Luigi dei Francesi, Rome. The window at the top of the painting is covered by parchment, often used by painters to diffuse light in their studios. This makes the intensity of light entering the room from the right especially remarkable.

The light that streams in from an unseen window at the upper right of the painting is almost palpable. It falls onto the table where the tax collector Levi (Saint Matthew's name before becoming one of Jesus' apostles) and his four assistants count the day's take, highlighting their faces and gestures. They are dressed not of Jesus' time, but of Caravaggio's, making it more possible for his audience to identify with them. With Saint Peter at his side, Christ enters from the right, a halo barely visible above his head. He reaches out with his index finger extended in a gesture derived from Adam's gesture toward God in the Sistine Chapel ceiling *Creation*—an homage, doubtless, by the painter to his namesake (see Fig. 15.11). One of the figures at the table—it is surely Levi, given his central place in the composition—points with his left hand, perhaps at himself, as if to say, "Who, me?" or perhaps at the young man bent over at the corner of the table intently counting money, as if to say, "You mean him?" All in all, he seems to find the arrival of Jesus uninteresting. In fact, the assembled group is so ordinary—reminiscent of gamblers seated around a table—that the transformation of Levi into Saint Matthew, which is imminent, takes on the aspect of a miracle, just as the light flooding the scene is reminiscent of the original miracle of creation: "And God said, 'Let there be light: and there was light'" (Gen. 1:3). The scene also echoes the New Testament, specifically John 8:12, where Christ says: "I am the light of the world; he that followeth me shall not walk in darkness, but shall have the light of life."

Caravaggio's insistence on the reality of his scene is thus twofold: He only depicts real people of his own day engaged in real tasks (by implication, Christ himself assumes a human reality as well), but he also insists on the reality of its psychological drama. The revelatory power of light—its ability to reveal the world in all its detail—is analogous, in Caravaggio's painting, to the transformative power of faith. Faith, for Caravaggio, fundamentally changes the way we *see* the world, and the way we *act* in it. Time and again, his paintings dramatize this moment of conversion through use of the technique known as **tenebrism** [TEN-uh-briz-um]. As

opposed to *chiaroscuro*, which many artists employ to create spatial depth and volumetric forms through slight gradations of light and dark, a tenebrist style is not necessarily connected to modeling at all. Tenebrism makes use of large areas of dark contrasting sharply with smaller brightly illuminated areas. In *The Calling of Saint Matthew*, Christ's hand and face rise up out of the darkness, as if his very gesture creates light itself—and by extension Matthew's salvation.

One of the clearest instances of Caravaggio's use of light to dramatize moments of conversion is the *Conversion of Saint Paul*, painted around 1601 (Fig. **21.14**). Though

Fig. 21.14 Caravaggio, *Conversion of Saint Paul*. ca. 1601. Oil on canvas, 90 $^1/_2$″ × 68 $^7/_8$″. Santa Maria del Popolo, Rome. This painting was designed to fill the right wall of the narrow Carasi family chapel in Santa Maria del Popolo. Caravaggio had to paint it to be seen at angle of about 45 degrees, a viewpoint that can be replicated by tipping this page inward about half open to an angle of 45 degrees to the reader's face. The resulting space is even more dramatic and dynamic.

LEARN MORE   Gain insight from a primary source document on Caravaggio at **www.myartslab.com**

painted nearly 50 years before Bernini's *Ecstasy of Saint Teresa* (see Fig. 21.6), its theme is essentially the same, as is its implied sexuality. Here, Caravaggio portrays the moment when the Roman legionnaire Saul (who will become Saint Paul) has fallen off his horse and hears the words, "Saul, Saul, why persecutest thou me?" (Acts 9:4). Neither Saul's servant nor his horse hears a thing. Light, the visible manifestation of Christ's words, falls on the foreshortened soldier. Saul reaches into the air in both a shock of recognition and a gesture of embrace. A sonnet, "Batter My Heart," by the English metaphysical poet John Donne [dun] (1572–1631), published in 1618 in his *Holy Sonnets*, captures Saul's experience in words (**Reading 21.3**):

READING 21.3

John Donne, "Batter My Heart" (1618)

Batter my heart, three-person'd God, for you
As yet but knock, breathe, shine, and seek to mend;
That I may rise and stand, o'erthrow me, and bend
Your force to break, blow, burn, and make me new.
I, like an usurp'd town to'another due,
Labor to'admit you, but oh, to no end;
Reason, your viceroy in me, me should defend,
But is captiv'd, and proves weak or untrue.
Yet dearly' I love you, and would be lov'd fain,
But am betroth'd unto your enemy;
Divorce me,'untie or break that knot again,
Take me to you, imprison me, for I,
Except you'enthrall me, never shall be free,
Nor ever chaste, except you ravish me.

There is no reason to believe the English poet—who was raised a Catholic but converted to the Anglican church for his own safety and prosperity—knew the Italian's painting, but the fact that the two men share so completely in the ecstasy of the moment of conversion, imaged as physical ravishment, suggests how widespread such conceits were in the seventeenth century. Both share with Teresa of Ávila a profound mysticism, the pursuit of achieving communion or identity with the divine through direct experience, intuition, or insight. All three believe that such experience is the ultimate source of knowledge or understanding, and they seek to convey that in their art. Such mystical experience, in its extreme physicality and naturalistic representation, also suggests how deeply the Baroque as a style was committed to sensual experience.

Caravaggio would openly pursue this theme in a series of homoerotic paintings commissioned by the same Cardinal del Monte [MON-tay] who arranged for the painting of *The Calling of Saint Matthew*. These paintings depict seminude young men, quite clearly youths from the streets of Rome, dressed in Bacchic [BAK-ik] costume. In his *Bacchus* (Fig. **21.15**), the slightly plump but also attractively muscular boy offers the viewer a glass of wine at the same time that he seems, with his right hand, to be undoing the belt of his robe. This is not the mythic Bacchus, but a boy dressed up as Bacchus, probably

Fig. 21.15 Caravaggio, *Bacchus.* ca. 1597. Oil on canvas, 37 $^3/_8$" × 33 $^1/_2$". Galleria degli Uffizi, Florence. One of the ways in which Caravaggio exhibits his skill in this painting is the handle of the wine goblet held by the boy. It is at once volumetric and transparent.

pulled off the street by Caravaggio to pose, as the dirt beneath his fingernails attests. The bowl of fruit in the foreground is a still life that suggests not only Caravaggio's virtuosity as a naturalistic painter, but, along with the wine, the pleasures of indulging the sensual appetites and, with them, carnal pleasure. In fact, paintings such as this one suggest that Caravaggio transformed the religious paintings for which he received commissions into images that he preferred to paint—scenes of everyday people, of erotic and dramatic appeal, and physical (not spiritual) beauty. These same appetites are openly celebrated, in the same spirit, in many of John Donne's poems, such as "The Flea" (see **Reading 21.4**, page 701).

Elisabetta Sirani and Artemisia Gentileschi: Caravaggisti Women

Caravaggio had a profound influence on other artists of the seventeenth century. Two of these were women. Like her sixteenth-century Bolognese [boh-loh-NEEZ] predecessor, Lavinia Fontana (see Chapter 20), Elisabetta Sirani [sih-RAH-nee] (1638–1665) was the daughter of a painter. Although trained in the refined, classical tradition, Sirani developed a taste for realism much like Caravaggio's and shared his willingness to depict the miracles of Christianity as if they were everyday events. Most of her paintings were for private patrons, and she produced more than 190 works before her early death at age 27; by then she had become a cultural hero and tourist attraction in Bologna for the easy way she could dash off a picture. She painted portraits, religious

Fig. 21.16 Elisabetta Sirani (1638–1665), *Virgin and Child.* **1663.** Oil on canvas, 34 ″ × 27 ¹/₂ ″. National Museum of Women in the Arts, Washington, D.C. Gift of Wallace and Wilhelmina Holladay. Conservation funds generously provided by the Southern California State Committee of the National Museum of Women in the Arts. The artist signed and dated this picture in gold letters as if sewn into the horizontal seam of the pillow.

works, allegorical works, and occasionally mythological works and stories from ancient history.

Sirani's *Virgin and Child* of 1663 portrays Mary as a young Italian mother, wearing a turban of the kind favored by Bolognese peasant women (Fig. **21.16**). The Virgin's white sleeve, thickly painted to emphasize the rough texture of homespun wool, is consistent with the lack of ornamentation in the painting as a whole. The only decorative elements are the pillow on which the baby sits and the garland with which he is about to crown his mother, in a gesture that seems nothing more than playful.

One of Caravaggio's most important followers, and one of the first women artists to achieve an international reputation, was Artemisia Gentileschi [jen-tee-LESS-key] (1593–1652/3). Born in Rome, she was raised by her father, Orazio, himself a painter and Caravaggisto. Orazio was among Caravaggio's closest friends. As a young girl, Artemisia could not have helped but hear of Caravaggio's frequent run-ins with the law—for throwing a plate of artichokes at a waiter, for street brawling, for carrying weapons illegally, and, ultimately, in 1606, for murdering a referee in a tennis match. Artemisia's own scandal would follow. It and much of her painting must be understood within the context of this social milieu—the loosely renegade world of Roman artists at the start of the seventeenth century. In 1612, when she was 19, she was raped by Agostino Tassi, a Florentine artist who worked in her father's studio and served as her teacher. Orazio filed suit against Tassi for injury and damage to his daughter. The transcript of the seven-month trial survives. Artemisia accused Tassi of repeatedly trying to meet with her alone in her bedroom and, when he finally succeeded, of raping her. When he subsequently promised to marry her, she freely accepted his continued advances, naïvely assuming marriage would follow. When he refused to marry her, the lawsuit followed.

At trial, Tassi accused her of having slept with many others before him. Gentileschi was tortured with thumbscrews to "prove" the validity of her testimony, and was examined by midwives to ascertain how recently she had lost her virginity. Tassi further humiliated her by claiming that Artemisia was an unskilled artist who did not even understand the laws of perspective. Finally, a former friend of Tassi's testified that Tassi had boasted about his exploits with Artemisia. Ultimately, he was convicted of rape but served only a year in prison. Soon after the long trial ended, Artemesia married an artist and moved with him to Florence. In 1616, she was admitted to the Florentine Academy of Design.

Beginning in 1612, Artemisia painted five separate versions of the biblical story of Judith and Holofernes [hol-uh-FUR-neez]. The subject was especially popular in Florence, which identified with both the Jewish hero David and the Jewish heroine Judith (both of whom had been celebrated in sculptures by Donatello and Michelangelo). When Artemisia moved there, her personal investment in the subject found ready patronage in the city. Nevertheless, it is nearly impossible to see the paintings outside the context of her biography. She painted her first version of the theme during and just after the trial itself, and the last, *Judith and Maidservant with Head of Holofernes*, in about 1625 (Fig. **21.17**), suggesting that in this series she transforms her personal tragedy in her painting. In all of them, Judith is a self-portrait of the artist. In the Hebrew Bible's Book of Judith, the Jewish heroine enters the enemy Assyrian camp intending to seduce their lustful leader, Holofernes, who has laid siege to her people. When Holofernes falls asleep, she beheads him with his own sword and carries her trophy back to her people in a bag. The Jews then go on to defeat the leaderless Assyrians.

Gentileschi lights the scene by a single candle, dramatically accentuating the Caravaggesque [kah-rah-vah-JESK] tenebrism of the presentation. Judith shades her eyes from its light, presumably in order to look out into the darkness that surrounds her. Her hand also invokes our silence, as if danger lurks nearby. The maid stops wrapping Holofernes's head in a towel, looking on alertly herself. Together, mistress and maid, larger than life-size and heroic, have taken their revenge on not only the Assyrians, but on lust-driven men in general. As is so often the case in Baroque painting, the space of the drama is larger than the space of the frame. The same invisible complement outside Bernini's *David* (see Fig. 21.7) hovers in the darkness beyond reach of our vision here.

Gentileschi was not attracted to traditional subjects like the Annunciation. She preferred biblical and mythological heroines and women who played major roles. In addition to Judith, she dramatized the stories of Susannah, Bathsheba, Lucretia, Cleopatra, Esther, Diana, and Potiphar. A good business woman, Gentileschi also knew how to exploit the taste for paintings of female nudes.

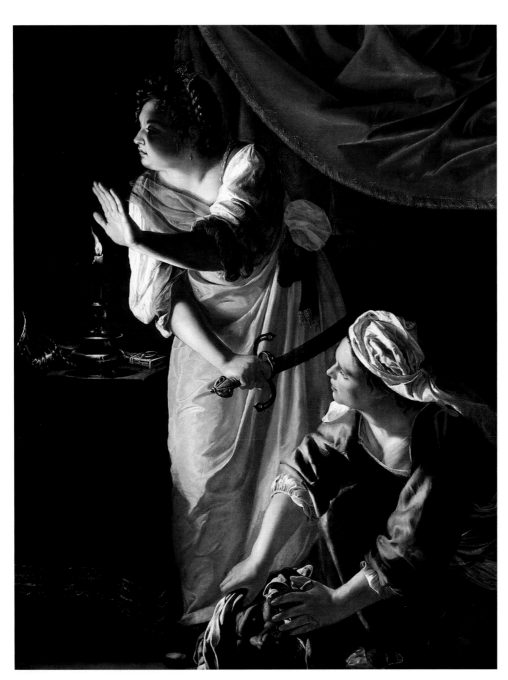

Fig. 21.17 Artemisia Gentileschi, *Judith and Maidservant with Head of Holofernes.* **ca. 1625.** Oil on canvas, 72 1/2″ × 55 3/4″. The Detroit Institute of Arts. Gift of Leslie H. Green. 52.253. Photo © 1984 Detroit Institute of Art. Judith is a traditional symbol of fortitude, a virtue with which Artemisia surely identified.

EXPLORE MORE Gain insight from a primary source document on Artemisia Gentileschi at **www.myartslab.com**

VENICE AND BAROQUE MUSIC

In the sixteenth century, the Council of Trent had recognized the power of music to convey moral and spiritual ideals. "The whole plan of singing," it wrote in an edict issued in 1552,

> should be constituted not to give empty pleasure to the ear, but in such a way that the words be clearly understood by all, and thus the hearts of the listeners be drawn to the desire of heavenly harmonies, in the contemplation of the joys of the blessed. . . . They shall also banish from church all music that contains, whether in the singing or in the organ playing, things that are lascivious or impure.

In other words, the Council rejected the use of secular music, which by definition it deemed lascivious and impure, as a model for sacred compositions. Renaissance composers such as Guillaume Dufay and Josquin des Prez (see Chapters 14 and 15) had routinely used secular music in composing their masses, and Protestants had adapted the chorales of their liturgy from existing melodies, both religious and secular.

The division between secular and religious music was far less pronounced in Venice, a city that had traditionally chafed at papal authority. As a result, Venetian composers felt freer to experiment and work in a variety of forms, so much so that in the seventeenth century, the city became the center of musical innovation and practice in Europe.

Giovanni Gabrieli and the Drama of Harmony

Venice earned its place at the center of the musical world largely through the efforts of Giovanni Gabrieli [gah-bree-AY-lee] (1556–1612), the principal organist at Saint Mark's Cathedral. Gabrieli composed many secular madrigals, but he also responded to the Counter-Reformation's edict to make church music more emotionally engaging. To do this, he expanded on the polychoral style that Adrian Willaert had developed at Saint Marks in the mid-1500s (see Chapter 15). Gabrieli located contrasting bodies of sound in different areas of the cathedral's interior, which already had two organs, one on each side of the chancel (the space containing the altar and seats for the clergy and choir). Playing them against one another, he was able to produce effects of stunning sonority. Four choirs—perhaps a boys' choir, a women's ensemble, basses and baritones, and tenors in another group—sang from separate balconies above the nave. Positioned in the alcoves were brass instruments, including trombones and cornetts. (A cornett was a hybrid wind instrument, combining a brass mouthpiece with woodwind finger technique. The nineteenth-century band instrument has a similar name but is spelled with a single "t.") Both the trombone and the cornett were staples of Venetian street

processions. And the street processions of the Venetian confraternities or *scuole* (see Chapter 15) are in many ways responsible for the development of instrumental music in Venice. By 1570, there were approximately 40 street processions a year, with each of the six confraternities participating. Each *scuola* was accompanied through the streets by singers, bagpipes, shawms (a double reed instrument similar to a bagpipe, but without the bag), drums, recorders, viols, flutes, and *pifarri*, or ensembles of wind instruments often composed of cornetts and trombones (two or three of each) (Fig. **21.18**). The Venetian love for these ensembles quickly led to the adaptation from secular ceremonies to religious ones (many of the *scuole* processions were associated with religious feast days in the first place).

Gabrieli was among the first to write religious music intended specifically for wind ensemble—music that was independent of song and that could not, in fact, be easily sung. One such piece is his 1597 *Canzona Duodecimi Toni* [kan-ZOH-na doo-oh-DAY-chee-me TOH-nee] (*Canzona in the Twelfth Mode [or Tone]*), in which two brass ensembles create a musical dialogue (track 21.1). A **canzona** is a type of instrumental contrapuntal work, derived from Renaissance secular song, like the madrigal, which was increasingly performed in the seventeenth century in church settings. It is particularly notable for its dominant rhythm, LONG-short-short, known as the "canzona rhythm." In Saint Mark's, the two ensembles would have been placed across from one another in separate lofts. The alternating sounds of cornett and trombone or, in other compositions, brass ensemble, choir, and organ coming from various parts of the cathedral at different degrees of loudness and softness create a total effect similar to stereo "surround sound."

HEAR MORE at www.myartslab.com

For each part of his composition, Gabrieli chose to designate a specific voice or instrument, a practice we have come to call **orchestration**. Furthermore, he controlled the **dynamics** (variations and contrast in force or intensity) of the composition by indicating, at least occasionally, the words *piano* ("soft") or *forte* ("loud"). In fact, he is the first known composer to specify dynamics. The dynamic contrasts of loud and soft in the *Canzona Duodecimi Toni*, mirroring the taste for tenebristic contrasts of light and dark in Baroque painting, is a perfect example of Gabrieli's use of dynamic variety. As composers from across Europe came to Venice to study, they took these terms back with them, and Italian became the international language of music.

Finally, and perhaps most important, Gabrieli organized his compositions around a central note, called the **tonic note** (usually referred to as the **tonality** or **key** of the composition). This tonic note provides a focus for the composition. The ultimate resolution of the composition into the tonic, as in the *Canzona Duodecimi Toni*, where the tonic note is C, the twelfth mode (or "tone") in Gabrieli's harmonic system, provides the heightened sense of harmonic drama that typifies the Baroque.

Fig. 21.18 Detail of Gentile Bellini, *Procession of the Reliquary of the True Cross in Piazza San Marco.* 1496. Oil on canvas, 12 $^1/_2$″ × 24′ 5 $^1/_4$″. Gallerie dell'Accademia, Venice. (See Fig. 15.23) The procession here includes six *trombe lunghe,* or long silver trumpets, followed by three shawms, and two trombonists.

Claudio Monteverdi and the Birth of Opera

A year after Gabrieli's death, Claudio Monteverdi [KLAU-dee-oh mohn-tay-VAIR-dee] (1567–1643) was appointed musical director at Saint Mark's in Venice. A violinist, Monteverdi had been the music director at the court of Mantua. In Venice, Monteverdi proposed a new relation of text (words) and music. Where traditionalists favored the subservience of text to music—"Harmony is the ruler of the text," proclaimed Giovanni Artusi, the most ardent defendant of the conservative position—Monteverdi proclaimed just the opposite: "Harmony is the mistress of the text!" Monteverdi's position led him to master a new, text-based musical form, the **opera**, a term that is the plural of *opus*, or "work." Operas are works consisting of many smaller works. (The term *opus* is used, incidentally, to catalogue the musical compositions of a given composer, usually abbreviated *op.*, so that "op. 8" would mean the eighth work or works published in the composer's repertoire.)

The form itself was first developed by a group known as the Camerata of Florence (*camerata* means "club" or "society"), a group dedicated to discovering the style of singing used by the ancient Greeks in their drama, which had united poetry and music but was known only through written accounts. The group's discussions stimulated the composer Giulio Caccini to write *New Works of Music.* Here, he describes what the Camerata considered the ancient Greek ideal of music (**Reading 21.5**):

Over the course of the 1580s and 1590s, Caccini and others began to write works that placed a solo vocal line above an instrumental line, known as the **basso continuo**, or "continuous bass," usually composed of a keyboard instrument (organ, harpsichord, etc.) and bass instrument (usually a cello), that was conceived as a supporting accompaniment, not as the harmonic equivalent, to the vocal line. This combination of solo voice and *basso continuo* came to be known as **monody**.

The inspiration for Monteverdi's first opera, *Orfeo* [or-FAY-oh] (1607), was the musical drama of ancient Greek theater. The **libretto** [lih-BRET-toh] (or "little book") for Monteverdi's opera was based on the Greek myth of Orpheus [OR-fee-us] and Eurydice [yoor-ID-ih-see]. In the opera, shepherds and nymphs celebrate the love of Orpheus and Eurydice in a dance that is interrupted by the news that Eurydice has died of a snake bite. The grieving Orpheus, a great musician and poet, travels to the underworld to bring Eurydice back. His plea for her return so moves Pluto, the god of the underworld, that he grants it, but only if Orpheus does not look back at Eurydice as they leave. But anxious for her safety, he does glance back and loses her forever. Monteverdi did, however, offer his audience some consolation (if not really a happy ending): Orfeo's father, Apollo, comes down to take his son back to the heavens where he can behold the image of Eurydice forever in the stars.

Although *Orfeo* is by no means the first opera, it is generally accepted as the first to successfully integrate music and drama. Monteverdi tells the story through a variety of musical genres—choruses, dances, and instrumental interludes. Two particular forms stand out—the **recitativo** [ray-chee-tah-TEE-voh] and the **aria** [AH-ree-uh]. *Recitativo* is a style of singing that imitates very closely the rhythms of speech. Used for dialogue, it allows for a more rapid telling of the story than might be possible otherwise. The *aria* would eventually develop into an elaborate solo or duet song that expresses the singer's emotions and feelings, expanding on the dialogue of the recitative (in Monteverdi's hands, the aria could still be sung in recitative style). "The modern composer," Monteverdi wrote, "builds his works on the basis of truth," and he means by this, most of all, the emotional truth that we have come to expect of the Baroque in general. Orfeo's *recitativo* after learning of the death of Eurydice is one of the most moving scenes in this opera (track **21.2**). He sings passionately first of his grief:

((•■ HEAR MORE at
www.myartslab.com

Tu se' morta, se' morta mia vita ed io respiro?	You are dead, my life, and I am still breathing?
Tu se' de me partita, se' da me partitat per mai piu, mia piu non tonare, ed io rimango?	You have left me, left me, Never more to return, and I remain here?

The melody imitates speech by rising at the end of each question. Then, when Orfeo decides to go back to the underworld and plead for Eurydice's return, the music reflects his shift from despair to determination. But even in this second section, as he expresses his dream of freeing

Eurydice, when he sings of the "lowest depths" (*profundi abissi* [pro-FOHN-dee ah-BEE-see]) of the underworld or of "death" (*morte* [MOR-tay]) itself, the melody descends to low notes in harmony with the words. Moment by moment, Monteverdi's music mirrors the emotional state of the character.

Orfeo required an orchestra of three dozen instruments—including ten viols, three trombones, and four trumpets—to perform the overture, interludes, and dance sequences, but generally only a harpsichord or lute accompanied the arias and recitatives so that the voice would remain predominant. For the age, this was an astonishingly large orchestra, financed together with elaborate staging by the Mantuan court where it was composed and first performed, and it provided Monteverdi with a distinct advantage over previous opera composers. He could achieve what his operatic predecessors could only imagine—a work that was both musically and dramatically satisfying, one that could explore the full range of sound and, with it, the full range of psychological complexity.

Arcangelo Corelli and the Sonata

The *basso continuo* developed by Caccini and others to support the solo voice also influenced purely instrumental music, especially in the sonatas of the Roman composer and violinist Arcangelo Corelli (1653–1713). The term **sonata** as we use it today, did not develop until the last half of the eighteenth century. In the Baroque era, it had a much more general meaning. In Italian, *sonata* simply means "that which is sounded," or played by instruments, as opposed to that which is sung, the *cantata*. By the end of the seventeenth century, the **trio sonata** had developed a distinctive form. As the word "trio" suggests, it consists of three parts: two higher voices, usually written for violins, but often performed by two flutes, or two oboes, or any combination of these, that play above a *basso continuo*. One of the results of this arrangement is that the *basso continuo* harmonizes with the higher voices, resulting in distinct chord clusters that often provide a dense textural richness to the composition.

There were two main types of sonata, a secular form, the **sonata da camera** (chamber sonata), and a religious form, the **sonata da chiesa** (church sonata). Corelli wrote both. The *sonata da camera* consists of a suite of dances, and the *sonata da chiesa* generally consists of four **movements**, or independent sections, beginning with a slow, dignified movement, followed by a fast, imitative movement, then slow and fast again. The distinctive feature of both forms is the primacy of a particular major or minor scale. At the least, the first and last movements of such works share the same key; in the case of the *sonata da camera*, every movement might be in the same key.

Corelli quickly adopted the form because it allowed him, as a virtuoso violinist, to compose pieces for himself that showcased his talents. It was further expected that virtuoso violinists would embellish their musical lines. The following, from a single piece of sheet music from Corelli's violin sonata, Opus no. 5, shows the *basso continuo* in the bass clef and the complex violin part, filled with intricate runs of musical notes, as Corelli actually played it in the treble clef:

From Arcangelo Corelli, Opus no. 5. Dagli Orti/Picture Desk, Inc./Klobal Collection.

Thus, against the clear notation of the melody in the music, the solo voice performs with rhythmic freedom.

Antonio Vivaldi and the Concerto

Corelli's instrumental flair deeply influenced Venice's most important composer of the early eighteenth century, Antonio Vivaldi [vee-VAHL-dee] (1678–1741). Vivaldi, son of the leading violinist at Saint Mark's, assumed the post of musical director at the Ospedale della Pietà [oh-spay-DAH-lay DAY-lah pee-ay-TAH] in 1703, one of four orphanages in Venice that specialized in music instruction for girls. (Boys at the orphanages were not trained in music since it was assumed they would enter the labor force.) As a result, many of the most talented harpsichordists, lutenists, and other musicians in Venice were female, and many of Vivaldi's works were written specifically for performance by Ospedali [oh-spay-DAH-lee] girl choirs and instrumental ensembles (Fig. 21.19). By and large, the Ospedali musicians were young girls who would subsequently go on to either a religious life or marriage, but several were middle-aged women who remained in the Ospedali, often as teachers, for their entire lives. The directors of the Ospedali hoped that wealthy members of the audience would be so dazzled by the performances that they would donate money to the orphanages. Audiences from across Europe attended these concerts, which were among the first in the history of Western music that took place outside a church or theater and were open to the public. And they were, in fact, dazzled by the talent of these female musicians; by all accounts, they were as skilled and professional as any of their male counterparts in Europe.

Fig. 21.19 Jacopo Guarana, *Apollo Conducting a Choir of Maidens*. 1776. Oil on canvas. Ospedaletto, Salla della Musica, Venice. The Ospedaletto church was the performance space for the girls of the orphanage of Santa Maria dei Derelitti. Although Apollo conducts in this painting, the ensemble director can be seen in yellow, just behind the right column, score in hand.

Vivaldi specialized in composing **concertos** [kun-CHAIR-tohs], a three-movement secular form of instrumental music, popular at court, which had already been established, largely by Corelli. Vivaldi systematized its form. The first movement of a concerto is usually *allegro* (quick and cheerful), the second slower and more expressive, like the pace of an opera aria, and the third a little livelier and faster than the first. Concertos usually feature one or more solo instruments that, in the first and third movements particularly, perform passages of material, called *episodes*, that contrast back and forth with the orchestral score—a form known as **ritornello** [re-tor-NEL-loh], "something that returns" (i.e., returning thematic material). At the outset, the entire orchestra performs the *ritornello* in the tonic—the specific home pitch around which the composition is organized. Solo episodes interrupt alternating with the *ritornello*, performed in partial form and in different keys, back and forth, until the *ritornello* returns again in its entirety in the tonic in the concluding section.

Ritornello

In the course of his career, Vivaldi composed nearly 600 concertos—for violin, cello, flute, piccolo, oboe, bassoon, trumpet, guitar, and even recorder. Most of these were performed by the Ospedale ensemble. The most famous is a group of four violin concertos, one for each season of the year, called *The Four Seasons*. It is an example of what would later come to be known as **program music**, or purely instrumental music in some way connected to a story or idea. The program of the first of these concertos, *Spring* (track **21.3**) is supplied by a sonnet, written by Vivaldi himself, at the top of the score. The first eight lines suggest the text for the first movement, and the last six lines, divided into two groups of three, the text for the second and third movements:

> Spring has arrived, and full of joy
> The birds greet it with their happy song.
> The streams, swept by gentle breezes,
> Flow along with a sweet murmur.
> Covering the sky with a black cloak,
> Thunder and lightning come to announce the season.
> When all is quiet again, the little birds
> Return to their lovely song.

The *ritornello* in this concerto is an exuberant melody played by the whole ensemble. It opens the movement, and corresponds to the poem's first line. Three solo violins respond in their first episode—"the birds greet it with their happy song"—imitating the song of birds. In the second episode, they imitate "streams swept by gentle breezes," then, in the third, "thunder and lightning," and finally the birds again, which "Return to their lovely song." The whole culminates with the *ritornello*, once again resolved in the tonic.

In its great rhythmic freedom (the virtuoso passages given to the solo violin, recalling the improvisational embellishments of Corelli) and the polarity between orchestra and solo instruments (the contrasts of high and low timbres, or sounds, such as happy bird song and clashing thunder), Vivaldi's concerto captures much of what differentiates Baroque music from its Renaissance predecessors. Gone are the balanced and flowing rhythms of the *prima prattica* and the polyphonic composition in which all voices are of equal importance. Perhaps most of all, the drama of beginning a composition in a tonic key, moving to different keys and then returning to the tonic—a process known as **modulation**—could be said to distinguish Baroque composition from what had come earlier. The dramatic effect of this modulation, together with the rich texture of the composition's chord clusters, parallels the dramatic lighting of Baroque painting, just as the embellishment of the solo voice finds its equivalent in the ornamentation of Baroque architecture.

As an instrumental composition, *The Four Seasons* naturally foregoes the other great innovation of the Baroque, the *secunda prattica*'s emphasis on an actual text, as found particularly in opera. Even in Rome, where sacred music dominated the scene, opera began to take hold. In 1632, an opera by Stefano Landi (1590–1639), with stage designs by Gian Lorenzo Bernini, premiered at a theater seating no fewer than 3,000 spectators inside the walls of the Barberini [bar-buh-REE-nee] palace, home of the Barberini pope Urban VIII (papacy 1622–1623). Like many of the Roman operas that followed, its subject was sacred, *Sant'Allessio* [sahnt-ah-LESS-ee-oh] (Saint Alexander), and it convinced the Church that sung theater could convey moral and spiritual ideas. This conviction would shortly give rise to a new genre of vocal music, the **oratorio** [or-uh-TOR-ee-oh]. Generally based on religious themes, the oratorio shared some of opera's musical elements, including the *basso continuo*, the aria, and the recitative, but it was performed without the dazzle of staging and costume. This development of Baroque music will be discussed in Chapter 24.

The End of Italian Ascendency

In France, the finance minister to King Louis [loo-EE] XIV was wise in matters far beyond finance. Jean-Baptiste Colbert [kohl-BAIR] counseled the king that "apart from striking actions in warfare, nothing is so well able to show the greatness and spirit of princes than buildings; and all posterity will judge them by the measure of those superb habitations which they have built during their lives." The king was looking for an architect to design a new east facade for the Palais du Louvre [pah-LAY dew loov] in Paris, which would house the new royal apartments. For such grand plans, the world's most famous—and original—architect, Gian Lorenzo Bernini, was the obvious choice. With the pope's permission, Bernini departed for Paris. Large and adoring crowds greeted him in every city through which he passed.

In Paris, he received a royal welcome, but the king was far from happy with Bernini's plans for the Louvre (Fig. 21.20). Although he accepted the plans, and foundations were poured, he concluded, after Bernini returned to Rome, that the Italian's design was too elaborate and ornate. Furthermore, French architects were protesting the award of such an important commission to a foreigner. The architect Louis Le Vau [loo-EE leh voh], the painter Charles Le Brun [sharl leh brun], and the physician, mathematician, and architectural historian Claude Perrault [peh-ROH] together designed a simpler, more classically inspired facade (Fig. 21.21), consisting of five

Fig. 21.20 Gianlorenzo Bernini, design for the east facade of the Palais du Louvre, Paris. 1664. Musée du Louvre, Paris.

Fig. 21.21 Louis Le Vau, Claude Perrault, and Charles Le Brun, east facade, Palais du Louvre, Paris. 1667–70.

units, centered by a triangular pediment and paired Corinthian colonnades. Louis was so pleased that he added paired colonnades to the other facades of the palace.

This debate between the ornate and the classical, the sensuous and the austere, would define the art of the eighteenth century. Baroque ornamentation, epitomized in the seventeenth century by Bernini, would become even more exaggerated in the eighteenth, transformed into the fanciful and playful decoration of the so-called Rococo style. Ironically, this happened especially at the French court. The forms of classical Greek and Roman architecture offered a clear alternative, countering what seemed to many an art of self-indulgence, even moral depravity. Painting, too, could abandon the emotional theatrics of the Baroque and appeal instead to the intellect and reason, assuming a solidity of form as stable as architecture.

Louis XIV's rejection of Bernini's plan marks the end of the ascendency of Italian art and architecture in European culture. From 1665 on, the dominant artists of Europe would be Northern in origin. Even in the field of music, northerners like Bach [bahk] and Handel, then Mozart [MOH-tzart] and Beethoven [BAY-toh-vun], were about to triumph. In Holland, France, and England, the Baroque would become an especially potent cultural force, permanently redefining the centers of European culture. ■

What is the Baroque?

As part of its strategy to respond to the Protestant Reformation, the Catholic Church in Rome championed a new Baroque style of art that appealed to the range of human emotion and feeling, not just the intellect. Bernini's majestic new colonnade for the square in front of Saint Peter's in Rome helped to reveal the grandeur of the basilica itself, creating the dramatic effect of the Church embracing its flock. How does his sculptural program for the Cornaro Chapel in Rome epitomize the Baroque? How are Baroque sensibilities reflected in his sculpture of the biblical hero David? How do action, excitement, and sensuality fulfill the Counter-Reformation objectives in Baroque religious art? What role do the senses play in the theological writings of Saint Ignatius? What role does art play in his set of "Rules"? How is this reflected in Andrea Pozzo's ceiling for the church of Sant'Ignazio?

One of the most influential pieces of Baroque architecture is Francesco Borromini's Church of San Carlo alle Quattro Fontane in Rome. Borromini replaces the traditions of Renaissance architecture with a facade of dramatic oppositions and visual surprises. How does the architecture of Bernini and Borromini express the theatrical urge to draw the viewer into the drama?

How does the Baroque style manifest itself in painting?

Caravaggio used the play of light and dark to create paintings of stunning drama and energy that reveal a new Baroque taste for vividly realistic detail. His followers, among them Elisabetta Sirani and Artemisia Gentileschi, inherited his interest in realism and the dramatic. What does Caravaggio share with the mystical writings of Teresa of Ávila and the poetry of Englishman John Donne? What social conditions and aesthetic values of the Italian Baroque particularly interested the artists Elisabetta Sirani and Artemisia Gentileschi?

How is the Baroque style manifest in music, particularly in Venice?

If Rome was the center of Baroque art and architecture, Venice was the center of Baroque music. Giovanni Gabrieli took advantage of the sonority of Saint Mark's Cathedral to create canzonas in which he carefully controlled the dynamics (loud/soft) of the composition and its tempo. What is a canzona? It was in Venice that a new form of musical drama known as *opera* was born in the hands of Claudio Monteverdi, who gave text precedence over harmony for the first time in the history of Western music. His opera *Orfeo* successfully married music and drama. What is an opera? The sonata, popularized as an instrumental genre by virtuoso violinist Arcangelo Corelli, provided a model for all instrumental music. Finally, Antonio Vivaldi perfected the concerto as a genre, and many of his concertos were performed by the women at the Ospedale della Pietà, where he was musical director. What are the chief features of the concerto? In general, what features of Venetian Baroque music are analogous to Baroque painting and sculpture?

PRACTICE MORE Get flashcards for images and terms and review chapter material with quizzes at **www.myartslab.com**

GLOSSARY

aedicule The architectural frame of an opening composed of an entablature and pediment supported by columns or pilasters.

aria An elaborate solo or duet song that expresses the singer's emotions and feelings.

baldachino A canopy.

balustrade A decorative railing.

basso continuo A "continuous bass" line that serves as the supporting accompaniment to the solo instrumental or vocal line above it; also, the performers playing that part.

canzona A type of instrumental contrapuntal work increasingly performed in the seventeenth century in church settings.

cartouche An oval frame.

concerto A three-*movement* secular form of instrumental music.

dynamics Variations and contrast in loudness or intensity.

invisible complement The space surrounding a sculpture, with which it often has an active relationship.

key The central note of a musical composition; also called *tonic note*.

libretto The text of a musical work such as an *opera*.

modulation The process of beginning a composition in a tonic *key*, moving to different keys and then returning to the tonic.

monody A work consisting of a solo voice supported by a *basso continuo*.

movements The independent sections of a composition.

opera A text-based musical drama.

oratorio A form of vocal music, generally on religious themes.

orchestration A musical arrangement in which each part of the composition has been designated with a specific voice or instrument.

piazza A space surrounded by buildings.

pilaster A flat column, usually in relief, which appears to support weight but is essentially ornamental..

program music Purely instrumental music connected in some way to a story or idea.

recitativo A style of singing that imitates very closely the rhythms of speech.

ritornello A musical passage in which an instrument performs episodes that contrast back and forth with the orchestral score.

sonata Literally, "that which is sounded," referring in the broadest sense to a work for an instrument or instruments in any combination.

sonata da camera Literally, a "sonata of the chamber," usually featuring dance-related movements.

sonata da chiesa Literally, a "sonata of the church," often composed of four movements, slow-fast-slow-fast.

tenebrism An exaggerated form of chiaroscuro.

tonality The key of a composition.

tonic note The central note of a musical composition; also called the *key*.

trio sonata A sonata for two instruments of a high range and a *basso continuo*.

volute A coiled or scrolled and counter-curved architectural element.

READINGS

READING 21.4

John Donne, "The Flea" (1633)

Donne's poetry is often labeled "metaphysical" because it borrowed words and images from seventeenth-century science. It reflects a Baroque taste for dramatic contrast and the ability to synthesize discordant images. This last is reflected particularly in the elaborate metaphor, or "conceit," of the following poem, first published posthumously, in which a flea is taken for the image of love's consummation.

Mark but this flea, and mark in this,
How little that which thou deny'st me is;
Me it sucked first, and now sucks thee,
And in this flea, our two bloods mingled be;[1]
Confess it, this cannot be said
A sin, or shame, or loss of maidenhead,
 Yet this enjoys before it woo,
 And pampered swells with one blood made of two,
 And this, alas, is more than we would do.
Oh stay, three lives in one flea spare,[2]   10
Where we almost, nay more than married are,
This flea is you and I, and this
Our marriage bed, and marriage temple is;
 Though parents grudge, and you, we are met,
And cloistered in these living walls of jet.[3]
Though use make you apt to kill me,
Let not to this, self murder added be,
 And sacrilege,[4] three sins in killing three.

Cruel and sudden, has thou since
Purpled thy nail, in blood of innocence? 20
In what could this flea guilty be,
Except in that drop which it sucked from thee?
Yet thou triumph'st, and say'st that thou
Find'st not thyself, nor me the weaker now;
 'Tis true, then learn how false, fears be;
 Just so much honour, when thou yield'st to me,
 Will waste, as this flea's death took life from thee.

READING CRITICALLY

How would you describe the tone of this poem? Is it sincere? Playful? How does this tone affect how we understand its argument?

---

[1]United in the flea are the flea itself, the lover, and the mistress, thus echoing the Trinity, an elaborate metaphor that continues on throughout the poem.
[2]The mistress is about to kill the flea.
[3]Jet: black; in other words, the living body of the flea.
[4]Sacrilege because the flea is portrayed as a "marriage temple."

22 | The Secular Baroque in the North
The Art of Observation

THINKING AHEAD

What forces were at work in Amsterdam in the seventeenth century?

How did developments in philosophy and science underpin the Dutch attention to visual detail?

How does the vernacular manifest itself in Dutch painting?

What are the characteristic features of Baroque keyboard music?

Seventeenth-century Amsterdam was arguably the best-known city in the world. In Europe, it might have competed for pre-eminence with Rome, Paris, Venice, and London, but in the far regions of the Pacific and Indian oceans, in Asia, Africa, and even South America, if you knew of Europe, you had heard of Amsterdam. No city was more heavily invested in commerce. No port was busier. The city's businessmen traded in Indian spices and Muscovy furs, grain from the Baltic, sugar from the Americas, Persian silk, Turkish carpets, Venetian mirrors, Italian maiolica, Japanese lacquerware, saffron, lavender, and tobacco. Tea from China, coffee from the Middle East, and chocolate from South America introduced the West to caffeine, the stimulant that would play a key role in igniting the Industrial Revolution a century later.

The Geographer (Fig. **22.1**), a painting by Dutch artist Jan Vermeer (1632–1675), celebrates Amsterdam's geographical self-esteem. A sea chart on the back wall shows "all the Sea coasts of Europe," a map published in Amsterdam. The globe above his head was also produced in Amsterdam. (So detailed is this painting that the viewer can read the dates and names of the manufacturers of the map and the globe.) He holds a set of dividers, used to mark distances on what must be a chart or map on the table in front of him; the table covering is bunched up behind it as if he has pushed it out of his way. With his left hand resting on a book, he stares intently to his right, as if caught up in a profound intellectual problem.

Vermeer's *Geographer* not only embodies the intellectual fervor of the age, but also many of the themes and strategies of Dutch vernacular painting in the seventeenth century. It reveals, first of all, a rigorous attention to detailed observation, which is why we can readily identify the originals of things like the map and globe. It actively seeks to capture something of the personality of the figure, increasingly the aim of Dutch portraiture. It represents a domestic interior—a favorite theme in Dutch painting—even as it suggests an interest, through the practice of geography, in the natural **landscape**.

◀ **Fig. 22.1 Jan Vermeer, *The Geographer*. 1668–69.** Oil on canvas, 20 1/8″ × 18 1/4″. Städelsches Kunstinstitut, Frankfurt. Courtesy Blauel/Gramm–ARTHOTEK, Peissenberg. The Granger Collection, New York. Many scholars believe this to be a portrait of the Dutch lens maker, Antoni van Leewenhoek, whose scientific investigations are discussed later in the chapter. One of the details supporting the notion that Leeuwenhoek served as a model for this image is the carpet draped across the front of the desk on which he works. Leeuwenhoek worked in the textile industry.

HEAR MORE Listen to an audio file of your chapter at **www.myartslab.com**

(The word "landscape" derives, in fact, from the Dutch *landschap*—that is, "land form.") And, in all likelihood, the painting possesses an allegorical or symbolic meaning in keeping with the strict Dutch Calvinist discipline: The geographer not only charts the landscape but, as he looks forward into the light of revelation, the proper course in life itself. The *Geographer* is also a simple expression of joy in the world of things—carpets, globes, even pictures—and the Dutch desire to possess them.

And yet, for all their wealth and knowledge of foreign lands, the Dutch remained somewhat conservative, as if the very flatness of the landscape, recovered from the sea, led the Netherlandish mind to a condition of restraint. Between 1590 and 1640, nearly 200,000 acres of land intersected by canals and dikes were created by windmills that pumped water out of the shallows and into the sea. The resulting landscape was an austere geometry of right angles and straight lines (Fig. **22.2**). The homes of the rich merchants of Amsterdam were distinguished by this same geometric understatement, their facades typically avoiding

Baroque asymmetry and ornamentation. In life as in architecture, in Calvinist Holland, the values of a middle class intent on living well but not making too public a show of it eclipsed the values of European court culture elsewhere. Especially avoided were what the Dutch deemed the lavish Baroque excesses of the Vatican in Rome.

This chapter outlines the forces that defined Amsterdam as the center of the more austere Baroque style that dominated northern Europe in the seventeenth century. As Amsterdam's port established itself as the center of commerce in the north, the city's economy thrived, sometimes too hotly, as when mad speculation sent the market in tulip bulbs skyrocketing. But this tendency to excess was balanced by the conservatism of the Dutch Reformed Church. The Calvinist fathers of the Dutch Reformed Church found no place for art in the Calvinist liturgy, by and large banning art from its churches. The populace as a whole, however, embraced a new vernacular art depicting the material reality and everyday activities of middle-class Dutch society. The art of portraiture was especially popular, as average citizens sought to affirm their well-being in art.

Fig. 22.2 Jan Christaensz-Micker, *View of Amsterdam.* **ca. 1630.** Oil on canvas, 39⅜″ × 54″. Collection Amsterdam Historical Museum, Amsterdam. By 1640, the city would expand well into the fields on both sides of this image and continue expanding throughout the century. Note the realism of the shadows of passing clouds falling over the city.

CALVINIST AMSTERDAM: CITY OF CONTRADICTIONS

Seventeenth-century Amsterdam was a city of contradictions. It was a society at once obsessed with the acquisition of goods of all kinds, yet rigidly austere in its spiritual life. It was intolerant of what it deemed religious heresy among Protestants, but tolerant of Catholics and Jews; its people avidly collected art for their homes but forswore art in the church. The city was also the curious beneficiary of its sworn enemy, Catholic Spain. Throughout the first three-quarters of the sixteenth century, the provinces of the Netherlands, which correspond roughly to modern-day Belgium and Holland, had been ruled by Charles I of Spain and then his son, Philip II, as part of their Habsburg kingdom (see Chapter 20). Antwerp was their banking center, and through its port passed much of the colonial bounty of the Western Hemisphere, especially from the great silver mines of Potosí, Bolivia (see Chapter 18), and Zacatecas, Mexico. At Potosí alone, a minimum of 7.6 million pesos, minted into coins near the mine, were produced annually between 1580 and 1650, all destined to pay off the ever-increasing debt of the Spanish royal family.

Map 22.1 The United Provinces of the Netherlands in 1648.

Gaining Independence from Spain

Charles I had been born in Flanders and spoke no Spanish when he assumed the Spanish throne in 1519 (see Chapter 20). But Philip II was born in Spain, and, in 1559, he left the Netherlands permanently for his native land, entrusting the northern provinces to the regency of Margaret of Parma, his half-sister. From Spain, Philip tried unsuccessfully to impose Catholic rule on the north by breaking down the traditional autonomy of the 17 Netherlands provinces and asserting rule from Madrid. To this end, he imposed the edicts of the Council of Trent (see Chapter 20) throughout the Netherlands and reorganized its churches under Catholic hierarchy. The Calvinists roundly rejected both moves, especially in the northern seven provinces of Holland centered at Amsterdam. Ten thousand mercenaries led by the Duke of Alba arrived in 1567 to force the Calvinist resistance into cooperation, but the Dutch opened their dikes, flooding the countryside in order to repulse the Spanish. Finally, in 1576, Spanish soldiers, rioting over lack of pay, killed 7,000 citizens in the streets of

Antwerp in a four-day battle that became known as the Spanish Fury. Appalled at the slaughter, the southern ten provinces of the Netherlands, which had remained Catholic up to this point, united with the north to form the United Provinces of the Netherlands (see Map **22.1**). The union lasted only three years, at which point five southern provinces made peace with Spain. Throughout this period, Protestants migrated in mass numbers out of the south, and out of Antwerp particularly, to the north. So did intellectuals and merchants. Of Antwerp's 100,000 inhabitants in 1570, no more than about 40,000 remained by 1590.

Meanwhile, in 1581, the northern provinces declared their independence from Spain, even as Philip reinvigorated his efforts to reconquer them. In 1584 and 1585, when the Spanish under Alessandro of Farnese captured Antwerp after a 14-month siege, the city's fate was sealed. The northern provinces felt that Antwerp was too closely associated with the Spanish for comfort. Thus, at the end of the Thirty Years' War, when the Treaty of Westphalia in 1648 permanently excluded Spain from meddling in Netherlands affairs, Amsterdam closed the port of Antwerp by closing off the river Scheldt to commerce. As Amsterdam clearly understood, no viable commercial enterprise could remain in the city. The wealth that had flowed through the port at Antwerp would thereafter flow through the port of Amsterdam. Amsterdam's prize of war was largely this: What Antwerp had been to the sixteenth century, Amsterdam would be to the seventeenth.

Tulipomania

No single incident captures Amsterdam's commercial success and the wealth at its disposal better than the great tulip "madness" of 1634 to 1637. During those three years, frenzied speculation in tulip bulbs nearly ruined the entire Dutch economy. The tulip had arrived in Europe in 1554, when the Austrian Habsburg ambassador to the court of Suleiman the Magnificent (1494–1566) in Constantinople shipped home a load of bulbs for the enjoyment of the royal court. Its Turkish origin lent the flower a certain exotic flavor (the word *tulip*, in fact, derives from the Turkish word for "turban"), and soon the tulip became the flower of fashion throughout northern Europe. The more flamboyant and extravagant a tulip's color, the more it was prized.

Especially valued were examples of what the Dutch called a "broken" tulip. Tulips, by nature, are a single color—red or yellow, for instance—but in any planting of several hundred bulbs, a single flower might contain feathers or flames of a contrasting hue. Offsets of these "broken" flowers would retain the pattern of the parent bulb, but they produced fewer and smaller offsets than ordinary tulips. Soon, the bulbs of certain strains—most notably the *Semper Augustus* [SEM-per aw-GUS-tus], with its red flames on white petals—became the closely guarded treasures of individual botanists.

We know, today, that a virus spread from tulip to tulip by the peach potato aphid causes the phenomenon of "breaking." The flower produces fewer and smaller offsets because it is diseased. As a result of this deterioration, by 1636 there were reportedly only two of the red-flamed *Semper Augustus* root bulbs in all of Holland. The one in Amsterdam sold for 4,600 florins [FLOR-inz] (fifteen or twenty times the annual income of a skilled craftsman), a new carriage and harness, and two gray horses. Some idea of what value these prices represent can

Fig. 22.3 From the Tulip Book of P. Cos. 1637. Wageningen University and Research Center Library, The Netherlands. In the first half of the seventeenth century, 34 "tulip books," cataloguing the flower's many varieties, were published in Holland.

be understood by looking at some of the "in-kind" dealings that transpired in the tulip trade. In his history of the Dutch seventeenth century, *The Embarrassment of Riches*, Simon Schama reports that one man, presumably a farmer leaping into the market, paid two *last* of wheat (approximately 4,000 pounds), four of rye, four fat oxen, eight pigs, a dozen sheep, two oxheads of wine, four tons of butter, a thousand pounds of cheese, a bed, some clothing, and a silver beaker, for a single Viceroy bulb, valued at 2,500 guilders [GILL-durz]. Presumably the farmer planned on planting it and selling its offsets for 2,500 guilders each.

We cannot know for certain what caused the burst of speculation in "broken" flowers, although the Dutch taste for beauty certainly contributed to the madness. Tulip books, illustrated nursery catalogues of available bulbs and the flowers they produced, added to the frenzy (Fig. 22.3). But by the autumn of 1635, trade in actual bulbs had given way to trade in promissory notes, listing what flowers would be delivered and at what price. At the stock exchange in Amsterdam and elsewhere in Holland, special markets were established for their sale. Suddenly, good citizens sold all their possessions, mortgaged their homes, and invested their entire savings in "futures"—bulbs not yet even lifted from the ground. In a matter of months, the price of a single Switsers bulb, a yellow tulip with red feathers, soared from 60 to 1,800 guilders. Speculation was so frenzied that the paper "futures" began to be traded, not the bulbs themselves, and when in the winter of 1637 the tulip market faced the prospect of fulfilling paper promissory notes with actual bulbs, it collapsed. Suddenly no one could sell a tulip bulb in Holland for any price.

In Amsterdam, the assembled deputies declared any debt incurred in the tulip market before November 1636 null and void, and the debt of any purchaser whose obligation was incurred after that date to be considered met upon payment of 10 percent. Those holding debts were outraged, but the court in Amsterdam unanimously ruled that any debt contracted in gambling, which they deemed the tulip market to be, was no debt at all under the law.

The Dutch Reformed Church: Strict Doctrine and Whitewashed Spaces

The excesses of Dutch society so evident in the tulip craze were strongly countered by the conservatism of the Calvinist Dutch Reformed Church, which actively opposed speculation in the tulip market. In the 1560s, as the Spanish had tried to impose Catholicism upon the region, many Dutch religious leaders, almost all of them Calvinist (see Chapter 17), fled the country. Finally, in October 1571, 23 of these Calvinist leaders gathered in Emden, Germany, and proclaimed the creation of the Dutch Reformed Church. By 1578, they had returned to Holland.

This strict Calvinist sect did not become, as many believe, an official state religion, but the state did require that any person in public service be a member of the Dutch Reformed Church. The Church was itself split over questions of doctrine: In the saving of souls, could good deeds overcome predestination? On one side were those who held that the faith and good deeds of the believer might to some extent affect the bestowal of grace and their ultimate salvation. Opposing them were those who believed that salvation was predestined by God. Those who would ascend to heaven (the elect) were numbered from the moment of birth, and no good works could affect the outcome of the damned. By 1618, this doctrinal conflict would erupt into what narrowly escaped becoming civil war, and those who believed in good works were soon expelled from the Reformed Church, their leader tried for treason and beheaded, and others imprisoned.

The doctrinal rigidity of the Reformed Church is reflected in the austerity of its churches. Ever since the Calvinist's iconoclastic destruction of religious imagery in 1566 (see Chapter 17), when van Eyck's *Ghent Altarpiece* at Saint Bavo Cathedral in Ghent (see Figs. 16.5 and 16.6) was dismantled

and hidden away, Dutch churches had remained devoid of paintings. A depiction of a different church dedicated to Saint Bavo, in Haarlem [HAR-lum] (Fig. **22.4**), painted by Pieter Saenredam [SAHN-ruh-dahm] (1597–1665) nearly a century after the removal of the *Ghent Altarpiece*, shows a typical Dutch Reformed interior stripped of all furnishings, its walls whitewashed by Calvinist iconoclasts. A single three-tiered chandelier hangs from the ceiling above three gentlemen whom Saenredam includes in the composition in order to establish the almost spiritual vastness of the medieval church's interior. This stripped-down, white space is meant to reflect the purity and propriety of the Reformed Church and its flock.

Fig. 22.4 Pieter Saenredam, *Interior of the Choir of Saint Bavo's Church at Haarlem.* 1660. Oil on panel, 27 $^7/_8$" × 21 $^5/_8$". Worcester Art Museum, Worcester, MA. The Bridgeman Art Library, New York. Charlotte E. W. Buffington Fund. 1951.29. The only adornments of the space are an escutcheon, bearing the coat of arms of Saint Bavo, hanging on the left wall, and a memorial tablet on the right.

THE SCIENCE OF OBSERVATION

As stark and almost barren as Saenredam's painting is, it nevertheless reveals an astonishing attention to detail, capturing even the texture of the whitewashed walls with geometric precision. This attention to detail, typical of Northern Baroque art, reflects both religious belief and scientific discovery. Protestants believed that all things had an inherent spiritual quality, and the visual detail in Northern art was understood as the worldly manifestation of the divine. But perhaps more significantly, new methods of scientific and philosophical investigation focused on the world in increasing detail. In the seventeenth century, newly invented instruments allowed scientists to observe and measure natural phenomena with increasing accuracy. Catholics and Protestants were equally appalled at many of the discoveries, since they seemed to challenge the authority of Scripture. Also problematic for both religions were new methods of reasoning that challenged the place of faith in arriving at an understanding of the universe. According to these new ways of reasoning, *Scientia*, the Latin word for "knowledge," was to be found in the world, not in religious belief.

Francis Bacon and the Empirical Method

One of the most fundamental principles guiding the new science was the proposition that, through the direct and careful observation of natural phenomena, one could draw general conclusions from particular examples. This process is known as **inductive reasoning**, and with it, scientists believed they could predict the workings of nature as a whole. When inductive reasoning was combined with scientific experimentation, it produced a manner of inquiry that we call the **empirical method.** The leading advocate of the empirical method in the seventeenth century was the English scientist Francis Bacon (1561–1626). His *Novum Organum Scientiarum* (*New Method of Science*), published in 1620, is the most passionate plea for its use. "One method of delivery alone remains to us," he wrote, "which is simply this: we must lead men to the particulars themselves, and their series and order; while men on their side must force themselves for a while to lay their notions by

CONTINUITY & CHANGE and begin to familiarize themselves
Aristotle, p. 159 with facts." The greatest obstacle to human understanding, Bacon believed, was "superstition, and the blind and immoderate zeal of religion." For Bacon, Aristotle represented a perfect example (see Chapter 5). While he valued Aristotle's emphasis on the study of natural phenomena, he rejected as false doctrine Aristotle's belief that the experience coming to us by means of our senses (things as they *appear*) automatically presents to our understanding things as they *are*. Indeed, he felt that reliance on the senses frequently led to fundamental errors.

A proper understanding of the world could only be achieved, Bacon believed, if we eliminate the errors in

reasoning developed through our unwitting adherence to the false notions that every age has worshiped. He identified four major categories of false notion, which he termed Idols, all described in his *Novum Organum Scientiarum* (*The New Method of Science*) (see **Reading 22.1,** page 729). The first of these, the Idols of the Tribe, are the common fallacies of all human nature, derived from the fact that we trust, wrongly, in our senses. The second, the Idols of the Cave, derive from our particular education, upbringing, and environment—an individual's religious faith or sense of his or her ethnic or gender superiority or inferiority would be examples. The third, the Idols of the Market Place, are errors that occur as a result of miscommunication, words that cause confusion by containing, as it were, hidden assumptions. For instance, the contemporary use of "man" or "mankind" to refer to people in general (common well into the twentieth century), connotes a worldview in which hierarchical structures of gender are already assumed. Finally, there are the Idols of the Theater, the false dogmas of philosophy—not only those of the ancients but those that "may yet be composed." The object of the empirical method is the destruction of these four Idols through intellectual objectivity. Bacon argued that rather than falling back on the preconceived notions and opinions produced by the four Idols, "Man, [using the last idol] being the servant and interpreter of Nature, can do and understand so much and so much only as he has observed in fact or in thought of the course of Nature; beyond this he neither knows anything nor can do anything."

Bacon's insistence on the scientific observation of natural phenomena led, in the mid-1640s, to the formation in England of a group of men who met regularly to discuss his new philosophy. After a lecture on November 28, 1660, by Christopher Wren, the Gresham College Professor of Astronomy and architect of Saint Paul's Cathedral in London (see Chapter 24), they officially founded "a College for the Promoting of Physico-Mathematicall Experimentall Learning." It met weekly to witness experiments and discuss scientific topics. Within a couple of years, the group became known as "The Royal Society of London for Improving Natural Knowledge," an organization that continues to the present day as the Royal Society. It is one of the leading forces in international science, dedicated to the recognition of excellence in science and the support of leading-edge scientific research and its applications.

René Descartes and the Deductive Method

Bacon's works circulated widely in Holland, where they were received with enthusiasm. As one seventeenth-century Dutch painter, Constantijm Huygens [HOY-guns] (1596–1687), put it in his *Autobiography*, Bacon offered the Dutch "most excellent criticism of the useless ideas, theorems, and axioms which, as I have said, the ancients possessed." But equally influential were the writings of the French-born René Descartes [day-CART] (1596–1650).

Descartes (Fig. **22.5**), in fact, lived in Holland for over 20 years, from 1628 to 1649, moving between 13 different cities, including Amsterdam, and 24 different residences. It was in Holland that he wrote and published his *Discourse on the Method of Rightly Conducting the Reason and Seeking for Truth in the Sciences* (1637). As opposed to Bacon's inductive reasoning, Descartes proceeded to his conclusions by the opposite method of **deductive reasoning**. He began with clearly established general principles and moved from those to the establishment of particular truths.

Like Bacon, Descartes distrusted almost everything, believing that both our thought and our observational senses can and do deceive us. In his *Meditations on the First Philosophy*, he draws an analogy between his own method and that of an architect (**Reading 22.2**):

READING 22.2

from René Descartes, *Meditations* (1641)

Throughout my writings I have made it clear that my method imitates that of the architect. When an architect wants to build a house which is stable on ground where there is a sandy topsoil over underlying rock, or clay, or some other firm base, he begins by digging out a set of trenches from which he removes the sand, and anything resting on or mixed in with the sand, so that he can lay his foundations on firm soil. In the same way, I began by taking everything that was doubtful and throwing it out, like sand.

Fig. 22.5 Frans Hals, *Portrait of René Descartes.* 1649. Oil on wood, 7 3/8″ × 5 1/2″. Musée du Louvre/RMN Réunion des Musées Nationaux, France. Erich Lessing/Art Resource, New York. Hals was renowned for his portraiture. Here he seems to reveal the very essence of Descartes. The philosopher appears to be thinking, with some evident amusement, perhaps about the prospect of any painter "capturing" his essence on canvas.

He wants, he says, "to reach certainty—to cast aside the loose earth and sand so as to come upon rock and clay." The first thing, in fact, that he could not doubt was that he was thinking, which led him to the inevitable conclusion that he must actually exist in order to generate thoughts about his own existence as a thinking individual, which he famously expressed in *Discourse on Method* in the Latin phrase "*Cogito, ergo sum*" [KOH-guh-toh er-goh sum] ("I think, therefore I am").

At the heart of Descartes's thinking—we refer to Descartes's method as *Cartesian*—is an absolute distinction between mind and matter, and hence between the metaphysical soul and the physical body, a system of oppositions that has come to be known as *Cartesian dualism*. The remarkable result of this approach is that, beginning with this one "first principle" in his *Discourse on Method*, Descartes comes to prove, at least to his own satisfaction, the existence of God. He would repeat this argument many times, most formally in his 1641 *Meditations*, but the logic, simply stated, is as follows: (1) I think, and I possess an idea of God (that is, the idea exists in me and I can be aware of it as an object of my understanding); (2) The idea

of God is the idea of an actually infinite perfect being; (3) Such an idea could only originate in an actually infinite perfect being ("it had been placed in me by a Nature which was really more perfect than mine could be, and which had within itself all the perfections of which I could form any idea"); and (4) Therefore, there is an infinitely perfect being, which we call God. This line of thinking established Descartes as one of the most important founders of **deism** (from the Latin *deus* [DAY-us], "god"), the brand of faith that argues that the basis of belief in God is reason and logic rather than revelation or tradition. Descartes's did not believe that God was at all interested in interfering in human affairs. Nor was God endowed, particularly, with human character. He was, in Descartes's words, "the mathematical order of nature." Descartes was himself a mathematician of considerable inventiveness, founding analytic geometry, the bridge between algebra and geometry crucial to the invention of calculus. The same year that he published *Discourse on Method*, Descartes also published a treatise entitled *Optics*. There, among other things, he used geometry to calculate the angular radius of a rainbow (42 degrees).

Johannes Kepler, Galileo Galilei, and the Telescope

Descartes's *Optics* was built upon the earlier discoveries in optics of the German mathematician Johannes Kepler [KEP-lur] (1571–1630). In fact, Descartes was so taken with Kepler's insights that he included Kepler's illustration of the working of the human eye in his *Optics* (Fig. **22.6**). Kepler had made detailed records of the movements of the planets, substantiating Copernicus's theory that the planets orbited the sun, not the Earth (see Chapter 20). The long-standing tradition of a **geocentric** (Earth-centered) cosmos was definitively replaced with a **heliocentric** (sun-centered) theory. Kepler also challenged the traditional belief that the orbits of the planets were spherical, showing that the five known planets moved around the sun in elliptical paths determined by the magnetic force of the sun and their relative distance from it. His interest in optics was spurred on when he recognized that the apparent diameter of the moon differed when observed directly and when observed using a **camera obscura** [ob-SKYOOR-uh], a device that temporarily reproduces an image on a screen or wall (Fig. **22.7**).

Meanwhile, in Italy, Kepler's friend Galileo Galilei [gal-uh-LAY] had improved the design and magnification of the telescope (invented by a Dutch eyeglass-maker, Hans Lippershey; see Chapter 24). Through the improved telescope, Galileo saw and described the craters of the moon, the phases of Venus, sunspots, and the moons of Jupiter. Galileo also theorized that light takes a certain amount of time to travel from one place to the next, and that either as a particle or as a wave, it travels at a measurable uniform speed. He proposed, too, that all objects, regardless of shape, size, or density, fall at the same rate of acceleration—the law of

Fig. 22.6 Illustration of the theory of the retinal image as described by Johannes Kepler. From René Descartes, ***Optics (La Dioptrique)*,** **Leiden, 1637.** Bancroft Library, Berkeley, CA. Descartes was more interested in what happened to the image in the brain after it registered itself on the retina, while Kepler was interested in the physical optics of the process itself.

Fig. 22.7 An artist drawing in a large camera obscura. Courtesy George Eastman House, Buffalo, NY. The camera obscura works by admitting a ray of light through a small hole that projects a scene, upside down, directly across from the hole. Recent studies have shown that Vermeer made extensive use of such a device.

falling bodies, or gravity. Inspired by Galileo's discoveries, Kepler wrote a study on the optical properties of lenses, in which he detailed a design for a telescope that became standard in astronomical research. Kepler's and Galileo's work did not meet with universal approval. The Church still officially believed that the Earth was the center of the universe and that the sun revolved around it. Protestant churches were equally skeptical. The theories of Kepler and Galileo contradicted certain passages in the Bible. Joshua, for instance, is described in the Old Testament as making the sun stand still, a feat that would be impossible unless the sun normally moved around the Earth: "So the sun stood still in the midst of the heaven, and hasted not to go down about a whole day. And there was no day like that before it or after it" (Joshua 10:13–14). Furthermore, it seemed to many that the new theories relegated humankind to a marginal space in God's plan. Thus, in 1615, when Galileo was required to defend his ideas before Pope Paul V in Rome, he failed to convince the pontiff. He was banned from both publishing and teaching his findings. When his old friend Pope Urban VIII was elected pope, Galileo appealed Paul's verdict, but Urban went even further. He demanded that Galileo admit his error in public and sentenced him to life in prison. Through the intervention of friends, the sentence was reduced to banishment to a villa outside Florence. Galileo was lucky. In 1600, when the astronomer Giordano Bruno had asserted that the universe was infinite and without center and that other solar systems might exist in space, he was burned at the stake.

Antoni van Leeuwenhoek, Robert Hooke, and the Microscope

In the last decade of the sixteenth century, two Dutch eyeglass-makers, Hans Lippershey and Zaccharias Janssen, discovered that if one looked through several lenses in a single tube, nearby objects appeared greatly magnified. This discovery led to the compound microscope (a microscope that uses more than one lens). Early compound microscopes were able to magnify objects only about 20 or 30 times their natural size. Another Dutch lens maker, Antoni van Leeuwenhoek [vahn LAY-ven-hook] (1632–1723), was able to grind a lens that magnified over 200 times. The microscope itself was a simple instrument, consisting of two plates with a lens between, which was focused by tightening or loosening screws running through the plates. Two inches long and one inch across, it could easily fit in the palm of one's hand. Leeuwenhoek was inspired by the 1665 work *Micrographia* by Robert Hooke, Curator of Experiments for the Royal Society of London. It was illustrated by drawings of Hooke's observations with his compound microscope: a flea that he said was "adorn'd with a curiously polish'd suite of sable Armour, neatly jointed," and a thin slice of cork, in which he observed "a Honey-comb [of] . . . pores, or cells"—actually, cell walls (Fig. **22.8**).

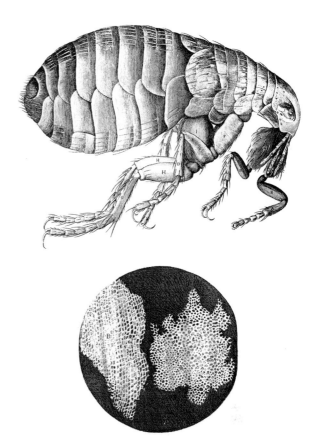

Fig. 22.8 Robert Hooke, illustrations from *Micrographia*: a flea (top), and a slice of cork (bottom). London. 1665. Courtesy the University of Virginia Library. Hooke was the first person to use the word *cell* to describe the basic structural unit of plant and animal life.

Leeuwenhoek wrote letters to the Royal Society of London to keep them informed about his observations. In his first letter, of 1673, he described the stings of bees. Then, in 1678, he wrote to the Royal Society with a report of discovering "little animals"—actually, bacteria and protozoa—and the society asked Hooke to confirm Leeuwenhoek's findings, which he successfully did. For the next 50 years, Leeuwenhoek's regular letters to the Royal Society, describing, for the first time, sperm cells, blood cells, and many other microscopic organisms, were printed in the Society's *Philosophical Transactions*, and often reprinted separately. In 1680, Leeuwenhoek was elected a full member of the Society.

Many scholars believe that Leeuwenhoek served as the model for the 1668 to 1669 painting by Jan Vermeer, *The Geographer* (see Fig. 22.1). Leeuwenhoek was interested in more than microscopes. A biographer described him six years after his death as equally interested in "navigation, astronomy, mathematics, philosophy, and natural science." He would serve as trustee for Vermeer's estate in 1676, and we know that Vermeer actively used a camera obscura to plan his canvases, so the painter shared something of Leeuwenhoek's fascination with lenses.

DUTCH VERNACULAR PAINTING: ART OF THE FAMILIAR

The prosperous Dutch avidly collected pictures. A visiting Englishman, John Evelyn, explained their passion for art this way, in 1641: "The reason of this store of pictures and their cheapness proceeds from want of land to employ their stock [wealth], so that it is an ordinary thing to find a common farmer lay out two or three thousand pounds in this commodity. Their houses are full of them and they vend them at their fairs to very great gains." If Evelyn exaggerates the sums invested in art—a typical landscape painting sold for only three or four guilders, still the equivalent of two or three days' wages for a Delft clothworker—he was accurate in his sense that almost everyone owned at least a few prints and a painting or two.

Despite Dutch Reformed distaste for religious history painting—commissions from the Church had dried up almost completely by 1620—about a third of privately owned paintings in the city of Leiden (one of the most iconoclastic in Holland) during the first 30 years of the seventeenth century represented religious themes. But other, more secular forms of painting thrived. Most Calvinists did not object to sitting for their portraits, as long as the resulting image reflected their Protestant faith. And most institutions wanted visual documentation of their activities, resulting in a thriving industry in group portraiture. Painting also came to reflect the matter-of-fact materialism of the Dutch character—its interest in all manner of things, from carpets, to furnishings, to clothing, collectibles, foodstuffs, and everyday activities. And the Dutch artists themselves were particularly interested in technical developments in the arts, particularly Caravaggio's dramatic lighting (see Fig. 21.13). To accommodate the taste of the buying public, Dutch artists developed a new visual vocabulary that was largely vernacular, reflecting the actual time and place in which they lived.

Fig. 22.9 Johannes Goedaert, *Flowers in a Wan-li Vase with Blue-Tit.* ca. 1660. Medium. Photo: Charles Roelofsz/RKD Images. Bob P. Haboldt & Co., Inc. Art Gallery, N.Y. The shell in the lower right corner is a symbol of worldly wealth, but as it is broken and empty, it is also a reminder of our vanity and mortality.

Still Lifes

Among the most popular subjects were **still lifes**, paintings dedicated to the representation of common household objects and food. At first glance, they seem nothing more than a celebration of abundance and pleasure. But their subject is also the foolishness of believing in such apparent ease of life. Johannes Goedaert's (1621–1668) *Flowers in a Wan-li Vase with Blue-Tit* (Fig. **22.9**) is, on the one hand, an image of pure floral exuberance. The arrangement contains four varieties of tulip—somewhat ominously, given the memories of tulipomania—and a wide variety of other flowers, including a Spanish iris, nasturtiums from Peru, fritallaria [FRIT-ul-air-ee-uh] from Persia, a striped York and Lancaster Rose—a whole empire's worth of blossoms. The worldliness of the blooms is underscored by the Wan-li vase in which they are placed, a type of Ming dynasty porcelain (see Fig. 18.20) that became popular with Dutch traders around the turn of the century. The short life of the blooms is suggested by the yellowing leaves, the impermanence of the scene by the fly perched on one of the tulips. But perhaps the most telling detail is the bird at the bottom left of the painting, a blue-tit depicted in the act of consuming a moth. Dutch artists of this period used such details to remind the viewer of the frivolous quality of human existence, our vanity in thinking only of the pleasures of the everyday. Such *vanitas* [VAN-ih-tahss] **paintings**, as they are called, remind us that pleasurable things in life inevitably fade, that the material world is not as long-lived as the spiritual, and that the spiritual should command our attention. They

Fig. 22.10 Jacob van Ruisdael, *View of Haarlem from the Dunes at Overveen.* ca. 1670. Oil on canvas, 22″ × 24³⁄₈″. Mauritshuis, The Hague. The play of light and dark across the landscape can be understood in terms of the rhythms of life itself.

are, in short, examples of the *momento mori*—reminders that we will die. Paintings such as Goedaert's were extremely popular. Displayed in the owner's home, they were both decorative and imbued with a moral sensibility that announced to a visitor the owner's upright Protestant sensibility.

Landscapes

Another popular subject was landscapes. Landscape paintings such as Jacob van Ruisdael's [vahn ROYS-dahl] (ca. 1628–1682) *View of Haarlem from the Dunes at Overveen* reflect national pride in the country's reclamation of its land from the sea (Fig. **22.10**). The English referred to the United Provinces as the "united bogs," and the French constantly poked fun at the baseness of what they called the *Pays-Bas* [PAY-ee bah] (the "Low Countries"). But the

Dutch themselves considered their transformation of the landscape from hostile sea to tame farmland, in the century from 1550 to 1650, as analogous to God's recreation of the world after the Great Flood.

In Ruisdael's landscape painting, this religious undertone is symbolized by the great Gothic church of Saint Bavo at Haarlem, which rises over a flat, reclaimed landscape where figures toil in a field lit by an almost celestial light. (See Fig. 22.4 for Pieter Saenredam's depiction of the interior of the church.) It is no accident that two-thirds of Ruisdael's landscape is devoted to sky, the infinite heavens. In flatlands, the sky and horizon are simply more evident, but more symbolically, the Dutch thought of themselves as *Nederkindren*, the "children below," looked after by an almighty God with whom they had made an eternal covenant.

Genre Scenes

Paintings that depict events from everyday life were another favorite of the Dutch public. *The Dancing Couple* (Fig. **22.11**) by Jan Steen (1626–1679) is typical of such **genre scenes**. Like many of Steen's paintings, it depicts festivities surrounding some sort of holiday or celebration. Steen was both a painter and a tavern keeper, and the scene here is most likely a tavern patio in midsummer. An erotic flavor permeates the scene, an atmosphere of flirtation and licentiousness. To the right, musicians play as a seated couple drunkenly watch the dancers. To the left, two men enjoy food at the table, a woman lifts a glass of wine to her lips, and a gentleman—a self-portrait of the artist—gently touches her chin. Steen thus portrays his own—and, by extension, the Dutch—penchant for merrymaking, but in typical Dutch fashion he also admonishes himself for taking such license. On the tavern floor lie an overturned pitcher of cut flowers and a pile of broken eggshells, both *vanitas* symbols. Together with the church spire in the distance, they remind us of the fleeting nature of human life as well as the hellfire that awaits those who have fallen into the vices so openly displayed in the rest of the painting.

One of the most popular genre painters of the day—and, incidentally, illustrator of a favorite tulip catalogue as well—was Judith Leyster [LY-ster] (1609–1660) of Haarlem (see Fig. 22.3). We do not know much about her life, but she was admitted to the Haarlem painter's guild in 1633, in her early twenties, and married another genre painter, Jan Miense Molenaer, in 1636. The moral severity of her 1631 painting *The Proposition* is unmistakable (Fig. **22.12**). Taking advantage of the contrast of light and dark, a Baroque technique probably learned from the example of Caravaggio (see Figs. 21.13 and 21.14), Leyster creates a small drama of considerable tension and opposition. A woman sits quietly, intent on her needlework, as a lusty man leans over her, grinning. His left hand rests on her shoulder and his right offers her a handful of coins. Even as she ignores his clear proposition, her virtue is compromised. Perhaps her physical safety is in jeopardy as well, for the man's good humor will probably crumble under her rejection of him—a premonition signaled by the tension, even pain, evident in her concentration. The painting is, furthermore, remarkable for contrasting the domestic world of women with the commercial world of men, associating the former with

Fig. 22.11 Jan Steen, *The Dancing Couple*. 1663. Oil on canvas, 40 $\frac{3}{8}$" × 56 $\frac{1}{8}$". National Gallery of Art, Washington, D.C., Widener Collection. 1942.9.81. Photograph © 2007 Board of Trustees, National Gallery of Art, Washington, D.C. Steen's paintings, whatever their moralizing undercurrents, remind us that the Dutch were a people of great humor and happiness. They enjoyed life.

Fig. 22.12 Judith Leyster, *The Proposition*. 1631. Oil on canvas, 11 7/8″ × 9 1/2″. Mauritshuis, The Hague. The Netherlands. SCALA/Art Resource, New York. The small size of the work underscores the intimacy of the scene, its detail almost as precise as the woman's needlework.

virtue and the latter with lust and greed. *The Proposition* stops short of submission, but Leyster frankly depicts the polarity of gender roles in Dutch society: the tension between private and social space, the awkward collision of domesticity and sexuality.

Johannes Vermeer and the Domestic Scene

As his painting *The Geographer* (see Fig. 22.1) suggests, Johannes Vermeer was, above all, a keen observer of his world. His paintings illuminate—and celebrate—the material reality of Dutch life. We know very little of Vermeer's life, and his painting was largely forgotten until the middle of the nineteenth century. But today he is recognized as one of the great masters of the Dutch seventeenth century. Vermeer painted only 34 works that modern scholars accept as authentic, and most depict intimate genre scenes that reveal a moment in the domestic world of women.

The example here is *Woman with a Pearl Necklace* (Fig. 22.13). Light floods the room from a window at the left, where a yellow curtain has been drawn back, allowing the young woman to see herself better in a small mirror beside the window. She is richly dressed, wearing an ermine-trimmed yellow satin jacket. On the table before her are a basin and a powder brush; she has evidently completed the process of putting on makeup and arranging her hair as

she draws the ribbons of her pearl necklace together and admires herself in the mirror. From her ear hangs a pearl earring, glistening in the light. The woman brims with self-confidence, and nothing in the painting suggests that Vermeer intends a moralistic message of some sort. While the woman's pearls might suggest her vanity—to say nothing of pride because of the way she gazes at them—they also traditionally symbolize truth, purity, even virginity. This latter reading is supported by the great, empty, and white stretch of wall that extends between her and the mirror. It is as if this young woman is a *tabula rasa* [TAB-yuh-luh RAHZ-uh], a blank slate, whose moral history remains to be written.

Vermeer's paintings of interiors are, for many art historians, a celebration of Dutch domestic culture. As much as anything else, they extol the comforts of home. In fact, the home is the chief form of Dutch architecture. Decorated with paintings and maps, furnished with comfortable furniture and carpets, its larder filled with foodstuffs from around the world, the home was the center of Dutch life.

The basic household consisted of a husband and wife, who married late, compared to the custom in other European countries: Men were generally over 26 and women over 23. Almost all families had at least one servant, usually a young

Fig. 22.13 Jan Vermeer, *Woman with a Pearl Necklace*. ca. 1664. Oil on canvas, 22 5/32″ × 17 3/4″. Post-restoration. Inv.: 912 B. Photo: Joerg P. Anders. Gemäldegalerie, Staatliche Museen zu Berlin, Berlin, Germany. Bildarchiv Preussischer Kulturbesitz/Art Resource, New York. The mirror can symbolize both vanity—self-love—and truth, the accurate reflection of the world.

Fig. 22.14 Jan Vermeer, *The Little Street*. ca. **1657–58.** Oil on canvas, 21 1/16″ × 17 1/8″. Rijksmuseum, Amsterdam. Note how the shape of the sky imitates the gables of the houses, but in reverse—an example of just how carefully Vermeer composed the piece.

woman who helped with domestic chores. She often was of the same social status as her employer and might stay on for eight to ten years, or until her own marriage. By working, she could accumulate a dowry large enough to contribute to the establishment of her own household when she married.

Vermeer's *The Little Street* (Fig. **22.14**) is a celebration of such domestic life. Seen from across the cobblestone street, the house is typical, presenting a symmetrical, step-gabled, and red-brick facade (against which Vermeer plays the asymmetry of his painting) that rises at a steep pitch to the central ridge of the roof. Its windows are rectangular but are set below decorative brick arches. Their shutters—on

the first floor, two green shut ones on the left, a open red one at the right—underscore the asymmetry of Vermeer's composition. Similarly, the doorways to the passageways that run between the two houses contrast dramatically, the one open and light-filled, the other closed and dark. (Notice, as well, that the closed door is arched and set in a rectangular niche, while the open door is rectangular and set in an arched niche.) The painting is an exercise in contrasts, and yet it presents a scene of quiet and peaceful harmony. By means of these contrasts—and such details as the whitewash that extends incompletely up the wall, and the mortar filling the cracked facade—Vermeer acknowledges the tensions of domestic life, even as he presents a scene of quiet harmony. A woman sits in the doorway, absorbed in her needlework. Children play at some game at the edge of the street. In the passageway that leads to an inner courtyard, the maidservant works at her chores. Not coincidentally, the vines growing on the house at the left are traditional symbols of love, fidelity, and marriage.

Marriage manuals were, in fact, extremely popular, even bestsellers. All advocated friendship between husband and wife as a major goal of a good marriage. The man was head of the household, his authority was absolute, and all external affairs were his responsibility. The woman maintained a certain status. She not only ruled over the workings of the house itself, but, as the marriage manuals uniformly suggested, was expected to be a true partner in her husband's affairs. She counseled him, encouraged him, and shared equally with him his burdens and successes. Probably the most popular of the marriage manuals was Jacob Cats's *Houwelick* (*Marriage*), first published in 1625, which devoted one chapter to each of six different roles in a woman's life: maiden, sweetheart, bride, housewife, mother, and widow. The book preached piety and virtue, but it also described, in tantalizing detail, the carnal acts that would inevitably lead to dire consequences. *Marriage* was, in short, a thinly disguised sex manual. Much like Dutch still-life painting, it was full of succulent treats and delicious morsels, but couched in the moral rhetoric of *vanitas*.

The Group Portrait

The leading portrait painter of early seventeenth-century Holland was Frans Hals (1581–1666) of Haarlem. Hals

worked quickly, probably without preliminary sketches (none survive), with the loose and gestural brushstrokes apparent in his lively portrait of Descartes (see Fig. 22.5). He avoided flattering his sitters by softening or altering their features, seeking instead to convey their vitality and personality. Hals was particularly successful at the **group portrait**, a large canvas commissioned by a civic institution to document or commemorate its membership at a particular time.

Between 1616 and 1639, Hals painted five enormous group portraits for the two Haarlem militias: the Civic Guard of Saint George and the Cluveniers, who were also known as the Civic Guard of Saint Adrian. This was a mammoth task, because the five canvases alone contain 68 portraits of 61 different prominent Haarlem citizens, plus one dog. Group portraits of the civic guards had been commissioned before, but these set a new standard. Until this series, such group portraits had tended to be little more than formal rows of individual portraits. In the first of these paintings, *Banquet of the Officers of the St. George Civic Guard*, Hals turns the group portrait into a lively social event, capturing in specific detail a fleeting moment at the farewell banquet for the officers who had completed their three-year stint (Fig. **22.15**). Despite the casualness of the scene, Hals shows the hierarchy of the company by arranging its highest officers under the tip of the flag that tops an imaginary pyramid of figures. Alone at the head of the table and closest to the viewer sits the colonel, with the provost marshal, the second in command, on his right. They are the highest-ranking officers. Three captains sit down along the side of the table to the

Fig. 22.15 Frans Hals, *Banquet of the Officers of the St. George Civic Guard*. 1616. Oil on canvas, 68 7/8" × 137 1/2". Frans Halsmuseum, Haarlem. The enormous scale of this painting reflects the Baroque taste for colossal theatrical settings. It is, in effect, the Northern vernacular equivalent in painting of Bernini's architectural colonnade for Vatican square (see Fig. 25.1)—both conceived essentially to consume the viewer within their space.

colonel's left, and three lieutenants sit at the far end of the table between the colonel and the provost. Three ensigns, not technically part of the officers' corps, stand at the right. Holding the flag at the back of the composition is a servant. So vigorous are Hals's portraits that this painting quickly became a symbol of the strength and healthy optimism of the men who established the new Dutch Republic.

Rembrandt van Rijn and the Drama of Light

In the hands of Rembrandt van Rijn (1606–1669), the group portrait took on an even more heightened sense of drama. The leading painter in Amsterdam and 25 years Hals's junior, Rembrandt learned much from the elder Dutchman, not least of all how to build up the figure with short dashes of paint or, alternately, long, fluid lines of loose, gestural brushwork. The result, paradoxically, is an image of extreme clarity, a clarity that has not always been apparent in his group portrait of *Captain Frans Banning Cocq Mustering His Company* (Fig. **22.16**). The enormous canvas (which was originally even larger) was so covered by a layer of grime and darkened varnish that for years it was thought to represent the Captain's company on a night patrol of Amsterdam's streets, and it was known, consequently, as *The Night Watch*. But after a thorough cleaning and restoration in 1975–76, its true subject revealed itself—the company forming for a parade in a side street of the city. Perhaps more important, the cleaning also revealed one of Rembrandt's important contributions to the art of portraiture— his use of light to animate his figures. Captain Cocq's hand extends toward us in the very center of the painting,

Fig. 22.16 Rembrandt van Rijn, *Captain Frans Banning Cocq Mustering His Company (The Night Watch).* **1642.**
Oil on canvas, 11′11″ × 14′4″ (3.63 × 4.37 m). Rijksmuseum, Amsterdam. Recently, Dutch scholar Dudok van Heel has made a convincing case that the main character in the painting is not Frans Banning Cocq but Frans Bannink Cocq, a member of a much richer and more influential family than Banning Cocq.

LEARN MORE Gain insight from a primary source document on Rembrandt van Rijn at **www.myartslab.com**

Fig. 22.17 Rembrandt van Rijn, *Christ Preaching* (the "Hundred-Guilder Print"). ca. 1648–50. Etching, 11″ × 15¹/₂″. Rijksmuseum, Amsterdam. Many of the figures in this etching were suggested by Spanish and Jewish refugees who crowded the streets of Amsterdam and whom Rembrandt regularly sketched.

casting a shadow across the lemon-yellow jacket of his lieutenant. Competing for our attention is a young woman, also dressed in yellow satin studded with pearls, to the Captain's right. A chicken hangs from her waist, and below it a money-bag, as if she has encountered the company on her way home from the market. She is such an odd addition to the scene that scholars have for years tried to account for her presence as, for instance, a symbolic representation of the company itself or, alternately, an ironic commentary on the company's relation to mercantile interests. That said, she certainly adds a dimension of liveliness to the scene, asserting herself as a dramatic presence who underscores the motion and action of the painting as a whole. Everyone seems to be looking in different directions; different conversations abound; the figure in red, at the left, seems to have just discharged his rifle; a dog barks at a drummer entering from the right. Compared to the sedentary group portrait of Hals (see Fig. 22.16), with its linear hierarchy, in which everybody seems literally to sit still for the portraitist, Rembrandt's group is animated, even noisy. As his figures move in and out of light and shadow, it seems as if the artist has barely managed to capture them.

In one of his most famous group portraits, *The Anatomy Lesson of Dr. Tulp* (see *Closer Look*, pages 720–721), Rembrandt would use this symbolic light for ironic effect. But in his religious works, especially, it would come to stand for the redemption offered to humankind by the example of Christ. This is especially apparent in his prints, where the contrast between rich darks and brilliant lights could be exploited to great effect. Among the greatest of these is *Christ Preaching* (Fig. **22.17**), also known as the "Hundred-Guilder Print" because it sold for 100 guilders at a seventeenth-century auction, at that time an unheard-of price for a print. The image illustrates the Gospel of Matthew, showing Christ addressing the sick and the lame, grouped at his feet and at his left, and the Pharisees, at his right. Always aware of Albrecht Dürer's great achievements in the medium (see Figs. 17.8 and 17.9), Rembrandt here constructs a triangle of light that seems to emanate from the figure of Christ himself, which seems to burst from the deep black gloom of the night. What the light is meant to offer, of course, is hope—and life.

Of all the artists of his era, Rembrandt was certainly the most interested in self-portraiture. A painter's own face is always freely available for study, and the self-portrait offered Rembrandt the opportunity to explore technical and compositional problems using himself as a means to do it. Over 60 self-portraits survive, most of them imbued with the same drama of light and dark that characterizes his other work. Beginning in 1640, he endured a series of tragedies, beginning with the death of his mother. Two years later, Rembrandt's wife Saskia died shortly after giving birth to Titus, the only one of their four children to survive to adulthood. Furthermore, Rembrandt lived notoriously beyond his means. In 1656, he was forced to declare bankruptcy, a public humiliation. The inventory of the collection he had put together to satisfy his eclectic taste is astonishing. There

EXPLORE MORE View a studio technique video about etching at **www.myartslab.com**

The *Anatomy Lesson of Dr. Tulp* was commissioned by Dr. Tulp to celebrate his second public anatomy demonstration performed in Amsterdam on January 31, 1632. Public dissections were always performed in the winter months in order to better preserve the cadaver from deterioration. The body generally was that of a recently executed prisoner. The object of these demonstrations was purely educational—how better to understand the human body than to inspect its innermost workings? By understanding the human body, the Dutch believed, one could come to understand God. As the Dutch poet Barlaeus put it in 1639, in a poem dedicated to Rembrandt's painting:

Listener, learn yourself! And while you proceed through the parts, believe that, even in the smallest, God lies hid.

Public anatomies, or dissections, were extremely popular events. Town dignitaries would generally attend, and a ticket-paying public filled the amphitheater. As sobering as the lessons of an anatomy might be, the event was also an entertaining spectacle. An example of the Dutch group portrait, this one was designed to celebrate Tulp's medical knowledge as well as his following. He is surrounded by his students, all of whom are identified on the sheet of paper held by the figure standing behind the doctor. Their curiosity underscores Tulp's prestige and the scientific inquisitiveness of the age.

Like Frans Hals's group portrait *Banquet of the Officers of the St. George Civic Guard* (see Fig. 26.16), the figures are arranged in a triangle. Dr. Tulp, in the bottom right corner, holds forceps that are the focus of almost everyone's attention. As is characteristic of Rembrandt's work, light plays a highly symbolic role. It shines across the room, from left to right, directly lighting the faces of the three most inquisitive students, suggesting the light of revelation and learning. And it terminates at Tulp's face, almost as if he himself is the source of their light. Ironically, the best-lit figure in the scene is the corpse. Whereas light in Rembrandt's work almost always suggests the kind of lively animation we see on the students' brightly lit faces, here it illuminates death.

Dr. Frans van Loenen points at the corpse with his index finger as he engages the viewer's eyes. The gesture is meant to remind us that we are all mortal.

The pale, almost bluish skin tone of the cadaver contrasts dramatically with the rosy complexions of the surgeons. Typically, the cadaver's face was covered during the anatomy, but Rembrandt unmasked the cadaver's face for his painting. In fact, we know the identity of the cadaver. He is Adriaen Adriaenszoon, also known as "Aris Kindt"— "the Kid"—a criminal with a long history of thievery and assault who was hanged for beating an Amsterdam merchant while trying to steal his cape. Dr. Tulp and his colleagues retrieved the body from the gallows. In another context, a partly draped nude body so well lit would immediately evoke the entombment of Christ with its promise of Resurrection. It is the very impossibility of that fate for Adriaen Adriaenszoon that the lighting seems to underscore here.

Dr. Tulp is displaying the flexor muscles of the arm and hand and demonstrating their action by activating various muscles and tendons. It is the manual dexterity enabled by these muscles that physically distinguishes man from beast.

Something to Think About . . .

While it is the hand that distinguishes man from beast, why would an artist like Rembrandt be especially drawn to representing its dissection?

SEE MORE For a Closer Look at Rembrandt van Rijn's *The Anatomy Lesson of Dr. Tulp*, go to **www.myartslab.com**

Dr. Hartman Hartmanszoon holds in his hand a drawing of a flayed body upon which someone later added the names of all the figures in the scene.

Dr. Tulp was born Claes Pieterszoon but took the name *Tulp*—Dutch for "tulip"—sometime between 1611 and 1614 when still a medical student in Leiden, where he encountered the flower in the botanical gardens of the university. Throughout his career, a signboard painted with a single golden yellow tulip on an azure ground hung outside his house.

This large book may be the *De humani corporis fabrica,* the first thorough anatomy, published in 1543 by the Dutch scientist Andreis van Wesel (1514–1564), known as Vesalius, who had taught anatomy at the University of Padua. Tulp thought of himself as *Vesalius redivivus,* "Vesalius revived."

Rembrandt van Rijn, ***The Anatomy Lesson of Dr. Tulp.*** **1632.** Oil on canvas, 5'3 ³/₄" × 7'1 ¹/₄" (169.5 × 216.5 cm).
Royal Cabinet of Paintings Maurithsuis Foundation, The Hague, Netherlands.

Fig. 22.18 Rembrandt van Rijn, *Slaughtered Ox.* **1655.** Oil on panel, 37″ × 27⅛″. Musée du Louvre/RMN Réunion des Musées Nationaux, France. Erich Lessing/Art Resource, New York. The painting lies fully within the tradition of Dutch still life (see Fig. 21.13), though it is much more starkly realistic than the norm.

Saskia—another 20,000 guilders. Within the context of these difficulties, he must have identified with the flayed body of the ox. Yet the image is also one of plenty and well-being—suggesting a feast to come. This reading is supported by the emergence from the doorway behind the crossbeams of a kitchen maid, bathed in a soft light. A similar optimism pervades all of Rembrandt's late work, perhaps because he saw light, a requirement of the painter's act of seeing, as inherently imbued with divine goodness, or at least its promise.

His *Self-Portrait* of 1658 tends to confirm this reading of the *Slaughtered Ox* as a kind of self-portrait (Fig. **22.19**). Here Rembrandt sits kinglike, dressed in rich robes, leaning forward in his chair, his legs wide apart, scepter or staff in hand, bathed in light. His hands, especially the left one, show the same ferocity and rough brushwork as the *Slaughtered Ox* and look quite meaty. In this painting, Rembrandt seems to rise above his impoverished condition long enough to play the part of the victor, not the vanquished. The ferocity of Rembrandt's brushwork suggests that the function of art is to transform mere flesh by the stroke of imagination, to wrest from the inevitable misfortune of humanity a certain dignity, even a kind of triumph. In the drama of light that pervades his art, he asserted both the psychological complexity of a profoundly individual personality and a more general, but deeply felt, compassion for humanity.

THE BAROQUE KEYBOARD

In the late eighteenth century, the philosopher and sometimes composer Jean-Jacques Rousseau [roo-SOH] (whose work will be discussed in Chapter 25) described Baroque music in the most unflattering terms: "A baroque music is that in which the harmony is confused, charged with modulation and dissonances, the melody is harsh and little natural, the intonation difficult, and the movement constrained." In many ways, the description is accurate, although Rousseau's negative reaction to these characteristics reveals more about the musical taste of his own later age than it does the quality of music in the Baroque era itself. Stylistically, the music of the Baroque era is as varied as the Baroque art of Rome and Amsterdam. Like the art created in both centers, it is purposefully dramatic and committed to arousing emotion in the listener. Religious music, particularly, was devoted to evoking the Passion of Christ. Also like Baroque art in both cities, Baroque music sought to be new and original, as Catholic and Protestant churches, north and south, constantly demanded new music for their services. At the same time, Baroque musicians created new secular forms of music as well. (See the discussion of Corelli and the *sonata da camera* in Chapter 21.) Perhaps most significant of all, the Baroque era produced more new instruments than any other. Additionally, even traditional instruments were almost totally transformed. This was the golden age of the organ. The deep intonations of this very ancient instrument, dating from the

were South American Indian costumes, shells, sponges, and coral from around the world's oceans, a stuffed New Guinea bird of paradise, Chinese ceramics, Turkish and Persian textiles, musical instruments of all kinds and from all periods, Javanese shadow puppets, and arms and armor. Works of art included sculpture busts of the Roman emperors from Augustus through Marcus Aurelius, "a little child by Michelangelo," and a huge collection of works on paper, including examples by Bruegel and Rubens, and a "precious book" (perhaps a collection of drawings) by Mantegna. He had used many of these items in his paintings. Suddenly he found himself without his things.

It is tempting to read his *Slaughtered Ox* of 1655, painted just before his bankruptcy, as a psychological self-portrait, reflecting the artist's anguish as he saw ruin approaching (Fig. **22.18**). Disemboweled and lashed to a wooden frame, its hind legs spread in some grotesque parody of the Crucifixion, the carcass is an exercise in the furious brushwork, the signature "rough style," for which Rembrandt was by now famous. At this point, he was over 13,000 guilders in debt, creditors were threatening to take his home, and he had spent all of Titus's inheritance from

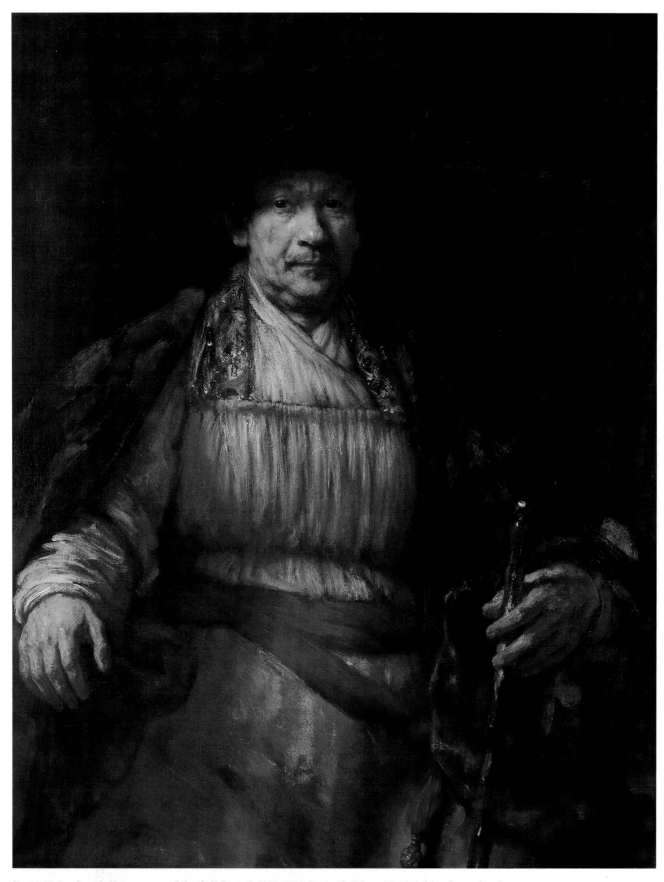

Fig. 22.19 Rembrandt Harmensz van Rijn, *Self-Portrait.* **1606–1669.** Dutch, "Self-Portrait". 1658. Oil on Canvas (lined)
52⅝″ × 40⅞″. (133.7 × 103.8 cm). Signed and dated on the arm of the chair at right: Rembrandt/f.1658. Purchased in 1906.
Acc #06.1.97. The Frick Collection, NY. Looking past the viewer, Rembrandt's gaze removes him from the cares of everyday life,
and transports him into an almost purely imaginative space.

third century BCE, reached new heights as it commanded the emotions of both Catholic and Protestant churchgoers alike. By the first half of the eighteenth century, the piano began to emerge as a vital instrument even as the harpsichord was perfected technically. And for the first time in the history of music, instrumental virtuosos, especially on violin and keyboard, began to rival vocalists in popularity.

One of the primary forms of entertainment at Dutch family gatherings was the performance of keyboard music by the lady of the house, and indeed most of the surviving compositions from the period are scores made for home use. In fact, Vermeer's several paintings of young women playing the virginal, a keyboard instrument, such as his *Lady at the Virginal with a Gentleman*, also known as *The Music Lesson* (Fig. 22.20), are emblems of domestic harmony. In Vermeer's painting, the idea of harmony is further asserted by the empty chair and bass viol behind the young woman, which, we can assume, the young gentleman will soon take up in a duet. Inscribed on the lid of the virginal are the words "MVSICA LETITIAE CO[ME]S MEDICINA DO-LOR[VM]" ("Music is the companion of joy and balm for sorrow"). In the context of Dutch domestic life, it would not be far-fetched to substitute *marriage* for *music*, so close is the analogy.

Jan Pieterszoon Sweelinck's Fantasies for the Organ

Amsterdam was home to one of the greatest keyboard masters of the seventeenth century, Jan Pieterszoon Sweelinck [SWAY-lingk] (1562–1621). As the official organist of Amsterdam, he performed on the great organ at the Oude Kerk (Old Church) for 40 years. Calvinist doctrine required that, at church services, he play standard hymns from the early years of the Reformation. Nevertheless, he was famous for his preludes and postludes to the services, which were virtuoso improvisations. These helped to draw large congregations on Sundays, and he routinely gave public concerts during the week as well. Students from all over Europe flocked to Amsterdam to study with Sweelinck, and, by the time of his death in 1621, he had transformed keyboard composition, especially in Germany. A long line of his pupils came to be regarded as members of the North German school.

Sweelinck was especially noted for his **fantasias**, keyboard works that lack a conventional structure but follow, or at least give the impression of following, the composer's free flight of fantasy. In fact, by the 1620s, when Sweelinck's compositions were in wide circulation, the terms *fantasia* and *prelude* were used interchangeably to refer to this purely instrumental form.

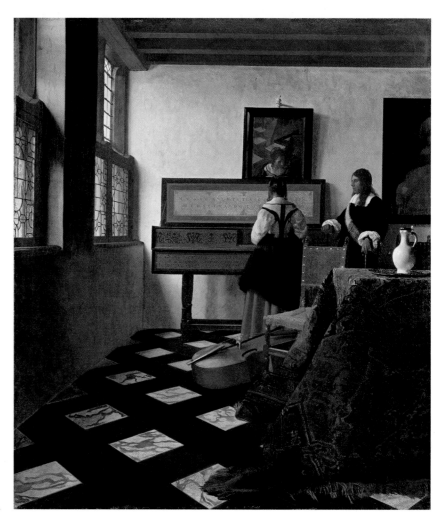

Fig. 22.20 Jan Vermeer, *Lady at the Virginal with a Gentleman (The Music Lesson).* ca. 1662–64. Oil on canvas, 29 1/8″ × 25 3/8″. Courtesy of Her Majesty Queen Elizabeth II. In the manner of van Eyck's *Giovanni Arnolfini and His Wife Giovanna Cenami* (see Fig. 20.11), Vermeer includes himself, or at least his easel, reflected in the mirror at the back of the painting.

In his 1597 *Plain and Easy Introduction to Practical Music*, the English composer Thomas Morley (1558–1602) described fantasias as follows:

> The most principal and chiefest kind of music which is made without a ditty [i.e., without words to be sung] is the Fantasy, that is when a musician taketh a point [i.e., a theme] at his pleasure and wresteth and turneth it as he list [chooses], making either much or little of it according as shall seem best in his own conceit. In this may more art be shown than in any other music because the composer is tied to nothing, but that he may add, diminish, and alter at his pleasure.

Sweelinck's displays of virtuosity were heightened by his use of the pedalboard. (The organ normally had two keyboards playable by the hands, and a third keyboard playable by the feet.) Using the pedalboard as an independent part of the composition allowed Sweelinck, and the many composers who followed his lead, to create highly dramatic works that, in Morley's words, "wresteth and turneth" in surprisingly original ways. In their variety of forms—"discords, quick motions, slow motions"—in the composer's ability "to add, diminish, and alter at his pleasure," but above all in their ability to surprise their audience, Sweelinck's compositions were the musical equivalent of the Baroque architecture embodied in Francesco Borromini's Church of San Carlo alle Quattro Fontane (see Fig. 21.10).

The North German School: Johann Sebastian Bach

Perhaps the greatest heir to Sweelinck's innovations was Johann Sebastian Bach [bakh] (1685–1750). Born 60 years after Sweelinck's death and at the end of the seventeenth century, Bach was very much a master of the keyboard in Sweelinck's Baroque tradition. Like Sweelinck, Bach sought to convey the devotional piety of the Protestant tradition through his religious music. And like Sweelinck, he was an organist, first in the churches of small German towns, then in the courts of the Duke of Weimar [VY-mahr] and the Prince of Cöthen, and finally at Saint Thomas's Lutheran Church in Leipzig [LIPE-zig]. There he wrote most of the music for the Lutheran church services, which were much more elaborate than the Calvinist services in Amsterdam.

Vocal Music For each Sunday service, Bach also composed a **cantata**, a multimovement musical commentary on the chosen text of the day sung by soloists and chorus accompanied by one or more instruments, usually the organ. The first half of the cantata was performed after the scriptural lesson and the second half after the sermon, concluding with a chorale, a hymn sung in the vernacular by the entire congregation. Like operas, cantatas include both recitative parts and arias.

Bach's cantatas are usually based on the simple melodies of Lutheran chorales, but are transformed by his genius for **counterpoint**, the addition of one or more independent melodies above or below the main melody, in this case the line of the Lutheran chorale. The result is an ornate musical texture that is characteristically Baroque. *Jesu, der du meine Seele* ("Jesus, It Is By You That My Soul") provides a perfect example, and it reveals the extraordinary productivity of Bach as a composer, driven as he was by the Baroque demand for the new and the original. He wrote it in 1724, a week after writing another entirely new cantata, and a week before writing yet another. (Bach was compelled to write them in time for his choir and orchestra to **HEAR MORE** at rehearse.) The opening chorus (track **22.1**) is **www.myartslab.com** based on the words and melody of a chorale that would have been familiar to all parishioners. That melody is always presented by the soprano, and is first heard 21 measures into the composition after an extended passage for the orchestra. Even the untrained ear can appreciate the play between this melody and the others introduced in counterpoint to it.

Over the course of his career, Bach composed more than 300 cantatas, or five complete sets, one for each Sunday and feast day of the church calendar. In addition, he composed large-scale **oratorios**. These are lengthy choral works, either sacred or secular, but without action or scenery, performed by a narrator, soloists, chorus, and orchestra (see Chapter 21) for Christmas and Easter. Bach's *Christmas Oratorio* is a unique example of the form. It consists of six cantatas, written to be sung on six separate days over the course of the Christmas season from 1734 to 1735, beginning on Christmas Day and ending on Epiphany (January 6). Based on the gospels of Saint Luke and Saint Matthew, the story is narrated by a tenor soloist in the role of an Evangelist. Other soloists include an Angel, in the second cantata, and Herod, in the sixth. The chorus itself assumes several roles: the heavenly host singing "Glory to God" in the second cantata; the shepherds singing "Let us, even now, go to Bethlehem" in the third; and, in the fifth, the Wise Men, singing "Where is this new-born child; the king of the Jews?" Solo arias interrupt the narrative in order to reflect upon the meanings of the story.

One of Bach's greatest achievements in vocal music is *The Passion According to Saint Matthew*, written for the Good Friday service in Leipzig in 1727. A **passion** is similar to an oratorio in form but tells the story from the Gospels of the death and Resurrection of Jesus. Composed of the sung texts of chapters 26 and 27 of the Gospel of Matthew, it narrates the events between the Last Supper and the Resurrection. It is a huge work, over three hours long. A double chorus assisted by a boys' choir alternates with soloists (representing Matthew, Jesus, Judas, and others) who sing arias and recitatives, all accompanied by a double orchestra and two organs. As in the *Christmas Oratorio*, the story is narrated by a tenor Evangelist. The words of Jesus are surrounded by a lush string accompaniment, Bach's way of creating a musical halo around them. All told, in the *Passion of Saint Matthew* Bach seems to have captured the entire range of human emotion, from terror and grief to the highest joy.

Instrumental Music Bach wrote instrumental music for almost all occasions, including funerals, marriages, and civic celebrations. Among his most famous instrumental works are the six *Brandenburg* concertos, dedicated to the Margrave of

Brandenburg in 1721. (A margrave was a German title, of lesser rank than a duke.) Each of the six is scored differently, and in fact Bach seems to have been intent on exploring the widest possible range of orchestral instruments in often daring combinations. Technically, concertos number one, two, four, and five are examples of the **concerto grosso** large concerts—which feature several solo instruments accompanied by a **ripieno** (Italian for "full") ensemble. The second, for instance, is scored for trumpet, recorder (often performed by a flute today), oboe, and violin as soloists. In the third movement of the second concerto, the main melody is stated by the solo trumpet and subsequently imitated in counterpoint by all the other soloists, and subsequently restated by both the violin and oboe, until at the conclusion the trumpet makes a final statement accompanied by all the soloists and the orchestra (track **22.2**). The third concerto is a **ripieno concerto**, a form which features no solo instruments at all and is scored for strings. The sixth is unique, calling for low strings (no violins or violas) to accompany two solo violas and two solo viola da gambas (a bass stringed instrument slightly smaller than a cello).

HEAR MORE at www.myartslab.com

One of Bach's great contributions to secular instrumental musical history is his *Well-Tempered Clavier.* It is an attempt to popularize the idea of **equal temperament** in musical tuning, especially the tuning of keyboard instruments like the harpsichord, the virginal (a smaller harpsichord), and the clavichord. The harpsichord is a piano-like instrument whose strings are plucked rather than struck as with a piano. A clavichord's brass or metal strings are struck by metal blades (Fig. **22.21**). Equal temperament consists in dividing the octave into 12 half-steps of equal size. *The Well-Tempered Clavier* is a two-part collection of musical compositions, the first part completed in 1722, and the second around 1740. Each part consists of 24 preludes and fugues, one prelude and one fugue in each of the 12 major and minor keys.

The **fugue** is a genre that carries a single thematic idea for the entire length of the work. As Bach wrote on the title page to the first part, the pieces were intended "for the profit and use of musical youth desirous of learning and especially for the pastime of those already skilled in this study." Bach's fugues, of which the *Fugue in D major* from Part II of *The Well-Tempered Clavier* is a remarkable example, consist of four independent parts (or occasionally three), one part, or *voice*, of which states a theme or melody—called a *subject*—and is then imitated by a succession of the other voices. The parts constantly overlap as the first voice continues playing in counterpoint, using material other than the main subject, while the second takes up the subject, and so on. The trick is to give each voice a distinctly independent line and to play all four voices simultaneously with two hands on a single instrument (track **22.3**). In the end, the fugues in *The Well-Tempered Clavier* are almost sublime examples of Cartesian rationalism. In his 1649 *The Passions of the Soul*, Descartes had argued that human emotions—love, hate, joy, sadness, or exaltation—were objective in nature and susceptible to rational description, particularly in the language of music. Bach's fugues are a demonstration of this, laying out a range of feeling with a virtually mathematical clarity.

HEAR MORE at www.myartslab.com

Fig. 22.21 Clavichord with painted images, Dirk Stoop (painter). ca. 1660–80. Painted musical instrument, $4'' \times 32\frac{1}{2}'' \times 10\frac{3}{4}''$. Collection Rijksmuseum, Amsterdam. Item # NM -9487. Clavichords were built as early as the fifteenth century, perhaps even earlier. It was at once the most personal and quietest of European keyboard instruments, perfect for the household chamber.

The Art of the People and the Tastes of the Court

If, as many believe, Rembrandt was the leading painter of the vernacular in Baroque Amsterdam, the leading court painter of the period is Peter Paul Rubens (1577–1640). Rubens's career in Antwerp, the Catholic city in the Spanish Netherlands, overlapped Rembrandt's in Amsterdam. Rubens was 30 years older than Rembrandt and had long been an international sensation by the time Rembrandt left Leiden for Amsterdam in 1631. The list of Rubens's accomplishments is long and impressive: chief painter to the Habsburg governors of Flanders, then in the 1620s to the Queen Mother of France, Marie de' Medici, and to Charles I of England; knighted in Brussels, London, and Madrid; successful diplomat who negotiated the treaty of peace between England and Spain in 1629 to 1630; and owner of what many considered the greatest collection of antique sculpture in the world, housed in what was also arguably the finest house in all Antwerp.

Across Europe in the seventeenth century, Rubens's exuberant style would dominate. It was a style more attuned to the lavish, even sensual lifestyle of the royal courts. The Dutch Reformists had managed to expel the excesses of Baroque style from Holland, but still, Rubens was the artist whom every young painter sought to emulate in the early seventeenth century. Rembrandt, despite his far more conservative and Protestant leanings, was no exception. What distinguished him was that he possessed the talent to compete with the master.

In 1633, at age 27, Rembrandt painted a *Descent from the Cross* (Fig. **22.22**) based directly on an engraving of Rubens's own *Descent from the Cross* in Antwerp Cathedral (Fig. **22.23**), painted 20 years earlier. The differences are more revealing than the similarities. For one thing, the scale of Rembrandt's intimate painting is much smaller than Rubens's original altarpiece, probably the result of Rembrandt's working from the etching. Furthermore, Rembrandt pushes the scene deeper into the space of the canvas, filling the foreground with shadow and deepening the picture plane so that viewers are more removed from the action. Many of his figures, too, are removed from the action, helplessly looking on, whereas in the Rubens everyone is engaged in the scene. The greatest difference, however, is that Rubens's *Descent* luxuriates in color and sensually curving line. Rembrandt's painting seems positively austere beside it. Nowhere in the seventeenth century can we more plainly see the tension between the art of the people, embodied in the taste of the middle-class Dutch, and the art of the royal courts of France, Spain, and England, the subject of the next chapter. ■

Fig. 22.22 Rembrandt van Rijn, *Descent from the Cross*. ca. 1633. Oil on panel, 35$\frac{1}{4}$" × 25$\frac{5}{8}$". Antwerp Cathedral, Belgium. SCALA/Art Resource, New York.

Fig. 22.23 Peter Paul Rubens, *Descent from the Cross*. 1611–14. Oil on panel, 13'9$\frac{5}{8}$" × 10'2". Alte Pinakothek, Munich, Germany. SCALA/Art Resource, New York.

What forces were at work in Amsterdam in the seventeenth century?

As Holland asserted its independence from Spain at the end of the sixteenth century, Amsterdam replaced Antwerp as the center of culture and commerce in the north. Its commercial ascendancy was underscored by the wealth at the city's disposal during the tulipomania, or tulip madness, of 1634 to 1637. How were the forces that drove the tulip craze balanced by the conservatism of the Dutch Reformed Church?

How did developments in philosophy and science underpin the Dutch attention to visual detail?

Developments in philosophy and science challenged the authority of both the Catholic and Protestant churches. In England, Francis Bacon developed the empirical method, a process of inductive reasoning. Bacon's writings circulated widely in Holland, where, for over 20 years, René Descartes developed a separate brand of philosophy based on deductive reasoning. What is the difference between inductive and deductive reasoning? Why would the Church—Catholic and Protestant alike—feel threatened by the philosophies of both Francis Bacon and René Descartes?

Scientific discoveries supported the philosophies of Bacon and Descartes. Johannes Kepler described functional properties of the human eye, the optical properties of lenses, and the movement of the planets in the solar system. His friend Galileo Galilei perfected the telescope, described the forces of gravity, and theorized the speed of light. How would the Church react to Galileo's discoveries? Meanwhile, in Holland, the microscope had been developed, and soon Antoni van Leeuwenhoek began to describe, for the first time, "little animals"—bacteria and protozoa—sperm cells, blood cells, and many other organisms.

How does the vernacular manifest itself in Dutch painting?

Still lifes, landscapes, and genre paintings, including many like Vermeer's that depict domestic life, were especially popular. Most popular of all, however, were portrait paintings, including large-scale group portraits, such as those by Hals and Rembrandt, commemorating the achievements of community leaders, civic militia, and the like. How does the Dutch taste in painting reflect Francis Bacon's philosophical principles? How do you account for the popularity of portraiture in Dutch society? How might you connect it to Descartes's sense of self? Rembrandt van Rijn's paintings are especially notable for their dramatic liveliness. How does his mastery of light and dark contribute to this?

What are the characteristic features of Baroque keyboard music?

Keyboard music was a prominent feature of Dutch domestic life. What role did it play in the home? In Amsterdam, Jan Pieterszoon Sweelinck, organist for 40 years at the Oude Kerk (Old Church), developed the distinctly Baroque brand of keyboard work known as the fantasy, or alternately, the prelude. These works were widely imitated across Europe, reaching a height in the composition of Johann Sebastian Bach in Germany. How would you characterize these keyboard works? Bach's many compositions reflect one of the distinct features of Baroque music, the drive to create new and original compositions at a sometimes unheard-of pace. What did his *Well-Tempered Clavier* contribute to secular musical history?

PRACTICE MORE Get flashcards for images and terms and review chapter material with quizzes at **www.myartslab.com**

GLOSSARY

camera obscura A device that anticipates the modern camera but lacks the means of capturing an image on film.

cantata A multimovement musical commentary on the chosen text of the day sung by soloists and chorus accompanied by one or more instruments, most often the organ.

concerto grosso A Baroque concerto featuring both soloists and a larger ensemble (the *ripieno*).

counterpoint The addition of one or more independent melodies above or below the main melody.

deductive reasoning A method that begins with clearly established general principles and proceeds to the establishment of particular truths.

deism The brand of faith that argues that the basis of belief in God is reason and logic rather than revelation or tradition.

empirical method A manner of inquiry that combines *inductive reasoning* and scientific experimentation.

equal temperament A system of tuning that consists of dividing the octave into 12 half-steps of equal size.

fantasias A keyboard work that possesses no conventional structure but follows, or at least gives the impression of following, the composer's free flight of fantasy.

fugue A contrapuntal work in which a musical theme is played by a series of musical lines, each in turn, until all the lines are playing at once.

genre scene A painting that depicts events from everyday life.

geocentric Earth-centered.

group portrait A large canvas commissioned by a civic institution to document or commemorate its membership at a particular time.

heliocentric Sun-centered.

inductive reasoning A process in which, through the direct and careful observation of natural phenomena, one can draw general conclusions from particular examples and predict the operations of nature as a whole.

landscape A painting that shows natural scenery.

oratorio A lengthy choral work of a sacred or secular nature but without action or scenery and performed by a narrator, soloists, chorus, and orchestra.

passion A musical setting, similar to an *oratorio*, that recounts the last days of the life of Jesus.

ripieno In Baroque music, the name for the large ensemble within a *concerto grosso*.

ripieno concerto A concerto for a large ensemble lacking any soloists.

still life A painting dedicated to the representation of common household objects and food.

***vanitas* painting** A type of painting that reminds the viewer that pleasurable things in life inevitably fade, that the material world is not as long-lived as the spiritual, and that the spiritual should command our attention.

READING

READING 22.1

from Francis Bacon, *Novum Organum Scientiarum (The New Method of Science)* (1620)

As a lawyer, member of Parliament and Queen's Counsel, the Englishman Francis Bacon wrote on questions of law, state, and religion, as well as on contemporary politics, but he is best known for his empirical essays on natural philosophy, including the Novum Organum Scientiarum (The New Method of Science). *In that work, he presents the following theory of "Idols," the false notions that must be purged from the mind before it can properly engage in the acquisition of knowledge. Empiricism is, in fact, the "new method of science" that will restore the senses by freeing them from the Idols.*

36 One method of delivery alone remains to us which is simply this: we must lead men to the particulars themselves, and their series and order; while men on their side must force themselves for a while to lay their notions by and begin to familiarize themselves with facts.

38 The idols and false notions which are now in possession of the human understanding, and have taken deep root therein, not only so beset men's minds that truth can hardly find entrance, but even after entrance is obtained, they will again in the very instauration[1] of the sciences meet and trouble us, unless 10 men being forewarned of the danger fortify themselves as far as may be against their assaults.

39 There are four classes of Idols which beset men's minds. To these for distinction's sake I have assigned names, calling the first class *Idols of the Tribe*; the second, *Idols of the Cave*; the third, *Idols of the Market Place*; the fourth, *Idols of the Theater*.

41 The Idols of the Tribe have their foundation in human nature itself, and in the tribe or race of men. For it is a false assertion that the sense of man is the measure of things. On the contrary, all perceptions as well of the sense as of the mind are according 20 to the measure of the individual and not according to the measure of the universe. And the human understanding is like a false mirror, which, receiving rays irregularly, distorts and discolors the nature of things by mingling its own nature with it.

42 The Idols of the Cave are the idols of the individual man. For everyone (besides the errors common to human nature in general) has a cave or den of his own, which refracts and discolors the light of nature, owing either to his own proper and peculiar nature; or to his education and conversation with others; or to the reading of books, and the authority of those whom he es- 30 teems and admires; or to the differences of impressions, accordingly as they take place in a mind preoccupied and predisposed or in a mind indifferent and settled; or the like. So that the spirit of man (according as it is meted out to different individuals) is in

fact a thing variable and full of perturbation, and governed as it were by chance. Whence it was well observed by Heraclitus[2] that men look for sciences in their own lesser worlds, and not in the greater or common world.

43 There are also Idols formed by the intercourse and association of men with each other, which I call Idols of the Market Place, on 40 account of the commerce and consort of men there. For it is by discourse that men associate, and words are imposed according to the apprehension of the vulgar. And therefore the ill and unfit choice of words wonderfully obstructs the understanding. Nor do the definitions or explanations wherewith in some things learned men are wont to guard and defend themselves, by any means set the matter right. But words plainly force and overrule the understanding, and throw all into confusion, and lead men away into numberless empty controversies and idle fancies.

44 Lastly, there are Idols which have immigrated into men's 50 minds from the various dogmas of philosophies, and also from wrong laws of demonstration. These I call Idols of the Theater, because in my judgment all the received systems are but so many stage plays, representing worlds of their own creation after an unreal and scenic fashion. Nor is it only of the systems now in vogue, or only of the ancient sects and philosophies, that I speak; for many more plays of the same kind may yet be composed and in like artificial manner set forth; seeing that errors the most widely different have nevertheless causes for the most part alike. Neither again do I mean this only of entire systems, 60 but also of many principles and axioms in science, which by tradition, credulity, and negligence have come to be received.

READING CRITICALLY

Can you identify, in your own place and time, an example of each of Bacon's "Idols" playing itself out and determining the way people think fallaciously?

[1] Reorganization or renewal.

[2] A Greek philosopher, ca. 500 BCE, who taught that nature was in a state of flux.

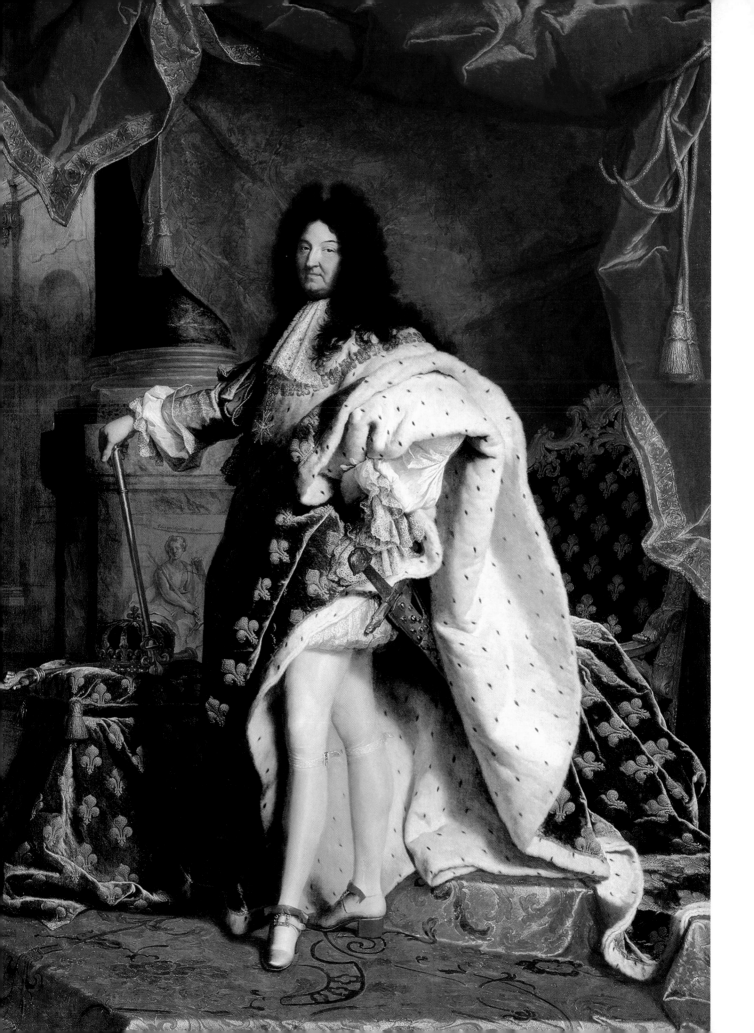

23 The Baroque Court
Absolute Power and Royal Patronage

THINKING AHEAD

What is absolutism?

What tastes in art competed for Louis XIV's favor?

How did political conflict affect the arts in England?

What role did the arts play in the Spanish court?

How did Native American traditions affect the Baroque style in the Americas?

Louis XIV (r. 1643–1715), King of France, thought of himself as *Le Roi Soleil* [leh wah so-LAY], "the Sun King," because like the sun (associated with Apollo, god of peace and the arts) he saw himself dispensing bounty across the land. His ritual risings and retirings (the *levée du roi* [leh-VAY dew wah] and the *couchée du roi* [koo-SHAY]) symbolized the actual rising and setting of the sun. They were essentially state occasions, attended by either the entire court or a select group of fawning aristocrats who eagerly entered their names on waiting lists.

Louis's sense of his own authority—to say nothing of his notorious vanity—is wonderfully captured in Hyacinthe Rigaud's [ree-GOH] (1659–1743) official state portrait of 1701 (Fig. 23.1). The king has flung his robes over his shoulder in order to reveal his white stockings and red high-heeled shoes. He designed the shoes himself to compensate for his 5-foot-4-inch height. He is 63 years old in this portrait, but he means to make it clear that he is still a dashing courtier.

Louis's control over the lives of his courtiers had the political benefit of making them financially dependent on him. According to the memoirs of the duc de Saint Simon, Louis de Rouvroy (1675–1755):

> He loved splendour, magnificence, and profusion in all things, and encouraged similar tastes in his Court; to spend money freely on equipages and buildings, on feasting and at cards, was a sure way to gain his favour, perhaps to obtain the honour of a word from him. Motives of policy had something to do with this; by making expensive habits the fashion, and, for people in a certain position, a necessity, he compelled his courtiers to live beyond their income, and gradually reduced them to depend on his bounty for the means of subsistence.

Louis, in fact, encouraged the noblewomen at court to consider it something of an honor to sleep with him; he had many mistresses and many illegitimate children. Life in his court was entirely formal, governed by custom and rule, so

◀ **Fig. 23.1 Hyacinthe Rigaud, *Louis XIV, King of France.* 1701.** Oil on canvas, 9'1" × 6'4³⁄₈". Musée du Louvre/RMN Réunion des Musées Nationaux, France. Herve Lewandowski/Art Resource, New York. In his ermine coronation robes, his feet adorned in red high-heeled shoes, Louis both literally and figuratively looks down his nose at the viewer, his sense of superiority fully captured by Rigaud.

SEE MORE For a Closer Look at Hyacinthe Rigaud's *Louis XIV*, go to **www.myartslab.com**

HEAR MORE Listen to an audio file of your chapter at **www.myartslab.com**

etiquette became a way of social advancement. He required the use of a fork at meal times instead of using one's fingers. Where one sat at dinner was determined by rank. Rank even determined whether footmen opened one or two of his palace's glass-paneled "French doors" as each guest passed through.

By the start of the eighteenth century, almost every royal court in Europe modeled itself on Louis XIV's court. Louis so successfully asserted his authority over the French people, the aristocracy, and the Church that the era in which he ruled has become known as the Age of Absolutism. **Absolutism** is a term applied to strong, centralized monarchies that exert royal power over their dominions, usually on the grounds of divine right. The principle had its roots in the Middle Ages, when the pope crowned Europe's kings, and went back even further to the man/god kings of ancient Mesopotamia and Egypt. But by the seventeenth century, the divine right of kings was assumed to exist even without papal acknowledgment. The most famous description of the nature of absolutism is by Bishop Jacques-Bénigne Bossuet [BOS-sway] (1627–1704), Louis's court preacher and tutor to his son. While training the young dauphin for a future role as king, Bossuet wrote *Politics Drawn from the Very Words of Holy Scripture*, a book dedicated to describing the source and proper exercise of political power. In it, he says the following:

> God is infinite, God is all. The prince, as prince, is not regarded as a private person: he is a public personage, all the state is in him; the will of all the people is included in his. As all perfection and all strength are united in God, so all the power of individuals is united in the person of the prince. What grandeur that a single man should embody so much! . . .

> Behold an immense people united in a single person; behold this holy power, paternal and absolute; behold the secret cause which governs the whole body of the state, contained in a single head: you see the image of God in the king, and you have the idea of royal majesty. God is holiness itself, goodness itself, and power itself. In these things lies the majesty of God. In the image of these things lies the majesty of the prince.

The role of absolutism in defining and controlling developments in the arts in the seventeenth century is the subject of this chapter. Although the monarchs of Europe were often at war with one another, they were united in their belief in the power of the throne and the role of the arts in sustaining their authority. In France, Louis XIV never missed an opportunity to use the arts to impress upon the French people (and the other courts of Europe) his grandeur and power. In England, the monarchy struggled to assert its divine right to rule as it fought for power against Puritan factions that denied absolutism. Royalist and Puritan factions each developed distinctive styles of art and literature. In Spain, the absolute rule of the monarchy was deeply troubled by the financial insolvency of the state. Nevertheless, royal patronage brought about what has been called the Golden Age of Spanish arts and letters. Finally, in the Americas, the Spanish monarch asserted his absolute authority by encouraging the creation of art and architecture as symbols of his divine right to rule over the two continents. In the Americas, the European Baroque merged with Native American decorative tastes to produce what is possibly the era's most elaborate expression of the Baroque.

Fig. 23.2 Grand facade, Palace of Versailles, France. 1669–85. Versailles could house over 10,000 people—servants, members of the court, and ambitious aristocrats on the rise.

Fig. 23.3 Jules Hardouin-Mansart and Charles Le Brun, Galerie des Glaces (Hall of Mirrors), Palace of Versailles. Begun 1678. The Galerie des Glaces is 233 feet long and served as a reception space for state occasions. It gets its name from the Venetian mirrors—extraordinarily expensive at the time—that line the wall opposite windows of the same shape and size, creating by their reflection a sense of space even vaster than it actually is.

VERSAILLES AND THE RISE OF ABSOLUTISM

From a young age, Louis had detested the Louvre, the royal palace in Paris that had been the seat of French government since the Middle Ages. He had assumed the throne at five years of age, and a year later, he had been forced to flee Paris after an angry mob broke into the Louvre and demanded to see their child king. (Louis in his bedchamber feigned sleep, and the mob left after simply looking at him.) But the episode made Louis feel unsafe in the Louvre. Thus, in 1661, when he was 23 years of age, he began construction of a new residence in the small town of Versailles [vair-SIGH], 12 miles southeast of Paris. For 20 years, some 36,000 workers labored to make Versailles the most magnificent royal residence in the world (Fig. **23.2**). When Louis permanently moved his court and governmental offices there in 1682, Versailles became the unofficial capital of France and symbol of Louis's absolute power and authority.

More than any other art, French architecture was designed to convey the absolute power of the monarchy. From the moment that Louis XIV initiated the project at Versailles, it was understood that the new palace must be unequaled in grandeur, unparalleled in scale and size, and unsurpassed in lavish decoration and ornament. It would be the very image of the king, in whose majesty, according to the bishop, "lies the majesty of God."

The elaborate design of the his new palace at Versailles was intended to leave the attending nobility in awe. Charles Le Brun, who had participated in designing the new east facade of the Louvre (see Fig. 21.21), now served as chief painter to the king, and directed the team of artists who decorated the palace's interior. The Hall of Mirrors (Fig. **23.3**) was begun in 1678 to celebrate the high point of Louis XIV's political career, the end of six years of war with Holland. With the signing of the Treaty of Nijmegen [NY-may-gun], France gained control of the Franche-Comté [frahnsh-cohn-tay] region of eastern France.

Louis asked Le Brun to depict his government's accomplishments on the ceiling of the hall in 30 paintings, framed by stuccowork, showing the monarch as a Roman emperor, astute administrator, and military genius. Le Brun balanced the 17 windows that stretch the length of the hall and overlook the garden with 17 arcaded mirrors along the interior wall, all made in a Paris workshop founded to compete with

Venice's famous glass factories. Originally, solid silver tables, lamp holders, and orange-tree pots adorned the gallery. Louis later had them all melted down to finance his ongoing war efforts. Such luxury was in stark contrast to how the common people lived throughout France. Louis's centralized government did not address the enemies of their daily lives: drought, famine, and plague.

Landscape architect André Le Nôtre [leh NOHT] was in charge of the grounds at Versailles. He believed in the formal garden, and his methodical, geometrical design has come to be known as the **French garden**. (See Chapter 25 for its counterpart, the English garden.) The grounds were laid out around a main axis, emphasized by the giant cross-shaped Grand Canal, which stretched to the west of the palace (Figs. **23.4** and **23.5**). Pathways radiated from this central axis, circular pools and basins surrounded it, and both trees and shrubbery were groomed into abstract shapes to match the geometry of the overall site. The king himself took great interest in Le Nôtre's work, even writing a guide to the grounds for visitors. Neat boxwood hedges lined the flower beds near the chateau, and a greenhouse provided fresh flowers to be planted in the gardens as the seasons changed. Over 4 million tulip bulbs, imported from Holland, bloomed each spring.

THE ARTS OF THE FRENCH COURT

Louis asserted control over the nobility in a number of subtle ways. First, he made sure that the nobility benefited from the exercise of his own authority, by creating the largest army in Europe, numbering a quarter of a million men, and he modernized the army as well. Where previously local recruits and mercenaries had lived off the land, draining the resources of the nobility and pillaging and stealing to obtain their everyday needs, now Louis's forces were well-supplied, regularly paid, and extremely disciplined. The people admired them, understanding that this new army was not merely powerful, but also designed to protect them and guarantee their well-being—another benefit of centralized, absolute authority. However, as the army was always a present threat, Louis made no effort to limit the authority of regional *parlements*, and he generally made at least a pretense of consulting with these provincial governmental bodies before making decisions that would affect them. He also consulted with the nobility

Fig. 23.4 André Le Nôtre, plan of the gardens and park, Versailles. Designed 1661–68, executed 1662–90. Drawing by Leland Roth after Delagive's engraving of 1746. To the right are the main streets of the town of Versailles. Three grand boulevards cut through it to converge on the palace itself.

Fig. 23.5 André Le Nôtre, north flower bed, formal French gardens, Versailles. 1669–85. The gardens are most formal near the palace and become increasingly less elaborate further out in the park. Louis's gardener had more than 2 million flowerpots at his disposal.

at court. In fact, he required their presence in court in order to prevent them from developing regional power bases of their own that might undermine his centralized rule. He barred them from holding high government positions as well, even as he cultivated them socially and encouraged them to approach him directly.

Louis also established his authority through his control of the arts. He was the absolute judge of taste at the French court and a great patron of the arts. He inherited some 200 paintings from his father but increased the royal collection tenfold during his reign. Over the course of his career, he established the national academies of painting and sculpture, dance, music, and architecture. His motives were simple enough: Championing the greatest in art would establish him as the greatest of kings. "Gentlemen," he is reputed to have said to a group of academicians, "I entrust to you the most precious thing on earth—my fame."

Louis's aesthetic standards modulated between the balance, harmony, and proportions of classical art and the decorative exuberance of the Italian Baroque. Both the new east facade of the Louvre (see Fig. 21.21) and the geometric symmetry and clarity of Versailles and its grounds reflect his identification with classical precedent, and by extension, the order, regularity, and rational organization of the Roman Empire. On the other hand, he fully understood the attractions of Baroque scale and decorative effect, its power to move, even awe, its audience. So Louis promoted an essentially classical architecture with Baroque dramatic effects, in the process creating a style that is something of a contradiction, the Classical Baroque.

It was in painting that the stylistic tensions of the French court found their most complete expression. These tensions—which by extension were philosophical and even moral—were between the rational clarity of the classical and the emotional drama of the Baroque, the rule of law and the rule of the heart. These styles shared the common ground of grandeur and magnificence. Furthermore, in private, the court tended to prefer the frank sensuality of the Baroque, but in public, for political reasons, it chose the rationality and clarity of the classical in order to present an image of moderation as opposed to excess.

The Painting of Peter Paul Rubens: Color and Sensuality

One of Louis's favorite artists was the Flemish painter Peter Paul Rubens (1577–1640), and although Rubens died when Louis was only 2 years of age, the taste for Rubens's painting dominated Louis's court. Louis's grandmother, Marie de' Medici [deh-MED-ih-chee], had commissioned Rubens in 1621 to celebrate her life in a series of 21 monumental paintings. This series was to be paired with

a similar (but never completed) series extolling Henry IV, her late husband. She was, by this time, serving as regent of France for her young son, Louis XIII—Louis XIV's father—and the cycle was conceived to decorate the Luxembourg Palace in Paris, which today houses the French Senate. Rubens was 44 years old, had spent eight formative years (1600–08) in Italy in the service of the Duke of Mantua, and had already provided paintings for numerous patrons in his native Flanders, especially altarpieces for Catholic churches in Antwerp (see Fig. 22.23). He had spent time in most of Europe's royal or princely courts fulfilling commissions for large-scale paintings and gaining an international reputation. The cycle took four years (1621–25) to complete with the help of studio assistants.

Rubens's pictorial approach to such self-promoting biographical commissions was through lifelike allegory. *The Arrival and Reception of Marie de' Medici at Marseilles* depicts the day Marie arrived in France from her native Italy on route to her marriage to King Henry IV (Fig. **23.6**). The figure of Fame flies above her, blowing a trumpet, while

Fig. 23.6 Peter Paul Rubens and his workshop, *The Arrival and Reception of Marie de' Medici at Marseilles.* 1621–25. Oil on canvas, 13′ × 10′. Musée du Louvre/ RMN Réunion des Musées Nationaux, France. Erich Lessing/Art Resource, New York. The point of view here is daringly low, perhaps in the water, or oddly floating above it. This creates a completely novel relationship between viewer and painting.

Fig. 23.7 Peter Paul Rubens, *The Kermis (La Kermesse)*. ca. 1635. Oil on canvas, 56⅝" × 102¾".
Musée du Louvre/RMN Réunion des Musées Nationaux, France. Erich Lessing/Art Resource, New York. In this painting, Rubens reveals his Flemish heritage, taking up the traditional subject matter of Bruegel and others, a genre scene of everyday life.

Neptune, god of the sea, and his son Triton, accompanied by three water nymphs, rise from the waves to welcome her. A helmeted allegorical figure of France, wearing a *fleur-de-lis* robe like that worn by Louis XIV in his 1701 portrait, bows before her. Marie herself, not known for her beauty, is so enveloped by rich textures, extraordinary colors, and sensuous brushwork, that she seems transformed into a vision as extraordinary as the scene itself.

The fleshy bodies of the nymphs in this painting are a signature stylistic component of Rubens's work In fact, Rubens's style is almost literally a "fleshing out" of the late Italian Renaissance tradition. It is so distinctive that it came be known as "Rubenesque." His nudes, which often startle contemporary viewers because we have developed almost entirely different standards of beauty, are notable for the way in which their flesh folds and drapes across their bodies. Their beauty rests in the sensuality of this flesh, which in some measure symbolizes the sensual life of self-indulgence and excess. Rubens pushed to new extremes the Mannerist sensibilities of Michelangelo's *Last Judgment* and Bronzino's *Allegory with Venus and Cupid*, the color and textures of the Venetian school as embodied in Titian's *Rape of Europa* (see Chapter 20 for all), and the play of light and dark of the Caravaggisti [kah-rah-vah-GEE-stee] (see Chapter 21). He brought to the Italian tradition a Northern appreciation for observed nature—in particular, the realities of human flesh—and an altogether inventive and innovative sense of

space and scale. Only rarely are Rubens's paintings what might be called frontal, where the viewer's position parallels the depicted action. Rather, the action moves diagonally back into space from either the front left or right corner of the composition. Rubens's 1611 to 1614 *Descent from the Cross*, created for Antwerp Cathedral, is an early example of these features (see Fig. 22.23).

In a painting like *The Kermis* [ker-miss], or *Peasant Wedding*, Rubens transforms a simple tavern gathering—a genre common to Northern painting (see Fig. 22.11)—into a monumental celebration (Fig. **23.7**). *The Kermis* is over 8 feet wide. Its wedding celebration spills in a diagonal out of the confines of the tavern into the panoramic space of the Flemish countryside. At the pinnacle of this sideways pyramid of entwined flesh, a young man and a disheveled woman, her blouse fallen fully from her shoulders, run off across the bridge, presumably to indulge their appetites behind some hedge. Like the Hall of Mirrors at Versailles, with its mathematical regularity overlaid with sumptuously rich ornamentation, Rubens's painting seems at once moralistic and libertine. Arms and legs interlace in a swirling, twirling riot that can be interpreted as either a descent into debauchery or a celebration of sensual pleasure, readings that Rubens seems to have believed were not mutually exclusive.

Such frank sensuality is a celebration of the simple joy of living in a world where prosperity and peace extend even to the lowest rungs of society. Yet in keeping with his northern roots, Rubens gave the painting moralistic overtones. The posture of the dog with its nose in the cloth-draped tub at the bottom center of the canvas echoes the form of the kissing couple directly behind it and the dancing couples above it and, once more, represents the base, animal instincts that dominate the scene. The nursing babes at breast throughout the painting do not so much imply abundance as animal hunger, the desire to be fulfilled. Rubens knew full well that the bacchanal was not merely an image of prosperity but also of excess. In his later years, excess enthralled him, and *The Kermis* is a product of this sensibility.

Some 50 years later, in April 1685, Louis XIV purchased *The Kermis* for Versailles. What did the monarch who turned down Bernini's design for the new east wing of the Louvre (see Fig. 21.20) because he found it too extravagant see in this painting? For one thing, it was probably important to the man who considered himself Europe's greatest king to possess the work of the artist widely considered to be Europe's greatest painter. For another, Louis must have appreciated the painting's frank sexuality, which the artist emphasized by his sensual brushwork and color. It recalled the king's own sexual exploits.

The Painting of Nicolas Poussin: Classical Decorum

By the beginning of the eighteenth century, 14 other Rubens paintings had found their way to the court of Louis XIV. Armand-Jean du Plessis [dewplay-SEE], duc de Richelieu [duh REESH-uh-lee-yuh] (1629–1715), the great-nephew of Cardinal Richelieu (1585–1642), who had served as artistic advisor to Marie de' Medici and Louis XIII, purchased 14 other paintings that had remained in Rubens's personal collection after his death in 1640. Before he acquired his own collection of Rubens's work, Richelieu had wagered and lost his entire collection of paintings by Nicolas Poussin [poo-SEHN] (1594–1665) against Louis's own collection of works by Rubens in a tennis match between the two. A debate had long raged at court as to who was the better painter—Poussin or Rubens. Charles Le Brun had gone so far as to declare Poussin the greatest painter of the seventeenth century. Although a Frenchman, Poussin had spent most of his life in Rome. He particularly admired the work of Raphael and, following Raphael's example, advocated a classical approach to painting. A painting's subject matter, he believed, should be drawn from classical mythology or Christian tradition, not everyday life. There was no place in his theory of painting for a genre scene like Rubens's *Kermis*, even if portrayed on a monumental scale. Painting technique itself should be controlled and refined. There could be no loose brushwork, no "rough style." Restraint and decorum had to govern all aspects of pictorial composition.

This *poussiniste* [poo-sehn-EEST] style is clearly evident in *The Shepherds of Arcadia* of 1638 to 1639 (Fig. 23.8). Three shepherds trace out the inscription on a tomb, *Et ego in Arcadia*, "I too once dwelled in Arcadia," suggesting that death comes to us all. The Muse of

Fig. 23.8 Nicolas Poussin, *The Shepherds of Arcadia* (also called *Et in Arcadia Ego*). 1638–39. Oil on canvas, 33 1/2" × 47 5/8". INV7300. Photo: Renè-Gabriel Ojèda. Musée du Louvre/RMN Réunion des Musées Nationaux, France. Art Resource, New York. Note how even the bands on the shepherds' sandals parallel other lines in the painting.

LEARN MORE Gain insight from a primary source document from Nicolas Poussin at **www.myartslab.com**

History, standing to the right, affirms this message. Compared to the often exaggerated physiques of figures in Rubens's paintings, the muscular shepherds seem positively understated. Color, while sometimes brilliant, as in the yellow mantle robe of History, is muted by the evening light. But it is the compositional geometry of horizontals and verticals that is most typically *poussiniste*. Note how the arms of the two central figures form right angles and how they all fit within the cubical space suggested by the tomb itself. This cubic geometry finds its counterpoint in the way the lighted blue fold of History's dress parallels both the red-draped shepherd's lower leg and the leftmost shepherd's staff. These lines suggest a diagonal parallelogram working both against and with the central cube.

Louis XIV was delighted when he defeated the duc de Richelieu at tennis and acquired his Poussins. But to Louis's surprise, Richelieu quickly rebuilt his collection by purchasing the 14 Rubens paintings and then commissioning

CONTINUITY & CHANGE

School of Athens, p. 505

Roger de Piles [deh peel] to write a catalogue describing his acquisitions. De Piles was a *rubeniste* [roo-bayn-EEST]. He argued that color was the essence of painting. Color is to painting as reason is to man, as he put it. The *poussinistes*, by contrast, were dedicated to drawing, what Vasari called *disegno*, particularly the art of Raphael (see *Closer Look*, pages 750–751).

Poussin's paintings addressed the intellect, Rubens's the senses. For Poussin, subject matter, the connection of the picture to a classical narrative tradition, was paramount; for Rubens, the expressive capabilities of paint itself were primary. In 1708, de Piles scored each painter on his relative merits. Rubens received 18 points for composition, 13 for design, 17 for color, and 17 for expression. Poussin earned 15 points for composition, 17 for design, 6 for color, and 15 for expression. By de Piles's count, Rubens won 65 to 53. In essence, Rubens represented Baroque decorative expressionism and Poussin, classical restraint—the two sides of the Classical Baroque. Both would have their supporters in the Academy over the course of the following decades.

Music and Dance at the Court of Louis XIV

Louis XIV loved the pomp and ceremony of his court and the art forms that allowed him to most thoroughly

Fig. 23.9 Louis XIV as the sun in the *Ballet de la Nuit.* 1653.
Bibliothèque Nationale, Paris. Louis, who was 15 years old at the time, appeared as himself wearing this costume during the ballet's intermezzo, a short musical entertainment between the main acts.

engage this taste: dance and music. The man largely responsible for entertaining the king at court was Jean-Baptiste Lully [lew-LEE] (1632–1687), who was born in Florence but moved to France in 1646 to pursue his musical education.

Jean-Baptiste Lully Lully composed a number of popular songs, including the famous "Au Clair de la Lune." By the 1660s, he had become a favorite of the king, who admired in particular his ***comédie-ballets*** [koh-may-DEE bah-LAY], performances that were part opera (see Chapter 21) and part ballet and that often featured Louis's own considerable talents as a dancer (Fig. 23.9). Louis commissioned many ballets that required increasingly difficult movements of the dancers. As a result, his Royal Academy of Dance soon established the rules for the five positions of ballet that became the basis of classical dance. They valued, above all, clarity of line in the dancer's movement, balance, and, in the performance of the troop as a whole, symmetry. But in true Baroque fashion, the individual soloist was encouraged to elaborate upon the classical foundations of the ballet in exuberant, even surprising expressions of virtuosity.

Lully used his connections to the king to become head of the newly established Royal Academy of Music, a position that gave him exclusive rights to produce all sung dramas in France. In this role, he created yet another new operatic genre, the **tragédie en musique** [trah-zhay-DEE on moo-ZEEK], also known as the *tragédie lyrique* [leer-EEK]. Supported and financed by the court, Lully composed and staged one of these *tragédies* each year from 1673 until 1687, when he died of gangrene after hitting his foot with the cane he used to pound out the beat while conducting.

Lully's *tragédies en musique* generally consist of:

- An overture, distinguished by a slow, homophonic melody (associated with the royal dignity) that built to a faster contrapuntal section, a form today known as the **French overture**
- An allegorical prologue, which established the drama's connection to recent events at court, always flattering to the king
- Five acts of sung drama, subdivided into several scenes
- A multitude of **intermezzi**—called **divertissements** [dee-ver-tees-MOHN] in France—short displays of dance, song, or instrumental music

Lully's *tragédies* seamlessly blended words and music. The meter of the music constantly shifts, but the rhythms closely follow the natural rhythms of the French language.

One of the most powerful scenes in Lully's repertoire occurs at the end of Act II of *Armide* [ar-MEED], first performed in Paris in 1686 and the last of his *tragédies*. Based on *Jerusalem Liberate*, an epic poem by Torquato Tasso [TAHS-so] (1544–1595), the story concerns the crusader knight Renaud [ruh-NOH], whose virtue, according to the allegorical prologue, is like that of Louis XIV. Renaud is desperately trying to resist the temptations of the sorceress Armida. But in a ballet sequence, demons disguised as satyrs and shepherds put him under a spell. Armida enters, intending to kill Renaud as he sleeps. But she is overcome by her love for him and decides, instead, to hold him forever in her power and to make him love her through the wiles of her sorcery. Her recitative

monologue, *Enfin, il est en ma puissance* [en-fan eel ay-t-on mah pwee-SAHNSS] ("At last, he is in my power"), is considered among the greatest of Lully's works (track **23.1**). One contemporary of Lully's, a French nobleman who saw the tragédie many times, recalls the scene's effect on its audience: "I have twenty times seen the entire audience in the grip of fear, neither breathing nor moving, their whole attention in their ears and eyes, until the instrumental air which concludes the scene allowed them to draw breath again, after which they exhaled with a murmur of pleasure and admiration." Lully's music, with its ever-intensifying repetitions, creates a dramatic tension fully in keeping with Baroque theatricality.

HEAR MORE at www.myartslab.com

Dance Forms Louis's love of the dance promoted another new musical form at his court, the **suite**, a series of dances, or dance-inspired movements, usually all in the same key, though varying between major and minor modes. Most suites consist of four to six dances of different tempos and meters. These might include the following:

- Allemande [ah-luh-MAHND], a dance of continuous motion in double meter (marked by two or a multiple of two beats per measure) and moderate tempo
- Bourrée [boo-RAY], a dance of short, distinct phrasing, in double meter and moderate to fast in tempo
- Courante [koo-RAHNT], a dance often in running scales, in triple meter, and moderate to fast in tempo
- Gavotte [gah-VOT], a "bouncy" dance, in double meter, and moderate to fast in tempo
- Gigue [zheeg], a very lively dance, fast in tempo, and usually employing a 6/8 meter
- Sarabande [sah-rah-BAHND], a slow and stately dance, with accent on the second beat, in triple meter

In a suite, two moderately fast dances—say, an allemande and a courante—might precede a slower, more elegant dance—perhaps a sarabande—and then conclude with an exuberant gigue. The structure is closely related to the *sonata da camera* (see Chapter 25). Although it did not commonly occur in the dance suites themselves, the most important of the new dance forms was the **minuet**, an elegant triple-time dance of moderate tempo. It quickly became the most popular dance form of the age.

To help the courtiers learn the fashionable dances, members of Louis's court developed a system of dance notation—a way of putting the steps of a dance down on paper. The notation system facilitated the adoption of French dances in other courts across Europe. The 1700 publication of *Choreography, or the Art of Describing Dance in Characters*, by Raoul-Auger Feuillet [oh-ZHAY foy-YAY] (ca. 1653–ca. 1710), catalogued the entire repertoire of dance steps. It was widely imitated across Europe. As a general rule, Feuillet noted, dancers should perform a *plié* [plee-AY], or bend, on the upbeats of the music, and an *élevé* [ay-luh-VAY], or rise, on the downbeats.

Elisabeth-Claude Jacquet de la Guerre One of Louis's favorite composers of dance suites was Elisabeth-Claude Jacquet de la Guerre [deh la ghair] (1665–1729), who performed for him beginning at age five. Her *Pièces de clavecin* [pee-ESS deh klav-SEHN] ("Pieces for the Harpsichord") was published in 1687, when she was just 22 years old. The courante in Jacquet de la Guerre's suite is, like most dances, in **binary form**—it has a two-part structure—and both sections are repeated (track **23.2**). This repetition derives from the primary function of social dance, which is not to challenge the dancer but to provide for interaction with one's partner. It consists of a prescribed pattern of dance steps repeated over and over. In addition, Jacquet de la Guerre's courante features what the French called a *double*—a second dance based on the first and essentially a variation on it. Always a court favorite for her skill at improvising on the harpsichord, Jacquet de la Guerre would become the first French

(((•● **HEAR MORE** at
www.myartslab.com

woman to compose an opera: *Cephale et Procris* [say-FAHL ay pro-KREE] (1694).

Theater at the French Court

When, in 1629, Louis XIII appointed Cardinal Richelieu as his minister of state, he coincidentally inaugurated a great tradition of French theater. This tradition would culminate in 1680 with the establishment of the *Comédie Française* [koh-may-DEE frahn-SEZ], the French national theater (Fig. **23.10**). It was created as a cooperative under a charter granted by Louis XIV to merge three existing companies, including the troupe of the playwright Molière [moh-lee-AIR].

Pierre Corneille Cardinal Richelieu loved the theater. When a comedy by Rouen lawyer Pierre Corneille [COR-nay] (1606–1684) was first performed in Paris soon after the cardinal's appointment, Richelieu urged the company to settle in Paris's Marais Theater, a former indoor tennis court. There, under Richelieu's direction, Corneille dedicated himself to writing tragedies in the classical manner

Fig. 23.10 The Comédie Française. Interior of the Comédie Française Theatre in 1791, color lithograph after an original nineteenth-century French watercolor. Bibliothèque Nationale, Paris, France, Archives Charmet/The Bridgeman Art Library. The feuding that marked the Parisian theater world led Louis XIV to establish the Comédie Française in 1680 as a cooperative venture among the three major companies.

based on Greek or Roman themes that alluded to contemporary events. Richelieu exerted a great deal of control over the plays. He outlined each idea and then asked his author to fill in the dialogue. But Corneille resisted Richelieu's direction and took liberties that the cardinal found to be appalling lapses of taste, and so the playwright struck out on his own.

In 1637, Corneille opened a new play, *Le Cid*. It was based on the legend of El Cid, a Spanish nobleman who conquered and governed the city of Valencia in the eleventh century. The play was an immediate hit, moving Louis XIII to send his compliments. But Richelieu was furious. Corneille had ignored the **classical unities**, a notion derived from Aristotle's *Poetics* that requires a play to have only one action that occurs in one place and within one day. At Richelieu's insistence, the Académie Française [ah-kah-day-MEE frahn-SEZ] officially condemned the play as "dramatically implausible and morally defective." Although deeply hurt by this censure, Corneille followed with three masterpieces: *Horace* [or-AHSS] (1640), which dramatizes the conflict between the ancient Romans and their Alban neighbors; *Cinna* (1641), which tells the story of a conspiracy against the first Roman emperor, Augustus Caesar; and *Polyeucte* (1643), perhaps his greatest work, telling the story of an Armenian nobleman newly converted to Christianity who finds that his wife is in love with another man. Twenty-one more plays followed. In their allusion to antiquity, Corneille's plays embrace the classical side of the French Classical Baroque. And while Richelieu found their highly complex plots dramatically implausible, the plays embrace the Baroque love for elaborate moral and emotional range and possibility.

CONTINUITY & CHANGE
Poetics, p. 160

Molière Meanwhile, comedy had taken center stage in Paris, pushing the moral vision of Corneille to the wings. The son of a court upholsterer, Molière had been touring France for 13 years with a troupe of actors when he was asked, in 1658, to perform Corneille's tragedy *Nicomède* [nee-koh-MED] before the young king Louis XIV. The performance was a miserable failure, but Molière asked if he might perform a farce of his own, *Le Docteur Amoureux* [leh DOK-ter ah-moo-REH] ("The Amorous Doctor"). The king was delighted with this comedy, and Molière's company was given what was intended to be a permanent home.

Molière's first play to be performed was *Les Précieuses Ridicules* [lay PRAY-see-erz ree-dee-KEWL] ("The Pretentious Ladies"), in 1659. It satirized a member of the French court named Madame de Rambouillet [deh RAHM-boo-yeh], who fancied herself the chief guardian of good taste and manners in Parisian society. At her Parisian home, ladies of the court routinely gather to discuss matters of love, reviving in particular the elegance, manners, and high moral character of Platonic courtly love as they imagined it was practiced in the medieval courts of figures such as Eleanor of Aquitaine (see Chapter 10). Molière scoffed at

their pretensions, and the success of the play soon led him to double the admission price. The king himself was so delighted that he honored the playwright with a large monetary reward. But not so, Madame de Rambouillet. Outraged, she tried to drive Molière from the city but succeeded only in having the company's theater demolished. The king struck back by immediately granting Molière the right to perform in the Théâtre du Palais Royal [tay-AT-ruh dew pah-LAY roy-AHL], in Richelieu's former palace, and there he staged his productions for the rest of his life.

Molière spared no one his ridicule, attacking religious hypocrisy, misers, hypochondriacs, pretentious doctors, aging men who marry younger women, the gullible, and all social parasites. (Ironically, he himself was capable of the most audacious flattery.) His play *Tartuffe* [tar-TEWF], or *The Hypocrite* (1664), concludes, for instance, with an officer praising the ability of the king to recognize hypocrisy of the kind displayed by Tartuffe in earlier scenes from the play (**Reading 23.1a**):

READING 23.1a

from Molière, *Tartuffe*, Act V (1664)

We serve a Prince to whom all sham is hateful,
A Prince who sees into our inmost hearts,
And can't be fooled by any trickster's arts.
His royal soul, though generous and human,
Views all things with discernment and acumen;
His sovereign reason is not lightly swayed,
And all his judgments are discreetly weighed.
He honors righteous men of every kind,
And yet his zeal for virtue is not blind,
Nor does his love of piety numb his wits   10
And make him tolerant of hypocrites.
'Twas hardly likely that this man could cozen
A King who's foiled such liars by the dozen.

These words undoubtedly warmed the heart of the king, described here as if he were a god. But until Molière's sudden death of an aneurysm during a coughing fit onstage, the playwright remained in disfavor with many in Louis's court who felt threatened by his considerable insight and piercing wit. They recognized what perhaps the king could not—the irony of flattering the king by saying he is above flattery.

The plot of *Tartuffe*, like most of Molière's plays, is relatively simple. Character, not plot, is its chief concern. Tartuffe himself is a great ego who disguises his massive appetites behind a mask of piety. He is completely amoral, and his false morality makes a mockery of all it touches. (For a selection from the play, in which Tartuffe tries to seduce Orgon's wife Elmire [el-MEER], **see Reading 23.1**, pages 761–763). While the hypocrite Tartuffe is himself a great comic creation, the naïve Orgon is almost as interesting. Why, the audience wonders, is he so blind to Tartuffe's true nature? What drives human beings to ignore the evil that surrounds them?

Jean Racine In 1664, Molière befriended the struggling young playwright Jean Racine [rah-SEEN] (1639–1699) and offered to stage his first play to be performed in Paris, a tragedy. Racine was disappointed in the quality of the production that Molière's comedic company was able to muster, so he offered his next play to another company after seducing Molière's leading actress and convincing her to join him. Molière was deeply offended and never spoke to Racine again.

Racine went on to write a string of successful tragedies, to the dismay of the aging and increasingly disfavored Corneille. The feud between those two reached its height in 1670, when, unknown to each other, both were asked to write a play on the subject of Bérénice, an empress from Cilicia, in love with the Roman emperor Titus. Well aware that Rome opposes Bérénice, Titus chooses to reject her. Corneille's play was unenthusiastically received, but Racine's proved a triumph. Of all his plays, it thoroughly embraces the classical unities, which Corneille had rejected. There is only one action in Racine's play—Titus's announcement to Bérénice that he is leaving her—but it takes place over five acts in the course of a single day. The audience knows his intentions from the outset, and the play reaches its climax at the end of the fourth act, when Titus explains that he must forsake his love for the good of the state. Bérénice at first rejects his decision, but in the fifth act, they both come to terms with their duty—and their tragic fate.

Such successes made Racine the first French playwright to live entirely on earnings from his plays. But he had also acquired a large number of powerful enemies, many of whom were offended by his seeming humiliation of Corneille and Molière. Determined to destroy Racine's career, these enemies conspired to buy tickets for the opening night of *Phèdre* [FED-ruh] (1677) and leave their seats unoccupied. This and the other intrigues of the court so depressed Racine that he retired from the theater altogether in that year and accepted a post as royal historiographer, chronicling the reign of Louis XIV.

THE ART AND POLITICS OF THE ENGLISH COURT

The arts in England were dramatically affected by tensions between the absolutist monarchy of the English Stuarts and the much more conservative Protestant population. As in France, throughout the seventeenth century, the English monarchy sought to assert its absolute authority, although it did not ultimately manage to do so. The first Stuart monarch, James I (1566–1625), succeeded Queen Elizabeth I in 1603. "There are no privileges and immunities which can stand against a divinely appointed King," he quickly insisted. His son, Charles I (1600–1649), shared these absolutist convictions, but Charles's reign was beset by religious controversy. Although technically head of the Church of England, he married a Catholic, Henrietta Maria, sister of the French king Louis XIII.

Charles proposed changes in the Church of England's liturgy that brought it, in the opinion of many, dangerously close to Roman Catholicism. Puritans (English Calvinists) increasingly dominated the English Parliament and strongly opposed any government that even remotely appeared to accept Catholic doctrine.

Parliament raised an army to oppose Charles, and civil war resulted, lasting from 1642 to 1648. The key political question was who should rule the country—the king or the Parliament? Led by Oliver Cromwell (1599–1658), the Puritans defeated the king in 1645, and, while peace talks dragged on for three years, Charles made a secret pact with the Scots. Cromwell retaliated by suppressing the Scots, along with other royalist brigades, in 1648. Charles was executed for treason on January 30, 1649, a severe blow to the divine right of kings, and hardly lost on young Louis XIV across the Channel in France.

Initially, Cromwell tried to lead a commonwealth—a republic dedicated to the common well-being of the people—but he soon dissolved the Parliament and assumed the role of Lord Protector. His protectorate occasionally called the Parliament into session, but only to ratify his own decisions. Cromwell's greatest difficulty was requiring the people to obey "godly" laws—in other words, Puritan doctrine. He forbade swearing, drunkenness, and cockfighting. No shops or inns could do business on Sunday. The country, used to the idea of a freely elected parliamentary government, could not tolerate such restriction, and when, in September 1658, Cromwell died, his system of government died with him. A new Parliament was convened, which issued an invitation to Prince Charles (1630–1685), who was exiled in the Netherlands, to return to his kingdom as Charles II.

The new king landed in Dover in May 1660. A predominantly royalist Parliament was elected, somewhat easing the king's relations with the people. The threat of the monarchy adopting Catholicism, however, continued to cause dissension among Puritans, especially after Charles's brother, James, converted to Catholicism in 1667. James became king (James II) in 1685, and quickly antagonized the Puritans by appointing Roman Catholics to the highest government posts and establishing a large standing army with Roman Catholics heading several key regiments. Finally, in September 1688, William of Orange, married to the Protestant daughter of James II, invaded Britain from Holland at the invitation of the Puritan population. James II fled, and what has come to be called the Glorious Revolution ensued. Parliament enacted a Bill of Rights endorsing religious tolerance and prohibiting the king from annulling parliamentary law. Constitutional monarchy was re-established once and for all in Britain, and the divine right of kings permanently suspended. Yet tensions between those who believed in the absolute power of the monarchy and those who believed in the self-determination of the people were by no means diffused.

Fig. 23.11 Anthony Van Dyck, *Portrait of Charles I Hunting*. **1635.** Oil on canvas, 8′ × 6′11″. Inv 1236. Musée du Louvre/RMN Réunion des Musées Nationaux, France. SCALA/Art Resource, New York. Charles's posture, his left hand on his hip, and his right extended outward where it is supported by a cane, adopts the positions of the arms in court dance.

Anthony Van Dyck: Court Painter

The tension between the Catholic-leaning English monarchy and the more Puritan-oriented Parliament is clearly visible in two portraits by Flemish artist Anthony Van Dyck [dike] (1599–1641), court painter to Charles I. Sometime in his teens, Van Dyck went to work in Rubens's workshop in Antwerp, and he led the studio by the time he was 17. Van Dyck's great talent was portraiture. After working in Italy in the 1620s, in 1632 he accepted the invitation of Charles I of England to come to London as court painter. He was knighted there in 1633. Van Dyck's *Portrait of Charles I Hunting* is typical of the work that occupied him (Fig. **23.11**). He often flattered his subjects by elongating their features and portraying them from below to increase their stature. In the case of the painting shown here, Van Dyck positioned Charles so that he stands a full head higher than the grooms behind him, lit in a brilliant light that glimmers off his silvery doublet. The angle of his jauntily cocked cavalier's hat is echoed in the trees above his head and the neck of his horse, which seems to bow to him in respect. He is, in fact, the very embodiment of the

Cavalier [kav-uh-LEER] (from the French *chevalier* [shuh-vahl-YAY], meaning "knight"), as his royalist supporters were known. Like the king here, Cavaliers were famous for their style of dress—long, flowing hair, elaborate clothing, and large, sometimes feathered hats.

Cavaliers are the very opposite in style and demeanor from the so-called **Roundheads**, supporters of the Puritan Parliament who cropped their hair short and dressed as plainly as possible. Just before his death in 1641, Van Dyck painted one such Roundhead, Alexander Henderson, one of the most important figures in the Church of Scotland in the early seventeenth century (Fig. **23.12**). Henderson was one of the authors of the National Covenant, a document that pledged to maintain the "true reformed religion" against the policies of Charles I. This portrait was probably painted when Henderson was in London negotiating with Charles I. Henderson's short-cropped hair and dark, simple clothing contrast dramatically with Van Dyck's portrait of Charles I, as does the shadowy interior of the setting. Henderson's finger holds his place in his Bible, seeming to announce that here is a man of the Book, little interested in things of this world.

Fig. 23.12 Anthony Van Dyck, *Alexander Henderson*. **ca. 1641.** Oil on canvas, 50′ × 41½″. National Galleries of Scotland. PG 2227. Van Dyck probably came to paint this portrait because Charles I admired Henderson for his forthrightness and honesty in their troubled negotiations over the liturgy.

Fig. 23.13 John Foster, *Richard Mather*. ca. 1670. Woodblock print, 50′ × 41 1/2″. Graphic Arts Division, Princeton University. Given in memory of Frank Jewett Mather Jr. by his wife, his son, Frank Jewett Mather III, and his daughter, Mrs. Louis A. Turner. GA 2006.00728. The Mather family was arguably the most prominent of the early Puritan settlers.

Portraiture in the American Colonies

The Puritans who arrived in America in the seventeenth century did not think of themselves as Americans but as subjects of the crown and Parliament. They brought with them the prejudices against ostentation that are embodied in Van Dyck's portrait of Alexander Henderson, as is evident in the first woodcut portrait printed in America, a portrait of Richard Mather (1569–1669) by John Foster, printed around 1670 to accompany the publication of *The Life and Death of that Reverend Man of God, Mr. Richard Mather* (Fig. 23.13). Richard Mather was born in Lancashire, England, where he was a clergyman until emigrating to Dorchester, Massachusetts, in 1635. The following year, he became the minister of the church in Dorchester, where, according to his grandson, Cotton Mather (1663–1728), "His way of preaching was very plain, studiously avoiding obscure and foreign terms and unnecessary citation of Latin sentences; and aiming to shoot his arrows not over the heads, but into the hearts of his hearers." Mather was also one of the translators of *The Whole Booke of Psalmes* (1640), commonly referred to as the *Bay Psalm Book*, the first book printed in the colonies.

Foster's portrait of Mather is as different from John Closterman's portrait of the American monarchist Daniel Parke II (Fig. 23.14) as Van Dyck's *Alexander Henderson* is from his *Charles I Hunting*. The two American paintings reflect the same debate between monarchists and Puritans that informs Van Dyck's two works, and they underscore as well a deep division in the American colonies that would have lasting impact on their history. Where New England was dominated by the Puritan sensibility, the southern colonies were led by men of Cavalier attitudes and tastes. Thus the political division that marks seventeenth-century England manifested itself as a regional division in the colonies—the simple, God-fearing people of the North versus the luxury-loving aristocracy of the South.

The portrait of Parke hung, as part of the largest portrait collection in the American colonies, in the home of William Byrd of Westover, Virginia, head of one of the most prominent Cavalier families in Virginia. Parke's daughter, Lucy, was Byrd's wife. In his portrait, Parke's elaborately embroidered vest and rich satin coat announce his taste for luxury and wealth. Both the king and his admirer sport long, curly locks and a jaunty air, and they look out of the canvas with a similar sense of haughtiness. Parke sought appointment as governor of Virginia from the king, but

Fig. 23.14 John Closterman, *Daniel Parke II*. 1706. Oil on canvas. Virginia Historical Society. Gift of Mr. and Mrs. D. Tennant Bryan, 1985. On his chest, Parke wears a miniature portrait of Queen Anne, the niece of Charles I, who ascended to the British throne in 1702, presented to him by the queen and set in a diamond frame.

Fig. 23.15 Artist unknown, *John Freake*. ca. 1671–74. Oil on canvas, 42 $\frac{1}{2}$″ × 36 $\frac{3}{4}$″. American School, seventeenth century/Worcester Art Museum, Massachusetts/The Bridgeman Art Library. Freake's portrait lacks objects, as if to understate his wealth and underscore his Puritan moderation.

Fig. 23.16 Artist unknown, *Elizabeth Freake and Baby Mary*. ca. 1671–74. Oil on canvas, 42 $\frac{1}{2}$″ × 36 $\frac{3}{4}$″. American School, seventeenth century/Worcester Art Museum, Massachusetts/The Bridgeman Art Library. Almost everything in this image was imported, suggesting the scope of the merchant trade in seventeenth-century Boston.

failing that was appointed governor of the Leeward Islands in the Caribbean. There, he was killed in 1710 by a rebellion among the island's planters, who resented, among other things, his ardent defense of royal rule, his suppression of smuggling, his uncompromising personality, and his "debauching many of the[ir] wives and daughters."

Still, however remote the sensibilities of a Parke might have seemed to the Puritan immigrants of New England, as those immigrants achieved a measure of prosperity, they celebrated their success in portraits commissioned from a growing group of portrait painters, most of whom remain anonymous. Prosperity was, after all, the reward a good Calvinist could expect in fulfilling his Christian duties in the world. Worldly effort—what we have come to call the Protestant work ethic—was a way to praise God, and prosperity was a sign that God was looking on one's effort with favor. (The term "Protestant work ethic" is a twentieth-century invention. German sociologist Max Weber used it to describe the forces that motivated individuals to acquire wealth in the Protestant West.)

We see something of this sensibility in a pair of portraits of John and Elizabeth Freake and their child Mary painted in Boston in the early 1670s (Figs. **23.15** and **23.16**). John Freake was born in England and came to

America in 1658. He was a merchant and lawyer, and owned a brewery, a mill, an interest in six ships, and two homes, including one of the city's finest. His wife, Elizabeth, was the daughter of another Boston merchant. While avoiding ostentation, the Freake portraits are careful to suggest their sitters' wealth. John's collar, of imported Spanish or Italian lace, is set off against a rich brown—not black—velvet coat. He holds a pair of gloves, symbolizing his status as a gentleman, and with his left hand, decorated with a large gold ring, he touches an ornate brooch that tops a row of silver buttons. His hair is Cavalier length, perhaps suggesting aristocratic sympathies but certainly aristocratic taste. Elizabeth's dress is made of French satin trimmed with rich brocade and topped by a beautiful lace collar. She wears three strands of pearls around her neck, a garnet bracelet, and a gold ring. She sits on what is known as a "Turkey-work" chair, so named because its upholstery imitates the designs of Turkish carpets. John owned over a dozen such chairs, the finest known in Boston in the seventeenth century. In this context, the child Mary, born after the paintings were begun and added late in the painting process, is another sign of the Freakes' prosperity, a sign of God's grace being bestowed upon them.

Puritan and Cavalier Literature

The debate between the monarchy and the Puritans had distinct literary ramifications. As the flamboyant style of Cavalier dress suggests, writers of a Cavalier bent were sensualists and often wrote frankly erotic works. These contrasted strongly with the moral uprightness of even the most emotional Puritan writing.

One of the most moving Puritan writers of the day was Anne Bradstreet (ca. 1612–1672), who was born in Northampton, England, but migrated to Massachusetts in 1630 to avoid religious persecution. In order to entertain herself in the wilderness of rural Massachusetts, she took to composing epic poetry, eventually publishing in England *The Tenth Muse Lately Sprung Up in America* (1650), the first volume of poetry written by an English colonist. But it is her personal poetry, most of it published after her death, for which she is renowned. Consider, for instance, "To My Dear and Loving Husband" (**Reading 23.2a**):

READING 23.2a

Anne Bradstreet, "To My Dear and Loving Husband" (1667)

If ever two were one, then surely we.
If ever man were loved by wife, then thee;
If ever wife was happy in a man,
Compare with me, ye women, if you can.
I prize thy love more than whole mines of gold
Or all the riches that the East doth hold.
My love is such that rivers cannot quench,
Nor ought but love from thee, give recompense.
Thy love is such I can no way repay,
The heavens reward thee manifold, I pray.   10
Then while we live, in love let's so persevere
That when we live no more, we may live ever.

This poem is a pious and direct statement of true affection from a devoted wife. While only the last line suggests its author's religious foundation, in its reference to an afterlife, Bradstreet's Puritan faith is a constant theme in many of her other poems, such as "Here Follows Some Verses upon the Burning of Our House" (**see Reading 23.2**, page 763). The poem narrates Bradstreet's conviction that she must give up all her worldly goods in order to pursue the path to salvation.

In its sense of progressing from the material world to spiritual redemption, Bradstreet's "Here Follows Some Verses . . ." anticipates what is perhaps the most influential Puritan text of the era, *The Pilgrim's Progress* by John Bunyan (1628–1688). After the Restoration of the monarchy in 1660, Bunyan spent 12 years in prison for his fiery preaching, during which time he wrote an autobiography, *Grace Abounding*. But it is *The Pilgrim's Progress*, first published in 1678, that established the symbolism of the Puritan quest for salvation. It narrates the allegorical story of Christian who, with friends Hopeful and Faithful, journeys to the Celestial City. On the way, they learn to resist the temptations

of Mr. Worldly Wiseman and Vanity Fair in the city of Vanity. They also navigate the Slough of Despond and endure a long dark night in the Doubting Castle. Their faith is tested at every turn. Eventually they realize they must deny the joys of family and society, all earthly security, and even physical well-being, to attain "Life, life, eternal life."

Except for the clarity of their diction, and their rejection of complicated metaphor, Bradstreet and Bunyan share almost nothing with the Cavalier poets of their generation. All were admirers of Ben Jonson (1572–1637), a playwright and poet who flourished during the reign of James I. His comedies *Volpone* (1605) and *The Alchemist* (1610) were immediate hits. Collaborating with the designer and architect Inigo Jones (1573–1652), Jonson also wrote a series of **masques** [masks], a type of performance that combined speech, dance, and spectacle. These were performed for James's court, and they are closely related to the *comedies en musique* composed by Lully for Louis XIV's court. The Cavalier poets of the next generation appreciated especially the erudition and wit of his lyric poetry. Robert Herrick's (1591–1674) Cavalier poem "To the Virgins, To Make Much of Time," descends directly from Jonson's example (**Reading 23.3**):

READING 23.3

Robert Herrick, "To the Virgins, To Make Much of Time" (1648)

Gather ye Rose-buds while ye may,
Old Time is still a flying:
And this same flower that smiles to-day,
To-morrow will be dying.

The glorious Lamp of Heaven, the Sun,
The higher he's a getting;
The sooner will his Race be run,
And neerer he's to Setting.

That Age is best, which is the first,
When Youth and Blood are warmer;   10
But being spent, the worse, and worst
Times, still succeed the former.

Then be not coy, but use your time;
And while ye may goe marry:
For having lost but once your prime,
You may for ever tarry.

First published in 1648 in a 1,200-poem volume called *Hesperides* [hess-PER-ih-deez], the poem addresses not merely young women but youth generally and is an example of a carpe diem [CAR-peh DEE-em] (Latin for "seize the day") poem admonishing the reader to make merry while one can. The poem is a forthright argument for making love. There is nothing of the traditional Renaissance conceit portraying the poet's love for his mistress as a metaphor for his higher love of God. Some Puritans saw Herrick's poem as a call to fornication, but it ends with a more traditional call to "marry." The poem's carpe diem argument is here turned to the purpose of Christian orthodoxy (although when heard out loud, "marry" would have been impossible to distinguish from a more high-spirited "merry").

The ribald Cavalier sensibility is most pronounced in Restoration drama. Here the sensual, "fleshy" spirit of Rubens's paintings was expressed on stage, in a theater made possible by the Restoration of the monarchy in 1660. For 18 years, under Cromwell and the Puritan Parliament, theater had been banned in England, but when Charles II lifted the ban, a lewd anti-Puritanical theater ascended to the stage. The most notorious of these plays is *The Country Wife*, written by William Wycherley (1640–1716) in 1675. For the first time in British history, women were allowed on stage. Like many of his Cavalier colleagues, Wycherley stunned audiences by having his female characters cross-dress as males, in tight-fitting breeches, and engage their male counterparts in sexual banter. *The Country Wife* itself revolves around the exploits of Harry Horner (the name is suggestive) who has spread a rumor throughout London male society that he is impotent so that he may more easily seduce respectable ladies. The play consists of a series of Horner's seductions, in which he is always at the brink of being found out but just manages to escape detection. In keeping with its libertine spirit, the play is totally unrepentant; even at the end, it is clear that Horner's behavior will never change.

Henry Purcell and English Opera

Just as they were of the theater, Puritans were suspicious of secular music in all its forms, and special contempt was reserved for opera. Even after the Restoration, the English resisted drama that consisted entirely of singing, preferring plays and masques that combined drama, song, and dance. One of the very few operas of its time is *Dido* [DY-doh] *and Aeneas* [uh-NEE-us], the work of Henry Purcell [PUR-sul] (ca. 1659–1695). *Dido and Aeneas* was first performed in 1689 by students at a school for young ladies in Chelsea, west of London, but was not performed again until 1700, after Purcell's death. King William, the foreign king, and Queen Mary, the native daughter of Charles I, may have suppressed it, finding the alliance of Aeneas and Dido a story too close to their own. But the opera's Roman subject is in keeping with the Classical Baroque. It is the same story that Virgil tells in the *Aeneid* (see Chapter 6). There, Aeneas falls in love with Dido, queen of Carthage, but knowing he must continue his journey and found Rome, he abandons her and she commits suicide. The final piece in Purcell's opera, known as "Dido's Lament," begins with a recitative, moves to an emotional aria, followed by a short orchestral conclusion. The lament itself is a ground bass aria, in which the melody is set over a repeated pattern in the bass (track **23.3**). The opening recitative moves steadily downward, setting the stage for the grief-stricken Dido's aria. Then the ground bass by itself descends by half steps, like some slowly accumulating sadness. It repeats 11 times during the course of the aria. Over it, Dido's

CONTINUITY & CHANGE
Aeneid, p. 209

HEAR MORE at www.myartslab.com

words repeat themselves for dramatic effect, and convey her increasingly despairing emotional state. At the lament's conclusion, Dido dies. Despite its ability to move the listener, Purcell's opera did not capture the English imagination until 1711, when it helped to inaugurate an English passion for opera as a form.

THE ARTS OF THE SPANISH COURT

Even as England endured its divisive religious wars, Spain remained dogmatically Catholic. Yet after the death of Philip II (see Chapter 22), and despite the wealth flowing into the country from its American empire, Spain entered a period of decline during which deteriorating economic and social conditions threatened the absolutist authority of its king. Severe inflation, a shift of population away from the countryside and into the cities, and a loss of population and tax revenue brought the absolutist Spanish court to bankruptcy. To make matters worse, if the reign of Philip III (r. 1598–1621) was marked by the corruption of his inner court, the regime of Philip IV (r. 1621–1665) was marked by disastrous, highly costly military campaigns. These culminated in 1659 when Spain accepted a humiliating peace with France and, in 1668, agreed to total independence for Portugal. As early as 1628, the Dutch had captured the entire Spanish treasure fleet in the Caribbean, taking 177,537 pounds of gold and silver valued at 4.8 million silver pesos. One might have suspected Spanish citizens to be angry with the Dutch, but in fact, they were delighted. As the painter Peter Paul Rubens, at work on a commission for Philip IV, reported, "Almost everyone here is very glad about it, feeling that this public calamity can be set down as a disgrace to their rulers." Nevertheless, even as the Spanish throne seemed to crumble, the arts flourished under the patronage of a court that recklessly indulged itself. So remarkable was the outpouring of Spanish arts and letters in the seventeenth century that the era is commonly referred to as the Spanish Golden Age.

Diego Velázquez and the Royal Portrait

The Spanish court understood that in order to assert its absolutist authority, it needed to impress the people through its patronage of the arts. So when Philip IV assumed the Spanish throne at the age of 16, his principal advisor suggested that his court should strive to rival all the others of Europe by employing the greatest painters of the day. The king agreed, hiring Rubens in the 1630s to paint a cycle of 112 mythologies for his hunting lodge. But when the 24-year-old Diego Rodríguez de Silva y Velázquez [vah-LASS-kez] (1599–1660) was summoned to paint a portrait of the king in the spring of 1623, both the king and his advisor recognized that one of the great painters of seventeenth-century Europe was homegrown. An appointment as court painter quickly followed, and Velázquez became the only artist permitted to paint the king.

Fig. 23.17 Diego Velázquez, *El Triumfo de Baco*, or *Los Borrachos (The Triumph of Bacchus*, or *The Drunkards)*. 1628–29. Oil on canvas, 65 1/8" × 87 1/2". Museo del Prado, Madrid, Spain. SCALA/Art Resource, New York. Velázquez's canvases consist of loosely painted layers of paint that appear totally coherent from even a few feet away, but which dissolve into a seemingly random amalgamation of individual brushstrokes when studied at close range. Dashes of white, lemon, and pale orange give the effect of light reflecting off the surface of his forms.

In 1628, when Rubens visited the Spanish court, Velázquez alone among artists in Madrid was permitted to visit with the master at work. And Velázquez guided Rubens through the royal collection, which included Bosch's *Garden of Earthly Delights* (see *Closer Look*, Chapter 16) and, most especially, Titian's *The Rape of Europa* (see Fig. 20.8), which had been painted expressly for Philip II. Rubens copied both. He also persuaded Velázquez to go to Italy in 1629 to 1630, where he studied the work of Titian in Venice. In Florence and Rome, Velázquez disliked the paintings of Raphael, whose linear style he found cold and inexpressive.

By the time Rubens met the young painter, he was already deeply affected by Caravaggio. The figure of Bacchus in *The Triumph of Bacchus*, also known as *Los Borrachos* [bor-RAH-chohs] (*The Drunkards*) (Fig. 23.17), painted around the time of Rubens's visit, is directly indebted to

Caravaggio's realistic and tightly painted treatments of the same mythological figure (see Fig. 21.15). And the peasants gathered around the youth are reminiscent of the ruddy working-class types that populate Caravaggio's canvases. But Rubens's own taste for bacchanalian themes was at work as well.

CONTINUITY & CHANGE

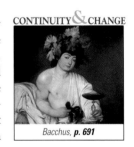

Bacchus, **p. 691**

Velázquez's chief occupation as painter to Philip IV was painting court portraits and supervising the decoration of rooms in the various royal palaces and retreats. Most were portraits of individuals, but *Las Meninas* [las may-NEE-nahss] (*The Maids of Honor*) is a life-size group portrait and his last great royal commission. It elevates the portrait to a level of complexity almost unmatched in the history of art.

The source of this complexity is the competing focal points of the composition (see *Closer Look*, pages 750–751). This work, with its unusual spatial scheme that includes a likeness of the painter and permits us into his studio, continues to inspire later artists.

The Literature of the Spanish Court

Under Philip III and Philip IV, the literary arts in Spain flourished as never before. Cervantes's great novel *Don Quixote* appeared in two parts, the first in 1605 and the second in 1615 (see Chapter 20). A transitional text, it represents the culmination of Renaissance thought even as it announces the beginning of an age of great innovation and originality. Especially influential was Cervantes's willingness to criticize, by means of good humor and satire, the social structures of Spanish society, particularly its aristocracy and religious institutions. Above all, the example of Cervantes freed Spanish writers to be entertaining.

The Plays of Lope de Vega and Calderón The Golden Age of Spanish drama lasted for nearly 100 years, spanning the years when Lope Félix de Vega [LOH-pay FAY-leeks day VAY-gah] (1562–1635) produced his first play in 1592, and 1681, when the playwright who succeeded him as the favorite of the Spanish court, Pedro Calderón de la Barca [PAY-droh kahl-day-ROHN day la BAR-kah] (1600–1681), died. Literally thousands of plays were written and produced in these years, an estimated 1,800 by Lope de Vega alone (only 500 of these are considered authentic), a pace of some 42 plays a year, or one every eight or nine days. As a rule, plays in Golden Age Spain were intended for a single performance, and yet despite the pace at which they were produced, which would tend to encourage formulaic and repetitive strategies, inventiveness was highly prized. Actors struggled to learn their lines and often begged forgiveness of their audiences for errors they committed. Set designers, many of them engineers imported from Italy, were encouraged to create as many changeable scenes as possible, and playwrights obliged them by creating plays of ten or more scene changes.

So extensive are Lope's writings in every genre—novels, short stories, epistles, epic poems, and lyric poetry in addition to plays—that a complete edition of his works has never been assembled. But beyond his extraordinary energy, his innovative approach to drama sets him apart. Before Lope, Spanish drama had been governed by strict observance of the classical unities. He offered instead a new model, the *comedia nueva* [koh-MAY-dee-ah noo-WAY-vah] ("new comedy"), fast-paced, romantic treatments taking as their themes national history or everyday Spanish life. According to Lope, the classical unities were to be abandoned. Furthermore, comedy and tragedy should be mixed in the same play, and noble and base characters intermingled. Puns, disguises, mistaken identities, and fixed types or caricatures should facilitate the plot. Finally, any theme was admissible. Lope's new comedies were a smashing success, performed again and again for both Philip III and Philip IV.

Calderón's temperament was very different from Lope's. He lived a quiet life dedicated to his books and thoughts. He wrote almost exclusively for the court, not the public, and produced some 120 plays, most of which followed models established by Lope. Some of them even recast Lope's original works. But it would be a mistake to think of Calderón as unoriginal. He was more philosophical and profound than Lope, and the beauty of his poetry far exceeded his mentor's. His so-called court-and-sword plays are especially interesting. His theme is the conflict between love and honor.

The point of honor (*pundonor* [poon-doh-NOR]) in Spanish society was based primarily on a notion of marital fidelity that extended to a man's entire household, including all women in the house, married or unmarried. Any violation of female honor had to be avenged as a matter of reputation and self-respect. In actual practice, the *pundonor* often led to horrific outcomes. If a wife was even suspected of infidelity, her husband was permitted to kill her and had to murder her suspected lover as well. Calderón's plays take full advantage of the dramatic possibilities of such a social code. He weaves the intrigues of lovers—and the accompanying disguises, mistaken identities, false accusations, and humiliating loss of honor—into complex and entangled plots that capture the sometimes horrid depths and sometimes glorious heights of Spanish passion.

The Satires of Francisco de Quevedo No writer of Golden Age Spain understood so well or confronted so thoroughly the country's political, economic, and moral bankruptcy as Francisco de Quevedo y Villegas [day kay-VAY-doh ee veel-YAY-gahss] (1580–1645). Most of his literary life was dedicated to exposing the corruption and weakness of the Spanish court, the foolish ways and misplaced values of his contemporaries, and especially the dishonesty and deceit of Spain's professional and merchant classes—lawyers, doctors, judges, barbers, tailors, and actors. His greatest work along these lines is *Sueños* [soo-AYN-yohss] (*Visions*). The work consists of five visions written between 1606 and 1622. In the first, *El Sueño del Juicio Final* [el soo-AY-noh del hoo-EE-see-oh fee-NAHL] (*The Vision of the Last Judgment*), Quevedo recalls a dream in which on the day of the Last Judgment, the dead rise from their graves. Their bones detached and scattered, the dead must reassemble themselves. While every soul finally gets it right, Quevedo witnesses considerable procrastination. A scribe pretends his own soul is not his own in order to be rid of it. Slanderers are slow to

Diego Velázquez's *Las Meninas*, or *The Maids of Honor*, is a painting remarkable in conception and extraordinary in execution. This group portrait captures in a passing moment ten individuals in the vast room that was the painter's studio in the royal palace of Spain. The competing focal points of the composition are the source of the work's complexity. At the very center of the painting, bathed in light, is the Infanta Margarita, beloved daughter of King Philip IV and Queen Mariana. In one sense, the painting is the Infanta's portrait, as she seems the primary focus. Yet the title *Las Meninas*, "The Maids of Honor," implies that her attendants are the painting's real subject. However, Velázquez has painted himself into the composition at work on a canvas, so the painting is, at least partly, also a self-portrait. The artist's gaze, as well as the gaze of the Infanta and her dwarf lady-in-waiting, and perhaps also of the courtier who has turned around in the doorway at the back of the painting, is focused on a spot outside the painting, in front of it, where we as viewers stand. The mirror at the back of the room, in which Philip and Mariana are reflected, suggests that the king and queen also occupy this position, acknowledging their role as Velázquez's patrons.

Difficult to see even in person, this painting on the back wall is a reproduction of Rubens's *Pallas and Arachne* of 1636 to 1637, commissioned by Philip IV, and is thus an homage to that painter.

The **red cross** on the artist's breast is the symbol of the Order of Santiago, to which the painter was nominated in 1658. The order had formerly banned membership to those who worked with their hands. In winning his nomination, Velázquez affirmed not only his own nobility, but also that of his craft. Philip IV ordered the addition of the cross in the painting after Velázquez's death in 1660.

No other Velázquez painting is as tall as *Las Meninas,* which suggests that the back of the canvas in the foreground is, in fact, *Las Meninas* itself. Velázquez thus paints himself painting this painting.

Something to Think About . . .

At the time that Velázquez was at work on *Las Meninas*, Jan van Eyck's painting *Giovanni Arnolfini and His Wife Giovanna Cenami* (see Fig. 16.7) was hanging in Philip IV's palace. How might van Eyck's painting have influenced Velázquez's?

One of two **maids of honor** who give the painting its title. The other stands just to the Infanta's left. This one hands the Infanta a terra-cotta jug on a gold plate. The jug probably contained cold, scented water.

SEE MORE For a Closer Look at Diego Velázquez's *Las Meninas,* go to **www.myartslab.com**

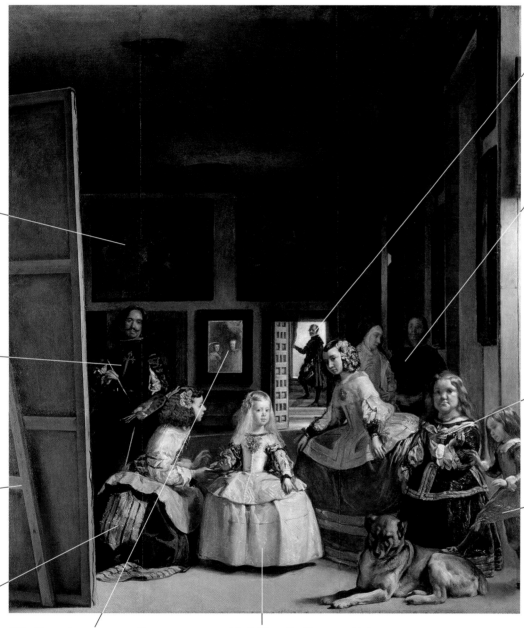

José Nieto, the queen's chamberlain, responsible for the day-to-day operations of the royal household. His gesture and the light that surrounds him draw attention to the mirror reflecting the king and queen.

The **nun and priest** emphasize the importance of the Catholic faith in the Spanish court.

Dwarfs were a common feature in the royal courts of Europe, a source of entertainment and amusement. They were dressed in fine costume, lavished with jewelry and gold, and shown off at court ceremonies and festivals. Often, they were presented as gifts to court dignitaries. Velázquez paints them with compassion, for their status in court was not much better than his own.

Court Jester Nicolasito, shown tormenting the huge dog in front of him by stepping on its back.

If the king and queen were really situated where the viewer stands, their reflection in the mirror at the back of the room would be much smaller. Velázquez is playing games with the space of the painting.

Infanta Margarita, five years old at the time of the painting, was heir to the Spanish throne.

Diego Velázquez. *Las Meninas (The Maids of Honor).* **1656.** Oil on canvas, 10′ $^3/_4$″ × 9′ $^3/_4$″. Museo del Prado, Madrid.

find their tongues, and the lustful fear to find their eyes lest these organs bear witness against them. Thieves and murderers spend hours trying to avoid their hands. Among the dead, Adam, Herod, Pilate, Judas, Mohammed, and Martin Luther are all tried and condemned until an astrologer arrives and declares that there is a great mistake—it is not Judgment Day at all. Devils promptly carry him off to Hell.

The other *Sueños* follow this same pattern. They are plotless catalogs of social types and historical characters, each exposed in succession to Quevedo's biting wit. Seeing themselves and their neighbors in Quevedo's sketches, and apparently capable of laughing at his often sardonic vision, Spaniards responded enthusiastically to the *Sueños*. Philip IV was less enthused. Perhaps that explains why Quevedo was arrested in 1639. He remained in prison until 1643 and died

profoundly pessimistic that Spain would long remain a force in world politics.

THE BAROQUE IN THE AMERICAS

Don Quixote, Cervantes's great character (see Chapter 20), is in part a spoof of the Spanish conquistador mentality that had taken control of the Americas and whose chivalry both Lope de Vega and Quevedo later likewise spoofed. The Americas were Spain's greatest source of wealth, and Spanish culture quickly took hold in both North and South America. This was a politically important enterprise, because it underscored that the absolute authority in the Americas was the Spanish monarchy. In Cuzco [KOOS-koh], Peru, the Spanish adopted the structures of the Inca to their own purposes, constructing their own buildings, as we saw in Chapter 11, on original Inca foundations. As we have seen, they even converted the most magnificent of the Inca sacred sites, the Temple of the Sun, into a Dominican church and monastery (see *Continuity & Change*, Chapter 11). Over time, Spanish leaders and missionaries believed, the distinction between worshiping the Inca gods and worshipping the sacred in general would become increasingly less clear, and Christianization of the native population would occur naturally.

The Cuzco School

In truth, the indigenous native populations Indianized the Christian art imposed upon them, creating a unique visual culture, part Baroque, part Indian. A case in point is the city of Lima, founded by the conquistador Francisco Pizarro in 1535 as capital of the Viceroyalty of Peru (see Map 23.1) on the coast, convenient to harbor and trade. As opposed to Cuzco, with its narrow, winding streets, Lima was laid out in a formal grid, with wide, open vistas, the very image of imperial order. By the start of the seventeenth century, the city was a fully Baroque testament to the Spanish culture of its founders. The stones for its mansions were shipped in from Panama as ballast for ships

Legend:
— Viceroyalty of Peru, 1542
Viceroyalty of New Granada, separated from Viceroyalty of Peru, 1717
Viceroyalty of La Plata, separated from Viceroyalty of Peru, 1776
Viceroyalty of Peru after 1776

Map 23.1 Spanish Viceroyalties in South America, 1542–1824.

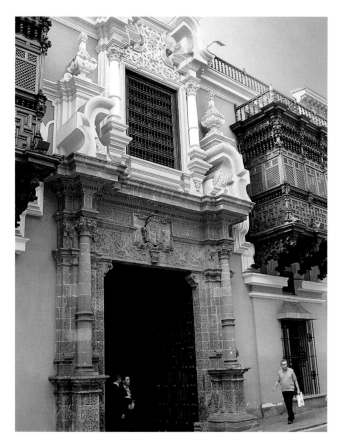

Fig. 23.18 Palacio Tore Tagle, Lima, Peru, 1735. Today the Palacio houses the Peruvian Foreign Ministry. Such ornately carved Baroque balconies were part of the facades of many colonial mansions in Lima.

from its center, take the shape of the curved blade and handle of the Inca ceremonial knife used in traditional sacrifices, a shape also worn as a pin by Inca princesses as a symbol of good luck. Thus Catholic and native traditions are compounded in a single image, a syncretism mirrored in the increasingly mestizo fabric of the population as a whole (see Chapter 18).

Baroque Music in the Americas: Sor Juana Inés de la Cruz

The syncretism in the work of the Cuzco artists is also evident in Baroque music as it developed in New Spain. As the Church sought to convert native populations to the Catholic faith, the musical liturgy became a powerful tool.

Fig. 23.19 Luis Niño (Bolivian), *Our Lady of the Victory of Málaga.* **Southern Cuzco school, Potosí, Bolivia. ca. 1740.** Oil on canvas overlaid with gold and silver, 59$\frac{1}{2}$″ × 43$\frac{3}{4}$″ Gift of John C. Freyer for the Frank Barrows Freyer Collection. Denver Art Museum, CO. This particular manifestation of the Virgin is associated with the Minimi order of the Catholic Church, founded in the fifteenth century by Francis of Paula (Italy). He was present at the Spanish victory over the Moors at Málaga in 1487, and claimed to have seen the Virgin appear. He was eventually sanctified by the pope, and was the patron saint of travelers, sailors, and navigators. A Minimi monastery was established in Peru in the seventeenth century.

that carried gold from the highlands and silver from Potosí (see Chapter 18) to Mexico and then on to Spain. The wood for its mansions, with their elaborately carved Baroque balconies (Fig. **23.18**), was imported oak and cedar.

The artisans who carved these Baroque panels were increasingly native, as were the metalworkers who created fine objects to satisfy colonists' tastes and the painters who decorated their churches. Especially in Cuzco, they brought to their work techniques and motifs from their Inca background. *Our Lady of the Victory of Málaga* (Fig. **23.19**) by Luis Niño (active 1730–1760) employs **brocateado** [broh-kah-tay-AH-doh], the application of gold leaf to canvas, a technique extremely popular among the Cuzco painters, especially for creating elaborate, brocadelike effects on saints' garments. Here the Virgin stands on a silver crescent moon above the tiled roofs and trees of the Cuzco countryside, recalling the Inca association of silver with religious worship of the moon, while the flat symmetry of the *brocateado* evokes the flat patterns of Inca textile design (see Fig. 11.34) and the Inca association of gold with worship of the sun. In fact, some scholars argue that the crescent at the virgin's feet, together with the two vertical red lines that rise straight up

As early as 1523, Spanish monks created a school for Native Americans in Texcoco, Mexico (just east of Mexico City), and began teaching music, including Gregorian chant, the principles of polyphony, and composition, on an imported organ. Throughout the sixteenth century, missionaries used music, dance, and religious dramas to attract and convert the indigenous population to Christianity. These forms were sometimes adapted to local conditions. For example, the religious drama *Battle of the Christians and Moors* became the *Battle of Pizarro and Atahuallpa* (see Chapter 18), a dance-drama still performed in Peru.

An interesting example of syncretism in the cultures of New Spain is in the work of Sor Juana Inés de la Cruz (1648–1695). The illegitimate daughter of an America-born mother of pure Spanish descent and a Basque father, she was recognized as a prodigy at an early age, and at 16 was named lady-in-waiting to the wife of the Spanish viceroy. Four years later, seeking freedom to pursue her education, she entered the Convent of San Jerónimo in Mexico City, where she spent the rest of her life. She is remembered today largely as the author of an important tract, *Reply to Sor Philotea* (1691), in which she defended the rights of women to pursue any form of education they might desire, and as a poet. Her sonnet "To Her Self-Portrait" is representative of her work (**Reading 23.4**):

READING 23.4

Sor Juana Inés de la Cruz, "To Her Self-Portrait" (posthumous publication 1700)

What you see here is colorful illusion,
an art boasting of beauty and its skill,
which in false reasoning of color will
pervert the mind in delicate delusion.
Here where the flatteries of paint engage
to vitiate the horrors of the years,
where softening the rust of time appears
to triumph over oblivion and age,
all is a vain, careful disguise of clothing,
it is a slender blossom in the gale,   10
it is a futile port for doom reserved,
it is a foolish labor that can only fail;
it is a wasting zeal and, well observed,
is corpse, is dust, is shadow, and is nothing.

The poem expresses the poet's profound distrust in what is apparent in the self-portrait only through the observational senses. If "well observed," she concludes, one should see there the inevitable fact of death, which the color, beauty, and skill of the portrait masks. The poem is a profound example of Baroque self-awareness, the product of a mind that loves beauty even as it recognizes its fleeting nature.

Many of Sor Juana's poems were originally songs written to be accompanied by music, the notation to which is now lost. Nevertheless, they tell us much about music in Baroque New Spain. Her hymn *Tocatîn*, written in the Aztec language of Nahuatl, in which she was fluent, aligns the Virgin Mary with the Aztec Earth Mother and was probably sung to the tune of a popular Spanish folk tune. Among her most popular musical productions are several collections of *villancicos*. The *villancico* is a form similar to the Italian *frottola* (see Chapter 14), and it developed in fifteenth- and sixteenth-century Spain. Simple polyphonic songs, on a light, rustic, or pastoral theme, in which the upper voice dominates while the lower voices fill in the polyphony, many early *villancicos* were originally written for voice and guitar. In New Spain, the form developed over the course of the next hundred years into a religious genre that made increasing use of recitative and aria, often employing as many as five solo voices. Because the New World *villancico* made use of vernacular texts and told popular stories, it was a particularly effective means of addressing the native populations.

In Sor Juana's hands, the *villancico* was a means to dramatize the diversity of language and culture in New Spain. In her suite of eight *villancicos* known as *San Pedro Nolasco* (1677), the story of a Mexican saint known for freeing slaves of both African and Indian descent, her soloists sang in three languages. An Aztec sang in Nahuatl. A female poet introduced and narrated the performance in proper Spanish. A common man of the street sang in less refined Spanish. An African-American slave also sang in Spanish, but in a very colloquial and African-inflected dialect. Finally, a student sang in Latin. All of these voices came together in a story of profound miscommunication about the possibilities of salvation. What the music might have sounded like is open to question, but it is likely that the different languages would have been sung in different rhythms with accents falling in different places. For instance, we know because the female poet narrator says so when she introduces him that the African-American slave's opening refrain was sung "to the music of a calabazo song," that is, a song accompanied by a percussive gourd. The introduction of a folk instrument into the religious *villancico* speaks to the heterogeneous complexity of Mexican Baroque music.

The Churrigueresque Style: *Retablos* and Portals in New Spain

The taste for elaborate decorative effects and complexity evident in the Cuzco Madonna and the Lima balconies as well as in Sor Juana's *villancicos* found its most extraordinary expression in large altarpiece ensembles, known as *retablos* [ray-TAH-blohs], which began to appear in the churches of Mexico in the late seventeenth century. In Spain, a family of architects and sculptors known as the Churriguera [choor-ree-GAY-rah] had introduced and given their name to an extremely lavish Baroque style called Churrigueresque [choor-ree gay-RESK], used to decorate *retablos* and church portals. (These Baroque

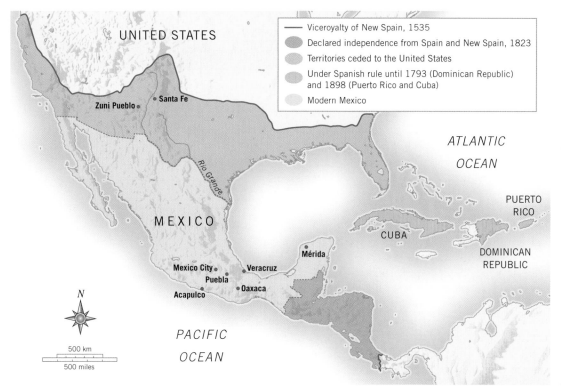

Map 23.2 The Viceroyalty of New Spain, 1535–1821.

— Viceroyalty of New Spain, 1535
Declared independence from Spain and New Spain, 1823
Territories ceded to the United States
Under Spanish rule until 1793 (Dominican Republic) and 1898 (Puerto Rico and Cuba)
Modern Mexico

Fig. 23.20 Jerónimo de Balbás, Altar of the Kings, principal *retablo* of the Cathedral, Mexico City. 1718–37. Polychrome and gilded wood, height 85′. Balbás was the first architect to employ the distinctive *estípite* column in Spanish-colonial America. Before coming to Mexico in 1717, Balbás had been a leading *retablo* maker in Seville.

retablos are distinct from the folk art *retablos* that originated in the late nineteenth century as devotional oil paintings sold to devout believers who displayed them in home altars to honor their patron saints.) In the Viceroyalty of New Spain, comprising most of modern Mexico, Central America, and the American Southwest (see Map **23.2**), Baroque *retablos* were at first the work of teams of European artists, then later *criollos* [kree-OHL-yoh], Mexican-born descendants of Spaniards. These *retablos* were generally designed to frame, in the most extravagant style, paintings and sculptures brought to the Americas from Europe.

A good example of the Churrigueresque *retablo* is the vast Altar of the Kings, designed by Jerónimo de Balbás [day bahl-BAHSS] (ca. 1680–1748) for the cathedral in Mexico City (Fig. **23.20**). Here artisans used gold leaf unsparingly in a radical vertical design distinguished by a new form of engaged column, narrow at the base and top, wider in the middle, known as the **estípite** [es-TEE-pee-tay] **column**. The column is constructed of segmented, upside-down, and tapered pyramids and other sculpted forms of the kind previously found

Fig. 23.21 San Xavier del Bac, near Tucson, Arizona 1783–97. Nearly 99 feet in length, the church is made of brick and mortar, instead of adobe (earth and straw), the usual building material of the Southwest. The material was probably chosen to assert the Church's permanence.

only on the finials of furniture. Surrounded by decorative scrolls, garlands, and sculptures of angels and saints, all gilded and flickering in the candlelight, these *estípite* columns rise column upon column to an awe-inspiring height of 85 feet!

The extravagance of the Mexico City *retablo* is hardly unique. On the one hand, *retablos* were designed to impress the indigenous population, which the Spanish missionaries were intent on converting to Christianity. Thus nearly every church of any size in New Spain possessed a *retablo* that aspired to the magnificence of the one in the Mexico City Cathedral. On the other hand, *retablos* were a manifestation of the extraordinary wealth that Mexico enjoyed as the center of a trade for precious metals. It coordinated a network of sources and outlets that through its Atlantic and Pacific ports linked the silver mines of Peru in the south, its own silver mines in the Sierra Madre of central Mexico, and other mining towns in the north, to Spain, the Philippines, and China. Thus, as far north as New Mexico and

Arizona, new missionary churches built in the seventeenth and eighteenth centuries were modeled on churches built in the same era to the south.

One of the most beautiful of these northern churches is San Xavier del Bac [sahn KSAH-vee-ay del bahk], just south of present-day Tucson, built in 1783 to 1797. The mission was founded in the early eighteenth century to serve the Tohono O'odham, or "Desert People," and the settlement these people called Bac, "place where the water appears." The name of the settlement refers to the fact that the Santa Cruz River, which runs underground for some distance, reappears on the surface nearby. Surrounding the church's portal are niches framed by *estípite* columns (Fig. **23.21**). Elaborate volutes, almost certainly deliberate echoes of the facade of Il Gésu, the Jesuit church in Rome (see Fig. 21.9), decorate the facade and support the two towers (one of which was mysteriously never completed). The magnificent *retablo* inside has unusual twin *estípite* columns that rise from floor to ceiling (Fig. **23.22**).

Despite Spain's program to convert Native Americans to Christianity, the Native American cultures of the Southwest never comfortably assimilated Western religion. In August 1680, the Pueblo peoples of present-day New Mexico and Arizona simultaneously revolted under the leadership of a San Juan Indian named Popé [POH-pay]. They killed 21 of the province's 33 Franciscans and 308 Spanish settlers, including men, women, and children.

Survivors fled south to El Paso del Norte [el–PAH-soh del NOR-tay].

Not until 1692 would the Spanish reassert control of the region, but they had learned their lesson. They no longer practiced *encomienda* or *repartimiento*, they formally recognized the Pueblos' rights to their lands, and they abandoned their attempt to force Christianity upon the population. As a result, the Pueblo peoples today still retain the greater part of their pre-Conquest culture. But interestingly, from 1692 on, the two traditions, native and

Fig. 23.22 Nave of San Xavier del Bac with *retablo*. 1783–97. The *retablo* was restored in 1992 to 1997, a project that included the delicate cleaning of its gold and silver leaf.

Christian, have stood side by side, especially in mission architecture and decoration, to create a composite and syncretic style.

The decorative program of the Church of San José at Old Laguna Pueblo, the first church to be rebuilt after the reconquest in 1699 to 1706, is a case in point (Fig. **23.23**). The altar and *retablo* are the work of an unknown artist known as the Laguna Santero, an itinerant Mexican artist who created altar ensembles from the 1780s to about 1810, not only at Laguna but also at Acoma, Zia, Santa Ana, and Pojoaque pueblos and for churches in Santa Cruz de la Cañada and Santa Fe. The high altar at Laguna is decorated with floral motifs—that may have once covered the walls to both right and left of the altar as well—probably meant to replicate the European woven tapestries found in the wealthier cathedrals to the south. The carved wooden *retablo* behind the high altar consists of four spiraling columns—reminiscent of the solomonic columns popular in European Baroque architecture in the seventeenth century—topped by a painting of the Holy Trinity. In the center of the columns is Saint Joseph (San José), the patron saint of the church, holding the Christ child in one arm. To the left is Saint John Nepomuk, sainted for refusing to violate the secrecy of the confessional, and to the right, Saint Barbara, patron saint of those who work with explosives, and hence associated with thunder and lightning. Attached to the top of the *retablo* and extending above the altar is a buffalo hide, painted with a sun on the left, a moon on the right, between them a rainbow and stars. Extending from the sun are zigzag lines that culminate in a triangular head, symbol of the Pueblo deity, the Horned Water Snake, god of lightning and rain. At each side of the altar are three mountains set beneath an overarching rainbow. Each possesses the eyes and mouth of a kachina. They echo the Holy Trinity at the top of the *retablo*, who stand beneath the overarching rainbow on the buffalo hide above and each of which is backed by a triangular green halo. Thus Pueblo and Christian traditions are unified in the design, and this syncretic impulse is underscored not only by the Pueblo designs which run the length of the nave but also by the fact that the Christ child in Saint Joseph's arms carries a green peyote button.

Fig. 23.23 The Laguna Santero, *Retablo* and high altar of the Church of San José, Old Laguna Pueblo. ca. 1780–1810. A *santero* is a New Mexico artist whose carvings and paintings depict saints, angels, or other religious figures.

Excess and Restraint

An underlying characteristic of the Baroque age is its ultimate trust in the powers of reason. Major breakthroughs in mathematics, astronomy, geology, physics, chemistry, biology, and medical science dominate the history of the age. These products of empirical reasoning constituted a so-called **Scientific Revolution** that transformed the way the Western mind came to understand its place in the universe.

It may seem odd that painters like Caravaggio, Rubens, and Rembrandt, who appealed to the emotional and dramatic, the sensual and the spectacular, should be products of the same age as the Scientific Revolution. It would seem more reasonable to say that the scientific energies of the age found their painterly expression more in the likes of Poussin than Rubens, their literary expression more in Corneille than Molière. And yet Rembrandt's *Anatomy Lesson of Dr. Tulp* (see Chapter 22 *Closer Look*, pages 720–721) clearly engages the scientific mind, and Rubens's swirling, flowing lines are the product of a mind confident that order and wholeness are the basic underpinnings of experience. In a very real sense, then, Rubens and Rembrandt, Molière and Wycherley, Calderón and Quevedo, can best be understood in terms of their ability to look beneath the surface of experience for the human truths that motivate us all. Their work—like the autobiographical writings of Montaigne in the sixteenth century—announces the dawn of modern psychology.

Still, the Baroque age does embody a certain tension between reason and emotion, decorum and excess, clearly defined in the contest between the *poussinistes* and the *rubenistes* for ascendancy in the arts. This tension is evident in a painting that shows Louis XIV visiting the Académie des Sciences in 1671 (Fig. **23.24**). Following the lead of King Charles II of England, who had chartered the Royal Society in 1662, Louis created the French Academy of Sciences in 1666. He stands surrounded by astronomical and scientific instruments, charts and maps, skeletal and botanical specimens. Out the window, the ordered geometry of a classical French garden dominates the view. At the same time, Louis seems alien to his surroundings. Decked out in all his ruffles, lace, ribbons, and bows, he is the very image of ostentatious excess. The tension he embodies will become a defining characteristic of the following century. In the next two chapters, we will examine the tension in the eighteenth century between the demands of reason, the value that defines the so-called Enlightenment, and the limits of excess, the aristocratic style that has come to be known as the Rococo. Both equally were the product of the Baroque age that precedes them. ■

Fig. 23.24 Henri Testelin, *Jean-Baptiste Colbert Presenting the Members of the Royal Academy of Science to Louis XIV*. **ca. 1667**. Oil on canvas. © Chateau de Versailles, France/Lauros/Giraudon/The Bridgeman Art Library.

What is absolutism?

The court and government of Louis XIV of France were centered at Versailles, the magnificent palace outside Paris designed by Charles Le Brun. André le Nôtre laid out the grounds in the geometric style called the French garden. In what ways does Versailles reflect Louis's sense of his absolute authority? What did he mean to suggest by calling himself *Le Roi Soleil*, "the Sun King"?

What tastes in art competed for Louis XIV's favor?

Various members of the court favored one or the other of two competing styles of art, represented, on the one hand, by the work of Peter Paul Rubens and, on the other, by that of Nicolas Poussin. What compositional features characterize the painting of Rubens, and how do they contrast with the painting of Poussin?

Louis indulged his taste for pomp and ceremony in music and dance, and especially entertainments written by Jean-Baptiste Lully, who created a new operatic genre, the *tragédie en musique*. What characterizes Lully's operas? Louis also strongly promoted dance, the most important form of which was the minuet.

Under a charter granted by Louis, the *Comédie Française*, the French national theater, was established. How did the plays of Pierre Corneille reflect the aesthetic tastes of Poussin? Molière's comedies, such as *Tartuffe*, spared no one from ridicule. What is the central focus of his works? Jean Racine wrote such successful tragedies that he became the first French playwright to live entirely on the earnings from his plays.

How did political conflict affect the arts in England?

The greatest artist of the English court was Anthony Van Dyck, who had worked in Rubens's studio as his chief assistant. His great talent was portraiture. How did the political climate in England—the rivalry between Roundhead Puritan factions and Cavalier royalists—complicate his career? Can you briefly describe the political maneuverings of the era? How did this rivalry

manifest itself in literature? And how did it manifest itself in the burgeoning art and literature of the American colonies?

What role did the arts play in the Spanish court?

Philip IV of Spain strove to rival the other great courts of Europe by employing the greatest painters of the day, including Peter Paul Rubens. The young court painter Diego Velázquez, already deeply influenced by Caravaggio, visited Rubens at work. Velázquez's greatest work is *Las Meninas*, ostensibly a portrait of the royal princess, but a self-portrait as well, and a complex realization of space. There are many different gazes that ricochet throughout Velázquez's painting *Las Meninas* and act as focal points. Describe as many of them as you can find. Under Philip III and Philip IV, the literary arts thrived, especially in the drama of Lope de Vega and Calderón, who were central to what has come to be known as the Golden Age of Spanish drama. What is the central theme of Calderon's work? What characterizes Lope de Vega's plays? What theme predominates the satires of Francisco de Quevedo?

How did Native American traditions affect the Baroque style in the Americas?

By the start of the seventeenth century, Lima, Peru, was a fully Baroque city. Native painters decorated their paintings of saints with elaborate *brocateado*. How does the technique reflect their Inca heritage? In New Spain, the poet Sor Juana Inés de la Cruz wrote *villancicos*. How would you describe these complex Baroque musical compositions? What do they celebrate? The Baroque found particular expression in the *retablos*, or altarpiece ensembles, in the churches of New Spain. What characterizes them? This style spread throughout the Viceroyalty of Mexico, as far north as San Xavier del Bac, near present-day Tucson, Arizona. After the Pueblo revolt of 1680, the Church became more tolerant of native traditions. How does the Church of San José at Old Laguna Pueblo reflect this new tolerance?

PRACTICE MORE Get flashcards for images and terms and review chapter material with quizzes at **www.myartslab.com**

GLOSSARY

absolutism A term applied to strong, centralized monarchies that exert royal power over their dominions, usually on the grounds of divine right.

binary form Having a two-part structure.

brocateado The application of gold leaf to canvas.

Cavalier The term for the aristocratic royalist supporters of Charles I of England.

classical unities The notion, derived from Aristotle's *Poetics*, that requires a play to have only one action that occurs in one place and within one day.

comédie-ballet A drama that is part opera and part ballet.

divertissement An intermezzo.

estípite column A form of engaged column, narrow at the base and top, wider in the middle, that is constructed of segmented, upside-down, and tapered pyramids and other sculpted forms.

French garden A style of formal garden that is characterized by a methodical, geometrical design.

French overture An overture distinguished by a slow, homophonic melody (associated with the royal dignity) that built to a faster contrapuntal section.

intermezzo A short display of dance, song, or instrumental music.

masque A type of performance that combined speech, dance, and spectacle.

minuet An elegant triple-time dance of moderate tempo.

retablo A large altarpiece ensemble.

Roundhead Supporter of the Puritan Parliament who cropped his hair short and dressed plainly.

Scientific Revolution A time of major breakthroughs in mathematics, astronomy, geology, physics, chemistry, biology, and medical science, all the result of empirical reasoning.

suite An ordered series of instrumental dances.

tragédie en musique An operatic genre that generally consists of an overture, an allegorical prologue, five acts of sung drama, and many intermezzos.

READINGS

READING 23.1

from Molière, *Tartuffe*, Act III, scenes 2 and 3 (1664)

A remarkable feature of Molière's play is that its central character, Tartuffe, does not come on stage until Act III, scene 2. Up to that point, however, he has been the focus of all conversation, and the family maid Dorine has tried valiantly to expose his calumny. In these two scenes, the perceptive Dorine mocks his hypocrisy even as she announces the arrival of Orgon's wife, Elmire, whom Tartuffe attempts to seduce.

SCENE II

TARTUFFE, LAURENT, DORINE

TARTUFFE *[Observing Dorine and calling to his manservant off stage]*
Hang up my hair shirt, put my scourge in place,
And pray, Laurent, for Heaven's perpetual grace.
I'm going to the prison now, to share
My last few coins with the poor wretches there.
DORINE *[Aside:]* Dear God, what affectation! What a fake!
TARTUFFE You wished to see me?
DORINE Yes . . .
TARTUFFE *[Taking a handkerchief from his pocket]*
For mercy's sake,
Please take this handkerchief, before you speak.
DORINE What? 10
TARTUFFE Cover that bosom, girl. The flesh is weak,
And unclean thoughts are difficult to control.
Such sights as that can undermine the soul.
DORINE Your soul, it seems, has very poor defenses,
And flesh makes quite an impact on your senses.
It's strange that you're so easily excited;
My own desires are not so soon ignited,
And if I saw you naked as a beast,
Not all your hide would tempt me in the least.
TARTUFFE Girl, speak more modestly; unless you do, 20
I shall be forced to take my leave of you.
DORINE Oh, no, it's I who must be on my way;
I've just one little message to convey:
Madame is coming down, and begs you, Sir,
To wait and have a word or two with her.
TARTUFFE Gladly.

DORINE *(Aside)* That had a softening effect!
I think my guess about him was correct.
TARTUFFE Will she be long?
DORINE No: that's her step I hear. 30
Ah, here she is, and I shall disappear.

SCENE III

ELMIRE, TARTUFFE

TARTUFFE May Heaven, whose infinite goodness we adore,
Preserve your body and soul forevermore,
And bless your days, and answer thus the plea
Of one who is its humblest votary.
ELMIRE I thank you for that pious wish. But please,
Do take a chair and let's be more at ease.
[They sit down.]
TARTUFFE I trust that you are once more well and strong?
ELMIRE Oh, yes: the fever didn't last for long.
TARTUFFE My prayers are too unworthy, I am sure, 40
To have gained from Heaven this most gracious cure;
But lately, Madam, my every supplication
Has had for object your recuperation.
ELMIRE You shouldn't have troubled so. I don't deserve it.
TARTUFFE Your health is priceless, Madam, and to preserve it
I'd gladly give my own, in all sincerity.
ELMIRE Sir, you outdo us all in Christian charity.
You've been most kind. I count myself your debtor.
TARTUFFE It was nothing. Madam. I long to serve you better. 50
ELMIRE There's a private matter I'm anxious to discuss.
I'm glad there's no one here to hinder us.

TARTUFFE I too am glad: it floods my heart with bliss
    To find myself alone with you like this.
    For just this chance I've prayed with all my power—
    But prayed in vain, until this happy hour.
ELMIRE This won't take long, Sir, and I hope you'll be
    Entirely frank and unconstrained with me.
TARTUFFE Indeed, there's nothing I had rather do
    Than bare my inmost heart and soul to you.   60
    First, let me say that what remarks I've made
    About the constant visits you are paid
    Were prompted not by any mean emotion.
    But rather by a pure and deep devotion.
    A fervent zeal . . .
ELMIRE No need for explanation.
    Your sole concern, I'm sure, was my salvation.
TARTUFFE *[Taking Elmire's hand and pressing her fingertips]*
    Quite so:
    and such great fervor do I feel . . .
ELMIRE Ooh! Please! You're pinching!
TARTUFFE 'T was from excess of zeal.   70
    I never meant to cause you pain, I swear.
    I'd rather . . .
    [He places his hand on Elmire's knee.]
ELMIRE What can your hand be doing there?
TARTUFF Feeling your gown; what soft, fine-woven stuff!
ELMIRE Please, I'm extremely ticklish. That's enough.
    [She draws her chair away; Tartuffe pulls his after her.]
TARTUFFE *[Fondling the lace collar of her gown]* My, my, what
    lovely lacework on your dress!
    The workmanship's miraculous, no less.
    I've not seen anything to equal it.
ELMIRE Yes, quite. But let's talk business for a bit.   80
    They say my husband means to break his word
    And give his daughter to you, Sir. Had you heard?
TARTUFFE He did once mention it. But I confess
    I dream of quite a different happiness.
    It's elsewhere, Madam, that my eyes discern
    The promise of that bliss for which I yearn.
ELMIRE I see: you care for nothing here below.
TARTUFFE Ah, well—my heart's not made of stone, you know.
ELMIRE All your desires mount heavenward, I'm sure,
    In scorn of all that's earthly and impure.   90
TARTUFFE A love of heavenly beauty does not preclude
    A proper love for earthly pulchritude;
    Our senses are quite rightly captivated
    By perfect works our Maker has created.
    Some glory clings to all that Heaven had made;
    In you, all Heaven's marvels are displayed.
    On that fair face, such beauties have been lavished.
    The eyes are dazzled and the heart is ravished;
    How could I look on you, O flawless creature,
    And not adore the Author of all Nature,   100
    Feeling a love both passionate and pure
    For you, his triumph of self-portraiture?
    At first, I trembled lest that love should be
    A subtle snare that Hell had laid for me;
    I vowed to flee the sight of you, eschewing
    A rapture that might prove my soul's undoing;
    But soon, fair being, I became aware
    That my deep passion could be made to square
    With rectitude, and with my bounden duty.
    I thereupon surrendered to your beauty.   110

    It is, I know, presumptuous on my part
    To bring you this poor offering of my heart,
    And it is not my merit, Heaven knows,
    But your compassion on which my hopes repose.
    You are my peace, my solace, my salvation;
    On you depends my bliss—or desolation;
    I bide your judgment and, as you think best,
    I shall be either miserable or blest.
ELMIRE Your declaration is most gallant, Sir.
    But don't you think it's out of character?   120
    You'd have done better to restrain your passion
    And think before you spoke in such a fashion.
    It ill becomes a pious man like you . . .
TARTUFFE I may be pious, but I'm human too:
    With your celestial charms before his eyes,
    A man has not the power to be wise.
    I know such words sound strangely, coming from me,
    But I'm no angel, nor was meant to be,
    And if you blame my passion, you must needs
    Reproach as well the charms on which it feeds.   130
    Your loveliness I had no sooner seen
    Than you became my soul's unrivaled queen;
    Before your seraph glance, divinely sweet,
    My heart's defenses crumbled in defeat,
    And nothing fasting, prayers, or tears might do
    Could stay my spirit from adoring you.
    My eyes my sighs have told you in the past
    What now my lips make bold to say at last,
    And if, in your great goodness, you will deign
    To look upon your slave, and ease his pain,—   140
    If in compassion for my soul's distress,
    You'll stoop to comfort my unworthiness,
    I'll raise to you, in thanks for that sweet manna,
    An endless hymn, an infinite hosanna.
    With me, of course, there need be no anxiety.
    No fear of scandal or of notoriety.
    These young court gallants, whom all the ladies fancy,
    Are vain in speech, in action rash and chancy;
    When they succeed in love, the world soon knows it;
    No favor's granted them but they disclose it   150
    And by the looseness of their tongue profane
    The very altar where their hearts have lain.
    Men of my sort, however, love discreetly,
    And one may trust our reticence completely.
    My keen concern for my good name insures
    The absolute security or yours;
    In short, I offer you, my dear Elmire,
    Love without scandal, pleasure without fear.
ELMIRE I've heard your well-turned speeches to the end,
    And what you urge I clearly apprehend.   160
    Aren't you afraid that I may take a notion
    To tell my husband of your warm devotion,
    And that, supposing he were duly told,
    His feelings toward you might grow rather cold?
TARTUFFE I know, dear lady, that your exceeding charity
    Will lead your heart to pardon my temerity;
    That you'll excuse my violent affection
    As human weakness, human imperfection;
    And that—O fairest!—you will bear in mind
    That I'm but flesh and blood, and am not blind.   170
ELMIRE Some women might do otherwise, perhaps,
    But I shall be discreet about your lapse;

I'll tell my husband nothing of what's occurred
If, in return, you'll give your solemn word
To advocate as forcefully as you can
The marriage of Valère and Mariane,
Renouncing all desire to dispossess
Another of his rightful happiness,
And . . .

READING CRITICALLY

Why do you suppose that Molière leaves it to the maid of the house to see through Tartuffe's hypocrisy, while the more educated members of the household seem blind to it?

READING 23.2

Anne Bradstreet, "Here Follows Some Verses upon the Burning of Our House, July 10th, 1666" (1667)

This poem is a poignant statement of the author's Puritan faith in the face of terrible personal tragedy. The opening lines, in which Bradstreet confesses her attraction to fire, refer not to the actual burning of her house, but to the day of judgment and the second coming of Christ. The poem then goes on to explore the tension between worldly desires and spiritual salvation.

In silent night when rest I took
For sorrow near I did not look
I wakened was with thund'ring noise
And piteous shrieks of dreadful voice.
That fearful sound of "Fire!" and "Fire!"
Let no man know is my desire.
I, starting up, the light did spy,
And to my God my heart did cry
To strengthen me in my distress
And not to leave me succorless.   10
Then, coming out, beheld a space
The flame consume my dwelling place.
And when I could no longer look,
I blest His name that gave and took,
That laid my goods now in the dust.
Yea, so it was, and so 'twas just.
It was His own, it was not mine,
Far be it that I should repine;
He might of all justly bereft
But yet sufficient for us left.   20
When by the ruins oft I past
My sorrowing eyes aside did cast,
And here and there the places spy
Where oft I sat and long did lie:
Here stood that trunk, and there that chest,
There lay that store I counted best.
My pleasant things in ashes lie,
And them behold no more shall I.
Under thy roof no guest shall sit,
Nor at thy table eat a bit.   30
No pleasant tale shall e'er be told,

Nor things recounted done of old.
No candle e'er shall shine in thee,
Nor bridegroom's voice e'er heard shall
In silence ever shall thou lie,
Adieu, Adieu, all's vanity.
Then straight I 'gin my heart to chide,
And did thy wealth on earth abide?
Didst fix thy hope on mold'ring dust?
The arm of flesh didst make thy trust?   40
Raise up thy thoughts above the sky
That dunghill mists away may fly.
Thou hast an house on high erect,
Framed by that mighty Architect,
With glory richly furnished,
Stands permanent though this be fled.
It's purchased and paid for too
By Him who hath enough to do.
A price so vast as is unknown
Yet by His gift is made thine own;   50
There's wealth enough, I need no more,
Farewell, my pelf, farewell my store.
The world no longer let me love,
My hope and treasure lies above.

READING CRITICALLY

In the middle of the poem, Bradstreet points to the places where her former possessions used to rest—"here" and "there." How is the "here" and "there" of the poem transformed in its second half?

24

The Rise of the Enlightenment in England
The Claims of Reason

THINKING AHEAD

Who were Hobbes and Locke?

What is satire, and how did it shape the Enlightenment in England?

What gave rise to the novel?

What was the purpose of Captain Cook's voyages to the Pacific Ocean?

L ondon, the city of elegance and refinement painted in 1747 by Venetian master of cityscapes Canaletto (Giovanni Antonio Canal; 1697–1768), was rivaled only by Paris as the center of European intellectual culture in the eighteenth century (Fig. **24.1**). Neither the map showing the growth of London from 1720 to 1820 (Map **24.1**) nor Canaletto's painting offers any hint that the city had been devastated by fire 80 years earlier. Before dawn on the morning of September 2, 1666, a baker's oven exploded on Pudding Lane in London. A strong east wind hastened the fire's spread until, by morning, some 300 houses were burning (Fig. **24.2**). In his private diaries, Samuel Pepys [peeps] (1633–1703) recorded what he saw on that fateful day:

> I rode down to the waterside, . . . and there saw a lamentable fire. . . . Everybody endeavoring to remove their goods, and flinging into the river or bringing them into lighters that lay off; poor people staying in their houses as long as till the very fire touched them, and then running into boats, or clambering from one pair of stairs by the waterside to another. . . .
>
> [I hurried] to [Saint] Paul's; and there walked along Watling Street, as well as I could, every creature coming away laden with goods to save and, here and there, sick people carried away in beds. Extraordinary goods carried in carts and on backs. At last [I] met my Lord Mayor in Cannon Street, like a man spent, with a [handkerchief] about his neck. . . . "Lord, what can I do? [he cried] I am spent: people will not obey me. I have been pulling down houses, but the fire overtakes us faster than we can do it." . . . So . . . I . . . walked home; seeing people all distracted, and no manner of means used to quench the fire. The houses, too, so very thick thereabouts, and full of matter for burning, as pitch and tar, in Thames Street; and warehouses of oil and wines and brandy and other things.

From Samuel Pepys, *Diary* (September 2, 1666)

◀ **Fig. 24.1 Canaletto, *London: The Thames and the City of London from Richmond House* (detail). 1747.** Oil on canvas, 44⁷⁄₈″ × 39³⁄₈″. Trustees of the Goodwood House, West Sussex, UK. From May 1746 until at least 1755, interrupted by only two visits to Venice in 1750 to 1751 and 1753 to 1754, the Venetian painter Canaletto occupied a studio in Beak Street, London. The geometric regularity and perspectival inventiveness of his paintings reflect the Enlightenment's taste for rationality. But his sense of grandeur and scale is, like Louis XIV's Versailles (see Chapter 27), purely aristocratic.

HEAR MORE Listen to an audio file of your chapter at **www.myartslab.com**

Map 24.1 The growth of London 1720 to 1820.

London in 1720
London in 1770
London in 1820
Church
Important building

The fire in these warehouses so fueled the blaze that over the course of the next two days it engulfed virtually the entire medieval city and beyond (Map 24.2). Almost nothing was spared. About 100,000 Londoners were left homeless. Eighty-seven churches had burned. Businesses, particularly along the busy wharves on the north side of the Thames, were bankrupted. Taken together with the Great Plague that had killed some 70,000 Londoners just the year before, John Evelyn, one of the other great chroniclers of the age, summed up the situation in what amounts to typical British understatement: "London was, but is no more."

Such devastation was both a curse and a blessing. While the task of rebuilding London was almost overwhelming, the fire gave the city the opportunity to modernize its center in a way that no other city in the world could even imagine. By 1670, almost all the private houses destroyed by the fire had been rebuilt, and businesses were once again thriving. Over the course of the next century, the city would prosper as much or more than any other city in the world, "London," as one writer put it, "is the centre to which almost all the individuals who fill the upper and middle ranks of society are successively attracted. The country pays its tribute to the supreme city."

This chapter surveys developments in London, the literary center of what would come to be known as the Age of Enlightenment. Across Europe, intellectuals began to advocate rational thinking as the means to achieving a comprehensive system of ethics, aesthetics, and knowledge. The rationalist approach owed much to scientist Isaac Newton (1642–1727), who in 1687 demonstrated to the satisfaction of just about everyone that the universe was an intelligible system, well ordered in its operations and guiding principles. The workings of human society—the production and consumption of manufactured goods, the social organization of families and towns, the functions of national governments, even the arts—were believed to be governed by analogous universal laws. The intellectuals of Enlightenment England thought of themselves as the guiding lights of a new era of progress that would leave behind, once and for all, the irrationality, superstition, and tyranny that had defined Western culture, particularly before the Renaissance. The turmoil that had led to Civil War in 1642 to 1648 was followed in 1688 by a bloodless "Glorious Revolution," the implementation of a Bill of Rights, and the establishment of a constitutional monarchy, all of which seemed proof that reason could triumph over political and religious intolerance. Still, recognizing that English society was deeply flawed, they also satirized it, attacking especially its aristocracy. At the same time, an expanding publishing industry and an increasingly literate public offered Enlightenment writers the opportunity to instruct their readers in moral behavior, even as they described English vice in prurient detail. Finally, the voyages of Captain James Cook (1728–1779) to the Pacific suggested that Enlightenment thinkers might have much to learn from the peoples of the world.

Fig. 24.2 *The Great Fire, 1666.* Engraving. The tower in the middle is Old Saint Paul's. It too would be destroyed. In the words of John Evelyn, "The stones of St. Paules flew like grenados, the Lead mealting down the streetes in a streame and the very pavements of them glowing with fiery rednesse, so as no horse, nor man, was able to tread on them."

Map 24.2 The spread of the Great Fire from September 2nd to 5th, 1666. From Roy Porter, *London: A Social History* (New York: Penguin Books, 1996), p. 86. Reproduced by permission. Porter's highly regarded history informs much of the discussion concerning England in these pages.

THE NEW LONDON: TOWARD THE ENLIGHTENMENT

After the Great Fire, architect Christopher Wren (1632–1723) proposed a grand redesign scheme that would have replaced the old city with wide boulevards and great squares. But the need to rebuild the city's commercial infrastructure quickly made his plan impractical, and each property owner was essentially left to his own devices.

Nevertheless, certain real improvements were made. Wood construction was largely banned; brick and stone were required. New sewage systems were introduced, and streets had to be at least 14 feet wide. Just a year after the fire, in a poem celebrating the devastation and reconstruction, "Annus Mirabilis" ("year of wonders"), the poet John Dryden (1631–1700) would equate London to the mythological Phoenix rising from its own ashes, reborn: "a wonder to all years and Ages . . . a *Phoenix* in her ashes." Moved by the speed of the city's

LEARN MORE Gain insight from a primary source document on the burning of Old Saint Paul's at **www.myartslab.com**

rebuilding, Dryden is sublimely confident in London's future. Under the rule of Charles II, the city would become even greater than before (**Reading 24.1**):

READING 24.1

from John Dryden, "Annus Mirabilis" (1667)

More great than human, now, and more august,[1]
New-deified she from her fires does rise:
Her widening streets on new foundations trust,
And, opening, into larger parts she flies. . . .

Now like the maiden queen, she will behold
From her high turrets, hourly suitors come:
The East with incense, and the West with gold,
Will stand like suppliants, to receive her doom.

[1]**Augusta,** the old name of London.

For Dryden, the Great Fire was not so much a disaster as a gift from God. And Charles II must have thought so as well, for as a way of thanking Dryden for the poem, the king named him poet laureate of the nation in 1668.

Although Christopher Wren's plans to redesign the entire London city center after the Great Fire proved impractical, he did receive the commission to rebuild 52 of the churches destroyed in the blaze. Rising above them all was Saint Paul's Cathedral, a complex yet orderly synthesis of the major architectural styles of the previous 150 years (see *Closer Look*, pages 770–771). According to Wren's son, "a memorable omen" occurred on the occasion of his father's laying the first stone on the ruins of the old cathedral in 1675:

> When the SURVEYOR in Person [Wren himself, in his role as King's Surveyor of Works] had set out, upon the Place, the Dimensions of the great Dome and fixed upon the centre; a common Labourer was ordered to bring a flat stone from the Heaps of Rubbish . . . to be laid for a Mark and Direction to the Masons; the Stone happened to be a piece of Grave-stone, with nothing remaining on the Inscription but the simple word in large capitals, RESURGAM [the Latin for "REBORN"].

"RESURGAM" still decorates the south transept of the cathedral above a figure of a phoenix rising from the ashes.

Something of the power of Wren's conception can be felt in Canaletto's view of *The Thames and the City of London from Richmond House* (see Fig. 24.1). The cathedral does indeed rise above the rest of the city, not least because, in rebuilding, private houses had been limited to four stories. Only other church towers, almost all built by Wren as well, rise above the roof lines, as if approaching the giant central structure in homage.

Absolutism versus Liberalism: Thomas Hobbes and John Locke

The new London was, in part, the result of the rational empirical thinking that dominated the Royal Society (see Chapter 26). Following the Civil War and the Restoration, one of the most pressing issues of the day was how best to govern the nation, and one of the most important points of view had been published by Thomas Hobbes [hobz] (1588–1679) in 1651, in *Leviathan; or the Matter, Forme, and Power of a Commonwealth, Ecclesiasticall and Civil* (Fig. **24.3**). His classical training had convinced Hobbes that the reasoning upon which Euclid's geometry was based could be extended to political and social systems. A visit to Galileo in Italy in 1636 reaffirmed that Galileo's description of the movement of the solar system—planets orbiting the central sun—could be extended to human relations—a people orbiting their ruler. Hobbes argued that people are driven by two things—the fear of death at someone else's hands and the desire for power—and that the government's role is to

Fig. 24.3 Frontispiece to *Leviathan*. 1651. Bancroft Library, Berkeley, CA. At the top of the image, the body of the king is composed of hundreds of his subjects. Below his outstretched arms holding sword and scepter, the world is orderly and peaceful.

check both of these instincts, which if uncontrolled would lead to anarchy. Given the context in which *Leviathan* was written—the English Civil War had raged throughout the previous decade—Hobbes's position is hardly surprising. Most humans, Hobbes believed, recognize their own essential depravity and therefore willingly submit to governance. They accept the **social contract**, which means giving up sovereignty over themselves and bestowing it on a ruler. They carry out the ruler's demands, and the ruler, in return, agrees to keep the peace. Humankind's only hope, Hobbes argued (see **Reading 24.2**, pages 793–794), is to submit to a higher authority, the "Leviathan" [luh-VY-uh-thun], the biblical sea monster who is the absolutist "king over all the sons of pride" (Job 41:34).

John Locke (1632–1704) disagreed. In his 1690 *Essay on Human Understanding*, Locke repudiated Hobbes, arguing that people are perfectly capable of governing themselves. The human mind at birth, he claimed, is a *tabula rasa*, a "blank slate," and our environment—what we learn and how we learn it—fills this slate (**Reading 24.3**):

READING 24.3

from Locke's *Essay on Human Understanding* (1690)

1. Idea is the object of thinking. Every man being conscious to himself that he thinks; and that which his mind is applied about whilst thinking being the ideas that are there, it is past doubt that men have in their minds several ideas—such as are those expressed by the words whiteness, hardness, sweetness, thinking, motion, man, elephant, army, drunkenness, and others: it is in the first place then to be inquired, How he comes by them? . . .

2. All ideas come from sensation or reflection. Let us then suppose the mind to be, as we say, white paper, void of all characters, without any ideas—How comes it to be furnished? Whence comes it by that vast store which the busy and boundless fancy of man has painted on it with an almost endless variety? Whence has it all the materials of reason and knowledge? To this I answer, in one word, from EXPERIENCE. In that all our knowledge is founded; and from that it ultimately derives itself. Our observation employed either, about external sensible objects, or about the internal operations of our minds perceived and reflected on by ourselves, is that which supplies our understandings with all the materials of thinking. These two are the fountains of knowledge, from whence all the ideas we have, or can naturally have, do spring.

3. The objects of sensation one source of ideas. First, our Senses, conversant about particular sensible objects, do convey into the mind several distinct perceptions of things . . . [and] thus we come by those ideas we have of yellow, white, heat, cold, soft, hard, bitter, sweet, and all those which we call sensible qualities. . . .

4. The operations of our minds, the other source of them. Secondly, the other fountain from which experience furnisheth the understanding with ideas, is the perception of the operations of our own mind within us, as it is employed about the ideas it has got; which operations, when the soul comes to reflect on and consider, do furnish the understanding with another set of ideas, which could not be had from things without. And such are perception, thinking, doubting, believing, reasoning, knowing, willing, and all the different actings of our own minds. . . .

Given this sense that we understand the world through experience, if we live in a reasonable society, it should follow, according to Locke's notion of the *tabula rasa*, that we will grow into reasonable people. In his *Second Treatise of Government* (see **Reading 24.4**, pages 794–796), also published in 1690, Locke went further. He refuted the divine rights of kings and argued that humans are "by nature free, equal, and independent." They agree to government in order to protect themselves, but the social contract to which they submit does not require them to surrender their own sovereignty to their ruler. The ruler has only limited authority that must be held in check by a governmental system balanced by a separation of powers. Finally, they expect the ruler to protect their rights, and if the ruler fails, they have the right to revolt in order to reclaim their natural freedom. This form of **liberalism**—literally, from the Latin, *liberare*, "to free"—sets the stage for the political revolutions that will dominate the Western world in the eighteenth and nineteenth centuries.

John Milton's *Paradise Lost*

The debate between absolutism and liberalism also informs what is arguably the greatest poem of the English seventeenth century, *Paradise Lost* by John Milton (1608–1674). Milton had served in Oliver Cromwell's government during the Commonwealth. (He had studied the great epics of classical literature, and he was determined to write his own, one which would, as he puts it in the opening verse of the poem, "justifie the wayes of God to men.") In 12 books, Milton composed a densely plotted poem with complex character development, rich theological reasoning, and long, wave-like sentences of blank verse. The subject of the epic is the Judeo-Christian story of the loss of Paradise by Adam and Eve and their descendents. As described in the Bible, the couple, enticed by Satan, disobey God's injunction that they not eat the fruit of the Tree of Knowledge. Satan had revolted against God and then sought to destroy humanity.

While occasionally virulently anti-Catholic, the poem is, among other things, a fair-minded essay on the possibilities of liberty and justice. In many ways, God assumes the position of royal authority that Hobbes argues for in his *Leviathan*. In Book 5 of Milton's poem, God sends the angel Raphael to Adam to warn him of the nearness of Lucifer

Christopher Wren, Saint Paul's Cathedral, London, western facade.
1675–1710. A statue of Saint Paul stands on top of the central portico, flanked by statues of Saint John (*right*) and Saint Peter (*left*). The sculptural detail in the portico pediment depicts the conversion of Paul following his vision on the road to Damascus.

Saint Paul's is the first cathedral ever built for the Anglican Church of England. It rises above the foundations of an earlier church destroyed in the Great Fire of London in 1666. In its design, architect Christopher Wren drew on classical, Gothic, Renaissance, and Baroque elements. Its imposing two-story facade is crowned by symmetrical twin clock towers and a massive dome. The floor plan—an elongated, cruciform (crosslike) design—is Gothic. The dome is Renaissance, purposefully echoing Bramante's Tempietto (see Fig. 15.6) but maintaining the monumental presence of Michelangelo's dome for Saint Peter's (see Fig. 15.7). The facade, with its two tiers of paired Corinthian columns, recalls the French Baroque Louvre in Paris (see Fig. 21.21). And the two towers are inspired by a Baroque church in Rome. Wren manages to bring all these elements together into a coherent whole.

lantern

conical brick-work dome

supporting timber framework

clerestory windows

inner dome

bell tower

west portico

Wren's Saint Paul's Cathedral

The church was laid out so that the congregation would directly face the sunrise on Easter morning, metaphorically revisiting the Resurrection itself. Rather than its ornamentation, the geometry of the building—especially the relationships established between geometric units—was at the heart of Wren's design. Notice the extraordinarily refined symmetry of the whole, particularly the relationships of the paired freestanding columns and the square embedded ones on the western facade. As Wren himself would write, "It seems very unaccountable that the generality of our late architects dwell so much on the ornamental, and so lightly pass over the geometrical, which is the most essential part of architecture." This reliance on geometric regularity is wholly consistent with Enlightenment thinking, reflecting Newton's description of the universe as an intelligible system, well-ordered in its operations and guiding principles.

SEE MORE For a Closer Look at Christopher Wren's Saint Paul's Cathedral, go to **www.myartslab.com**

Something to Think About . . .

If Wren believed that the overall design should reflect a classical sense of balance, symmetry, and proportion, he also believed that within that framework there was room for a variety of features. How does the facade of St. Paul's reflect Wren's sense of variety and diversity?

Cutaway illustrations of the outer shell and ground floor of Saint Paul's Cathedral, London. Designed 1675. Wren's dome transforms the relatively small scale of Bramante's Tempietto into monumental space. It is some 102 feet in diameter, spanning both nave and side aisles, and rises 366 feet to the top of the lantern cross (only Saint Peter's is higher, at 405 feet). The dome itself is a triple-layer construction. The outer dome or shell is made of timber, covered with lead sheathing. A hidden central dome, conical in shape and made of brick, supports the outer shell and, with the help of iron bands, the lantern, ball, and cross at the top of the building as well. The inner dome—the dome viewed by the congregation—is made of light brick and is decorated with a trompe l'oeil representation of the heavens.

(Satan) and to explain how Lucifer became God's enemy. Raphael recounts how God had addressed the angels to announce that he now had a son, Christ, whom all should obey as if he were God, and he did so with the authority of hereditary kingship (**Reading 24.5a**):

READING 24.5a

from John Milton, *Paradise Lost*, Book 5 (1667)

"Hear all ye angels, Progeny of Light,
Thrones, Dominations, Princedoms, Virtues, Powers,
Hear my Decree, which unrevoked shall stand.
This day I have begot whom I declare
My only Son, and on this holy hill
Him have anointed, whom ye now behold
At my right hand; your head I him appoint;
And by my Self have sworn to him shall bow
All knees in heav'n, and shall confess him Lord."

Lucifer, formerly God's principal angel, is not happy about the news of this new favorite. Motivated by his own desire for power, he gathers the angels loyal to him, and addresses them in terms more in the spirit of Locke than Hobbes. He begins his speech as God had begun his, invoking the imperial titles of those present; he reminds them, "which assert / Our being ordain'd to govern, not to serve" (**Reading 24.5b**):

READING 24.5b

from John Milton, *Paradise Lost*, Book 5 (1667)

Thrones, Dominations, Princedoms, Virtues, Powers,
If these magnific titles yet remain
Not merely titular, since by decree
Another now hath to himself engrossed
All power, and us eclipsed under the name
Of King anointed. . . .

Will ye submit your necks, and choose to bend
The supple knee? ye will not, if I trust
To know ye right, or if ye know yourselves
Natives and sons of heav'n possessed before
By none, and if not equal all, yet free,
Equally free; for orders and degrees
Jar not with liberty. . . .

Who can in reason then or right assume
Monarchy over such as live by right
His equals, if in power and splendor less,
In freedom equal?

Lucifer's is a "reasonable" argument. Like Locke, he thinks of himself and the other angels as "by nature free, equal, and independent." The battle that ensues between God and Lucifer (see **Reading 24.5**, pages 796–797) is reminiscent of the English Civil War, with its complex protagonists, its councils, and its bids for leadership on both sides. It results in Lucifer's expulsion from Heaven to Hell, where he is henceforth known as Satan. While many readers understood God as a figure for the Stuart monarchy, and Satan as Cromwell, it is not necessary to do so in order to understand the basic tensions that inform the poem. The issues that separate God from Satan are clearly the issues dividing England in the seventeenth century: the tension between absolute rule and the civil liberty of the individual.

THE ENGLISH ENLIGHTENMENT

Under the rule of William and Mary, the turmoil that had marked British political life for at least a century was replaced by a period of relative stability. The new king and queen moved quickly to reaffirm the Habeas Corpus Act, passed during the reign of Charles II in 1679. The act required a warrant for the arrest of anyone, detailing the reasons for the arrest, and the right to a speedy trial. It was a revolutionary abridgement of royal power. At least since the time of Henry VIII, English kings had imprisoned their enemies—or their suspected enemies—for as long as they liked without a trial. Parliament also passed a Bill of Rights, guaranteeing that no Catholic could ever rule England and no British king could ever marry a Catholic. Additionally, it required monarchs to obey the law like other British citizens, and banned them from raising taxes without the consent of Parliament. The Toleration Act provided Puritans with the freedom to worship as they chose, though neither Puritans nor Roman Catholics were allowed to hold positions in the government or attend universities. By the middle of the 1690s, the royal privilege of press censorship was permanently abandoned.

As royal power was being curtailed, Parliament also brought the succession of the monarchy under the rule of law. The Settlement Act of 1701 provided for the peaceful succession of the English crown. The act named Anne, Mary's younger sister, as heir to the throne upon William's death (Mary had died of smallpox in 1694). Should none of Anne's children survive her (and in fact none did), the act called for the Protestant House of Hanover in Germany to succeed to England's throne. Anne succeeded William in 1702, and upon her death, in 1714, George I, who spoke only German at the time, became King of England.

Even before George assumed the throne, Parliament's two factions, the Whigs and the Tories, had been at odds. The Whig faction tended to support constitutional monarchy as opposed to absolutism, and non-Anglican Protestants, such as the Presbyterians. The Tories tended to support the Anglican church and English gentry. Naturally, they preferred a strong monarchy, while the Whigs favored Parliament retaining final sovereignty. Nevertheless, the Whigs gained favor with George, and so, when he assumed the throne, George was predisposed to the Whigs and to their leading the government. For the next 40 years, the Whigs had access to public office and enjoyed royal patronage, and the Tories were effectively eliminated from public life. The end result was that Whig leadership, chiefly that of Robert Walpole (1676–1745), who can be regarded as the first English prime minister and who dominated the English political scene from 1721 to 1742, was consistent and predictable. Nothing could have fostered the Enlightenment more. Above all else, England's transformation from a state in near chaos to one in comparative harmony demonstrated what is probably the fundamental principle of Enlightenment thought—that social change and political reform are not only desirable but possible.

Satire: Enlightenment Wit

Not every Englishman was convinced that the direction England was heading in the eighteenth century was for the better. London was a city teeming with activity; Canaletto's painting (see Fig. 24.1) was an idealized view of city life. Over the course of the eighteenth century, the rich and the middle class largely abandoned the city proper, moving west into present-day Mayfair and Marylebone, and even to outlying villages such as Islington and Paddington. At the start of the century, these villages were surrounded by meadows and market gardens, but by century's end they had been absorbed into an ever-growing suburbia (see Map 24.1).

In the heart of London, a surging population of immigrants newly arrived from the countryside filled the houses abandoned by the middle class, which had been subdivided into tenements. The very poor lived in what came to be called the East End, a semicircle of districts surrounding the area that extended from Saint Paul's in the west to the Tower of London in the East (the area contained by the old London Wall). Here, in the neighborhoods of Saint Giles, Clerkenwell, Spitalfields, Whitechapel, Bethnal Green, and Wapping, the streets were narrow and badly paved, the houses old and constantly falling down, and drunkenness, prostitution, pickpocketing, assault, and robbery were the norm. On the outer edges, pig keepers and dairymen labored in a landscape of gravel pits, garbage dumps, heaps of ashes, and piles of horse manure.

Whatever the promise offered by the social order established by Robert Walpole and the Georgian government, thoughtful, truly enlightened persons could look beneath the surface of English society and detect a cauldron of social ferment and moral bankruptcy. By approaching what might be called the "dark side" of the Enlightenment and exposing it to all, dissenting writers and artists like William

Hogarth (1697–1764), Jonathan Swift (1667–1745), and Alexander Pope (1688–1744) believed they might, by means of irony and often deadpan humor that marks their satire, return England to its proper path.

Hogarth and the Popular Print By 1743, thousands of Londoners were addicted to gin, their sole means of escape from the misery of poverty. In 1751, just four years after Canaletto painted his view of London, William Hogarth published *Gin Lane*, a print that illustrated life in the gin shops (Fig. **24.4**). In the foreground, a man so emaciated by drink that he seems a virtual skeleton lies dying, half-naked, presumably having pawned the rest of his clothes. A woman takes snuff on the stairs as her child falls over the railing beside her. At the door to the thriving pawnshop behind her, a carpenter sells his tools, the means of his livelihood, as a woman waits to sell her kitchen utensils, the means of her nourishment. In the background, a young woman is laid out in a coffin, as her child weeps beside her.

Fig. 24.4 William Hogarth, *Gin Lane*. 1751. Engraving and etching, third state, 14″ × 11 7/8″
Copyright The Trustees of the British Museum, London/Art Resource, New York. In his *Autobiographical Notes*, Hogarth wrote: "In gin lane every circumstance of its [gin's] horrid effects are brought to view; nothing but Idleness, Poverty, misery, and ruin are to be seen . . . not a house in tolerable condition but Pawnbrokers and the Gin shop."

Fig. 24.5 William Hogarth, *The Countess's Levée*, or *Morning Party*, from *Marriage à la Mode*. 1743–45. Oil on canvas, 27" × 35". The National Gallery, London. The reproductions on the wall tell us much about the sexual proclivities of the Countess and her court. Those directly above the Countess are Correggio's *Jupiter and Io* (see Figure 22.7) and a representation of Lot's seduction by his daughters. On the table between the Countess and Silvertongue is a French pornographic novel.

A building comes tumbling down, a man parades down the street with a bellows on his head and a child skewered on his staff—an allegorical if not realistic detail. In the top story of the building on the right, another man has hanged himself. At the lower left, above the door to the Gin Royal, one of the only buildings in good condition, are these words: "Drunk for a penny / Dead drunk for two pence / Clean Straw for Nothing."

In *Gin Lane*, Hogarth turned his attention, not to the promise of the English Enlightenment, but to the reality of London at its worst. He did so with the savage wit and broad humor that marks the best social satire. And he did so with the conviction that his images of what he called "modern moral subjects" might not only amuse a wide audience, but would influence that audience's behavior as well. Hogarth usually painted his subjects first, but recognizing the limited audience of a painting, he produced engraved versions of them for wider distribution. Hogarth recognized

that his work appealed to a large popular audience, and that by distributing engravings of his works he might make a comfortable living by entertaining it.

A successful engraving had to sell enough impressions to pay for its production and earn a profit for its maker, who was not usually the artist. Before Hogarth's time, British printmakers had kept most of the profits from an illustration. But Hogarth marketed his prints himself by means of illustrated subscription tickets, newspaper advertisements, and broadsides, and kept the profits. Especially popular were three series of prints, each telling a different tale. One of the series, *Marriage à la Mode* [ah-luh-moad], was produced as both one-of-a-kind paintings and a subscription series of engravings. In six images, the series tells the story of a marriage of convenience between the son of a bankrupt nobleman, the Earl of Squanderfield, and the daughter of a wealthy tradesman. The moral bankruptcy of British society—not just the poor—is Hogarth's subject.

His **caricature**—a portrait that exaggerates each person's peculiarities or defects—of each of his cast of characters is underscored by their names: Squanderfield, Silvertongue, and so on. The loveless couple is sacrificed to the desires of their parents, for money or social position, and the results of this union go from bad to worse. By the time we arrive at the fourth image, *The Countess's Levée* [luh-VAY], or *Morning Party* (Fig. **24.5**), which encapsulates the morning ritual of the young wife, the moral depravity of the couple's lifestyle is clear. An Italian *castrato* [kah-STRAH-toh]—a singer castrated in his youth so that he might retain his high voice—sings to the inattentive crowd, accompanied by his flautist. Next to them, a hanger-on with his hair in curlers sips his tea. The lady of the house listens attentively to her illicit lover Silvertongue, the family lawyer, whose portrait overlooks the room. Below them, a black child-servant points to a statue of Actaeon. (In classical mythology, Actaeon was a hunter who was transformed into a stag for having observed the goddess Diana bathing. His horns traditionally signify a cuckold, a man whose wife is unfaithful.)

The Satires of Jonathan Swift Perhaps the most biting satirist of the English Enlightenment was Jonathan Swift. In a letter to fellow satirist and friend Alexander Pope, Swift confided that he hated the human race for having misused its capacity for reason simply to further its own corrupt self-interest. After a modestly successful career as a satirist in the first decade of the eighteenth century, Swift was named Dean of Saint Patrick's Cathedral in Dublin in 1713, and it was there that he wrote his most famous works, *Gulliver's Travels*, published in 1726, and the brief, almost fanatically savage *A Modest Proposal* in 1729. There, reacting to the terrible poverty he saw in Ireland, Swift proposed that Irish families who could not afford to feed their children breed them to be butchered and served to the English. With a tongue perhaps never before so firmly lodged in his cheek, Swift concludes (Reading 24.6):

READING 24.6

from Jonathan Swift, "A Modest Proposal" (1729)

I am not so violently bent upon my own opinion as to reject any offer proposed by wise men, which shall be found equally innocent, cheap, easy and effectual. But before something of that kind shall be advanced in contradiction to my scheme, and offering a better, I desire the author or authors will be pleased maturely to consider two points. First, as things now stand, how they will be able to find food and raiment for 100,000 useless mouths and backs. And secondly, there being a round million of creatures in human figure throughout this kingdom, whose whole subsistence put into a common stock would leave them in debt 2,000,000£ sterling, adding those who are beggars by profession to the bulk of farmers, cottagers, and labourers, with the wives and children who are beggars in effect; I desire those politicians who dislike my overture, and may perhaps be so bold as to attempt an answer, that they will first ask the parents of these mortals, whether they would not at this day think it a great happiness to have been sold for food at a year old in the manner I prescribe, and thereby have avoided such a perpetual scene of misfortunes as they have since gone through by the oppression of landlords, the impossibility of paying rent without money or trade, the want of common sustenance, with neither house nor clothes to cover them from the inclemencies of the weather, and the most inevitable prospect of entailing the like or greater miseries upon their breed for ever.

I profess, in the sincerity of my heart, that I have not the least personal interest in endeavouring to promote this necessary work, having no other motive than the *public good of my country, by advancing our trade, providing for infants, relieving the poor, and giving some pleasure to the rich.* I have no children by which I can propose to get a single penny; the youngest being nine years old, and my wife past child-bearing.

Such a solution to the problem of starving Irish families—they would, as it were, breed for profit—is meant to be understood as the symbolic equivalent of what was actually happening to Irish families and their children. In fact, many Irishmen worked farms owned by Englishmen who charged them such high rents that they were frequently unable to pay them, and consequently lived on the brink of starvation. As Dean of the Cathedral in Dublin, Swift was in a position to witness their plight on a daily basis. For all practical purposes, Swift believed, England was consuming the Irish young, if not literally then figuratively, sucking the lifeblood out of them by means of its oppressive economic policies.

In *Gulliver's Travels*, Swift's satire is less direct. Europeans were familiar with the accounts of travelers' adventures in far-off lands at least since the time of Marco Polo, and after the exploration of the Americas, the form had become quite common. Swift played off the travel adventure narrative to describe the adventures of one Lemuel Gulliver as he moves among lands peopled by miniature people, giants, and other fabulous creatures. But Swift employs his imaginary peoples and creatures to comment on real human behavior. In Book 1, the Lilliputians, a people that average 6 inches in height, are "little people" not just physically but ethically. In fact, their politics and religion are very much those of England, and they are engaged in a war with a neighboring island that very closely resembles France. Swift's strategy is to reduce the politics of his day to a level of triviality. In Book 4, Gulliver visits Houyhnhnms, a country of noble horses whose name sounds like a whinnying horse and is probably pronounced *hwinnum*. Gulliver explains that "the word Houyhnhnm, in their tongue, signifies a horse, and, in its etymology, the perfection of nature." Their ostensible nobility contrasts with the bestial and degenerate behavior of their human-looking slaves, the Yahoos. Of course, Gulliver resembles a Yahoo as well. At one point, Gulliver's Houyhnhnm host compliments him, saying "that he was sure I must have been born of some noble family, because I far exceeded in shape, colour, and cleanliness, all the Yahoos of his nation." Gulliver's response is a model of Swift's satiric invective (**Reading 24.7**):

READING 24.7

from Jonathan Swift, *Gulliver's Travels*, Book IV, Chapter VI (1726)

I made his Honour my most humble acknowledgments for the good opinion he was pleased to conceive of me, but assured him at the same time, "that my birth was of the lower sort, having been born of plain honest parents, who were just able to give me a tolerable education; that nobility, among us, was altogether a different thing from the idea he had of it; that our young noblemen are bred from their childhood in idleness and luxury; that, as soon as years will permit, they consume their vigor, and contract odious diseases among lewd females; and when their fortunes are almost ruined, they marry some woman of mean birth, disagreeable person, and unsound constitution (merely for the sake of money), whom they hate and despise. That the productions of such marriages are generally scrofulous, rickety, or deformed children; by which means the family seldom continues above three generations, unless the wife takes care to provide a healthy father, among her neighbours or domestics, in order to improve and continue the breed. That a weak diseased body, a meager countenance, and sallow complexion, are the true marks of noble blood; and a healthy robust appearance is so disgraceful in a man of quality, that the world concludes his real father to have been a groom or a coachman. The imperfections of his mind run parallel with those of his body, being a composition of spleen, dullness, ignorance, caprice, sensuality, and pride.

Gulliver's Travels was an immediate best-seller, selling out its first printing in less than a week. "It is universally read," said his friend Alexander Pope, "from the cabinet council to the nursery." So enduring is Swift's wit that names of his characters and types have entered the language as descriptive terms—"yahoo" for a coarse or uncouth person, "Lilliputian" for anything small and delicate.

The Classical Wit of Alexander Pope The English poet Alexander Pope shared Swift's assessment of the English nobility. For 12 years, from 1715 until 1727, Pope spent the majority of his time translating Homer's *Iliad* and *Odyssey*, and producing a six-volume edition of Shakespeare, projects of such popularity that he became a wealthy man. But in 1727, his literary career changed directions and, as he wrote, he "stooped to truth, and moralized his song"—he turned, in

short, to satire. His first effort was the mock epic *Dunciad* [DUN-see-ad], published in 1728 and dedicated to Jonathan Swift. The poem opens with a direct attack on the king, George II (r. 1727–1760), who had recently succeeded his father, George I, to the throne. For Pope, this suggested the goddess Dullness reigned over an England where "Dunce the second rules like Dunce the first." Pope's dunces are the very nobility that Swift attacks in the fourth book of Gulliver—men of "dullness, ignorance, caprice, sensuality, and pride"—and the writers of the day whom Pope perceived to be supporting the policies of Walpole and the king.

Against what he believed to be the debased English court, Pope argues for honesty, charity, selflessness, and the order, harmony, and balance of the classics, values set forth in *An Essay on Man*, published between 1732 and 1734. Pope intended the poem to be the cornerstone of a complete system of ethics that he never completed. His purpose was to show that despite the apparent imperfection, complexity, and rampant evil of the universe, it nevertheless functions in a rational way, according to natural laws. The world appears imperfect to us only because our perceptions are limited by our feeble moral and intellectual capacity. In reality, as he puts it at the end of the poem's first section (**Reading 24.8**):

READING 24.8

from Alexander Pope, *An Essay on Man* (1732)

All Nature is but Art, unknown to thee;
All Chance, Direction, which thou canst not see;
All Discord, Harmony not understood;
All partial Evil, universal good;
And, spite of Pride in erring Reason's spite,
One truth is clear: WHATEVER IS, IS RIGHT.

Pope does not mean to condone evil in this last line. Rather, he implies that God has chosen to grant humankind a certain imperfection, a freedom of choice that reflects its position in the universe. At the start of the second section of the poem, immediately after this passage, Pope outlines humankind's place:

Know then thyself, presume not God to scan;
The proper study of Mankind is Man.
Placed on this isthmus of a middle state,
A Being darkly wise, and rudely great;
With too much knowledge for the Sceptic side,
With too much weakness for the Stoic's pride.
He hangs between, in doubt to act, or rest;
In doubt to deem himself a God, or Beast;
In doubt his Mind or Body to prefer;
Born but to die, and reas'ning but to err;
Alike in ignorance, his reason such,
Whether he thinks too little, or too much:

Chaos of Thought and Passion, all confused;
Still by himself abused, or disabused;
Created half to rise, and half to fall;
Great lord of all things, yet a prey to all;
Sole judge of Truth, in endless Error hurled:
The glory, jest, and riddle of the world!

In the end, for Pope, humankind must strive for good, even if in its frailty it is doomed to fail. But the possibility of success also looms large. Pope suggests this through the very form of his poem—**heroic couplets**, rhyming pairs of iambic pentameter lines (the meter of Shakespeare, consisting of five short-long syllabic units)—that reflect the balance and harmony of classical art and thought.

Isaac Newton: The Laws of Physics

In 1735, eight years after the death of the great English astronomer and mathematician Isaac Newton (1642–1727), Pope wrote a heroic couplet epitaph, "Intended for Sir Isaac Newton":

Nature and Nature's laws lay hid in night;
God said, Let Newton be! and all was light.

With the 1687 publication of his *Mathematical Principles of Natural Philosophy*, more familiarly known as the *Principia* [prin-CHIP-ee-uh], from the first word of its Latin title, Newton had demonstrated to the satisfaction of almost everyone that the universe was an intelligible system, well-ordered in its operations and guiding principles. This fact appealed especially to the author of *An Essay on Man*, Pope. First and foremost, Newton computed the law of universal gravitation in a precise mathematical equation, demonstrating that each and every object exerts an attraction to a greater or lesser degree on all other objects. Thus, the sun exercises a hold on each of the planets, and the planets to a lesser degree influence each other and the sun. The Earth exercises a hold on its moon, and Jupiter on its several moons. All form a harmonious system functioning as efficiently and precisely as a clock or machine. Newton's conception of the universe as an orderly system would remain unchallenged until the late nineteenth and early twentieth centuries, when the new physics of Albert Einstein and others would once again transform our understanding.

Newton's *Principia* marked the culmination of the forces that had led, earlier in the century, to the creation of the Royal Society in England and the Académie des Sciences in France. Throughout the eighteenth century, the scientific findings of Newton and his predecessors—Kepler and Galileo, in particular—were widely popularized and applied to the problems of everyday life. Experiments demonstrating the laws of physics became a popular form of entertainment. In his *An Experiment on a Bird in the Air-Pump* (Fig. **24.6**), the English painter Joseph Wright (1734–1797) depicts a scientist conducting an experiment before the members of a middle-class household. He stands in his red robe behind an

Fig. 24.6 Joseph Wright, *An Experiment on a Bird in the Air-Pump.* 1768.
Oil on canvas, 6′ × 8′. The National Gallery, London. The resurrection of apparently dead birds was a popular entertainment of the day, a trick usually performed by self-styled magicians. In this painting, however, Wright takes the idea seriously, demonstrating to his audience the power of science.

air pump, normally used to study the properties of different gases but here employed to deprive a white cockatoo of oxygen by creating a vacuum in the glass bulb above the pump. The children are clearly upset by the bird's imminent death, while their father points to the bird, perhaps to demonstrate that we all need oxygen to live.

Wright had almost certainly seen such an experiment conducted by the Scottish astronomer James Ferguson, who made scientific instruments in London and toured the country, giving lectures. However, Ferguson rarely used live animals. As he explains in the 1760 edition of his lecture notes:

> If a fowl, a cat, rat, mouse or bird be put under the receiver, and the air be exhausted, the animal is at first oppressed as with a great weight, then grows convulsed, and at last expires in all the agonies of a most bitter and cruel death. But as this experiment is too shocking to every spectator who has the least degree of humanity, we substitute a machine called the "lung-glass" in place of the animal; which, by a bladder within it, shows how the lungs of animals are contracted into a small compass when the air is taken out of them.

Wright illustrated the crueler demonstration, and the outcome is uncertain. Perhaps, if the bird's lungs have not yet collapsed, the scientist can bring it back from the brink of death. Whatever the experiment's conclusion, life or death, Wright not only painted the more horrific version of the experiment but drew on the devices of Baroque painting—dramatic, nocturnal lighting and chiaroscuro—to heighten the emotional impact of the scene. The painting underscores the power of science to affect us all.

The Industrial Revolution

Among Wright's closest friends were members of a group known as the Lunar Society. The Society met in and around Birmingham each month on the night of the full moon (providing both light to travel home by and the name of the society). Its members included prominent manufacturers, inventors, and naturalists. Among them were Matthew Boulton (1728–1809), whose world-famous Soho Manufactory produced a variety of metal objects, from buttons and buckles to silverware; James Watt (1736–1819), inventor of the steam engine, who would team with Boulton to produce it; Erasmus Darwin (1731–1802), whose writings on botany and evolution anticipate by nearly a century his grandson Charles Darwin's famous conclusions; William Murdock (1754–1839), inventor of gas lighting; Benjamin Franklin (1706–1790), who was a corresponding member; and Josiah Wedgwood (1730–1795), Charles Darwin's other grandfather and the inventor of mass manufacturing at his Wedgwood ceramics factories. From 1765 until 1815, the group discussed chemistry, medicine, electricity, gases, and any and every topic that might prove fruitful for industry. It is fair to say that the Lunar Society's members inaugurated what we think of today as the **Industrial Revolution**. The term itself was invented in the nineteenth century to describe the radical changes in production and consumption that had transformed the world.

Wedgwood opened his first factory in Burslem, Staffordshire, on May 1, 1759, where he began to produce a highly durable cream-colored earthenware (Fig. **24.7**). Queen Charlotte, wife of King George III, was so fond of these pieces that Wedgwood was appointed royal supplier of dinnerware. Wedgwood's production process was unique. Instead of shaping individual pieces by hand on the potter's wheel—the only way ceramic ware had been produced—he cast liquid clay in molds and then fired it. This greatly increased the speed of production, as did mechanically printing decorative patterns on the finished china rather than painting them. The catalog described Queen's Ware, as it came to be known, as "a species of earthenware for the table, quite new in appearance . . . manufactured with ease and expedition, and consequently cheap." It was soon available to mass markets in both Europe and America, and Wedgwood's business flourished.

Wedgwood's Queen's Ware is an exemplary product of the Industrial Revolution. New machinery in new factories created a supply of consumer goods unprecedented in history, answering an ever-increasing demand for everyday items, from toys, furniture, kitchen utensils, and china, to silverware, watches, and candlesticks. Textiles were in particular demand, and in many ways, advances in textile manufacture could be called the driving force of the Industrial Revolution. At the beginning of the eighteenth century, textiles were made of wool from sheep raised in the English Midlands. A thriving

Fig. 24.7 Transfer-printed Queen's Ware. ca. 1770. The Wedgwood Museum, Barlaston, England. Elaborate decorations such as the one on this coffee pot were mechanically printed on ceramic tableware at Wedgwood's factory. Queen's Ware became so popular that pattern books, showing the available designs, were available across Europe by the turn of the century.

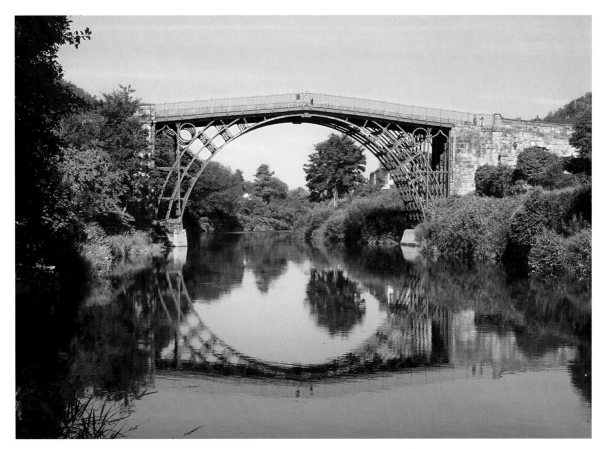

Fig. 24.8 Thomas Farnolls Pritchard, Iron Bridge, Coalbrookdale, England. 1779. Cast iron. Pritchard was keenly aware that the reflection of the bridge would form a visual circle, a form repeated in the ironwork at the corners of the bridge.

LEARN MORE Gain insight from an architectural simulation on cast iron at **www.myartslab.com**

cottage industry, in which weavers used handlooms and spinning wheels, textile manufacture changed dramatically in 1733 when John Kay in Lancashire invented the flying shuttle. Using this device, a weaver could propel the shuttle, which carries the yarn that forms the weft through the fibers of the warp, beyond the weaver's reach. Cloth could be made both wider and more rapidly. Invention after invention followed, culminating in 1769 when Richard Arkwright (1732–1792) patented the water frame, a waterwheel used to power looms. With their increased power, looms could operate at much higher speeds. Arkwright had duped the actual inventors out of their design, and in 1771 installed the water frame in a cotton mill in Derbyshire, on the river Derwent. These first textile mills, needing water power to drive their machinery, were built on fast-moving streams like the Derwent. But after the 1780s, with the application of Watts's steam power, mills soon sprang up in urban centers. In the last 20 years of the eighteenth century, English cotton output increased 800 percent, accounting for 40 percent of the nation's exports.

Another important development was the discovery of techniques for producing iron of unprecedented quality in a cost-effective manner. Early in the century, Abraham Darby (1678–1717) discovered that it was possible to fire cast iron with coke—a carbon-based fuel made from coal. Darby's grandson, Abraham Darby III (1750–1791), inherited the patent rights to the process; to demonstrate the structural strength of the cast iron he was able to manufacture, he proposed to build a single-arch cast-iron bridge across the River Severn, high enough to accommodate barge traffic on the river. The bridge at Coalbrookdale (Fig. **24.8**) was designed by a local architect, while its 70-foot ribs were cast at Darby's ironworks. The bridge's 100-foot span, arching 40 feet above the river, demonstrated once and for all the structural potential of iron. A century later, such bridges would carry railroad cars, as the need for transporting new mass-produced goods exploded.

Handel and the English Oratorio

The sense of prosperity and promise created by the Industrial Revolution in England found expression, particularly, in the music of German-born George Frederick Handel (1685–1759). Handel had studied opera in Italy for several years, and was serving as Master of the Chapel in the Hanover court when George I was named king of England. He followed the king to London in the autumn of 1712. He was appointed composer to the Chapel Royal in 1723, became a British citizen in 1727, and, when George II was crowned in 1728, composed four anthems for the ceremony. Over the course of his career, Handel composed several orchestral suites (musical series of thematically related movements) that remain preeminent examples of the genre. *Water Music* was written for a royal procession down the River Thames in 1717, and *Music for the Royal Fireworks* (1749) celebrated the end of a war with Austria. He wrote concertos for the oboe and the organ, performing the latter himself between acts of his operas and oratorios at London theaters. Opera was, in fact, his chief preoccupation—he composed 50 in his lifetime, 46 in Italian and 4 in German—but it was the oratorio, the same genre that so attracted Johann Sebastian Bach (see Chapter 26), that made his reputation.

An **oratorio** is a lengthy choral work, usually employing religious subject matter, performed by a narrator, soloists, choruses, and orchestra. It resembles opera in that it includes arias, recitatives, and choruses (see Chapter 25), but unlike opera, it does not have action, scenery, or costumes. To compensate for the lack of action, a narrator often connected threads of the plot. Handel composed his oratorios in English rather than Italian, the preferred opera language at that time. It is not clear just why he wrote oratorios, but a displeased bishop of London may have had something to do with it. The bishop banned Handel's biblical opera, *Esther,* in 1732, asserting that a stage production of the Bible was inappropriate. By using the oratorio form, Handel could treat biblical themes decorously.

Handel's greatest achievement is the oratorio *Messiah.* Written in 24 days, the work premiered in Dublin, Ireland, in 1742, as a benefit for Irish charities. It is probably the best known of all oratorios, although it is thoroughly atypical of the genre: The *Messiah* has no narrator, no characters, and no plot. Instead, Handel collected loosely related verses from the Old and New Testaments. It was an immediate success. Many Englishmen thought of their country as enjoying God's favor as biblical Israel had in the Old Testament, and Handel tapped into this growing sense of national pride. It recounts, in three parts, the biblical prophecies of the coming of a Savior, the suffering and death of Jesus, and the Resurrection and redemption of humankind. *Messiah* is sometimes remarkable in its inventiveness. When, for instance, Handel scored the text "All we, like sheep, have gone astray," he made the last words scatter in separate melodies across the different voices, mimicking the scattering referred to in the text. This technique, known as *word painting,* had been used during the Renaissance—the mood of the musical elements imitated the meaning of the text (see Chapter 15). Tradition has it that in 1743 when

((•● **HEAR MORE** at George II first heard the now famous "Hallelujah www.myartslab.com Chorus" (track **24.1**), which concludes the second part of the composition, he rose from his seat—whether in awe or simply because he was tired of sitting, no one knows—a gesture that has since become standard practice for all English-speaking audiences. For the rest of Handel's

life, he performed *Messiah* regularly, usually with a chorus of 16 voices and an orchestra of 40, both relatively large for the time.

LITERACY AND THE NEW PRINT CULTURE

Since the seventeenth century, literacy had risen sharply in England, and by 1750 at least 60 percent of adult men and between 40 and 50 percent of adult women could read. Not surprisingly, literacy was connected to class. Merchant-class men and women were more likely to read than those in the working class. And among the latter, city dwellers had higher literacy rates than those in rural areas. But even the literate poor were often priced out of the literary marketplace. Few had enough disposable income to purchase even a cheap edition of Milton, which cost about 2 shillings at mid-century. (At Cambridge University, a student could purchase a week's meals for 5 shillings.) And even though, by the 1740s, circulating libraries existed in towns and cities across Britain, the poor generally could not afford the annual subscription fees. Nevertheless, libraries broadened considerably the periodicals and books—particularly, that new, increasingly popular form of fiction, the novel—available to the middle class. Priced out of most books and libraries, the literate poor depended on an informal network of trading books and newspapers. Sharing reading materials was so common, in fact, that the publisher of one popular daily periodical estimated "twenty readers to every paper." The publisher was Joseph Addison (1672–1719), who with Richard Steele (1672–1729) published the periodical *The Spectator* every day except Sunday from March 1711 to December 1712.

The Tatler and *The Spectator*

Since their schooldays in London, Addison and Steele, men of very different temperaments, had been friends. Addison was reserved and careful, Steele impulsive and flamboyant. Addison was prudent with his money, Steele frequently broke. In fact, it was Steele's need for money that got him into the newspaper business in April 1709 when he launched *The Tatler* under the assumed name of Isaac Bickerstaff. Published three times a week until January 1711, *The Tatler,* its name purposefully evocative of gossip so that it might appeal to a female audience, mixed news and personal reflections and soon became popular in coffeehouses and at breakfast tables throughout London. Steele wrote the vast majority of *Tatlers,* although Addison and other friends occasionally contributed. *The Spectator* began its nearly 2-year run 2 months after the last *Tatler* appeared, with Addison assuming a much larger role.

Addison and Steele invented a new literary form, the **journalistic essay,** a form perfectly suited to an age dedicated to the observation of daily life, and drawing from life's experiences, in Locke's terms, an understanding of the world. Forced daily to describe—and reflect upon—English society, Addison and Steele's *Spectator* left almost no aspect of their culture unexamined. They instructed their readership in good manners, surveyed the opportunities that London offered the prudent shopper, and described the goings-on at the Royal Exchange, the city's financial center, where, in Addison's words, one could witness "an assembly of countrymen and foreigners consulting together . . . and making this metropolis a kind of emporium for the whole earth." They reviewed the city's various entertainments, both high and low, offered brief, usually fictionalized biographies of both typical and atypical English citizens, and very often expounded upon more literary and philosophical issues, such as John Locke's reflections upon the nature of wit.

One of Addison and Steele's greatest creations in *The Spectator* was the Tory eccentric Sir Roger de Coverley. Described by Steele in the second issue of the newspaper, Sir Roger was "a gentleman very singular in his behavior . . . [whose] humor creates him no enemies . . . [and who is] now in his fifty-sixth year, cheerful, gay, and hearty; keeps a good house both in town and in country; a great lover of mankind . . . [with] such a mirthful cast in his behavior that he is rather beloved than esteemed." Sir Roger is the ancestor of many similar characters that inhabit English fiction. In fact, the cast of characters that inhabit Addison and Steele's *Spectator* anticipate, to an astonishing degree, those found in English fiction as a whole.

The Rise of the English Novel

The novel as we know it was not invented in eighteenth-century England—Cervantes's *Don Quixote*, written a century earlier, is often considered the first example of the form in Western literature (see Chapter 20). But the century abounded in experiments in fiction writing that anticipate many of the forms that novelists have employed down to the present day. Works that today are called novels (from the French *nouvelle* and Italian *novella*, meaning "new") were rarely called "novels" in the eighteenth century itself. That term did not catch on until the very end of the century. Typically, they were referred to as "histories," "adventures," "expeditions," "tales," or—Hogarth's term—"progresses." They were read by people of every social class. What the novel claimed to be, and what appealed to its ever-growing audience, was a realistic portrayal of contemporary life. It concentrated almost always on the trials of a single individual, offering insight into the complexities of his or her personality. It also offered the promise, more often than not, of upward social mobility through participation in the expanding British economy and the prospect of prosperity that accompanied it. As London's population swelled with laborers, artisans, and especially young people seeking fame and fortune, and as the Industrial Revolution created the possibility of sudden financial success for the inventive and imaginative, the novel endorsed a set of ethics and a morality that were practical, not idealized. Above all, the novel was entertaining. Reading novels offered some respite from the drudgery of everyday life and, besides, was certainly a healthier addiction than drinking gin.

Daniel Defoe's Fictional Autobiographies One of the first great novels written in English is *Robinson Crusoe* by Daniel Defoe [dih-FOH] (1660–1731). Published in 1719, the full title of this sprawling work is *The Life and Strange Surprising Adventures of Robinson Crusoe of York, Mariner; Who lived Eight and Twenty Years, all alone in an un-inhabited Island on the coast of America, near the Mouth of the Great River of Oronoque; Having been cast on Shore by Shipwreck, wherein all the Men perished but himself. With An Account how he was at last as strangely deliver'd by Pirates. Written by Himself* (Fig. 24.9). The last three words are crucial, for they establish Defoe's claim that this novel is actually an autobiography.

Fig. 24.9 Frontispiece to *The Life and Strange Surprising Adventures of Robinson Crusoe of York, Mariner . . .*, by Daniel Defoe. London: W. Taylor, 1719. First edition. No other book in the history of Western literature has spawned more editions and translations, including Eskimo, Coptic, and Maltese.

Defoe's audience was used to reading accounts of real-life castaways that constituted a form of voyage literature. But far from falling into the primitive degradation and apathy of the average castaway, Robinson Crusoe rises above his situation, realizing, in his very ability to sustain himself, his God-given human potential. So many of Defoe's readers felt isolated and alone, like castaways, in the sea of London. For them, Crusoe represented hope and possibility.

This theme of the power of the average person to survive and flourish is what assured the novel's popularity and accounted for four editions by the end of the year. Defoe followed *Robinson Crusoe* with a series of other fictitious autobiographies of adventurers and rogues—*Captain Singleton* (1720), *Moll Flanders* (1722), *Colonel Jack* (1722), and *Roxanna* (1724). In all of them, his characters are in one way or another "shipwrecked" by society and as determined as Crusoe to overcome their situations through whatever means—not always the most virtuous—at their disposal.

The Epistolary Novel: Samuel Richardson's *Pamela* One of the most innovative experiments in the new novelistic form was devised by Samuel Richardson (1689–1761). He fell into novel writing as the result of his work on a "how-to" project commissioned by two London booksellers. Aware that "Country Readers" could use some help with their writing, the booksellers hired Richardson to write a book of "sample letters" that could be copied whenever necessary. Richardson was both a printer and the author of a history based on the letters of a seventeenth-century British ambassador to Constantinople and India. He had never written fiction before, but two letters in his new project suggested the idea of a novel—"A Father to a Daughter in Service, on hearing of her Master's attempting her Virtue," and "The Daughter's Answer." Richardson wrote *Pamela, or Virtue Rewarded*, in just over two months. It is the first example of what we have come to call the **epistolary novel**—that is, a novel made up of a series of "epistles," or letters. It was published in two volumes in 1740.

Pamela is a poor servant girl, of even poorer parents, in the service of a good lady who dies on page one. The good lady's son, Mr. B., promises to take care of her and all of his mother's servants: "For my Master said," Pamela reports in a letter home, "I will take care of you all, my Lasses; and for you, Pamela (and took me by the Hand; yes he took me by the Hand before them all) for my dear Mother's sake, I will be a Friend to you, and you shall take care of my Linen." From the outset, then, Richardson established Pamela's naiveté through the ambiguity implied in his "friendship" and, particularly, the word "linen," which includes, in the meaning of the day, his underwear. Indeed, Mr. B. abducts Pamela to his estate in Lincolnshire, where she is kept a prisoner and is continuously accosted to surrender her virginity. Thus virtue

confronts desire, a confrontation that over the course of the novel is compounded by Pamela's own growing desire for Mr. B. (**Reading 24.9**):

READING 24.9

from Samuel Richardson's *Pamela* (1740)

My dear master is all love and tenderness. He sees my weakness, and generously pities and comforts me! I begged to be excused [from] supper; but he brought me down himself from my closet, and placed me by him. . . . I could not eat, and yet I tried, for fear he should be angry. . . . Well, said he, if you won't eat with me, drink at least with me: I drank two glasses by his over-persuasions, and said, I am really ashamed of myself. Why, indeed, said he, my dear girl, I am not a very dreadful enemy, I hope! I cannot bear any thing that is the least concerning to you. Oh, sir! said I, all is owing to the sense I have of my own unworthiness!—To be sure, it cannot be any thing else.

He rung for the things to be taken away; and then reached a chair, and sat down by me, and put his kind arms about me, and said the most generous and affecting things that ever dropt from the honey-flowing mouth of love. All I have not time to repeat: some I will. And oh! indulge your foolish daughter, who troubles you with her weak nonsense; because what she has to say, is so affecting to her; and because, if she went to bed, instead of scribbling, she could not sleep.

Finally, after more than 1,000 pages of letters, Pamela's high moral character is rewarded by her marriage to her would-be seducer, Mr. B., and the novel's subtitle is justified. The success of Richardson's novel rested not only on the minute analysis of its heroine's emotions but also in the combination of its high moral tone and the sexual titillation of its story, which readers found irresistible.

The Comic Novels of Henry Fielding The morality of Richardson's *Pamela* was praised from church pulpits, recommended to parents skeptical of the novel as a form, and generally celebrated by the more Puritan elements of British society, who responded favorably to the heroine's virtue. Pamela herself asked a question that women readers found particularly important: "How came I to be his Property?" But the novel's smug morality (and the upward mobility exhibited by the novel's heroine) offended many, most notably Richardson's contemporary Henry Fielding (1707–1754), who responded, a year after the appearance of *Pamela*, with *Shamela*. Fielding's title tips the reader off that his work is a **parody**, a form of satire in which the style of an author or work is closely imitated for comic effect or ridicule. In Fielding's parody, his lower-class heroine's sexual appetite is every bit a match for her Squire

Booby's—and from Fielding's point of view, much more realistic (**Reading 24.10**):

READING 24.10

from Henry Fielding, *Shamela* (1741)

I was sent for to wait on my Master. I took care to be often caught looking at him, and then I always turn'd away my Eyes, and pretended to be ashamed. As soon as the Cloth was removed, he put a Bumper of Champagne into my Hand, and bid me drink—O la I can't name the Health. . . . I then drank towards his Honour's good Pleasure. Ay, Hussy, says he, you can give me Pleasure if you will; Sir, says I, I shall be always glad to do what is in my power, and so I pretended not to know what he meant. Then he took me into his Lap.—O Mamma, I could tell you something if I would—and he kissed me—and I said I won't be slobber'd about so, so I won't; and he bid me get out of the Room for a saucy Baggage, and said he had a good mind to spit in my Face.

Sure no Man ever took such a Method to gain a Woman's Heart.

Fielding presents Pamela's ardent defense of her chastity against her upper-class seducer as a sham; it is simply a calculated strategy, an ambitious hussy's plot to achieve financial security.

Fielding's greatest success came with the publication in 1749 of *The History of Tom Jones, a Foundling*. Fielding's model was Cervantes's *Don Quixote*, a loosely structured picaresque plot in which its outcast hero wanders through England and the streets of London. Fielding called it "a comic epic-poem in prose," which contrasts its generous, good-natured, and often naïve hero with cold-hearted and immoral British society. As Fielding himself explained, his purpose was to show "not men, but manners; not an individual, but a species." His characters are generally products, not of individual psychology, but of class. As opposed to Richardson, in Fielding's novels, plot takes precedence over character, the social fabric over individual consciousness. This is crucial to the comedy of his narrative. If readers were to identify too closely with Fielding's characters, they might not be able to laugh at them. It is, after all, the folly of human behavior that most intrigues Fielding himself.

The World of Provincial Gentry: Jane Austen's *Pride and Prejudice* Not all readers were charmed and entertained by Fielding's lavish portraits of vice. Many found his narratives deplorable. These readers found an antidote to Fielding in the writings of Jane Austen (1775–1817). Although Austen's best-known novels were published in the first quarter of the nineteenth century, she was more in tune with the sensibilities of the late eighteenth century, especially with Enlightenment values of sense, reason, and self-improvement.

None of Austen's heroines better embodies these values than the heroine of *Pride and Prejudice* (1813), Elizabeth Bennett, one of five daughters of a country gentlemen whose wife is intent on marrying the daughters off. The novel famously opens (**Reading 24.11a**):

READING 24.11a

from Jane Austen, *Pride and Prejudice*, Chapter 1 (1813)

It is a truth universally acknowledged, that a single man in possession of a good fortune, must be in want of a wife.

However little known the feelings or views of such a man may be on his first entering a neighbourhood, this truth is so well fixed in the minds of the surrounding families, that he is considered the rightful property of some one or other of their daughters.

The level of Austen's irony in these opening sentences cannot be overstated, for while she describes the fate that awaits any single, well-heeled male entering a new neighborhood, these lines are a less direct, but devastating reflection upon the possibilities for women in English society. Their prospect in life is to be married. And if they are not themselves well-heeled and attractive—that is, marriageable—their prospects are less than that.

Austen first told this story in *First Impressions* (1796–97), in the form of an exchange of letters between Elizabeth and Fitzwilliam Darcy, an English gentleman. When we first meet him in *Pride and Prejudice*, Austen describes him as follows: "He was looked at with great admiration for about half the evening, till his manners gave a disgust which turned the tide of his popularity; for he was discovered to be proud, to be above his company, and above being pleased; and not all his large estate in Derbyshire could then save him from having a most forbidding, disagreeable countenance. . . ." The novel's plot revolves around the two words of its title, *pride* and *prejudice*. Where Elizabeth at first can only see Darcy's pride, she comes to realize that her view is tainted by her prejudice. Darcy's disdain for country people and manners is a prejudice that Elizabeth's evident pride helps him to overcome. Together, they come to understand not only their own shortcomings but their society's.

This reconciliation begins when Elizabeth tours Darcy's estate at Pemberley in the company of her aunt and uncle, the Gardiners. The scene Austen describes is quite literally the quintessential English garden, a new form of landscape design (see Chapter 25), but it is also an extended metaphor for its owner (**Reading 24.11b**):

READING 24.11b

from Jane Austen, *Pride and Prejudice*, Chapter 43 (1813)

Elizabeth, as they drove along, watched for the first appearance of Pemberley Woods with some perturbation; and when at length they turned in at the lodge, her spirits were in a high flutter.

The park was very large, and contained great variety of ground. They entered it in one of its lowest points, and drove for some time through a beautiful wood, stretching over a wide extent.

Elizabeth's mind was too full for conversation, but she saw and admired every remarkable spot and point of view. They gradually ascended for half a mile, and then found themselves at the top of a considerable eminence, where the wood ceased, and the eye was instantly caught by Pemberley House, situated on the opposite side of a valley, into which the road, with some abruptness, wound. It was a large, handsome, stone building, standing well on rising ground, and backed by a ridge of high woody hills;—and in front, a stream of some natural importance was swelled into greater, but without any artificial appearance. Its banks were neither formal nor falsely adorned. Elizabeth was delighted. She had never seen a place for which nature had done more, or where natural beauty had been so little counteracted by an awkward taste. They were all of them warm in their admiration; and at that moment she felt that to be mistress of Pemberley might be something!

They descended the hill, crossed the bridge, and drove to the door; and, while examining the nearer aspect of the house, all her apprehensions of meeting its owner returned.

By subtly identifying Darcy with his estate, Austen affirms the commonly held belief that a man's estate and grounds were a reflection of the man himself. The description is certainly analogous to Elizabeth's aunt's assessment of Darcy toward the end of the chapter: "There is something a little stately in him to be sure . . . but it is confined to his air, and is not unbecoming. I can now say with the housekeeper, that though some people may call him proud, *I* have seen nothing of it." Austen's language here prepares us in fact for Darcy's own "large" and "handsome . . . eminence."

The subtle manipulation of descriptive language apparent in this passage is indicative of Austen's great talent. Her novels track, with uncanny precision, distinctions of class, rank, and social standing that mark her times. And she looks upon the English class system with a sense of both irony and compassion, and with a sensitivity to the pressures challenging it in her own day. But perhaps above all, she understands the weight that individual words can bear, how mere description—the use of the word "large," for instance—can influence and manipulate feeling.

Samuel Johnson: Stylist and Moralist The English novel, and the state of the society reflected in it, was of special concern to Samuel Johnson (1709–1784) (Fig. **24.10**). Johnson was editor of two coffeehouse magazines, *The Rambler* (1750–52) and *The Idler* (1758–60), author of the groundbreaking *Dictionary of the English Language*, published in 1755, the moral fable *Rasselas, Prince of Abyssinia* (1759), and the critical and biographical text *The Lives of the Most Eminent English Poets* (ten volumes, 1779–81), as well as editor of a completely annotated edition of Shakespeare's plays (1765). He was also subject of what is arguably the first great biography of the modern era, *The Life of Samuel Johnson* by James Boswell (1740–1795), published in 1791, and unique in its inclusion of conversations among Johnson and his contemporaries that Boswell recorded in his journals at the time.

Born to a poor bookseller in Lichfield, Stratfordshire, he had been forced to leave Oxford for lack of funds and arrived in London penniless in 1737. For three decades, he supported himself by his writing, until awarded a government pension in 1762. Three years later, he received an honorary doctorate from Trinity College, Dublin, and another from

Fig. 24.10 Sir Joshua Reynolds, *Samuel Johnson*. 1756–57. Oil on canvas, 50¼" × 40". National Portrait Gallery, London. Given by an anonymous donor, 1911. NPG 1597. Reynolds was a close associate of Johnson's. The most prolific portrait painter of the era, he produced over 1,500 portraits of the English nobility and was the first president of the English Royal Academy.

Oxford ten years after that—which explains his commonly used title, Dr. Johnson.

Johnson's concerns about the novel are best articulated in an essay on fiction that appeared in *The Rambler*, an essay that demonstrates Johnson's considerable talents as a literary critic (**Reading 24.12**):

READING 24.12

from Samuel Johnson, *The Rambler* No. 4, Saturday, March 31, 1750

The works of fiction with which the present generation seems more particularly delighted are such as exhibit life in its true state, diversified only by accidents that daily happen in the world, and influenced by passions and qualities which are really to be found in conversing with mankind.

This kind of writing may be termed, not improperly, the comedy of romance. . . . Its province is to bring about natural events by easy means, and to keep up curiosity without the help of wonder: it is therefore precluded from the machine and expedients of the heroic romance, and can neither employ giants to snatch away a lady from the nuptial rites, nor knights to bring her back from captivity; it can neither bewilder its personages in deserts, nor lodge them in imaginary castles. . . .

The task of our present writers . . . requires, together with that learning which is to be gained from books, that experience which can never be attained by solitary diligence, but must arise from general converse and accurate observation of the living world. . . . These books are written chiefly to the young, the ignorant, and the idle, to whom they serve as lectures of conduct, and introductions into life. They are the entertainment of minds unfurnished with ideas, and therefore easily susceptible of impressions; not fixed by principles, and therefore easily following the current of fancy; not informed by experience, and therefore open to every false suggestion and partial account. . . .

I cannot discover why there should not be exhibited the most perfect idea of virtue; of virtue not angelical, nor above probability (for what we cannot credit, we shall never imitate), but the highest and purest humanity can reach, which, exercised in such trials as the various revolutions of things shall bring upon it, many, by conquering some calamities and enduring others, teach us what we may hope, and what we can perform. Vice (for vice is necessary to be shown), should always disgust. . . . Wherever it appears, it should raise hatred by the malignity of its practices, and contempt by the meanness of its stratagems. It is therefore to be steadily inculcated that virtue is the highest proof of understanding, and the only solid basis of greatness; and that vice is the natural consequence of narrow thoughts; that it begins in mistake, and ends in ignominy.

This last paragraph sums up what Johnson disliked in Fielding's novels, whose characters, he complained, were "of very low life."

Perhaps Johnson's most important contribution to English letters is his *Dictionary of the English Language*, published in 1755. A quintessential Enlightenment effort, it represents an attempt to standardize the English language, especially its wildly inconsistent spelling. Johnson's *Dictionary* consists of definitions for some 40,000 words, illustrated with about 114,000 quotations gathered from English literature. This dictionary has served as the basis for all English dictionaries since. Occasionally, Johnson's considerable wit surfaces in the text. His definition of "patron," for example, reads: "Patron: One who countenances, supports, or protects. Commonly a wretch who supports with insolence, and is repaid with flattery." "Angling" is treated even more amusingly: "A stick and a string, with a worm on one end and a fool on the other."

Johnson is notorious for the **aphorisms**—concise and clever observations—which are scattered throughout his essays. Here are a few examples:

> Promise, large promise, is the soul of an advertisement. (from *The Idler*)
> Language is the dress of thought. (from *The Lives of the English Poets*)
> Marriage has many pains, but celibacy has no pleasures. (from *Rasselas*)

With his piercing wit, Johnson expressed his deep skepticism regarding the perfectibility of human nature. Humanity needed to be saved from itself, and doing that required a strict social and moral order. Most of the great thinkers of the Enlightenment shared his view.

EXPLORATION IN THE ENLIGHTENMENT

When, on August 26, 1768, Captain James Cook (1728–1779) set sail on the *Endeavor* from Plymouth, England, for the uncharted waters of the South Pacific, both his sponsors, the Royal Society and the British Admiralty, and Cook himself believed the enterprise to be consistent with the aims of the Enlightenment. While Cook would claim new territories for the British crown, his primary mission was to extend human knowledge: to map the South Seas, record his observations, and otherwise classify a vast area of the world then unknown to European civilization. Although he was careful to document the lives of the people he encountered, his primary mission was to visit Tahiti in order to chart the transit of Venus, that moment in time when the planet Venus crosses directly between the sun and the Earth. This phenomenon occurs twice, eight years apart, in a pattern that repeats every 243 years; in the eighteenth century, that was in 1761 and 1769. (Astronomers around the world watched in fascination when it occurred in June 2004, and will study it again in June 2012.) The measurement of the transit of Venus was understood to be useful in calculating the size of the solar system.

The Royal Society knew of Tahiti because one of its members, the Frenchman Louis-Antoine de Bougainville [deh boo-gahn-VEEL] (1729–1811), had landed on its shores just months before, in April 1768. Bougainville's descriptions of Tahitian life, published in 1771 as *Voyage around the World*, captured the Enlightenment's imagination. Denis Diderot [dee-DROH] (see Chapter 25) quickly penned a *Supplement* to Bougainville's text, arguing that the natives of Tahiti were truly Rousseau's "noble savages." They were free from the tyrannical clutches of social hierarchy and private property—in Diderot's words, "no king, no magistrate, no priest, no laws, no 'mine' and 'thine.'" All things were held for the common good, including the island's women, who enjoyed, in Diderot's eyes, the pleasures of free love. By following their natural instincts, these people had not fallen into a state of degradation and depravity, as Christian thinkers would have predicted, but rather formed themselves into a nation of gentleness, general well-being, and harmonious tranquility.

Cook, upon his return, took exception to Diderot's picture of Tahitian life. The careful observer would have noticed, he pointed out, a highly stratified social hierarchy of chiefs and local nobility, that virtually every tree on the island was the private property of one of the natives, and that the sexual lives of the Tahitians were in general as morally strict as those of the English (although women in port were as likely in Tahiti as in Plymouth to sell their sexual favors to visiting sailors). But if Cook's position seems at odds with that of the Enlightenment, it was, in its way, also consistent. Enlightenment philosophers had argued that human nature and behavior were the same all over the world, and in his view the Tahitians proved that point. In addition, Enlightenment economists had argued that private property and social stratification were the basic features of a complex and flourishing society. Cook found both in Tahitian society, and this accounted for the general well-being of their society, he believed.

Cook's Encounters in the South Pacific

The islands of the South Pacific that Cook and others explored in the late eighteenth century consist of three primary groups and the continent of Australia (Map **24.3**). Melanesia is a long crescent of relatively large islands stretching east from Indonesia and including New Guinea, the largest. Micronesia consists of many smaller islands to the north, most formed from coral reefs growing over submerged volcanoes. Polynesia, meaning "many islands," is a large, triangular area in the central Pacific Ocean defined by New Zealand in the southwest, Easter Island in the southeast, and the Hawaiian Islands in the north.

New Zealand The people that Bougainville and Cook encountered in Tahiti had arrived in the islands around 200 CE from the vicinity of Tonga and Samoa to the west. Easter Island, the easternmost island in Polynesia, was first inhabited in about 300 CE, probably by Marquesas [mar-KAY-zuz] islanders. The peoples of Hawaii, the northernmost islands of Polynesia, arrived there about 100 years later, probably from the Marquesas also. A second wave of Tahitians populated the Hawaiian Islands between about 900 and 1200 CE. Finally, New Zealand, the western- and southernmost islands of Polynesia, was inhabited by the Maori [MAUR-ee] in about 900 CE. The Maori also may have come from Tahiti. In the course of his three voyages to the South Seas, beginning in 1768 and ending 11 years later, Cook visited all of these islands.

One of the most distinctive art forms that Cook and his crew encountered in Polynesia was tattooing, a word derived from *tatau* [ta-ta-OO], the Tahitian term for the practice. One of Cook's crew, Sydney Parkinson, a young draftsman on board to record botanical species, captured the tattooed face of a Maori warrior during the first voyage

Map 24.3 The islands of the South Pacific.

Fig. 24.11 Sydney Parkinson, *Portrait of a Maori*. 1769. Wash drawing, 15 1/2″ × 11 5/8″, later engraved and published as Plate XVI in Parkinson's *Journal*, 1773. The British Library, London. Add. 23920 f.55. Parkinson's drawings provide some of the earliest archeological records of Polynesian life.

(Fig. **24.11**). The Maori had imported the practice from the Polynesian islands to the north.

Tattooing is an aspect of complex sacred and ritual traditions found throughout the Pacific Islands. The islanders believed that individuals, many places, and a great many objects are imbued with **mana** [MAH-nah], a spiritual substance that is the manifestation of the gods on earth. Chiefs, considered descendants of the gods, were supposedly born with considerable quantities of *mana*, nobility with less, and commoners with almost none. Anything or anyone possessing *mana* was protected by *tapu*, a strict state of restriction indicating that an object or person cannot be touched or a place entered. A chief's food might be protected by *tapu*. A person might increase his or her *mana* by skillful or courageous acts, or by wearing certain items of dress, including tattoos. Thus, the warrior depicted by Parkinson possesses considerable *mana*. This derives from the elegance of his tattoo, from his headdress and comb, his long earring, probably made of greenstone (a form of jade), and his necklace. From it hangs a *hei-tiki*, a stylized carving of a human figure, a legendary hero or ancestor figure whose *mana* the warrior carries with him.

Among the Maori, the most sacred part of the body was the head, and so it was the most appropriate place for a tattoo. All high-ranking Maori were tattooed, including women (although less elaborately). The first tattoos were inscribed during the rituals marking the passage into adulthood.

Tattoos generally consisted of broad, curving, parallel lines from nose to chin, spiral forms on the cheeks, and broad, parallel lines between the bridge of the nose and the ears following the curve of the brow. Their design mirrors the human form and is meant to celebrate it. The design was almost always bilaterally symmetrical, but each one was so distinctive that, after coming in contact with Western practice, many Maori began signing documents with them. The tattoo artist possessed great skill and thus considerable *mana*, and was also *tapu*, in no small part because the process was extremely painful. Using a bone chisel, the tattoo artist cut deeply into the skin. Pigment made from burnt Kauri gum or burnt vegetable caterpillars was then pushed into the cuts by tapping, the sound of which, "ta-ta," gives the process its name.

Easter Island Cook arrived on Easter Island in 1794, where he discovered monumental heads with torsos known as **moai** [moe-eye] (Fig. **24.12**), the remains of an abandoned civilization. Like the *hei-tiki* figures in Maori culture, the *moai* may well represent ancestors' figures. Around 1000 CE, the Easter Islanders began erecting *moai* on stone platforms, called *ahu*, around the steep hillsides of the island facing the sea or turned away from the sea overlooking villages. They were probably designed to protect the island's people, and they possessed great *mana*, but not until inlaid coral and stone eyes were set in place (today, these eyes exist only in a few restorations). The *ahu* average about 190 feet in

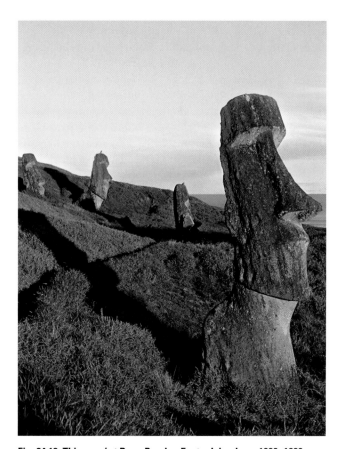

Fig. 24.12 Thin *moai* at Rano Raraku, Easter Island. ca. 1000–1600 CE. Rano Raraku is a volcanic crater with a crater lake in its center. Of the 394 *moai* at Rano Raraku, approximately 150 lie unfinished in the quarry.

length and 15 feet in height, and the *moai* range from 6 to about 70 feet in height. *Moai* of between 12 and 20 feet high are common. Carved out of compressed volcanic ash at Rano Raraku, a quarry where 394 *moai* are still visible today, the majority weigh between 18 and 20 tons, the largest as much as 80 or 90 tons.

The *moai* were carved out of large rock outcroppings that were still attached to the hillside as if lying on their backs, face up. Working from the front of the face and around the side to the back, the artists gradually carved out the entire form until only a narrow spine of stone connected the sculpture to the rock outcrop. Once cut free from the hill, the sculptures were transported around the island on sledges or rollers, and levered into place on the *ahu*.

The quarries in Rano Raraku appear to have been abandoned abruptly, with many incomplete statues still in place. Deforestation was at least partly responsible, since it became increasingly difficult to create the rollers and levers necessary to erect the statues. Some scholars believe that the religious or social system responsible for erecting the *moai* was overthrown by a cult that identified itself with bird imagery and that exercised rituals to ensure the fertility of the land. The deforestation associated with creation of the *moai* might have been perceived by this new cult as a threat. Whatever the reason, by the nineteenth century, within a few years of Captain Cook's visit to the island in 1774, the standing *moai* had all been toppled to lie on their faces and sides on the hillsides.

Melanesia The largest island in Melanesia, and the second largest island in the world after Australia, is New Guinea, which Cook first visited in 1778. Here he encountered an extremely hostile and fearless native population. The eastern half of the island is Papua, known for its elaborate displays of ritual objects in ceremonial houses where young farmers are initiated into agricultural cults dedicated especially to growing yams as large as 7 feet long. The Asmat people of Irian Jaya, the western half of the island, were headhunters, and it is likely that it was the Asmat whom Cook first encountered in New Guinea. The Asmat created monumental sculptures in connection with the rituals surrounding the act of headhunting. They believed that in displaying the head of an enemy warrior, they could possess that warrior's strength.

Elaborate *bis* poles (Fig. **24.13**), carved in connection with the Asmat funeral rituals, reflect each step in the headhunting process. First a tree is cut (symbolic of the decapitation of the enemy), its bark removed (skinning the victim), and its sap allowed to run like blood. Then artists carve various images into the poles. In addition to images of deceased ancestors, there are birds eating fruit, which symbolize the headhunter eating the brains of his victim. Hollows at the base of the poles were meant to hold the heads of enemies. Long, elaborately carved elements project from the groins of the topmost figures, whose bent knees are meant to suggest the praying mantis. (The female praying mantis eats the head of its mate—symbolic to the Asmat of headhunting.) The projections are called *tsjemen*

Fig. 24.13 *Bis* **poles. Mid-twentieth century. New Guinea, Irian Jaya, Faretsj River, Omadesep village, Asmat people.** Wood, paint, fiber, height 18′. The Michael C. Rockefeller Memorial Collection, Bequest of Nelson A. Rockefeller, 1979 (1979.206.1611). © The Metropolitan Museum of Art/Art Resource, New York. After the *bis* ceremonies were concluded, the poles were moved to groves of sago palms, the primary food source of the Asmat. There, the poles were allowed to decay and nourish the palms.

(literally "enlarged penis") and symbolize the virility and strength of the warrior and his ancestors. The ceremonies involving these poles were meant to restore balance to the Asmat village after the death of one or more of their members created an imbalance.

Australia Captain Cook first sailed along the eastern coast of Australia in 1770, claiming it for the British crown. He and his crew were the first Westerners to encounter the Australian Aboriginal culture. The British established their first permanent settlement there in 1788, in New South Wales, and the colony's first governor, Arthur Philip, reported seeing Aboriginal rock art (Fig. **24.14**), which represents the longest continuously practiced artistic tradition anywhere in the world. In Arnhem Land, in northern Australia, a great many rock formations and caves are decorated with rock art dating from the earliest periods (40,000–6,000 BCE) to works created within living memory. The earliest works are sticklike figures that represent ancestral spirits, or *mimis*. Some of these are visible behind the kangaroo in Figure 24.14. According to Arnhem legend, *mimis* made the earliest rock paintings and taught the art to present-day Aborigines, who, in painting such figures, release the power of the *mimis*. Aboriginal artists do not believe that they create or invent their subjects; rather, the *mimis* give them their designs, which they then transmit for others to see. The act of painting creates a direct link between the present and the past.

The kangaroo in this prehistoric rock painting is rendered in what has come to be known as the *x-ray style*, where the skeletal structure, heart, and stomach of an animal are painted over its silhouetted form as if the viewer can see the life force of the animal through its skin. Painting of this kind was still prevalent when European settlers arrived in the nineteenth century, and even today bark painters from western Arnhem Land continue to work in the x-ray style. Although two centuries of contact with European culture significantly altered Aboriginal culture, many of their long-standing traditions and rituals survive.

Fig. 24.15 *Kukailimoku*, Hawaii. ca. 1790–1810. Wood, height 77″. The British Museum, London. Gift of W. Howard. Ethno 1839, 4-26.8. © The Trustees of the British Museum. The figure is probably a vehicle for the god to enter and make himself present in the temple.

Hawaii On his last voyage in the Pacific, in January 1778, Cook visited the Hawaiian Islands for the first time. It was the middle of the rainy season and the Hawaiians at first treated him with reverence and awe, believing him to be an incarnation of the rain god Lono, father of waters and god of thunder and lightning, which they probably associated with his guns and cannon. From Hawaii, Cook traveled along the western coast of North America, all the way to the Bering Sea, and then returned to Hawaii. At first he was treated with the same respect and honor he had encountered previously, but his overreaction to the Hawaiians' theft of one of his small boats and the demands of his company upon the diminishing food supplies of the natives turned the islanders against him. On February 14, 1779, he was clubbed and stabbed to death in a skirmish on the beach at Kealakekua Bay on the Kona coast of the Island of Hawaii, the so-called Big Island.

Legend has it that among the warriors who attacked Cook was a young Kamehameha I (ca. 1758–1819), the Hawaiian king who first consolidated the islands under one rule. In Hawaiian society, each man worshiped a specific deity related to his work. The king worshiped the war god Kukailimoku ("Ku, Snatcher of Islands"), and Kamehameha was dedicated to him. A well-preserved wood statue of Kukailimoku captures the god's ferocity (Fig. 24.15). The god's head is disproportionately large because it is the site of his *mana*. His nostrils flare menacingly, and his mouth, surrounded by what may be tattoos or scarification, is ferociously open, perhaps in a war cry, suggesting his *tapu*. Small, stylized pigs, possibly symbols of wealth, decorate his headdress. The statue is meant to convey the ferocity of Kamehameha I himself, the ferocity that was required in bringing all of the islands of Hawaii under his rule, "snatching" them, as Kukailimoku's name suggests.

Cook in the North Pacific

Cook's expedition to the northern reaches of the Pacific Basin, which occurred between his two visits to Hawaii, were inspired by the hope that he might find a "Northwest Passage" connecting the Atlantic and the Pacific Oceans. As always on his voyages, Cook was accompanied by illustrators and scientists. On the island of Unalaska (called by Cook "Oonalashka") in the Aleutian Chain, approximately 800 miles southwest of present-day Anchorage, artist John Webber captured the likeness of a native Aleut, his lower lip pierced with bead-covered bones (Fig. **24.16**). Here, he also made contact with Russian fur traders, who were making a considerable fortune selling furs in China.

Taking particular notice of the possibilities of the fur trade was Connecticut-born John Ledyard (1751–1789), who would publish his *Journal of Captain Cook's Last Voyage in the Pacific* in Hartford, Connecticut in 1783. Recalling the wealth of furs the Cook expedition had encountered in Nootka Sound off Vancouver Island, he wrote (**Reading 24.13**):

READING 24.13

from John Ledyard, *A Journal of Captain Cook's Last Voyage* (1783)

The light in which this country will appear most to advantage respects the variety of its animals, and the richness of their furr. They have foxes, sables, hares, marmosets, ermines, weazles, bears, wolves, deer, moose, dogs, otters, beavers, and a species of weazel called the glutton; the skin of this animal was sold at Kamchatka, a Russian factory on the Asiatic coast for sixty rubles, which is near 12 guineas, and had it been sold in China it would have been worth 30 guineas. . . . Neither did we purchase a quarter part of the beaver and other furr skins we might have done, and most certainly should have done had we known of meeting the opportunity of disposing of them to such an astonishing profit.

By 1784, Ledyard was in Paris, where he was quickly befriended by Thomas Jefferson, at that time American ambassador to France. Jefferson suggested that he attempt to be the first person to cross the American continent by foot, leaving France to cross Russia, continue across the Bering Strait to Alaska, and eventually reach Virginia. Ledyard in

fact set out from St. Petersburg in June 1787 and made it as far as the Siberian capital of Irkutsk before Catherine the Great of Russia had him arrested as a spy and deported. He died of fever in Cairo, at the age of 37, while attempting to organize an expedition across Africa from the Red Sea to the Atlantic Ocean. But Ledyard's dream of crossing the continent became, almost obsessively, Jefferson's own, and it would inspire, finally, Jefferson's persuading the United States Congress to finance the expedition of Meriweather Lewis and William Clark across the continent and back in 1804 to 1806 after Jefferson's purchase of the Louisiana Territory in 1803. And Ledyard's sense of the potential of a fur trade with China would soon be realized by John Jacob Astor (1763–1848), who founded the American Fur Company in 1808 and, in 1811, opened a trading post at the mouth of the Columbia River, Fort Astor, at the site of present-day Astoria, Oregon. Astor would become America's first millionaire.

A MAN of OONALASHKA.

Fig. 24.16 John Webber (ca. 1752–1798), artist, William Sharp (1749–1825), engraver, *A Man of Oonalashka*. ca. April 1778. Engraving, from the atlas volume of James Cook's *A Voyage to the Pacific Ocean. Undertaken, by the Command of His Majesty, for Making Discoveries in the Northern Hemisphere. To Determine the Position and Extent of the West Side of North America; Its Distance from Asia; and the Practicability of a Northern Passage to Europe. . . .* (London: Printed by W. and A. Strahan, for G. Nicol, Bookseller to His Majesty, in the Strand, and T. Cadell in the Strand, 1784). Wisconsin Historical Society, Madison, WI. Cook wrote of the Native Americans he met in Alaska: "In this wretched extremity of earth, situated beyond everything that we conceived to be most barbarous and inhospitable, and, as it were, out of the very reach of civilization, barricaded with ice, and covered with summer snow . . . we met with feelings of humanity, joined to a greatness of mind, and elevation of sentiment, which would have done honour to any nation or climate."

The Growing Crisis of the Slave Trade

The most troubling instance of cross-cultural encounter during the Enlightenment revolved around slavery. Since the Portuguese introduced the slave trade in the sixteenth century (see Chapter 18), hundreds of thousands of Africans had been forcibly transported to the Americas in conditions so appalling that many, even most, died in transit. Those who survived the voyage then experienced the brutality of slavery itself.

American slave owners sought to suppress their slaves' identification with their African heritage. Rarely were slaves from the same locales in Africa allowed to work on the same plantation. Even more radically, slave families were generally broken up—men, women, and children sold separately—in order to undermine their ability to carry on African traditions and practices.

Many leading Enlightenment thinkers in America defended the institution of slavery. Thomas Jefferson wrote in his *Notes on the State of Virginia*, "Comparing [blacks] by their faculties of memory, reason, and imagination, it appears to me that in memory they are equal to whites; in reason much inferior. . . . I advance it . . . as a suspicion only, that the blacks, whether originally a distinct race, or made distinct by time and circumstances, are inferior to the white in the endowments both of body and mind. . . . This unfortunate difference of color, and perhaps of faculty, is a powerful obstacle to the emancipation of these people." Nevertheless, Jefferson did attempt, unsuccessfully, to incorporate a paragraph condemning slavery in his Declaration of Independence, one of the great documents of Enlightenment thought—although he owned 187 slaves of his own.

In Britain, Jefferson was considered a hypocrite, and that hypocrisy would come to play a major role in the Revolutionary War. The British, as we will see in the next chapter, could not understand how the Declaration's call for "life, liberty, and the pursuit of happiness" was consistent with the defense of slavery as an institution. And, although the British were deeply involved in the slave trade, an increasingly large number of English Enlightenment thinkers had come to condemn it. John Zoffany's double portrait of Dido Elizabeth Belle Lindsay and Lady Elizabeth Murray (Fig. **24.17**) underscores the difference between British and American attitudes. Nothing like this portrait exists in eighteenth- or nineteenth-century American painting. Dido was the daughter of an English Captain and an enslaved African woman. Dido was raised by the Captain's uncle, Lord Chief Justice William Murray, First Earl of Mansfield, together with another of Mansfield's nieces, Elizabeth Murray. The girls were best friends and apparently equal in all things. When the colonial governor of Massachusetts, Thomas Hutchinson, saw them arm in arm at Mansfield's estate, Kenwood House on Hampstead Heath, he was shocked and outraged. ∎

Fig. 24.17 John Zoffany, *Dido Elizabeth Belle Lindsay and Lady Elizabeth Murray.* 1779–81. Oil on canvas, 35^1/$_2$″ × 28^1/$_4$″. From the Collection of the Earl of Mansfield, Scone Place, Scotland.

Who were Hobbes and Locke?

On September 2, 1666, the better part of London was destroyed by fire. Among the achievements of this rebuilding campaign is Christopher Wren's Saint Paul's Cathedral (and indeed the 51 other churches that he rebuilt). At the same time, English intellectuals began to advocate rational thinking as the means to achieve a comprehensive system of ethics, aesthetics, and knowledge. Political strife inevitably raised the question of who should govern and how. In *Leviathan*, Thomas Hobbes argued that ordinary people were incapable of governing themselves and should willingly submit to the sovereignty of a supreme ruler. John Locke argued in opposition that humans are "by nature free, equal, and independent." Can you provide two or three examples of how their positions play out in the politics of the era? How do they play out in John Milton's *Paradise Lost*?

What is satire, and how did it shape the Enlightenment in England?

Deeply conscious of the fact that English society fell far short of its ideals, many writers and artists turned to satire. William Hogarth's prints, produced for a popular audience, satirized the lifestyles of all levels of English society. Jonathan Swift aimed the barbs of his wit at the same aristocracy and lambasted English political leaders for their policies toward Ireland in his *Modest Proposal*. Alexander Pope's *Dunciad* took on not only the English nobility, but the literary establishment that supported it. In a more serious vein, his *Essay on Man* attempts to define a complete ethical system in classical terms of balance and harmony.

After the Glorious Revolution, in fact, English politics settled into a state of comparative harmony. How did the scientific discoveries of Isaac Newton contribute to Enlightenment thinking? How did the Lunar Society, the group that arguably launched what we think of today as the Industrial Revolution, reflect this same thinking?

In music, composer George Frederick Handel's oratorio *Messiah* captured Britain's sense of identification with biblical Israel. What distinguishes the *Messiah* from most other oratorios?

What gave rise to the novel?

The growing literacy of the English population, matched by an explosion in publishing, gave rise to new genres of writing. Newspapers such as Joseph Addison and Richard Steele's *The Tatler* and *The Spectator* introduced the journalistic essay, which described and reflected upon all aspects of English society. Fiction writers experimented with many types of novel, from Daniel Defoe's fictive autobiographies to Samuel Richardson's epistolary works, Fielding's "comic epic-poems in prose," and Jane Austen's novels extolling the virtues of good sense, reason, and self-improvement. In what ways does Samuel Johnson's assessment of the novel in his *Rambler* essay of 1850 apply to the works of Defoe, Richardson, and Fielding?

What was the purpose of Captain Cook's voyages to the Pacific Ocean?

The peoples of the South Seas were seen by many Enlightenment thinkers to be unfettered by social hierarchy and private property. But Captain Cook saw things otherwise. How does Cook's thinking equally reflect Enlightenment values?

In New Zealand, Cook encountered the Maori, whose tattoo practices were connected to the *mana*, or invisible spiritual force, a manifestation of the gods on earth, with which, the culture believed, certain individuals, places, and objects were endowed. How did the concept of *mana* influence the cultural production of the South Seas islanders? On Easter Island, Cook discovered the remnants of a culture that had erected *moai*, monumental heads with torsos, since about 1000 CE. In the western half of New Guinea, he encountered the Asmat, headhunters. Why did these peoples display the heads of enemy warriors on *bis* poles? In Australia, Cook was the first to encounter Australian Aborigines, whose rock art represents the longest continuously practiced artistic tradition in the world.

Before Cook was killed in Hawaii, he traveled to the northern Pacific, up the Canadian and Alaska coasts, as far as the Bering Sea. For what was he searching? What possibilities for trade did his expedition discover?

PRACTICE MORE Get flashcards for images and terms and review chapter material with quizzes at **www.myartslab.com**

GLOSSARY

aphorism A concise and clever observation.

caricature A portrait that exaggerates a person's peculiarities or defects.

epistolary novel A novel made up of a series of epistles, or letters.

heroic couplet A rhyming pair of iambic pentameter lines.

Industrial Revolution The term used to describe a change in practices of production and consumption that occurred in the nineteenth century.

journalistic essay A reportorial set of observations of current events or other issues of interest to the author.

liberalism A political theory that argues that people are by nature free, equal, and independent and that they consent to government for protection but not by surrendering sovereignty to a ruler.

mana Among the Maori, an invisible spiritual substance that is the manifestation of the gods on earth.

moai Monumental heads with torsos found on Easter Island that probably represent ancestral figures.

oratorio A lengthy choral work, usually religious, performed by a narrator, soloists, choruses, and orchestra.

parody A form of satire in which a serious author or work is ridiculed or mocked in a humorous way through exaggerated imitation.

social contract An agreement by which a person gives up sovereignty over him- or herself and bestows it on a ruler.

READINGS

READING 24.2

from Thomas Hobbes, *Leviathan* (1651)

Leviathan argues that the "natural condition of mankind" is a state of nature where life is "solitary, poor, nasty, brutish, and short." Born into this condition, human beings are motivated only by fear of violent death and accept the governance of a higher authority only to be protected from it and to guarantee their peace and security. When Leviathan *was published, just 2 years after England's antiroyalist faction had beheaded Charles I, Hobbes's treatise shocked his contemporaries and caused others, such as John Locke, to construct very different theories in open opposition to it.*

PART I CHAPTER 13: OF THE NATURAL CONDITION OF MANKIND AS CONCERNING THEIR FELICITY AND MISERY

Nature has made men so equal in the faculties of the body and mind as that, though there be found one man sometimes manifestly stronger in body or of quicker mind than another, yet, when all is reckoned together, the difference between man and man is not so considerable as that one man can thereupon claim to himself any benefit to which another may not pretend as well as he. For as to the strength of body, the weakest has strength to kill the strongest, either by secret machination or by confederacy with others that are in the same danger with himself. . . .

From this equality of ability arises equality of hope in the at- 10 taining of our ends. And therefore if any two men desire the same thing, which nevertheless they cannot both enjoy, they become enemies; and in the way to their end, which is principally their own conservation, and sometimes their delectation only, endeavor to destroy or subdue one another. And from hence it comes to pass that where an invader has no more to fear than another man's single power, if one plant, sow, build, or possess a convenient seat, others may probably be expected to come prepared with forces united to dispossess and deprive him, not only of the fruit of his labor, but also of his life or liberty. 20 And the invader again is in the like danger of another. . . .

So that in the nature of man we find three principal causes of quarrel: first, competition; secondly, diffidence; thirdly, glory.

The first makes men invade for gain, the second for safety, and the third for reputation. The first use violence to make themselves masters of other men's persons, wives, children, and cattle; the second, to defend them; the third, for trifles, as a word, a smile, a different opinion, and any other sign of undervalue, either direct in their persons or by reflection in their kindred, their friends, their nation, their profession, or their name. 30

Hereby it is manifest that, during the time men live without a common power to keep them all in awe, they are in that condition which is called war, and such a war as is of every man against every man. For WAR consists not in battle only, or the act of fighting, but in a tract of time wherein the will to contend by battle is sufficiently known; and therefore the notion of *time* is to be considered in the nature of WAR as it is in the nature of weather. For as the nature of foul weather lies not in a shower or two of rain but in an inclination thereto of many days together, so the nature of war consists not in actual fighting but in 40 the known disposition thereto, during all the time there is no assurance to the contrary. All other time is PEACE.

Whatsoever, therefore, is consequent to a time of war where every man is enemy to every man, the same is consequent to the time wherein men live without other security than what their own strength and their own invention shall furnish them withal. In such condition there is no place for industry, because the fruit thereof is uncertain; and consequently no culture of the earth; no navigation nor use of the commodities that may be imported by sea; no commodious building; no instruments 50 of moving and removing such things as require much force; no knowledge of the face of the earth; no account of time; no arts; no letters; no society; and, which is worst of all, continual fear and danger of violent death; and the life of man solitary, poor, nasty, brutish, and short. . . .

PART II CHAPTER 17: OF THE CAUSES, GENERATION, AND DEFINITION OF A COMMONWEALTH

The final cause, end, or design of men, who naturally love liberty and dominion over others, in the introduction of that restraint upon themselves in which we see them live in 60 commonwealths, is the foresight of their own preservation, and of a more contented life thereby—that is to say, of getting themselves out from that miserable condition of war which is necessarily consequent . . . to the natural passions of man when there is no visible power to keep them in awe and tie them by fear of punishment to the performance of their covenants and observations of [the] laws of nature. . . .

For the laws of nature—as *justice, equity, modesty, mercy,* and, in sum, *doing to others as we would be done to*—of themselves, without the terror of some power to cause them to be observed, are contrary to our natural passions, that carry us to partiality, pride, revenge, and the like. And covenants without the sword are but words, and of no strength to secure a man at all. Therefore, notwithstanding the laws of nature . . . if there be no power erected, or not great enough for our security, every man will—and may lawfully—rely on his own strength and art for caution against all other men. . . .

The only way to erect such a common power as may be able to defend them from the invasion of foreigners and the injuries of one another, and thereby to secure them in such sort as that by their own industry and by the fruits of the earth they may nourish themselves and live contentedly, is to confer all their power and strength upon one man, or upon one assembly of men that may reduce all their wills, by plurality of voices, unto one will; which is as much as to say, to appoint one man or assembly of men to bear their person, and everyone to own and acknowledge to himself to be author of whatsoever he that so bears their person shall act or cause to be acted in those things which concern the common peace and safety, and therein to submit their wills every one to his will, and their judgments to his judgment. This is more than consent or concord; it is a real unity of them all in one and the same person, made by covenant of every man with every man, in which manner as if every man should say to every man, *I authorize and give up my right of governing myself to this man, or to this assembly of men, on this condition, that you give up your right to him and authorize all his actions in like manner.* This done, the multitude so united in one person is called a COMMONWEALTH, in Latin CIVITAS. This is the generation of that great LEVIATHAN (or rather, to speak more reverently, of that *mortal god*) to which we owe, under the *immortal God*, our peace and defense. For by this authority, given him by every particular man in the commonwealth, he has the use of so much power and strength conferred on him that, by terror thereof, he is enabled to form the wills of them all to peace at home and mutual aid against their enemies abroad. And in him consists the essence of the commonwealth, which, to define

it, is *one person, of whose acts a great multitude, by mutual covenants one with another, have made themselves every one the author, to the end he may use the strength and means of them all as he shall think expedient for their peace and common defense.* And he that carries this person is called SOVEREIGN and said to have *sovereign power,* and everyone besides, his SUBJECT.

The attaining to this sovereign power is by two ways. One, by natural force. . . . The other is when men agree among themselves to submit to some man or assembly of men voluntarily, on confidence to be protected by him against all others. This latter may be called a political commonwealth, or commonwealth by *institution,* and the former a commonwealth by *acquisition.* . . .

PART II CHAPTER 30: OF THE OFFICE OF THE SOVEREIGN REPRESENTATIVE

The office of the sovereign, be it a monarch or an assembly, consists in the end for which he was trusted with the sovereign power, namely, the procuration of the *safety of the people,* to which he is obliged by the law of nature, and to render an account thereof to God, the author of that law, and to none but him. But by safety here is not meant a bare preservation but also all other contentments of life which every man by lawful industry, without danger or hurt to the commonwealth, shall acquire to himself.

And this is intended should be done, not by care applied to individuals further than their protection from injuries when they shall complain, but by a general providence contained in public instruction, both of doctrine and example, and in the making and executing of good laws, to which individual persons may apply their own cases.

And because, if the essential rights of sovereignty . . . be taken away, the commonwealth is thereby dissolved and every man returns into the condition and calamity of a war with every other man, which is the greatest evil that can happen in this life, it is the office of the sovereign to maintain those rights entire, and consequently against his duty, first, to transfer to another or to lay from himself any of them. For he that deserts the means deserts the ends. . . .

READING CRITICALLY

How does the figure of the Leviathan, the mythological marine monster described in the Bible, contribute to the power of Locke's thesis?

READING 24.4

from John Locke, *The Second Treatise of Government* (1690)

As opposed to Thomas Hobbes, John Locke argued that human beings can attain their maximum development only in a society free of the unnatural constraints placed upon them by absolute rulers. In his Two Treatises on Civil Government, *published the same year as his* Essay Concerning Human Understanding, *as something of a practical companion to the more philosophical* Essay, *and as a kind of applied theory, Locke argued that government must rest upon the consent of the governed. The work would deeply influence many thinkers in the eighteenth century, not least of all Thomas Jefferson, who drew heavily upon the work in drafting the American Declaration of Independence (see Chapter 26).*

From Chapter II: Of the State of Nature

4.   To UNDERSTAND political power right and derive it from its original, we must consider what state all men are naturally in, and that is a state of perfect freedom to order their actions and dispose of their possessions and persons as they think fit, within the bounds of the law of nature, without asking leave or depending upon the will of any other man.

A state also of equality, wherein all the power and jurisdiction is reciprocal, no one having more than another; there being nothing more evident than that creatures of the same species and rank, promiscuously born to all the same advantages of nature and the use of the same faculties, should also be equal one amongst another without subordination or subjection; unless the lord and master of them all should, by any manifest declaration of his will, set one above another, and confer on him by an evident and clear appointment an undoubted right to dominion and sovereignty.

From Chapter V: Of Property

26.   God, who has given the world to men in common, has also given them reason to make use of it to the best advantage of life and convenience. The earth and all that therein is given to men for the support and comfort of their being. And though all the fruits it naturally produces and beasts it feeds belong to mankind in common, as they are produced by the spontaneous hand of nature; and nobody has originally a private dominion exclusive of the rest of mankind in any of them, as they are thus in their natural state; yet, being given for the use of men, there must of necessity be a means to appropriate them some way or other before they can be of any use or at all beneficial to any particular man. The fruit or venison which nourishes the wild Indian, who knows no enclosure and is still a tenant in common, must be his, and so his, i.e., a part of him, that another can no longer have any right to it before it can do him any good for the support of his life.

27.   Though the earth and all inferior creatures be common to all men, yet every man has a property in his own person; this nobody has any right to but himself. The labor of his body and the work of his hands, we may say, are properly his. Whatsoever then he removes out of the state that nature has provided and left it in, he has mixed his labor with, and joined to it something that is his own, and thereby makes it his property.

From Chapter VIII: Of the Beginning of Political Societies

95.   MEN BEING, as has been said, *by nature all free, equal, and independent, no one can be put out of this estate and subjected to the political power of another without his own consent.* The only way whereby any one divests himself of his natural liberty and puts on the bonds of civil society is by agreeing with other men to join and unite into a community for their comfortable, safe, and peaceable living one amongst another, in a secure enjoyment of their properties and a greater security against any that are not of it. This any number of men may do, because it injures not the freedom of the rest; they are left as they were in the liberty of the state of nature. When any number of men have so consented to make one community or government, they are thereby presently incorporated and make one body politic wherein the majority have a right to act and conclude the rest.

96.   For when any number of men have, by the consent of every individual, made a community, they have thereby made that community one body, with a power to act as one body, which is only by the will and determination of the majority . . . And therefore we see that in assemblies impowered to act by positive laws, where no number is set by that positive law which impowers them, the act of the majority passes for the act of the whole and, of course, determines, as having by the law of nature and reason the power of the whole.

97.   And thus every man, by consenting with others to make one body politic under one government, puts himself under an obligation to every one of that society to submit to the determination of the majority and to be concluded by it; or else this original compact, whereby he with others incorporates into one society, would signify nothing, and be no compact, if he be left free and under no other ties than he was in before in the state of nature.

From Chapter IX: Of The Ends of Political Society and Government

123.   IF MAN in the state of nature be so free, as has been said, if he be absolute lord of his own person and possessions, equal to the greatest, and subject to nobody, why will he part with his freedom, why will he give up his empire and subject himself to the dominion and control of any other power? To which it is obvious to answer that though in the state of nature he has such a right, yet the enjoyment of it is very uncertain and constantly exposed to the invasion of others; for all being kings as much as he, every man his equal, and the greater part no strict observers of equity and justice, the enjoyment of the property he has in this state is very unsafe, very unsecure. This makes him willing to quit a condition which, however free, is full of fears and continual dangers; and it is not without reason that he seeks out and is willing to join in society with others who are already united, or have a mind to unite, for the mutual preservation of their lives, liberties, and estates, which I call by the general name "property."

124.   The great and chief end, therefore, of men's uniting into commonwealths and putting themselves under government is the preservation of their property.

From Chapter XVIII: Of Tyranny

199.   As USURPATION is the exercise of power which another has a right to, so tyranny is the exercise of power beyond right, which nobody can have a right to. And this is making use of the power any one has in his hands, not for the good of those who are under it, but for his own private separate advantage—when the governor, however entitled, makes not the law, but his will, the rule, and his commands and actions are not directed to the preservation of the properties of his people, but the satisfaction of his own ambition, revenge, covetousness, or any other irregular passion . . .

202.   Wherever law ends, tyranny begins if the law be transgressed to another's harm. And whosoever in authority exceeds the power given him by the law, and makes use of the force he has under his command . . . ceases in that to be a magistrate and, acting without authority, may be opposed as any other man who by force invades the right of another.

203.   May the commands, then, of a prince be opposed? May he be resisted as often as any one shall find himself aggrieved, and but imagine he has not right done him? This will

unhinge and overturn all polities, and, instead of government and order, leave nothing but anarchy and confusion.

204. To this I answer that force is to be opposed to nothing but to unjust and unlawful force; whoever makes any opposition in any other case draws on himself a just condemnation both from God and man; and so no such danger or confusion will follow, as is often suggested.

READING CRITICALLY

Without looking forward to Jefferson's Declaration of Independence, what aspects of Locke's argument here do you recognize as fundamental to your own definition of American liberty?

from John Milton, *Paradise Lost,* Book 6 (1667)

The following section opens Book 6 of Milton's epic poem. The passage opens with the angel Abdiel, referred to in the book's first line as the "dreadless" or fearless angel because in the previous book he had refused to join Satan's rebellion and had prophesized his downfall, flying about heaven as the other angels gather to confront Satan under the leadership of Gabriel and Michael. The passage takes us up to the moment that the two armies meet. The ensuing battle, in which Abdiel and Michael engage in hand-to-hand combat with Satan, is purposefully reminiscent of Homer's Iliad *(see Chapter 4).*

All night the dreadless angel unpursued
Through heav'n's wide champaign held his way, till Morn,
Waked by the circling Hours, with rosy hand
Unbarred the gates of light. There is a cave
Within the mount of God, fast by his throne,
Where light and darkness in perpetual round
Lodge and dislodge by turns, which makes through heav'n
Grateful vicissitude, like day and night;
Light issues forth, and at the other door
Obsequious darkness enters, till her hour   10
To veil the heav'n, though darkness there might well
Seem twilight here; and now went forth the Morn
Such as in highest heav'n, arrayed in gold
Empyreal; from before her vanished night,
Shot through with orient beams: when all the plain
Covered with thick embattled squadrons bright,
Chariots and flaming arms, and fiery steeds
Reflecting blaze on blaze, first met his view:
War he perceived, war in procinct, and found
Already known what he for news had thought   20
To have reported: gladly then he mixed
Among those friendly Powers who him received
With joy and acclamations loud, that one
That of so many myriads fall'n, yet one
Returned not lost: on to the sacred hill
They led him high applauded, and present
Before the seat supreme; from whence a voice
From midst a golden cloud thus mild was heard.

"Servant of God, well done, well hast thou fought
The better fight, who single hast maintained   30
Against revolted multitudes the cause
Of truth, in word mightier than they in arms;
And for the testimony of truth hast borne
Universal reproach, far worse to bear
Than violence: for this was all thy care
To stand approved in sight of God, though worlds
Judged thee perverse: the easier conquest now
Remains thee, aided by this host of friends,
Back on thy foes more glorious to return
Than scorned thou didst depart, and to subdue   40
By force, who reason for their law refuse,
Right reason for their law, and for their King
Messiah, who by right of merit reigns.
Go Michael of celestial armies prince,
And thou in military prowess next
Gabriel, lead forth to battle these my sons
Invincible, lead forth my armed saints
By thousands and by millions ranged for fight;
Equal in number to that godless crew
Rebellious, them with fire and hostile arms   50
Fearless assault, and to the brow of heav'n
Pursuing drive them out from God and bliss,
Into their place of punishment, the gulf
Of Tartarus, which ready opens wide
His fiery chaos to receive their fall."

---

[3]**Hours:** four beautiful daughters of love, goddesses of the seasons and guards of the gates of heaven.

[8]**vicissitude:** (L. *vicissim* in turn, *vicis* change, alternation) alternating succession of contrasting things.

[10]**Obsequious:** (L *ob* toward + *sequi* to follow) compliant.

[14]**Empyreal:** (CK *pyr* fire) heavenly.

[16]**embattled:** in battle array.

[19]**in procinct:** prepared.

[29]**Servant of God:** the literal meaning of the Hebrew word *abdiel*. Cf Matt. 25.21: "His lord said unto him. Well done, thou good and faithful servant." 2 Tim. 4.7: "I have fought a good fight, I have finished my course, I have kept the faith."

[33]–[34]Cf. Ps. 69.7: "Because for thy sake I have borne reproach."

[36]Cf. 2 Tim. 2.15: "Study to show thyself approved unto God."

So spake the Sovran Voice, and clouds began
To darken all the hill, and smoke to roll
In dusky wreaths reluctant flames, the sign
Of wrath awaked: nor with less dread the loud
Ethereal trumpet from on high gan blow: 60
At which command the powers militant,
That stood for heav'n, in mighty quadrate joined
Of union irresistible, moved on
In silence their bright legions, to the sound
Of instrumental harmony that breathed
Heroic ardor to advent'rous deeds
Under their godlike leaders, in the cause
Of God and his Messiah. On they move
Indissolubly firm; nor obvious hill,
Nor strait'ning vale, nor wood, nor stream divides   70
Their perfect ranks; for high above the ground
Their march was, and the passive air upbore
Their nimble tread; as when the total kind
Of birds in orderly array on wing
Came summoned over Eden to receive
Their names of thee; so over many a tract
Of heav'n they marched, and many a province wide
Tenfold the length of this terrene: at last
Far in th' horizon to the north appeared
From skirt to skirt a fiery region, stretched   80
In battailous aspect, and nearer view
Bristled with upright beams innumerable
Of rigid spears, and helmets thronged, and shields
Various, with boastful argument portrayed,
The banded powers of Satan hasting on
With furious expedition; for they weened
That selfsame day by fight, or by surprise
To win the mount of God, and on his throne
To set the envier of his state, the proud

Aspirer, but their thoughts proved fond and vain   90
In the mid-way: though strange to us it seemed
At first, that angel should with angel war,
And in fierce hosting meet, who wont to meet
So oft in festivals of joy and love
Unanimous, as sons of one great Sire
Hymning th' Eternal Father: but the shout
Of battle now began, and rushing sound
Of onset ended soon each milder thought.
High in the midst exalted as a god   100
Th' Apostate in his sun-bright chariot sat
Idol of majesty divine, enclosed
With flaming Cherubim, and golden shields;
Then lighted from his gorgeous throne, for now
'Twixt host and host but narrow space was left,
A dreadful interval, and front to front
Presented stood in terrible array
Of hideous length: before the cloudy van,
On the rough edge of battle ere it joined,
Satan with vast and haughty strides advanced,   110
Came tow'ring, armed in adamant and gold;
Abdiel that sight endured not, where he stood
Among the mightiest, bent on highest deeds,
And thus his own undaunted heart explores. . . .

READING CRITICALLY

How do the opening 20 lines, with their description of
darkness and light, reminiscent of the opening lines of
the Book of Genesis in the Bible, contribute to both the
emotional and moral thrust of the poem as the angels
prepare for battle?

[58]**reluctant:** L *re* back + *luctari* to struggle.
[62]**quadrate:** a square military formation in close order.
[69]**obvious:** standing in the way of.
[78]**terrene:** (an adjective used as a noun) terrain.
[81]**battailous:** warlike.
[83–84]On the shields were drawn heraldies emblems with their mottoes.
[86]**furious:** (L *furia tage*) rushing expedition: speed

[90]**fond:** (ME. *fon* fool) foolish vain; L *vanus* empty.
[93]**hosting:** hostile encounter.
[100]**Apostate:** Gk *apo* out from, against + *stēnai* to stand.

25

The Rococo and the Enlightenment on the Continent

Privilege and Reason

THINKING AHEAD

What is the Rococo?

Who are the philosophes*?*

What are the characteristics of Classical music?

How did China and the West influence one another?

Until his death in 1715, Louis XIV had opened his private apartments in Versailles three days a week to his courtiers, where they entertained themselves by playing games. After his death, such entertainments continued, only not at Versailles but in the *hôtels*—or Paris townhouses—of the French nobility, where the same crowd who had visited the king's apartments now entertained on their own. The new king, Louis XV, was only 5 years old, and so there was no point in staying so far out of town in the rural palace where the Sun King had reigned supreme.

The *hôtels* all had a salon, a room designed especially for social gatherings. Very soon the term *salon* came to refer to the social gathering itself. A number of these rooms still survive, including the Salon de la Princesse, which was designed by Germain Boffrand to commemorate the 1737 marriage of the 80-year-old prince de Soubise to the 19-year-old Marie-Sophie de Courcillon (Fig. 25.1). Decorated around the top of the room with eight large paintings by Charles-Joseph Natoire [nah-TWAHR] (1700–1777) depicting the story of Cupid and

Psyche from Ovid's *Metamorphoses* (Fig. 25.2), the room embodies the eroticism that dominated the art of the French aristocracy in the eighteenth century.

These **salons** became the center of French culture in the eighteenth century, and by 1850 they were emulated across Europe (see Map **25.1**). The new princesse de Soubise was perhaps too young to be herself an active ***salonnière*** [sah-lohn-YAIR], one of the hostesses who presided over the weekly gatherings that soon dominated Parisian social life. Among the most popular salons were those of Jeanne-Julie-Eleonore de Lespinasse [deh less-peen-AHSS] (1732–1776). In his memoirs, Friedrich Melchior, Baron von Grimm (1723–1807), a frequent guest, recalls the ambiance:

> Her circle met daily from five o'clock until nine in the evening. There we were sure to find choice men of all orders in the State, the Church, the Court—military men, foreigners, and the most distinguished men of letters. Every one agrees that though the name of M. d'Alembert [an intellectual who lived with Julie de Lespinasse, and

◀ **Fig. 25.1 Germain Boffrand, *Salon de la Princesse de Soubise (Salon ovale)*, Hôtel de Soubise, Paris. ca. 1740.** Oval shape, 33′ × 26′. Photo: Bulloz. Reunion des Musees Nationaux/Art Resource, New York. In his 1745 *Livre d'architecture* (*Book on Architecture*), Boffrand compared architecture to theater, arguing that it had both a tragic and pastoral mode. In the lightness of its ornament and the eroticism of its paintings, the Salon de la Princesse is an example of the pastoral mode.

HEAR MORE Listen to an audio file of your chapter at **www.myartslab.com**

Fig. 25.2 Charles-Joseph Natoire, *Cupid and Psyche*, Salon de la Princesse, Hôtel de Soubise, Paris. 1738.
Oil on canvas, 5′7³/₄″ × 8′6³/₈″. Peter Willi/The Bridgeman Art Library. Here Psyche has been brought to the palace
of Love where Cupid, under cover of darkness, has consummated their union. Psyche had promised never to seek to
know his identity. Here she breaks her oath by lighting her lamp to reveal Cupid's face.

who is discussed later in the chapter] may have drawn
them thither, it was she alone who kept them there. Devoted wholly to the care of preserving that society, of
which she was the soul and the charm, she subordinated
to this purpose all her tastes and all her personal intima-
cies. She seldom went to the theatre or into the country,
and when she did make an exception to this rule it was an
event of which all Paris was notified in advance. . . . Politics, religion, philosophy, anecdotes, news, nothing was
excluded from the conversation, and, thanks to her care,
the most trivial little narrative gained, as naturally as possible, the place and notice it deserved. News of all kinds
was gathered there in its first freshness.

The baron numbered among his friends many of the
most influential Parisian thinkers of the day, the so-
called *philosophes* [FILL-loh-sof], "philosophers," who
frequented the salons and dominated the intellectual
life of the French Enlightenment, a movement that
emphasized reason and rationality and sought to develop a systematic understanding of divine and natural
law. Not philosophers in the strict sense of the word
because they did not concentrate on matters metaphysical,

but turned their attention to secular and social concerns, the *philosophes* were almost uniformly alienated
from the Church, despising its hierarchy and ritual.
They were also if not totally committed to the abolition of the monarchy, which they saw as intolerant,
unjust, and decadent, then at least deeply committed
to its reform.

The tension in the eighteenth century between the
philosophes, who aspired to establish a new social order
of superior moral and ethical quality, and the French
courtiers, whose taste favored a decorative and erotic
excess that the *philosophes* abhorred, is the subject of
this chapter. The two often collided at the salons. Consider, for instance, the salons of Madame de Pompadour
[mah-DAHM deh pohm-pah-DOOR] (1721–1764),
born into a middle-class family involved in Parisian financial circles. She was a great defender of the
philosophes, but she was also mistress to Louis XV after
he assumed full power in 1743. She blocked efforts to
have the works of the *philosophes* suppressed by censors
and was successful in keeping works attacking the
philosophes out of circulation. And yet, she was also the
king's trusted advisor and the subject of many erotic

Map 25.1 Europe in 1750.

paintings done at court depicting her as Venus. The competing styles of Louis XIV's Baroque court survived into the eighteenth century, but now were no longer united or comfortable together. Whereas at Versailles essentially classical architecture was embellished with Baroque ornamentation, the nobility now appreciated only an ever-more-elaborate decoration and ornament, while the *philosophes* shunned ornamentation altogether, preferring the order, regularity, and balance of the classical tradition. These tensions were apparent across Europe, particularly in Prussia, where an absolutist monarchy consciously emulated the courts of Louis XIV and XV. In painting, the absolutist courts preferred a sensual style of painting indebted to Rubens, while the *philosophes* admired paintings that were representational and conveyed emotional truth. In France, Germany, and England, a taste soon developed for gardens dominated by winding and circuitous paths, inspired by the curvilinear ornamentation of the Baroque, as opposed to the geometric regularity of the French gardens at Versailles. By the middle of the eighteenth century, these Baroque gardens were made even more exotic with the addition of elements inspired by Western interaction with China. In fact, a taste for all things Chinese became one of the chief characteristics of the age. And in music, the intricate and charming melodies of the court composers gave way to Classical form and structure, while *opera seria* gave way to *opera buffa* and to a hybrid form called *dramma giocoso*.

THE ROCOCO

The decorative style fostered by the French court in the eighteenth century and quickly emulated by royal courts across Europe was known as the **Rococo** [ruh-KOH-koh]. The term is thought to derive from the French word *rocaille* [roh-KYE], a type of decorative rockwork made from round pebbles and curvilinear shells. But it also derives from *barocco*, the Italian word for "baroque." In fact, the Rococo style is probably best understood as the culmination of developments in art and architecture that began in the late work of Michelangelo and progressed through Mannerism and the Baroque into the eighteenth century. Along the way, the style became increasingly elaborate, with architectural interiors employing a vocabulary of S- and C-curves, shell, wing, scroll, and plant tendril forms, and rounded, convex, often asymmetrical surfaces surrounded by elaborate frames, called **cartouches** [car-TOOSH]. In its decorative excess, the Rococo is related to the ornate *retablos* of Mexican churches (see Chapter 23). But, even if the style sometimes found its ways into religious architecture, it is more a secular decorative tradition, conceived for the residences and palaces of Europe's nobility and for the art and objects that filled them.

Rococo Painting in France: The *Fête Galante* and the Art of Love

Most eighteenth-century French painters still relied on the court for commissions. But once the courtiers had moved back from Versailles to the comfort of their Paris townhouses and country estates, they were less interested in commissioning paintings that glorified them than those that entertained. The new Rococo style as applied to French painting suited this domestic goal perfectly. Its subject matter is often frivolous, emphasizing the pursuit of pleasure, particularly love. Its compositions were generally asymmetrical, and its color range was light, emphasizing gold, silver, and pastels.

Jean-Antoine Watteau The Rococo found its most eloquent expression in France in the paintings of Jean-Antoine Watteau [wah-TOH] (1684–1721). This is ironic because he did not have aristocratic patrons and was little known during his lifetime beyond a small group of bourgeois buyers, such as bankers and dealers. One of his most famous paintings in fact served as a signboard for the shop of a Paris art dealer (see *Closer Look*, pages 804–805).

In a very short time, however, Watteau's work became a favorite of the Prussian ruler Frederick the Great (discussed in the next section of this chapter), and a great many of his paintings entered Frederick's collection.

Watteau was best known for his paintings of *fêtes galantes* [fet gah-LAHNT]—gallant, and by extension amorous, celebrations or parties enjoyed by an elite group in a pastoral or garden setting. The erotic overtones of these *fêtes galantes* are immediately apparent in *The Embarkation from Cythera* in the pedestal statue of Venus at the right side of the painting and the flock of winged cupids darting about among the revelers (Fig. **25.3** and see detail, page 674). The scene is the island of Cythera, the mythical birthplace of the goddess. Below her statue, which the pilgrims have decked with garlands of roses, a woman leans across her companion's lap as three cupids try to push the two closer together. Behind them, a gentleman leans toward his lady to say words that will be overheard by another woman behind them, who gathers roses with her lover as she leans over them both. Further back in the scene, a gentleman helps his lady to her feet while another couple turns

Fig. 25.3 Jean-Antoine Watteau, ***The Embarkation from Cythera.*** **ca. 1718–19.** Oil on canvas, 50³/₄″ × 76³/₈″. Staatliche Museen, Schloss Charlottenburg, Berlin. This painting and the one in *Closer Look* (pages 804–805) were purchased by Frederick the Great of Prussia for his own collection. Frederick often staged *fêtes galantes* at Sanssouci.

LEARN MORE Gain insight from a primary source document on Antoine Watteau at **www.myartslab.com**

to leave, the woman looking back in regret that they must depart the garden island.

François Boucher Madame de Pompadour's favorite painter was François Boucher [BOO-shay] (1703–1770), who began his career, in the mid-1720s, copying the paintings of Watteau owned by Jean de Jullienne, the principal collector of Watteau's works in France. Jullienne, a manufacturer of dyes and fine fabrics, had conceived the idea of engraving Watteau's work so that a wider public could enjoy it, and Boucher was easily the best of Jullienne's copyists. Boucher himself felt he needed more training, so he set off for Rome with his profits from Jullienne. Once there, he found the work of Raphael "trite" and that of Michelangelo "hunchbacked," perhaps a reference to the well-developed musculature of his figures. By the time Madame de Pompadour established herself as Louis XV's mistress, Boucher had returned from Rome and was firmly established as Watteau's heir, the new master of *fêtes galantes*.

In the 33 years since the death of Louis XIV, the court had enjoyed relatively free reign, and the younger king, Louis XV, essentially adapted himself to its carefree ways. He felt free to take a mistress. Madame de Pompadour was by no means the first, though by 1750 the king had apparently left her bed because, so the story went, her health was frail. But she remained his closest and probably most trusted advisor, and she happily arranged for other women to take her place in the king's bed. Given this context, it is hardly surprising that many of Boucher's portraits of Madame de Pompadour are like the portrait of 1756, which portrays her as an intellectual supporter of the French Enlightenment, reading a book, her writing table nearby with her quill inserted in the inkwell (Fig. **25.4**). What *is* somewhat surprising are his many paintings of nude goddesses in which the nude bears a striking resemblance to the king's mistress. (Boucher was notoriously famous for such nudes.) *The Toilet of Venus*, for instance, was commissioned by Madame de Pompadour for the bathing suites of the château of Bellevue, one of six residences just outside Paris that Louis built for her (Fig. **25.5**). She had played the title role in a production called *La Toilette de Vénus* staged at Versailles a year earlier, and evidently this is a scene—or more likely an idealized version—of one from that production. The importance of the work is that it openly acknowledges both Madame de Pompadour's sexual role in the court and the erotic underpinnings of the Rococo as a whole.

Jean-Honoré Fragonard Boucher's student Jean-Honoré Fragonard [frah-goh-NAHR] (1732–1806) carried his

Fig. 25.4 François Boucher, *Madame de Pompadour*. 1756. Oil on canvas, 79$^1/_8$″ × 61$^7/_8$″. The Bridgeman Art Library. Bayerische Hypo und Vereinsbank, Alte Pinakothek, Bayerische Staatsgemäldesammlungen, Munich. Boucher's playful and fragile imagery, evident here in the elaborate frills decorating Madame's dress and in the decorative details on the column behind her, was miniatured within gold cartouches on the surfaces of the vases and urns of the Royal Porcelain Manufactory at Sevres, Madame de Pompadour's pet project.

Fig. 25.5 François Boucher, *The Toilet of Venus*. 1751. Oil on canvas, 42$^5/_8$″ × 33$^1/_8$″. Signed and dated (lower right): f-Boucher-1751. Bequest of William K. Vanderbilt, 1920 (20.155.9). Photograph © 1993. The Metropolitan Museum of Art, New York. Boucher's contemporaries likened his palette, which favored pinks, blues, and soft whites, to "rose petals floating in milk."

Jean-Antoine Watteau's *The Signboard of Gersaint* [zhair-SAHNT], painted in about 1721, is quite literally a signboard. A little over 5 feet high and 10 feet long, it was commissioned to hang outside Gersaint's art gallery in Paris, and later, in about 1744, it entered the collection of Frederick the Great of Prussia. Gersaint called his gallery Au Grand Monarque ("At the Sign of the Great King"), and in this painting the artist alludes to the recently departed Sun King by showing gallery workers putting a portrait of Louis XIV, probably painted by Hyacinthe Rigaud, into a box for storage. A woman in a pink satin gown steps over the threshold from the street, ignoring, for a moment, her companion's outstretched hand to gaze down at the portrait as it descends into its coffinlike confines. It is as if she is taking one last look at the fading world of Louis XIV before turning her back on it once and for all. In fact, just one day after Louis's death, the aristocracy abandoned the palace and returned to Paris.

Jean-Antoine Watteau, ***The Signboard of Gersaint.*** **ca. 1721.** Oil on canvas, 5'4" × 10'1". Staatliche Museen zu Berlin, Preussischer Kulturbesitz, Verwaltung der staatl. Schlösser und Gärden Kunstsammlungen. After it was sold, the work was cut in two halves and displayed as two separate paintings. Its two halves were reunited in the twentieth century.

Watteau's painting is really the signboard of a social world dominated by the leisure, elegance, and refinement of the aristocratic Parisian elite. But here, he adds an ominous note. An unkempt passerby, stick in hand, stands just to the left of the crate. He, too, stares down at the Grand Monarque's picture as it is lowered into place, but with a certain disdain. He is the other France, the France that, so marginalized, will erupt in revolution in 1789.

A portrait of King Louis XIV, probably one of several painted by Hyacinth Rigaud (see Fig. 23.1), is deposited in a storage crate.

Something to Think About . . .

What do the dog, on the far right side of the painting, and the working-class passerby, on the far left, have in common? How do they frame, both literally and figuratively, the world of the painting?

Watteau was a great admirer of Rubens and copied his work often. He shared with Rubens a great love of painting flesh, as well as the ability to reflect in the sensuality of his brushwork and color the sensuality of his subject matter. In *The Signboard of Gersaint*, for instance, Watteau fills the room with Rubeniste canvases. One canvas appears to depict a drunken Silenus, a figure from Greek mythology who is the rotund, older tutor of the god of wine, Dionysius, a scene very much in the spirit of Rubens's many paintings of the same theme. Beside it is a reclining nude.

Two customers are being shown a reclining nude in the painting with magnifying glasses, emphasizing the eroticism of the exchange between viewer and painting.

The dog is an echo of Rubens's frequent use of a dog as an emblem of the sensual appetites. Art historian Svetlana Alpers has, in fact, identified Watteau's dog as an outright copy, in reverse, of one painted by Rubens in *The Coronation of Marie de' Medici*, one of the 21 paintings in the series commissioned to celebrate the life of the queen (see Fig. 23.6).

Peter Paul Rubens, *The Coronation of Marie de' Medici*. 1622–25. Oil on canvas, 12′ 11″ × 23′10″. Musée du Louvre, Paris.

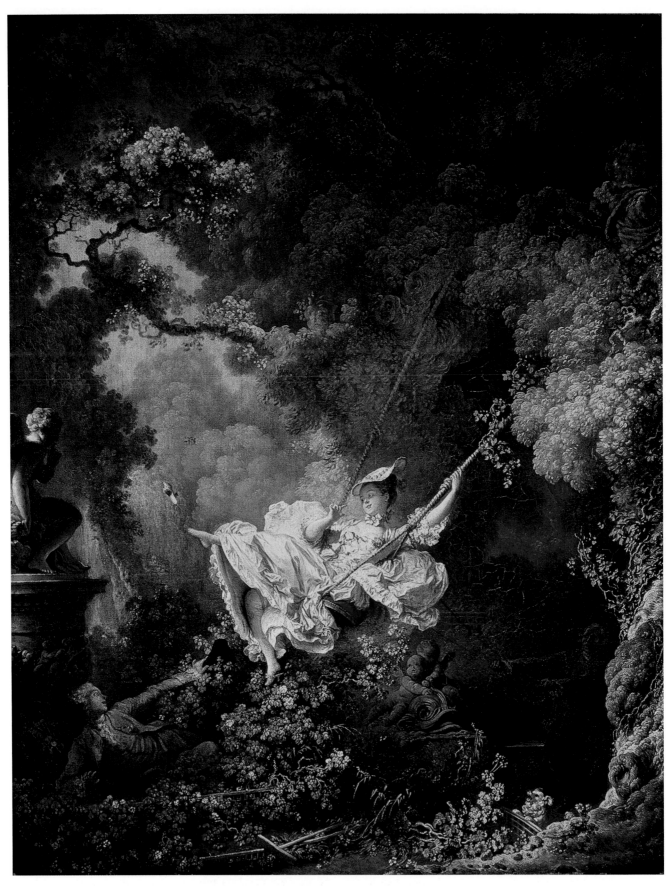

Fig. 25.6 Jean-Honoré Fragonard, *The Swing*. 1767. Oil on canvas, $32\frac{5}{8}$" × 26". Wallace Collection, London. Contributing to the erotic overtones of the composition is the lush foliage of the overgrown garden into which the male lover has inserted himself.

master's tradition into the next generation. Fragonard's most important commission was a series of four paintings for Marie-Jeanne Bécu, comtesse du Barry [kohn-TESS dew bah-REE], the last mistress of Louis XV. Entitled *The Progress of Love*, it was to portray the relationship between Madame du Barry and the king, but in the guise of young people whose romance occurs in the garden park of the countess's château at Louveciennes, itself a gift from Louis.

The most famous painting in the series, *The Swing*, suggests an erotic intrigue (Fig. **25.6**) between two lovers. It implies as well the aesthetic intrigue between the artist and the patron, a conspiracy emphasized by the sculpture of Cupid to the left, holding his finger to his mouth as if to affirm the secrecy of the affair. The painting's subject matter was in fact suggested by another artist, Gabriel-François Doyen (1726–1806), who was approached by the baron de Saint-Julien to paint his mistress "on a swing which a bishop is setting in motion. You will place me in a position in which I can see the legs of the lovely child and even more if you wish to enliven the picture." Doyen declined the commission but suggested it to Fragonard.

Much of the power of the composition lies in the fact that the viewer shares, to a degree, the voyeuristic pleasures of the reclining lover. The entire image is charged with an erotic symbolism that would have been commonly understood at the time. For instance, the lady on the swing lets fly her shoe—the lost shoe and naked foot being a well-known symbol of lost virginity. The young man reaches toward her, hat in hand—the hat that in eighteenth-century erotic imagery was often used to cover the genitals of a discovered lover. Even more subtly, and ironically, the composition echoes the central panel of Michelangelo's Sistine Ceiling, the *Creation of Adam* (see Fig. 15.11). The male lover assumes Adam's posture, and the female lover God's, although she reaches toward Adam—to bring him to life, as it were—with her foot, not her hand.

Rococo Architecture and Landscape Design in Central Europe and England

Rococo architecture, as the Salon de la Princesse at the Hôtel de Soubise in Paris (see Fig. 25.1) demonstrates,

CONTINUITY & CHANGE

Plan of San Carlo alle Quattro Fontane, p. 688

is both a refined and exaggerated realization of the curvilinear Baroque architecture of such seventeenth-century masters as Borromini (see Fig. 21.11.) By the 1690s, architects in the Catholic regions of Central Europe began to explore the possibilities of this elaborate curvilinear style in a series of buildings designed to glorify the princes of the many small states that comprised the region, some of which, like Prussia, were extremely

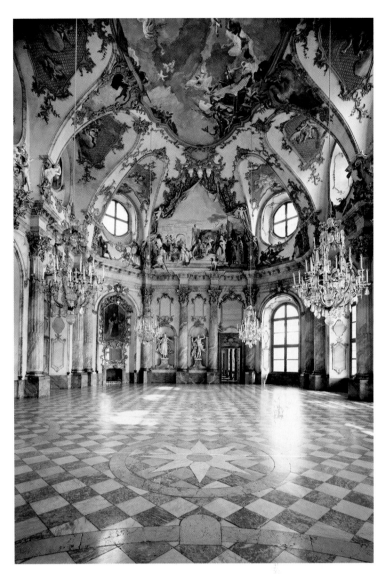

Fig. 25.7 Balthasar Neumann, Kaisersaal, Residenz, Würzburg, Germany. 1719–44. Frescoes by Giovanni Battista Tiepolo, 1751–52. The chandeliers were specially designed to contribute to the overall effect.

powerful. They turned their attention to the grounds as well, where a new type of garden design that had originated in England captured the Rococo imagination.

Balthasar Neumann and Giovanni Tiepolo in Bavaria One of the most magnificent statements of the Rococo in Central Europe is the Residenz (Episcopal Palace) for the prince-bishop of Würzburg in Bavaria. It is the work of Balthasar Neumann (1687–1753), a military engineer turned designer. To complete the work, the prince-bishop sent him to Paris and Vienna in 1723 to consult with the leading architects. Ribbonlike moldings that rise above columns and pilasters that serve no structural purpose dominate the decorative scheme for the oval-shaped Kaisersaal [kye-zur-ZAHL], or Imperial Hall (Fig. **25.7**). The entire white surface of the interior is covered with irregular cartouches and garlands of floral motifs.

Fig. 25.8 Giovanni Battista Tiepolo, ceiling fresco (detail). 1751. Kaisersaal, Residenz, Würzburg. Ninety percent of Würzburg was destroyed in an Allied bombing raid in March 1945. Tiepolo's paintings were saved by a U.S. Army officer whose assignment was to protect and save threatened art objects. He temporarily replaced the vital section of the Residenz roof, which had burned to ashes, and so prevented rain water from pouring through into the vault beneath.

The paintings decorating the room seem to open the interior to the sky. They are the work of the Italian painter Giovanni Battista Tiepolo [tee-EH-po-lo] (1696–1770). The central panel is remarkable for its pastel colors and asymmetrical organization, in which a few figures seem to poke out from behind the clouds and even the frame of the **cartouche** itself (Fig. **25.8**). Notice, for instance, how the two small openings at the top of the composition seem continuous with the space of the main painting, making the ceiling seem weightless and expansive. Yet the work feels remarkably different from ceiling paintings of the earlier Baroque, with their avalanches of figures propelled into space by dramatic bursts of light.

Prussia and the Rococo The Kingdom of Prussia, with its two royal capitals of Berlin and Potsdam (Map **25.2**), exerted an almost uncanny power over Europe in the eighteenth century. As a state, Prussia demanded obedience to its rulers, the Hohenzollern [ho-un-TSOLL-urn] family. They had controlled the German territory of Brandenburg since 1417 and, over the next couple of centuries and through the good fortune of inheritance, had acquired additional scattered holdings in the west along the Rhine to New East Prussia in the east as far as present-day Lithuania, including most of northern Poland. By 1740, it was a

Map 25.2 Prussia in the late eighteenth and early nineteenth centuries.

military giant, its army numbering almost 80,000 men, the third largest in Europe. Its values were, at least to some degree, military: Discipline was valued above all else. The Prussian social elite was the officer corps, which was composed largely of Junkers, the sons of the German nobility.

The first Prussian ruler to assert himself in European affairs was Frederick William (r. 1640–1688), known as the Great Elector (an elector was one of the princes who elected the Holy Roman emperor). It was the Great Elector who first began to build a sizable Prussian army. His son, Frederick (r. 1701–1713), put this army at the disposal of the Habsburg Holy Roman Emperor in 1701, and in return was permitted to call himself "King Frederick I in Prussia"—that is, king in Prussia, but not beyond its bounds, and not to be confused with the emperor. He passed this title on to his son, King Frederick William I (r. 1713–1740).

Frederick I's personal taste leaned toward ostentation and extravagance. During his first year in power, he used more than half the state's annual revenue to support his Berlin court. But he balanced this tendency for pomp with an almost intolerant style of bureaucratic austerity and discipline. For instance, he disbanded the prestigious Berlin court orchestra, putting many musicians out of work. (This delighted Johann Sebastian Bach, who hired seven of the best ones to work with him in the small town of Coethen, where he was chapel master, and provide him with the musicianship required for what would later come to be known as the Brandenburg Concertos.) Following in his father's footsteps, Frederick William I created a centralized bureaucracy, known as the General Directory. He imposed taxes on the nobility and enforced them by means of his army, which included his personal bodyguards. Known as the "Tall Fellows" for their extraordinary stature, the tallest among them was an Irishman who at nearly 7 feet was one of the tallest men of the age. In 1730, when the 18-year-old Crown Prince Frederick attempted to flee his father's tyrannical rule with a friend, Frederick William ordered the friend executed in front of the prince as a lesson in obedience.

This same crown prince would himself become Frederick II (r. 1740–1786), more commonly known as Frederick the Great. He assumed this mantle following a series of campaigns against the Habsburg province of Silesia (see Map 29.1), home of Maria Theresa (1717–1780), who had succeeded to the Habsburg throne in 1740. In defeating the House of Habsburg, which up to this time had been the leading power in Central Europe, and expanding his own holdings by over a third, Frederick II established Prussia as a force at least equal to the Habsburgs. But whereas his father had focused largely on matters of state, Frederick II turned his attention to the arts. For instance, the construction in Berlin that his father had overseen consisted of a series of meticulously laid out streets with houses that one contemporary described as looking like "a line of soldiers, their bay windows resembling grenadiers' caps." By contrast, Frederick the Great, immediately upon assuming the throne, ordered construction of a new opera house, and he added an elaborate new wing to the Charlottenburg Palace, his principal residence in the city. Voltaire [vohl-TAIR], the French intellectual with whom Frederick had been corresponding since the 1730s (and who is discussed later in the chapter), described the change through a simple analogy with the two most important city-states of ancient Greece: "Things changed visibly: Sparta became Athens." In other words, Spartan and militaristic Prussia became a center of culture on a par with Athenian and artistic Paris.

The taste for elegance, luxury, and the arts that exemplified Frederick the Great's court in fact derived largely from Paris during the Rococo period. This is most evident at the palace of Sanssouci [sahn-soo-SEE], Frederick's summer residence in the countryside outside Potsdam. Georg Wenzeslaus von Knobelsdorff (1699–1753) designed it between 1745 and 1747 so that Frederick might escape the pomp and ceremony of the Berlin court. Frederick lavished his attention on the palace. The music room was decorated with mirrors opposite its windows—a trick learned, perhaps, from the Hall of Mirrors at Versailles (see Fig. 23.3) to increase the amount of light in an age still illuminated by candles (Fig. **25.9**). Here, musicians daily entertained Frederick, who often joined in on his own flute—"my best friend," he called it. Alternating with paintings depicting Ovid's *Metamorphoses*, the mirrors reflected the surrounding gardens, visually doubling the size of the room.

The most notable feature of the music room is its elaborate gilded stucco decorations. Executed under the direction of Johann August Nahl (1710–1781), whom Frederick

Fig. 25.9 Concert hall, Sanssouci Palace, Potsdam. ca. 1746–47. The wall painting depicts a scene from Ovid's *Metamorphoses* by French painter Antoine Pesne, who had settled in Prussia by 1735.

Fig. 25.10 Johann Friedrich Schleuen, after Friedrich Zacarias Saltzmann, general plan of Sanssouci Palace, Potsdam. 1772. Etching, colored, 18 1/8″ × 32 3/8″. Stiftung Preussische Schlösser und Gärten, Berlin-Brandenburg, Plansammlung, Potsdam. The original palace, with its terraced vineyards, is at the right. The pleasure garden extends to the left, ending before the much larger New Palace, constructed between 1763 and 1769.

appointed director of ornaments in 1741, they are among the finest examples of the Rococo style. The relationship between these interior details and the natural world is explicit in the general plan of Sanssouci, with its cartouche title at top center (Fig. **25.10**). It shows the original palace and vineyard at the right and the larger New Palace at the left, joined by an extensive pleasure garden. In the pleasure garden, there are none of the straight paths and manicured flowerbeds of the formal gardens of Versailles (see Figs. 23.4 and 23.5). Instead, the left-to-right axis is framed by two winding and serpentine paths that contain a lightly forested deer park. The ensemble appeared entirely rural and natural but was actually "put into order by artistic means." These paths contrast dramatically with the architectural symmetry and geometry of the old and new palaces. They suggest a growing awareness of the need to acknowledge or balance the conflicting claims of order, reason, and intellect with those of the senses, pleasure, and the imagination—between what might be called the *useful*, or practical, and the *aesthetic*, or beautiful.

For Frederick the Great, the conflict amounted to the tension between what he called the "abominable work" of state—at which he was, incidentally, very skilled—and the pleasure of decorating his palaces and grounds, every detail of which he oversaw. So the architectural regularity and symmetry of Frederick's palaces represented an emblem of his public life—a symbol of the state and its orderly workings—whereas the interior rooms and the grounds suggested his private life. And indeed this monarch had a powerful imagination, for in 1746 he composed his own

Symphony in D Major (a genre discussed later in the chapter), for two flutes (one part expressly for himself), two oboes, two horns, string orchestra, and bass continuo.

The English Garden The inspiration for Frederick's garden park at Sanssouci was a new kind of garden that became very popular in England beginning in about 1720 and that aspired to imitate rural nature. Instead of the straight, geometrical layout of the French garden, the walkways of the **English garden** are, in the words of one garden writer of the day, "serpentine meanders . . . with many twinings and windings." The English found precedent for this new garden in the pastoral poetry of Virgil and Horace (see Chapter 8) and, especially, in Pliny's descriptions of the gardens of his Roman contemporaries, translated in 1728 by Robert Castell in *Villas of the Ancients Illustrated*. According to Castell, Pliny described three styles of Roman garden: the plain and unadorned; the "regular," laid out "by the Rule and Line"; and the *Imitatio Ruris*, or the imitation of rural landscapes. This last consisted of "wiggly" paths opening on "vast amphitheaters such as could only be the work of nature." But Castell understood that such landscapes were wholly artificial. For him, the *Imitatio Ruris* was

> . . . a close Imitation of Nature; where, tho' the Parts are disposed with the greatest Art, the Irregularity is still preserved; so that their Manner may not improperly be said to be an artful Confusion, where there is no Appearance of that Skill which is made use of, their Rocks, Cascades, and Trees, bearing their natural Forms.

Fig. 25.11 Henry Flitcroft and Henry Hoare, the park at Stourhead, Wiltshire, England. 1744–65. Each vista point along the Stourhead path looks over an artificial ruin that tells the story of Aeneas's visit to the underworld in Books 3 through 6 of Virgil's *Aeneid*.

The ideal estate was to be "thrown open" in its entirety to become a vast garden, its woods, gardens, lakes, and marshes all partaking of a carefully controlled "artificial rudeness" (in the sense of raw, primitive, and undeveloped).

The gardens at Stowe, in Buckinghamshire, are exemplary. Prior to about 1730, they were composed of straight pathways bordering geometrically shaped woods and by lakes with clearly defined linear forms, including, at the bottom of the hill below the house, an octagonal pool. These more regular gardens were adorned by artificial Greek temples designed by James Gibbs (1682–1754) and William Kent (1685–1748). Kent's Temple of Ancient Virtue, built in 1734, contained life-size statues of Homer, Lycurgus (a Spartan lawgiver), Socrates, and Epaminondas (a Theban general and statesman). Across the valley, on lower ground, was a Shrine of British Worthies, containing the busts of 16 famous Englishmen, including Shakespeare, Isaac Newton, and John Locke. After 1740, Lancelot "Capability" Brown (1716–1783) took over the gardens' design. Brown was nicknamed "Capability" because, he argued, any landscape is capable of improvement.

Brown was inspired by the gardens at Stourhead, built in the 1740s by wealthy banker Henry Hoare (Fig. **25.11**). Hoare had built dams on several streams to raise a lake, around which he created a serpentine path offering many views and vistas. These included a miniature Pantheon that he probably modeled after similar buildings in the landscape paintings of the seventeenth-century French artist Claude Lorrain [klohd loh-REHN]. His Italian pastoral landscapes, with their winding streams and arched bridges framed by ruins and deftly placed trees, were widely popular in England (Fig. **25.12**).

Fig. 25.12 Claude Lorrain, *The Rest on the Flight into Egypt (Noon)*. 1661. Oil on canvas, 45⅝" × 62⅞". Hermitage Museum, Saint Petersburg, Russia. The Bridgeman Art Library. Collection of Empress Josephine, Malmaison, 1815. Note how the artist makes the viewer's eye move through the painting from the grouping at the lower right diagonally, across the bridge (following the shepherd boy and his dog) toward the ruin at the left, then in a zigzag down the road and over the arched bridge into the hazy light of the distant landscape. This serpentine organization directly inspired English garden design.

Fig. 25.13 Charles Bridgeman and Lancelot "Capability" Brown, Plan of the Gardens of the Most Noble Marquis of Buckingham at Stowe, from the *Visitor's Guide Book*. 1797. Lithograph. English School (eighteenth century). Private collection. The Bridgeman Art Library. This reflects the site plan of Stowe as it has appeared since the mid-eighteenth century. Although the landscape looks completely natural, it is as thoroughly designed as a modern-day golf course.

"Capability" Brown, too, was inspired by Claude. By the early 1750s, the edges of the lakes at Stowe, once neatly regular, were completely naturalized, and the landscape had been reformed into an almost entirely pastoral setting, with wide vistas and broad views. Brown's site plan for the garden shows this more natural-looking arrangement (Fig. **25.13**).

Aristocratic visitors to Stowe would have arrived at the estate with their special "Claude" glasses, tinted yellow so that the landscape would glow with the same warmth as a Claude painting. On the one hand, they would have admired the classical ruins and the classical facade of the manor house itself. On the other, they would have discovered, in the grounds, a space in which they might escape emotionally, as Frederick the Great did at Sanssouci, from the very civilization that classical architecture symbolized. The English garden, in other words, embodied many of the same contradictions as the Parisian salon, where the demands of reason championed by the *philosophes* confronted the excesses of the French court.

THE *PHILOSOPHES*

When in 1753 the French painter Jean-Baptiste-Siméon Chardin [shar-DEHN] (1699–1779) exhibited his *Philosopher Occupied with His Reading* in Paris, one French commentator described the painting (Fig. **25.14**) as follows:

> This character is rendered with much truth. A man wearing a robe and a fur-lined cap is seen leaning on a table and reading very attentively a large volume in bound parchment. The painter has given him an air of intelligence, reverie, and obliviousness that is infinitely pleasing. This is a truly philosophical reader who is not content merely to read, but who meditates and ponders, and who appears so deeply absorbed in his meditation that it seems one would have a hard time distracting him.

In short, this is the very image of the French *philosophe*.

Most *philosophes* were **deists** [DEE-ists], who accepted the idea that God created the universe but did not believe he had much, if anything, to do with its day-to-day workings. Rather, the universe proceeded according to what they termed **natural law**, law derived from nature and binding upon human society. In Newtonian terms, God had created a great clock, and it ran like clockwork, except for the interference of inept humanity. So humans had to take control of their own destinies. Deists viewed the Bible as a work of mythology and superstition, not the revealed truth of God. They scoffed at the idea of the divine right of kings. The logic of their position led the *philosophes* to a simple proposition, stated plainly by the *philosophe* Denis Diderot (1713–1784): "Men will not be free until the last king is strangled with the entrails of the last priest."

Denis Diderot and the *Encyclopédie*

The crowning achievement of the *philosophes* was the *Encyclopédie* [on-see-kloh-pay-dee], begun in 1751 and completed in 1772. Its editors were the teacher and translator Denis Diderot and Jean le Rond d'Alembert [DAHL-ohm-behr] (1717–1783), a mathematician who was in charge of the articles on mathematics and science. Both were active participants in salon society, and d'Alembert in fact lived with the great hostess Julie de Lespinasse. The work was unpopular in the French court: Louis XV claimed that the *Encyclopédie* was doing "irreparable damage to morality and religion" and twice banned its printing. But despite the opposition, the court's salons proved useful to the Encyclopedists. In his memoirs, d'Alembert would recall a conversation with Madame Geoffrin [zhoh-fren] (1699–1777), the hostess who was Julie de Lespinasse's mentor:

> As she had always among the circle of her society persons of the highest rank and birth, as she appeared even to seek an acquaintance with them, it was supposed that this flattered her vanity. But here a very erroneous opinion

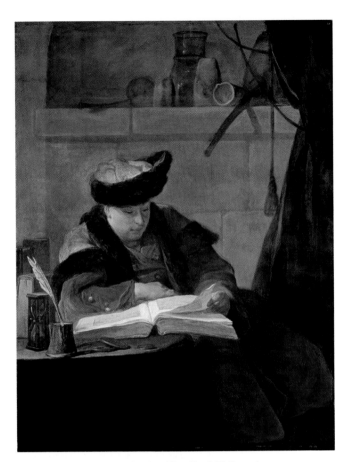

Fig. 25.14 Jean-Baptiste-Siméon Chardin, *A Philosopher Occupied with His Reading.* 1734. Oil on canvas, 54 3/8″ × 41 3/8″ Photo: Hervè Lewandowski/ Musee du Louvre/RMN Reunion des Musees Nationaux, France. SCALA/Art Resource, New York. This is actually a portrait of Joseph Aved, a painter who was a friend of Chardin's.

was formed of her; she was in no respect the dupe of such prejudices, but she thought that by managing the humours of these people, she could render them useful to her friends. "You think," said she, to one of the latter, for whom she had a particular regard, "that it is for my own sake I frequent ministers and great people. Undeceive yourself,—it is for the sake of you, and those like you who may have occasion for them."

It is very likely that d'Alembert was the "friend" to whom she addressed these words.

Although the *Encyclopédie* was rather innocently subtitled a *Classified Dictionary of the Sciences, Arts, and Trades,* the stated intention of the massive 35-volume text, which employed more than 180 writers, was "to change the general way of thinking." Something of the danger that the *Encyclopédie* presented to the monarchy is evident in the entry on natural law written by French lawyer Antoine-Gaspard Boucher d'Argis [boo-SHAY dar-ZHEES] (1708–1791) (**Reading 25.1**):

READING 25.1

from "Law of Nature or Natural Law," from Diderot's *Encyclopédie* (1751–72)

LAW OF NATURE, OR NATURAL LAW, in its most extended sense, refers to certain principles inspired only by nature that are common to men and to animals: on this *law* are based the union of male and female, the procreation of children and concern for their education, the love of liberty, the conservation of one's own person, and the effort each man makes to defend himself when attacked by others.

But it is an abuse of the term *natural* law to use it to refer to the impulses that govern the behavior of animals; for they have not the use of reason and are therefore incapable of perceiving any law or justice.

More frequently, we mean by *natural* law certain rules of justice and equity, which natural reason alone has established among men, or to put it better, which God has engraved in our hearts.

Such are the fundamental precepts of *law* and of all justice: to live honestly, to offend no one, and to render unto every man what belongs to him. From these general precepts are derived many other particular rules, which nature alone, that is to say reason and equity, suggests to men.

Such thinking was fundamental to the Enlightenment's emphasis on human liberty and would fuel revolutions in both America and France. Similar thinking could be found in the sections of the *Encyclopédie* on political science written by the baron de Montesquieu (1689–1755), a deep believer in the writings of John Locke and England's parliamentary democracy. In his 1748 treatise *The Spirit of the Laws,* he had argued for the separation of powers, dividing government into executive, legislative, and judicial branches—an argument that would provide one of the foundations for the American Constitution in the 1780s. Freedom of thought was, in fact, fundamental to the transmission of knowledge, and any state that suppressed it was considered an obstacle to progress. So when Louis XV's censors halted publication of the *Encyclopédie* in 1759, the *philosophes* affirmed the despotism of the French state, even if other government officials, prompted by the salon hostesses, secretly worked to ensure the work's continued viability.

Funded by its 4,000 subscribers, the *Encyclopédie* was read by perhaps 100 times that many people, as private circulating libraries rented it to customers throughout the country. In its comprehensiveness, it represents a fundamental principle of the Enlightenment, also evident in Samuel Johnson's *Dictionary of the English Language* (see Chapter 24), to accumulate, codify, and preserve human knowledge. Like the *Histoire Naturelle* (*Natural History*) of Georges-Louis Leclerc (1707–1788) [leh-kler], published in 36 volumes from 1749 to 1788, which claimed to include everything known about the natural world up to the moment of publication, the *Encyclopédie* claimed to be a collection of "all the knowledge scattered over the face of the earth." The principle guiding this encyclopedic impulse is **rational humanism**, the belief that through logical, careful thought, progress is inevitable. In other words, the more people knew, the more likely they would invent new ways of doing things. Thus, the *Encyclopédie* illustrated manufacturing processes in the most careful detail, imagining that astute readers might recognize better, more efficient methods of manufacturing even as the processes were demystified (Fig. **25.15**).

Jean-Jacques Rousseau and the Cost of the Social Contract

Another contributor to the *Encyclopédie* was Jean-Jacques Rousseau [roo-SOH] (1712–1778), an accomplished composer originally hired by Diderot to contribute sections on music. Rousseau had been born Protestant, in Geneva, was orphaned early in life, and converted to Catholicism while wandering in Italy. He eventually arrived in Paris. Published after his death, the *Confessions* is an astonishingly frank account of his troubles, from sexual inadequacy to a bizarre marriage, including his decision to place each of his five children in an orphanage soon after birth (see **Reading 25.2**, pages 832–833). More forthcoming and revealing than any autobiography previously written, it explains in large part the origins of Rousseau's tendency to outbursts of temper and erratic behavior, and makes it very clear why he eventually fell out with the other *philosophes*. Rousseau was not a social being, even though his writings on social issues were among the most influential of the age.

In the semifictional work *Émile* [ay-MEEL], published in 1762, Rousseau created a theory of education that would influence teaching to the present day. He believed that the education of a child begins at birth. *Émile*'s five books correspond to the five stages of its hero's social development. The first two books outline the youth's growth to age 12, what Rousseau calls the Age of Nature. The third and fourth books describe his adolescence, and the fifth, the Age of Wisdom, his growing maturity between age 20 to 25. The most important years, Rousseau believed, were early adolescence, from age 12 to 15. Entering the teenage years, the child, named Émile by Rousseau, begins formal education, turning his attention to only what he finds "useful" or "pleasing." As a result, the child finds education a pleasurable and exciting experience that naturally leads his imagination to the enjoyment and contemplation of beauty. In his early twenties, Émile is introduced to the corrupting forces of society. Not until he has absorbed these lessons is it safe for Émile to enter society without fear of submitting to its corrupting influence.

As advanced as Rousseau was in his ideas about education, he saw little reason to educate women in the same manner as men. In Book V, Émile encounters woman, in the form of Sophie, Émile's ideal mate: "Her education is in no way exceptional. She has taste without study, talents without art, judgment without knowledge. Her mind is still vacant but has been trained to learn; it is well-tilled land only waiting for the grain. What a pleasing ignorance! Happy is the man destined to instruct her." Within a very few years, women would reject such thinking and assert their equal right to liberty and education.

As *Émile* demonstrates, Rousseau believed in the natural goodness of humankind, a goodness corrupted by society and the growth of civilization. Virtues like unselfishness and kindness were inherent—a belief that

Fig. 25.15 *A Brazier's Workshop,* **illustration from the** *Encyclopédie,* **edited by Denis Diderot. 1751–72.** The metalsmiths at work are making hunting horns. In the center, a worker pounds copper around a rod to make the horn's tube. Behind him, a worker standing above a fireplace pours molten lead into the tube to make it more malleable. At the left, the flared end of the horn is soldered to the tube. And at the right, a worker curves the horn into its final, snail-like form.

gives rise to what he termed the "noble savage"—but he strongly believed that a new social order was required to foster them. In *The Social Contract*, published in 1762, Rousseau describes an ideal state governed by a somewhat mystical "General Will" of the people that delegates authority to the organs of government as it deems necessary. In Chapter 4, "Slavery," Rousseau addresses the subjugation of a people by their monarch (**Reading 25.3**):

READING 25.3

from Jean-Jacques Rousseau, *The Social Contract*, Book 1, Chapter 4 ("Slavery") (1762)

No man has a natural authority over his fellow, and force creates no right. . . .

If an individual . . . can alienate his liberty and make himself the slave of a master, why could not a whole people do the same and make itself subject to a king? There are in this passage plenty of ambiguous words which would need explaining; but let us confine ourselves to the word *alienate*. To alienate is to give or to sell. Now, a man who becomes the slave of another does not give himself; he sells himself, at the least for his subsistence: but for what does a people sell itself? A king is so far from furnishing his subjects with their subsistence that he gets his own only from them; and, according to Rabelais, kings do not live on nothing. Do subjects then give their persons on condition that the king takes their goods also? I fail to see what they have left to preserve.

It will be said that the despot assures his subjects civil tranquility. Granted; but what do they gain, if the wars his ambition brings down upon them, his insatiable avidity, and the vexatious conduct of his ministers press harder on them than their own dissensions would have done? What do they gain, if the very tranquility they enjoy is one of their miseries? Tranquility is found also in dungeons; but is that enough to make them desirable places to live in? The Greeks imprisoned in the cave of the Cyclops lived there very tranquilly, while they were awaiting their turn to be devoured.

To say that a man gives himself gratuitously, is to say what is absurd and inconceivable; such an act is null and illegitimate, from the mere fact that he who does it is out of his mind. To say the same of a whole people is to suppose a people of madmen; and madness creates no right.

Even if each man could alienate himself, he could not alienate his children: they are born men and free; their liberty belongs to them, and no one but they has the right to dispose of it. Before they come to years of discretion, the father can, in their name, lay down conditions for their preservation and well-being, but he cannot give them irrevocably and without conditions: such a gift is contrary to the ends of nature, and exceeds the rights of paternity. It would therefore be necessary, in order to

legitimise an arbitrary government, that in every generation the people should be in a position to accept or reject it; but were this so, the government would be no longer arbitrary.

To renounce liberty is to renounce being a man, to surrender the rights of humanity and even its duties.

This passage explains the famous opening line of *The Social Contract*: "Man is born free, and everywhere he is in chains." What Rousseau means is that humans have enslaved themselves, and in so doing have renounced their humanity. He is arguing here, in many ways, against the precepts of the Enlightenment, for it is their very rationality that has enslaved humans.

Even though he was a contributor to it, Rousseau came to reject the aims of the *Encyclopédie*, especially its celebration of manufacturing and invention. In his 1755 *Discourse on the Origin of Inequality among Men*, he writes (**Reading 25.4**):

READING 25.4

from Jean-Jacques Rousseau, *Discourse on the Origin of Inequality among Men* (1755)

As long as men were content with their rustic huts, as long as they confined themselves to sewing their garments of skin with thorns or fish-bones, and adorning themselves with feathers or shells, to painting their bodies with various colors, to improving or decorating their bows and arrows; and to using sharp stones to make a few fishing canoes or crude musical instruments; in a word, so long as they applied themselves only to work that one person could accomplish alone and to arts that did not require the collaboration of several hands, they lived as free, healthy, good and happy men. . . . but from the instant one man needed the help of another, and it was found to be useful for one man to have provisions enough for two, equality disappeared, property was introduced, work became necessary, and vast forests were transformed into pleasant fields which had to be watered with the sweat of men, and where slavery and misery were soon seen to germinate and flourish with the crops.

Given such thinking, it is hardly surprising that Rousseau ultimately withdrew from society altogether, suffering increasingly acute attacks of paranoia, and died insane.

Voltaire and French Satire

The third great figure among the Parisian *philosophes* was François-Marie Arouet, known by his pen name, Voltaire (1694–1778). So well-schooled, so witty, and so distinguished was Voltaire that to many minds he embodies all the facets of a very complex age. He wrote voluminously—plays, novels, poems, and history. More than any other *philosophe*, he saw the value of other, non-Western cultures and traditions and encouraged his fellow *philosophes* to follow his lead (Fig. **25.16**). He was a man of science and an advisor to both Louis XV and Frederick the Great of Prussia. He believed in an enlightened monarchy, but even as he served these rulers, he satirized them. This earned him a year in the Bastille prison in 1717 to 1718, and later, in 1726, another year in exile in London.

Voltaire's year in England convinced him that life under the British system of government was far preferable to life under what he saw as a tyrannical French monarchy. He published these feelings in his 1734 *Philosophical Letters*. Not surprisingly, the court was scandalized by his frankness, so in order to avoid another stint in prison, Voltaire removed himself to the country town of Cirey, home of his patroness the marquise du Châtelet [dew SHAHT-lay], a woman of learning who exerted an important intellectual influence on him. In 1744 he returned once again to court, which proved tedious and artificial, but in 1750 he discovered in the court of Frederick the Great what he believed to be a more congenial atmosphere. While there he published his greatest historical work, *Le Siècle de Louis XIV* (*The Century of Louis XIV*; 1751). In four brief years he wore out his welcome in Prussia and had to remove himself to the countryside once again. From 1758 to 1778, he lived in the village of Freney in the French Alps. Here he was the center of what amounted to an intellectual court of artists and intellectuals who made regular pilgrimages to sit at his feet and talk.

Voltaire did not believe in the Bible as the inspired word of God. "The only book that needs to be read is the great book of nature," he wrote. He was, more or less, a Deist. What he championed most was freedom of thought, including the freedom to be absolutely pessimistic. This pessimism dominates his most famous work, *Candide* [kahn-DEED], or *Optimism* (1758). It is a prose satire, based in part on the philosophical optimism of Alexander Pope's *Essay on Man* (see Chapter 28). Voltaire's work tells the tale of Candide, a simple and good-natured but star-crossed youth, as he travels the world struggling to be reunited with his love, Cunegonde.

Candide's journey leads from Germany to Portugal to the New World and back again, as he follows the belief

Fig. 25.16 Anicet-Charles-Gabriel Lemonnier, after a drawing by François Boucher, *Reading of Voltaire's Tragedy 'L'orphelin de la Chine' at the Salon of Madame Geoffrin in 1755*. 1812. Oil on canvas. Photo: D. Arnaudet. Châteaux de Malmaison et Bois-Preau, Rueil-Malmaison, France. RMN Reunion des Musees Nationaux/Art Resource, New York. Here Jean le Rond d'Alembert reads Voltaire's new play *L'Orphélin de Chine* (*The Orphan of China*), a tragedy based on an actual fourteenth-century Chinese play brought to Paris by a Jesuit priest in 1735. Voltaire's bust looks on from the back of the room.

that, in the words of German philosopher Gottfried Leibniz, "everything is for the best in the best of all possible worlds." This is a sentiment Candide learns from Dr. Pangloss, his tutor. Pangloss, whose name with its first syllable *pan* ("all" in Latin) suggests the ability to gloss over everything, lacks the clear vision needed to see life's darker sides. On his journey Candide finds himself beset by disasters of all kinds, including the 1755 Lisbon earthquake (see **Reading 25.5,** pages 834–835). He discovers a world filled with stupidity, plagued by evil, mired in ignorance, and completely boring. Although Candide survives his adventures—a testament to human resilience—and eventually finds his Cunegonde, the book concludes with the famous sentiment: "We must cultivate our garden." We must, in other words, give up our naïve belief that we live in "the best of all possible worlds," tend to the small things that we can do well—thus keeping total pessimism at bay—and leave the world at large to keep on its incompetent, evil, and even horrific way.

Art Criticism and Theory

One of the "gardens" most carefully cultivated by the French intellectuals (and those with intellectual pretensions) was art. By the last half of the eighteenth century, it was becoming increasingly fashionable for educated upper-class people to experience what the English called the Grand Tour and the French and Germans referred to as the Italian Journey. Art and architecture were the focal points of these travels, along with picturesque landscapes and gardens. A new word was coined to describe the travelers themselves—*tourist.*

Tourists then, as they do today, wanted to understand what they were seeing. Among the objects of their travel were art exhibitions, particularly the Paris Salon—the official exhibition of the French Royal Academy of Painting and Sculpture. It took place in the Salon Carré [kah-ray] of the Louvre, which lent the exhibition its name. It ran from August 25 until the end of September almost every year from 1737 until 1751, and every other year from 1751 to 1791. But few visitors were well-equipped to appreciate or understand what they were seeing, so a new brand of writing soon developed in response: art criticism.

Diderot's *Salons* Denis Diderot began reviewing the official exhibitions of the Paris Salon in 1759 for a private newsletter circulated to a number of royal houses outside France. Many consider these essays (there are nine of them) the first art criticism. Boucher and his fellow Rococo artists were the object of his wrath. In 1763, Diderot asked, "Haven't painters used their brushes in the service of vice and debauchery long enough, too long indeed?" Painting, he argued, ought to be "moral." It should seek "to move, to educate, to improve us, and to induce us to virtue." And in his *Salon of 1765,* Diderot would complain about Boucher:

I don't know what to say about this man. Degradation of taste, color, composition, character, expression, and drawing have kept pace with moral depravity. . . . And then there's such a confusion of objects piled one on top of the other, so poorly disposed, so motley, that we're dealing not so much with the pictures of a rational being as with the dreams of a madman.

An artist who did capture his imagination was the still-life and genre painter Jean-Baptiste-Siméon Chardin (1699–1779) (see Fig. 25.14). Considering the small Chardin still life *The Brioche* (Fig. **25.17**), a painting of the famous French bread or cake eaten at the breakfast table, Diderot in the *Salon of 1767* wrote: "One stops in front of a Chardin as if by instinct, as a traveler tired of his journey sits down almost without being aware of it in a spot that offers him a bit of greenery, silence, water, shade, and coolness." What impressed Diderot most was Chardin's use of paint: "Such magic leaves one amazed. There are thick layers of superimposed color and their effect rises from below to the surface. . . . Come closer, and everything becomes flat, confused, and indistinct; stand back again, and everything springs back into life and shape." What Diderot valued especially in Chardin's work was its detail, what amounts to an almost encyclopedic attention to the everyday facts of the world. As opposed to the Rococo artists of the court, whose *fêtes galantes,* he complained, conveyed only the affected and therefore false manners and conventions of polite society, Chardin was able to convey the truth of things. "I prefer rusticity to prettiness," Diderot proclaimed.

Despite Diderot's preference for subject matter of a "truthful" kind, he was fascinated with the individual work of art. He expressed this fascination in his description of its painterly surface beyond whatever "subject matter" it

Fig. 25.17 Jean-Baptiste-Siméon Chardin, *The Brioche (The Dessert).* *1763.* Oil on canvas, 18$\frac{1}{2}$″ × 22″. Photo: Hervè Lewandowski. Musee du Louvre/RMN Reunion des Musees Nationaux, France. SCALA/Art Resource, New York. Chardin painted from dark to light, the brightest parts of the canvas coming last.

might possess. This fascination was part of a broader change in the way that the eighteenth century approached the arts in general.

Gotthold Ephraim Lessing's *Laocoön* At the beginning of the century, painting, sculpture, architecture, poetry, and music had begun to separate themselves from the traditional "liberal arts," to be recast as the "fine arts." In the process, these fine arts began to distinguish themselves from each other, most notably in the writings of Gotthold Ephraim Lessing [LESS-ing] (1729–1781), a native of Frederick the Great's Prussia. His major work, written while serving as secretary to a Prussian general, is *Laocoön: or, An Essay upon the Limits of Painting and Poetry*, published in 1766.

Since the Renaissance, painting and poetry had been considered "sister arts." The saying "*ut pictura poesis*" ("as is painting so is poetry") of the ancient Roman Horace in his

Laocoön, **p. 165**

Ars Poetica had prevailed. Lessing took a different approach. Basing his argument on his understanding of the famous Hellenistic statue *Laocoön* (see Fig. 5.26), he argued that the visual arts and poetry were essentially different. "Painting," and by extension a sculpture like *Laocoön*, "can use only one single moment of the action, and must therefore choose the most pregnant, from which what precedes and follows will be most easily apprehended." On the other hand, poetry consists of a *series* of actions in time. Images unfold in space, texts in time. While the distinction is a bit superficial since it takes time to look at a painting carefully, it was deeply influential. The German Romantic playwright, poet, and novelist Johann Wolfgang von Goethe (see Chapter 27) was only 17 when the book was published, but he would later recall its impact. "It lifted us up from the region of miserably limited observation into the wide open spaces of thought," he wrote. "That long misunderstood dictum, *ut pictura poesis*, was instantly dispensed with; the difference between plastic and verbal arts was now clear."

ROCOCO AND CLASSICAL MUSIC

The growing distaste for the Rococo and the moral depravity associated with it was epitomized in the eighteenth century in the rise of what we have come to call **Classical music**. It would almost completely supplant Rococo music, which was characterized by pieces written for the harpsichord, a keyboard instrument the strings of which are plucked rather than struck with hammers as on a piano. Its sound, as a result, is delicate and light. The two most important Rococo composers were French: François Couperin [koop-uh-RAN] (1668–1733) and Jean-Philippe Rameau [rah-MOH] (1683–1764). Their harpsichord music was composed of graceful melodies, many of them dance pieces with charmingly simple harmonies displayed in intricate and complex rhythms that mirror the Rococo's taste for

ornamentation. Their work epitomized what came to be known as the **style galant** [steel gah-LAHN], the perfect accompaniment to the *fêtes galantes* of Rococo art. At least one of Couperin's pieces in the *style galant*, "The Chimes of Cythera," directly evokes Watteau. Rameau, in addition, composed dramatic operas that featured ballet sequences for a large corps of dancers, as Lully's had for the court of Louis XIV (see Chapter 27). These operas exploit the sexual tensions inherent in their stories, just as so much Rococo art did.

The style of music we have come to call Classical, on the other hand, developed first in Vienna about 1760, and lasted into the nineteenth century. It represents an almost total rejection of the values associated with the Rococo and Baroque. In fact, we call this style Classical because it shares with Greek and Roman art the essential features of symmetry, proportion, balance, formal unity, and, perhaps above all, clarity. This clarity was a direct result of the rise of a new musical audience, a burgeoning middle class that demanded from composers a more accessible and recognizable musical language than found in the ornate and complex structures of Baroque and Rococo music.

The Symphonic Orchestra

The most important development of the age, designed specifically to address the new middle-class audience, was the **symphonic orchestra**. This musical ensemble was much larger than the ensemble used by Baroque composers such as Vivaldi (see Chapter 21). Its basic structure was established in the 1740s by Johann Stamitz [SHTAH-mits] (1717–1757), concertmaster and conductor of the orchestra in Mannheim, located in the Rhine Palatinate (now southwestern Germany). Although Renaissance and Baroque instruments were already organized into families of instruments, the relatively large size of Stamitz's ensemble set it apart (Fig. **25.18**).

Stamitz divided his orchestra into separate sections according to type of instrument: the *strings*, made up of violins, violas, cellos, and double basses; *woodwinds*,

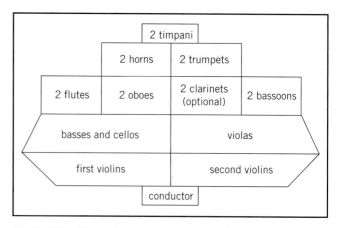

Fig. 25.18 The Classical symphonic orchestra in the time of Mozart and Haydn. From Jay Zorn, *Listening to Music*, second edition. Used by permission of Prentice Hall, Inc.

Fig. 25.19 The Classical symphonic orchestra today. From Jay Zorn, *Listening to Music*, second edition. Used by permission of Prentice Hall, Inc. Over the years, the symphonic orchestra has added new instruments as composers increasingly experimented with them, and larger numbers of traditional instruments as they sought a fuller and richer sound. V-1: first violin; V-2: second violin; Vla: viola; C: cello; Db: double bass; Ob: oboe; Fl: flute; Cl: clarinet; Bn: bassoon; Hn: French horn; Tpt: trumpet; Tbn: trombone; Tba: tuba.

consisting of flutes, oboes, clarinets, and bassoons; a *brass* section of trumpets and French horns (by the end of the century, trombones were added); and a *percussion* section, featuring the kettledrums and other rhythm instruments. Gradually the piano, invented around 1720, was increasingly refined in design until it replaced the clavichord and harpsichord as the favored solo instrument at the heart of the orchestra. This improved piano was known as the **pianoforte** because it could play both soft (*piano*) and loud (*forte* [FOR-tay]), which the harpsichord could not. The composer himself usually led the orchestra and often played part of the composition on the piano or harpsichord in the space now reserved for the conductor. The modern symphony orchestra (Fig. **25.19**) is a dramatically enlarged version of Stamitz's.

Stamitz's orchestra was the first to use an overall **score**, which indicated what music was to be played by each instrument. This let the composer view the composition as a whole. In addition, each instrument section was given its own individual part. The **time signature** (number of beats per measure), **key signature** (showing the scale upon which the piece will be played), **dynamics** (*forte*, for instance, for loud, *piano* for soft), **pace** (*allegro* [uh-LEG-roh], for fast; *lento* [LEN-toe], for slow), and interpretative directions (*affettuoso* [ah-fet-too-OH-soh] for "with feeling") were indicated both in the score as a whole and the individual parts. These devices have remained part of the vocabulary of Western musical composition ever since (Fig. **25.20**).

Fig. 25.20 Devices of standard musical notation.

Symphonic Form

The music most often played by the symphonic orchestra was the **symphony**. The term derives from the Italian *sinfonia*—the three-movement, fast–slow–fast, introduction or overture to Italian operas. In Mannheim, however, Stamitz began to popularize a four-movement form, consisting of a first movement played in a fast tempo (*allegro*); a second movement that is slow (*adagio* [ah-DAHZ-oh] or *andante* [ahn-DAHN-tay]) and reflective; a third that picks up the pace again, often in the stately rhythms of the minuet; and a fourth movement which is generally *allegro* once again, spirited and lively. The predictability of the form is the source of its drama, since audiences anticipated the composer's inventiveness as the composition proceeded through the four movements. The first *allegro* movement (and occasionally the fourth) possessed its own distinct **sonata form**, a kind of small form within the larger symphonic form.

Each movement in the sonata form was divided into three parts: exposition, development, and recapitulation (Fig. **25.21**). In the *exposition*, the composer "exposes" the main theme in the composition's "home" key and then contrasts it with a second theme in a different key. In the *development*, the composer further develops the two themes in contrasting keys, and then, in the *recapitulation*, restates the two themes, but both now in the home key. Use of the home key in the restatement resolves the tension between the two themes. A short *coda* (or "tail") is often added to bring the piece to a definitive end, typically with a strong harmonic closing (called by musicians a *cadence*).

There were several other important forms at the disposal of Classical composers in which they might write an individual movement of a composition. The most important of these are theme-and-variations form, aria form, minuet-and-trio form, and rondo form. One main musical theme dominates the theme-and-variations form. The theme repeats throughout the movement, each succeeding section presenting a variation or modification of it, but still in recognizable form so that its transformations are easy to follow. Aria form was a popular choice for slow movements, and it has already been discussed in connection with opera. However, in the symphony it is an instrumental not a vocal form. It consists of three parts, ABA. A slow, lyrical opening section (A), often in triple meter, is followed by a central section in a new key (B), and, finally, by a repeat of the opening section (A), usually with variation of some kind.

The minuet-and-trio form was favored for the third movement of symphonies. It originates in the minuet dance form so popular in the Baroque courts. In the Classical symphony, minuet-and-trio movements are always in ¾ meter, played at a moderate tempo, and consist of three sections: a minuet (in two parts, each repeated, AABB); a trio, which

follows the same pattern (CCDD), contrasting with the minuet in instrumentation, texture, dynamics, key, or some combination of these. Then the first minuet is played again, often without repeats (AABB, or simply AB):

MINUET	TRIO	MINUET
AABB	CCDD	AABB, or AB

The final form common to the Classical symphony is rondo form. It consists of a lively or catchy tune, played at a relatively fast pace, that keeps on returning or coming round again (hence the name "rondo"). Between occurrences of this main theme (A), contrasting episodes occur (ABACADA). Composers seeking a more balanced or symmetrical form often repeat the first episode just before the last occurrence of the main theme (ABACABA).

Although individual composers often modified and played with these main forms, the most common structure of a four-movement symphony would generally follow the scheme shown here.

Symphonic Movement	Form
I	Sonata
II	Aria, Sonata, or Theme and Variations
III	Minuet and Trio
IV	Rondo or Sonata

Some symphonies reverse the position of the middle two movements, putting the slower movement third instead of second. Sonata form was sometimes used twice, once for the first movement and then again, often in the fourth movement.

Fig. 25.21 Sonata form.

The String Quartets of Joseph Haydn

One of the most important contributors to the development of the symphonic form was the composer Joseph Haydn [HY-din] (1732–1809). In 1761, at the age of 29, he was appointed musical director to the court of the Hungarian nobleman Prince Paul Anton Esterházy. Haydn worked for Esterházy for nearly 30 years, isolated at Esterháza Palace in Eisenstadt, about 30 miles south of Vienna. The palace, modeled on Versailles, included two theaters (one for opera) and two concert halls. In these surroundings, Haydn composed an extraordinary amount of music: operas, oratorios, concertos, sonatas, overtures, liturgical music, and above all, the two genres that he was instrumental in developing—the classical symphony and the string quartet. (He composed 106 of the former and 67 of the latter.) He also oversaw the repair of instruments, trained a chorus, and rehearsed and performed with a symphony of about 25 musicians.

The **string quartet**, the first of the new Classical genres that Haydn played such a large role in developing, features four string instruments: two violins, a viola, and a cello. Since all the instruments are from the same family, the music has a distinctly uniform sound. Its form closely followed that of the symphony. The string quartet was a product of the Classical age of music, performed almost exclusively in private settings, such as salons, for small audiences that understood the form to be a musical variation of their own conversations, an intimate exchange among friends.

Haydn was able to create new genres such as the string quartet precisely because Esterházy gave him the freedom to do so. "I could make experiments," Haydn told a biographer, "observe what elicited or weakened an impression, and thus correct, add, delete, take risks. I was cut off from the world . . . and so I had to become original." When Esterházy died in 1790, his son disbanded the orchestra and a London promoter, Johann Peter Salomon, invited Haydn to England. There he composed his last 12 symphonies for an orchestra of some 60 musicians. Among the greatest of the London symphonies is *Symphony No. 94*, the so-called *"Surprise" Symphony*. It was so named for a completely unanticipated *fortissimo* [for-TIS-uh-mo] ("very loud") percussive stroke that occurs on a weak beat in the second movement of the piece. This moment was calculated, so the story goes, to awaken Haydn's dozing audience, since concerts usually lasted well past midnight.

HEAR MORE at www.myartslab.com The third movement of *Symphony No. 94* (track **25.1**) is in minuet and trio form. It is among Haydn's greatest works. In the very first section of the movement, the graceful cadences of the minuet last for only about 13 seconds, but in that short span, Haydn changes dynamics four times. He then repeats this first section, so that in the first 30 seconds of the composition, a total of eight changes in dynamics occur. The violins alone play the quiet, or *piano*, passages, and the full orchestra the loud, or *fortissimo*, passages. This opening theme, with all its contrasting elements, is followed by the second theme of the opening minuet, after which the first theme briefly repeats, followed in turn by a repetition of the entire second theme. The trio manipulates the themes of the first minuet, lending them an entirely different texture, as first horns and violins alternate and then oboes and bassoons replace the horns, adding a sudden and surprising shift to a minor key. Finally, the entire minuet repeats exactly. The full effect is one of almost stunning emotional range.

Wolfgang Amadeus Mozart: Classical Complexity

The greatest musical genius of the Classical era was Haydn's younger contemporary and colleague, Wolfgang Amadeus Mozart [MOHT-sart] (1756–1791). Mozart wrote his first original composition at age six, in 1762, the year after Haydn assumed his post with Prince Esterházy. When he was just eight, the prodigy penned his first symphony. Over the course of his 35-year life, he would write 40 more, plus 70 string quartets, 20 operas, 60 sonatas, and 23 piano concertos. (All of Mozart's works were catalogued and numbered in the nineteenth century by Ludwig von Köchel, resulting in each of them being identified with the letter *K*.) Haydn told Mozart's father that the boy was simply "the greatest composer I know in person or by name," and in 1785 Mozart dedicated six string quartets to the older composer. On several occasions the two met at parties, where they performed string quartets together, Haydn on the violin, Mozart on the viola.

By the time Mozart was six years old, his father, Leopold, began taking him and his sister, Anna, also a talented keyboard player, on concert tours throughout Europe (Fig. **25.22**). The tours exposed the young genius to virtually every musical development in eighteenth-century Europe, all of which he absorbed completely. As Mozart grew into adulthood, he suffered from depression and illness. He was unable to secure a position in the Habsburg court in Vienna until late in his life, when he was given the minor task of writing new dances for New Year's and other celebrations, so he was forced to teach composition to supplement his income. By the mid-1780s, he had also begun to perform his piano concertos in public concerts, from which he derived some real income.

Despite the stunning successes of his operas, Mozart's music was generally regarded as overly complicated, too demanding emotionally and intellectually for a popular audience to absorb. When the Habsburg Emperor Joseph II commented that the opera *Don Giovanni* was beautiful "but no food for the teeth of my Viennese"—meaning too refined for their taste—Mozart reportedly replied, "Then give them time to chew it." Indeed, his work often took time to absorb. Mozart could pack more distinct melodies into a single movement than most composers could write for an entire symphony, and each line would arise and grow naturally from the beginning to the end of the piece. But the reaction of Joseph II to another of his operas is typical: "Too many notes!" Ironically, it is exactly this richness that we value today.

Fig. 25.22 Michel Barthélémy Ollivier, *Tea at Prince Louis-François de Conti's in the Temple, Paris.* **1766.** Oil on canvas. Musée du Louvre, Paris. The painting depicts an actual salon in the summer of 1766, during Mozart's second visit to Paris when he was about ten years old. The prodigy is seated at the harpsichord, about to accompany the singer Pierre Jéylotte, seen tuning his guitar.

An example of Mozart's complexity is his *Symphony No. 40*, composed in the course of eight weeks in the summer of 1788. Unlike Haydn, who had a standing orchestra at his disposal, Mozart had no compelling reason to compose symphonies on a regular basis. *Symphony No. 40* and the two others he wrote in 1788 were probably undertaken with an eye toward an upcoming trip to London, where he planned to showcase his talents. The symphony is marked by almost perfect balance and control, and although its sonata form is easy to hear and follow, it is also easy to hear the ways in which Mozart manipulates the form in order to play with his audience's expectations. In the first movement, Mozart uses the sonata form in a way that is very easy for the listener

HEAR MORE at to hear, and yet the movement is full of small— www.myartslab.com and sometimes larger—surprises (track **25.2**). The composition shifts dramatically between loud and soft passages, woodwinds and strings, rising and falling phrasings, and major and minor keys. Particularly dramatic is the

way Mozart leads the listener to anticipate the beginning of the recapitulation, only to withhold it. As developed in the clear forms originated by Haydn and Mozart, the Classical symphony is nearly the antithesis of the delicately ornate *style galant* of the Rococo. As such, it announces the demise of the Rococo style.

The Popularization of Opera

The musical form that most clearly announces the death of the Rococo is opera. Its chief genre in the seventeenth and eighteenth centuries was ***opera seria*** ("serious opera"), a very formal kind of opera characterized by mythological or historical subjects and complex arias. *Opera seria* developed in Italy after Monteverdi's initial example (see Chapter 21). Sung almost exclusively in Italian, its tragic mode had found favor throughout Europe.

By the middle of the eighteenth century, the conventions of *opera seria* had come under attack. As early as 1728, in London, *The Beggar's Opera* by John Gay (1685–1732) openly lampooned them. Instead of mythological figures or historical heroes, it portrayed common criminals. Where in France, opera always opened with an overture honoring the king, Gay began his with a song attacking the prime minister. The setting (a prison as opposed to a grand hall) and score (69 songs, including 28 English ballads) stand in marked contrast to the elaborate scenery (including mechanical devices for grand spectacles) and arias and recitative of *opera seria*. In fact, Gay dispensed with recitative altogether, substituting spoken dialogue.

The Beggar's Opera was an instant success, so popular that it was soon performed in the American colonies. It is said to have been George Washington's favorite opera. For the remainder of the eighteenth century it was performed in one city or another throughout the English-speaking world at least once a year.

Opera Seria versus Opera Buffa Meanwhile, a new style of opera had developed in Italy—*opera buffa* ("comic opera")—which, like the novel or Gay's *Beggar's Opera*, took everyday people for its characters and their more or less everyday activities for its plot. Its melodies, like Gay's, were generally simple and straightforward, unlike the complex solo arias that mark *opera seria*.

But even those who were dedicated to *opera seria* sought to reform it. Leading the way was Christoph Willibald Gluck (1714–1787). A prolific composer of operas himself, he resolved "to free [Italian opera] from all the abuses which have crept in either through ill-advised vanity on the part of the singers or through excessive complaisance on the part of composers." The **da capo aria**, which comprised the vast majority of *opera seria* arias, particularly annoyed him. Meaning "from the head," or, as we would say today, "from the top," or the beginning, the da capo aria had an ABA form. Singers were expected to embellish the A section in its repetition, transforming long notes into runs, adding new higher notes, and generally showing off their singing skills. When an aria ended, the singer usually left the stage, thus allowing for curtain calls and even encores. A singer who performed the A section the second time around with little or no change would be booed off the stage or pelted with rotten vegetables. The way in which the audience interrupted the flow of the performance as it expressed its approval or disapproval frustrated Gluck. He therefore proposed replacing the da capo aria with a more syllabic setting of text to music. This would eliminate needless embellishment and make the words more intelligible. He also advocated simpler and more flowing melodies.

Opera buffa accepted Gluck's propositions and went even further, eliminating the chief practitioners of the da capo aria. These practitioners were **castrati**, men who were subjected to castration in their youth in order to preserve their high voices. The best of them enjoyed great financial success, comparable to a modern-day rock star. Their disproportionately long limbs and extremely high voices left

them open to broad satire, which contributed to the growing image of *opera seria* as an "unnatural" or artificial art form. By eliminating castrati from its productions, *opera buffa* underscored the closeness of its comedies to real life.

Mozart's Stylistic Synthesis Mozart wrote five *opera seria*, but in his last four great operas—*The Marriage of Figaro, Don Giovanni, Cosi fan tutte,* and *The Magic Flute*—he united *opera seria* and *opera buffa*. Mozart referred to these four operas as **dramma giocoso**, "comic drama." The first three bring together nobles and commoners in stories that are at the same time comic and serious. What distinguishes them most, however—and the Italian librettist Lorenzo da Ponte (1749–1838) must be given some credit for this—is the depth of their characters. From the lowest to the highest class and rank, all are believable as they sort out their stormy relationships and love lives.

Based on the legend of Don Juan, a seducer of women who killed the father of one of his noble conquests and then got his comeuppance when the father's funerary statue accepted the Don's playful invitation to dinner and dragged the Don down to Hell, Mozart's *Don Giovanni* is a tour de force. The lead character is at once attractive and repulsive, a defier of all social convention and ethical norms. Opposite him are two noble female leads, Donna Anna and Donna Elvira, and a peasant girl, Zerlina, whom Don Giovanni is also intent on seducing.

As the curtain rises, Don Giovanni's servant Leporello guards the courtyard outside the bedroom where his master is trying to seduce Donna Anna. His opening aria is a complaint lamenting the wicked ways of his master yet asserting the desire to be a "gentleman" himself. Harmonically, rhythmically, and melodically simple, it sets a distinct *opera buffa* tone. But no sooner does Leporello finish than the noblewoman Donna Anna and Don Giovanni himself sing a duet of an entirely different tone. The Don has evidently failed to seduce Donna Anna and is trying to escape her cries of alarm, but she pursues him. Leporello, standing safely apart but observing the interchange, soon makes the duet a trio, commenting on the action and predicting his master's behavior will lead to his ultimate ruin. Donna Anna's father, the Commendatore, answers his daughter's cries and challenges Don Giovanni to a duel. The Don reluctantly agrees and quickly kills the Commendatore, who dies slowly as Leporello comments on his master's behavior again, this time even more despondently. When Donna Anna returns with her fiancé, Don Ottavio, to find her father dead, the two swear to avenge the murder.

So the opera's comic opening is transformed into a drama of high seriousness and consequence. Throughout this scene, Mozart does not provide a single moment in which the audience can applaud. In the next scene, the *opera buffa* tone resumes as Leporello mockingly consoles Donna Elvira, whom Don Giovanni has already seduced and deserted. His aria, "Madamina," sometimes called the "Catalog Aria," enumerates Don Giovanni's numerous

((⦁ HEAR MORE at
www.myartslab.com conquests throughout Europe and is a master-piece of comic composition (track **25.3**). As nobility confront peasantry, and then work together to bring Don Giovanni to justice, the concerns of *opera seria* and *opera buffa* coalesce into highly entertaining drama.

After debuting triumphantly in Prague, *Don Giovanni* was received with less enthusiasm in Vienna, at least at first. But Haydn loved it. "If every music-lover, especially among the nobility, could respond to Mozart's inimitable works with the depth of emotion and understanding which they arouse in me, the nations would compete to have such a jewel within their frontiers."

CHINA AND EUROPE: CROSS-CULTURAL CONTACT

Unlike the cultures of the South Pacific, which were unknown to Europeans until the expeditions of Cook and Bougainville, China and India were well known (Map **25.3**). The *philosophes* were especially attracted to China. They recognized that in many respects, China was more advanced than any society in the West. Its people were better educated, with over a million graduates of its highly sophisticated educational system, and its industry and commerce more highly developed. It was also a more egalitarian society (at least for males) than any in the West, for, although a wealthy, landed nobility did exist, it was subject to a government of scholar-bureaucrats drawn from every level of society.

The first Portuguese trading vessels had arrived in China in 1514 (see Chapter 18), and by 1715, every major

Fig. 25.23 Jean-Étienne Liotard. *Still Life: Tea Set.* **ca. 1781–83.** Oil on canvas mounted on board, 14 7/8″ × 20 5/16″. The J. Paul Getty Museum, Los Angeles, CA. The lacquer tray upon which the tea service is set was probably made in Europe in imitation of Chinese lacquerware.

European trading nation had an office in Canton. Chinese goods—porcelains, wallpapers, carved ivory fans, boxes, lacquerware, and patterned silks—flooded the European markets, creating a widespread taste for what quickly became known as **chinoiserie** [sheen-WAHZ-ree] (meaning "all things Chinese"). Jean-Étienne Liotard's (1702–1789) *Still Life: Tea Set* (Fig. **25.23**) captures the essence of chinoiserie taste. Central to the image is tea itself, the trade in which was dominated by the Dutch. Across Europe, tea consumption rose from 40,000 pounds in 1699 to an annual average

Map 25.3 The Far East. ca. 1600–1799.

SEE MORE View a Closer Look about Chinoiserie at **www.myartslab.com**

Fig. 25.24 **William Marlow,** *View of the Wilderness at Kew,* **1763.** Watercolor; sheet: 11 $^{1}/_{16}$″ × 17 $^{17}/_{16}$″. Metropolitan Museum of Art, New York. The Chinese pagoda built by Chambers in 1761 still stands in the gardens today.

of 240,000 pounds by 1708. The Chinese tea service that is Liotard's primary focus was made in China for export to Europe.

The craze for chinoiserie even reached the English garden (Fig. **25.24**). A Chinese pagoda in London's Kew Gardens was designed by Sir William Chambers (1726–1796). Chambers visited China in the 1740s, and his work on garden architecture, published in 1762 as *Dissertation on Oriental Gardening*, was widely influential, creating a craze that swept France at the end of the eighteenth century—the *jardin anglo-chinois*, the English–Chinese garden. Likewise, blue-on-white porcelain ware—"china" as it came to be known in the West— was especially desirable (see Fig. 18.21) and before long ceramists at Meissen [MY-sen], near Dresden [DREZ-den], Germany, had learned how to make their own porcelain. This allowed for almost unbounded imitation and sale of Chinese designs on European-manufactured ceramic wares. Even the Rococo court painter François Boucher imitated the blue-on-white Chinese style in oil paint (Fig. **25.25**). The scene is simply a *fête galante* in Chinese costume. A balding Chinese man bends to kiss

Fig. 25.25 **François Boucher,** *Le Chinois Galant.* **1742.** Oil on canvas, 41″ × 57″. The David Collection, inv.B275. Photo: Pernille Klemp. Boucher also created a suite of tapestries on Chinese themes for the king. The style of both this painting and the tapestries is decidedly Rococo, including, here, an elaborate Rococo cartouche border.

the hand of his lady, who sits with her parasol beneath a statue, not of Venus (as might be appropriate in a European setting), but of Buddha. A blue-on-white Chinese vase of the kind Boucher is imitating rests on a small platform behind the lady, and the whole scene is set in a Rococo-like cartouche.

European thinkers were equally impressed by Chinese government. In his *Discourse on Political Economy*, 1755, Jean-Jacques Rousseau praised the Chinese fiscal system, noting that in China, "taxes are great and yet better paid than in any other part of the world." That was because, as Rousseau explained, food was not taxed, and only those who could afford to pay for other commodities were taxed. It was, for Rousseau, a question of tax equity: "The necessaries of life, such as rice and corn, are absolutely exempt from taxation, the common people are not oppressed, and the duty falls only on those who are well-to-do." And he believed the Chinese emperor to be an exemplary ruler, resolving disputes between officials and the people according to the dictates of the "general will"—decidedly different from the practices of the French monarchy.

Likewise, in his 1756 *Essay on the Morals and Customs of Nations*, Voltaire praised the Chinese emperors for using government to protect civilization, creating a social stability unmatched in Europe and built upon Confucian principles of respect and service. He somewhat naively believed that the Chinese ruling class, in cultivating virtue, refined manners, and an elevated lifestyle, set an example that the rest of its people not only followed but revered. In England, Samuel Johnson praised China's civil-service examination system as one of the country's highest achievements, far more significant than their invention of the compass, gunpowder, or printing. He wished Western governments might adopt it.

The Arts in the Qing Dynasty (1644–1911)

The China that the West so idealized was ruled by Qing [ching] ("clear" or "pure") Manchus, or Manchurians, who had invaded China from the north, capturing Beijing in 1644. They made Beijing their capital and ruled China continuously until 1911, but they solidified their power especially during the very long reign of the Qianlong emperor (r. 1736–1795). By 1680, the Qing rulers had summoned many Chinese artists and literati to the Beijing court, and under the Qianlong, the imperial collections of art grew to enormous size, acquired as gifts or by confiscating large quantities of earlier art. (Today the collection is divided between the National Palace

Fig. 25.26 Jean Denis Attiret, *The Presentation of Uigur Captives.* **From** *Battle Scenes of the Quelling of Rebellions in the Western Regions, with Imperial Poems.* **ca. 1765–74; poem dated 1760.** Etching, mounted in album form, 16 leaves plus 2 additional leaves of inscriptions; 51 × 87 cm. © The Cleveland Museum of Art, John L. Severance Fund. 1998.103.14. In order to indicate his pride in the Qing military, the Qianlong emperor wrote a poem to accompany each etching.

Fig. 25.27 Detail of porcelain punch bowl, painted in overglaze enamels in Guangzhou (Canton) with a copy of William Hogarth's print, *The Gates of Calais.* **ca. 1750–55.** Diameter 16″. Board of Trustees of the Victoria and Albert Museum, London (Basil Ionides Bequest), C. 23–1951.

Museum in Taipei and the Palace Museum in Beijing.) The collection was housed in the Forbidden City (see Figs. 18.18 and 18.19), which the Qing emperors largely rebuilt.

While many court artists modeled their work on the earlier masterpieces collected by the emperor, others turned to the study of Western techniques introduced by the Jesuits. Among these Jesuits were Giuseppe Castiglione [kah-steel-YOH-nay] (1688–1766) and Jean Denis Attiret [ah-teer-RAY] (1702–1768), both of whom had been trained as painters of religious subjects before being sent to China in 1715. Once there, Castiglione virtually abandoned his religious training and worked in the court, where he was known as Lang Shi'ning. He painted imperial portraits, still lifes, horses, dogs, and architectural scenes, and even designed French-style gardens on the model of Versailles. A series of prints made for the Qianlong emperor celebrated the suppression of rebellions in the Western provinces (present-day Xingjiang). The print illustrated here, *The Presentation of Uigur*

Captives, from the series *Battle Scenes of the Quelling of Rebellions in the Western Regions, with Imperial Poems,* is a fine example of the representation of space through careful scientific perspective, a practice virtually unknown in Chinese painting before 1700 (Fig. **25.26**). It is the kind of work that made painters like Castiglione and Attiret extremely popular in the Qianlong court, for it combines an Eastern appreciation for the order of the political state with the Western use of perspective.

But it was not at court that Western conventions were most fully expressed. In the port cities such as Yangzhou and Guangzhou, throughout the eighteenth century, Chinese artists created images for export to both the West and Japan. At the same time, Westernized ceramics became very popular with the increasingly wealthy Chinese mercantile class. Local commercial artists decorated ceramic wares with images provided by European traders, such as the bowl illustrating Hogarth's print of *The Gates of Calais* [kah-LAY] (Fig. **25.27**). As Western trading companies placed large orders to meet the European demand for ceramics,

Chinese artists mastered the art of perspective. Especially popular were aerial views of cities (Fig. 25.28). Perspectival space appealed to the Chinese audience because it was both novel and exotic. The Western audience, used to perspective, found the views of urban China exotic in themselves.

As much as the Qianlong emperor enjoyed Western artistic conventions, he valued traditional Chinese art more. He commissioned large numbers of works painted in the manner of earlier masters, especially those of the Song [soong] dynasty (see Chapter 11). A perfect example is *A Thousand Peaks and Myriad Ravines* (Fig. **25.29**), painted by Wang Hui [wahng hwee] (1632–1717). In typical literati fashion, the artist has added a poem at the top of the painting, by Li Cheng [lee-chung], a Tang dynasty master:

> Moss and weeds cover the rocks and mist hovers over the water
> The sound of dripping water is heard in front of the temple gate.
> Through a thousand peaks and myriad ravines the spring flows,
> And brings the flying flowers into the sacred caves.

Below these lines Wang Hui states his artistic sources:

> In the fourth month of the year 1693, in an inn in the capital, I painted this based on a Tang dynasty poem in the manner of the [painters] Dong [Yuan] and Ju[ran].

Both poem and painting display the conventional elements of Chinese painting. Mountains rise over the valley

Fig. 25.28 Anonymous, *View of Suzhou Showing the Gate of Changmen*. 1734. Color print from woodblock, 42 3/4″ × 22″ (108 × 56 cm). Ohsha'joh Museum of Art, Hiroshima, Japan. Suzhou was a center of printmaking and luxury manufactured goods and was a popular tourist destination. Notice the three-masted Western ship in the harbor.

Fig. 25.29 Wang Hui, *A Thousand Peaks and Myriad Ravines*. Qing dynasty. 1693. Hanging scroll, ink on paper, 8′ 2 1/2″ × 3′ 4 1/2″. National Palace Museum, Taipei, Taiwan. Wang Hui was known, even in his own day, for his ability to synthesize the techniques of the old masters.

as prominently as the emperor overseeing his people (see *Closer Look,* Chapter 11, pages 366–367). A vast cosmic flow of river and stream, cascading waterfalls, jagged rock, and trees ready to flower dwarf all evidence of human life, including a temple on the right bank in the middle distance and the barely noticeable fishermen, wandering scholars, and priests who fill the scene.

Celebrating Tradition: The Great Jade Carving

The Qianlong emperor had already celebrated the conquest of the far western city of Khotan [koe-THAN] by commissioning a series of etchings from the Jesuit artists in his court (see Fig. 25.26). Not long after, in the late 1770s, he would have reason to celebrate again. Digging not far from Khotan, workers unearthed the largest single boulder of jade ever discovered. It was 7 feet 4 inches high, over 3 feet in diameter, and it weighed nearly 6 tons. It took three years to bring the stone to Beijing, transported on a huge wagon drawn by 100 horses, and a retinue of 1,000 men to construct the necessary roads and bridges.

The Qianlong emperor immediately understood the stone's value—not just as an enormous piece of jade, but as a natural wonder of potentially limitless propagandistic value. He himself picked the subject to be carved on the stone: it would be based on an anonymous Song painting in his collection depicting the mythical emperor Yu [yoo] the Great (2205–2197 BCE) taming a flood. In this way, it would connect the Qianlong emperor to one of the oldest emperors in Chinese history and, implicitly, establish the continuity of the Qing dynasty with all that had preceded it.

The Qianlong court kept meticulous records of the jade's carving. Workers first made a full-size wax model of the stone. Then artists in the imperial household carved it to resemble what was to be the finished work. The emperor personally viewed and approved the carved model. Then, because he felt that Beijing jade-carvers were not as accomplished as those in Yangzhou [yahng-joe], the center of luxury goods manufacturing, he decided to ship the model south. But fearing that the excessive heat of Yangzhou's southern climate would melt the wax model, he ordered another model to be made in wood. A team of Yangzhou craftsmen carved the stone in 7 years, 8 months—a total of 150,000 working days!

Meanwhile, the wooden model was shipped back to Beijing, where the emperor tried it out in various locations around the palace. When the actual jade returned in 1787, he placed it in the spot in the palace where it still stands today (Fig. **25.30**). On the base of the stone, a carved inscription eulogized both Yu the Great and the great stone itself, and linked them to the magnificence of the Qianlong emperor himself.

The story of Yu the Great first appears in *The Book of History,* a collection edited by Confucius in the fourth century BCE (see Chapter 4). When the farmlands of the Yellow River valley were inundated by a great flood, the emperor Shun ordered Yu to device some means of controlling it. With the help of all the princes who ruled in the valley, Yu organized an army of people who, over the course

Fig. 25.30 *Yu the Great Taming the Waters.* **Qing Dynasty, completed 1787.** Jade carving, $7'1/_4'' \times 3'1^3/_4''$. Collection of The Palace Museum, Beijing. The black area at the sculpture's base, full of swirling waves, represents the waters that Yu the Great is in the process of taming. The implication is that as the water recedes, the green plenty of the earth (represented by the green jade) will be restored.

of 13 years, cut channels in the land to drain the flood waters into the sea. *Yu the Great Taming the Waters* is not, in other words, the representation of a miracle, but a celebration of hard work, organizational skill, and dedicated service to one's ruler—traditional Confucian [kun-FYOO-shun] values. It is hard to say just which of the many humans carved onto the surface of the stone is Yu, because all are equally at work, digging, building, and pumping the waters of the Yellow River to the sea. Formally, in the way that a set of flowing curves seem to hold the strong diagonals of the jade and broad sweeps of stone balance its intimate detail, the sculpture also suggests the overall unity of purpose that characterizes the ideal Chinese state.

The End of the Rococo

A major talent of the Rococo era was the painter Marie-Louise-Elisabeth Vigée-Lebrun (1755–1842), whose career spanned two centuries. By 1775, when she was only 20 years old, her paintings were commanding the highest prices in Paris. Vigée-Lebrun painted virtually all the famous members of the French aristocracy, including on many occasions Marie-Antoinette, Louis XVI's queen, for whom she served as official portraitist.

Vigée-Lebrun was an ardent royalist, deeply committed to the monarchy. When she submitted *Marie-Antoinette en chemise* (Fig. **25.31**) to the Salon of 1783, she was asked to withdraw it, because many on the committee thought the very expensive gown the queen wore in the painting was lingerie—*chemise*, in French usage, refers to undergarments. But the queen herself adored the painting, with its soft curves and petal-like textures. It presents her as the ideal Rococo female, the *fête galante*'s very object of desire.

Within six years, the French nation was convulsed by revolution and Marie-Antoinette had fallen completely from grace. When Jacques-Louis David (1748–1825)

sketched her from a second-story window as she was transported by cart to the guillotine on October 16, 1793, she was dressed in a much humbler chemise and cap (Fig. **25.32**). Her chin is thrust forward in defiance and perhaps a touch of disdain, but her erect posture hints at the aristocratic grandeur she once enjoyed. David was one of the great painters of the period, and his career, like Vigée-Lebrun's, spanned two centuries. In fact, and as we shall soon see, his large-scale paintings with their classical structure and balance explicitly reject the Rococo values of the French monarchy. Instead, they embrace the moral authority of the French people who overthrew so corrupt a court.

Meanwhile, Marie-Antoinette's favorite painter, Vigée-Lebrun, escaped from Paris, traveling first to Italy, then Vienna, and finally Saint Petersburg. In all of these places, she continued to paint for royal patrons in the Rococo style she had used in France. Finally, in 1802, after 255 fellow artists petitioned the government, she was allowed to return to France, where, ever the ardent royalist, she lived in obscurity for the next 40 years. ∎

Fig. 25.31 Elisabeth-Louise Vigée, *Marie-Antoinette en* **Chemise. 1783.** Oil on canvas, 33 ¹/₂″ × 28 ¹/₄″. Hessische Hausstiftung (Hessian House Foundation) Museum Schloss Fasanerie.

Fig. 25.32 Jacques-Louis David, *Marie-Antoinette conduite au supplice* (*Queen Marie-Antoinette on the way to the guillotine*). 1793. Ink drawing. DR 3599 Coll. Rothschild. Musee du Louvre/RMN Reunion des Musees Nationaux, France. SCALA/Art Resource, New York.

What is the Rococo?

The Rococo is a decorative style of art that originated in the *hôtels* and salons of Paris. It is characterized by S- and C-curves, shell, wing, scroll, and plant tendril forms, and cartouches. Parisian court life was conducted in the Rococo salons of the city's hostesses, where *philosophes*, artists, and intellectuals gathered, and where there was a continuing tension between the aims and values of the French monarchy and the Enlightenment views of the *philosophes*. On the one hand, artists, such as Jean-Antoine Watteau, captured the court's Rococo style in paintings of *fêtes galantes*. How would you characterize the emotional content of Watteau's *fêtes galantes*? How is this emotional content carried forward in the paintings of François Boucher and his pupil, Jean-Honoré Fragonard?

Across the royal courts of Europe, the Rococo style of the French court was widely emulated. In Germany at Würzburg, the architect Balthasar Neumann and the painter Giovanni Tiepolo created an elaborate Rococo interior for the prince-bishop's Residenz. In Prussia, Frederick the Great decorated his country palace of Sanssouci in a Rococo style. The palace's surrounding gardens forsook the straight and geometrical layout of the French garden, substituting the new English garden design. What are the characteristics of the English garden?

Who are the philosophes*?*

In France, the *philosophes* carried the ideals of the Enlightenment forward, often in open opposition to the absolutist French court. What were the primary sources of the conflict between the *philosophes* and the French court? The *philosophes* were mostly deists, who accepted the idea that God created the universe but did not have much, if anything, to do with its day-to-day workings. What was the guiding principle of Diderot's *Encyclopédie*? In what ways was Jean-Jacques Rousseau's profoundly personal autobiography, *Confessions,* antagonistic to Enlightenment ideals? How, nevertheless, did his other writings—like *Émile* and *The Social Contract*—influence Enlightenment thinking? Finally, the satirist Voltaire challenged all the forms of absolutism and fanaticism that he saw in the world, especially in his satirical narrative *Candide.* How would you compare Voltaire's satires to those of his English contemporaries such as Jonathan Swift and Alexander Pope?

The *philosophes* also contributed to the development of art criticism and theory. In his critical reviews called *Salons*, Diderot declared Boucher's work depraved. Why did he champion the paintings of Jean-Baptiste-Siméon Chardin? It was at this time that the fine arts began to distinguish themselves from the liberal arts, and that Gotthold Ephraim Lessing distinguished between the visual arts and poetry in his treatise *Laocoön*. What, according to Lessing, distinguishes the one from the other?

What are the characteristics of Classical music?

Rococo musical taste centered on light, airy tunes with intricate and complex rhythms generally played on the harpsichord in what came to be known as the *style galant.* François Couperin and Jean-Philippe Rameau were its chief proponents. Classical music is very different and developed in opposition to the Rococo style. It shares with Greek and Roman art the essential features of symmetry, proportion, balance, formal unity, and clarity. The symphony orchestra, the primary vehicle of Classical music, was first conceived by Johann Stamitz in the 1740s. What are the major structural divisions of the Classical symphony? Two of the greatest composers of symphonies were Joseph Haydn and Wolfgang Amadeus Mozart. Haydn was also instrumental in developing the form of the string quartet. Mozart was able to bring competing musical elements into a state of classical balance like no composer before him, but why was it criticized in his own day? Mozart also synthesized the two contrasting types of opera most popular at the time: *opera seria* and *opera buffa.* What is the difference between the two? Mozart called the new form *opera giocoso* and used it in four operas, of which *Don Giovanni* is a good example. How does the popularity of opera reflect the decline of the Rococo?

How did China and the West influence one another?

Trade with China brought luxury goods from Asia to European markets in vast quantities, creating a widespread taste in Europe for "things Chinese"—chinoiserie. How would you define *chinoiserie*? European thinkers such as Rousseau and Voltaire thought that China offered a model of exemplary government, and Samuel Johnson believed that the West should adopt the Chinese civil-service examination system. During the Qing dynasty, the West influenced China as well. What Western art technique did the Jesuit priest Giuseppe Castiglione introduce to the court of the Qianlong emperor? Traders also introduced Western conventions of representation as they gave Chinese artisans images for reproduction on ceramic ware and other luxury goods destined for Europe. But the Qianlong emperor valued traditional Chinese art above all else. His court painters copied the masters of the Song era, and the emperor modeled his giant jade carving of *Yu the Great Taming the Waters* on Song precedents.

PRACTICE MORE Get flashcards for images and terms and review chapter material with quizzes at **www.myartslab.com**

GLOSSARY

cartouche An elaborate frame.

castrato A male singer who, in order to retain his high voice, was castrated before puberty.

chinoiserie A term used to define the European taste for "all things Chinese."

Classical music A style of music that developed in Europe about 1760 and lasted into the nineteenth century as an alternative to and rejection of the Rococo and Baroque; it shares with Greek and Roman art the essential features of symmetry, proportion, balance, formal unity, and, perhaps above all, clarity.

da capo aria A type of aria in the ABA form in which the singer was expected to embellish the music, especially in the return of the A.

deist One who accepts the idea that God created the universe but does not believe that God is actively involved in its day-to-day workings.

dramma giocoso Literally "comic drama," Mozart's name for his last four operas, which combine both *opera seria* and *opera buffa* styles.

dynamics A notation in a musical score that indicates relative loudness (for example, *forte* for loud; *piano* for soft).

English garden A type of garden design of artificial naturalness that became popular in England beginning in the early 1700s with irregular features and winding walkways.

fête galante A gallant and, by extension, amorous celebration or party.

key signature The scale upon which a piece is based.

natural law Law derived from nature and binding upon human society.

opera buffa Comic opera, featuring everyday characters.

opera seria Literally "serious opera," emphasizing virtuoso singing, featuring themes from ancient history and mythology.

pace A notation in a musical *score* that indicates rate of movement (for example, *allegro*, for fast; *lente*, for slow).

philosophes The "philosophers" who dominated the intellectual life of the French Enlightenment and who frequented *salons*.

pianoforte A type of piano that could play both soft (*piano*) and loud (*forte*) sounds.

rational humanism The belief that through logical, careful thought, progress is inevitable.

Rococo The highly decorative and ornate style employed by the French court that was quickly emulated by royal courts across Europe, especially in Germany.

salon A room designed especially for social gatherings; later, also referred to the social gathering itself.

salonnière The hostess of a French salon.

score A musical composition that indicates what music is to be played by each instrument.

sonata form A kind of small form within the larger symphonic form.

string quartet A group of musicians playing four instruments from the same family—two violins, a viola, and a cello—thus lending the music a distinctly homogenous sound.

style galant A *Rococo* style of music characterized by graceful melodies, many of them dance pieces with charmingly simple harmonies.

symphony A musical composition typically consisting of a first movement played in a fast tempo (*allegro*); a second movement that is slow (*adagio* or *andante*) and reflective; a third that picks up the pace again; and a fourth that is generally *allegro* once again, spirited and lively.

symphonic orchestra A large ensemble that organized the orchestra into separate sections according to type of instrument: strings, woodwinds, brass, and percussion.

time signature The number of beats per measure.

READINGS

READING 25.2

from Jean-Jacques Rousseau, *Confessions*, Book 1 (completed 1770, published 1780)

The first two paragraphs of Confessions *set out the author's intention of total revelation, which he claims is totally new. In fact,* Confessions *does reveal more about the writer's private self than any other work before it. Only Montaigne's* Essais *come close. The* Confessions *are sometimes almost unbearably honest. In the longer excerpt below, Rousseau reveals his "spanking" fetish. Above all, the* Confessions *stands out as a supreme example of the autobiographical impulse in Enlightenment thought, the need to know oneself in as much detail as possible.*

[1712–1719]—I am commencing an undertaking, hitherto without precedent, and which will never find an imitator. I desire to set before my fellows the likeness of a man in all the truth of nature, and that man myself.

Myself alone! I know the feelings of my heart, and I know men. I am not made like any of those I have seen; I venture to believe that I am not made like any of those who are in existence. If I am not better, at least I am different. Whether Nature has acted rightly or wrongly in destroying the mold in which she cast me, can only be decided after I have been read. . . . 10

As Mademoiselle Lambercier had the affection of a mother for us, she also exercised the authority of one, and sometimes carried it so far as to inflict upon us the punishment of children when we had deserved it. For some time she was content with threats, and this threat of a punishment that was quite new to me appeared very terrible; but, after it had been carried out, I found the reality less terrible than the expectation; and what was still more strange, this chastisement made me still more devoted to her who had inflicted it. It needed all the strength of this devotion and all my natural docility to keep myself from doing something which would have deservedly brought upon me a repetition of it; for I had found in the pain, even in the disgrace, a mixture of sensuality which had left me less afraid than desirous of experiencing it again from the same hand. No doubt some precocious sexual instinct was mingled with this feeling, for the same chastisement inflicted by her brother would not have seemed to me at all pleasant. But, considering his disposition, there was little cause to fear the substitution; and if I kept myself from deserving punishment, it was solely for fear of displeasing Mademoiselle Lambercier; for, so great is the power exercised over me by kindness, even by that which is due to the senses, that it has always controlled the latter in my heart.

The repetition of the offense, which I avoided without being afraid of it, occurred without any fault of mine, that is to say, of my will, and I may say that I profited by it without any qualm of conscience. But this second time was also the last; for Mademoiselle Lambercier, who had no doubt noticed something which convinced her that the punishment did not have the desired effect, declared that it tired her too much, and that she would abandon it. Until then we had slept in her room, sometimes even in her bed during the winter. Two days afterwards we were put to sleep in another room, and from that time I had the honor, which I would gladly have dispensed with, of being treated by her as a big boy.

Who would believe that this childish punishment, inflicted upon me when only eight years old by a young woman of thirty,[1] disposed of my tastes, my desires, my passions, and my own self for the remainder of my life, and that in a manner exactly contrary to that which should have been the natural result? When my feelings were once inflamed, my desires so went astray that, limited to what I had already felt, they did not trouble themselves to look for anything else. In spite of my hot blood, which has been inflamed with sensuality almost from my birth, I kept myself free from every taint until the age when the coldest and most sluggish temperaments begin to develop. In torments for a long time, without knowing why, I devoured with burning glances all the pretty women I met; my imagination unceasingly recalled them to me, only to make use of them in my own fashion, and to make of them so many Mlles. Lambercier.

Even after I had reached years of maturity, this curious taste, always abiding with me and carried to depravity and even frenzy, preserved my morality, which it might naturally have been expected to destroy. If ever a bringing-up was chaste and modest, assuredly mine was. My three aunts were not only models of propriety, but reserved to a degree which has long since been unknown amongst women. My father, a man of pleasure, but a gallant of the old school, never said a word, even in the presence of women whom he loved more than others, which would have brought a blush to a maiden's cheek; and the respect due to children has never been so much insisted upon as in my family and in my presence. In this respect I found M. Lambercier equally careful; and an excellent servant was dismissed for having used a somewhat too free expression in our presence. Until I was a young man, I not only had no distinct idea of the union of the sexes, but the confused notion which I had regarding it never presented itself to me except in a hateful and disgusting form. For common prostitutes I felt a loathing which has never been effaced: the sight of a profligate always filled me with contempt, even with affright. My horror of debauchery became thus pronounced ever since the day when, walking to Little Sacconex[2] by a hollow way, I saw on both sides holes in the ground, where I was told that these creatures carried on their intercourse. The thought of the one always brought back to my mind the copulation of dogs, and the bare recollection was sufficient to disgust me.

This tendency of my bringing-up, in itself adapted to delay the first outbreaks of an inflammable temperament, was assisted, as I have already said, by the direction which the first indications of sensuality took in my case. Only busying my imagination with what I had actually felt, in spite of most uncomfortable effervescence of blood, I only knew how to turn my desires in the direction of that kind of pleasure with which I was acquainted, without ever going as far as that which had been made hateful to me, and which, without my having the least suspicion of it, was so closely related to the other. In my foolish fancies, in my erotic frenzies, in the extravagant acts to which they sometimes led me, I had recourse in my imagination to the assistance of the other sex, without ever thinking that it was serviceable for any purpose than that for which I was burning to make use of it.

In this manner, then, in spite of an ardent, lascivious and precocious temperament, I passed the age of puberty without desiring, even without knowing of any other sensual pleasures than those of which Mademoiselle Lambercier had most innocently given me the idea; and when, in course of time, I became a man, that which should have destroyed me again preserved me. My old childish taste, instead of disappearing, became so associated with the other, that I could never banish it from the desires kindled by my senses; and this madness, joined to my natural shyness, has always made me very unenterprising with women, for want of courage to say all or power to do all. The kind of enjoyment, of which the other was only for me the final consummation, could neither be appropriated by him who longed for it, nor guessed by her who was able to bestow it. Thus I have spent my life in idle longing, without saying a word, in the presence of those whom I loved most. Too bashful to declare my taste, I at least satisfied it in situations which had reference to it and kept up the idea of it. To lie at the feet of an imperious mistress, to obey her commands, to ask her forgiveness—this was for me a sweet enjoyment; and, the more my lively imagination heated my blood, the more I presented the appearance of a bashful lover. It may be easily imagined that this manner of making love does not lead to very speedy results, and is not very dangerous to the virtue of those who are its object. For this reason I have rarely possessed, but have none the less enjoyed myself in my own way—that is to say, in imagination. Thus it has happened that my senses, in harmony with my timid disposition and my romantic spirit, have kept my sentiments pure and my morals blameless, owing to the very tastes which, combined with a little more impudence, might have plunged me into the most brutal sensuality.

READING CRITICALLY

One of the great questions Rousseau's *Confessions* raises concerns the quality of its purported honesty. Is such self-revelation evidence of Rousseau's sincerity and humility or the manifestation of a kind of perverse pride?

---

[1] Actually, at the time described, Mlle. Lambercier was about 38 and Rousseau about 11.

[2] A village on the outskirts of Geneva.

from Voltaire, *Candide* (1758)

The following excerpt narrates a few of the many adventures of Candide and Dr. Pangloss. In Chapter 6, the Inquisition punishes Candide and Pangloss, blaming them for the earthquake that destroyed Lisbon on November 1, 1755. Pangloss is hanged, and Candide believes the philosopher to be dead. Not until Chapter 28 does he learn otherwise, when the two are reunited and Pangloss tells him how he narrowly escaped death. These two passages convey Voltaire's conviction that religion is based in superstition and illusion even as they satirize the foolishness of Pangloss's philosophical optimism.

CHAPTER 6

HOW THE PORTUGUESE MADE A SUPERB AUTO-DA-FÉ TO PREVENT ANY FUTURE EARTHQUAKES, AND HOW CANDIDE UNDERWENT PUBLIC FLAGELLATION

After the earthquake which had destroyed three-quarters of the city of Lisbon[1] the sages of that country could think of no means more effectual to preserve the kingdom from utter ruin, than to entertain the people with an *auto-da-fé*,[2] it having been decided by the University of Coimbra that burning a few people alive by a slow fire, and with great ceremony, is an infallible secret to prevent earthquakes.

In consequence thereof they had seized on a Biscayan for marrying his godmother, and on two Portuguese for taking out the bacon of a larded pullet they were eating.[3] After dinner, they came and secured Dr. Pangloss, and his pupil Candide; the one for speaking his mind, and the other for seeming to approve what he had said. They were conducted to separate apartments, extremely cool, where they were never incommoded with the sun. Eight days afterwards they were each dressed in a *fanbenito*,[4] and their heads were adorned with paper mitres. The mitre and *fanbenito* worn by Candide were painted with flames reversed, and with devils that had neither tails nor claws; but Dr. Pangloss's devils had both tails and claws, and his flames were upright. In these habits they marched in procession, and heard a very pathetic sermon, which was followed by a chant, beautifully intoned. Candide was flogged in regular cadence, while the chant was being sung; the Biscayan, and the two men who would not eat bacon, were burnt, and Pangloss was hanged, although this is not a common custom at these solemnities. The same day there was another earthquake, which made most dreadful havoc.[5]

Candide, amazed, terrified, confounded, astonished, and trembling from head to foot, said to himself, 'If this is the best of all possible worlds, what are the others? If I had only been whipped, I could have put up with it, as I did among the Bulgarians; but, O my dear Pangloss! thou greatest of philosophers! that ever I should live to see thee hanged, without knowing for what!

CHAPTER 28

WHAT BEFELL CANDIDE, CUNEGUNDE, PANGLOSS, MARTIN, &C.

"But how happens it that I behold you again, my dear Pangloss?" said Candide.

"It is true," answered Pangloss, "you saw me hanged, though I ought properly to have been burnt; but you may remember that it rained extremely hard when they were going to roast me. The storm was so violent that they found it impossible to light the fire; so they hanged me because they could do no better. A surgeon purchased my body, carried it home, and prepared to dissect me. He began by making a crucial incision from my navel to the clavicle. It is impossible for any one to have been more lamely hanged than I had been. The executioner of the Holy Inquisition was a subdeacon, and knew how to burn people very well, but as for hanging, he was a novice at it, being quite out of the way of his practice; the cord being wet, and not slipping properly, the noose did not join. In short, I still continued to breathe; the crucial incision made me scream to such a degree that my surgeon fell flat upon his back; and imagining it was the devil he was dissecting, ran away, and in his fright tumbled downstairs. His wife hearing the noise flew from the next room, and, seeing me stretched upon the table with my crucial incision, was still more terrified than her husband. She took to her heels and fell over him. When they had a little recovered themselves, I heard her say to her husband, 'My dear, how could you think of dissecting an heretic? Don't you know that the devil is always in them? I'll run directly to a priest to come and drive the evil spirit out.' I trembled from head to foot at hearing her talk in this manner, and exerted what little strength I had left to cry out, 'Have mercy on me!' At length the Portuguese barber took courage, sewed up my wound, and his wife nursed me; and I was upon my legs in a fortnight's time. The barber got me a place as lackey to a Knight of Malta who was going to Venice; but finding my master had no money to pay me my wages, I entered into the service of a Venetian merchant, and went with him to Constantinople."

"One day I happened to enter a mosque, where I saw no one but an old imam and a very pretty young female devotee, who was

---

[1] Lisbon was destroyed by an earthquake on November 1, 1755.
[2] An *auto-da-fé*, literally, an "act of faith." In the Inquisition, it was the announcement of judgment generally followed by execution.
[3] By marrying his godmother, the Biscayan is guilty of spiritual incest. By not eating bacon, the two Portuguese are assumed to be Jews.
[4] A long yellow garment worn by the criminals of the Inquisition.
[5] Lisbon suffered a second earthquake on December 21, 1755.

saying her prayers; her neck was quite bare, and in her bosom she had a beautiful nosegay of tulips, roses, anemones, ranunculuses, hyacinths, and auriculas. She let fall her nosegay. I ran immediately to take it up, and presented it to her with a most respectful bow. I was so long in delivering it, that the imam began to be angry; and, perceiving I was a Christian, he cried out for help; they carried me before the cadi, who ordered me to receive one hundred bastina-does, and sent me to the galleys. I was chained in the very galley, and to the very same bench with my lord the Baron. On board this 80 galley there were four young men belonging to Marseilles, five Neapolitan priests, and two monks of Corfu, who told us that the like adventures happened every day. The Baron pretended that he had been worse used than myself; and I insisted that there was far less harm in taking up a nosegay, and putting it into a woman's bo-som, than to be found stark naked with a young Icoglan. We were

continually in dispute, and received twenty lashes a-day with a thong, when the concatenation of sublunary events brought you on board our galley to ransom us from slavery."

"Well, my dear Pangloss," said Candide to him, "when you 90 were hanged, dissected, whipped, and tugging at the oar, did you continue to think that every thing in this world happens for the best?"

"I have always abided by my first opinion," answered Pan-gloss; "for, after all, I am a philosopher …

READING CRITICALLY

In what way does Pangloss's philosophical optimism directly contradict the philosophy of John Locke and by extension other Enlightenment thinkers?

The BLOODY MASSACRE perpetrated in King—t—Street BOSTON on March 5th 1770, by a party of the 29th REG.t

BUTCHER'S HALL

CUSTOM HOUSE

Engrav'd Printed & Sold by PAUL REVERE BOSTON

happy BOSTON! see thy Sons deplore,
y hallow'd Walks besmear'd with guiltless Gore:
ile faithless P—n and his savage Bands,
th murd'rous Rancour stretch their bloody Hands;
ke fierce Barbarians grinning o'er their Prey,
pprove the Carnage, and enjoy the Day.

If scalding drops from Rage from Anguish Wrung
If speechless Sorrows lab'ring for a Tongue,
Or if a weeping World can ought appease
The plaintive Ghosts of Victims such as these:
The Patriot's copious Tears for each are shed,
A glorious Tribute which embalms the Dead.

But know, FATE summons to that awful Goal,
Where JUSTICE strips the Murd'rer of his Soul:
Should venal C—ts the scandal of the Land,
Snatch the relentless Villain from her Hand,
Keen Execrations on this Plate inscrib'd,
Shall reach a JUDGE who never can be brib'd.

The unhappy Sufferers were Messrs SAML GRAY SAML MAVERICK, JAMS CALDWELL, CRISPUS ATTUCKS & PATK CARR
Killed. Six wounded, two of them (CHRISTR MONK & JOHN CLARK) Mortally

26

The Rights of Man
Revolution and the Neoclassical Style

THINKING AHEAD

What do the American and French Revolutions have in common? How do they differ?

How did women respond to the promise of revolution?

What is Neoclassicism?

What values shaped Napoleonic France?

How did the issue of slavery undermine the idealism of the era?

On March 5, 1770, an angry mob of Bostonians attacked a small band of British troops stationed at the Boston Custom House to protect its customs agents and tax collectors. Five years earlier, in 1765, the British had challenged the American colonies' growing sense of independence by imposing a Stamp Act, which taxed all sorts of items, from legal documents to playing cards, calendars, liquor licenses, newspapers, and academic degrees. The colonists were infuriated, calling the Stamp Act a "manifest" example of the British desire "to subvert the rights and liberties of the colonies." Tensions finally erupted at the Boston Customs House. The mob was yelling "Kill them! Kill them!" when the British troops opened fire, killing five, including Crispus Attucks, an African American who had escaped slavery 20 years earlier. The silversmith and engraver Paul Revere (1735–1818) quickly produced a print depicting the event called *The Bloody Massacre* (Fig. **26.1**). It was widely distributed, arousing the colonists

to even greater resistance, although its depiction of the troops' brutally attacking a defenseless crowd misrepresented the facts.

By the last half of the eighteenth century, the demand for freedom had become a rallying cry in America and throughout Europe. In Germany, in fact, the philosopher Immanuel Kant (1724–1804) argued in his essay "What Is Enlightenment?" (1784) that the very precondition of the Enlightenment was freedom:

> *Dare to know!* "Have the courage to use your own understanding"—that is the motto of Enlightenment. . . .
>
> [T]hat the public should enlighten itself is more possible; indeed, if only freedom is granted enlightenment is almost sure to follow. For there will always be some independent thinkers, even among the established guardians of the great masses, who, after throwing off the yoke of tutelage from their own shoulders, will

◀ **Fig. 26.1 Paul Revere, after Henry Pelham, *The Bloody Massacre*. 1770.** Hand-colored engraving, $8^{15}/_{16}$″ × $10^{3}/_{16}$″. The Metropolitan Museum of Art, New York. © Massachusetts Historical Society, Boston, MA. The Bridgeman Art Library. Though it served to inflame the nation, Revere's print was largely fiction. John Adams defended the British troops in court, arguing that the soldiers had been attacked by a mob. "Facts are stubborn things," he concluded, "and whatever may be our wishes, our inclinations, or the dictums of our passions, they cannot alter the state of facts and evidence." The jury acquitted the British commander and six of the eight soldiers.

HEAR MORE Listen to an audio file of your chapter at **www.myartslab.com**

Map 26.1 North America in 1763, after the conclusion of the Seven Years' War.

disseminate the spirit of the rational appreciation of both their own worth and every man's vocation for thinking for himself. It is more nearly possible, however, for the public to enlighten itself; indeed, if it is only given freedom, enlightenment is almost inevitable. . . .

For this enlightenment, however, nothing is required but freedom, and indeed the most harmless among all the things to which this term can properly be applied. It is the freedom to make public use of one's reason at every point.

Enlightenment historian Peter Gay sums up the driving forces of the era as "freedom from arbitrary power, freedom of speech, freedom of trade, freedom to realize one's talents, freedom of aesthetic response, freedom, in a word, of moral man to make his way in the world."

The drive for these freedoms, first expressed in violence at the Boston Custom House, was repeated in May 1773, when the British introduced another law allowing direct importation of tea into the Americas without the usual colonial tax. It was met with opposition not only

because it thus reduced an important colonial revenue stream without the colonists' consent, but also because it removed colonial middlemen from participation in the tea trade. The following December, Massachusetts Bay colonists gathered at the Boston waterfront and cheered as a group of men dressed as Native Americans, almost all of them with a financial stake in the tea market, emptied three ships of thousands of pounds of tea, dumping it into the harbor. The so-called Boston Tea Party outraged the British, and they soon retaliated. The Revolutionary War was about to begin.

In Paris, 16 years later, on July 14, 1789, a mob gathered outside the Bastille, a prison on the eastern edge of the city, upset by rumors, probably true, that King Louis XVI (r. 1774–1792) was about to overthrow the National Assembly. The prison governor panicked and ordered his guard to fire on the crowd. In retaliation, the mob stormed the Bastille, decapitating the prison governor and slaughtering six of the guards. The only practical effect of the battle was to free a few prisoners, but the next day Louis XVI asked if the incident had been a riot. "No, your majesty," was the reply, "it was a revolution."

The social changes produced by these two revolutions strongly influenced world history, and would spur the nineteenth-century revolutions in South America, again in France, and, in 1848, all across Europe. The American Revolution was essentially the revolt of an upper class that felt disenfranchised by its distant king, while the French Revolution was a revolt against an absolute monarch whose abuse of power had disenfranchised his own people. But both the French and the Americans looked to classical antiquity for models upon which to build their new societies. Theirs would be Neoclassical societies—stable, balanced, and rational cultures that might imitate their admittedly idealized view of Rome and Athens. In the arts, classical traditions were expressed in a style known as Neoclassicism, literally a "new classicism." The style was most eloquently expressed in Britain, in the architectural and interior designs of Robert Adam and in the decorative ceramics of Josiah Wedgwood. Both were widely imitated in the fledgling United States, where Thomas Jefferson was Neoclassicism's principal advocate. Jefferson designed his own home at Monticello, the Virginia capital, and even laid out the new national capital of Washington, D.C., using the trademarks of the Neoclassical style—balance and order. Leading the way in France were painters Jacques-Louis David [dah-VEED] (1748–1825), probably the most influential artist of the era, and Angelica Kauffmann (1741–1807), probably the most popular.

The idealism embodied in Neoclassicism, its call for order, balance, and proportion, was countermanded in America by the inequalities embodied in the slave trade, and in France by the chaos and terror that followed hard upon the Revolution of 1789. By 1700, the slave trade had helped make England the wealthiest nation in the world, and the economy of the American South depended

Fig. 26.2 John Trumbull, *The Declaration of Independence, 4 July 1776*. 1786–97. Oil on canvas, 21 $^1/_8$″ × 31$^1/_8$″. Trumbull Collection. 1832.3, Yale University Art Gallery, New Haven, CT/Art Resource, New York. The canvas portrays 47 of the 56 delegates who signed the Declaration of Independence, and Trumbull painted 36 of them from life. Standing in front of John Hancock are, from left to right, John Adams, Roger Sherman, Robert R. Livingston, Thomas Jefferson, and Benjamin Franklin.

on it, to say nothing of the port cities of the North, particularly Providence and Boston. But no one could long ignore the hypocrisy of demanding human rights and freedom for some while subjugating others to abject misery and enslavement. And women, in both France and America, argued for their own equality in the same terms. Were they not, they argued, entitled to the same freedoms as their husbands and brothers? In France, the revolution deposed the monarchy, executing both Louis XVI and his queen, Marie Antoinette, and, as a result, Europe's other monarchies—especially those in Germany—threatened it from without even as royalists from within worked to reinstate the crown. France soon fell into a state of mutual distrust and vindictive retribution. Hardly anyone was exempt from the charge of betraying the revolution—and from the sentence of execution by guillotine. Not until Napoleon Bonaparte, a young military leader risen from within the army's ranks, took control of the country was order restored and with it the values of Neoclassicism.

THE AMERICAN AND FRENCH REVOLUTIONS

The American Declaration of Independence was signed on July 4, 1776 (Fig. **26.2**), and the French Declaration of the Rights of Man and Citizen on August 26, 1789. The two documents are monuments of Enlightenment thinking, both looking to the writings of John Locke for inspiration (see Chapter 24), and the French Declaration of the Rights of Man and Citizen influenced as well by the American Declaration.

The Road to Revolt in America: War and Taxation

Since August 1774, representatives from the 13 British colonies in North America (see Map **26.1**) had periodically gathered in the city of Philadelphia to consider what action the colonies might take against the tyrannical behavior of the British king. Philadelphia was the largest city in the colonies, boasting 7 newspapers, 23 printing presses, 30 bookstores, and over 60 taverns and coffee-houses. It produced more goods than any other American city—from hardware to carriages to the Franklin stove. That stove's inventor, Benjamin Franklin (1706–1790), had founded the American Philosophical Society in the city in 1743. (The Society predated the English Lunar Society, which had many of the same aims as its American counterpart.) (See Chapter 24.) The American Philosophical Society was dedicated, Franklin wrote, to the study of anything that might "let light into the nature of things . . . all new-discovered plants, herbs, roots, and methods of propagating them. . . . New methods of curing or preventing diseases. . . . New mechanical inventions for saving labor. . . . All new arts, trades, manufacturers, etc. that may be proposed or thought of." Therefore, when the 48 representatives of the 13 colonies gathered in Philadelphia's State House, now known as Independence Hall, on July 4, 1776, to sign the Declaration of Independence from Britain, the city was the center of the burgeoning nation's economic prosperity and a dominant force in shaping its ideas and policies. The revolt of the colonies followed nearly 200 years of British rule, but the most recent tensions began with the Seven Years' War (1756–1763) fought by Britain and France. The war spread to North America, where the two powers were competing for land and control.

Britain's victory left it the most powerful colonial power in the Americas. The British felt that they had saved the colonists from the French. They had borne almost the entire cost of the war themselves, and they continued to provide protection from Indian uprisings on the western frontier. Consequently, they felt entitled to tax the colonies as needed. The colonists did not agree. The battle at the Boston Custom House and the Boston Tea Party were the expression of their frustration.

The so-called Boston Tea Party especially outraged the British. In 1774, they deeded all the land west of the Alleghenies to Canada and passed what soon became known as the Intolerable Acts, closing the port of Boston to trade, suspending elections in Massachusetts colony, allowing British troops to be quartered in private homes, and providing for the trials of customs officials to take place in England. The colonists responded by forming the First Continental Congress. Meeting in Philadelphia, the Congress declared the Intolerable Acts unconstitutional and called for the people to begin organizing for war. The first gunshots of the Revolutionary War were fired at Lexington and Concord, in Massachusetts, on April 19, 1775, when the British sent a regiment to confiscate arms and arrest revolutionaries. A Second Continental Congress in that year created the Continental Army under the leadership of George Washington and attempted to reconcile with the king, but failed.

In January 1776, in Philadelphia, an anonymous pamphlet written by an English immigrant named Thomas Paine argued for a new **republicanism**. The only solution to the colonists' problems with Britain, he wrote, was independence followed by a republican form of government. Such a government would have a chief of state who is not a monarch. Paine asked, "Why is it that we hesitate? . . . The birthday of a new world is at hand." The pamphlet was called *Common Sense*, and within a matter of months, 100,000 copies were in circulation. Colony-wide war was inevitable. Six months later, the colonies ratified the Declaration of Independence.

The Declaration of Independence

The American Declaration of Independence is one of the Enlightenment's boldest assertions of freedom. The chairman of the committee that prepared the document and its chief drafter was Thomas Jefferson (1743–1826) of Virginia. Jefferson's argument came from his reading of English philosopher John Locke's vigorous denial of the divine rights of kings (see Chapter 24). In *Two Treatises on Government* (1689), Locke asserted that humans are "by nature free, equal, and independent." Jefferson's denunciation of the monarchy was further stimulated by Rousseau's *Social Contract* (1763), and its principal point: "No man has a natural authority over his fellow," wrote Rousseau, "and force creates no right" (see Chapter 29). Jefferson was influenced, too, by the writings of many of his colleagues in the Continental Congress, who were themselves familiar with the writings of Locke and Rousseau. George Mason (1725–1792) had written: "All men are born equally free and independent and have certain inherent natural rights . . . among which are the enjoyment of life and liberty." An even greater source of inspiration came from the writings of Jefferson's friend John Adams (1735–1826), whose Preamble to the Massachusetts State Constitution (1779) reflects their common way of thinking:

> The end of the institution, maintenance, and administration of government is to secure the existence of the body politic; to protect it; and to furnish the individuals who compose it with the power of enjoying, in safety and tranquility, their natural rights and the blessings of life; and whenever these great objects are not obtained, the people have a right to alter the government, and to take measures necessary for their safety, happiness, and prosperity.

But as powerful as the thinking of Mason and Adams might be, neither man could rise to the level of Jefferson's eloquence (**Reading 26.1**):

READING 26.1

from The Declaration of Independence (1776)

When in the Course of human events, it becomes necessary for one people to dissolve the political bands which have connected them with another, and to assume among the powers of the earth, the separate and equal station to which the Laws of Nature and of Nature's God entitle them, a decent respect to the opinions of mankind requires that they should declare the causes which impel them to the separation.

We hold these truths to be self-evident, that all men are created equal, that they are endowed by their Creator with certain unalienable Rights, that among these are Life, Liberty and the pursuit of Happiness.— That to secure these rights, Governments are instituted among Men, deriving their just powers from the consent of the governed,—That whenever any Form of Government becomes destructive of these ends, it is the Right of the People to alter or to abolish it, and to institute new Government, laying its foundation on such principles and organizing its powers in such form, as to them shall seem most likely to effect their Safety and Happiness.

As indebted as it is to John Locke's *Two Treatises of Government*, Jefferson's Declaration extends and modifies Locke's arguments in important ways. While Locke's writings supported a government *for* the people, he did not reject the idea of a monarchy per se. The people would tell the king what he should do, and the king was obligated to respect their rights and needs. But Jefferson rejected the idea of a monarchy altogether and argued that the people were themselves sovereign, that theirs was a government not *for* the people but *of* and *by* the people. Where Locke, in his *Two Treatises*, had argued for "life, liberty, and property," Jefferson argued for "Life, Liberty, and the pursuit of Happiness." Locke's basic rights are designed to guarantee justice. Jefferson's are aimed at achieving human fulfillment, a fulfillment possible only if the people control their own destiny.

After reading Jefferson's document, John Adams wrote to his wife, Abigail, that he was "delighted with its high tone and [the] flights of oratory with which it abounded." When it was read in New York the day after its first presentation in Philadelphia, an enthusiastic mob pulled down a larger-than-life equestrian statue of England's King George III (r. 1760–1820). Later, in August, when the text finally made its way south to Savannah, Georgia, the largest crowd in the colony's history gathered for a mock burial of George III. The document had the power to galvanize the colonies to revolution.

A year after the colonists signed the Declaration of Independence, they adopted the Articles of Confederation, combining the 13 colonies into a loose confederation of sovereign states. The war itself continued into the 1780s and developed an international scope. France, Spain, and the Netherlands supported the revolutionaries with money and naval forces in order to dilute British power. This alliance was critical in helping the Americans defeat the British at Yorktown, Virginia, in 1781. This victory convinced the British that the war was lost and paved the way for the Treaty of Paris, signed on September 3, 1783. The war was over.

The Declaration of the Rights of Man and Citizen

In France, the situation leading to the signing of the Declaration of the Rights of Man and Citizen was somewhat more complicated. It was, in fact, the national debt that abruptly brought about the events leading to revolution, the overthrow of the royal government, and the country becoming a republic. In the 15 years after Louis XVI ascended to the throne in 1774, the debt tripled. In 1788, fully one-half of state revenues were dedicated to paying interest on debt already in place, despite the fact that two years earlier, bankers had refused to make new loans to the government. The cost of maintaining Louis XVI's court was enormous, so the desperate king attempted to levy a uniform tax on all landed property. Riots, led by aristocrat and bourgeois alike, forced the king to bring the issue before an Estates General, an institution little used and indeed half-forgotten (it had not met since 1614).

The Estates General convened on May 5, 1789, at Versailles. It was composed of the three traditional French **estates**. The First Estate was the clergy, which comprised a mere 0.5 percent of the population (130,000 people) but controlled nearly 15 percent of French lands. The Second Estate was the nobility, consisting of only 2 percent of the population (about 500,000 people) but controlling about 30 percent of the land. The Third Estate was the rest of the population, composed of the bourgeoisie (around 2.3 million people), who controlled about 20 percent of the land, and the peasants (nearly 21 million people), who controlled the rest of the land, although many owned no land at all.

Traditionally, each estate deliberated separately and each was entitled to a single vote. Any issue before the Estates General thus required a vote of at least 2:1—and the consent of the crown—for passage. The clergy and nobility usually voted together, thus silencing the opinion of the Third Estate. But from the outset, the Third Estate demanded more clout, and the king was in no position to deny it. The winter of 1788 to 1789 had been the most severe in memory. In December, the temperature had dropped to −19° Celsius (or −2° Fahrenheit), freezing the Seine over to a considerable depth. The ice blockaded barges that normally delivered grain and flour to a city already filled by unemployed peasants seeking work. With flour already in short supply after a violent hailstorm had virtually destroyed the crop the previous summer, the price of bread almost doubled. As the Estates General opened, Louis was forced to appease the Third Estate in any way he could. First he "doubled the third," giving the Third Estate as many deputies as the other two estates combined. Then he was pressured to bring the three estates together to debate and "vote by head," each deputy having a single vote. Louis vacillated on this demand, but on June 17, 1789, the Third Estate withdrew

Fig. 26.3 Jacques-Louis David, *The Tennis Court Oath*. 1789–91. Pen and brown ink and brown wash on paper, 26″ × 42″. Musée National du Château, Versailles. MV 8409: INV Dessins. Photo: Gerard Blot. RMN Réunion des Musées Nationaux/Art Resource, New York. Note how the figures in this painting, all taking an oath, stretch out their hands in the manner of David's earlier Neoclassical masterpiece, *The Oath of the Horatii* (see Fig. 26.17).

from the Estates General, declared itself a National Assembly, and invited the other two estates to join them.

A number of the First Estate, particularly parish priests who worked closely with the common people, accepted the Third Estate's offer, but the nobility refused. When the king banned the commoners from their usual meeting place, they gathered nearby at the Jeu de Paume [zhurd pohm], an indoor tennis court at Versailles that still stands, and there, on June 20, 1789, swore an oath never to disband until they had given France a constitution. Jacques-Louis David recreated the scene a year later in a detailed sketch for a painting that he would never finish, as events overtook its subjects (Fig. 26.3). David's plan, like Trumbull's celebration of the signing of the Declaration of Independence, was to combine exact observation (he drew the major protagonists from life) with monumentality on a canvas where everyone would be life-size (many of his subjects would soon fall out of favor with the revolution itself and be executed). The "winds of freedom" blow in through the windows as commoners look on. At the top left, these same winds turn an umbrella inside out, signaling the change to come. In the middle of the room, the man who would soon become mayor of Paris reads the proclamation aloud. Below him a trio of figures, representing

each of the three estates, clasp hands as equals in a gesture of unity. At the actual event, all of the members of the National Assembly marched in alphabetical order and signed the Tennis Court Oath, except for one. He signed, but wrote after his name the word "opposed." David depicts him, an object of ridicule, seated at the far right, his arms folded despairingly across his chest. Faced with such unanimity, Louis gave in, and on June 27 ordered the noble and clerical deputies to join the National Assembly.

But the troubles were hardly over. While the harvest was good, drought had severely curtailed the ability of watermills to grind flour from wheat. Just as citizens were lining up for what bread was available, a false rumor spread through the Paris press that the queen, Marie Antoinette, had flippantly remarked, on hearing that the people lacked bread, "Let them eat cake!" The antiroyalists so despised the queen that they were always willing to believe anything negative said about her. Peasant and working-class women, responsible for putting bread on the table, had traditionally engaged in political activism during times of famine or inflation, when bread became too expensive, and would march on the civic center to demand help from the local magistrates. But now, on October 5, 1789, about

Fig. 26.4 *To Versailles, To Versailles, October 5, 1789.* Engraving. Musée de la Ville de Paris, Musée Carnavalet, Paris. The despair on the face of the aristocratic woman at the left contrasts sharply with the determined working-class women heading for Versailles.

7,000 Parisian women, many of them armed with pikes, guns, swords, and even cannon, marched on the palace at Versailles demanding bread (Fig. **26.4**). The next day, they marched back to the city with the king and queen in tow. The now essentially powerless royal couple lived as virtual prisoners of the people in their Paris palace at the Tuileries.

The National Assembly, which also relocated to Paris after the women's march on Versailles, had passed, on August 26, 1789, the Declaration of the Rights of Man and Citizen. It was a document deeply influenced by Jefferson's Declaration of Independence, as well as the writings of John Locke. It listed 17 "rights of man and citizen," among them these first three, which echo the opening of the American document (**Reading 26.2**):

READING 26.2

from The Declaration of the Rights of Man and Citizen (1789)

1. Men are born and remain free and equal in rights. . . .
2. The aim of every political association is the preservation of the natural and imprescriptible [inherent or inalienable] rights of man. These rights are liberty, property, security, and resistance to oppression.
3. The principle of all sovereignty resides essentially in the nation. No body nor individual may exercise authority which does not proceed from the nation.

Due process of law was guaranteed, freedom of religion was affirmed, and taxation based on the capacity to pay was announced.

For a time, the king managed to appear as if he were cooperating with the National Assembly, which was busy drafting a constitution declaring a constitutional monarchy on the model of England. Then, in June 1791, just a couple of months before the new constitution was completed, Louis tried to flee France with his family, an act that seemed treasonous to most Frenchmen. The royals were evidently planning to join a large number of French nobility who had removed themselves to Germany, where they were actively seeking the support of Austria and Russia in a counterrevolution. A radical minority of the National Assembly, the **Jacobins** [zhak-oh-behns], had been lobbying for the elimination of the monarchy and the institution of egalitarian democracy for months. Louis's actions strengthened their position. When the Constitutional Convention convened, it immediately declared France a republic, the only question being just what kind. Moderates favored executive and legislative branches independent of one another and laws that would be submitted to the people for approval. But Jacobin extremists, led by Maximilien Robespierre [rohbz-pee-YAIR] (1758–1794), argued for what he called a "Republic of Virtue," a dictatorship led by a 12-person Committee for Public Safety, of which he was one of the members. A second Committee for General Security sought out enemies of the republic and turned them over to the new Revolutionary Tribunal, which over the course of the next three years executed as many as 25,000 citizens of France. These included not only royalists and aristocrats, but also good republicans whose moderate positions were in opposition to Robespierre. Louis XVI himself was tried and convicted as "Citizen Louis Capet" (the last of the Capetian dynasty) on January 21, 1793, and his queen, Marie Antoinette, referred to as "the widow

Fig. 26.5 Anne-Louis Girodet-Trioson, *Jean-Baptiste Bellay, Deputy from Santo Domingo.* 1797. Oil on canvas, 63″ × 45″. Musée National du Château de Versailles, France. Art Resource/Réunion des Musées Nationaux. Bellay delivered a strong speech to the Constitutional Convention pledging the support of his people to the French Revolution and asking the Convention to abolish slavery. His efforts helped convince the Convention to declare the liberty of all black people.

Capet," was executed ten months later (see Fig. 25.32). As Robespierre explained, defending his Reign of Terror:

> If virtue be the spring of popular government in times of peace, the spring of that government during a revolution is virtue combined with terror. . . . Terror is only justice prompt, severe and inflexible; it is then an emanation of virtue. . . .
>
> It has been said that terror is the spring of despotic government. . . . The government in revolution is the despotism of liberty against tyranny.

The Constitutional Convention instituted many other reforms as well. Some bordered on the silly—expunging the king and queen from the deck of cards and eliminating use of the formal *vous* ("thou") in discourse, substituting the informal *tu* ("you") in its place. Others were of greater import. The delegates banned slavery in all the French colonies, inspired by the contributions of representatives such as Jean-Baptiste Bellay [beh-LAY] (Fig. **26.5**, a former slave and one of three black delegates from Santo Domingo (now Haiti),

where slaves led by freed slave Toussaint-Louverture [too-SEHN loo-vair-tyoor] (ca. 1743–1803) had revolted in 1791. His portrait in the Neoclassical style by Anne-Louis Girodet [zhee-roh-DAY] (1767–1824), a student of Jacques-Louis David's, shows Bellay dressed in the French fashion and leaning against a bust of the Abbé Reynal [reh-NAHL]. With the assistance of *philosophe* Denis Diderot, Reynal had written a six-volume *Philosophical and Political History of the Settlements and Trades of the Europeans* (1770), which openly asserted the right of oppressed peoples in the colonies to revolt. Reynal's thinking paved the way for the convention's ban on slavery in the colonies. The painting is important as a tribute to Reynal and Bellay's egalitarian principles rather than as a great portrait of Bellay himself.

Another reform was the de-Christianization of the country, which required that all churches become "Temples of Reason." The calendar was no longer to be based on the year of the birth of Christ, but on the first day of the Republic. Year one began, then, on September 21, 1792. New names, associated with the seasons and the climate, were given to the months. "Thermidor," for instance, was the month of Heat, roughly late July through early August. Finally, the idea of the Sunday sabbath was eliminated, and every tenth day was a holiday.

Tensions remained high. On July 13, 1793, the day before the celebration honoring the storming of the Bastille, the Jacobin hero and fiery editor of *The Friend of the People*, Jean-Paul Marat (1743–1793), was assassinated in his bath, where he normally spent hours to treat a severe case of eczema. The assassin was Charlotte Corday [KOR-day], a young royalist who believed she was the new Joan of Arc, destined to liberate France from Jacobin radicalism. The Jacobins of the National Assembly asked David to paint a *Death of Marat* (Fig. **26.6**). This work is notable for its seemingly unflinching depiction of its hero at the moment of his brutal death and for David's ability to turn a lowly bathroom setting into a monumental image.

Marat had specifically designed a desk to fit over the bath to allow him to conduct business while attending to his terrible skin disease. The pose David chose for him is an instance of using a religious device for a secular image, for the revolutionary patriot confronts the viewer in a position reminiscent of the dead Christ at the Lamentation, traditionally depicted with his right arm dropping to his side. David also pushes Marat to the front of the picture plane so that the viewer seems to be in the same room with the body. Marat holds in one hand the letter from Corday that had gained her entry, and in the other his pen, with which he had been writing the note that hangs over the edge of the crate he used as a desk. The letter of introduction from Corday to Marat is partly legible. Translated from the French, it reads, "My unhappiness alone suffices to give a right to your good will." Her "unhappiness" was her distaste for Marat and the antiroyalist politics he represented, but Corday understood full well that Marat would misinterpret her meaning, supposing that she was complaining about the monarchy, not representing its interests.

When David presented the painting, on October 16, 1793, the day before Marie Antoinette was guillotined, he addressed the assembly in a remarkable speech:

> Hurry, all of you! Mothers, widows, orphans, oppressed soldiers, all whom he defended at the risk of his life, approach and contemplate your friend; he who was so vigilant is no more; his pen, the terror of traitors, his pen has slipped from his hand! Grieve! Our tireless friend is dead. He died giving you his last piece of bread; he died without even the means to pay for his funeral. Posterity, you will avenge him; you will tell our descendants how he could have possessed riches if he had not preferred virtue to fortune. . . .

In this image of self-enforced poverty, David has purposefully contrasted Marat's pen, which he holds in his right hand, with Corday's knife, on the floor beside him. The pen, "the terror of traitors," David seems to say, is mightier than the sword.

Marat's self-imposed poverty is represented by the *assignat* [ah-seen-YAH], French paper money, that lies on the writing table beside him. The accompanying note, translated, says, "You will give this *assignat* for the defense . . ." of a widow with five children whose father had died for his country, indicating that Marat is voluntarily giving up money for a noble cause. The *assignat* is a sign of the same faith and conviction in the future of the republic that led Marat unsuspectingly to admit Charlotte Corday to his rooms.

The Reign of Terror ended suddenly in the summer of 1794. Robespierre pushed through a law speeding up the work of the Tribunal, with the result that in six weeks some 1,300 people were sent to death. Finally, he was hounded out of the Convention to shouts of "Down with the tyrant!" and chased to city hall. Here he tried to shoot himself but succeeded only in shattering his lower jaw. He was executed the next day with 21 others.

The last act of the convention was to pass a constitution on August 17, 1795. It established France's first bicameral (two-body) legislature, consisting of the Council of Five Hundred (modeled on the ancient Athenian Council of Five Hundred) and the Council of Elders. Only men who owned or rented property worth between 100 and 200 days' labor could serve as electors to choose the Councils, effectively limiting the number of voters to 30,000 people. The Council of Five Hundred nominated a slate of candidates to serve on a five-person executive Directory, and the Council of Elders, a smaller body, chose the five. Over the next four years, the Directory improved the lot of French citizens, but its relative instability worried moderates. So, in 1799, the successful young commander of the army, Napoleon Bonaparte (1769–1821), conspired with two of the five directors in the *coup d'état* that ended the Directory's experiment with republican government. This put Napoleon in position to assume control of the country.

THE RIGHTS OF WOMAN

It was obvious to most women in both revolutionary France and America that although the rights of "man" were forcefully declared, the rights of women were wholly ignored. Abigail Adams, in a letter to her husband in the spring of 1776, reminded him that

> if particular care and attention is not paid to the ladies we are determined to foment a rebellion, and will not hold ourselves bound by any laws in which we have no voice or representation.
>
> That your sex are naturally tyrannical is a truth so thoroughly established as to admit of no dispute, but such of yours as wish to be happy willingly give up the harsh title of master for the more tender and endearing one of friend. Why then not put it out of the power of the vicious and the lawless to use us with cruelty and indignity with impunity. Men of sense in all ages abhor those customs which treat us only as vassals of your sex. Regard us then as being placed by providence under your protection and in imitation of the Supreme Being make use of that power only for our happiness.

Sentiments such as these represent the dawn of the modern movement for gender equality. Although Adams expressed her feelings privately to her husband, other women, such as Olympe de Gouges in France and Mary Wollstonecraft in England, took a more public stand.

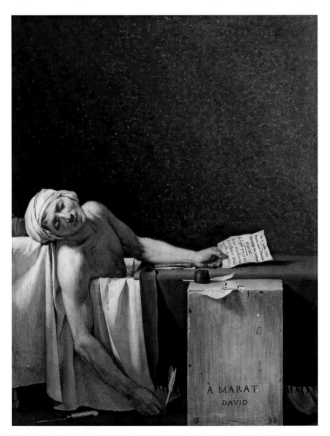

Fig. 26.6 Jacques-Louis David, *The Death of Marat*. 1793. Oil on canvas, 65″ × 50¹/₂″. Musée Royal des Beaux-Arts, Brussels. David inscribed the makeshift writing table in trompe-l'oeil fashion, as if carved into the wood, "À MARAT DAVID" —"To Marat David"—his own name in smaller capital letters than his hero's, suggesting his own humility and that the work is an homage to the greater man.

Olympe de Gouges: The Call for Universal Rights

Olympe de Gouges [duh goozh] (1748–1793) was one of the victims of the Reign of Terror. Born in the south of France to a butcher and a washerwoman, she moved to Paris after the death of her husband and began to write essays, manifestos, and plays concerning social injustice. She greeted the start of the French Revolution with enthusiasm, but when it became clear that equal rights to vote and hold political office were not being extended to women, she became disenchanted. In 1791 she joined a group of advocates for women's rights. In particular, they called for more liberal divorce laws that would grant women equal rights to sue for divorce, and for a revision of inheritance laws that would grant women equal rights in inheriting family property. In this haven of Enlightenment thinking de Gouges declared, "A woman has the right to mount the scaffold. She must possess equally the right to mount the speaker's platform." In that same year, she wrote a *Declaration of the Rights of Woman and the Female Citizen*, modeled on the Declaration of the Rights of Man and Citizen. It begins as follows (**Reading 26.3**):

READING 26.3

from Olympe de Gouges, *Declaration of the Rights of Woman and the Female Citizen* (1791)

Article I. Woman is born free and lives equal to man in rights. . . .

Article II. The purpose of any political association is the conservation of the natural and imprescriptible [inherent or inalienable] rights of woman and man; these rights are liberty, property, security, and especially resistance to oppression.

Article III. The principle of all sovereignty rests essentially with the nation, which is nothing but the union of woman and man; no body and no individual can exercise any authority which does not come expressly from it [the nation].

Article IV. Liberty and justice consist of returning all that belongs to others; thus, the only limits on the exercise of the natural rights of woman are perpetual male tyranny wielded; these limits are to be reformed by the laws of nature and reason. . . .

De Gouges also published a *Social Contract*, an intentionally radical revision of Jean-Jacques Rousseau's work of the same name proposing marriage based on male and female equality. De Gouges tirelessly lobbied the Constitutional Convention for passage of her *Declaration*, and as her efforts appeared fruitless, she became more vehement in her writings about injustice. (Most revolutionary males followed the thinking of Rousseau in *Émile* [see Chapter 25] and believed that the proper role for women remained in the home.) In 1793, the convention banned all women's clubs, ostensibly because of fights between women's club members and market women over proper revolutionary costume, but in reality because of widespread distaste for women's involvement in political activity. Four days later the government put de Gouges to death. She was guillotined as a counterrevolutionary, for authoring a pamphlet arguing that the future government of the country should be determined by popular referendum, not by the National Convention.

Mary Wollstonecraft: An Englishwoman's Response to the French Revolution

Even as de Gouges was pleading her case before the Constitutional Convention, in England one of the great defenders of the French Revolution was Mary Wollstonecraft (1759–1797). She published *A Vindication of the Rights of Woman* in 1792, just a year before publishing her *History and Moral View of the Origin and Progress of the French Revolution*. The immediate incentive for the first of these two important publications was certain policies of the French Revolution unfavorable to women that were inspired by Rousseau. She accused Rousseau and others who supported traditional roles for women of trying to restrict women's experience and narrow their vision, thus keeping them as domestic slaves of men. Wollstonecraft, like Olympe de Gouges, broadened the agenda of the Enlightenment by demanding for women the same rights and liberties that male writers had been demanding for men. The tone of her attack is apparent in the following extract from the Introduction to *A Vindication* (**Reading 26.4**):

READING 26.4

from Mary Wollstonecraft, Introduction to *A Vindication of the Rights of Woman* (1792)

My own sex, I hope, will excuse me, if I treat them like rational creatures, instead of flattering their fascinating graces, and viewing them as if they were in a state of perpetual childhood, unable to stand alone. I earnestly wish to point out in what true dignity and human happiness consists—I wish to persuade women to endeavour to acquire strength, both of mind and body, and to convince them that the soft phrases, susceptibility of heart, delicacy of sentiment, and refinement of taste, are almost synonymous with epithets of weakness, and that those beings who are only the objects of pity and that kind of love, which has been termed its sister, will soon become objects of contempt.

Dismissing then those pretty feminine phrases, which the men condescendingly use to soften our slavish dependence, and despising that weak elegancy of mind, exquisite sensibility, and sweet docility of manners, supposed to be the sexual characteristics of the weaker vessel, I wish to show that elegance is inferior to virtue, that the first object of laudable ambition is to obtain a character as a human being, regardless of the distinction of sex. . . .

Liberty is the mother of virtue, and if women be, by their very constitution, slaves, and not allowed to breathe the sharp, invigorating air of freedom, they must ever languish like exotics, and be reckoned beautiful flaws in nature. . . .

Wollstonecraft's own personal life was not nearly as clearly organized as her arguments in *A Vindication*. During a turbulent affair with an American timber merchant, she mothered an illegitimate child and attempted suicide on at least two occasions. She married the novelist William Godwin (1756–1836) when she became pregnant by him, giving birth to a daughter Mary (1797–1851), the future wife of poet Percy Bysshe Shelley (1792–1822) and author of the novel *Frankenstein* (see Chapter 27). The placenta remained in Wollstonecraft's womb after the birth, and in 1797, at the age of 38, she died of blood poisoning resulting from her physician's attempt to remove it. But however troubled her personal life, the *Vindication of the Rights of Woman*, in contrast to the writings of her French contemporary Olympe de Gouges, was deeply influential. In many ways, Wollstonecraft fashioned the main points of what would later become the liberal feminist movement, arguing not for a radical restructuring of society, but for the right of women to access the same social and political institutions as men. She demanded, simply, equal opportunity.

THE NEOCLASSICAL SPIRIT

By the end of the eighteenth century, Neoclassicism had in many ways become an international style, dominating taste across Europe and extending to the newly formed United States. That a taste for classical order and calm would grow to major proportions in the last half of the eighteenth century is hardly surprising. Europe and America both needed a respite from the political and social chaos of the period. In Paris, Neoclassicism supplanted the ornate, decorative—and, in some minds, dissolute—styles of the Baroque and Rococo, the styles that, in fact, had been the hallmark of monarchical taste. In the United States, the classical style was seen as the direct expression of democracy itself.

Neoclassicism in Britain and America

The founders of the newly created United States of America modeled their new republic on classical precedents. Theirs would be a Neoclassical society—a stable, balanced, and rational culture that might imitate their admittedly idealized view of Rome and Athens. After the Federal Convention presented the states with a new constitution to replace the six-year-old Articles of Confederation on October 27, 1787, a series of 85 articles appeared that came to be known as *The Federalist*, arguing for ratification. They were signed "Publius," a collaborative pseudonym in honor of Publius Valerius Publicola (d. 503 BCE), whose surname means "friend of the people" and who is generally considered one of the founding fathers of the Roman Republic. The authors were actually Alexander Hamilton (1757–1804), John Jay (1745–1829), and James Madison (1751–1836). More than any other delegate to the convention, Madison had been responsible for drafting the constitution itself, and his inspiration came from ancient Greece and Rome. (Among his papers was a list of books he thought were essential for understanding the American political system, among them Edward Gibbon's *On the Decline of the Roman Empire*, Basil Kennett's *Antiquities of Rome*, Plutarch's *Lives*, Plato's *Republic*, and Aristotle's *A Treatise on Government*.)

Federalist No. 10, written by Madison, sums up the chief issue facing adoption of his new constitution—its argument for a centralized and strong federal government. To many, this appeared to be nothing short of a sure path to despotism. The country had fought a war in order to shake off one strong government. Why should it put itself under the yoke of another? Madison's key contribution revolved around his analysis of "factions": "A zeal for different opinions concerning religion, concerning Government and many other points . . . an attachment to different leaders ambitiously contending for pre-eminence and power . . . have divided mankind into parties, inflamed them with mutual animosity, and rendered them much more disposed to vex and oppress each other, than to co-operate for their common good." But Madison understood that in a large republic, these factions counteract each other. As a result, at the heart of the constitution was a system of checks and balances to guarantee that no faction or branch of government—each of which was vested with different, and sometimes opposing powers—could wield undue power over any other.

The fledgling United States also embraced Neoclassicism as an architectural style, both as a reflection of its classically inspired political system and to give a sense of ancient stability to the new republic. Many of the founding fathers had traveled extensively in Europe, where they viewed the antiquities of Greece and Rome and many of the later works inspired by them. As a young man, Thomas Jefferson had dreamed of taking the Grand Tour, the capstone experience of any Briton's formal education. The Grand Tour could last anywhere from a few months to a few years. It included visits to Paris, Florence, Pisa, Bologna, and Venice, followed by a journey to Rome, Naples, and the ruins of Herculaneum and Pompeii. Travelers would then go on to German-speaking cities, Holland, and Belgium. Although Jefferson never completed the Grand Tour, after his appointment as minister to the court of the French king, Louis XVI, in 1784, he traveled extensively. With John Adams, he toured the gardens and estates of England, visiting Stowe (see Chapter 25), Alexander Pope's garden at Twickenham, and other sites. Later, Jefferson visited Northern Italy and France, where he marveled at the Roman ruins (and also developed a deep enthusiasm for French wine). Jefferson also well knew that the next best thing to visiting the sights of Europe was to read about them.

Among the recently published books that described the antiquities of Rome and Athens, one of the most compelling was Johann Winckelmann's *History of Ancient Art* (1764)—the first book to include the words *history* and *art* in its title. While working as the Prefect of Papal Antiquities in Rome, Winckelmann (1717–1768) saw and described the vast collection of antique classical art at the Vatican as possessing "a noble simplicity and quiet grandeur." Capturing this same simplicity and grandeur became the primary aim of artists and architects whose works came to be known as Neoclassical. In fact, the taste for these values was enormous, and so was the market for classical objects.

The British Influence: Robert Adam and Josiah Wedgwood

The rise of Neoclassical architecture in the United States was directly inspired by the architectural practice of Robert Adam (1728–1792) in England. Adam and his brother James had taken the Grand Tour in 1754, including visits to Pompeii and Herculaneum. What they saw inspired an

*Arch of Constantine, **p. 256***

architectural style that interpreted and organized classical architectural forms and decorative motifs in innovative new ways. Adam's designs were so popular that he became the most sought-after architect of the day. He and his brother James employed a permanent staff that designed every detail of a house, both outside and in. His work was so influential that his Neoclassical style became more commonly known in England as the **Adam style**.

Adam's motifs came from a variety of antique sources. His facade for the south front of Lord Scarsdale's country house, Kedleston [KED-ul-stun] Hall in Derbyshire [DAR-bee-shir] (Fig. **26.7**), for instance, is a direct copy of the Arch of Constantine in Rome (see Fig. 8.7) but elevated on a platform with wings on each side and approached by a magnificent open-ended oval staircase. Adam filled the interior with opulent marbles, stucco decoration, Corinthian colonnades, and alcoves to contain sculpture copied from the ancients. He also decorated the walls with copies of ancient medallions, plaques, and other motifs that evoked what he labeled his "antique style." He placed a replica of the *Apollo Belvedere* at the far end of the Marble Hall (Fig. **26.8**), designed to suggest the open courtyard of a Roman villa. (See Fig. 6.27.)

Very often Adam decorated his interiors with the ceramics of Josiah Wedgwood, not the common earthenware that Wedgwood mass-produced known as Queen's Ware (see Chapter 24), but his stoneware known as **jasperware**, ornamented in Neoclassical style with a white relief on a colored ground. His primary markets were his native England, Russia, France, and North America. The latter was especially lucrative, as Wedgwood explained in a letter to a friend: "For the islands of North America we cannot make anything too rich and costly."

CONTINUITY & CHANGE

*House of the Silver Wedding, **p. 203***

Fig. 26.7 Robert Adam, south front of Kedleston Hall, Derbyshire, England. ca. 1765–70. Not only did the Adam architectural firm design every aspect of a house—at no small expense—it also owned interests in timber, brick, cast iron, stone, stucco, and sand businesses. In essence, the firm was a high-end developer, employing over 2,000 people.

Fig. 26.8 Robert Adam, interior of the Marble Hall, Kedleston Hall, Derbyshire, England. ca. 1765–1770. 67′ × 42′. John Bethell. The Bridgeman Art Library. The *Apollo Belvedere*, which stands in the left niche at the end of the hall, was perhaps the most copied statue from Greek and Roman antiquity. Above the niches and door are panels with classical subjects.

Most of the relief designs on the vases were by sculptor and draftsman John Flaxman (1755–1826). Flaxman's design for a vase depicting the Muses (Fig. **26.9**) was modeled on an ancient Roman household altar. The design is divided into six sections by columns. The three Muses—Thalia, Urania, and Erato—fill three of these sections, alternating with symbols representing Jupiter (thunderbolt), Mars (spear and helmet), and Mercury (caduceus, or winged staff). Flaxman's designs echo the flat vase painting of the original designs in their own extreme linearity and their extremely low relief, barely raised sculptural surfaces. This planarity and linearity became synonymous with Neoclassicism itself as the Wedgwood manufacity popularized the Neoclassical look.

American Neoclassical Architecture The Neoclassical style of architecture dominated the architecture of the new American republic, where it became known as the **Federal style**. Its foremost champion was Thomas Jefferson. Like almost all leaders of the American colonies, Jefferson was well educated in the classics and knew well such works as Stuart and Revett's *Antiquities of Athens* (1758) and Adam's

Fig. 26.9 John Flaxman, Wedgwood vase. Late eighteenth century, ca. 1780–1800. Made by Josiah Wedgwood and Sons, Etruria/Staffordshire, England. Jasperware: height 6 $^1/_2$″; diameter 5 $^1/_8$″. Metropolitan Museum of Art, New York, Rogers Fund, 1909 (09.194.79). Depicted here is Urania, muse of astronomy, contemplating a globe.

Fig. 26.10 Thomas Jefferson, Monticello, Charlottesville, VA. 1770–84, 1796–1806. The colonnade at the entrance to Jefferson's Monticello, itself modeled on the work of Robert Adam, would inspire the architecture of countless antebellum Southern mansions.

Works in Architecture (3 volumes, 1773–82). His taste for the classical would affect the design, the furniture, and even the gardens at his home outside Charlottesville, Virginia (Fig. **26.10**). For the convenience of getting goods to the marketplace, most American estates had been located near rivers. Jefferson located his on the top of a hill, the traditional site for a Greek or Roman temple. He called the place Monticello [mon-tih-CHEH-loh], or "little mountain." He designed the building himself after the villas of Andrea Palladio (see Fig. 15.30) but augmented with features he had seen in France when he served as American minister there, such as French doors and tall, narrow windows, and the use of a balustrade above the cornice to mask the second story. The facade, with its six Corinthian columns and classical pediment, is modeled on the work of Robert Adam. He also decorated the fireplace of the Monticello dining room with Wedgwood panels (Fig. **26.11**).

The house was surrounded by an English garden similar to the one he had seen at Stowe (see Fig. 25.13) when he traveled with his friend John Adams. Its meandering hilltop pathway opened to vistas of the surrounding Virginia countryside. An accomplished gardener, in characteristic Enlightenment fashion, Jefferson documented the plants and animals of the entire Virginia region, cataloguing his findings in a volume that remains useful to Virginia gardeners to this day.

Jefferson's Neoclassical tastes were not limited to his private life. He designed the Virginia State Capitol in Richmond, Virginia, which was, first of all, a "capitol," the very name derived from Rome's Capitoline Hill. The building

Fig. 26.11 Thomas Jefferson, dining room with Wedgwood reliefs, Monticello, Charlottesville, VA. 1770–1784, 1796–1806. Jefferson kept books on this mantelpiece, and often read into the evening in front of this fireplace.

Fig. 26.12 Benjamin Henry Latrobe, *View of Richmond Showing Jefferson's Capitol from Washington Island*. 1796. Watercolor on paper, ink and wash, 7″ × 10³/₈″. Maryland Historical Society, Baltimore. No view of an American capitol in the eighteenth century better captures the almost audacious aspirations of the new nation.

(Fig. 26.12) is a literal copy of the Maison Carrée [may-ZOHN kah-RAY] in Nîmes [neem], France, a Roman temple built in the first century BCE (Fig. 26.13). The view of Richmond by Jefferson's disciple, architect Benjamin Henry Latrobe (1764–1820), gives some idea of the lack of harmony between the American landscape, in all its rustic and undeveloped expanse, and Jefferson's Neoclassical and highly cultivated vision. To prevent other such incongruities, Jefferson had proposed in 1785 that Congress pass a land ordinance requiring all new communities to be organized according to a grid. The measure—actually a call to order—resulted in a regular system of land survey across the American continent. It effectively installed a Neoclassical pattern on the American landscape.

The nation's new capitol in Washington, D.C., would, however, modify Jefferson's rectilinear scheme. President Washington believed that the swampy, humid site along the Potomac River required something more magnificent, so he hired Major Pierre-Charles L'Enfant [lahn-FAHN] (1754–1825) to create a more ambitious design. The son of a court painter at Versailles, L'Enfant had emigrated to America from Paris in 1776 to serve in the

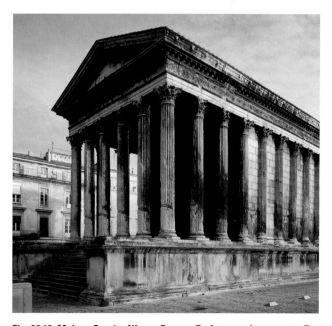

Fig. 26.13 Maison Carrée, Nîmes, France. Early second century CE. The six Corinthian columns across the front of this ancient temple may also have inspired the entrance to Monticello.

Fig. 26.14 Pierre-Charles L'Enfant, plan for Washington, D.C. (detail). 1791. Published in the *Gazette of the United States*, Philadelphia, January 4, 1792. The Bridgeman Art Library. Engraving after the original drawing, Library of Congress, Washington, D.C. The architect, L'Enfant, had served as a volunteer in the Revolutionary War. He also designed Federal Hall in New York City, which hosted the first Continental Congress in 1789.

Continental Army. His plan (Fig. **26.14**) is a conscious echo of the diagonal approaches and garden pathways at Versailles (see Fig. 23.4), superimposed upon Jefferson's grid. The result is an odd mixture of angles and straightaways that mirrored, though unintentionally, the complex workings of the new American state. Visiting in 1842, a half century later, English novelist Charles Dickens would be struck by the city's absurdity: "Spacious avenues . . . begin in nothing, and lead nowhere; streets, mile-long, that only want houses, roads, and inhabitants; public buildings that need but a public to be complete." It was, he wrote, a city of "Magnificent Intentions," as yet unrealized. Like the Latrobe painting of the capitol in Richmond, the city somewhat oddly combined Neoclassical cultivation with what might be called rural charm. Latrobe, in fact, was hired to rebuild the Capitol Building

CONTINUITY & CHANGE

*Corinthian capital, **p. 115***

after the British burned it during the War of 1812. He invented a new design for the capitals of the Corinthian columns in the vestibule and rotunda of the Senate wing, substituting corncobs and tobacco for the Corinthian's acanthus leaves (Fig. **26.15**).

Neoclassical Sculpture in America During Jefferson's stay in France as minister to the court of Louis XVI, he became acquainted with the work of the two great Neoclassical sculptors of the day, the Italian Antonio Canova (1757–1822) and his French rival Jean-Antoine Houdon [oo-DOHN] (1741–1828). At Jefferson's recommendation, the Virginia Assembly commissioned Houdon in 1785 to create a full-length marble statue of George Washington for the Virginia State Capitol at Richmond. Convinced that a true likeness could only be achieved from life, Jefferson insisted that Houdon sail to America from France. Houdon traveled to Mount Vernon, Washington's Virginia estate, to make a cast of the general's bust in plaster; the rest of the body would be created from traditional plaster models. He finished the sculpture in Paris in 1788, the year before Washington's inauguration as the first president of the United States (Fig. **26.16**). Although Washington wears contemporary clothing, Houdon presents him as Cincinnatus [sin-sih-NAH-tus], the ancient Roman general who had returned to farming after a life of military service for his country, in the same way that the Roman poet Horace had done (see Chapter 6). The medal of the Order of Cincinnatus, an organization created by retiring officers after the Revolutionary War, projects from under Washington's waistcoat. He leans against a column of 13 *fasces*, or rods, symbols of Roman political office as well as the 13 colonies of the new nation. Behind him is a plowshare, beaten from a sword, signifying his role as a warrior who has brought peace and prosperity to his people. Washington's relaxed *contrapposto* pose and serene but dignified facial expression derive from classical statues and suggest the high moral purpose, or *gravitas*, of a Roman senator; they successfully link the father of his country—*pater patriae*, "father of the fatherland"—with the ancient leaders who preceded him.

Fig. 26.16 Jean-Antoine Houdon, *George Washington.* 1788. Marble, life-size. Virginia State Capitol, Richmond. Houdon also sculpted busts of Benjamin Franklin and Thomas Jefferson.

CONTINUITY&CHANGE

*Head of a Man, **p. 182***

Years later, when the North Carolina legislature decided to place a sculpture of Washington in the rotunda of their state house, Jefferson recommended

Fig. 26.15 Benjamin Henry Latrobe, tobacco leaf capital for the U.S. Capitol, Washington, D.C. ca. 1815. Despite this unique design, Latrobe used more traditional capitals elsewhere in the Capitol. For the Supreme Court area of the building, he designed Doric capitals in proportions similar to those at Paestum (see Fig. 4.16).

another sculptor, Canova. Jefferson insisted that the sculpture should depict Washington as a Roman senator, since, he wrote, "Our boots and regimentals have a very puny effect." Since the hall of the capitol in Raleigh was only 16 feet high, Washington was to be seated, attired in senatorial toga and sandals, signing the letter relinquishing command of the army, his sword at his feet. The sculpture stood in the capitol for ten years, until a fire destroyed both. But early in the twentieth century, Canova's original model was discovered and the Italian government donated the plaster replica to North Carolina.

Jacques-Louis David and the Neoclassical Style in France

No artist more fully exemplifies the values of Neoclassicism in France than the painter Jacques-Louis David (1748–1825). His career stretches from pre-Revolutionary Paris, through the turmoil of the Revolution and its aftermath, and across the reign of Napoleon Bonaparte. He was, without doubt, the most influential artist of his day. "I do not feel an interest in any pencil but that of David," Thomas Jefferson wrote in a flush of enthusiasm from Paris during his service as minister to the court of Louis XVI from 1785 to 1789. And artists flocked to David's studio for the privilege of studying with him. In fact, many of the major artists of the following century had been his students, and those who had not been such defined themselves against him.

David abandoned the traditional complexities of composition that had defined French academic history painting since at least the time of Rubens's series of paintings depicting the life of Marie de' Medici (see Fig. 23.6) and substituted a formal balance and simplicity that is fully Neoclassical. His work has a frozen quality to emphasize rationality, and the brushstrokes are invisible, to create a clear focus and to highlight details. At the same time, his works have considerable emotional complexity. A case in point is his painting *The Oath of the Horatii* (Fig. **26.17**), commissioned by the royal government in 1784 to 1785. The story derives from a play by French playwright Corneille (see Chapter 23), and is a sort of parable or example of loyal devotion to the state. It concerns the conflict between early Rome, ruled by Horatius [hor-AY-shus], and neighboring Alba, ruled by Curatius [kyoor-AY-shus]. In order to spare a war that would be more generally destructive, the two

Fig. 26.17 Jacques-Louis David, *The Oath of the Horatii*. 1784–85. Oil on canvas, 10′10″ × 13′11¹/₂″. Musée du Louvre, Paris. RMN Réunion des Musées Nationaux, France/Art Resource, New York. Corneille's play *Horace* inspired the painting (see Chapter 23).

LEARN MORE Gain insight from a primary source document on Jacques-Louis David at **www.myartslab.com**

leaders agreed to send their three sons—the Horatii [hor-AY-shee-eye] and the Curatii [kyoor-AY-shee-eye]—to battle each other. David presents the moment *before* the battle when the three sons of Horatius swear an oath to their father, promising to fight to the death. The sons on the left, the father in the middle, and the sisters to the right are each clearly and simply contained within the frame of one of three arches behind them. Except for Horatius's robe, the colors are muted and spare, the textures plain, and the paint itself almost flat. The male figures stand rigidly in profile, their legs extending forward tensely, as straight as the spear held by the foremost brother, which they parallel. Their orderly Neoclassical arrangement contrasts with that of the women, who are disposed in a more conventional, Baroque grouping. Seated, even collapsing, while the men stand erect, the women's soft curves and emotional despair contrast with the male realm of the painting. David's message here is that civic responsibility must eclipse the joys of domestic life, just as reason supplants emotion and classical order supplants Baroque complexity. Sacrifice is the price of citizenship (a message that Louis XVI would have been wise to heed).

David's next major canvas, *The Lictors Returning to Brutus the Bodies of his Sons*, was painted in 1789, the year of the Revolution but before it had begun. It is a more complex response to the issues of sacrifice for the state. The painting shares with the *Oath of the Horatii* the theme of a stoic father's sacrifice of his sons for the good of the state, as

Brutus's lictors (the officers in his service as ruler) return the sons' bodies to him after their execution. Although received by the public in 1789 as another assertion of the priority of the republic over the demands of personal life, the painting is emotionally far more complex. That is, it seems to question the wisdom of such acts of heroism (see *Closer Look*, pages 856–857). Although, as we have seen, David would serve the new French Republic with verve and loyalty as its chief painter after the Revolution, his paintings are rarely as straightforward as they at first appear. In David's work, it would seem, the austerity of the Neoclassical style is something of a mask for an emotional turbulence within, a turbulence that the style holds in check.

Angelica Kauffmann and Neoclassical Motherhood.

Cornelia Pointing to Her Children as Her Treasures, painted in 1785 by Swiss-born Angelica Kauffmann (1741–1807), depicts a popular subject among late-eighteenth-century Neoclassical painters (Fig. **26.18**). Cornelia was the daughter of the Roman hero Scipio Africanus, the Roman general who defeated Hannibal in 202 BCE, and she is remembered as the model of Roman motherhood. In this painting, Cornelia responds to a visiting lady who had been showing Cornelia her jewels. When the visitor asks to see Cornelia's jewels, Cornelia points to her two sons and says, "These are my most precious jewels." The two sons, as Kauffmann's audience knew, would one day be great reformers of the Roman Republic, leading the effort to

Fig. 26.18 Angelica Kauffmann (born Swiss, 1741–1807), *Cornelia Pointing to Her Children as Her Treasures.* **ca. 1785.** Oil on canvas, 40 in. H × 50 in. W (101.6 × 127.0 cm). Signed on base of column at right: Angelica Kauffmann Pinx. Virginia Museum of Fine Arts, Richmond. The Adolph D. and Wilkins C. Williams Fund. Photo: Ann Hutchison. © Virginia Museum of Fine Arts. 75.22/50669.2. Kauffmann is unique in being the only female artist of the eighteenth century who became a successful history painter.

The French monarchy commissioned Jacques-Louis David to create *The Lictors Returning to Brutus the Bodies of His Sons*, and it was exhibited in 1789, just six weeks after the storming of the Bastille. As a result, the public closely identified it with the cause of the French Republic. The hero of the historical tale that is the subject of this painting is the founder of the Roman Republic, Lucius Junius Brutus (sixth century BCE; not to be confused with the Brutus who would later assassinate Julius Caesar). He had become head of Rome and inaugurated the republic by eliminating the former monarch, Tarquinius, who himself had assumed the throne by conspiring with the wife of the former king. She murdered her husband, and he his own wife, and the two married. Brutus's sons had conspired to restore the monarchy—their mother was related to Tarquinius—and under Roman law Brutus was required not only to sentence them to death but to witness the execution.

In David's painting, Brutus sits in shadow at the left, his freshly beheaded sons passing behind him on stretchers carried by his lictors (officers who served rulers). Brutus points ignominiously at his own head, as if affirming his responsibility for the deed, the sacrifice of family to the patriotic demands of the state. In contrast to the darkened shadows in which Brutus sits, the boys' mother, nurse, and sisters await the bodies in a fully lighted stage space framed by a draperied colonnade. The mother reaches out in a gesture reminiscent of Horatius's in the *Oath of the Horatii*. The nurse turns and buries her head in the mother's robe. One of the sisters appears to faint in her mother's arms, while the other shields her eyes from the terrible sight. Their spotlit anguish emphasizes the high human cost of patriotic sacrifice, whereas the *Oath of the Horatii* more clearly celebrates the patriotic sacrifice itself.

This shift in David's emphasis can be at least partly explained by his own biography. Early in 1888, his favorite apprentice, Jean-Germain Drouais, died of smallpox at the age of 25 (see Fig. 32.6). David was devastated by this loss of one of the best young painters in France. (Drouais was a winner of the Prize of Rome, which sent him to study in that city for five years.) *The Lictors* probably reflects the strength of David's feelings for his young companion.

Jacques-Louis David, details from *The Lictors Returning to Brutus the Bodies of His Sons*. 1789. Oil on canvas, 10′7 1/4″ × 13′10 1/4″. Musée du Louvre, Paris. RMN Réunion des Musées Nationaux, France. Gerard Blot/C. Jean/Art Resource, New York. Brutus's emotional exile from his proper place at the table as patriarch is emphasized by the subtle analogy that David draws between Brutus's own toes and the scrolling decoration at the base of the table where once he sat.

SEE MORE For a Closer Look at Jacques-Louis David's *The Lictors Returning the Bodies of His Sons,* go to **www.myartslab.com**

The **statue of Roma** represents the state and is darkened to suggest the turmoil that Rome is enduring.

The **Doric order** of the architecture underscores the severity of the scene and represents the reasonable and rational order of the Roman Republic—the very model of the new French Republic about to be born.

David reverses the structure of the *Horatii* by having Brutus's wife extend her hand as Horatius does in the earlier painting. Now the women stand, and the males sit (or lie dead). Female emotion stands triumphant over the demands of reason.

Much of the emotional tension of the painting derives from the contrast between the rigorous scientific perspective of the composition, most explicit in the floor tiles, and the soft, falling curves of the drapes and women's clothing.

This **central column** extends to the top of the painting, separating Brutus from his family and emphasizing the great gulf between them.

The graceful curve that defines the back of the empty chair in front of the central column suggests the powers of human feeling, compassion, and love. The chair is surely Brutus'sown, from which he has been exiled.

The relief portraying the legend of the founders of Rome, **Romulus and Remus,** suckled by a wolf suggests how, at its origin, the Roman republic was integrally connected to the importance of family, especially after the rise of Augustus.

Something to Think About . . .

How would you compare the emotional impact of this painting to that of David's *Death of Marat* (see Fig. 26.6)? How might the original audience of *Death of Marat*, depending upon its politics, have found itself in a position similar to either Brutus or his family?

Jacques-Louis David, ***The Lictors Returning to Brutus the Bodies of His Sons.*** **1789.** Oil on canvas, 10′7 1/4″ × 13′10 1/4″. Musée du Louvre, Paris. RMN Réunion des Musées Nationaux, France. Gerard Blot/C. Jean/Art Resource, New York.

redistribute to the poor the public lands that had been taken over by the rich.

Cornelia is at the center of the composition, balancing the painting's two halves. This balance is emphasized by the fold down the front of her dress, the line of which extends directly up the side of the square column behind her. Cornelia recognizes that her children represent the future of the state and hence her care for them is her greatest civic responsibility. What most distinguishes Kauffmann's painting is that it thus carries the weight and force of historical narrative even as it extols the virtues of motherhood.

Kauffmann was a great portraitist herself, in fact one of the most sought-after of the day. With Sir Joshua Reynolds, she was also one of the founding members of England's Royal Academy of the Arts. Kauffmann and her husband were employed by the architect Robert Adam (see Chapter 31) to decorate the homes he designed for the English aristocracy with ceiling and wall paintings illustrating historical themes. It is her dedication to painting historical subjects that earned her the admiration of her contemporaries, a rare feat for women artists in the eighteenth century.

NAPOLEON AND NEOCLASSICAL PARIS

Women's dissatisfaction with the outcome of the French Revolution was one of many problems facing the government. In fact, turbulence was the political reality of post-Revolutionary France. The Directory was not providing stability. On November 9 and 10, 1799, Napoleon Bonaparte staged a veritable **coup d'état** (violent overthrow of government) and forced three of the Directory's five directors to resign, barely managing to persuade the councils to accept himself and the two remaining directors. It was the threat of economic and international chaos—including a new coalition formed against France by England, Austria, Russia, and the Ottomans—that guaranteed his success. Order was the call of the day, and Napoleon was bent on restoring it. To this purpose he turned to models from classical antiquity.

The Consulate and the Napoleonic Empire: 1799–1814

Napoleon's coup d'état was intended to overthrow the existing constitution that the Directory had approved. The new constitution that he put in its place created a very strong executive called the Consulate, modeled on ancient Roman precedents. Composed of himself and the two directors, it established Napoleon as First Consul of the French Republic, relegating the other two to mere functionary status. The constitution also established something of a sham legislature composed of four bodies: a Council of State to propose laws; a Tribunate to debate them (though not vote on them); a Legislative Corps to vote (though not debate); and a Senate, which possessed the right to veto any legislation. The First Consul appointed the Council of State, and thus it proposed laws as Napoleon decreed. It was understood that the duty of the other three bodies was to "rubber stamp" the First Consul's wishes. France's experiment with a republican form of government was over.

By 1802, Napoleon had convinced the legislators to declare him First Consul of the French Republic for life, with the power to amend the constitution as he saw fit. In 1804, he instigated the Senate to go a step further and declare that "the government of the republic is entrusted to an emperor." This created the somewhat paradoxical situation of a "free" people ruled by the will of a single individual.

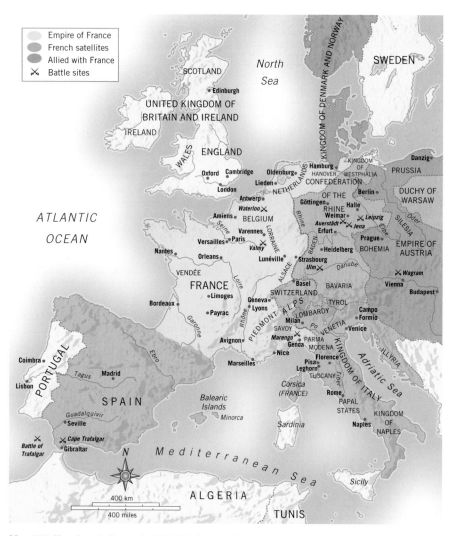

Map 26.2 Napoleonic Europe in 1807. Only Portugal, Britain, and Sweden were free of Napoleonic domination. Sicily and Sardinia, in the Mediterranean, were protected by the British fleet.

But Napoleon was careful to seek the consent of the electorate in all of these moves. When he submitted his constitution and other changes to the voters in a plebiscite, they ratified them by an overwhelming majority.

Napoleon justified voter confidence by moving to establish stability across Europe by force. To this end, in 1800 he crossed into Italy and took firm control of Piedmont and Lombardy. After establishing a position in Italy, he prepared to invade England, his chief enemy. Financed in no small part by the sale of the Louisiana Territory to the United States in 1803 for 80 million francs (roughly $16 million), Napoleon assembled over 100,000 troops and a thousand landing craft on the straits of Dover. His tactics were arguably flawless, but they were not executed as planned. In order to cross the Channel, he needed to lure away Vice Admiral Horatio Nelson (1758–1805), commander of the British fleet. To this end, in the fall of 1805, he dispatched the French fleet to the West Indies under the command of Admiral Pierre de Villeneuve. The plan was for Villeneuve to give Nelson the slip and return to escort the French army across the Channel. But Nelson caught up to Villeneuve off Cape Trafalgar near the southwest corner of Spain in October and, at the cost of his own life, destroyed nearly half the French fleet without the loss of any of his own ships.

Although Napoleon never defeated the British navy—and thus never controlled the seas—from 1805 to 1807 he launched a succession of campaigns against Britain's allies, Austria and Prussia. He defeated both, and by 1807 the only European countries outside Napoleon's sphere of influence were Britain, Portugal, and Sweden. Through ten years of war and short periods of armed truce, Napoleon changed the map of Europe (see Map **26.2**). Everywhere he was victorious, he brought the reforms that he had established in France and overturned much of the old political and social order. Eventually the subdued lands became resentful. A series of military defeats, including the so-called Battle of the Nations at Leipzig in October 1813, led to his abdication and exile and then final defeat by the English under the Duke of Wellington and the Prussians under Field Marshall von Blücher at Waterloo, Belgium, on June 18, 1815.

Art as Propaganda: Painting, Architecture, Sculpture

Napoleon celebrated major events by commissioning paintings, sculpture, and architecture. The paintings and sculptures were prominently displayed in public settings and the architecture was situated at important junctions in Paris. All were meant to present the physically small but extremely ambitious man as hero and leader of France or to remind the public of his efforts on their behalf. The Neoclassical style was perfect for these purposes. It was already associated with the republicanism and liberty of the French Revolution, and it could easily be adapted to the needs of empire and authority. So Napoleon adopted it as First Consul and continued to

Fig. 26.19 Jacques-Louis David, _Napoleon Crossing the Saint-Bernard_. 1800–01. Oil on canvas, 8'11" × 7'7". Musée National du Château de la Malmaison, Rueil-Malmaison, France. RMN Réunion des Musées Nationaux/Art Resource, New York. David would claim to everyone, "Bonaparte is my hero!" This is one of five versions of the painting, which differ significantly in color, painted by David and his workshop. There are also many copies in French museums and elsewhere done by others.

do so after he crowned himself emperor in 1804. Contributing to these efforts were the painters Jacques-Louis David and Jean-Auguste-Dominique Ingres [eng], the architect Pierre-Alexandre Vignon [veen-YOHN], and the sculptor Antonio Canova [kuh-NOH-vah].

David as Chronicler of Napoleon's Career David, who had survived the revolutionary era and painted many of its events, went on to portray many of the major moments of Napoleon's career. He celebrated the Italian campaign in _Napoleon Crossing the Saint-Bernard_ (Fig. **26.19**). Here he depicts Napoleon on horseback leading his troops across the pass at Saint-Bernard in the Alps. In its clearly drawn central image and its emphasis on right angles (consider Napoleon's leg, the angle of his pointing arm to his body, the relation of the horse's head and neck, and the angle of its rear legs), the painting is fully Neoclassical. In the background, as is typical of David, is a more turbulent scene as Napoleon's troops drag a cannon up the pass. In the foreground, inscribed on the rocks, are the names of the only generals who crossed the Alps into Italy: Hannibal, whose brilliance in defeating the Romans in the third century BCE Napoleon sought to emulate; Karolus Magnus (Charlemagne); and Napoleon.

Actually, Napoleon did not lead the crossing of the pass but crossed it with his rear guard, mounted on a mule led by a peasant. So the work is pure propaganda, designed to create a proper myth for the aspiring leader. Though still four years from crowning himself emperor, the First Consul's aspirations to unite Europe and rule it are made clear in his identification with the great Frankish emperor of the Holy Roman Empire, Charlemagne. Napoleon was boldly creating a myth that is probably nowhere better expressed than by the great German philosopher Georg Wilhelm Friedrich Hegel [HAY-gul] (1770–1831) in a letter of October 13, 1806: "I have seen the emperor, that world soul, pass through the streets of the town on horseback. It is a prodigious sensation to see an individual like him who, concentrated at one point, seated on a horse, spreads over the world and dominates it."

Ingres's Glorification of the Emperor No image captures Napoleon's sense of himself better than the 1806 portrait by Jean-Auguste-Dominique Ingres (1780–1867) of *Napoleon on His Imperial Throne* (Fig. **26.20**). Ingres was David's student, a winner of the Rome prize, and a frequent exhibitor at the annual Salon of the French Academy of Fine Arts. He sought a pure form of classicism, characterized by clarity of line, a dedication to detail, and a formal emphasis on balance and symmetry.

In this commission from Napoleon, Ingres depicts him as a monarch who embodies the total power of his country. Ingres combines two well-known frontal images of the deities Jupiter, or Zeus, and God the Father with the imperial attributes of the historical emperors Charlemagne and Charles V of Spain. The Jupiter image was a lost sculpture known only in gemstone but attributed to Phidias, the master of the Greek Golden Age. The God the Father image was in Jan van Eyck's *Ghent Altarpiece* (see Figure 16.6), which Napoleon had taken from Ghent during his Prussian campaign and installed in the Louvre. Ingres establishes the emperor's identification with Charlemagne by the sword beneath his left forearm and the ivory hand of justice, both of which were believed to have originally belonged to Charlemagne. And he evokes the Habsburg Holy Roman Emperor Charles V of Spain through the scepter in Napoleon's right hand, thus symbolically uniting France and Austria for the first time since Charlemagne's reign in the early Middle Ages. Like David's portrait, *Napoleon Crossing the Saint-Bernard*, Ingres's painting is a conscious act of propaganda, cementing in the public mind the image of the emperor as nearly godlike in his power and dominion. The David and Ingres portraits underscore the fact that Napoleon understood quite well the ability of art to move and control the popular imagination.

Fig. 26.20 Jean-Auguste-Dominique Ingres, *Napoleon on His Imperial Throne*. 1806. Oil on canvas, 102″ × 64″. Musée de l'Armée, Paris. The carpet at Napoleon's feet is an imperial eagle flanked by signs of the zodiac, including Scorpio, Libra, and Virgo, at the left, and Pisces and Taurus at the right, as if the emperor's fame were written in the stars.

Vignon's La Madeleine Napoleon reasoned that if he was now the new emperor, Paris should be the new Rome. The city already tended to be dominated by Neoclassical architecture, from the east facade of the Louvre to Sainte-Geneviève (see Fig. 32.1) rising above the Left Bank. Napoleon sought to extend the sense of order and reason these buildings suggested. He soon commissioned the construction of Roman arches of triumph and other classically inspired monuments to commemorate his victories and convey the political message of the glory of his rule. One of

Fig. 26.21 Pierre-Alexandre Vignon, La Madeleine, Paris. 1806–42. Length, 350', width 147', height of podium 23', height of columns 63'. The church of La Madeleine was built to culminate a north–south axis that began on the left bank of the Seine at the Chamber of Deputies (newly refurbished with a facade of Corinthian columns), crossing a new bridge northward into the Place de la Concorde.

the most impressive works was the redesign of a church that had been started under Louis XVI but that Napoleon wanted to see reinterpreted as a new Temple of the Glory of the Grand Army. This work, commissioned in 1806 from Pierre-Alexandre Vignon (1763–1828), was to have been identified by the following dedicatory inscription: "From the Emperor to the soldiers of the Great Army." It was another of the many Parisian churches, like Sainte-Geneviève, that were converted to secular temples during this epoch. Ironically, Napoleon reversed his decision to honor the army in 1813 after the unfortunate Battle of Leipzig and the loss of Spain. Although work continued on the building, its original name, the church of La Madeleine, was restored.

Not completed until after Napoleon's downfall, but nevertheless to Vignon's original design, La Madeleine is imperially Roman in scale and an extraordinary example of Neoclassical architecture (Fig. **26.21**). Eight 63-foot-high Corinthian columns dominate its portico, and 18 more rise to the same height on each side. Beneath the classical roofline of its exterior, Vignon created three shallow interior domes that admit light through oculi at their tops that are hidden by the roofline. They light a long nave without aisles that culminates in a semicircular apse roofed by a semidome. This interior evokes traditional Christian architecture, even as the exterior announces its classicism through the Roman temple features.

Canova and the Bonapartes Napoleon did not limit his propagandistic commissions to French artists and architects. In 1802 he had invited to Paris the highly reputed Italian sculptor Antonio Canova (1757–1822) to model a larger-than-life-size marble statue of him to celebrate his being named consul for life. Napoleon expected a portrait of himself in full military dress, but the artist believed that he should be depicted in the nude as the

modern embodiment of Mars, the Roman god of war (Fig. **26.22**). As it turned out, by the time Canova's sculpture arrived in Paris in 1811, Napoleon was embroiled in the military campaigns that would end his career, and he rejected the statue, understanding that as a nude its propagandistic uses were limited. For Napoleon understood quite well the role of Neoclassical art in the service of the state: In its order and majesty it projected, like the sculpture of Caesar Augustus at the Primaporta (see Fig. 6.13), his own dignity and power. To present himself to the public in the nude, however idealized, would be to subject himself to ridicule. Ironically, the sculpture would eventually be purchased by the British government as a gift—and sort of trophy—for the Duke of Wellington, who defeated Napoleon at the Battle of

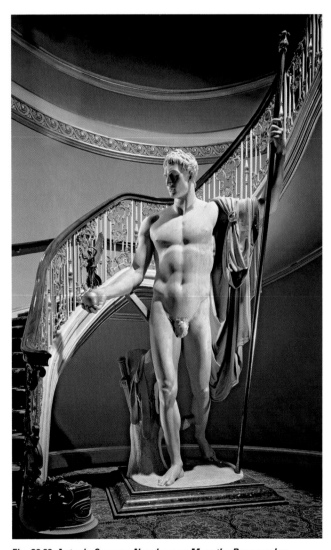

Fig. 26.22 Antonio Canova, *Napoleon as Mars the Peacemaker.* **1802–06.** Marble, height 10'8". The Wellington Collection, Apsley House, London. Napoleon had argued with Canova about being portrayed in the nude and the sculptor had replied: "We, like the poets, have our own language. If a poet introduced into a tragedy, phrases and idioms used habitually by the lower classes in the public streets, he would be rightly reprimanded. . . . We sculptors cannot clothe our statues in modern costume without deserving a similar reproach."

Fig. 26.23 Antonio Canova, *Paolina Borghese as Venus.* 1808. Marble, life-size. Galleria Borghese, Rome. Canova's sculpture was originally mounted on a pivot so that it might be turned toward the window for viewing in natural light or adjusted at night to be illuminated in torchlight from within.

Waterloo on June 18, 1815. Wellington would place it in the stairwell of his house in London.

In 1808, by which time the consul had had himself crowned as emperor, Canova had less trouble convincing Napoleon's sister, Paolina Bonaparte Borghese [bor-GAY-zeh] (1780–1825), to allow him to depict her in the nude as well. Perhaps this was because she understood that her sexuality was the means by which she had attained her position as the wife of one of the richest men in all of Europe, Prince Camillo Borghese.

Canova was bent on showing that his art was equal if not superior to that of the ancients. Following the recommendations of Winckelmann, he searched for beauty in clear forms, harmonious lines, and all-around viewpoints. His portrait busts and sculptural groups ranged from delicately lyric to formal and symbolic. His sculpture of Paolina Borghese (Fig. **26.23**) is life-size, and its pedestal is a different-colored marble, replicating a chaise

(reclining chair). She holds an apple, the traditional symbol of Venus, and thus, like her brother, appropriates mythical status, the personification of a goddess, untouchable by mortal hands. In its elegant contours and astonishingly smooth representation of flesh (unequaled by any of Canova's many imitators), the work aspires to the noble simplicity and calm grandeur that Winckelmann found in ancient classical sculpture (see Fig. 5.20).

Paolina Borghese never intended this sculpture to be viewed by a public any wider than her immediate social circle, and then only at night, under the dramatic lighting of torchlight. Thus, the sculpture is a sort of dramatic set piece, unlike the statue of her brother, which had a political intent. Her nudity was understood to suggest a goddess of antiquity and thus be aristocratic, not demeaning. It was a form of *personal* propaganda that belied her beginnings as the daughter of a poor family of lesser nobles.

THE ISSUE OF SLAVERY

In America, the high-minded idealism reflected in the adoption of Neoclassicism in art and architecture was clouded, from the outset, by the issue of slavery. In the debates leading up to the revolution, slavery had been lumped into the debate over free trade. Americans had protested not only the tax on everyday goods shipped to the colonies from Britain, including glass, paint, lead, paper, and tea, but the English monarchy's refusal to allow the colonies to trade freely with other parts of the world, and that included trade in enslaved Africans.

The Atlantic slave trade followed an essentially triangular pattern (Map **26.3**). Europe exported goods to Africa, where they were traded for African slaves (see Chapter 18), who were then taken to the West Indies and traded for sugar, cotton, and tobacco; these goods were then shipped either back to Europe or north to New England for sale. Since the slaves provided essentially free labor for the plantation owners, these goods, when sold, resulted in enormous profits. Although a port like Boston might seem relatively free of the slave trade, Boston's prosperity and the prosperity of virtually every other port on the Atlantic depended on slavery as an institution. And the American taste for Neoclassical art, epitomized by Wedgwood's assertion that for "North America we cannot make anything too rich and costly," was in very large part made possible by the slave trade.

No nation had profited more from the slave trade than England. It had been late to get into the business, leaving it largely to the Portuguese until 1672. By then, the English government needed labor for its sugar plantations in the Caribbean and its tobacco plantations in Virginia. England chartered the Royal African Company, granting it a monopoly in the slave trade. From 1680 to 1686, the company traded approximately 5,000 slaves a year. In 1698, Parliament yielded to the demands of English merchants eager to share in the Royal African Company's profits and opened the slave trade to all. The trafficking of African slaves on English ships increased fourfold to an average of more than 20,000 a year, and by the start of the eighteenth century, England's was the largest slave trade in the world.

Throughout the eighteenth century, slaves continued to be sold in Britain, especially in Bristol and Liverpool, which the trade had turned into boom towns. In fact, it became fashionable among aristocratic British women to have a black child servant. (See the black child at the lower right-hand corner of the The Countess's Levée in Hogarth's Marriage À la Mode series, Fig. 24.5.)

Map 26.3 The slave trade triangle.

Autobiographical and Fictional Accounts of Slavery

The conditions on board slave ships have been described by Olaudah Equiano [ay-kee-AH-noh], a native of Benin [ben-EEN], in West Africa, who was kidnapped and enslaved in 1756 at age 11 (Fig. **26.24**). Freed in 1766, he traveled widely, educated himself, and mastered the English language. In his autobiography, published in England in 1789 (see **Reading 26.5**, pages 871–873, for a fuller account of this passage), he describes the transatlantic journey (**Reading 26.5a**):

READING 26.5a

from Olaudah Equiano, *The Interesting Narrative of the Life of Olaudah Equiano, or Gustavus Vassa the African* (1789)

The stench of the hold while we were on the coast [of Africa] was so intolerably loathsome that it was dangerous to remain there for any time, and some of us had been permitted to stay on the deck for the fresh air, but now that the whole ship's cargo were confined together it became absolutely pestilential. The closeness of the place and the heat of the climate, added to the number in the ship, which was so crowded that each had scarcely room to turn himself, almost suffocated us. This produced copious perspirations, so that the air soon became unfit for respiration from a variety of loathsome smells, and brought on a sickness among the slaves, of which many died, thus falling victims to the improvident avarice, as I may call it, of their purchasers. This wretched situation was again aggravated by the galling of the chains, now become insupportable; and the filth of the necessary tubs, into which the children often fell and were almost suffocated. The shrieks of the women and the groans of the dying soon rendered the whole a scene of horror almost inconceivable.

Recent biographical discoveries cast doubt on Equiano's claim that he was born and raised in Africa and that he endured the Middle Passage (the name given to the slave ships' journey across the Atlantic Ocean) as he describes. Baptismal and naval records suggest, instead, that he was born around 1747 in South Carolina. Still, if Equiano did fabricate his early life, it appears that he did so based on the verbal accounts of his fellow slaves, for the story he tells, when compared to other sources, is highly accurate. Whatever the case, Equiano's book became a bestseller among the over 100 volumes on the subject of slavery published the same year, and it became essential reading for the ever-growing abolitionist movement in both England and the Americas.

The lot of the slaves, once they were delivered to their final destination, hardly improved. One of the most interesting accounts is *Narrative of a Five Years' Expedition against the Revolted Negroes of Surinam, in Guiana, on the Wild Coast of South America, from the Year 1772 to 1777*, written by John Gabriel Stedman (1747–1797) and illustrated by William Blake (1757–1827) (Figs. **26.25** and **26.26**). Blake was already an established engraver and one of England's leading poets. Stedman had been hired by the Dutch to suppress rebel slaves in Guiana, but once there, he was shocked to see the conditions the slaves were forced to endure. Their housing was deplorable, but worse, they were routinely whipped, beaten, and otherwise tortured for the nonperformance of impossible tasks, as a means of instilling a more general discipline. Female slaves endured sexual abuses that were coarse beyond belief. The planters maintained what amounted to harems on their estates and freely indulged their sexual appetites.

Even as Stedman moved on from Guiana to Surinam, Phillis Wheatley (ca. 1753–1784) became the first black American to publish a book. Wheatley had been kidnapped as a child in Senegal and raised in Boston by John Wheatley along with his own children, where she was also a maidservant to Wheatley's wife. Wheatley had begun writing poems when she was 13 and was regarded as a

Fig. 26.24 *Stowage of the British Slave Ship "Brookes" Under the Regulated Slave Trade (Act of 1788).* 1788. Conditions on slave ships were appalling. Food was bad, space so cramped that movement was virtually impossible, and disease devastating.

Fig. 26.25 William Blake, *Negro Hung Alive by the Ribs to a Gallows*, engraved illustration to John Gabriel Stedman's *Narrative of a Five Years' Expedition against the Revolted Slaves of Surinam . . .* 1796. Library of Congress, Catalog no. 1835. Private Collection, Archives Charmet/The Bridgeman Art Library. Blake executed the etchings for Stedman's volume after original drawings by Stedman himself. Stedman was impressed that the young man being tortured here stoically endured the punishment in total silence.

A Surinam Planter in his Morning Dress.

Fig. 26.26 William Blake, *A Surinam Planter in His Morning Dress*, engraved illustration to John Gabriel Stedman's *Narrative of a Five Years' Expedition against the Revolted Slaves of Surinam . . .* 1796. Library of Congress, Catalog no. 1835. Of the plantation owners, Stedman wrote: "Such absolute power . . . cannot help but be peculiarly delightful to a man who was, in all probability, in his own country, Europe, a nothing."

prodigy in Boston. When she went to England with the Wheatleys in 1773, she achieved great popularity, perhaps most of all because she seemed to have so thoroughly accepted and adopted the attitudes of her new culture. It was in England that she published her *Poems on Various Subjects: Religious and Moral* in 1773. Most of Phillis Wheatley's poems reflect her religious and classical New England upbringing and stress the theme of Christian salvation. She accepts her plight as divinely ordained, but in one of her poems she argues for equality with others and the ability of her race to attain the "refinement" of her European contemporaries. The poem, in fact, reflects what many in America and Britain, both pro-slavery and abolitionist, would hold up as the ideal aspiration of all African-Americans (**Reading 26.6**):

Soon after Phillis Wheatley returned home from England, she was given her freedom. The beneficent treatment of Wheatley is, however, rare in the annals of American slavery, and more often than not, the Christianity of the kind she adopted and her acceptance of its values were seen by other slaves as hypocritical, even as a betrayal of her race. As Olaudah Equiano put it in his autobiography (see Reading 31.3): "O, ye nominal Christians! might not an African ask you—learned you this from your God, who says unto you, Do unto all men as you would men should do unto you?"

One of the earliest accounts of slavery is the short novel *Oroonoko* by Aphra Behn (1640–1689) published in 1688. As author of 20 plays for the stage, Behn was the first woman in the Western world to have made her living as a writer. *Oroonoko* tells the story of an African prince and the woman he loves, both of whom are sold separately into slavery and carried to Surinam, where Behn, a white woman, had lived for a time and where the British had begun importing slaves for the sugar cane plantations. In Surinam the two lovers are reunited, and Oroonoko, exerting his royal nature, organizes a slave revolt, for which he is punished by the deputy governor with public execution by dismemberment. Although Behn never criticizes slavery as an institution, she portrays her hero as a natural king and clearly superior to the whites around him (see **Reading 26.7** page 873).

Like Stedman, Behn is conflicted about her relationship to slavery. Although she was a lifelong militant royalist and opposed to democracy in favor of a strong king, she clearly identified as a woman with her hero's oppression by a sadistic deputy governor. But she was equally convinced of her own English culture's social superiority, even if some of her kind were capable of the Surinam deputy governor's act of atrocity.

The Economic Argument for Slavery and Revolution: Free Trade

In an odd conflict of interests and allegiances, slavery pitted abolitionist sentiments against freethinking economic theory. Free-trade economists, such as Adam Smith (1723–1790), would argue that people should be free to do whatever they might to enrich themselves. Thus Smith would claim that a **laissez-faire** [lay-say-FAIR], "let it happen as it will," economic policy was the best. "It is the maxim of every prudent master of a family," Smith wrote in *The Wealth of Nations*, published in 1776, "never to make at home what it will cost him more to make than to buy. . . . What is prudence in the conduct of every private family, can scarce be folly in that of a great kingdom. If a foreign country can supply us with a commodity cheaper than we ourselves can make it, better buy it of them." Labor, it could be argued, was just such a commodity and slavery its natural extension. At the same time, ironically, Smith was against the very tariffs and taxes that England had imposed on its colonies. He argued that free trade among nations, which the British had denied the colonies by asserting their own right to the accumulation of wealth over and above that of the colonists, should be the basis of economic policy.

Thus, in 1776, the arguments both for and against slavery as an institution seemed, to many people, to balance each other out. Economics and practicality favored the practice of slavery, while human sentiment and, above all, the idea of freedom, denied it. Although at the time he wrote the Declaration of Independence, Jefferson himself owned about 200 slaves and knew that other Southern delegates supported slavery as necessary for the continued growth of their agricultural economy, in his first draft he had forcefully repudiated the practice. Abigail Adams (1744–1818), who, like her husband John, knew and respected Jefferson, but unlike him owned no slaves, was equally adamant on the subject: "I wish most sincerely," she wrote her husband in 1774, as he was attending the First Continental Congress in Philadelphia, "that there was not a slave in the province. It always seemed a most iniquitous scheme to me—fight for ourselves what we are daily robbing and plundering from those who have as good a right to freedom as we have."

The Abolitionist Movement in Britain and America

Many Britons, looking from across the Atlantic at the American Revolution, shared Abigail Adams's sentiments. As long as the colonies tolerated slavery, their demand for their own liberty seemed hypocritical. The English poet Thomas Day (1748–1789) described the typical American as "signing resolutions of independence with one hand, and with the other brandishing a whip over his affrighted slaves."

Abolitionist opposition to slavery in both England and the American colonies began to gain strength in 1771

Fig. 26.27 William Hackwood, for Josiah Wedgwood, "Am I Not a Man and a Brother?" 1787. Black-and-white jasperware, $1^3/_8$" × $1^3/_8$". The Wedgwood Museum, Barlaston, Staffordshire, England. The image illustrated Erasmus Darwin's poem "The Botanic Garden," which celebrates not only the natural world, but also the rise of British manufacturing at the dawn of the Industrial Revolution. The poem nevertheless severely criticized British involvement in the slave trade, which it deemed highly "unnatural."

Fig. 26.28 John Singleton Copley, *Watson and the Shark*. 1778. Oil on canvas, 71 $^3/_4$" × 90 $^1/_2$". Museum of Fine Arts, Boston. Ferdinand Lammot Belin Fund. Photograph © 2006 Board of Trustees, National Gallery. The shark-infested waters are perhaps a metaphor for slavery itself, especially since it was well known that some slave traders threw slaves overboard into shark-infested waters in order to collect insurance.

when Granville Sharp pled the case of an escaped American slave, James Somerset, before the Lord Chief Justice, Lord Mansfield. Somerset's American owner had recaptured him in England, but the Lord Chief Justice set Somerset free, ruling that the laws governing another country carried no weight in England. Leading the fight against slavery were the Quakers as well as the members of the Lunar Society (see Chapter 24). In 1787, Josiah Wedgwood made hundreds of ceramic cameos of a slave in chains, on bent knee, pleading, "Am I Not a Man and a Brother?" (Fig. 26.27). He distributed them widely, and the image quickly became the emblem for the abolitionist movement as a whole. In Philadelphia, Benjamin Franklin, president of the Philadelphia Abolitionist Society, received a set.

The sentiments of Wedgwood's cameo find expression even in paintings that seem to have no direct reference to slavery. *Watson and the Shark* by John Singleton Copley (1738–1815) is a case in point (Fig. **26.28**). The painting

was commissioned by its subject, Brook Watson, a wealthy English merchant and Tory leader who was deeply opposed to slavery. As a young man, in 1749, Watson had lost his leg when a shark attacked him as he swam in Havana harbor. The ship he had been serving on had been involved with the triangular slave trade described earlier. It carried timber, dried fish, and other goods from Boston to Africa, where it had exchanged this merchandise for slaves, who were in turn traded in the West Indies for sugar and molasses, commodities then brought back to Boston. Even as Copley was at work on this painting, Watson was attacking the colonists in Parliament for the hypocrisy of their position. The black man who forms the focus of the composition serves an interesting purpose. Though the man's attitude seems ambiguous—as if not quite sure he should go so far as to save a white man—he holds the lifeline that has been thrown to Watson. Their relationship is thus affirmed, even as its complexities and tensions are openly acknowledged.

Fig. 26.29 Thomas Coram (American, 1756–1811), *View of Mulberry House and Street.* **ca. 1800.** Oil on paper. Gibbes Museum of Art/Carolina Art Association, 1968. 1968.18.01. The steep-pitched roofs of the slave quarters allowed rain to wash rapidly off the roof, a fact that in Africa helped prevent the thatched roofs from leaking.

The African Diaspora

All told, about 14 million Africans survived the Atlantic crossing, the largest forced scattering of a people in history and now known as the **African diaspora**. In some places, particularly in Brazil and the Caribbean, people from the same African homelands and speaking the same language were gathered together on plantations, where they were able to revive and continue cultural practices from their native lands. For instance, the Haitian religious practice known as Vodou combines recognizable elements from Yoruba, Kongo, and Dahomey. (The commonly used term *Voodoo* is considered offensive by practicing communities.) But in North America, slaveholders made a conscious effort to gather together only Africans of differing cultural and linguistic backgrounds, believing this would reduce the possibility of rebellion. Still, many forms of African culture survived. A late eighteenth-century painting of the Mulberry Plantation in South Carolina (Fig. **26.29**) depicts slave houses with steeply pitched roofs similar to the thatched roof houses of the same era found in West Africa. The roof comprises over half the height of the house, allowing warm air to rise in the interior and trapping cooler air beneath it—a distinct advantage in the hot climate of both Africa and the Carolinas.

The cultural form that most thoroughly survived the African diaspora was music. Sub-Saharan African cultures, despite their enormous size and diversity, all shared certain fundamental characteristics. Almost all of these cultures played drums, in an array of rhythms and tones that may involve several rhythms produced simultaneously or two or more interwoven melodies (see Chapter 23). In addition, almost all of these cultures played one form or another of **mbira** [em-BEER-ah], an instrument made of a small wooden box or gourd that acts as a resonator, attached to which is a row of thin metal strips that vibrate when plucked. Music performed on the drum or the mbira is largely improvisational, each performance involving a lengthy combination of repetition and gradual variation. Like drum music, mbira music displays the African fascination with complex rhythms and melodies HEAR MORE at (track **26.1**). In the mbira musical selection www.myartslab.com on the CD, two traditional songs of the Shona people of Zimbabwe, the widely popular *Chemutengure* and *Mudendero* (a children's song accompanying circle games), combine in a slow pattern of repetition and gradual variation. In this we can hear the patterns and movements that would, in the West, survive in American jazz.

The Romantics and Napoleon

On February 8, 1807, during a fierce blizzard near the town of Eylau, Russia's General Bennigsen, with an army of 74,500 men, engaged Napoleon Bonaparte and his much smaller army of less than 50,000 in battle. Napoleon struck first, knowing that he had reinforcements in the wings. But the blizzard hampered both sides. The Russians withdrew, and Bonaparte claimed victory. There were 23,000 Russian casualties who had died for their emperor, Alexander I, but the battlefield was also strewn with 22,000 dead and wounded French.

Five weeks after Napoleon's "victory," a competition was announced in France for a painting commemorating the great day. The director of French museums declared that it should depict "The moment . . . when, His Majesty visiting the battlefield at Eylau in order to distribute aid to the wounded, a young Lithuanian hussar, whose knee had been shot off, rose up and said to the Emperor, 'Caesar, you want me to live. . . . Well, let them cure me and I will serve you as faithfully as I did Alexander!'" Antoine Jean Gros [groh] (1771–1835) won the competition with the painting illustrated here (Fig. **26.30**). The painting made an odd piece of official propaganda. The larger-than-life-size pile of bodies, frozen blue, at the bottom of the painting is so terrifying and so openly hostile to the idea of victory that it seems impossible Napoleon would have approved it. Yet he did, just as he would ignore the advice of his aides in the fall of 1812 not to push into Russia, where his army "took" the city of Moscow, even as the Russians burned it. Napoleon abandoned his troops to return to Paris. He had begun his march into Russia with over 1 million men. Only about 100,000 returned. Never before had the term "heroism" seemed more hollow.

The promise of Napoleon—his ability to impose classical values of order, control, and rationality upon a French society that had been wracked with revolution and turmoil—was thus undermined by a darker reality. The Romantics, whose fascination with the powers of individual intuition and creativity had led them to lionize Napoleon, would react to his failure and to the ensuing disorder that marked the first half of the nineteenth century. Artists, composers, and writers would express in their works a profound pessimism about the course of human events. The optimistic spirit we find in Wordsworth and Constable, Emerson and Thoreau, would be challenged, not merely by the sense of darkness and foreboding expressed by Coleridge and Melville, but by a pessimism that undermined the Romantics' faith in the powers of nature to heal and restore humanity's soul. ∎

Fig. 26.30 Antoine Jean Gros, *Napoleon at Eylau.* **1808.** Oil on canvas 17′5 $^1/_2$″ × 26′3″. Musée du Louvre, Paris. RMN Réunion des Musées Nationaux, France. Erich Lessing/Art Resource, New York.

*What do the American and French Revolutions have
in common? How do they differ?*

The idea of human freedom was fundamental to the Enlightenment, finding two of its greatest expressions in the
Declaration of Independence, ratified by the 13 colonies
on July 4, 1776, and, in France, the Declaration of the
Rights of Man and Citizen, passed by the National Assembly in August 1789. Jefferson's argument that the American colonies should be self-governing was preceded by
British taxation of the colonies. In France, the national
debt, and taxes associated with paying it, produced events
leading to revolution. What do you think accounts for the
fact that in America, revolution was followed with relative
stability, while in France, chaos and terror followed?

How did women respond to the promise of revolution?

While the rights of "man" had been boldly asserted in
both the American and French revolutions, the rights of
women had been ignored. In France, Olympe de Gouges
wrote a *Declaration of the Rights of Women*, for which she was
sent to the guillotine. In England, Mary Wollstonecraft
quickly followed with *A Vindication of the Rights of Woman*.
For Wollstonecraft, how were women in eighteenth-
century society equivalent to African slaves?

What is Neoclassicism?

The founders of the newly created United States modeled their republic on classical precedents and embraced
Neoclassicism as an architectural style. What specific aspects of Neoclassical art and architecture attracted
Thomas Jefferson to the Neoclassical style? Why did it become known in America as the "Federal style," and why
did it seem so appropriate for governmental architecture?
In France, Jacques-Louis David, the premier painter of the
day, readily adopted the style in his painting *The Oath of
the Horatii*, in which he champions heroism and personal
sacrifice for the state. How do "gender politics" inform
David's painting? How do they compare to David's treatment of similar issues in *The Lictors Returning to Brutus
the Bodies of His Sons* and Angelica Kauffmann's treatment

of gender in *Cornelia Pointing to Her Children as Her
Treasures*?

What values shaped Napoleonic France?

As Napoleon took greater and greater control of
French political life in the opening decade of the nineteenth century, he turned to antiquity, modeling his government particularly upon the military and political
structures of the Roman Empire. He commissioned paintings of himself that served the propagandistic purpose of
cementing his image as an invincible, nearly godlike
leader. In what ways is David's *Napoleon Crossing the Saint-
Bernard* a work of propaganda? How does Ingres's *Napoleon
on His Imperial Throne* continue this propagandistic tradition? Convinced that Paris was the new Rome, Napoleon
commissioned architectural monuments based on Roman
precedents. He hired the Italian sculptor Antonio Canova
to celebrate his being named consul for life. How did
Canova's Neoclassicism impress Napoleon?

*How did the issue of slavery undermine
the idealism of the era?*

Autobiographical and fictional accounts of slavery intensified abolitionist sentiments in both Europe and
North America. Olaudah Equiano exposed the conditions on board slave ships in his *Travels*, and John Gabriel
Stedman revealed the shocking treatment of slaves in
Guiana. The black poet Phillis Wheatley accepted her
plight as divinely ordained, while novelist and playwright
Aphra Behn, in *Oroonoko*, the first English novel to show
blacks in a sympathetic light, identified with her hero's
oppression despite her own sense of racial superiority. By
1700, England had become the largest trafficker of slaves
in the world, and its own economy depended heavily on
the trade. In what ways does John Singleton Copley's
painting *Watson and the Shark* reflect the issues raised by
slavery? How did African slaves, despite their circumstances, adapt the cultures of their native lands to their
American conditions?

PRACTICE MORE Get flashcards for images and terms and review chapter material with quizzes at **www.myartslab.com**

GLOSSARY

Adam style   The term for the Neoclassical style in England, where it became closely associated with the work of the architect Robert Adam.

African diaspora   The forced scattering of millions of Africans as a result of the Atlantic crossing.

coup d'état   A violent overthrow of government.

estate   One of three traditional groups that comprised the Estates General in France. The First Estate was the clergy; the Second Estate was the nobility; and the Third Estate was the rest of the population, composed of the bourgeoisie and the peasants.

Federal style   The term for the Neoclassical style as it appeared in the United States.

Jacobin   A member of a radical minority of France's National Assembly who favored the elimination of the monarchy and the institution of egalitarian democracy.

jasperware   A type of stoneware produced by Josiah Wedgwood that was ornamented in Neoclassical style with a white relief on a colored ground.

laissez-faire   Literally "let it happen as it will," this economic policy argues that people should be free to do whatever they might to enrich themselves.

mbira   An instrument made of a small wooden box or gourd—to which is attached a row of thin metal strips that vibrate when plucked—that acts as a resonator.

republicanism   Sympathy for a republican form of government, that is, a government having a chief of state who is not a monarch.

READINGS

READING 26.5

from *The Interesting Narrative of the Life of Olaudah Equiano* (1789)

The following passage concludes Chapter 2 of Equiano's autobiography, entitled "Kidnapping and Enslavement," and it describes Equiano's passage to the Americas. Born in Benin, Equiano reports that he was first kidnapped (by fellow Africans) at the age of 11 and sold repeatedly to a succession of West African tribal families until finally sold to slavers bound for the Americas. Recent research has brought his account into question, but he undoubtedly captures experiences shared by many. The majority of his narrative concerns his life in the Americas, first on a Virginia plantation, then in the service of a British naval officer (who helped educate him), and then as the slave of a Philadelphia merchant, who finally helped him purchase his freedom. By the time he published his autobiography, he was a permanent resident in England, working for the abolition of slavery.

The first object that saluted my eyes when I arrived on the coast was the sea, and a slave ship, which was then riding at anchor, and waiting for its cargo. These filled me with astonishment, that was soon converted into terror, which I am yet at a loss to describe, and much more the then feelings of my mind when I was carried on board. I was immediately handled and tossed up to see if I was sound, by some of the crew; and I was now persuaded that I had got into a world of bad spirits, and that they were going to kill me. Their complexions too, differing so much from ours, their long hair, and the language they spoke, which was very different from any I had ever heard, united to confirm me in this belief. Indeed such were the horrors of my views and fears at the moment, that if ten thousand worlds had been my own, I would have freely parted with them all to have exchanged my condition with the meanest slave in my own country. When I looked round the ship too, and saw a large furnace or copper boiling and a multitude of black people, of every description, chained together, every one of their countenances expressing dejection and sorrow, I no longer doubted of my fate; and, quite overpowered with horror and anguish, I fell motionless on the deck, and fainted. When I recovered a little, I found some black people about me, who I believed were some of those who brought me on board, and had been receiving their pay: they talked to me in order to cheer me, but all in vain. I asked them if we were not to be eaten by those white men with horrible looks, red faces, and long hair. They told me I was not: and one of the crew brought me a small portion of spirituous liquor in a wine glass; but, being afraid of him, I would not take it out of his hand. One of the blacks therefore took it from him and gave it to me, and I took a little down my palate, which, instead of reviving me, as they thought it would, threw me into the greatest consternation at the strange feeling it produced, having never tasted any such liquor before.

Soon after this the blacks who brought me on board went off, and left me abandoned to despair. I now saw myself deprived of all chance of returning to my native country, or even the least glimpse of gaining the shore, which I now considered as friendly; and I even wished for my former slavery, in preference to my present situation, which was filled with horrors of every kind, still heightened by my ignorance of what I was to undergo. I was not long suffered to indulge my grief. I was soon put down under the decks, and there I received such a salutation in my nostrils as I had never experienced in my life: so that, with the loathsomeness of the stench, and with my crying together, I became so sick and low that I was not able to eat, nor had I the least desire to taste any thing. I now wished for the last friend, death, to relieve me; but soon, to my grief, two of the white men offered me eatables; and, on my refusing to eat, one of them held me fast by the hands, and laid me across, I think, the windlass, and tied my feet, while the other flogged me severely. I had never experienced any thing of this kind before, and although, not being used to the water, I naturally feared that element the first time I saw it, yet nevertheless, could I have got over the nettings, I would have jumped over the side, but I could not; and besides the crew used to watch us very closely, who were not chained down to decks, lest we should leap into the water. I have seen some of these poor African prisoners most severely cut for attempting to do so, and hourly whipped for not eating. This indeed was often the case with myself. In a little time after, amongst the poor chained men, I found some of my own nation, which in a small degree gave ease to my mind. I inquired of these what was to be done with us. They gave me to understand we were to be carried to these white people's country to work for them. I was then a little revived, and thought if it were no worse than working, my situation was not so desperate. But still I feared I should be put to death, the white people looked and acted, as I thought, in so savage a manner; for I had never seen among any people such instances of brutal cruelty: and this is not only shewn towards us blacks, but also to some of the whites themselves. One white man in particular I saw, when we were permitted to be on deck, flogged so unmercifully with a large rope near the foremast, that he died in consequence of it; and they tossed him over the side as they would have done a brute. This made me fear these people the more; and I expected nothing less than to be treated in the same manner. I could not help expressing my fearful apprehensions to some of my countrymen; I asked them if these people had no country, but lived in this hollow place, the ship. They told me they did not, but came from a distant one. 'Then,' said I, 'how comes it, that in all our country we never heard of them?' They told me, because they lived so very far off. I then asked, where their women were: had they any like themselves. I was told they had. And why, said I 'do we not see them?' They answered, because they were left behind. I asked how the vessel could go. They told me they could not tell; but that there was cloth put upon the masts by the help of the ropes I saw, and then the vessel went on; and the white men had some spell or magic they put in the water, when they liked, in order to stop the vessel. I was exceedingly amazed at this account, and really thought they were spirits. I therefore wished much to be from amongst them, for I expected they

would sacrifice me; but my wishes were in vain, for we were so quartered that it was impossible for any of us to make our escape.

While we stayed on the coast I was mostly on deck; and one day, to my great astonishment, I saw one of these vessels coming in with the sails up. As soon as the whites saw it, they gave a great shout, at which we were amazed; and the more so as the vessel appeared larger by approaching nearer. At last she came to an anchor in my sight, and when the anchor was let go, I and my countrymen who saw it, were lost in astonishment to observe the vessel stop, and were now convinced it was done by magic. Soon after this the other ship got her boats out, and they came on board of us, and the people of both ships seemed very glad to see each other. Several of the strangers also shook hands with us black people, and made motions with their hands, signifying, I suppose, we were to go to their country; but we did not understand them. At last, when the ship, in which we were, had got in all her cargo, they made ready with many fearful noises, and we were all put under deck, so that we could not see how they managed the vessel.

But this disappointment was the least of my grief. The stench of the hold, while we were on the coast, was so intolerably loathsome, that it was dangerous to remain there for any time, and some of us had been permitted to stay on the deck for the fresh air; but now that the whole ship's cargo were confined together, it became absolutely pestilential. The closeness of the place, and the heat of the climate, added to the number in the ship, being so crowded that each had scarcely room to turn himself, almost suffocated us. This produced copious perspirations, so that the air soon became unfit for respiration, from a variety of loathsome smells, and brought on a sickness among the slaves, of which many died, thus falling victims to the improvident avarice, as I may call it, of their purchasers. This deplorable situation was again aggravated by the galling of the chains, now become insupportable; and the filth of necessary tubs, into which the children often fell, and were almost suffocated. The shrieks of the women, and the groans of the dying, rendered it a scene of horror almost inconceivable. Happily, perhaps, for myself, I was soon reduced so low here that it was thought necessary to keep me almost continually on deck; and from my extreme youth, I was not put in fetters. In this situation I expected every hour to share the fate of my companions, some of whom were almost daily brought upon deck at the point of death, and I began to hope that death would soon put an end to my miseries. Often did I think many of the inhabitants of the deep much more happy than myself; I envied them the freedom they enjoyed, and as often wished I could change my condition for theirs. Every circumstance I met with served only to render my state more painful, and heighten my apprehensions and my opinion of the cruelty of the whites. One day they had taken a number of fishes; and when they had killed and satisfied themselves with as many as they thought fit, to our astonishment who were on the deck, rather than give any of them to us to eat, as we expected, they tossed the remaining fish into the sea again, although we begged and prayed for some as well as we could, but in vain; and some of my countrymen, being pressed by hunger, took an opportunity, when they thought no one saw them, of trying to get a little privately; but were discovered, and the attempt procured for them some very severe floggings.

One day, when we had a smooth sea and moderate wind, two of my wearied countrymen, who were chained together (I was near them at the time), preferring death to such a life of misery, somehow made through the nettings and jumped into the sea: immediately another quite dejected fellow, who on account of his illness was suffered to be out of irons also followed their example; and I believe many more would very soon have done the same, if they had not been prevented by the ship's crew, who were instantly alarmed. Those of us who were the most active were in a moment put down under the deck; and there was such a noise and confusion amongst the people of the ship as I never heard before, to stop her and get the boat out to go after the slaves. However, two of the wretches were drowned; but they got the other, and afterward flogged him unmercifully, for thus attempting to prefer death to slavery. In this manner we continued to undergo more hardships than I can now relate, hardships which are inseparable from this accursed trade. Many a time we were near suffocation from the want of fresh air, being deprived thereof for days together. This, and the stench of the necessary tubs, carried off many.

READING CRITICALLY

Several times in this passage Equiano refers to magic, yet he clearly understands that what he describes is not magical. What is he seeking to convey to the reader, and why?

READING 26.7

from Aphra Behn, *Oroonoko, or The Royal Slave* (1688)

Behn's Oroonoko *is a "history" written during the time when the novel was just beginning to be defined as a form, and when the word "history" could mean any story true or false. To a certain degree, Behn's history is probably true. She was in the new sugar colony of Surinam, where much of this narrative takes place, in 1664. Whether she witnessed a slave rebellion while there, let alone met anyone resembling the displaced African prince Oroonoko, is a matter of pure conjecture. We can, though, be certain of her idealization of the "primitive." The following passage, from early in the narrative, describes Oroonoko's many virtues, virtues that more "civilized" Christians often fall short of matching.*

I have often seen and convers'd with this great Man and been a Witness to many of his mighty Actions; and do assure my Reader, the most Illustrious Courts cou'd not have produc'd a braver Man, both for Greatness of Courage and Mind, a Judgment more solid, a Wit more quick, and a Conversation more sweet and diverting. He knew almost as much as if he had read much: He had heard of, and admir'd the *Romans*; he had heard of the late Civil Wars in *England*, and the deplorable Death of our great Monarch[1] and wou'd discourse of it with all the Sense, and Abhorrence of the Injustice imaginable. He had an extream good and graceful Mien, and all the Civility of a well-bred great Man. He had nothing of Barbarity in his Nature, but in all Points address'd himself, as if his Education had been in some *European* Court.

This great and just character of *Oroonoko* gave me an extream Curiosity to see him, especially when I knew he spoke *French* and *English*, and that I cou'd talk with him. But though I had heard so much of him, I was as greatly surpriz'd when I saw him, as if I had heard nothing of him; so beyond all Report I found him. He came into the Room, and addresse'd himself to me, and some other Women, with the best Grace in the World. He was pretty tall, but of a Shape the most exact that can be fancy'd: The most famous Statuary cou'd not form the Figure of a Man more admirably turn'd from Head to Foot. His Face was not of that brown, rusty Black which most of that Nation are, but a perfect Ebony, or polish'd Jett. His Eyes were the most awful that cou'd be seen, and very piercing; the White of 'em being like Snow as were his Teeth. His Nose was rising and *Roman*, instead of *African* and flat. His Mouth, the finest shap'd that cou'd be seen; far from those great turn'd Lips, which are so natural to the rest of the *Negroes*. The whole Proportion and Air of his Face was so noble, and exactly form'd that bating[2] his Colour there cou'd be nothing in Nature more beautiful, agreeable and handsome. There was no one Grace wanting, that bears the Standard of true Beauty: His Hair came down to his Shoulders, by the Aids of Art; which was, by pulling it out with a Quill, and keeping it comb'd; of which he took particular Care. Nor did the Perfections of his Mind come short of those of his Person; for his Discourse was admirable upon almost any Subject; and who-ever had heard him speak, wou'd have been convinc'd of their Errors, that all fine Wit is confin'd to the *White* Men, especially to those of *Christendom*; and wou'd have confess'd that *Oroonoko* was as capable even of reigning well, and of governing as wisely, had as great a Soul, as politick Maxims, and was as sensible of Power as any Prince civiliz'd in the most refin'd Schools of Humanity and Learning, or the most Illustrious Courts.

This Prince, such as I have describ'd him, whose Soul and Body were so admirably adorn'd, was (while yet he was in the Court of his Grandfather) as I said, as capable of Love, as 'twas possible for a brave and gallant Man to be; and in saying that, I have nam'd the highest Degree of Love; for sure, great Souls are most capable of that Passion.

READING CRITICALLY

Behn presents Oroonoko as a royalist or at least as a man sympathetic to the English royalist cause. Why does she portray the African prince in this way?

[1]Charles I

[2]excepting

Romanticism, Realism, and Empire

1800 TO 1900

Detail of Eugéne Delacroix, *Liberty Leading the People.* **1830.** Oil on canvas, 8′ 6″ × 10′ 7″. Photo: Hervè Lewandowski. Musée du Louvre/RMN Réunion des Musées Nationaux, France. SCALA/Art Resource, New York. (See Fig. 28.15)

The nineteenth century is dominated by two crucial social transformations—the emergence of industrial society, supplanting the predominantly agricultural way of life that had defined Western society for centuries, and the extension of European and American control over the native cultures of Africa, Asia, and the Americas. These two forces—industrialization and imperialism—gave rise, especially in the last half of the century, to many of the characteristics that still define Western culture today. More people began living in cities than in the country. Big business emerged, and trade unions organized to resist them. Liberals, recognizing that labor was consistently mistreated by industry, worked for reform, laying the foundations of the welfare state.

Socialism, which decried the control of production by the wealthy few, became a central force in the political life of the West. Seeking work, literally millions of workers emigrated, especially from Eastern Europe to the United States, where, by 1890, fully three quarters of the population was foreign-born. In Europe, the working class increasingly found itself pushed out of the city, as in Paris, or removed to one side, as in London. Where tenements had once stood, the new bourgeois middle class gentrified the cityscape, creating parks, wide streets, and shopping districts. For the first time in history, a large percentage of the population had the time and money to indulge in leisure entertainment and activities, like sailing on the Seine, painting in the open air, or strolling on the island of La Grande Jatte outside Paris on a Sunday afternoon. Increasingly, the populations of the West began to assert their ethnic, linguistic, and cultural identities, and the nation-state as we know it began to take shape. Italy and Germany were unified. France, England, Germany, Russia, and even Belgium all competed to assert their national supremacy by gaining control of vast reaches of Africa and Asia. This was taking place even as, in the Americas, the United States moved to assert its supremacy over the American continent, driving the Native American population into reservations and its own Southern states, who tried to assert their own national identity by seceding from the Union, into subjugation. All this required great military expenditure, and the foundations of modern warfare were laid in place.

In the arts, such developments were not received uncritically. Reacting against the Neoclassical quest for order and control that was epitomized by the figure of Napoleon Bonaparte, the Romantic movement in art and literature sought to broaden its understanding of human experience, to recognize the tumultuous power of human emotion and imagination. Sentimentality, melancholy, and longing, as well as triumph and joy, all were symptomatic of the Romantic cast of mind. The darker side of the imagination also revealed itself—one tormented by the horrors of war, the destructive power of the human will, and the frightening prospects of nightmare and fantasy. In poetry, in painting, and in music, this new investigation into the subjective reaches of the self opened new realms of feeling and experience.

To some, such investigations were merely self-indulgent, especially given the sordid realities of working-class life that would lead, in 1848, to more than a hundred revolutions across the European continent. Some writers chose to parody the Romantic frame of mind. Painters and writers celebrated the quiet heroism of the working class, even as they lambasted the ruling class and the blind eye it turned toward suffering. Idealism came to seem something of a sham, a retreat from the human condition—or what one author called the "human comedy." Forces larger than the self—biological and social—seemed to determine the course of existence. But art could also turn its eye to the bourgeoisie and celebrate its good life, as the Impressionist painters would come to paint not work but leisure.

Beginning in the 1880s, artists and thinkers begin to believe in the necessity of pushing aside previous norms and standards entirely, instead of merely revising past knowledge in light of current techniques, a process that suggests a nascent, burgeoning modernism. As one writer remarked, "It is essential to be thoroughly modern in one's tastes." The drive to be "modern" involved the self-conscious rejection of tradition, which very often asserted itself at major art exhibitions. In literature, the Symbolist movement would have a tremendous influence on the development of modernist poetry, and the first great modernist painters of the next century would develop directly out of a Symbolist tradition in painting. And philosophers and intellectuals in their abandonment of convention and tradition announced the liberation of modern consciousness.

1806
Georg Wilhelm Friedrich Hegel, *The Philosophy of History*

1817–1818
Caspar David Friedrich, *The Wanderer above the Mists*

1814–1815
Goya's *Third of May, 1808*

1824
Beethoven, Ninth Symphony

1823–1839
Katsushika Hokusai's *Thirty-six Views of Mount Fuji*

1832
Goethe's play *Faust*

1835
Thomas Phillips, *Portrait of Byron*

1839
The first photographs

1848
Karl Marx and Friedrich Engel, *The Communist Manifesto*

1849
Gold discovered in California; Henry David Thoreau writes *Civil Disobedience*

1850s
Florence Nightingale establishes nursing as a profession

1853
Admiral Perry initiates contact with Japan

1853–1870s
Baron Haussmann redesigns Paris

1857
Charles Baudelaire's book of poems *Les Fleurs du mal*

1859
Charles Darwin, *The Origin of Species*

1888–1889
Auguste Rodin's *The Kiss*

1880s–90s
European "Scramble for Africa"

1883
U.S. Supreme Court nullifies Civil Rights Act, enabling Jim Crow laws in South

1885
Mark Twain's novel *Huckleberry Finn*

1892
Walt Whitman's final edition of *Leaves of Grass*

1897–1898
Louis Sullivan's Bayard (Condict) Building, New York

1902–1904
Paul Cezanne's *Mont Sainte-Victoire*

LEARN MORE Explore an interactive timeline on **www.myartslab.com**

27 | The Romantic World View
The Self in Nature and the Nature of Self

THINKING AHEAD

What is Romanticism?

How does landscape painting reflect a Romantic worldview?

What is Transcendentalism?

What are the characteristics of the Romantic hero?

What experience shaped Goya's worldview?

What insight lies at the heart of Herman Melville's novel Moby Dick*?*

What is Romantic music?

intern Abbey is a ruined medieval monastery on the banks of the Wye River north of Bristol in South Wales, England (Fig. **27.1**). For centuries, its roofless buildings had been open to the air and its skeletal Gothic arches overgrown with weeds and saplings. In the late eighteenth century, it was common for British travelers to tour the beautiful Wye River, and the final destination of the journey was the Abbey (Map **27.1**). In 1798, a British magazine writer assigned a degree of importance to the *Wye Tour* (as it was known) that might surprise the modern reader:

> The enchanting beauties of the River Wye are by this time pretty generally known among the lovers of the picturesque . . . [C]uriosity has been inflamed by poetry and by prose, by paintings, prints, and drawings. . . . An excursion on the Wye has become an essential part of the education . . . of all who aspire to the reputation of elegance, taste, and fashion.

That a "tour" of English scenery should be "essential" to one's education suggests that there is more to the picturesque than just the "view" it offers. The River Wye offered larger lessons.

This chapter surveys the growing taste for the natural world in the late eighteenth and first half of the nineteenth centuries in Europe, particularly England and Germany, and in America, where a loosely knit group known as the Transcendentalists sought to discover the "transcendent" order of nature. Unifying principles could be found in the natural world, which became a sacred space that pointed to the immanent presence of the divine. During this period, poets, painters, essayists, and composers increasingly came to view nature itself as the greatest teacher, the defining center of culture, and the pivotal force that determined and guided human experience. London and New York might well have been the Western hubs of commerce, Washington, D.C., and Paris the focal

◀ **Fig. 27.1 J. M. W. Turner,** *Interior of Tintern Abbey.* **1794.** Watercolor, 12 ⁵/₈ × 9 ⁷/₈″. The Trustees of the Victoria and Albert Museum, London, Art Resource, New York. Turner toured South Wales and the Wye Valley in 1792, when he was 19 years old. This watercolor is based on a sketch made on that trip.

HEAR MORE Listen to an audio file of your chapter at **www.myartslab.com**

points of political life, but it was to nature that artists turned for inspiration.

Romantic artists revolted against the classical values of order, control, balance, and proportionality championed by Neoclassical artists, many of whom—Jacques-Louis David, for instance (see Chapter 26)—were their contemporaries. They approached the world instead with an outpouring of feeling and emotional intensity that came to be called *Romanticism* [roh-MAN-tih-siz-um]. Originally coined in 1798 by the German writer and poet Friedrich von Schlegel [SHLAY-gul] (1772–1829), "Romanticism" was an overt reaction against the Enlightenment and classical culture of the eighteenth century. For Schlegel, Romanticism refers mainly to his sense that the common cultural ground of Europe—the Classical past from which it had descended, and the values of which it shared—was disintegrating, as Europeans formed new nation-states based on individual cultural identities.

Schlegel's own thinking was deeply influenced by the philosopher Immanuel Kant [kahnt] (1724–1804). In his *Critique of Judgment* (1790), Kant defined the pleasure we derive from art as "disinterested satisfaction." By this he meant that contemplating beauty, whether in nature or in a work of art, put the mind into a state of free play in which things that seemed to oppose each other—subject and object, reason and imagination—are united. Schlegel was equally influenced by Johann Winckelmann's perspective on Greek art (see Chapter 26). What the Greeks offered were not works of art to be slavishly imitated, in the manner of Neoclassical artists. For Winckelmann, and for Schlegel, the Greeks provided a new way for the Romantic artist to approach nature: The Greeks studied nature in order to discover its essence. Nature only occasionally rises to moments of pure beauty. The lesson taught by the Greeks, Winckelmann argued, was that art might capture and hold those rare moments.

Late in his life, the French *philosophe* Jean-Jacques Rousseau, who had argued in *Émile* (1762) for the centrality of preserving the "natural" in every child's education (see Chapter 25), anticipated the Romantic engagement with such "rare moments" in his *Reveries of the Solitary Walker* (**Reading 27.1**):

Map 27.1 Romantic England.

READING 27.1

from Jean-Jacques Rousseau, *Reveries of the Solitary Walker* (1782)

Everything is in constant flux on this earth. But if there is a state where the soul can find a resting-place secure enough to establish itself and concentrate its entire being there, with no need to remember the past or reach into the future, where time is nothing to it, where the present runs on indefinitely but this duration goes unnoticed, with no sign of the passing of time, and no other feeling of deprivation or enjoyment, pleasure or pain, desire or fear than the simple feeling of existence, a feeling that fills our soul entirely, as long as this state lasts, we can call ourselves happy, not with a poor, incomplete and relative happiness such as we find in the pleasures of life, but with a sufficient, complete and perfect happiness which leaves no emptiness to be filled in the soul. Such is the state which I often experienced on the Island of Saint-Pierre in my solitary reveries, whether I lay in a boat and drifted where the water carried me, or sat by the shores of the stormy lake, or elsewhere, on the banks of a lovely river or a stream murmuring over the stones.

Dedicated to the discovery of just such moments in nature, the Romantics rejected the truth of empirical observation, which John Locke and other Enlightenment thinkers had championed. The objective world mattered far less to them than their subjective experience of it. The poet Samuel Taylor Coleridge, one of the founders of the Romantic movement, offered a pithy summary in a letter to a friend: "My opinion is this—that deep Thinking is attainable only by a man of deep Feeling, and that all Truth is a species of Revelation." Knowing the exact distance between Earth and its moon mattered far less than how it *felt* to look at the moon in the dark sky. And it must be remembered that for Romantics, the night was incomparably more appealing, because it was more mysterious and unknowable, than the daylight world.

Nor did they believe that the human mind was necessarily a thinking thing, as Descartes had argued, when he wrote, "I think, therefore I am." For the Romantics, the mind was a feeling thing, not distinct from the body as Descartes had it, but intimately connected to it. Feelings, they believed, led to truth, and most of the major writers and artists of the early nineteenth century used their emotions as a primary way of expressing their imagination and creativity.

Indeed, since nature stimulated the emotions as it did the imagination, the natural world became the primary subject of Romantic poetry, and landscape the primary genre of Romantic painting. Because nurturing one's feelings restored human beings to their own true nature, examining the emotional life of the self in relation to the world characterized Romantic fiction. In nature the Romantics discovered not just the wellspring of their own creativity, but the very presence of God, the manifestation of the divine on earth.

THE EARLY ROMANTIC IMAGINATION

In July 1798, the same year the British writer claimed that the Wye Tour was essential to everyone's education, the 28-year-old poet William Wordsworth (1770–1850) visited Wye Valley, accompanied by his sister Dorothy. There he experienced something akin to the same moments of reverie as Rousseau on his walks on the Island of Saint-Pierre and composed a poem that for his entire generation would come to embody the very idea of the Romantic.

The Idea of the Romantic: William Wordsworth's "Tintern Abbey"

The Wordsworth poem that had such a major impact is generally known by the shortened title "Tintern Abbey." Its complete title is "Lines Composed a Few Miles above Tintern Abbey, on Revisiting the Banks of the Wye during a Tour, July 13, 1798" (see **Reading 27.2**, pages 915–916, for the complete poem). The poet had visited the valley five years before, and he begins his poem by thinking back to that earlier trip:

> Five years have passed; five summers, with the length
> Of five long winters! and again I hear
> These waters, rolling from their mountain-springs
> With a soft inland murmur. —Once again
> Do I behold these steep and lofty cliffs,
> That on a wild secluded scene impress
> Thoughts of more deep seclusion; and connect
> The landscape with the quiet of the sky.

The implication is that the scene evokes thoughts "more deep" than mere appearance, thoughts in which landscape and sky—and perhaps the poet himself—are all connected, united together as one.

After describing the scene before him at greater length, the poet then recalls the solace that his memories of the place had brought him in the five intervening years as he had lived "in lonely rooms, and 'mid the din / Of towns and cities." His memories of the place, he says, brought him "tranquil restoration," but even more important "another gift," in which "the weary weight / Of all this unintelligible world, / Is lightened" by allowing the poet to "see into the life of things." Wordsworth does not completely comprehend the power of the human mind here. What the mind achieves at such moments remains to him something of a "mystery." But it seems to him as if his breath and blood, his very body—that "corporeal frame"—is suspended in a "power / Of harmony" that informs all things.

Wordsworth next describes how he reacted to the scene as a boy. The scene, he says, was merely "an appetite." But now, as an adult, he looks on the natural world differently. He finds in nature a connection between landscape, sky, and thought that is intimated in the opening lines of the poem. Humankind and Nature are united in total harmony:

> A motion and a spirit, that impels
> All thinking things, all objects of all thought,
> And rolls through all things.

In this perception of the unity of all things, Wordsworth is able to define nature as his "anchor" and "nurse," "The guide, the guardian of my heart, and soul / Of all my mortal being." Wordsworth's vision is informed not just by the scene itself, but by his memory of it, and by his imagination's understanding of its power. As the poem moves toward conclusion, Wordsworth turns to his sister beside him, praying that she too will know, as he does, that "Nature never did betray / The heart that loved her." Indeed, Wordsworth's prayer for his sister Dorothy is really intended as a prayer for us all. We should each of us become, as he is himself, "a worshipper of Nature."

"Tintern Abbey" can be taken as one of the fullest statements of the Romantic imagination. In the course of its 159 lines, it argues that in experiencing the beauty of nature, the imagination dissolves all opposition. Wordsworth suggests that the mind is an active participant in the process of human perception rather than a passive vessel. There is an ethical dimension to aesthetic experience, a way to stand above, or beyond, the "dreary intercourse of daily life," both literally and figuratively on higher ground. Perhaps most of all, the poem provides Wordsworth with the opportunity for communion, not merely with the natural world, but with his sister beside him, and by extension his readers as well. In individual experience, Wordsworth makes contact with the whole.

A Romantic Experiment: Lyrical Ballads

On his way to Tintern Abbey and the River Derwent [DUR-wunt] in 1798, Wordsworth had stopped in Bristol to drop off a book of poems at Joseph Cottle's publishing house. He had co-written the book *Lyrical Ballads* with his friend, Samuel Taylor Coleridge [KOLE-rij] (1772–1834). Coleridge had published with Cottle already, but *Lyrical Ballads* was published anonymously. As Coleridge put it, "Wordsworth's name is nothing—[and] to a large number of persons mine stinks." At the last moment, on his way back from South Wales, Wordsworth added "Tintern Abbey" to the volume.

For its next editions, in 1800 and 1802, the book was significantly revised and augmented, and Wordsworth included an important preface that discussed why poetry should attempt to reflect what he called "the language of conversation" (**Reading 27.3**):

READING 27.3

from William Wordsworth, "Preface" to
***Lyrical Ballads* (1800)**

The principal object . . . proposed in these Poems was to choose incidents and situations from common life, and to relate or describe them, throughout, as far as was possible, in a selection of language really used by men. . . . Humble and rustic life was generally chosen, because, in that condition, the essential passions of the heart find a better soil in which they can attain their maturity, are less under restraint, and speak a plainer and more emphatic language; because in that condition of life our elementary feelings co-exist in a state of greater simplicity, and, consequently, may be more accurately contemplated, and more forcibly communicated; because the manners of rural life germinate from those elementary feelings; and, from the necessary character of rural occupations, are more easily comprehended, and are more durable; and lastly, because in that condition the passions of men are incorporated with the beautiful and permanent forms of nature. The language, too, of these men is adopted . . . because such men hourly communicate with the best objects from which the best part of language is originally derived; and because . . . they convey their feelings and notions in simple and unelaborated expressions.

Although the Wordsworth of "Tintern Abbey" is no humble rustic, the aim of the poem is precisely that of the *Lyrical Ballads* as a whole, to discover that moment when "the passions of men are incorporated with the beautiful

and permanent form of nature." Wordsworth further defines poetry as "the spontaneous overflow of powerful feelings" resulting from "emotion recollected in tranquility," emotions like those he recollected overlooking Tintern Abbey. The poet, Wordsworth writes, "considers man and nature as essentially adapted to each other, and the mind of man as naturally the mirror of the fairest and most interesting qualities of nature."

In 1799, Wordsworth and his sister moved to the northern Lake District, where they had grown up. Over the course of the next seven years, he wrote some of his greatest poems, such as "The Rainbow," a favorite subject of both Romantic poets and painters (Fig. **27.2**) and published in 1807 as *Poems in Two Volumes* (Reading **27.4**):

READING 27.4

William Wordsworth, "The Rainbow" (1802)

My heart leaps up when I behold
A rainbow in the sky:
So was it when my life began,
So is it now I am a man,
So be it when I shall grow old,
Or let me die!
The child is the father of the man;
And I could wish my days to be
Bound each to each by natural piety.

Wordsworth wrote "The Rainbow" in 1802, while he was working on the first draft of *The Prelude*, the book-length autobiographical poem not published until after his death in 1850 in which he traced "the growth of a poet's mind." So, despite its shortness—only nine lines—"The Rainbow" has packed into it much of the thinking that went into the later, much longer poem. Both poems express the idea that his poetic occupation had been foreordained in his childhood. In "The Rainbow," the poet is reaching back into his childhood in order to begin his quest for the unity of self. The poem's first line brings together feeling

Fig. 27.2 John Constable, ***Landscape and Double Rainbow.*** **1812.** Oil on paper mounted on canvas, 13$\frac{1}{4}$" × 15". Victoria and Albert Museum, London/Art Resource, New York. 328-1888. Near the end of his life, Constable would copy Wordsworth's poem into his notebooks. Constable himself wrote: "Nature in all the varied aspects of her beauty exhibits no feature more lovely nor any that awakens a more soothing reflection than the rainbow."

SEE MORE For a Closer Look at William Wordsworth's poem "The Rainbow" go to **www.myartslab.com**

("my heart leaps up") and vision ("when I behold"); the subjective and objective are unified in a single moment. The rainbow itself serves as a traditional symbol of renewal, a renewal founded in Judeo-Christian tradition, where God says to Noah after the Flood: "I do set my bow in the cloud, and it shall be a covenant between me and the earth." Yet here, it symbolizes the bridge between the secular world and the spiritual realm. Wordsworth's covenant is not between God and humanity, but between himself and nature. This is what he means by "natural piety," a reverence for nature of which he longs to be reminded each and every day.

Romanticism as a Voyage of Discovery: Samuel Taylor Coleridge

Wordsworth's statements in the Preface to *Lyrical Ballads* could not be further from the mind-sets of the characters created by his friend Coleridge. In fact, the Mariner in Coleridge's "Rime of the Ancient Mariner," a long narrative poem which opened *Lyrical Ballads*, is a man wholly at odds with nature. In Part 1 of the poem, the Mariner senselessly kills the albatross that had been his shipmates' companion at sea (see **Reading 27.5**, pages 917–918). He and his shipmates come to see this act as bringing them the worst luck a ship can have, to be floating in the middle of the ocean until they run out of food and water (**Reading 27.5a**):

READING 27.5a

from Samuel Taylor Coleridge, "Rime of the Ancient Mariner," Part II (1797)

Day after day, day after day,
We stuck, nor breath nor motion;
As idle as a painted ship
Upon a painted ocean.

Water, water, everywhere,
And all the boards did shrink;
Water, water, everywhere,
Nor any drop to drink.

In fact, a death ship arrives in this unnatural sea, taking all the crew but leaving the Mariner alone in a kind of living death (**Reading 27.5b**):

READING 27.5b

from Samuel Taylor Coleridge, "Rime of the Ancient Mariner," Part IV (1797)

Alone, alone, all, all alone,
Alone on a wide wide sea!
And never a saint took pity on
My soul in agony.

His salvation comes only when he recognizes that even the watersnakes that surround him are "living things" (**Reading 27.5c**):

READING 27.5c

from Samuel Taylor Coleridge, "Rime of the Ancient Mariner," Part IV (1797)

A spring of love gushed from my heart,
And I blessed them unaware:
Sure my kind saint took pity on me,
And I blessed them unaware. . . .

The self-same moment I could pray;
And from my neck so free
The Albatross fell off, and sank
Like lead into the sea.

Although the Mariner still faces many trials, this is the turning point of his life. His redemption seems possible.

The supernatural and mystical character of Coleridge's imagination—fueled not incidentally by his addiction to opium—helped to define Romantic art as a voyage of discovery. Indeed, Coleridge's poem contains a clear moral lesson. The Mariner's killing of the albatross is an act of bad faith, an attack on the natural world that puts him at odds with it. Only after he blesses the watersnakes, creatures even more monstrous than the albatross, can he redeem himself, reuniting himself with nature as a whole.

Classical versus Romantic: The Odes of John Keats

The odes of John Keats (1795–1821) represent the essence of Romantic poetry. An **ode** is a poem of exaltation, exhibiting deep feeling. Keats's life was tragically short. Most of his greatest poems were written in one year (September 1818 to September 1819) when he was deeply in love with a young woman and was simultaneously diagnosed with tuberculosis, the disease that had killed his mother.

Keats's "Ode to a Nightingale" is typical of the Romantic's contemplation of nature. "My heart aches, and a drowsy numbness pains / My sense, as though of hemlock I had drunk," it begins, but the song of the Nightingale awakens his senses. Still, he says, "I have been half in love with easeful Death, / Call'd him soft names in many a mused rhyme." But he recognizes something eternal in the song of the nightingale (**Reading 27.6**):

READING 27.6

from John Keats, "Ode to a Nightingale" (1819)

Thou wast not born for death, immortal Bird!
No hungry generations tread thee down;

The voice I hear this passing night was heard
In ancient days by emperor and clown:
Perhaps the self-same song that found a path
Through the sad heart of Ruth, when, sick for home,
She stood in tears amid the alien corn;[1]
The same that oft-times hath
Charm'd magic casements,[2] opening on the foam
Of perilous seas, in faery lands forlorn. . . .

[1] In proclaiming the immortality of the nightingale, Keats alludes to the biblical Ruth. As a widow, she relocated to Bethlehem to care for her mother-in-law, Naomi, and ended up tending fields of grain in an alien land. She ultimately married the landowner, Boaz, and was great-grandmother to King David of Israel. Ruth attained immortality through her good deeds.
[2] Casements are windows.

Keats comes to an awareness here of the eternal beauty and continuity of the nightingale's song. This is also the clear implication of Keats's "Ode on a Grecian Urn"—the beauty of art lives on. In the poem, Keats contemplates a Greek vase covered with figures whose joy in the fleeting pleasures of life is, paradoxically, permanently immortalized in the design of the vase (**Reading 27.7**):

READING 27.7

John Keats, "Ode on a Grecian Urn" (1819)

Thou still unravish'd bride of quietness,
Thou foster-child of silence and slow time,
Sylvan historian, who canst thou express
A flowery tale more sweetly than our rhyme:
What leaf-fring'd legend haunt about thy shape
Of deities or mortals, or of both,
In Tempe or the dales of Arcady?
What men or gods are these? What maidens loth?
What mad pursuit? What struggle to escape?
What pipes and timbrels? What wild ecstasy?

Heard melodies are sweet, but those unheard
Are sweeter: therefore, ye soft pipes, play on;
Not to the sensual ear, but, more endear'd,
Pipe to the spirit ditties of no tone:
Fair youth, beneath the trees, thou canst not leave
Thy song, nor ever can those trees be bare;
Bold lover, never, never canst thou kiss,
Though winning near the goal—yet, do not grieve;
She cannot fade, though thou hast not thy bliss,
For ever wilt thou love, and she be fair!

Ah, happy, happy boughs! that cannot shed
Your leaves, nor ever bid the spring adieu;
And, happy melodist, unwearied,
For ever piping songs for ever new;
More happy love! more happy, happy love!
For ever warm and still to be enjoy'd,
For ever panting, and for ever young;
All breathing human passion far above,
That leaves a heart high-sorrowful and cloy'd,
A burning forehead, and a parching tongue.

Who are these coming to the sacrifice?
To what green altar, O mysterious priest,
Lead'st thou that heifer lowing at the skies,
And all her silken flanks with garlands drest?
What little town by river or sea shore,
Or mountain-built with peaceful citadel,
Is emptied of this folk, this pious morn?
And, little town, thy streets for evermore
Will silent be; and not a soul to tell
Why thou art desolate, can e'er return.

O Attic shape! Fair attitude! with brede
Of marble men and maidens overwrought,
With forest branches and the trodden weed;
Thou, silent form, dost tease us out of thought
As doth eternity: Cold Pastoral!
When old age shall this generation waste,
Thou shalt remain, in midst of other woe
Than ours, a friend to man, to whom thou say'st,
"Beauty is truth, truth beauty,"—that is all
Ye know on earth, and all ye need to know.

Contemplating a Greek vase—probably a composite "ideal" vase made up of scenes derived from those in the collection of the British Museum—Keats admits ignorance about the symbolism of the decorative motifs and what "deities or mortals, or both" are painted on it. Yet the vase's scenes come alive in his imagination and are all the more poignant for being eternal, unchangeable, and silent. The melodies being played by the musicians illustrated on the vase, if anyone were to hear them, would, of course, be beautiful, "but those unheard / Are sweeter." The trees can never lose their leaves. And though the lover will never succeed in kissing his love, thus painted, he can take solace in the fact that she "cannot fade" and will be forever fair. He imagines that the people who populate the vase have been drawn out of some "little town," the streets of which are now forever silent. Then, to conclude, the poet addresses the vase directly: "O Attic shape," he says, when we are dead, you shall remain a "friend to man." The vase imparts an important message to humankind:

"Beauty is truth, truth beauty,"—that is all
Ye know on earth, and all ye need to know.

These last two lines are possibly the most discussed and debated in English poetry. They suggest that the vase, and by extension the poem itself, is a higher form of nature than mortal life. This is, of course, a traditional theme of poetry—think of Shakespeare's sonnets (see Chapter 19)—but in the context of Keats's own tragic struggle with tuberculosis and his imminent death, it takes on a stunningly poignant and deeply Romantic tone. Rather than being terrified by the prospect of mortality, the individual contests death and exalts in the confrontation. Perhaps the poem's greatest achievement is that it dissolves the greatest opposition of them all, uniting life and death in the circularity of the "leaf-fring'd legend" that draws the viewers' eyes around the vase's shape. In February 1821, a few months after his twenty-fifth birthday, Keats died in Rome, survived only by his posthumously published poems.

THE ROMANTIC LANDSCAPE

The most notable landscape painting in Europe had developed in Italy and the Netherlands 200 years earlier. Even the term *landscape* derives from the Dutch word *landschap*, meaning a patch of cultivated ground. Although influenced by Italian artists' use of light and color, the great seventeenth-century Dutch landscape painters, including Jacob van Ruisdael (see Chapter 22), were also inspired by a dramatically changing physical geography sparked by the reclamation of hundreds of thousands of acres of land along the coasts. The Dutch landscape painters in turn influenced later English landscape painters. Two seventeenth-century French painters, Nicolas Poussin and Claude Lorrain, also influenced the British artists (see Figs. 23.8 and 25.12). Lorrain's use of light and color, in particular, inspired the young John Constable, among the most popular of the English Romantic painters.

John Constable: Painter of the English Countryside

Tension between the timeless and the more fleeting aspects of nature deeply informs the paintings of John Constable (1776–1837). Constable focused most of his efforts on the area around the valley of the Stour River in his native East Bergholt, Suffolk. Like Wordsworth, he felt his talents depended on "faithful adherence to the truth of nature." In 1802, he complained that he had been too busy looking at the work of others: "I have been running after pictures, and seeking the truth at second hand." He acknowledged that "one's mind may be elevated, and kept up to what is excellent, by the works of the great masters," but believed that he needed to look to nature, for "Nature is the fountain's head, the source from which all originally must spring."

Like Wordsworth, Constable believed that his art could be traced back to his childhood on the Stour, to places that he had known his whole life. "I should paint my own places best," he wrote to a friend in 1821, "I associate my 'careless boyhood' to all that lies on the banks of the Stour. They made me a painter (& I am grateful)." A painting like *The Stour Valley and Dedham Village* could almost illustrate the opening lines of Wordsworth's "Tintern Abbey," with its "plots of cottage grounds," "orchard tufts," "hedge rows," and "pastoral farms" (Fig. 27.3). Like Wordsworth, Constable also wished to depict incidents and situations from common life, including villages, churches, farmhouses, and cottages. But most of all, the painting captures Constable's sense that he was, like Wordsworth, "a worshipper of Nature," a religious sentiment underscored by the presence of the Dedham parish church in the distance. As Constable

Fig. 27.3 John Constable, *The Stour Valley and Dedham Village.* 1814. Oil on canvas, 21$\frac{3}{4}$" × 30$\frac{3}{4}$". Photograph © 2008 Museum of Fine Arts, Boston. William W. Warren Fund, 1948 (48.226). The workers in the foreground are loading manure onto a cart for spreading in the fields.

wrote in a letter of May 1819, "Every tree seems full of blossom of some kind & the surface of the ground seems quite living—every step I take & on whatever object I turn my Eye that sublime expression of the Scripture 'I am the resurrection and the life' &c, seems verified about me." In fact, the cathedral at the center of so many Constable landscapes symbolizes the permanence of God in nature.

Constable sketched endlessly. His drawing of *Willy Lott's House, East Bergholt* is typical (Fig. **27.4**). Lott, a farmer, lived in this house his entire 80 years, spending only four nights of his life away from it. For Constable, the house symbolized a stability and permanence that contrasts dramatically with the impermanence of the weather, the constant flux of light and shadow, sun and cloud. The drawing served as the basis for one of *The Hay Wain* (Fig. **27.5**), one of a

Fig. 27.4 John Constable, *Willy Lott's House, East Bergholt*. ca. 1820. Graphite on paper (drawing made up of three sheets of paper), $9^7/_8'' \times 11^1/_8''$. Courtauld Institute of Art Gallery, London. For Constable, this farmhouse symbolized a stability and permanence that contrasted dramatically with the unpredictability of weather, the constant flux of light and shadow, sun and cloud.

Fig. 27.5 John Constable, *The Hay Wain*. 1821. Oil on canvas, $51^3/_8'' \times 73''$. The National Gallery, London. Constable failed to sell *The Hay Wain* when it was exhibited at the Royal Academy in 1821, though he turned down an offer of £70 for it.

LEARN MORE Gain insight from a primary source document from John Constable at **www.myartslab.com**

series of major paintings that he referred to as his "six-footers" and that he worked on from 1819 to 1825. All six canvases depict scenes on the Stour painted in his London studio from sketches and drawings done earlier. Constable felt that a sketch reflected just one emotion. "A sketch," he wrote, "will not serve more than one state of mind & will not serve to drink at it again & again—in a sketch there is nothing but one state of mind—that which you were in at the time." This critique of the sketch goes a long way toward explaining the power of Constable's painting. It contains more than one state of mind—the passing storm, indicated by the darkened clouds on the left, contrasts with the brightly lit field below the billowing clouds at the right, the longevity of the tree behind the house with its massive trunk contrasts with the freshly cut hay at the right, the gentleman fisherman contrasts with the hard-working cart drivers.

When the painting was first exhibited at the Royal Academy in 1821, Londoners could not accept that this was a "finished" painting because it had been painted in economic, almost abstract terms. Constable used short, broken strokes of color in a variety of shades and tints to produce a given hue (the green of foliage, for example). Nor did they understand how such a common theme deserved such a monumental canvas. Constable subsequently complained to a friend, "Londoners with all their ingenuity as artists know nothing of the feeling of a country life (the essence of Landscape)—any more than a hackney coach horse knows of pasture."

Joseph Mallord William Turner: Colorist of the Imagination

The other great English landscape painter of the day, Joseph Mallord William Turner (1775–1851), was closer in temperament to Coleridge than to Wordsworth. He freely explored what he called "the colors of the imagination." Even his contemporaries recognized, in the words of the critic William Hazlitt (1778–1830), that Turner was interested less in "the objects of nature than . . . the medium through which they are seen." In Turner's paintings, earth and vegetation seem to dissolve into light and water, into the very medium—gleaming oil or translucent watercolor—with which he paints them. In *The Upper Falls of the Reichenbach* [RY-khun-bahk], for instance, Turner's depiction of the falls, among the highest in the Swiss Alps, seems to animate the rocky precipice (Fig. 27.6). Turner draws our attention not to the rock, cliff, and mountain, but to the mist and light through which we see them.

Fig. 27.6 J. M. W. Turner, *The Upper Falls of the Reichenbach.* ca. 1810–1815. Watercolor, $10^7/_8''$ × $15^7/_{16}''$. Yale Center for British Art, Paul Mellon Collection. The Bridgeman Art Library. Turner achieved the transparent effect of the rainbow and the spray rising from the falls by scraping away the watercolor down to the white paper beneath.

Perhaps the best way to understand the difference between Constable and Turner is to consider the *scale* of their respective visions. Constable's work is "close," nearby and familiar, with an abundance of human associations. Turner's is exotic, remote, and even alienating. The human figure in Constable's paintings is an essential and elemental presence, uniting man and nature. The human figure in Turner's paintings is minuscule, almost irrelevant to the painting except insofar as its minuteness underscores nature's very indifference. Not only is *The Upper Falls of the Reichenbach* removed from the close-at-hand world of Constable's paintings, but the cowherd and his dog, barely visible at the lower left of the painting, are dwarfed by the immensity of the scene. Cattle graze on the rise at the bottom middle, and another herd is on the ridge across the gorge. The effect is similar to that described by Wordsworth in "Tintern Abbey":

And I have felt
A presence that disturbs me with the joy
Of elevated thought; a sense sublime
Of something far more deeply interfused,
Whose dwelling is the light of setting suns,
And the round ocean and the living air
And the blue sky, and in the mind of man:
A motion and a spirit, that impels
All thinking things, all objects of all thought,
And rolls through all things.

We must keep in mind, though, that the sublime is never altogether benign or kind. In *The Fall of an Avalanche in the Grisons* [gree-SOHNZ], for example, (Fig. **27.7**), there is no human figure, only a mountain hut about to be crushed beneath a giant thumb of rock and debris. The viewer has nowhere to stand, except in the path of this mammoth demonstration of nature's force. Turner himself wrote lines to accompany the painting in the exhibition catalogue:

The downward sun a parting sadness gleams,
Portentous lurid thro' the gathering storm'
Thick drifting snow on snow,
Till the vast weight bursts thro' the rocky barrier;
Down at once, its pine clad forests,
And towering glaciers fall, the work of ages
Crashing through all! extinction follows,
And the toil, the hope of man—o'erwhelms.

The painting suggests the "extinction" of the very "hope of man"—a sentiment far removed from Constable's pastoral landscapes or Wordsworth's "natural piety." Turner had never been to the Grisons, and this painting seems to have been inspired by an avalanche that occurred there in 1808, crushing a chalet beneath huge rocks propelled by a giant mass of snow. The painting is an act of pure imagination. It anticipates his great paintings of the 1840s, in which he focused on the immersion of the self (and the viewer) into the primal forces of nature.

Fig. 27.7 J. M. W. Turner, *The Fall of an Avalanche in the Grisons.* 1810. Oil on canvas, 35⅝" × 47¼". Clore Collection, Tate Gallery, London/Art Resource, New York. This and Fig. 27.6 were influenced by Turner's tour of the Alps in 1802.

One of the most daring of these later masterpieces was *Snow Storm—Steam-Boat off a Harbour's Mouth* (1842), originally subtitled *The author was in this storm on the night the Ariel left Harwich* (Fig. **27.8**). "I wished to show," Turner said, "what such a scene was like. I got the sailors to lash me to the mast to observe it . . . and I did not expect to escape: but I felt bound to record it if I did." We have no evidence confirming a ship named *Ariel*. Most likely, Turner imagined this scene of a maelstrom of steam and storm that deposits us at its very heart. Turner's depiction of the raw experience of nature in its most elemental form clearly represents a Romantic view of the world. This view is the opposite of the Enlightenment ideal of the natural world characterized by clarity, order, and harmony.

The Romantic in Germany: Friedrich and Kant

Although Constable and Turner's approaches are very different, both believed that nature provoked their imaginations. In the German Romantic tradition, the imagination is also the fundamental starting point. The painter Caspar David Friedrich [FREED-rikh] (1774–1840) represents the imaginative capacities of the Romantic mind by placing figures, often solitary ones, before sublime landscapes (see *Closer Look*, pages 888–889). In *Monk by the Sea* (Fig. **27.9**), a figure stands alone, engulfed in the vast expanse of sand and storm, as if

Fig. 27.8 J. M. W. Turner, ***Snow Storm—Steam-Boat off a Harbour's Mouth.*** **1842.** Oil on canvas, 36″ × 48″. Clore Collection, Tate Gallery, London/Art Resource, New York. Turner bequeathed 19,049 drawings and watercolors to the British nation. Many of these works anticipate the gestural freedom of this painting, with its sweeping, linear rhythms.

facing the void. His is a crisis of faith. How do I know God? he seems to ask. And how, in the face of this empty vastness, do I come to belief? Can I even believe?

These sentiments echo the philosopher Immanuel Kant's *Critique of Pure Reason* (1781), in which Kant had argued that the mind is not a passive recipient of information—not, that is, the "blank slate" that Locke had claimed. For Kant, the mind was an active agent in the creation of knowledge. He believed that the ways we understand concepts like space, time, quantity, the relations among things, and, especially, quality, are innate from birth. We come to understand the world through the operation of these innate mental abilities as they perceive the various aspects of experience. Each of our experiences is various as well, and so each mind creates its own body of knowledge, its own world. No longer was the nature of reality the most important question. Instead, the mind confronting reality was paramount. Kant shifted the basic question of philosophy, in other

Fig. 27.9 Caspar David Friedrich, ***Monk by the Sea.*** **1809–1810.** Oil on canvas, 47 1/2″ × 67″. Inv.: NG 9/85. Nationalgalerie, Staatliche Museen zu Berlin, Berlin, Germany. Joerg P. Anders/Bildarchiv Preussischer Kulturbesitz/Art Resource, New York. Schloss Charlottenburg, Berlin. Bildarchiv Preussischer Kulturbesitz. Some art historians believe that the monk is Friedrich himself, which makes this a self-portrait.

In his 1756 *Philosophical Enquiry into the Origin of Our Ideas of the Sublime and the Beautiful,* the philosopher Edmund Burke (1729–1797) wrote that "the passion caused by the great and sublime in nature is astonishment." "Astonishment," Burke continues, "is that state of the soul in which all its motions are suspended, with some degree of horror." The **sublime,** in short, is the prospect of anything beyond the ability of the human mind to comprehend it fully. Thus, "the sublimity of the ocean is due to the fact that it is an object of no little terror," and "infinity fills the mind with that sort of delightful horror which is the truest test of the sublime." French art historian Jean Clay notes that "the sublime is evoked through monuments too colossal to be apprehended except by fragments," monuments such as that portrayed in Hubert Robert's *Pyramids.* As Burke argued, "Let it be considered that hardly anything can strike the mind with its greatness, which does not make some sort of approach towards infinity; which nothing can do whilst we are able to perceive its bounds."

Great mountain ranges stretching as far as the eye can see, such as the Alps or the American Rockies, evoke the same feelings. As late as 1681, Thomas Burnet, writing in his *Sacred Theory of the Earth,* could feel confident in condemning mountains:

> They are placed in no Order one with the other, that can either respect Use or Beauty; and if you consider them singly, they do not consist of any Proportion of Parts that is referable to any Design. . . . There is nothing in Nature more shapeless or ill-figured, and all that variety that is among them, is but the many various Modes of Irregularity. . . . They are the greatest examples of Confusion that we know in Nature.

Order, regularity, proportion, and design—these are the hallmarks of beauty to Burnet. And these remain the standards of the beautiful for Burke. The beautiful is self-contained. It can manifest itself as an discreet object—as a building like the Parthenon, or a perfectly proportioned body. But the sublime is limitless, unbounded. In his *Critique of Judgment,* written some 33 years after Burke's *Philosophical Enquiry,* in 1790, Immanuel Kant would put it this way: "The beautiful in nature is a question of the form of the object, and this consists in limitation, whereas the sublime is to be found in an object even devoid of form, so far as it immediately involves, or else by its presence provokes, a representation of *limitlessness.*"

Occupying a middle ground between the sublime and the beautiful is the **picturesque.** It finds its roots in the English Garden movement (see Chapter 25), itself inspired by Pliny's descriptions of the gardens of his Roman contemporaries, which were translated by Robert Castell in the 1728 *Villas of the Ancients Illustrated.* Here, the very disorder and irregularity that Burnet abhorred not half a century earlier are the very substance of a garden's appeal. For Castell, the ideal garden takes

> the form of a beautiful Country, Hills, Rocks, Cascades, Rivulets, Woods, Buildings &c. [which] were possibly thrown into such an agreeable Disorder, as to have pleased the Eye for several Views, like so many beautiful Landskips . . . where, tho' the Parts are disposed with the greatest Art, the Irregularity is still preserved; so that their Manner may not improperly be said to be an artful Confusion.

Over the course of the eighteenth century, the principles guiding Castell would come to define the picturesque. Late in the century, Uvedale Price defined the term in his *Essays on the Picturesque* (1794–1801), as "roughness and sudden

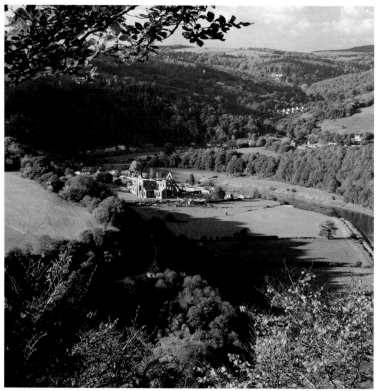

Tintern Abbey, Wye Valley, Monmouthshire, Wales. Robert Harding Picture Library.

Hubert Robert, *Pyramids.* **ca. 1750.** Oil on canvas, 24″ × 28 ¹/₂″. Smith College Museum of Art, Northampton, MA.

variation joined to irregularity." In fact, the very Wye Tour that had drawn William Wordsworth to Tintern Abbey had been recommended by William Gilpin in his *Three Essays: On Picturesque Beauty; On Picturesque Travel; and on Sketching Landscape* (1792), and more specifically in the *Wye Tour* (1782). Other picturesque tours included the *Lakes Tour* (1786) and the *Highlands Tour* (1789), and all were designed to introduce their readers to the pleasures of the picturesque. Standing on the hill above Tintern Abbey, Wordsworth would have been inspired by a picturesque view not unlike the one reproduced here.

Something to Think About . . .

As William Gilpin's travel books make clear, seeking out the picturesque lies at the heart of what would become, in the nineteenth century, the tourist industry. But how might you argue that in the United States, and in its national park system in particular, the sublime supplanted the picturesque as tourism's primary motive?

Fig. 27.10 Caspar David Friedrich, *The Wanderer above the Mists*. ca. 1817–18. Oil on canvas, 37 $\frac{1}{4}$" × 29 $\frac{1}{2}$". Inv.: 5161. On permanent loan from the Foundation for the Promotion of the Hamburg Art Collections. Photo: Elke Walford. Hamburger Kunsthalle, Hamburg, Germany. Bildarchiv Preussischer Kulturbesitz/Art Resource, New York. The artist's identification with nature is underscored by the analogy Friedrich establishes between the figure's head and the distant rock at the right.

words, from What do we know? to How do we know?—even to How do we know that we know?

The theme of doubt is a constant in Friedrich's paintings, but more as a stimulant to the imagination than a source of anxiety and tension. In his *Wanderer above the Mists*, Friedrich pictures a lone man with windblown hair positioned directly in front of the viewer on a rocky promontory (Fig. **27.10**). Like the monk, we can view him as a projection of ourselves. His view is interrupted by the vast expanse of mist, just as ours is cut off by the outcropping of rock. The full magnificence of the scene is only hinted at, a vague promise of eventual revelation. Friedrich, in fact, had this to say about the value of uncertainty:

If your imagination is poor, and in fog you see nothing but gray, then an aversion to vagueness is understandable. All the same, a landscape enveloped in mist seems vaster, more sublime, and it animates the imagination while also heightening suspense—like a veiled woman. The eye and the imagination are generally more intrigued by vaporous distances than by a nearby object available to the eye.

The viewer's imagination is further stimulated by the contrast between near and far, between the rock in the foreground and the ethereal atmosphere stretching into the distance—that is, between the earthly and spiritual realms.

The American Romantic Landscape

In America, the Romantic landscape was literally shaped by the presence of vast tracts of wilderness. One of the foremost American landscape painters of the time was an Englishman, Thomas Cole (1801–1848). Cole immigrated to the United States when he was 18 years old, and he returned to London ten years later, where he studied the paintings of Constable and Turner. Traveling on to Paris and Florence, he came to recognize that "in civilized Europe the primitive features of scenery have long since been destroyed or modified." In America, on the other hand,

> . . . nature is still predominant, and there are those who regret that with the improvements of cultivation the sublimity of the wilderness should pass away; for those scenes of solitude from which the hand of nature has never been lifted, affect the mind with a more deep toned emotion than aught which the hand of man has touched. Amid them the consequent associations are of God the creator—they are his undefiled works, and the mind is cast into the contemplation of eternal things.

Cole's painting, *The Oxbow*, of a famous bend in the Connecticut River in Massachusetts, describes the boundary between those lands "which the hands of man has touched" and the "undefiled" wilderness (Fig. **27.11**). Cole paints himself into the scene—he is at his easel below the rocks to the left of his pack and umbrella—where he acts as mediator between the neatly defined fence rows and sunny fields of the valley below and the rugged wilderness behind him, symbolized by the blasted tree stump and the dark clouds of the thunderstorm in the distance.

Cole painted most often in the Catskill Mountains up the Hudson River halfway between Albany and New York. He was the most prominent artist in what became known as the Hudson River School. His pupil, Frederic Edwin Church (1826–1900), began construction of his own home, Olana, in 1860, overlooking the Hudson River and the Catskills from a ridge high over Hudson, New York.

By then Church had taken two trips to South America, which resulted in a number of enormous paintings of the Andes Mountains. After seeing these canvases, one British reviewer commented that "the mantle of our greatest painter [i.e., Turner] appears to us to have fallen" on

Fig. 27.11 Thomas Cole, *The Oxbow (View from Mount Holyoke, Northampton, Massachusetts, After a Thunderstorm).* 1836. Oil on canvas, 4'3 $^1/_2$" × 6'4". The Metropolitan Museum of Art, New York. Gift of Mrs. Russell Sage, 1908 (08.228). The painting suggests, as the storm departs to the left, that civilization will eventually overwhelm the wilderness, a prospect Cole anticipated with distress.

Fig. 27.12 Frederic Edwin Church, *Twilight in the Wilderness*. 1860. Oil on canvas, 40″ × 60″. The Cleveland Museum of Art, Mr. and Mrs. William H. Marlatt Fund. The Bridgeman Art Library. As was true of almost all Church's major paintings of the era, this one was exhibited by itself as a paid-entrance event in New York City, where it became enormously popular.

Church. But for what many consider to be his masterpiece, Church turned to his native land. *Twilight in the Wilderness* lacks any human presence (Fig. **27.12**). The painting suggests that its subject is not merely twilight *in* the wilderness, but twilight *of* the wilderness. This spot, above the glassy lake, might be among the last such places on the continent. Indeed, there was a growing interest in preserving such spaces. In 1864, President Lincoln signed an act which declared that Yosemite Valley in California "be held for public use, resort, and recreation . . . inalienable for all time." Eight years later, in 1872, Congress established Yellowstone as the nation's first national park.

TRANSCENDENTALISM AND THE AMERICAN ROMANTICS

Just as the American landscape inspired the Romantic sensibilities of artists, it provoked in the minds of writers what Cole had described as "the contemplation of eternal things." American writers of a Romantic sensibility shared with the painters like Church a wonder at the natural world with which they felt an ecstatic communion. In many ways, they were shaped by the nation's emphasis on individualism and

individual liberty. Free to think for themselves, their imaginations were equally free to discover the self in nature.

The Philosophy of Romantic Idealism: Emerson and Thoreau

In 1834, a 31-year-old minister, disenchanted with institutionalized religion and just back from England, where he had encountered Coleridge and heard Wordsworth recite his poetry, moved to the village of Concord, Massachusetts. Over the next several years, Ralph Waldo Emerson (1803–1882), a Unitarian minister, wrote his first book, *Nature*, published anonymously in 1836. The book became the intellectual beacon for a group of Concord locals, mostly ministers, that became known as the "Transcendental Club." It took its name from the *System of Transcendental Idealism*, written by Friedrich Schelling [SHELL-ing] (1775–1854), which argued that scientific observation and artistic intuition were complementary, not opposed, modes of thought. "Nature," Schelling wrote, "is visible Spirit; Spirit is invisible Nature."

This sense of the spirit's oneness with nature informs the most famous passage of *Nature*, when Emerson outlines the fundamental principle of transcendental thought: In the direct experience of nature, the individual is united with God, thus transcending knowledge based on empirical observation (**Reading 27.8**):

READING 27.8

from Ralph Waldo Emerson, *Nature*, Chapter 1 (1836)

Crossing a bare common, in snow puddles, at twilight, under a clouded sky, without having in my thoughts any occurrence of special good fortune, I have enjoyed a perfect exhilaration. Almost I fear to think how glad I am. In the woods too a man casts off his years, as the snake his slough, and at what period soever of life, is always a child. In the woods, is perpetual youth. Within these plantations of God, a decorum and sanctity reign, a perennial festival is dressed, and the guest sees not how he should tire of them in a thousand years. In the woods, we return to reason and faith. There I feel that nothing can befall me in life,—no disgrace, no calamity (leaving me my eyes,) which nature cannot repair. Standing on the bare ground,—my head bathed by the blithe air, and uplifted into infinite space,—all mean egotism vanishes. I become a transparent eye-ball. I am nothing. I see all. The currents of the Universal Being circulate through me; I am part or particle of God. The name of the nearest friend sounds then foreign and accidental. To be brothers, to be acquaintances,—master or servant, is then a trifle and a disturbance. I am the lover of uncontained and immortal beauty. In the wilderness, I find something more dear and connate [i.e., congenial] than in streets or villages. In the tranquil landscape, and especially in the distant line of the horizon, man beholds somewhat as beautiful as his own nature.

The sense of the self at the center of experience—the "eye/I" is also the sense of individualism and self-reliance fundamental to transcendental experience. In fact, in one of his most famous essays, "Self-Reliance," Emerson would declare, "Whoso would be a man must be a nonconformist. . . . Nothing is at last sacred but the integrity of your own mind." Of all Emerson's contemporaries, none fits this description better than Henry David Thoreau [thor-OH] (1817–1862). Educated at Harvard, Thoreau was fiercely independent. He resigned his first job as a schoolteacher in Concord because he refused to inflict corporal punishment on his students. He became one of the nation's most vocal abolitionists and was briefly jailed for refusing to pay a poll tax to a government that tolerated slavery. But most famously, for two years, from 1845 to 1847, he lived in a small cabin that he built himself, on Emerson's property at Walden Pond. This experience spawned *Walden, or Life in the Woods*, a small book published in 1854, dedicated to teaching the satisfactions and virtues of living simply and wisely in communion with nature (Fig. **27.13**). Thoreau's woods are the same woods that Emerson extols in *Nature*. Thoreau writes (**Reading 27.9**):

READING 27.9

from Henry David Thoreau, *Walden, or Life in the Woods*, Chapter 2 (1854)

I went to the woods because I wished to live deliberately, to front only the essential facts of life, and see if I could not learn what it had to teach, and not, when I came to die, discover that I had not lived. . . . I wanted to live deep and suck out all the marrow of life, to live so sturdily and Spartan-like as to put to rout all that was not life. . . . Time is but the stream I go a-fishing in. I drink at it; but while I drink I see the sandy bottom and detect how shallow it is. Its thin current slides away, but eternity remains.

Fig. 27.13 Original title page to the 1854 edition of *Walden*, by Henry David Thoreau. This is as accurate a depiction of Thoreau's cabin at Walden Pond as we have.

The eccentricities of Thoreau's life are matched by the inventiveness of his prose, and in the end, Thoreau's argument is for what he calls "the indescribable innocence and beneficence of Nature."

As powerful and as transformative as nature was, Thoreau viewed it as vulnerable to human encroachment, an insight that proved him far ahead of his time. He worried, for instance, that the railroad had destroyed the old scale of distances, a complaint shared by many of his contemporaries. His understanding of the environment's vulnerability and humanity's role in conserving or degrading it illustrates Thoreau's other enduring influence on American literary culture—as a powerful social conscience and spokesman for unpopular causes. Rebelling against unjust war in his essential essay "Civil Disobedience," against slavery as an active supporter of the Underground Railroad, and against conformism in his work as a writer and educator, Thoreau was both highly individualistic as well as a committed social activist. In his essay "Life without Principle," drawn from a series of lectures in 1854, Thoreau pondered "the way we spend our lives," and the negative effect it had on the natural world as well as our human nature (**Reading 27.10**):

READING 27.10

from Henry David Thoreau, "Life without Principle" (1854)

This world is a place of business. What an infinite bustle! I am awaked almost every night by the panting of the locomotive. It interrupts my dreams. . . . It would be glorious to see mankind at leisure for once. It is nothing but work, work, work. I cannot easily buy a blank-book to write thoughts in; they are commonly ruled for dollars and cents. . . . If a man was tossed out of a window when an infant, and so made a cripple for life, or scared out of his wits by the Indians, it is regretted chiefly because he was thus incapacitated for— business! I think that there is nothing, not even crime, more opposed to poetry, to philosophy, ay, to life itself, than this incessant business. . . . If a man walk in the woods for love of them half of each day, he is in danger of being regarded as a loafer; but if he spends his whole day as a speculator, shearing off those woods and making earth bald before her time, he is esteemed an industrious and enterprising citizen. As if a town had no interest in its forests but to cut them down!

Thoreau's sense of individualistic conscience is most evident in his 1849 essay "Civil Disobedience," written after his brief imprisonment for refusing to pay a poll tax (a tax levied on every male adult voter) as a protest against the Mexican-American war and slavery (**Reading 27.11**):

READING 27.11

from Henry David Thoreau, "Civil Disobedience" (1849)

Must the citizen ever for a moment, or in the least degree, resign his conscience to the legislator? Why has every man a conscience, then? I think that we should be men first, and subjects afterward. It is not desirable to cultivate a respect for the law, so much as for the right. The only obligation which I have a right to assume is to do at any time what I think right. . . . Under a government which imprisons any unjustly, the true place for a just man is also a prison. The proper place to-day, the only place which Massachusetts has provided for her freer and less desponding spirits, is in her prisons. . . . It is there that the fugitive slave, and the Mexican prisoner on parole, and the Indian come to plead the wrongs of his race, should find them; on that separate, but more free and honorable ground, where the State places those who are not *with* her, but *against* her—the only house in a slave State in which a free man can abide with honor.

ROMANTICISM'S DARKER REALITIES

In May 1798, Napoleon set sail for Egypt, accompanied by some 35,000 troops. His army soon took Cairo and installed a French administration in the country. But they were cut off from Europe. In August, the British Navy, under the command of Admiral Horatio Nelson, destroyed the French fleet in the Bay of Aboukir, which lies between Alexandria and the mouth of the Nile. Recognizing Napoleon's vulnerability, the Ottoman Turks declared war on France in early 1799, but Napoleon took the initiative, leading an army of 13,000 north into Syria. At the port city of Jaffa (today incorporated into Tel Aviv, but then part of Ottoman Syria), his troops quickly overwhelmed the Ottoman defenses, but then engaged in a senseless bloodbath. Low on ammunition, they bayoneted some 2,000 Turkish soldiers who were trying to surrender, then they turned on the town. Some 3,500 men, women, and children were murdered and raped, their homes and businesses looted and burned. Three days later, faced with the alternative of feeding and guarding another 2,000 to 3,000 Turkish troops who had surrendered to his adjutants, Napoleon ordered that they be executed en masse on the beach.

Within a matter of a couple of days, things turned even more gruesome. Bubonic plague began to spread quickly among Napoleon's troops. Realizing that his troops' morale was in jeopardy, Napoleon decided to visit his infected troops at the hospital, a converted mosque, where his doctors were treating the disease. Five years later, Jean Antoine Gros would celebrate the visit in an enormous painting designed, in many ways, to divert public attention from the horrors of what had really occurred at Jaffa (Fig. **27.14**). Napoleon is

Fig. 27.14 Antoine Jean Gros, *Napoleon in the Pesthouse at Jaffa*. 1804. Oil on canvas, 17′5″ × 23′7″. Musée du Louvre, Paris. Gros accompanied Napoleon on the Italian campaign in 1797 and would then become one of the most important of those chosen to officially chronicle Napoleon's campaigns (see Fig. 26.30).

bathed in light in the center of the painting, laying hands, Christ-like, on an infected soldier. The composition is inspired by David's *Oath of the Horatii* (see Fig. 26.17), its shallow foreground space set in front of an a wall of arched porticos, and Napoleon's hand, like Horatius's, the focal point of the painting. But as much as Napoleon must be admired for putting himself (and his staff, which accompanied him) at risk, before he left Syria, he ordered that those too weak to retreat south—around 50 sick and perhaps already dying soldiers—be poisoned. In all, French casualties in the campaign amounted to around 1,200 killed in action, 2,500 ill or seriously injured, and about 2,000 dead from the plague. Still besieged by the French navy, Napoleon left for France on his own, leaving his army in Egypt.

The Romantic Hero

So stunningly successful were so many of Napoleon's other military campaigns, so fierce was his dedication to the principles of liberty, fraternity, and equality (abolishing serfdom throughout much of Europe), and so brilliant was his reorganization of the government, the educational system, and civil law, that in the first years of the nineteenth century, he seemed to many a savior. Ultimately, Napoleon was the very personification of the Romantic hero as well as a French national icon, a man of common origin who had risen, through sheer wit and tenacity, to dominate the world stage.

But the promise of Napoleon—his ability to impose classical values of order, control, and rationality upon a French society that had been wracked with revolution and turmoil—was undermined by the darker reality of events like those that transpired at Jaffa. The Romantics, whose fascination with the powers of individual intuition and creativity had led them to lionize Napoleon, would react to his ultimate defeat and to the ensuing disorder that marked the first half of the nineteenth century with a profound pessimism about the course of human events.

To the Romantic imagination, Napoleon was something of a figure for Prometheus [pro-MEE-thee-us]. In Greek myth, Prometheus is a member of the race of deities known as Titans. Prometheus stole fire, the source of wisdom and creativity, from the sun and gave it to humankind, to whom Zeus, ruler of the Gods, had denied it. For this crime Zeus chained him to a rock, where an eagle fed daily on his liver, which was restored each night, so that he might suffer the same fate each day. On the one hand, the Romantics revered him as the all-suffering but ever noble champion of human freedom. But on the other, in his reckless ambition to achieve his goals by breaking the laws imposed by supreme authority, as well as in his endless suffering, they also recognized in Prometheus a certain futility and despair.

The Hegelian Dialectic and the "Great Man" Theory of History German philosopher Georg Wilhelm Friedrich Hegel (1770–1831) looked at the Promethean Napoleon in an almost entirely positive light. He was, for Hegel, the force driving the world toward an absolute freedom embodied in the laws and institutions of a great European nation-state. From Hegel's point of view, the entire world is governed by a single divine nature, which he alternately called "absolute mind" or "world-spirit." Napoleon, whom Hegel termed "that world soul," personified this "absolute mind," which in seeking to know its own nature initiates a process known as the **dialectic**. At any given moment, the prevailing set of ideas, which Hegel termed the "thesis," finds itself opposed by a conflicting set of ideas, the "antithesis." For instance, chaotic revolutionary forces in France found themselves opposed by the call for order and rule of law embodied by Napoleon. This conflict resolves itself in a "synthesis," which inevitably establishes itself as the new thesis, generating its own new antithesis, with the process always moving forward, ever closer to the ultimate goal—spiritual freedom. Each period in history is necessary to the next, driven by conflict, which Hegel viewed as a positive and productive force rather than a damaging or destructive one.

Hegel, along with English philosopher-historian Thomas Carlyle (1795–1881), is also responsible for what is commonly called the **"Great Man" theory**, which asserts that human history is driven by the achievement of men (and men only) who lead humankind forward because they have sensed by intuition the "world-spirit" (**Reading 27.12**):

READING 27.12

from Georg Wilhelm Friedrich Hegel,
Philosophy of History (1805–06)

Such are all great historical men . . . they may be called Heroes, inasmuch as they have derived their purposes and their vocation, not from the calm, regular course of things, sanctioned by the existing order, but from a concealed fount—one which has not attained to phenomenal, present existence—from that inner Spirit, still hidden beneath the surface, which, impinging on the

outer world as on a shell, bursts it in pieces. . . . Such individuals had no consciousness of the general Idea they were unfolding . . . but at the same time they were thinking men, who had an insight into the requirements of the time—what was ripe for development.

Hegel's primary emphasis here is the same as that of the Romantic writers and philosophers—history is driven by the spiritual rather than the material—but unlike the Romantics, he believed that world history revealed a rational process. "Reason is the Sovereign of the World," declared Hegel, and it was only through men such as Alexander, Charlemagne, or Napoleon that the world-spirit could manifest itself in an orderly process. The "Great Man" theory has many shortcomings, the most obvious being that women have no political or historical role. Neither do the common people and workers, a deficiency that one of Hegel's astute students, Karl Marx, would address several decades later when he revised Hegel's "dialectic" by contending that the struggle between social classes moves history forward (see Chapter 29).

The Promethean Idea in England: Lord Byron and the Shelleys For poet George Gordon, Lord Byron (1788–1824), Prometheus was the embodiment of his own emphatic spirit of individualism. Byron was a prodigious traveler to foreign countries, a sexual experimenter, and a champion of oppressed nations. In his 1816 ode "Prometheus," Byron rehearses the myth as described in Aeschylus's play *Prometheus Bound*, and then addresses his mythical hero (**Reading 27.13**):

READING 27.13

from George Gordon, Lord Byron,
"Prometheus" (1816)

Thou art a symbol and a sign
To Mortals of their fate and force;
Like thee, Man is in part divine,
A troubled stream from a pure source;
And Man in portions can foresee

His own funereal destiny;
His wretchedness, and his resistance,
And his sad unallied existence:
To which his Spirit may oppose
Itself—an equal to all woes,

And a firm will, and a deep sense,
Which even in torture can descry
Its own concentred recompense,
Triumphant where it dares defy,
And making Death a Victory.

Prometheus's daring to oppose the Olympian gods was, for Byron, the same daring that he saw in Napoleon. In *Childe Harold's Pilgrimage*, the long narrative poem that established his reputation, Byron addressed Napoleon directly (**Reading 27.14**):

Childe Harold's Pilgrimage essentially recounts Byron's own Grand Tour, his own restless travels through Spain, Portugal, Greece, Turkey, and Albania, where he purchased the costume in which he posed for Thomas Phillips (Fig. **27.15**). Barely distinguishable from his chief character, Byron in succeeding years would add new cantos to the poem, relating his travels through Belgium, Switzerland, the Alps, and Italy.

In Italy, Byron met up with the English poet Percy Bysshe Shelley (1792–1822) and his wife Mary Godwin Shelley (1797–1851), daughter of the philosopher and writer William Godwin and author Mary Wollstonecraft

(see Chapter 26). Shelley was also working on a Prometheus project, a four-act play entitled *Prometheus Unbound*. It concerns Prometheus's final release from captivity, and in it Shelley departs from tradition in choosing to have that release follow the overthrow of Zeus rather than precede a reconciliation between the hero and his tyrannical oppressor. A revolutionary text that champions free will, goodness, and idealism in the face of oppression, *Prometheus Unbound* is Shelley's answer to the mistakes of the French Revolution and its cycle of replacing one tyrant with another. Shelley declares his beliefs as a poet and revolutionary in the epilogue (**Reading 27.15**):

Shelley also shared with Byron a deep belief in the immortality of art. In his 1819 "Ode to the West Wind," a five-stanza lyric poem in which the Wind is the vehicle for spreading the word of reform and change, Shelley addressed the Wind as the enduring power of human expression (**Reading 27.16**):

Fig. 27.15 Thomas Phillips, *Lord Byron Sixth Baron in Albanian Costume.* 1835. Oil on canvas, 29 $^1/_2$" × 24 $^1/_2$". National Portrait Gallery, London. The Bridgeman Art Library. This is Phillips's own copy of the original 1813 painting, which hangs in the British Embassy in Athens. Bryon's dashing good looks and his exotic costume, the Albanian shawl wrapped round his head like a turban, underscore the poet's Romantic individualism.

For Shelley, poets were, as he wrote in *A Defense of Poetry*, "the unacknowledged legislators of the world" who sought to change the world with their writing. In the lines above, he exhorts the Wind to give life to his message of reform and revolution by spreading his words over the world.

Mary Shelley (1797–1851) was as galvanized by the Prometheus myth as her husband and Byron, but her attitude toward it was more ambivalent. When Byron arrived in Italy, she had already begun her novel *Frankenstein; or the Modern Prometheus*. The novel is narrated by an English explorer in the Arctic, whose ice-bound ship takes on a man in terrible condition named Victor Frankenstein, and reports the passenger's story. Dr. Frankenstein had learned the secret of endowing inanimate material with life.

Dr. Frankenstein subsequently created a monster of giant proportion and supernatural strength from assembled body parts taken from graveyards, slaughterhouses, and dissecting rooms. But as soon as the creature opened his eyes, the scientist realized that he had not so much created a miracle as a horror, a creature doomed to a miserable existence of exile from normal society. Dr. Frankenstein flees his laboratory (Fig. **27.16**), leaving the creature to fend for himself (see **Reading 27.17**, pages 918–919, for this episode). What follows is the story of the monster's revenge—a series of murders that adversely affect Frankenstein and his family.

Fig. 27.16 Theodor M. von Holst, illustration from *Frankenstein* by Mary Shelley. 1831. Engraving. Private Collection. The Bridgeman Art Library.

So, like Prometheus, Dr. Frankenstein is punished for the acquisition of powerful knowledge. Promethean ambition and power, Mary Shelley tells us, can step beyond the bounds of reason and the human capacity to manage the consequences—as Napoleon had demonstrated.

In July 1823, Byron sailed to Greece to aid the Greeks in their War of Independence from the Ottoman Turks. Greece was for Byron a Promethean country, longing to be "unbound." Now he would come to its aid himself. But he never did face any action. Instead, he died in 1824 of fever and excessive bleeding, the result of his doctor's mistaken belief that bleeding would cure him. He was buried in his family vault in England, except for his heart and lungs, which were interred at Missolonghi, where he had perished. Keats had died of tuberculosis in 1821, Shelley had drowned in a boating accident in 1822. Of all the great English Romantic poets, only Wordsworth and Coleridge were still alive by the mid-1820s.

The Romantic Hero in Germany: Johann Wolfgang von Goethe's *Werther* and *Faust* One of the great ironies in the development of Romanticism is that two of its greatest heroes, Werther [VER-tur] and Faust (rhymes with "oust"), were the creation of an imagination that defined itself as classical. The creator of these two heroes, Johann Wolfgang von Goethe [GUH-tuh] (1749–1832), had strong classical tastes and is often categorized as a "classical" author. He had moved to Weimar [VY-mar], one of the great cultural centers of Europe, in 1775, and later filled his house there with Greek and Roman statuary. His most famous portrait, painted by J. H. W. Tischbein [TISH-bine] in 1787, presents him in a pilgrim's garb before an array of Roman ruins (Fig. **27.17**), and, indeed, he found Romanticism abhorrent. In a famous letter of 1829, Goethe wrote a friend, "The classical I call healthy, the Romantic sick . . . [the Romantic] is weak, sickly, ill, and the [classical] is strong, fresh, cheerful . . ."

Goethe himself occasionally descended into what he called these "other darker places." As he admitted, the German poet Friedrich Schiller (1759–1805) had "demonstrated to me that I myself, against my will, was a Romantic." This ill-defined border between Goethe's "classical" and "Romantic" approaches to literature reminds us that labeling artistic and literary styles is helpful in gaining some basic understanding of their context, but does not produce ironclad, fixed categories.

Early in his career, Goethe had written what was, for the age, the quintessential Romantic novel, *The Sorrows of Young Werther*. It told the story of a young man who feels increasingly disillusioned with life, even as he finds himself hopelessly in love with a happily married woman. This much was semiautobiographical—Goethe had fallen in love with his law partner's fiancée. But where Goethe's Werther ends his life by committing suicide, Goethe simply left town and turned his experiences into a best-selling novel, establishing a precedent for alienated, ambitious young artists for the next two centuries.

Fig. 27.17 J. H. W. Tischbein, *Johann Wolfgang von Goethe in the Roman Campana.* **1787.** Oil on canvas, 64 1/2″ × 81″. Location: Staedelsches Kunstinstitut, Frankfurt am Main, Germany. Kavaler/Art Resource, New York. Tischbein painted this portrait during Goethe's first visit to Rome, which lasted from September 1786 until June 1788, during which time the two shared an apartment.

suicide, copies of the book in their pockets. It is, no doubt, these young men to whom Goethe refers when he says that the Romantic is "sick."

Goethe well understood that the Romantic aspirations of his fictional hero Werther represented the same feelings described by his friend, the poet Georg Friedrich Philipp von Hardenberg (1772–1801), who wrote under the pen name Novalis [noh-VAH-lis]. Novalis defined the process of creating art from the Romantic perspective: "Insofar as I give the common an elevated meaning, the usual a secret perspective, the known the value of the unknown, the finite an infinite appearance—I thus romanticize." Goethe expanded on this theme, arguing that "Great works of art are comparable to the great works of nature; they have been created by men according to true and natural laws. Everything arbitrary, imaginary collapses. Here is necessity, here is God." While great art is transcendent, Goethe suggests, it is, ultimately, subject to God's grand design and the natural laws that govern the universe, a point of view similar to that of the Enlightenment *philosophes.*

Goethe conceived his greatest character and hero, Faust, in the 1770s, but did not start writing the work until 1800, and completed it just before his death in 1832. It is a 12,000-line verse play based on a sixteenth-century German legend about an actual traveling physician named Johann or Georg Faust, who was reputed to have sold his soul to the devil in return for infinite knowledge. To Goethe, he seemed an ideal figure for the Romantic hero—driven to master the world, with dire consequences.

Faust is a man of great learning and breadth of knowledge—like Goethe himself—but bored with his station in life and longing for some greater experience. He wants the kind of knowledge that does not always come from books (**Reading 27.19a**):

Werther is happiest when by himself, in nature: "I am so happy, my friend," he writes in one of the first letters in the book, ". . . when the lovely valley surrounds me in mist, and the sun at noon lingers on the surface of the impenetrable darkness of my woods, and only a few rays steal into the inner sanctum. . . . [then] the entire heavens come to rest in my soul, like the form of a beloved." But when he actually falls in love, he finds nothing but torment (**Reading 27.18**):

READING 27.18

from Johann Wolfgang von Goethe, *The Sorrows of Young Werther* **(1774)**

When I have spent several hours in her company, till I feel completely absorbed by her figure, her grace, the divine expression of her thoughts, my mind becomes gradually excited to the highest excess, my sight grows dim, my hearing confused, my breathing oppressed as if by the hand of a murderer, and my beating heart seeks to obtain relief for my aching senses.

Such sentiments were a revelation for readers at the time. Even Napoleon later admitted to Goethe that he had enthusiastically read *Young Werther* several times. Across Europe, young men began to wear the blue jacket and yellow trousers that Goethe describes as Werther's habitual dress, and some of these, disappointed like their hero, committed

from Johann Wolfgang von Goethe, *Faust*, Part 1 (1808)

> FAUST . . .
> Here stand I, ach, Philosophy
> Behind me and Law and Medicine too
> And, to my cost, Philosophy—
> All these I have sweated through and through
> And now you see me a poor fool
> As wise as when I entered school!
> They call me Master, they call me Doctor,
> Ten years now I have dragged my college
> Along by the nose through zig and zag
> Through up and down and round and round
> And this is all that I have found—
> The impossibility of knowledge!
> . . .
> Besides, I have neither goods nor gold,
> Neither reputation nor rank in the world;
> No dog would choose to continue so! . . .
> Oh! Am I still stuck in this jail?
> This God-damned dreary hole in the wall
> Where even the lovely light of heaven
> Breaks wanly through the painted panes!

In essence, Faust is profoundly bored, suffering from one of the great afflictions of the Romantic hero, **ennui** [ahn-wee], a French term that denotes both listlessness and a profound melancholy. He longs for something that will challenge the limits of his enormous intellect. That challenge appears, not long after, in the form of Mephistopheles [mef-ih-STOFF-uh-leez]—the devil—who arrives in Faust's study dressed as a dandy (Fig. **27.18**), a nineteenth-century man of elegant taste and appearance (**Reading 27.19b**):

Fig. 27.18 Eugène Delacroix, *Mephistopheles Appearing to Faust in His Study*. Illustration for Goethe's *Faust*. 1828. Lithograph, 10¾″ × 9″. Private Collection. The Stapleton Collection. The Bridgeman Art Library. Delacroix's illustrations were Goethe's favorite representations of his work.

from Johann Wolfgang von Goethe, *Faust*, Part 1 (1808)

> MEPHISTOPHELES . . . We two, I hope, we shall be good friends . . .
> I am here like a fine young squire today,
> In a suit of scarlet trimmed with gold
> And a little cape of stiff brocade,
> With a cock's feather in my hat
> And at my side a long sharp blade,
> And the most succinct advice I can give
> Is that you dress up just like me,
> So that uninhibited and free
> You may find out what it means to live.

Mephistopheles makes a pact with Faust: He promises Faust "ravishing samples of my arts" which will satisfy his greatest yearnings, but in return, if Faust agrees that he is satisfied, Mephistopheles will win Faust's soul. As Faust leaves to prepare to accompany Mephistopheles, the fiend contemplates the doctor's future:

> MEPHISTOPHELES . . . We just say go—and skip.
> But please get ready for this pleasure trip.
> *[Exit Faust]*
>   Only look down on knowledge and reason,
> The highest gifts that men can prize,
> Only allow the spirit of lies
> To confirm you in magic and illusion,
> And then I have you body and soul.
> Fate has given this man a spirit
> Which is always pressing onwards, beyond control,
> And whose mad striving overleaps
> All joys of the earth between pole and pole.
> Him I shall drag through the wilds of life
> And through the flats of meaninglessness,
> I shall make him flounder and gape and stick
> And to tease his insatiableness
> Hang meat and drink in the air before his watering lips;
> In vain he will pray to slake his inner thirst,
> And even had he not sold himself to the devil
> He would be equally accursed.

Mephistopheles recognizes Faust as the ultimate Promethean hero, a man "always pressing onwards, beyond control," whose insatiable ambition will inevitably lead him to "overleap" his limitations. After a tumultuous love affair with a young woman named Gretchen—"Feeling is all!" he proclaims—he abandons her, which causes her to lose her mind and murder their illegitimate child. For this she is condemned to death, but the purity of her love wins her salvation in the afterlife.

In Part 2, Faust follows Mephistopheles into the "other dark worlds" of the Romantic imagination, a nightmare world filled with witches, sirens, monsters, and heroes from the distant past, including Helen of Troy, with whom he has a love affair. But, in Goethe's ultimately redemptive story, Faust is unsatisfied with this unending variety of experiences. What begins to quench his thirst, ironically, is good works, namely, putting knowledge to work in a vast land-reclamation project designed to provide good land for millions of people. (This reminds us of Prometheus's desire to benefit humanity through the gift of fire.) Before achieving his dream, Faust dies, but without ever having actually declared his satisfaction. So, despite Mephistopheles's attempt to grab Faust's soul as it leaves his body, a band of angels carry Faust to heaven with the divine Gretchen at their head. She is what Goethe calls the "Eternal Womanhead"—both nature itself and the redeeming power of love—and so the poem ends as follows (**Reading 27.19c**):

READING 27.19c

from Johann Wolfgang von Goethe,
***Faust*, Part 2 (1832)**

All that is past of us
Was but reflected;
All that was lost in us
Here is corrected;
All indescribables
Here we descry;
Eternal Womanhead
Leads us on high.

In the end, Goethe's *Faust* is an extremely ambiguous figure, a man of enormous ambition and hence enormous possibility, and yet, like Frankenstein, his will to power is self-destructive. We see these ambiguities in the poem's high seriousness countered by ribald comedy, and in Faust's great goodness countered by deep moral depravity.

Fig. 27.19 Francisco Goya, *The Sleep of Reason Produces Monsters*, from the *Caprichos*. 1796–98. Etching and aquatint on paper, 8$\frac{1}{2}$" × 6". The Hispanic Society of America, New York. Goya offered 300 sets of the *Caprichos* series for sale in 1799, only to withdraw them two days later, presumably because the Church, which he portrayed in unflattering ways throughout, threatened to bring him before the Inquisition.

SEE MORE For a Closer Look at Francisco Goya's *The Sleep of Reason Produces Monsters*, go to **www.myartslab.com**

GOYA'S TRAGIC VISION

The impact of Napoleon's Promethean ambition, and the human tragedy associated with it, extended across Europe and into Spain especially. The Spanish painter Francisco Goya [GOY-ah] (1746–1828) was, at first, enthusiastic about Napoleon's accession to power in France. Yet he, too, came to see through the idealistic veil of the emperor's ostensible desire to establish a fair and efficient government in a still-feudal country that was debased, corrupt, and isolated from the rest of Europe. Indeed, Goya came simply to hate the emperor, as most Spaniards did.

Goya before Napoleon: Social Satire

Under the rule of Charles III, from 1759 to 1788, Spain had instituted many liberal reforms, but the French Revolution frightened his successor, Charles IV. This monarch reinstated the Inquisition and went so far as to ban the importation of books from France. Goya was angered at this abandonment of reform, and between 1796 and 1798 he executed a series of prints, called the *Caprichos* [kah-PREE-chohss], or *Caprices*, that expressed this sentiment. *The Sleep* [or Dream] *of Reason Produces Monsters* (Fig. **27.19**)

was originally designed as a title page to the series. According to biographers, it shows Goya himself asleep at his work table as winged creatures swarm in the darkness behind him. An owl, a symbol of wisdom, takes up Goya's pen as if urging him to depict the monsters of his dreams. Throughout the series, Goya shows the follies of Spanish society, including the ruling class who employed him—social injustice, prostitution, vanity, greed, snobbery, and superstition (accounting for the many images depicting witches and monsters). In Goya's view, Spanish society, although in no way Promethean in its ambition, similarly steps beyond the bounds of reason without any capacity to manage the consequences. For this reason, he presents it as a parody of the Promethean myth, in the same way that Miguel de Cervantes's delusional Don Quixote (see Chapter 20) is a parody of the ideal knight.

The Third of May, 1808: Napoleon's Spanish Legacy

When Napoleon decided to send a French army across the Iberian Peninsula to force Portugal to abandon its alliance with Britain, he did not foresee a problem since Spain had been his ally since 1796. At first, Napoleon's army was unopposed, but by the time the troops reached Saragossa, the Spanish population rose up against the invaders in nationalistic fervor. For the next five years, the Spanish conducted a new kind of warfare, engaging the French in innumerable *guerrillas* [gay-REE-yahs], or "little wars," from which derives the concept of guerrilla warfare.

In March 1808, Napoleon made a fatal error. Maneuvering the Spanish royal family out of the way through bribery, he named his brother, Joseph Bonaparte

Fig. 27.20 Francisco Goya, *The Third of May, 1808*. 1814–15. Oil on canvas, 8′9½″ × 13′4½″. Museo del Prado, Madrid. Goya was later asked why he had painted the scene with such graphic reality. His reply was simple: "To warn men never to do it again."

Grande hazaña ! Con muertos!

Fig. 27.21 Francisco Goya, *Grande hazara! Con muertos! (Great courage! Against corpses!)*, from *The Disasters of War*, *No. 39*. 1810–14. Etching. Private Collection. The Bridgeman Art Library. The series was not published in Goya's lifetime—and not until 1863—probably because the government in Spain persecuted liberals after the return of Ferdinand VII in 1815.

(r. 1808–1814), to the Spanish throne. This gesture infuriated the Spanish people. The crown was *their* crown, after all, not Napoleon's. Even as the royal family was negotiating with Napoleon, rumors had spread that Napoleon was planning to execute them. On May 2, 1808, the citizens of Madrid rose up against Napoleon's troops, resulting in hundreds of deaths in battle, with hundreds more executed the next day on a hill outside Madrid. Six years later, in 1814, after Napoleon had been deposed and Ferdinand reinstated as king, Goya commemorated the events of May 2 and 3 in two paintings, the first depicting the battle and the second the executions of the following day. *The Third of May, 1808* is one of the greatest testaments to the horrors of war ever painted (Fig. **27.20**). The night after the events of May 2, Napoleon's troops set a firing squad and executed hundreds of Madrileños—anyone caught bearing weapons of any kind. The only illumination comes from a square stable lantern that casts a bright light on a prisoner with his arms raised wide above his head in a gesture that seems at once a plea for mercy and an act of heroic defiance. Below him the outstretched arms of a bloody corpse mirror his gesture. To his left, in the very center of the painting, another soon-to-be casualty of the firing squad hides his eyes in terror, and behind him stretches a line of victims to follow. Above them, barely visible in the night sky, rises a solitary, darkened church steeple.

Much of the power of the painting lies in its almost Baroque contrast of light and dark and its evocation of Christ's agony on the cross, especially through the cruciform pose of the prisoner. The soldier-executioners represent the grim reality of loyalty to one's state, as opposed to loyalty to one's conscience. Goya documented the realities of war in other works, including *The Disasters of War*, a series of etchings begun in 1810 and completed about the same time as *The Third of May, 1808*. These prints testify to the brutality of Napoleon's army, which, by all accounts, saw the Spanish people as little better than animals. In one of these prints, satirically entitled *Great courage! Against corpses!* Goya shows that in the hands of the French troops, the human body is no longer human (Fig. **27.21**).

The Black Paintings

Goya's sense that his world had abandoned reason dominated his final works. In 1819, when Goya was 72 years old, he moved into a small two-story house outside Madrid. The

Fig. 27.22 Francisco Goya, *Saturn Devouring One of His Children.*
1820–1823. Oil on plaster transferred to canvas, 57 7/8″ × 32 5/8″. All rights
reserved. © Museo Nacional del Prado, Madrid. The painting reflects Goya's
increasing disgust with Spanish politics. In 1824, he finally gave up on
Ferdinand VII's Spain and, under the pretense of needing to visit the thermal
baths, moved to Bordeaux, France, where he remained in self-exile until his
death in 1828.

Quinta del sordo. Today they are known as the "black paintings." There is no record that Goya ever explained them to any friend or relative, nor did he title them in any written form. Among these works are a painting of a woman who is evidently Leocadia, leaning on a tomb; two men dueling with cudgels; a pilgrimage of terrifying and hideous figures through a nocturnal landscape; a convocation of these same figures in a witch's sabbath around a giant he-goat; two skeletal old people eating soup; and most terrifying of all, the painting today known as *Saturn Devouring One of His Children* (Fig. **27.22**). Derived from the story of Kronos [KROH-noss] eating his children, it is among the legends associated with the pre-Olympian Titans. Saturn is the Latin form of the Greek Kronos.

At the Quinta del sordo, the *Saturn* faced the main door, and it seems likely that Goya did not intend the Saturn myth as a "welcoming" image. His horrific giant with skinny legs, massive shoulders, wild hair, and crazed eyes is perhaps more an image of society as a whole, the social order, even Spain itself, devouring its own people. It is worth recalling that even as Goya was painting the *Saturn*, Beethoven was completing the Ninth Symphony. These works represent two sides of the Romantic imagination. Both share a profound sense of despair, isolation, and loneliness, but where Beethoven overcomes this condition and rises to a statement of hope and affirmation, Goya descends into a world of near-madness and fear.

HERMAN MELVILLE: THE UNCERTAIN WORLD OF *MOBY DICK*

Perhaps the image of the Promethean hero finds nowhere more dark an expression than in the sensibility of Herman Melville (1819–1891). Melville had worked as a ship's cabin boy, and later as a crew member on a whaler bound for the South Pacific. His experiences at sea led him to view the natural world (and the humans who inhabited it) as a severe challenge rather than a calm gateway to inspiration. After abandoning the whaling ship because of its intolerable conditions, Melville was taken prisoner by cannibals in the Marquesas Islands. Once rescued, he survived by taking menial jobs in Tahiti and Hawaii in the 1840s.

Melville's hardscrabble years as a sailor would inform his great novel *Moby Dick*. Published in 1851, the novel tells the story of Captain Ahab's [AY-hab] vengeful quest across the vast reaches of the Pacific Ocean for an elusive white whale to whom he had lost his leg.

Melville knew and appreciated Turner's work, collecting engravings of *Snow Storm—Steam-Boat off a Harbour's Mouth* (see Fig. 27.8). He was also aware that Turner had painted a number of whaling pictures, based on Thomas Beale's *Natural History of the Sperm Whale* (1839), which

move was inspired at least in part by his relationship with his 30-year-old companion, Leocadia Weiss, which scandalized more conservative elements of Madrid society. It was also a more general expression of Goya's growing preference for isolation.

Goya spent the next four years executing a series of 14 oil paintings directly on the plaster walls of this house,

Fig. 27.23 J. M. W. Turner, *The Whale Ship.* ca. 1845. Oil on canvas, 36 1/8″ × 48 1/4″. The Metropolitan Museum of Art, New York. Catharine Lorillard Wolfe Collection, Wolfe Fund, 1896 (96.29). Image © The Metropolitan Museum of Art. This painting was exhibited at the Royal Academy in 1845 with the caption "Vide Beale's Voyage p. 175." This refers to a passage in a book written by Thomas Beale, describing the harpooning of a large sperm whale off Japan in 1832.

he himself used as a source for the novel. Among them is the 1845 *Whale Ship*, depicting a whale breaching in a fury of foam and spray, harpoonists approaching from its right (Fig. **27.23**). In fact, early in *Moby Dick*, its narrator, Ishmael [ISH-may-el], having decided to go to sea, arrives at the Spouter Inn in New Bedford, Massachusetts, where he encounters a picture hanging in the entry (**Reading 27.20a**):

READING 27.20a

from Herman Melville, *Moby Dick*, Chapter 3, "The Spouter Inn" (1851)

. . . a very large oil painting so thoroughly besmoked, and every way defaced, that in the unequal crosslights by which you viewed it, it was only by diligent study and a series of systematic visits to it, and careful inquiry of the neighbors, that you could any way arrive at an understanding of its purpose.

. . .What most puzzled and confounded you was a long, limber, portentous, black mass of something hovering in the centre of the picture over three blue, dim, perpendicular lines floating in a nameless yeast. A boggy, soggy, squitchy picture truly, enough to drive a nervous man distracted. Yet was there a sort of indefinite, half-attained, unimaginable sublimity about it that fairly froze you to it. . . . Ever and anon a bright, but, alas, deceptive idea would dart you through.—It's the Black Sea in a midnight gale.—It's the unnatural combat of the four primal elements.—It's a blasted heath.—It's a Hyperborean [hy-pur-BOR-ee-un] winter scene.—It's the breaking-up of the icebound stream of Time. But at last all these fancies yielded to that one portentous something in the picture's midst. . . . But stop; does it not bear a faint resemblance to a gigantic fish? even the great leviathan himself?

In fact, the artist's design seemed this. . . . The picture represents a Cape-Horner in a great hurricane; the half-foundered ship weltering there with its three dismantled masts alone visible; and an exasperated whale, purposing to spring clean over the craft, is in the enormous act of impaling himself upon the three mast-heads.

As long as the painting is mysterious, as long as its meaning escapes definition, then, like Friedrich's mist, "it animates the imagination." It is alive with sublime possibility. In this sense, the painting is analogous to Ahab's white whale, possessed of a whiteness that is at once "innocent" and "pure" and like Coleridge's albatross, "pale dread . . . that white phantom [that] sails in all imaginations." Readers have interpreted the white whale in countless ways since *Moby Dick* was published. It symbolizes both good and evil, as well as elements of the natural world that cannot be controlled by humans—that are truly wild.

As much as it reflects a Romantic sensibility, in many ways, Melville's book is a challenge to American transcendentalism and the Romantic imagination. This is most evident in his chapter entitled, "The Mast-Head," in which Ishmael describes his first watch from the top of the ship's mast looking for whales. "There," he says, "you stand, lost in the infinite series of the sea, with nothing ruffled but the waves. The tranced ship indolently rolls; the drowsy trade winds blow; everything resolves you into languor." It is, he says, the perfect place for a young man with a Romantic sense of melancholy to find himself, even if it means that no whales will be spied on account of the watchman's reverie (**Reading 27.20b**):

READING 27.20b

from Herman Melville, *Moby Dick*, Chapter 35, "The Mast-Head" (1851)

And let me in this place movingly admonish you, ye ship-owners of Nantucket! Beware of enlisting in your vigilant fisheries any lad with lean brow and hollow eye; given to unseasonable meditativeness. . . . Beware of such an one, I say: your whales must be seen before they can be killed; and this sunken-eyed young Platonist will tow you ten wakes round the world, and never make you one pint of sperm the richer. Nor are these monitions at all unneeded. For nowadays, the whale-fishery furnishes an asylum for many romantic, melancholy, and absent-minded young men . . .

Very often do the captains of such ships take those absent-minded young philosophers to task, upbraiding them with not feeling sufficient "interest" in the voyage; half-hinting that they are so hopelessly lost to all honorable ambition, as that in their secret souls they would rather not see whales than otherwise ". . . Why, thou monkey," said a harpooneer to one of these lads, "we've been cruising now hard upon three years, and thou hast not raised a whale yet. Whales are scarce as hen's teeth whenever thou art up here." Perhaps they were; or perhaps there might have been shoals of them in the far horizon; but lulled into such an opium-like listlessness of vacant, unconscious reverie is this absent-minded youth by the blending cadence of waves with thoughts, that at last he loses his identity; takes the mystic ocean at his feet for the visible image of that deep, blue, bottomless soul, pervading mankind and nature . . .

Here Melville indicates sensibly that the precarious sailor's perch on the mast of a ship is no place for deep thoughts of "romantic, melancholy, and absent-minded young men." They are lost "in the round ocean and the living air / And the blue sky" that Wordsworth describes in "Tintern Abbey," and risk falling to their death. In *Moby Dick*, Ishmael's Romantic vision is definitely limited. It cannot grasp the complexity of experience, just as Ahab cannot grasp the meaning of the whale that he longs to destroy. This is the darkest side of the Romantic imagination.

BEETHOVEN AND THE RISE OF ROMANTIC MUSIC

Fascination with the Promethean hero was not limited to literature. It was reflected in music, and especially that of Ludwig van Beethoven (1770–1827), the key figure in the transition from the Classical to the Romantic era. His Third Symphony, which came to be known as the *Eroica* [eh-ROH-ee-kah]—Italian for the "Heroic"—was originally dedicated to Napoleon because of the composer's admiration for the French leader as a champion of freedom. But when, on December 2, 1804, Napoleon had himself crowned as emperor, Beethoven changed his mind, saying to a friend: "Is he then, too, nothing more than an ordinary human being? Now he, too, will trample on all the rights of man and indulge only his ambition. He will exalt himself above all others, become a tyrant!" Thus, on the title page of the symphony he crossed out the words "*Intitulata* [in-tee-too-LAH-tah] *Bonaparte*," "Entitled Bonaparte."

Beethoven remained ambivalent about the emperor. Even as Napoleon occupied Vienna in 1809 in his second taking of the city (the first had been in 1805 without a battle when the citizens greeted him with interest), Beethoven had chosen to conduct the *Eroica* at a charity concert for the theatrical poor fund, probably in hopes of attracting the emperor to the performance. (Napoleon, it turns out, had left town the day before.) And as late as October 1810, he wrote a note to himself: "The Mass [in C, op. 86] could perhaps be dedicated to Napoleon." Bonaparte thus embodied the type of contradiction that always fueled Beethoven's imagination. The composer viewed the emperor as at once the enlightened leader and tyrannical despot, as did most of Europe.

Early Years in Vienna: From Classicism to Romanticism

Beethoven's music is a direct reflection of his life's journey, his joys and sorrows, and, in turn, an indication of the shift from the formal structural emphases of Classical music to the expression of more personal, emotional feelings in Romantic music. Other, earlier composers had expressed emotion in their works, but not in the personal, autobiographical way that Beethoven did. Arriving in Vienna from Bonn, Germany, in November 1792, just a month before his twenty-second birthday, Beethoven gained wide acclaim for his skills as a pianist.

The city of Mozart and Haydn was deeply aware of its musical preeminence. In fact, Haydn would serve as the young Beethoven's teacher during his first 14 months in the city. Although their relationship was stormy, Haydn's emphasis on formal inventiveness within the framework of Classical clarity guided Beethoven's development as an artist in his first decade in Vienna. The city was one of extraordinary contradiction. At the turn of the century, it was still contained within its medieval walls, and it would remain so contained until 1827. Still, as the capital of the

Austrian-Hungarian Empire, it was one of the most rapidly growing cities in Europe. This extraordinary growth was accompanied by a near-collapse in infrastructure—its water system was probably the worst in Europe—even as it gained an ever greater reputation for its cultural sophistication. As the century progressed, the city dismantled its elaborate system of defensive walls and constructed gardens, parks, and broad boulevards that allowed for urban expansion and a gradual transition to the surrounding suburbs. Yet even before the medieval walls came down, the streets of Vienna were lined with dance halls, theaters, coffeehouses, and wine bars. An English traveler, John Owen, reported in 1792, the year that Beethoven arrived, "good cheer is, indeed, pursued here in every quarter, and mirth is worshiped in every form."

It was in this atmosphere that Beethoven began every day at his desk, working until midday. After his noontime dinner, he took a long walk around the city, often spending the entire afternoon in the streets until, in the early evening, he made his way to a favorite tavern like the White Swan Inn (Fig. **27.24**). Located across the city square from the inn was Mehlgrube [MEHL-groo-beh] Hall, where, on April 2, 1800, Beethoven premiered his First Symphony. Mozart had performed a series of six concerts in the Mehlgrube in 1785. Yet in Beethoven's First and Second Symphonies, completed in 1802, there is a sense that he consciously intended to recapitulate and summarize the Classical tradition, preparing to move on to more exciting breakthroughs. A personal crisis, brought on by his increasing deafness, instigated an extraordinary period of creativity for Beethoven over the next decade, in which he produced six symphonies, four concertos, and five string quartets, leaving the Classical tradition behind.

The Heroic Decade: 1802–1812

In April 1802, Beethoven left Vienna for the small village of Heiligenstadt [HY-lig-en-shtaht], just north of the city. Though his hearing had been deteriorating for some time, what had started as humming and buzzing was becoming much worse. Moody and temperamental by nature, his deafness deeply depressed him. His frustrations reached a peak in early October as he contemplated ending his life. His feelings are revealed in a remarkable document found among his papers after his death, a letter to his brothers today known as the *Heiligenstadt Testament* (**Reading 27.21**):

READING 27.21

from Ludwig van Beethoven, *Heiligenstadt Testament* (1802)

From childhood on, my heart and soul have been full of the tender feeling of goodwill, and I was ever inclined to accomplish great things. But, think that for six years now I have been hopelessly afflicted, made worse by senseless physicians, from year to year deceived with hopes of improvement, finally compelled to face the prospect of a lasting malady . . . Though born with a fiery, active temperament, even susceptible to the diversions of society, I was soon compelled to withdraw myself, to live life alone . . . It was impossible for me to say to people, "Speak louder, shout, for I am deaf." Ah, how could I possibly admit an infirmity in the one sense which ought to be more perfect in me than in others. . . . I must live almost alone, like one who has been banished . . . If I approach near to

Fig. 27.24 Carl Schütz, colored engraving of Neuer Markt ("New Market"), Vienna. ca. 1785. Colored engraving. Wien Museum Karlsplatz, Vienna, Austria. Erich Lessing, Art Resource, New York. The building at the far end is the Schwarzenberg Palace, where, among other works, Beethoven would premier his String Quintet in C, op. 29, in 1801. To the left of it is the Mehlgrube, literally "flour store," so called because it had served that function in the Middle Ages. Here, Beethoven premiered his Symphony No. 1, on April 2, 1800. Beethoven's favorite tavern, the White Swan Inn, is at the right.

people a hot terror seizes upon me, and I fear being exposed to the danger that my condition might be noticed. . . . What a humiliation for me when someone standing next to me heard a flute in the distance and I heard nothing, or someone heard a shepherd singing and again I heard nothing. Such incidents drove me almost to despair; a little more of that and I would have ended my life—it was only my art that held me back . . .

Beethoven soon reconciled himself to his situation, recognizing that his isolation was, perhaps, the necessary condition to his creativity. His sense of self-sufficiency, of an imagination turned inward, guided by an almost pure state of subjective feeling, lies at the very heart of Romanticism. Beethoven's post-Heiligenstadt works, often called "heroic" because they so thoroughly evoke feelings of struggle and triumph, mark the first expression of a genuinely Romantic musical style. When composer and author E. T. A. Hoffmann said, in 1810, that Beethoven's music evokes "the machinery of awe, of fear, of terror, of pain"—he meant that it evokes the *sublime*. To this end, it is much more emotionally expressive than its Classical predecessors. In Beethoven's groundbreaking compositions, this expression of emotion manifests itself in three distinct ways: long, sustained *crescendos* that drive the music inexorably forward; sudden and surprising key changes that always make harmonic sense; and both loud and soft repetitions of the same theme that are equally, if differently, poignant.

The *Eroica* Beethoven's Third Symphony, the *Eroica*, is the first major expression of this new style in his work. Much longer than any previous symphony, the 691 measures of the first movement alone take approximately 19 minutes to play compared to 8 minutes for the first movement

((•● HEAR MORE at www.myartslab.com

of Mozart's Symphony No. 40 in G minor (see track **25.2**). In fact, the first movement is almost as long as an entire Mozart symphony! Dramatically introducing the main theme and recapitulating it after elongated melodies, this movement ends in a monumental climax, es-

((•● HEAR MORE at www.myartslab.com

tablishing the Romantic, Promethean mood of the piece. The second movement (track **27.1**), with its strong, repetitive beat of double basses imitating military drums, signals the start of the main theme, a solemn funeral march. At the end of the movement, the clockwork sound of the violins suggests the passing of time, while the return of the solemn theme in fragmented form suggests to many listeners the sighing of a dying man. This movement expresses despair with a few hints of consolation. For the third movement, Beethoven relaxed the tension and substituted a **scherzo [SKER-tso]**—an Italian term meaning "joke," denoting a type of musical composition, especially one that is fast and vibrant and presents a surprise—for the courtly measures of the traditional minuet, which had faded in popularity. The finale brings together the themes and variations of the first movement in a broad, triumphant conclusion

featuring a majestic horn. Ultimately, this symphony dramatizes Beethoven's own descent into despair at Heiligenstadt (figured in the second movement), his inward struggle, and his ultimate triumph through art.

The Fifth Symphony Beethoven's Fifth Symphony, like the *Eroica*, brings musical form to the triumph of art over death, terror, fear, and pain. Premiering on December 22, 1808, the symphony's opening four-note motif, with its short-short-short-long rhythm, is in fact the basis for the entire symphony (for the first movement, track **27.2**):

Throughout the symphony's four movements, this rhythmic unit is used again and again, but never in a simple repetition. Rather, the rhythm seems to grow from its minimal opening phrasings into an expansive and monumental theme by the symphony's end.

A number of startling innovations emerge as a counterpoint to this theme: an interruption of the opening motif by a sudden oboe solo; the addition of piccolo and double bassoons to the woodwind sections and of trombones in the finale; the lack of a pause between the last two movements; the surprising repetition of the scherzo's theme in the finale; and the ending of the piece in a different key than it began—a majestic C major rather than the original C minor. In fact, the Fifth Symphony ends with one of the longest, most thrilling conclusions Beethoven ever wrote. Over and over again it seems as if the symphony is about to end, but instead it only gets faster and faster, until it finally comes to a rest on the single note C, played *fortissimo* [for-TISS-eh-moh] by the entire orchestra.

The Late Period: The Romantic in Music

Although initially Beethoven's musical innovations startled his public, by the end of the "Heroic Decade," Beethoven was the most famous composer of instrumental music in Europe. His prominence in the Viennese musical scene always attracted an audience to see him perform or conduct. At the height of his popularity, in 1815, as he seemed to be rebounding from a hopeless romantic affair with a friend's wife, his brother Casper Carl died of tuberculosis, leaving a widow, Johanna, and a nine-year-old son, Karl, under Beethoven's protection. For five years, Johanna and Beethoven contested in court the guardianship of young Karl, which Beethoven finally won in 1820. During this time, the composer was at first unproductive, but beginning in 1818, even as the court battle raged, he composed 23 of the *Diabelli* [dee-ah-BEH-lee] *Variations* for piano, brought the *Missa Solemnis* [MIS-sah soh-LEM-nis] a long way toward completion (Fig. **27.25**), and began sketching what would be his final great symphony, the Ninth. Once again,

Fig. 27.25 Joseph Carl Stieler, *Beethoven*. 1820. Oil on canvas, 24 ³⁄₈″ × 19 ³⁄₈″. Beethoven Haus, Bonn, Germany. The Bridgeman Art Library. This portrait shows Beethoven writing the *Missa Solemnis* and was commissioned by Antonie Brentano, who kept a miniature copy of it on ivory.

out of the chaos of his personal life, Beethoven gained new energy and artistic vision.

One of the most remarkable of Beethoven's last works HEAR MORE at is the Piano Sonata No. 30 in E Major, op. 109, www.myartslab.com which he completed in 1820 (track **27.3**). Beethoven's 32 piano sonatas are almost uniformly original, and many of them have acquired nicknames: the *Moonlight* Sonata, so named by a critic who was reminded of moonlight on a lake; *Les Adieux* ("The Farewell"), so named by Beethoven himself to commemorate the exile and return of his pupil and patron the Archduke Rudolph; and the *Appassionata,* which derives its name from the passionate tone of the first and last movements. The Piano Sonata No. 30 in E Major, one of three he composed in his late period, lacks a nickname but, like the other sonatas, is completely original and untraditional in form. In Sonata No. 30, Beethoven alters the standard number and order of movements. In contrast to the traditional four-movement, fast-slow-minuet-fast sonata structure, he presents only three movements: *Vivace* ("Lively"), *Prestissimo* ("Very fast"), and *Andante molto cantabile ed espressivo* ("Quite slow, lyrical, and expressive"). In addition to its Italian tempo marking, the last movement has a direction in German: *Gesangvoll mit*

innigster Empfundung ("Songlike with the innermost feeling"). The animated but quiet first movement is interrupted by a slow passage that culminates in an explosive and passionate outburst. The short second movement creates a sense of powerful and dramatic tension. But the long third movement—at nearly 15 minutes, it is nearly twice as long as the other two movements combined—is completely unanticipated. In the form of a theme and variations, it moves between extreme simplicity and profound, almost dreamlike feeling, culminating in a sense of peace and harmony.

The Ninth Symphony returns to the heroic style of the first decade of the nineteenth century. Simply put, it is a statement of faith in humanity, a utopian vision. The great innovation of the symphony is that in its finale, it turns to song, introducing a vocal chorus into HEAR MORE at www.myartslab.com the symphonic form (track **27.4**). For this reason, the work is also known as the *Choral Symphony*. For the text, Beethoven adapted Friedrich Schiller's 1785 poem "An die Freude" [ahn dee FROY-duh] ("To Joy"), known to English-speaking audiences as the "Ode to Joy," a celebration of the joy of universal brotherhood:

Freude, schöner Götterfunken,	Joy, beauteous spark of divinity,
Tochter aus Elysium,	Daughter of Elysium,
Alle Menschen werden Brüder	All men become brothers
Wo dein sanfter Flügel weilt.	Where your gentle wing abides.

Ninety voices performed the piece at its May 7, 1824, premiere. This, Beethoven's final expansive gesture, was designed to explore the full, expressive, and Romantic possibilities of the symphonic form.

Romantic Music after Beethoven

Beethoven's musical explorations of individual feelings were immensely influential on the Romantic composers who succeeded him. They strove to find new ways to express their own emotions. Some focused on the symphony as the vehicle for their most important statements. Others found a rich vehicle in piano music and song.

Hector Berlioz and Program Music French composer Hector Berlioz [BER-lee-ohz] (1803–1869) was the most startlingly original of Beethoven's successors, both musically and personally. His compositions were frankly autobiographical; Berlioz attracted attention with new approaches to symphonic music and instrumentation. He wrote three symphonies: the *Symphonie fantastique* [SAM-foh-nee FAHN-tahss-teek] (1830); *Harold en Italie* [AH-rold ahn EE-tah-lee] (1834), based on Byron's *Childe Harold;* and *Roméo et Juliette* [ROH-may-oh ay joo-lee-ET] (1839). All are notable for their inventiveness and novelty, and especially for the size of the orchestras Berlioz enlisted to play them. The enormity of the sound could be deafening (Fig. **27.26**). The symphonies are also instances of program music, which suggests a sequence of images or incidents and may be prefaced with a text identifying these themes (see Chapter 21). As large as the orchestras were and as intricate as their narrative structure was, Berlioz was able to unify his symphonies by introducing recurring themes that provided continuity through the various movements.

The *Symphonie fantastique*, subtitled "Episode in the Life of an Artist," was inspired by the composer's passionate love affair with Irish Shakespearean actress Harriet Smithson. In the notes for the first movement, entitled "Reveries, Passions," Berlioz joyously describes the infatuation of young lovers (track **27.5**). Berlioz insisted on the importance of his written program notes. He believed it essential that the audience read the text in advance of the performance "in order," he wrote, "to provide an overview of the dramatic structure of this work." Here is his description of the first movement's dramatic structure:

(((•● HEAR MORE at
www.myartslab.com

The author imagines that a young musician . . . sees for the first time a woman who embodies all the charms of the ideal being of his dreams, and he falls hopelessly in love with her. By bizarre peculiarity, the image of the beloved always presents itself to the soul of the artist with a musical idea that incorporates a certain character he bestows to her, passionate but at the same time noble and shy.

This melodic image pursues the young musician ceaselessly as a double **idée fixe** [EE-day feex] ("fixed idea"), the term Berlioz gave to the leading theme or melody in his work. This is the reason for the persistent appearance, in every movement of the symphony, of the melody that begins the opening Allegro. The transition from this state of melancholic reverie (interrupted by a few spasms of unfounded joy) to one of delirious passion (with its animations of fury, jealousy, return to tenderness, and tears) is the theme of the first movement.

As Berlioz's idée fixe changes appearance through the course of the symphony, it mirrors the progress of the

**Fig. 27.26 Andrew Geiger,
A Concert of Hector Berlioz in 1846.
1846.** Engraving. Musée de l'Opera, Paris, France. The Bridgeman Art Library. Berlioz was famous for his extraordinary hairstyle, which was as audacious as the loudness of his orchestras.

composition. In the second movement, "A Ball," the composer sees his beloved dancing a concert waltz. The third movement, "Scene in the Country," mixes hope and fear, as the artist seeks the solace of nature. In the fourth movement, "March to the Scaffold," the artist hallucinates on opium, dreaming that he kills his beloved and is witness to his own execution. Finally, in the symphony's last movement, "Dream of a Witches' Sabbath," his beloved appears on her broomstick, accompanied by a virtual pandemonium of sound and a symphonic shriek of horror, echoing Faust's adventures with Mephistopheles. The emphasis on overwhelming emotion, passion, and otherworldly scenes marks Berlioz as a key figure in the Romantic movement of the nineteenth century.

Felix Mendelssohn and the "Meaning" of Music Program music was an important part of the work of another Romantic composer after Beethoven. As a young man, Felix Mendelssohn [MEN-dul-zohn] (1809–1847) was befriended by Goethe, and their great friendship convinced the composer, who was recognized as a prodigy, to travel widely across Europe from 1829 to 1831. These travels inspired many of his orchestral compositions. These include the *Italian Symphony* (1833), which with its program has become his most popular work; the *Scottish Symphony* (1842), which is the only symphony he allowed to be published in his lifetime; and the *Hebrides* (1832), also known as *Fingal's Cave*. The last is a **concert overture**, a form that grew out of the eighteenth-century tradition of performing opera overtures in the concert hall. It consists of a single movement and is usually connected in some way with a narrative plot known to the audience, and in this sense is programmatic. The *Hebrides* Overture, however, does not tell a story. Rather, it sets a scene—one of the first such compositions in Western music—the rocky landscape and swell of the sea that inspired Mendelssohn when he visited the giant cave carved into basalt columns on an island off the Scottish coast.

Mendelssohn himself played both piano and violin. For the piano he composed 48 "Songs without Words," published in eight separate books that proved enormously popular. The works challenge the listener to imagine the words that the compositions evoke. When asked by a friend to provide descriptive titles to the music, he replied:

> I believe that words are not at all up to it [the music], and if I should find that they were adequate I would stop making music altogether. . . . So if you ask me what I was thinking of, I will say: just the song as it stands there. And if I happen to have had a specific word or specific words in mind for one or another of these songs, I can never divulge them to anyone, because the same word means one thing to one person and something else to another, because only the song can say the same thing, can arouse the same feelings in one person as in another—a feeling that is not, however expressed by the same words.

The meaning of music, in other words, lies for Mendelssohn in the music itself. It cannot be expressed in language. The music creates a feeling that all listeners share, even if no two listeners would interpret it in the same terms.

One of Mendelssohn's most beautiful and popular works is the Concerto in E Minor for Violin and Orchestra, composed in 1844 (track **27.6**). HEAR MORE at www.myartslab.com Its lyrical beauty is matched by the dazzling virtuosity Mendelssohn's score demands of the soloist. Throughout the composition, the violinist is required to finger and bow two strings simultaneously, a technique known as "double-stopping." This allows performers not only to demonstrate their skill but also to assert, in a manner consonant with Romantic individualism, their own expressive genius. The work is also innovative compositionally. Most notably, each movement follows the previous one without break, and in contrast to the Classical concerto, the violin states each melody first instead of the orchestra.

Song: Franz Schubert and the Schumanns Not all Romantic composers followed Beethoven in concentrating on the symphonic form to realize their most important innovations and to communicate most fully their personal emotions. Since the middle of the eighteenth century, German composers had been intrigued with the idea of setting poetry to music, especially the works of Schiller and Goethe. Called **lieder** [LEE-der] (singular *lied* [leet]), these songs were generally written for solo voice and piano. Their popularity reflected the growing availability and affordability of the piano in middle-class households and the composers' willingness to write compositions that were within the technical grasp of amateur musicians. This early expansion of the market for music freed composers from total reliance on the patronage of the wealthy.

The *lieder* of Franz Schubert [SHOO-burt] (1797–1828) and Robert Schumann [SHOO-mahn] (1810–1856) were especially popular. Schubert's life was a continual struggle against illness and poverty, and he worked feverishly. In his brief career, he composed nearly 1,000 works, 600 of which were *lieder*, as well as 9 symphonies and 22 piano sonatas. Schubert failed to win international recognition in his lifetime, for which his early death by typhoid was partially to blame. But his melodies, for which he had an uncanny talent, seemed to capture, in the minds of the many who discovered him after his death, the emotional feeling and depth of the Romantic spirit.

Before he married Clara Schumann (1819–1896) in 1840, Robert Schumann had permanently damaged his hands by constant over-practice. He turned from performance to composition and journalism, founding and editing one of the most important journals of its kind, still published today, the *Neue Zeitschrift für Musik* [NOY-uh TSITE-shrift fur MOO-zeek] (*New Journal of Music*), even as he struggled to write music. His success was directly tied to his moods. In the decade before marrying Clara, he never wrote more than five pieces in a given year. In the year of his marriage, however, he composed 140 songs, including his wedding gift to Clara, the poem *Du bist wie eine Blume* [doo beest vee EYE-nuh BLOO-muh], "You Are Like a Flower," and another song performed at their wedding, *Widmung* [VEED-moong], "Dedication," which begins "You are my soul, / you are my heart," and ends with a brief musical quotation from Schubert (track **27.7**). So Clara was the inspiration for much of her husband's most moving music.

By the age of 20, Clara Schumann was so well known as a piano virtuoso that the Viennese court had given her the title Royal and Imperial Virtuosa. She was one of the most famous and respected concert pianists and composers of her day, despite her difficult marriage to Robert Schumann. Like her husband, she specialized in performing piano works known as **character pieces**, works of relatively small dimension that explore the mood or "character" of a person, emotion, or situation. Robert's greatest piano music comprises thematically related suites of such miniatures, including his 1835 *Carnaval*. After Robert's death, Clara supported her family by performing lengthy concert tours and was among the first artists to do this on a regular basis.

Piano Music: Frédéric Chopin Performance of character pieces often occurred at **salon concerts**, in the homes of wealthy music enthusiasts. Among the most sought-after composer/performer pianists of the day was the Polish-born Frédéric Chopin [SHOH-pan] (1810–1849), a good friend of the painter Eugène Delacroix, who painted his portrait in 1838 (Fig. **27.27**) and whose work we will consider in the next chapter. He composed almost exclusively for the piano. Among his most impressive works are his **études** [ay-TOOD], or "studies," which address particular technical challenges on the piano; **polonaises** [poh-loh-NEZ], stylized versions of the Polish dance; **nocturnes** [NOK-turns], character pieces related to the tradition of the serenade performed outside a loved one's window; and larger-scale works, particularly the four **ballades** [bah-LAHD], dramatic narrative forms that are among his most famous works. Focusing on melodramatic romance, supernatural events, and stormy emotion, Chopin's ballades are rich and complex, synthesizing contemporary poetry and diverse moods.

The *Fantasie impromptu* [fahn-tah-ZEE em-prohm-TOO] showcases the expressive range Chopin was capable of even in a brief composition (track **27.8**). Like other pianists of the day, Chopin enhanced the emotional mood of the piece by using *tempo rubato* [TEM-poh roo-BAH-toh] (literally "robbed time"), in which the tempo of the piece accelerates or decelerates in a manner "akin to passionate speech" as described by one of his students. While the word *fantasie* connotes creativity, imagination, magic, and the supernatural, the word *impromptu* suggests spontaneous improvisation, though, of course, the piece was written down. Combining impulsive, spur-of-the-moment creativity and imaginary and fantastical effects, Chopin's work is the very definition of Romanticism.

Fig. 27.27 Eugène Delacroix, *Frédéric Chopin*. 1838. Oil on canvas, 18 3/4" × 14 3/4". Musée du Louvre, Paris. Delacroix's loose and gestural brushwork is completely in keeping with Chopin's impromtu musical style.

From Romanticism to Realism

The Romantic imagination as embodied in the works of Beethoven, Goethe, and Goya is profoundly subjective, the product of an interior world that was intent, like Faust, on developing itself to the fullest. Beethoven spoke regretfully on his deathbed of his failure to set Goethe's *Faust* to music not because he approved of Faust as a man, but because he recognized in the sweep of the character's ambition something of his own expansive spirit.

However, it was not to the subjective imagination alone that the nineteenth-century imagination turned. We are witness again and again in the art of the century to the reality of contemporary events. In such works, the painter accepts the role of a newspaper reporter and attempts to convey, if not the actuality, then the emotional reality of events. The career of Théodore Géricault [ZHAY-ree-koh] (1791–1824) testifies to this shift. Trained in Paris in a Neoclassical style, by the last years of Napoleon's reign, he was painting largely military subjects that increasingly reflected a growing recognition of the emperor's limitations. By 1816, he was engaged in a full critique of the French government in his monumental canvas *The Raft of the Medusa* (see Fig. 28.10). In the years just before his death, in 1824, Géricault produced a series of paintings, none of which were discovered until a half century after his death, that are today known as his portraits of the insane (Fig. **27.28**). What motivated Géricault to paint these portraits remains a mystery, but they reveal an interest in the most intimate side of human emotion, depicting their subjects with something approaching deep reverence for their psychological fragility. These are not subjective paintings, but they are *about* subjectivity—or more precisely, about the subjective mind's inability to come to grips with its world. And they suggest, in the isolation of each figure within the confined dark space of traditional portraiture, that we are not witness to personalities—the traditional subject of portraiture—but to figures emptied of their personalities.

These paintings amount to an extended study of the impact of nineteenth-century society on the downtrodden, the forgotten, and the all-too-often-alienated masses. They are one of the first expressions of what would in the coming years be a redirection of artistic attention away from the personal turmoil and dramas of the Romantic self and toward the plight of those unable to manage for themselves in a quickly changing industrial world. Reacting to images like these—and there would soon be others—the arts would come to the service of those demanding social reform. And the reformists themselves, impatient for change, would foment revolution. A new realism would be born, one dedicated to righting social wrongs. ■

Fig. 27.28 Théodore Géricault, *Portrait of an Insane Man.* 1822–23. Oil on canvas, 24″ × 19 ³/₄″. Museum voor Schone Kunsten, Ghent, Belgium. The Bridgeman Art Library.

What is Romanticism?

The Romantics were dedicated to the discovery of beauty in nature through their subjective experience of it. William Wordsworth's poem "Tintern Abbey" embodies the growing belief in the natural world as the source of inspiration and creativity that marks the early Romantic imagination. Wordsworth's poem was included in *Lyrical Ballads*, a book he co-authored with Samuel Taylor Coleridge in 1798 as a self-conscious experiment dedicated to presenting "incidents and situations from common life . . . in a selection of language really used by men." How do Wordsworth and Coleridge differ as poets? Of all Romantic poetry, perhaps the odes of John Keats most fully embody the Romantic imagination's ability to transcend even death, which Keats faced when he realized at age 23 that he was dying of tuberculosis. In a nightingale's song or a Grecian urn, Keats discovers the essence of a beauty that represents a form of nature higher than mortal life itself.

How does landscape painting reflect a Romantic worldview?

Landscape painters in the nineteenth century saw the natural world around them as the emotional focal point or center of their own artistic imaginations. John Constable, painting in the valley of the Stour River in his native Suffolk, considered himself "a worshipper of Nature." What is the "transcendence" that Wordsworth and Constable find in nature? J. M. W. Turner specialized in capturing light, not the objects of nature so much as the medium through which they are seen. What is Turner's conception of the "sublime"? In Germany, the painter Caspar David Friedrich often places solitary figures before sublime landscapes that constantly raise the theme of doubt. Why does doubt excite Friedrich's imagination? In America, the Romantic imagination found itself at home in the untamed wilderness. What tensions do the paintings of Thomas Cole and Frederic Edwin Church explore?

What is Transcendentalism?

The American writers of Romantic sensibility were, like the painters, free to discover the self in nature. Ralph Waldo Emerson codified their thinking in his 1836 treatise *Nature*. His contemporary, Henry David Thoreau, sought to experience nature firsthand by retreating to a small cabin in the woods on Emerson's property, where he wrote *Walden, or Life in the Woods*, first published in 1854. How do Emerson's "transparent eyeball" and Thoreau's "stream of time" compare?

What are the characteristics of the Romantic hero?

Almost everyone recognized that even if Napoleon personified the Romantic hero, he also possessed a darker side. In many eyes, he was a modern Prometheus. What are the different views of Prometheus? in Hegel? in the poems of Lord Byron and Percy Bysshe Shelley? in Mary Shelley's *Frankenstein*? How does Johann Wolfgang von Goethe view his Promethean figure Faust? Despite its darker side, what are the attractions of the Promethean figure?

What experiences shaped Goya's worldview?

The Spanish painter Francisco Goya was at first enthusiastic about Napoleon, but quickly changed his mind after the emperor's invasion of Spain in 1808. How did he see Spanish society? How did the royal family reflect their culture? How did Napoleon's invasion confirm his pessimism?

What insight lies at the heart of Herman Melville's novel *Moby Dick*?

Romantic thinking was more problematic for the novelist Herman Melville. While many of the characters in his *Moby Dick* reflect a deeply Romantic sensibility, Melville challenges their way of approaching the world as overly simplistic and even dangerously so. How does the world he portrays in *Moby Dick* compare to that presented in the paintings of Caspar David Friedrich?

What is Romantic music?

Beethoven's musical career can be divided into three eras. In the early years, he was deeply influenced by the Classical music of Mozart and Haydn. In the so-called "Heroic Decade," after coming to the brink of suicide in 1802 due to his increasing deafness, he was guided by an almost pure state of subjective feeling. In great symphonies like the *Eroica* and the Fifth, he defined the Romantic style in music. How would you describe that style? After undergoing much personal anguish related to his family, Beethoven entered his late period, during which he completed three uniquely structured piano sonatas and his triumphal Ninth Symphony in 1824. Beethoven's approach to the Romantic style in music required innovation and originality. Succeeding generations of composers followed his lead by expanding the musical vocabulary of orchestras and developing new symphonic forms. What are the innovations of Hector Berlioz and Felix Mendelssohn? Other composers, such as Franz Schubert and Robert and Clara Schumann, set the poems of Romantic poets such as Schiller and Goethe to music in compositions called *lieder*. Frédéric Chopin composed almost solely for the piano and was famous especially for his *études*, studies that address particular technical challenges.

PRACTICE MORE Get flashcards for images and terms and review chapter material with quizzes at **www.myartslab.com**

GLOSSARY

ballade A highly dramatic narrative form.

character piece A piano work of relatively small dimension that explores the mood or "character" of a person, emotion, or situation.

concert overture A programmatic form that grew out of the eighteenth-century tradition of performing opera overtures in the concert hall and that consists of a single movement usually connected in some way with a narrative plot known to the audience.

dialectic An evolutionary process in which the prevailing set of ideas, called the "thesis," finds itself opposed by a conflicting set of ideas, the "antithesis." This conflict resolves itself in a "synthesis," which inevitably establishes itself as the new thesis.

ennui A French term that denotes both listlessness and a profound melancholy.

étude In music, a study that addresses particular technical challenges.

"Great Man" theory A theory asserting that human history is driven by the achievement of men who lead humankind forward because they have sensed by intuition the "world-spirit."

idée fixe A French term meaning "fixed idea," or an idea that dominates one's mind for a prolonged period.

lieder Songs, generally written for solo voice and piano.

nocturne In music, a character piece evocative of the night.

ode A lyric poem of exaltation, exhibiting deep feeling.

picturesque A view defined by "roughness and sudden variation joined to irregularity."

polonaise A stylized version of the Polish dance.

salon concert A concert held in the homes of wealthy music enthusiasts.

scherzo An Italian term meaning "joke," denoting a type of musical composition, especially one that is fast and vibrant and that may present a surprise. In the symphony, the scherzo replaced the minuet.

sublime The prospect of anything beyond the ability of the human mind to comprehend it fully.

READINGS

READING 27.2

from William Wordsworth, "Lines Composed a Few Miles above Tintern Abbey, on Revisiting the Banks of the Wye during a Tour, July 13, 1798" (1798)

"Tintern Abbey" is the product of Wordsworth's visit to the medieval abbey's ruins on the banks of the Wye River in 1798. The 159-line poem is typical of Wordsworth's poetry in the way that it swings back and forth between his observation of an external scene and his contemplation of the feelings generated by that scene, between the past and the present, and between his personal experience ("I") and more universal and general experience ("we").

Five years have passed; five summers, with the length
Of five long winters! and again I hear
These waters, rolling from their mountain-springs
With a soft inland murmur.—Once again
Do I behold these steep and lofty cliffs,
That on a wild secluded scene impress
Thoughts of more deep seclusion; and connect
The landscape with the quiet of the sky.
The day is come when I again repose
Here, under this dark sycamore, and view   10
These plots of cottage-ground, these orchard-tufts,

Which at this season, with their unripe fruits,
Are clad in one green hue, and lose themselves
'Mid groves and copses. Once again I see
These hedge-rows, hardly hedge-rows, little lines
Of sportive wood run wild: these pastoral farms,
Green to the very door; and wreaths of smoke
Sent up, in silence, from among the trees!
With some uncertain notice, as might seem
Of vagrant dwellers in the houseless woods,   20
Or of some Hermit's cave, where by his fire
The Hermit sits alone.
        These beauteous forms,

Through a long absence, have not been to me
As is a landscape to a blind man's eye:
But oft, in lonely rooms, and 'mid the din
Of towns and cities, I have owed to them
In hours of weariness, sensations sweet,
Felt in the blood, and felt along the heart;
And passing even into my purer mind,   30
With tranquil restoration:—feelings too
Of unremembered pleasure: such, perhaps,
As have no slight or trivial influence
On that best portion of a good man's life,
His little, nameless, unremembered, acts
Of kindness and of love. Nor less, I trust,
To them I may have owed another gift,
Of aspect more sublime; that blessed mood,
In which the burthen of the mystery,
In which the heavy and the weary weight   40
Of all this unintelligible world,
Is lightened:—that serene and blessed mood,
In which the affections gently lead us on,—
Until, the breath of this corporeal frame
And even the motion of our human blood
Almost suspended, we are laid asleep

In body, and become a living soul:
While with an eye made quiet by the power
Of harmony, and the deep power of joy,
We see into the life of things.   50
    If this
Be but a vain belief, yet, oh! how oft—
In darkness and amid the many shapes
Of joyless daylight; when the fretful stir
Unprofitable, and the fever of the world,
Have hung upon the beatings of my heart—
How oft, in spirit, have I turned to thee,
O sylvan Wye! thou wanderer thro' the woods,
How often has my spirit turned to thee!
And now, with gleams of half-extinguished thought,   60
With many recognitions dim and faint,
And somewhat of a sad perplexity,
The picture of the mind revives again:
While here I stand, not only with the sense
Of present pleasure, but with pleasing thoughts
That in this moment there is life and food
For future years. And so I dare to hope,
Though changed, no doubt, from what I was when first
I came among these hills; when like a roe
I bounded o'er the mountains, by the sides   70
Of the deep rivers, and the lonely streams,
Wherever nature led: more like a man
Flying from something that he dreads, than one
Who sought the thing he loved. For nature then
(The coarser pleasures of my boyish days,
And their glad animal movements all gone by)
To me was all in all.—I cannot paint
What then I was. The sounding cataract
Haunted me like a passion: the tall rock,
The mountain, and the deep and gloomy wood,   80
Their colours and their forms, were then to me
An appetite; a feeling and a love,
That had no need of a remoter charm,
By thought supplied, nor any interest
Unborrowed from the eye.—That time is past,
And all its aching joys are now no more,
And all its dizzy raptures. Not for this
Faint I, nor mourn nor murmur, other gifts
Have followed; for such loss, I would believe,
Abundant recompence. For I have learned   90
To look on nature, not as in the hour
Of thoughtless youth; but hearing oftentimes
The still, sad music of humanity,
Nor harsh nor grating, though of ample power
To chasten and subdue. And I have felt
A presence that disturbs me with the joy
Of elevated thoughts; a sense sublime
Of something far more deeply interfused,
Whose dwelling is the light of setting suns,
And the round ocean and the living air,   100
And the blue sky, and in the mind of man;
A motion and a spirit, that impels
All thinking things, all objects of all thought,
And rolls through all things. Therefore am I still
A lover of the meadows and the woods,
And mountains; and of all that we behold
From this green earth; of all the mighty world
Of eye, and ear,—both what they half create,

And what perceive; well pleased to recognise
In nature and the language of the sense,   110
The anchor of my purest thoughts, the nurse,
The guide, the guardian of my heart, and soul
Of all my moral being.
    Nor perchance,
If I were not thus taught, should I the more
Suffer my genial spirits to decay:
For thou art with me here upon the banks
Of this fair river; thou my dearest Friend,
My dear, dear Friend; and in thy voice I catch
The language of my former heart, and read   120
My former pleasures in the shooting lights
Of thy wild eyes. Oh! yet a little while
May I behold in thee what I was once,
My dear, dear Sister! and this prayer I make,
Knowing that Nature never did betray
The heart that loved her; 'tis her privilege,
Through all the years of this our life, to lead
From joy to joy: for she can so inform
The mind that is within us, so impress
With quietness and beauty, and so feed   130
With lofty thoughts, that neither evil tongues,
Rash judgments, nor the sneers of selfish men,
Nor greetings where no kindness is, nor all
The dreary intercourse of daily life,
Shall e'er prevail against us, or disturb
Our cheerful faith, that all which we behold
Is full of blessings. Therefore let the moon
Shine on thee in thy solitary walk;
And let the misty mountain-winds be free
To blow against thee: and, in after years,   140
When these wild ecstasies shall be matured
Into a sober pleasure; when thy mind
Shall be a mansion for all lovely forms,
Thy memory be as a dwelling-place
For all sweet sounds and harmonies; oh! then,
If solitude, or fear, or pain, or grief,
Should be thy portion, with what healing thoughts
Of tender joy wilt thou remember me,
And these my exhortations! Nor, perchance—
If I should be where I no more can hear   150
Thy voice, nor catch from thy wild eyes these gleams
Of past existence—wilt thou then forget
That on the banks of this delightful stream
We stood together; and that I, so long
A worshipper of Nature, hither came
Unwearied in that service: rather say
With warmer love—oh! with far deeper zeal
Of holier love. Nor wilt thou then forget,
That after many wanderings, many years
Of absence, these steep woods and lofty cliffs,   160
And this green pastoral landscape, were to me
More dear, both for themselves and for thy sake!

READING CRITICALLY

At the heart of Wordsworth's poem is his sense that nature is not merely a scene but is infused with a moral value comparable to divinity itself. In what ways does he describe his growing realization that this is so?

from Samuel Taylor Coleridge, "Rime of the Ancient Mariner," Part 1 (1798)

Coleridge's poem in seven parts is set on the foreboding ocean. It reveals truths about nature that seem, at first, the total opposite of Wordsworth's nurturing landscapes. In Coleridge's poem, nature is an indomitable force, a ruthless power. Yet, even in its most horrific aspects, it possesses an inherent value and beauty. In the first book of the poem, which sets up the tragic tale, the Mariner's destructive act in killing the albatross symbolizes humanity's destructive relation to the natural world as a whole. In the subsequent parts, the Mariner's regeneration and salvation come as he accepts responsibility for his actions.

ARGUMENT

How a Ship having passed the Line was driven by storms to the cold Country towards the South Pole; and how from thence she made her course to the tropical Latitude of the Great Pacific Ocean; and of the strange things that befell; and in what manner the Ancyent Marinere came back to his own Country.

PART I

An ancient Mariner meeteth three Gallants bidden to a wedding-feast, and detaineth one.

It is an ancient Mariner,
And he stoppeth one of three.
'By thy long beard and glittering eye,
Now wherefore stopp'st thou me?

The Bridegroom's doors are opened wide,   10
And I am next of kin;
The guests are met, the feast is set:
May'st hear the merry din.'

He holds him with his skinny hand,
'There was a ship,' quoth he.
'Hold off! unhand me, grey-beard loon!'
Eftsoons his hand dropt he.

The Wedding-Guest is spell-bound by the eye of the old seafaring man, and constrained to hear his tale.

He holds him with his glittering eye—
The Wedding-Guest stood still,
And listens like a three year's child: 20
The Mariner hath his will.

The Wedding-Guest sat on a stone:
He cannot choose but hear;
And thus spake on that ancient man,
The bright-eyed Mariner.

'The ship was cheered, the harbour cleared,
Merrily did we drop
Below the kirk, below the hill,
Below the lighthouse top.

The Mariner tells how the ship sailed southward with a good wind and fair weather, till it reached the Line.

The Sun came up upon the left,   30
Out of the sea came he!
And he shone bright, and on the right
Went down into the sea.

Higher and higher every day,
Till over the mast at noon—'
The Wedding-Guest here beat his breast,
For he heard the loud bassoon.

The Wedding-Guest heareth the bridal music; but the Mariner continueth his tale.

The bride hath paced into the hall,
Red as a rose is she;
Nodding their heads before her goes   40
The merry minstrelsy.

The Wedding-Guest he beat his breast,
Yet he cannot choose but hear;
And thus spake on that ancient man,
The bright-eyed Mariner.

The ship driven by a storm toward the south pole.

'And now the STORM-BLAST came, and he
Was tyrannous and strong:
He struck with his o'ertaking wings,
And chased us south along.

With sloping masts and dipping prow,   50
As who pursued with yell and blow
Still treads the shadow of his foe,
And forward bends his head,
The ship drove fast, loud roared the blast,
The southward aye we fled.

And now there came both mist and snow,
And it grew wondrous cold:
And ice, mast-high, came floating by,
As green as emerald.

The land of ice, and of fearful sounds where no living thing was to be seen.

And through the drifts the snowy cliffs   60
Did send a dismal sheen:
Nor shapes of men nor beasts we ken—
The ice was all between.

The ice was here, the ice was there,
The ice was all around:
It cracked and growled, and roared and howled,
Like noises in a swound!

Till a great sea-bird, called the Albatross, came through the snow-fog, and was received with great joy and hospitality.

At length did cross an Albatross,
Through the fog it came;
As if it had been a Christian soul,   70
We hailed it in God's name.

It ate the food it ne'er had eat,
And round and round it flew.
The ice did split with a thunder-fit;
The helmsman steered us through!

And lo! the Albatross proveth a bird of good omen, and followeth the ship as it returned northward through fog and floating ice.

And a good south wind sprung up behind;
The Albatross did follow,
And every day, for food or play,
Came to the mariner's hollo!

In mist or cloud, on mast or shroud,
It perched for vespers nine;
Whiles all the night, through fog-smoke white,
Glimmered the white Moon-shine.'

80

The ancient Mariner inhospitably killeth the pious bird of good omen.

'God save thee, ancient Mariner!
From the fiends, that plague thee thus!—
Why look'st thou so ?'—With my cross-bow
I shot the ALBATROSS.

READING CRITICALLY

The Mariner narrates his tale to a wedding guest, who in the fourth stanza "listens like a three years' child." Why do you suppose Coleridge wants the Mariner's audience to listen with childlike attentiveness?

READING 27.17

from Mary Shelley, *Frankenstein*, Chapter 5 (1818)

Mary Shelley's Frankenstein *was begun in 1816 at a villa in Switzerland after the English poet Lord Byron proposed to his companions that they compete in writing ghost stories.* Frankenstein *is an epistolary novel, a series of letters written by an English explorer in the Arctic whose ice-bound ship takes on a man in terrible condition, Victor Frankenstein, who narrates his own story to the explorer. Here, Frankenstein describes the horror he felt after creating a monster when he had dreamed of creating a creature of unparalleled beauty.*

It was on a dreary night of November that I beheld the accomplishment of my toils. With an anxiety that almost amounted to agony, I collected the instruments of life around me, that I might infuse a spark of being into the lifeless thing that lay at my feet. It was already one in the morning; the rain pattered dismally against the panes, and my candle was nearly burnt out, when, by the glimmer of the half-extinguished light, I saw the dull yellow eye of the creature open; it breathed hard, and a convulsive motion agitated its limbs.

How can I describe my emotions at this catastrophe, or how delineate the wretch whom with such infinite pains and care I had endeavoured to form? His limbs were in proportion, and I had selected his features as beautiful. Beautiful!—Great God! His yellow skin scarcely covered the work of muscles and arteries beneath; his hair was of a lustrous black, and flowing; his teeth of a pearly whiteness; but these luxuriances only formed a more horrid contrast with his watery eyes, that seemed almost of the same colour as the dun white sockets in which they were set, his shriveled complexion and straight black lips.

The different accidents of life are not so changeable as the feelings of human nature. I had worked hard for nearly two years, for the sole purpose of infusing life into an inanimate body. For this I had deprived myself of rest and health. I had desired it with an ardour that far exceeded moderation; but now that I had finished, the beauty of the dream vanished, and breathless horror and disgust filled my heart. Unable to endure the aspect of the being I had created, I rushed out of the room, and continued a long time traversing my bedchamber, unable to compose my mind to sleep. At length lassitude succeeded to the tumult I had before endured; and I threw myself on the bed in my clothes, endeavouring to seek a few moments of forgetfulness. But it was in vain: I slept, indeed, but I was disturbed by the wildest dreams. I thought I saw Elizabeth, in the bloom of health, walking in the streets of Ingolstadt. Delighted and surprised, I embraced her; but as I imprinted the first kiss on her lips, they became livid with the hue of death; her features

10

20

30

appeared to change, and I thought that I held the corpse of my dead mother in my arms; a shroud enveloped her form, and I saw the grave-worms crawling in the folds of the flannel. I started from my sleep with horror; a cold dew covered my forehead, my teeth chattered, and every limb became convulsed: when, by the dim and yellow light of the moon, as it forced its way through the window shutters, I beheld the wretch—the miserable monster whom I had created. He held up the curtain of the bed; and his eyes, if eyes they may be called, were fixed on me. His jaws opened, and he muttered some inarticulate sounds, while a grin wrinkled his cheeks. He might have spoken, but I did not hear; one hand was stretched out, seemingly to detain me, but I escaped, and rushed down stairs. I took refuge in the courtyard belonging to the house which I inhabited; where I remained during the rest of the night, walking up and down in the greatest agitation, listening attentively, catching and fearing each sound as if it were to announce the approach of the demoniacal corpse to which I had so miserably given life.

40

50

Oh! no mortal could support the horror of that countenance. A mummy again endued with animation could not be so hideous as that wretch. I had gazed on him while unfinished; he was ugly then; but when those muscles and joints were rendered capable of motion, it became a thing such as even Dante could not have conceived.

60

I passed the night wretchedly. Sometimes my pulse beat so quickly and hardly that I felt the palpitation of every artery; at others, I nearly sank to the ground through languor and extreme weakness. Mingled with this horror, I felt the bitterness of disappointment; dreams that had been my food and pleasant rest for so long a space were now become a hell to me; and the change was so rapid, the overthrow so complete!

Morning, dismal and wet, at length dawned, and discovered to my sleepless and aching eyes the church of Ingolstadt, its white steeple and clock, which indicated the sixth hour. The porter opened the gates of the court, which had that night been

70

my asylum, and I issued into the streets, pacing them with quick steps, as if I sought to avoid the wretch whom I feared every turning of the street would present to my view. I did not dare return to the apartment which I inhabited, but felt impelled to hurry on, although drenched by the rain which poured from a black and comfortless sky.

I continued walking in this manner for some time, endeavouring, by bodily exercise, to ease the load that weighed upon my mind. I traversed the streets, without any clear conception of where I was, or what I was doing. My heart palpitated in the sickness of fear; and I hurried on with irregular steps, not daring to look about me: . . .

80

READING CRITICALLY

Why does Frankenstein reject his creation? Why does his dream turn to nightmare? Why did Mary Shelley leave so many questions unanswered?

28 Industry and the Working Class

A New Realism

THINKING AHEAD

How did industrialization shape the urban environment in the nineteenth century?

How did reformers react to industrialization?

What is literary realism?

Who defined the direction of French painting during the nineteenth century?

What is photography's role in the rise of a realist art?

What is The Origin of the Species?

During the life of the great English novelist Charles Dickens (1812–1870), London was both the capital of a nation of ever-increasing wealth and international preeminence and a city mired in poverty, crime, and urban blight. In part, Dickens saw London through the lens of a trained reporter. He had covered endless, unproductive debates in Parliament about social reform that left him impressed only by that august body's inability to act in any meaningful way. But he also viewed the vast city from the perspective of his harsh childhood, details of which were so awful that he kept them secret his entire life. Two days after his twelfth birthday, he went to work in a boot-blacking factory, from 8:00 AM to 8:00 PM, for a wage of 6 shillings a week. (Twenty shillings equaled a British pound—worth approximately $5 at the time—so Dickens earned less than $2 per week.) Shortly afterward, his father was arrested and committed to debtors' prison. The family moved into the prison cell with him, as was common at the time. These events so indelibly marked young Charles that, later in life, he would become one of the English reform movement's most active speakers. As a novelist, he portrayed the lives of children whose suffering mirrored his own. These novels, published in serialized chapters in the London press beginning when Dickens was in his twenties, attracted hundreds of thousands of readers. In depicting the lives of the English lower classes with intense sympathy and great attention to detail, Dickens became a leading creator of a new type of prose fiction, **literary realism**.

◀ **Fig. 28.1 Anonymous, *Old Hetton Colliery, Newcastle*. ca. 1840.** Beamish, North of England Open Air Museum, Durham, UK. The Bridgeman Art Library. The industrialization of Europe changed the nature of work and with it the nature of society, especially in England. While it created vast wealth for a few, industrialization forced the vast majority of men and women to work in factories where conditions were grim, the workday long, and wages low.

HEAR MORE Listen to an audio file of your chapter at **www.myartslab.com**

Dickens's novels illuminated the enormous inequities of class that existed in nineteenth-century England, with his heroes and heroines, villains and scoundrels, often approaching the point of caricature. While his sentimentalism sometimes verged on the maudlin, Dickens also had an unparalleled ability to describe England vividly. Take, for instance, his description of industrial Birmingham in his 1840 novel *The Old Curiosity Shop*, a scene very much like the one depicted in the anonymous *Old Hetton Colliery, Newcastle* (Fig. **28.1**) painted at about the same time that Dickens wrote these words:

> A long suburb of red brick houses—some with patches of garden-ground, where coal-dust and factory smoke darkened the shrinking leaves, and coarse rank flowers, and where the struggling vegetation sickened and sank under the hot breath of kiln and furnace, making them by its presence seem yet more blighting and unwholesome than in the town itself—a long, flat, straggling suburb passed . . . where not a blade of grass was seen to grow, where not a bud put forth its promise in the spring, where nothing green could live. . . . On every side, and far as the eye could see into the heavy distance, tall chimneys, crowding on each other, and presenting that endless repetition of the same dull, ugly form, which is the horror of oppressive dreams, poured out their plague of smoke, obscured the light, and made foul the melancholy air. On mounds of ashes by the wayside, sheltered only by a few rough boards, or rotten pent-house roofs, strange engines spun and writhed like tortured creatures; clanking their iron chains, shrieking in their rapid whirl from time to time . . . . Dismantled houses here and there appeared, tottering to the earth, propped up by fragments of others that had fallen down, unroofed, windowless, blackened, desolate, but yet inhabited.
>
> Men, women, children, wan in their looks and ragged in attire, tended the engines, fed their tributary fire, begged upon the road, or scowled half-naked from the doorless houses. Then came more of the wrathful monsters, whose like they almost seemed to be in their wildness and their untamed air, screeching and turning round and round again; and still, before, behind, and to the right and left, was the same interminable perspective of brick towers, never ceasing in their black vomit, blasting all things living or inanimate, shutting out the face of day, and closing in on all these horrors with a dense dark cloud.

Fig. 28.2 Gustave Doré, *Orange Court—Drury Lane.* **1869.**
Illustration for Gustave Doré and Blanchard Jerrold. *London: A Pilgrimage*, 1872. Accompanied by policemen from Scotland Yard, Doré went around the city, including the East End and Whitechapel, making sketches on the spot. Though executed some 36 years after Dickens penned *Sketches by Boz*, Doré's drawings capture the poverty that Dickens describes, at the same time proving how enduring poverty was.

As the number of factories in and around cities such as London exploded over the course of the century (Map **28.1**), not just the landscape, but the nature of work and with it the nature of human society, changed dramatically. Although industrialization created wealth for a few, it forced the vast majority of men and women into jobs as low-paid laborers. In the southern United States, where work was conducted by slaves, conditions in rural areas were often even more horrifying. In England, France, Russia, and the United States, many artists and writers called for social reform. Some depicted the actual conditions of the working class in increasingly realistic works of art and literature; others demanded the reinvention of society itself. The new medium of photography allowed uniquely accurate representations of people, objects, and landscapes. The increasing emphasis on realism in the arts—depicting the world as it actually was rather than idealizing it—was mirrored by the growing popularity of the scientific methodology to investigate rigorously every facet of human experience and the natural world. In fact, Auguste Comte (1798–1857), an enormously influential French thinker, elevated science to a kind of religion, developing the philosophy of "positivism." According to Comte, society passes through three successive stages in its quest for knowledge of any subject—theological (religious), metaphysical (abstract, philosophical), and positive (scientific). It was only through the application of the scientific method that truth could be obtained about the natural world, technology, or human society. This chapter ends by summarizing the achievements of one of the century's most creative scientists, Charles Darwin. By challenging established theories, Darwin set the stage for viewing nature and the universe as part of a dynamic, ever-changing process.

Map. 28.1 London in 1898: Factories with over 100 workers.

THE INDUSTRIAL CITY: CONDITIONS IN LONDON

In his earliest published book, writing under the pen name Boz, Dickens describes one of the worst slums in London, on Drury Lane (**Reading 28.1**). A century earlier, it had been a good address, but by the beginning of the 1800s, it was dominated by prostitution and gin houses (Fig. **28.2**):

READING 28.1

from Dickens, *Sketches by Boz* (1836)

The filthy and miserable appearance of this part of London can hardly be imagined by those (and there are many such) who have not witnessed it. Wretched houses with broken windows patched with rags and paper; every room let out [rented] to a different family, and sometimes two or even three—fruit and "sweet stuff" manufacturing in the cellars, barners and red-herring vendors in the front parlours, cobblers in the back; a bird fancier in the first floor, three families on the second, starvation in the attics, Irishmen in the passage, a "musician" in the front kitchen, and a charwoman and five hungry children in the back one—filth everywhere—a gutter before the houses and a drain behind—clothes drying, and slops emptying from the windows, girls of fourteen or fifteen, with matted hair, walking about barefoot, and in white great-coats, almost their only covering; boys of all ages, in coats of all sizes and no coats at all; men and women, in every variety of scanty and dirty apparel, lounging, scolding, drinking, smoking, squabbling, fighting, and swearing.

The writing style is pure Dickens. Descriptions pile up in detail after detail, in one long sentence, so that the reader, almost breathless at its conclusion, feels overwhelmed, as the author tries to make the unimaginable real. His aim is not simply to entertain, but to advocate reform. Dickens was hardly alone in criticizing the fruits of "progress" of Western civilization. The plight of the poor, coupled with the indolence of the wealthy, was a matter of great concern for many writers and artists in mid-nineteenth-century England. Thomas Carlyle (1795–1881), the foremost essayist and social critic of the day, put it this way (**Reading 28.2**):

from Thomas Carlyle, *Past and Present* (1843)

The condition of England . . . is justly regarded as one of the most ominous, and withal one of the strangest, ever seen in this world. England is full of wealth, of multifarious produce, supply for human want in every kind; yet England is dying of inanition [exhaustion, lack of social, moral vigor]. With unabated bounty the land of England blooms and grows; waving with yellow harvests; thick-studded with workshops, industrial implements, with fifteen millions of workers, understood to be the strongest, the cunningest and the willingest our Earth ever had; these men are here; the work they have done, the fruit they have realised is here, abundant, exuberant on every hand of us: and behold, some baleful fiat as of Enchantment has gone forth, saying, "Touch it not, ye workers, ye master-workers, ye master-idlers; none of you can touch it, no man of you shall be the better for it; this is enchanted fruit!" . . . Of these successful skilful workers some two millions, it is now counted, sit in Workhouses, Poor-Law Prisons; or have "out-door relief" flung over the wall to them,—the workhouse Bastille [referring to the infamous Paris prison that triggered the French revolution in 1789] being filled to bursting, and the strong Poor-law broken asunder by a stronger. They sit there, these many months now; their hope of deliverance as yet small. In workhouses, pleasantly so-named, because work cannot be done in them. Twelve-hundred-thousand workers in England alone; their cunning right-hand lamed, shut in by narrow walls. They sit there, pent up, as in a kind of horrid enchantment; glad to be imprisoned and enchanted, that they may not perish starved. . . .

Carlyle argued that while the natural guardians of the poor, the English aristocracy, were out fox hunting and shooting game, poverty was exploding around them. The upper classes and much of the government were blind to the horrors that were everywhere evident if they bothered to look. Those horrors penetrated all aspects of urban living: water, housing, labor, and family life.

Water and Housing

Carlyle and Dickens saw, every day, that the river Thames was little more than an open sewer. A petition of 1827 to the House of Commons advised against its use:

> The water taken from the River Thames at Chelsea, for the use of the inhabitants of the western part of the metropolis, [is] being charged with the contents of the great common sewers, the drainings from dunghills, and laystalls [collections of human waste], the refuse of hospitals, slaughter houses, colour, lead and soap works, drug mills and manufactures, and with all sorts of decomposed animal and vegetable substances, rendering the said water offensive and destructive to health, ought no longer to be taken up by any of the water companies from so foul a source.

Among the lethal bacteria that thrived in this water was cholera, and its principal victims were the poor. Where they lived, one in three children died before the age of one. After several devastating cholera epidemics in the 1830s and 1840s, a municipal waterworks was finally established in London in 1855, charged with the construction of "a system of sewerage which should prevent . . . any part of the sewage within the metropolis from passing into the Thames in or near the metropolis." Contributing to London's water pollution problem was the extraordinarily rapid growth of the population (Map **28.2**). As the city's boundaries expanded, high-density neighborhoods grew as well.

At the end of the eighteenth century.

In the 1830s.

In the 1870s.

Map 28.2 The growth of London, 1800–1880. After Roy Porter, *London: A Social History* (New York: Penguin Books, 1994). London's population in 1800 was about 1 million. By 1881, the population had more than quadrupled, growing to 4.5 million, dwarfing the industrial cities to the north. Social services were unable to keep up with this rapid growth.

Because laborers needed to walk to their jobs in urban factories, living in the countryside was no longer possible. As the poor crowded into buildings already stressed by age and disrepair, whole neighborhoods turned into slums. Map 28.1 shows factories employing more than 100 workers in London in 1898, with most of them concentrated in the inner city. Rent for an entire house cost about 7 shillings 6 pence a week, around $2.00, though most working families could afford only to rent a single room in a central London house. The 1841 census found 27 houses in Goodge Place, a poor neighborhood but no slum, occupied by 485 people, many practicing their trade in the same room where they lived!

Labor and Family Life

As a result of industrialization, the British workforce increasingly became **proletariat**—a class of workers who neither owned the means of production (tools and equipment) nor controlled their own work. Trades such as clothing and shoemaking that had flourished in the West End of London, close to the homes of wealthy customers in the eighteenth century, were replaced by factories, producing goods for the proletariat itself. The introduction of machine manufacture into the textile industry, especially, required fewer skilled workers, and more unskilled workers, mostly single young women and widows, who worked for lower wages than men. Some women turned to prostitution as a way to supplement their meager wage income. In addition, the sexual exploitation of low-paid, uneducated women workers by their male supervisors was commonplace.

Children of poor families often worked as assistants in the factories. The English Factory Act of 1833 banned employment of children under the age of nine. Children 9 to 13 years of age could work a 9-hour day (down from 12 hours), and employers had to provide 2 hours of education to child workers each day. Not surprisingly, these conditions radically altered family life. Before the nineteenth century, families had often worked together in textile production, usually at home. But as married women were displaced from the workforce and their husbands' wages allowed families to live on a single income, wives became solely responsible for domestic life—child-rearing, food preparation, and housekeeping. Gender-determined roles, which had previously been the rule only among the relatively small middle class and the aristocracy, now characterized the working-class family as well.

REFORMISTS RESPOND: UTOPIAN SOCIALISM, MEDIEVALISM, AND CHRISTIAN REFORM

Faced with the reality of working-class life, reformist thinkers and writers across Europe reacted by writing polemical works that are meant to be understood as critiques of industrial society. Chief among their targets were the economic engine of the industrial state—its desire to reap a profit at whatever human cost—and the unbridled materialism that, in turn, seemed to drive industrialism's economic engine. This world seemed life-consuming and soul-destroying, a world in which the pulse of machinery was supplanting the pulse of the human heart.

For many humanist thinkers, London's social conditions were directly tied to economics. Ever since Adam Smith's *Wealth of Nations* (see Chapter 26), economists had argued that a nation achieved economic growth by free enterprise and a marketplace unimpeded by governmental regulation. Competition would naturally result in the marketplace governing itself. By the 1820s, however, many began to question the free-market system, especially its low wages, unequal distribution of goods, and hollow materialism. Social critics deplored a system that permitted the factory owners, the "haves," to enjoy leisure and comfort at the expense of the impoverished working class who "had not." They argued that human society could be better organized as a cooperative venture, with each person working for the good of the whole.

Utopian Socialism

Among the critics of free enterprise were those who envisioned ideal communities, where production would be controlled by society as a whole rather than owned by individuals. In France, for instance, Charles Fourier [sharl foo-ree-AY] (1772–1837) argued for the establishment of phalanxes, communities that would liberate individuals to live freely rather than follow the drudgery of industrial life. Phalanxes would be located in the countryside, where no person performed the same kind of work for the entire day, where there was sexual freedom for the young (marriage was to be reserved for later life), and where all residents would be free to pursue pleasure. Scholars have come to call Fourier and those who sought to create such communities *utopian socialists*.

British industrialist Robert Owen (1771–1858), owner of one of the largest British cotton factories, developed a more practical scheme. At his factory at New Lanark, Scotland, he provided his workers with good quarters, recreational opportunities, education for their children, and classes for adults. In 1824, Owen left England for the United States, where he intended to found a series of communities in which factory and farm workers might live and work together. After purchasing the town of New Harmony, Indiana, for $135,000, Owen hired architect Stedman Whitwell to design a city plan, and invited people to apply for the 800 spaces that were available. Although New Harmony attracted hundreds of settlers, most found themselves unable to adapt to life in the community, and most lacked the skills to either farm or otherwise contribute meaningfully to the economy. By 1828, Owen's New Harmony experiment had failed.

A. W. N. Pugin, Architecture, and the Medieval Model

In 1836 (the same year that Dickens published his *Sketches by Boz*), the architect Augustus Welby Northmore Pugin [PYOO-jin] (1812–1852) published a book called *Contrasts*. Pugin compared medieval and modern buildings, aiming to show the decay of taste over time. He contrasted a contemporary poorhouse to a medieval one, run with compassion by the Church (Fig. **28.3**). The rag-clad, miserable tenants of the nineteenth-century poorhouse were subjected to a whip-carrying master, a meager diet of bread and gruel, barren cells, and a sense of imminent death. In contrast, medieval tenants had had a beneficent master, a garden setting, and a bountiful supply of mutton, beef, bread, and ale. Such nostalgia for medieval life was rooted in the Romantic taste for Gothic ruins—Turner's view of the

Fig. 28.3 A. W. N. Pugin, *Contrasted Residences for the Poor,* from *Contrasts: or, a Parallel Between the Noble Edifices of the Fourteenth and Fifteenth Centuries, and similar Buildings of the Present Day; showing the Present Decay of Taste: Accompanied by Appropriate Text.* 1836. Pugin contrasts the harsh treatment of the Poor Law to the charitable good works of the medieval church.

Interior of Tintern Abbey (see Fig. 27.1), for instance. Tales of adventure and love set in medieval times such as Sir Walter Scott's historical novel *Ivanhoe*, which described the late twelfth-century Crusades, also inspired the Romantics.

Yet Pugin found such Romantic medievalism shallow, even vacuous. He saw in medieval architecture not so much a style to be imitated as the expression of a way of life that would help reform nineteenth-century English society. "We do not want to revive a facsimile of the works of style of any particular individual or even period," he wrote—"*but it is the devotion, majesty, and repose of Christian art, for which we are contending; it is not a style, but a principle.*" For the Catholic Pugin, the advantage of medieval society was that it was guided by Christian principles. These principles had long since been lost to English society. The problems inherent in industrialization, mechanization, and materialism, he believed, were created by society's lack of the ethical foundations provided by the Church. Pugin believed that architecture served not just a functional purpose, but also a moral one. The building itself embodied a spirit of ethical conduct.

Many found Pugin's ideas attractive, but his most celebrated commission came when architect Sir Charles Barry (1795–1860) asked him to design the interiors and ornamentation for London's new Houses of Parliament. (A fire had destroyed the old buildings in 1834.) To be consistent with Westminster Abbey, which it abutted, the new Parliament needed Gothic ornamentation (Fig. **28.4**). Barry's basic plan is classical—a symmetrical layout meant to suggest the balance of powers inherent in the British system of government. Pugin's ornamentation follows from what he called the "two great rules" of architecture: "first that there should be no features about a building which are not necessary for convenience, construction, or propriety; second, that all ornament should consist of enrichment of the essential structure of the building." Nevertheless, Pugin's scheme for decorative ornament was hardly restrained, as he also believed that legislators surrounded by "glorious" and elaborate ornament would deliberate with "the faith, the zeal, and, above all, the unity, of our ancestors."

LITERARY REALISM

Faced with the reality of working-class life, reformist thinkers and writers across Europe reacted by writing polemical works that criticized industrial society. Chief among their targets were the economic engine of the industrial state—its desire to reap a profit at whatever human cost—and the unbridled materialism that seemed to drive industrialism's economic engine. Industrialized society seemed life-consuming and soul-destroying, a society in which the pulse of machinery was supplanting the pulse of the human heart. Even while essayists like Carlyle argued forcefully for social reforms in the new industrialized economic system, most reformists felt some ambivalence toward the Industrial Revolution. It seemed to

Fig. 28.4 Charles Barry and A. W. N. Pugin, Houses of Parliament, London. 1836–60. Length 940'. Barry was in charge of the structural floor plan while Pugin took care of the decorative plan. The tower of Westminster Abbey is at the far left.

promise both hope and despair. Probably nothing embodied this uncertainty more than the steam locomotive. London's first railway began operating in December 1836, with the London & Greenwich Railway running 4 miles southeast from London Bridge. A virtual railroad mania followed as company after company vied to build new and competing lines. For Charles Dickens, writing in *Dombey and Son*, which appeared at the height of the mania between 1846 and 1848, the steam engine offered untold potential even as he imaged it as a kind of monster (**Reading 28.3**):

READING 28.3

from Dickens, *Dombey and Son* (1846–1848)

The miserable waste ground, where the refuse matter had been heaped of yore, was swallowed up and gone, and in its frowsy [ill-smelling] stead were tiers of warehouses, crammed with rich goods and costly merchandise. . . . The carcasses of houses, and beginnings of new thoroughfares, had started off upon the line at steam's own speed, and shot away into the country in a monster train. To and from the heart of this great change, all day and night, throbbing currents

rushed and returned incessantly like its life's blood. Crowds of people and mountains of goods, departing and arriving scores upon scores of times in every four-and-twenty hours, produced a fermentation in the place that was always in action. The very houses seemed disposed to pack up and take trips. Wonderful Members of Parliament, who, little more than twenty years before, had made themselves merry with the wild railroad theories of engineers . . . [now] went . . . north with their watches in their hands, and sent on messages before by the electric telegraph, to say that they were coming. . . .

Night and day the conquering engines rumbled at their distant work, or, advancing smoothly to their journey's end, and gliding like tame dragons into the allotted corners grooved out to the inch for their reception, stood bubbling and trembling there, making the walls quake, as if they were dilating with the secret knowledge of great powers yet unsuspected in them, and strong purposes not yet achieved.

Even as the coming of the railroad transformed the "waste ground" of the inner city into "warehouses crammed with rich goods" and "costly merchandise," clearing out the "carcasses of houses" to make way for new rails, Dickens knew there was a price to pay. Its "monstrous" effect was to displace thousands, perhaps as many as 100,000, of the poor from their homes.

"The poor are displaced," *The Times* of London warned in 1861, "but they are not removed. They are shovelled out of one side of the parish, only to render more overcrowded the stifling apartments in another part." In fact, construction of the London and Blackwall Railway engine caused almost 3,000 homes to be destroyed in 1836 alone, and the railway companies had no obligation to provide alternate housing for any of their residents.

The price of progress is the subject of J. M. W. Turner's 1844 painting *Rain, Steam, and Speed—The Great Western Railway* (Fig. **28.5**). We stare over the river Thames across the Maidenhead Bridge, the Great Western Railway barreling toward us. To the left, a boat floats gently on the river before an arched bridge on the far shore. To the right of the boat, strokes of white paint suggest a group of bathers. To the left lies the preindustrial world, to the right postindustrial modernity. Rain and fog and machine-made vapor combine with a new factor,

the blurring effects of speed, to leave the landscape largely undefined and indefinable. The rational architecture of the bridge and the railway—the very images of progress rendered in a strict two-point, linear perspective—are consumed in a Romantic light that renders the world at once beautiful and murky. "What price progress?" the painting ultimately asks.

Dickens's *Hard Times*

This question dominates the work of the writers whose novels probed the realities of life in the new industrial world. Nothing exasperated Dickens more than the promise of the Industrial Revolution to improve life and its ability to do just the opposite—to make life miserable for so many. None of his novels so openly address this issue as *Hard Times*, which appeared during the spring and summer of 1854 in weekly segments in *Household Words*, a periodical edited by Dickens himself.

Designed to satirize industrialists known as Utilitarians, who sought to create the greatest good for the greatest number of people, the novel portrayed them as aiming to

Fig. 28.5 J. M. W. Turner, *Rain, Steam, and Speed—The Great Western Railway*. 1844. Oil on canvas, 33 $\frac{3}{4}$″ × 48″. National Gallery, London, Great Britain. Erich Lessing/Art Resource, New York. Although not easily seen in reproduction, a hare races down the tracks in front of the train. A traditional symbol of natural speed, the hare is about to be overcome by the train speeding at 50 miles per hour.

create wealth for the upper and middle classes at the expense of the majority—the poor working class. Dickens describes Utilitarians as "those who see figures and averages, and nothing else." In *Hard Times*, they are represented by the "eminently practical" Mr. Thomas Gradgrind, who views literature as "destructive nonsense," emotion as "unmanageable thought," and "Fact"—statistics in particular—as the only truth. Dickens resolved to "strike the heaviest blow in my power" for those who worked in the inhuman conditions created by Utilitarian-endorsed industries.

Probably no passage in the novel better summarizes Dickens's beliefs about the social consequences of Utilitarianism than his description of the novel's fictional Coketown, an industrial wasteland that is an amalgam of his observations of all British industrial cities (**Reading 28.4**):

READING 28.4

from Dickens, *Hard Times* (1854)

It was a town of red brick, or of brick that would have been red if the smoke and ashes had allowed it; but as matters stood it was a town of unnatural red and black like the painted face of a savage. It was a town of machinery and tall chimneys, out of which interminable serpents of smoke trailed themselves for ever and ever, and never got uncoiled. It had a black canal in it, and a river that ran purple with ill-smelling dye, and vast piles of buildings full of windows where there was a rattling and a trembling all day long, and where the piston of the steam-engine worked monotonously up and down like the head of an elephant in a state of melancholy madness. It contained several large streets all very like one another, and many small streets still more like one another, inhabited by people equally like one another, who all went in and out at the same hours, with the same sound upon the same pavements, to do the same work, and to whom every day was the same as yesterday and tomorrow, and every year the counterpart of the last and the next.

In this setting, Gradgrind, a retired wholesale hardware dealer, runs a Utilitarian school. His closest friend is Josiah Bounderby, manufacturer, banker, and mill owner, "a man perfectly devoid of sentiment." As is often the case in Dickens's fiction, their lack of feeling is contrasted sharply with that of another character, Sissy, partially educated but also the irrepressible product of her life in the circus, a young woman full of imagination and hope.

Their story is told in three parts, "Sowing," "Reaping," and "Garnering," ironic references to agriculture rather than industry as well as to the biblical verse, "Whatever a man sows, this he will also reap." Given what Gradgrind and Bounderby have sown in creating Coketown, Dickens must have delighted in manufacturing their demise: Gradgrind abandons his Utilitarian philosophy, which draws the wrath of his fellow members of Parliament whom he so

admires, while Bounderby dies in a fit in the street one day, having squandered his fortune. Yet in the end, Dickens never really questions the ultimate wisdom of industrialization. Rather, the novel seems to argue that in the hands of more humane industrialists, who cared about the well-being of their workers, the industrialization of England might be good for everyone.

French Literary Realism

Literary realism was not restricted to England, although elsewhere in Europe writers rarely confronted the effects of the Industrial Revolution as forcefully as Dickens had. As in England, the work of French novels often appeared in serial form, designed to appeal to a growing middle-class audience. However, French authors aimed at creating fully rounded characters and were less inclined to caricature than Dickens was. French realists claimed to examine life scientifically, without bias, and to describe what they saw in a straightforward manner. The writings of Honoré de Balzac and Gustave Flaubert [floh-BAIR] are the foremost examples.

Balzac's *Human Comedy* "I am not deep," the novelist Honoré de Balzac (1799–1850) once said, "but very wide." In 1833, he decided to link together his old novels so that they would reflect the whole of French society. He would come to call this series of books *The Human Comedy*. Balzac's plan eventually resulted in 92 novels, which include more than 2,000 characters. Among the masterpieces are *Eugénie Grandet* [er-ZHEN GRAHN-deh] (1833); *Father Goriot (Père Goriot)* [pair GOH-ree-oh] (1835); the trilogy *Lost Illusions* (1837–43); and *Cousin Bette* [koo-ZHEN bet] (1846). The primary setting is Paris, with its old aristocracy, new wealth, and the rising culture of the **bourgeoisie** (middle-class shopkeepers, merchants, and business people, as distinct from laborers and wage-earners). The novel is populated by characters from all levels of society—servants, workers, clerks, criminals, intellectuals, courtesans, and prostitutes. Certain individuals make appearances in novel after novel, for instance Eugène Rastignac [eh-ZHEN RAH-steen-yak], a central figure in *Father Goriot*, who comes from an impoverished provincial family to Paris to seek his fortune, and Henri de Marsay [ahn-REE deh mar-ZAY], a dandy who appears in 25 of the novels.

Balzac drew his characters from direct observation: "In listening to these people," he wrote of those he encountered in the Paris streets, "I could espouse their lives. I felt their rags on my back. I walked with my feet in their tattered shoes; their desires, their wants—everything passed into my soul." The story goes that he once interrupted one of his friends, who was telling about his sister's illness, by saying, "That's all very well, but let's get back to reality: to whom are we going to marry Eugénie Grandet?"

Father Goriot is an adaptation of Shakespeare's play *King Lear*. Rastignac falls in love with Delphine [DEL-feen], one of two daughters of old Goriot, a father who has sacrificed everything for his children. Both daughters have married into the French aristocracy, but they rely on their father's excessive paternal love to bail them out of the financial crises that constantly confront them through their husbands' profligacy. The novel contrasts the poverty of the boarding house, where both Goriot and Rastignac live, to their daughters' glittering social world, to which Rastignac aspires. Goriot dies penniless, and Rastignac is forced to pay for his funeral. When the funeral is over, Rastignac contemplates the possibilities that Paris offers (**Reading 28.5**):

READING 28.5

from Balzac, *Father Goriot* (1834)

He went a few paces further, to the highest point of the cemetery, and looked out over Paris and the windings of the Seine; the lamps were beginning to shine on either side of the river. His eyes turned almost eagerly to the space between the column of the Place Vendome [plahss vahn-DOME] and the cupola of the Invalides [en-vah-LEED]; there lay the shining world that he had wished to reach. He glanced over that humming hive, seeming to draw a foretaste of its honey, and said magniloquently:

"Henceforth there is war between us."

This comment ends the novel and is the very heart of serialization. It is the bone Balzac throws to his audience to create a sense of anticipation of more to come, another novel, and then another and another, in which Rastignac declares that he will take on French society. He will, as it turns out, have many lovers and a gambling problem of his own, before becoming a successful politician.

Flaubert's *Madame Bovary* The novel *Madame Bovary*, written by Gustave Flaubert [floh-BAIR] (1821–1880) at mid-century, is at its core a realist attack on Romantic sensibility. But Flaubert had a strong Romantic streak as well, for which his Parisian friends strongly condemned him. They suggested that he should write a "down-to-earth" novel of ordinary life, and further, that he base it on the true story of Delphine Delamare [del-MAR], the adulterous wife of a country doctor who had died of grief after deceiving and ruining him. Flaubert agreed, and *Madame Bovary*, first published in magazine installments in 1856, is the result.

The realism of the novel is born of Flaubert's struggle not to be Romantic. He would later say, "Madame Bovary—*c'est moi!*" [say mwah] ("Madame Bovary—that's me!) in testament to his deep understanding of the bourgeois, Romantic sensibility that his novel condemns. Toward the middle of the novel, Emma imagines she is dying. She has been ill for two months, since her lover Rodolphe ended their affair.

Now, she romanticizes what she thinks are her last moments, experiencing a rapturous ecstasy of the kind portrayed by Bernini in *The Ecstasy of St. Teresa* (**Reading 28.6**; also see Fig. 21.6):

READING 28.6

from Flaubert, *Madame Bovary* (1856)

One day, when at the height of her illness, she had thought herself dying, and had asked for the communion; and, while they were making the preparations in her room for the sacrament, while they were turning the night table covered with syrups into an altar, and while Felicite was strewing dahlia flowers on the floor, Emma felt some power passing over her that freed her from her pains, from all perception, from all feeling. Her body, relieved, no longer thought; another life was beginning; it seemed to her that her being, mounting toward God, would be annihilated in that love like a burning incense that melts into vapour. The bedclothes were sprinkled with holy water, the priest drew from the holy pyx [small box containing the sacrament] the white wafer . . . The curtains of the alcove floated gently round her like clouds, and the rays of the two tapers burning on the night-table seemed to shine like dazzling halos. Then she let her head fall back, fancying she heard in space the music of seraphic harps, and perceived in an azure sky, on a golden throne in the midst of saints holding green palms, God the Father, resplendent with majesty.

In an 1852 letter describing a dinner conversation between Leon and Emma earlier in the book, Flaubert wrote: "I'm working on a conversation between a young man and a young lady on literature, the sea, the mountains, music—in short, every poetic subject there is. It could be taken seriously and I intend it to be totally absurd." The same could be said of Emma's faint in which her paroxysm of religious experience is as staged as her illness itself. Words and phrases such as "an azure sky, on a golden throne" are examples of what Flaubert called *le mot juste* [leh moh joost], "the right word," exactly the precise usage to capture the essence of each situation, in this case a level of cliché that underscores the dramatic absurdity of Emma's experience. Flaubert felt he was proceeding like the modern scientist, investigating the lives of his characters through careful and systematic observation.

Literary Realism in the United States: The Issue of Slavery

It was, in fact, the "terrible truth" of slavery that most haunted American realist writers. They were inspired largely by the abolitionist movement. While the movement had been active in both Europe and America ever since the 1770s (see Chapter 26), it didn't gain real momentum in the United States until the establishment of the American Anti-Slavery Society in 1833. The Society organized lecture tours by abolitionists, gathered petitions, and printed and distributed antislavery propaganda. By 1840, it had 250,000 members in 2,000 local chapters and was publishing more than 20 journals.

Proslavery forces were given an unanticipated lift by the scientific theories of Louis Agassiz [AG-uh-see] (1807–1873), arguably the most respected scientific figure of the day, whose studies of glaciology, for instance, had led him to be the first to propose that the earth had once endured an Ice Age. In 1850, four years after moving to the United States in order to assume the position as professor of zoology and geology at Harvard University, Agassiz commissioned J. T. Zealy to take a series of photographs of slaves on a plantation in South Carolina to use as scientific visual evidence to support his theories on the physical differences among the races (Fig. 28.6). He believed that the different races arose separately in the different climatic zones of the world, and that they were by no means equal. "Each species," Agassiz wrote, "is a thought of the Creator," and each race was, for him, a separate species. In fact his photographs were believed to demonstrate the inferiority of black Africans and, by extension, the racial superiority of the white race.

Zealy was asked to take two kinds of photographs: a series of physiognomic shots showing this models in the nude from the front, side, and rear; and a phrenological series focusing specifically on the head and torso. The first were designed to demonstrate body shape, proportions, and posture; the latter, the size and shape of the head—the larger the brain, it was mistakenly believed, the greater the intelligence and, it followed, moral capacity.

Agassiz's influence was by no means inconsequential. He was one of the 11 original founders, in 1856, of the so-called Saturday Club, which included in its ranks Ralph Waldo Emerson (see Chapter 27), the poet Henry Wadsworth Longfellow, and Nathanial Hawthorne, author of *The Scarlet Letter*. It is, of course, by no means possible to ascribe Agassiz's feelings to his fellow club members, but Agassiz had written, in 1846, upon seeing African Americans for the first time in Philadelphia:

> It is impossible for me to repress the feeling that they are not the same blood as us. In seeing their black faces with their thick lips and grimacing teeth, the wool on their head, their bent knees, their elongated hands, the large curved nails, and especially the livid color of the palms of their hands, I could not take my eyes off their faces in order to tell them to stay far away. . . . What unhappiness for the white race—to

**Fig. 28.6 *Renty, Congo. Plantation of B. F. Taylor, Esq.* Daguerreotype taken by J. T. Zealy, Columbia, SC, March 1850. Peabody Museum, Harvard University. The slaves who were the subjects of Zealy's photographs—both men and women—were brought to his studio where they were stripped and photographed in the nude.

have tied their existence so closely with that of negroes in certain countries! God preserve us from such a contact!

The South Carolina plantation photographs testify to the fact that by 1850 Agassiz's attitudes had hardly changed. And though he pled disinterest in the political events leading up to the American Civil War, the simple truth is within ten years of moving to the United States, Agassiz had, in the words of his biographer, Edward Lurie, "provided racial extremists with primary arguments . . . and permitted his reputation to support doctrines of social and racial inequality."

Frederick Douglass Countering the likes of Agassiz were the testimonials of slaves themselves. When William Lloyd Garrison (1805–1879), head of the Anti-Slavery Society, heard a speech delivered by a 24-year-old former slave in Nantucket in 1841, he was so impressed that he immediately enlisted him as a lecturer. The young man's name was

Frederick Douglass (1817–1895) (Fig. **28.7**). He never knew his father, a white man, and was separated from his mother, a slave, while still very young. His account of life under slavery was so compelling that the society helped him publish his autobiography, *Narrative of the Life of Frederick Douglass: An American Slave*, in 1845.

The book moves from Douglass's first clear memory, the whipping of his Aunt Hester, which he describes as his "entrance into the hell of slavery" (see **Reading 28.7**, pages 955–957), to the book's turning point, when he resolves to stand up and fight his master. "From whence came the spirit I don't know," Douglass writes. "You have seen how a man was made a slave; you shall see how a slave was made a man," he says before summing up the fight's outcome" (**Reading 28.7a**):

Fig. 28.7 Portrait of Frederick Douglass. 1847. Daguerreotype. National Portrait Gallery, Smithsonian Institution, Washington, D.C. Collection William Rubel. After publishing his *Narrative*, Douglass lectured in England and Ireland for two years, fearing recapture under the Fugitive Slave Act.

READING 28.7a

from *Narrative of the Life of Frederick Douglass* (1845)

This battle with Mr. Covey was the turning point in my career as a slave. It rekindled the few expiring embers of freedom, and revived within me a sense of my own manhood. It . . . inspired me again with a determination to be free. The gratification afforded by the triumph was a full compensation for whatever else might follow, even death itself. . . . I felt as I never felt before. It was a glorious resurrection, from the tomb of slavery, to the heaven of freedom. My long-crushed spirit rose, cowardice departed, bold defiance took its place; and I now resolved that, however long I might remain a slave in form, the day had passed forever when I could be a slave in fact. I did not hesitate to let it be known of me, that the white man who expected to succeed in whipping, must also succeed in killing me.

Douglass guesses at the reason Covey spares him being beaten at the whipping post for raising his hand against a white man: "Mr. Covey enjoyed the most unbounded reputation for being a first-rate overseer and negro-breaker," he says, ". . . so, to save his reputation, he suffered me to go unpunished." The rest of the book recounts Douglass's escape to New York, and then to New Bedford, Massachusetts, up to the moment that he meets Garrison in Nantucket.

Douglass eventually broke with the Anti-Slavery Society because "its doctrine of 'no union with slaveholders,' carried out, dissolves the Union, and leaves the slaves and their masters to fight their own battles, in their own way. This I hold to be an abandonment of the great idea . . . to free the slave. It ends by leaving the slave to free himself." Douglass argued the issue with Abraham Lincoln in print during the early phases of the Civil War. Initially Lincoln was reluctant to emancipate the slaves, because he feared that emancipation would divide the Union. Lincoln finally agreed with Douglass, whom he welcomed to the White House several times, and issued the Emancipation Proclamation at the end of 1862.

Slave Narratives More than 100 book-length slave narratives were published in the 1850s and 1860s. Besides

Douglass's, one of the other most important of these was the *Narrative of Sojourner Truth*, dictated by an illiterate former slave to her friend Olive Gilbert. Sojourner Truth (ca. 1797–1883) (Fig. **28.8**) was born Isabella Baumfree to slave parents in Ulster County, New York, and was sold four times before she was 30 years old. In 1843, inspired by a spiritual revelation, she changed her name to Sojourner Truth and became a preacher advocating "God's truth and plan for salvation." She often tied her lessons to her own experiences as a slave, and she championed both abolition and the woman's suffrage movement.

Because Olive Gilbert tells Truth's story in the third person, occasionally quoting her subject's much more colloquial speech, it is hard to say just how much of the work is Gilbert's and how much Truth's. This question also surrounds Truth's most famous speech, "Ain't I a Woman?" delivered to a Women's Convention in Akron, Ohio in 1851. Unpublished until 1863, it still offers evidence of the rhetorical persuasiveness of Truth—and her undeniable wit (**Reading 28.8**):

READING 28.8

from Sojourner Truth, "Ain't I a Woman?" (1851)

Well, children, where there is so much racket there must be something out of kilter. I think that 'twixt the

Fig. 28.8 Sojourner Truth Seated with Knitting. 1864. Sophia Smith Collection, Smith College Archives, Northampton, Massachusetts. In 1863, it occurred to Truth to earn money by selling photographs of herself. As she explained, "I'll sell the Shadow to support the Substance."

negroes of the South and the women at the North, all talking about rights, the white men will be in a fix pretty soon. But what's all this here talking about?

That man over there says that women need to be helped into carriages, and lifted over ditches, and to have the best place everywhere. Nobody ever helps me into carriages, or over mud-puddles, or gives me any best place! And ain't I a woman? Look at me! Look at my arm! I have ploughed and planted, and gathered into barns, and no man could head me! And ain't I a woman? I could work as much and eat as much as a man—when I could get it—and bear the lash as well! And ain't I a woman? I have borne thirteen children, and seen most all sold off to slavery, and when I cried out with my mother's grief, none but Jesus heard me! And ain't I a woman? . . .

Obliged to you for hearing me, and now old Sojourner ain't got nothing more to say.

Like so many others in the abolitionist movement, Truth saw the cause of women's rights as part of the effort to end slavery. The growing conviction that women—white and black—endured a brand of slavery of their own is one of the most important subtexts of the Civil War.

In fact, the Anti-Slavery Society was a leader in this effort. Sarah Grimke (1792–1873), daughter of a slave-holding judge from Charleston, South Carolina, publicly called for women "to rise from that degradation and bondage to which the faculties of our minds have been prevented from expanding." With help from some in the Society, she published the groundbreaking *Letters on the Equality of the Sexes* in 1838. Other members were not at all pleased by the society's advocacy of women's rights, and when three women were elected to the executive committee, many withdrew, contending that "To put a woman on the committee with men is contrary to the usages of civilized society."

Harriet Beecher Stowe's *Uncle Tom's Cabin* The daughter of a minister and reformer who spoke out against slavery, Harriet Beecher Stowe (1811–1896) was raised with strong abolitionist convictions. She would write the best-selling antislavery novel of the day, *Uncle Tom's Cabin*, becoming the symbol of the abolitionist movement in America. Writing to a woman who admired the book, she connects its themes to the grief she endured after her young son died of cholera in 1849 (**Reading 28.9**):

READING 28.9

Letter from Harriet Beecher Stowe, Andover to Mrs. E[liza] L[ee] Follen, 16 December 1852

My Dear Madam,
So you want to know something about what sort of woman I am! . . . To begin, then, I am a little bit of a woman,—somewhat more than 40—about as thin and dry as a pinch of snuff—never very much to look at in my best days—& looking like a used up article now. I was married when I was 25 years old to a man rich in Greek and Hebrew and Latin and Arabic, and alas! rich in nothing else. . . .

But then I was abundantly enriched with wealth of another kind. I had 2 little curly headed twin daughters to begin with, & my stock in this line has gradually increased, till I have been the mother of 7 children, the most beautiful of which, & the most loved, lies buried near my Cincinnati residence. It was at *his* dying bed, & at *his* grave that I learned what a poor slave mother may feel when her child is torn away from her. In the depths of sorrow which seemed to me immeasurable, it was my only prayer to God that such anguish might not be suffered in vain! There were circumstances about his death of such peculiar bitterness, of what might seem almost cruel suffering, that I felt that I could never be consoled for it unless it should appear that this crushing of my own heart might enable me to work out some great good to others.

I allude to this now because I have often felt that much that is in this book had its root in the awful scenes & bitter sorrows of that summer. It has left now, I trust, no trace in my mind except a deep compassion for the sorrowful, especially for mothers who are separated from their children. . . .

Uncle Tom's Cabin is a narrative concerning the differing fates of three slaves—Tom, Eliza, and George—whose life in slavery begins together in Kentucky. Although Eliza and George are married, they are owned by different masters. In order to live together they escape to free territory with their little boy. Tom meets a different fate. Separated from his wife and children, he is sold by his first owner to a kind master, Augustine St. Clare, and then to the evil Simon Legree, who eventually kills him. Serialized in 1851 in the abolitionist newspaper *The National Era*, and published the year after, the book sold 300,000 copies in the first year after its publication. Stowe's depiction of the plight of slaves like Tom roused antislavery sentiment worldwide and it eventually became the best-selling novel of the nineteenth century. Only the Bible could compete, although it could be argued that Stowe's book was equally pious. The scene of Little Eva reading from the Bible to Tom (Fig. **28.9**) as Stowe sets it up in Chapter 22 of the novel is deeply romanticized (**Reading 28.10**):

READING 28.10

from Harriet Beecher Stowe, *Uncle Tom's Cabin* (1852)

It is now one of those intensely golden sunsets which kindles the whole horizon into one blaze of glory, and makes the water another sky. The lake lay in rosy or golden streaks, save where white-winged vessels glided hither and thither, like so many spirits, and little golden stars twinkled through the glow, and looked down at themselves as they trembled in the water. . . .

At first, she read to please her humble friend; but soon her own earnest nature threw out its tendrils, and wound itself around the majestic book; and Eva loved it, because it woke in her strange yearnings, and strong, dim emotions, such as impassioned, imaginative children love to feel.

Fig. 28.9 Robert S. Duncanson, *Uncle Tom and Little Eva.* 1853. Oil on canvas, 27$^1/_4$″ × 38$^1/_4$″. The Detroit Institute of Arts, Detroit, MI. The Bridgeman Art Library. Duncanson was the first African-American artist to receive international fame.

This passage points to a central mission of the abolitionist movement. Abolitionists felt the duty to enlighten the darkened souls of slaves by asserting Christian beliefs. Notice how light is used as a metaphor in the passage. But the condescension apparent to the modern reader—both Tom and Eva are depicted as children—together with Tom's sentimental attachment to both Eva and her pious Christianity—would eventually make the term "Uncle Tom" a derogatory label referring to anyone who is servile or deferential to white people.

Mark Twain's *Adventures of Huckleberry Finn* A patronizing tone dominates representations of African Americans by whites in the nineteenth and twentieth centuries, and it informs *Adventures of Huckleberry Finn*, arguably one of the greatest American novels. Published in 1885 by Samuel L. Clemens (1835–1910), whose pen name was Mark Twain, the novel tells the story of a young boy, Huck Finn, and Jim, an escaped slave, as they make their way by raft down the Mississippi River from Hannibal, Missouri. They intend to turn north at the juncture of the Ohio River so that Jim might reach freedom in Cincinnati. (Ohio was a slave-free state.) Set in the years just before the Civil War, the book is vigorously opposed to slavery, and portrays those who supported it in a uniformly unflattering light, designed precisely to expose them. When, for instance, Huck and Jim are anticipating arriving at Cairo, where the Ohio meets the Mississippi, Huck is anguished by his role in helping Jim escape (**Reading 28.11a**):

READING 28.11a

from Mark Twain, *Huckleberry Finn* (1885)

Jim said it made him all over trembly and feverish to be so close to freedom. Well, I can tell you it made me all over trembly and feverish, too, to hear him, because I begun to get it through my head that he was most free—and who was to blame for it? Why, me. I couldn't get that out of my conscience, no how nor no way. It got to troubling me so I couldn't rest; I couldn't stay still in one place. It hadn't ever come home to me before, what this thing was that I was doing. But now it did; and it stayed with me, and scorched me more and more. I tried to make out to myself that I warn't to blame, because I didn't run Jim off from his rightful owner; but it warn't no use, conscience up and says, every time, "But you knowed he was running for his freedom, and you could a paddled ashore and told somebody." That was so—I couldn't get around that noway. That was where it pinched. Conscience says to me, "What had poor Miss Watson done to you that you could see her nigger go off right under your eyes and never say one single word? What did that poor old woman do to you that you could treat her so mean? Why, she tried to

learn you your book, she tried to learn you your manners, she tried to be good to you every way she knowed how. That's what she done." I got to feeling so mean and so miserable I most wished I was dead. I fidgeted up and down the raft, abusing myself to myself, and Jim was fidgeting up and down past me. We neither of us could keep still. Every time he danced around and says, "Dah's Cairo!" it went through me like a shot, and I thought if it was Cairo I reckoned I would die of miserableness.

Huck is torn between the tenets of his upbringing, in which, of course, slaves were the legal property of their owner, and his affection for Jim as a human being. In helping Jim, he believes he is stealing from Miss Watson, one of the two sisters who have adopted him.

Twain put words into the mouths of his characters that are realistic for the time but offensive today. Thus, when Aunt Sally asks if anyone was hurt in a steamboat accident, Huck replies, "No'm. Killed a nigger." Twain fully intends the word to signify racist dehumanization of African Americans by whites, but Huck is speaking exactly as a young boy raised in the slaveholding South would. Part of Twain's great achievement is to allow his readers the chance to see the specter of racism rise up in otherwise basically good people, and along with Huck discover that presence in themselves. The triumph of *Huckleberry Finn*, then, lies in the fact that the reader joins Huck in coming to understand and appreciate Jim's humanity. Huck's realization occurs as he contemplates redeeming himself, becoming "washed clean of sin" by informing Miss Watson of his whereabouts, seeking the posted reward, and therefore returning "property" to its rightful owner (**Reading 28.11b**):

READING 28.11b

from Mark Twain, *Huckleberry Finn* (1885)

. . . And got to thinking over our trip down the river; and I see Jim before me all the time: in the day and in the night-time, sometimes moonlight, sometimes storms, and we a-floating along, talking and singing and laughing. But somehow I couldn't seem to strike no places to harden me against him, but only the other kind. I'd see him standing my watch on top of his'n, 'stead of calling me, so I could go on sleeping; and see him how glad he was when I come back out of the fog. . . . and how good he always was; and at last I [remember] I saved him by telling the men we had small-pox aboard, and he was so grateful, and said I was the best friend old Jim ever had in the world, and the *only* one he's got now; and then I happened to look around and see that paper [the note informing his owner of his whereabouts].

It was a close place. I took it up, and held it in my hand. I was a-trembling, because I'd got to decide, forever, betwixt two things, and I knowed it. I studied a minute, sort of holding my breath, and then says to myself:

"All right, then, I'll *go* to hell"—and tore it up.

It was awful thoughts and awful words, but they was said. And I let them stay said; and never thought no more about reforming.

Thus Mark Twain, in a fictional setting, follows the path set by Thoreau in *Civil Disobedience* a quarter century earlier, forcefully rejecting the conventional morality of society that saw slaves as legal property. Rather than conforming to the law, Huck followed the dictates of his conscience, thinking "no more about reforming" and vowing to steal Jim out of slavery again if necessary because "as long as I was in, and in for good, I might as well go the whole hog."

FRENCH PAINTING: THE DIALOGUE BETWEEN IDEALISM AND REALISM

After the fall of Napoleon in 1815, the battle between Neoclassicism and Romanticism raged within France, fueled by political factionalism. Bourbon rule had been restored when Louis XVIII (r. 1814–1824), the deposed Louis XVI's brother, assumed the throne. Royalists, who favored this return of the monarchy, championed the more conservative Neoclassical style. Liberals identified with the new Romantic style, which from the beginning had allied itself with the French Revolution's radical spirit of freedom and independence.

The new king could not ignore the reforms implemented by both the revolution and Napoleon. His younger brother, the Count of Artois [AR-twah], disagreed, and almost immediately a so-called Ultraroyalist movement, composed of families who had suffered at the hands of the revolution, established itself. Advocating the return of their confiscated estates and the abolition of revolutionary and Napoleonic reforms, the Ultraroyalists imprisoned and executed

Fig. 28.10 Théodore Géricault, *The Raft of the "Medusa."* 1818. First oil sketch. Oil on canvas, 16′1″ × 23′6″. Musée du Louvre, Paris. Photo: Hervé Lewandowski. Inv.: RF 2229. © Réunion des Musées Nationaux/Art Resource, New York. The painting today is much darker than it was originally because Géricault used bitumen, an organic carbon-based material, in his pigment.

hundreds of revolutionaries, Bonaparte's sympathizers, and Protestants in southern France. (David, who had supported Napoleon, was in exile during this period.) In order to solidify his control, Louis dissolved the largely Ultraroyalist Chamber of Deputies and called for new elections, which resulted in a more moderate majority.

Relative calm prevailed in France for the next four years, but in February 1820, the son of the Count of Artois, who was the last of the Bourbons and heir to the throne, was assassinated, initiating ten years of repression. The education system was placed under the control of Roman Catholic bishops, press censorship was inaugurated, and "dangerous" political activity banned. At the death of Louis XVIII, the Count of Artois assumed the throne as Charles X (r. 1824–1830).

Théodore Géricault: Rejecting Classicism

Against this political backdrop, the young painter Théodore Géricault [ZHAY-ree-koh] (1791–1824) inaugurated his career. Trained in Paris in a Neoclassical style, by the last years of Napoleon's reign, he was painting largely military subjects that reflected a growing recognition of the emperor's limitations. In fact, perhaps seeking some way to retrieve what was evidently lost, Géricault joined the Royal Musketeers in 1815, assigned to protect the future Louis XVIII from Napoleon. But events quickly overcame Géricault's brief royalist career. On July 2, 1816, a government frigate named the *Medusa*, carrying soldiers and settlers to Senegal, was shipwrecked on a reef 50 miles off the coast of West Africa. The captain and crew saved themselves, leaving 150 people, including a woman, adrift on a makeshift raft. Only 15 survived the days that followed, days marked by insanity, mutilation, famine, thirst, and finally cannibalism. Géricault was outraged. An inexperienced captain, commissioned on the basis of his noble birth and connections to the monarchy, saved himself, providing a profound indictment of aristocratic privilege.

Géricault set himself the task of rendering the events. He interviewed survivors, and painted mutilated bodies in the Paris morgue. The enormous composition of *The Raft of the "Medusa"* is organized as a double triangle (Fig. **28.10**). The mast and the two ropes supporting it form the apex of one triangle, and the torso of the figure waving in the direction of the barely visible *Argus*, the ship that would eventually rescue the castaways, the apex of the other. The opposing diagonals form a dramatic "X" centered on the kneeling figure whose arm reaches upward in the hope of salvation. Ultimately, however, the painting makes a mockery of the idea of deliverance, just as its rigid geometric structure parodies the ideal order of Neoclassicism. Like Byron, Géricault's Romanticism assumed a political dimension

through his art. He had himself become a Promethean hero, challenging the authority of the establishment.

The Aesthetic Expression of Politics: Delacroix versus Ingres

When Géricault's *The Raft of the "Medusa"* was exhibited at the French Academy of Fine Arts Salon of 1819, it was titled simply *A Shipwreck Scene*, in no small part to avoid direct confrontation with the Bourbon government. Royalist critics dismissed it. The conservative press wrote that the painting was "not fit for moral society. The work could have been done for the pleasure of vultures." But its sense of immediacy, its insistence on depicting current events (but not how the castaways actually looked after 13 days adrift), made an enormous impression on another young painter, Eugène Delacroix (1798–1863), who actually had served as the model for the facedown nude in the bottom center of the *Raft*. Soon after Géricault's accidental death, Delacroix exhibited his *Scenes from the Massacres at Chios* at the Salon of 1824 (Fig. **28.11**).

The full title of the painting—*Scenes from the Massacres at Chios; Greek Families Awaiting Death or Slavery, etc.—See Various Accounts and Contemporary Newspapers*—reveals its close association with journalistic themes. It depicts events

Fig. 28.11 Eugène Delacroix, ***Scenes from the Massacres at Chios.*** **1824.** Oil on canvas, 165″ × 139′ 1/4″. Musée du Louvre, Paris. Photo: Le Mage. © Réunion des Musées Nationaux/Art Resource, New York. Delacroix relied on the testimony of a French volunteer in the Greek cause for the authenticity of his depiction.

Fig. 28.12 Jean-Auguste-Dominique Ingres, *The Vow of Louis XIII.* **1824.** Oil on canvas, 165³/₄" × 103¹/₈". Montauban Cathedral, Montauban, France, Lauros. Giraudon/The Bridgeman Art Library, New York. The plaque in the hands of the putti reads "Louis XIII puts France under the protection of the Virgin, February 1638."

of April 1822, after the Greeks had initiated a War of Independence from Turkey, a cause championed by all of liberal Europe. In retaliation, the sultan sent an army of 10,000 to the Greek island of Chios [KY-oss], just several miles off the west coast of Turkey. The troops killed 20,000 and took thousands of women and children into captivity, selling them into slavery across North Africa. In the left foreground, defeated Greek families await their fate. To the right a grandmother sits dejectedly by what is perhaps her dead daughter, even as her grandchild tries to suckle at its dead mother's breast. A prisoner vainly tries to defend a Greek woman tied to a triumphant Turk's horse. The vast space between the near foreground and the far distance is startling, almost as if the scene transpires before a painted tableau.

The stark contrast between Delacroix's *Scenes from the Massacres at Chios* and a traditional painting by Ingres entitled *The Vow of Louis XIII* (Fig. **28.12**) at the Salon of 1824 emphatically underscored Delacroix's Romanticism. Especially in the context of the times, Ingres's painting is a deeply royalist work. It depicts Louis XIII placing France under the protection of the Virgin in February 1638 in order to end a Protestant rebellion. The painting is divided into two distinct zones, the religious and the secular, or the worlds of church and state. The king kneels in the secular space of the foreground, painted in almost excruciating detail. Above him, the Virgin, bathed in a spiritual light, is a monument to Renaissance classicism, directly referencing the Madonnas of Raphael. In every way, the painting is a monument to tradition, to the traditions of the Bourbon throne, the Catholic Church, and classical art.

In his paintings, Ingres never hesitated to adjust the proportions of the body to the overall composition. A good example is his *Grand Odalisque* of 1814 (Fig. **28.13**). An **odalisque** is a female slave or concubine in a Middle Eastern, particularly Turkish, harem. When it was exhibited at

Fig. 28.13 Jean-Auguste-Dominique Ingres, *La Grande Odalisque.* **1814.** Oil on canvas, 35⁷/₈" × 63". Musée du Louvre, Paris. Inv. RF1158. The painting was commissioned by Napoleon's sister, Caroline Murat, Queen of Naples.

LEARN MORE Gain insight from a primary source document from Jean-Auguste-Dominique Ingres at **www.myartslab.com**

Fig. 28.14 Eugène Delacroix, *Odalisque*. **1845–50**. Oil on canvas, 14 $^7/_8$″ × 18 $^1/_4$″. © Fitzwilliam Museum, Universtiy of Cambridge, England. The Bridgeman Art Library.

the Salon of 1819, viewers immediately recognized that his figure's back is endowed with too many vertebrae, that her right arm extends to too great a length, as if disjointed at the elbow, and that her right foot appears amputated from a rather too-distant right knee. Ingres could hardly have cared less. For him, the composition demanded the sweeping curve of both back and arm, the curve of which continues into the folds of the hanging drapery, even as it crosses and works against the emphatic diagonal created by his figure's legs. Equally appealing to him was the dramatic contrast between the dark background and the brilliantly lit flesh of the body, his stunningly realistic realization of satin and silk, and the almost palpable sense of touch elicited by the peacock-feather fan—all rendered without so much as the trace of a brushstroke.

The odalisque continued to occupy Ingres for the rest of his career, as in fact it did nineteenth-century French artists as a group (see *Closer Look*, pages 940–941). But when

Delacroix took up the theme in an *Odalisque* painted in 1845–50 (Fig. **28.14**), the effect is dramatically different. Both employ the standard iconography of the harem—the unkempt bed, the hashish pipe, or hookah, the curtained room. Both figures address the viewer with their eyes. But where the cool blues of Ingres's painting underscore the equally cool, even icy sexual aloofness of his model, the reds of Delacroix's are charged with an intense eroticism, underscored by the fact that his model is turned toward the viewer rather than away. In fact, where Ingres's odalisque seems untainted, almost pure, Delacroix's appears lasciviously postcoital. And Delacroix's brushwork, the wild, energetic gesture of his touch, is the very opposite of Ingres's traceless mark. In 1854, Delacroix wrote in his journal, "I pity those who work tranquilly and coldly [by whom he means Ingres]. I am convinced that everything they do can only be cold and tranquil." Delacroix preferred what he called "the fury of the brush," a fury especially evident in

CLOSER LOOK

n 1978, Edward Said [seye-EED] (1935–2003), a professor of English and comparative literature at Columbia University, published a book entitled simply *Orientalism*. At the most basic level, his title was meant to evoke a long-standing academic discipline in the West that had focused on "the Orient" generally as opposed to "the Occident," and specifically on the Middle East. Among the earliest examples of this Orientalist scholarship was the 24-volume *Description de l'égypte* initiated by Napoleon's campaign in Egypt in 1798 to 1799 (see Fig. 27.14) and published in Paris between 1809 and 1822. Photographic collections such as Maxine Du Camp's *Egypte, Nubia, Palestine et Syrie* (Paris, 1852) (see Fig. 28.26 later in the chapter) would also contribute to the ever-growing body of Orientalist studies in the nineteenth century.

What struck Said about these and later Western studies of the region was their distance from a Middle East that, as a Palestinian born in Jerusalem and living much of his young life in Egypt, he had come to know. Thus, the "Orientalism" that Said wished to study was how Orientalist scholarship was, in fact, an "institution for dealing with the Orient—dealing with it by making statements about it, authorizing views of it, describing it, by teaching it, settling it, ruling over it: in short, Orientalism as a Western style for dominating, restructuring, and having authority over the Orient."

In nineteenth-century painting, this Orientalism manifested itself particularly in paintings of the harem and the odalisque, and the most significant contributors to this Orientalist style were Ingres, his student Théodore Chassériau [chaz-sair-ee-OH] (1819–1856), and Jean-Léon Gérome [jair-OHM] (1824–1904), a fervent admirer of Ingres. Ingres's *Turkish Bath* is perhaps Orientalist painting's fullest expression. It exploits, particularly, the deep-seated Western male belief in and envy of the Orientalist male dominance of the female in the harem. Here is a field of play over which

Something to Think About . . .

How might a painting such as Ingres's *Turkish Bath* be seen as a reaction to writers such as Olympe de Gouges and Mary Wollstonecraft (see Chapter 26)?

the Western male might gaze unperturbed by the strictures of Western moral order. For, in fact, before such a painting, the viewer, always implicitly male, might indulge his most libidinous dreams even as he maintained the decorum of his position—he was, after all, simply enjoying great art.

In Said's terms, the position of the viewer in front of such works is a position of mastery. He controls the situation with his gaze, and it is hardly a coincidence that this gaze is culturally contemporaneous with the British and French colonial occupation of North Africa and the Middle East. His is a look of cultural superiority, strength, and domination. His gaze is, in short, an exercise in power.

Jean-Auguste-Dominique Ingres, *The Valpinçon Bather.* **1808.** Oil on canvas, 57 $^1/_2$" × 38 $^1/_8$". Musée du Louvre, Paris.

Ingres's *Turkish Bath* is an inventory of the five senses and their role in sensual experience. Here is the sense of touch.

Here a woman sprays herself with perfume—the sense of smell.

Ingres represents the sense of sight by both the open eyes of the reclining nude and the closed eyes of the woman lying beside her.

The seated, turbaned nude plays a lute, eliciting the sense of hearing. Ingres worked on this figure his entire life, beginning in 1808 with *The Valpinçon Bather* (named, incidentally, after one of its nineteenth-century owners). Here many of the anatomical anomalies that bothered Ingres's early critics are resolved by the simple strategy of seating the figure cross-legged. Her left leg also echoes the curve of Ingres's circular frame.

A small table bearing currants, coffee, and other delicacies represents the sense of taste.

Ingres never drew from the live model. This figure is, in fact, a composition of circles, echoing the circular format of the painting as a whole—round belly, round breasts, round face, round eyes. And her entire left side parallels the curve of the frame.

Jean-Auguste-Dominique Ingres, *The Turkish Bath*. 1862. Oil on canvas on wood, diameter 42$\frac{1}{2}$". Musée du Louvre, Paris.

paintings such as this one. Described by a contemporary as "plunged deep like sword thrusts," his brushwork in this painting is indeed almost violently sexual.

Thus, Delacroix and Ingres reenact the aesthetic debate that marked French painting since the time of Louis XIII, the debate between the intellect and emotion, between the school of Poussin and the school of Rubens (see Chapter 23). But Ingres's Neoclassicism and Delacroix's Romanticism entered into this debate not merely as expressions of aesthetic taste but as a political struggle, which already in 1830 had erupted again in a revolution that Delacroix would celebrate in his monumental painting *Liberty Leading the People* (Fig. **28.15**).

Three years earlier, after liberals won a majority in the Chamber of Deputies, King Charles X responded by relaxing censorship of the press and government control of education. But these concessions irked him, and in the spring of 1830, he called for new elections. The liberals won a large majority, but Charles was not to be thwarted. On July 25, he dissolved the new Chamber, reinstituted censorship of the press, and restricted the right to vote to the wealthiest French men. The next day, rioting erupted as workers took to the streets, erected barricades, and confronted royalist troops. In the following days, 1,800 people died. Soon after, Charles abdicated the throne and left France for England. In his place, the Chamber of Deputies named the Duke of Orléans, Louis-Philippe [loo-EE-fee-LEEP], king of their new constitutional monarchy. The two-century-old Bourbon dynasty had fallen.

In the end, the French workers may have overthrown the Bourbon dynasty, but their new king, Louis-Philippe, was hardly an improvement. He instructed the workers that

Fig. 28.15 Eugène Delacroix, *Liberty Leading the People*. 1830. Oil on canvas, 8'6" × 10'7". Photo: Hervé Lewandowski. Musée du Louvre/RMN Réunion des Musées Nationaux, France. SCALA/Art Resource, New York. Note one of the towers of Notre Dame Cathedral in the right background of the painting, which contributes to the realism of the image.

if they displayed sufficient energy, they need not fear being poor, but he did nothing concrete to help them. As early as 1831, he ordered troops to suppress a worker's revolt in Lyons, and a year later, he ordered the army to do the same in Paris, where they killed or wounded more than 800 workers. And in 1834, he crushed a silkworkers' strike, again in Lyons.

Eugène Delacroix's version of the events of July 1830, *Liberty Leading the People*, is an allegorical representation with realistic details, an emotional call to political action. A bare-breasted Lady Liberty, symbolic of freedom's nurturing power, strides over a barricade, the tricolor flag of the revolution in hand, accompanied by a young street ruffian waving a pair of pistols. On the other side is a middle-class gentleman in his top hat and frock coat, and beside him a man wielding a sabre. A worker, dressed in the colors of the revolution, rises from below the barricade. The whole triangular structure of the composition rises from the bodies of two French royalist guards, both stripped of their shoes and one of his clothing by the rioting workers. These figures purposefully recall the dead at the base of both Gros's *Napoleon at Eylau* (see Fig. 26.30) and Géricault's *Raft of the "Medusa"* (see Fig. 28.10).

To the middle-class liberals who had fomented the 1830 revolution, the painting was frighteningly realistic. The new king, Louis-Philippe, ordered that it be purchased by the state, and then promptly put it away so that its celebration of the commoners would not prove too inspiring. In fact, the painting was not seen in public again until 1848, when Louis-Philippe was himself deposed by yet another revolution, this one ending the monarchy in France forever.

Caricature and Illustration: Honoré Daumier

Despite strict censorship, the press quickly made Louis-Philippe an object of ridicule. Honoré Daumier [DOH-mee-ay] (1808–1879), an artist known for his political satire, regularly submitted cartoon drawings to daily and weekly newspapers. The development of the new medium of **lithography** (see *Materials & Techniques*, page 945), made Daumier's regular appearance in newspapers possible. He could literally create a drawing and publish it the same day. In a cartoon that appeared in the weekly paper, *La Caricature*, Daumier depicted the king—recognizable due to his pear-shaped head—as Gargantua (Fig. **28.16**), the sixteenth-century character created by the French writer Rabelais, who had a giant body and an equally gigantic appetite (see Chapter 17). The drawing shows the king gorging himself with taxes that are carried up a ramp to his waiting mouth. The poor offer up their last coins to the corrupt king while an impoverished woman at the far right tries to breast-feed her baby. As the king digests the taxes, he evacuates a series of laws and regulations.

Louis-Philippe was not amused. Daumier, his publisher, and their printer were charged with inciting contempt and

Fig. 28.16 Honoré Daumier, *Gargantua*. 1831. Lithograph, $10^3/_8$″ × 12″. Fine Arts Museums of San Francisco, Museum purchase, Herman Michels Collection, Vera Michels Bequest Fund, 1993.48.1. Daumier produced over 4,000 lithographs for Paris newspapers and journals over the course of his career, often publishing as many as three images a week.

Fig. 28.17 Honoré Daumier, *Rue Transnonain, April 15, 1834*. 1834. Lithograph, 11 $\frac{1}{2}$" × 17 $\frac{5}{8}$". Inv. A 1970–67. Kupferstichkabinett, Staatliche Kunstsammlungen, Dresden, Germany Erich Lessing/Art Resource, New York. A few days after the police killed the residents of 12 rue Transnonain, Daumier exhibited this image in the window of a Paris store, drawing huge crowds.

hatred of the French government and with insulting the king. Daumier was sentenced to six months in jail and fined 100 francs, but he continued to publish political cartoons. His *Rue Transnonain* [roo trahns-noh-NAN] is not a caricature but direct reportage of the killings committed by government troops during an insurrection by Parisian workers in April 1834 (Fig. **28.17**). After a sniper's bullet killed one of their officers, the police claimed it had come from 12 rue Transnonain and they killed everyone inside. Daumier's illustration shows the father of the family, who had been sleeping, lying dead by his bed, his child crushed beneath him, his dead wife to his right and an elder parent to his left. The strong diagonal of the scene draws us into its space, a working-class recasting of Géricault's *Raft of the "Medusa"* (see Fig. 28.10). The impact of such images on the French public was substantial, as the king clearly understood. Louis-Philippe eventually declared that freedom of the press extended to verbal but not pictorial representation.

Realist Painting: The Worker as Subject

In his focus on ordinary life, Daumier openly lampooned the idealism of both Neoclassical and Romantic art. No longer

was the object of art to reveal some "higher" truth. What mattered instead was the truth of everyday experience. In his paintings, such as *The Third-Class Carriage* (Fig. **28.18**), Daumier clearly demonstrates his interest in the daily lives of working people. The painting conveys a sense of unity and continuity with the men gathered in the background, apparently engaged in conversation, while a young mother breast-feeds her child, her own mother beside her, a basket (presumably of food) on her lap, and her young son asleep beside his grandmother.

The subject of Daumier's painting is typical of French realist painting as a whole. By focusing on laborers and common country folk rather than on the Parisian aristocracy and bourgeoisie, the painting is implicitly political. It reflects the social upheaval that in 1848 rocked almost all of Europe (see Chapter 29).

It was not only this new subject matter that was transforming the idea of what was acceptable as art. It was the new and rapid methods artists used as well—Daumier with his crayon in lithography, for instance, and Jean-François Millet [mee-YAY] (1814–1875) with his brush. In *The Sower*, Millet's broad brushstrokes of dark paint mirror the

Lithography

Lithography, which literally means "stone writing," is a printing process that depends on the fact that oil and water do not mix. The process was discovered accidentally by a young German playwright named Alois Senefelder [AH-lo-us zay-nuh-FEL-dur]. Senefelder published his plays by writing them backward on a copper plate and then etching the text. But seeking a less expensive material, he chose a piece of Kelheim [KEL-hime] limestone, the material used to line the Munich streets and abundantly available. One day his laundry woman arrived to pick up his clothes and, with no paper or ink on the premises, he jotted down what she had taken in wax on the prepared limestone. It dawned on him to bathe the stone with nitric acid and water, and when he did so, he found that the acid had etched the stone and left his writing raised in relief above its surface. Here, at last, was an extraordinarily cheap—and quick—reproductive process.

Recognizing the commercial potential of his invention, by 1798 he had discovered that if he drew directly on the stone with a greasy crayon and then treated the entire stone with nitric acid, water, and gum arabic (a very tough substance obtained from the acacia tree that attracts and holds water), then ink, applied with a roller, would stick only to the greasy drawing. He also discovered that the acid and gum arabic solution did not actually *etch* the limestone. As a result, the same stone could be used again and again. So it would be possible to pull multiple prints from one stone.

In the lithographic process, the prepared stone is rolled with ink that sticks only to the crayon image. Then a layer of damp paper is placed over the stone and both are pressed together with a scraper, later replaced by a press. This transfers the image from the stone to the paper, thereby creating the lithograph. Lithography became an important commercial reproduction process and a popular artists' medium. The French artists Daumier, Géricault, and Delacroix dominated the early history of lithography.

EXPLORE MORE: View a studio technique about lithography at **www.myartslab.com**

Fig. 28.18 Honoré Daumier, *The Third-Class Carriage*. ca. 1862. Oil on canvas, 25 3/4" × 35 1/2". Bequest of Mrs. H. O. Havemeyer, 1929. The H. O. Havemeyer Collection. © 1922 The Metropolitan Museum of Art, New York. Without glass windows, third-class carriages were open to smoke, cinders, and the cold.

Fig. 28.19 Jean-François Millet, *The Sower*. 1850. Oil on canvas, 40″ × 32¹/₂″. Museum of Fine Arts, Boston. Gift of Quincy Adams Shaw through Quincy A. Shaw, Jr., and Mrs. Marian Shaw Haughton, 17.1485. Photograph © 2008 Museum of Fine Arts, Boston. Millet painted in the village of Barbizon, south of Paris. An artists' colony there was known for its nostalgic view of the simplicity and innocence of rural life. Millet was far less sentimental.

physical exhaustion of the peasant in the fields, working until daylight is completely gone (Fig. **28.19**). On the horizon, a yoke of oxen till the field, bathed in the light of the setting sun. Following the tiller, the sower, cast in shadow, seems to emerge out of the very soil he sows, almost literally a "man of the earth." Birds flock behind the sower, eating his seed, allowing us a glimpse into the hard and futile work of the rural poor. When they were first exhibited, Millet's paintings were interpreted as political statements, in part because of the massive scale of his figures, which fill most of the picture frame. Objectionable to many aristocratic and bourgeois viewers was his apparent desire to romanticize his rural subjects. In *The Sower* and in Millet's most famous painting, *The Gleaners* (1857), he renders them in such heroic terms that they seem to rise to the level of poetry.

Gustave Courbet: Against Idealism

The leading realist painter of the era was undoubtedly Gustave Courbet (1819–1877). A farmer's son and self-taught artist, Courbet's goal was to paint the world just as he saw it, without any taint of Romanticism or idealism. "To know in order to be able to create," Courbet wrote in his Realist Manifesto of 1855, "that was my idea. To be in a position to translate the customs, the ideas, the appearance of my epoch, according to my own estimation; to be not only a painter, but a man as well; in short, to create living art—this is my goal." In fact, he rejected the traditional political and moral dimensions of realism in favor of a more subjective and apolitical approach to art. This new brand of realism would dominate the art of the following generations.

But when the public first saw his work at the Salon of 1850–51, they were astonished by the monumental scale of his paintings. Such a grand size was usually reserved for paintings of historical events, but Courbet's subjects were the mundane and the everyday. Both *The Stonebreakers* (Fig. **28.20**) and *A Burial at Ornans* (Fig. **28.21**) are enormous paintings, all the figures in each life-size. In *The Stonebreakers*, Courbet depicts two workers outside his native Ornans, a town at the foot of the Jura Mountains near the Swiss border. They are pounding stones to make gravel for a road. Everything in the painting seems to be pulled down by the weight of physical labor—the strap pulling down across the boy's back, the basket of stones resting on his knee, the hammer in the older man's hand descending downward, the stiff, thick cloth of his trousers pressing against his thigh, even the shadows of the hillside behind them descending toward them. Only a small patch of sky peeks from behind the rocky ridge in the upper right-hand corner, the ridge itself following the same downward path as the hammer. Together, the older man and his younger assistant seem to suggest the unending nature of their work, as if their back-breaking work has afflicted generation after generation of Courbet's rural contemporaries—"a complete expression of human misery," as Courbet explained it.

Perhaps Courbet's most daring effort to address ordinary life without expressing sentimentalism of any kind is a nearly 22-foot-wide painting of 1849 to 1850, *A Burial at Ornans*. Critics disliked Courbet's monumental treatment of a common country burial. The scene depicts the actual residents of Ornans at the funeral of a local farmer, the painter's great uncle, Claude-Etienne Teste. The rock cliffs in the background are the same ones beneath which the men work in *The Stonebreakers*. The funeral procession of pallbearers, choirboys, and priests on the left side of the painting is headed by two beadles (lay church officers), one a vine-grower and the other a shoemaker. Dressed in red, they add

Fig. 28.20 Gustave Courbet, *The Stonebreakers*. 1849. (Salon of 1850–51). Oil on canvas, 5'3" × 8'6". (Destroyed in 1945), Galerie Neue Meister, Dresden, Germany, © Staatliche Kunstsammlungen Dresden. The Bridgeman Art Library. The painting is believed to have been destroyed during the American fire-bombing of Dresden in World War II.

Fig. 28.21 Gustave Courbet, *A Burial at Ornans,* 1849–50 (Salon of 1850–51). Oil on canvas, 10'3¹⁄₂" × 21'9". Hervé Lewandowski/Musée d'Orsay, Paris, France. RMN Réunion des Musées Nationaux/Art Resource, New York. Both the blue gaiters (knee-socks) and the old-fashioned culotte (knee-breeches) of the man standing to the right of the grave identify him as a survivor of the French Revolutionary era—that is, he brackets the revolutions of both 1789 and 1849.

SEE MORE For a Closer Look at Gustave Courbet's *A Burial at Ornans,* go to **www.myartslab.com**

a comic air to the scene, and their flushed faces suggest that they have recently been sampling the vintner's wine—or perhaps the wine reserved for the Eucharist at the local church. Courbet's black-and-white color scheme was meant, at least in part, to evoke the realist medium of photography. The shroud over the coffin, with its black crossbones and tears, is an imaginative transformation of the usual coffin shroud design of black with gold or white crossbones and tears. The contrast between the white dog and the black mourning dresses of the funeral attendees underscores the dominant contrast between black and white in the painting, as well as its other tensions—between the green gaiters of the veteran and the red robes of the beadles, between the sky at the top of the painting and the hard reality of the earth at its bottom, between the idea of transcendence implied by the crucifix rising above the horizon and the matter-of-factness of burial imaged in the open grave.

Such a vast canvas was traditionally reserved for depicting historical events, considered the highest form of painting. By using a broad horizontal composition, with rows of 52 life-size mourners arranged without a hierarchy of importance, Courbet presents the scene in a matter-of-fact way. The crucifixion rises above the scene with no more authority than another spectator. No eye meets any other. In fact, like the dog who turns to look at something outside the frame, the entire work is a study in collective distraction. Even as the town gathers together in ritual mourning, each individual seems alone. Just as there is no single focal point in the painting, the community as a whole lacks focus. It is as if all unifying feelings, all shared beliefs, have been lost. As Courbet explained, his new realism was "the negation of the ideal . . . [and] *A Burial at Ornans* was in reality the burial of Romanticism."

PHOTOGRAPHY: REALISM'S PENCIL OF LIGHT

It is no coincidence that the invention of photography coincides with the rise of realism in the arts. The scientific principles required for photography had been known in Europe since at least 1727 when Johann Heinrich Schulze (1684–1744), a German physician, showed that certain chemicals, especially silver halides, turn dark when exposed to light. And the optical principle employed in the camera is essentially the same as that used in the camera obscura, which Leonardo da Vinci described and Johannes Vermeer used in his paintings (see Fig. 22.14). While the camera obscura could capture an image, it could not preserve it. But in 1839, inventors in England and France discovered a means to fix the image. It was as if the world could now be drawn by a pencil made of light itself.

In England, William Henry Fox Talbot presented a process for fixing negative images on paper coated with light-sensitive chemicals, which he called **photogenic drawing** (Fig. 28.22). In France, a different process, which yielded a positive image on a polished metal plate, was named the **daguerreotype** [duh-GAIR-oh-type], after one of its inventors, Louis-

Fig. 28.22 William Henry Fox Talbot, *Wrack*. 1839. Photogenic drawing (salted paper print), 8 $^{11}/_{16}$″ × 8 $^{7}/_{8}$″. Harris Brisbane Dick Fund, 1936 (36.37.20). Image copyright © The Metropolitan Museum of Art/Art Resource, New York. Fox Talbot discovered that by placing an image, such as that of the wrack (or seaweed) shown here, on sensitized paper and exposing both to sunlight, a latent image was etched onto the paper and could be brought out by dipping the paper in gallic acid. This calotype process is the basis of modern photography.

Jacques-Mandé Daguerre [dah-GAIR] (1789–1851). Wildly enthusiastic public reaction followed, and the French and English presses reported each advance in great detail.

When the French painter Paul Delaroche [deh-lah-ROSH] saw his first daguerreotype, he exclaimed, "From now on, painting is dead!" Delaroche overreacted, but he understood the potential of photography to seize painting's historical role of representing the world. Photographic portraiture quickly became a successful business, with daguerreotype images of individuals costing 15 francs in Paris. This new medium made personalized pictures available not only to the wealthy but to the middle- and working classes. By 1849, a decade after the process was discovered, 100,000 daguerreotype portraits were sold in Paris each year.

At the time Daguerre first announced his discovery, imprinting an image on a metal plate took 8 to 10 minutes in bright summer light. His photo of *Le Boulevard du Temple* was exposed for so long that none of the people or traffic moving in the street left any impression, except for one solitary figure at the lower left who is having his shoes shined (Fig. **28.23**). By 1841, the discovery of so-called chemical "accelerators" had made it possible to expose the plate for only 1 minute, but a sitter, such as Daguerre himself (Fig. **28.24**), could not move for fear of blurring the image. The process remained cumbersome, requiring considerable time to prepare, expose, and develop the plate. Iodine was vaporized on a copper sheet to create light-sensitive silver iodide, and the picture developed by suspending it face down in heated mercury, The unexposed silver iodide was dissolved with salt and the plate was then carefully rinsed and dried.

**Fig. 28.23 Louis-Jacques-Mandé Daguerre, *Le Boulevard du Temple.*
1839.** Daguerreotype. Bayerisches National Museum, Munich. Daguerre was
a painter who made his living producing panoramic dioramas, room-size
backlit paintings that appeared to change from daylight to dusk as the
illumination behind them decreased. Daguerre composed these large painted
scenes with a camera obscura, a tedious process requiring hours of tracing.
His interest in photography stemmed from his desire to speed up his painting
process. This daguerreotype was taken from the roof of the building that
housed his diorama attraction.

**Fig. 28.24 Charles Richard Meade, portrait
Louis-Jacques-Mandé Daguerre. 1848.**
Daguerreotype, hand-colored half-plate,
8′ $^{11}/_{16}$″ × 7′. The J. Paul Getty Museum, Los
Angeles. 84.XT.953. Unaware that Daguerre very
much disliked having his own portrait made, Charles
Richard Meade traveled to France in 1848 to make a
photograph that would show American audiences
what Daguerre looked like. Meade visited Daguerre
at his country home, where he finally succeeded in
making five portraits of the inventor.

Fig. 28.25 William Henry Fox Talbot, *The Open Door.* 1843. Salted paper print from a calotype negative 5⅝″ × 7⅝″. Museum of Modern Art, New York. Gilman Paper Company Collection (L.1995.2.7). Talbot's experiments with photography were sparked by the fact that he drew poorly and yet wanted to record his impressions of landscape.

The daguerreotype process resulted in a single, unreproducible image, but the invention of lithography had demonstrated that there was a market for mass-produced prints. Fox Talbot, whose photogenic drawings used paper instead of a metal plate, led the way to making multiple prints of an image. Talbot also discovered that sensitized paper, exposed for even a few seconds, held a latent image that could be brought out and developed by dipping the paper in gallic acid. This **calotype** [KAL-uh-type] process is the basis of modern photography. In 1843, Talbot's picture, which he called *The Open Door* (Fig. **28.25**), made it apparent that calotypes could become works of art in their own right. The power of the image rests in the contrast between light and dark, the visible and the unseen. Talbot published the image in *The Pencil of Nature* (1844–45), the first book fully illustrated by photographs. It was accompanied by the following caption: "A painter's eye will often be arrested where ordinary people see nothing remarkable. A casual gleam of sunshine, or a shadow thrown across his path, a time-withered oak, or a moss-covered stone may awaken a train of thought and feelings. . . ." Thus, for Talbot, photography was a realist medium that might evoke Romantic sentiment. But the medium's ability to document current events quickly overshadowed its more artistic possibilities in the public mind.

Very quickly, the public's taste for views of the world's architectural and scenic wonders gave rise to the practice of commercial photography. Among the first and most successful of these was Maxine Du Camp [do kawmp] (1822–1894), who traveled in Egypt extensively, together with the French novelist Flaubert, from 1849 to 1852. Since enlarging was not yet feasible, a relatively large picture, such as his *Westernmost Colossus of the Temple of Re, Abu Simbel* (Fig. **28.26**), required transporting glass plates the same size as the print, and a large folding wooden camera, into the field. Usually commercial photographers such as Du Camp outfitted themselves with traveling darkrooms consisting of wagons and dark-tents that had to be set up within a three-minute walk from where the glass plate would be exposed. Du Camp was particularly fond of photographing locations at sunrise and sunset, when raking light highlighted the monuments' features. He also almost

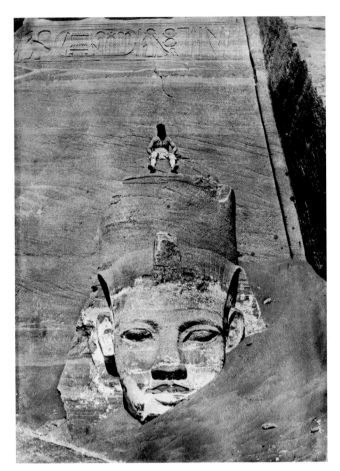

Fig. 28.26 Maxine Du Camp, *Westernmost Colossus of the Temple of Re, Abu Simbel*. 1850. Salted paper print form a calotype negative, 8 $7/8''$ × 6 $5/16''$. Gilman Paper Company Collection, New York. This was plate 107 of Du Camp's album *Egypte, Nubia, Palestine et Syrie* (Paris, 1852), one of the first photography books issued in France. It contained 122 calotypes.

always included a human figure in the composition in order to indicate scale. Such techniques would become standard photographic practice.

CHARLES DARWIN: THE SCIENCE OF OBJECTIVE OBSERVATION

The emphasis on direct observation and the objective reporting of real conditions that is so evident in realist literature and painting is reflected as well in the science of the nineteenth century, especially in the work of Charles Darwin (1809–1882). In December 1831, the 22-year-old Darwin, grandson of Josiah Wedgwood and Erasmus Darwin, founding members of the Lunar Society (see Chapter 24), set sail on the H. M. S. *Beagle* (Fig. **28.27**), to serve as naturalist on the ship's survey of South America. On his five-year journey, he kept a daily diary, the basis for his *Journal of Researches into the Geology and Natural History of the Various Countries Visited by H. M. S. Beagle* (1839), commonly known as *The Voyage of the Beagle*. There he

recorded his detailed observations of the geology, flora, and fauna of the region, from the rainforests of Brazil, "undefaced by the hand of man," to the barren landscape of Tierra del Fuego, and finally, the volcanic islands of Galapagos, just below the equator off the South American coast. Darwin was astonished at what he found there (**Reading 28.12**):

READING 28.12

from Darwin, *Voyage of the Beagle* (1839)

The natural history of these islands is eminently curious, and well deserves attention. Most of the organic productions are aboriginal creations, found nowhere else; there is even a difference between the inhabitants of the different islands; yet all show a marked relationship with those of America, though separated from that continent by an open space of ocean, between 500 and 600 miles. . . . The archipelago is a little world within itself, or rather a satellite attached to America, whence it has derived a few stray colonists. . . . Considering the small size of the islands, we feel the more astonished at the number of their aboriginal beings, and at their confined range. . . .

The circumstance, that several of the islands possess their own species of the tortoise, mockingthrush, finches, and numerous plants, these species having the same general habits, occupying analogous situations, and obviously filling the same place in the natural economy of this archipelago, that strikes me with wonder. . . . Reviewing the facts here given, one is astonished at the amount of creative force, if such an expression may be used, displayed on these small, barren, and rocky islands; and still more so, at its diverse yet analogous action on points so near each other. I have said that the Galapagos Archipelago might be called a satellite attached to America, but it should rather be called a group of satellites, physically similar, organically distinct, yet intimately related to each other, and all related in a marked, though much lesser degree, to the great American continent.

Twenty years later, Darwin would publish his analysis of the vast amount of data he had collected. In *The Origin of the Species by Means of Natural Selection, or the Preservation of the Favored Races in the Struggle for Life* (1859), he concluded that similar flora and fauna, in similar habitats, but isolated from each other, developed in a relatively brief period of time—geologically speaking—into distinct species. Darwin was on the way to understanding the "mystery of mysteries," the origin of life itself.

In the *Origin of Species*, Darwin argued that through the process of natural selection, certain organisms are able to increase rapidly over time by retaining traits conducive to their survival and eliminating those that are less favorable to survival. A given species' ability to *adapt to its environment*, then, is fundamental to its survival. A species' ability

Fig. 28.27 Conrad Martens, *The Beagle Laid Ashore for Repairs,* from Charles Darwin, *Journal of Researches into the Geology and Natural History of the Various Countries Visited by H. M. S. Beagle,* Henry Colburn Publishers, London, 1839. The artist Conrad Martens sailed for South America from England in May 1833. When his ship docked at Rio de Janeiro, he heard that the *Beagle*, refitting at Montevideo, needed an artist. Martens was hired and served as the artist on board the *Beagle* until July 1834.

to repel predators—including environmental challenges such as drought or flood—enhances its chances for procreation and determines its "fitness" to survive. And, in the end, only the "fittest" survive, an idea that, misunderstood and misapplied, would have an enormous impact on social theory later in the century.

Darwin's theory met with instant resistance. In its picture of nature as a theater of competition and struggle, a process of local adaptation with no intrinsic drive toward a higher state or greater good, propelled not by some higher force but by sexual instinct, the theory was profoundly alienating, especially to Christians. Chief among these was the same Louis Agassiz who, as we have seen earlier in the chapter, had argued for the innate inferiority of black Africans and the superiority of whites. In his 1857 *Essay on Classification* (a second revised version of which was published in 1859, just three months before the publication the Darwin's *Origin of the Species*), Agassiz maintained, that "the plan of creation has not grown out of the necessary action of physical laws, but was the free conception of the Almighty Intellect, matured in his thought before it was manifested in tangible, external forms." Have not, he asked, the taxonomic divisions of the species "been instituted by

the Divine Intelligence?" To his mind, it was indisputably the fact that the systems of classification of the species were "but translations, into human language, of the thoughts of the Creator."

Some members of Boston's Saturday Club to which, as we have seen, Agassiz belonged together with the likes of Ralph Waldo Emerson and Nathanial Hawthorne, found Agassiz's appeal to a divine creator especially appealing. Richard Henry Dana, Jr., for instance, author of the memoir *Two Years before the Mast* and, ironically, a prominent abolitionist, found Agassiz's arguments especially appealing. Edward Waldo Emerson (1844–1930), Ralph Waldo's youngest son, wrote in his 1918 history of *The Early Members of the Saturday Club*, that Dana "especially abhorred Darwinism, and the godlessness that he found in the scientific theories of later investigators. Agassiz's religious feeling and struggle against Darwin must have been a comfort to him." Yet by 1862, when Darwin published a paper on the fertilization of orchids by insects and hummingbirds, he had convinced many that his theories were correct. Today, the science of molecular genetics—the study of the information stored in our DNA—provides biological confirmation of Darwin's theories, although no one has as yet fully explained the origins of life itself.

Documenting War

One of the earliest efforts to document war photographically was undertaken by Roger Fenton (1819–1869) on the Crimean peninsula in the northern reaches of the Black Sea in 1855. The Crimean War—among the many global confrontations that mark the era, one of the costliest in terms of human life—had been precipitated by a series of misjudgments and miscalculations, all revolving around the imperial aspirations of Britain, France, Russia, and Turkey. Initially Russia and Turkey had come into conflict over which nation controlled the Orthodox Church. Russia seized the opportunity to extend its reach into the Mediterranean by defeating the Ottoman Empire. England and France sided with Turkey in order to protect their trade in the eastern Mediterranean and beyond to India. To that end, in September 1854, British and French troops sailed north across the Black Sea to the Crimean peninsula intent on the destruction of Russia's naval base at Sebastopol.

A painter of no particular distinction, Fenton had begun taking photographs in about 1851, and by early 1854, he had begun to photograph the British royal family. Perhaps because of those connections, he was given permission to undertake a commercial expedition to photograph the war, and in November 1854, he purchased a wine merchant's wagon and converted it into a mobile darkroom. In February 1855, with his mobile studio in tow, he set sail for the Crimea.

From March 8 to June 26, 1855, he produced 360 photographs documenting the war. None of them depict the action of battle (lengthy exposure times made such shots impossible). And none of them show the dead or wounded (and there were literally hundreds of thousands of both). Perhaps Fenton was working under an agreement with the British government to refrain from photographing anything that might be used to question the war effort, or perhaps Fenton's own sense of propriety restrained him. Or his publisher may not have thought photographs of the dead would sell. At any rate, his photograph of *The Valley of Shadow of Death* (Fig. **28.28**) is as close as he comes to documenting the actual horrors of war—something that American photographers would begin to do during the American Civil War eight years later, as discussed in the next chapter. British soldiers had so named the long ravine after the Twenty-Third Psalm of the Bible. As Fenton described the scene: ". . . incoming to a ravine called the valley of death, the sight passed all imagination: round shot and shell lay like a stream at the bottom of the hollow all the way down, you could not walk without treading upon them." The cannonballs are scattered across the completely barren landscape, stretching down the road almost as far as the eye can see—metaphors for those who had died where they lay. ■

Fig. 28.28 Roger Fenton, *The Valley of the Shadow of Death*. 1855. Salt print, $10^7/_8$″ × $13^3/_4$″. The Getty Center, Los Angeles. Fenton had originally intended to advance much farther up the road, but danger forced him to retreat to this spot.

How did industrialization shape the nineteenth century?

During much of the nineteenth century, industrialization created wealth for a few but left the vast majority of men and women living bleak and unhealthy lives. They worked long hours for low wages in an environment plagued by smoke and soot. In London, their drinking water was taken from the river Thames, which was little better than an open sewer. Cholera and other contagious diseases thrived in the rapidly growing urban areas of Britain, Europe, and the United States, causing millions of deaths. Housing was cramped at best, owing to the fact that workers needed to live near the factories in which they worked. As single women increasingly entered the workforce—sometimes resorting to prostitution to supplement their wages—married women were driven out, leaving men as the sole breadwinners for the family. How did Dickens and Carlyle react to these conditions?

How did reformers react to industrialization?

In France and England, the horrific conditions brought about by industrialization led socialist thinkers such as Charles Fourier and Robert Owen to argue for the creation of utopian communities where work and wealth would be shared by all. Other humanists called for a return to medieval values. Augustus Pugin was chief among those who argued that restoring Christian values to art and architecture would instill those principles into the social fabric of nations. How did Pugin see Gothic art and architecture as contributing to social reform?

What is literary realism?

Humanist writers attacked the problems afflicting the working class by addressing their plight in realistic terms, describing in minute detail the material conditions and psychological impact wrought by unhealthy surroundings. How does Charles Dickens address industrialization in *Hard Times*?

In France, realist writers such as Honoré de Balzac depicted the full breadth of French society, from its poor to its most wealthy. In the 92 novels that make up Balzac's *Human Comedy*, some 2,000 characters come to life for the reader. In the novel *Madame Bovary*, Gustave Flaubert attacked the Romantic sensibilities to which he was himself strongly attracted. How does this French brand of realist writing differ from that of Dickens?

In the United States, slavery was the chief target of realist writers, even as intellectuals such as Louis Agassiz argued for the cultural inferiority of black Africans. Such arguments were countered, at least in part, by the slaves themselves, who recounted the horrors of their lives in autobiographical narratives such as those by Frederick Douglass and Sojourner Truth. Truth saw the cause of women's rights to be intimately connected with the effort to end slavery. How do Truth's arguments compare to those of Olympe de Gouges and Mary Wollstonecraft (see Chapter 26)? One of the most important attacks on the institution of slavery and

the most widely read novel of the era was Harriet Beecher Stowe's *Uncle Tom's Cabin*. Even so, Stowe's novel adopts a patronizing tone in its treatment of African Americans. How does Mark Twain address attitudes such as Stowe's in his great novel *Huckleberry Finn*?

Who defined the direction of French painting during the nineteenth century?

After Napoleon's defeat in France, the monarchy was restored. Painters like Théodore Géricault became increasingly disenchanted with the monarchy and rejected their classical training. His *Raft of the "Medusa,"* based on the wreck of a government frigate and the abandonment of its passengers, represents a new direction in Romantic painting by depicting with a sense of urgency and immediacy a disturbing contemporary event. How did Géricault's student Eugène Delacroix do the same in his *Scenes from the Massacres at Chios*, which was exhibited at the Salon of 1824? How does Delacroix's painting compare to Ingres's *Vow of Louis XIII*, exhibited at the same Salon? Delacroix's *Liberty Leading the People* was received by the public as both a threat to the aristocracy and an attack on the middle class. How was it viewed as both realist and idealist?

A full-blown French realism found its first expression in Honoré Daumier's cartoon work for daily and weekly newspapers. Daumier constantly held the French court of King Louis-Philippe up to ridicule, even as he depicted the plight of working people in a series of paintings not exhibited until near the end of his life. Working-class life became an increasingly popular subject. How do Jean-François Millet's and Gustave Courbet's realist paintings challenge traditional notions about the nature of art?

What is photography's role in the rise of a realist art?

The new art of photography arose in the context of the rise of realism in the arts. In England, William Henry Fox Talbot developed a process for fixing a negative image on paper at the same time that in France Louis-Jacques Mandé Daguerre invented the daguerreotype, a process yielding a positive image on a metal plate. Daguerre's process, which produced single images that could not be reproduced, quickly revolutionized the art of portraiture, while Fox Talbot's calotype process offered a way of making multiple prints, and it was not long before commercial photographers such as Maxine Du Camp took advantage of the new process to sell images of the world's architectural and natural wonders. How would you describe the calotype process? What were its limitations?

What is The Origin of the Species?

Charles Darwin's voyage on the H. M. S. *Beagle* to the Galapagos Islands led him to develop a theory of evolution, published in 1859 as *The Origin of the Species*. What do Darwin's theories have in common with the fiction of Dickens, Flaubert, and Twain? How did Louis Agassiz counter Darwin's theories?

PRACTICE MORE Get flashcards for images and terms and review chapter material with quizzes at **www.myartslab.com**

GLOSSARY

bourgeoisie Middle-class merchants, shopkeepers, and businessmen.

calotype An early photographic process in which sensitized paper, exposed for a few seconds, holds a latent image that is brought out and developed by dipping the paper in gallic acid.

daguerreotype A photographic process developed in 1839 that yielded a positive image on a polished metal plate; named after one of its two inventors, Louis-Jacques-Mandé Daguerre.

literary realism The depiction of contemporary life emphasizing fidelity to everyday experience and the facts and conditions of everyday life.

lithography Literally "stone writing," this printing process depends on the fact that oil and water do not mix.

odalisque A female slave or concubine in a Middle Eastern, particularly Turkish, harem.

photogenic drawing A process for fixing negative images on paper coated with light-sensitive chemicals, developed by William Henry Fox Talbot in 1839.

proletariat A class of workers lacking ownership of the means of production (tools and equipment) and control over both the quality and price of their own work.

READINGS

READING 28.7

from the *Narrative of the Life of Frederick Douglass: An American Slave,* Chapter 1 (1845)

There are over 6,000 narratives recounting the pre–Civil War experience of slaves, many of them interviews and essays, and nearly 100 of them book-length works. Frederick Douglass's Narrative of the Life of Frederick Douglass, An American Slave, *is generally considered the greatest of these. In Chapter 1, Douglass recounts his witnessing, as a young boy, of the beating of his Aunt Hester by Mr. Plummer, the overseer of a small plantation in Maryland. The story inaugurates the first half of the book, what he refers to as his descent into "the hell of slavery."*

CHAPTER 1

I was born in Tuckahoe, near Hillsborough, and about twelve miles from Easton, in Talbot county, Maryland. I have no accurate knowledge of my age, never having seen any authentic record containing it. By far the larger part of the slaves know as little of their ages as horses know of theirs, and it is the wish of most masters within my knowledge to keep their slaves thus ignorant. I do not remember to have ever met a slave who could tell of his birthday. They seldom come nearer to it than planting-time, harvest-time, cherry-time, spring-time, or fall-time. A want of information concerning my own was a source [10] of unhappiness to me even during childhood. The white children could tell their ages. I could not tell why I ought to be deprived of the same privilege. I was not allowed to make any inquiries of my master concerning it. He deemed all such inquiries on the part of a slave improper and impertinent, and evidence of a restless spirit. The nearest estimate I can give makes me now between twenty-seven and twenty-eight years of age. I come to this, from hearing my master say, some time during 1835, I was about seventeen years old.

My mother was named Harriet Bailey. She was the daughter [20] of Isaac and Betsey Bailey, both colored, and quite dark. My mother was of a darker complexion than either my grandmother or grandfather.

My father was a white man. He was admitted to be such by all I ever heard speak of my parentage. The opinion was also whispered that my master was my father; but of the correctness of this opinion, I know nothing; the means of knowing was withheld from me. My mother and I were separated when I was but an infant—before I knew her as my mother. It is a common custom, in the part of Maryland from which I ran away, [30] to part children from their mothers at a very early age. Frequently, before the child has reached its twelfth month, its mother is taken from it, and hired out on some farm a considerable distance off, and the child is placed under the care of an old woman, too old for field labor. For what this separation is done, I do not know, unless it be to hinder the development of the child's affection toward its mother, and to blunt and destroy the natural affection of the mother for the child. This is the inevitable result.

I never saw my mother, to know her as such, more than four [40] or five times in my life; and each of these times was very short in duration, and at night. She was hired by a Mr. Stewart, who lived about twelve miles from my home. She made her journeys to see me in the night, travelling the whole distance on foot, after the performance of her day's work. She was a field hand, and a whipping is the penalty of not being in the field at sunrise, unless a slave has special permission from his or her master to the contrary—a permission which they seldom get, and one that gives to him that gives it the proud name of being a kind master. I do not recollect of ever seeing my mother by the light [50] of day. She was with me in the night. She would lie down with me, and get me to sleep, but long before I waked she was gone. Very little communication ever took place between us. Death soon ended what little we could have while she lived, and with it her hardships and suffering. She died when I was about seven years old, on one of my master's farms, near Lee's Mill. I was not allowed to be present during her illness, at her death, or burial. She was gone long before I knew any thing about it. Never having enjoyed, to any considerable extent, her soothing presence, her tender and watchful care, I received the tidings of her death with much the same emotions I should have probably felt at the death of a stranger.

Called thus suddenly away, she left me without the slightest intimation of who my father was. The whisper that my master was my father, may or may not be true; and, true or false, it is of but little consequence to my purpose whilst the fact remains, in all its glaring odiousness, that slaveholders have ordained, and by law established, that the children of slave women shall in all cases follow the condition of their mothers; and this is done too obviously to administer to their own lusts, and make a gratification of their wicked desires profitable as well as pleasurable; for by this cunning arrangement, the slaveholder, in cases not a few, sustains to his slaves the double relation of master and father.

I know of such cases; and it is worthy of remark that such slaves invariably suffer greater hardships, and have more to contend with, than others. They are, in the first place, a constant offence to their mistress. She is ever disposed to find fault with them; they can seldom do any thing to please her; she is never better pleased than when she sees them under the lash, especially when she suspects her husband of showing to his mulatto children favors which he withholds from his black slaves. The master is frequently compelled to sell this class of his slaves, out of deference to the feelings of his white wife; and, cruel as the deed may strike any one to be, for a man to sell his own children to human flesh-mongers, it is often the dictate of humanity for him to do so; for, unless he does this, he must not only whip them himself, but must stand by and see one white son tie up his brother, of but few shades darker complexion than himself, and ply the gory lash to his naked back; and if he lisp one word of disapproval, it is set down to his parental partiality, and only makes a bad matter worse, both for himself and the slave whom he would protect and defend.

Every year brings with it multitudes of this class of slaves. It was doubtless in consequence of a knowledge of this fact, that one great statesman of the south predicted the downfall of slavery by the inevitable laws of population. Whether this prophecy is ever fulfilled or not, it is nevertheless plain that a very different-looking class of people are springing up at the south, and are now held in slavery, from those originally brought to this country from Africa; and if their increase do no other good, it will do away the force of the argument, that God cursed Ham, and therefore American slavery is right. If the lineal descendants of Ham are alone to be scripturally enslaved, it is certain that slavery at the south must soon become unscriptural; for thousands are ushered into the world, annually, who, like myself, owe their existence to white fathers, and those fathers most frequently their own masters.

I have had two masters. My first master's name was Anthony. I do not remember his first name. He was generally called Captain Anthony—a title which, I presume, he acquired by sailing a craft on the Chesapeake Bay. He was not considered a rich slaveholder. He owned two or three farms, and about thirty slaves. His farms and slaves were under the care of an overseer. The overseer's name was Plummer. Mr. Plummer was a miserable drunkard, a profane swearer, and a savage monster. He always went armed with a cowskin and a heavy cudgel. I have known him to cut and slash the women's heads so horribly, that even master would be enraged at his cruelty, and would threaten to whip him if he did not mind himself. Master, however, was not a humane slaveholder. It required extraordinary barbarity on the part of an overseer to affect him. He was a cruel man, hardened by a long life of slave-holding. He would at times seem to take great pleasure in whipping a slave. I have often been awakened at the dawn of day by the most heart-rending shrieks of an own aunt of mine, whom he used to tie up to a joist, and whip upon her naked back till she was literally covered with blood. No words, no tears, no prayers, from his gory victim, seemed to move his iron heart from its bloody purpose. The louder she screamed, the harder he whipped; and where the blood ran fastest, there he whipped longest. He would whip her to make her scream, and whip her to make her hush; and not until overcome by fatigue, would he cease to swing the blood-clotted cowskin. I remember the first time I ever witnessed this horrible exhibition. I was quite a child, but I well remember it. I never shall forget it whilst I remember any thing. It was the first of a long series of such outrages, of which I was doomed to be a witness and a participant. It struck me with awful force. It was the blood-stained gate, the entrance to the hell of slavery, through which I was about to pass. It was a most terrible spectacle. I wish I could commit to paper the feelings with which I beheld it.

This occurrence took place very soon after I went to live with my old master, and under the following circumstances. Aunt Hester went out one night,—where or for what I do not know,—and happened to be absent when my master desired her presence. He had ordered her not to go out evenings, and warned her that she must never let him catch her in company with a young man, who was paying attention to her belonging to Colonel Lloyd. The young man's name was Ned Roberts, generally called Lloyd's Ned. Why master was so careful of her, may be safely left to conjecture. She was a woman of noble form, and of graceful proportions, having very few equals, and fewer superiors, in personal appearance, among the colored or white women of our neighborhood.

Aunt Hester had not only disobeyed his orders in going out, but had been found in company with Lloyd's Ned; which circumstance, I found, from what he said while whipping her, was the chief offence. Had he been a man of pure morals himself, he might have been thought interested in protecting the innocence of my aunt; but those who knew him will not suspect him of any such virtue. Before he commenced whipping Aunt Hester, he took her into the kitchen, and stripped her from neck to waist, leaving her neck, shoulders, and back, entirely naked. He then told her to cross her hands, calling her at the same time a d–d b–h. After crossing her hands, he tied them with a strong rope, and led her to a stool under a large hook in the joist, put in for the purpose. He made her get upon the stool, and tied her hands to the hook. She now stood fair for his infernal purpose. Her arms were stretched up at their full length, so that she stood upon the ends of her toes. He then said to her, "Now, you d–d b—h, I'll learn you how to disobey my orders!" and after rolling up his sleeves, he commenced to lay on the heavy cowskin, and soon the warm, red blood (amid heart-rending shrieks from her, and horrid oaths from him) came dripping to the floor. I was so terrified and horror-stricken at the sight, that I hid myself in a closet, and dared not venture out till long after the bloody transaction was over. I expected it would be my turn next. It was all new to me. I had never seen any thing like it before. I had always lived with my grandmother on the outskirts of the plantation, where she was put to raise the children of the younger women. I had

180

therefore been, until now, out of the way of the bloody scenes that often occurred on the plantation.

READING CRITICALLY

Near the end of this chapter, Douglass makes the somewhat startling claim, "It was all new to me." How does this claim help the reader to identify with Douglass's plight?

29 Global Confrontation and Civil War

Challenges to Cultural Identity

THINKING AHEAD

What events did Karl Marx and Friedrich Engels foresee in their Communist Manifesto?

How did the American Civil War affect popular attitudes toward warfare?

What is imperialism?

How did imperialism affect Egypt?

What is Japonisme?

Between 1800 and 1848, the city of Paris doubled in size, to nearly 1 million people. Planning was nonexistent. The streets were a haphazard labyrinth of narrow, stifling passageways, so clogged with traffic that pedestrians were in constant danger. The gutters were so full of garbage and raw sewage that cesspools developed overnight in low-lying areas. The odor they produced was often strong enough to induce vomiting. And they bred rats and fleas, and the diseases they carried, such as cholera, dysentery, typhus, and typhoid fever. One epidemic in Paris during 1848 and 1849 killed more than 19,000 people. Further complicating the situation, no accurate map of the streets existed prior to 1853, so to venture into them was to set out into unknown and dangerous territory.

By 1848, these conditions prevailed throughout urban areas in Europe, made worse by food shortages and chaos in the agricultural economy. The potato famine in Ireland, which killed a million people, was merely the worst of a widespread breakdown. The agricultural crisis in turn triggered bankruptcies and bank closings, particularly in places where industrial expansion had not been matched by the growth of new markets. In France, prices plummeted, businesses failed, and unemployment was rampant. The situation was ripe for revolution. Soon the streets of Paris were filled with barricades, occupied by workers demanding the right to earn a livelihood and determine their own destiny. The brutal street fighting was so disturbing to Parisians that even such a traditional salon painter as Ernst Meissonier (me-saw-NYEY) (1815–1891), who spent his entire career celebrating French military history, was moved, for once, to depict the truth of war (Fig. **29.1**). In other European capitals, workers quickly followed the Parisians' lead (Map **29.1**).

This chapter explores the revolutions of 1848 in Europe and their aftermath. At the heart of these conflicts

◀ **Fig. 29.1 Ernest Meissonier,** *Memory of Civil War (The Barricades)* . **1849 (Salon of 1850–51).** Oil on canvas, 11$\frac{1}{2}$″ × 8$\frac{1}{4}$″. Inv. RF1942-31. Location: Louvre, Paris, France. Musée du Louvre/RMN Réunion des Musées Nationaux, France. SCALA/Art Resource, New York. Meissonier served as a captain of the Republican Guard defending the Hôtel de Ville in the June Days and witnessed the bloodshed with his own eyes. The result is this painting, which a contemporary called an "omelette of men." It is Delacroix's *Liberty Leading the People* (see Fig. 28.15) stripped bare of all its glory.

HEAR MORE Listen to an audio file of your chapter at **www.myartslab.com**

Map 29.1 Revolutionary activity in Europe in 1848.

North Sea

Baltic Sea

PRUSSIA

Berlin

BELGIUM

Frankfurt

Paris

Prague

Bayreuth

BOHEMIA

MORAVIA

Vienna

Munich

AU

Buda

HU

FRANCE

Milan

Venice

PAPAL STATES

Rome

OTT

were two ideologies that were sometimes compatible and sometimes not: liberalism and nationalism. Liberal belief was founded in Enlightenment values—the universal necessity for equality and freedom at the most basic level. The nationalist agenda, however, focused on regional autonomy, cultural pride, and freedom from monarchical control, especially that of the Habsburgs, who controlled much of central, eastern, and southern Europe. Liberal politics were transnational; nationalism rested upon claims of distinct regional, even local, ethnic and linguistic identity.

The cultural identities of non-Western cultures were, however, severely challenged as Western nations, revitalized by effective new military, communication, and naval technologies, sought to expand their influence and reap new economic and political power in far-distant lands during the nineteenth century. The confrontation of Western civilization with other peoples whose values were often dramatically opposed to the West's own— the cultures of China, India, and Japan in particular— suggests that by the dawn of the twentieth century, the tradition and sense of centeredness that had defined indigenous cultures for hundreds, even thousands, of years was either threatened or in the process of being destroyed. Worldwide, non-Western cultures suddenly found that they were defined as outposts of new colonial empires developed by Europeans, resulting in the weakening of traditional cultural practices, political leadership, and social systems that had been in place for centuries.

THE REVOLUTIONS OF 1848: FROM THE STREETS OF PARIS TO VIENNA AND BEYOND

Although the working classes suffered most from the miserable living conditions in European cities, they were not the initial cause of the revolutionary turmoil of 1848. It was the middle-class (bourgeois) political thinkers who most strongly argued for representative government and civil liberties. They considered themselves to be *liberal*, espousing legal equality, religious toleration, and freedom of the press. They generally believed, like Enlightenment writers John Locke and Thomas Jefferson, that government emanated from the people, who freely consented to its rule and had the power to oust unwanted leaders. The people expressed this consent through the election of representatives, and they protected their rights through written constitutions. Many liberals supported the ideas of Adam Smith, who argued (see Chapter 26) that government should keep its nose out of economics and trade. Many were, in fact, self-serving capitalists, partisans of unregulated economic life, and opponents of tyranny of any government that threatened their self-interest. When they allied themselves with the working classes— generally more predisposed to violence—it was more a matter of convenience than conviction. Nineteenth-century liberalism thus expressed the French Revolution's principle, "*Liberté, Égalité, Fraternité*," in less strident terms, but with the same concern for individual rights and common morality.

Marxism

There were, however, more radical thinkers whose convictions were untarnished by self-interest and who, furthermore, did not shy away from proposing violence to attain their goals. Karl Marx (1818–1883) and Friedrich Engels [EN-gulz] (1820–1895) were two young, middle-class Germans who believed that since the conditions in which one earns a living determined all other aspects of life—social, political, and cultural—capitalism must be eliminated because of its inherent unfairness. Reform was pointless—only a revolution of the working people would succeed in achieving meaningful change. In fact, Marx and Engels believed revolution was inevitable, following the logic of the philosopher Georg Wilhelm Friedrich Hegel's dialectic (see Chapter 27). The struggle between the bourgeoisie—which Engels defined as "the class of modern capitalists, owners of the means of production and employers of wage labor"—and the proletariat (working class) amounted to the conflict between thesis and antithesis. (The term *bourgeoisie* generally referred to the capitalist or merchant class.) The resolution lay in the synthesis of a classless society, a utopian society at "the end of history," since the dialectic forces that drive history would be finally and permanently resolved.

The collaboration of Marx and Engels would ultimately help shape nineteenth- and twentieth-century history across the globe. Their epochal partnership began rather simply in a Parisian café in August 1844, where Marx first met Engels. Marx had been editing a German newspaper and Engels was the heir to his father's textile factory in Manchester, England. The following year, Engels published his *Conditions of the Working Class in England*, a scathing indictment of industrial life, and in early 1848, the two had co-authored and published a manifesto for the newly formed Communist League in London. The term *communist* at the time suggested a more radical approach to communal politics than *socialist*. In the *Communist Manifesto* (see **Reading 29.1**, pages 987–988, for Part I, "Bourgeois and Proletarians"), Marx and Engels argued that class struggle characterized all past societies and that industrial society simplified these class antagonisms. "Society as a whole is splitting up more and more into two great hostile camps, into two great classes directly facing each other: Bourgeoisie and Proletariat."

In its most controversial phrases, the *Communist Manifesto* called for "the forcible overthrow of all existing social conditions," and concluded, "The proletarians have nothing to lose but their chains. They have a world to win. WORKING MEN OF ALL COUNTRIES, UNITE." This simplistic call-to-arms would gain support steadily through the ensuing decades, even though Marx and Engels failed to anticipate capitalism's ability to adapt to change and slowly improve the lot of "the proletariat." However, the *Manifesto*, as well as Marx's later *Das Kapital* (*Capital*), offered an important testament of the living conditions of the proletariat and an incisive interpretation of the way capitalism operated. Ironically, this forceful critique of the effects of the free market became an influential factor in advancing reforms in working conditions, as well as providing higher wages and greater social equality.

The Streets of Paris

In February 1848, rioters overthrew Louis-Philippe, who had ruled since 1830. Tension among the bourgeoisie, the intellectual liberals, and the working people who fought beside them was evident from the first. In his *History of the Revolution of 1848*, writer and politician Alphonse de Lamartine [lah-mar-TEEN] (1790–1869) describes the scene just before the overthrow (**Reading 29.2**):

READING 29.2

from Alphonse de Lamartine, *History of the Revolution of 1848* (1849)

These two classes exhibited a characteristic difference of air and costume. The one was composed of young men belonging to the rich and refined mercantile classes, to the schools, to trade . . . to literature, and . . . to the periodical press. These harangued the people, inflamed popular indignation against the king, the minister, and the chambers; spoke of the humiliation of France before the foreigner, of the diplomatic treasons of the court, and the insolent corruption and servility of deputies, who had sold themselves to the sovereign will of Louis-Philippe. . . . The numerous promenaders and bystanders, whose curiosity was excited by whatever was new, crowded around these orators, and applauded their expressions. The other class was composed of the lower orders [workers], summoned within the last two days, from their shops, by the sound of firing; clad in their working dress, with their blue shirts open, and their hands still blackened with the smoke of the forge. These came down in silence, in little knots. . . . One or two workmen, better dressed than the rest, with long skirted cloth coats, walked before them, addressed them in a low tone, and seemed to be giving them the word of command. These were the heads of the sections of the Rights of Man and of Families [a reference to the French Revolution of the 1790s].

Within several days, King Louis-Philippe fled to exile in England. A provisional government for the Second French Republic was installed by voice vote of a crowd that shouted its judgment for each name read by Alphonse de Lamartine.

The June Days in Paris: Worker Defeat and Rise of Louis-Napoleon

The mob that day had made one thing clear—it demanded the "right to work." The provisional government quickly acted to form *Ateliers Nationaux* [ah-tuh-lee-AY nah-see-oh-NOH], "National Workshops," to provide employment. Enrollment in these workshops quickly jumped from 10,000 in March to 120,000 in June. Unable to provide useful employment for such numbers, the government discovered it had inadvertently created a vast army eager to support almost every radical cause. On June 22, the National Workshops were officially terminated and disillusioned workers took up arms in response. The so-called June Days—three days of the bloodiest street fighting in nineteenth-century European history—followed, as workers built and occupied barricades in the streets (Fig. **29.2**; and see Fig. 29.1). The army quickly overcame the workers at the cost of 10,000 dead and wounded. Eleven thousand more so-called leaders of the revolution were deported to France's new colony of Algiers [al-JEERZ], in North Africa.

Many members of the middle class were convinced that they had barely survived the complete collapse of social order. What came to be known as the Red Fear, an almost paranoid distrust of the working class, gripped France. Conservatives succeeded in passing legislation that curbed freedom of the press and limited political association. A new constitution provided for the election of a president who could deal with any future rebellions without interference.

In the December 1848 election for president, Charles-Louis-Napoleon Bonaparte (1808–1873) was the victor. Known as Louis-Napoleon [loo-EE-nah-poh-lay-OHN], this nephew of Napoleon I was awkward and spoke French with a German accent, but his name proved attractive to the electorate. When, in 1851, the assembly refused to amend the constitution to allow the president to run for a second term, Louis-Napoleon staged a *coup d'état*. On December 2 of that year, the anniversary of his uncle's great victory at Austerlitz, he ordered his troops to disperse the assembly. Hundreds were killed resisting the coup, 26,000 people were arrested, and 10,000 deported to Algeria. A year later, Louis-Napoleon was proclaimed Emperor Napoleon III, again approved by an overwhelming popular plebiscite (a "yes or no" vote). The conservative bourgeoisie, or as Marx would term them, the capitalists, were firmly entrenched in power. An autocrat, Louis-Napoleon was popular with monarchists and the middle class as a force for restoring order. To the working class, he promised economic progress for all, while the rural population revered him as Napoleon Bonaparte's nephew.

No image better illustrates the repressive role of the state in Paris after 1848 than *What Is Called Vagrancy* (Fig. **29.3**) by the Belgian painter Alfred Stevens (1823–1906), working in Paris. On a street in Vincennes [van-SEN], on the outskirts of Paris, troops of Napoleon III arrest for vagrancy a woman with a baby in her arms and a humiliated little boy at her skirt. A more elegantly dressed woman tries to intercede, but she is rebuffed by the threatening gesture of a soldier. An elderly disabled worker has already given up and turns away. Posters on the wall behind them emphasize the disparity between rich and poor—one announces a court auction of buildings (presumably for default) and the other a "*Bal*" [bahl] or dance. When Napoleon III saw this painting, he was outraged, believing such spectacles could stir up conflict. He ordered that vagrants should be transported to prison in closed coaches.

Fig. 29.2 Thibault, *The Barricades on the rue Saint-Maur-Popincourt before the Attack by General Lamoricière's Troops on Sunday, 25 June 1848.* Daguerreotype, $4^5/_8$″ × $5^7/_8$″. Musée d'Orsay, Paris. Published in *L' Illustration* of July 1–8, 1848 and in the special issue of the magazine *Journées illustrées de la révolution de 1848*, published in August 1848, this scene is regarded as the first photograph used to illustrate a newspaper story.

Fig. 29.3 Alfred Stevens, *What Is Called Vagrancy*. 1855 (1855 Exposition Universal). Oil on canvas, 52″ × 63 ¾″. Musée d'Orsay, Paris, France. Photo: Hervé Lewandowski/Réunion des Musées Nationaux. Art Resource, New York. The painting was also known in the mid-nineteenth century by the telling title *The Hunters of Vincennes*.

The Haussmannization of Paris

In July 1853, Napoleon III chose Baron Georges-Eugène Haussmann [ohss-MAHN] (1809–1891) to supervise a daunting task—planning the modernization of Paris by destroying the old city and rebuilding it anew—a process that has come to be known as **Haussmannization**. They shared a dream: to rid Paris of its medieval character, transforming it into the most beautiful city in the world. By 1870, their reforms were largely completed, resulting in improved housing, sanitation, and increased traffic flow, all of which encouraged growth in the city's shopping districts. But the vast renovation served another important purpose as well: to prevent the possibility of out-of-control street riots leading to revolutions—like those of 1830 and 1848—from ever happening again.

By widening the streets, Haussmann made it harder to build barricades. By extending long, straight boulevards across the capital, he made it easier to move troops and artillery rapidly within the city (see Map **29.2**). And he integrated each project into a larger-scale city planning strategy. After demolishing the labyrinth of ancient streets and dilapidated buildings that were home to the rebellious working class—25,000 buildings between 1852 and 1859 and after 1860 another 92,000—the government installed enormous new sewer lines before extending impressively wide boulevards atop them. Great public parks were developed. Before 1848, there were perhaps 47 acres of parkland in Paris, most of it along the Champs-Élysées [shahnz-ay-lee-ZAY], but Emperor Louis-Napoleon soon opened to the public all the previously private gardens, including the Jardin des Plantes [zhar-DEHN deh plahnt], the Luxembourg [luks-om-BOOR] Gardens, and the royal gardens. Haussmann amplified this gesture by creating a series of new parks,

Fig. 29.4 Felix Thorigny, *Demolition of the rue de la Barillerie to allow for construction of the Boulevard de Sébastopol, Paris, 1st arrondissement.* 1859. Engraving. Bibliothèque Nationale, Paris. Here thirteenth- and fourteenth-century streets and houses on the Right Bank are shown being cleared away.

squares, and gardens. These included the massive re-design of the Bois de Boulogne [bwah deh boo-LOHN] on the city's western edge and the conversion of the old quar-ries in the working-class neighborhoods into a huge park with artificial mountains, streams, waterfalls, and a lake, all overlooked by new cafés and restaurants. By 1870, Hauss-mann had increased the total land dedicated to parks in the city by nearly 100 times, to 4,500 acres.

But the wholesale destruction of working-class neighbor-hoods throughout Paris (Fig. **29.4**) had other consequences as well. Almost all of the less expensive housing for workers was erected on the outskirts of the city, and many residents of the demolished areas were subsequently moved to new working-class suburbs. As much as Haussmann wanted to open the city to air and light, he wanted to rid it of crowd-ing, crime, and political disaffection. "Rue Transnonain," he bragged, referring to the site of Daumier's famous litho-graph of 1834 (see Fig. 28.17), "has disappeared from the map of the city." The working-class exodus to the outskirts of Paris resulted in a city inhabited almost exclusively by the bourgeoisie and the upper classes. To further facilitate the exodus of the working class, Haussmann banned large-scale industry (as opposed to artisan workshops) from the city altogether. By the last quarter of the nineteenth century, Paris became a city of leisure, as discussed in Chapter 30, a

city of the good life, surrounded by a ring of industrial and working-class suburbs, as it remains to the present day.

Revolution across Europe: The Rise of Nationalism

The Paris uprising of February 1848 triggered a string of suc-cessive revolts in Austria, many of the lesser German states, and throughout Italy, spreading northward from Sicily, Sardinia, and Naples to the Papal States, Tuscany, and the northern regions under Austrian rule (see Map 29.1). One of the most important factors contributing to revolution was na-tionalism, the exaltation of one's home territory. National groups across Eastern Europe sought to replace the rule of the Prussian and the Austrian Habsburgs with smaller indepen-dent states. First, in Vienna, Magyar [MAG-yar] nationalists called for the independence of Hungary, even as Czech [chek] nationalists demanded the right to create an autonomous Slavic [SLAH-vik] state in Bohemia [boh-HEE-mee-uh] and Moravia [mor-AY-vee-uh]. In early June, the first Pan-Slavic Congress, including Poles, Croats [KROH-ats], Slovenes [SLOH-veenz], and Serbs, met in Prague [prahg] and issued a manifesto that protested the repression of all Slavic peoples. By June 12, as the Congress closed, an anti-government riot broke out, and the Habsburgs' military smashed the radicals, thus temporarily ending the drive toward a Pan-Slavic state.

Map 29.2 Paris. ca. 1870. The map shows (in red) the street work done by Haussmann between 1850 and 1870.

Meanwhile, in Italy, revolution against Habsburg domination began in Milan and moved southward. In Rome, radicals rose up against papal control, forcing the pope to appoint a new ministry. Republican nationalists from across Italy, including Giuseppe Mazzini [mah-TZEE-nee] (1805–1872) and Giuseppe Garibaldi [gah-ree-BAHL-dee] (1807–1882), converged on the city hoping to unite the rest of Italy behind the example of this new Republic of Rome. But by June 1849, 10,000 French troops, sent by Louis-Napoleon, laid siege in support of continued papal control, and by the end of the month, the Roman Republic was dissolved.

In mid-March 1848, popular disturbances also erupted in Berlin, forcing the Prussian king, Frederick William IV (r. 1840–1861), to install a liberal government. But again the forces of reform were thwarted, and in April 1849, the Prussian monarch forced the liberal assembly to resign and proclaimed his own constitution. Elsewhere in Germany, the liberal Frankfurt Parliament offered the crown of a united Germany to Frederick William IV, who refused it. The Frankfurt Parliament, hopelessly caught between its fear of the working classes and its dependence on the troops of conservative monarchs, dissolved.

Given the nationalists' opposition to the monarchist (and papal) governments that controlled most of the rebelling regions, it is hardly surprising that they often found themselves allied with liberals. But important differences existed between the two camps. In fact, on many questions nationalism was distinctly at odds with liberal political values. Nationalist groups often defined themselves in direct opposition to other ethnic groups whom they considered their cultural inferiors. The Hungarian Magyars, for instance, sought authoritarian control over all other ethnic groups living within the historical boundaries of Hungary, including Romanians, Croatians, and Serbs.

One group that appeared to benefit from the revolutions of 1848 was the Jews, who had historically been subject to great repression throughout Europe. In Scandinavia, Italy, Germany, Belgium, and Holland, Jews attained full rights of citizenship after 1848, and in 1867, Austria-Hungary extended them the same rights. By 1858, Jews were permitted to sit in Parliament in England. As a result, Jewish participation in European cultural life increased dramatically. For the first time, Jews were able to enter art and music schools, and subsequently they became leaders in science and education. From 1850 until about 1880, Jews lived their lives in relative freedom from persecution and discrimination.

Only in Russia and other parts of Eastern Europe did anti-Semitism continue unabated. In Russia, Jews were confined to designated ghettos, from which they could leave only with internal passports. They were banned from state service and most forms of higher education, and publication of Jewish texts was severely restricted. The police regularly led *pogroms* [POH-grums] (organized and violent riots) against Jewish neighborhoods and villages. As a result, hundreds of thousands of Jews emigrated from the East to Western Europe as well as the United States.

Despite the anti-Semitic atmosphere in Russia, a new transnational Jewish literature began to surface, written in Yiddish, a German dialect using the Hebrew alphabet. Among its most notable authors is Sholem Yakov Rabinovitsh [SHOH-lem YAH-kov rah-bin-o-vits], widely known as Sholem Aleichem [ah-LAY-khum] (1859–1916). His stories about Tevye the Milkman would later inspire the Broadway musical and film *Fiddler on the Roof*.

THE AMERICAN CIVIL WAR

There was a great cultural and geographical distance between Paris and the rural South of the United States, yet as the nineteenth-century world became increasingly interdependent, there were also important connections between the two areas. Cotton textiles were enormously important to Europeans, and much of their supply came from the American South. So there was great consternation in Britain, France, Germany, and other European states when, in 1860, the Civil War loomed. From the European point of view, the causes that led to that war (1861–1865) seemed all too familiar. On the one hand, it appeared that the Union (Northern) states were insisting on the abolition of slavery in the tradition of liberal ideology. On the other hand, the Confederate (Southern) states, a predominantly agricultural society based on slavery, desired, in typical nationalist ideological form, to become a sovereign state of its own.

Both the British and French textile industries, and indeed, the entire economies of both nations, depended heavily on the imports of Southern cotton. As a result, they sided with the South insofar as it fought, in the antebellum [an-tee-BELL-um] [prior to the Civil War] Congress, to uphold free-trade policies while the North pushed for protective tariffs. The South felt confident that out of economic necessity Britain, and possibly France, would side with it in any conflict. But abolitionist sentiment ran high in Europe. Harriet Beecher Stowe's *Uncle Tom's Cabin* (see Chapter 28) was a best-seller across the Continent, and, besides, both the British and French governments were not disposed to support an uprising that appeared even vaguely nationalist. Both nations were busily acquiring colonial possessions in Asia and Africa, and were uncomfortable with nationalist sentiment. To the South's surprise, both maintained neutrality throughout the conflict, despite continued Confederate attempts to draw Europeans to their side.

Romanticizing Slavery in Antebellum American Art and Music

Many in Europe and across the globe were surprised that war erupted in the United States, believing that some sort of compromise was likely. In no small part, this delusion resulted from a romanticized view of slavery embedded even in abolitionist literature such as *Uncle Tom's Cabin*. For every Simon Legree there is an Augustine Saint Clare and his daughter, Little Eva; for every abused slave, a grateful Christian convert.

Eastman Johnson: The Ambiguity of *Negro Life in the South* A prime example of blindness to the full implications of slavery in antebellum America is evident in the painting *Negro Life in the South* by Eastman Johnson (1824–1906) (Fig. **29.5**). The painting achieved instant success when exhibited in 1859 in New York. Much of its realism was contributed by the models Johnson employed—the household slaves owned by his father in Washington, D.C.

Negro Life in the South was a curious painting in that it was highly ambiguous—it could be read as either for or against slavery. For some, Johnson's painting seemed to depict slaves as contented with their lot. A banjo-picker plays a song for a mother and child who are dancing together. A young man and woman flirt at the left, while another woman and child look out on the scene from the window above. The white mistress of the house steps through the gate at the left as if to join in the party. However, to an abolitionist, the contrast between the mistress's gown and the more ragged clothing of the slaves, between the dilapidated shed and the finer house behind, demonstrates the sorry plight of the slaves.

Stephen Foster and the Minstrel Song Of all representations of African Americans before the Civil War, perhaps the most popular was the **minstrel show**, a theatrical event that presented black American melodies, jokes, and impersonations, usually performed by white performers in blackface. It evolved out of two types of common entertainment in the early nineteenth century: theatrical or circus skits in which white actors impersonated black banjo-playing street musicians. In 1828, Thomas Dartmouth "Daddy" Rice, a white man, began performing as an old slave named Jim Crow, and his song-and-dance show soon had many imitators. By the 1840s, a group of white performers in New York were performing in blackface as the Virginia Minstrels. The instruments they used to accompany themselves—bone castanets, violin, banjo, and tambourine—quickly became standard. The Virginia Minstrels' success led to the formation of the Christy Minstrels, headed by white actor Edwin P. Christy, whose show included songs, often referred to as "Ethiopian" melodies, usually set in the South and rendered in black dialect, as well as crude, racist jokes. The stereotypes perpetrated by the minstrel shows—African Americans as fun-loving, carefree people likely to break out in joyful song but also as ignorant, lazy, and superstitious buffoons—became a staple of American entertainment. And by the 1850s, songs about escaped slaves longing to return to their kindly masters were standard fare.

In 1848, the Christy Minstrels performed a song that quickly became a national hit: "Oh! Susanna," written by Stephen Foster (1826–1864), a young Pittsburgh bookkeeper. Foster realized that the minstrel stage was the key to securing an audience for his songs, but he also wanted

Fig. 29.5 Eastman Johnson, _Negro Life in the South (Kentucky Home)_. 1859. Oil on canvas, 36″ × 45″.
© Collection of the New York Historical Society/The Bridgeman Art Library. Johnson studied in Europe from 1849
to 1855, culminating in Paris in the studio of Thomas Couture, where Édouard Manet was also a student.

to write a new kind of music for it. Rather than trivializing the hardships of slavery, he wanted to humanize the characters in his work and create songs that communicated to all people. Foster was also a music-business pioneer, becoming a professional songwriter in an era when selling sheet music through a publisher was the only way to earn money from his wildly popular tunes.

In the next several decades, Foster wrote all kinds of songs, including "Camptown Races" (1850) (track **29.1**). The near-nonsense dialect of "Camptown Races" reinforces the portrayal of the black as a fool. Foster's so-called **plantation melodies** were also written in dialect but were quite different—depicting blacks as capable of a full range of human emotion. His 1849 song "Nelly Was a Lady," for instance, made popular by the Christy Minstrels, portrays a black man and woman as loving husband and wife. In "Nelly," Foster did something previously unheard of, allowing the husband to call his wife a "lady," a term heretofore reserved for well-born

((• HEAR MORE at
www.myartslab.com

white women. Other famous Foster tunes included "Old Folks at Home" ("Swanee River") (1851) and "My Old Kentucky Home" (1853). Finally, Foster wrote a number of parlor songs—so-called because they were to be performed in parlors—including "Jeanie with the Light Brown Hair" (1854) and "Beautiful Dreamer" (1862).

Eastman Johnson's _Negro Life in the South_ was so closely associated with Foster's music that the painting quickly became known by another name—_Kentucky Home_. Together they sum up the complexities of antebellum attitudes about slavery. What they make apparent is how America before the Civil War was dominated by the mythologized, unrealistic, and romanticized view of slavery.

Representing the War

On October 16, 1859, relations between whites and slaves in America changed dramatically when John Brown (1800–1859), a white abolitionist, led twenty-one followers, five of them African Americans, on a raid to capture the federal arsenal at Harpers Ferry, West Virginia. Their intention was to set off a revolt of slaves throughout the South, but two days later, Lieutenant Colonel Robert E. Lee (1807–1879) recaptured the arsenal. Ten of Brown's men were killed in the battle, and he and the rest were hanged.

The prospect of a general slave insurgency, aided and abetted by abolitionists, convinced many in the South that the North was intent on ending slavery, a belief that the election of Abraham Lincoln (1809–1865) as president in November 1860 seemed to confirm. The images of contented slaves such as Eastman Johnson had painted in his *Negro Life* seemed to vanish instantly. After the war began in the spring of 1861, Johnson himself began to accompany Union troops to the front. His *A Ride for Liberty: The Fugitive Slaves*, which Easton painted in 1862

to 1863 from an incident he had witnessed, is entirely different in mood and handling from his earlier painting (Fig. **29.6**). The previous summer, the Confederate army had soundly defeated the North at Bull Run, a stream near Manassas [man-ASS-uss], Virginia. Ever since that defeat, the Northern and Confederate armies had stood their ground between Manassas and Washington, D.C., with only minor skirmishes between the two forces. This delay gave Union commander George B. McClellan the opportunity to train a new Army of the Potomac. His intention in the spring of 1862 was to press on to Richmond, Virginia, and capture the Southern capital. In fact, in late June, before Johnson's painting was completed, now General Robert E. Lee would drive McClellan away from Richmond, back through Manassas, defeating him once more at Bull Run and moving forward to the outskirts of Washington.

Fig. 29.6 Eastman Johnson, *A Ride for Liberty: The Fugitive Slaves*. ca. 1862–63. Oil on board, 22″ × 26 $\frac{1}{4}$″. © Brooklyn Museum of Art, New York/The Bridgeman Art Library Nationality. Gift of Gwendolyn O. L. Conkling. The image of a family in flight inevitably evoked associations in viewers' minds with the flight of Mary, Joseph, and the baby Jesus into Egypt, though this is a family of four, not three. (Barely visible is a small child in the arms of its mother.) During the Civil War, over half a million slaves fled from the South, though 4 million remained.

Fig. 29.7 After Winslow Homer, *The Army of the Potomac—A Sharpshooter on Picket Duty*. 1862. Wood engraving on paper, 9 1/8″ × 13 13/16″. Gift of International Machines Corp. Location: Smithsonian American Art Museum, Washington, D.C. Art Resource, New York. This is the first of many wood engravings published in *Harper's Weekly* that were based on paintings that Homer would sometimes execute first, as is the case with Fig. 36.17 (on page 1194). More often, the engravings were done before the painting was completed, as in this instance, serving as advertisements for the paintings to come.

In Johnson's painting, smoke fills the darkening sky. Under the muzzle of the horse, reflections flash off the barrels of the rifles of the advancing Union army. The myth of happy slave families living on Southern plantations is nowhere to be seen as the father urges his horse on, desperate to save his wife and children from the battle. Their drive for liberty, Johnson seems to say, made possible by McClellan's advance, is what the war is all about.

The American Civil War changed the nature of warfare and in response the nature of representing war. It was an intensely modern event, mechanized and impersonal in a way that no previous war had been—with hand-to-hand battles, face-to-face, bayonet-on-bayonet, being the exception, not the rule. The traditional pageantry of war, "long lines advancing and maneuvering, led by generals in cocked hats and by bands of music," as one contemporary put it, were soon a thing of the past. When in the summer of 1861 the Union and Confederate armies clashed at Manassas, across the Potomac from Washington, D.C., ladies and gentlemen from the capital drove out to the battleground to picnic and observe the conflict in their carriages. They quickly realized their mistake as the Union army retreated in panic, forcing its way through the wagons and buggies of the terror-stricken civilians. Still, a deep desire to know what was happening at the

front consumed Americans. In response, a number of newspapers and journals began to send "special artists" to the battlegrounds to picture events. One of these was a 25-year-old illustrator for *Harper's Weekly*, Winslow Homer (1836–1910).

Winslow Homer's Magazine Illustrations Homer immediately understood that this new war presented unique challenges. The battlefields were large—too large to represent—and death arrived not from near at hand but from the distance, from some cannon or rifle beyond the range of normal vision. The wood engraving *The Army of the Potomac—A Sharpshooter on Picket Duty* depicts this reality, with snipers hidden in the branches atop pine trees and using a telescopic sight capable of hitting a target more than a mile away (Fig. **29.7**). Death came without warning: "Our loss of officers," a Union officer said in 1862, ". . . has been awfully disproportioned, and indeed entirely unprecedented; and it may be attributed wholly to the presence of sharpshooters, who, by the brilliant uniforms which our generals wore, were enabled to pick them off like so many partridges." "Brilliant uniforms," like so many other traditional accoutrements of war, soon were relics of the past.

Once, in April 1862, at Yorktown, Homer looked through the scope of a sharpshooter's rifle, and the image he saw, of an officer in the rifle's sights, "struck me as being as near murder as anything I could think of." This wood engraving, then, is for the artist an icon of murder and horror. It resonates with a particular irony through the near classical formality of Homer's setting: the sharpshooter in a visual square defined by the vertical trunk of the tree opposite his back and the horizontal line of his rifle and boot. The calm structure of the composition is a dramatic contrast with the terrible violence it describes.

Mathew Brady's Photographers It was the terror of war that increasingly impressed itself upon the American national consciousness. Given the mechanistic nature of modern warfare, this fear was, appropriately and accurately, captured by yet another machine—the camera. On September 19, 1862, Alexander Gardner, an employee of the photographer Mathew Brady (1823–1896), visited the battlefield at Antietam [an-TEET-um], Maryland. Twenty-six thousand Northern and Southern troops had just died in a battle that had no particular significance and decided nothing. Until that day, no American battlefield had ever been photographed before the dead were properly buried, but Gardner took many photographs of the scene. He even rearranged the bodies of the dead for photographic effect—in part a necessity created by the technical limitations of photographing on a smoky battlefield. Gardner's manipulation of scenes for the camera was understood as an attempt to record a more accurate sense of the whole. Brady displayed Gardner's photographs in his New York gallery on Broadway in October—and took full credit for them, to Gardner's dismay. Within a month, Brady was selling the pictures in both album-card size and stereoscopic views.

In July 1863, Gardner, now working on his own, went to the site of the Battle of Gettysburg with an assistant, Timothy O'Sullivan, who shot the most famous photograph to come out of the war, *A Harvest of Death, Gettysburg, Pennsylvania* (Fig. **29.8**). It was published after the war in 1866 in *Gardner's Photographic Sketchbook of the War*, probably the first book-length photo essay. It is a condemnation of the horrors of war, with the battle of Gettysburg at its center. O'Sullivan's matter-of-fact photograph is accompanied by the following caption:

> The rebels represented in the photograph are without shoes. These were always removed from the feet of the dead on account of the pressing need of the survivors. The pockets turned inside out also show that appropriation did not cease with the coverings of the feet. Around is scattered the litter of the battle-field, accoutrements, ammunitions, rags, cups and canteens, crackers, haversacks, and letters that may tell the name of the owner, although the majority will surely be buried unknown by strangers, and in a strange land.

In O'Sullivan's photograph, both foreground and background are purposefully blurred to draw attention to the central corpses. Such focus was made possible by the introduction of albumen paper, which retained a high degree of sharpness on its glossy surface. "Such a picture," Gardner wrote, "conveys a useful moral: It shows the blank horror and reality of war, in opposition to the pageantry. Here are the dreadful details! Let them aid in preventing such another calamity falling upon the nation." These sentiments were echoed in Abraham Lincoln's famous Gettysburg Address, one of the most powerful, and shortest, speeches ever made (see **Reading 29.3**, pages 988–989).

Reconstruction Because most of the war was fought in the South, the region was devastated physically, economically, and socially. So the next decade became known as the era of Reconstruction. The South also was home to nearly 4 million African Americans who suddenly found themselves free. The federal government es-

Fig. 29.8 Timothy O'Sullivan (negative) and Alexander Gardner (print), *A Harvest of Death, Gettysburg, Pennsylvania, July 1863,* **from Alexander Gardner's** *Gardner's Photographic Sketchbook of the War.* **1866.** Albumen silver print (also available as a stereocard), 6 $\frac{1}{4}$" $\times$ 7 $\frac{13}{16}$". Location: The New York Public Library, New York/Art Resource, New York. The battle of Gettysburg was the decisive land battle of the American Civil War. O'Sullivan's photograph is meant to show something of the human cost of a battle that left 51,000 casualties—dead, wounded, captured, or missing—in three days of fighting.

Fig. 29.9 Winslow Homer, *The Veteran in a New Field*. 1865. Oil on canvas, 24 $\frac{1}{8}$" × 38 $\frac{1}{8}$". The Metropolitan Museum of Art, New York. Bequest of Adelaide Milton de Groot (1876–1967), 1967 (67.187.131). Image copyright © The Metropolitan Museum of Art. In the "New Field" of Homer's title, the veteran leaves behind the "field of battle." Homer was thinking of the biblical passage from Isaiah 2:4: "they shall beat their swords into plowshares, and their spears into pruning hooks," a theme also informing Jean-Antoine Houdon's famous statue of George Washington (see Fig. 26.16).

tablished the Freedmen's Bureau to provide food, clothing, and medical care to refugees in the South, especially freed slaves. It also set up schools for African Americans, and teachers from the North and South worked to help young and old become literate. Additionally, Congress passed two amendments to the Constitution to give blacks equal rights with whites. The Fourteenth Amendment gave African Americans citizenship and struck down discriminatory state laws. Before they could be readmitted to the union, Southern states were ordered to ratify the amendment. Another amendment to the Constitution, the Fifteenth, gave African American men the right to vote. Meanwhile, to maintain order, Union troops remained in the South.

African-American emancipation, which advanced rapidly in the years immediately following the Civil War, would soon suffer setbacks, eliminating whatever gains had been made until the civil rights movement arose during the 1950s and 1960s. In 1877, Union troops withdrew from the South, and Southern whites who had never accepted African Americans as equals quickly restored their control of the region. Groups such as the Ku Klux Klan openly terrorized the African-American community, and lynching became commonplace. In 1883, the Supreme Court nullified the Civil Rights Act, and in 1896, the courts allowed segregation

in the railroads, and thus, by extension, in all public services. These new laws that destroyed the legality of the postwar constitutional amendments for freed blacks were called Jim Crow laws. By 1900, African Americans were once again almost totally disenfranchised from American life.

The postwar North, where hundreds of thousands of Union soldiers returned home, was a region of almost unfettered optimism. As Mark Twain and Charles Dudley Warner described it in *The Gilded Age*, their best-seller of 1873, "the air [was] full of money, nothing but money, money floating through the air." One of the first painted images of the Reconstruction era—Winslow Homer's *The Veteran in a New Field* (1865)—also points to the possibilities of a prosperous future (Fig. **29.9**). It depicts a Union soldier at work in his agricultural field and so recently returned home that his canteen and army uniform jacket are visible at the lower right. The painting glows with golden light, the promise of a harvest of plenty. But the veteran is also the grim reaper with his scythe, and his harvest is the same harvest of death that O'Sullivan and Gardner recorded at Gettysburg. It is as if the veteran is slashing, not so much at grain as at his memories, and the realities of Reconstruction would continue to haunt Homer in other paintings as well (see *Closer Look*, pages 972–973).

As a painting like *Veteran in a New Field* (see Fig. 29.9) makes clear, Winslow Homer's feelings about the end of the Civil War and the possibilities of Reconstruction were complicated. Sometime in early 1877, after the 1876 withdrawal of federal troops from the South officially ended Reconstruction, Homer left his studio in New York and traveled south to Virginia, making numerous sketches of African Americans that served as the basis for a series of paintings that he completed that same year. *A Visit from the Old Mistress* is one of these.

The composition is not new; it is a reworking of what, in 1877, was still his most famous painting, and the one that had established his reputation, the 1866 *Prisoners from the Front*. A Union officer—the Civil War hero, General Francis Channing Barlow—is depicted receiving three Confederate prisoners, probably after troops under his command had captured a division of Confederate soldiers and two generals at the battle of Spotsylvania in 1864. The painting is anything but neutral in its characterization of its figures. The critic for the *New York Evening News* described the figures in terms that almost all viewers immediately understood. "On one side," he wrote, "the hard, firm-faced New England man, without bluster, and with dignity of a life animated by principle, confronting the audacious, reckless, impudent young Virginian . . .; next to him the poor bewildered old man, . . . scarcely able to realize the new order of things about to sweep away the associations of his life; back of him the 'poor white,' stupid, stolid, helpless, yielding to the magnetism of superior natures and incapable of resisting authority."

Thus, by disposing his figures in *A Visit from the Old Mistress* in the same manner as in *Prisoners*, Homer is purposefully evoking something of the same cultural gulf that separates them. But where in the earlier painting they were all men, now they are all women. And where the tension before was between the victorious North and the defeated South, now it is between freed slaves and dispossessed mistress. And where the relationship between the two sides is quite clear in *Prisoners*, it is demonstrably problematic in *A Visit*. In her 2002 book *Winslow Homer: The Nature of Observation*, art historian Elizabeth Johns has pointed out that we don't know whether the old mistress was "a tyrant or a guardian . . . a firm disciplinarian or a sympathetic nurse." We don't know why she has decided to visit her former slaves. We don't know how they view her. We do know that Homer means two things by calling the visitor the "old" mistress—she is both an *aging* woman and the slaves' *former* owner. She represents, in other words, a past that is no longer relevant to the present. Or does she? Already, by 1877, when this picture was painted, the black population of the South was discovering itself subjugated to the same conditions of at least virtual slavery that had existed before their emancipation. Perhaps, in other words, the "old mistress" is announcing, even by her presence, a return to the "old ways." Perhaps she is attempting to assert the same authority over her former chattel that General Barlow asserted, in *Prisoners from the Front*, over the defeated Confederate Army. But if so, her authority possesses no moral footing. And the defiance we sense in the white-aproned central figure is the very opposite of the "audacious, reckless, impudent young Virginian" in *Prisoners*. Her defiance is wholly merited. It may be that she stands for the promise of a future—surely represented by her grandchild behind her—that the old mistress threatens to sweep away.

Winslow Homer, *Prisoners from the Front*. 1866. The Metropolitan Museum of Art, New York. Gift of Mrs. Frank B. Porter, 1922.

As many as four generations of the black family are included in the scene—the great-grandmother seated at the left, the mother meeting the old mistress in the center, her daughter and granddaughter behind her. The contrast between the close-knit family and the lone "old mistress" underscores the differences between them. It also, rather remarkably, underscores the centrality of women to the social stability of the family and American culture as a whole. As we will see in Chapter 32, Homer continuously explored the issue of woman's place in American society.

In order to heighten the tension of the scene, Homer has dressed the white woman in black and given the black woman, across the gulf that divides them, a white scarf and apron. In addition, and of course ironically, the black woman is dressed in red, white, and blue.

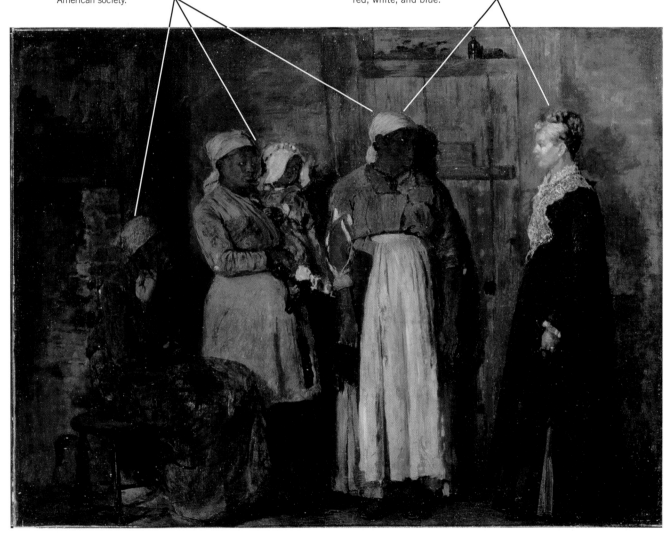

Winslow Homer, *A Visit from the Old Mistress.* **1876.** National Museum of American Art, Smithsonian Institution. Gift of William T. Evans, 1909.7.28.

Something to Think About. . .

Note that the central figure in *A Visit from the Old Mistress* stands in the same place as the Union guard in *Prisoners from the Front*. What does this suggest to you?

Fig. 29.10 Attributed to Tingqua, _Shop of Tingqua, the Painter_. ca. 1855. Watercolor on paper, $10\frac{1}{2}''$ × $13\frac{3}{4}''$.
Photograph courtesy Peabody Essex Museum. Note that Tingqua depicted his shop in Western perspective.

THE BRITISH IN CHINA AND INDIA

Westerners also posed dire threats to the two most popu-
lous and culturally influential Asian nations during the
course of the eighteenth and nineteenth centuries.
While not posing a threat to the actual existence of
China and India, Western nations sought to dominate
them through aggressive military and economic policies
aimed at transferring wealth to their own countries and
limiting their sovereignty. During the eighteenth century, both the English East India Company and the
French Compagnie des Indes [kohm-pahn-YEE dayz-
ahnd] (French East India Company) vied for control of
trade with India and the rest of Asia even as they engaged in ruthless competition in Europe and North
America. In fact, India's trade was seen as the stepping-
stone to even larger markets in China, whose silks,
porcelains, and teas were highly valued throughout
Europe and America. Rather than being mutually beneficial, however, trade with the West was a profound
threat to local, regional, and national leaders in both
China and India. Before the end of the nineteenth century, both countries would become outposts in new colonial empires developed by Europeans, resulting in the
weakening of traditional cultural practices, political
leadership, and social systems.

China and the Opium War

From the seventeenth century onward, the Chinese tolerated Western traders while also imposing strict controls on
the people they called _fanqui_ ("foreign devils"). By 1793, the
tide was beginning to shift in favor of the West, with proud
emperor Ch'ien-lung [chee-EN-loong] (r. 1735–1796) sending a defiant message to the English King George III
(r. 1760–1820) concerning this trade:

> Our Empire produces all that we ourselves need. But
> since our tea, rhubarb and silk seem to be necessary to
> the very existence of the barbarous Western peoples, we
> will, imitating the clemency of Heaven, Who tolerates
> all sorts of fools on this globe, condescend to allow a
> limited amount of trading through the port of Canton.

The Chinese policy of admitting foreign ships to Canton
[kant-ON] (modern Guangzhou [gwahng-JOE]) and con-
fining traders to a narrow strip of land where they lived and
did business in buildings or factories dated from the early
eighteenth century. Chinese entrepreneurs quickly set up
shops in the narrow lanes between the factories, selling

silks, teas, porcelains, lacquerware, screens, chessboards, carvings, boxes, and pictures to satisfy the European taste for chinoiserie (see Chapter 25). The shops of Lampqua and his younger brother Tingqua were famous for copying European engravings and for producing paintings of the daily life and ceremonies of the Chinese, along with scenes of Macao and Canton for export (Fig. **29.10**).

More important to the Westerners than these wares was the opium trade. In order to compensate for the gold and silver spent on the purchase of tea, porcelains, and silks, the British East India Company began selling to the Chinese large quantities of opium, which it grew in India. Produced at a very low cost, opium was a very profitable trade item for the British. Unfortunately for the Chinese, opium addiction rapidly became a severe social problem. In 1839, after the emperor's son died an opium-related death, the Chinese moved to ban the drug.

However, by this time, the British were increasingly impatient with the traditional trade restrictions in China as well as the new attempts to limit the opium trade. Since the English military and naval technologies were far superior to those of the Chinese, the nineteenth-century aphorism "Might makes right" can summarize the ensuing British course of action. The parallel with the antagonistic policies of the American government toward indigenous Americans during this period is clear.

A Chinese official, Commissioner Lin Zexu (1785–1850), even sought the help of Queen Victoria (r. 1837–1901) in a plea that invoked ethical and moral principles:

Let us ask, where is your conscience? I have heard that the smoking of opium is very strictly forbidden by your country; that is because the harm caused by opium is clearly understood. Since it is not permitted to do harm in your own country, then even less should you let it be passed on to the harm of other countries—how much less to China! Of all that China exports to foreign countries, there is not a single thing which is not beneficial to people. . . . Suppose there were people from another country who carried opium for sale to England and seduced your people into buying and smoking it; certainly you honorable ruler would deeply hate it and be bitterly aroused. . . . Now after this communication has been dispatched and you have clearly understood the strictness of the prohibitory laws of the Celestial Court, certainly you will not let your subjects dare again to violate the law.

Whether the Queen read the letter is unknown, but in fact, opium addiction was rampant in London during her reign. She certainly supported British merchants in their refusal to cooperate with the Chinese prohibition after Lin confiscated all the opium he could find and destroyed it in the spring and summer of 1839.

Curiously, the British acknowledged that Lin had the right to prohibit the Chinese from using opium, but they considered his ban on trading it an unlawful violation of the freedom of commerce. They declared war and subsequently crushed China, attacking most of its coastal and river towns (Fig. **29.11**). In the resulting Treaty of Nanjing [nan-JING],

Fig. 29.11 Edward Duncan, *The Iron Steam Ship HMS* Nemesis, *Commanded by Lieutenant W. H. Hall, with Boats from the* Sulphur, Calliope, Larne *and* Starling, *Destroying the Chinese War Junks in Anson's Bay, on 8 January 1841*. 1843. Color engraving.

China ceded Hong Kong to Britain and paid an indemnity of 21 million silver dollars (roughly equivalent to $2 billion today). Chinese ports and markets were opened to Western merchants, and by 1880, the import of cheap machine-made products resulted in the collapse of the Chinese economy. It would not recover for over a century.

Indentured Labor and Mass Migration

While the coffers of British government and merchants were enriched, the declining Chinese economy produced a number of unforeseen consequences, typical of the interactions between Westerners and indigenous peoples during this period. First, ever-worsening economic conditions drove many Chinese to emigrate in order to earn a living. Tens of thousands were attracted to California after gold was discovered there in 1849. Mostly single men, many worked for several years in the mines and then returned home. By 1852, 20,000 Chinese a year arrived in California, although that number declined in the ensuing decades. San Francisco, the port of entry to most Asian immigrants, soon boasted a growing "Chinatown," which offered further employment opportunities as immigrant entrepreneurs built new businesses. America's "melting pot" of cultures was continuing to grow.

The Chinese were also an important source of labor for the Central Pacific Railroad as it constructed railroad lines across the Western United States. By 1867, 90 percent of the workers on the railroad were Chinese. Hired for 30 percent less than the cost of hiring whites, they soon organized and struck for better wages. After the Burlingame Treaty of 1868, in which the United States and China established friendly relations, Chinese immigration to the United States increased to approximately 16,000 a year. By 1882, however, the threat to the American workforce posed by immigrant Chinese

labor in a time of economic downturn led to the passing of the Chinese Exclusion Act, which outlawed further immigration and denied citizenship to those already in the country.

The Chinese did not emigrate only to the United States (Map **29.3**), and they generally encountered much worse treatment elsewhere. They were technically indentured workers—laborers working under contract, generally for from 5 to 8 years, to pay off the price of their passage, usually for no pay, just food and accommodation. In 1873, the Chinese government conducted an investigation of Chinese emigration to Cuba. There it discovered horrific conditions as a Chinese plantation worker testified: "We labor 21 hours out of 24 and are beaten. . . . On one occasion I received 200 blows, and though my body was a mass of wounds I was still forced to continue labor. . . . A single day becomes a year. . . . And our families know not whether we are alive or dead."

East Indian indentured workers faced similarly harsh conditions. In the 1860s and 1870s, more than 50,000 Indians were shipped to French colonies in the Caribbean, where they were kept in "perpetual servitude." Just a century earlier, India had been one of the most productive economies in the world. In the 1760s, for instance, Britain imported most of its best cast steel from India, where hundreds of thousands were employed in mills and mines. But by the end of the eighteenth century, India lost its European markets for finished goods after the British East India Company bought Indian raw materials at exploitatively low prices and then undercut Indian manufacturers by selling finished textiles in India at low prices. Backed by the force of the British Army and increasingly efficient mechanized factories in Britain, English merchants profited handsomely at the expense of traditional economic production in

Map 29.3 The movement of indentured labor in the late nineteenth century.

Fig. 29.12 Sheikh Muhammad Amir, *A Horse and Groom.* 1830–50. Calcutta, India. Pencil and opaque watercolor with touches of white and gum arabic, 11″ × 17 ½″. Arthur M. Sackler Gallery. Smithsonian Institution, Washington, D.C. Purchase, S1999.121. Note the carefully realized rocks and grasses in the foreground and the way the trees occupy perspectival space.

India. So, instead of manufacturing cast steel, India found itself producing only iron ore; instead of manufacturing finished textiles, it exported raw cotton. In this economy, from which manufacturing had been almost completely eliminated, work became a scarce commodity. As its population increased in the second half of the nineteenth century, India experienced an unprecedented series of intensive famines, as well as widespread unemployment and poverty. As a result, over the course of the late nineteenth and early twentieth centuries, nearly 1.5 million Indians sold themselves into indentured servitude. Having produced 25 percent of the world's industrial output in 1750, India by 1900 contributed only 2 percent.

Company School Painting in India

In the early seventeenth century, the Mogul court in India had already expressed an interest in Western art, especially the degree of realism that could be accomplished through modeling and perspective (see Chapter 18). Yet most Indian artists considered European art an exotic oddity, and well into the nineteenth century, traditional modes of picture making almost completely dominated Indian artistic production. Gradually, as the British Westernized India, they commissioned and purchased Indian art, and the subcontinent's artists responded by incorporating Western techniques and pictorial traditions.

The British East India Company employed Indian artists as draftspersons, instructing them in European techniques, with others assigned to work as assistants to European artists. In art schools, Indians began to study and copy European prints. Thus encouraged and employed by the East India Company, they soon became known as the Company School.

The subjects favored by their European patrons tended to be images featuring Indian costumes and dress, and depictions of Indians at work—a weaver at his loom or a potter at his wheel. Europeans were also fascinated by the "curiosities" of Indian culture, particularly religious practices, which seemed exotically foreign. Indian artists also specialized in depicting the domestic lives of the British themselves. Among the greatest of the Company School painters was Sheikh Muhammad Amir of Karraya (a suburb of Calcutta [kal-CUT-tuh]). In depicting horses with their grooms, Sheikh Muhammad added newly adopted Western techniques—shading, texture, and accurately depicted anatomy—to the traditional subject matter (Fig. **29.12**). By the last decades of the century, the British were able to document their lives in India more effectively by means of photography, and so the Company School came to an end.

THE RISE AND FALL OF EGYPT

The occupation of Egypt in 1798 to 1799 by Napoleon's army, and the study of the country that it initiated, the 24-volume *Description de l'Égypte* published in Paris between 1809 and 1822 (see *Closer Look*, Chapter 28), inspired French officials to support Mehmet Ali [MEH-meht ah-lee] (1769–1849), whose family would rule Egypt until 1953, in the rapid industrialization of the country. An Ottoman Turk who had arrived in Egypt in 1801 in order to consolidate Ottoman authority, Ali soon established himself as the country's titular viceroy, ostensibly reporting to the Ottoman Empire but effectively ruling the country on his own. Ali desired nothing more than to put Egypt on an equal economic footing with Europe, and to that end he enlisted the services of European

Fig. 29.13 Edouard Riou, *A Turkish Paddle Steamer Going Up the Suez Canal*, 1869. Watercolor for a souvenir album to commemorate the *Voyage of Empress Eugenie* to the inauguration of the canal in 1869. Château de Compiègne, Compiègne, France.

experts, by and large French, to help him industrialize the country. Soon munitions factories (many of which had been opened by Napoleon's armies in 1798 to 1799), steelworks, shipyards, and, above all, cotton mills filled the Nile Delta.

Cotton soon became Egypt's chief cash crop. In 1817, Ali invited Louis Alexis Jumel (1785–1823) to Egypt to set up a spinning and weaving mill. Once there, Jumel discovered a cotton bush, being used only by a few local Cairo women, that produced remarkably long and exceptionally strong fibers. Ali ordered farmers, who had previously been growing wheat, to convert their fields to cotton, and he ordered 500 steam-operated looms from Britain. When, in 1823, Egypt began exporting the cotton, it attracted some of the highest prices in Europe, and by the mid-1830s, Egypt was producing 1,200,000 bolts of cotton a year. It was in gratitude to the French that Ali presented them with the obelisk from Luxor that still stands in the Place de la Concorde in Paris today (see Fig. 2.22).

But Britain, with a thriving cotton industry of its own (dependent on the export of raw cotton from the American South), chafed at Egyptian competition. In 1838, Ali informed both the French and British that he intended to declare Egypt's independence from the Ottoman Empire, and a year later, he invaded Turkey, believing that he would have assistance from the French. The French demurred, and Britain forced Egypt to abandon the protective tariffs on its cotton industry. Before long, Egypt, like India and the American South, no longer exported manufactured cotton products, but only the raw product. Egypt's attempt at modernization had failed.

But Ali's grandson, Khedive Ismail (heh-DEEV ihs-mah-EEL] (r. 1863–1879), would try again. "My country," he said in 1874, "is no longer in Africa; we are now part of Europe. It is therefore natural for us to abandon our former ways and to adopt a new system adapted to our social conditions." To that end, Ismail borrowed heavily from European banks, at sometimes extraordinary interest. He greatly expanded Cairo, building an entire new city on the old city's western edge modeled on Haussmann's Paris, with wide boulevards and modern hotels. To celebrate the opening of the Suez Canal (Fig. **29.13**), he hired Italian architects to build an opera house modeled after La Scala in Milan, and commissioned Giuseppe Verdi (discussed in Chapter 30) to write an opera, *Aida*, to be premiered at his new theater. French financing and French engineers were responsible for cutting the canal through from the Mediterranean to the Red Sea, and France owned a majority interest in the project. But the simple truth was that, owing to Ismail's extravagances (including an ill-fated attempt to conquer Ethiopia), Egypt was virtually bankrupt. In 1875, Britain purchased the Egyptian share in the canal, and in 1879, European debtors forced him to abdicate. A large portion of Egypt's revenue was assigned to pay off foreign debt, and Britain, responding to a minor rebellion in the Egyptian military, quickly stepped in to occupy the country. As Sir Alfred Milner, Egyptian Finance Minister from 1889 to 1892, later put it, with typical end-of-the-century imperialist bravado: "Let it always be remembered that Great Britain did save Egypt from anarchy, and all European nations interested in Egypt from incalculable losses in blood and treasure, to say nothing of the deep dishonour which those losses . . . would have brought on civilized mankind."

THE OPENING OF JAPAN

As India was rapidly changing under the British colonial regime in the mid-nineteenth century, Japan sought to accommodate Western industrialization while maintaining the most important aspects of its cultural traditions. Until the American Commodore Matthew Perry sailed into Tokyo Bay on July 8, 1853, the archipelago had been closed to the West for 250 years. Seeking to gain the Japanese government's assistance in opening trade as well as providing safe havens for stranded sailors, Perry demanded and received concessions. His expedition ultimately led to the Treaty of Kanagawa (1854) and the Harris Treaty (1858) between the United States and Japan, which opened diplomatic and trade relations between the two countries and brought large quantities of Japanese goods to the West for the first time. The Japanese realized that they had to accommodate Perry, the immediate threat, as well as cope with the longer-term challenge from Western nations. Their goal was to modernize along Western lines but maintain sovereignty as well as their ancient cultural traditions. Visitors arriving in Japan in the late nineteenth and early twentieth centuries had to follow carefully laid out itineraries if they wished to venture beyond the "treaty ports" of Yokohama [yoh-koh-HAH-mah], just south of Tokyo; Kobe [KOH-bee], just outside Osaka; and Nagasaki [nah-gah-SAH-kee]. The Japanese by this means tried to control the image of their country that visitors took home.

Industrialization: The Shifting Climate of Society

At first, Japan focused on closing the technology gap between its army and navy and Western military powers. Samuel Williams, the Perry expedition's interpreter, described the Japanese army as it appeared to him in July 1853: "Soldiers with muskets and drilling in close array," but also, "soldiers in petticoats, sandals, two swords, all in disorder." But pressure for change was growing, and by 1868, a historic shift occurred, as the Tokugawa Shogunate, which had held power since 1603, was replaced by a new coalition led by leaders of the Satsuma and Choshu provinces, who aimed to restore direct imperial rule. A new emperor, Meiji, had ascended the throne the year before, and the new government took his name, despite the fact that his role was largely symbolic. The new rulers, however, were determined to centralize power and decrease the influence of the previous shogun's clan, the *daimyo* (regional provincial leaders and warlords), and the samurai class, the military nobility that had little practical purpose in a modern society. In order to modernize their society, the new Meiji government had to industrialize, which they commenced without delay.

Exports of traditional Japanese products—raw silk (which accounted for more than a third of Japan's export trade), tea, cotton yarn, buttons (before 1853 unknown in Japan), and even woodblock prints—financed the

Fig. 29.14 *Shimbashi Station, Tokyo,* from *Famous Places on the Tokaido: A Record of the Process of Reform.* **1875.** The Tokyo–Yokohama railway, the first long-distance railway in the country, was built in 1872 with the aid of foreign engineers.

industrialization process. The state took an active role, developing the railway lines within several years of the replacement of the Tokugawa Shogunate in order to, first, expand and speed up food-distribution networks throughout the mountainous terrain of the country and, second, assist in centralizing political power. By 1872, the emperor presided over the opening of the first long-distance railway from Tokyo to Yokohama (Fig. **29.14**), and by 1900, the nation boasted 5,000 miles of track. Shipyards used to build warships in the 1850s and 1860s were converted to the production of iron and steel for other industries. Many of the large corporations that still dominate Japanese economic life, such as Mitsui and Mitsubishi, originated in this period as co-partners with the Japanese state.

Eiichi Shibusawa (1840–1931) was the father of Japanese capitalism. Founder of the National Bank of Japan and in charge of national industrialization until 1873, he admitted that he first believed that only the military and political classes could lead the nation. Traditionally, merchants had always been at the bottom of the Japanese social hierarchy, but Shibusawa changed

Fig. 29.15 Suzuki Harunobu, *Two Courtesans, Inside and Outside the Display Window*. Edo period, ca. 1768–69. Woodblock print (*nishiki-e*), ink and color on paper, 26 $^3/_8$" × 5 $^1/_{16}$". Museum of Fine Arts, Boston. Denman Waldo Ross Collection, 1906.06.1248. One of the subtler features of this print is the display of the courtesan's foot as she stands in her *geta* (wooden clogs). The foot and toes were considered highly erotic.

his mind when he visited the 1867 World Exposition in Paris as a member of the Japanese delegation. "Then," Shibusawa wrote, "I realized that the real force of progress lay in business." Born to a poor farming family, Shibusawa rose to enormous political and economic power, and embodied the shifting climate of Japanese society.

Japanese Printmaking

By the late nineteenth century, the Japanese economy was booming, as was the art of woodblock printing, a tradition that had developed steadily in Japan since the beginning of the Tokugawa era (1603–1868). The export trade in prints was a vital part of the economy, and Western artists, particularly the Impressionists, were captivated by the effects Japanese printmakers were able to achieve. Very popular among the urban classes in Edo (Tokyo) since the 1670s, woodblock printing had gained new potential a century later when a Chinese painting manual, *The Mustard Seed Garden*, accelerated the shift to polychrome printing, which produced multicolored woodblock prints. The resulting images, known as **nishiki-e** [nee-shee-kee-ay] or "brocade pictures"—so named because they were felt to resemble brocade fabrics—were, at first, commissioned by a group of wealthy Japanese who, among various other intellectual pursuits, routinely exchanged elaborately decorated calendars on each New Year's Day. Since the government held a monopoly on the printing of all calendars, the artists making these *nishiki-e* calendars went to elaborate lengths to disguise their efforts, and the symbols for the months were introduced into the compositions in the most subtle ways.

The first and most prominent of the artists to produce *nishiki-e* calendars was Suzuki Harunobu [har-OON-oh-boo] (1724–1770). So admired were his designs that by 1766 they were widely distributed commercially—minus, of course, their calendar symbols. Before his death in 1770, Harunobu produced hundreds of *nishiki-e* prints, many of them dedicated to illustrating the most elegant aspects of eighteenth-century Japanese life, and his prints were, if not the first, then certainly the most influential early examples of what would soon become known as **ukiyo-e** [oo-kee-oh-ay], "pictures of the transient world of everyday life." He was especially renowned for his ability to portray women of great beauty, and some of his favorite subjects were the beautiful courtesans in the Yoshiwara pleasure district of Edo (modern Tokyo), of which *Two Courtesans, Inside and Outside the Display Window* (Fig. **29.15**) is a striking example. The display window, or *harimise*, is the lattice-windowed area in the front of a brothel where the potential client might choose the courtesan of his pleasure. This print is remarkable for both its graphic simplicity and its subtle evocation of traditional Japanese culture and values. Instead of showing the entirety of the window, Harunobu depicts just one section, creating a powerfully realized grid structure into which he has placed his figures. In other words, the delicate, rounded lines of the courtesans' features and clothing contrast dramatically with the broad two-dimensional structure of the *harimise*. This graphic contrast, equally realized in the contrast between the inside and outside of the *harimise*, as well as the fact that one courtesan stands while the other sits, reflects the philosophy embodied in the traditional Japanese principle of complementarity, which itself originates in Chinese Taoist philosophy. Representing unity within diversity, opposites organized in perfect harmony, the ancient symbol for this principle is the famous *yin* and *yang* (see Fig. 7.5). In the play of opposites that dominates the composition—especially the assertively masculine structure of the *harimise* versus the passively soft lines of the women—Harunobu's print is thus not merely a depiction of everyday life in the Yoshiwara pleasure district, but a subtle philosophical defense of the era's sexual mores.

But Harunobu did not limit his production to depictions of daily life. Another of his most favorite subjects was the life of the most beautiful poet of the Heian court, Ono no Komachi [oh-noh noh koh-MAH-chee] (ca. 833–857). By the eighteenth century, the Heian period (785–1185) was considered the classical age of Japanese culture, a period of extraordinary refinement and style (see Chapter 11). In the famous scene from Komachi's life represented here (Fig. **29.16**), she has promised a would-be lover that if he could visit her house for one hundred consecutive nights without looking upon her, she would grant him a rendezvous. She stands on the veranda, looking down upon a servant who counts the days on her fingers. After ninety-nine successful nights spent on the mounting block of Komachi's carriage, he has, in fact, failed to appear due to the untimely death of his father, and the box above the servant's head is Komachi's poem to the absent lover:

> In the early dawn
> You marked up a hundred nights
> On the mounting block—
> But the night you failed to come
> It was I who counted that

The poem surrounds a small picture of a man shielding himself under an umbrella, a traditional symbol of male sexuality, as if shielding himself also from his desire. Note how Harunobu sets the two women in an architecture that, rising as it does straight up from the servant's head to the image above, implies the presence of the male principle in the scene very much in the manner of the window frame in Fig. 29.15.

Woodblock prints were mass-produced and thus affordable to artisans, merchants, and other city dwellers. They depicted a wide range of Japanese social and cultural activity, including the daily rituals of life, the theatrical world of actors and geisha, sumo wrestlers, and artisans along with landscapes and nature scenes. Incorporating

Fig. 29.16 Suzuki Harunobu, *Visiting (Kayoi)*, from the series *Seven Komachi in Fashionable Disguise*. Edo period, ca. 1766–67. Woodblock print (*nishiki-e*), ink and color on paper, 12 1/16″ × 5 5/16″. Museum of Fine Arts, Boston. William Sturgis Bigelow Collection, 1911. 11.16497. Komachi holds a long tobacco pipe in her hand. Pipe smoking entered Japan in 1600, introduced by an Englishman named William Adams, and it quickly became standard courtesan paraphernalia.

traditional themes from literature and history, such as the life of Ono no Komachi, the prints were also notable for introducing contemporary tastes, fads, and fashions, thus forming an invaluable source of knowledge on the Japanese culture over the more than two centuries of its development.

Traditionally, the creation of a Japanese print was a team effort, and the publisher, the designer, the woodblock carver, and the printer were all considered equal in the process. The publisher conceived of the ideas for the prints, financing individual works or series of works that the public would, in his estimation, be likely to buy. Another of the leading artists of the era, Kitagawa Utamaro [oo-tah-MAH-roh] (1753–1808), illustrated the process of developing a colored woodblock print in a triptych entitled *Utamaro's Studio* (Fig. **29.17**). The print is a *mitate*, or fanciful picture. Each of the workers in the studio is a pretty girl—hence, the print's status as a *mitate*—and they are engaged, according to the caption on the print, in "making the famous Edo color prints." Utamaro depicts himself at the right, dressed in women's clothing and holding a finished print. His publisher, also dressed as a woman, looks on from behind his desk.

The process begins, at the left, with the workers preparing paper. They are *sizing* it—that is, brushing the surface with an astringent crystalline substance called *alum* that reduces the absorbency of the paper so that ink will not run along its fibers—then hanging the sized prints to dry. The paper was traditionally made from the inside of the bark of the mulberry tree mixed with bamboo fiber, and, after sizing, it was kept damp for six hours before printing.

In the middle section of the print, the block is actually prepared. In the foreground, a worker sharpens her chisel on a stone. Behind her is a stack of blocks with brush drawings by Utamaro stuck face-down on them with a solution of rice starch dissolved in water. The woman seated at the desk in the middle rubs the back of the drawing to remove several layers of fiber. She then saturates what remains with oil until it becomes transparent. At this point, the original drawing looks as if it were drawn on the block.

Next, in the middle section, workers carve the block, and we see large white areas being chiseled out of the block by the woman seated in the back. Black-and-white prints of this design are made and then returned to the artist, who indicates the colors for the prints, one color to a sheet. The cutter then carves each sheet on a separate block. The final print is, in essence, an accumulation of the individually colored blocks, each color requiring a separate printing.

Utamaro's depiction of *The Fickle Type*, from his series *Ten Physiognomies of Women*, embodies the sensuality of the urban world that *ukiyo-e* prints often reveal (Fig. **29.18**). But probably the most famous series of Japanese prints is *Thirty-Six Views of Mount Fuji* by Katsushika Hokusai

Fig. 29.17 Kitigawa Utamaro (Japanese, 1754–1806), *How the Famous Brocade Prints of Edo are Produced* **(Edo Meibutsu Nishiki-e Kosaku) ca. 1790.** Ink and color on paper, 38.3 × 74.3 cm. Clarence Buckingham Collection. 1939.2141. © The Art Institute of Chicago. All rights reserved. Each of the workers is pictured as a pretty girl—which gives the print its status as a *mitate*, or "fanciful picture"—workers in print shops were not normally pretty young women. To further the fancifulness of the image, Utamaro depicts himself at the right, holding a finished print and dressed in women's clothing. His publisher, also dressed as a woman, looks on from behind his desk.

Fig. 29.18 Kitigawa Utamaro, *The Fickle Type*, from the series *Ten Physiognomies of Women*. ca. 1793. Color woodblock print with mica, 14$^{13}/_{16}$" × 9$^3/_4$". Miriam and Ira D. Wallach Division. The New York Public Library/Art Resource, New York. Utamaro captures the woman's fickleness by having her glance over her shoulder as she returns from the bath, evidently hoping to catch the interested eye of her suitor.

[HO-koo-sigh] (1760–1849). The print in that series known as *The Great Wave* has achieved almost iconic status in the art world (Fig. **29.19**). It depicts two boats descending into a trough beneath a giant crashing wave that hangs over the scene like a menacing claw. In the distance, above the horizon, rises Mount Fuji [FOO-jee], symbol to the Japanese of immortality and of Japan itself, framed in a vortex of wave and foam. Though the wave is visually larger than the distant mountain, the viewer knows it will imminently collapse and that Fuji will remain, illustrating both the transience of human experience and the permanence of the natural world. The print also juxtaposes the perils of the moment, as represented by the dilemma of the boatmen, and the enduring values of the nation, represented by the solidity of the mountain. Those values can be understood to transcend the momentary troubles and fleeting pleasures of daily life.

Fig. 29.19 Katsushika Hokusai, *The Great Wave*, from the series *Thirty-Six Views of Mount Fuji*. ca. 1823–39. Color woodblock print, 10$^1/_8$" × 14$^1/_4$". © Historical Picture Archive/CORBIS. The boatsmen can be understood as working in harmony with the powers of nature, something like samurai of the sea.

SEE MORE For a Closer Look at Katsushika Hokusai's *The Great Wave*, go to **www.myartslab.com**

In 1867, the Japanese Pavilion at the Exposition Universelle in Paris highlighted the *ukiyo-e* along with other cultural artifacts, attracting much attention from the Western public and inaugurating the style known as **Japonisme**, the imitation of Japanese art. The Impressionists, who are discussed in Chapter 31, were fascinated by the multilayered complexity of the *ukiyo-e*, which nevertheless remained commercial products rather than the artistic masterpieces that we consider them today. Claude Monet, it was said, spotted the prints being used as wrapping material in a shop in Amsterdam in 1871 and walked out with the first of a collection that eventually numbered over 200. But the artist most enthusiastic about Japanese prints was probably Vincent van Gogh. He owned prints by the hundreds, and on numerous occasions he copied them directly. *Japonaiserie: The Courtesan (after Kesai Eisen)* (Fig. 29.20) is an example (van Gogh has misspelled Eisen's first name). The central figure in the painting is copied from a print by

Keisai Eisen (1790–1848) that van Gogh saw on the cover of a special Japanese issue of *Paris Illustré* published in May 1886 (Fig. 29.21). All the other elements of the painting are derived from other Japanese prints, except perhaps the boat at the very top, which appears Western in conception. The frogs were copied from Yoshimaro's *New Book of Insects*, and both the cranes and the bamboo stalks are derived from prints by Hokusai. Van Gogh's intentions in combining all these elements become clear when we recognize that the central figure is a courtesan (her tortoiseshell hair ornaments signify her profession), and that the words *grue* (crane) and *grenouille* (frog) were common Parisian slang for prostitutes. Van Gogh explained his interest in Japanese prints in a letter written in September 1888: "Whatever one says," he wrote, "I admire the most popular Japanese prints, colored in flat areas, and for the same reasons that I admire Rubens and Veronese. I am absolutely certain that this is no primitive art."

Fig. 29.20 (left) Vincent van Gogh, *Japonaiserie: The Courtesan (after Kesai Eisen)*. 1887. Oil on canvas, 41 3/8 × 24 in. (105.5 × 60.5 cm.). Van Gogh Museum, Amsterdam (Vincent van Gogh Foundation); **Fig. 29.21 (above) "Le Japon," cover of *Paris Illustré*. May 1886.** Van Gogh Museum, Amsterdam (Vincent van Gogh Foundation). The color of Gogh's painting is much bolder than the original, suggesting that he was using the "flat areas" that he so admired in Japanese prints as a way to study the interaction of colors (see Chapter 31).

Painting Modern Life

In July 1864, the French painter Édouard Manet [mah-NAY] traveled from Paris to Boulogne-sur-Mer [boo-LOHN ser mair] on the English Channel expressly to paint the U.S.S. *Kearsarge* [KEER-sarj], a small warship ideal for coastal defense. The *Kearsarge* had sunk the Confederate sloop-of-war *Alabama* off Cherbourg [shair-BOOR], on the Norman coast, on June 19. The *Alabama* had been fitted with supplies and repaired at Cherbourg after nearly two years of roving the seas, from Brazil to Singapore. During that time, it had sunk 65 Union merchant ships. The *Kearsarge* patiently waited for the *Alabama* to leave French waters, and then attacked, sinking it.

Manet relied on newspaper accounts to paint *The Battle of the "Kearsarge" and the "Alabama"* (Fig. 29.22), exhibiting it only 26 days after the battle. Soon after, he traveled to Boulogne-sur-Mer to see the victorious ship in person.

Manet was, above all, the painter of a new, self-consciously modern bourgeois France. Under Napoleon III, the emperor who had come to power after the revolution of 1848, France, and England too, openly sympathized with the Confederacy. Both the French and English textile industries depended on Southern cotton, and the Union blockade of the Confederate ports had crippled them. Manet felt differently. He did not believe in placing economic self-interest above the cause of human equality and freedom. *The Battle of the "Kearsarge" and the "Alabama"* is, thus, a deeply political statement. Manet's painting challenges the complicity of the French government and the bourgeois culture supporting it with the Southern cause.

The painting, finally, epitomizes the dawning modern age, an age of revolution and civil war when tensions surrounding questions of freedom and equality, self-determination and national identity, erupted in violence. As revolution threatened, the bourgeoisie tightened its control of European society, and the attitudes and tastes of modern bourgeoisie culture are the constant targets of Manet's art. ■

Fig. 29.22 Édouard Manet, *The Battle of the "Kearsarge" and the "Alabama."* 1864. Oil on canvas, 54$\frac{1}{4}$" × 50$\frac{3}{4}$". John G. Johnson Collection, 1917. Philadelphia Museum of Art, Philadelphia, Pennsylvania. Art Resource, New York.

What events did Karl Marx and Friedrich Engels foresee in their Communist Manifesto*?*

By the middle of the nineteenth century, living conditions in Paris and across Europe had deteriorated to an intolerable point. In 1848, in Paris, workers revolted with their battle cry "the right to work," and across Europe other revolutions quickly followed. Karl Marx and Friedrich Engels had anticipated these uprisings in the *Communist Manifesto*. What did they see as the solution to the problems facing the working class? In Paris, the bourgeois middle class was convinced that it had barely survived the complete collapse of the social order, and so it elected the nephew of Napoleon I, Charles-Louis-Napoleon Bonaparte, president and subsequently proclaimed him Emperor Napoleon III. Napoleon hired the Baron Georges-Eugène Haussmann to modernize the city of Paris. What is Haussmannization, and what factors other than the urge to modernize motivated it? One of the most important factors contributing to revolutions elsewhere in Europe was nationalism. What is nationalism?

How did the American Civil War affect popular attitudes toward warfare?

From Europe, the American Civil War appeared to be a contest between liberal Northern values and nationalist Southerners. Until the outbreak of hostilities, compromise seemed possible, especially in light of the mythologized and romanticized view of slavery of antebellum America. How did Stephen Foster and Eastman Johnson romanticize slavery?

The outbreak of the Civil War in 1861 quickly extinguished such an outlook. The war was an intensely modern event, mechanized and impersonal as no other war had been, and the nature of representation changed with it. Artists like Eastman Johnson and Winslow Homer followed troops into the field, as did photographers, who documented what Americans had never before witnessed—the battlefield before the dead had been properly buried. How did Abraham Lincoln's Gettysburg Address reflect these images? After the war, nearly 4 million African Americans in the South suddenly found themselves free as the federal government inaugurated a process of reconstruction, reforms that by 1900 were almost completely abandoned until the late1950s and 1960s. How did Winslow Homer react to reconstruction and its aftermath?

What is imperialism?

With their scientific and technological advances providing a decided edge in military and economic competition, Western nations sought to dominate the resources and economies of Asia and Africa in order to transfer wealth to their own countries. Britain proved the most successful at this through the policy of imperialism, which included using aggressive military and economic policies to take control either directly or indirectly of non-Western nations. Colonists played a major role by establishing plantations, other economic enterprises, and colonial governments in order to transfer effective sovereignty to Britain and other colonial powers, such as France, Germany, and Belgium. What role did opium play in British relations with China? How was India's economy damaged by British policies?

How did imperialism affect Egypt?

After Mehmet Ali established himself as viceroy of Egypt, he attempted to put the country on an equal footing with Europe. What role did cotton play in his efforts? Why did Ali's attempts to modernize Egypt fail? How did his grandson, Khedive Ismail, fare in his own attempts at modernization?

What is Japonisme?

Japan was one of the few Asian nations never colonized by the West. After the forced "opening" of Japan by American Commodore Matthew Perry in 1853, Japan embarked on new trade and diplomatic relationships with Europe and the United States, while also beginning a rapid effort to modernize its own economy and government. After 1868, Japanese industrialization quickened, and a flood of Japanese products reached the West for the first time.

Among the most distinctive of those exports were woodblock prints. What are *nishiki-e* prints? How did they contribute to the *ukiyo-e* tradition of printmaking? How did they both contribute to the fascination for things Japanese, known as *Japonisme*, in the West?

PRACTICE MORE Get flashcards for images and terms and review chapter material with quizzes at **www.myartslab.com**

GLOSSARY

Haussmannization The term used to describe Baron Haussmann's approach to urban redevelopment, including the mass destruction of working-class neighborhoods.

Japonisme The imitation of Japanese art.

minstrel show A theatrical event presenting a program of black American melodies, jokes, and impersonations, usually performed by white performers in blackface.

nishiki-e "Brocade pictures"—so named because they were felt to resemble brocade fabrics.

plantation melody A type of song written in dialect, the lyrics of which depicted blacks as capable of a full range of human emotion.

ukiyo-e Japanese woodblock prints ("pictures of the transient world of everyday life") often referred to as "pictures of the floating world."

READINGS

Karl Marx and Friedrich Engels, *The Communist Manifesto*, Part I, from "Bourgeois and Proletarians" (1848; English edition 1888; trans. Samuel Morse)

Marx and Engels began their collaboration in 1844 in Paris. In 1847, they were invited by a leftist group in London to write their program for them, which they did during December 1847 and January 1848. The group changed its name to the Communist League and adopted Marx and Engels's 12,000-word program as their manifesto. The following is the first part, which describes the tensions between the proletariat (working class) and the modern bourgeoisie.

The history of all hitherto existing society is the history of class struggles.

Freeman and slave, patrician and plebeian, lord and serf, guild-master and journeyman, in a word, oppressor and oppressed, stood in constant opposition to one another, carried on uninterrupted, now hidden, now open fight, a fight that each time ended, either in a revolutionary reconstitution of society at large, or in the common ruin of the contending classes.

In the earlier epochs of history we find almost everywhere a complicated arrangement of society into various orders, a manifold gradation of social rank. In ancient Rome we have patricians, knights, plebeians, slaves; in the Middle Ages, feudal lords, vassals, guild-masters, journeymen, apprentices, serfs; in almost all of these classes, again, subordinate gradations.

The modern bourgeois society that has sprouted from the ruins of feudal society has not done away with class antagonisms. It has but established new classes, new conditions of oppression, new forms of struggle in place of the old ones.

Our epoch, the epoch of the bourgeoisie, possesses, however, this distinctive feature; it has simplified the class antagonisms. Society as a whole is more and more splitting up into two great hostile camps, into two great classes directly facing each other: Bourgeoisie and Proletariat.

From the serfs of the Middle Ages sprang the chartered burghers of the earliest towns. From these burgesses the first elements of the bourgeoisie were developed.

The discovery of America, the rounding of the Cape, opened up fresh ground for the rising bourgeoisie. The East Indian and Chinese markets, the colonization of America, trade with the colonies, the increase in the means of exchange and in commodities generally, gave to commerce, to navigation, to industry, an impulse never before known, and thereby, to the revolutionary element in the tottering feudal society, a rapid development.

The feudal system of industry, under which industrial production was monopolized by close guilds, now no longer sufficed for the growing wants of the new market. The manufacturing system took its place. The guild-masters were pushed on one side by the manufacturing middle class; division of labor between the different corporate guilds vanished in the face of division of labor in each single workshop.

Meantime the markets kept ever growing, the demand ever rising. Even manufacture no longer sufficed. Thereupon, steam and machinery revolutionized industrial production. The place of manufacture was taken by the giant Modern Industry, the place of the industrial middle-class, by industrial millionaires, the leaders of whole industrial armies, the modern bourgeois.

Modern industry has established the world-market, for which the discovery of America paved the way. This market has given an immense development to commerce, to navigation, to communication by land. This development has, in its turn, reacted on the extension of industry; and in proportion as industry, commerce, navigation, railways extended, in the same proportion the bourgeoisie developed, increased its capital, and pushed into the background every class handed down from the Middle Ages.

We see, therefore, how the modern bourgeoisie is itself the product of a long course of development, of a series of revolutions in the modes of production and of exchange.

Each step in the development of the bourgeoisie was accompanied by a corresponding political advance of that class. An oppressed class under the sway of the feudal nobility; an armed and self-governing association in the medieval commune, (here independent urban republic, as in Italy and Germany, there taxable "third estate" of the monarchy, as in France); afterwards, in the period of manufacture proper, serving either the semi-feudal or the absolute monarchy as a counterpoise against the nobility, and in fact cornerstone of the great monarchies in general—the bourgeoisie has at last, since the establishment of modern industry and of the world-market, conquered for itself, in the modern representative state, exclusive political sway. The executive of the modern state is but a committee for managing the common affairs of the whole bourgeoisie.

The bourgeoisie, historically, has played a most revolutionary part.

The bourgeoisie, wherever it has got the upper hand, has put an end to all feudal, patriarchal, idyllic relations. It has pitilessly torn asunder the motley feudal ties that bound man to his "natural superiors," and has left no other nexus between man and man than naked self-interest, than callous "cash payment." It has drowned the most heavenly ecstasies of religious fervor, of chivalrous enthusiasms, of philistine sentimentalism, in the icy water of egotistical calculation. It has resolved personal worth into exchange value, and in place of the numberless indefeasible chartered freedoms, has set up that single, unconscionable freedom—Free Trade. In one word, for exploitation, veiled by religious and political illusions, it has substituted naked, shameless, direct, brutal exploitation.

The bourgeoisie has stripped of its halo every occupation hitherto honored and looked up to with reverent awe. It has converted the physician, the lawyer, the priest, the poet, the man of science, into its paid wage laborers.

The bourgeoisie has torn away from the family its sentimental veil, and has reduced the family relation to a mere money relation. . . .

The need of a constantly expanding market for its products drives the bourgeoisie over the whole surface of the globe. It must elbow-in everywhere, settle everywhere, establish connections everywhere.

The bourgeoisie has through its exploitation of the world-market given a cosmopolitan character to production and consumption in every country. To the great chagrin of reactionists, it has drawn from under the feet of industry the national ground on which it stood. All old-established national industries have been destroyed or are daily being destroyed. They are dislodged by new industries, whose introduction becomes a life and death question for all civilized nations, by industries that no longer work up indigenous raw material, but raw material drawn from the remotest zones; industries whose products are consumed, not only at home, but in every quarter of the globe. In place of the old wants, satisfied by the productions of the country, we find new wants, requiring for their satisfaction the products of distant lands and climes. In place of the old local and national seclusion and self-sufficiency, we have intercourse in every direction, universal interdependence of nations. And as in material, so also in intellectual production. The intellectual creations of individual nations become common property. National onesidedness and narrowmindedness become more and more impossible, and from the numerous national and local literatures there arises a world-literature. . . .

In proportion as the bourgeoisie,—that is, as capital, is developed, in the same proportion is the proletariat, the modern working class, developed, a class of laborers who live only so long as they find work, and who find work only so long as their labor increases capital. These laborers, who must sell themselves piece-meal, are a commodity, like every other article of commerce, and are consequently exposed to all the vicissitudes of competition, to all the fluctuations of the market . . . .

The various interests and conditions of life within the ranks of the proletariat are more and more equalized, in proportion as machinery obliterates all distinctions of labor, and nearly everywhere reduces wages to the same low level. The growing competition among the bourgeois, and the resulting commercial crises, make the wages of the workers ever more fluctuating; the unceasing improvement of machinery, ever more rapidly developing, makes their livelihood more and more precarious; the collisions between individual workmen and individual bourgeois take more and more the character of collisions between two classes. Thereupon the workers begin to form combinations (trade unions) against the bourgeois; they club together in order to keep up the rate of wages; they found permanent associations in order to make provision beforehand for these occasional revolts. Here and there the contest breaks out into riots.

Now and then the workers are victorious, but only for a time. The real fruit of their battle lies not in the immediate result, but in the ever expanding union of workers. . . .

The first step in the revolution by the working class is to raise the proletariat to the position of ruling class, to win the battle of democracy.

The proletariat will use its political supremacy to wrest, by degrees, all capital from the bourgeoisie, to centralize all instruments of production in the hands of the state,—that is, of the proletariat organized as a ruling class; and to increase the total productive forces as rapidly as possible. . . .

When, in the course of development, class distinctions have disappeared, and all production has been concentrated in the hands of a vast association of the whole nation, the public power will lose its political character. Political power, properly so called, is merely the organization power of one class for oppressing another. If the proletariat during its contest with the bourgeoisie is compelled, by the force of circumstances, to organize itself as a class, if, by means of a revolution, it makes itself the ruling class, and, as such, sweeps away by force the old conditions of production, then it will, along with these conditions, have swept away the conditions for the existence of class antagonisms, and of classes generally, and will thereby have abolished its own supremacy as a class.

In place of the old bourgeois society, with its classes and class antagonisms, we shall have an association in which the free development of each is the condition for the free development of all.

READING CRITICALLY

What leads Marx and Engels to believe that the conflict between the bourgeoisie and the proletariat will have a different result from history's previous class conflicts?

READING 29.3

from Abraham Lincoln, Address Delivered at the Dedication of the Cemetery at Gettysburg (1863)

Abraham Lincoln became president of the United States on March 4, 1861, just over a month before fighting between the Union and the Confederacy commenced, on April 12, 1861, when Confederate troops attacked the federal military installation at Fort Sumter, South Carolina. Lincoln exercised executive authority in a manner unprecedented in American history, an authority achieved, in no small part, by the persuasiveness of his rhetoric. At once lofty and colloquial, eloquent and down-to-earth, his speeches, which appeared within days of their delivery in almost every newspaper in the North, served to unite Northerners in their fight against the South. The Gettysburg Address was delivered on November 19, 1863, at the site of the decisive Battle of Gettysburg in which the Union's 90,000 men defeated 70,000 Southern troops in a three-day battle that ended in General Robert E. Lee's retreat to Virginia on July 3, 1863. The Union dead totaled 3,155, the Confederate dead 4,708. With combined wounded and missing soldiers standing at 46,000, Lincoln delivered his address at the Union Cemetery.

Four score and seven years ago our fathers brought forth on this continent, a new nation, conceived in Liberty, and dedicated to the proposition that all men are created equal.

Now we are engaged in a great civil war, testing whether that nation, or any nation so conceived and so dedicated, can long endure. We are met on a great battle-field of that war. We have come to dedicate a portion of that field, as a final resting place for those who here gave their lives that that nation might live. It is altogether fitting and proper that we should do this.

But, in a larger sense, we can not dedicate—we can not consecrate—we can not hallow—this ground. The brave men, living and dead, who struggled here, have consecrated it, far above our poor power to add or detract. The world will little note, nor long remember what we say here, but it can never forget what they did here. It is for us the living, rather, to be dedicated here to the unfinished work which they who fought here have thus far so nobly advanced. It is rather for us to be here dedicated to the great task remaining before us—that from these honored dead we take increased devotion to that cause 20 for which they gave the last full measure of devotion—that we here highly resolve that these dead shall not have died in vain—that this nation, under God, shall have a new birth of freedom—and that government of the people, by the people, for the people, shall not perish from the earth.

READING CRITICALLY

Part of the power of this speech rests in its brevity. How does that serve to make it more forceful?

30 In Pursuit of Modernity

Paris in the 1850s and 1860s

THINKING AHEAD

Who was George Sand?

How did poet Charles Baudelaire initiate modernism?

What made painter Édouard Manet so notorious?

How would you define Émile Zola's naturalism?

What new directions in opera developed in the mid-nineteenth century?

Soon after the fighting had stopped in the streets of Paris in 1848, Pierre-Joseph Proudhon [proo-DOHN] (1809–1865), the French journalist who was the first to call himself an "anarchist" and famously coined the phrase "property is theft," wrote: "We have been beaten and humiliated . . . scattered, imprisoned, disarmed, and gagged. The fate of European democracy has slipped from our hands." Political and moral idealism seemed vanquished. In their place remained only the banal prosperity of the triumphant bourgeoisie. In fact, the political, moral, and religious emptiness of the bourgeoisie became the targets of a new realism, which critiqued what Proudhon called the "fleshy, comfortable" bourgeois lifestyle.

The physical embodiment of this new lifestyle were Haussmann's *grands boulevards* [grahn bool-uh-VAHR], along whose broad sidewalks the bourgeoisie promenaded (Map 30.1). Of all the boulevards, the broad avenue de l'Opéra connecting the Louvre to Charles Garnier's new Paris Opéra (see Fig. 30.9), was Haussmann's favorite.

The project was not completed until 1877, but the vista Haussmann created was of stunning scale, inspiring many artists, such as Camille Pissarro [pee-SAH-roo], to paint it (Fig. 30.1). The greatest wealth of the city was concentrated along such promenades, and so was the city's best shopping. In a memoir of his visit to the Paris Exposition of 1867, Edward King, an American, described how those seeking the trappings of bourgeois life were drawn to these new public venues:

> The boulevards are now par excellence the social centre of Paris. Here the aristocrat comes to lounge, and the stranger to gaze. Here trade intrudes only to gratify the luxurious. . . . On the grands boulevards you find porcelains, perfumery, bronzes, carpets, furs, mirrors, the furnishings of travel, the copy of Gérome's latest picture, the last daring caricature in the most popular journal, the most aristocratic beer, and the best flavored coffee.

◀ **Fig. 30.1 Camille Pissarro, *Avenue de l'Opéra, Sunlight, Winter Morning.* ca. 1880.** Oil on canvas, 28³/₄″ × 35⁷/₈″. Musée Saint-Remi, Reims, France. Noticeably absent in this view of the avenue, looking northwest from the Hôtel de Louvre toward Charles Garnier's Opéra at the other end of the street, are the trees that line the other grand boulevards of Paris. The Baron Georges-Eugène Haussmann forbade planting any in order to maintain what he called the "dignity" of the avenue, his monument to Louis-Napoleon's Second Empire.

HEAR MORE Listen to an audio file of your chapter at **www.myartslab.com**

Map 30.1 The grand boulevards of Paris. The grand boulevards are composed of a continuous arc that changes its name every few blocks, running across the front of the Opéra. They begin in the west at the Church of La Madeleine with the Boulevard de la Madeleine, then the Boulevard des Capucines, then the Boulevard des Italiens, and finally bending eastward to become the Boulevard Montmartre.

Haussmann understood full well that the boulevards appealed to tourists, and so in 1860, as he was busy adding sidewalks, gas streetlights, and trees to the boulevard des Capucines, he facilitated the demolition of old buildings to make way for the 700-room Grand Hôtel [grahnd oh-TEL]. Occupying a full block, it was a short walk to the city's most famous cafés, restaurants, and theaters.

The youthful painter Gustave Caillebotte [ky-BOTT] (1848–1894) grew up in Haussmann's Paris, and when, at age 28, he painted *Paris Street, Rainy Day* (Fig. **30.2**), he took its broad avenues and squares for granted. The casual elegance of the painting, the rhythms of the curved umbrellas and rounded shoulders of its pedestrians, play off the complex perspective of the scene. Here it seems as though Haussmann has bequeathed the good life—even on rainy days—to the city's inhabitants. Citizens and tourists alike enjoyed miles of new sidewalks with over 100,000 trees planted beside them. The eight new bridges that spanned the river Seine and pathways and roads along its banks further expanded the scenic vistas of the city's architectural treasures.

GEORGE SAND: POLITICS AND THE FEMALE VOICE

If any figure can be said to have anticipated the artistic sweep and direction of French society in the 1850s, it is George Sand (1804–1876), pen name for Aurore-Lucile Dupin [doo-PAHN]. She was 44 years of age when the Revolution of 1848 occurred and was already famous for some 30 novels and novelettes that she had written since her first success, the novel *Indiana*, published in 1831. So respected was Sand, in fact, that she was appointed Minister of Propaganda of the new republican government. As editor (and principal author) of the *Bulletins of the Republic*, the official publication of the new government, distributed throughout the country, she advanced the cause of socialism. In *Bulletin No. 12*, published in August 1848, she argued that, of all the oppressed, it was women who "have of necessity been the principal victims of the wretchedness that overwhelmingly oppresses body and soul. . . . The privileged classes have always mocked and disdained women's courage and self-sacrifice. The working-class man knows that if he falls in battle, his wife and children will remain on the barricade until his death has been avenged." But when the dreams of the republic—her own dreams, after all—were shattered by the coup d'état of Louis-Napoleon, she did not react with Proudhon's pessimism. Rather, she arranged to meet with the newly proclaimed prince-president and asked him to free the republicans he had imprisoned, and he acquiesced. Like so many before her, she believed, simply but wholeheartedly, in freedom. When, for instance, the French edition of *Uncle Tom's Cabin* appeared in 1853, she wrote, by way of introduction, "Where will we find creations more complete, types more vivid, situations more touching, more original, than in *Uncle Tom?*"

Over the course of her career, Sand wrote over 100 volumes of prose—fiction, travel books, essays, plays, and a 10-volume autobiography published in 1854 to 1855, and the publication of her correspondence with the leading figures of the age—Gustave Flaubert chief among them—has been published in 26 volumes, averaging nearly 1,000 pages each. As a result of the publication of her letters, we know a good deal more about her life than did her contemporaries, but she was still, even in her own day, a notorious libertine. She was married, but legally separated, and had two children, a son by her husband and a daughter by the first of her many lovers, among them composer Frédéric Chopin (see Chapter 27), with whom she had an affair that lasted from 1838 to 1847, and before that, the poet Alfred de Musset, a relationship she frankly, and somewhat scandalously, described in her 1858 novel *Elle et lui* (*She and He*). Having taken a man's name for her nom de plume, dressing in top hat and top coat of the kind the men are wearing in Caillebotte's *Paris Street, Rainy Day*, and smoking cigars, she challenged every sexual stereotype of her day. "Men and women are so much the same," she wrote to Flaubert in 1867, "that one can hardly understand the mass of differentiations and the subtle arguments upon which all

Fig. 30.2 Gustave Caillebotte (French 1848–1894), *Paris Street, Rainy Day.* **1877.** Oil on canvas, 83 ¹/₂″ × 108 ³/₄″ (212.2 × 276.2 cm). Charles H. and Mary F. S. Worcester Collection, 1964.336. Photograph © 2006, The Art Institute of Chicago. All Rights Reserved. This view of the place de Dublin, near the Saint-Lazare railroad station, shows one of Haussmann's favorite devices, the so-called *places-carrefours,* or "crossroad-squares," where multiple boulevards converge.

societies have been nourished on this matter. I observed the childhood and maturation of both my daughter and my son. My son was I—that is to say, a woman—much more than my daughter, who was an unsuccessful man."

Her chief subject was, in fact, relations between the sexes—even more than that, love itself, and passionate love at that. In her autobiography, *Histoire de ma vie* (*History of My Life*), she explains the theoretical basis of her fiction (**Reading 30.1**):

READING 30.1

from George Sand, *Histoire de ma vie* (1854–55)

A novel is as much a work of poetry as of analysis. True and even real situations and characters are needed, grouped around a character intended to sum up the feeling or the main idea of the book. The character usually embodies the passion called "love." . . . [L]ove, and consequently the character, must be idealized . . . and the writer should not fear to grant him exceptional importance in life, uncommon powers, charm, or suffering beyond what is normal for a human being, even beyond what most minds would consider credible.

In her own time, Sand's novels were thus classified as "idealist," as opposed to the "realist" novels of the likes of Balzac (see Chapter 28). As one nineteenth-century critic put it, her novels viewed life through an imagination "enamoured of beauty, truth, [and] happiness." But if the love she wrote about was, as she admits, idealized, she could quite easily see the world through different lenses. One of the most remarkable of her characters is the courtesan/prostitute Pulchérie in the 1833 novel *Lélia*. Pulchérie is, in fact, the sister of the title character, and they meet at a costume ball in Paris just after the 30-year-old Lélia has broken off her affair with 20-year-old Sténio. At the ball, Sténio mistakes

Pulchérie for her sister. At the center of the novel is a dialogue between Pulchérie and Lélia in which the "sinful" sister defends her occupation (**Reading 30.2**):

READING 30.2

from George Sand, *Lélia* (1832)

Unlike you, I have known no disappointments because I have never asked more of life than it could give me. My aim has been limited to knowing how to enjoy things as they are. I have made a virtue out of not despising them, and my wisdom has been not to hanker after anything more. . . . [D]efiance of shame is my virtue, my power, just as yours is the avoidance of it; I tell you that this is my wisdom which leads me to my ends, overcomes all obstacles, outlives constantly recurring anxieties, and pleasure is my reward for these struggles. This is my ray of sunlight after the storm, the enchanted island upon which the tempest throws me, and though I may be degraded, at least I am not ridiculous, to be ridiculous is worse than to be infamous; to serve no purpose in the world is more despicable than to serve the most debasing one. . . . What, then, does God ask of us here on earth? . . . To live, surely? And what does society demand of us? Not to steal. Society is so constructed that many people have no other way of making a living but by a trade which the social body sanctions, yet at the same time stigmatizes with the hateful name of vice. Do you realize of what temper of steel a poor woman must be made to live this way? With how many insults people try to make her pay for the weaknesses she has discovered and the brutalities she has satisfied? Under what burdens of ignominy and injustice must she learn to sleep, to live, to be lover, mistress, and mother, three aspects of the female destiny from which no woman can escape, whether she sell herself as a prostitute or through a marriage contract? . . . You see, if there be a heaven and a hell, then heaven will be for those who will have suffered most and have managed, on their bed of pain, to find a few smiles of joy and blessing to bestow on God; hell will be for those who, having seized the best things of life, have failed to appreciate their worth. In the midst of the horrors of social degradation, the courtesan Zinzolina [Pulchérie's working name] will have made a profession of faith by remaining true to sensual pleasure, while the ascetic Lélia, under a life of austerity and respectability will have repudiated God every moment by closing her eyes and her soul to the blessings of life.

No female character in fiction before this ever dared utter such libidinous words—and none for many years after, either. But Sand is of two minds about Pulchérie's position. In fact, Lélia and Pulchérie are doubles, two sides of Sand herself. Lélia has come to the masked ball in male dress. She is the masculine to Pulchérie's feminine. "Had I been a man," Lélia declares, "I would have loved combat, the odor of blood, the pressures of danger. . . . As a woman I had only

Fig. 30.3 Thomas Couture, *George Sand*. 1859. Bistre ink on canvas, 24″ × 15 ³/₄″. Musée national des châteaux de Versailles et de Trianon. Versailles, France. © Direction des Musées de France, 1986. Photo: © Gérard Blot, Réunion des musées nationaux. In August 1866, Sand wrote to Flaubert: "On going home yesterday, I found Couture to whom I said on your behalf that HIS portrait of me was, according to you, the best that anyone had made. He was not a little flattered."

one noble destiny on earth, which was to love. I love *valiantly*." But she had loved in horror of the sexual act, as an idealist removed from the realities of the sexual life that Pulchérie frankly enjoys. In other words, the two sisters represent ideal love (doomed, it would seem, to failure) and sexual pleasure (fated, apparently, to be loveless). In the end, Lélia is strangled by a sex-crazed priest; Pulchérie seduces Sténio in a sex-filled scene at her house.

Lélia can be read as a sort of moral allegory of the impossible position of women in mid-nineteenth-century French culture, and, in broader terms, as a condemnation of French culture as a whole. When Sand's friend, the painter Thomas Couture [coo-TUR] (1815–1879), whose portrait of her (Fig. **30.3**) Sand considered the best anyone had ever done, exhibited his mammoth *Romans during the Decadence of the Empire* (Fig. **30.4**) in 1847, critics immediately understood it to be just such an allegory, calling it "The Decadence of the French under Louis-Philippe."

But if Sand and Couture meant to critique bourgeois culture under Louis-Philippe, it was not apparent to everyone.

Fig. 30.4 Thomas Couture, *Romans during the Decadence of the Empire*. 1847. Oil on canvas, 15'5$^3/_4$" × 25'3$^7/_8$". Musée d'Orsay, Paris. © RMN (Musée d'Orsay) / Hervé Lewandowski. At its inaugural exhibition, the painting was glossed by a quotation from Juvenal's "Sixth Satire: The Women," which in Latin read: "We are all suffering today from the fatal results of a long peace more damaging than arms, / Luxury has rushed upon us and avenges the universe."

Just a year before, the poet Charles Baudelaire [boh-deh-LAIR] (1821–1867) had dedicated his *Salon of 1846*, an art review of the official government-sponsored exhibition of painting and sculpture by living artists held at the Louvre, to the bourgeoisie in an address saturated with irony (**Reading 30.3**):

READING 30.3

from Charles Baudelaire,
"To the Bourgeoisie," in *Salon of 1846* (1846)

The government of the city is in your hands, and that is just, for you are the force. But you must also be capable of feeling beauty; for as not one of you today can do without power, so not one of you has the right to do without poetry. . . .

Very well, you need art.

Art is an infinitely precious good, a draught both refreshing and cheering which restores the stomach and the mind to the natural equilibrium of the idea.

You understand its function, you gentlemen of the bourgeoisie—whether lawgivers or businessmen—when the seventh or eighth hour strikes and you bend your tired head towards the embers of your hearth or the cushions of your arm-chair.

This is the time when a keener desire and a more active reverie would refresh you after your daily labors.

Baudelaire recognized the bourgeoisie as his audience, but their hypocrisy was his constant target. His admonitions that they should love art masks his feelings that they are incapable of understanding true artistic innovation. As for Sand, he wrote: "She is stupid, heavy and garrulous. Her ideas on morals have the same depth of judgment and delicacy of feeling as those of janitresses and kept women. . . ." She was, from his point of view, not against, but *of* the bourgeoisie he so despised.

CHARLES BAUDELAIRE AND THE POETRY OF MODERN LIFE

Baudelaire's own sense of the beautiful, the true, and the marvelous is nowhere more apparent than in his poetry, which was passionately attacked for its unconventional themes and subject matter, chosen to shock bourgeois minds. When Flaubert's *Madame Bovary* first appeared in magazine installments in 1856 (see Chapter 28), its author had been brought to trial, charged with giving "offense to public and religious morality and to good morals." Eight months later, in August 1857, Baudelaire faced the same charge for his book of 100 poems, *Les Fleurs du mal* [lay fler doo mahl], usually translated "Flowers of Evil." Unlike Flaubert, Baudelaire lost his case, was fined, and was forced to remove six poems concerning lesbianism and vampirism, all of which remained censored . . . for the next century!

The poems in *Les Fleurs du Mal* unflinchingly confront the realities of this "underworld" and of life itself. In the poem "Carrion," for example, Baudelaire recalls strolling with his love one day (**Reading 30.4**):

READING 30.4

Charles Baudelaire, "Carrion," in *Les Fleurs du mal* (1857) (translation by Richard Howard)

Remember, my soul, the thing we saw
that lovely summer day?
On a pile of stones where the path turned off,
the hideous carrion—

legs in the air, like a whore—displayed
indifferent to the last,
a belly slick with lethal sweat
and swollen with foul gas.

the sun lit up that rottenness
as though to roast it through,
restoring to Nature a hundredfold
what she had here made one.

And heaven watched the splendid corpse
like flower open wide—
you nearly fainted dead away
at the perfume it gave off.

The poem is an attack on the romanticized view of death that marks, for instance, Emma Bovary's illusory ecstasy (see Chapter 28). To look at such reality unflinchingly, with open eyes is, for Baudelaire, the central requirement of modern life.

The lover in "Carrion" is Jeanne Duval [zhun doo-VAHL], Baudelaire's Haitian-born mistress with whom he had a tumultuous on-again-off-again relationship for 20 years. His painter friend Édouard Manet (1832–1883) would paint her in 1862 sitting on a sofa, her enormous crinoline (hoop-skirt) dress spread around her (Fig. **30.5**). In his 1863 essay "The Painter of Modern Life," Baudelaire writes: "What poet, in sitting down to paint the pleasure caused by the sight of a beautiful woman, would venture to separate her from her costume?" Such sentiments define the attitude that would soon

create the Paris fashion industry, the tradition of *haute couture* [oht koo-TOOR] that has come down to the present day.

Many critics and scholars have objected to Manet's rather unflattering depiction of his sitter. The work suggests that the woman and the dress embrace a larger unity, incorporating both attraction and repulsion. Nevertheless, both the painting and the many poems Baudelaire wrote about Jeanne openly address the attractions of her sexuality (**Reading 30.5**):

READING 30.5

Charles Baudelaire, "The Head of Hair," in *Les Fleurs du mal* (1857) (translation by Richard Howard)

Ecstatic fleece, that ripples to your nape
And reeks of negligence in every curl!
To people my dim cubicle tonight
with memories shrouded in that head of hair,
I'd have it flutter like a handkerchief!

For torpid Asia, torrid Africa,
—the wilderness I thought a world away—
survive at the heart of this dark continent.
As other souls set sail to music, mine
O my love! embarks upon your redolent hair.

Take me, tousled current, to where men
as mighty as the trees they live among
submit like them to the sun's long tyranny;
ebony sea, you bear a brilliant dream
of sails and pennants, mariners and masts.

A harbor where my soul can slake its thirst,
for color, sound and smell—where ships that glide
among the seas of golden silk throw wide
their yardarms to embrace a glorious sky
palpitating in eternal heat.

Drunk, and in love with drunkenness, I'll dive
into this ocean where the other lurks,
and solaced by these waves, my restlessness
will find a fruitful lethargy at last,
rocking forever at aromatic ease.

Poetry has rarely addressed sexual pleasure more openly, but Baudelaire also acts out what we can recognize today as imperialist imagery: Jeanne Duval's body becoming at once China and Africa, her harbors open to the colonizing fleet of his desire.

Édouard Manet: The Painter of Modern Life

In 1863, Baudelaire called for an artist "gifted with an active imagination" to actively pursue a new artistic goal: describing the modern city and its culture. Édouard Manet most clearly embodies this new vision of the artist as a recorder of

Fig. 30.5 Édouard Manet, *Baudelaire's Mistress Reclining* (*Study of Jeanne Duval*). ca. 1862. Oil on canvas, 35 $^3/_8$″ × 44 $^1/_2$″. Museum of Fine Arts (Szépmuvészeti Muzeum), Budapest, Hungary. Giraudon/Art Resource, New York. Baudelaire referred to this dark-skinned actress, whom he first met in 1842, as his "Black Venus."

everyday city life, since he, like Baudelaire, was a *flâneur*. The *flâneur* was a man-about-town, with no apparent occupation, strolling the city, studying and experiencing it coolly, dispassionately. Moving among its crowds and cafés in fastidious and fashionable dress, the *flâneur* had an acute ability to understand the subtleties of modern life and the ability to create art, according to a definitive essay by Baudelaire (**Reading 30.6**):

READING 30.6

from Charles Baudelaire, "The Painter of Modern Life" (1863)

Be very sure that this man, such as I have depicted him—this solitary, gifted with an active imagination, ceaselessly journeying across the great human desert—[aims for] . . . something other than the fugitive pleasure of circumstance. He is looking for that quality which you must allow me to call "modernity". . . By "modernity" I mean the ephemeral, the fugitive, the contingent. . . . This transitory, fugitive element, whose metamorphoses are so rapid, must on no account be despised or dispensed with. By neglecting it, you cannot fail to tumble into the abyss of an abstract and indeterminate beauty.

According to Baudelaire, the *flâneur* is distinguished by one other important trait: his attitude toward the bourgeoisie. He holds their vulgar, materialistic lifestyle in contempt, and his greatest devotion is to shocking them. "*Il faut Épater le bourgeois*" [eel foh ay-pah-TAY leh boor-ZHWAH] ("One must shock the bourgeoisie"), he said. Thus, it came as no surprise to Manet when *Le*

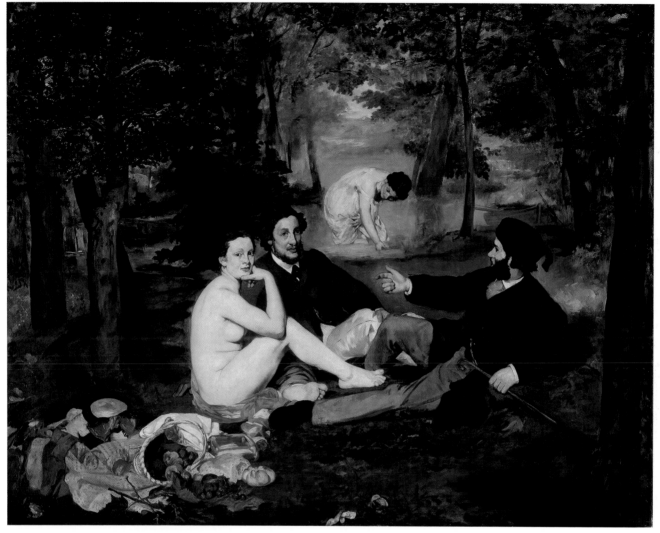

Fig. 30.6 Édouard Manet, *Le Déjeuner sur l'herbe* (*Luncheon on the Grass*). 1863. Oil on canvas, 7′ × 8′10″. Musee d'Orsay, Paris. RMN Réunion des Musées Nationaux/Art Resource, New York. © 2008 Artists Rights Society (ARS), New York. The model for the reclining young man on the right, whose gesture seems to point simultaneously at both female figures, was Manet's future brother-in-law.

Déjeuner sur l'herbe [leh day-zhur-NAY sur lerb] (*Luncheon on the Grass*) was rejected by the jury for the Salon of 1863 (Fig. **30.6**). It was not designed to please them. The Salon drew tens of thousands of visitors a day to the Louvre and was the world's most prominent art event. The public also reacted with outrage when Manet's painting appeared at the Salon des Refusés [sah-LOHN day reh-foo-ZAY], an exhibition hurriedly ordered by Louis-Napoleon after numerous complaints arose about the large number of rejected artworks. While many of the paintings included in the Salon des Refusés were of poor quality, others, including *Le Déjeuner sur l'herbe* by Manet and *The White Girl, Symphony in White, No. 1* by American artist James McNeill Whistler, were vilified because of their supposedly scandalous content or

challenging style. The Paris newspapers lumped them all together: "There is something cruel about this exhibition: people laugh as they do at a farce. As a matter of fact it is a continual parody, a parody of drawing, of color, of composition."

Manet's painting evokes the *fêtes galantes* of Watteau (see Fig. 25.3) and a particular engraving executed by Marcantonio Raimondi [ray-MOHN-dee] (Fig. **30.7**) after a lost painting designed by Raphael, *The Judgment of Paris* (1520). Manet's three central figures assume the same poses as the wood nymphs seated at the lower right of Raimondi's composition, and so Manet's painting can be understood as a "judgment of Paris" in its own right— Manet judging Paris the city in all its bourgeois decadence, as in fact Thomas Couture had in his *Romans*

Fig. 30.7 Marcantonio Raimondi after Raphael, _The Judgment of Paris._ ca. 1520. Engraving. Inv. 4167LR. Rothschild Collection. Musée du Louvre/RMN Réunion des Musées Nationaux, France. SCALA/Art Resource, New York. Paris judges which of the goddesses—Aphrodite, Hera, or Athena—is the most beautiful. His choice has profound impact, leading as it does to the Trojan War.

during the Decadence of the Empire (see Fig. 30.4). It is no accident that Manet had studied with Couture in the 1850s. And it is no accident that Manet's nude gazes directly at the viewer as does Couture's reclining central figure, although the gaze of Manet's nude is somewhat less languid, less remote. Her fully clothed male companions, who seem engaged in a conversation wholly at odds with the sexualized circumstances, discomfited the painting's audience. Manet's assault on his fellow Parisians' sensibilities continued in 1863 with _Olympia_ (see _Closer Look_, pages 1000–1001), though the painting was not exhibited until the Salon of 1865, where once again it was the object of public scandal and ridicule.

ÉMILE ZOLA AND THE NATURALIST NOVEL

Early in 1867, the novelist Émile Zola [ay-MEEL zoh-LAH] (1840–1902) came to the defense of his friend Manet and _Olympia_ in particular in a short book entitled simply _Édouard Manet._ Manet, he said, painted "in a way which is contrary to the sacred rules taught in schools." He continues (**Reading 30.7**):

READING 30.7

from Émile Zola, _Édouard Manet_ (1867)

He has made us acquainted with Olympia, a contemporary girl, the sort of girl we meet every day on the pavements, with thin shoulders wrapped in a flimsy faded woolen shawl. The public as usual takes good care not to understand the painter's intentions. Some people tried to find philosophic meaning in the picture, others, more lighthearted, were not displeased to attach an obscene significance to it. . . . But I know that you have succeeded admirably in doing a painter's job, the job of a great painter; I mean to say you have forcefully reproduced in your own particular idiom the truths of light and shade and the reality of objects and creatures.

Manet's *Olympia* is a courtesan, or, more properly, not quite a courtesan. For she possesses the slightly stocky body of the working class—a *petite fabourienne* [puh-TEET fah-boor-ee-EN], one critic of the day called her, a "little factory girl." Perhaps she is one of the many factory girls who, in 1863, found themselves out of work in Paris, a casualty of the American Civil War. Unable to get raw cotton from the South, the cotton mills of Paris had to shut down. Many girls turned to prostitution in order to survive. Viewers at the Salon of 1865 were disturbed by her class—a courtesan satisfied upper-class tastes, prostitutes did not—by the position of her left hand, and, above all, by her gaze. Not only is her gaze as direct as the nude in *Le Déjeuner* (Manet used the same model in both); it is confidently directed downward toward us, the viewers. It is as if we have just arrived on the scene, bringing flowers that we have handed to the black maid. We are suddenly Olympia's customers. And if her body is for sale, then we have entered as well into the economy in which human beings are bought and sold—the economy of slavery.

SEE MORE For a Closer Look at Édouard Manet's *Olympia*, go to **www.myartslab.com**

Critics particularly criticized Manet's treatment of this hand, its fingers smudged and unformed, seeming to lack joints. Its rendering appeared simply incompetent to them, but it announces that Manet's realism is something other than photographic. He is more interested in the social realities that inform the scene.

We know that Manet was acutely aware of the politics of slavery. At age 16, in 1848, he set sail for Brazil aboard a merchant marine ship. From Rio de Janeiro, he wrote his mother:

> In this country all the Negroes are slaves; they all look downtrodden; it's extraordinary what power whites have over them; I saw a slave market, a rather revolting spectacle for people like us. The Negresses are generally naked to the waist, some with a scarf tied at the neck.

Here, in all likelihood, is the original contact with slavery that 15 years later would be realized in *Olympia* itself.

Titian, *Reclining Nude (Venus of Urbino)*. ca. 1538. Oil on canvas, 47″ × 65″. Galleria degli Uffizi, Florence.

In the 1980s, this very bracelet and medallion were found in France. In the medallion was a lock of hair and a note, apparently written by Manet's niece, Julie Manet. The note claimed that the hair was Édouard Manet's at the age of 15 months.

Something to Think About . . .

Manet's *Olympia* could be said to possess something of the same sense of bravado as George Sand's Pulchérie in the novel *Lélia* (see Reading 30.2). How would you compare the two?

Manet's painting mirrors the structure of Titian's *Reclining Nude* (left), but where Titian portrays two ladies-in-waiting in the deep architectural space of the right side, Manet paints a single, barely lit window. This suggests that where Titian's painting takes place in daylight, Manet's takes place at night in a room lit by artificial light and may be a comment on the nature of love and beauty in Manet's Paris. In Titian's *Reclining Nude* a dog, symbolizing fidelity, lies at the nude's feet. Here a black cat, symbolizing promiscuity, arches its back as if to hiss in protest at the viewer's arrival.

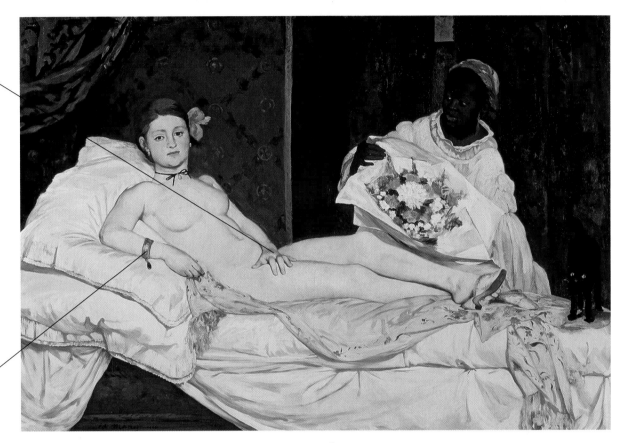

Édouard Manet. *Olympia*. 1863 (Salon of 1865). Oil on canvas, 51″ × 74 ³/₄″. Inv. RF 2772. Hervé Lewandowski/Musée d'Orsay, Paris, France. RMN Réunion des Musées Nationaux/Art Resource, New York. © 2008 Édouard Manet/Artists Rights Society (ARS), New York.

Alexandre Cabanel, *The Birth of Venus*. Salon of 1863. Oil on canvas, 52″ × 90″. P. Selert/Musée d'Orsay, Paris, France. Réunion des Musées Nationaux/Art Resource, New York. Just how radical Manet's painting must have seemed in 1865 can be understood by comparing it to this painting. The notoriously prurient Napoleon III, who had called Manet's *Le Déjeuner* "immodest," purchased it at the Salon of 1863. Cabanel's nude passively invites the gaze of the viewer, but does not meet it. The flock of cupids busy blowing conch shells above her head establishes the propriety of her nudity. She exists in mythological space, unlike Olympia, who rests firmly in the real.

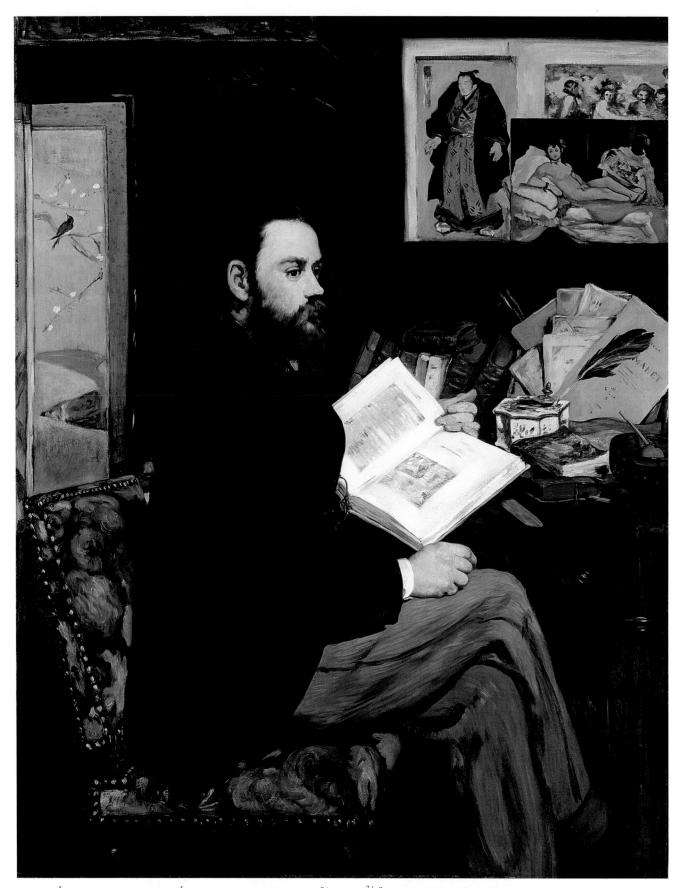

Fig. 30.8 Édouard Manet, *Portrait of Émile Zola.* 1868. Oil on canvas, 56⅝" × 44⅞". RF2205. Musée d'Orsay, Paris, France. Photo: Hervé Lewandowski. Reunion des Musées Nationaux/Art Resource, New York. The Japanese woodblock print in the painting has been identified as a portrait of a sumo wrestler by Kuniaki II. It was just the year before, in 1867, that Japanese woodblock prints had been introduced at the Universal Exposition in Paris (see Chapter 29).

A year after Zola's defense, Manet painted his friend's portrait (Fig. **30.8**). On the wall behind him is a black-and-white reproduction of *Olympia*—perhaps a subtle tribute to Zola's claim that Manet was interested in portraying "the truths of light and shade." Zola himself was anything but disinterested in the gritty realities of modern life. He practiced a brand of literary realism called *naturalism*—that is, in his words, "nature seen through a temperament." It is distinct from realism because it does not pretend to objective reporting. Zola was, in other words, completely aware that the artist's own personality definitively influenced the work and his view of the world (**Reading 30.8**):

READING 30.8

from Émile Zola, "The Moment in Art" (1867)

There are, in my opinion, two elements in a work: the element of reality, which is nature, and the personal element, which is man. The element of reality, nature, is fixed, always the same; it is given equally to all men. . . . The personal element, man, is, on the other hand, infinitely variable; there are as many possible works as there are different minds. . . . The word "realist" means nothing to me, since I am determined to subordinate the real to temperament. . . . For it is equally ridiculous to believe that in matters of artistic beauty, there is one absolute and eternal truth. The single and whole truth is no good for us, since we construct new truths each morning and have worn them out by the evening. . . . This means that the works of tomorrow cannot be the same as those of today. . . .

Zola also believed that all human beings (including authors and artists) are products of hereditary and environmental factors over which they have no control but which very much determine their lives. He applied this belief in such novels as *Thérèse Raquin* [tay-REZ rah-KEHN] (1867). The Thérèse of the title begins a love affair with a friend of her husband. The lovers drown the husband, only to find that their guilt makes life together intolerable, leading them to plot each other's murder. Zola described his strategy in the novel's preface (**Reading 30.9**):

READING 30.9

from Émile Zola, Preface to *Thérèse Raquin*, 2nd edition (1868)

I set out to study, not characters, but temperaments. Therein lies the whole essence of the book. I chose to portray individuals existing under the sovereign dominion of their nerves and their blood, devoid of free will and drawn into every act of their lives by the inescapable laws of their physical nature. Thérèse and Laurent are human animals, nothing more. I have endeavored to follow these animals through the devious working of their passions, the compulsion of their instincts, and the mental unbalance resulting from a nervous crisis. . . . I had only one desire: given a highly-sexed man and an unsatisfied woman, to uncover the animal side of them and see that alone, then throw them together in a violent drama and note down with scrupulous care the sensations and actions of these creatures. I simply applied to two living bodies the analytical method that surgeons apply to corpses.

Such naturalism reached its most powerful expression in Zola's 1885 novel *Germinal* [zher-mee-NAHL], about the lives of France's coal miners (see **Reading 30.10**, pages 1013–1015, for an extended passage). Permanently fatigued, anemic, emaciated by the coal dust they ceaselessly breathe, the miners live their lives in perpetual gloom (**Reading 30.10a**):

READING 30.10a

from Émile Zola, *Germinal* (1885)

They all hammered away, and nothing could be heard but these irregular blows, muffled, seemingly far-off. The sounds took on a harsh quality in the dead, echoless air, and it seemed as if the shadows created a mysterious blackness, thickened by the flying coal dust and made heavier by the gas which weighed down their eyes. The wicks of their lamps displayed only glowing red tips through their metal screens. You couldn't make out anything clearly. The work space opened out into a large chimney, flat and sloping, on which the soot of ten winters had created a profound night. Ghostly forms moved about, random light beams allowing a glimpse of the curve of a thigh, a brawny arm, a savage face, blackened as if in preparation for a crime. . . .

Zola experienced these brutal realities firsthand when, in researching the novel, he descended into a mineshaft and took detailed notes. The scene could also be summed up as Zola's effort to capture "the truths of light and shade and the reality of objects and creatures," as he had written of Manet's *Olympia*. But it is the novel's intense documentary-like exposé of the living conditions his characters must endure that is most notable. The plight of the proletariat had never been so clearly depicted.

Nationalism and the Politics of Opera

Popular taste in Napoleon III's Second Empire was antithetical to the realism of a Courbet (see Chapter 31) and the naturalism of artists like Manet and Zola. It preferred the Romanticism of an earlier generation, as illustrated by Emma Bovary's voracious consumption of romantic novels.

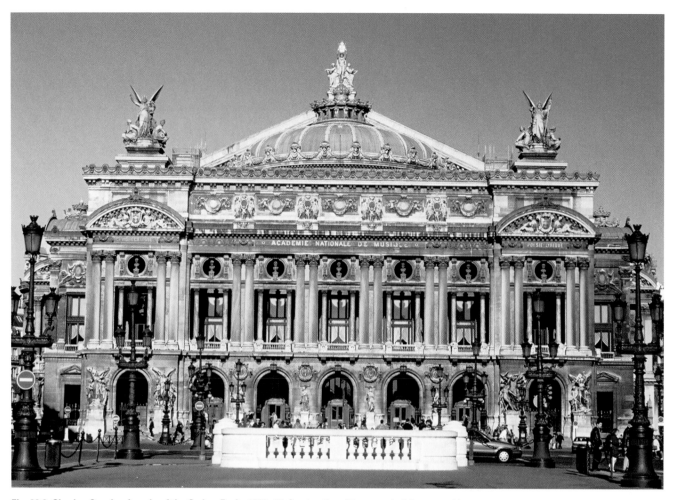

Fig. 30.9 Charles Garnier, facade of the Opéra, Paris. 1860–75. Construction of the opera building started in 1862, but was slowed because of the high water table under the gigantic stage and fly tower. The water was drained, a massive concrete well was built to carry the stage and fly tower, and it was filled with water to counter the water pressure. This is the underground lake made famous in Paul Leroux's play *The Phantom of the Opera*.

SEE MORE For an architectural panorama of Charles Garnier's Paris Opéra, go to **www.myartslab.com**

The dynamics of this confrontation between bourgeois taste and what we have come to call the **avant-garde** [ah-vunt-GARD]—any group, including artists, on the cutting edge—played itself out in the Second Empire most surprisingly at the opera. As a musical form favored by the aristocracy, and increasingly by the bourgeoisie, opera played an important social as well as musical role in Paris. Established by Louis XIV in 1669, the Académie Nationale de Musique (National Academy of Music) encompassed opera, music, and ballet. The opera was at once a state institution, a symbol of French culture and sovereignty, and a reminder of the country's royal heritage. In a period of rapid change during a century when the aristocracy lost its hold on power throughout Europe, the opera house seemed to be an oasis of conservative stability and aristocratic values. Or it should have been, thought its longtime aristocratic patrons and the nouveau riche (newly rich) bourgeois audience.

Yet change did arrive at the opera in the form of the most creative composers of the period, many of whom were associated with the revolutions of 1848 and the fervent nationalism sweeping the Continent. Since the aristocracy and the bourgeoisie shared a sense of hostility toward liberal nationalism and its notions of social equality and individual rights, a clash between opera's practitioners and audience was bound to happen.

Ever since Beethoven stopped writing his dynamic and tempo directions in Italian, replacing them with German, nationalism had become a growing force in music. Frédéric Chopin (see Chapter 27), a native of Poland, wrote many mazurkas and polonaises—traditional Polish folk dance forms—while living in Paris as part of a group of Poles forced into exile after the Russians had taken control of their country. The composer Robert Schumann immediately recognized Chopin's works as political compositions. If the Russian czar "knew what a dangerous enemy threatened him in Chopin's works," Schumann wrote, "in the simple tunes of his mazurkas, he would forbid this music. Chopin's works are cannons buried in flowers."

Fig. 30.10 Édouard Detaille, *Inauguration of the Paris Opera House, January 5, 1875: Arrival of Lord Maire (with entourage) from London, Greeted by Charles Garnier.* Gouache on paper. Photo: Gerard Blot. Châteaux de Versailles et de Trianon, Versailles, France. Réunion des Musées Nationaux/Art Resource, New York. At the staircase's base, the two bronze torchères, large female figures brandishing bouquets of light, were illuminated by the new technological innovation of gaslight, as were the large sconces in front of the marble columns.

The confrontation between nationalism and the aristocracy played out, in Paris, at the new Paris Opéra [oh-pay-RAH], designed by Charles Garnier and constructed between 1860 and 1875 (Fig. **30.9**). Its facade is a unique marriage of the Neoclassical and the Baroque, conceived to reflect a new imperial style. A Corinthian colonnade of paired columns tops a closed arcade of arches at the entrance, the whole embellished with exotic carved decorations. At the head of the new, broad Avenue de l'Opéra running at a diagonal from the rue de Rivoli and the Louvre, the Opéra literally commanded the center of Paris. Its Grand Staircase, rising to a height of 98 feet, is itself a theater within the theater, designed to allow the aristocrats and the bourgeoisie to display themselves (Fig. **30.10**). So too were the loges, multi-seat boxes where women typically sat forward, in their finest evening wear, to show off their social position and wealth.

Giuseppe Verdi and the Grand Opera The Italian composer Giuseppe Verdi [VER-dee] (1813–1901) led the way in politicizing opera compositions. Verdi believed that opera should be, first of all, dramatically realistic. No longer were arias, duets, or quartets merely displays of the singers' technical virtuosity; rather, they dramatically expressed the characters' temperament or situation in magnificent sustained melodies. A case in point is Verdi's *Rigoletto* [ree-goh-LET-toh], a tragic opera in three acts, first performed in Venice in 1851, in which the womanizing Duke of Mantua [MAHN-too-ah], disguised as a student, pays court to Gilda, who, unknown to him is the daughter of his

Fig. 30.11 The Quartet from Act III of Verdi's *Rigoletto*. This stage drawing demonstrates how lighting might underscore the contrasting feelings of the duke trying to seduce Maddalena inside the inn while Rigoletto and Gilda watch in darkness from the outside.

hunchbacked court jester, Rigoletto. When Rigoletto learns that the duke has seduced her, he conspires to have him killed by a professional assassin, but the plan goes awry when the assassin's sister, Maddalena [mad-uh-LEH-nah], pleads for the duke's life. Because the assassin needs a victim in order to justify his payment, Gilda, who has overheard their conversation, sacrifices her own life to save the duke. For Act III, Verdi composed a quartet in which each of the characters conveys contrasting emotions (track **30.1**). Two scenes are presented simultaneously. The duke tries to seduce Maddalena inside the inn while Rigoletto and Gilda watch from the outside (Fig. **30.11**). Rigoletto is demonstrating to the innocent Gilda the duke's moral depravity, and she reacts with shock and dismay. Here a wide range of human emotion occurs in a single scene.

As Italy struggled to achieve national unity, Verdi's operas came to symbolize Italian nationalism. Any time a female

lead in his operas would yearn for freedom, the audience would understand her as a symbol of Italian unification, and it would erupt in a frenzy of applause. Even Verdi's name came to be identified with nationalist politics, as an acronym for the constitutional monarchy established in 1861 of Victor Emanuel—V[ictor], E[manuel], R[e] d'I[talia], "Victor Emanuel, King of [a unified] Italy."

To have his operas produced in Paris, Verdi was forced to make changes to satisfy the censors, who were sensitive to nationalist references. He had to accommodate French taste as well. Since all Paris operas traditionally included a second-act ballet, he inserted a gypsy dance around a campfire at an appropriate spot in *Il Trovatore* [eel troh-vah-TOR-eh] (*The Troubadour*). *Il Trovatore* (originally premiered in Rome in 1853) was set in Spain and centered on the Count di Luna's young brother, kidnapped and brought up by a gypsy woman, whose own mother had been burned as a witch by the count's father. The second-act ballet was a requirement of the Jockey Club, an organization of French aristocrats who came to the opera after dinner, long after the opera had begun, and expected a ballet when they arrived. As the French journalist Alfred Delvau [del-VOH] explained: "One is more deliciously stirred by the sight of the ballet corps than by the great arias of the tenor in vogue or the reigning prima donna." So Verdi, the most popular opera composer of the day, who also viewed himself as a pragmatist, went along with the idiosyncratic Paris tradition. Considering the large number of Verdi performances in Paris in the 1850s, his changes must have met with success. (In the 1856–1857 season, the Théâtre des Italiens in Paris offered 87 performances—54 of them Verdi operas.)

Wagner's Music Drama Meets the Jockey Club The Jockey Club's ability to dictate taste and fashion—which the bourgeoisie anxiously copied—extended, in a notorious example, to Richard Wagner's opera *Tannhäuser* [than-HOY-zur] in March 1861. Declaring that his was "the art of the future," Richard Wagner [VAHG-ner] (1813–1883) had arrived in Paris in 1859, where Wagner reported that the press found him "arrogant" and guilty of "repudiating all existing operatic music." Nonetheless, he managed to secure Louis-Napoleon's support for a production of *Tannhäuser*, an opera in three acts. Because of the Paris Opéra's rule that foreign works be presented in French, Wagner set about having the opera translated into French.

Tannhäuser's protagonist is a legendary knight minstrel (*Minnesinger*), the German equivalent of a medieval troubadour. When other minstrels gather for a tournament of song in the great hall of the Wartburg [vart-boorg] castle, near the Venusberg [VEH-noos-berg], a hill in which Tannhäuser has taken refuge for a year under the magic spell of Venus, goddess of love, he insists on returning to earth in order to compete. Once again he meets his beloved, Elisabeth, who sings to him the famous aria ((•)) HEAR MORE at *Dich, teure Halle* [dikh toy-ruh hah-leh] www.myartslab.com ("Thou, Beloved Hall") (track **30.2**), welcoming him back to the great hall where he formerly sang. She is excited that this beautiful space will once again resonate with music.

Traditionally, the operatic voice carries the melody and the orchestra provides accompaniment. As a result, Wagner felt, the music overwhelmed the text. So, in order to make the text understandable, Wagner shifted the melodic element from the voice to the orchestra. Elisabeth thus sings in a declamatory manner that lies somewhere between aria and recitative, and the orchestra carries the melody, following Elisabeth's shift in mood from ecstatic welcome to sad remembrance of her year-long loss. So radical was this change, the orchestra more or less taking over from the vocalist the primary responsibility for developing the melodic character of the work, that French audiences found

Wagner's music almost unrecognizable as opera. A cartoon in a Parisian newspaper of 1869 shows Wagner literally assaulting the eardrums of his audience (Fig. **30.12**)

For a French audience, the music was too new to appreciate fully, and the plot, derived directly from German folklore, was hopelessly foreign. The opera seemed aimed at inflaming French/German hostility. Wagner was informed, furthermore, of the necessity of writing a ballet for the opening of the second act. He refused, though he did agree to *begin* the opera with a ballet. Already unhappy that an expensive production of a German work was to be staged in *their* opera, the Jockey Club was doubly outraged that its composer refused to insert the ballet in its traditional place. Wagner seemed nothing short of a liberal nationalist deliberately trying to provoke his conservative French audience.

Fig. 30.12 André Gill, *Richard Wagner*. April 18, 1869. Caricature in *L'Éclipse*, Paris. 18″ × 12″. *L'Éclipse* was published in Paris between 1868 and 1876 and lampooned the most famous artists of the day. Because of government restriction, it consisted of only one page per issue.

As rehearsals progressed, the Jockey Club provided its members with silver whistles engraved with the words "Pour Tannhaeuser." They used these whistles in defense of their aristocratic privileges on opening night, March 13, 1861. With Louis-Napoleon present in his box, the Jockey Club interrupted the music for as much as 15 minutes at a time as they hissed and whistled. "The Emperor and his consort stoically kept their seats throughout the uproar caused by their own courtiers," Wagner noted. The opera received the same reception at both its second and third performances. Paris was divided. The composer Berlioz found no virtue in the music, while Baudelaire admired it. After the third performance, which included several lengthy fights and continued whistling from the Jockey Club, Wagner demanded that the opera be withdrawn from performance. The French government accepted their financial losses and agreed.

Wagner's Music Drama The theme of *Tannhäuser*—the conflicting claims of sexual pleasure and spiritual love—is hopelessly Romantic, which might have appealed to bourgeois and aristocratic French taste, but its music and its approach to the opera as a form did not. Like Verdi, Wagner sought to convey realism, so that his recitatives, arias, and choruses made dramatic sense. And he considered his work a new genre—**music drama**—in which the actions performed on stage are the visual and verbal manifestations of the drama created by the instruments in the orchestra, "deeds of music made visible," as he put it. This he accomplished by the **leitmotif** [LITE-moh-teef], literally a "leading motive." For Wagner, this meant a brief musical idea connected to a character, event, or idea that recurs throughout the music drama each time the character, event, or idea recurs. However, as characters, events, and ideas change throughout the action, so do the leitmotifs, growing, developing, and transforming. Berlioz's idée fixe is a similar device in Romantic orchestral music (see Chapter 27).

A clear example of the leitmotif is in the Prelude to HEAR MORE at www.myartslab.com Wagner's 1865 opera in three acts, *Tristan und Isolde* (track **30.3**). The opera is based on the medieval legend of the ill-fated love of the Cornish knight Tristan and the Irish princess Isolde, whom Tristan's uncle, King Mark, wishes to marry against her will and for which purpose he has sent Tristan to Ireland to bring her back to Cornwall. Tristan's allegiance to King Mark is compromised by the fact that many years earlier, Isolde, not knowing his identity as the man who had killed her fiancé and suffered wounds in the battle, had saved his life by nursing him back to health. When she did learn his identity, she could not bring herself to take vengeance. And so, as their ship sails for Cornwall, the two, unable to admit their mutual attraction but acknowledging the debt owed to Isolde, agree to drink poison before the ship lands. However, Isolde's maid substitutes a love potion for the poison, which frees the pair to admit their love. The leitmotif associated with drinking the love potion constitutes the first phrases of the Prelude:

At the first sounding of this leitmotif—known as both the "love potion" motif and the "yearning" motif—the audience does not understand its significance. The motif repeats throughout the Prelude in various forms and pitches. Not until it recurs, in Act I, as Tristan and Isolde are about to drink what they believe to be poison, does its full significance become clear. The longing that the leitmotif conveys is largely dependent on harmonic dissonance of the opening chord, which, as the very first harmony of the work, audiences found particularly disconcerting. The chord does not resolve itself, but rather changes into an equally dissonant harmony followed by a long silence. This refusal to resolve the leitmotif represents the lovers' unresolved longing.

Wagner's greatest realization of the leitmotif idea occurs in four music dramas dating from 1848 to 1874, titled collectively *Der Ring des Nibelungen* [der ring des nee-beh-LOONG-un] (*The Ring of the Nibelung*). The "*Ring*" forms an epic cycle based on Norse mythology involving the quest for a magical but accursed golden ring, the possessor of which can control the universe. Collectively, it represents Wagner's dream of composing a **Gesamtkunstwerk** [geh-SAHMT-koonst-verk], or total work of art, synthesizing music, drama, poetry, gesture, architecture, and painting (the latter two through stage design). The *Ring* features more than 20 leitmotifs that Wagner weaves into an intricate web, the four music dramas being performed over the course of four days. For instance, the hero, Siegfried, is associated with his famous horn call, and other leitmotifs represent the ring itself or a place like Valhalla (home of the gods), emotional states like love's awakening, and concepts like redemption. The cycle premiered in 1876 in Bayreuth, a small city in Bavaria. Here, with the help of his patron Ludwig II of Bavaria, Wagner oversaw the building of a *Festspielhaus* [FESHT-peel-hows], or "festival drama house," that he hoped might help to unify Germany both culturally and politically (Fig. **30.13**). In his appeal for funds to underwrite construction, Wagner makes the political motives of his project plain:

> In Hellas [ancient Greece], the supreme flowering of the State went hand in hand with that of Art; so too the resurrection of the German Empire should be accompanied

Fig. 30.13 Richard Wagner, cross-section of the Bayreuth Festspielhaus. 1872–76. From Frederic Spotts, *Bayreuth: A History of the Wagner Festival* (New Haven: Yale University Press, 1994). © 2003 Yale University Press/Spotts, BAYREUTH: A History of the Wagner Festival (1994), image p. 9. The design puts the orchestra beneath the stage, thus drawing the audience closer to the performance and projecting the orchestra's music directly toward it, all resulting in acoustics ideal for the integration of orchestral and vocal parts.

by a massive artistic monument to the German intellect. In the field of politics, the German mission in the history of the world has recently enjoyed its second triumph [the victory over France in the 1870 Franco-Prussian war]—now its spiritual victory is to be celebrated, through the German Festival in Bayreuth.

It was this spirit of German nationalism that would lead Adolf Hitler to lionize Wagner's music during the Third Reich [rykh] 60 years later.

Operetta: Jacques Offenbach and Musical Satire As Wagner's experience suggests, serious opera was not particularly well received in Paris, the center of the art and music world during the 1860s. But the comic operas that played at the Opéra-Comique [oh-pay-RAH-koh-MEEK] were widely popular, enjoyed by Baudelaire and almost everyone else in Paris, aristocrats, the bourgeoisie, and the working class alike. Far and away the most admired of those writing comic operas was Jacques Offenbach [OFF-un-bahk] (1819–1880), a Jewish composer.

This fact must have appalled the virulently anti-Semitic Richard Wagner, who in 1850 had composed a polemic entitled "Jewry in Music," the chief target of which was composer Felix Mendelssohn. The tract makes clear that Wagner's feelings were driven largely by his nationalism. As a speaker of German he is offended by Yiddish, which he calls "intolerably jumbled blabber." From Wagner's point of view, Jewish speech necessarily rendered the Jews incapable of producing music. Of Offenbach's music in particular, Wagner would simply say that it "gives off the heat of the manure in which all the pigs of Europe have come to wallow."

Born in Germany, Offenbach did not care what Wagner thought of his music. After all, Wagner was a failure in Paris, while he, Offenbach, was a success. He dominated the fashionable music scene of the Second Empire, satirizing the politics of Louis-Napoleon's reign and capturing its cosmopolitan atmosphere and loose morals in light operas that he called **operettas**. This genre of musical theater usually mixed spoken dialogue with sung numbers that might include rowdy music from the dance halls of the day, including the "can-can." His hit of 1866, *La Vie Parisienne* [lah vee pah-ree-zee-EN] (*The Parisian Life*), has a baron and baroness bamboozled by two veterans of the boulevards as they enjoy the plays, cafés, and amorous entertainments the city has to offer (Fig. 30.14). His hit of the following year, *The Grand Duchess of Gérolstein* [zhay-roll-SHTINE], was originally entitled simply *The Grand Duchess*, but censors objected on the grounds that Russia might take offense, thinking that Offenbach was satirizing Catherine II, which in fact he was. (*Grand Duchess* was her title upon marrying Grand Duke Peter.) At one point, the duchess lines up her troops for inspection: "Oh, how I love the military," she sings, "Their sexy uniforms, / Their mustaches and their plumes." Upon seeing a handsome young soldier named Fritz, she promotes him to sergeant, then lieutenant, captain, and ultimately commander-in-chief to replace General Boum [boom], a man who, instead of taking snuff, shoots off his pistol periodically and inhales the smoke from its barrel. In an amusing way, and under the guise of mindless entertainment, Offenbach effectively mocked the political and military authorities. Indeed, within three years, the farcical war that Fritz wages—no one gets killed because he gets the enemy drunk—would suddenly become a reality in Paris, but no longer a farce, this time a tragedy led by the tyrant Louis-Napoleon, who precipitated the Franco-Prussian War (see Chapter 31). In later life, Offenbach tried to bridge the gulf between serious and light opera that he had helped to create in the five-act opera *The Tales of Hoffmann*.

Verdi, Wagner, and Offenbach all played an important role in transforming opera from a staid bastion of aristocrats and conservative values to a popular art form. By the end of the century, Verdi and Wagner were firmly placed in the pantheon of national heroes of their countries alongside leaders and revolutionaries such as Garibaldi, Mazzini, and Bismarck. And by the end of the nineteenth century, aristocrats, bourgeoisie, and workers across Europe were enthralled by a nationalist ideology that would, little more than a decade later, lead to an epochal conflict that would kill 10 million—World War I.

Fig. 30.14 Jules Cheret, poster for Offenbach's *La Vie Parisienne*. 1866. Cheret, one of the great poster artists of the day, captures something of the operetta's comedy.

Impressionist Paris

In the early 1870s, Édouard Manet befriended a number of young painters whom he would deeply influence and who would in turn come to be known as the Impressionists. Chief among his new, younger colleagues were Claude Monet, Pierre Renoir [ruh-NWAHR], Gustave Caillebotte [ky-BOTT], Edgar Degas, and Berthe Morisot [bairt-mo-ree-ZOH], who was married to Manet's brother. Starting in 1874, the Impressionists organized their own group exhibitions, in which Manet politely declined to participate, choosing instead to pursue recognition in the official Salons. Nevertheless, he came to be widely regarded as a pre-Impressionist if not the first Impressionist.

Manet never abandoned the complex social commentary that informs his earlier painting. In his *The Gare Saint-Lazare* [gahr san-luh-ZAHR] (Fig. **30.15**), his model is the same woman as in *Le Déjeuner sur l'herbe* and *Olympia*. The little girl is the daughter of Manet's friend Alphonse Hirsch, in whose garden the scene is set; she gazes through the fence at the tracks, obscured by the smoke of a passing train in the new train station of Saint-Lazare. The station

was the work of the Baron Georges Eugène Haussmann, who had "modernized" the city by broadening its avenues, demolishing its worst neighborhoods, and building vast gardens and railway stations. By 1868, the station was receiving more than 13 million passengers a year, many of whom were workers, clerks, and laborers commuting in from the suburbs. The station and the bridge above the surrounding streets would become a favorite subject of the Impressionist painters. The front door to Manet's own studio from 1872 to 1878 can be seen through the railings behind the woman's head. In 1877, Claude Monet rented a studio nearby in order to paint a series of views of the station itself.

Manet's painting is a bouquet of contrasts. The little girl is dressed in white with blue trim, while the older woman, posed here as her mother, or perhaps her nanny, is in blue with white trim. The one sits, regarding us; the other stands, gazing through the fence railing. The nanny's hair is down, the little girl's up. The nanny's angular collar is countered by the soft curve of the little girl's neckline. The black choker around the one's neck finds its way to the other's hair. The older woman sits with her puppy on her lap, a symbol of her contentment. The little girl is eating grapes (beside her on the ledge), which have bacchanalian associations. The older escapes into her novel, perhaps a Romantic one, while the younger looks out at the trains leaving the station, possibly dreaming of adventure.

Manet's painting suggests that the little girl will grow up into the woman beside her. The painting implicitly portrays the limits of women's possibilities in French society. As the nineteenth century progressed, women like the Impressionist painters Mary Cassatt and Berthe Morisot would strive to eliminate those limitations as they increasingly demanded equality and respect, not only in their work, but also in their lives. ∎

Fig. 30.15 Édouard Manet, *The Gare Saint-Lazare.* 1873. Oil on canvas, 36 3/4″ × 45 1/8″.
Gift of Horace Havemeyer in memory of his mother, Louisine W. Havemeyer. 1956.10.1. Image © 2007.
Board of Trustees, National Gallery of Art, Washington, D.C. © 2008 Artists Rights Society (ARS), New York.

Who was George Sand?

Even before the revolution of 1848, French intellectuals had begun attacking the bourgeois lifestyle. George Sand, born Aurore-Lucile Dupin, was concerned particularly with the position of women in French society. Why was Sand labeled an "idealist"? How do characters like Pulchérie in the novel *Lélia* challenge Sand's idealism?

How did poet Charles Baudelaire initiate modernism?

While his *Salon of 1846* was an ironic plea to the bourgeoisie to value art, the poet Charles Baudelaire was certain that they would ignore him. In his poems, he sought to shock them, using imagery that ranged from exotic sexuality to the grim reality of death in the modern city. How did he define the ideal painter of modern life? Baudelaire styled himself a *flâneur*. What is a *flâneur*?

What made painter Édouard Manet so notorious?

Manet was Baudelaire's "Painter of Modern Life." Why did depictions of women in his paintings of the 1860s, particularly *Le Déjeuner sur l'herbe* and *Olympia*, shock his bourgeois audience?

How would you define Émile Zola's naturalism?

On what grounds did the novelist Émile Zola champion Manet's paintings? He believed that all human beings are products of hereditary and environmental factors over which they have no control but which determine their lives. How does his naturalism differ from realism? How would you say his vision differs from George Sand's?

What new directions in opera developed in the mid-nineteenth century?

In music, the nationalist tendencies of the era played themselves out in the Paris opera. Giuseppe Verdi's *Rigoletto* and other works by him came to symbolize Italian nationalism, and the Parisian Jockey Club ostracized the German composer Richard Wagner on nationalist grounds when he tried to produce his opera *Tannhäuser*. What did the Jockey Club object to in particular about Wagner's work? What new genre did Wagner believe he had invented? Wagner shifted the melodic element from the voice to the orchestra and organized his opera dramas around the leitmotif. What is a leitmotif? He also believed that he might create a *Gesamtkunstwerk*. What is a *Gesamtkunstwerk*? What work did he believe realized his dream and why? The Opéra Comique was, however, the most popular form of opera in Paris and the composer Jacques Offenbach its most popular artist. How would you characterize Offenbach's opera?

PRACTICE MORE Get flashcards for images and terms and review chapter material with quizzes at **www.myartslab.com**

GLOSSARY

avant-garde Literally the "advanced guard," this military term is used to describe artists and other creative groups on the cutting edge.

flâneur A French version of the aristocratic English dandy. A man-about-town, with no apparent occupation, strolling the city, studying and experiencing it dispassionately.

Gesamtkunstwerk A total work of art, one that synthesizes music, drama, poetry, gesture, architecture, and painting.

leitmotif In opera, a brief musical idea connected to a character, event, or idea that recurs throughout the work.

music drama A musical genre in which the actions on stage are the visual and verbal manifestations of the drama created by the instruments in the orchestra.

operetta Light musical drama usually incorporating spoken dialogue.

READINGS

from Émile Zola, *Germinal* (1885)

Germinal is an unflinching depiction of life among the coalminers of northern France in the 1860s. It is generally considered Zola's masterpiece. In the following scene, the novel's central character, Étienne Lantier, is taken through the mine by the miner Maheu, who works with his teenage daughter, Catherine. Despite its uncompromising condemnation of life in the mines, Germinal *is, in the end, a hopeful book. Its title,* Germinal, *was the name of the seventh month of the French Revolutionary calendar, which occurred in the spring, as new life began to germinate and with it the possibility of hope.*

"Damn! It's not warm here," muttered Catherine, shivering.

Etienne simply nodded. He found himself before the shaft, in the center of a huge hall swept by drafts. Of course he thought of himself as brave, yet an unpleasant emotion caused his throat to contract among the thundering of the carts, the clanking of the signals, the muffled bellowing of the megaphone, facing the continuously flying cables, unrolling and rolling up again at top speed on the spools of the machine. The cages rose and fell, slithering like some nocturnal animal, continually swallowing men that the hole seemed to drink down. It was his turn now. He was very cold. He kept silent out of nervousness which made Zacharie and Levaque snicker, for both disapproved of the hiring of this stranger—Levaque especially, hurt because he had not been consulted. So Catherine was happy to hear her father explaining things to the young man.

"Look, up on top of the cage; there's a parachute and iron hooks that catch in the guides in case the cable breaks. It works . . . most of the time. . . . Yes, the shaft is divided into three vertical compartments, sealed off by planks from top to bottom. In the center are the cages; on the left the ladder-well."

But he broke off to complain, without daring to speak very loudly, "What the hell are we doing waiting here, for God's sake? How can they let us freeze here like this?"

Richomme, the foreman, who was also going down, his open miner's lamp hanging from a nail in his leather cap, heard him complaining.

"Be careful; the walls have ears!" he muttered paternalistically, as a former miner who still sided with the workers.

"They've got to make the adjustments . . . See? Here we are, get in with your team."

And in fact, the cage, banded with sheet iron and covered by a fine-meshed screen, was waiting for them, resting on its catches. Maheu, Zacharie, Levaque, and Catherine slid into a cart at the back; and since it was supposed to hold five people, Étienne got in as well; but all the good places were taken and he had to squeeze in beside the young girl, whose elbow poked into his belly. His lamp got in his way; he was advised to hang it from a buttonhole of his jacket. He didn't hear this advice and kept it awkwardly in his hand. The loading continued, above and below, a jumbled load of cattle. Couldn't they get going? What was happening? It seemed as if he'd been waiting for a long time. Finally a jolt shook him and everything fell away, the objects around him seemed to fly past while he felt a nervous dizziness that churned his guts. This lasted as long as he was in the daylight, passing the two landing levels, surrounded by the wheeling flight of the timbers.

Then, falling into the blackness of the pit, he remained stunned, no longer able to interpret his feelings.

"We're off," said Maheu tranquilly.

They seemed relaxed. He, however, wondered at moments whether he was going down or up. There were moments at which they seemed immobile, when the cage was dropping straight down without touching the guides; then brusquely there were shudders, a sort of dancing between the planks, which made him fear a catastrophe was going to happen. In addition, he couldn't make out the walls of the shaft behind the grill to which his face was pressed. The lamps only dimly lit the heap of bodies at his feet. Alone, the open lamp of the foreman shone from the next cart like a beacon.

"This one is fifteen feet wide," continued Maheu, instructing him. "The casing needs to be redone; water's leaking everywhere. . . . Listen, we're down at the water level. Can you hear it?"

Étienne had just been asking himself what this sound of a downpour could be. A few big drops had splashed first on the roof of the cage, like at the beginning of a storm; and now the rain grew, streamed, was transformed into a real deluge. The roof must have had a hole in it, for a trickle of water, flowing onto his shoulder, was soaking him to the skin. The cold became glacial; they entered a damp blackness, then there was a blinding flash and a glimpse of a cave where men were moving about. But already they were plunging back into nothingness.

Maheu said:

"That's the first landing. We're a hundred feet down now . . . Look how fast we're going."

Lifting his lamp, he lit up a guide timber flying past like the rail beneath a train running full steam ahead; beyond that, nothing else could be seen. Three other platforms flew out of the shadows.

"How deep it is!" murmured Étienne.

The fall seemed to have lasted for hours. He was suffering because of the awkward position he was in, not daring to move, above all tortured by Catherine's elbow. She didn't say a word; he only felt her pressed against him, warming him. When the cage finally halted at the bottom, at 12,828 feet, he was astonished to learn that the descent had lasted just one minute. But the sound of the catches taking hold and the feeling of something solid underneath him suddenly cheered him up. . . .

The cage was emptying; the workers crossed the landing dock, a room carved out of the rock vaulted over with bricks lit by three huge lamps with open flames. The loaders were violently shoving full carts across the cast-iron floor. A cellar-like odor seeped from the walls, a chilly smell of saltpeter traversed by warm gusts from the stable nearby. Four galleries gaped into the opening.

"This way," said Maheu to Étienne. You're not there yet. We have another good mile and a quarter to go. . . ."

The miners were separating, disappearing by groups into these black holes. Some fifteen of them had just entered the one on the left; and Étienne walked behind them following Maheu, who led Catherine, Zacharie and Levaque. It was a good tunnel for hauling the carts, cutting through a layer of rock so solid that only partial timbering had been necessary. They walked single file, walking always onward, without a word, led by the tiny flames in their lamps. The young man stumbled at every step, catching his feet in the rails. Suddenly a muffled sound worried him, the distant noise of a storm whose violence seemed to grow, coming from the bowels of the earth. Was it the thunder of a cave-in which would crush down onto their heads the enormous mass cutting them off from the light of day . . .?

The further they went, the more narrow the gallery became, lower, with an uneven ceiling forcing them constantly to bend over.

Étienne bumped his head painfully. If he hadn't been wearing a leather cap, his skull would have been cracked. Yet he had been following closely the smallest movements of Maheu ahead of him, his somber silhouette created by the flow of the lamps. None of the workers bumped into anything; they must have known every hump in the ground, every knot in the timbers, every protrusion in the rock. The young man was also bothered by the slippery ground, which was getting more and more damp. Sometimes he passed through virtual seas which he discovered only as his feet plunged into the muddy mess. But what surprised him the most were the abrupt changes in temperature. At the bottom of the shaft it was very cold, and in the haulage tunnel, through which all the air in the mine flowed, a freezing wind was blowing, like a violent storm trapped between narrow walls. Further on, as they gradually traveled down other passageways which got less ventilation, the wind dropped and the warmth increased, creating a suffocating, leaden heat.

Maheu had not said another word. He turned right into a new gallery saying only to Étienne, without turning around, "The Guillaume vein."

This was the vein whose coal face they were to work. After a few steps Étienne bruised his head and elbows. The sloping roof descended so far that they had to walk doubled over for fifty or a hundred feet at a time. The water reached his ankles. They went on in this way for more than 600 feet when suddenly, Levaque,

Zacharie and Catherine disappeared, seemingly swallowed by a tiny crack that opened in front of him.

"You have to climb up," said Maheu. "Hang your lamp from a buttonhole and hang on to the timbers."

He too disappeared. Étienne had to follow him. This chimney was left for the miners to allow them to reach all the secondary passageways, just the width of the coal vein, barely two feet. Fortunately the young man was thin: still clumsy, he drew himself up with a wasteful expense of strength, pulling in his shoulders and buttocks, hand over hand, clinging to the timbers. Fifty feet higher up they came to the first secondary passageway, but they had to go on; the work area of Maheu and his team was at the sixth level, "in Hell" as they said, and every fifty feet there was another passageway to be crossed. The climb seemed to go on forever, through this crack which scraped against his back and chest. Étienne gasped as if the weight of the rocks were crushing his limbs; his hands were skinned, his legs bruised. Worst of all, he was suffocating, feeling as if the blood was going to burst out through his skin. He could vaguely see down one of the passageways two animals crouched down, one small and one large, shoving carts ahead of them: Lydie and La Mouquette, already at work. And he still had to clamber up two more levels! Sweat blinded him, he despaired of catching up to the others whose agile legs he could hear constantly brushing against the rock.

"Come on; here we are!" said Catherine's voice. . . .

Little by little the veins had filled, the faces were being worked at each level, at the end of each passageway. The all-devouring mine had swallowed its daily ration of men, more than 700 workers laboring now in this giant ant heap, burrowing through the earth in every direction, riddling it like an old piece of wood infested by worms. And in the midst of this heavy silence, under the crushing weight of these deep layers of earth, could be heard—if you put your ear to the rock—the movement of these human insects at work, from the flight of the cable raising and lowering the extraction cage to the bite of the tools digging into the coal at the bottom of the mine. . . .

The four cutters had stretched out one above the other across the sloping coal face. . . . Maheu was the one who suffered most. High up where he was, the temperature was as high as 95°, the air did not circulate, and eventually you would suffocate. In order to see clearly he had had to hang his lamp on a nail near his head; but this lamp broiled his skull, making his blood seethe. His torture was worsened above all by the damp. Water kept flowing over the rock above him a few inches from his face; and huge drops kept rapidly, continuously, in a maddening rhythm, falling, always on the same spot. It was no use twisting his neck or bending his head, the drops fell on his face, beating at him, splattering endlessly. After a quarter of an hour he was soaked, covered with his own sweat, steaming like a laundry tub. He didn't want to stop cutting and gave huge blows which jolted him violently between the two rocks, like a flea caught between the pages of a book, threatened by being completely crushed.

Not a word was spoken. They all hammered away, and nothing could be heard but these irregular blows, muffled, seemingly far-off. The sounds took on a harsh quality in the dead, echoless air, and it seemed as if the shadows created a mysterious blackness, thickened by the flying coal dust and made heavier by the gas which weighed down their eyes. The wicks of their lamps displayed only glowing red tips through their 200 metal screens. You couldn't make out anything clearly. The work space opened out into a large chimney, flat and sloping, on which the soot of ten winters had created a profound night. Ghostly forms moved about, random light beams allowing a glimpse of the curve of a thigh, a brawny arm, a savage face, blackened as if in preparation for a crime. Sometimes blocks of coal stood out, suddenly lit up, their facets glinting like crystals.

Then everything was plunged back into darkness, the picks beating out their heavy, dull blows; and there was nothing but the sound of heavy breathing, groans of pain and fatigue 210 beneath the weight of the air and the showers from the underground streams.

READING CRITICALLY

In his research of the coal-mining industry, Zola had taken careful notes about the elevator, or cage, in which workers were lowered into and raised out of the shaft. His description is thus meticulously realistic. But how does his writing exceed mere realistic description?

The Promise of Renewal

Hope and Possibility in Late Nineteenth-Century Europe

THINKING AHEAD

What is Impressionism?

How was Russian nationalism reflected in literature, art, and music?

How did the Crystal Palace and Pre-Raphaelite artists express the spirit of social reform?

In July 1870, Otto von Bismarck (1817–1898), prime minister of the Kingdom of Prussia, goaded the French Emperor Napoleon III into declaring war. Two months later, at the Battle of Sedan, the Germans soundly defeated the French army. The French emperor was imprisoned and exiled to England, where he died three years later. Meanwhile Bismarck marched on Paris, setting siege to the city, forcing its government to surrender in January 1871 after four months of ever-increasing famine during which most of the animals in the Paris zoo were killed and consumed by the public.

Soon Paris would find itself once again embroiled in civil war, and once again barricades would fill the streets, as Édouard Manet records in a drawing finished shortly after the events themselves (Fig. **31.1**). The new French National Assembly elected in February 1871, at the conclusion of the Franco-Prussian war, was dominated by monarchists. The treaty it negotiated with Bismarck required France to pay its invader a large sum of money and give up the eastern provinces of Alsace and part of Lorraine. Most Parisians felt that the assembly had betrayed the true interests of France. In March, they elected a new city government, which they dubbed

the Paris Commune, with the intention of governing Paris separately from the rest of the country. In a prelude to civil war, the National Assembly quickly struck back, ordering troops, led by General Lecomte [leh-KOHNT], to seize the armaments of the Commune. By the end of the day, angry Paris crowds seized Lecomte and summarily shot him. By nightfall, the National Assembly's troops, and the Assembly itself, had withdrawn to Versailles.

But the National Assembly was not about to let Paris go. Their troops surrounded the city and on May 8 bombarded it. Paris remained defiant, even festive. Edmond de Goncourt [ed-MOHN deh gohn-KOOR] (1822–1896), a chronicler of Parisian life, recalled: "I go into a café at the foot of the Champs-Élysées; and while the shells are killing up the avenue . . . men and women with the most tranquil, happy air in the world drink their beer and listen to an old woman play songs by Thérésa on a violin." Finally, on May 21, as hundreds of musicians entertained crowds in the Tuileries, 70,000 of the Assembly's troops stormed the city. Caught unawares, the Communards began erecting barricades, only to discover that Haussmannization allowed the army to outflank them and clear the

◄ **Fig. 31.1 Édouard Manet, *The Barricade*. ca. 1871.** Pencil ink, wash, watercolor, and gouache, 18¼″ × 12¾″ Szépüvészeti Múzeum, Budapest. Here Manet intentionally conflates "the bloody week" of May 1871 with the Civil War of 1848, the narrow street recalling especially Meissonier's 1849 *Memory of Civil War (The Barricades)* (see Fig. 29.1).

HEAR MORE Listen to an audio file of your chapter at **www.myartslab.com**

Fig. 31.2 Édouard Manet, *The Execution of Maximilian.* **1868–69.** Oil on canvas, 99 ¼″ × 120″.
Stadische Kunsthalle, Mannheim, Germany. This painting was not exhibited in France until 1905.

broad streets with artillery. By May 22, the city was ablaze, and a series of executions began as government troops arrested and killed anyone who seemed even vaguely sympathetic to the Commune. In what become known as "the bloody week," May 21 through 28, 1871, approximately 20,000 to 25,000 Parisians died. The Commune was crushed, and with it, the dreams of an independent Paris.

Whether Manet was actually in Paris that week is unknown. What is certain is that his drawing of the barricades is not an eye-witness account. Rather, it is derived from a painting of 1869, *The Execution of Maximilian* (Fig. **31.2**), an expression of Manet's outrage at Louis-Napoleon's humiliating imperial adventure in Mexico. In 1862, the emperor had sent 10,000 French troops to depose the first indigenous president ever elected, Benito Juarez [hwar-EZ] (1806–1872). Louis-Napoleon seethed at Juarez's independent policies, and his troops placed Maximilian

(1832–1867), brother of the Austrian emperor, on the throne as a puppet ruler. Under severe criticism at home in 1867, Louis-Napoleon withdrew all French forces from Mexico, abandoning Maximilian, who was captured by Juarez's troops and summarily executed.

Manet illustrated his displeasure with Louis-Napoleon's autocratic reign by depicting the scene in three full-scale paintings, an oil sketch, and a lithograph, none of which the government allowed to be exhibited at the time. The largest and most ambitious of these works is *The Execution of Maximilian.* The painting's most obvious influence is Francisco Goya's *The Third of May, 1808* (see Fig. 27.20), which Manet had probably seen in person in his August 1865 visit to Spain. Like the quasi-religious light shining on Goya's victims, Maximilian's sombrero encircles his head like a halo, an iconic symbol of martyrdom. The crowd leaning over the wall to observe the execution is reminiscent of many of Goya's bullfighting illustrations, lending the scene an aura of a bullfight's ritualistic death. But it is the point-blank range of the execution that most startles viewers, together with the evident coldness of the soldier in the red hat, who loads his rifle to deliver the final, mortal shot. (Manet read reports that the initial fusillade had failed to kill Maximilian—two more shots were required to finish him off.) Here Manet paints death as the matter-of-fact outcome of the emperor's own imperial ambitions.

The 1870s thus began, in France, in a mood that was anything but hopeful. The emperor of the bourgeoisie had been deposed, the country had been humiliated by Prussia, blood had filled the gutters of Paris's streets once again, flowing with the very hopes of the Commune into the sewers that Haussmann had built to make the city a more livable and attractive place. Haussmann himself had been dismissed by Louis-Napoleon in January of 1870 because of the questionable financial schemes he had arranged to fund his massive reconstruction projects. As for Manet, after the

defeat of the Commune, he traveled to Bordeaux, the seat of the National Assembly, and attended a session with a friend who had been elected as a delegate. Manet was amazed: "I never imagined France could be represented by such doddering old fools, not excepting that little twit Thiers [Louis Adolphe Thiers (1797–1877), former Prime Minister under King Louis-Philippe and after the Commune provisional President until 1873, when the National Assembly accepted his resignation after a vote of no confidence] who I hope will drop dead one day in the middle of a speech and rid us of his wizened little person." Manet then experienced a bout of severe depression and was unable to work again until the spring of 1872.

But work again he would, inspired by a group of painters a generation younger than himself who were determined to begin anew. As a group portrait by Henri Fantin-Latour [fahn-tan-law-TOOR] (1836–1904) makes clear, they already saw Manet as their leader (Fig. 31.3). And like Manet, they saw the entire apparatus of the

Fig. 31.3 Henri Fantin-Latour, *A Studio in the Batignolles*. 1870 (Salon of 1870). Oil on canvas, 6′ 8 1/4″ × 8′ 11 3/4″. Musée d'Orsay, Paris. From left to right are: Otto Schölderer, a German painter who had come to France to get to know Courbet's followers; the red-bearded Manet, sitting at his easel; Auguste Renoir, wearing a hat; Zacharie Astruc, who had written a poem to accompany the 1865 exhibition of *Olympia*; Émile Zola, the great defender of Manet's painting; Edmond Maître, a civil servant at the Town Hall; the painter Frédéric Bazille, who was killed a few months later during the 1870 war, at 26 years of age; and at the far right, Claude Monet.

French art world—the École des Beaux Arts [ay-KOHL deh bohz AHR], the Salon, and the Salon des Refusés—as hopelessly mired in the politics that had led to the disaster of the Commune. Many writers called for the arts to lead the way in rebuilding French culture: "Today, called by our common duty to revive France's fortune," the editor of the *Gazette des Beaux-Arts* wrote, "we will devote more attention to . . . the role of art . . . in the nation's economy, politics, and education." Across Europe—in Russia and England particularly—the same sense of hope and renewal, spawned by the arts, was taking hold. This drive for renewal is the subject of this chapter.

Moved by such rhetoric, in France a *Société anonyme* [soh-see-ay-TAY ah-noh]—literally, a public corporation—for painters, sculptors, and other artists was founded in December 1873. Membership was open to anyone who contributed 60 francs per year (about $12, or about $72 today). Among the founders were the painters Claude Monet (1840–1926) and Camille Pissarro (1830–1903); Pierre-Auguste Renoir [ruh-NWAHR] (1841–1919); Edgar Degas [deh-GAH] (1834–1917); and Berthe Morisot [moh-ree-SOH] (1841–1895), initially the lone woman in the group. Many of them had served

in the military, and their close friend and fellow painter Frédéric Bazille [bah-ZEEL] (1841–1870) had been killed during the war with Prussia. On April 15, 1874, they held the first of eight exhibitions. The last was held in 1886, by which time the Société had forever changed the face of French painting. In fact, it had transformed Western painting altogether.

FRENCH IMPRESSIONISM

From the outset, critics recognized that a distinguishing feature of this new group of painters was its preference for painting out-of-doors, **en plein air** [plen air] ("in open air"). The availability of paint in metal tubes, introduced between 1841 and 1843, is in part responsible. Now paints could be easily transported out-of-doors without danger of drying. It was the natural effects of light that most interested these younger painters, which they depicted using new synthetic pigments consisting of bright, transparent colors. Before they were ever called Impressionists, they were called the École de Plein Air, although the term *Impressionist* was in wide use by 1876, when poet Stéphane Mallarmé [mahl-ar-MAY]

Fig. 31.4 Claude Monet, *The Regatta at Argenteuil*. ca. 1872. Oil on canvas, 19″ × 29¹/₂″. Musée d'Orsay, Paris, France. Erich Lessing/Art Resource, New York. Monet moved to Argenteuil, a suburb on the Seine just north of Paris, in December 1871, perhaps to leave memories of the Commune behind.

Fig. 31.5 Claude Monet, *Impression: Sunrise*. 1873. Oil on canvas, 19 $\frac{5}{8}$" × 25 $\frac{1}{2}$". Musée Marmottan-Claude Monet, Paris, France. Erich Lessing/Art Resource, New York. The painting is a view of the harbor in Le Havre, France, on the English Channel.

(1842–1898) published his essay "Impressionism and Édouard Manet." (Manet, although generally considered the leader of the Impressionists, repeatedly declined invitations to exhibit with them.)

Plein air painting implied, first of all, the artist's abandonment of the traditional environment of the studio. Of all the Impressionists, Claude Monet was the most insistent that only *en plein air* could he realize the full potential of his artistic energy. In rejecting the past, the painters of the Société cultivated the present moment, emphasizing improvisation and spontaneity. Each painting had to be quick, deliberately sketchy, in order to capture the ever-changing, fleeting effects of light in a natural setting. Although Monet habitually reworked his paintings in the studio, he would tell a young American artist: "When you go out to paint, try to forget what objects you have before you—a tree, a house, a field, or whatever. Merely think, here is a little square of blue,

here an oblong of pink, here a streak of yellow, and paint it just as it looks to you, until it gives you your own naïve impression of the scene before you." It is not surprising, then, that in Monet's *The Regatta at Argenteuil* [ar-zhan-TOY-eh] the reflection of the landscape in the water disintegrates into a sketchy series of broad dashes of paint (Fig. 31.4). On the surface of the water, the mast of the green sailboat seems to support a red-and-green sail, but this "sail" is really the reflection of the red house and cypress tree on the hillside. Monet sees the relationship between his painting and the real scene as analogous to the relationship between the surface of the water and the shoreline above. Both of these surfaces—canvas and water—reflect the fleeting quality of sensory experience.

Two paintings by Monet in the first Impressionist exhibition offer different perspectives on this new approach to art. The first, *Impression: Sunrise*, went a long way toward giving Impressionism its name (Fig. **31.5**). The artist applied the paint in brushstrokes of pure, occasionally unmixed, color that evoke forms in their own right. He rendered waves in staccato bursts of horizontal dashes, the reflection of the rising sun on the water in swirls of orange brushstrokes highlighted with white. Violets and blues contrast with yellows and oranges as if to capture the prismatic effects of light. Most of all, one feels the very presence of the painter at work, his hand racing across the surface of the canvas before the morning light vanished. Although Monet would often work and rework his paintings, they seem "of the moment," as immediate as a photograph.

In the second painting, *Boulevard des Capucines*, we look out over the *grands boulevards* with the two top-hatted men who lean forward out the window at the right (Fig. **31.6**). The building at the left is the Grand Hôtel, and between it and the next building, the space compressed by Monet's perspective, is the Place de l'Opéra. We are, in fact, standing in the exhibition space of the first Impressionist show, and this is a work of art about its own marketplace. Monet's brushwork, capturing the play of light on the leaves of the trees and the crowds in the street, is even looser and freer than in *Impression: Sunrise*. Writing in *Paris-Journal* in May 1874, the critic Ernest Chesneau [shay-noh] recognized the painting's significance:

The extraordinary animation of the public street, the crowd swarming on the sidewalks, the carriages on the pavement, and the boulevard's trees waving in the dust and light—never has movement's elusive, fugitive, instantaneous quality been captured and fixed in all its tremendous fluidity as it has in this extraordinary, marvelous sketch. . . . At a distance, one hails a masterpiece in this stream of life, this trembling of great shadow and light, sparkling with even darker shadows and brighter lights. But come closer, and it all vanishes. There remains only an indecipherable chaos of palette scrapings. . . . It is necessary to go on and transform the sketch into a finished work. But what a bugle call for those who listen carefully, how it resounds far into the future!

Fig. 31.6 Claude Monet, *Boulevard des Capucines*. 1873. Oil on canvas, 24″ × 31 ¹/₂″. Pushkin Museum of Fine Arts, Moscow, Russia. Scala/Art Resource, New York. There are two paintings by this name, both executed in 1873. The other is a winter scene. It is unclear which of these two was exhibited at the first Impressionist exhibition, but Chesneau's description points toward this one.

Fig. 31.7 Claude Monet. *Grainstack (Snow Effect).* **1891.** Oil on canvas, 25³/₄″ × 36³/₈″. Museum of Fine Arts, Boston. Gift of Miss Aimee and Rosamond Lamb in memory of Mr. and Mrs. Horatio A. Lamb, 1970.253. Photograph © 2008 Museum of Fine Arts, Boston. This painting has a simple geometric structure—a triangle set on a rectangle, both set on a rectangular ground.

Chesneau failed to understand that this "sketch" was already "finished." But he was right that it was a painting of the future. It would not take long for the public to understand that this "chaotic" brushwork was the very mark of a new sensibility, one dedicated to capturing what the French call *le temps* [tahn], a word that refers to the "time of day," "the weather," and "the age" all at once.

Monet's Escape to Giverny

After the Commune, except for a brief stint in Paris in 1876 to 1877 when he painted a series of works on the Gare Saint-Lazare train station, Monet continually sought to escape the city for the pleasures of the countryside. In December 1871, he had moved to Argenteuil, an idyllic little village on the Seine downriver from Paris and where he lived for seven years. Then, faced with the suburb's increasing industrialization and urbanization, he moved farther downriver to Vétheuil [vay-TOY], another little town with a tiny population, no railroads, no industry, no pollution, and no weekend Parisian crowds. Finally, in April 1883, he moved farther downriver again, to Giverny [zhee-vair-NEE]. Monet's determined flight from the distraction of crowds is an announcement of the rapid growth of suburbs and outlying towns surrounding Paris (and every other growing metropolis) in the last quarter of the century.

Monet did not begin painting at Giverny immediately. Instead, he traveled—to the south of France, to the Côte d'Azur [koht dah-ZOOR], to Brittany and the Normandy coast, and to locations all across France. Monet's sojourn through the countryside points to the increased opportunities for leisurely travel afforded by the ever-expanding railroad networks in France. Indeed many of the towns and scenes he painted were tourist locales, frequented by the prosperous Parisian middle class that the Impressionists sought to cultivate. Many of his contemporaries attacked the master of Impressionism for the shallowness of his themes and his apparent instantaneous rendering of light effects. But the painting was anything but instantaneous. "The more I go on," Monet wrote in a letter to a friend, "the more I see that I must work a lot to succeed in rendering what I am looking for: 'instantaneity' . . . more than ever I'm disgusted by easy things that come without effort."

In the autumn of 1888, Monet began using a different series format than before, painting the same subject at different times of day and in different atmospheric conditions. In addition to a series on a line of poplar trees and on Rouen Cathedral, he painted a series of grainstacks in the nearby farmer's field. In May 1891, he exhibited 15 grainstack paintings in Paris. They were a spectacular success (Fig. **31.7**). In a preface to

LEARN MORE Gain insight from a primary source document about Claude Monet at **www.myartslab.com**

the catalog for the exhibition, art critic and Monet friend's Gustave Geffroy describes their effect on the viewer:

> These stacks in this deserted field are transient objects whose surfaces, like mirrors, catch the mood of the environment, the states of the atmosphere with the errant breeze, the sudden glow. Light and shade radiate from them, sun and shadow revolve around them in relentless pursuit; they reflect its dying heat, its last rays; they are shrouded in mist, soaked with rain, frozen with snow, in harmony with the distant horizon, the earth, the sky. . . .

Each painting in the series, then, becomes a fragment in the duration of the whole, and Geffroy's reading of the works transforms Monet into an artist who in rendering nature also depicts his own interior landscape. As he continued to work—almost daily until his death in 1926—he turned his attention to his gardens at Giverny, creating some of the most monumental paintings in the history of art (see Chapter 33).

Morisot and Pissarro: The Effects of Paint

Monet's willingness to break his edges with feathery strokes of paint was even more radically developed in the work of Berthe Morisot. Born to a socially connected bourgeois family (she was the granddaughter of the Rococo painter Fragonard, noted for his rapid brushwork) (see Fig. 25.6), Morisot received an education that included lessons in drawing and painting from the noted landscape artist Camille Corot. She became a professional painter and a highly regarded colleague to male artists of her generation. Morisot was the sister-in-law of Manet, and it was she who convinced him to adopt an Impressionist technique of his own. But no one could match her "vaporous and barely drawn lines," as one critic put it. "Here are some young women rocking in a boat," writes a critic of her painting *Summer's Day*, ". . . seen through fine gray tones, matte white, and light pink, with no shadows, set off with little multi-colored daubs . . ." (Fig. **31.8**). She drapes her bourgeois figures, out for a little recreation, in clothing that is often barely distinguishable from the background, like those worn by the woman in the middle of the boat. She shuns outline

Fig. 31.8 Berthe Morisot, *Summer's Day*. 1879. Oil on canvas, 18″ × 29³/₄″. National Gallery, London. Note the almost arbitrary brushwork that defines the bottoms of the dresses worn by both women, one a set of zigzags, the other a patchwork of straight strokes, emphasizing the distance and difference between the two.

Fig. 31.9 Camille Pissarro, _Red Roofs_, or _The Orchard, Côtes Saint-Denis at Pontoise_. 1877. Oil on canvas, 21½" × 25⅞". Musée d'Orsay, Paris, France. Erich Lessing/Art Resource, New York. When Bismarck advanced on Paris, Pissarro abandoned his home in Louveciennes, on the outskirts of the city, and Bismarck's forces moved in. On rainy days, they created a path across the courtyard with Pissarro's paintings to keep their feet from getting wet. As a result, few of his paintings from before 1871 survive.

altogether—each of the ducks in the water is realized in several broad, quick strokes.

If Morisot's paintings seem to dissolve into a uniform white light, Camille Pissarro's landscapes give us the impression of a view never quite fully captured by the painter. In _Red Roofs_, a random patchwork of red and green, orange and blue appears through a veil of tree branches that interrupt the viewer's vision (Fig. **31.9**). Pissarro was deeply interested in the new science of color theory, and he paid close attention to the 1864 treatise of Michel-Eugène Chevreul [shev-RULL] (1786–1889), _On Colors and Their_

Applications to the Industrial Arts. Chevreul argued that complementary colors of pigment (that is, colors directly opposite each other on the traditional color wheel)—like red and green, yellow and violet, blue and orange—intensify each other's hue when set side by side. Pissarro adopted a later scheme by American physicist Ogden Rood (1831–1902), in which the primary colors of light, rather than pigment, were red, green, and blue-violet. In this he anticipated the color theories that would stimulate Neo-Impressionist painters of the next generation like Georges Seurat [suh-RAH] and Paul Signac [seen-YAK] (see Chapter 33).

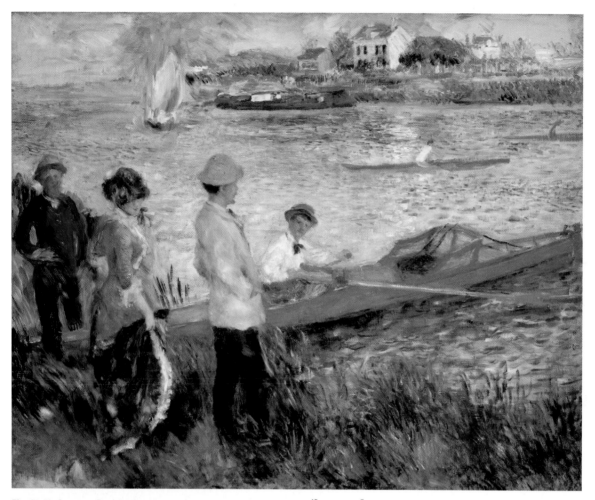

Fig. 31.10 Auguste Renoir, *Oarsmen at Chatou*. 1879. Oil on canvas, 31 $^{15}/_{16}$" × 39 $^{7}/_{16}$". National Gallery of Art, Washington, D.C. Gift of Sam A. Lewisohn. 1951.5.2 The man in the boat may be Renoir's brother Edmond.

Leisure and Work: Renoir, Degas, and Caillebotte

While Monet and Pissarro concentrated on landscape painting, Auguste Renoir and Edgar Degas preferred to paint the crowd in the cafés and restaurants, at entertainments of all kinds, and in the countryside, to which the middle class habitually escaped on weekends via the ever-expanding railroad lines. Renoir was especially attracted to Chatou [shah-TOO], a small village on the Seine frequented by rowers. No longer reserved for the upper class, Chatou and other riverside towns became retreats for a diverse crowd of Parisian artists, bourgeoisie, and even workers. Weekend escapes centered on cafés, dance halls, boating, and swimming. Renoir was particularly fond of the Maison and Restaurant Fournaise [foor-NEZ], a lodging house and restaurant on an island in the river, which served as the setting of *Luncheon of the Boating Party* (see *Closer Look*, pages 1028–1029). In *Oarsmen at Chatou* (Fig. **31.10**), the Restaurant Fournaise is behind us. On the opposite bank of the river is another well-known restaurant, La Mère Lefranc. A sailboat, two single sculls, and a working barge make their way upriver. In the foreground, a rower holds a two-person gig, designed for a rower and a passenger who would steer the boat with two lines attached to the rudder. He gestures as if inviting one of the group on the bank to join him. The man in white is the painter Gustave Caillebotte, whose *Paris Street, Rainy Day* we saw in the last chapter (see Fig. 30.2). The woman is Aline Charigot [shah-ree-GOH], Renoir's future wife. As the great historian of French Impressionism, Robert L. Herbert, has said of this painting: "Lushness is the word for Renoir's color, as well as the setting: saturated oranges and orange reds against blues and greens. . . .The picture has the air of a fable, of an ideal world of leisure without work, of sensual pleasure without tarnish." But despite the lushness of Renoir's palette and the loose freedom of his brushwork, the painting, like so many of Renoir's best pictures, is tightly composed. The four figures on the left, together with the sailboat directly above them, form an almost perfect pentagon, from the feet of the two forward figures to the top of the sail. That geometric symmetry contrasts dramatically with the random horizontals and diagonals that make up the right side of the painting. Here is one of the great secrets of Impressionist painting—the looseness and freedom of the brush held in check by orderly design.

Edgar Degas was as dedicated as Renoir to the careful construction of his paintings. *Dance Class* depicts 21 dancers awaiting their turn to be evaluated by the ballet master, who stands leaning on a tall cane in the middle ground watching a young ballerina making her salute to an imaginary audience (Fig. **31.11**). The atmosphere is unpretentious, emphasizing the elaborate preparations and hard work necessary to produce a work of art that will appear effortless on stage. The dancers form an arc, connecting the foreground to the middle ground and drawing the eye quickly through the space of the painting. Degas draws the viewer's attention to the complex structure of his composition—that is, to the fact that he too has *worked* long and hard at it.

Fig. 31.11 Edgar Degas, *Dance Class*. ca. 1874. Oil on canvas, 32 $^3/_4$″ × 30 $^1/_4$″. The Metropolitan Museum of Art. Bequest of Mr. and Mrs. Harry Payne Bingham, 1986 (1987.47.1). Image © The Metropolitan Museum of Art. The dance instructor is Jules Perrot, the most famous male dancer of the middle third of the century, whose likeness Degas took from a photograph of 1861.

Renoir's *Luncheon of the Boating Party* required the painter to take a slightly different tack than was usual for him. We can identify many of the figures from his circle of friends and acquaintances at Chatou, including members of the Fournaise family at whose restaurant the painting is set. To represent such recognizable figures, Renoir had to abandon the gestural brushwork of Monet and Pissarro except in the background landscape. He composed his figures with firm outlines and modeled them in subtle gradations of light and dark, which clearly define their anatomical and facial features. And he carefully structured the group in a series of interlocking triangles, the largest of which is made up of Aline Charigot, his future wife, sitting at the table holding her dog. Scholars believe that the painting, begun in the summer of 1880, may represent Renoir's response to Émile Zola's critique in his review of the 1880 Salon charging the Impressionists with selling "sketches that are hardly dry" and challenging them to make more complex paintings that would be the result of "long and thoughtful preparation." For this reason, the theory goes, Renoir assimilates into this single work landscape, still life, and genre painting in a manner probably intentionally recalling seventeenth-century Dutch and Flemish paintings like Rubens's *The Kermis* (see Fig. 23.7), which Renoir would have seen at the Louvre.

Grounding the interplay of triangles upon which Renoir's painting is based is the still-life composition of three bottles in the center of the table. Outlined here are the various sets of triangular relationships determined by groupings of figures and their visual or verbal interchanges. While the entire composition moves off into space at an angle from left to right, another compositional pyramid is formed by the angles of Caillebotte's and Charigot's hats, meeting roughly at the top of the post supporting the awning at the top middle of the painting.

Something to Think About . . .

Given the wide variety of people in this composition, how might you describe its social politics? In other words, what sort of broader society does it suggest?

Renoir's *Luncheon of the Boating Party*

Auguste Renoir, *Luncheon of the Boating Party*. 1880–81. Oil on canvas, 51 1/4″ × 69 1/8″ (130.18 × 175.58 cm). Acquired 1923. Phillips Collection, Washington, D.C.

The Italian journalist Adrien Maggiolo, the only male not wearing a hat, leans over an actress by the name of Angèle Legault and the painter Gustave Caillebotte. Maggiolo was a writer for *Le Triboulet* (*The King's Dunce*), a journal dedicated to theater and cabaret in Paris.

Alphonsine Fournaise, the proprietor's daughter, rests her elbow on the railing. She is talking with Baron Raoul Barbier, Renoir's friend and a notorious womanizer.

Charles Euphussi, in the top hat, editor of the *Gazette des Beaux-Arts* and an avid art collector, chats with a young man in a mariner's cap, perhaps the poet Jules Laforgue, who served as Euphussi's personal secretary.

The actress Jeanne Samary, a star of the Comédie Française, covers her ears as two of Renoir's best friends, the writer Paul Lhote, in the red-striped hat, and Eugène Pierre Lestringuez, who had known Renoir since childhood, flirt with her.

Leaning against the rail and overseeing the entire luncheon is Alphonse Fournaise, son of the restaurant's proprietor.

Renoir would marry Aline Charigot in 1890. Serving as their witnesses were Lhote and Lestringuez, depicted in the opposite corner of the painting flirting with the actress Jeanne Samary.

The actress Ellen Andrée was a close friend of Aline Charigot. She performed in the most avant-garde plays of the day, those of Swedish playwright Henrik Ibsen (see Chapter 33), at the Théâtre-Libre.

At age 32, when Renoir painted this scene, Caillebotte was the youngest of the Impressionists. He was also by far the wealthiest, having inherited his father's considerable fortune, and he thought it his God-given duty to support his Impressionist colleagues. As a result, he amassed a very substantial collection of works by Degas, Cézanne, Manet, Monet, Pissarro, Renoir, and Sisley, which he bequeathed to the state upon his death in 1894. His bequest—Renoir was his estate's executor—became the basis for the great collection of Impressionist painting today housed in the Musée d'Orsay in Paris.

Work is, in fact, one of Degas's primary themes, and it is no accident that the ballet master leans on a cane—as a former dancer, he is understood to be physically impaired from a dance injury. Degas understood that the young women he depicted were, in fact, full-time child workers, mired in the monotony of *répétition*, which in French is the word for both "repetition" and "rehearsal." Almost all were from lower-class families and normally entered the ballet corps at age seven or eight when their schooling ceased, leaving most of them illiterate. They had to pass examinations, such as the one Degas depicts here, in order to continue. By the time they were nine or ten, they might earn 300 francs a year (approximately $60 in 1870, with a buying power of about $400 today). If and when they rose to the level of performing brief solos in the ballet, they might earn as much as 1,500 francs—more than most of their fathers, who were shop clerks, cab drivers, and laborers. Should they ever achieve the status of *première danseuse* [pruh-mee-YAIR dahn-SUZ], in their late teens, they might earn as much as 20,000 francs, a status like today's richly compensated professional athlete that few reached but all dreamed of. Thus, Degas's *Dance Class* presents young women in a moment of great stress, struggling in a Darwinian world in which only the fittest survived.

Work was also the theme of the first painting that Gustave Caillebotte exhibited with the Impressionists at their exhibition in April 1876, *The Floor-Scrapers* (Fig. **31.12**). Degas would later claim that he had introduced Caillebotte to the group. Together with another Impressionist, it was Renoir who invited him to exhibit in the show. As in Degas's images of dancers, Caillebotte's theme is the monotony of repetition, the rhythm of parallel lines of flooring reinforcing the theme. It was Caillebotte's subject matter that most startled reviewers: "In his *Floor-Scrapers*, Caillebotte declares himself to be a Realist as crude and intelligent, in his own way, as Courbet, as violent and precise, again in his own way, as Manet," wrote one critic. The painting is instructive because, in its absolutely traditional

Fig. 31.12 Gustave Caillebotte, *The Floor-Scrapers*. 1875. Oil on canvas, 40 $^1/_8$″ × 57 $^1/_2$″. Musée d'Orsay, Paris. Gift of the artist's heirs, 1894. RF 2718. When, as executor of Caillebotte's estate, Renoir arranged for the state to accept Caillebotte's bequest of his collection of Impressionist paintings, he suggested that *The Floor-Scrapers* accompany the bequest, and thus it eventually entered the collection of the Musée d'Orsay.

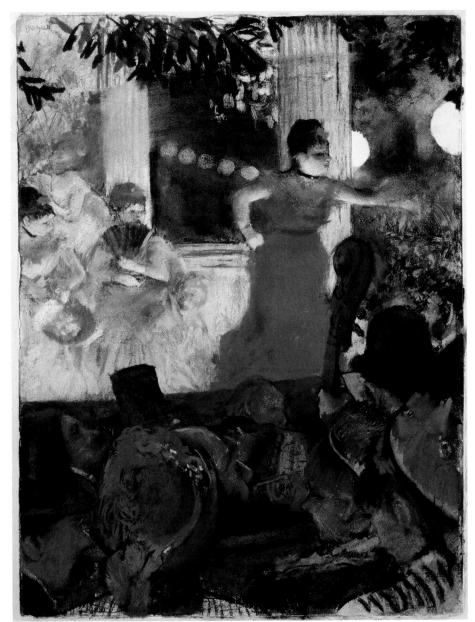

handling of paint, it suggests that subject matter, more than technique—the signature Impressionist loose, almost sketchy brushwork—was at least initially what defined Caillebotte as a member of the group. By the 1880s, Caillebotte would adopt the looser Impressionist style, but at the time, Émile Zola complained in a review that Caillebotte's painting was "bourgeois in its precision."

Degas was the most radical of the Impressionists in experimenting with new media. He was especially stimulated by **pastels**—sticks of powdered pigment bound with resin or gum. The soft effects of pastel could simulate the gaslit atmosphere of Paris's café-concerts in the outdoor pavilions behind cafés such as the Café des Ambassadeurs, in the park at the base of the Champs-Élysées. Degas's

Aux Ambassadeurs, displayed at the 1877 Impressionist exhibition, places the viewer in the audience close to the orchestra and behind three ladies and a gentleman (Fig. **31.13**). Onstage is the *chanteuse* ("singer"), her arm extended toward the audience as she sings. Behind her is the *corbeille* [kor-BAY], a term meaning "flowerbed" or "basket" but used figuratively to refer to the dress circle at the theater. In fact, the *corbeille* was composed of women of questionable repute hired to sit on the stage and look attractive and who communicated with admirers in the audience with a sign language, visible in Degas's pastel. Degas's taste for depicting such pleasure-seekers—on the stage and in the audience—is similar to Manet's earlier "judgments" of Paris.

Manet's Impressionism

Throughout the 1870s the influence of Manet's sister-in-law, Berthe Morisot, caused Manet increasingly to adopt the Impressionist techniques of the younger generation, particularly the loose application of paint and the emphasis on capturing the effects of light. But whereas the Impressionists tended to celebrate the good life, Manet never gave up his penchant for critiquing it in terms much more direct than the subtle "judgments" offered by Degas. Manet's *A Bar at the Folies-Bergère* [foh-LEE-ber-ZHER], the last major painting he finished before his death in 1883, situates the viewer in a higher-class environment than Degas's café-concert (Fig. 31.14). The viewer faces a barmaid standing behind her marble counter on a balcony in front of a mirror reflecting the Folies theater in front of her. She is more or less in the same position as the barmaid at the lower right of Jules Chéret's 1875 poster for the Folies, which reveals the entertainment of the moment: a trapeze artist flying across the space (Fig. 31.15). The same trapeze artist's feet are visible at the top left of Manet's painting.

What really captures viewer attention in this painting is the barmaid's eyes. Instead of gazing directly at the viewer, as in *Le Déjeuner sur l'herbe* (see Fig. 30.6) or *Olympia* (see *Closer Look*, Chapter 30), the eyes look past us, perhaps even inward in thought. In the midst of the crowd, the barmaid seems totally alone. The oddity of this is compounded by the barmaid's reflection in the mirror, improbably shifted to the right. For, in fact, the barmaid is facing a gentleman, who stands before her in the place we occupy as viewers. She is the object of his gaze (and our own), and he affirms her status, in his own eyes at least, as a server of consolation. Manet's Impressionism, then, incorporates the viewer into its "atmosphere," which like the illusion of depth provided by the mirror is actually impenetrable.

Fig. 31.14 Édouard Manet, *A Bar at the Folies-Bergère*. 1881–82. Oil on canvas, 37 ³/₄″ × 51 ¹/₈″. The Samuel Courtauld Trust, The Courtauld Gallery, London. Manet's model was actually a waitress at the Folies-Bergère named Suzon.

SEE MORE For a Closer Look at Edouard Manet's *A Bar at the Folies-Bergère,* go to **www.myartslab.com**

Fig. 31.15 Jules Chéret, *Aux Folies-Bergère*. 1875. Poster. Mention obligatoire Les Arts Decoratifs, Paris (Inv. 7972); Musée de la Publicité (Inv. 10531); Photo: Laurent Sully Jaulmes. Tous droits reserves. The Folies-Bergère opened as a department store specializing in bedding in 1860, but a "salle des spectacles" at the back of the store became so successful that by 1869, the store had given up the bedding business to concentrate solely on entertainment.

RUSSIAN REALISM AND THE QUEST FOR THE RUSSIAN SOUL

Ever since Catherine the Great made French the official language of the Russian court in the eighteenth century, unabashed Francophiles [FRANK-oh-files]—lovers of all things French—had dominated cultural life in Saint Petersburg. By the turn of the century, Moscow merchants Sergei Shchukin (1854–1936) and Ivan Morozov (1871–1921) had amassed important collections of Impressionist paintings. Shchukin purchased Camille Pissarro's *Avenue de l'Opéra* (see Fig. 30.1) as well as paintings from Claude Monet's *Grainstacks*, *Rouen Cathedral*, and *Water Lilies* series. Morozov purchased Monet's *Boulevard des Capucines* (see Fig. 31.6) and several important Renoirs. Such collecting was motivated, at least in part, by political beliefs. Those who turned to France and Germany for inspiration, known as Westernizers, believed that Russia was hopelessly backward, epitomized by the continuation of serfdom. They believed that only by adopting Western values could the nation be saved.

But many Russians disagreed, arguing that the country possessed a spirit uniquely its own. These so-called Slavophiles [SLAHV-oh-files]—Russian nationalists—rejected the West as a source of inspiration in favor of Old Russian traditions and the Orthodox Church. They prided themselves on their spirituality. These values were shared by Fyodor Dostoyevsky [dust-uh-YEF-skee] (1821–1881) and Leo Tolstoy (1828–1910). Russian nationalism found expression in art and music too. Underlying all Russian culture—Francophile and Slavophile alike—was the plight of the Russian serfs, 22 million souls who were essentially slaves who worked the fields of their landlords for their entire lives with little or no compensation.

The Writer and Artist under the Tsars

Under the rule of Nicholas I (1825–1855), literary culture in Russia was severely stifled. Constantly on guard against rebellion, the tsar exercised strict control over education, publishing, and all public entertainment. Nicholas's successor, Alexander II (r. 1855–1881), was as autocratic as his father, but he instituted a series of reforms, including the emancipation of the serfs in 1861. This act would profoundly affect the cultural life of his country, creating a sense of hope and possibility where before there had been none.

The Psychological Realism of Dostoyevsky Troubled by the European revolutions of 1848, Nicholas abolished the study of philosophy at the University of Saint Petersburg and arrested members of a radical discussion group called the Petrashevsky Circle. One of those detained was the 27-year-old novelist Fyodor Dostoyevsky. Found guilty of subversive activities, he, like his colleagues, was sentenced to death. On December 22, 1849, Dostoyevsky and the others were led before the firing squad, but at the last minute, the tsar issued a reprieve. Dostoyevsky was sentenced to four years in a Siberian labor camp, followed by six years in the army in Mongolia. He would describe his experiences in prison in the short novel *The House of the Dead* (1862) as "A period of burial alive, I was put in a coffin. The torture was unutterable and unbearable."

However, Dostoyevsky slowly came to admire his fellow inmates—murderers, thieves, and social outcasts. And the question he began to contemplate, which would occupy him for the rest of his life, was this: Can we love the damned? Are we not obligated to face the horrors of life to which the damned are condemned? As one of his characters in *The Insulted and Injured* (1861) puts it: "It thrills the heart to realize that the most downtrodden man, the lowest of the low, is also a human being and is called your brother."

Dostoyevsky was not allowed to return to Saint Petersburg until 1859, four years after the death of Nicholas I. Two years later, in 1861, when the new tsar, Alexander II, ordered the emancipation of Russia's serfs, Dostoyevsky felt the impact personally. His domineering and alcoholic father, a retired military surgeon and doctor at a hospital for the poor in Moscow, may have been murdered by his own serfs in 1839. Dostoyevsky's greatest and last novel, *The Brothers Karamazov* (1880), would have as a central figure an abusive father who is killed by his sons.

The complexity of psychological guilt is the theme of his 1866 novel, *Crime and Punishment*, as is the basic question: "Can immoral means justify worthy ends?" Its hero, Rodion Petrovich Raskolnikov—Rodya, for short—is tormented by his senseless axe murder of a despised pawnbroker and her more likable sister. Prior to the murder, Raskolnikov, an intellectual, had written an article dividing the world into ordinary people and gifted heroes (like Napoleon) who are above the law (see **Reading 31.1**, page 1045). Like all of Dostoyevsky's heroes, Raskolnikov is driven by an idea, not by hereditary or environmental causes. Dostoyevsky called his style a "higher realism" because it is so infused with the anxieties, conflicts, and tensions that comprise modern consciousness. Raskolnikov believes himself to be the embodiment of his idea, as a gifted hero above the law. It was, in fact, a misguided attempt to assert individual freedom and to escape humanity's enslavement to scientific rationalism, capitalism, and industrialism. Dostoyevsky's hero, then, has damned himself—like Goethe's Faust (see Chapter 27). In a bold gambit, the author asks you, the reader, to comprehend that Raskolnikov is also "your brother."

After the murder, Raskolnikov barely escapes detection at the pawnbroker's home, then makes his way through the streets of Saint Petersburg. A short excerpt captures the drama that characterizes Dostoyevsky's style (**Reading 31.1a**):

READING 31.1a

from Fyodor Dostoyevsky, *Crime and Punishment*, **Part I, Chapter 7 (1866)**

No one was on the stairs, nor in the gateway. He passed quickly through the gateway and turned to the left in the street.

He knew, he knew perfectly well that at that moment they were at the flat, that they were greatly astonished at finding it unlocked, as the door had just been fastened, that by now they were looking at the bodies, that before another minute had passed they would guess and completely realise that the murderer had just been there, and had succeeded in hiding somewhere, slipping by them and escaping. They would guess most likely that he had been in the empty flat, while they were going upstairs. And meanwhile he dared not quicken his pace much, though the next turning was still nearly a hundred yards away. "Should he slip through some gateway and wait somewhere in an unknown street? No, hopeless! Should he fling away the axe? Should he take a cab? Hopeless, hopeless!"

At last he reached the turning. He turned down it more dead than alive. Here he was half way to safety, and he understood it; it was less risky because there was a great crowd of people, and he was lost in it like a grain of sand. But all he had suffered had so weakened him that he could scarcely move. Perspiration ran down him in drops, his neck was all wet. . . .

He was only dimly conscious of himself now, and the farther he went the worse it was. . . . He was not fully conscious when he passed through the gateway of his house! he was already on the staircase before he recollected the axe. And yet he had a very grave problem before him, to put it back and to escape observation as far as possible in doing so. He was of course incapable of reflecting that it might perhaps be far better not to restore the axe at all, but to drop it later on in somebody's yard. . . . Scraps and shreds of thoughts were simply swarming in his brain, but he could not catch at one, he could not rest on one, in spite of all his efforts. . . .

The drama continues to heighten as the detective, Porfiry Petrovich, persistently pecks away at Raskolnikov and as Sonya, a young woman driven to prostitution by her alcoholic father, tries to persuade him to confess. He does finally confess his guilt and is sentenced to imprisonment in Siberia, where Sonya faithfully accompanies him. By the novel's end, Raskolnikov realizes he is not a superhuman hero above the law, and he dreams that his nihilism was a deadly plague advancing on Russia and Europe. Rejecting his former beliefs, Raskolnikov undergoes a spiritual rebirth, accepting the necessity of religion as well as love:

> Life had stepped into the place of theory and something quite different would work itself out in his mind. . . . He did not know that the new life would not be given him for nothing, that he would have to pay dearly for it, that it would cost him great striving, great suffering. But that is the beginning of a new story—the story of the gradual renewal of a man, the story of his gradual regeneration, of his passing from one world into another, of his initiation into a new unknown life.

In this renewal, Raskolnikov discovers his connection with the common people and so the essence of his Russian soul.

The Historical Realism of Tolstoy If Dostoyevsky's realism turned inward to the psychology of his tormented Russian heroes, Leo Tolstoy's realism turned outward, to the epic stage of Russian history. Slightly younger than Dostoyevsky, Tolstoy was born to privilege and wealth, and he began publishing short stories in the mid-1850s, while serving in the army. These dealt with childhood memories and his military career and helped him establish a literary reputation. Yet no one anticipated the two great novels he would write after his return to the family estate, 100 miles south of Moscow: *War and Peace* (1869) and *Anna Karenina* [kuh-REN-ih-nuh] (1877). Although both novels focus on the lifestyle of the Russian aristocracy, they also critique it.

War and Peace surveys Russian life in the early nineteenth century, telling the story of five aristocratic families as they come to terms with Napoleon's 1812 invasion of their country. Two major male characters, the intellectual but pessimistic Prince Andre Bolkonsky and the spiritual, questing Pierre Bezukhov, represent conflicting moral positions: the Romantic desire to fully realize the self versus dedication to others. Against the backdrop of war, each falls in love with Natasha Rostov, the young daughter of a noble Moscow family whose fortunes are failing. Andre is prevented from marrying her by his father, while Pierre, after having been taken prisoner by the French, finally succeeds. Their story illustrates the triumph of the Russian soul over the logical Western mind of Napoleon, whose disastrous decision to invade Russia initiates his downfall.

There are scores of characters in *War and Peace*, but Natasha Rostov is one of the great characters in all of fiction. Along with his brilliant accounts of war, Tolstoy's depiction of her is the hallmark of his realist style. We first meet her in Chapter 11 of the novel as a 13-year-old who, on her name-day (the day of the year associated with her name), bursts into the sitting room where her parents, the count and countess, have been receiving guests (**Reading 31.2**):

READING 31.2

from Leo Tolstoy, *War and Peace*, Part I, Chapter 11 (1869)

The countess looked at her callers, smiling affably, but not concealing the fact that she would not be distressed if they now rose and took their leave. The visitor's daughter was already smoothing down her dress with an inquiring look at her mother, when suddenly from the next room were heard the footsteps of boys and girls running to the door and the noise of a chair falling over, and a girl of thirteen, hiding something in the folds of her short muslin frock, darted in and stopped short in the middle of the room. It was evident that she had not intended her flight to bring her so far. . . .

The count jumped up and, swaying from side to side, spread his arms wide and threw them round the little girl who had run in. "Ah, here she is!" he exclaimed laughing. "My pet, whose name day it is. My dear pet!"

"Ma chere, there is a time for everything," said the countess with feigned severity. "You spoil her, Ilya," she added, turning to her husband.

"How do you do, my dear? I wish you many happy returns of your name day," said the visitor. "What a charming child," she added, addressing the mother.

This black-eyed, wide-mouthed girl, not pretty but full of life—with childish bare shoulders which after her run heaved and shook her bodice, with black curls tossed backward, thin bare arms, little legs in lace-frilled drawers, and feet in low slippers—was just at that charming age when a girl is no longer a child, though the child is not yet a young woman. Escaping from her father she ran to hide her flushed face in the lace of her mother's mantilla—not paying the least attention to her severe remark—and began to laugh.

The exuberance of the young girl, her ability to dominate any room into which she walks, is immediately established. From this moment, Natasha lives life boldly, determined to enjoy it to the fullest, and over the course of the novel, she grows into a woman of real wisdom and understanding.

The scope of Tolstoy's next novel, *Anna Karenina*, is narrower than in *War and Peace*, even as its representation of human feeling and emotions is more fully realized. It tells the story of the adulterous love affair of Anna, who is married to a government official in Saint Petersburg, and Count Vronsky [VRON-skee], a dashing young cavalry officer. Anna's "double" in the book is Constantine Levin. He shares her intensity and passion, but unlike Anna does not easily fit into Saint Petersburg's social swirl and so chooses to live instead on his country estate, dedicating himself to farming and the lives of the peasants who work for him. Tortured by doubts about the meaning of his life throughout most of the book, he experiences a spiritual revelation at the novel's end that reveals his reason for being. By contrast, Anna's more carnal passion leads to her destruction, the inevitable victim of her society's double standards.

It is possible to see Tolstoy's own spiritual autobiography in Levin's struggle with God. Tolstoy experienced many religious crises in his life, struggling to find a way of living religiously without endorsing the hypocrisies and greed of the Russian Orthodox Church, from which he was eventually excommunicated. Most of his writing after *Anna Karenina* consisted of educational articles and pamphlets, the ideas of which are most clearly formulated in his 1886 *What Then Must We Do?* In the interest of leading an exemplary life, he gave up smoking and drinking alcohol, became a vegetarian, dressed in peasant clothes, engaged in hard labor (Fig. **31.16**), and renounced sexual relations with his wife, with whom he had fathered 13 children. Yet all of Tolstoy's spiritual striving and rationally constructed religious doctrine could not ensure a happy family life. Arguments continually flared between his wife and the leader of a group of his followers. Finally, in 1910, he determined to leave

society altogether and lead a hermit's life. He died of pneumonia a few days after leaving his ancestral estate.

The Travelers: Realist Painters of Social Issues Dostoyevsky's and Tolstoy's rigorous examination of Russian society was sustained by 13 visual artists who organized a society known as the Travelers dedicated to presenting art exhibitions throughout the country in 1870. All were students at the Saint Petersburg Academy, which emphasized traditional European standards of beauty and the production of painting and sculpture depicting mythological subjects in Neoclassical style. Several of the students were from peasant or working-class families and were more interested in addressing social issues than pursuing the Academy's more traditional, and less threatening, artistic agenda. Realism, they believed, was the only stylistic choice available to them. Like their literary predecessors, they addressed the inequities of Russian society in their paintings, often depicting peasants at work.

Ilya Repin (1844–1930), who painted the portrait of *Tolstoy Ploughing* (see Fig. 31.16), visited Western Europe many times over the course of his career, and the fluid brushwork of the Impressionists is evident in his paintings. Ivan Kramskoy's [KRAM-skoys] (1837–1887)

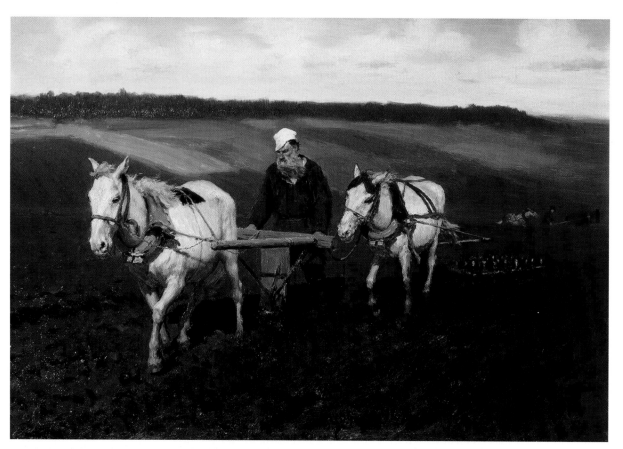

Fig. 31.16 Ilya Repin, *Leo Tolstoy Ploughing*. 1887. Oil on canvas. Photo: Roman Beniaminson. Tretyakov Gallery, Moscow, Russia. Bildarchiv Preussischer Kulturbesitz/Art Resource, New York. This portrait of Tolstoy by his friend and admirer Ilya Repin shows the writer and landowner engaged in the kind of manual labor that he believed it was his duty to perform so as not to take advantage of others.

Fig. 31.17 Ivan Nikolaevich Kramskoy, *Ivan I. Shishkin*. 1880. Oil on canvas, 46″ × 33¹/₂″. © 2009. State Russian Museum, St. Petersburg. As a young man, Kramskoy worked as a retoucher for a traveling photographer.

portrait of another member of the group, landscape painter Ivan Shishkin [SHIS-kin] (1832–1898), achieves a virtually photographic realism (Fig. 31.17). In every detail, from the links in Shishkin's watch chain to the curls in his beard and hair, we feel as if we are looking at something more than a painting or a photograph—we are gazing into the eyes of an actual man.

The real force of the work of the Travelers group, however, lies in their means of exhibiting it. Previously, art exhibitions had been restricted to Saint Petersburg and Moscow, but as their name suggests, the Travelers "traveled," taking their paintings across the country for the peasantry to see and appreciate. Their desire to spread the message of social reform to the Russian countryside would be emulated by the Russian revolutionary movement in the twentieth century.

Russian Nationalist Music and Ballet

The quest to express the fundamental essence of Russia was reflected in the nation's music as well. Here too, a group of five musicians known as "the Mighty Handful" led the way, finding strength in unified action. The primary method by which they expressed their Slavic

pride was through the incorporation of Russian folklore, folk songs, and native instruments such as the balalaika into their compositions. The most ardent of these nationalists was Modest Mussorgsky [moos-ORG-skee] (1839–1881), whose 1869 opera *Boris Godunov* was about a sixteenth-century tsar of Russia who ascended the throne after murdering the rightful heir and who eventually died of guilt.

Never included in their number—because they considered him too cosmopolitan—was Pyotr Ilyich Tchaikovsky [chy-KOF-skee] (1840–1893). But Tchaikovsky's nationalism is clearly apparent in his *1812 Overture*, written in 1880 and commemorating Napoleon's retreat from Moscow. It is one of the most nationalistic works ever composed, capturing in music the same drama as Tolstoy's **HEAR MORE at www.myartslab.com** *War and Peace* (track **31.1**). The work opens with a Russian hymn, "God Preserve Thy People." As horns and drums imitate Napoleon's march on Moscow, strains of the French national anthem, "The Marseillaise," are heard. (Ironically, the anthem could not have been heard during Napoleon's actual invasion, since he had banned its use. It was restored as the French national anthem in 1879, just the year before Tchaikovsky wrote his overture.) After a day of battle, there is a traditional Russian lullaby and folk song, then, after a more furious battle, the hymn "God Save the Tsar" (again ironically, the Russian national anthem in 1880, but not in 1812), as bells chime to rifle and cannon fire. When the *Overture* was first performed in 1882 in front of Moscow's Cathedral of Christ the Redeemer, first conceived by Tsar Alexander I to celebrate his victory over Napoleon but still not completed in 1882, the orchestra did not fire off actual rifles and cannons for the finale as Tchaikovsky's score required. In fact, it was not performed as written until it was recorded with cannon, church bells, and brass band by Antal Doráti conducting the Minneapolis Symphony Orchestra in 1954.

Tchaikovsky's real fame came from his ballet music, a very popular form in Europe, particularly in France. After dancing *en pointe* [on pwahnt] (on the tips of one's toes) was introduced early in the nineteenth century, costumes became skimpier, even skintight, showcasing the human form. Tchaikovsky's lyrical melodies and rich orchestrations in *Swan Lake* (1876), *Sleeping Beauty* (1889), and *The Nutcracker* (1892) raised ballet music to a new level, matching the groundbreaking choreography of Marius Pepita (1818–1910), ballet master of the Imperial Ballet in Saint Petersburg. (Pepita is often called the father of classical ballet.) In *The Nutcracker*, based on a story by Prussian writer E. T. A. Hoffmann, a young girl named Clara receives a magical nutcracker in the form of a soldier as a Christmas present. At night it comes to life and leads an army of toy soldiers into battle with an army of mice. When Clara saves the Nutcracker's life, he is transformed into a handsome youth. He takes her on a magical journey to the Land of the Sugar Plum Fairy, where she encounters a variety of exotic dance images, including a French café, an Arabian dance, a

Chinese tea party, and the Waltz of the Flowers, all culminating in her meeting the Sugar Plum Fairy herself. For this dance, Tchaikovsky contrasts the delicate sound of the celesta, a keyboard instrument similar to a glockenspiel, and the rich depth of a bass clarinet. So memorable is *The Nutcracker* that its music has found a permanent place in modern consciousness, with annual performances scheduled at Christmastime throughout the Western world.

BRITAIN AND THE DESIGN OF SOCIAL REFORM

In Great Britain, Haussmann's modernization of Paris did not go unnoticed. Nor did the revolution in painting that Impressionism represented escape the British. Yet the Impressionist interest in depicting light had been heralded by the work of J. M. W. Turner, and its looseness in depicting landscape by John Constable (see Chapter 27). In fact, both had influenced the Impressionist approach to painting. As for Haussmann, experience had taught the British that public works had little power to effect social reform. London, after all, had rebuilt itself after the Great Fire of 1666 (see Chapter 24), and that had done little to alleviate social suffering, perhaps even exaggerated it, until the early nineteenth century, when a program of reconstruction began. Aided by an ongoing series of sanitary improvements, along with accelerated clearing of slums and new building projects in the 1850s, London rivaled Paris in setting the standard upon which European cities were judged. British thinkers like Thomas Carlyle and A. W. N. Pugin argued, however, that the problems inherent in industrialization, mechanization,

and materialism could also be solved through increased attention to moral values connected with Christianity. And there were other, more secular approaches to reform as well.

The answer appeared to many to lie in the question of design itself—so that as civil servant Henry Cole (1808–1882) argued, the "harmony of beauty and utility" would help the public understand the virtue of moderation and restraint. Cole argued for the creation of government-sponsored design schools—of which he became the director—and for the creation of the *Journal of Design*. Finally, in order to demonstrate the *lack* of standards in British design, he proposed an Exhibition of the Art and Industry of All Nations in London, which was held in 1851. To house the more than 14,000 exhibitors, half of whom were from outside Britain, a remarkable new type of building, designed by Joseph Paxton (1801–1865), was constructed in Hyde Park. Known as the Crystal Palace, it was made of glass and cast- and wrought iron (Figs. **31.18** and **31.19**). Distinctly modern, the Crystal Palace seemed to reflect the lack of standards that Cole ascribed to British design in general. Nevertheless, it revolutionized architectural design.

Resembling a horticultural greenhouse but of gigantic dimensions, the Crystal Palace called for 900,000 square feet of glass (about one-third of Britain's annual production). All its components were standardized, modular, and factory-made, brought together on site and requiring a minimum of traditional building skills to assemble. The three-story structure, 1,848 feet long (the length of about six football fields) and 408 feet wide, was built over a period of months. Its vast expanses of glass solved the problem of lighting individual exhibits and aisles (an especially

Fig. 31.18 Joseph Paxton's Crystal Palace. 1851. Iron, glass, and wood. Lithograph by Charles Burton with *Aeronautic View of the Palace of Industry for All Nations*, from *Kensington Gardens*, published by Ackerman (1851). Guildhall Library, City of London. The Bridgeman Art Library. Paxton described the roof as a "table and cloth"—the cast- and wrought-iron trusses providing a rigid "table" over which an external lightweight "cloth" of glass was draped. In summer, the roof was covered by retractable canvas awnings, which were sprayed with cool water.

Fig. 31.19 The interior of Joseph Paxton's Crystal Palace. 1851. Institut für Theorie der Architektur an der ETH, Zürich. The vault was high enough to allow for elm trees on the Hyde Park site to remain in place.

difficult issue in the era before electricity). It even incorporated the park's trees into its wide, open interiors. Above all, Paxton's design made clear that industrial mass production, prefabrication, and systematic site assembly had the potential to revolutionize architecture and construction.

Morris, the Guild Movement, and the Pre-Raphaelites

Although the Great Exhibition, as it became known, was a roaring success, not everyone appreciated its implications. If it bred confidence in the speed and utility of technological innovation, it also demonstrated, in the words of Owen Jones (1809–1874), an architect who was the director of the Fine Arts exhibits, "no principles, no unity . . . novelty without beauty, beauty without intelligence, and all work without faith."

A young student preparing for the clergy at Oxford University named William Morris (1834–1896) conceived of a different way to attack the problem of design. Morris was deeply affected by the writings of John Ruskin [RUSS-kin] (1819–1900), who argued in his essay "On the Nature of Gothic" that the benefits of mass production were illusory (**Reading 31.3**):

READING 31.3

from John Ruskin, "On the Nature of Gothic," in *The Stones of Venice* (1851–53)

In mass manufacture people were deprived of the satisfaction of making a thing from start to finish. "We have much studied and much perfected, of late, the great civilized invention of the division of labor . . . It is not, truly speaking, the labor that is divided; but the men: divided into mere segments of men—broken in small fragments and crumbs of life. . . . All the stamped metals, and artificial stones, and imitation woods and bronzes, over the invention of which we hear daily exaltation—all the short, and cheap, and easy ways of doing that whose difficulty is its honor—are just so many new obstacles in our already encumbered road. They will not make one of us happier or wiser—they will extend neither the pride of judgment nor the privilege of enjoyment. They will only make us shallower in our understandings, colder in our hearts, and feebler in our wits.

To rectify this situation, in 1855, Morris and a group of friends created a new design firm, the first task of which was to produce the furnishings for Morris's new home in Kent, i once a king and chief·now am the tree·barks thief :

ever twixt trunk and leaf · chasing the prey · ·

Fig. 31.20 Morris and Company, *The Woodpecker*. 1885. Wool tapestry designed by Morris. William Morris Gallery, Walthamstow, England. The great contradiction in Morris and Company is that its beautifully crafted furnishings were beyond the means of the workers who made them.

the Red House, designed by Philip Webb. "At this time," Morris wrote, "the revival of Gothic architecture was making great progress in England. . . . I threw myself into these movements with all my heart; got a friend [Webb] to build me a house very medieval in spirit . . . and set myself to decorating it." Morris longed to return to a handmade craft tradition, in which workers, as with the medieval craft guilds, would no longer be alienated from their labor. In effect, he was declaring war on the Industrial Revolution. The firm soon was turning out high-quality tapestries, embroideries, chintzes, wallpapers, ceramic tiles and bowls, stained-glass windows, and furniture of all kinds.

In his designs, Morris constantly emphasized two principles: simplicity and utility. However, it is difficult to see "simplicity" in work such as *The Woodpecker*, a wool tapestry meant to decorate a wall and keep out drafts as they had in medieval palaces (Fig. **31.20**). For Morris, however, the natural and organic were by definition simple. Thus the pattern possesses, in Morris's words, a "logical sequence of form, this growth looks as if it could not have been otherwise." Anything, according to Morris, "is beautiful if it is in accord with nature." And just as Henry Cole believed that "harmony of beauty and utility" would transform public taste, Morris argued that "simplicity of taste" worked hand in hand with "simplicity of life"—all in accord with nature.

To assist him in creating the most beautiful designs possible, Morris hired many of his artist friends, among them Dante Gabriel Rossetti [roh-SET-tee] (1828–1882) and Edward Burne-Jones (1833–1898). Rossetti had been leader and spokesperson of a group at the Royal Academy named the Pre-Raphaelite Brotherhood, who denounced contemporary art as well as all painting done after the early work of Raphael—including the work of Leonardo da Vinci and Michelangelo, whose techniques they found appalling. (The Pre-Raphaelites knew Michelangelo primarily through the unrestored, grimy painted ceiling of the Sistine Chapel.) Instead, they admired the work of fifteenth-century Flemish artist Jan van Eyck, whose texture and clarity of detail they tried to emulate (see Chapter 16), and the linear contours of fifteenth-century Italian painter Sandro Botticelli (see Chapter 14), whose work had been almost entirely forgotten until they rediscovered him.

CONTINUITY & CHANGE

Botticelli, *Primavera*, **p. 478**

Although the Pre-Raphaelite Brotherhood officially dissolved by 1860, Rossetti continued to champion the spiritual values of medieval and early Renaissance culture, values that he imparted both to Morris and his friend Edward Burne-Jones. Modernity intruded, however, in the form of an undercurrent of erotic tension in Rossetti's work. The subject of his painting *Mariana*, for example, is a minor character in Shakespeare's play *Measure for Measure* who has been spurned by Angelo, her fiancé, because her dowry was lost in a shipwreck (Fig. **31.21**). Unbeknownst to Angelo, Mariana substitutes herself, in the darkness of Angelo's bedroom, for Isabella, whom Angelo has convinced to sleep with him. Rossetti's model in the painting is Jane Morris (1839–1914), William Morris's wife. Janey, as she was known, and her sister Bessie were the preeminent embroiderers at Morris's design company, producing many of the finest pieces themselves, as well as supervising the other workers. Rossetti portrays her here at work on a piece of embroidery of the kind that would be sold by the firm. Rossetti was obsessed with Jane, and there is good reason to believe that the two were romantically involved. In her role as Mariana, Jane's gaze directly

Fig. 31.21 Dante Gabriel Rossetti, *Mariana*. 1870. Oil on canvas, 43¼" × 35⅝". Aberdeen Art Gallery and Museums, Aberdeen, Scotland. Acc. No. ABDAG002900. The richness of the fabrics in this painting are typical of Morris and Co.'s own production.

addresses the painter. Behind her a boy, playing a lute, sings to her, a moment from the opening of Act 4 of Shakespeare's play:

> Take, oh take those lips away,
> that so sweetly were forsworne. . .

Rossetti inscribed these words on the frame of the painting, suggesting the undercurrent of sexual tension that informs the scene.

Burne-Jones, who regularly illustrated many of the books produced by Morris's press, including the famous *Kelmscott Chaucer*, was even more devoted to medieval culture than Rossetti. *Laus Veneris* (*In Praise of Venus*) depicts a scene from the legend of Tannhäuser, the hero of Wagner's opera (see Chapter 30), who falls in love with Venus and lives with her, seduced by carnal pleasures, which he comes to understand as sinful (Fig. **31.22**). At this point, Tannhäuser has abandoned Venus, but the four maidens on the left, flute and clavichord in hand, are about to sing her praises, as she slumps in her chair on the right. The painting was inspired by a poem of the same name written four years earlier, in 1866, by the English poet Algernon Charles Swinburne (1837–1909). Swinburne describes Venus in terms that Burne-Jones captures in the painting (**Reading 31.4**):

READING 31.4

from Algernon Charles Swinburne, "Laus Veneris" (1866)

Her little chambers drip with flower-like red,
Her girdles, and the chaplets of her head,
Her armlets and her anklets; with her feet
She tramples all that wine-press of the dead.

Her gateways smoke with fume of flowers and fires,
With loves burnt out and unassuaged desires;
Between her lips the steam of them is sweet,
The languor in her ears of many lyres.

Venus's languorous sexuality has evidently captivated the knights outside the window, who gaze in longingly. The tapestry behind her shows her mounted on a chariot with

Fig. 31.22 Edward Burne-Jones, *Laus Veneris (In Praise of Venus)*, 1873–78. Oil on canvas, 48¾" × 74¼". Laing Art Gallery, Newcastle-upon-Tyne, England. The design of the tapestry on the right of the painting was created in 1861 by Burne-Jones as a design for tiles produced by Morris and Co. and in 1898 realized as an actual tapestry by the firm.

Cupid, whose arrow is aimed at another victim. Like Rossetti's works, Burne-Jones's painting seethes with repressed sexuality and longing.

The influence of Morris's design company was enormous, fostering a guild movement throughout England intent on producing quality handcrafted goods. A socialist, Morris dreamed of a society "in which all men would be living in equality of condition." But despite the fact that female sexuality was something of an obsession of the company's designers—or perhaps precisely because they were so obsessed and thus unable to see women as anything more than sexual beings—this equality did not extend to women. Morris and Company employed women, but only to make embroidered wall hangings. As already noted, the embroidery workshop was at first managed by Morris's wife, Jane, and then, after 1885, by their daughter, May, then 23 years old. (Many of the designs attributed to her father after 1885 were actually her own. Apparently, she thought it important, at least from a commercial point of view, to give her father the credit.) May Morris (1862–1938) would continue to practice her craft (Fig. **31.23**), helping to found the Women's Guild of Art in 1907, the purpose of which was to create a "centre and a bond for the women who were doing decorative work and all the various crafts." A successful businesswoman, author, and lecturer, she became an important role model for women in early-twentieth-century England.

The Fight for Women's Rights: Mill's *Subjection of Women*

That socialists were not so liberal in their thinking about women was common. Many reformers felt that women were inherently conservative, unduly controlled by the clergy. So, too, upper-class women, sensitive to their own economic interests, often lacked the inclination to support feminist causes. But some liberals and reformers did provide intellectual support for women's causes. An essential text in this regard was *The Subjection of Women*, an 1860 essay by John Stuart Mill (1806–1873).

Mill was an advocate of **utilitarian** theory—believing that the goal of any action should be to achieve the greatest good for the greatest number. By that logic, it was evident that in assigning an inferior role to women, society was wasting an enormous resource. Thus, the essay opens with the following argument (**Reading 31.5**):

> ## READING 31.5
>
> ### from John Stuart Mill, *The Subjection of Women* (1869)
>
> The principle which regulates the existing social relations between the two sexes—the legal subordination of one sex to the other—is wrong itself, and now one of the chief hindrances to human improvement; and . . . it ought to be replaced by a principle of perfect equality, admitting no power or privilege on the one side, nor disability on the other.

Mill further points out that for centuries, women have been subordinate to men, excluded from the kinds of individual choices that naturally follow from the principle of liberty, which decrees "over himself, over his own body and mind, the individual is sovereign."

Mill wrote *The Subjection of Women* in collaboration with his wife, Harriet Taylor Mill, and after his wife's death in 1854, with her daughter from an earlier marriage, Helen Taylor. Scholars are divided as to how much Mill relied on these women—some go so far as to suggest that the work was actually "ghost-written" by them. Although Mill never accepted his wife's contention that women should be able to work outside the home after marriage, there is no question that she and her daughter's ideas greatly influenced Mill's version of feminism. Whatever the case, the feminist sensibility defined by Mill reflects not only the spirit of reform that has been the focus of this chapter, but also the evolving lifestyle of the increasingly affluent class populating Europe's capitals. In an age demanding freedom, it is hardly surprising that women should take up the call.

Fig. 31.23 May Morris (1862–1938), Bed Hangings (Two Curtains). 1917 or earlier. Embroidered wool on linen, each panel 76 $^3/_4$ × 27 in. Collection of Cranbrook Art Museum, Bloomfield Hills, Michigan. Gift of George Gough Booth and Ellen Scripps Booth. Photo: R. H. Hensleigh. (CAM 1955.402). The two halves of the embroidery are identical except for the birds at the lower left.

The Prospect of America

One of Edgar Degas's closest friends in Paris was the American expatriate painter Mary Cassatt (1845–1926), who began exhibiting with the Impressionists in 1867. Cassatt, like Monet, Degas, and van Gogh, was fascinated with Japanese prints (see Chapter 29). She was especially impressed with its interest in the intimate world of women, the daily routines of domestic existence. Consciously imitating works like Utamaro's *Shaving a Boy's Head* (Fig. 31.24), her *The Bath* exploits the same contrasts between printed textiles and bare skin (Fig. 31.25). One of ten prints inspired by an April 1890 exhibition of Japanese woodblock prints at the École des Beaux-Arts in Paris, *The Bath* is a set of flatly silhouetted shapes against a bare ground, devoid of the traditional shading and tonal variations that create the illusion of depth in Western art.

American tastes were, in fact, deeply attracted to all things exotic, and France itself seemed attraction enough. Certainly, France appeared to offer Americans a kind of liberation from the cramped Puritan morality they found at home. And so creative people in particular were drawn to work and study there. The painter Theodore Robinson (1852–1896) went to France in 1884 to study with Monet at his home in Giverny. Other Americans came to sit at Monet's feet as well—Phillip Leslie Hale (1865–1931), who stayed at Giverny for four or five summers beginning in 1888, Lilla Cabot Perry (1848–1933), who spent nine summers there, and Theodore Earl Butler (1861–1936), who married Monet's stepdaughter.

These painters as well as more famous ones—including Cassatt, James Abbott McNeill Whistler (1834–1903), and John Singer Sargent (1856–1925)—as well as writers like Henry James (1843–1916) and Henry Adams (1838–1918), grandson of President John Quincy Adams—all came to Europe in the last half of the nineteenth century intent on immersing themselves in its cultural fervor. They admired what they saw in Europe. By comparison, when they turned their eyes back upon their own country, they saw only vulgarity and superficiality, moneymaking and materialism, boss-ridden politics, sanctimonious hypocrisy, and blind acceptance of social convention and conformity. It was Mark Twain who named this era in America the "Gilded Age," as opposed to a utopian Golden Age, and the name stuck.

The gilt covered, among other things, deep social unrest among the working poor, the continuing subjugation of women, the gradual elimination of all rights that African Americans had gained in the Civil War (see Chapter 29), the removal of Native Americans to reservations, and, under the guise of enlightening the backward peoples of the world, the vast territorial theft of Africa and Asia by the imperial powers of Europe. But Europe offered many artists a way to ignore these realities, just as to those who stayed at home the thriving American economy offered a sense of well-being that enabled them to ignore the darker realities beneath the gilt. ∎

Fig. 31.24 Kitagawa Utamaro (Japan 1753–1806), *Shaving a Boy's Head.* 1801 (Edo Period, 18th Century). Color woodblock print, 14 $^{15}/_{16}$ × 9 $^{13}/_{16}$ in. (38 × 25 cm) (image) 15 $^{3}/_{8}$ × 10 $^{1}/_{4}$ in. (39 × 26 cm) (sheet). Signed Utamuro hitsu. Bequest of Richard P. Gale. The Minneapolis Institute of Arts. Utamaro was noted for his depictions of beautiful women, especially his 1793 *Ten Physiognomies of Women.*

Fig. 31.25 Mary Stevenson Cassatt, *The Bath.* 1890–91. Drypoint and aquatint on laid paper, plate: 12 $^{3}/_{8}$" × 9 $^{3}/_{4}$"; sheet: 17 $^{13}/_{16}$" × 12". Rosenwald Collection. Photograph © Board of Trustees, National Gallery of Art, Washington, D.C. Photo: Dean Beasom.

What is Impressionism?

The renovation of Paris came to a temporary halt in 1870 during the Franco-Prussian war. Embarrassed by the failure of his imperial adventuring in Mexico, where his hand-picked leader was executed by revolutionaries, Louis-Napoleon entered into war with Prussia. He was soundly defeated by Otto von Bismarck and exiled to England. After Bismarck laid siege to Paris, which surrendered in January 1871, the newly declared Third Republic granted generous concessions to its citizens. In March, they created their own municipal government, the Commune. The National Assembly's army attacked, and after a bloody week the Commune was crushed. In what ways was Impressionism borne out of this political climate? Many of these young artists who were identified as Impressionists preferred painting out-of-doors to capture the natural effects of light. What technological innovations made such an approach to painting possible? Monet, Pissarro, Renoir, Degas, and Morisot were the founders of the group. Although he never exhibited with them, Manet was considered by many to be their leader. In what ways did Impressionism undercut conventional assumptions about the style and content of painting?

How was Russian nationalism reflected in literature, art, and music?

In Russia, Francophiles followed developments in Paris carefully, but Slavophiles rejected the pro-Western bias and those Westernizers who believed that Russia was hopelessly mired in the medieval past. Slavophiles tended to be nationalists and saw Russian culture and its spirituality (or "soul") as essentially different from that of the West. How did Fyodor Dostoyevsky's novel *Crime and Punishment* reflect the Russian soul? What was novelist Leo Tolstoy's approach? In painting, a group of young Russian painters called the Travelers created highly realistic works that celebrated peasant life. In music, the nationalist spirit manifested itself in the use of folklore and folk songs, particularly in the compositions of Modest Mussorgsky. How did Tchaikovsky's *1812 Overture* reflect a nationalist spirit?

How did the Crystal Palace and Pre-Raphaelite artists express the spirit of social reform?

The lack of standards of beauty in British industrial design was symptomatic of the country's social inequities, according to English civil servant and designer Henry Cole. Why did Cole propose a Universal Exposition for London's Hyde Park in 1850? The Exposition took place at Joseph Paxton's Crystal Palace. How did the Crystal Palace revolutionize architectural construction?

William Morris took a different approach to the problem. With a group of friends he founded the design firm Morris and Company in 1855. Modeled on the medieval guilds, the company made everything from tapestries and ceramic tiles to stained glass and furniture, all handcrafted. In his employ were the Pre-Raphaelite painters Daniel Gabriel Rossetti and Edward Burne-Jones, whose work was both medieval in spirit and highly charged with erotic tension. Why did these artists and designers turn to medieval models? How does Morris's exclusion of women from higher-level production and design positions in his firm compare with John Stuart Mill's 1869 essay *The Subjection of Women*, which argued against the continued subjugation of women in Western society?

PRACTICE MORE Get flashcards for images and terms and review chapter material with quizzes at **www.myartslab.com**

GLOSSARY

en plein air French for "in open air" and referring to painting out-of-doors in front of the subject rather than in the studio.

pastel Stick of powdered pigment bound with resin or gum.

utilitarian A person who believes that the goal of any action should be to achieve the greatest good for the greatest number.

READINGS

from Fyodor Dostoyevsky, *Crime and Punishment,* Part 3, Chapter 5 (1866)

Dostoyevsky's novel describes the actions of a poor, young student, Raskolnikov, who is driven by the idea that extraordinary individuals, such as himself, have the right to commit immoral acts in the pursuit of greatness. As a result, he rationalizes the murder of an old woman and her younger sister. His crime goes unsolved, but a Saint Petersburg detective, Porfiry Petrovich, suspects him. The following scene demonstrates Dostoyevsky's fondness for developing character through dialogue. Note the way that Porfiry's "innocent" questions allow Raskolnikov to say more than he intends. Even more important, in explaining his "thesis," Raskolnikov exposes its very absurdity.

"All these questions about crime, environment, children, recall to my mind an article of yours which interested me at the time. 'On Crime' . . . or something of the sort, I forget the title, I read it with pleasure two months ago in the *Periodical Review.*"

"My article? In the *Periodical Review*?" Raskolnikov asked in astonishment. "I certainly did write an article upon a book six months ago when I left the university, but I sent it to the *Weekly Review.*"

"But it came out in the *Periodical.*" . . .

Raskolnikov had not known.   10

"Why, you might get some money out of them for the article! What a strange person you are! You lead such a solitary life that you know nothing of matters that concern you directly. It's a fact, I assure you." . . .

"How did you find out that the article was mine? It's only signed with an initial."

"I only learnt it by chance, the other day. Through the editor; I know him. . . . I was very much interested."

"I analysed, if I remember, the psychology of a criminal before and after the crime."   20

"Yes, and you maintained that the perpetration of a crime is always accompanied by illness. Very, very original, but . . . it was not that part of your article that interested me so much, but an idea at the end of the article which I regret to say you merely suggested without working it out clearly. There is, if you recollect, a suggestion that there are certain persons who can . . . that is, not precisely are able to, but have a perfect right to commit breaches of morality and crimes, and that the law is not for them."

Raskolnikov smiled at the exaggerated and intentional distortion of his idea. . . .   30

"No, not exactly because of it," answered Porfiry. "In his article all men are divided into 'ordinary' and 'extraordinary.' Ordinary men have to live in submission, have no right to transgress the law, because, don't you see, they are ordinary. But extraordinary men have a right to commit any crime and to transgress the law in any way, just because they are extraordinary. That was your idea, if I am not mistaken?" . . .

Raskolnikov smiled again. He saw the point at once, and knew where they wanted to drive him. He decided to take up the challenge.   40

"That wasn't quite my contention," he began simply and modestly. "Yet I admit that you have stated it almost correctly; perhaps, if you like, perfectly so." (It almost gave him pleasure to admit this.) "The only difference is that I don't contend that extraordinary people are always bound to commit breaches of morals, as you call it. In fact, I doubt whether such an argument could be published. I simply hinted that an 'extraordinary' man has the right . . . that is not an official right, but an inner right to decide in his own conscience to overstep . . . certain obstacles, and only in case it is essential for the practical fulfilment of his idea   50 (sometimes, perhaps, of benefit to the whole of humanity). . . ."

"Thank you. But tell me this: how do you distinguish those extraordinary people from the ordinary ones? Are there signs at their birth? I feel there ought to be more exactitude, more external definition. . . ."

"Oh, you needn't worry about that either," Raskolnikov went on in the same tone. "People with new ideas, people with the faintest capacity for saying something *new*, are extremely few in number, extraordinarily so in fact. . . . The man of genius is one of millions, and the great geniuses, the crown of humanity, ap-   60 pear on earth perhaps one in many thousand millions. . . ."

"Yes, yes." Porfiry couldn't sit still. "Your attitude to crime is pretty clear to me now. . . ."

READING CRITICALLY

Dostoyevsky sets up this exchange between Raskolnikov and Porfiry in the form of a Socratic dialogue (see Chapter 7), with Raskolnikov taking the part of Socrates. What is the author's purpose in doing this?

32

The Course of Empire
Expansion and Conflict in America

THINKING AHEAD

How did territorial expansion affect Native Americans in North America?

How were the contradictions of economic expansion expressed by American artists?

What is ragtime?

What is an expatriate?

What ideal of America was exhibited at the Columbian Exposition?

The first consistent interactions between native peoples and Europeans in North America occurred during the seventeenth century and were confined mostly to the eastern part of the continent. In the aftermath of the Revolutionary War and Jefferson's purchase of the Louisiana Territory in 1803, the movement westward accelerated, first into the Ohio Valley, then the Midwest and South Central regions (Indiana, Illinois, Kentucky), and last, the Great Plains, Rocky Mountain, and Pacific regions. Images such as *The Rocky Mountains, Lander's Peak* (Fig. **32.1**) by Albert Bierstadt [BEER-shtaht] (1830–1902) reinforced in the national consciousness the wisdom of Jefferson's purchase. First exhibited in New York in April 1864 at a public fair, the painting's display was accompanied by performances by Native Americans, who danced and demonstrated their sporting activities in front of it. However, the scenes depicted by the painting were almost entirely fictional. Although commonly believed at the time to be a representation of Lander's Peak in the

Wind River Range, the mountain rising in the center of the painting does not bear even a vague resemblance to any Rocky Mountain, let alone Lander's Peak. It is instead an illustration of a mountain from the Alps, a none-too-disguised version of the Matterhorn. Bierstadt presents the American West through a European lens, perhaps because he both understood that view was what his audience expected and saw the world through that lens himself. As Bierstadt wrote in 1859, describing a journey to the American Rockies:

> The mountains are very fine; as seen from the plains, they resemble very much the Bernese Alps, one of the finest ranges of mountains in Europe, if not in the world. . . . The color of the mountains and of the plains, and, indeed of the entire country, reminds one of the color of Italy; in fact, we have here the Italy of America in primitive condition.

By "primitive," Bierstadt means pure, untainted, and unfallen, as if it were another biblical Garden of Eden before Eve ate of the apple of knowledge. The Native Americans

◀ **Fig. 32.1 Albert Bierstadt, *The Rocky Mountains, Lander's Peak*. Detail. 1863.** Oil on panel, 73 1/2″ × 120 3/4″. The Metropolitan Museum of Art, Rogers Fund, 1907 (07.123). Image © The Metropolitan Museum of Art. This painting established a visual rhetoric that Bierstadt applied in painting after painting—the bucolic foreground with a clear lake at the base of a waterfall that drops from the heights of the mountains beyond. It presented a myth of landscape and of the Native American presence within it.

HEAR MORE Listen to an audio file of your chapter at **www.myartslab.com**

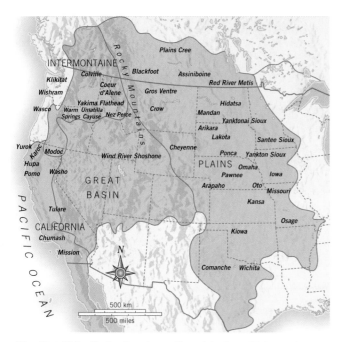

Map 32.1 Major Native American tribes of the Great Plains and Mountain West.

westward growth was driven by the desire for land and the determination to prevail over any obstructions posed by indigenous peoples, whether through legal means (agreements and treaties) or extralegal methods (ignoring those same treaties and agreements).

The onslaught of Western settlers is epitomized by Emanuel Leutze's [LOYT-zuh] (1816–1868) painting *Westward the Course of Empire Takes Its Way (Westward Ho!)* (Fig. **32.2**). Leutze, a German painter specializing in American subjects, conveys the expansion into the Louisiana Territory as a matter of national pride. Commissioned by Congress, the mural for which the painting was a precursor decorates a stairwell of the Capitol building in Washington, giving it a kind of official seal of approval from the U.S. government. *Westward Ho!* depicts miners, trappers, scouts, and families in wagon trains converging on the golden promise of the sun setting in the West. (See Fig. 32.28 for a similar image.) At the base of the painting is a panorama depicting the end of the trail, Golden Gate Bay and San Francisco harbor, flanked by portraits of two original American pioneers, Daniel Boone and explorer William Clark, dressed in a buckskin jacket and animal-fur headdress.

The trickle of settlers moving west at the beginning of the nineteenth century soon became a torrent: From 1790 to 1860, the population density of nonnative Americans

in the foreground are similarly "primitive," the "noble savages" that Rousseau so admired (see Chapter 25), at peace in a place as yet untouched by white settlement. But in the pamphlet accompanying the painting's exhibition as it toured the country, Bierstadt wrote that he hoped that, one day, in the area occupied by the Native American encampment, "a city, populated by our descendants, may rise, and in its art-galleries this picture may eventually find a resting-place."

Before Jefferson's Louisiana Purchase, it would not have occurred to the Native Americans who inhabited the region (Map **32.1**) that it was either France's to sell or Jefferson's to buy. This massive expanse of land extending from Canada to the gulf of Mexico and from the Mississippi River to the Rocky Mountains cost Jefferson a mere $15 million, or about four cents an acres. The nation's third president had effectively doubled the size of the United States of America and greatly accelerated the opening of the Western frontier, which now extended to the Pacific coast. In setting the stage for the ensuing century of expansion, Jefferson was only dimly aware of the hundreds of Native-American tribes that would be obliterated or forever changed as European-American settlers moved westward, staking their claim on the "empty" land.

The true extent of the devastation of Native American cultures was little understood at the time because invisible microbes that spread infectious diseases for which indigenous peoples had no immunity caused much of the damage. So too, the brutal nineteenth-century policy of "Indian Removal," the subsequent Indian Wars, and attempts to "civilize" Native Americans stemmed from the lack of awareness by Americans like Jefferson and his successors of the ancient preliterate cultures of indigenous Americans. Yet much of America's nineteenth-century

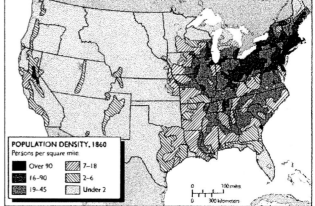

Map 32.2 Population density of nonnative peoples in the United States in 1820 (a) and 1860 (b). After G. B. Tindall and D. E. Shea, *America: A Narrative History.*

Fig. 32.2 Emanuel Leutze, Study for *Westward the Course of Empire Takes Its Way (Westward Ho!)*. 1861. Oil on canvas, 33 1/4″ × 43 3/8″. Smithsonian American Art Museum, Washington, D.C./Art Resource, New York. When Leutze transferred this image to the wall of the Capitol in 1862, he added, in the center foreground, a black man leading a white woman and child on a mule. Although Leutze's abolitionist sentiments were well known, he probably meant to suggest that blacks as well as whites might enjoy freedom in the West. It is notable, however, that the black man remains in a subservient position to the mother and child.

increased from 4 million to 31 million. Nearly half of them moved to territory west of the Atlantic coast states, but the other half were concentrated in the urban centers of the east coast, with New York City as its focal point (Map **32.2**). New York's port handled most of America's imports and roughly 50 percent of the country's exports. As the nation's financial center, the city teemed with lawyers, architects, engineers, and entrepreneurs of every nationality. In 1892, 30 percent of all millionaires in the United States lived in Manhattan and Brooklyn, side by side with millions of the nation's working-class immigrants. By 1900, fully three-quarters of the city's population was foreign-born, having arrived via Ellis Island, which opened in 1892. Italians, Germans, Poles, and waves of Jews from Hungary, Romania, Russia, and Eastern Europe sought the unlimited opportunities they believed were to be found in America. Together immigrants, wealthy industrialists, ambitious merchants, and flagrantly corrupt politicians struggled to gain a share of the American Dream. This dream—usually expressed in dollars and the things those dollars could buy—was so often built on a framework of fraud and exploitation that Mark Twain gave this era the compelling name "The Gilded Age."

Meanwhile, America's frontier shifted into regions where the possibilities (and natural resources) seemed limitless. It was as if America's future lay somewhere out past the pointing finger of Leutze's trapper. "Go West, young man, and grow up with the country," Indiana journalist John Soule had advised in 1851. Influential New York journalist Horace Greeley (1811–1872) took up the first part of the refrain, and soon it became obvious that the American West would be central to America's self-identity. The nature of that identity, fashioned by expansion, both economic and territorial, is the subject of this chapter.

THE NATIVE AMERICAN IN MYTH AND REALITY

Western expansion made conflict with Native Americans inevitable. The most visible dimension of a multifaceted clash of cultures was the fight over land—who owned it and who had the right to live on it. The settlers thought of the land as something to organize, control, and own. (As early as 1784, Thomas Jefferson had proposed surveying public lands in the West in geographic units that were 10 miles square, based on the decimal system. This was later replaced by townships of 6 miles square.) They saw the land as central to their own economic well-being and as a resource to exploit to their own benefit. Land was also fungible, like money—that is, it could be traded like any other commodity, and disposed of as well. The Native Americans, on the other hand, saw themselves as one element in the whole of nature, not privileged in relation to the natural world but part of its delicate balance. Their primary responsibility was to live in harmony with nature rather than transforming, trading, or altering it in a fundamental way.

The Indian Removal Act

In 1830, at the request of President Andrew Jackson (held office 1829–1837), Congress passed "An Act to provide for an exchange of lands with the Indians residing in any of the states or territories, and for their removal west of the river Mississippi." Jackson had provided Congress with the rationale in a speech the previous year:

> Their present condition, contrasted with what they once were, makes a most powerful appeal to our sympathies. Our ancestors found them the uncontrolled possessors of these vast regions. By persuasion and force they have been made to retire from river to river and from mountain to mountain, until some of the tribes have become extinct and others have left but remnants to preserve for awhile their once terrible names. Surrounded by the whites with their arts of civilization, which by destroying the resources of the savage doom him to weakness and decay, the fate of the Mohegan, the Narragansett, and the Delaware is fast overtaking the Choctaw, the Cherokee, and the Creek. That this fate surely awaits them if they remain within the limits of the states does not admit of a doubt. Humanity and national honor demand that every effort should be made to avert so great a calamity.

Jackson's apparent concern for the Native Americans' well-being was insincere, to put it mildly. As a military leader during the War of 1812, he had brutally suppressed the Creek tribal nation, which occupied much of the southeast United States, then afterward negotiated a treaty that took more than half of Creek lands. He also spearheaded the movement to grant Native Americans individual ownership of land, inciting competition, and breaking down ancient traditions of communal landholding.

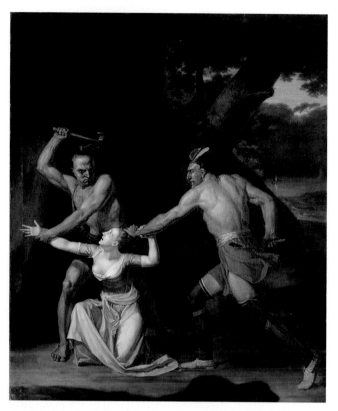

Fig. 32.3 John Vanderlyn (American, 1775–1852), *The Murder of Jane McCrea*. 1803–04. Oil on canvas, 32″ × 26 ¹/₂″. Courtesy Wadsworth Atheneum Museum of Art, Hartford, Connecticut. Purchased by subscription. Jane McCrea's plight symbolized colonial vulnerability, but also warned about the fate of women who disobeyed the wishes of their families.

Jackson's presidential policies mirrored George Washington's idea of "civilizing" the Native Americans by teaching them to farm and build homes, educating their children, and helping them embrace Christianity. But many Americans viewed indigenous cultures more negatively, drawing from a wealth of lurid images that depicted them as morally depraved and violent. One of the most revealing of these portrayals was prompted by President Jefferson's envoy to France, Joel Barlow, who commissioned John Vanderlyn (1775–1852) [VAN-der-lin] to paint *The Murder of Jane McCrea* (1803–04), which occurred in 1777 (Fig. **32.3**). The painting depicts Jane McCrea, daughter of a Presbyterian minister in upstate New York, who followed her Loyalist fiancé to Canada against the wishes of her pro-Revolutionary brother and was captured, killed, and scalped by Native Americans fighting for the British. Jane became an instant symbol of vulnerable colonials preyed upon by diabolical and savage Native Americans, and her story helped galvanize American colonists to resist the British troops and Native-American allies.

Such images, etched on the national consciousness, provoked the likes of Henry Clay, who served as secretary of state (1824–1828) under John Quincy Adams and who was nearly elected president 20 years later, to contend that the Native Americans' "disappearance from the human family would be no great loss to the world." Even a "civilized" tribe like the Cherokee in Georgia was subject to Jackson's

Removal Act. An 1825 census revealed that the tribe, with a population of little over 13,000, owned 2,486 spinning wheels, 2,923 plows, 69 blacksmith shops, 13 sawmills, 33 grist mills, and 1,277 black slaves—signs of Western acculturation—but the Cherokee made the fatal mistake of insisting on their sovereignty. Jackson therefore assented to the eviction of the Cherokee and the other "civilized" tribes of the Southeast—the Choctaw, Chickasaw, Creek, and Seminole [SEM-ihn-ohl]—from their homes and farms. In the winter of 1838, the Cherokee were forced to march across the country, many without shoes or moccasins, to their newly assigned homes in Oklahoma on a journey that would become known as the Trail of Tears. Over 4,000 Cherokee died en route. By 1838, 46,000 Native Americans from the Cherokee and other southeastern nations had been removed from their homelands, opening 25 million acres in Georgia, Alabama, and Mississippi to white settlement.

Recording Native Americans: Catlin's Ethnographic Enterprise

In 1830, George Catlin (1796–1872), a successful portrait painter from the East Coast, headed west to St. Louis. He would make five trips in six years into the territory west of the Mississippi to record the costumes and practices of the Native Americans. On Catlin's historic but unheralded journeys, he encountered cultures of vast diversity and represented more than 40 different tribes in 470 portraits and portrayals of daily life: Osage [OH-sage], Kickapoo, Iowa, Ojibwa [oh-JIB-wah], Pawnee [PAW-nee], and Mandan [MAN-dan], to name just a few. In 1832, Catlin discussed his reasons for painting the Native American peoples that he encountered:

> I have, for many years past, contemplated the noble races of red men who are now spread over these trackless forests and boundless prairies, melting away at the approach of civilization, their rights invaded, their morals corrupted, their lands wrested from them, their customs changed, and therefore lost to the world; and they at last sunk into the earth, and the ploughshare turning the sod over their graves, and I have flown to their rescue—not of their lives or of their race (for they are "doomed" and must perish), but to the rescue of their looks and their modes, at which the acquisitive world may hurl their poison . . . and trample them down and crush them to death; yet, phoenix-like, they may rise from the "stain on a painter's palette," and live again upon canvas, and stand forth for centuries yet to come, the living monuments of a noble race.

While Catlin assumes too much power for his art to resurrect the vanishing tribes, his contribution to Native-American ethnography—the scientific description of individual cultures—is indisputable. His depiction of *The Last Race, Part of Okipa Ceremony* is one of several representing a four-day Mandan ceremony linking all of creation to the seasons (Fig. **32.4**). According to legend, the Mandan sprang from the earth like corn, the mainstay of their diet. Their ceremonial life revolved around the "Old Woman Who Never Dies," keeper of the corn seed, who oversees the agricultural well-being and hunting success of the tribe. Performed each year, before and after the summer buffalo hunt, the Okipa Ceremony was designed to dramatize the tribe's

Fig. 32.4 George Catlin, *The Last Race, Part of Okipa Ceremony (Mandan).* 1832. Oil on panel, 23 3/8″ × 28 1/8″. Smithsonian American Art Museum, Washington, D.C./Art Resource, New York. Beginning in 1837, Catlin toured with his paintings, including a trip in 1839 to London and Paris. The Okipa Ceremony paintings were especially popular, but even as he began his tour, a plague of smallpox almost completely wiped out the Mandan themselves.

myths and to provide an opportunity for young men to be initiated into manhood. The young men of the village fasted for a prolonged period, then suspended themselves from a central platform in the ceremonial lodge by thongs attached to the pierced skin of the back or chest. In the "last race" of the ceremony, they ran around outside the lodge pulling buffalo skulls similarly attached to the skin of their legs and arms, a ritual clearly depicted in the foreground of Catlin's painting.

Huron Moccasins: The Influence of European Styles on Native-American Art

Although he was not above eliminating details that, in his words, "interfered with the grace and simplicity" of his figures, Catlin's ethnography remains an important source of our knowledge about the Native American cultures of the Great Plains, especially those, like the Mandan, who succumbed to disease introduced by the explorers and subsequent settlers. But perhaps more important are objects made by the Native American cultures themselves. In many of these we can see the impact of European contact on Native American arts, even the emergence of new, syncretic styles.

A particularly fine example is a pair of moccasins dating from about 1835 and originating in the Huron cultures of Ontario's Georgian Bay (Fig. 32.5). As early as the 1640s, many of the Huron had adopted Christianity as they sought refuge from the warring Iroquois by seeking protection of the French colonists—predominantly, in the seventeenth century, Catholic missionaries. French Catholic nuns offered embroidery courses to the Huron women, which they adapted to moccasin designs, weaving floral patterns adopted from colonial folk art with dyed moose hair. Although many of these products were used by the Huron themselves, by the 1830s, much of their work was made for sale to European visitors and British army officers who had been stationed in the region since the British defeat of the French in the Seven Years' War in 1764.

Plains Narrative Painting: Picturing Personal History and Change

Unlike almost all other Native American tribes in North America, the Native Americans of the Great Plains developed a strong sense of history. They recorded their history as a narrative in relatively flat semiabstract images on buffalo-hide robes, the exterior hides of teepees, shields, and muslin cloths. In these designs, humans are generally stick figures, and events are described in selective detail. Both served as memory aids that would help the wearer in relating his family's history through the traditional art of storytelling.

Some tribes, particularly the Lakota and Kiowa, recorded family or band history in what is known as a "**winter count**" (Fig. 32.6). Marking the passing of years in winters—the Lakota designated a year as the time elapsed from first snowfall to first snowfall—tribal artists created pictographic images, one for each year, which would, in effect, stir the collective memory of what else happened in the year. They then arranged the pictographs in a pattern, often circular, reading from the center outward, but also in linear designs as seen here, reading from left to right in the first row, then right to left in the second, and so on. This particular winter count covers the years 1776 to 1879. As the buffalo disappeared in the last decades of the nineteenth century, Plains artists turned to drawing on cloth. This winter count was probably copied to muslin cloth from an original count on hide. White men are depicted in black, wearing hats, and sometimes bearded. Their first appearance in this winter count is in the middle of the third row, followed immediately by an drawing of a pox-covered figure—note, however, that the first pox-covered figures occur in the top row, in about 1780.

Fig. 32.5 Huron moccasins. ca. 1835. Black-dyed hide; dyed moosehair, silk ribbon, length 9". Warnock Collection WC9605008. In addition to moccasins, Huron women decorated mittens, caps, pincushions, and other items for sale to tourists.

Fig. 32.6 Sioux Winter Count. ca. 1900. Muslin, wax crayon, 69 1/4″ × 35 1/4″. Warnock Collection WC8708499. One of the most interesting figures this winter count is at the end of the sixth row—a teepee surrounded by crosses representing stars. The winter count year is 1833–34, when on November 12, 1833, the Leonid meteor shower occurred.

Women's Arts on the Plains: Quillwork and Beadwork

The artwork of women was greatly respected in the Plains and Intermountain tribal cultures. Among the Cheyenne, women who worked on the construction, design, and decoration of teepees held some of the most prestigious positions in the tribe. However, the two main art forms practiced by women were quillwork and beadwork. Quillwork, first practiced by Eastern Woodlands tribes, spread to the Plains, where it was considered a sacred art (Fig. **32.7**). Using porcupine quills that range from 2 1/2 to 5 inches in length,

quillworkers sorted them according to size, dyed them in batches, then softened and made them flexible for use by the artist, who repeatedly pulled the quills through her teeth as she stitched them into hides. Among the Lakota, a woman received an ornamented stick for each piece of work quilled, and the four women with the greatest number of sticks were honored by being seated in places of honor and being served food before all others. This reward system, in which valued accomplishments were often signified in elevated status rather than in material goods, was emblematic of many aspects of Native American social and economic life. It was a major difference from the value system of white settlers and colonists.

Quillwork design was quickly adapted to beadwork after the introduction of glass beads by explorers and traders. Before large numbers of whites came to the region, glass beads were so valuable that 100 of them were approximately equivalent to the value of a horse. Their bright, permanent colors were believed by many to be preferable to the softer tones attainable in quillwork. Nonetheless, artists imitated the quillwork stitch by creating what is known as a "lazy stitch," stringing about seven beads on each thread. Another seven beads are strung on the thread and laid parallel to the first seven, back and forth until a complete band is realized. In both quillwork and beadwork—and in the textile arts as well—Native tribes believed that artistic skill coexisted with divine and supernatural powers. This belief lent the artist a unique and immeasurable authority. Like the indigenous system of rewards, this power was largely invisible to Westerners.

Fig. 32.7 Baby carrier, from the Upper Missouri River area, Eastern Sioux. Nineteenth century. Board, buckskin, porcupine quill, length 31″. Smithsonian Institution Libraries, Washington, D.C. Woven into the carrier are three bands of thunderbirds, symbols of protection capable of warding off supernatural harm as well as human adversaries.

Weaving and Basketry

We can learn most about the traditions of the Pueblo peoples of the Southwest through their arts. Among the Navajo, weaving, basketry, and pottery are practiced today very much as they were in pre-colonial times. Anthropologists believe that the Navajo, or Diné'é [din-AY], meaning "the People," migrated south from Northeastern Canada and Alaska about 1000 CE. They are not Pueblos, but they learned to weave with domestic cotton and native grasses from their Pueblo neighbors. They took up weaving with wool sometime in the middle of the sixteenth century, after the introduction of sheep into the Americas by the Spanish, and by as early as 1706 they had their own flocks.

For the Navajo, weaving is a sacred activity that stretches back to creation itself when the universe was woven on an enormous loom by their mythic female ancestor, Spider Woman. In turn, Spider Woman taught Changing Woman, whose very name underscores the importance of transformation to Navajo culture, the art of weaving. When First Man and First Woman first discovered Changing Woman on the top of a sacred mountain, she was clothed in materials of the cosmos that Spider Woman had woven for her—clouds laced together with lightning, rainbows, and sunbeams. She is, thus, the embodiment of the natural world, renewing herself each spring in a garment of grasses and vegetation. When the Navajo weaver works, she imitates Changing Woman, transforming plants (wood used to construct the loom and vegetal dyes), animals (sheep wool), and human skill into the finished rug or *serape* [suh-RAH-pay], or poncho.

When, after years of war, the Navajo people were defeated by the United States in 1863, they were force-marched on what became known as "the Long Walk" to Bosque Redondo on the Pecos River in eastern New Mexico. There they remained until 1868. Their herds of sheep were destroyed, and they were forced to buy factory-made wools, principally from commercial mills in Germantown, Pennsylvania, which were especially popular because of the

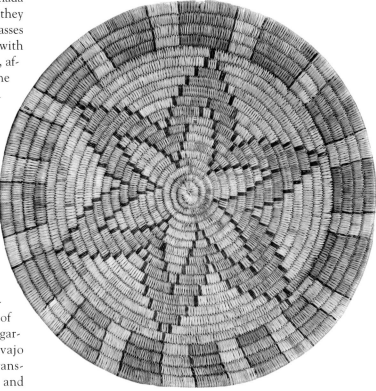

Fig. 32.9 Mescalero Apache coiled basket. Early twentieth century. Arizona State Museum, University of Arizona, Tucson. The image on the basket is a star suggesting that the basket was intended to hold the bounty of the cosmos—especially food.

brilliant colors. Germantown yarns were more uniform in diameter than the handspun Navajo yarns, and as a result, weavers were able to create complex arrangements of small zigzag patterns. Known as "eye-dazzlers" (Fig. **32.8**) for the bright colors of their densely woven patterns, these blankets became the first widely collected Native-American artifacts in the Southwest.

The Navajo and Pueblo facility with weaving probably originated in the grass-weaving techniques used for centuries by their forebears. The art of basketry is, of course, a fiber-weaving art, practiced throughout the Southwest but particularly honored among the Apache peoples of Arizona, where the native materials of the desert environment—willow, cottonroot, black devil's claw, and red yucca root—are used to create elaborate designs of mazes, animals, stars, and interlocking geometric forms.

Because natural grasses and fibers are so susceptible to decay, early examples are rare, but thousands of baskets from the nineteenth and early twentieth centuries survive (Fig. **32.9**). During that time, basket collecting became a literal craze among white collectors, even spawning a quarterly journal in the early 1900s called *The Basket: The Journal of the Basket Fraternity or Lovers of Indian Baskets and Other Good Things*. In fact, as we will see in Book Six, the rebirth of pottery arts in the Southwest and the rejuvenation of Northwest Coast arts have both contributed to the survival of Indian arts (and, to a certain extent, the Indian traditions embodied in their art). The economic benefits resulting from commercial sales of artwork have stimulated the Native Americans' own desire to preserve the cultural integrity and traditions of their people.

The End of an Era

The ultimate fate of Plains tribes was inextricably linked to the fate of the buffalo. By the 1870s, the military was pursuing an unofficial but effective policy of Native American extermination, and it encouraged the slaughter of the buffalo as a shortcut to this end. Echoing President Andrew Jackson 40 years earlier, General Philip Sheridan (1831–1888) urged that white settlers hasten the killing of buffalo herds, thereby undercutting the Native American supply of food. The effort to build a transcontinental railroad helped Sheridan's wish to be realized, as more than 4 million buffalo were slaughtered by meat hunters for the construction gangs, by hide hunters, and by tourists. In the late summer of 1873, railroad builder Granville Dodge reported that "the vast plain, which only a short twelve-month before teemed with animal life, was a dead, solitary, putrid desert." The end of the buffalo signaled the end of Native American culture.

By 1889, the crisis had come to a head. A Paiute holy man by the name of Wavoka declared that if the Indian peoples lived peaceably, if they performed a new circle dance called the Ghost Dance, the world would be transformed into what it once had been, populated by great herds of buffalo and the ancestral dead. White people

Fig. 32.10 Arapaho artist, Ghost Dance dress. 1890s. Deerskin and pigments. Field Museum of Natural History, Chicago, Illinois. (Neg. No. # A113021c). Although this dress is made of deerskin, by the 1890s, hides had become scarce enough that many Ghost Dance dresses were made of cloth—even old flour sacks.

would disappear, and with them alcohol, disease, and hunger. Across the West, the message was adopted by various tribes, and the costumes associated with the dance were particularly beautiful. An Arapaho Ghost Dance dress (Fig. **32.10**) is decorated with five-pointed stars, no doubt derived, in their design, from the American flag, but also a long-standing symbol in Native American culture of the cosmos. The yoke is decorated with a woman and two eagles, one on each side of her. She holds a peace pipe in one hand and a branch in the other. The turtle above the hem refers to a myth of origin, in which the turtle brings soil for the world's creation out of the primal waters. The birds on the skirt, magpies in this case, represent messengers to the spirit world. Many Plains Indians also believed that the Ghost Dance costumes had the power to protect them from harm, and thus left them immune to gunfire or other attack.

That belief would come to an end at Wounded Knee Creek, South Dakota, on December 29, 1890. The white population, paying little attention to the fact that their presumed "disappearance" was predicted to be wholly nonviolent, soon reacted with fear and hostility. More than 200 participants in the Ghost Dance were massacred by the Seventh Cavalry of the U.S. Army at Wounded Knee that day, despite their dress. At least symbolically, Native American culture on the Great Plains came to an end. A Crow warrior named Two Legs put it this way: "Nothing happened after that. We just lived. There were no more war parties, no capturing horses from the Piegan (tribe) and the Sioux, no buffalo to hunt. There is nothing more to tell."

WALT WHITMAN'S AMERICA

The United States' treatment of the Native American populations was, of course, nothing short of deplorable, even criminal, but at the same time a more positive side of American identity was asserting itself, and there is no better human symbol for the restless, ambitious American spirit in the nineteenth century than the poet Walt Whitman (1819–1892) (Fig. **32.11**). Whitman revolutionized American literature as he linked the Romantic, Transcendental, and Realist movements. Born into a working-class Brooklyn household (his father was a carpenter), Whitman went to work full time as an office boy at age 11. Within a year he was a printer's devil (an apprentice who did odd jobs around print shops), soon contributing the occasional story.

After an unhappy five-year stint as a teacher beginning in his late teens, Whitman spent the next two decades working in the newspaper trade as a printer and journalist, refining his writing skills. He also sharpened his powers of observation, as he gained a thorough knowledge of New York and its surrounding regions (Map **32.3**). Whitman became an ardent opponent of slavery in this period—even getting fired at one point by a conservative newspaper publisher who could not tolerate his views.

During a brief but memorable residence in New Orleans in 1846, where he helped set up a new newspaper, Whitman encountered a kaleidoscope of colorful characters and immersed himself in the city's exotic mixture of Indian,

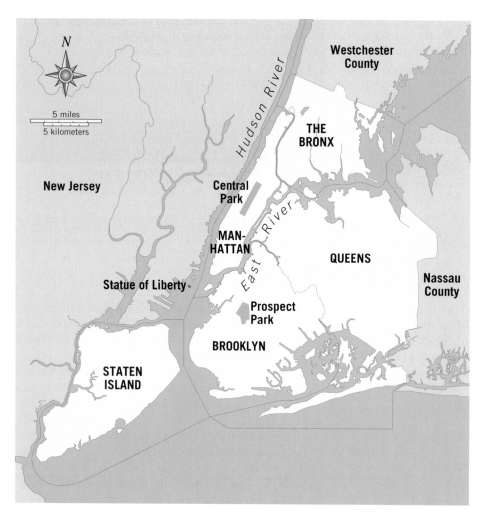

Map 32.3 New York City and its boroughs. ca. 1900.

Fig. 32.11 Frontispiece of the 1855 edition of *Leaves of Grass*. Often accused of egotism, Whitman picked an image of himself to grace the first edition of the poem that seems to capture the poem's opening line: "I CELEBRATE myself."

French, and African-American culture. He liked the French market and the amazing variety of people and goods, and he enjoyed the strong coffee he purchased from a "Creole mulatto woman." Near his lodging house, Whitman also witnessed a less pleasant spectacle—slave auctions, which were a common occurrence in the American South. He would never forget the sight, and he kept an auction poster displayed in his room for years afterward to remind him of the degrading scene. More than a decade later, Whitman would make a slave auction the setting of one of his most famous poems, "I Sing the Body Electric."

As much as he appreciated the dynamism and unique appeal of New Orleans, Whitman was a confirmed New Yorker. He eventually gained fame with his portraits of the city's environment and people. He celebrated the sense of urgency and vigor conveyed by the urban atmosphere in "Crossing Brooklyn Ferry" (**Reading 32.1**):

READING 32.1

from Walt Whitman, "Crossing Brooklyn Ferry" (1856)

Come on, ships from the lower bay! pass up or down,
    white-sail'd schooners, sloops, lighters!
Flaunt away, flags of all nations! be duly lower'd at
    sunset!
Burn high your fires, foundry chimneys! cast black
    shadows at nightfall! cast red and yellow light
    over the tops of the houses! . . .
Thrive, cities—bring your freight, bring your shows,
    ample and sufficient rivers,
Expand. . . .

New York City was the very embodiment of the vast American possibilities Whitman celebrated in *Leaves of Grass*, the long and complex volume of poems that he self-published in 1855 and continuously revised until 1892. It started out as a slim volume of 12 poems and grew to more than 400 as the author's life changed and as he grew into his self-defined role as "the American poet," speaking for the common man. In the first few years, *Leaves* was not received favorably and it did not sell many copies. But within a decade, new editions became a commercial success and the foundation of his growing reputation as the nation's most important poet. In "Song of Myself," the first and eventually longest of the poems, Whitman spoke to his own and the country's diverse experiences (**Reading 32.2a**):

READING 32.2a

from Walt Whitman, "Song of Myself," in *Leaves of Grass* (1867)

I am large, I contain multitudes. . . .
Of every hue and cast am I, of every rank and religion,
A farmer, mechanic, artist, gentleman, sailor, quaker,
Prisoner, fancy-man, rowdy, lawyer, physician, priest.

Whitman openly embraced all Americans in "Song of Myself," from immigrants to African Americans and Native Americans, from male to female, and heterosexual to homosexual. He celebrated all forms of sexuality, a fact that shocked many readers. One early reviewer called *Leaves* "a mass of stupid filth" and its author a pig rooting "among a rotten garbage of licentious thoughts." And in 1865, Whitman, who worked at the U.S. Interior Department as a clerk, was fired by his boss, the Secretary of Interior, for having violated in that work "the rules of decorum and propriety prescribed by a Christian Civilization."

"Song of Myself" consists of 52 numbered sections with the "I" of the narrator serving as a literary device for

Fig. 32.12 Childe Hassam, *The Manhattan Club (The Stewart Mansion)*. ca. 1891. Oil on canvas, 18 1/4″ × 22 1/8″. Santa Barbara Museum of Art, California. Gift of Mrs. Sterling Morton to the Preston Morton Collection. 1960.62. At the northwest corner of 34th Street and Fifth Avenue, the Manhattan Club was originally the home of A. T. Stewart, owner of a department store on Broadway specializing in "feminine attire." It was the largest iron structure in the United States and contained 55 rooms, most with 19-foot ceilings.

viewing the experiences of one man as representative of multitudes. *Leaves of Grass* is therefore a subjective epic. "Remember," Whitman would tell a friend late in his life, "the book arose out of my life in Brooklyn and New York.... absorbing a million people for fifteen years, with an intimacy, an eagerness, an abandon, probably never equaled." (See **Reading 32.2**, pages 1079–1080, for a lengthy excerpt.)

Whitman loved equally the finery of New York's upper classes and the city's "newly-come immigrants." He appreciated the elegant lifestyle depicted by the American Impressionist painter Childe Hassam [child HASS-um] (1859–1935) in such works as *The Manhattan Club* (Fig. **32.12**) and how it contrasted with the impoverished lifestyle of the city's working class as depicted in George Bellows's painting *Cliff Dwellers* (Fig. **32.13**), a street scene in Lower Manhattan on a hot summer afternoon. "The pleasures of heaven are with me," Whitman writes in "Song of Myself," "and the pains of hell are with me, / the first I graft and increase upon myself, the latter I translate into a new tongue."

Whitman developed a **free verse** style of writing poetry, based on irregular rhythmic patterns as opposed to conventional meter. Rhymes are rare in his work, but the "song" of the poems derives from his liberal use of alliteration, assonance (similar, repeated vowel sounds in successive words), and other forms of repetitive phrasing.

The style owes much to the opera arias that Whitman admired so much. As he wrote in "Song of Myself" (**Reading 32.2b**):

READING 32.2b

from Walt Whitman, "Song of Myself," in *Leaves of Grass* (1867)

I hear the sound I love, the sound of the human voice,
I hear sounds running altogether, combined, fused or
　following,
Sounds of the city and sounds out of the city, sounds
　of the day and night . . .
I hear the chorus, it is a grand opera,
Ah this indeed is music—this suits me.

By the time Whitman issued his final ("deathbed") edition of *Leaves of Grass*, the work had grown from 96 printed pages in the 1855 edition to 438. He would come to anguish over the personal suffering of the soldiers who fought in the Civil War in "Drum Taps," and mourn the death of Abraham Lincoln in "When Lilacs Last in the Dooryard Bloom'd," both added to the 1867 edition. To celebrate the opening of the Suez Canal, he added to the 1876 edition the long "Passage to India." *Leaves of Grass*, in other words, was as expansive and as ever-changing as its author.

But it is finally in Whitman's feelings for New York City that we can best understand the complexity of his feelings for America. In a paragraph from a lengthy pamphlet in 1871 that argued for the necessity of reinvigorating American democracy, he tells of his feelings for the city (**Reading 32.3**):

from Walt Whitman, *Democratic Vistas* (1871)

After an absence, I am now again (September, 1870) in New York City and Brooklyn, on a few weeks' vacation. The splendor, picturesqueness, and oceanic amplitude and rush of these great cities, the unsurpass'd situation, rivers and bay, sparkling sea-tides, costly and lofty new buildings, facades of marble and iron, of original grandeur and elegance of design, with the masses of gay color, the preponderance of white and blue, the flags flying, the endless ships, the tumultuous streets, Broadway, the heavy, low, musical roar, hardly ever in-termitted, even at night; the jobbers' houses, the rich shops, the wharves, the great Central Park, and the Brooklyn Park of hills (as I wander among them this beautiful fall weather, musing, watching, absorbing)—

the assemblages of the citizens in their groups, conversations, trades, evening amusements, or along the by-quarters—these, I say, and the like of these, completely satisfy my senses of power, fulness, motion, &c., and give me, through such senses and appetites, and through my esthetic conscience, a continued exaltation and absolute fulfilment. Always and more and more, . . . I realize . . . that not Nature alone is great in her fields of freedom and the open air, in her storms, the shows of night and day, the mountains, forests, seas—but in the artificial, the work of man too is equally great—in this profusion of teeming humanity—in these ingenuities, streets, goods, houses, ships—these hurrying, feverish, electric crowds of men, their complicated business genius, . . . and all this mighty, many-threaded wealth and industry concentrated here.

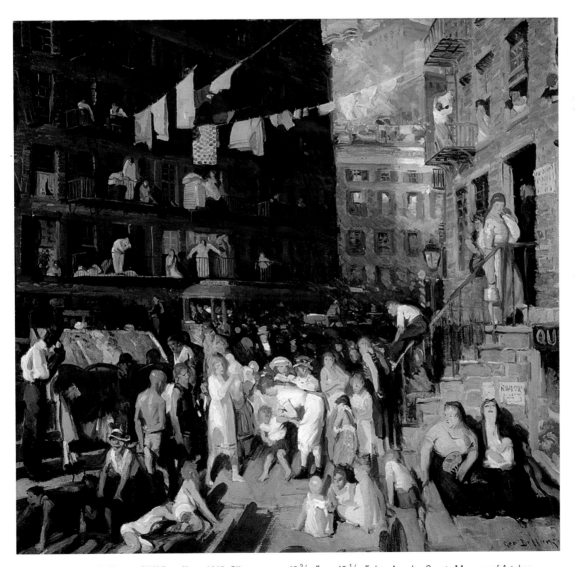

Fig. 32.13 George Bellows, *Cliff Dwellers*. 1913. Oil on canvas, 40 $^3/_{16}$″ × 42 $^1/_{16}$″. Los Angeles County Museum of Art. Los Angeles County Fund. Photograph © 2007 Museum Associates/LACMA. A preparatory drawing for this painting in *The Masses*, a socialist magazine published in New York from 1911 to 1917, was entitled "Why Don't They All Go to the Country for Vacation?" The painting's name comes from a remark reportedly made by a Fifth Avenue socialite observing the scene.

In the Interest of Liberty: An Era of Contradictions

Whitman's essential optimism, his genuine belief in the egalitarian promise of democracy, was put to the test during Reconstruction. As he wrote in *Democratic Vistas*, the promise that he saw in New York's streets and harbors remained unfulfilled: "With such advantages at present fully, or almost fully, possess'd—the Union just issued, victorious, . . . and with unprecedented materialistic advancement—society, in these States, is canker'd, crude, superstitious, and rotten." As if to prove his point, the Supreme Court nullified the Civil Rights Act in 1883. Lynchings of African Americans became almost commonplace across the South as white-controlled state legislatures passed laws designed to rob blacks of their civil rights. Legally sanctioned segregation ("Jim Crow" laws) prevented blacks from using public facilities such as restrooms, hotels, and restaurants, and from attending school with whites.

The Statue of Liberty and Tammany Hall Even as African Americans were losing their freedoms, the nation celebrated liberty when wealthy businessmen and politicians raised the necessary funds for a pedestal to support a French gift to the American people sculpted by Frédéric-Auguste Bartholdi [bar-tohl-DEE] (1834–1904), *Liberty Enlightening the World*. Known simply as the Statue of Liberty—a broken chain under Liberty's foot alludes to the emancipation of the slaves—it was positioned on an island in New York Harbor and dedicated in 1886. At the ceremony, President Grover Cleveland (held office 1885–1889) noted, with no irony intended, "Instead of grasping in her hand the thunderbolts of terror and death, she holds aloft the light that illumines the way to man's enfranchisement." Former slaves and their descendants, along with all American women, might have objected to the grand sentiments, since the prospect of gaining the vote or a voice in democracy was far in the future.

However it was perceived, democracy was a complicated and imperfect process of self-governance, and especially so in large urban areas with diverse populations. Organizations like the Tammany [TAM-uh-nee] Society, founded in the eighteenth century for social purposes, now used working-class and immigrant votes to gain and keep power indefinitely. By offering those at the bottom of society's ladder assistance in gaining citizenship, jobs, and housing, Tammany leaders such as William "Boss" Tweed (1823–1878) were able to create a self-sustaining system of patronage, whereby favors would be traded in return for political loyalty.

By the 1860s, the Tammany Society, which was closely aligned with the Democratic Party, completely controlled the city's political life. Under the leadership of Boss Tweed, City Hall became known as Tammany Hall. In his role as commissioner of public works, Tweed not only helped workers and immigrants, but also enriched himself and his cronies through swindling the city government. He purchased 300 benches for $5 each, which he turned around and resold to the city for $600 apiece. Tweed commissioned his friends to do work for the city. One carpenter received $360,747 for a month's labor, and a supplier of furniture and carpets was paid over $5 million.

Boss Tweed was not alone in helping to corrupt democratic government. President Ulysses S. Grant (held office 1868–1876) and his cabinet were implicated in a number of dubious schemes, leading to notorious scandals. It was just such corruption that led Mark Twain to remark in a *New York Tribune* newspaper column in 1871: "What is the chief end of man?—to get rich. In what way?—dishonestly if we can; honestly if we must."

Economic Depression, Strikes, and the Haymarket Riot

Widespread fraud and corruption contributed to the impoverishment of the working class, but so did the profit motive that drove the industrial sector of the economy. By 1890, 11 million of the nation's 12 million families had an average annual income of $380, well below the poverty line ($380 would buy about the same as $7,600 in today's dollars). Sudden, unexpected events also precipitated widespread economic hardship, as occurred in September 1873, when a Philadelphia banking firm failed, causing investors to panic, banks to shut down, and the New York Stock Market to close for ten days. The "Panic of 1873" triggered the "Long Depression," which lasted four years. In this period, over 20,000 American businesses failed and a quarter of the nation's 364 railroads went bankrupt. (The downturn also affected other countries, particularly in Europe and Britain.)

Millions of American workers found themselves without jobs in the 1870s, while business owners began cutting wages—an oversupply of employees meant cheaper labor. Many lost their savings as well as their jobs when unregulated banks, insurance companies, and investment firms went out of business while federal and state governments stood by. As the unemployment rate in New York and other cities passed 25 percent, famine and starvation in the land of opportunity became a reality.

It should not be surprising that workers developed new forms of collective action in this harsh economic environment. Impromptu strikes, walkouts, and the beginnings of organized labor unions signaled the changing economic and social climate. When the Baltimore & Ohio Railroad cut wages in 1877, its workers staged spontaneous strikes, which spread rapidly to other railroads. In Baltimore, the state militia shot and killed 11 strikers and wounded 40 others. In Pittsburgh, the head of the Pennsylvania Railroad wryly suggested that strikers be given "a rifle diet for a few days and see how they like that kind of bread." Perhaps in response to his suggestion, troopers began firing at the unarmed crowd—leaving at least 20 dead. In Philadelphia, strikers burned down much of the downtown before federal troops stepped in. But despite the widespread strikes and development of labor organizations, workers were largely unsuccessful because of the power and wealth of those united against them.

Fig. 32.14 Robert Koehler, *The Strike*. 1886. Oil on canvas, 71 $^5/_8$" × 9' $^5/_8$". Deutsches Historisches Museum, Berlin, Germany/The Bridgeman Art Library, New York. Koehler's father was a machinist, and he identified with the plight of the working class. The painting was exhibited at the National Academy of Design in 1886, to general approval.

Owners of railroads and other corporations together with the political leaders they supported made sure wage reductions remained in place. The federal government aided them when the U.S. War Department created the National Guard as a quick reaction force to put down future disturbances. It was an era of unparalleled political unrest, and *The Strike* by Robert Koehler [KOH-lur] (1850–1917) suggests something of the mood of the workers and their bosses, as well as the grim environment of industrial-age America (Fig. **32.14**). The painting depicts an angry crowd confronting an employer, demanding a living wage from the stern top-hatted man and a worried younger man standing behind him. An impoverished woman with her children looks on at the left; another woman, more obviously middle-class, tries to talk with one of the workers, but behind him a striker bends down to pick up a stone to throw. Koehler's realism is evident in the diversity of his figures, each possessing an individual identity. But the background of the work, with its smoky, factory-filled landscape on the horizon, owes much to the Impressionist style.

The May 1, 1886, issue of *Harper's Weekly* included the painting as its central feature. On the same day, a national strike called for changing the standard workday from 12 hours to 8. More than 340,000 workers stopped work at 12,000 companies across the country. In Chicago, a bomb exploded as police broke up a labor meeting in Haymarket Square. A police officer was killed by the blast and police retaliated, firing into the crowd of workers, killing one and wounding many more. Four labor organizers were charged with the policeman's death and subsequently hanged, demoralizing the national labor movement and energizing management to resist labor's demands.

The American Woman

Women as well as working-class whites and blacks felt the contradictions and limitations of American democracy. In the post–Civil War years, women became the public face of social reform as they led the suffrage movement, aimed at gaining the right to vote, and the temperance movement, which sought to moderate (or cease) the consumption of alcohol. Both

Fig. 32.15 Thomas Wilmer Dewing, *A Reading*. 1897. Oil on canvas, 20 $^{1}/_{4}$″ × 30 $^{1}/_{4}$″. Bequest of Henry Ward Ranger through the National Academy of Design. Smithsonian American Art Museum, Washington, D.C./Art Resource, New York. For Dewing and many of his contemporaries, repose was therapeutic. His paintings were intended to evoke that state in the viewer.

movements met formidable opposition. At the dedication of the Statue of Liberty, officials barred the New York State Woman Suffrage Association from participating. The New York "suffragettes" sailed out to Bedloe's Island anyway and invited the public onboard their ship, where their president, Lillie Devereux Blake, spoke: "In erecting a Statue of Liberty embodied as a woman in a land where no woman has political liberty, men have shown a delightful inconsistency which excites the wonder and admiration of the opposite sex."

Yet women were making *some* gains. After the Civil War, they had assumed a growing role in education, as state-run schools trained women as teachers. And during the war, many had followed the lead of England's Florence Nightingale (1820–1910), who established nursing as an honored profession during the Crimean War in the 1850s. By the end of the century, nursing schools, usually associated with the nation's medical schools, had opened across the country, although physician training was still reserved for men. By 1900, fully 80 percent of the nation's colleges, universities, and professional schools were admitting women, though in small numbers. And the literacy rate of white women equaled that of white men.

If women were the symbols of social reform in Gilded Age America, they increasingly embodied education and literacy in art and literature as well. In *A Reading* by Thomas Dewing (1851–1938), created by a painter who worked with his wife, also an artist, in a professional partnership, we see women in the act of reading (Fig. **32.15**). It is even fair to say that women became the favorite subject of American painters in the last decades of the nineteenth century.

Formal portraits of society women were an important source of income for many painters, but artists also showed women in more relaxed settings. Thomas Dewing, for example, painted women almost exclusively, bathing them in a gauzy light, as in *A Reading*, a technique that he learned from the Impressionists during his training at the Académie Julian in Paris in the 1870s, which was, incidentally, one of the few places where women could study art from the live model. Such scenes are double-edged since on one hand, they celebrate the intellectual capacity of women, but on the other, they insulate these same women from the harsh world of labor and business by showing them sitting comfortably in their home, safely domestic. In short, nothing about such artworks challenged the status quo. Male painters of the Gilded Age depicted women as almost always passive—sitting, lounging, reading, writing a letter—and rarely physically active. Flowers are often present in these images, with the women sometimes contemplating a bloom, as in Dewing's painting. The ever-present cut rose might symbolize fallen virtue, while daffodils were associated with the innocence of spring.

Impressionist painting in France influenced paintings such as this, but the contrast between female passivity and male action was much more pronounced in American painting than in European art. And with the possible exception of Thomas Eakins's [AY-kinz] *Agnew Clinic* (see *Closer Look*, pages 1064–1065), no painting embodies the tension between genders more than Winslow Homer's *The Life Line* (Fig. **32.16**). Immediately recognized as a masterpiece when exhibited at the National Academy in 1884, it depicts a woman's rescue from a ship wrecked in a storm. A review in the *New York Times* summarizes the painting's attraction to its New York audience:

> The coast guard is a well-drawn muscular figure with face hidden. . . . The hiding of his features concentrates the attention very cleverly on his comrade, who has fainted or is numb with fright. She has nothing on but her shoes, stockings, and dress, while the skirt of the latter has been so torn that her legs are more or less shown above the knees. Then, the drenching she has received makes her dress cling to bust and thighs, outlining her whole form most admirable. She is a buxom lassie, by no means ill-favored in figure and face. Her disordered hair, torn skirt, drenched dress, and set face call for sympathy; a redness of the skin, above the stockings hints at a cruel blow, and puts the climax on one's pity; at the same time, one cannot forget her beauty.

This is the very image of the strong, active male in whose embrace the weak, passive female is rescued. And part of her attractiveness is her passivity and vulnerability. That the painting appealed to the prurient interests of its audience—in some other context, the couple might be seen as lovers embracing—sealed its success. But above all, the painting positions woman in a condition of total dependency on a man, which is precisely where the American male, in the last quarter of the nineteenth century, thought she should be.

Fig. 32.16 Winslow Homer, *The Life Line*. 1884. Oil on canvas, 28 5/8″ × 44 3/4″. The George W. Elkins Collection, 1924. The Philadelphia Museum of Art, Philadelphia/Art Resource, New York. In the first days that the painting was exhibited, the rescuer's face was visible. However, Homer apparently felt that it detracted from the composition, so he painted in the windblown red shawl to cover him while the exhibition was in progress.

Thomas Eakins (1844–1916) was an American Realist who began teaching at the Pennsylvania Academy of Fine Art in Philadelphia in 1876 and became its director in 1882. Always controversial, he was dismissed from the Academy in 1886 for removing a loincloth from a nude male model in a studio where female students were present. Among his most notable—and controversial—works are two portraits of surgeons, *The Gross Clinic* and *The Agnew Clinic*, painted 14 years apart, in 1875 and 1889 respectively. Although anticipated in seventeenth-century European paintings such as Rembrandt's *Anatomy Lesson of Dr. Tulp* (see *Closer Look*, Chapter 22), the subject was relatively unknown in American art and so not considered an appropriate subject for a painting. In addition, Eakins's graphic realization of both surgeries shocked the public.

The Gross Clinic is the product of the painter's own desire to paint Dr. Samuel D. Gross (1805–1884) in his surgical clinic, which he had attended when he studied anatomy a year before at the Jefferson Medical College in Philadelphia. It shows Dr. Gross standing in his surgical amphitheater, scalpel in hand, explaining a procedure to his students. Like Rembrandt's *Anatomy Lesson*, the composition is pyramidal in structure, with Dr. Gross at its apex. Light bathes the surgeon's head and hand and the surgery itself, emphasizing the intellectual capacity and physical dexterity of the surgeon. He and his colleagues are in the process of removing a piece of dead bone from the leg of a patient suffering from osteomyelitis, a bone disease that until the nineteenth century had been treated by amputation. Eakins evidently understood the shock the scene would cause his viewers because behind Dr. Gross he has depicted a woman, probably a relative of the patient, recoiling in horror from the scene. The era's prototypical weak woman, she is a far cry

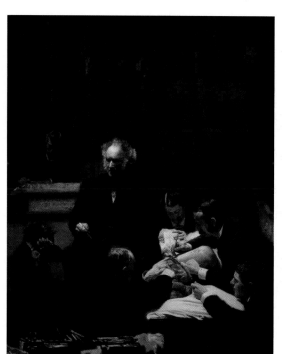

Thomas Eakins, *The Gross Clinic*. 1875. Oil on canvas, 96″ × 78 ¹/₂″. Philadelphia Museum of Art on loan from the University of Pennsylvania School of Medicine. The brightest color in this painting is the red of oozing blood on the patient's wound and on the surgeon's hands and linens.

from the stoic nurse who watches Dr. Agnew's surgery in *The Agnew Clinic*.

The Agnew Clinic was a commission from the students of Dr. D. Hayes Agnew (1818–1892), who expected merely a portrait of their retiring mentor. Eakins, however, wanted to survey advances in medicine since his last effort and offered to paint all of Agnew's students and colleagues into a work echoing *The Gross Clinic*. The painting, the largest Eakins ever painted and depicting surgery on a young woman, was rejected by the Pennsylvania Academy—it had asked him to submit it to their annual exhibition—and then subsequently by the Society for American Artists. It was finally displayed at the Chicago World's Columbian Exhibition in 1893. Oblivious to the fact that Eakins was celebrating American medical advancement, one critic wrote: "It is impossible to escape from Mr. Eakins's ghastly symphonies in gore and bitumen. Delicate or sensitive women or children suddenly confronted by the portrayal of these clinical horrors might receive a shock from which they would never recover." Nevertheless, in *The Agnew Clinic* Eakins had replaced the fear and blood of *The Gross Clinic* with professionalism and detachment.

Something to Think About . . .

In his *Agnew Clinic*, Eakins makes much more of the contrast between light and dark than he does in the earlier *Gross Clinic*. What does this dramatic contrast suggest to you? How does it reinforce the themes of the painting?

HEAR MORE For a Closer Look at Thomas Eakins' *Gross Clinic* and *Agnew Clinic,* go to **www.myartslab.com**

Eakins's *Gross Clinic* and *Agnew Clinic*

The doctors wear white coats, unlike the surgeons in *The Gross Clinic*. This indicated that in the 14 years separating the two paintings, principles of *antisepsis*—the destruction or minimization of germs and other microorganisms—had been introduced into the surgical arena. The figures are also much better lit by artificial lighting, whereas in *The Gross Clinic* the light enters the auditorium through skylights above.

The figure of Eakins himself stands in the doorway, listening as a colleague of Agnew's whispers to him, possibly explaining the procedure. Eakins's wife Susan added his likeness to the painting.

Dr. Agnew was professor of surgery at the University of Pennsylvania School of Medicine. His students described him, according to the Latin motto carved on the finished work's frame, as "the most experienced surgeon, the clearest writer and teacher, the most venerated and beloved man." At Dr. Agnew's request there is no blood shown on him or his patient.

The female patient is undergoing a mastectomy, or breast removal—still an experimental procedure—to combat her breast cancer. The doctor at her head administers chloroform as an anesthetic, another experimental technique. Poor men and women from almshouses were regularly recruited to undergo such experimental procedures in return for free medical care.

The nurse is Mary V. Clymer, at the top of her nursing class at the University of Pennsylvania. She serves a double function: overseeing the propriety of the male doctors' handling of the female patient and representing the new profession of nursing as a whole. While women were still not admitted to medical schools (an exclusion strongly supported by Dr. Agnew), the University of Pennsylvania was one of the first American universities to inaugurate a school of nursing. It was only three years old at the time of Eakins's painting.

Thomas Eakins, *The Agnew Clinic*. 1889. Oil on canvas, 84 ³/₈″ × 118 ¹/₈″. Jefferson College, Philadelphia/The Bridgeman Art Library. Today, this painting is reproduced on the diplomas of all graduates of the University of Pennsylvania School of Medicine.

Emily Dickinson: The Poetry of Enigma As a result of the broadly condescending attitude toward women and the fierce resistance to the fledgling women's-rights and suffrage movements, the achievements of women in the nineteenth century were often individual ones. A remarkable example is the work of Emily Dickinson (1830–1886), who lived in her father's Amherst, Massachusetts, home almost her entire life. Here she gardened, baked bread—her chief talent in her father's eyes—and read voluminously. Dickinson also wrote continuously, corresponding with a small circle of friends and composing some of the most remarkable poetry in the history of American literature. Her work is characterized by passion, simplicity, and an economy and concentration of style. She summarized her life in 1862, at age 31, when she wrote a letter to Thomas Higginson, at *Atlantic Monthly* magazine, responding to his published essay that offered advice to young authors:

> You ask of my Companions Hills—Sir—and the Sundown—and a Dog—large as myself, that my Father bought me—They are better than Beings—because they know—but do not tell—and the noise in the Pool, at Noon—excels my Piano. I have a Brother and Sister— My Mother does not care for thought—and Father, too busy with his Briefs—to notice what we do—He buys me many Books—but begs me not to read them—because he fears they joggle the Mind. They are religious—except me—and address an Eclipse every morning—whom they call their "Father." But I fear my story fatigues you—I would like to learn—Could you tell me how to grow—or is it unconveyed—like Melody—or Witchcraft?

Higginson could not, in fact, tell her how to grow as an author. He found her unconventional verse curious, and even powerful, but decidedly unorthodox. It was in this lack of orthodoxy, however, that Dickinson found her own form of freedom and her resemblance to Whitman. Even in the isolation of her Amherst home, her poetry awakened her senses, as she explained, in a poem: "I am alive— because / I am not in a Room— / The Parlor . . ." (In the New England parlor one met with one's visitors, and Dickinson studiously avoided visiting.) Dickinson so avoided the parlor (and the visitors in them) that she remained something of a mystery to her neighbors—and to us. In fact, there are only two known photographs of her (Fig. **32.17**).

Yet one day in 1882, in that dreaded parlor, Emily's mother read some of her daughter's poems to a young neighbor, Mabel Loomis Todd, who found them "full of power." Encouraged by Emily's sister, Todd undertook the task of transcribing them. By letter, Dickinson and Todd developed "a very pleasant friendship," even though they never actually met. In 1890, four years after Dickinson's death, Todd persuaded Thomas Higginson to publish a collection of Dickinson's poems, followed by a second series in 1891, and a third in 1896. They seemed to embody the

Fig. 32.17 Emily Dickinson. ca. 1848–1853. Albumen photograph copy of an original daguerreotype, $5\,^1/_2" \times 3\,^7/_8"$. Until Professor Gura of the University of North Carolina purchased this photograph on eBay, only one other photograph of the reclusive Dickinson was known to exist. Asked at age 31 to supply a photograph of herself, she replied, "Could you believe me—without? I had no portrait, now, but am small, like the Wren, and my Hair is bold, like the Chestnut Bur—and my eyes, like the Sherry in the Glass, that the Guest leaves—Would this do just as well?"

pent-up imagination of the nineteenth-century American woman, and they became popular almost immediately.

The crisp, sharp imagery and economy of statement in poems like Dickinson's "Wild Nights" contrasts dramatically with its great emotional intensity. As is typical of Dickinson's work, her brevity seems to charge the poem, fuel its ambiguity, and contribute to the fierceness of her vision (**Reading 32.4a**):

READING 32.4a

Emily Dickinson, "Wild Nights" (as published in 1953)

Wild Nights—Wild Nights!
Were I with thee
Wild Nights should be
Our luxury!

Futile—the Winds—
To a Heart in port—
Done with the Compass—
Done with the Chart!

Rowing in Eden—
Ah, the Sea!
Might I but moor—Tonight—
In Thee!

The poem contrasts the safety and repose of a port and the wildness of the open seas, which are metaphors for the poet's emotional state. It opens with the poet longing for the "wild nights" that would evidently be assured if she were with "thee." The second stanza seems to describe the circumstances of a heart safely harbored in port. It has no need of compass or chart and the winds do not stir it. She is "Rowing in Eden," in a paradise-like calm. But she rejects such calm, for it is "wildness" that the poet desires. The peace of Eden offers no risk, none of the passion represented by the wild seas.

The poem can also be read in terms of sexual encounter, adding to the ambiguity. We know that Dickinson used an 1844 dictionary that linked *luxury* with its Latin origins in wantonness, sexual desire, and riotous living. However, the poem remains enigmatic and suggestive rather than clear and detailed. The reader's imagination is as free to play as Dickinson's own. (See **Reading 32.4**, pages 1080–1081, for several other Dickinson poems.)

Kate Chopin and the New Feminist Novel Unlike the writings of Emily Dickinson, which were almost unknown in her lifetime, the works of writer Kate Chopin [SHOH-pan] (1851–1904), of St. Louis, Missouri, were well known. Having taken up writing in 1884 after the death of her husband, Chopin's first two books of stories, *Bayou Folk* (1894) and *A Night in Arcadie* (1897), were praised for their attention to local custom and dialect. *Vogue* magazine and other commercial publications featured her work. But when her short novel *The Awakening* (1899) appeared, she was harshly criticized for its frank treatment of female marital infidelity.

In its celebration of sensuality and its positive attitude toward the sexual desire of its central character, Edna Pontellier [pohn-tell-ee-AY], *The Awakening* owes much to Walt Whitman, whose work Chopin greatly admired.

Set in New Orleans and Grand Isle, a summer resort on the Louisiana coast, *The Awakening* opens as Edna is falling in love with Robert Lebrun [luh-BRUHN], a young Creole [KREE-ohl] whose family owns the resort. From the story's very first moments, it becomes apparent that the author intends to challenge the viability of Edna's marriage. In the following passage, Mr. Pontellier watches her return from the beach with her new object of affection (**Reading 32.5a**):

READING 32.5a

from Kate Chopin, *The Awakening*, Chapter 1 (1899)

Mr. Pontellier finally lit a cigar and began to smoke, letting the paper drag idly from his hand. He fixed his gaze upon a white sunshade that was advancing at snail's pace from the beach. He could see it plainly between the gaunt trunks of the water-oaks and across the stretch of yellow camomile. The gulf looked far away, melting hazily into the blue of the horizon. The sunshade continued to approach slowly. Beneath its shelter were his wife, Mrs. Pontellier, and young Robert Lebrun. . . .

"What folly! to bathe at such an hour in such heat!" exclaimed Mr. Pontellier. . . . "You are burnt beyond recognition," he added, looking at his wife as one looks at a valuable piece of personal property which has suffered some damage.

Edna is as seduced by the sea as she is by young Robert Lebrun. When he takes her to the beach a few chapters later, Edna begins to experience the "awakening" that will free her from her marriage (**Reading 32.5b**):

READING 32.5b

from Kate Chopin, *The Awakening*, Chapter VI (1899)

A certain light was beginning to dawn dimly within her,—the light which, showing the way, forbids it. . . .

In short, Mrs. Pontellier was beginning to realize her position in the universe as a human being, and to recognize her relations as an individual to the world within and about her. . . .

But the beginning of things, of a world especially, is necessarily vague, tangled, chaotic, and exceedingly disturbing. How few of us ever emerge from such beginning. How many souls perish in its tumult!

The voice of the sea is seductive; never ceasing, whispering, clamoring, murmuring, inviting the soul to wander for a spell in abysses of solitude; to lose itself in mazes of inward contemplation.

The voice of the sea speaks to the soul. The touch of the sea is sensuous, enfolding the body in its soft, close embrace.

And so Edna learns to swim, both literally and figuratively, to fend for herself, free of her husband, in a new-found world of sensual, even carnal pleasure. No other writer of the era even tried to describe the feelings a woman experiences as she discovers her own sexual being and, more important, her own identity. The novel's commercial and critical failure, in fact, mirrored Edna's own inability, once she has in fact fully awakened to herself, to fit into her society. The author fared better than her character, and Chopin turned to writing more commercially acceptable short stories. Illustrating the changing social and literary environment, Kate Chopin was recognized in the first edition of Marquis *Who's Who* (1900), which includes concise biographies of "distinguished Americans."

RAGTIME AND THE BEGINNINGS OF JAZZ

Edna Pontellier was not the kind of woman that Americans were used to encountering personally. But Chopin had carefully chosen New Orleans as Edna's place of awakening. New Orleans was still a French city, but it was also African-American, Spanish, Haitian, Creole, and Caucasian. At the end of the nineteenth century, it was probably the most cosmopolitan city in America. Out of this mixture a thriving musical culture developed, which included opera and chamber music, as well as a new form of music that evolved in the city's bars, dance halls, streets, and brothels. The bands that

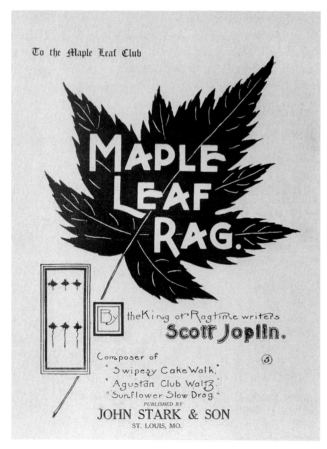

Fig. 32.18 Title page to an early edition of Scott Joplin's *Maple Leaf Rag*. ca. 1899. Joplin received $50 plus royalties for the work.

played at festivals, dances, and weddings, in the bars and in parades, and at political rallies and funerals, gained inspiration from African and Caribbean dance and drumming traditions. Combining these traditions with the brass bands and syncopated musical tunes that gained popularity in the 1880s, New Orleans gave birth to a new musical tradition that has come to be known as **jazz**.

Jazz is characterized by a steady rhythm that plays off against a rhythmic **syncopation**—the accentuation of "off-beats." **Ragtime** piano music is one of the earliest manifestations of this principle, although it appears in popular dance music in the nineteenth century—in the waltz, for instance—and in 4/4 music such as the march, another kind of "movement music" and one source of ragtime, where the accents are on the odd-numbered beats (1 and 3). A musician "rags" by playing a classical or popular melody in a syncopated style. The left hand maintains a steady, marchlike tempo, while the right plays the melody in syncopated rhythm. The most famous ragtime pianist was Scott Joplin, whose *Maple Leaf Rag* (Fig. 32.18) sold hundreds of thousands of copies after 1899 (track **32.1**).

HEAR MORE at
www.myartslab.com

To many, more puritanical Americans, the loose rhythms of ragtime suggested loose morals, and ragtime was subjected to the same harsh criticisms as Chopin's novel, published in the same year that Joplin's tune was released. One American music critic, for instance, urged readers to "take a united stand against the Ragtime Evil. . . . In Christian homes, where purity of morals is stressed, ragtime should find no resting place. . . . Let us purge America and the Divine Art of Music from this polluting nuisance." Such sentiments, which would later also be aimed at jazz (in the 1920s and 1930s) and rock-and-roll (in the 1950s and 1960s), were often motivated by racism. However, more open-minded white audiences were attracted to the music's fresh spontaneity. Ragtime—and, later, jazz in general—represented a new, authentic form of American expression, a synthesis of diverse traditions that transcended the classical symphony, ballet, and opera musical forms that originated in Europe.

THE AMERICAN ABROAD

As much as New Orleans offered Americans the prospect of a colorfully complex urban atmosphere, the rest of the world also beckoned, available as never before for exploration. Novelist Henry James remarked, "The world is shrinking to the size of an orange." He meant that it had become easy for Americans to travel to and live in London, Paris, and Rome. In fact, by the end of the nineteenth century, there were 17 companies with over 173 steamships regularly sailing between New York and Europe. With the advent of steam turbine engines, screw propellers, and steel hulls, it took less than a week to cross the Atlantic. (Fifty years earlier, it had taken two to three weeks, and in Benjamin Franklin's time, it took from six weeks to three months.)

Another innovation that made international travel even more inviting was the development of ocean liners, ships that measured up to a thousand feet long with lavish accommodations for (some of) their passengers. Ocean liners had three classes of rooms for its customers, with the third or "steerage" class (originally referring to those housed in cargo holds of ships) comprising the greatest number, and the first and second classes supplying the majority of profits. European immigrants moving westward with dreams of a better life filled the steerage compartments, while newly rich Americans traveled eastward toward Britain and the Continent. In Europe, wealthy Americans, who would sometimes stay for months and years, took in the history and culture, spent their money freely, sometimes married (or dallied with) aristocrats, and generally indulged in behavior that would draw scorn from their more puritanical families and friends as well as from the scandal-seeking press in the United States.

Henry James and the International Novel

Perhaps the best-traveled and most cosmopolitan American writer in the nineteenth century was Henry James (1843–1916). His first years were spent in Paris—his first memory, he claimed, was of the Place Vendôme [vahn-DOME] with its Napoleonic column—and he was educated there as well as in Geneva, Switzerland, and Bonn, Germany. American schooling was not up to his father's high standards. On his first European tour, undertaken when he was 26 years of age in 1869 to 1870, James met the intellectual elite of England: William Morris, Dante Gabriel Rossetti, Edward Burne-Jones, John Ruskin, and Charles Darwin. He then traveled on to Paris and to Switzerland; from there he hiked into Italy, then on to Milan, Venice, and Rome. He took his aunt and sister on a second tour in 1872 to 1874, returned to Paris in 1875, meeting writers Gustave Flaubert and Émile Zola, among others, and then settled in England in 1876. "My choice is the Old World," he wrote in his diary, "my choice, my need, my life."

James often depicted the drama of American innocence confronting European experience in his novels. In *Portrait of a Lady* (1881), for instance, Isabel Archer, a young woman freed by her inheritance to travel wherever she pleases, follows in James's footsteps to England and France, marrying a morally bankrupt American expatriate. Her relationship with him tests every fiber of her innocence and moral being. In *The Ambassadors*, Lambert Strether is sent to Europe to free Chad Newsome, his fiancée's son, from the perceived clutches of the older, more experienced Madame de Vionnet [vee-oh-NAY]. Yet he himself is transformed by his acquaintance, in London and Paris, with Maria Gostrey, an American émigré, and by Chad's new circle of friends. Over a period of weeks, Strether recognizes that Chad has in fact "improved," gaining new sophistication, and knows that something similar has occurred to himself.

Painters Abroad: The Expatriate Vision

Henry James was as socially active as a hardworking writer could be. His network of friends and acquaintances included many British and European artists, as well as dozens of American expatriates. *The Ambassadors* began from a germ of an idea that the author captured in his notebook in October 1895 when he recorded how fellow American author William Dean Howells (1837–1920), standing in a Paris garden, sermonized to a young man that he must live to the fullest while young. The Parisian home where the garden was located belonged to American expatriate painter James Abbott McNeill Whistler (1834–1903), who maintained a friendship with James for almost two decades.

The painter had notoriously sued English critic John Ruskin for libel after Ruskin published a scathing review of Whistler's *Nocturne in Black and Gold: The Falling Rocket* (Fig. **32.19**). In his review, Ruskin berated the artist for asking "two hundred guineas for flinging a pot of paint in the public's face." The trial verged on high comedy, as the jury was shown the offending picture upside-down, and "experts" of all persuasions testified to the painting's worth. Whistler eventually won but was awarded only a farthing (the least valuable English coin), a far cry from the cost of the legal action, which eventually drove him into bankruptcy.

The painting at the center of the controversy is a kind of radical impressionistic illustration of a seaside fireworks display, so deeply atmospheric that its subject matter is hard to

Fig. 32.19 James Abbott McNeill Whistler, *Nocturne in Black and Gold: The Falling Rocket.* **ca. 1874.** Oil on oak panel, 23 3/4″ × 18 3/8″. The Detroit Institute of Arts. Gift of Dexter M. Ferry, Jr. 46.309. The Bridgeman Art Library. The painting depicts fireworks falling over Cremorne Gardens, the popular resort on the banks of the Thames.

SEE MORE Gain insight from a primary source document about James Abbott McNeill Whistler at **www.myartslab.com**

fathom. Whistler was an admitted **aesthete**—someone who valued art for art's sake, for its beauty, not for its content. In an 1890 collection of essays called *The Gentle Art of Making Enemies*, he explained the philosophy behind **aestheticism**:

> [Art] should be independent of all clap-trap—should stand alone and appeal to the artistic sense of ear or eye, without confounding this with emotions entirely foreign to it, as devotion, pity, love, patriotism and the like. All these have no kind of concern with it, and that is why I insist on calling my works "arrangements" and "harmonies."

Whistler wanted the public to understand that the painter had a right to alter objective truth in order to conform to his or her own subjective standards of beauty. A work created in this way was not incompetent. It was, rather, of the highest order of art.

Another American painter who spent much of his life in Europe was John Singer Sargent (1856–1924). Born in Florence and trained in Italy and France, Sargent was Whistler's rival, though 22 years his junior. He took Whistler's old studio in London after Henry James convinced the young artist to leave Paris in 1886, and it was

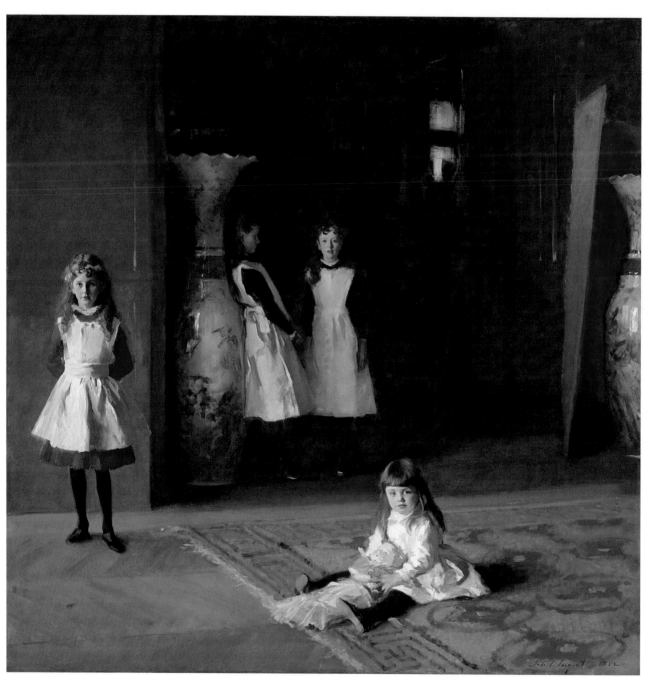

Fig. 32.20 John Singer Sargent, *The Daughters of Edward Darley Boit*. 1882. Oil on canvas, 87 3/8″ × 87 5/8″. Gift of Mary Louisa Boit, Julia Overing Boit, Jane Hubbard Boit, and Florence D. Boit in memory of their father, Edward Darley Boit, 19.124 Photograph © 2008 Museum of Fine Arts, Boston. The unusual, almost square canvas is probably something of a pun on the "Boit" name since *boîte*, in French, means "box."

there that Sargent did most of his work. Sargent specialized in portraits of the aristocracy and the wealthy, and he was noted for his stylish, bravura brushwork. James and Sargent moved in similar social circles, becoming fast friends after James's review of the 26-year-old painter's work in *Harper's Weekly*.

In the *Harper's* article, James took special note of Sargent's *The Daughters of Edward Darley Boit*, exhibited in Paris at the Salon of 1883 (Fig. **32.20**). The painting depicts the four daughters of an expatriate patrician couple from Boston, Edwin Darley Boit and Mary Louisa Cushing Boit, in the entry to their apartment in Paris. In the foreground, Julia, the youngest child, aged four, sits on the floor with her doll between her legs. To the left, facing the viewer forthrightly, but gazing just to the viewer's left, is Mary Louisa, aged eight. In the shadows of the doorway, Jane, aged 12, looks directly at us, while Florence, the eldest, aged 14, leans, as if unwilling to cooperate with the painter, against one of two enormous Chinese vases that lend the scene something of an "Alice in Wonderland" effect.

James first described this painting as "a rich, dim, rather generalized French interior (the perspective of a hall with a shining floor, where screens and tall Japanese vases shimmer and loom), which encloses the life and seems to form the happy play-world of a family of charming children." But gradually he perceived in this work the same mysterious depth that he tried to convey in his own fiction—"the sense," he called it, "of assimilated secrets." At least at some level, the painting is a parable of the coming of age of young women in late nineteenth-century society, from the innocence of youth to the privacy and alienation of adolescence. As in James's fiction, there is always more than meets the eye, and this is the lesson that James continually impressed upon Americans who traveled or lived abroad.

One of the most successful of the American expatriate painters was Mary Cassatt, who moved to Paris in 1874 and was befriended by one of the founders of Impressionism, Edgar Degas. Participating in the Impressionist exhibitions

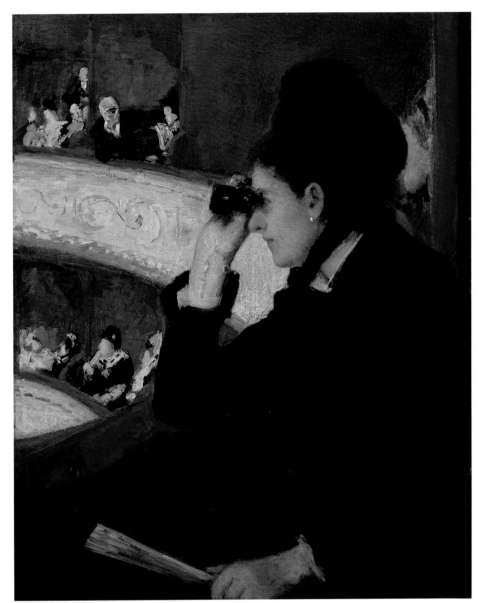

Fig. 32.21 Mary Stevenson Cassatt, *In the Loge*. 1879. Oil on canvas, 32″ × 26″. Museum of Fine Arts, Boston. The Hayden Collection—Charles Henry Hayden Fund, 10.35. Photograph © Museum of Fine Arts, Boston. This was the first of Cassatt's Impressionist paintings to be displayed in the United States. American critics thought the picture a promising sketch, but not, as the Impressionist Cassatt intended, a finished painting.

in 1879, 1880, and 1881, Cassatt was a figure painter, concentrating almost exclusively on women in domestic and intimate settings. Among her most famous works are paintings of women at the Paris Opéra. *In the Loge* is a witty representation of Opéra society (Fig. **32.21**). A woman respectably dressed all in black peers through her binoculars in the direction of the stage. Across the way, a gentleman in the company of another woman leans forward to stare through his own binoculars in the direction of the woman in black. Cassatt's woman, in a bold statement, becomes as active a spectator as the male across the way. Cassatt continually explored new styles and methods of painting, including, as we have seen, works inspired by Japanese woodblock prints (see Fig. 31.25) .

Fig. 32.22 Mary Stevenson Cassatt, *Modern Woman*, central panel, in the Hall of Honor, Woman's Building, World's Columbian Exposition, Chicago, 1893 (destroyed). Mural, 13' × 58'. Reproduced in *Harper's New Monthly Magazine*, Vol. 86, Issue 516, May 1893, p. 837. At the opposite end of the Hall of Honor was a mural entitled *Primitive Woman*, painted by Mary Fairchild Macmonnies, an American artist who had moved to Paris in 1888 and spent each summer near Monet at Giverny.

CHICAGO AND THE COLUMBIAN EXPOSITION OF 1893

An influential artist in Europe and America, Mary Cassatt played an integral part in the 1893 Columbian Exposition (an early world's fair) in Chicago. The U.S. Congress selected Chicago as the site for this massive exhibition to mark the four-hundredth anniversary of the arrival of Christopher Columbus in the Americas. The exposition was intended to demonstrate the economic, technological, and cultural progress of the country. Chicago was a logical choice, since it had grown from a village of 250 people in 1833 to, 60 years later, the nation's second-largest city, with a population of almost 1 million, most of them foreign-born. West Coast cities like San Francisco, though also growing swiftly in population, were still too rough, too much like frontier towns, to make the right impression.

Cassatt's mural for the fair, entitled *Modern Woman*, was displayed in the Hall of Honor in the Woman's Building. It was designed as an allegorical triptych (three-paneled work of art). The left and right panels depicted *Young Girls Pursuing Fame* and *Arts, Music, Dancing*. She represented the allegorical figure of Fame as a flying female figure, her nudity emblematic of the necessity of abandoning conventional social constraints. Three girls chase Fame, and a gaggle of geese chase them in turn. The three self-confident and assured women at the other side of the central panel demonstrated that women are accomplished in their own right, not just the creative muses of men.

The central panel, entitled *Young Women Plucking the Fruits of Knowledge or Science*, drew the most attention. Here Cassatt offers a positive reinterpretation of the theme of Eve

Fig. 32.23 Mary Stevenson Cassatt, *Gathering Fruit*. ca. 1893. Drypoint, softground etching, and aquatint printed in color from three plates, 16⁷/₈″ × 15³/₈″. Gift of William Emerson and The Hayden Collection—Charles Henry Hayden Fund, 41.813. Photograph © 2008 Museum of Fine Arts, Boston. This is one of several prints by Cassatt related to the theme of the Hall of Honor mural.

Fig. 32.24 Charles Graham, *Sophia Hayden's Woman's Building*, World's Columbian Exposition, Chicago. 1893. Watercolor, 17″ × 27 ¹/₂″. The Granger Collection, New York. Graham included a gondola in the lake to express the fair's Venetian theme.

in the Garden of Eden, as women pass on knowledge, imaged as fruit, from one generation to the next. Although the mural does not survive, we know it from reproductions in contemporary periodicals (Fig. **32.22**). In *Gathering Fruit*, a print from the same era as the mural, Cassatt combined the primary theme of the central panel with a baby, an element from the mural's border, which was decorated with several plump infants (Fig. **32.23**).

Cassatt's murals coincided with the early development of the women's movement in America and Europe. The 1878 International Congress of Women's Rights, held in Paris, advocated for free and compulsory education for women through secondary school, a measure that the French in fact implemented in the 1880s. The meeting also focused on the important role women play in nurturing and educating their children—the theme, indeed, of Cassatt's central panel at the Chicago Exposition and one that she would paint continuously in her domestic scenes of mothers tending their children.

As plans for the Columbian Exposition were being made, the all-male World's Columbian Commission appointed a "Board of Lady Managers," headed by a Chicago socialite, to design a building where women could meet at the fair. When it became apparent that women would have difficulty exhibiting elsewhere, the project was transformed into the pavilion where Cassatt's painting and

other women's artwork was displayed. Designed by the first female graduate of the Massachusetts Institute of Technology to earn a degree in architecture, Sophia Hayden (1868–1953), the two-story Women's Building was of Neoclassical design, with a central arcade flanked by pavilions at each end and a two-story pediment over the main entrance (Fig. **32.24**). Hayden, sadly, would never design another building. Constant interference by the all-male Board of Architects, a meager budget, and confused guidance led to a nervous breakdown and Hayden's withdrawal from her profession.

The fair was situated on 700 acres of swampland at the edge of Lake Michigan planned to resemble a Venetian park, complete with waterways and gondolas. Like all of the other buildings, the Woman's Building was steel-framed, with its plaster-of-Paris facade painted white, an effect that lent the fairgrounds their nickname—the White City. It was a white city in more ways than one. Although African Americans tried mightily to be represented at the fair, actively seeking membership on the planning committees and employment at its venues, they were systematically excluded from participation. They could attend the fair only on select days, even though on the mile-long Midway Plaisance [play-ZAHNSS] the fair's official Department of Ethnology, simulated African, Laplander, Turkish, Chinese, Pacific Island, and

Japanese villages. Men from Dahomey [dah-HOH-may] populated the African village, brought to the fair by an eccentric French entrepreneur. Other indigenous peoples from America, Asia, and North Africa were also included in this "outdoor museum" of "primitive peoples." (Such ethnographic exhibits were already standard at European world fairs.) Frederick Douglass, appalled by the fair's segregationist admission policies, its indifference to African-American job-seekers, and its representation of "the Negro as a repulsive savage," joined Ida B. Wells in writing a scathing review of the exposition, "The Reason Why the Colored American Is Not in the World's Columbian Exposition."

Louis Sullivan and the Chicago School of Architecture

One of the main reasons Chicago was so attractive as a venue for the Columbian Exposition was the sheer volume and impressiveness of its original, contemporary architecture. Ironically, the origin of the city's vast expanse of modern buildings was due to a catastrophic accident. On Sunday evening, October 8, 1871, a fire began in the cow barn at the rear of the Patrick O'Leary cottage on Chicago's West Side. By midnight, the city's business district was in flames. By Monday evening, as rains helped to douse the blaze, 300 residents of Chicago were dead, 90,000 were homeless, and the property loss was estimated at $200 million. The entire central business district of Chicago was leveled.

While devastating, the fire also contributed substantially to Chicago's economic boom as the city raced to rebuild. This provided an extraordinary opportunity for architectural innovation. Four factors contributed to what became known as the Chicago School of architecture. First, there was an urgent need to rebuild with fireproof materials. Second, Chicago was a world leader in the manufacture and production of steel. Third, the hydraulic elevator was invented the same year that the fire occured. And fourth, there was a growing conviction that because land in the downtown district was so expensive, buildings should be built higher.

Until the 1880s, the height of buildings was restricted to 10 stories because of the structural limitations of masonry bearing walls, even with cast iron built into them. The solution was metal-frame construction, first developed for building bridges in England (see Fig. 24.8). The frame supported the entire load of the building, with the **curtain wall** (a non-load-bearing wall applied to keep out the weather) carried on the structural skeleton. In Chicago, where the bearing capacity on soil at the edge of Lake Michigan was extremely poor and could not support the weight of a brick building over 10 stories high, the lightness of iron- and then steel-frame construction became a driving force in rebuilding the downtown after the great fire of 1871.

Fig. 32.25 Louis H. Sullivan, Bayard (Condict) Building, New York. 1897–98. For Sullivan, the foremost problem that the modern architect had to address was how the building might transcend the "sinister" urban conditions out of which, of necessity, it had to rise.

Iron- and steel-frame construction also opened the curtain wall to ornamentation and large numbers of exterior windows. One of the leading proponents of this new method of design and construction was the Chicago architect Louis H. Sullivan (1856–1924). For Sullivan, the building's identity lay in its ornamentation. As he put it in his satirically titled 1901 to 1902 *Kindergarten Chats*, ornamentation was the "spirit" that enhanced the architectural idea. Inorganic, rigid, and geometric lines of the steel frame would flow through the ornamental detail that covered it into "graceful curves," and angularities would "disappear in a mystical blending of surface." So at the top of Sullivan's Bayard Building in New York, the vertical columns that rise between the windows blossom in an explosion of floral decoration (Fig. **32.25**).

Such ornamentation might seem to contradict the aphorism for which Sullivan is most famous: "Form ever follows function." If the function of the urban building is to provide a well-lighted and ventilated place in which to work, the steel-frame structure and the abundance of windows on the building's facade make sense. But how does the ornamentation follow from the structure's function?

Down through the twentieth century, Sullivan's original meaning has largely been forgotten. He was not promoting a notion of design akin to the sense of practical utility found in the first mass-produced automobile, the Model T Ford. For Sullivan, "the function of all functions is the Infinite Creative Spirit," and it could be revealed in the rhythm of growth and decay that we find in nature. Thus the elaborate organic forms that cover his buildings were intended to evoke nature and the creative impulse. For Sullivan, the primary function of a building was to

elevate the spirit of those who worked in it. No architect would have a greater influence on modern architecture in the twentieth century. He is at once the father of the skyscraper, and, perhaps most important, the teacher of one of the twentieth century's most influential architects, Frank Lloyd Wright.

Frederick Law Olmsted and the Invention of Suburbia

Sullivan's buildings reflect the same motivation that inspired the parks movement inaugurated by Central Park in New York City and other parks throughout the country—the desire to bring the spirit of nature to the urban environment. In order to allow the rapidly growing population to escape the rush of urban life, New York City in 1856 acquired an 840-acre tract of land for a park in the still largely undeveloped regions north of 59th Street. It hired Frederick Law Olmsted [OLM-sted] (1822–1903) and Calvert Vaux [voh] (1824–1895) to effect the transformation (Fig. **32.26**). The two men modeled what is now known as Central Park on the English garden (see Chapter 25) with, in Olmsted's words, "gracefully curved lines, generous spaces, and the absence of sharp corners, the idea being to suggest and imply leisure, contemplativeness, and happy tranquility." Here, immigrants

Fig. 32.26 John Bachman, *View of Central Park*. ca. 1870. Color lithograph. (fl.1850-77). © Museum of the City of New York/The Bridgeman Art Library. Frederick Law Olmsted and Calvert Vaux designed the park, and construction began in 1857. For Olmsted, the park was an educational environment in which poor immigrants could mingle freely with the upper classes and learn how to "comport" themselves properly.

from the hundreds of blocks of tenement housing in Manhattan could stroll side by side with the wealthy ladies and gentlemen whose homes lined Fifth Avenue facing the park. Sheep grazed in one area of the park, and in another, the Dairy, children could sip milk fresh from the cows that grazed nearby. In this artificial rural environment, city dwellers could forget that they were even *in* the city.

So successful was Central Park that, in 1866, Olmsted and Vaux collaborated on the design of Prospect Park, across the East River, in Brooklyn. And after Vaux's dissolution of their partnership in 1872, Olmsted went on to design many other public commons, including South Park in Chicago, the parkway system of the City of Boston, Mont Royal in Montreal, and the grounds at Stanford University and the University of California at Berkeley. Moreover, Olmsted was able to foresee that the increasing population density of cities required the growth of suburbs, a residential community within commuting distance of the city. "When not engaged in business," Olmsted wrote, "[the worker] has no occasion to be near his working place, but demands arrangements of a wholly different character. Families require to settle in

certain localities which minister to their social and other wants, and yet are not willing to accept the conditions of town-life . . . but demand as much of the luxuries of free air, space and abundant vegetation as . . . they can be enabled to secure."

As early as 1869, Olmsted and Vaux laid out a general plan for the city of Riverside, Illinois, situated nine miles outside Chicago and one of the city's first suburbs (Fig. 32.27). The plan incorporated the railroad as the principal form of transportation into the city, making it one of the very first commuter suburbs in America. The plan provided for the best-engineered streets of the time, with cobblestone gutters for proper drainage, sewers, water lines, gas lines, and gas street lamps. Olmsted strove to create a communal spirit by subdividing the site into small "village" areas linked by drives and walks, all intended to have "the character of informal village greens, commons and playgrounds." Together with Forest Hills in New York, Llewellyn Park in New Jersey, and Lake Forest, also outside Chicago, Olmsted's design for Riverside set the standard for suburban development along with a new pattern of living for Americans.

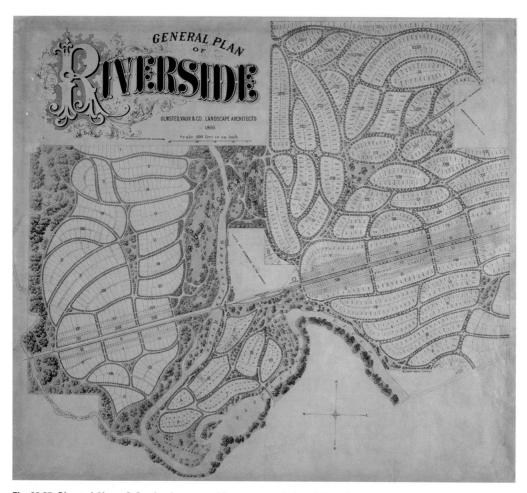

Fig. 32.27 Olmsted, Vaux, & Co., landscape architects, general plan of Riverside, Illinois. 1869. Francis Loeb Library, Graduate School of Design, Harvard University. In the Preliminary Report for Riverside, Olmsted remarks, "The city [of Chicago] as yet has no true suburb in which rural and urban advantages are agreeably combined."

The "Frontier Thesis" of Frederick Jackson Turner

Coinciding with the Columbian Exposition of 1893 was the American Historical Association's yearly convention, where Frederick Jackson Turner (1861–1932) presented one of the most influential essays on the American West ever written. Entitled "The Significance of the Frontier in American History," Turner argued that the frontier was "the meeting point between savagery and civilization." He further contended that "the existence of an area of free land, its continuous recession, and the advance of American settlement westward explain American development." Twenty years earlier, painter John Gast (b. 1842) had essentially illustrated this argument in his widely popular painting *American Progress* (Fig. **32.28**). As trains, a covered wagon, a stagecoach, riders, miners, trappers, and farmers push westward driving bear, buffalo, and Indians before them, the frontiersmen are inspired by the allegorical figure of Progress. So when, in 1890, the U.S. Census Bureau proclaimed the frontier closed, Turner understood that a defining era in American history had passed. The frontier, according to Turner, had produced a "dominant individualism," men "of coarseness and strength . . . acuteness and inquisitiveness, [of a] practical and inventive turn of mind . . . [with] restless and nervous energy . . . [and the] buoyancy and exuberance which comes with freedom."

From the beginning, he continued, this "frontier individualism . . . promoted democracy." Yet he also warned that

the democracy born of free land, strong in selfishness and individualism, intolerant of administrative experience and education, and pressing individual liberty beyond its proper bounds, has its dangers as well as its benefits. Individualism in America has allowed a laxity in regard to governmental affairs which has rendered possible the spoils system and all the manifest evils that follow from the lack of highly developed civic spirit. In this connection may be noted also the influence of frontier conditions in permitting lax business honor, inflated paper currency and wildcat banking. . . . He would be a rash prophet who should assert that the expansive character of American life has now entirely ceased . . . [but] now, four centuries from the discovery of America, at the end of a hundred years of life under the Constitution, the frontier has gone, and with its going has closed the first period of American history.

Turner ignored the important role women played in settling the West, the role of slave labor in creating a productive economy, and perhaps most of all, the price Native Americans paid for the "free" land that Americans claimed as their own. Nevertheless, even as Buffalo Bill was performing his "Wild West Show" to tens of thousands of people just outside the Columbian Exposition's gates, Turner had articulated the seminal American myth. True or false, his "frontier thesis" affirmed the role that most people thought individualism would have to play if the nation were to continue to progress forward and meet the challenges of its increasing global presence. ∎

Fig. 32.28 John Gast, *American Progress*. 1872. Oil on canvas, 20 ^{1}/₄" × 30 ^{1}/₄". (fl.1872). Private Collection. Photo © Christie's Images/The Bridgeman Art Library. The allegorical figure of Progress unravels telegraph wire as Indians and buffalo flee before her. At the right is Manhattan Island, the twin towers of the Brooklyn Bridge just visible over the East River. Construction on the suspension bridge, designed by engineer John Augustus Roebling, had begun in 1869 but would not be completed until 1883.

How did territorial expansion affect Native Americans in North America?

The confrontation between white settlers and indigenous Americans accelerated after the Louisiana Purchase in 1803, effectively doubling the size of the United States. American presidents like Washington and Jefferson emphasized the importance of "civilizing" Native Americans by converting them to Christianity, teaching them to farm, and educating their children. President Jackson claimed to believe in the same things, but how did his practices counter that position? How would you describe the difference between Native American attitudes about the land and those of the white settlers of North America?

American artists of the nineteenth century offered a range of mythic interpretations of the frontier experience. How do the visions of Albert Bierstadt contrast to those of John Vanderlyn? What were George Catlin's intentions as an artist?

Native American artists offered unique testament to their cultures and the rapid changes that overtook them by the end of the century. How do their arts—as evidenced in Huron moccasins, Sioux winter counts, Plains beadwork, Navajo blankets, and Apache basketry—reflect European influence? What eventually led to the demise of the Plains tribes?

How were the contradictions of economic expansion expressed by American artists?

As New York City grew to over 3 million people in the last decades of the nineteenth century, poet Walt Whitman celebrated the city's— as well as the nation's— sense of energy, excitement, and unlimited possibility. How would you describe his subject matter? What significant stylistic innovation did he introduce? The quintessential New Yorker, Whitman fully recognized the corruption that characterized New York's Tammany Hall and the plight of the working class, which in 1877 erupted in a series of strikes across the country. What caused these strikes?

Women of the era continued to be disenfranchised, but they did make gains, as state-run schools trained women as teachers and nurses. In the last decades of the century, women became one of the favorite subjects of male American painters. How did male painters generally depict women?

Women often made significant individual contributions to the culture, in the arts as well as in the fledgling women's-rights movement. Emily Dickinson's poetry, although little known in her lifetime, was widely read and admired by century's end. How do the contrasting styles and content of Whitman's and Dickinson's verse define the American culture of their era? How does Kate Chopin challenge the traditional place of women did her novel *The Awakening*?

What is ragtime?

By the end of the century, New Orleans was one of the nation's most cosmopolitan cities. In the city's bars and dance halls, at its political rallies, weddings, and funerals, a new kind of music developed that has come to be known as jazz. What characterizes the ragtime piano music popularized by Scott Joplin?

What is an expatriate?

Many Americans left home to travel to Europe for lengthy sojourns. Based on their life and works, why do you think Henry James, James McNeill Whistler, Mary Cassatt, and John Singer Sargent chose to be expatriates?

What ideal of America was exhibited at the Columbian Exposition?

The Columbian Exposition in Chicago in 1893 marked the four-hundredth anniversary of the arrival of Christopher Columbus in the Americas. How were women represented at the Columbian Exposition? What point of view did they try to express?

Part of what attracted the fair's organizers to Chicago was its advanced architecture, represented particularly in the skyscrapers of Louis Sullivan. What was new and unique in Sullivan's design and construction? Frederick Law Olmsted and Calvert Vaux designed New York's Central Park, begun in 1857. Olmsted and Vaux also designed Riverside, Illinois, one of the very first commuter suburbs in the nation, creating a parklike city with "informal village greens, commons and playgrounds." How do the buildings of Sullivan and the parks of Olmstead help to express the Columbian Exposition's ideal?

PRACTICE MORE Get flashcards for images and terms and review chapter material with quizzes at **www.myartslab.com**

GLOSSARY

aesthete One who values art for art's sake, for its beauty rather than its content.

aestheticism A devotion to beauty in art.

curtain wall A non-load-bearing wall applied in front of a framed structure, often for decorative effect.

free verse Poetry based on irregular rhythmic patterns as opposed to conventional meter.

jazz A uniquely American form of music that developed out of ragtime's rhythmic accentuation of the "off-beats" but with greater freedom of syncopation and orchestration.

ragtime A genre of popular music in which the musician takes a classical or popular melody and plays it in a syncopated way; see *syncopation*.

syncopation The accentuation of "off-beats."

winter count A Plains tribe history marking the passing of the years from first snowfall to first snowfall with a single image designed to stir the tribe's collective memory of events.

READING 32.2

from Walt Whitman, "Song of Myself," in *Leaves of Grass* (1867)

From the time of its first edition in 1855, Leaves of Grass *constantly changed over the course of Whitman's lifetime. Its many revisions and additions reflect the changing course of American democracy, including the tragedy of the Civil War, the expansion of the nation into the West, and the industrialization of the eastern seaboard. At the center of the book is Whitman's "Song of Myself." It consists of 52 parts, reflecting the 52 weeks of the year. In the following passages, something of the range of Whitman's vision can be understood: his individualism in Part 1, his sexuality in Part 2, the development of his central metaphor, the grass, in Part 6, and his all-encompassing inclusiveness in Part 15.*

1

I CELEBRATE myself, and sing myself,
And what I assume you shall assume,
For every atom belonging to me as good belongs to you.

I loafe and invite my soul,
I lean and loafe at my ease observing a spear of summer grass.

My tongue, every atom of my blood, form'd from this soil,
  this air,
Born here of parents born here from parents the same, and
  their parents the same,
I, now thirty-seven years old in perfect health begin,   10
Hoping to cease not till death.

Creeds and schools in abeyance,
Retiring back a while suffced at what they are, but never
  forgotten,
I harbor for good or bad, I permit to speak at every hazard,
Nature without check with original energy.

2

Houses and rooms are full of perfumes, the shelves are
  crowded with perfumes,
I breathe the fragrance myself and know it and like it,
The distillation would intoxicate me also, but I shall not let it. 20

The atmosphere is not a perfume, it has no taste of the
  distillation, it is odorless,
It is for my mouth forever, I am in love with it,
I will go to the bank by the wood and become undisguised
  and naked,
I am mad for it to be in contact with me. . . .

6

A child said *What is the grass?* fetching it to me with full hands,
How could I answer the child? I do not know what it is any
  more than he.

I guess it must be the flag of my disposition, out of hopeful 30
  green stuff woven.

Or I guess it is the handkerchief of the Lord,
A scented gift and remembrancer designedly dropt,
Bearing the owner's name someway in the corners, that we
  may see and remark, and say *Whose*?

Or I guess the grass is itself a child, the produced babe of
  the vegetation.

Or I guess it is a uniform hieroglyphic,
And it means, Sprouting alike in broad zones and narrow zones,
Growing among black folks as among white,   40
Kanuck, Tuckahoe, Congressman, Cuff, I give them the same,
  I receive them the same.

And now it seems to me the beautiful uncut hair of graves. . . .
All goes onward and outward, nothing collapses,
And to die is different from what any one supposed, and
  luckier. . . .

15

The pure contralto sings in the organ loft,
The carpenter dresses his plank, the tongue of his foreplane
  whistles its wild ascending lisp,
The married and unmarried children ride home to their   50
  Thanks giving dinner,
The pilot seizes the king-pin, he heaves down with a strong arm,
The mate stands braced in the whale-boat, lance and
  harpoon are ready,
The duck-shooter walks by silent and cautious stretches,
The deacons are ordain'd with cross'd hands at the altar,
The spinning-girl retreats and advances to the hum of the big
  wheel,
The farmer stops by the bars as he walks on a First-day loafe
  and looks at the oats and rye,   60
The lunatic is carried at last to the asylum a confirm'd case,

(He will never sleep any more as he did in the cot in his
    mother's bedroom;)

The jour printer with gray head and gaunt jaws works at his
    case,

He turns his quid of tobacco while his eyes blurr with the
    manuscript;

The malform'd limbs are tied to the surgeon's table,

What is removed drops horribly in a pail;   70

The quadroon girl is sold at the auction-stand, the drunkard
    nods by the bar-room stove,

The machinist rolls up his sleeves, the policeman travels his
    beat, the gate-keeper marks who pass,

The young fellow drives the express-wagon, (I love him,
    though I do not know him;)

The half-breed straps on his light boots to compete in the race,

The western turkey-shooting draws old and young, some
    lean on their rifles, some sit on logs,

Out from the crowd steps the marksman, takes his position, 80
    levels his piece;

The groups of newly-come immigrants cover the wharf or
    levee,

As the woolly-pates hoe in the sugar-field, the overseer
    views them from his saddle,

The bugle calls in the ball-room, the gentlemen run for their
    partners, the dancers bow to each other,

The youth lies awake in the cedar-roof'd garret and harks to
    the musical rain,

The Wolverine sets traps on the creek that helps fill the Huron, 90

The squaw wrapt in her yellow-hemm'd cloth is offering
    moccasins and bead-bags for sale,

The connoisseur peers along the exhibition-gallery with
    half-shut eyes bent sideways. . . .

The city sleeps and the country sleeps,

The living sleep for their time, the dead sleep for their time,

The old husband sleeps by his wife and the young husband
    sleeps by his wife;

And these tend inward to me, and I tend outward to them,

And such as it is to be of these more or less I am,   100

And of these one and all I weave the song of myself.

READING CRITICALLY

In the selection from Part 6, Whitman refers to the grass
as "the flag of my disposition, out of hopeful green stuff
woven." How does Part 15 develop that sentiment?

READING 32.4

**from Emily Dickinson, *Poems* (as published in *The Complete Poems of Emily Dickinson*,
ed. T. H. Johnson, 1953)**

*Dickinson wrote almost 2,000 poems in her lifetime. It was not until 1953 that all of her known poems were
published—and, for the first time, as she wrote them, without editorial changes. The following three poems circulate
around the theme of death, that greatest of all enigmas. Even in so small a selection, they give a fair idea of the scope
of her mind.*

465

I heard a Fly buzz—when I died—
The Stillness in the Room
Was like the Stillness in the Air—
Between the Heaves of Storm—

The Eyes around—had wrung them dry—
And Breaths were gathering firm
For that last Onset—when the King
Be witnessed—in the Room—

I willed my Keepsakes—Signed away
What portion of me be   10
Assignable—and then it was
There interposed a Fly—

With Blue—uncertain stumbling Buzz—
Between the light—and me—
And then the Windows failed—and then
I could not see to see—

712

Because I could not stop for Death—
He kindly stopped for me—
The Carriage held but just Ourselves—
And Immortality.   20

We slowly drove—He knew no haste
And I had put away
My labor and my leisure too,
For His Civility—

We passed the School, where Children strove
At Recess—in the Ring—
We passed the Fields of Gazing Grain—
We passed the Setting Sun—

Or rather—He passed Us—
The Dews drew quivering and chill—   30
For only Gossamer, my Gown—
My Tippet—only Tulle—

We paused before a House that seemed
A Swelling of the Ground—
The Roof was scarcely visible—
The Cornice—in the Ground—

Since then—'tis Centuries—and yet
Feels shorter than the Day
I first surmised the Horses' Heads
Were toward Eternity –   40

754

My Life had stood—a Loaded Gun—
In Corners—till a Day
The Owner passed—identified—
And carried Me away—

And now We roam in Sovereign Woods—
And now We hunt the Doe—
And every time I speak for Him—
The Mountains straight reply—

And do I smile, such cordial light
Upon the Valley glow—   50

It is as a Vesuvian face
Had let its pleasure through—

And when at Night—Our good Day done—
I guard My Master's Head—
'Tis better than the Eider-Duck's
Deep Pillow—to have shared—

To foe of His—I'm deadly foe—
None stir the second time—
On whom I lay a Yellow Eye—
Or an emphatic Thumb—   60

Though I than He—may longer live
He longer must—than I—
For I have but the power to kill,
Without—the power to die—

READING CRITICALLY

One of Dickinson's preferred thematic forms was the riddle. How do these
three poems reflect that preference?

The Fin de Siècle

Toward the Modern

THINKING AHEAD

What was the significance of the 1889 Exposition Universelle in Paris?

What is the fin de siècle?

What is Post-Impressionism?

How does Symbolism manifest itself outside of France?

How did developments in Africa reflect European beliefs and sensibilities?

Paris's Exposition Universelle of 1889 was a fitting postscript to the nineteenth century as well as a precursor to the twentieth. It commemorated imperial supremacy, modern technology, and national pride exactly one century after the beginning of the French Revolution, all symbolized by the marvel of architecture and technology at the heart of the fair—the Eiffel Tower (Fig. **33.1**). Further, the exposition showcased France's cultural heritage and confirmed the status of Paris as one of the world's great centers of art. As he opened the fair, French President Sadi Carnot hailed the "new era in the history of mankind" that the revolutionary events of 1789 initiated, and the "century of labor and progress" that had unfolded since then.

But Carnot had little inkling of the darker side of technology and nationalism that would be unleashed over the next 50 years when two world wars killed over 60 million people with unparalleled efficiency. Ideologies also grew more strident and dangerous in the ensuing decades, becoming virulently transnational in scope and as dangerous as technology if unrestrained. France's

president himself would become a victim of a new ideology five years later when an Italian anarchist assassinated him to avenge the execution of several French anarchists who had participated in bombings. It seems that while nationalism held an increasing, often irrational sway over human behavior, political theories such as anarchism and, later, fascism and communism, would also lead to violent and destructive actions by individuals and groups aiming to reshape society to their own standards.

This chapter surveys the era just before and after the 1889 Exposition, now labeled the fin de siècle [fen duh see-EKL], or "end of the century," but implying much more. The 1890s were characterized by an atmosphere of opulence, decadence, and anticipation as Europeans prepared to enter the twentieth century. Paris was widely acknowledged as the center of the fin de siècle spirit and one of the centers of artistic and literary innovation. The progression of Western cultural movements and styles chronicled in this chapter—Art Nouveau, Symbolism, and Post-Impressionism—reveal a deeper mood

◀ Fig. 33.1 *Les Fêtes de Nuit à la Exposition.* **1900.** From *L'Exposition de Paris* (1900). Smithsonian Institution, Washington, D.C. The 1889 and 1900 expositions in Paris drew visitors from around the world to celebrate the centennial of the French Revolution and the beginning of a new century. In 1900, Paris was lit for the first time by electric light, and the Eiffel Tower, erected for the Exposition of 1889, was the centerpiece of "les fêtes de nuit," the nighttime celebrations at the fair. It was as if darkness was evaporating, both literally and figuratively, and that a new light was about to dawn.

HEAR MORE Listen to an audio file of your chapter at **www.myartslab.com**

of uncertainty about the world. Doubts about human rationality and about positivism—the belief that the scientific approach could explain and solve problems of the individual and society, were key elements of this uncertainty. In the realm of politics, revolution after revolution had promised a brighter future, but the rise of the bourgeois middle class proved unsettling, for its values seemed crassly materialistic, self-centered, and hypocritical. Even as scientific and technological innovation was everywhere apparent, artists found it difficult to reflect that spirit of innovation in their own work. A "new" modern art was struggling to be born, seemingly against the tide of popular culture and opinion.

THE PARIS EXPOSITION OF 1889

The social and political problems of the next century were certainly not in the minds of the 28 million people who visited the Paris fair in 1889. They excitedly circulated among the artistic, commercial, and engineering marvels displayed by more than 6,000 exhibitors on over 235 acres and thought about a future embodied by the Eiffel Tower. The past was also represented at the fair in the form of a village of 400 native Africans and similar displays of numerous other indigenous peoples from Asia and Africa in a "colonial" section. Together with reproductions of housing from around the world, the fair's "colonies" attested to the seemingly limitless ambition and power of imperial nations such as France to command the world's resources and peoples (Fig. 33.2).

The future was the chief attraction of the Paris Exposition, and *invention* was the key word of the day. In the Palace of Machines, Thomas Edison exhibited 493 new devices, including a huge carbon-filament electric lamp made from many smaller lamps. The magic of electricity made it possible to illuminate all 235 acres of the exposition. His phonograph was also a great attraction as thousands of visitors lined up each day to hear the machine. Other inventions fascinated the public—in the Telephone pavilion, one could listen to live performances of the Comédie Française through two earphones that created a convincing stereo effect.

The most popular "exhibit," however, was Gustav Eiffel's tower, a 984-foot-tall open-frame structure at the entrance of the fair that dominated the city. Almost twice the height of any other building in the world, the tower was meant "to raise to the glory of modern science and to the greater honor of French industry, an arch of triumph," according to Eiffel. One of the main challenges he faced was how to protect the tower from the wind, which he solved by designing three levels of wrought-iron piers to provide efficient wind resistance. Once the tower was completed, spotlights positioned on the third level illuminated various Paris monuments. One of the world's first electric beacons on the top of the tower flashed a brilliant light, visible for more than 100 miles, into the night sky. Electricity also allowed fair visitors to ascend to an observation platform at the top of the tower in a hydraulic elevator designed by the Otis Elevator Company, which in turn allowed Louis Sullivan to build his skyscrapers in America (see Fig. 32.25).

Fig. 33.2 Japanese house (left) and Chinese house (right) in the History of Habitation exhibit, Exposition Universelle, Paris. 1889. Library of Congress, Washington, D.C. LC-US262-106562. The juxtaposition of East and West underscores the growing decentralization of culture throughout the nineteenth century.

Not everyone was pleased with the project. From the early 1880s, when the tower was under consideration, to 1887, when construction began, a fusillade of angry resistance issued forth from architects, artists, and people who lived in the vicinity of the project. Three hundred prominent artists and writers submitted the *Protestation des artistes* to the Minister of Public Works, forcefully arguing that the erection of the tower was a violation of the city's beauty:

> Writers, painters, sculptors, architects, passionate lovers of the heretofore intact beauty of Paris, we come to protest with all our strength, with all our indignation, in the name of betrayed French taste, in the name of threatened French art and history, against the erection in the heart of our capital of the useless and monstrous Eiffel Tower.

Charles Garnier, the designer of the Paris Opéra (see Fig. 30.9) and spokesperson for traditional architecture, was one of the key opponents; the tower's extraordinarily high profile eclipsed his own buildings at the fair. Garnier's "History of Habitation" exhibit attempted to portray the progressive evolutionary history of humans through the buildings they lived in. The 33 buildings he carefully built to exacting historical standards illustrated how humans had improved their habitats over time through ingenious technology and architectural planning. However, Garnier's admiration for progress only went so far—and certainly did not include approval of the Eiffel Tower's mere "framework," as he ridiculed it.

If a writer like Guy de Maupassant [moh-pah-SOHN] lunched at the restaurant in the tower, it was not because he liked the food—he didn't—but because "It's the only place in Paris where I don't have to see it." Nevertheless, the tower quickly became one of the city's landmarks. Gradually, through the last decade of the century, the Eiffel Tower came to symbolize not only Paris itself, but modernity. It was a very popular symbol of "the new."

THE FIN DE SIÈCLE: FROM NATURALISM TO SYMBOLISM

Although its meaning was never exact, *fin de siècle* came to refer to the last decade of the nineteenth century's climate of decadence and world-weariness, and the dawn of a new kind of modernism in art. It was against the prevailing, popular spirit of progress and optimism as represented in the bourgeois values of the era. Max Nordau [NOR-dow], a Hungarian-born physician and Jewish leader, offered an eloquent and elaborate identification of the term in 1892:

> *Fin de siècle* is French, for it was in France that the mental state so entitled was first consciously realized . . . and Paris is the right place in which to observe its manifold

expressions. . . . It means a practical emancipation from traditional discipline. . . . To the voluptuary, this means unbridled lewdness, the unchaining of the beast in man; . . . to the sensitive nature yearning for aesthetic thrills, it means the vanishing of ideals in art, and no more power in its accepted forms to arouse emotion. . . .

> One epoch of history is unmistakably in its decline, and another is announcing its approach. . . . Things as they are totter and plunge, and they are suffered to reel and fall, because man is weary, and there is no faith that it is worth an effort to uphold them. . . . Men look with longing for whatever new things are at hand . . .

While Nordau's popular essay bemoans the loss of "traditional views of custom and morality" and openly deplores the art of the era, it accurately captures European society's sense of being trapped between the end of one era and the start of another. The art of the era seems similarly caught in a state of "in between"—between a tradition whose values it rejects and a future that it cannot quite see but is struggling to define.

Art Nouveau

One of the most pervasive and influential new artistic styles beginning in the 1880s was Art Nouveau ("new art"), the name of which was derived from the Paris interior design shop of Siegfried Bing (1838–1905), named Maison de l'art nouveau. As with most artistic styles, Art Nouveau was associated with a number of contemporary trends, from the Arts and Crafts movement in England (see Chapter 31) to Symbolism, which endeavored to elevate feelings, imagination, and the power of dreams as creative inspiration. While Bing saw his galleries as displaying a wide range of art of the future, from fabrics by William Morris to jewelry, glassware, and furniture, not everyone agreed. A Norwegian visitor put it this way:

> Rather than the rising sun of the coming century, this "new art" appears to symbolize the evening twilight of refinement, which has settled over French intellectual life and which, with a worn but still not worn out catchword, calls itself "fin de siècle."

In fact, Art Nouveau was a transitional style, one caught between fin de siècle decadence and the innovations of modernity; between the nineteenth century's dedication to complex decorative designs and more abstract visions of the twentieth.

The fin de siècle era itself was transitional, and as an entrepreneur, Bing realized that he could take advantage of the materialistic desires of the middle class by selling them a fashionable *art nouveau*. He was already the chief dealer of Japanese prints in Paris when he traveled to the United States in 1894 at the request of the French government to report on American art. While there, he visited the New York studios of Louis Comfort Tiffany (1848–1933), son of the founder of the famous New York

Fig. 33.3 Louis Comfort Tiffany, stained-glass window. ca. 1894. Glass, 43″ × 27 ¹/₂″. Mention obligatoire Les Arts Decoratifs, Paris (Inv. 7972); Musee de la Publicite (Inv. 10531); Photo: Laurent Sully Jaulmes. Tous droits reserves. Tiffany's stained-glass and iridescent *favrile* glass vases, made by mixing different colors of glass together while hot (a process Tiffany patented in 1894), were widely popular in France. The Musée des Art Décoratifs purchased this window soon after it arrived at Bing's galleries in 1895.

jewelry house. Tiffany's decorative stained glass, Bing felt, might provide a model for French design (Fig. **33.3**). Bing began to import Tiffany's designs and sell them, along with furniture by Émile Gallé [gal-LAY] and Eugène Gaillard [guy-YAHR], and ceramics by Georges de Feure [fehr], among others, in his new showrooms. So successful was his enterprise that he built his own pavilion at the 1900 Exposition Universelle, entitled L'art nouveau Bing. Consisting of six rooms—dining room, bedroom, sitting room, lady's boudoir, parlor, and foyer—this new, modern house was filled with decorative items from Bing's workshop, where he supervised every aspect of the design and production.

As an international movement, Art Nouveau included architecture, glassware, textiles, furniture, and painting, and its practitioners could be found almost everywhere in Europe as well as in America's major cities. In one of the most important early innovations,

Belgian architect Victor Horta [HOR-tuh] (1861–1947) incorporated the Art Nouveau style into architecture. Commissioned to design the Brussels home of scientist Emile Tassel, the traditionally trained Horta used floral patterns and designs resembling the tendrils and shoots of young plants to decorate the ironwork, walls, and floor tile of the house (Fig. **33.4**). Such decorative effects spread rapidly across Europe, manifest in the long, flowing locks of female figures on posters, the peacock feathers on vases designed by Tiffany, budding, flower-like forms of glasswork, and the designs of furniture and metalwork.

When viewing the poster design for Delftsche Slaolie salad oil (Fig. **33.5**) by Belgian painter Jan Toorop (1858–1928), one can easily understand how the whiplike tendrils, buds, and flowers of Art Nouveau could be interpreted not as a celebration of growth and rebirth but as decadent and suggestively sexual. The two women are preparing a salad, but in the undulating rhythms of their flowing robes and hair, they elevate the mundane task "to the level of almost mystic rite," according to the Rijksmuseum in Amsterdam. As the best-known example of Dutch Art Nouveau, this commercial poster is now considered a

Fig. 33.4 Victor Horta, Tassel House, Brussels. 1892–93. From a calyxlike capital (calyxes are green and leaflike parts of a flower that enclose the petals), the iron columns sprout slender iron strips to support the floor above.

Fig. 33.5 Jan Toorop, *Delftsche Slaolie*. 1894. Lithograph, 37 3/4″ × 21 1/4″. Dutch advertisement poster. Scala/Art Resource, New York. The undulating curvilinear rhythms of this poster advertising salad oil were widely emulated across Europe.

masterpiece in the collection of one of Europe's greatest museums. Toorop's use of dynamic flowing lines, organic forms, color, and abstract designs to celebrate and enliven everyday life highlights an important aspect of the Art Nouveau movement. Rather than being confined to either the sphere of fine art or the practical applied designs of household objects and furniture, Art Nouveau encompassed a wide range of types of design.

Exposing Society's Secrets: The Plays of Henrik Ibsen

In the world of literature, the fin de siècle spirit was apparent in the later works of Norwegian playwright Henrik Ibsen (1828–1906), whose plays were performed across Europe in the last decades of the century. French author Émile Zola [zoh-LAH] introduced Ibsen's work to Paris and considered the playwright a naturalist (see Chapter 30), who saw his world through an intensely acute and realistic

lens. Ibsen's 1879 play *A Doll's House* was a sensation for its scathing depiction of Victorian marriage, with its oppression of women and cruelty of men. The heroine of the story, Nora, finally awakens to the truth of her existence, for although she lives a pampered, sheltered life, she is continually patronized and humiliated, treated like a child—or a doll—by her husband, Torvald (**Reading 33.1**):

READING 33.1

from Henrik Ibsen, *A Doll's House*, Act III (1878)

Nora: . . . While I was still at home I used to hear Father airing his opinions and they became my opinions; or if I didn't happen to agree, I kept it to myself—he would have been displeased otherwise. He used to call me his doll-baby, and played with me as I played with my dolls. Then I came to live in your house . . . from Father's hands I passed into yours. You arranged everything according to your tastes, and I acquired the same tastes, or I pretended to—I'm not sure which—a little of both, perhaps. Looking back on it all, it seems to me I've lived here like a beggar, from hand to mouth. I've lived by performing tricks for you, Torvald. But that's the way you wanted it. You and Father have done me a great wrong. You've prevented me from becoming a real person. . . . Our home has never been anything but a play-room. I've been your doll-wife, just as at home I was Papa's doll-child. And the children, in turn, have been my dolls. I thought it fun when you played games with me, just as they thought it fun when I played games with them. And that's been our marriage, Torvald.

In her weariness and her despair, Nora found a symbolic image—the doll's house—that offers expression to her previously inarticulate feelings. When, at the end of the play, she leaves home forever with a slam of the door, she has become the symbol of individual freedom, a whole person who declares as she leaves: "I cannot be satisfied any longer with what most people say, and with what is in books. I must think over things for myself, and try to get clear about them."

In Ibsen's play, Nora represents the future, Torvald the past, and the reaction of European audiences to the play reveals just how resistant nineteenth-century European society was to the possibility of meaningful social change. Like the American audiences who reacted negatively to Kate Chopin's *The Awakening* (see Chapter 32), Europeans were outraged. To admit that a woman might reject her familial duties to satisfy her own needs was unthinkable. In fact, the actress who played Nora in the first German production refused to play the final scene of the play, as Nora says to Torvald, "I'm sure I'll think of you often, and about the children and the house here." The German actress loudly protested, "*I* would never leave *my* children," abruptly ending the play with Nora unable to leave her children, sinking to the floor of their room in despair.

Ibsen was a realist, and he presented the hidden truths of European society as no one before had ever dared. In *Ghosts* (1881), which followed *A Doll's House*, he took on the problematic issues of children born out of wedlock, venereal disease, infidelity, and incest. Again the reaction was outrage for what was perceived as Ibsen's affront to public decency. In *Hedda Gabler* (1890) he explored the world of a neurotic woman at the edge of insanity, who successfully schemes to sabotage an academic rival to her husband. By destroying her husband's rival, however, Hedda also destroys herself, illuminating the powerful influence of irrational, sometimes unconscious motivations and values upon our lives. Ibsen, in short, revealed the lies behind the seemingly upright facade of contemporary European society, lies that many of his critics clearly wished he had kept secret. While Ibsen's work heralded new cultural trends that would come to fruition in the twentieth century, it also had many attributes of popular nineteenth-century literary styles, particularly realism. His emphasis on realistic dramas with complex moral questions would become central to the world of drama (and eventually film) in the new century.

The Symbolist Imagination in the Arts

With *The Master Builder* (1892), Ibsen began a series of four interrelated plays that explored the lives of powerful men who come to recognize their failures and shortcomings. Culminating with *When We Dead Awaken* (1899), they abandon the realism of his earlier work and explore the dreams and fantasy worlds of their protagonists. This focus on the subjective experience and the often irrational impulses that rule human behavior signaled a new emphasis on introspection and the realization that human behavior was difficult, if not impossible, to quantify. Increasingly, Ibsen reflected the Symbolist aesthetic that in the last decade came to dominate the European imagination. The Symbolists aimed to "objectify the subjective . . . instead of subjectifying the objective," according to the poet Gustave Kahn (1859–1936). By describing transitory feelings of people through symbolic language and images, Symbolists hoped to convey the essential mystery of life.

Symbolism distinguished itself from naturalism as practiced by Émile Zola by downplaying the need to convey meaning through direct and accurate representation. Instead, it favored *suggesting* the presence of meaning in order to express the inexpressible. This movement away from the physical world and into the realm of impressionistic experience lays the groundwork for the modern in art because, detached as it is from tangible reality, it takes a first step toward abstraction.

The Sculpture of Rodin The transition from realism to Symbolism is notable in the expressive sculptures of Auguste Rodin [roh-DAN] (1840–1917), whose style matured in the years after 1877. In many ways, Rodin was thought of as a realist—many people believed that some of his pieces must have been the result of a mold being applied to a living model. Like the Impressionist painters who were his contemporaries, Rodin depended on the play of light upon surfaces for the energy of his works. And just as they worked *en plein air* [ahn plen air], Rodin based his sculpture on direct observation, which accounted for its smooth realization and considerable impact on critics and the public at large.

However, *The Kiss* (1888–1889), one of Rodin's most famous sculptures, is more than simply a sharply realistic portrayal of two bodies embracing (Fig. **33.6**). It is the very embodiment of ecstatic abandon in which the woman is clearly as active a participant as the man. The work was a purposeful homage to the opposite sex, according to Rodin. When it was exhibited at the Salon of 1886, viewers found it immodest and shocking. At the 1893 Columbian Exposition in Chicago (see Chapter 32), a bronze version of *The Kiss* was considered too scandalous for public display.

Rodin's monumental homage to Balzac, a full-length representation of the writer in his dressing gown, also depicts a source of creative power, in this case artistic

Fig. 33.6 Auguste Rodin,
***The Kiss.* 1888–89.** Marble,
$54^1/_2'' \times 43^1/_2'' \times 46^1/_2''$.
Musée Rodin, Paris. The sculpture was originally conceived as a depiction of Paolo and Francesca, the adulterous lovers whom Dante encounters in the Second Circle of Hell in *The Divine Comedy*.

Fig. 33.7 Auguste Rodin, *Monument to Balzac*. 1898. Bronze, 106$\frac{1}{4}$" × 47$\frac{1}{4}$" × 50$\frac{3}{8}$". Garden of the Museum, Musée Rodin, Paris. When a model of the sculpture was first exhibited, it was dismissed as a "colossal fetus," a "colossal clown," and a "snowman." The Society of Men of Letters refused to accept it, and Rodin was forced to return payments for it that had already been made.

(Fig. **33.7**). Rodin was grateful for the commission from the French literary organization of which Zola, an admirer of Rodin, was president. He immediately proceeded to study his subject in as much depth as Zola had studied the French mining industry for *Germinal* (see Chapter 30). He traveled to Balzac's hometown of Tours in order to study the physical types of the city's inhabitants. He tracked down Balzac's tailor to find out his measurements so that he could model the artist's dressing gown to exact specifications. He viewed portraits, lithographs, and daguerreotypes of the writer. He modeled an imaginary Balzac nude so that he would know the body that he was to fit under the robe. But the finished nine-foot-tall work is not realistic. It is recognizably Balzac, but a Balzac whose features have been exaggerated in the quest to illustrate the process of artistic creativity, enfolded in its robes. It is finally, as one contemporary critic has noted, as much Rodin's portrait as Balzac's, "the symbolic celebration, through Balzac, of the vigour and heroism of prolific genius."

Rodin, Lautrec, and the World of Montmartre In the early 1890s, a number of artists residing in Paris engaged in artistic experiments that combined music, dance, painting, and the new electrical lighting technology. Rodin was at the center of this community. He had always been attentive to the movement of the human body, and he allowed his models—often dancers—to wander around the studio, striking poses at will (Fig. **33.8**). Gustav Kahn described Rodin's technique:

> She can sit, stand, lie down, stretch, and, according to her fancy or fatigue, propose a movement, an attitude, a letting go, and one of these images will be stopped by Rodin and captured in a drawing that seems to emerge almost instantaneously. Sometimes he does not even make her stop, but makes a cursive notation, for the rare movement he seeks is a transition between two movements. . . . The series of drawings furnishes him with an encyclopedia of human movements. . . . The huge sketchbook consulted by the artist takes on full meaning when he seeks the confirmation of a freshly-sprouted idea. The simplest movement, or observation of a physical attitude can give rise to an idea too.

Fig. 33.8 Auguste Rodin, *Dancing Figure*. 1905. Graphite with orange wash, 12$\frac{7}{8}$" × 9$\frac{7}{8}$". Gift of Mrs. John W. Simpson. 1942.5.36. Image © 2007 Board of Trustees, National Gallery of Art, Washington, D.C. Rodin's drawings are characterized by their extreme simplicity, the outline of the body flowing continuously, without shadow or modeling. Broad bands of wash create a sense of volume.

Fig. 33.9 Henri de Toulouse-Lautrec, *Miss Loïe Fuller*. 1893. Color lithograph, sheet: 15 1/8" × 11 1/16". Rosenwald Collection. 1947.7.185 Image © 2007 Board of Trustees, National Gallery of Art, Washington, D.C. Each of the approximately 60 impressions in the series is unique. Toulouse-Lautrec used five different lithographic stones in the process, inking them in a wide range of colors. He dusted some of the prints, including this one, with gold or silver powder, attempting to imitate the play of electric light on Fuller's dance.

Rodin's ideas inspired a close friend, the American dance sensation Loïe Fuller (1862–1928). She had arrived in Paris in 1892, bringing with her electricians skilled at devising dramatic lighting techniques. Within a short time, she was dazzling audiences at the Folies-Bergère with a juxtaposition of colored lighting and dances marked by long, flowing, transparent fabrics swirling around her body. In 1893, French painter and printmaker Henri de Toulouse-Lautrec [too-LOOZ-loh-TREK] (1864–1901) executed a series of 60 lithographs of Fuller dancing, each hand-colored in order to capture the full effect of her inventive show (Fig. 33.9). An early champion of Rodin, Fuller helped organize the first exhibition of his work in New York in 1903.

Another popular dance of the era was the can-can, made infamous in 1890s Paris by La Goulue [goo-LEW] ("The Greedy One"), the stage name of Louise Weber (1866–1929). She was named La Goulue after her habit of dancing past café tables and quickly downing the drinks of the seated customers. When she danced the can-can, she lifted her skirts to reveal a heart embroidered on her panties. Then, with a high kick, she would flip a man's hat off with her toe. She performed regularly at the Moulin Rouge (Red Windmill), a cabaret in the Parisian red-light district in the Montmartre section of the city.

Such places and the people in them—gamblers, prostitutes, and circus performers—were Toulouse-Lautrec's favorite subjects. Severely deformed, the victim of a rare bone disease, Toulouse-Lautrec depicts himself walking with a tall cousin in the background of *At the Moulin Rouge* (Fig. 33.10). Behind the two, La Goulue herself adjusts her red hair. At the table, a coterie of cabaret regulars, including the entertainer La Macarona, her face powdered in stark white makeup, and the dancer Jane Avril [ah-VREEL], noted for her long, red hair, share a drink. Toulouse-Lautrec's portrayals of the nightlife of Paris—in many ways a counterpart to Tokyo's "floating world" of courtesans, actors, and artists—helped define the fin de siècle era in lithographs and paintings. Although generally considered a Post-Impressionist (discussed in the following section), Toulouse-Lautrec is hard to categorize. He influenced the Art Nouveau movement with his posters and lithographs, and also influenced the Symbolists. Perhaps the clearest assessment of Toulouse-Lautrec came from a German art historian who affirmed that "in his skilled hands, the denizens of Montmartre . . . are transformed into symbols of themselves. Toulouse-Lautrec's art is simultaneously realistic and symbolic. The figures are stripped of accidental detail and reduced to the essence of character. They are an essence distilled from reality by a great artist."

Mallarmé's Poetry Like Rodin and Toulouse-Lautrec, the Symbolist poet Stéphane Mallarmé [mah-lar-MAY] (1842–1898) was immediately enraptured by Loïe Fuller. She is "at once an artistic intoxication and an industrial achievement," he wrote, referring to her lighting effects, "fusing the swift changes of color that vary their limelit phantasmagoria of twilight and grotto with rapidly changing passions—delight, mourning, anger." If, for Mallarmé, to name a thing was to destroy it and to suggest it was to bring it to life, it was the dancer, not the lighting, that was the most important ingredient in Fuller's colorful show. "The dancer," he wrote,

> . . . does not dance, but suggests, by prodigies of bending and of leaping, by a corporeal writing, what would require paragraphs of prose, both dialogue and description, to express in words: a poem freed from all the machinery of the writer.

Because Mallarmé believed that a poem was somehow hindered by the writer's words and syntax—and that poetry might be freed of the necessity of words—it is not surprising that in his own works what is said is less important than how the poems evoke feelings. Their mysterious suggestions and overtones take precedence over the logic of grammar, replaced by a sensual web of

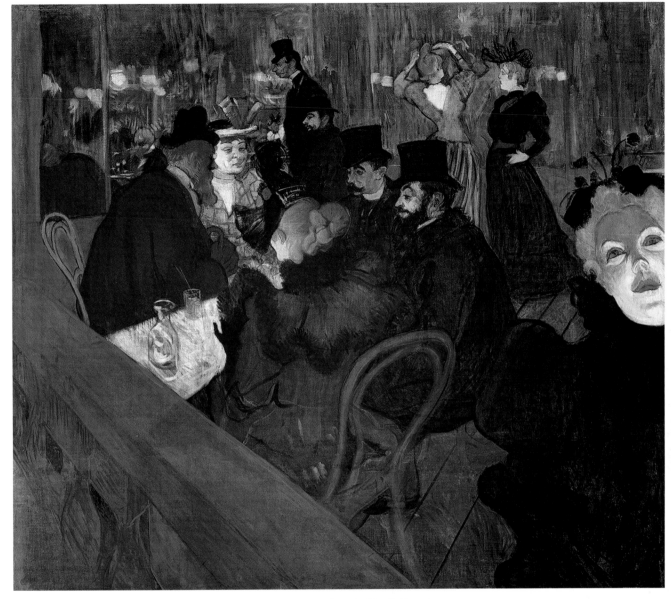

Fig. 33.10 Henri Marie Raymond de Toulouse-Lautrec (1864–1901 French), *At the Moulin Rouge.*
1892–95. Oil on canvas, 4' $^3/_8$" × 4' 7$^1/_4$" (23 × 141 cm). Helen Birch Bartlett Memorial Collection, 1928.610.
Photograph © 2006, The Art Institute of Chicago. All rights reserved. The faces of Toulouse-Lautrec's figures
border on caricature, as if to mock traditional canons of beauty.

free association. In one of his most famous poems,
"L'Après-midi d'un faune" [lah-pray-mee-DEE dun
fohn] ("The Afternoon of a Faun"), the faun—part-
man, part-goat—wakes from a dream to remember his
afternoon tryst with a group of nymphs (female goddesses, spirits of nature). The poem was inspired by the
Ovidian myth of the god Pan's attempt to seduce the
beautiful nymph Syrinx [SUR-inks], who is rescued
from his clutches. Regretting his loss, Pan discovers the
beauty of music by blowing air through the reeds into
which Syrinx has been transformed. While Mallarmé
takes many liberties with the myth, he maintains most
of the core elements, and leaves the ending ambiguous
(**Reading 33.2**):

READING 33.2
_____

**from Stéphane Mallarmé, "L'Après-midi d'un
faune" ("The Afternoon of a Faun") (1876)**

Ah well, towards happiness others will lead me
With their tresses knotted to the horns of my brow:
You know, my passion, that, purple and just ripe,
The pomegranates burst and murmur with bees;
And our blood, aflame for her who will take it,
Flows for all the eternal swarm of desire.
At the hour when this wood's dyed with gold and
    with ashes
A festival glows in the leafage extinguished:

It is clear that this passage is charged with sexual symbolism. The juxtaposition of "passion," "purple," and "just ripe" seems to suggest physical as well as imaginative readiness, and the pomegranate is a traditional symbol of fertility, bursting with seed. Above all, the poetry is suggestive, not definitive, creating a mood, an impression, an atmosphere, more than a clear image.

The Music of Debussy The most notable missing element in any translation of Mallarmé's poetry is the sound of the French language—the music of his words. Something of their effect, however, was translated into instrumental music by the composer Claude Debussy [duh-boo-SEE] (1862–1918), who began attending Mallarmé's Tuesday salons in about 1892, when he was 30 years old. Mallarmé's friends and associates—the international cast of artists and intellectuals who met on Tuesdays (*mardi* in French)—became known as les Mardistes. They included the Irish poet William Butler Yeats, the German poet Rainer Maria Rilke, and French poet Paul Verlaine. Two years later, Debussy composed one of his most famous and important pieces, *Prélude à l'après-midi d'un faune*, which many consider a defining moment in the history of music (track 33.1).

((•● HEAR MORE at
www.myartslab.com

Before its first performance on December 22, 1894, Debussy invited Mallarmé to attend: "I need not say how happy I would be if you were kind enough to honour with your presence the arabesque which, . . . I believe to have been dictated by the flute of your faun." Mallarmé was evidently delighted and responded with a short poem:

If you would know with what harmonious notes
Your flute resounds, O sylvan deity,
Then harken to the light that shall be breathed
There unto by Debussy's magic art.

Music's ability to bring to mind a torrent of images and thoughts without speech is almost perfectly realized in Debussy's composition, first by an opening flute solo that is shaped as a series of rising and falling arcs and then later by oboes, clarinets, and more flutes that develop the theme further. Debussy adds textures to this melody with harp, muted horns, the triangle, and lightly brushed cymbals, backed by orchestral accompaniment that provides atmospheric tone. The use of **chromatic scales**, which move in half-steps through all the black and white keys on a keyboard, lends *Prélude à l'après-midi d'un faune* a sense of aimless wandering.

As with other efforts by the fin de siècle artists, *Prélude* was a controversial work. More than 20 years after the premiere, another major French composer, Camille Saint-Saëns

(1835–1921), declared: "The *Prelude to the Afternoon of a Faun* has a pleasing sonority, but one finds in it scarcely anything that could properly be called a musical idea. It is to a work of music what an artist's palette is to a finished painting." Indeed, because Debussy's music lacks clear-cut cadences and tonal centers, it has often—and somewhat erroneously—been labeled Impressionist, with which he disagreed at the time. His 1905 composition *La Mer* [mair] (*The Sea*) seems to be a clearly impressionistic evocation of water. It consists of three sections. They illustrate the play of light on the surface of the water in the first, the movement of waves in the second, and the sound of wind on the water in the third. Superficially, it seems similar to the observation of the shimmering effects of water in Monet's *Regatta at Argenteuil* (see Fig. 31.4).

Some have made the point that Debussy's music is more Symbolist than Impressionist in nature because of the subtle but important difference between the words *impression* and *suggestion*. *Impression* is a received image and *suggestion* is a created effect. If *La Mer* were Impressionist, it would recreate the way in which the composer literally viewed the sea. But it is Symbolist, suggesting the way that Debussy feels about the sea, expressing the profound mysteries of its unseen depths.

POST-IMPRESSIONIST PAINTING

As we have seen, Toulouse-Lautrec has been labeled a Post-Impressionist, which refers to the generation of painters who followed the eight Impressionist Exhibitions in Paris, which ended in 1886. The other painters we think of as Post-Impressionists include Paul Cézanne, Paul Gauguin, and Georges Seurat, all of whom exhibited at various Impressionist shows. Rather than creating Impressionist works that captured the optical effects of light and atmosphere and the fleeting qualities of sensory experience, they sought to capture something transcendent in their act of vision, something that captured the essence of their subject. This is similar to the goal of Symbolist artists. The Post-Impressionists saw themselves as inventing the future of painting, of creating art that would reflect the kind of sharply etched innovation that, in their eyes, defined modernity.

Pointillism: Seurat and the Harmonies of Color

One of the most talented of the Post-Impressionist painters was Georges Seurat [suh-RAH] (1859–1891), who exhibited his masterpiece, *A Sunday on La Grande Jatte*, in 1886 when he was 27 years old (Fig. **33.11**). It depicts a Sunday crowd of Parisians enjoying the weather on the island of La Grand Jatte in the Seine River just northeast of the city. The subject matter is typically Impressionist, but it lacks that style's sense of spontaneity and the immediacy of its brushwork. Instead, *La Grande Jatte* is a carefully controlled, scientific application of tiny dots of color—*pointilles* [pwahn-TEE], as Seurat called them—and his method of painting became known as

Fig. 33.11 Georges Seurat (French 1859–1891), *A Sunday on La Grande Jatte*. 1884-86. Oil on canvas, 81³/₄″ × 121¹/₄″ (207.5 × 306.1 cm). Helen Birch Bartlett Memorial Collection, 1926.224. Combination of quadrant captures F1, F2, G1, G2. Photograph © 2006, The Art Institute of Chicago. All rights reserved. Capuchin monkeys like the one held on a leash by the woman on the right were a popular pet in 1880s Paris.

SEE MORE For a Closer Look at Georges Seurat's *A Sunday on La Grande Jatte,* go to **www.myartslab.com**

pointillism [POIN-tih-lizm] to some, and neo-impressionism to others.

Seurat tried to incorporate systematically the theories of Michel Eugène Chevreul's *Principle of Harmony and Contrast of Colors* (1839) and Ogden N. Rood's *Modern Chromatics* (1879) into his paintings to better use combinations of colors. Chevreul, in particular, had established the value of employing red, yellow, and blue as *primary* colors, through which most other colors can be mixed, and orange, green, and violet as *secondary* colors, produced by the mixing of two primaries. Rood's ideas were more sophisticated than Chevreul's and more useful to the painter, because he recognized that there was a significant difference between colored light and colored pigments. Not only did light possess a different set of primary and secondary colors—red, blue, and green—but the laws governing the mixture of these colors were dissimilar as well. Mixing together the colors of pigment is a *subtractive* process—that is, mixing together all three primary pigments ultimately creates black, the absence of color. But mixing light is an *additive* process—when all the primary colors of light are mixed,

they create white, which has all colors in it. This is illustrated when light refracting through the moisture in the air becomes a rainbow.

One of the most difficult tasks Seurat and other painters faced was imitating in the subtractive medium of pigments the additive effects of colored light observed in nature. In Rood's observation, placing "a quantity of small dots of two colors very near each other . . . allowing them to be blended by the eye placed at the proper distance. . . . [produces] true mixtures of colored light." The theory, it turns out, was not quite right, so while some found Seurat's painting to be luminous, others complained that "one could hardly imagine anything dustier or more dull." Ultimately, in pointillist paintings, dots of yellow-orange, meant to create a sensation of bright sunlight, will appear to be gray from a distance of even 15 feet.

Nevertheless, in setting his "points" of color side by side across the canvas, Seurat determined that color could be mixed, as he put it, in "gay, calm, or sad" combinations. Lines extending upward could also reflect these

Fig. 33.12 Georges Seurat (French 1859-1891), *Les Poseuses* (*The Models*). 1886–88. Oil on canvas, 78 3/4" × 98 3/8". The Barnes Foundation, Merion, Pennsylvania. Seurat unites the elements of this painting through color. Note, for instance, how the green stockings and green bag hanging on the wall echo the greens of *La Grande Jatte*, the huge painting on the wall to the left of the models, while the red umbrella, lying against a polka-dot dress, echoes the little girl in red running in the painting.

same feelings, he explained, imparting a cheerful tone, as do warm and luminous colors of red, orange, and yellow. Horizontal lines that balance dark and light, warmth and coolness, create a sense of calm. Lines reaching in a downward direction and the dark, cool hues of green, blue, and violet evoke sadness.

With this symbolic theory of color in mind, we can see much more in Seurat's *La Grande Jatte* than simply a Sunday crowd enjoying a day at the park. There are 48 people of various ages depicted, including soldiers, families, couples, and singles, some in fashionable attire, others in casual dress. A range of social classes is present as well, illustrating the mixture of diverse people on the city's day of leisure. Although overall the painting balances its lights and darks and the horizontal dominates, thus creating a sense of calm, all three groups in the foreground shadows are bathed in the melancholy tones of blue, violet, and green. With few exceptions—a running child, and behind her a couple—almost everyone in the painting is looking either straight ahead or downward. Even the tails of the pets turn downward. This solemn feature is further heightened by the toy-soldier rigidity of the figures. Like a Symbolist poem, Seurat's painting *suggests* more than it portrays—and his intentions are even more clearly revealed

in *Les Poseuses* [pose-URZ] (*The Models*) (1888), a painting of his studio in which *La Grande Jatte* functions as a sort of painting-within-the-painting (Fig. **33.12**). A critic of the time had written of *La Grande Jatte*, "one understands then the rigidity of Parisian leisure, tired and stiff, where even recreation is a matter of striking poses." *Les Poseuses* affirms this view. Some of the clothes in the foreground—notably the hats, the red umbrella, and the blue gown—are recognizably costumes used in the *La Grande Jatte*, and Seurat's models seem to be changing out of them into their street clothes. But the key element here is the title itself. As art historian Linda Nochlin has pointed out, *poseuse* is not the usual term employed by the French to describe an artist's model—*modèle* [moh-DELL] is. *Poseuse* rather means "one who seeks to attract attention by an artificial or affected manner." Seurat, then, in *Les Poseuses*, calls attention to the artificiality and affectation of the figures in *La Grande Jatte*.

Symbolic Color: Van Gogh

Seurat's influence on French painting was profound. Indeed many, including prominent critics of his era, considered him the founder of "neo-impressionism." Even Impressionist Camille Pissarro (see Chapter 31) would take up the

Fig. 33.13 Vincent van Gogh, *Night Café*. 1888. Oil on canvas, 28 1/2″ × 36 1/4″. Yale University Art Gallery, 1961.18.34. New Haven, Connecticut/Art Resource, New York. Van Gogh frequented this café on the place Lamartine in Arles. Gas lighting, only recently introduced, allowed it to stay open all night. Drifters and others with no place to stay would frequent it at night. Notice how many patrons seem to be asleep at the tables.

style for a time. Seurat's student Paul Signac would advance his theories by making his *pointilles* larger—passing on this innovation to twentieth-century painters such as Henri Matisse [mah-TEES] (see Chapter 34). And perhaps the most famous of the nineteenth-century artists, Dutch painter Vincent van Gogh (1853–1890), also studied Seurat's paintings while living in Paris in 1886–87. (He worked there for Siegfried Bing selling Japanese prints [see Chapter 29].) Van Gogh experimented extensively with Seurat's color combinations and pointillist technique, which extended even to his drawings, as a means to create a rich textural surface.

Van Gogh was often overcome with intense and uncontrollable emotions, an attribute that played a key role in the development of his unique artistic style. Profoundly committed to discovering a universal harmony in which all aspects of life were united through art, van Gogh found Seurat's emphasis on contrasting colors appealing. It became another ingredient in his synthesis of techniques. He began to apply complementary colors in richly painted zones using dashes and strokes that were much larger than Seurat's *pointilles*. In a letter to his brother Theo in 1888, van Gogh described the way the complementary colors in *Night Café* (Fig. **33.13**) work to create visual tension and emotional imbalance:

> In my picture of the *Night Café* I have tried to express the idea that the café is a place where one can ruin oneself, run mad, or commit a crime. I have tried to express the terrible passions of humanity by means of red and green. . . . Everywhere there is a clash and contrast of the most alien reds and greens. . . . So I have tried to express, as it were, the powers of darkness in a low wine shop, and all this in an atmosphere like a devil's furnace of pale sulphur. . . . It is a color not locally true from the point of view of the stereoscopic realist, but color to suggest the emotion of an ardent temperament.

Color, in van Gogh's paintings, becomes symbolic, charged with feelings. Added to the garish conflict of colors is van Gogh's peculiar point of view, elevated above the room that sweeps away from the viewer in exaggerated and unsettling perspective. *Night Café* in this regard reflects not just a mundane view of the interior of a café lit by lamps, but van Gogh's "ardent" reaction to it.

For many viewers and critics, van Gogh's paintings are the most personally expressive in the history of art, offering unvarnished insights into the painter's unstable psychological state. As he was painting *Night Café*, van Gogh was living in the southern French town of Arles, where, over the course of 15 months, he produced an astounding quantity of work: 200 paintings, over 100 drawings and watercolors, and roughly 200 letters. Many of these letters, especially those addressed to his brother Theo, help us to interpret his paintings, which have become treasured masterpieces, each selling for tens of millions of dollars. Yet at the time he painted them, almost no one liked them, and he sold almost none of his art.

To viewers at the time, the dashes of thickly painted color, an effect known as *impasto*, seemed thrown onto the canvas as a haphazard and unrefined mess. And yet, the

Fig. 33.14 Vincent van Gogh, *The Starry Night*. 1889. Oil on canvas, $28^3/_4" \times 36^1/_4"$. Acquired through the Lillie P. Bliss Bequest. (472.1941). Digital Image © The Museum of Modern Art/Licensed by Scala/Art Resource, New York. Saint-Rémy, where van Gogh painted this work, lies at the foot of a small range of mountains between Arles and Aix-en-Provence. This part of France is plagued in the winter months by the mistral, strong winds that blow day after day out of the Alps down the Rhône River valley. The furious swirls of van Gogh's sky and the blowing cypress trees suggest that he might be representing this wind known to drive people mad, in contrast to the harmonies of the painting's color scheme.

SEE MORE For a Closer Look at Vincent van Gogh's *The Starry Night,* **www.myartslab.com**

staccato rhythms of this brushwork seemed to van Gogh himself deeply autobiographic, capturing almost stroke by stroke the pulse of his own volatile personality.

In December 1888, van Gogh's personal emotional turmoil reached a fever pitch when he sliced off a section of his earlobe and presented it to an Arles prostitute as a present. After a brief stay at an Arles hospital, he was released, but by the end of January, the city received a petition signed by 30 townspeople demanding his committal. In early May, he entered a mental hospital in Saint-Rémy, not far from Arles, and there he painted *Starry Night*, perhaps his most famous composition (Fig. **33.14**). Unlike the violent contrasts that dominate the *Night Café*, here the swirling cypresses (in which red and green lie harmoniously side by side) and the rising church steeple unite earth and sky. Similarly, the orange and yellow stars and moon unite with the brightly lit windows of the town. Describing his thoughts about the painting in a letter to his brother, van Gogh wrote, "Is it not emotion, the sincerity of one's feeling for nature, that draws us?"

The Structure of Color: Cézanne

The French painter Paul Cézanne [say-ZAHN] (1839–1906) might have written the same words as van Gogh with respect to Impressionism. He certainly had similar thoughts regarding the colors of the south of France. Writing in 1876 to another Impressionist painter, Camille Pissarro, he described the village of L'Estaque [less-TAHK] on the Gulf of Marseilles [mar-SAY]:

> It's like a playing card. Red roofs against the blue sea. . . . The sun here is so tremendous that it seems to me that the objects are defined in silhouette, not only in black, but in blue, in red, in brown, in violet. I may be mistaken, but it seems to me to be the antithesis of modeling.

So it seems hardly accidental that Cézanne's *The Gulf of Marseilles, Seen from l'Estaque* (Fig. **33.15**) reds and blues that van Gogh uses in paintings like *Night Café* and *Starry Night*. Nevertheless, Cézanne did not much care for van Gogh's work. Indeed, Cézanne's color is not symbolic, like van Gogh's, but is used instead to structure the space of the canvas.

Of all the Post-Impressionists, Cézanne was the only one who continued to paint *en plein air*. In this regard, he remained an Impressionist, and he continued to paint what he called "optics." The duty of the painter, he said, was "to give the image of what we see," but innocently "forgetting everything that has appeared before." The result of this vision is a representation of nature as a series of patches of color that tend to flatten the surface of his paintings. (For an examination of this topic in regard to Cézanne's still-life paintings, see *Closer Look*, pages 1098–1099.) In *The Gulf of Marseilles*, for instance, the roofs and walls of the houses seem to lose the sense of having been drawn in proper perspective as swaths of yellow, orange, red, and green lie against one an-

Fig. 33.15 Paul Cézanne (French 1839–1906), *The Gulf of Marseilles, Seen from l'Estaque*. ca. 1885. Oil on canvas, 31 1/2″ × 39 1/4″ (80.2 × 106.6 cm). Mr. and Mrs. Martin A. Ryerson Collection. 1933.1116. Reproduction, The Art Institute of Chicago. All rights reserved. Note the way in which the brightly lit side wall of the building at the lower right seems to parallel the picture plane rather than recede at an angle away from it.

other. The uniform saturation of the blue color of the sea contradicts the illusion of spatial recession into deep space, causing the sea to hang like a curtain over the village.

Similar to Monet at Giverny [zhee-ver-NEE], Cézanne returned to the same theme continually—Mont Sainte-Victoire, the mountain overlooking his native Aix-en-Provence [eks-ahn-proh-VAHNSS] in the south of France (Fig. **33.16**). In the last decade of his life, the mountain became something of an obsession, as he climbed the hill behind his studio to paint it day after day. He especially liked to paint after storms, when the air was clear and the colors of the landscape were at their most saturated and uniform intensity. Cézanne acknowledges the illusion of space of the mountain scene by means of three bands of color. Patches of gray and black define the foreground, green and yellow-orange the middle ground, and violets and blues the distant mountain and sky. Yet in each of these areas, the predominant colors of the other two are repeated—the green brushstrokes of the middle ground in the sky, for instance—all with a consistent intensity. The distant colors possess the same strength as those closest. Together with the uniform size of Cézanne's brushstrokes—his patches do not get smaller as they retreat into the distance—this use of color makes the viewer very aware of the surface qualities and structure of Cézanne's composition. It is this tension between spatial perspectives and surface flatness that would become one of the chief preoccupations of modern painting in the forthcoming century.

Fig. 33.16 Paul Cézanne, *Mont Sainte-Victoire*. 1902–04. Oil on canvas, 28 3/4″ × 36 3/16″ (73 × 91.9 cm). Photo: Graydon Wood. Philadelphia Museum of Art: The George W. Elkins Collection, 1936. E1936-1-1. Cézanne painted this from the top of the steep hill known as Les Lauves, just north of Aix-en-Provence but within walking distance of the city center. He built his own studio on a plot of land halfway up the hill, overlooking the city.

In the late nineteenth century, few artists challenged the traditions of Western painting more dramatically than Paul Cézanne. In no painting is that challenge more explicit than *Still Life with Plaster Cast*, painted in about 1894. While the painting includes a plaster copy of a Cupid sculpted by Pierre Puget [poo-ZHAY] (1620–1694), it is also a commentary on the natural and artificial worlds. Since the Renaissance, Western art had been dedicated to representing the world as the eye sees it—that is, in terms of perspectival space. But Cézanne realized that we see the world in far more complex terms than just the retinal image before us. We see it through the multiple lenses of our lived experience. This multiplicity of viewpoints, or perspectives, is the dominant feature of Cézanne's paintings.

Cézanne consciously manipulates competing points of view in *Still Life with Plaster Cast*. Nothing in the composition is spatially stable. Instead we wander through the small space in the corner of Cézanne's studio just as the painter's eye would do. His viewpoint constantly moves, contemplating its object from this angle, then that one. In *Still Life with Plaster Cast* as well as other Cézanne still lifes, we experience the very uncertainty of vision. These still lifes consistently abandon Renaissance certainties about the position of objects in space in favor of a new, uncertain view, in which even a still life is animated. In French, the term for a "still life" is *nature morte* [nah-TOOR mort], literally "dead nature." Cézanne sought to reanimate vision, to bring "still life" back to life.

Something to Think About . . .

In the early years of the twentieth century, Pablo Picasso would think of Cézanne and, perhaps surprisingly, Jean-Auguste-Dominique Ingres as his two most interesting nineteenth-century predecessors. What do Cézanne and Ingres have in common?

Paul Cézanne, *The Peppermint Bottle*. 1893–95. Oil on canvas, 26″ × 32 3/8″. Image © 2007 Board of Trustees, National Gallery of Art, Washington, D.C. Chester Dale Collection. This is one of several paintings stacked against the wall of the painter's studio in *Still Life with Plaster Cast* that contribute to the visual complexity of that work. At the left side of *Still Life with Plaster Cast,* a blue cloth, under the plate of apples, seems to rise up off the table to support what we can now see are actually two apples in the right side of *The Peppermint Bottle,* where they appear ready to fall forward into the lap of the viewer. They are in motion, like Cézanne's eye and mind, and perhaps our frenetic modern lives.

Cézanne's *Still Life with Plaster Cast*

The edges of a canvas behind the statue visually reinforces the Cupid's posture, even as it seems to position him in the space of that canvas. This heightens the spatial confusion of the composition. What is in back seems to come forward. What is in front seems to fall back. Nothing is spatially stable.

If this is a green apple in the corner of the studio, it is far too large, larger than a grapefruit. Although we know that objects in the distance appear smaller than objects close at hand, Cézanne represents the apple not how it appears to us, but how we know it to be—the same size as the apple on the table directly below it.

The studio floor seems oddly to angle away to the left and also to tilt up. In fact, to the left of the Cupid, Cézanne appears to be looking at the floor from across the table, where as to the right of the Cupid, he seems to be looking down at the floor from above. Although the painting seems disjointed left to right, Cézanne seems to be suggesting that we never view the world from a single point of view. So he presents two different points of view here.

The two red onions are of radically different size, echoing the difference in size of the green apple on the floor at the corner of the room and the apples on the table. Yet, since both onions are on the same plane, it seems likely that this difference in size is real, which highlights Cézanne's manipulation of scale.

The Cupid is a highly ironic element. It has associations with traditional art and the Western ideal of love, which derives from Greco-Roman classical tradition. However, in the context of the apples that surround it, the Cupid also alludes to Christian tradition and Eve's eating of the fruit of knowledge.

Paul Cézanne, *Still Life with Plaster Cast.* **ca. 1894.** Oil on paper on board, 26$^1/_2$″ × 32$^1/_2$″. The Samuel Courtauld Trust, Courtauld Institute of Art Gallery, London.

The apple is modeled by radical shifts in color rather than gradations from light to dark (traditional chiaroscuro). The shaded areas are red, the lighted areas yellow. Furthermore, this apple and the other objects are outlined, which tends to flatten them, emphasizing their two-dimensional shape rather than their three-dimensional mass.

SEE MORE For a Closer Look at Paul Cezanne's *Still Life with Plaster Cast,* go to **www.myartslab.com**

Escape to Far Tahiti: Gauguin

Cézanne's self-exile from Paris to the solitude of his native Aix-en-Provence is also characteristic of the Symbolists, who valued the comparative quiet of the countryside over the turmoil of cities. The belief that silence allowed for contemplation of the essence of things and that solitude further enhanced this introspection provided the Symbolists with a reason to escape, an urge to retreat from the hectic pace of modern life.

In 1891, the painter Paul Gauguin [goh-GAN] (1848–1903) left France for the island of Tahiti, part of French Polynesia, in the South Pacific. A frustrated businessman and father of five children, he had taken up art with a rare dedication a decade earlier, studying with Camille Pissarro and Paul Cézanne. Gauguin was also a friend of van Gogh, with whom he spent several months painting in Arles during the Dutch artist's most productive period. He had also been inspired by the 1889 Exposition Universelle, where indigenous peoples and housing from around the world were displayed. "I can buy a native house," he wrote his friend Émile Bernard, "like those you saw at the World's Fair. Made of wood and dirt with a thatched roof." To other friends he wrote, "I will go to Tahiti and I hope to finish out my life there . . . far from the European struggle for money . . . able to listen in the silence of beautiful tropical nights to the soft murmuring music of my heartbeats in loving harmony with the mysterious beings in my entourage."

Gauguin's first trip to Tahiti was not everything he dreamed it would be, since by March 1892 he was penniless. When he arrived back in France, he had painted 66 pictures but had only four francs (about $12 today) to his name. He spent the next two years energetically promoting his work and writing an account of his journey to Tahiti, entitled *Noa Noa* (*noa* means "fragrant" or "perfumed"). It is a fictionalized version of his travels and bears little resemblance to the details of his journey that he honestly recorded in his letters. But *Noa Noa* was not meant to be true so much as sensational, with its titillating story of the artist's liaison with a 13-year-old Tahitian girl, Tehamana, offered to him by her family. He presents himself as a *primitif*—a word that

Fig. 33.17 Paul Gauguin, *Mahana no atua* (*Day of the God*). 1894. Oil on canvas, $27^{3}/_{8}"\times 35^{5}/_{8}"$ (69.5 × 90.5 cm). The Art Institute of Chicago. Helen Birch Bartlett Memorial Collection (1926.198). Photograph © 2007 The Art Institute of Chicago. All Rights Reserved. There is no record of Gauguin ever exhibiting this work. It was first exhibited at the Boston Art Club in 1925.

in French suggests a primal, original, or irreducible essence—and his paintings as visionary glimpses into the primal forces of nature.

Gauguin arranged for two exhibitions at a Paris gallery in November 1893 and another in December 1894. He opened a studio of his own, painted olive green and a brilliant chrome yellow, and decorated it with paintings, tropical plants, and exotic furnishings. He initiated a regular Thursday salon where he lectured on his paintings and regaled guests with stories of his travels, as well as playing music on a range of instruments.

In this studio, he painted *Mahana no atua* (*Day of the God*) of 1894 (Fig. **33.17**). Based on idealized recollections of his escape to Tahiti, the canvas consists of three zones. In the top zone or background, figures carry food to a carved idol, representing a native god, a musician plays as two women dance, and two lovers embrace beside the statue of the deity. Below, in the second zone, are three nude figures. The one to the right assumes a fetal position suggestive of birth and fertility. The one to the left appears to be daydreaming or napping, possibly an image of reverie. The middle figure appears to have just emerged from bathing in the water below that constitutes the third zone. She directs her gaze at the viewer and, so, suggests an uninhibited sexuality. The bottom, watery zone is an irregular patchwork of color, an abstract composition of sensuous line and fluid shapes. As in van Gogh's work, color is freed of its representational function to become an almost pure expression of the artist's feelings.

Gauguin returned to Tahiti in June 1895 and never came back to France, completing nearly 100 paintings and more than 400 woodcuts in the eight remaining years of his life. He moved in 1901 to the remote island of Hivaoa [hee-vah-OH-uh], in the Marquesas [mar-KAY-suz], where in the small village of Atuona [aht-uh-WOH-nuh] he built and decorated what he called his House of Pleasure. Taking up

with another young girl, who, like Tehamana, gave birth to his child, Gauguin alienated the small number of priests and colonial French officials on the islands but attracted the interest and friendship of many native Marquesans, who were fascinated by his nonstop work habits and his colorful paintings. Having suffered for years from heart disease and syphilis, he died quietly in Hivaoa in May 1903.

Escape to Giverny: The Late Monet

In 1893, Claude Monet bought the tract of land adjacent to the river and across the railroad tracks from his property in Giverny, the small village on the Seine where he had retreated in 1883 to escape the urbanization of Paris. The parcel included a pond, which he proceeded to expand, planting it with water lilies and building a Japanese bridge after the model found in any number of Japanese prints, which he had collected for years. Then he began to paint the ensemble repeatedly. The garden at Giverny became a sort of dream world for him, its reflections a metaphor for his own thoughts, his own self-reflections.

Beginning the series in 1902, Monet often repainted the canvases, destroying some in frustration. But in 1909, he exhibited 48 *Water Lilies* paintings in Paris. And in 1914, encouraged by his friend and neighbor Georges Clemenceau (1841–1929), prime minister of France, he began a series of mural-sized versions of the paintings, which he agreed to donate to the state. He worked on them continuously for the rest of this life, managing to ignore, as best he could, even the horrible battles of World War I, despite his close friendship with Clemenceau, who led the country during the war. In 1927, the year after he died, the paintings were finally installed, encircling the viewer in two rooms of the Orangerie [or-ohn-zhuh-REE], a building at the top of the Tuileries gardens (Fig. **33.18**).

Standing in the midst of Monet's panoramic cycle, the viewer's eye is driven randomly through the space of the

Fig. 33.18 Claude Monet, *Setting Sun*. ca. 1921–22. Panel from the *Water Lilies* murals. Oil on canvas, 6' 6³/₄" × 19' 8³/₈". Musée de l'Orangerie, Paris, France. Erich Lessing/Art Resource, New York. The painting is actually designed to curve around the end of a room at the Orangerie as shown in Fig. 33.19

Fig. 33.19 Room 1 of the *Water Lilies*. Photo: Gèrard Blot/Hervè Lewandowski. Musée de l'Orangerie, Paris, France. Réunion des Musées Nationaux/Art Resource, New York. In their scale, Monet's paintings anticipate the abstract painting of Jackson Pollock. In their simultaneously transparent and opaque fields of color, they look forward to the color-field paintings of Mark Rothko. (Pollock and Rothko are discussed in Chapter 38.)

paintings (Fig. **33.19**). It is as if one is standing on an island in the middle of the pond itself. Without a single focal point, the viewer organizes the visual experience through personal acts of perception and movement. The paintings verge on abstraction, as if the objective world is about to evaporate into a field of color and paint.

TOWARD THE MODERN

As a turn-of-the-century artistic movement, Symbolism was in many ways a revolt against reason, for to describe the world as it appears is to ignore the subjective experience of human beings—everything from belief and faith to intuition, the creative impulse, and the dream world. Symbolism represented a sort of return to spirituality, but without formalized religion, and especially its attendant moral rules. Symbolists practiced a kind of religion of the self, freed of social constraint. What further distinguishes that self from the Romantic self is that it does not merely seek the truth, even subjective truth—it attempts to *create* it.

Outside of Paris, artists and writers quickly adopted Symbolism as the style of the day. In Oslo, Norway, Henrik Ibsen's friend Edvard Munch [moongk] (1863–1944) adopted to his own explorations of the primordial forces of the human psyche the brushwork of Vincent van Gogh, whose paintings he had viewed in the early 1890s. In Vienna, Gustave Klimt (1862–1918) founded a movement dedicated to liberating art from the bonds of conventional morality. Perhaps the most influential thinker of the day was the German philosopher Friedrich Nietzsche [NEE-chuh] (1844–1900), whose new moral philosophy served to support the Symbolist movement.

The New Moral World of Nietzsche

Nietzsche's first important work was the *Birth of Tragedy from the Spirit of Music* (1872), which he dedicated to German composer Richard Wagner. Here he challenged Socrates' appeal for rationality in human affairs and outlined the turbulent conflict between what he called the "Apollonian" and "Dionysian" forces at work in Greek art and in the tragedies of Aeschylus and Sophocles (see Chapter 5). The Apollonian leads to the art of sculpture, the beautiful illusion of the ideal form, while the Dionysian expresses itself in music and dance, with their ability to excite the senses (**Reading 33.3**):

READING 33.3

from Friedrich Nietzsche, *The Birth of Tragedy*, section 1 (1872)

In song and in dance man expresses himself as a member of a higher community; he has forgotten how to walk and speak and is on the way toward flying into the air, dancing. His very gestures express enchantment. Just as the animals now talk, and the earth yields milk and honey, supernatural sounds emanate from him too: he feels himself a god, he himself now walks about enchanted, in ecstasy, like the gods he saw walking in his dreams. He is no longer an artist, he has become a work of art.

Apollonian and Dionysian tendencies usually run parallel to each other, but when they join together, they generate Athenian dramatic tragedies, with the Dionysian "spirit of music" in the chorus supplemented by Apollonian dialogue. Socratic philosophy, particularly in the plays of Euripides, eliminated the Dionysian from the stage (by reducing the use of the chorus), destroying the delicate balance between Dionysus and Apollo that is fundamental to Athenian tragedy. *The Birth of Tragedy*, then, is a call to bring the Dionysian back into art and life, something Nietzsche sees occurring in the operas of Wagner, whose *Gesamtkunstwerk* brings together song, music, dance, theater, and art (see Chapter 30).

In his subsequent books, including *The Gay Science* (1882—the title refers to the medieval troubadour art of writing poetry), *Beyond Good and Evil* (1886), *The Genealogy of Morals* (1887), *Twilight of the Idols* (1888), and *Thus Spoke Zarathustra* (1882–1893), Nietzsche would reject organized religion for subjecting humanity to "slave morality." In *The Gay Science*, he announces the death of God, and in *Beyond Good and Evil*, he defines the greatest men as those "who can be the loneliest, the most hidden, the most deviating," and the philosopher as one who seeks to live where everyone else is "least at home." (For excerpts from these two texts, see **Reading 33.4**, pages 1111–1112.) Democracy, according to Nietzsche, was a pretense, no more than a guarantee of mediocrity.

Following in the footsteps of Hegel's "Great Man" theory of history (see Chapter 27), Nietzsche called for a society led by an *Übermensch* [oo-ber-MENCH], or "higher man," a hero of singular vision and courage who could produce a new "master" morality. Nietzsche's ideas were bold, but in many ways they were also dangerous. For in empowering the individual in an industrial society, they left open the possibility of catastrophic evil being unleashed upon the world in a way that would be difficult to stop. In the twentieth century, Adolph Hitler would misconstrue Nietzsche's ideas to justify his notion of a master race of Germans, leading to mass genocide and a world war that killed more than 50 million people.

Nietzsche also argued that God was dead and that conventional morality was life-denying rather than life-affirming. In an argument directed particularly at social Darwinists, discussed later in the chapter, that also echoes the sentiments of English reformers like A. W. N. Pugin (see Chapter 28), he argued that progress was an illusion: "Mankind does not represent a development toward something better or stronger or higher in the sense accepted today. . . . The European of today is vastly inferior in value to the European of the Renaissance."

On the Cusp of Modern Music: Mahler and Brahms

Viennese composers and conductors Gustav Mahler [MAH-lur] (1860–1911) and Johannes Brahms (1833–1897) dominated the music scene of Vienna in the last years of the nineteenth century. Although temperamentally somewhat different, the two men recognized each other's genius, and Mahler often visited the older master.

Brahms, for his part, would call Mahler "king of the revolutionaries," but not without a hint of sarcasm.

Mahler was an avid student of Nietzsche's, and the influence of *The Birth of Tragedy* and the philosopher's other writings on Mahler's work was extensive. The first movement of his lengthy 95-minute Symphony No. 3 is a Dionysian procession, and the fourth movement is vocal, based on a song written by Nietzsche, the so-called "Drunken Song," from *Thus Spoke Zarathustra*. In fact, Mahler named the whole symphony *The Gay Science—A Summer Morning's Dream*, after Nietzsche's 1882 book. Though Mahler's symphonies are in many ways traditional nineteenth-century orchestral works, inspired by Beethoven, they are also evocations of Nietzsche's Dionysian spirit and so are clear assertions of modernity.

Mahler's Symphony No. 1 is a case in point. Originally called *Titan*, after Nietzsche's observation in *The Birth of Tragedy* that "the effects wrought by the Dionysian also seemed 'titanic,'" the symphony moves from struggle to triumph across its four movements. The third movement is a funeral march in the manner of the second movement of Beethoven's *Eroica* (see Chapter 27), but it is a parody, based on the French children's song "Frère Jacques" (track **33.2**). As Mahler explained in his program notes:

HEAR MORE at *www.myartslab.com*

> The composer found the external source of inspiration in the burlesque picture of the hunter's funeral procession in an old book of fairy tales known to all children in South Germany. The animals of the forest escort the dead forester's coffin to the grave. Hares carry flags; a band of gypsy musicians, accompanied by cats, frogs, crows, all making music, and deer, foxes, and other four-footed and feathered creatures of the woods, leads the procession in farcical postures.

Mahler introduces the movement with a solo double bass playing the march at a high range, one that challenges all double bass players to this day. The melody soon shifts to a minor mode in a variation of the "Frère Jacques" tune. This is followed in turn by so-called **klezmer music**, of Eastern European Jewish origin, characterized by its notable bass sound—"like a parody," Mahler indicates in the score—and the shrill sound of a clarinet. Soon the march metamorphoses into a lyrical song of great beauty, "The Two Blue Eyes of My Beloved," written by Mahler a few years earlier, and accompanied by a harp. Such contrasts were jarring to Mahler's audience, verging, many felt, on vulgarity, but the sense of conflict and tension he evoked by this means anticipated the modern and its rapid-fire juxtapositions of sensory images.

In both composing and conducting, Brahms at first seems more conservative than Mahler. For one thing, he was absolutely dedicated to building on the Classical example of Beethoven and Mozart, and he reached even further back into Western musical tradition to the examples of Bach, Handel, and even Palestrina. So his works are rich in musical allusions. His lushly lyric Symphony No. 4 of 1885 is a case in point, with its many references to Beethoven's compositions. The fourth and final movement, marked *allegro energico e passionato* ("energetically fast and passionate"), ((•• HEAR MORE at www.myartslab.com reaches even further back to an old-fashioned Baroque form (track **33.3**). Its basic structure is a series of 30 variations in triple time, each eight measures long and of increasing intensity, based on a theme in the finale of Bach's Cantata No. 150 that is clearly stated by trombones in the first eight notes of the movement. The next variation makes only minor changes on the first, but as the movement progresses, each variation seems to grow increasingly complex, as they seem to explore the entire range of human emotion and feeling.

Despite its traditional sources—the triple-time variation form was very popular among Baroque composers in Bach's time—the Fourth Symphony is startlingly modern, full of a wide variety of harmonies and dissonances, competing rhythms and meter changes. For this reason, many critics found Brahms's work as difficult to understand—and as modern—as Mahler's. But the final movement of the symphony is, above all, distinctly fin de siècle in tone, world-weary and pessimistic even as it seems to yearn for—and discover—the new.

The Painting of Isolation: Munch

By the time the Norwegian painter Edward Munch arrived in Paris in the early 1890s, he was deeply immersed in the writings of both Fyodor Dostoyevsky (see Chapter 31) and Friedrich Nietzsche. (After Nietzsche's death in 1900, Munch was commissioned to paint a portrait of the philosopher.) Their writings captured the sense of extreme isolation that seemed the inevitable fate of people of genius in the materialist world of bourgeois European culture. Equally moved by the paintings of Gauguin and van Gogh, Munch expressed his debt to his artistic heroes in *The Scream*, painted in 1893 after moving to Berlin (Fig. **33.20**). From Gauguin he took a sensuous curvilinear patterning of color and form (see Fig. 33.17). From van Gogh's work, he took the Dutch artist's intense brushwork and color, as well as his disorienting perspective. Compare, for instance, the up-tilted walkway in *The Scream* to the floor of van Gogh's *Night Café* (see Fig. 33.13).

Munch's depiction of the horrifying anxiety of modern life is unmatched in the work of any previous painter. His grotesquely contorted figure in *The Scream* clasps its skull-like head as if to close its ears to its own anguished cry, which funnels out and sweeps across the landscape behind it. The blood-red sky elevates this cry to a fever pitch. Ironically, the two figures walking farther down the way and the single ship moored in the bay intensify rather than diminish the figure's isolation, as if distancing themselves from the scene.

There is good reason to believe that the color of the scene was prompted by the 1883 eruption of the Indonesian volcano Krakatoa, which could be heard for 1,500 miles, and the ashes of which circled the globe, creating brilliant red sunsets for many months afterward. On a gouache version of the painting, Munch wrote:

Fig. 33.20 Edvard Munch. *Skrik (The Scream.)* **1893.** Tempera and wax crayon on cardboard, 36″ × 29″ (91.00 × 73.50 cm). Nasjonalgalleriet, Oslo. Photo: J. Lathion Nasjonalgalleriet 02. © 2010 Artists Rights Society (ARS), New York/ADAGP, Paris. The painting was stolen from the museum in August 2004, then recovered, severely damaged, and will be restored.

> I was out walking with two friends—the sun began to set—suddenly the sky turned blood red—I paused, feeling exhausted, and leaned on the fence—there was blood and tongues of fire above the blue-black fjord and the city—my friends walked on, and I stood there trembling with anxiety—and I sensed an endless scream passing through nature.

Munch would later include the painting in a series entitled *The Frieze of Life*, designed to occupy four walls of a Berlin exhibition in 1902. Each of the four walls, hung with four or five paintings, had its own title: *Love's Awakening, Love Blossoms and Dies, Fear of Life* (where he hung *The Scream*), and, finally, *Death*. He called *Frieze* "a poem of love, anxiety, and death." The trajectory of Munch's series is the opposite of a Mahler symphony. Where Mahler, like Beethoven, moves from struggle to triumph, Munch sees triumph as fleeting, and his work moves, always, toward despair. In fact, *Despair* was *The Scream*'s original title.

The Vienna Secession: Klimt

The painters of Mahler's Vienna, another European capital city with a high concentration of artists and intellectuals, largely avoided the pessimism of Munch. They turned toward a frank investigation of human sexuality in their work. One of the most important Viennese painters, Gustav Klimt (1862–1918), was a master of the erotic. Like Nietzsche, Klimt sought to liberate art from the confines of conventional morality, believing that human life was driven by sexual desire. His paintings therefore seek to explore not only the sexual instincts of his sitters and models, but his own—and the viewer's.

By 1897, at age 35, Klimt, a traditionally trained academic painter, had led a group of mostly younger artists out of the established art academy in order to form an organization they called the Secession. They called themselves *die Jungen*, "the Youth," and the journal they founded called *Vers Sacrum* (*Sacred Spring*) was named after the Roman ritual of consecrating youth in times of national danger. In 1898, they built themselves a new exhibition space, designed by Josef Olbrich [OHL-breekh] (1867–1908), called the House of the Secession. It was to serve as a retreat from daily life, a sanctuary that, in Olbrich's words, "would offer the art-lover a quiet place of refuge." Over the portal of the building these words were inscribed:

TO THE AGE ITS ART,
TO ART ITS FREEDOM.

The Secession would be dedicated, it proclaimed, to the proposition of showing "modern man his true face."

Klimt's *Judith I*, based on the biblical story of the Jewish heroine Judith and the Assyrian general Holofernes [hoh-luh-FER-neez], is the very embodiment of the Secessionist revolt (Fig. **33.21**). Klimt's Judith, caressing with her right hand Holofernes's head, which she has just severed, is no biblical heroine. She is a contemporary wealthy Viennese woman, clothed—or half-clothed—

CONTINUITY & CHANGE

Judith and Maidservant, p. 693

and adorned in a jewel-studded gold choker. She is at once the malevolent femme fatale, a danger to any male who might desire her—the violent Orientalist male "other" turned woman—as well as a symbol of the liberation of the newly emancipated woman of the twentieth century. Klimt's painting suggests that behind the facade of social decorum, and underneath the fine dresses worn by modern women, lies the earthy, elemental spirit of the heroic Judith. It also shows the continuing power of a theme that had been explored for many centuries.

Through his paintings, Klimt believed, he had begun to set society free of its inhibitions. This Secessionist spirit of liberation mirrored earlier artistic gestures of rebellion, such as Courbet's establishment of his own exhibit across the street from the 1855 Exposition Universelle, the Salons des Refusés established in the 1860s, and the Impressionist Exhibitions of the 1870s and 1880s. It would become a dominant theme of the arts in the century to come. This spirit of rebellion—and the artist's Nietzschean self-definition as one who lives where everyone else is "least at home," pushing the bounds of

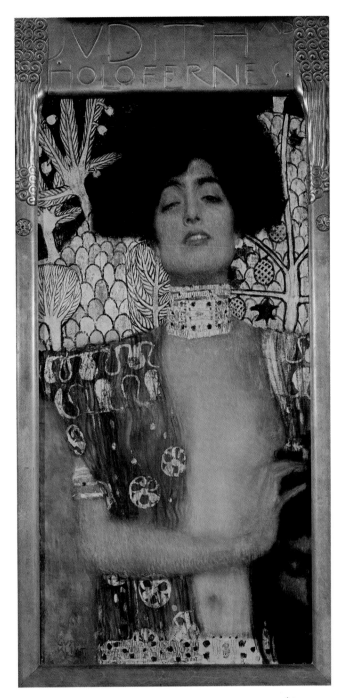

Fig. 33.21 Gustav Klimt, *Judith I*. 1901. Oil on canvas, 33″ × 16¹/₂″. Österreichische Galerie, Vienna. The frame identifies the subject of Klimt's painting as the biblical figures Judith and Holofernes.

accepted taste and tradition—would come to dominate not just the dawning century's visual arts, but its music, literature, and philosophy as well.

AFRICA AND EMPIRE

To those intellectuals most aware of the larger political climate of the late nineteenth century, the greatest cause for alarm rested not in Vienna, or Paris, or London, but in

Africa, specifically in the imperial policies that the European powers were exercising on that continent. During the second half of the nineteenth century, European nations competed with each other in acquiring territories in Asia, Africa, Latin America, and elsewhere around the world. In some cases, their management of these areas was direct, with a colonial political structure supervising the governance of the territory. In other cases, control was indirect, focusing on economic domination. In either case, the world is still living with the consequences more than a century later. There is probably no more overt statement of the principle than when the British, in 1858, declared Queen Victoria to be the empress of India.

By the beginning of the twentieth century, Western powers had established cultural, political, and economic hegemony (control or domination) over much of the world. They were motivated by economic and strategic self-interest—that is, the control of natural resources and trade routes—and the fates of India and Egypt are cases in point (see Chapter 29). Fierce nationalism, and a Europe-centered belief in the superiority of Western culture (as well as the white race), also fueled imperialism. Another important facet of the imperialist philosophy emphasized the humanitarian desire to "improve the lot" of indigenous peoples everywhere. By the last quarter of the century, the African continent was the focal point of imperialist competition.

European Imperialism

A quick glance at a map of Africa illustrates the spread of European domination of the continent after 1880 (Map **33.1**). The scramble for control of the continent had begun with the opening of the Suez Canal in 1869, and, by the 1880s, Britain's seizure of control of Egypt as a whole (see Chapter 29). Then, to further "protect" Egypt, it advanced into the Sudan. Beyond Africa's key strategic placement, its vast land area and untapped natural resources proved an irresistible lure for European nations.

France's direct control of Algeria in North Africa dated from 1834, when it formally annexed much of the region. Originally motivated by the desire to thwart piracy in the Mediterranean, France added Tunisia, much of West Africa, and Madagascar (the large island nation off the east coast of Africa) to its colonies by the 1880s. Not to be left behind, and motivated by a desire to appear at least as powerful as Britain and France, Belgium, Portugal, Spain, and Italy all began to expand previous colonies or acquire new ones. To counter this expansion, and to protect trade routes around the Cape of Good Hope, Britain expanded into present-day Zimbabwe and Zambia.

Looking at the situation in Africa, Germany's Chancellor Bismarck decided to acquire Southwest Africa, Namibia, Togoland, the Cameroons, and East Africa

Map 33.1 Imperial expansion in Africa to 1880 (a) and from 1880 to 1914 (b). Until 1880, European occupation of Africa was limited to a few colonies that facilitated shipping along the coast. Between 1880 and 1914, European countries came to control almost the entire continent, with only Liberia and Abyssinia (present-day Ethiopia) remaining independent.

(Tanzania). His motives were purely political, designed to improve his relations with Britain in his never-ending struggles with France and Russia. "My map of Africa lies in Europe," he said. "Here is Russia, and there is France, and here in the middle are we. That is my map of Africa." By and large, European imperial expansion in Africa and Southeast Asia was the nationalist expression of the desire of European countries to assert and expand their own political power.

Economic wealth was also at stake, for the exploitable resources of the African continent made Europe wealthy. France extracted phosphates from Morocco; Belgium acquired gems, ivory, and rubber from the Congo; and England obtained diamonds from South Africa. In this way, Europe's African colonies became (like India) primarily focused on producing large quantities of raw materials—a commodity-based export economy that left most Africans in dire poverty. The social dislocation created by the South African diamond mines is a case in point. In 1866, an African shepherd found a massive diamond of 83.5 carats, quickly dubbed the Star of Africa, on the Orange River. As news of the find spread, Europeans arrived in droves to Kimberley, South Africa, seeking their fortune. Mining was focused around the farm of Diederik Arnoldus de Beer, an Afrikaner (Dutch emigrant to South Africa). Gradually, these small, individual plots were bought up by Cecil Rhodes (1853–1902), and in 1880, he founded the DeBeers Mining Company. By 1914, Rhodes's Kimberley mine was the largest artificial crater on earth, and he controlled as much as 80 percent of the world's diamonds.

The diamond mines required huge amounts of labor, and native Africans supplied it. Between 1871 and 1875, an estimated 50,000 Africans arrived every year at the diamond mines, replacing roughly the same number who left each year. In a newspaper article published in 1874, Reverend Tyamzashe, an African clergyman, described the scene:

> There are San, Khoikhoi, Griquas, Batlhaping, Damaras, Barolong, Barutse . . . Bapedi, Baganana, Basutu, Maswazi, Matonga, Matabele, Mabaca, Mampondo, Mamfengu, Batembu, Maxosa etc. many of these [people] can hardly understand each other. . . . Those coming from far up in the interior . . . come with the sole purpose of securing guns. Some of them therefore resolve to stay no longer here than is necessary to get some six or seven pounds for the gun. Hence you will see hundreds of them leaving the fields, and as many arriving from the North almost every day.

So the peoples of southern Africa were diffused and reunited around a diamond mine in the South African Central Plateau, before dispersing, presumably with enough money to buy Western weapons to deal with their enemies. Laborers lived in closed compounds designed to control theft but actually closer to prisons. Workers left the compound each morning and returned to it each evening after work, when they were searched for diamonds hidden on their persons. These European-designed structures were also a sure way to control potentially unruly Africans. Christian missionaries such as Reverend Tyamzashe were encouraged to start congregations in the compounds to aid in the same policy of control. Their task, as Cecil Rhodes saw it, was to educate and prepare Africans for a future within British colonial society, however limited that might be. These compounds also effectively separated black Africans from the white residents of Kimberley, an enforced separation that in many respects marks the beginning of South African **apartheid** [uh-PAR-tite] (literally "separateness" in Afrikaans, the dialect of Dutch spoken by Afrikaners).

Social Darwinism: The Theoretical Justification for Imperialism

In the extended title of the groundbreaking work *On the Origin of Species by Means of Natural Selection, or the Preservation of Favored Races in the Struggle for Life* (see Chapter 28), Charles Darwin's use of the word *race* became a critical ingredient in the development of a new nineteenth-century ideology, **social Darwinism**. To those who desired to validate imperialism and the colonial regimes it fostered in Africa and Asia, social Darwinism explained the supposed social and cultural evolution that elevated Europe (and the white race) above all other nations and races. Europeans, it was argued, were the "fitter" race, and thus were destined not merely to survive but to dominate the world. While still a student at Oxford, Cecil Rhodes had written a "Confession of Faith" in which he clearly articulated the imperialists' faith in their ability to dominate the world:

> Why should we not form a secret society with but one object, the furtherance of the British Empire and the bringing of the whole civilized world under British rule for the recovery of the United States, for making the Anglo-Saxon race but one Empire? What a dream, but yet it is probable, it is possible.

Such grandiose thinking would later characterize the demented ambitions of Adolf Hitler in Germany. Social Darwinism seemed to overturn traditional Judeo-Christian and Enlightenment ethics, especially those pertaining to compassion and the sacredness of human life. It seemed at once to embrace moral relativism, the belief that ethical positions are determined not by universal truths but by social, political, or cultural conditions (such as the imperial imposition of its values upon another culture) and to support the superior evolutionary "fitness" and superiority of the Aryan (interpreted to mean Anglo-Saxon) race.

Darwin himself meant nothing of the kind. Recognizing the ways in which his theories were being misapplied to social conditions, he published *The Descent of Man* in 1871. In it, he offered a theory of conscience that had a distinctly more ethical viewpoint. Darwin contended that our ancestors, living in small tribal communities, and competing with one another ruthlessly, came to recognize the advantages to successful propagation of the tribe. Over generations, the tribe whose members exhibited selfless behavior that benefited the whole group would tend to survive and prosper over tribes whose members pursued more selfish and individualistic goals. "There can be no doubt," he wrote, "that a tribe including many members who, from possessing in a high degree the spirit of patriotism, fidelity, obedience, courage, and sympathy, were always ready to give aid to each other and to sacrifice themselves for the common good, would be victorious over most other tribes, and this would be natural selection." This is not the ethical philosophy that motivated imperialism.

Darwin's ideas were not the last word on the issue, however, and social Darwinism continually evolved. English philosopher and political theorist Herbert Spencer (1820–1903) offered extensive interpretations of social evolution that were influenced by Darwin but that equated change with constructive progress. Francis Galton (1822–1911) advocated human intervention in evolution, through selective breeding. His theory of **eugenics** focused on eliminating undesirable and less fit members of society by encouraging the proliferation of intelligent and physically fit humans. Galton's theories emphasized eliminating "inferior" humans through increased breeding of the most fit members of society by means of such state intervention as tax and other incentives. Later his theories mutated into the dark ideologies that developed into Nazism in the twentieth century.

Joseph Conrad's *Heart of Darkness*

No fiction writer examined European imperialist schemes in Africa—and the negative consequences of social Darwinism—more critically than Joseph Conrad (1857–1924). Born Józef Teodor Konrad Korzeniowski in Poland, Conrad began his career as a sailor, joined the British merchant marine in 1886 (at that point anglicizing his name and becoming a British citizen), and worked in the British merchant fleet until 1894. His many novels and stories are based largely on his experiences at sea, and although he did not speak English fluently until he was in his twenties—and never spoke the language without an accent—he is considered by many to be one of the greatest prose stylists in the English language.

In 1889, Conrad became captain of a river steamboat in what was then the Belgian Congo, and his experiences in that job form the basis of his novella *Heart of Darkness*. The story begins with the narrator (presumably Conrad) sitting with five other men on the deck of a yawl in the Thames River just downstream from London waiting for the tide to turn. Among them is one "Marlow," who presently begins to ruminate on the nature of Roman imperial adventuring in England nearly two thousand years earlier, which leads him, then, to entertain the group with the story of his experiences in the Congo on a mission to relieve a man named Kurtz from his duties as the Belgian government's most successful ivory trader (for the introductory section of the novella, see **Reading 33.5**, pages 1112–1113). *Heart*

of Darkness is thus a framed tale about Africa, narrated by Marlow, as he and his companions sit on the yawl as the sun sets and the evening comes on just outside of London.

The themes of Conrad's story are first articulated in Marlow's introductory remarks about the Romans. They were, he says, "men enough to face the darkness." He imagines some "decent young citizen in a toga" rowing up the Thames, surrounded presumably by native Britons who had never dreamed, let alone heard, of Rome. He would, Conrad writes (**Reading 33.5a**):

READING 33.5a

from Joseph Conrad, *Heart of Darkness* (1899)

Land in a swamp, march through the woods, and in some inland post feel the savagery, the utter savagery, had closed round him—all that mysterious life of the wilderness that stirs in the forest, in the jungles, in the hearts of wild men. There's no initiation either into such mysteries. He has to live in the midst of the incomprehensible, which is also detestable. And it has a fascination, too, that goes to work upon him. The fascination of the abomination . . .

This describes, rather precisely, Kurtz's experience in Africa, where Kurtz is transformed from an idealist dedicated to the proposition of civilizing Africa into a brutal, immoral tyrant, subjugating African natives to his dissipated will. What Marlow comes to understand through Kurtz's example is that colonialism is a dehumanizing enterprise, that in the dynamics of social superiority built into the social Darwinist view of the world is an inherent distaste and disregard for those one considers one's inferiors. In what amounts to an act of premonition, he sees in Kurtz's call to "exterminate all the brutes" the acceptance of the possibility, even inevitability of genocide. As Marlow says in the introductory section, "The conquest of the earth, which mostly means the taking it away from those who have a different complexion or slightly flatter noses than ourselves, is not a pretty thing when you look into it too much."

Heart of Darkness, as its title suggests, is stylistically dependent on contrasting patterns of light and dark, white Europeans and black Africans, but never in any set pattern of good and evil. Rather the meaning of both is ambiguous, never certain, and always at issue. Ambiguity, in fact, lies at the heart of the story—"darkness" itself being a metaphor for a world without clarity. The most famous line in the book occurs at Kurtz's death: "He cried in a whisper at some image, at some vision—he cried out twice, a cry that was no more than a breath—'The horror! The horror!'" It is not clear—purposefully so—whether the horror lies in the world that surrounds Kurtz, or in himself. Or, as the twentieth century was about to suggest, in both.

Freud and the Unconscious

In 1910, having lost his virility upon discovering that his young wife, Alma Schindler Mahler, was having an affair, Mahler sought out the Viennese psychoanalyst Sigmund Freud (1856–1939). On August 26, the two spent four hours walking through the streets of Leiden, Holland, discussing Mahler's "condition." Mahler recalled for Freud an "especially painful scene" between his parents, which caused him to run out of the house where he encountered a barrel organ playing the popular song, *Ach, du lieber Augustin* [akh doo LEE-bur OW-goos-ten]. According to Freud, the tension between the tragic episode between his parents and the banality of the organ grinder's song was permanently imprinted on Mahler's mind for life—the very stuff of the third movement of his Symphony No. 1.

If, by 1910, Freud was not the most famous man in Vienna, he was one of the most notorious. He had opened a medical practice there in 1886, specializing in psychic disorders. Just a year earlier, he had gone to Paris to study with the famous neurologist Jean-Martin Charcot [shar-KOH], and in his new practice, he began using Charcot's techniques—hypnosis, massage, and pressure on the head to get patients to call up thoughts related to their symptoms. In 1895, in collaboration with Josef Breuer [BROY-ur], another Viennese physician, he published *Studies in Hysteria*. But even then he was changing his techniques. He began to ask his patients to say whatever crossed their minds, a practice he called **free association**. With free association, he was able to abandon hypnosis, as he discovered that patients tended to relate their particular neurotic symptoms to earlier, usually childhood experiences when freed to talk spontaneously about themselves.

For Freud, free association required interpretation, and he came more and more to focus on the obscure language of the unconscious. By 1897, he had formulated a theory of infantile sexuality based on the proposition that sexual drives and energy already exist in infants. Childhood could no longer be considered innocent. One of the keys to understanding the imprint of early sexual feeling upon adult neurotic behavior was the interpretation of dreams. Freud was convinced that their apparently irrational content could be explained rationally and scientifically. He concluded that dreams allow unconscious wishes, desires, and drives that are censored by the conscious mind to exercise themselves. "The dream," he wrote in his 1900 *The Interpretation of Dreams*, "is the (disguised) fulfillment of a (suppressed, repressed) wish." So seminal was this idea that when Italian painter Ciorgio de Chirico [day KEER-ee-koh] (1888–1978) exhibited his work *The Child's Brain* (Fig. **33.22**) in Paris in the early 1920s, it was immediately understood as reflecting Freud's beliefs, despite the fact that de Chirico was barely familiar with Freud's writings.

Freud's work would become enormously influential, as we will see in Book Six, but as much as Freud was one of the innovative thinkers of the twentieth century, he is also a product of the nineteenth century's growing obsession with self-knowledge. He is also, in some measure, a Symbolist. Like Mallarmé, van Gogh, and Gauguin, for Freud the symbol is a vehicle for indirect expression. It is suggestive, elusive. In a manner of speaking, the entire dream life of an individual could be thought of as a Symbolist poem. ■

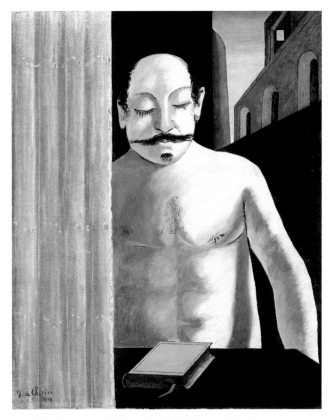

Fig. 33.22 Giorgio de Chirico, *The Child's Brain.* **1914.** Oil on canvas, 31 1/8″ × 25 5/8″. Moderna Museet, Stockholm. The Italian de Chirico would become a force in modern art after an exhibition of his work arranged in Paris in March 1922 by Paul Guillaume, where his paintings were understood as reflecting deep psychological profundity.

THINKING BACK

What was the significance of the 1889 Exposition Universelle in Paris?

When the Exposition Universelle opened in Paris in the spring of 1889, it heralded a new era of Western technological innovation and political and social superiority as displayed in the fair's thousands of exhibits. The most prominent exhibit was also the symbol of the exposition, and would soon become the embodiment of Paris itself—the Eiffel Tower. What, more specifically, did it symbolize? The fair's many exhibits displayed a wide range of technological innovations, including hundreds of inventions from Thomas Edison's laboratories, as well as an ambitious collection of houses from across the globe. How were France's imperial ambitions represented?

What is the fin de siècle?

The fin de siècle (French for "end of the century") is the period just before and after the two great Paris expositions of 1889 and 1900, marked—from the point of view of those who looked at it with disfavor—by a degenerate abandonment in art and culture of the ideals of the past. It was also an era marked by a spirit of innovation. How did Art Nouveau embody both aspects? How can Henrik Ibsen's Realist drama be characterized as fin de siècle theater?

The transition from Realism to Symbolism, also characteristic of the period, appears in the sculpture of Rodin, who came to value music and dance as the most Symbolist of art forms. How does Symbolism differ from Realism? Why are dance and music quintessential Symbolist media?

What is Post-Impressionism?

The generation of painters that followed the Impressionist exhibitions was dedicated to advancing art in innovative directions. What were Seurat's particular contributions? What did van Gogh contribute in terms of color and paint application? What tension particularly informs Cézanne's paintings? Finally, Gauguin reflected the *primitif*. What do we mean by this?

How does Symbolism manifest itself outside of France?

The Symbolist spirit manifested itself in Germany in the philosophy of Friedrich Nietzsche. In *The Birth of Tragedy*, he argued for a return of the Dionysian spirit. What is the Dionysian spirit? In *The Gay Science*, Nietzsche announced—not in his own words, but in the words of a madman—the death of God. And in *Beyond Good and Evil*, he argued that the true philosopher must live where everyone else is "least at home." What negative impacts did Nietzsche's writings have?

Deeply influenced by Nietzsche, composer Gustav Mahler created music distinguished by its jarring contrasts of melody and mood. How does his music contrast with that of his near-contemporary, Johannes Brahms? In Oslo, the painter Edvard Munch, influenced by van Gogh, Gauguin, and Nietzsche, captured the anguish of modern experience in works like *The Scream*, while in Vienna, Gustav Klimt revolted from tradition by painting deeply erotic works designed to set society free of its inhibitions. The Vienna Secession was dedicated to showing "modern man his true face." What is the significance of this?

How did developments in Africa reflect European beliefs and sensibilities?

Beginning with the opening of the Suez Canal in 1869, Africa proved an irresistible lure for European colonial and imperialist interests, particularly for Britain, France, Germany, and Belgium. At stake were the exploitable natural resources of the African continent, including phosphates, gems, ivory, and rubber. Europe's African colonies were mostly used to produce large quantities of raw materials at the lowest possible price, which left most Africans in dire poverty.

Europe's imperialists justified their policies through the philosophy of social Darwinism. What is social Darwinism? How did Charles Darwin himself counter its theories? How does Joseph Conrad react to the theory in his novella *Heart of Darkness*?

PRACTICE MORE Get flashcards for images and terms and review chapter material with quizzes at **www.myartslab.com**

GLOSSARY

apartheid A policy that promotes or is founded on racial segregation, especially as occurred in South Africa.

chromatic scale Scale that moves in half-steps through all the black and white keys on a keyboard.

eugenics A theory focused on eliminating undesirable and less fit members of society by encouraging the proliferation of intelligent and physically fit humans.

free association The practice developed by Sigmund Freud of directing patients to say whatever came to mind.

klezmer music A type of music of Eastern-European Jewish origin characterized by its *oompah, oompah* bass sound and the shrill sound of a clarinet.

pointilles Tiny dots of color and the building blocks of the pointillist style of painting.

social Darwinism An extension of Darwin's theory of evolution positing that nations and societies advance according to the rule of "the survival of the fittest."

READINGS

from Friedrich Nietzsche, *The Gay Science*, "The Madman" (1882), and *Beyond Good and Evil*, Section 212 (1888)

Nietzsche composed both of these works as a series of several hundred aphorisms the typical lengths of which range from a line or two to a page or two. The selection from The Gay Science *is a parable entitled "The Madman," in which Nietzsche announces the possibility that God is dead. Written in 1888,* Beyond Good and Evil *was designed to give the reader an overview of Nietzsche's philosophy as it had developed to this point. Subtitled* Prelude to a Philosophy of the Future, *it projects the terms of a new philosophy that has gotten rid of blind acceptance of Christian values and morality.*

THE MADMAN

Have you not heard of that madman who lit a lantern in the bright morning hours, ran to the market place, and cried incessantly: "I seek God! I seek God!"—As many of those who did not believe in God were standing around just then, he provoked much laughter. Has he got lost? asked one. Did he lose his way like a child? asked another. Or is he hiding? Is he afraid of us? Has he gone on a voyage? emigrated?—Thus they yelled and laughed.

The madman jumped into their midst and pierced them with his eyes. "Whither is God?" he cried; "I will tell you. *We have killed him*—you and I. All of us are his murderers. But how did we do this? How could we drink up the sea? Who gave us the sponge to wipe away the entire horizon? What were we doing when we unchained this earth from its sun? Whither is it moving now? Whither are we moving? Away from all suns? Are we not plunging continually? Backward, sideward, forward, in all directions? Is there still any up or down? Are we not straying, as through an infinite nothing? Do we not feel the breath of empty space? Has it not become colder? Is not night continually closing in on us? Do we not need to light lanterns in the morning? Do we hear nothing as yet of the noise of the gravediggers who are burying God? Do we smell nothing as yet of the divine decomposition? Gods, too, decompose. God is dead. God remains dead. And we have killed him.

"How shall we comfort ourselves, the murderers of all murderers? What was holiest and mightiest of all that the world has yet owned has bled to death under our knives: who will wipe this blood off us? What water is there for us to clean ourselves? What festivals of atonement, what sacred games shall we have to invent? Is not the greatness of this deed too great for us? Must we ourselves not become gods simply to appear worthy of it? There has never been a greater deed; and whoever is born after us—for the sake of this deed he will belong to a higher history than all history hitherto."

Here the madman fell silent and looked again at his listeners; and they, too, were silent and stared at him in astonishment. At last he threw his lantern on the ground, and it broke into pieces and went out. "I have come too early," he said then; "my time is not yet. This tremendous event is still on its way, still wandering; it has not yet reached the ears of men. Lightning and thunder require time; the light of the stars requires time; deeds, though done, still require time to be seen and heard. This deed is still more distant from them than most distant stars—*and yet they have done it themselves.*"

It has been related further that on the same day the madman forced his way into several churches and there struck up his *requiem aeternam deo.* Led out and called to account, he is said always to have replied nothing but: "What after all are these churches now if they are not the tombs and sepulchers of God?"

BEYOND GOOD AND EVIL, SECTION 212

WE SCHOLARS

More and more it seems to me that the philosopher, being *of necessity* a man of tomorrow and the day after tomorrow, has always found himself, and *had* to find himself, in contradiction to his today: his enemy was ever the ideal of today. So far all these extraordinary furtherers of man whom one calls philosophers, though they themselves have rarely felt like friends of wisdom but rather like disagreeable fools and dangerous question marks, have found their task, their hard, unwanted, inescapable task, but eventually also the greatness of their task, in being the bad conscience of their time.

By applying the knife vivisectionally to the chest of the very *virtues of their time*, they betrayed what was their own secret: to know of a *new* greatness of man, of a new untrodden way to his enhancement. Every time they exposed how much hypocrisy, comfortableness, letting oneself go and letting oneself drop, how many lies lay hidden under the best honored type of their contemporary morality, how much virtue was *outlived.* Every time they said: "We must get there, that way, where *you* today are least at home."

Facing a world of "modern ideas" that would banish everybody into a corner and "specialty," a philosopher—if today there could be philosophers—would be compelled to find the greatness of man, the concept of "greatness," precisely in his range and multiplicity, in his wholeness in manifoldness. He would even determine value and rank in accordance with how much and how many things one could bear and take upon himself, how *far* one could extend his responsibility.

Today the taste of the time and the virtue of the time weakens and thins down the will; nothing is as timely as weakness of the will. In the philosopher's ideal, therefore, precisely strength of the will, hardness, and the capacity for long-range decisions must belong to the concept of "greatness" —with as much justification as the opposite doctrine and the ideal of a dumb, renunciatory, humble, selfless humanity was suitable for an opposite age, one that suffered, like the sixteenth century, from its accumulated energy of will and from the most savage floods and tidal waves of selfishness.

In the age of Socrates, among men of fatigued instincts, among the conservatives of ancient Athens who let themselves go—"toward happiness," as they said; toward pleasure, as they acted—and who all the while still mouthed the ancient pompous words to which their lives no longer gave them any right, *irony* may have been required for greatness of soul, that Socratic sarcastic assurance of the old physician and plebeian who cut ruthlessly into his own flesh, as he did into the flesh and heart of the "noble," with a look that said clearly enough: "Don't dissemble in front of me! Here—we are equal."

Today, conversely, when only the herd animal receives and dispenses honors in Europe, when "equality of rights" could all too easily be changed into equality in violating rights—I mean, into a common war on all that is rare, strange, privi- 100 leged, the higher man, the higher soul, the higher duty, the higher responsibility, and the abundance of creative power and masterfulness—today the concept of greatness entails being noble, wanting to be by oneself, being able to be different, standing alone and having to live independently. And the

philosopher will betray something of his own ideal when he 110 posits: "He shall be greatest who can be loneliest, the most concealed, the most deviant, the human being beyond good and evil, the master of his virtues, he that is overrich in will. Precisely this shall be called *greatness*: being capable of being as manifold as whole, as ample as full." And to ask it once more: today—is greatness *possible*?

READING CRITICALLY

It is important to recognize that the man who calls for the death of God is a "madman." But can you see a relation between this madman and Nietzsche's new philosopher as described in the section from *Beyond Good and Evil*?

READING 33.5

from Joseph Conrad, *Heart of Darkness* (1899)

Heart of Darkness is framed by a narrator who introduces the novella's main narrator, Marlow, as he begins to recount one of many "inconclusive experiences," an encounter with a man named Kurtz in the interior of Belgian Congo. The selection excerpted here is the beginning of the novella, before Marlow begins in earnest. It encapsulates many of the remaining story's themes, but it is especially important in setting out a visual imagery of light and dark—"gloom" and luminosity—that informs the entire narrative.

The NELLIE, a cruising yawl, swung to her anchor without a flutter of the sails, and was at rest. The flood had made, the wind was nearly calm, and being bound down the river, the only thing for it was to come to and wait for the turn of the tide.

The sea-reach of the Thames stretched before us like the beginning of an interminable waterway. In the offing the sea and the sky were welded together without a joint, and in the lu-minous space the tanned sails of the barges drifting up with the tide seemed to stand still in red clusters of canvas sharply peaked, with gleams of varnished sprits. A haze rested on the 10 low shores that ran out to sea in vanishing flatness. The air was dark above Gravesend, and farther back still seemed condensed into a mournful gloom, brooding motionless over the biggest, and the greatest, town on earth.

The Director of Companies was our captain and our host. We four affectionately watched his back as he stood in the bows looking to seaward. On the whole river there was nothing that looked half so nautical. He resembled a pilot, which to a seaman is trustworthiness personified. It was difficult to realize his work was not out there in the luminous estuary, but behind 20 him, within the brooding gloom.

Between us there was, as I have already said somewhere, the bond of the sea. Besides holding our hearts together through long periods of separation, it had the effect of making us toler-ant of each other's yarns—and even convictions. . . . We felt meditative, and fit for nothing but placid staring. The day was ending in a serenity of still and exquisite brilliance. The water shone pacifically; the sky, without a speck, was a benign immen-sity of unstained light; the very mist on the Essex marsh was like a gauzy and radiant fabric, hung from the wooded rises inland, 30 and draping the low shores in diaphanous folds. Only the gloom to the west, brooding over the upper reaches, became more sombre every minute, as if angered by the approach of the sun.

And at last, in its curved and imperceptible fall, the sun sank low, and from glowing white changed to a dull red without rays and without heat, as if about to go out suddenly, stricken to death by the touch of that gloom brooding over a crowd of men.

Forthwith a change came over the waters, and the serenity became less brilliant but more profound. The old river in its broad reach rested unruffled at the decline of day, after ages of 40 good service done to the race that peopled its banks, spread out in the tranquil dignity of a waterway leading to the utter-most ends of the earth. We looked at the venerable stream not in the vivid flush of a short day that comes and departs for ever, but in the august light of abiding memories. And indeed nothing is easier for a man who has, as the phrase goes, "followed the sea" with reverence and affection, that to evoke the great spirit of the past upon the lower reaches of the Thames. The tidal cur-rent runs to and fro in its unceasing service, crowded with memories of men and ships it had borne to the rest of home or 50 to the battles of the sea. It had known and served all the men of whom the nation is proud, from Sir Francis Drake to Sir John Franklin, knights all, titled and untitled—the great knights-errant of the sea. It had borne all the ships whose names are like jew-els flashing in the night of time, from the GOLDEN HIND return-ing with her rotund flanks full of treasure, to be visited by the Queen's Highness and thus pass out of the gigantic tale, to the EREBUS and TERROR, bound on other conquests—and that never returned. It had known the ships and the men. They had sailed from Deptford, from Greenwich, from Erith—the adven- 60 turers and the settlers; kings' ships and the ships of men on 'Change; captains, admirals, the dark "interlopers" of the East-ern trade, and the commissioned "generals" of East India fleets. Hunters for gold or pursuers of fame, they all had gone out on that stream, bearing the sword, and often the torch, messengers of the might within the land, bearers of a spark from the sacred fire. What greatness had not floated on the ebb of that river into the mystery of an unknown earth! . . . The dreams of men, the seed of commonwealths, the germs of empires.

The sun set; the dusk fell on the stream, and lights began to appear along the shore. The Chapman light-house, a three-legged thing erect on a mud-flat, shone strongly. Lights of ships moved in the fairway—a great stir of lights going up and going down. And farther west on the upper reaches the place of the monstrous town [London] was still marked ominously on the sky, a brooding gloom in sunshine, a lurid glare under the stars.

"And this also," said Marlow suddenly, "has been one of the dark places of the earth." . . .

His remark did not seem at all surprising. It was just like Marlow. It was accepted in silence. No one took the trouble to grunt even; and presently he said, very slow—

"I was thinking of very old times, when the Romans first came here, nineteen hundred years ago—the other day. . . . Light came out of this river since . . . like a running blaze on a plain, like a flash of lightning in the clouds. We live in the flicker—may it last as long as the old earth keeps rolling! But darkness was here yesterday. Imagine the feelings of a commander of a fine—what d'ye call 'em? —trireme in the Mediterranean, ordered suddenly to the north; run overland across the Gauls in a hurry; put in charge of one of these craft the legionaries—a wonderful lot of handy men they must have been, too—used to build, apparently by the hundred, in a month or two, if we may believe what we read. Imagine him here—the very end of the world, a sea the colour of lead, a sky the colour of smoke, a kind of ship about as rigid as a concertina—and going up this river with stores, or orders, or what you like. Sand-banks, marshes, forests, savages,—precious little to eat fit for a civilized man, nothing but Thames water to drink. No Falernian wine here, no going ashore. Here and there a military camp lost in a wilderness, like a needle in a bundle of hay—cold, fog, tempests, disease, exile, and death—death skulking in the air, in the water, in the bush. They must have been dying like flies here. Oh, yes—he did it. Did it very well, too, no doubt, and without thinking much about it either, except afterwards to brag of what he had gone through in his time, perhaps. They were men enough to face the darkness. And perhaps he was cheered by keeping his eye on a chance of promotion to the fleet at Ravenna by and by, if he had good friends in Rome and survived the awful climate. Or think of a decent young citizen in a toga—perhaps too much dice, you know—coming out here in the train of some prefect, or tax-gatherer, or trader even, to mend his fortunes. Land in a swamp, march through the woods, and in some inland post feel the savagery, the utter savagery, had closed round him—all that mysterious life of the wilderness that stirs in the forest, in the jungles, in the hearts of wild men. There's no initiation either into such mysteries. He has to live in the midst of the incomprehensible, which is also detestable. And it has a fascination, too, that goes to work upon him. The fascination of the abomination—you know, imagine the growing regrets, the longing to escape, the powerless disgust, the surrender, the hate."

He paused.

"Mind," he began again, lifting one arm from the elbow, the palm of the hand outwards, so that, with his legs folded before him, he had the pose of a Buddha preaching in European clothes and without a lotus-flower—"Mind, none of us would feel exactly like this. What saves us is efficiency—the devotion to efficiency. But these chaps were not much account, really. They were no colonists; their administration was merely a squeeze, and nothing more, I suspect. They were conquerors, and for that you want only brute force— nothing to boast of, when you have it, since your strength is just an accident arising from the weakness of others. They grabbed what they could get for the sake of what was to be got. It was just robbery with violence, aggravated murder on a great scale, and men going at it blind—as is very proper for those who tackle a darkness. The conquest of the earth, which mostly means the taking it away from those who have a different complexion or slightly flatter noses than ourselves, is not a pretty thing when you look into it too much. What redeems it is the idea only. An idea at the back of it; not a sentimental pretence but an idea; and an unselfish belief in the idea—something you can set up, and bow down before, and offer a sacrifice to. . . ."

He broke off. Flames glided in the river, small green flames, red flames, white flames, pursuing, overtaking, joining, crossing each other—then separating slowly or hastily. The traffic of the great city went on in the deepening night upon the sleepless river. We looked on, waiting patiently—there was nothing else to do till the end of the flood; but it was only after a long silence, when he said, in a hesitating voice, "I suppose you fellows remember I did once turn fresh-water sailor for a bit," that we knew we were fated, before the ebb began to run, to hear about one of Marlow's inconclusive experiences.

READING CRITICALLY

Conrad clearly draws an analogy between Roman imperialism and the imperialism of his own time. But he also distinguishes between the two. How are they different?

Modernism and the Globalization of Cultures

1900 TO THE PRESENT

Detail of Diego Rivera, *Man, Controller of the Universe*. 1934. Fresco, main panel 15'11" × 37'6". Palacio de Bellas Artes, Mexico City, D. F. Mexico. © 2003 Banco de Mexico Diego Rivera & Frida Kahlo Museums Trust. Av. Cinco de Mayo No. 2, Col. Centro, Del. Cuauhtemoc 06059, Mexico, D. F. Reproduction authorized by the Instituto Nacional de Bellas Artes y Literatura. Photo credit: Schalkwijk/Art Resource, New York. (See Fig. 37.15.)

The twentieth century began in a frenzy of creativity and invention. If we think of the 1890s as a sort of prologue—during which the motion picture, the rubber bicycle tire, the diesel engine, the typewriter, the tape recorder, the carburetor, and even the zipper were all invented—then the first 14 years of the new century amount to a revolution in human life. Flight was, perhaps, the first emblem of this revolution. July 2, 1900, marked the first successful flight of a steerable airship, Ferdinand Zeppelin's dirigible, at Lake Constance in the south of Germany, and on December 17, 1903, Orville and Wilbur Wright flew a powered aircraft on four separate flights at Kitty Hawk, North Carolina—the longest of the day lasting 59 seconds and covering 852 feet of ground. On July 25, 1909, Louis Blériot [blay-ree-OH] crossed the 22 miles of the English Channel between Calais and Dover in a plane of his own design in 37 minutes.

But those first years of the new century were more than just a technological revolution. Science itself was transformed, and the knowable universe with it. It seemed possible, suddenly, to conceive of space in four, not three, dimensions, and to think of physics not as a system of coherence and truth, but rather as a condition of contradiction and uncertainty. And the traditions of science were by no means the only thing transformed. Rhymed verse gave way to "free verse," representational painting to abstraction. Music based on a tonal system was abandoned for atonal composition. Narrative became internalized into what was called stream of consciousness.

But this period of unbridled creativity was soon followed by what resembled nothing more than a long, sustained tragedy. The faith in human progress that had shaped the nineteenth century was thrown into doubt first by World War I, in which civilized Europe committed a kind of self-genocide, and then by the rise of totalitarian states, themselves intent on committing genocide on their own. The fruits of "progress" seemed to be guns, tanks, poison gas, and, ultimately, the atomic bomb. Disillusion and doubt were the inevitable result. The Cold War followed World War II, the Vietnam War added fuel to the Cold War, and the specter of war seemed unending. Sigmund Freud, who had begun his investigation of dreams at the end of the nineteenth century, posited a strong death wish in humankind's psychic makeup. The French existentialists, led by Jean-Paul Sartre, argued that the universe lacked both divine guidance and moral absolutes. Humans are thus "condemned to be free," he wrote, their condition one of perpetual anxiety, their only truth the inevitability of death.

But if humanity is condemned to freedom, many soon realized that freedom was theirs to gain. Anything seemed possible. Youth led the way—in the civil rights movement in the United States, the antiwar movement protesting U.S. involvement in Vietnam, the drug and music cultures of the 1960s and 1970s, and the growing feminist movement. Between 1944 and 1960, nation after nation—in Africa, Asia, and Southeast Asia—won their liberty from Britain, France, the Netherlands, Belgium, and Italy. The grip of the United States and Spain over the Western Hemisphere was loosened, most notably through the example of the Cuban Revolution.

By the beginning of the twenty-first century, many argued that, despite the continued existence of authoritarian rule in many parts of the world, a new form of power had substituted itself for the political control exercised in earlier times. A culture defined by an explosion in creative and technological ingenuity that seemed determined to break down borders and barriers between peoples began to emerge, based on the rise of the personal computer, the Internet, and digital media. This new culture seemed to close the brackets on the era from the outbreak of World War I in 1914 to the fall of the Soviet Union in 1989. Its promise—realizable or not—was a global culture of extraordinary diversity and plurality in which people throughout the world struggled to find their unique cultural and personal identities—and to express their identities through their art.

1903
W.E.B. Du Bois, *The Souls of Black Folk*

1905
Albert Einstein proposes theory of relativity

1907
Pablo Picasso, *Les Demoiselles d'Avignon*

1910
Stravinsky's *Firebird* performed in Paris

1917
Marcel Duchamp, *Fountain*

1917
Russian Revolution

1922
James Joyce, *Ulysses*

1924–29
The Harlem Renaissance

1924
Andre Breton, *Surrealist Manifesto*

1929
Stock market crash leads to Great Depression

1933–45
Adolf Hitler and Nazi Party rule Germany

1945
Lee Miller, *Buchenwald, Germany*

1950
Jackson Pollack, *Number 27*

1953
Karl Stockhausen composes first synthesized music

1954
Godzilla destroys Tokyo

1954
Samuel Beckett, *Waiting for Godot*

1963
Martin Luther King, Jr., "Letter from Birmingham Jail", Betty Friedan, *The Feminine Mystique*

1969
Woodstock music festival

1972
Robert Venturi, Denise Scott Brown, Steve Izenour write, *Learning from Las Vegas* advocating architectural postmodernism

1989–90
Collapse of U.S.S.R.

1994
Shirin Neshat, *Rebellious Silence*
2001
Terrorist attacks on United States; United States attacks Afghanistan

2003
United States attacks Iraq

LEARN MORE Explore an interactive timeline on **www.myartslab.com**

34

The Era of Invention
Paris and the Modern World

THINKING AHEAD

What are Cubism, Fauvism, and Futurism?

What is German Expressionism?

What innovations distinguish the literary world in the first years of the twentieth century?

What are the origins of cinema?

If the rhythm of life had been regulated by the physiology of a man or a horse walking, or, on a sailing voyage, by the vagaries of weather (calm, storm, and wind direction), after 1850 it was regulated by the machine—first by the steam engine and the train, then, in 1897, by the automobile, and then, finally, by the airplane. At the dawn of the twentieth century, the world was in motion. As early as 1880, one French advertising company boasted that it could post a billboard ad in 35,937 municipalities in five days' time—a billboard of the kind advertising Astra Construction in *The Cardiff Team* (Fig. **34.1**), a painting by Robert Delaunay [duh-lawn-AY] (1885–1941). The painting depicts the men of the Cardiff (Wales) rugby team leaping up at a rugby ball in the center of the painting. They represent the internationalization of sport; the first modern Olympic Games had taken place in 1896 in Athens, followed by the 1900 Games in Paris, staged in conjunction with the Exposition Universelle, and rugby was a medal sport in each. The rugby ball is framed by the famous Grande Roue de Paris. Built for the 1900 Exposition Universelle, at 100 meters (328 feet) in height, it was the tallest Ferris wheel in the world, surpassing by 64 feet the original Ferris wheel, built for Chicago's Columbian Exposition in 1893 (see Chapter 32), and although it would be demolished in 1920, the Grande Roue remained the world's tallest Ferris wheel until it was surpassed by three Japanese Ferris wheels in the 1990s. On July 1, 1913, the year that Delaunay painted *The Cardiff Team*, a signal was broadcast from the top of the Eiffel Tower, seen towering over Delaunay's work, establishing worldwide Standard Time. By 1903, Orville Wright had been airborne 59 seconds, and by 1908, he would fly for 91 minutes. A year later, Blériot crossed the English Channel by plane (though it would be another 18 years until Charles Lindbergh would cross the Atlantic by air). The aeroplane in Delaunay's painting is a "box kite" design built in a Paris suburb beginning in 1907 by the Voisin brothers, Gabriel and Charles, the first commercial airplane manufacturers in Europe. Finally, the signboard "MAGIC" refers to Magic City, an enormous dance-hall near the Eiffel Tower. Delaunay's *Cardiff Team* captures the pulse of Paris in the first decades of the twentieth century, and the heartbeat of modern life.

◀ **Fig. 34.1 Robert Delaunay, *L'Equipe de Cardiff (The Cardiff Team)*. 1913.** Oil on canvas, 10′ 8⅜″ × 6′10″. Collection Van Abbemuseum © L & M Service B.V. The Hague 20100903. Everything in the painting seems to rise into the sky as if, for Delaunay, the century is "taking off" much like the aeroplane. Even the construction company's name, "Astra," refers to the stars.

HEAR MORE Listen to an audio file of your chapter at **www.myartslab.com**

Delaunay called his work Simultanism, a term derived from Michel Eugène Chevreul's 1839 book on color *The Principle of Harmony and Contrast of Colors* (see Chapter 33)—in the original French title the word translated as "harmony" is *simultanée*—but the term signifies more than just an approach to color theory. The name referred to the immediacy of vision, and suggested that in any given instant, an infinite number of states of being existed in the speed and motion of modern life. Everything was in motion, including the picture itself.

The still photograph suddenly found itself animated in the moving picture, first in 1895 by the Brothers Lumière, in Paris, and then after 1905, when the Nickelodeon, the first motion-picture theater in the world, opened its doors in Pittsburgh, Pennsylvania. By 1925, Russian filmmaker Sergei Eisenstein would cram 155 separate shots into a four-minute sequence of his film *The Battleship Potemkin*—a shot every 1.6 seconds. In 1900, France had produced 3,000 automobiles; by 1907, it was producing 30,000 a year. The technological advances represented by the automobile were closely connected to the development of the internal combustion engine, pneumatic tires, and, above all, the rise of the assembly line. After all, building 30,000 automobiles a year required an efficiency and speed of production unlike any ever before conceived. Henry Ford (1863–1947), the American automobile maker, attacked the problem. Ford asked Frederick Taylor (1856–1915), the inventor of

"scientific management," to determine the exact speed at which the assembly line should move and the exact motions workers should use to perform their duties; in 1908, assembly-line production as we know it was born.

Amid all this speed and motion, the world also suddenly seemed a less stable and secure place. Discoveries in science and physics confirmed this. In 1900, German physicist Max Planck (1858–1947) proposed the theory of matter and energy known as quantum mechanics. In quantum mechanics, the fundamental particles are unknowable, and are only hypothetical things represented by mathematics. Furthermore, the very technique of measuring these phenomena necessarily alters their behavior. Faced with the fact that light appeared to travel in absolutely contradictory ways, as both particles and waves, depending upon how one measured it, in 1913, Danish physicist Niels Bohr (1885–1962) built on quantum physics to propose a new theory of complementarity: two statements, apparently contradictory, might at any moment be equally true. At the very end of the nineteenth century, in Cambridge, England, J. J. Thompson detected the existence of separate components in the previously indivisible atom. He called them electrons, and by 1911, Ernest Rutherford had introduced a new model of the atom—a small, positively charged nucleus containing most of the atom's mass around which electrons continuously orbit. Suddenly matter itself was understood to be continually in motion. Meanwhile, in 1905, Albert Einstein had published his theory of relativity

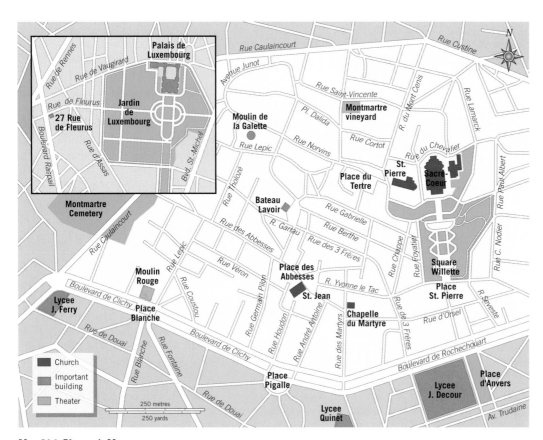

Map 34.1 Picasso's Montmartre.

and by 1915 had produced the *General Principles of Relativity*, with its model of the non-Euclidean, four-dimensional space-time continuum. Between 1895 and 1915, the traditional physical universe had literally been transformed—and it was not a universe of entities available to the human eye.

In the arts, the Spanish-born Pablo Picasso [pee-KAH-soh] (1881–1973) stood at the center of the new spirit of change and innovation that is the subject of this chapter. Picasso's studio in Paris was quickly recognized by artists and intellectuals as the center of artistic innovation in the new century. From around Europe and America, artists flocked to see his work, and they carried his spirit—and the spirit of French painting generally—back with them to Italy, Germany, and America, where it influenced the arts there. New art movements—new "isms," including Delaunay's Simultanism—succeeded one another in rapid fire. Picasso's work also encouraged radical approaches to poetry and to music, where the discordant, sometimes violent distortions of his paintings found their expression in sound.

PABLO PICASSO'S PARIS: AT THE HEART OF THE MODERN

Picasso's Paris was centered at 13 rue Ravignon [rah-veen-YOHN], at the Bateau-Lavoir [bah-TOH lah-VWAHR] ("Laundry Barge"), so nicknamed by the poet Max Jacob. It was Picasso's studio from the spring of 1904 until October 1909, and he continued to store his paintings there until September 1912. Anyone wanting to see his work would have to climb the hill topped by the great white cathedral of Sacre Coeur [sah-KRAY ker] in the Montmartre [mohn-MART] quarter, beginning from the Place Pigalle [plahss pee-GAHL], and finally climb the stairs to the great ramshackle space, where the walls were piled deep with canvases (see Map **34.1**). Or they might see his work at the Saturday evening salons of expatriate American writer and art collector Gertrude Stein [stine] (1874–1946) at 27 rue de Fleurus [fler-OOS] behind the Jardin du Luxembourg [zhar-DEHN due louks-em-BOOR] on the Left Bank of the Seine. If you knew someone who knew someone, you would be welcome enough. Many Picassos hung on her walls, including his portrait of her, painted in 1906 (Fig. **34.2**).

In her book *The Autobiography of Alice B. Toklas* (1932)—actually her own memoir disguised as that of her friend and lifelong companion—Stein described the making of this picture in the winter of 1906 (**Reading 34.1**):

Fig. 34.2 Pablo Picasso, *Gertrude Stein.* Winter–Autumn 1906. Oil on canvas, 39 ³/₈″ × 32″. Bequest of Gertrude Stein, 1946 (47.106). The Metropolitan Museum of Art, New York. Image © The Metropolitan Museum of Art/Art Resource, New York. © Art Rights Society (ARS), New York. According to Stein, in painting her portrait, "Picasso passed [on] . . . to the intensive struggle which was to end in Cubism."

> Gertrude had never thought of having her portrait painted, and they do not know either of them how it came about. Anyway, it did, and she posed for this portrait ninety times. There was a large broken armchair where Gertrude Stein posed. There was a couch where everybody sat and slept. There was a little kitchen chair where Picasso sat to paint. There was a large easel and there were many canvases. She took her pose, Picasso sat very tight in his chair and very close to his canvas and on a very small palette, which was of a brown gray color, mixed some more brown gray and the painting began. All of a sudden one day Picasso painted out the whole head. I can't see you anymore when I look, he said irritably, and so the picture was left like that.

Picasso actually finished the picture early the following fall, painting her face in large, masklike masses in a style very different from the rest of the picture. No longer relying on the visual presence of the sitter before his eyes, Picasso painted not his view of her, but his idea of her. When Alice B. Toklas later commented that some people thought the painting did not look like Stein, Picasso replied, "It will."

The Aggressive New Modern Art:
Les Demoiselles d'Avignon

In a way, the story of Gertrude Stein's portrait is a parable for the birth of modern art. It narrates the shift in painting from an optical art—painting what one sees—to an imaginative construct—painting what one thinks about what one sees. The object of painting shifts, in other words, from the literal to the conceptual. The painting that most thoroughly embodied this shift was *Les Demoiselles d'Avignon* [lay dem-wah-ZELL dah-veen-YOHN], which Picasso began soon after finishing his portrait of Stein (Fig. **34.3**).

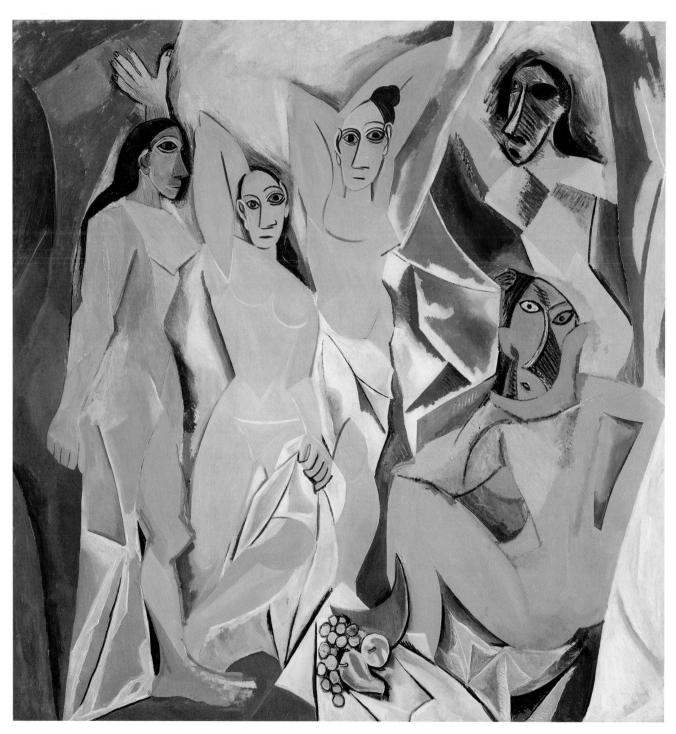

Fig. 34.3 Pablo Picasso, *Les Demoiselles d'Avignon*. May–July 1907. Oil on canvas, 95 ¹/₈″ × 91 ¹/₈″. Acquired through the Lillie P. Bliss Bequest. The Museum of Modern Art/Licensed by SCALA/Art Resource, New York. © 2008 Artists Rights Society (ARS), New York. Central to Picasso's composition is the almond shape, first used for Gertrude Stein's eyes and repeated in the eyes of the figures here and in other forms—thighs and arms particularly. The shape is simultaneously rounded and angular, reinforcing the sense of tension in the painting.

SEE MORE For a Closer Look at Pablo Picasso's *Les Demoiselles d'Avignon*, go to **www.myartslab.com**

Completed in the summer of 1907, *Les Demoiselles d'Avignon* was not exhibited in public until 1916. So if you wanted to see it, you had to climb the hill to the Bateau-Lavoir. And many did because the painting was notorious, understood—correctly—as an assault on the idea of painting as it had always been understood. At the Bateau-Lavoir, a common insult hurled by Picasso and his friends at one another was "Still much too symbolist!" No one said this about *Les Demoiselles*. It seemed entirely new in every way.

The painting represents five prostitutes in a brothel on the carrer d'Avinyo (Avignon Street) in Picasso's native

Olympia, **p. 1001**

Barcelona. As the figure on the left draws back a curtain as if to reveal them, the prostitutes address the viewer with the frankness of Manet's *Olympia* (see *Closer Look*, Chapter 30), a painting Picasso greatly admired. In fact, in January 1907, as Picasso was planning *Les Demoiselles*, *Olympia* was hung, for the first time, in the Louvre, to much public comment and controversy. It was placed, not coincidentally, alongside Ingres's

Grande Odalisque, **p. 938**

Grande Odalisque (see Fig. 28.13). Both figures turn to face the viewer, and the distortions both painters work upon their figures—Manet's flat paint, Ingres's elongated spine and disconnected extremities—probably inspired Picasso to push the limits of representation even further.

Also extremely important to Picasso was the example of Cézanne, who, a year after his death in October 1906, was honored with a huge retrospective at the 1907 Salon d'Automne [doh-TUN]. Cézanne, Picasso would say, "is the father of us all." In the way Picasso shows one object or figure

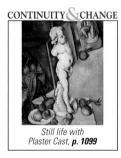

Still life with Plaster Cast, **p. 1099**

from two different points of view, the compressed and concentrated space of *Les Demoiselles* is much like Cézanne's (see *Still Life with Plaster Cast* in *Closer Look*, Chapter 33). Consider the still-life grouping of melon, pear, apple, and grapes in the center foreground. The viewer is clearly looking down at the corner of a table, at an angle completely inconsistent with the frontal view of the nude who is parting the curtain. And note the feet of the nude second from the left. Could she possibly be standing? Or is she, in fact, reclining, so that we see her from the same vantage point as the still life?

Picasso's subject matter and ambiguous space were disturbing to viewers. Even more disturbing were the strange faces of the left-hand figure and the two to the right. X-ray analysis confirms that originally all five of the figures shared the same facial features as the two in the middle left, with their almond eyes and noses drawn in an almost childlike profile. But sometime in May or June 1907, after he visited

the ethnographic museum at the Palais du Trocadéro [pah-LAY due troh-kah-DAY-roh], across the river from the Eiffel Tower, Picasso painted over the faces of the figure at the left and the two on the right, giving them instead what most scholars agree are the characteristics of African masks. But equally important to Picasso's creative process was a retrospective of Gauguin's painting and sculpture at the 1906 Salon d'Automne with their Polynesian imagery (see Fig. 33.17). At any rate, Picasso's intentions were clear. He wanted to connect his prostitutes to the seemingly authentic—and emotionally energizing—forces that

Mahana no atua, **p. 1100**

Gauguin had discovered in the "primitive." Many years later, he described the meaning of African and Oceanic masks to *Les Demoiselles*:

> The masks weren't just like any other pieces of sculpture. Not at all. They were magic things. . . . They were against everything—against unknown, threatening spirits. I always looked at fetishes. I understood; I too am against everything. I too believe that everything is unknown, that everything is an enemy! . . . All the fetishes were used for the same thing. They were weapons. To help people avoid coming under the influence of spirits again, to help them become independent. They're tools. If we give spirits a form, we become independent. . . . I understood why I was a painter. All alone in that awful museum [the Trocadéro] with masks, with dolls made by the redskins, dusty manikins. *Les Demoiselles d'Avignon* must have come to me that very day, but not because of the forms; because it was my first exorcism painting—yes absolutely!

Les Demoiselles, then, was an act of liberation, an exorcism of past traditions, perhaps even of painting itself. It would allow Picasso to move forward into a kind of painting that was totally new.

Picasso scholar Patricia Leighten has argued convincingly that the African masks in *Les Demoiselles* are designed not only to challenge and mock Western artistic traditions but also to evoke and critique the deplorable exploitation by Europeans of black Africans, particularly in the Congo—a theme, as we have seen, taken up by Joseph Conrad in his *Heart of Darkness* (see Chapter 33). A scandal had erupted in 1905 when the French government's administrators in the Congo, Gaud and Toqué, were accused of a wide variety of atrocities. In addition to their salaries, these administrators received bonuses for rubber collected under them, and they coerced natives to furnish them with rubber by pillaging their villages, executing "lazy" or uncooperative villagers, kidnapping their wives and children, and even more scandalous assaults. Gaud and Toqué were accused specifically of dynamiting an African guide in celebration of Bastille Day and of forcing one of their servants to drink soup they had made

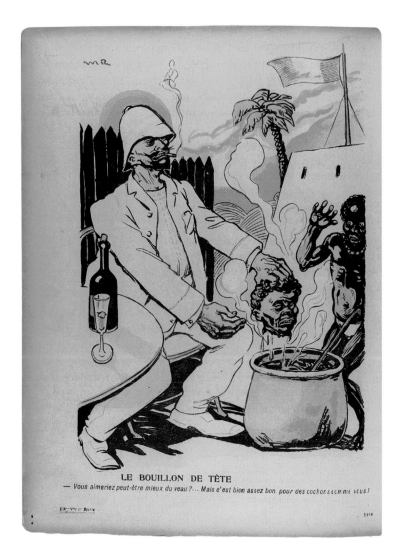

LE BOUILLON DE TÊTE
— Vous aimeriez peut-être mieux du veau ?... Mais c'est bien assez bon pour des cochons comme vous !

L'Assiette au Beurre.

Fig. 34.4 Maurice Radiguez, "Le Bouillon de Tête." *L'Assiette au beurre*, **March 11, 1905.** Photo: Morris Library, University of Delaware. The caption reads: "You'd perhaps like veal better? Well, it's plenty good enough for pigs like you!"

In fact, it verges on becoming an illustration for Mallarmé's *L'Après-midi d'un faune* (see Chapter 33). And not long before he painted *The Joy of Life*, Matisse had titled one of his large canvases *Luxe, calme, et volupté* (*Luxury, Calm, and Pleasure*), taken from Baudelaire's poem "L'invitation au voyage":

Là, tout n'est qu'ordre et beauté,	There, all is only order and beauty,
Luxe, calme, et volupté.	Luxury, calm, and pleasure.

Twelve years older than Picasso, Matisse was the favorite of Gertrude Stein's brother Leo. He had established himself, at the Salon des Indépendants in 1904, as the leader of a radical new group of experimental painters known as the Fauves [fohvz]—or "Wild Beasts." **Fauvism** [FOHV-izm] was known for its radical application of arbitrary, or unnatural, color, anticipated in a few of van Gogh's paintings and in the pool of color in the foreground of Gauguin's *Mahana no atua* (see Fig. 33.17). The fractured angularity of Picasso's *Demoiselles*, its subdued coloration, its shallow space, and its childlike as opposed to sensuous use of line, are diametrically opposed to the circular, undulating, and frankly erotic space of Matisse's field of color in *The Joy of Life*. The tension that dominates Picasso's painting—the way it pulls the viewer into the scene even as it repels entry—is totally absent in the Matisse, where harmony rules. It is as if Picasso consciously rejected Matisse's modernism.

Picasso and Matisse saw each other regularly at the Steins' apartment, but their relationship was competitive. In fact, it is useful to think of Matisse's monumental *Dance II* (Fig. **34.6**) as something of a rebuttal to the upstart Picasso's *Demoiselles*. For one thing, Matisse's circle dance consists of six figures that were in the distant yellow field of *Joy of Life*, but when Matisse repeats the motif in *Dance II*, the number is five, like Picasso's five prostitutes. Matisse also replaces Picasso's squared and angular composition with a circular and rounded one. Where Picasso's painting seems static, as if we are asked to hold our breath at the scene before us, Matisse's is active, moving as if to an unheard music. Most astonishing is Matisse's color—vermillion (red-orange), green, and blue-violet, the primary colors of light. In effect, Matisse's modernism takes place in the light of day, Picasso's in the dark of night; Matisse's with joy, Picasso's with fear and trepidation.

from a native's head. These atrocities were illustrated in a March 11, 1905, special issue of the Parisian political journal, *L'Assiette au beurre* (*The Butter Plate*), entitled "The Torturers of Blacks" (Fig. **34.4**). Thus Picasso's painting confronts a variety of idealizations: the idealization of the world as reflected in traditional European art, the idealization of sexuality—and love—and the idealization of the colonizing mission of the European state. It acknowledges, in other words, the artist's obligation to confront the horrific truths that lie behind and support bourgeois complacency.

Matisse and the Fauves: A New Color

When the painter Henri Matisse [mah-TEES] saw *Les Demoiselles*, he is said to have considered it an "audacious hoax," an "outrage [ridiculing] the modern movement." It is little wonder as the two painters' aesthetic visions were diametrically opposed. Gertrude Stein had introduced the two men in April 1906, just after Matisse had exhibited his *The Joy of Life* at the Salon des Indépendants [en-day-pahn-DAHN] (Fig. **34.5**). The painting is a sensual celebration of Symbolist sexuality, conceived under the sway of Baudelaire and Mallarmé.

Fig. 34.5 **Henri Matisse,** *Bonheur de vivre* (*The Joy of Life*). **1905–06.** Oil on canvas, 69 $\frac{1}{8}$″ × 94 $\frac{7}{8}$″. © 1995 The Barnes Foundation. 2008 Succession H. Matisse, Paris/Artists Rights Society (ARS), New York. Note how Matisse balances the scene's eroticism with a relaxed, almost innocent sense of nudity.

Fig. 34.6 **Henri Matisse,** *Dance*. **1910.** Oil on canvas, 8′ 5 $\frac{5}{8}$″ × 12′ 9 $\frac{1}{2}$″ (260 × 391 cm). Inv. No. 9673. The State Hermitage Museum, St. Petersburg, Russia. © 2008 Succession H. Matisse/Artists Rights Society (ARS), New York. This work and another similarly colored painting of musicians called *Music* were commissioned by the Russian collector Sergei Shchukin to decorate the staircase of his home in Moscow.

The Invention of Cubism:
Braque's Partnership with Picasso

When the French painter Georges Braque [brahk] (1882–1963) first saw *Les Demoiselles*, in December 1907, he said that he felt burned, "as if someone were drinking gasoline and spitting fire." He was, at the time, a Fauve, painting in the manner of Matisse, but like Picasso, he was obsessed with Cézanne, so much so that he planned to paint the following summer in Cézanne's l'Estaque (see Fig. 33.15). When he returned to Paris in September, he brought with him a series of landscapes, among them *Houses at l'Estaque* (Fig. **34.7**). Picasso was fascinated with their spatial ambiguity and cube-like shapes. Note in particular the central house, where (illogically) the two walls that join at a right angle are shaded on both sides of the corner, yet are similarly illuminated. And the angle of the roofline does not meet at the corner, thus flattening the roof. Details of windows, doors, and moldings have been eliminated, as have the lines between planes so that one plane seems to merge with the next in a manner reminiscent of Cézanne. The tree that rises on the left seems to merge at its topmost branch into the distant houses. The curve of the bush on the left echoes that of the tree, and its palmlike leaves are identical to the trees rising between the houses behind it. The structure of the foreground mirrors that of the houses. All this serves to flatten the composition even as the lack of a horizon causes the whole composition to appear to roll forward toward the viewer rather than recede in space.

Seeing Braque's landscapes at a gallery in November 1908, the critic Louis Vauxcelles [voh-SELL] wrote: "He [Braque] is contemptuous of form, reduces everything, sites and figures and houses to geometric schemas, to cubes." But the movement known as **Cubism** was born out of collaboration. "Almost every evening," Picasso later recalled, "either I went to Braque's studio or Braque came to mine. Each of us had to see what the other had done during the day." The two men were inventors, brothers—Picasso even took to calling Braque "Wilbur," after the aeronautical brothers Orville and Wilbur Wright. When Picasso returned to Paris from Spain in the fall of 1909, he brought

Fig. 34.7 Georges Braque, *Houses at l'Estaque*. 1908. Oil on canvas, 28 3/4″ × 23 3/4″. Peter Lauri/Kunstmuseum Bern. Estate of George Braque © 2008 Artists Rights Society (ARS), New York/ADAGP, Paris. Hermann and Margit Rupf Foundation. Braque's trip to l'Estaque in the summer of 1908 was a form of homage to Cézanne, whose style he consciously radicalized in works such as this.

Fig. 34.8 Pablo Picasso, *Houses on the Hill, Horta de Ebro*. 1909. Oil on canvas, 25 ⁵/₈″ × 31 ⁷/₈″. Jens Ziehe/Nationalgalerie, Museum Berggruen, Staatliche Museen zu Berlin, Berlin, Germany. Bildarchiv Preussischer Kulturbesitz/Art Resource, New York. © Artists Rights Society (ARS), New York. This is one of a series of some 15 paintings executed at Horta de Ebro (known today as Horta de Sant Joan) in the hills above Valencia during the summer of 1909.

with him landscapes that showed just how much he had learned from Braque (Fig. **34.8**).

Picasso and Braque pushed on, working so closely together that their work became indistinguishable to most viewers. They began to decompose their subjects into faceted planes, so that they seem to emerge down the middle of the canvas from some angular maze, as in *Violin and Palette* (Fig. **34.9**). Gradually they began to understand that they were questioning the very nature of reality, the nature of "truth" itself. This is the function of the trompe-l'oeil nail casting its shadow onto the canvas at the top of Braque's painting. It announces its own artifice, the practice of illusionistically representing things in three-dimensional space. But the nail is no more real than the violin, which is about to dissolve into a cluster of geometric forms. Both are painted illusions, equally real as art.

From 1910 to 1912, Picasso and Braque took an increasingly abstract approach to depicting reality through painting. They were so experimental, in fact, that the subject nearly disappeared. Only a few cues remained to help viewers understand what they were seeing—a moustache, the scroll of a violin, a treble clef.

Increasingly, they added a few words here and there. Picasso used words from a popular song "*Ma Jolie*" ("My pretty one") to identify portraits of his current lover, or "*Jou*," to identify the newspaper *Le Journal*. "*Jou*" was also a pun on the word *jeu* ("play"), and it symbolized the play between the reality of the painting as an object and the reality of the world outside the frame. This kind of ambiguity led Braque and Picasso to introduce actual two- and three-dimensional elements into the space of the canvas, in what Picasso

Fig. 34.9 Georges Braque, *Violin and Palette*. Autumn 1909. Oil on canvas, 36 ¹/₈″ × 16 ⁷/₈″. Solomon Guggenheim Museum. 54.1412. George Braque © 2008 Artists Rights Society (ARS), New York/ADAGP, Paris. As in Picasso's *Les Demoiselles*, the primary tension in the painting is created by the juxtaposition of the rounded and angular forms.

and Braque came to call **collage** [kuh-LAHZH], from the French *coller* [koll-AY], "to paste or glue" (see *Closer Look*, pages 1126–1127). These elements—paper, fabric, rope, and other material—at least challenged, if they did not completely obliterate, the space between life and art.

Late in the summer of 1912, wandering through Avignon, Braque came upon a decorator's shop selling wallpaper with a simulated wood-grain pattern. He bought it and pasted it onto a drawing called *Fruit Dish and Glass*, where it stood for both the wooden wall in the background and the drawer of a table. It was at once real wallpaper and fake wood. Now, the real and the recognizable had reentered the Cubist vocabulary in the form of ***papiers-collés***,

meaning "pasted paper." It was as if modern life had erupted into the space of painting, interrupting what had been the increasing abstraction and subjectivity of the Cubist project. Picasso saw *Fruit Dish and Glass* when he returned to Paris from the south of France in September. "The bastard," Picasso later joked. "He waited until I'd turned my back." Soon Picasso was incorporating paper objects into his works, as in *Violin*.

The spiral scroll at the top of the violin is drawn from two points of view, in profile and three-quarter. The spiral has special significance. It occurs throughout Cubist painting and not only on violins. It can be found at the end of armrests on armchairs, as rope, and so on. It signifies the interplay between two and three dimensions, flat design versus the sculptural vortex or coil.

These two pieces of newspaper are cut from the same page. The one on top is the reverse side of the one on the bottom and, like a jigsaw puzzle piece, would fit into the left side of the bottom piece if it were turned over. So the two pieces reveal simultaneously the front and back of the same thing. The bottom piece also represents the body of the violin (note Picasso's drawing at its top left), while the upper piece, cupping the scrollwork, becomes the background or shadow.

Picasso depicts the *f*-holes of the violin in completely different ways. The one on the left is a small, simple line, while the one on the right is a much larger, fully open and fully realized form. It is as if we see the right one from the front, and the left one as if it were swiveled away to a three-quarter view and deeper in space.

Pablo Picasso, *Violin.* **Late 1912.** Charcoal and *papiers-collés* on canvas, 24 ³/₈″ × 18 ¹/₂″. Musée National d'Art Moderne. Centre National d'Art et de Culture. Georges Pompidou Paris, France. CNAC/MNAM/Réunion des Musées Nationaux/Art Resource, New York. © 2008 Artists Rights Society (ARS), New York.

Pablo Picasso, *Guitar, Sheet Music, and Wine Glass.* **1912.** Charcoal, gouache, and *papiers-collés*, 18 $\frac{7}{8}$" × 14 $\frac{3}{8}$". The McNay Art Museum, San Antonio, Texas. Bequest of Marion Koogler McNay. © 2008 Estate of Pablo Picasso/Artists Rights Society (ARS), New York. The newspaper fragment at the bottom of the painting derives from the front page of *Le Journal*, November 18, 1912, reproduced below.

Picasso challenged the subjectivity of the creative act by including newspaper fragments in the painting. Newspaper insists on the inescapable reality of daily life. By admitting this element of pop culture into the space of art, Picasso and Braque defined painting as the setting in which the forces of the high and low, art and the real world, must engage one another.

Thus in Picasso's 1912 *Guitar, Sheet Music, and Wine Glass*, at the bottom of the page, the headline of *Le Journal* reads, "*La bataille s'est engagé*," "The battle is joined." Literally, it refers to a battle in the Balkans, where Bulgaria attacked the Turks, November 17 through 19. But the "battle" is also metaphorical, the battle between art and reality (and perhaps between Braque and Picasso as they explored the possibilities of collage). Similarly, the background's trellis-and-rose wallpaper is no more or less real than the fragment of the actual musical score, the *faux-bois* ("false wood") guitar, and the Cubist drawing of a goblet, cut out of some preexisting source as the other *papier-collé* elements in the work. Collage is the great equalizer in which all the elements are united on the same plane, both the literal plane of the canvas and the figurative plane of reality.

Something to Think About . . .

How is the drawing of the wine glass in *Guitar, Sheet Music, and Wine Glass* typically Cubist?

SEE MORE For a Closer Look at Pablo Picasso's collages, go to **www.myartslab.com**

Futurism: The Cult of Speed

News of the experimental fervor of Picasso and Braque spread quickly through avant-garde circles across Europe, and other artists sought to match their endeavors in independent but related ways. On February 20, 1909, for instance, the front page of the Paris newspaper *Le Figaro* [fee-gah-ROH] published the *Founding and Manifesto of Futurism*, written by the Italian Filippo Marinetti [mahree-NET-tee] (1876–1944). Reflecting the same antitraditional feelings that motivated Picasso's *Les Demoiselles* and the same distaste for a bourgeoisie seemingly secure in its complacency, Futurism rejected the political and artistic traditions of the past and called for a new art. Marinetti quickly attracted a group of painters and sculptors to invent it. These included the Italian artists Giacomo Balla [BAHL-lah] (1871–1958), Umberto Boccioni [boch-ee-OH-nee] (1882–1916), Carlo Carrà [KAH-rah] (1881–1966), Luigi Russolo [roo-SOH-loh] (1885–1947), who was also a musician, and Gino Severini [sev-eh-REE-nee] (1883–1966). The new style was called Futurism. The Futurists repudiated static art and sought to render what they thought of as the defining characteristic of modern urban life—speed. But it was not until Marinetti took Boccioni, Carrà, and Russolo to Paris for two weeks in the fall of 1911, arranging for visits to the studios of Picasso and Braque, that the fledgling Futurists discovered *how* they might represent it—in the fractured idiom of Cubism.

However, the work they created was philosophically remote from Cubism. It reflected Marinetti's *Manifesto* (see **Reading 34.2**, page 1141), which affirmed not only speed, but also technology and violence. In the manifesto, Futurism is born out of a high-speed automobile crash in the "maternal ditch" of modernity's industrial sludge, an intentionally ironic image of rebirth and regeneration. Where the Cubist rejection of tradition had largely been the invention of two men working in relative isolation, the Futurist rejection was public, bombastic, and political. As the Futurists traveled around Europe between 1910 and 1913 promoting their philosophy in public forums and entertainments, their typical evening featured insult-slinging and scuffles with the audience, usually an arrest or two, and considerable attention in the press.

Marinetti's artists turned to a variety of subjects for inspiration but particularly focused on the car, the plane, and the industrial town, all of which represented for the Futurists the triumph of humankind over nature. Balla painted a cycle of between 15 and 20 paintings representing speeding cars. Carrà was particularly sympathetic with Marinetti's poetic endeavors and Russolo's ideas about music, the former desiring to create "words-in-freedom . . . destroying the canals of syntax," and the latter a music of "noise-sounds." His *Interventionist Demonstration*, he said, celebrates "a love for modern life in its essential

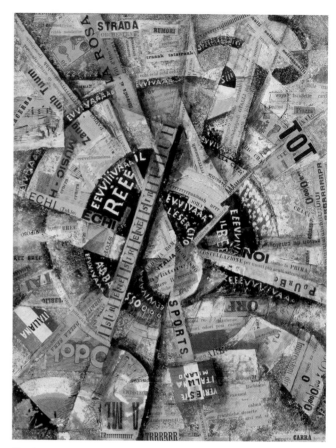

Fig. 34.10 Carlo Carrà, *Interventionist Demonstration*. 1914.
Tempera and collage on cardboard, 15 1/8″ × 11 7/8″. Collezione Mattioli, Milan, Italy. Scala/Art Resource, New York. © 2008 Artists Rights Society (ARS), New York. Carrà's inspiration for this image was a flurry of leaflets being dropped from an airplane flying over the Piazza del Duomo in Florence. The image is composed of sounds as much as words, suggesting a raucous political demonstration.

dynamism—its sounds, noises and smells" (Fig. **34.10**). It takes the form, essentially, of a spinning phonograph, its "music" represented by collaged elements from the newspaper.

One of the great masterpieces of Futurist art is Boccioni's *Unique Forms of Continuity in Space* (Fig. **34.11**), a work oddly evocative of the very *Nike of Samothrace* (see Fig. 5.24) that Marinetti in his manifesto found less compelling than a speeding car. Boccioni probably intended to represent a nude, her musculature stretched and drawn out as she moves through space. "What we want to do," he explained, "is show the living object in its dynamic growth."

CONTINUITY & CHANGE

Nike of Samothrace, p. 163

LEARN MORE Gain insight from a primary source document about Futurism at **www.myartslab.com**

tryman Vaslav Nijinsky [nih-JIN-skee] (1890–1950), who had performed, a year earlier, as the faun in Debussy's *L'Après-midi d'un faune* (*Afternoon of a Faun*). The performance was a scandal. Together with the Futurists' confrontational performances and, earlier, the public outrage at Manet's *Luncheon on the Grass* and *Olympia* in the earlier 1860s, it helped to define modern art as antagonistic to public opinion and an affront to its values.

The events of that evening surprised everyone. The night before, a dress rehearsal performed before an audience, in Stravinsky's words, "of actors, painters, musicians, writers, and the most cultured representatives of society," had proved uneventful. But on the night of the public premiere, the first chords of Stravinsky's score evoked derisive laughter. Hissing, booing, and catcalls followed, and at such a level that the dancers could not hear the music. Diaghilev ordered the lights to be turned on and off, hoping to quiet the crowd, but that just incensed the audience further. Finally the police had to be called, as Stravinsky himself crawled to safety out a backstage window.

What seemed most radically new to Stravinsky's audience was the music's angular, jarring, sometimes violent rhythmic inventiveness. The ballet's story—subtitled *Pictures from Pagan Russia*—centers on a pre-Christian ritual welcoming the beginning of spring that culminates in a human sacrifice. The music reflects the brutalism of the pagan rite with savage dissonance. Part 1 of the work, The Adoration of the Earth, culminates in a spirited dance of youths and maidens in praise of the earth's fertility. In Part 2, The Sacrifice, one of the maidens is chosen to be sacrificed in order to guarantee the fertility celebrated in Part 1. All dance in honor of the Chosen One, invoking the blessings of the village's ancestors, culminating in the frenzied Sacrificial Dance of the Chosen One herself (track **34.1**). Just before the dancer collapses and dies, Stravinsky shifts the meter eight times in 12 measures (see the score below); the men then carry the Chosen One's body to the foot of a sacred mound and offer her up to the gods.

HEAR MORE at www.myartslab.com

Sometimes different elements of the orchestra play different meters simultaneously. Such **polyrhythms** contrast

Modernist Music and Dance: Stravinsky and the Ballets Russes

The dynamism and invention evident in both Cubism and Futurism also appeared in music and dance. On May 29, 1913, the Ballets Russes, a company under the direction of impresario Sergei Diaghilev [dee-AH-ghee-lev] (1872–1929), premiered the ballet *Le Sacre du printemps* (*The Rite of Spring*) at the Théâtre des Champs-Élysées in Paris. The music was by the cosmopolitan Russian composer Igor Stravinsky [strah-VIN-skee] (1882–1971) and the choreography by his coun-dramatically with other passages where the same rhythmic pulse repeats itself persistently—such as when at the end of the ballet's first part the orchestra plays the same eighth-note chords 32 times in succession. (This technique is known as *ostinato*—Italian for "obstinate.") In addition to its rhythmic variety, Stravinsky's ballet was also **polytonal**: Two or more keys are sounded by different instruments at the same time, and the traditional instruments of the orchestra are used in startlingly unconventional ways, so that they sound raw and strange. Low-pitched instruments, such as bassoons, play at the top of their range, for instance, and clarinets at the gravelly bottom of their capabilities. Integrated across these jarring juxtapositions are passages of recognizable Russian folk songs. Stravinsky's music was enormously influential on subsequent composers, who began to think about rhythmic structure in a totally different way.

If his first Paris audience found Stravinsky's music offensive—more than one critic thought he was a disciple of the Futurists' "noise-sound"—Nijinsky's choreography seemed a downright provocation to riot: "They repeat the same gesture a hundred times over," wrote one critic, "they paw the ground, they stamp, they stamp, they stamp, they stamp and they stamp. . . . Evidently all of this is defensible; it is prehistoric dance." It certainly was not recognizable as ballet. It moved away from the traditional graceful movements of ballerinas dancing *en pointe* (on their toes in boxed shoes) toward a new athleticism. Nijinsky's choreography called for the dancers to assume angular, contorted positions that at once imitated ancient bas-relief sculpture and Cubist painting, hold these positions in frozen stillness, and then burst into wild leaps and whirling circle dances.

THE EXPRESSIONIST MOVEMENT: MODERNISM IN GERMANY AND AUSTRIA

Like Stravinsky, Nijinsky, and Diaghilev, by 1910, almost every European artist had turned to Paris for inspiration. German artists were no exception. We call the modernist style they created Expressionism, though no group of artists actually called itself Expressionist. We can think of German Expressionism as combining the Fauves' exploration of the emotional potential of color with Nijinsky's choreographic representation of raw primitivism and sexual energy. Like the Fauves, the Expressionists' interest in color can be traced to the art of van Gogh and Gauguin, while the sexual expressivity of their work has its roots in the art of the Vienna Secession (see Chapter 33). Their subject matter was often drawn from their own psychological makeup. They laid bare in paint the torment of their lives. There were Expressionist groups throughout Europe that encompassed the visual arts and other media, but the most important in Germany were Die Brücke, originally based in Dresden but moving later to Berlin; Der Blaue Reiter, based in Munich; and the musicians of the Second Viennese School.

Die Brücke: The Art of Deliberate Crudeness

In 1905, four young artists from Dresden calling themselves Die Brücke [dee BROO-kuh] ("The Bridge") exhibited new work in an abandoned chandelier factory. They took the name from a passage in Nietzsche's *Thus Spoke Zarathustra* where Zarathustra calls for humanity to assert its potential to "bridge" the gulf between its current state and the condition of the *Ubermensch*, the "higher man," who is the embodiment of the ideal future (see Chapter 33).

The original four artists were Karl Schmidt-Rottluff (1884–1976), Erich Heckel (1883–1970), Fritz Bleyl (1880–1966), and Ernst Ludwig Kirchner (1880–1938). In 1906, Emile Nolde [NOHL-duh] (1867–1956) and Max Pechstein [PEK-shtine] (1881–1955) joined them. They believed that through jarring contrasts of color and jagged, linear compositions—they admired, especially, the gouging, splintered effects that could be achieved in woodblock printing, a deliberately crude but more "direct" and unmediated medium—they could free the imagination from the chains that enslaved it. Kirchner's *Self-Portrait with Model* (Fig. **34.12**) embodies the raw, almost aggressive

Fig. 34.12 Ernst Ludwig Kirchner, *Self-Portrait with Model*. 1910. Oil on canvas, 58 ⅝" × 39". Photo: Elke Walford. Hamburger Kunsthalle, Hamburg, Germany. Bildarchiv Preussischer Kulturbeisitz/Art Resource, New York. Die Brücke exhibited as a group in Berlin, Darmstadt, Dresden, Dusseldorf, Hamburg, and Leipzig, as well as in traveling exhibitions to smaller German communities.

Fig. 34.13 Franz Marc, *The Large Blue Horses*. 1911. Oil on canvas, 3′5 ³/₈″ × 5′11 ¹/₄″ (1.05 × 1.81 m). Walker Art Center, Minneapolis. Gift of T. B. Walker Collection, Gilbert M. Walter Fund, 1942. The painting is meant to contrast the beauty of the untainted natural world to the sordidness of modern existence, very much in the spirit of Gauguin.

energy of Die Brücke's style. The artist stands in his striped robe, his masklike face contemplating his painting (unseen but in the space occupied by the viewer). He grips his wide paintbrush (implicitly a symbol for his own sexuality) in a manner that could only result in slashing, almost uncontrolled bands of color, as in fact exist in the painting itself. Behind him, possibly seated on a bed, is his model, dressed in her underwear, present (as in almost all Die Brücke work) solely as the eroticized object of male sexual desire.

Der Blaue Reiter: The Spirituality of Color

Der Blaue Reiter [dair BLAU-uh RY-tur] ("The Blue Rider") did not come into being until 1911. It was headed by the Russian émigré Wassily Kandinsky [kan-DIN-skee] (1866–1944) and by Franz Marc (1880–1916), an artist especially fond of painting animals, because he believed they possessed elemental energies. They were joined by a number of other artists, including Auguste Macke [MAH-kuh] (1887–1914) and Gabriele Münter [MUN-tur] (1877–1962), who met Kandinsky when she was his student in Munich in 1902.

These artists had no common style, but all were obsessed with color. "Color," Kandinsky wrote in *Concerning the Spiritual in Art*, first published in 1912 in the *Blaue Reiter Almanac*, "directly influences the soul. Color is the keyboard, the eyes are the hammers, the soul is the piano with many strings. The artist is the hand that plays . . . to cause vibrations of the soul." The color blue, Kandinsky wrote, is "the typical heavenly color." Marc saw in blue what he thought of as the masculine principle of spirituality. So his *The Large Blue Horses*, with its seemingly arbitrary color

Fig. 34.14 Gabriele Münter, *The Blue Gable*. 1911. Oil on canvas, 34 ¹⁵/₁₆″ × 39 ⁵/₈″. Krannert Art Museum, University of Illinois, Champaign. Gift of Albert L. Arenberg 1956-13-1. Münter lived in Murnau until her death in 1962. During World War II, she preserved her collection of Blaue Reiter works in the cellar of her house, hiding them first from the Nazis, who thought her work "degenerate," then from the occupying U.S. troops.

and interlocking rhythm of fluid curves and contours, very much influenced by Matisse, is the very image of the spiritual harmony in the natural world (Fig. **34.13**).

Yellow, on the other hand, was the female principle, a fact that deeply informs Gabriel Münter's *The Blue Gable* (Fig. **34.14**). Münter was one of the most original of the Blaue Reiter artists. At a time when, especially in Germany,

Fig. 34.15 Wassily Kandinsky, *Composition VII*. 1913. Oil on canvas, 6′6 ³/₄″ × 9′11 ¹/₈″. Tretyakov Gallery, Moscow.
Among practitioners of nonfigurative abstract art, Kandinsky was perhaps unique in not forcing his point of view on his colleagues.
If his was what he called "the Greater Abstraction," theirs was "the Greater Realism," equally leading to "the spiritual in art."

it was widely believed that women were not capable of artistic creation, she created a body of totally original work while involved in a relationship with Kandinsky that was emotionally painful for her. Eleven years her senior, he had seduced her as his student, promising to divorce his wife and marry her. Kandinsky never did marry her, though after he went to Russia in 1914, aspiring to help create a new revolutionary Russian art, he did divorce his wife and marry another woman. Münter remained deeply in love with Kandinsky and bought a summer house for them in the town of Murnau [MUR-now] in the foothills of the Bavarian Alps. At Murnau, she began to collect and emulate the Bavarian folk art of reverse-glass painting. The dark outlines of her forms in *The Blue Gable* function like leading in stained glass. A winter view of Murnau, it seems to suppress all the Blaue Reiter's coloristic tendencies, except for the yellow house and the deep blue gable. Given Kandinsky and Marc's color theory, the blue was probably a symbol of the masculine, even a symbol of Kandinsky himself. The yellow (feminine) house stands crookedly beside it, behind the tilted diagonals of a fence. In the foreground, a giant snow-covered rock and a jagged, leafless tree stand guard,

suggesting the opposite of Marc's natural harmony. On a symbolic level, they seem to reflect tensions that existed between Münter and Kandinsky.

Kandinsky's chief theme was the biblical Apocalypse, the moment when, according to a long tradition in the Byzantine church, Moscow would become the New Jerusalem. "Der Reiter," in fact, was the popular name for Saint George, patron saint of Moscow, and the explosions of contrasting colors across *Composition No. 7* (Fig. **34.15**) suggest that the fateful moment has arrived. Earthly yellow competes with heavenly blue, and red with green. Red, he wrote, "rings inwardly with a determined and powerful intensity," while green "represents the social middle class, self-satisfied, immovable, narrow." Linear elements, Kandinsky felt, were equivalent to dance, and the painting can be interpreted as a rendering of dance set to music. But *Composition No. 7* is the last of a series of "compositions"— the title in fact refers to music—the biblical themes of war and resurrection, deluge and apocalypse, with each painting becoming more and more abstract. Certain passages, however, remain legible, especially when seen in light of the earlier works, such as a boat with three oars at the

LEARN MORE Gain insight from a primary source document about Wassily Kandinsky at **www.myartslab.com**

bottom left which is, for Kandinsky, an emblem for the deluge. But above all, the painting remains a virtually nonobjective orchestration of line and color.

A Diversity of Sound: Schoenberg's New Atonal Music versus Puccini's Lyricism

On January 2, 1911, Kandinsky and Marc heard the music of Arnold Schoenberg [SHERN-berkh] (1874–1951) at a concert in Munich. Schoenberg was from Vienna, where he led a group of composers, including Alban Berg and Anton Webern, who believed that the long reign of tonality, the harmonic basis of Western music, was over. Marc later wrote to a friend, "Can you imagine a music in which tonality is completely suspended? I was constantly reminded of Kandinsky . . . . Schoenberg seems, like [ourselves], to be convinced of the irresistible dissolution of the European laws of art and harmony."

Schoenberg did in fact abandon **tonality**, the organization of the composition around a home key (the tonal center). In its place, he created a music of complete **atonality**, a term he hated (since it implied the absence of musical tone altogether), preferring instead "pantonal." His 1912 setting for a cycle of 21 poems by Albert Giraud, *Pierrot lunaire* [pee-yair-OH lune-AIR], is probably the first atonal composition to be widely appreciated, though to many it repre-

sented, as one critic put it, "the last word in cacophony and musical anarchy" (track **34.2**). Pierrot is a character from the Italian commedia dell'arte [kom-MAY-dee-ah dell-AR-tay], the improvisational traveling street theater that first developed in the fifteenth century. He is a moonstruck clown whose mask conceals his deep melancholy, brought on by living in a state of perpetually unrequited desire. (Picasso often portrayed himself as Pierrot, especially early in his career.) In *Pierrot lunaire*, five performers play eight instruments in various combinations in accompaniment to a voice that does not sing but instead employs a technique that Schoenberg calls *Sprechstimme* [SHPREK-shtim-muh] or "speech-song." "A singing voice," Schoenberg explained, "maintains the pitch without modification; speech-song does, certainly, announce it [the pitch], only to quit it again immediately, in either a downward or an upward direction." In the *Madonna* section of *Pierrot lunaire*, which addresses Mary at the moment of the pietà, when she mourns over the dead body of her son, the lyrics focus on the blood of Christ's wounds, which "seem like eyes, red and open." The atonality of Schoenberg's music reflects this anguish with explosive force.

Creating long works without the resources of tonality was a very real challenge to Schoenberg—hence the usefulness of 21 short works in the *Pierrot lunaire* series. By 1924, Schoenberg had introduced a system in which none of the 12 tones of the chromatic scale could be repeated by a given instrument until each of the other 11 had been played— they could, however, be repeated in counterpoint by another instrument. This **12-tone system** reflected his belief that every tone was equal to every other. The 12 notes in their given order are called a **tone row**, and audiences soon grew

accustomed to not hearing a tonal center in the progression and variation of the tone row as it developed in Schoenberg's increasingly **serial composition**. The principal tone row can be played upside down, backward, or upside down and backward. While the possibilities for writing an extended composition with a single tone row and its variations might at first seem limited, by adding rhythmic and dynamic variations, as well as contrapuntal arrangements, the development of large-scale works became feasible.

The radical nature of Schoenberg's composition can best be understood by comparing it to its opposite, the emotional lyricism of the Italian opera composer Giacomo Puccini (1858–1924). So Romantic is Puccini's music, and so Realist are his librettos, that in many ways, he is closer to Romantic and Realist writers and painters of the nineteenth century than to those of the twentieth. His first two great operas, *Manon Lescaut* and *La Bohème*, both love stories set in France, date from the last decade of the nineteenth century, 1893 and 1896 respectively, but the rest of his output dates from the twentieth century. *Tosca* (1900) is a passionate love story that ends in murder and suicide. *Madama Butterfly* (1904) describes the betrayal of a Japanese geisha by an American sailor, and her eventual suicide. *The Girl of the Golden West* (1910) is set in the American "Wild West" and features saloons, gunfights, and a manhunt. Puccini looked to Beijing, China, for the story of *Turandot*, an opera that is based on a Chinese folk tale. The opera was not quite finished when Puccini died in 1924, and the last two scenes were completed by a colleague for its premiere in 1926. These operas and their continued popularity demonstrate the enduring power of tradition over both composers and listeners throughout the twentieth century and down to the present day.

Two arias, *Un bel dì* ("One Fine Day") from *Madama Butterfly* and *Nessun dorma* ("Let No One Sleep") from *Turandot*, embody Puccini's extraordinary
melodic gifts (tracks **34.3** and **34.4**). *Madama Butterfly* tells the story of an American sailor, Lieutelnant Benjamin Franklin Pinkerton, who has rented a house in Japan for 999 years. As part of the deal, he is also given a bride, Cio-Cio-San ("Butterfly"). Pinkerton does not take the marriage seriously and soon returns to America, promising to return. Cio-Cio-San gives birth to a son and fully expects the boy's father to return to them. Pinkerton has no such plan and marries an American woman. When he returns to Japan with his wife three years later, the devastated Cio-Cio-San kills herself. Cio-Cio-San sings *Un bel dì* ("One Fine Day") near the beginning of Act II, after Pinkerton has left for America, as she tries to convince herself that her husband will one day return.

The aria *Nessun dorma* ("Let No One Sleep") occurs in the last act of *Turandot*. Turandot is a beautiful princess whose hatred of men has led her to declare that any suitor who does not correctly answer three riddles that she poses must die. Calàf, a prince from Tartary, is smitten by Turandot's beauty, and surprises her by answering each riddle correctly. Turandot is horrified, but Calàf offers her an out: If she can discover his name by dawn, he will forfeit his life. She immediately orders that no one shall sleep until Calàf's identity is discovered, and in *Nessun dorma*, Calàf's aria, he expresses his certainty that no one will discover his name.

The music of both Schoenberg and Puccini shares an emotionally charged expressivity, but there could be no greater contrast to Schoenberg's *Sprechstimme* than Puccini's lyricism. "Without melody," Puccini said, "there can be no music." If Schoenberg agreed, he differed in believing that melody could exist exclusive of harmony.

EARLY-TWENTIETH-CENTURY LITERATURE

If one word could express the literature of the early twentieth century, it would be *innovation*. Like visual artists and composers, writers too were drawn to uncharted ground and experimented with creating new forms in an effort to embrace the multiplicity of human experience. Like Picasso in his *Demoiselles d'Avignon*, they sought a way to capture the simultaneous and often contradictory onslaught of information and feelings that characterized the fabric of modern life. And writers understood that these multiple impulses from the real world struck the brain randomly, inharmoniously, in rhythms and sounds as discordant as the music of Stravinsky and Schoenberg.

Guillaume Apollinaire and Cubist Poetics

Picasso's good friend and a champion of his art, Guillaume Apollinaire [ah-pol-ee-NAIR] (1880–1918), was one of the leaders in the "revolution of the word," as this new approach to poetry and prose has been called. Modeling his work on the example of Picasso, Apollinaire quickly latched on to the principle of collage. In his poem "Lundi, rue Christine" [lun-DEE rue kree-STEEN] ("Monday in the rue Christine"), snatches of conversation overheard on a street in Paris, not far from the École des Beaux Arts [ay-KOHL day bohz-AR], follow one another without transition or thematic connection (**Reading 34.3**):

READING 34.3

from Guillaume Apollinaire, "Lundi, rue Christine" (1913)

Those pancakes were divine
   the water's running
Dress black as her nails
It's absolutely impossible
Here sir
The malachite ring
The ground is covered with sawdust

Then it's true
The red headed waitress eloped with a book seller.

A journalist whom I really hardly know
Look Jacques it's extremely important what I'm going
   to tell you
Shipping company combine

In this short, representative fragment from the poem, Apollinaire has transformed this collage of voices into poetry by the act of arranging each phrase into poetic lines.

He would feel free, as well, to reorganize poetic lines into visual images. In "Il Pleut" [eel pleh] ("It's Raining") (Fig. 34.16), Apollinaire deployed the following lines in loose vertical columns down the page to represent wind-blown sheets of rain (**Reading 34.4**):

READING 34.4

Guillaume Apollinaire, "Il Pleut" (1914)

It is raining women's voices as if they were dead even
   in memory
you also are raining down marvelous encounters of
   my life o little drops
and these rearing clouds are beginning to whinny a
   whole world of auricular towns
listen to it rain while regret and disdain weep an old
   fashioned music
listen to the fall of all the perpendiculars of your existence

---

Apollinaire called such visual poems **calligrammes** [kah-lee-GRAHM], a word of his own invention related to *calligraphy* and meaning, literally, "something beautifully written." The poem purposefully combines sound and sight, imaging, for instance, clouds as rearing horses neighing, "auricular towns"—that is, towns addressed to the ear, the noise of the modern urban street. As we listen to "an old fashioned music" verse/poetry, but also tradition as a whole—we also hear the "fall of all the perpendiculars" of our existence, everything generally considered "upright" both physically and morally. In Apollinaire's image of the poem, the voices of the old world literally rain down on us to give way to the new.

Ezra Pound and the Imagists

Apollinaire's strategy of juxtaposing fragments of speech heard simultaneously thereby juxtaposing two (or more) unlike words, objects, or images was, in fact, a fundamental strategy of modern art. It informs, as well, the poetry of the Imagists, a group of English and American poets who sought to create precise images in clear, sharp language. Imagism was the brainchild of American poet Ezra Pound (1885–1972), who in October 1912 submitted a group of poems under the title *Imagiste* to the new American journal *Poetry*. The poet and critic F. S. Flint would succinctly define the Imagist poem in the March 1913 issue of the magazine. Its simple rules were:

1. Direct treatment of the "thing," whether subjective or objective.
2. To use absolutely no word that does not contribute to the presentation.
3. As regarding rhythm: to compose in sequence of the musical phrase, not in sequence of the metronome.

It's Raining

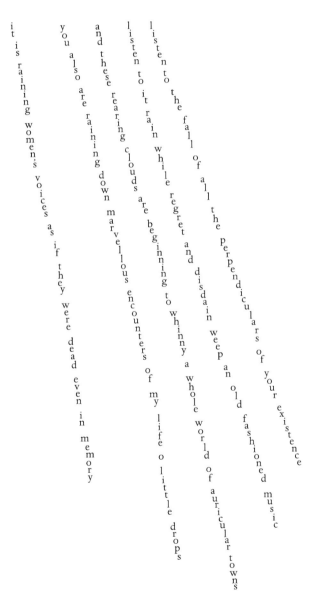

Fig. 34.16 Guillaume Apollinaire, "Il Pleut" (It's Raining). 1914.
Translated in its original form by Oliver Bernard. From *Selected Poems of Apollinaire*, trans. Oliver Bernard. (Vancouver, British Columbia: Anvil Press, 2003). Apollinaire's book *Les peintres cubistes* (*The Cubist Painters*), published in 1913, helped to define the aims of Picasso and Braque for a broader, more general audience.

Pound's "In a Station of the Metro" (**Reading 34.5**) which first appeared in *Poetry* in 1913, is in many ways the classic Imagist poem:

READING 34.5
Ezra Pound, "In a Station of the Metro" (1913)

The apparition of these faces in the crowd;
Petals on a wet, black bough.

Pound was an avid scholar of Chinese and Japanese poetry, and the poem is influenced both by the Japanese *waka* tradition, with its emphasis on the changing seasons, and formally, in its brevity at least, by the *haiku* tradition (see Chapter 11). (Haiku normally consist of 3 lines in 17 syllables, while Pound's poem is made up of 19 syllables in 2 lines.) The poem's first line seems relatively straightforward—except for the single word "apparition." It introduces Pound's predisposition, his sense that Paris is inhabited by the "living dead." It contrasts dramatically with the poem's second and final line, which is an attractive picture of nature. The first line's six-beat iambic meter—da-duh, da-duh, and so on—is transformed into a five-beat line that ends in three long strophes—that is, single beats—"wet, black bough." The semicolon at the end of the first line acts as a kind of hinge, transforming the bleak vision of the moment into a vision of possibility and hope, the implicitly "white" apparition of the faces of the ghostlike crowd transformed into an image of spring itself, the petals on the wet, black bough. The poem moves from the literal subway underground, from burial, to life, reborn in the act of the poetic vision itself. It captures that moment, as Pound said, when a thing "outward and objective" is transformed into a thing "inward and subjective."

Pound was also self-consciously working in the shadow of Walt Whitman (see Chapter 32), who, Pound believed, had opened poetry to the vast expanse and multiplicity of American culture. The poem "A Pact," also published in 1913 in *Poetry*, addresses Whitman (**Reading 34.6**):

CONTINUITY & CHANGE
"Song of Myself", **p. 1079**

READING 34.6
Ezra Pound, "A Pact" (1913)

I make truce with you, Walt Whitman—
I have detested you long enough.
I come to you as a grown child
Who has had a pig-headed father;
I am old enough now to make friends.
It was you that broke the new wood,
Now is a time for carving.
We have one sap and one root—
Let there be commerce between us.

Pound clearly recognizes in Whitman the poetic force that liberated poetry to address the world in all its multiplicity. But he feels he must whittle Whitman's voluminous work down to a more manageable size—to the single image, in fact. As it would turn out, over the course of his career, Pound would write a poem even longer than Whitman's *Leaves of Grass*, the massive *Cantos*, which would occupy him until his death (see Chapter 32). In fact, the legacy Whitman left for twentieth-century American poetry was not only the freedom to invent, but the propensity to write the long poem.

THE ORIGINS OF CINEMA

In 1894, a book called *Movement* was published in Paris. It was a treatise on human and animal locomotion written by Étienne-Jules Marey [mah-RAY] (1830–1904), a French physiologist who had long been fascinated by the possibility of breaking down the flow of movement into isolated data that could be analyzed. Marey himself had seen the series of photographs of a horse trotting published by his exact contemporary, the American photographer Eadweard Muybridge [MY-brij] (1830–1904), in the French journal *La Nature* [nah-CHOOR] in 1878 (Fig. **34.17**). Muybridge had used a trip-wire device in an experiment commissioned by California governor Leland Stanford to settle a bet about whether there were moments in the stride of a trotting or galloping horse when all four feet are off the ground. Intrigued by Muybridge's photographs, Marey began to use the camera himself, dressing models in black suits with white points and vertical stripes on the side that allowed him to study, in images created out of a rapid succession of photographs, the flow of their motion. He called them *chronophotographs*, literally "photographs of time."

Not long after Muybridge and Marey published their work, Thomas Edison (1847–1931) and W. K. Laurie Dickson (1860–1935) invented the Kinetoscope [kih-NET-oh-skope], the first continuous-film motion-picture viewing machine. After visiting with Marey in 1889, Edison had become convinced that a motion picture was possible, especially if he used celluloid film, the new invention of George Eastman (1854–1932) that came on a roll. Eastman had introduced his film in 1888 for a new camera called the Kodak. Dickson devised a sprocket wheel that would advance the regularly perforated roll of film, and Edison decided on a 35mm width (eventually the industry standard) for the film strip of their new motion-picture camera, the Kinetograph. But Edison's films were only viewable on the Kinetoscope through a peephole by one person at a time. Although viewing parlors first appeared in 1894, the commercial possibilities of film seemed limited since each of Edison's motion pictures lasted for only about 20 seconds.

The Lumière Brothers' Celluloid Film Movie Projector

The first projected motion pictures available to a large audience had their public premiere on December 28, 1895, in Paris. That night, August and Louis Lumière (1862–1954, 1864–1948) showed 10 films that lasted for about 20 minutes through their Cinématographe [see-nay-may-toh-GRAHF], a hand-cranked camera that, when connected to the equipment used for "magic lantern" shows (early "slide" shows), served as a projector as well. The program began with *Workers Leaving the Lumière Factory*, a film that conveyed, if nothing else, the large size of the Lumière brothers' operation.

Fig. 34.17 Eadweard Muybridge, *Annie G, Cantering Saddled*. December 1887. Collotype print, sheet 19″ × 24″, image 7″ × 16″. Philadelphia Museum of Art: City of Philadelphia, Trade & Convention Center, Dept. of Commerce (Commercial Museum). From photographs such as this, especially others showing the human body in motion, the science of physiology was born.

Fig. 34.18 Poster for the Cinématographe, with the Lumière brothers' film _L'Arroseur arrosé_ (_Waterer and Watered_) on screen. 1895. British Film Institute. Notable in this poster is the audience. From the beginning, cinema defined itself as family entertainment.

Two of their most famous films were not shown that night, _Arrival of a Train at La Ciotat_ [see-oh-TAH] and _Waterer and Watered_ (Fig. **34.18**). The first film depicts, in a single shot, a train arriving at a station—and the story goes that original audience members panicked as the train got closer to the camera because it seemed so real to them. The second film introduced comedy to the medium. A boy steps on a gardener's hose, stopping the flow of water; when the gardener looks at the nozzle, the boy steps off the hose, and the gardener douses himself. A brief chase ensues, with both boy and gardener leaving the frame of the stationary camera for a full two seconds.

The Nickelodeon: Movies for the Masses

By the turn of the century, the motion picture had established itself as little more than an interesting novelty. That would change when at first a few and then hundreds of entrepreneurs understood where the real audience for motion pictures was. By the turn of the century, thousands of immigrants to the United States, mostly from southern and central Europe, were living in overcrowded tenements in miserable city slums. They could not afford to pay much for entertainment, but they could afford a nickel (approximately $1 in today's money)—and so by 1905, the nickelodeon theater was born. By 1910, there were more than 10,000 nickelodeons in the United States. With names like the World's Dream Theater, they catered to the aspirations of the working class, and most often to women and children (though even before Prohibition, the movies would pull so many men out of saloons that thousands of bars around the country closed down). The nickelodeons showed a wide variety of films. Vitagraph [VIGH-tah-graf], an early producer, released a military film, a drama, a Western, a comedy, and a special feature each week. Civil

War films were popular (though not as popular as Westerns, which European audiences also adored). There were also so-called quality films: adaptations of Shakespeare, biblical epics, and the like.

Although by 1909 motion picture companies were increasingly using **intertitles**—printed text that could announce a scene change, provide lines of dialogue, or even make editorial comment—to aid in the presentation of their narratives, by and large, silent films were particularly accessible to working-class, immigrant audiences whose often rudimentary grasp of the English language was thus not a major obstacle to enjoying what remained primarily a visual medium.

D. W. Griffith and Cinematic Space

The need for a weekly supply of films to satisfy the nickelodeon audience dictated, at first, the length of films. Most were one-reelers—that is, a single film spool holding about 1,000 feet of film—and their running time was 10 to 15 minutes. But by 1914, more than 400 films of four reels or more had been produced in the United States (few survive), and audiences soon demanded longer narrative experiences.

This demand was met by D. W. Griffith (1875–1948), the foremost single-reel director of the day. In January 1915, his 13-reel epic _The Birth of a Nation_ premiered, released with its own score, to be played by a 40-piece orchestra, and with an admission price of $2, the same as for legitimate theater. A film about the Civil War and Reconstruction, its unrepentant racism, culminating in a tightly edited sequence in which a white woman tries to fend off the sexual advances of a black man as the Ku Klux Klan rides to her rescue, led the newly formed NAACP (National Association for the Advancement of Colored People) to seek to have it banned. Riots broke out in

Fig. 34.19 D. W. Griffith, battle scene from *The Birth of a Nation*. 1915. The Museum of Modern Art, Film Stills Archive. Griffith was the son of a Confederate colonel, which sheds light on his racism.

Boston and Philadelphia, while Chicago, Denver, Pittsburgh, St. Louis, Minneapolis, and eight states denied its release. Nevertheless, its box office receipts were among the largest in film history (partly due to its large admission fee), grossing nearly $18 million by the late 1920s, when the advent of talking films made it more or less obsolete. If nothing else, *The Birth of a Nation* demonstrated the viability of what came to be called the feature film, a film of multiple reels that ran for at least 40 minutes; they were "featured" with prominent billing and shown after several shorts, including newsreels and animated cartoons.

An even more important aspect of *The Birth of a Nation* was the large repertoire of camera shots that Griffith used to create visual variety in a film of such length. A *shot* is a continuous strip of motion picture film that portrays a subject and runs for an uninterrupted period of time. As the contemporary American film critic Roger Ebert has put it, "Griffith assembled and perfected the early discoveries of film language, and his cinematic techniques have influenced the visual strategies of virtually every film made since; they have become so familiar we are not even aware of them." Griffith's film techniques created a new sense of space, what might be called "cinematic space," as he combined his shots in innovative ways. His repertoire included the *full shot*, showing the actor from head to toe; the *medium shot*, from the waist up; the *close-up* of the head and shoulders; and the *extreme close-up* of a portion of the face. The *pan* is a name given to the panoramic vista in which the camera moves across the scene from one side to the other. Griffith also invented the *traveling shot*, in which the camera moves from back to front or from front to back. Related to the traveling shot is the *long shot*, a shot that takes in a wide expanse and many characters at once, as in the rather remarkable battle scene (Fig. **34.19**). Figure 34.19 is also an example of an *iris shot*, which involves the frame slowly opening in a widening circle as a scene begins, or slowly blacking out in a shrinking circle to end a scene.

Griffith arranged all of these shots by editing them in innovative ways as well. He incorporated intertitles in ways that interfered minimally with narrative action. The *flashback*, in which the film cuts to narrative episodes that are supposed to have taken place before the start of the film, is now standard in film practice, but it was entirely original when Griffith first used it. And he was a master at *cross-cutting*, in which the film moves back and forth between two separate events in ever shorter sequences, the rhythm of the shots eventually becoming furiously paced. The alternating sequence at the end of *The Birth of a Nation*, of an endangered maiden and the Ku Klux Klan riding to her rescue, is a classic example. The technique would become a staple of cinematic chase scenes.

It is almost impossible to imagine what it must have been like for early audiences to see, for the first time, a film jump from, say, a full shot of a couple embracing to an extreme close-up of their lips kissing. But audiences rapidly learned Griffith's skillful cinematic language. Here, they must have recognized, was a medium for the new age—a dynamic, moving medium, embodying the change and speed of the times.

The Prospect of War

In his collages of 1912 and 1913, Picasso brought not only the "real" world into the space of the canvas, but also an edge of dread and foreboding. The subject of his still life, *Bottle of Suze* (Fig. **34.20**), is a tabletop at some Parisian café on which stand a bottle of aperitif, a glass, and newspaper. But what would appear to be a metaphor for a comfortable autumn morning, the good life in Paris, is not. The war in the Balkans, which everyone feared would erupt into a larger, pan-European conflict (as indeed it did), is the real theme of this collage. Suze is a Balkan aperitif. Injecting a serious note into the pleasantries of café culture, the upside-down newspaper reports a cholera epidemic at the front. It begins:

Before long I saw the first corpse still grimacing with suffering and whose face was nearly black. Then I saw two, four, ten, twenty; then I saw a hundred corpses. They were stretched out there where they had fallen during the march of the left convoy, in the ditches or across the road, and the files of cars loaded with the almost dead everywhere stretched themselves out on the devastated route.

To the left of the bottle is another article, right side up, reporting on a mass socialist/pacifist/anarchist meeting attended by an estimated 50,000 citizens. The third speaker to address the crowd is represented only by his opening words: "In the presence of the menace of a general [Euro]pean war . . ." Here Picasso's scissors have terminated the report.

The prospect of a general war was real enough. Raymond Poincaré (1860–1934), who became France's premier and foreign minister in 1912, quickly began to ready for a war with Germany, which, he predicted, would be "short but glorious." As is so often the case, the war, which would officially begin on August 4, 1914, was far worse than expected. Within a month, the first major fight, the battle of the Marne, was underway, resulting in a half million casualties on each side. By the time the war was over, in November 1918, it had cost Germany 3.5 million men. The Allies—England and America had joined forces with France—had lost over 5 million.

The day after the British entered the war, the novelist Henry James wrote a friend:

The plunge of civilization into this abyss of blood and darkness . . . is a thing that gives away the whole long age during which we have supposed the world to be, with whatever abatement, gradually bettering, that to have to take it all now for what the treacherous years were all the while really making for and meaning is too tragic for words.

The myth of progress had ground to a halt. The technological advances that had driven the era of invention now seemed only preparation for wholesale human slaughter. The airplane, which had seemed so promising a machine, flying heavenward, was now an agent of death. The world had turned upside down. ∎

Fig. 34.20 Pablo Picasso, *Glass and Bottle of Suze (Le Bouteille de Suze)*. 1912. Pasted papers, gouache, and charcoal on paper. 25 $\frac{2}{5}$" × 19 $\frac{2}{3}$" (64.5 × 50 cm). Mildred Lane Kemper Art Museum, Washington University in St. Louis. University purchase, Kende Sale Fund, 1946. © Succession Picasso/DACS 1998. © 2008 Estate of Pablo Picasso/Artists Rights Society (ARS), New York.

What are Cubism, Fauvism, and Futurism?

The new century was marked by technological innovation epitomized by the automobile (and its speed), the motion picture, the airplane, and, perhaps most of all, by new discoveries in physics, to quantum mechanics, the theory of complementarity, and the theory of relativity. The focal point of artistic innovation was Pablo Picasso's studio in Paris. There, in paintings like the large canvas *Les Demoiselles d'Avignon*, he transformed painting. In what ways is *Les Demoiselles* a radical departure from then-contemporary art? Picasso's project was quickly taken up by Georges Braque, and the two worked together to create the style that came to be known as Cubism. What are the primary features of Cubism? How would you describe collage as a technique? Henri Matisse meanwhile helped to create the Fauve movement. What is Fauvism's chief concern? How would you compare the paintings of Matisse and Picasso? The Futurists, led by Filippo Marinetti, would introduce the idea of speed and motion into painting. How is their work an attack on traditional values? In music and dance, composer Igor Stravinsky and the Ballets Russes of impresario Sergei Diaghilev would shock Paris with the performance of *Le Sacre du printemps* in May 1913. How would you describe Stravinsky's music and Diaghilev's dance?

What is German Expressionism?

German Expressionism combined the Fauves' exploration of color with the primitivism of Nijinsky's choreography in an art that centered on the psychological makeup of its creators. The two chief groups in painting were Die Brücke and Der Blaue Reiter. What are the primary characteristics of each? How do Wassily Kandinsky's theories about color inform the paintings of the Blaue Reiter group? In music, the Viennese composer Arnold Schoenberg, who exhibited his own self-portrait paintings with the Der Blaue Reiter, dispensed with traditional tonality, the harmonic basis of Western music,

and created new atonal works. What is the 12-tone system that he used? What is *Sprechstimme*, and how did he use it? Nothing could be further from the lyrical compositions of his near-contemporary, Giacomo Puccini, whose operas—and a number of arias in particular—are nearly without parallel for the beauty of their melodies. Despite their differences, what beliefs do both Schoenberg and Puccini share?

What innovations distinguish the literary world in the early years of the twentieth century?

Like the visual arts and music, a spirit of innovation dominated the literary scene as well. The French poet Guillaume Apollinaire experimented with poetic forms. What characterizes his *calligrammes*? What techniques does he share with his friend Picasso? Ezra Pound and the Imagists sought to capture the moment, in the most economic terms, when the "outward and objective" turns "inward and subjective." What was Walt Whitman's influence on Pound?

What are the origins of cinema?

The invention of cinema is anticipated in the photographic work of Étienne-Jules Marey and Eadweard Muybridge. What was the primary focus of their work? The Kinetoscope, the first continuous-film motion-picture viewing machine, was invented by Thomas Edison and W. K. Laurie Dickson. It used celluloid film on a roll introduced by George Eastman in 1888 for the new Kodak camera. The first projected motion pictures available to a large audience had their public premiere on December 28, 1895, in Paris when August and Louis Lumière showed 10 films that lasted for about 20 minutes. When entrepreneurs realized the potential market of the thousands of immigrants who had arrived from southern and central Europe, the nickelodeon was born. In January 1915, D. W. Griffith introduced his 13-reel epic, *The Birth of a Nation*. What possibilities for cinema did this film propose? What visual vocabulary did it introduce?

PRACTICE MORE Get flashcards for images and terms and review chapter material with quizzes at **www.myartslab.com**

GLOSSARY

atonality The absence of a home key (tonal center).

calligrammes Literally, "something beautifully written," this term was invented by the poet Guillaume Apollinaire to describe his visual poems that purposefully conflate sound and vision.

collage The technique of pasting cut-out or found elements into the work of art.

Cubism An art style developed by Pablo Picasso and Georges Braque noted for the geometry of its forms, its fragmentation of the object, and its increasing abstraction.

Fauvism A style in art known for its bold application of arbitrary color.

intertitle Text inserted between scenes in a film to announce a change of location, provide dialogue lines, or make editorial comment.

ostinato The repetition of the same rhythmic pulse with the same or different notes.

papiers-collés Literally "pasted paper," the technique that is the immediate predecessor of collage in Cubism.

polyrhythm A musical technique in which different elements of an ensemble might play different meters simultaneously.

polytonal Occurs when two or more keys are sounded by different instruments at the same time.

serial composition Extending the potential of the prime tone row by inversion (playing it upside down so that a rise of a major third in the prime row becomes the fall of a major third in its inversion); the row may also be played backward (retrograde) or upside down and backward (retrograde inversion).

Sprechstimme Literally "speaking tone," a technique between speech and song, in which a text is enunciated in approximated pitches.

tonality The organization of a composition around a home key (the tonal center).

tone row The 12 chromatic notes in their chosen order in a musical composition.

12-tone system In its most basic form, a system developed by the composer Arnold Schoenberg in which none of the 12 tones of the chromatic scale could be repeated in a composition until each of the other 11 had been played.

READINGS

READING 34.2

from Filippo Marinetti, *Founding and Manifesto of Futurism* (1909)

Filippo Marinetti published the Founding and Manifesto of Futurism *on the front page of the Paris newspaper* Le Figaro *on February 20, 1909. The manifesto is a form of attack particularly suited to bombast and bravura, provocation and propaganda. Marinetti's first Futurist manifesto—many more would follow—is all of these. He thought of himself as "the caffeine of Europe," dedicated to keeping conservative culture awake all night with worry. He was also, as this excerpt from the document makes clear, something of an anarchist, desirous of overthrowing all traditions.*

We had stayed up all night, my friends and I, under hanging mosque lamps with domes of filigreed brass, domes starred like our spirits, shining like them with the prisoned radiance of electric hearts. For hours we had trampled our atavistic ennui into rich oriental rugs, arguing up to the last confines of logic and blackening many reams of paper with our frenzied scribbling . . . . Suddenly we jumped, hearing the mighty noise of the huge double-decker trams that rumbled by outside, ablaze with colored lights . . . . Under the windows we suddenly heard the famished roar of automobiles. "Let's go!" I said. "Friends, away! Mythology and the Mystic Ideal are defeated at last . . . . We went up to the three snorting beasts, to lay amorous hands on their torrid breasts. I stretched out on my car like a corpse on its bier, but revived at once under the steering wheel, a guillotine blade that threatened my stomach. The raging broom of madness swept us out of ourselves and drove us through streets as rough and deep as the beds of torrents. Here and there, sick lamplight through the window glass taught us to distrust the deceitful mathematics of our perishing eyes . . . . And on we raced . . . . Death, domesticated, met me at every turn, gracefully holding out a paw, or once in a while hunkering down, making velvety caressing eyes at me from every puddle. "Let's give ourselves utterly to the Unknown, not in desperation but only to replenish the deep wells of the Absurd!!" The words were scarcely out of my mouth when I spun my car around with the frenzy of a dog trying to bite its tail, and there, suddenly, were two cyclists coming toward me, shaking their fists . . . . I stopped short and to my disgust rolled over into a ditch with my wheels in the air . . . . Oh! Maternal ditch, almost full of muddy water! Fair factory drain! I gulped down your nourishing sludge . . . . When I came up—torn, filthy, and stinking—from under the capsized car, I felt the white-hot iron of joy deliciously pass through my heart . . . . And so, faces smeared with good factory muck—plastered with metallic waste, with senseless sweat, with celestial soot—we, bruised, our arms in slings, but unafraid, declared our high intentions to all the *living* of the earth:

MANIFESTO OF FUTURISM

1. We intend to sing the love of danger, the habit of energy and fearlessness.

2. Courage, audacity, and revolt will be essential elements of our poetry . . . .

4. We say that the world's magnificence has been enriched by a new beauty; the beauty of speed. A racing car whose hood is adorned with great pipes, like serpents of explosive breath—a roaring car that seems to ride on grapeshot is more beautiful than the *Victory of Samothrace*.

. . .

8. Time and space died yesterday. We already live in the absolute, omnipresent speed.

9. We will glorify war—the world's only hygiene—militarism, patriotism, the destructive gesture of freedom-bringers, beautiful ideas worth dying for, and scorn for women.

10. We will destroy the museums, libraries, academies of every kind. . . .

11. We will sing of great crowds excited by work, by pleasure, and by riot; we will sing of the multicolored, polyphonic tides of revolution in the modern capitals; we will sing of the vibrant nightly fervor of arsenals and shipyards blazing with violent electric moons; greedy railway stations that devour smoke-plumed serpents; factories hung on clouds by the crooked lines of their smoke; bridges that stride rivers like giant gymnasts, flashing in the sun with a glitter of knives . . . and the sleek flight of planes whose propellers chatter in the wind like banners and seem to cheer like an enthusiastic crowd.

READING CRITICALLY

To many readers, one of the most appalling aspects of Marinetti's manifesto is its worship of war, "the world's only hygiene." Why might that be more a rhetorical strategy than an actual position?

The Great War and Its Impact

A Lost Generation and a New Imagination

THINKING AHEAD

What were the effects of trench warfare on the European imagination?

What is Dada?

How did the arts respond to the Russian Revolution?

How does Freudian psychology manifest itself in the Surrealist art movement?

What is the stream-of-consciousness style of writing?

On June 28, 1914, a young Bosnian nationalist assassinated Archduke Francis Ferdinand, heir to the Austrian throne, in the Bosnian capital of Sarajevo. Europe was outraged, except for Serbia, which had been at war with Bosnia for years. Austria suspected that Serbian officials were involved (as in fact they were). With Germany's support, Austria declared war on Serbia, Russia mobilized in Serbia's defense, and France mobilized to support its ally, Russia. Germany invaded Luxembourg and Belgium, and then pushed into France. Finally, on August 4, Britain declared war on Germany, and Europe was consumed in battle.

Though the Germans advanced perilously close to Paris in the first month of the war, the combined forces of the British and French stopped them. From then on, along the Western Front on the French/Belgian border, both sides dug in behind zigzagging rows of trenches protected by barbed wire that stretched from the English Channel to Switzerland (Map **35.1**), some 25,000 miles of them. In the three years after its establishment, the Western Front moved only a few miles either east or west.

Stagnation accompanied the carnage. Assaults in which thousands of lives were lost would advance the lines only a couple of hundred yards. Poison mustard gas was introduced

Map 35.1 The Western Front, 1914–18. The stars represent the sites of major battles.

in the hope that it might resolve the stalemate, but it changed nothing, except to permanently maim and kill thousands upon thousands of soldiers. Mustard gas blinded those who encountered it, but it also slowly rotted the body from within and without, causing severe blistering and damaging the

◄ **Fig. 35.1 Ernst Ludwig Kirchner, *Self-Portrait as a Soldier*. 1915.** Oil on canvas, 27 ¼" × 24". The Allen Memorial Art Museum, Oberlin College, Oberlin, OH. Charles F. Olney Fund, 1950. 1950.29. This painting contrasts dramatically with his self-confident *Self-Portrait with Model* (Fig. 34.12), painted before the war.

HEAR MORE Listen to an audio file of your chapter at **www.myartslab.com**

bronchial tubes, so that its victims slowly choked to death. Most affected by the gas died within four to five weeks. British troops rotated trench duty. After a week behind the lines, a unit would move up, at night, to the front-line trench, then after a week there, back to a support trench, then after another week back to the reserve trench, and then, finally, back to a week of rest again. Attacks generally came at dawn, so it was at night, under the cover of darkness, that most of the work in the trenches was done—wiring, digging, moving ammunition. It rained often, so the trenches were often filled with water. The troops were plagued by lice, and huge rats, which fed on cadavers and dead horses, roamed through the encampments. The stench was almost as unbearable as the weather, and lingering pockets of gas might blow through at any time. As Germany tried to push both east and west (Map **35.2**), the human cost was staggering.

By the war's end, casualties totaled around 10 million dead—it became impossible to count accurately—and somewhere around twice that many wounded. Among the dead and maimed were some of the artists and writers discussed in the last chapter: Auguste Macke, Franz Marc, and Umberto Boccioni died; Braque was severely wounded and Apollinaire suffered a serious head wound in 1916. Ernst Ludwig Kirchner served as a driver in the artillery, and the experience overwhelmed him. In 1915, he was declared unfit for service. While recuperating in eastern Germany, he painted himself in the uniform of the Mansfelder Field Artillery Regiment Nr. 75 (Fig. **35.1**), cigarette dangling from his mouth, his eyes flat and empty, his right hand a bloody stump. He was not literally wounded, but the painting is a metaphorical expression of his fears—his sense of both creative and sexual impotence in the aftermath of war. Three years later, John Singer Sargent painted *Gassed* (Fig. **35.2**) after witnessing soldiers maimed by a mustard gas attack. The nobility and heroism of the Hellenic *Dying Gaul* (see Fig. 5.23) has been replaced by the kind of brutal realism we saw earlier in the foreground of Antoine Jean Gros's celebration of Napoleon's victory in *Napoleon at Eylau* (see Fig. 26.30).

CONTINUITY & CHANGE

Dying Gaul, p. 162

This chapter explores the effect of the war on the Western imagination. After 1918, Western art and literature seemed fundamentally different from art before the war. For one thing, the spirit of optimism that marked the era of invention and innovation in the years before 1914 had evaporated. In its place, the art and literature of the period reflect an increasing sense of the absurdity of modern life, the fragmentation of experience, and the futility of even daring to hope. The war created such a sense of alienation that Gertrude Stein would say of those who had gone to war and survived, "You are all a lost generation"—aimless and virtually uncivilized. The term stuck.

Nevertheless, in Russia, the war years brought a sense of possibility, as revolution overturned centuries of imperial domination by the tsars and the Russian nobility. There, experimentation with new means of expression, including film, flourished. And in fact, the spirit of experimentation

Map 35.2 World War I, 1914–1918.

Fig. 35.2 John Singer Sargent (1856–1925), *Gassed,* an Oil Study. 1918–19. Oil on canvas, 7 ½′ × 20′. Private Collection. Imperial War Museum, Negative Number Q1460. In 1918, Sargent (see Fig. 32.20) was commissioned to paint a large canvas commemorating British/American cooperation in the war. He went to France, where he saw this scene of troops blinded by mustard gas being evacuated from the field as others lay waiting to be led away.

that marked the years before the war carried on afterward unabated, but tempered now with a sense of crisis, doubt, and despair. But perhaps it was the war's nightmare aspect that most profoundly affected the arts after 1918. Psychoanalysis and therapy, used to treat shell-shocked troops (what today we call post-traumatic stress syndrome), provided insights into the workings of the human mind, and artists and writers soon explored these insights in their work.

TRENCH WARFARE AND THE LITERARY IMAGINATION

At the outset of the war, writers responded to the conflict with buoyant enthusiasm, along with thousands of others, their patriotic duty calling them to arms. Theirs was, after all, a generation raised on heroic poetry of the likes of Alfred, Lord Tennyson [TEN-ih-sen] (1809–1892), whose "Charge of the Light Brigade" celebrates the suicidal charge of the British cavalry at the Battle of Balaclava (Ukraine) in the Crimean War, fought in the last century (see *Continuity & Change,* Chapter 28) (**Reading 35.1**):

READING 35.1

from Alfred, Lord Tennyson, "Charge of the Light Brigade" (1854)

Cannon to right of them,
Cannon to left of them,
Cannon behind them
Volley'd and thunder'd;
Storm'd at with shot and shell,

While horse & hero fell,
They that had fought so well
Came thro' the jaws of Death,
Back from the mouth of Hell,
All that was left of them,
Left of six hundred.

When can their glory fade?
O the wild charge they made!
All the world wonder'd.
Honour the charge they made!
Honour the Light Brigade,
Noble six hundred!

Life in the trenches soon brought the meaninglessness of such rhetoric crashing down around this new generation of soldiers. Words like *glory* and *honor* suddenly rang hollow. The tradition of viewing warfare as a venue in which heroes exhibit what the Greeks called *areté,* or virtue (see Chapter 4)—that is, an arena in which men might realize their full human potential—no longer seemed applicable to experience, and a new kind of writing about war, an antiwar literature far removed from the heroic battle scenes of poems like Homer's *Iliad,* soon appeared.

The American novelist Ernest Hemingway served as a Red Cross ambulance driver on the Italian Front, and on his first day on duty was required to pick up the remains, mostly those of female workers, who were blown to pieces when the ammunition factory at which they worked was blown up. He was himself later wounded by mortar fragments and machine-gun fire while delivering supplies to the troops. German soldiers like novelist Erich Maria Remarque shared similar stories. The titles alone of the poems that came out of the war speak volumes: "Suicide in Trenches" by Siegfried Sassoon; "Dead Man's Dump" by

Isaac Rosenberg, who was killed on the Western Front in 1918; or "Disabled," a poem about a former athlete, with both legs and one arm gone, by Wilfred Owen.

Wilfred Owen: "The Pity of War"

In fact, the poetry of 25-year-old Wilfred Owen (1893–1918), killed in combat just a week before the armistice was signed in 1918, caused a sensation when it first appeared in 1920. "My subject is War, and the pity of War," he wrote in a manuscript intended to preface his poems, "and the Poetry is in the pity." The poems drew immediate attention for Owen's horrifying descriptions of the war's victims, as in "Dulce et Decorum Est," its title drawn from Ode 13 of the Roman poet Horace (see Chapter 6), "It is sweet and fitting to die for one's country." But Owen's reference to Horace is bitterly ironic (**Reading 35.2**):

CONTINUITY & CHANGE
Ode 13, p. 211

READING 35.2

Wilfred Owen, "Dulce et Decorum Est" (1918)

Bent double, like old beggars under sacks,
Knock-kneed, coughing like hags, we cursed through
  sludge,
Till on the haunting flares we turned our backs
And towards our distant rest began to trudge.
Men marched asleep. Many had lost their boots
But limped on, blood-shod. All went lame; all blind;
Drunk with fatigue; deaf even to the hoots
Of disappointed shells that dropped behind.

GAS! Gas! Quick, boys!—An ecstasy of fumbling,
Fitting the clumsy helmets just in time;
But someone still was yelling out and stumbling
And floundering like a man in fire or lime.—
Dim, through the misty panes and thick green light
As under a green sea, I saw him drowning.

In all my dreams, before my helpless sight,
He plunges at me, guttering, choking, drowning.

If in some smothering dreams you too could pace
Behind the wagon that we flung him in,
And watch the white eyes writhing in his face,
His hanging face, like a devil's sick of sin;
If you could hear, at every jolt, the blood
Come gargling from the froth-corrupted lungs,
Obscene as cancer, bitter as the cud
Of vile, incurable sores on innocent tongues,—
My friend, you would not tell with such high zest
To children ardent for some desperate glory,
The old Lie: Dulce et decorum est
Pro patria mori.

The quotation from Horace in the last lines is, notably, labeled by Owen a "lie." And the fact is, Owen's intent is that the reader should share his horrific dreams. His rhetorical strategy is to describe the drowning of this nameless man in a sea of green gas in such vivid terms that we cannot forget it either.

In the Trenches: Remarque's *All Quiet on the Western Front*

The horror of trench warfare is probably nowhere more thoroughly detailed than in *All Quiet on the Western Front*, a novel by Erich Maria Remarque [ruh-MARK], a German soldier who had witnessed it firsthand. Remarque had fought and been wounded by grenade fragments on the front. In the preface to the novel, he writes that his story "is neither an accusation nor a confession, and least of all an adventure, for death is not an adventure to those who stand face to face with it. It will simply try to tell of a generation of men, who, even though they may have escaped its shells, were destroyed by the war." Remarque's narrator, Paul Baumer [BOW-mur], recounts a moment when, in the midst of battle, under bombardment in a cemetery, the British launch poisonous gas in their direction (**Reading 35.3**):

READING 35.3

from Erich Maria Remarque, *All Quiet on the Western Front* (1928)

I reach for my gas-mask. . . . The dull thud of gas-shells mingles with the crashes of the high explosives. A bell sounds between the explosions, gongs, and metal clappers warning everyone—Gas—Gas—Gaas.

Someone plumps down beside me, another. I wipe the goggles of my mask clear of the moist breath. . . . These first minutes with the mask decide between life and death: is it tightly woven? I remember the awful sights in the hospital: the gas patients who in day-long suffocation cough their burnt lungs up in clots.

Cautiously, the mouth applied to the valve, I breathe. The gas creeps over the ground and sinks into all the hollows. Like a big, soft jelly-fish it floats into our shell-hole and lolls there obscenely . . . .

Inside the gas-mask my head booms and roars—it is nigh bursting. My lungs are tight. They breathe always the same hot, used-up air, the veins on my temples are swollen, I feel I am suffocating.

A grey light filters through to us. I climb out over the edge of the shell-hole. In the dirty twilight lies a leg torn clean off; the boot is quite whole, I take that all in at a glance. Now someone stands up a few yards distant. I polish the windows, in my excitement they are immediately dimmed again, I peer through them, the man there no longer wears his mask.

I wait some seconds—he has not collapsed—he looks around and makes a few paces—rattling in my throat I tear my mask off too and fall down, the air streams into me like cold water, my eyes are bursting, the wave sweeps over me and extinguishes me.

All Quiet on the Western Front sold more than a million copies in Germany the first year of its publication in 1928, and millions more read the book after it was translated into other languages and distributed outside Germany. In the United States, the film based on the novel won the Academy Award for Best Picture. The Nazi government considered the novel's antimilitarism disloyal and banned it in 1933; five years later, Remarque was stripped of his citizenship.

William Butler Yeats and the Specter of Collapse

The impact of the war unmoored the European poetic imagination from its earlier Symbolist reveries (see Chapter 33). The Symbolists favored *suggesting* the presence of meaning in order to express the inexpressible, and turned away from the physical world to explore the realm of imaginative experience. In his youth, the Irish poet William Butler Yeats [yates] (1865–1939) had longed to escape to an imaginary landscape that he dubbed the Lake Isle of Innisfree (**Reading 35.4**).

READING 35.4

William Butler Yeats, "The Lake Isle of Innisfree" (1893)

I will arise and go now, and go to Innisfree,
And a small cabin build there, of clay and wattles made:
Nine bean-rows will I have there, a hive for the honey-bee,
And live alone in the bee-loud glade.

And I shall have some peace there, for peace comes
   dropping slow,
Dropping from the veils of the morning to where the
   cricket sings;
There midnight's all a glimmer, and noon a purple glow,
And evening full of the linnet's wings.

And I will arise and go now, for always night and day
I hear the lake water lapping with low sounds by the shore;
While I stand on the roadway, or on the pavements gray,
I hear it in the deep heart's core.

Innisfree is the symbolic home of the poet's spirit, the source of his poetic inspiration, and although in the next-to-last line he acknowledges his physical presence in the everyday world, Innisfree remains for Yeats, as the memory of Tintern Abbey remains for Wordsworth a century earlier (see Reading 27.2), an imaginative reality in which he is literally attuned to the music and rhythms of nature.

But now, writing in 1919, Yeats imagines a much darker world. Apocalypse—if not the literal Second Coming of Christ predicted in the Bible's Book of Revelation, then its metaphorical equivalent—seemed at hand (**Reading 35.5**):

READING 35.5

William Butler Yeats, "The Second Coming" (1919)

Turning and turning in the widening gyre
The falcon cannot hear the falconer;
Things fall apart; the centre cannot hold;
Mere anarchy is loosed upon the world,
The blood-dimmed tide is loosed, and everywhere
The ceremony of innocence is drowned;
The best lack all conviction, while the worst
Are full of passionate intensity.

Surely some revelation is at hand;
Surely the Second Coming is at hand.
The Second Coming! Hardly are those words out
When a vast image out of Spiritus Mundi
Troubles my sight; somewhere in sands of the desert
A shape with lion body and the head of a man,
A gaze blank and pitiless as the sun,
Is moving its slow thighs, while all about it
Reel shadows of indignant desert birds.
The darkness drops again; but now I know
That twenty centuries of stony sleep
Were vexed to nightmare by a rocking cradle,
And what rough beast, its hour come round at last,
Slouches towards Bethlehem to be born?

The poem's opening image, of the falcon circling higher and higher in wider and wider circles, is a metaphor for history itself spinning further and further from its origin until it is out of control. In another poem written at about the same time, "A Prayer for My Daughter," Yeats had asked, "How but in custom and ceremony / Are innocence and beauty born?" Now, he despairs, custom and ceremony, those things that connect us to our origins, have been abandoned and "mere anarchy is loosed upon the world." In their place, a beast resembling the Sphinx at Giza (see Fig. 3.7) rises in the desert, possibly an image of the anti-Christ, the embodiment of Satan who in some biblical traditions anticipates the second coming of Christ himself. This beast is the new Spiritus Mundi [SPIR-ih-toos MOON-dee], or collective spirit of mankind, the specter of life in the new postwar era, insentient, pitiless, and nightmarish.

T. S. Eliot: The Landscape of Desolation

The American poet T. S. (Thomas Sternes) Eliot (1888–1965) was studying at Oxford University in England when World War I broke out. Eliot had graduated from Harvard with a degree in philosophy and the classics, and his poetry reflects both the erudition of a scholar and the depression of a classicist who feels that the tradition he so values is in jeopardy of being lost. In Eliot's poem *The Waste Land*, the opening section, called "The Burial of the Dead," is a direct reference to the Anglican burial service, performed so often during and after the war. "April is the cruelest month," the poem famously begins (**Reading 35.6a**).

READING 35.6a

from T. S. Eliot, *The Waste Land* (1921)

April is the cruelest month, breeding
Lilacs out of the dead land, mixing
Memory and desire, stirring
Dull roots with spring rain.
Winter kept us warm, covering
Earth in forgetful snow, feeding
A little life with dried tubers.

The world, in short, has been turned upside down. Spring is cruel, winter consoling. Eliot sees London as an "Unreal City" populated by the living-dead:

Unreal City,
Under the brown fog of a winter dawn,
A crowd flowed over London Bridge, so many,
I had not thought death had undone so many.
Sighs, short and infrequent, were exhaled,
And each man fixed his eyes before his feet.
Flowed up the hill and down King William Street,
To where Saint Mary Woolnoth kept the hours
With a dead sound on the final stroke of nine.

In the crucial middle section of the poem, Eliot describes modern love as reduced to mechanomorphic tedium (see **Reading 35.6**, page 1169). And in the poem's last section, "What the Thunder Said," the poet describes a landscape of complete emotional and physical aridity, a land where there is "no water but only rock," "sterile thunder without rain," and "red sullen faces sneer and snarl / From doors of mudcracked houses." At first Eliot dreams of the possibility of rain:

If there were rock
And also water
And water
A spring
A pool among the rock
If there were the sound of water only
Not the cicada
And dry grass singing
But sound of water over a rock
Where the hermit-thrush sings in the pine trees
Drip drop drip drop drop drop drop
But there is no water.

Finally, as the poem nears conclusion, there is "a flash of lightning. Then a dry gust / Bringing rain." What this signifies is difficult to say—hope certainly, but hope built on what premise? The poem is richly allusive—the passages excerpted here are among its most accessible—and the answer seems to reside in the weight of poetic and mythic tradition to which it refers, from Shakespeare to the myth of the Holy Grail and Arthurian legend, what Eliot calls at the poem's end, the "fragments I have shored against my ruin." Eliot resolves, apparently, as the critic Edmund Wilson put it, "to claim his tradition and rehabilitate it."

ESCAPE FROM DESPAIR: DADA IN THE CAPITALS

Some writers and artists—Picasso, for instance—simply waited out the war. Many others openly opposed it and vigorously protested the social order that had brought about what seemed to them nothing short of mass genocide, and some of these soon formed the movement that named itself *Dada*. The Romanian poet Tristan Tzara [TSAH-rah] (1896–1963) claimed it was his invention. The German Richard Huelsenbeck [HULL-sen-bek] (1892–1972) claimed that he and poet Hugo Ball (1886–1927) had discovered the name randomly by plunging a knife into a dictionary. Whatever the case, Tzara summed up its meaning best (**Reading 35.7**):

READING 35.7

Tristan Tzara, "Dada Manifesto 1918" (1918)

DADA DOES NOT MEAN ANYTHING . . . We read in the papers that the Negroes of the Kroo race call the tail of a sacred cow: dada. A cube, and a mother, in certain regions of Italy, are called: dada. The word for hobbyhorse, a children's nurse, a double affirmative in Russian and Romanian, is also: DADA.

Dada was an international signifier of negation. It did not mean anything, just as, in the face of war, life itself had come to seem meaningless. In fact, Tzara could be far more strident in the negativity of his claims for the movement. His *Monsieur Antipyrine's Manifesto* is a case in point (**Reading 35.8**):

READING 35.8

Tristan Tzara, "Monsieur Antipyrine's Manifesto" (1916)

dada is life with neither bedroom slippers nor parallels; it is against and for unity and definitely against the future; we are wise enough to know that our brains are going to become flabby cushions, that our antidogmatism is as exclusive as a civil servant, and that we cry liberty but are not free. . . . dada remains within the framework of

---

European weaknesses, it's still shit, but from now on we want to shit in different colors so as to adorn the zoo of art with all the flags of all the consulates . . . . This is Dada's balcony, I assure you. From there you can hear all the military marches, and come down cleaving the air like a seraph landing in a public bath to piss and understand the parable.

Tzara's "parable" is intentionally nonsensical. But its dissatisfaction with modern European life—its outright repugnance for its era—is palpable.

Dada came into being at the Cabaret Voltaire in Zurich, founded in February 1916 by a group of intellectuals and artists escaping the conflict in neutral Switzerland, including Tzara, Huelsenbeck, Ball, Jean Arp (1896–1966), and the poet, dancer, and singer Emmy Hennings (1885–1948). At the end of May, Ball created a "concert bruitiste" [brwee-TEEST] or "noise concert," inspired by the Futurists, for a "Grand Evening of the Voltaire Art Association." Language, Ball believed, was irrevocably debased. After all, the vocabulary of nationalism—the uncritical celebration of one's own national or ethnic identity—had led to the brutality of the War. Ball replaced language with sounds, whose rhythm and volume might convey feelings that would be understood on at least an emotional level. Dressed in an elaborate costume, so stiff that he could not walk and had to be carried onto the stage, he read (**Reading 35.9**):

READING 35.9
from Hugo Ball, "Gadji beri bimba" (1916)

gadji beri bimba
glandridi lauli lonni cadori
gadjama bim beri glassala
glandridi blassala tuffm i zimbrabim
blass galassasatuffm i zimbrabim. . . .

Soon the entire Cabaret Voltaire group was composing such sound poems, which they viewed as a weapon against convention, especially the empty rhetoric of nationalism that had led to the War. Those who believed in the War—notably Apollinaire, in Paris—accused them in turn of nihilism, anarchism, and cowardice.

In March 1917, the group opened the Galerie Dada. Arp's relief wall pieces—they were something between sculpture and painting—were among the most daring works on display (Fig. **35.3**). They were constructed "according to the laws of chance." His procedure was to draw random doodles on paper, allowing his pencil to move without any conscious intervention. He would then send these drawings to a carpenter who would cut them out in wood. The pieces were variously painted, then piled—again quite randomly—one on top of another and secured in place. Arp delighted in giving the resulting relief names, of usually two or more words with no logical connection—*Flower Hammer*, for instance.

Fig. 35.3 Hans Arp, *Fleur Manteau* (*Flower Hammer*). 1916. Painted paper, 24 ³/₈" × 19 ⁵/₈". Fondation Arp. Clamart, France. © 2008 Artists Rights Society (ARS), New York. Arp was from the sometimes German, sometimes French region of Alsace, and spoke both French and German, referring to himself sometimes as Jean (French), sometimes as Hans (German).

Such works, in their willful denial of the artist's aesthetic sensibilities, were considered by many used to thinking of art in more serious, high-minded terms as "anti-art." These more serious minds were especially offended by the so-called ready-mades of Marcel Duchamp [doo-SHAHM] (1887–1968). The term itself derived from the recent American invention, ready-made (as opposed to tailor-made) clothes, and Duchamp adopted it soon after arriving in New York in 1915, where he joined a group of other European exiles, including his close colleague Francis Picabia [peh-KAH-bee-ah] (1879–1953), in still-neutral America. He was already notorious for his *Nude Descending a Staircase* (Fig. **35.4**), which had been the focus of critical debate in February 1913 at the International Exhibition of Modern Art at the 69th Infantry Regiment Armory in New York. Known simply as the Armory Show, the exhibit displayed nearly 1,300 pieces, including

Fig. 35.5 Marcel Duchamp, *Fountain*. 1917; replica 1963. Porcelain, height 14 ″. Purchased with assistance from the Friends of the Tate Gallery 1999. Tate Gallery, London, Great Britain. © 2008 Artists Rights Society (ARS), New York. It is important to recognize that Duchamp has turned the urinal on its back, thus undermining its utility.

17 Matisses, 7 Picassos, 15 Cézannes (plus a selection of lithographs), 13 Gauguins (plus, again, a number of lithographs and prints), 18 van Goghs, 4 Manets, 5 Monets, 5 Renoirs, 2 Seurats, a Delacroix, and a Courbet. It was the first time that most Americans were able to view French modernist painting. One newspaper writer called Duchamp's *Nude* "an explosion in a shingle factory." The *American Art News* called it "a collection of saddlebags" and offered a $10 reward to anyone who could locate the nude lady it professed to portray. President Theodore Roosevelt compared it to the Navajo rug in his bathroom. Considering the European artists shown at the exhibition as a whole, he concluded that they represented the "lunatic fringe." But if Duchamp's nude seemed inexplicable to Americans in 1913, today we can easily identify several influences that shaped the work. Duchamp was familiar with Picasso and Braque's Cubist reduction of the object into flat planes (see Figs. 34.7 and 34.8). He also knew of the Futurists' ideas about depicting motion, and, perhaps more important, he was familiar with new developments in photography that captured moving figures on film, especially Étienne-Jules Marey's book *Movement* (see Chapter 34).

Thus, when Duchamp introduced his ready-mades, the New York art world was prepared to be shocked. And *Fountain* (Fig. **35.5**) shocked them indeed. A urinal purchased by Duchamp in a New York plumbing shop, laid on its back and signed with the pseudonym "R. Mutt," it was submitted by Duchamp to the New York Society of Independent Artists exhibition in April 1917. The exhibition committee, on which Duchamp served, had agreed that all work submitted would be shown, and was therefore unable

Fig. 35.4 Marcel Duchamp, *Nude Descending a Staircase, No. 2*. 1912. Oil on canvas, 58″ × 35″. Philadelphia Museum of Art, Louise and Walter Arenberg Collection. Photo: Graydon Wood, 1994. © 2008 Artists Rights Society (ARS), New York. Interestingly, when Duchamp submitted this painting to the 1912 Salon des Indépendants in Paris, the selection committee objected to its literal title and traditional subject matter.

SEE **MORE** For a Closer Look at Marcel Duchamp's *Nude Descending the Staircase, No. 2*, go to **www.myartslab.com**

Fig. 35.6 Marcel Duchamp, *Mona Lisa (L.H.O.O.Q.)*. 1919. Rectified Readymade (reproduction of Leonardo da Vinci's *Mona Lisa* altered with pencil), 7 ³/₄″ × 4 ¹/₈″. The Louis and Walter Arensberg Collection. Lynn Rosenthal, 1988/ Philadelphia Museum of Art. © 2007 Artists Rights Society (ARS), New York. The fact that this image is a postcard underscores Duchamp's sense that painting was little more than just another commodity to be bought and sold at will.

to reject the piece. To Duchamp's considerable amusement, they decided instead to hide it behind a curtain. Over the course of the exhibition, Duchamp gradually let it be known that he was "R. Mutt," and in a publication called *The Blind Man* defended the piece:

> Whether Mr Mutt with his own hands made the fountain or not has no importance. He CHOSE it. He took an ordinary article of life, placed it so that its useful significance disappeared under the new title and point of view—created a new thought for the object.

By the end of the war, it was clear to most observers that Duchamp had given up painting altogether—to play chess, he claimed. He nevertheless continued on throughout his career with a number of projects, ranging from film to installation. But his disregard for painting, which seemed to him the embodiment of bourgeois taste, is particularly manifest in his "rectified-readymade," *L.H.O.O.Q.* (Fig. **35.6**), a poster of Leonardo da Vinci's *Mona Lisa* to which he has added a mustache and goatee.

The title is a pun—pronounced in French, the letters sound like "*Elle a chaud au cul,*" (She's hot in the ass"). The pun was, in fact, one of his favorite things. It was the very embodiment of the simultaneity of opposites. Like Bohr's theory of complementarity (see Chapter 34), the pun meant to refer to mutually exclusive and contradictory things simultaneously.

Duchamp's antiestablishment sensibilities were reflected across the Dada scene. Even before the end of the war in November 1918, Huelsenbeck had attacked Expressionist painting, objecting to its subjective soul-searching. He called, instead, for "artists who every hour snatch the tatters of their bodies out of the frenzied cataract of life." Artists, he believed, could literally "snatch the tatters" of German life out of the everyday press, and they did, by snipping photographs from newspapers and recombining them as collages. His new *Club Dada* began publishing work that exploited the possibilities offered by this new technique, known as **photomontage**. In *The Art Critic* (Fig. **35.7**), Hausmann has placed a disproportionately large head, blinded in both eyes, on a brown-suited bourgeois body identified as that of his friend and Dada colleague George Grosz. The figure carries a large Venus pencil projecting phalluslike in front of him and stands before a section of a pink sound poem-poster created by Hausmann to be pasted on the walls of Berlin. Behind him is a German banknote, suggesting that his opinions are for sale. On his forehead a shoe steps on a German postage

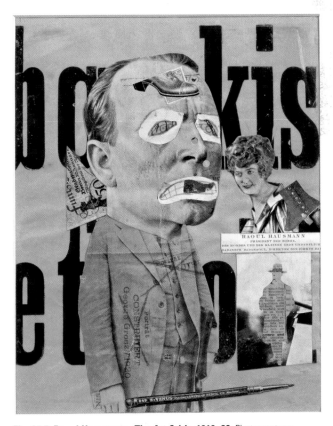

Fig. 35.7 Raoul Hausmann, *The Art Critic*. 1919–20. Photomontage, 12 ¹/₂″ × 10″. Tate Museum, London. T01918. Hausmann's business card is pasted below the woman. It identifies him as a "Dadasoph," as opposed to a "philosophe."

stamp. For all its rejection of the contemporary art world, the work's humor also reflects the survival of a positive energy in the face of devastation and despair. Like all of Dada, it offers up an arena in which the creative impulse might not only survive, but thrive.

RUSSIA: ART AND REVOLUTION

In 1914, Russia entered the war ill-prepared for the task before it; within the year, Tsar Nicholas II (1868–1918) oversaw the devastation of his army. One million men had been killed, and another million soldiers had deserted. Famine and fuel shortages gripped the nation. Strikes broke out in the cities, and in the countryside, peasants seized the land of the Russian aristocrats. The tsar was forced to abdicate in February 1917.

Vladimir Lenin and the Soviet State

Through a series of astute, and sometimes violent, political maneuvers, the Marxist revolutionary Vladimir Ilyich Lenin (1870–1924) assumed power the following November. Lenin headed the most radical of Russian postrevolutionary groups, the Bolsheviks. Like Marx, he dreamed of a "dictatorship of the proletariat," a dictatorship of the working class. Marx and Lenin believed that the oppression of the masses of working people resulted from capitalism's efforts to monopolize the raw materials and markets of the world for the benefit of the privileged few. He believed that all property should be held in common, that every member of society would work for the benefit of the whole and would receive, from the state, goods and products commensurate with their work. "He who does not work," he famously declared, "does not eat."

Lenin was a utopian idealist. He foresaw, as his socialist state developed, the gradual disappearance of the state: "The state," he wrote in *The State and Revolution* (1917), "will be able to wither away completely when society has realized the rule: 'From each according to his ability: to each according to his needs,' *i.e.*, when people have become accustomed to observe the fundamental rules of social life, and their labor is so productive that they voluntarily work *according to their ability*." But he realized that certain pragmatic changes had to occur as well. He emphasized the need to electrify the nation: "We must show the peasants," he wrote, "that the organization of industry on the basis of modern, advanced technology, on electrification . . . will make it possible to raise the level of culture in the countryside and to overcome, even in the most remote corners of land, backwardness, ignorance, poverty, disease, and barbarism." And he was, furthermore, a political pragmatist. When, in 1918, his Bolshevik party received less than a quarter of 1 percent of the vote in free elections, he dissolved the government, eliminated all other parties, and put the Communist party into the hands of five men, a committee called the Politburo, with himself at its head. He also systematically eliminated his opposition: Between 1918 and 1922, his secret police arrested and executed as many as 280,000 people in what has come to be known as the Red Terror.

The Arts of the Revolution

Before the Revolution in March 1917, avant-garde Russian artists, in direct communication with the art capitals of Europe, particularly Paris, Amsterdam, and Berlin, established their own brand of modern art. Most visited Paris, and saw Picasso and Braque's Cubism in person, but Kasimir Malevich [muh-LAY-vich] (1878–1935), perhaps the most inventive of them all, never did. By 1912, he had created Cubo-Futurism, a style that applied modernist geometric forms to Russian folk themes. But Malevich was soon engaged, he wrote, in a "desperate attempt to free art from the ballast of objectivity." To this end, he says, "I took refuge in the square," creating a completely nonobjective painting, in 1913, consisting of nothing more than a black square on a white ground. He called his new art Suprematism, defining it as "the supremacy of . . . feeling in . . . art."

Fig. 35.8 Kasimir Malevich, *Painterly Realism: Boy with Knapsack - Color Masses in the Fourth Dimension.* **1915.** Oil on canvas, 28″ × 17 ¹/₂″. Museum of Modern Art, New York. 1935 Acquisition confirmed in 1999 by agreement with the Estate of Kazimir Malevich and made possible with funds from the Mrs. John Hay Whitney Bequest (by exchange). 816.1935. Malevich always insisted that he painted not in three, but in four dimensions—that time, in other words, played a role in creating a work. Later, he claimed to work in five dimensions, the fifth being "economy," or minimal means.

Fig. 35.9 Photograph of work by Malevich in "0,10: The Last Futurist Exhibition of Painting." Petrograd, 1915. © 2006, State Russian Museum, St Petersburg. Visible here are 22 of the 38 works Malevich painted for the exhibition.

From Suprematism to Constructivism The "feeling" of which Malevich speaks is not the kind of personal or private emotion that we associate with, say, German Expressionism. Rather, it lies in what he believed was the revelation of an absolute truth—a utopian ideal not far removed from Lenin's political idealism—discovered through the most minimal means. Thus, his *Painterly Realism: Boy with Knapsack - Color Masses in the Fourth Dimension* (Fig. **35.8**) is not really a representation of a boy with a knapsack, nor is it an example of realism. The title is deeply ironic, probably intended to jolt any viewer expecting to see work like that of the Travelers (see Fig. 31.17). The painting is, rather, about the two forms—a black square and a smaller red one—that appear to float above a white ground, even, it seems, at different heights. The painting was first exhibited in December 1915 at an exhibition in Petrograd entitled "0,10: The Last Futurist Exhibition of Painting," where it can be seen in the photographic documentation of the event just above and to the left of the chair (Fig. **35.9**). The exhibition's name refers to the idea that each of the ten artists participating in the show were seeking to articulate the "zero degree"—that is, the irreducible core—of painting. What, in other words, most minimally makes a painting? In this particular piece, Malevich reveals that in relation, these apparently static forms—two squares set on a rectangle—are energized in a dynamic tension.

Malevich's installation of his works at the "0,10" exhibition is notable as well for the fact that what is probably the most "zero degree" of all his works, *Black Square*, is placed high in the corner of the room in the place usually reserved in traditional Russian houses for religious icons. The work is, in part, parodic, replacing images designed to invoke deep religious feeling with what Malevich referred to as a "void," a space empty of meaning or feeling. But, at the same time, and paradoxically, Malevich felt that it contained all feeling. As he wrote in his treatise, *The Non-Objective World* (**Reading 35.10**):

READING 35.10

from Kasimir Malevich *The Non-Objective World* (1921)

When, in the year 1913, in my desperate attempt to free art from the ballast of objectivity, I took refuge in the square form and exhibited a picture which consisted of nothing more than a black square on a white field, the critics and, along with them, the public sighed, "Everything which we loved is lost. We are in a desert . . . . Before us is nothing but a black square on a white background!" . . . But a blissful sense of liberating nonobjectivity drew me forth into the "desert," where nothing is real except feeling . . . and so feeling became the substance of my life. This was no "empty square" which I had exhibited but rather the feeling of nonobjectivity. . . . The black square on the white field was the first form in which nonobjective feeling came to be expressed. The square = feeling, the white field = the void beyond this feeling. Yet the general public saw in the nonobjectivity of the representation the demise of art and failed to grasp the evident fact that feeling had here assumed external form. The Suprematist square and the forms proceeding out of it can be likened to the primitive marks (symbols) of aboriginal man which represented, in their combination, not ornament, but a feeling of rhythm. Suprematism did not bring into being a new world of feeling but, rather, an altogether new and direct form of representation of the world of feeling.

At the end of the Russian Revolution in 1917, Malevich and other artists in his circle were appointed by the Soviet government to important administrative and teaching positions in the country. Malevich went to the Vitebsk [vih-TEPSK] Popular Art School in 1919, soon becoming its director. In 1921, he wrote to one of his pupils that Suprematism should adopt a more "Constructive" approach to reorganizing the world. By this he meant that art should turn to small-scale abstract works in three dimensions. He considered this "laboratory" work, explorations of the elements of form and color, space and construction, that would eventually serve some practical social purpose in the service of the revolution.

Malevich's thinking was inspired in part by Lazar Lissitzsky [lih-SIT-skee] (1890–1941), known as El Lissitzsky, a teacher of architecture and graphics at Vitebsk Popular Art School when Malevich arrived. For his part, El Lissitzsky quickly adopted Malevich's Suprematist designs to revolutionary ends. His poster *Beat the Whites with the Red Wedge* (Fig. 35.10) refers to the conflict between the Bolshevik "Reds" and the "White" Russians who opposed Lenin's party. As in Malevich's *Suprematist Painting*, a triangle crosses over into another form, this time a circle. The wedge is symbolically male, forceful and aggressive as opposed to the passive (and womblike) white circle, which it penetrates both literally and figuratively from the "left." Here design is in the service of social change.

The New Russian Cinema One of the greatest of Russia's revolutionary innovators was the filmmaker Sergei Eisenstein [EYE-zen-shtine] (1898–1948). After the Revolution, he had worked on the Russian agit-trains, special propaganda trains that traveled the Russian countryside bringing "agitational" materials to the peasants. ("Agitational," in this sense, means to present a political point of view.) The agit-trains distributed magazines and pamphlets, presented political speakers and plays, and, given the fact that the Russian peasantry was largely illiterate, perhaps most important of all presented films, known as *agitkas*. These films were characterized by their fast-paced editing style, designed to keep the attention of an audience that, at least at first, had never before seen a motion picture.

Out of his experience making *agitkas*, Lev Kuleshov (1899–1970), one of the founders of the Film School in Moscow in the early twenties, developed a theory of **montage**. He used a close-up of a famous Russian actor and combined it with three different images—a bowl of soup, a dead woman lying in a coffin, and a girl playing with a teddy bear. Although the image of the actor was the same in each instance, audiences believed that he was hungry with the soup, sorrowful with the woman, joyful toward the girl—a phenomenon that came to be known as the *Kuleshov effect*. Shots, Kuleshov reasoned, acquire meaning through their relation to other shots. Montage was the art of building a cinematic composition out of such shots.

Fig. 35.10 El Lissitzsky, *Beat the Whites with the Red Wedge.* 1919.
Lithograph. Collection: Stedelijk Van Abbemuseum, Eindhoven, Holland. © 2007 Artists Rights Society (ARS), New York/VG Bild-Kunst, Bonn. The diagonal design of the composition gives the red wedge a clear "upper hand" in the conflict.

Eisenstein learned much from Kuleshov, though he disagreed about the nature of montage. Rather than using montage to build a unified composition, Eisenstein believed that montage should be used to create tension, even a sense of shock, in the audience, which he believed would lead to a heightened sense of perception and a greater understanding of the film's action. His aim, in a planned series of seven films depicting events leading up to the Bolshevik revolution, was to provoke his audience into psychological identification with the aims of the revolution.

None of his films accomplishes this better than *The Battleship Potemkin* [puh-TEM-kin], the story of a 1905 mutiny aboard a Russian naval vessel and the subsequent massacre of innocent men, women, and children on the steps above Odessa harbor by tsarist troops. The film, especially the famous "Odessa Steps Sequence," which is a virtual manifesto of montage, tore at the hearts of audiences and won respect for the Soviet regime around the world (see *Closer Look*, pages 1156–1157).

FREUD, JUNG, AND THE ART OF THE UNCONSCIOUS

Eisenstein's emphasis on the viewer's psychological identification with his film was inspired in no small part by the theories of Viennese neurologist Sigmund Freud. By the start of World War I, Freud's theories about the nature of the human psyche and its subconscious functions (see *Continuity & Change*, page 1109) were gaining wide acceptance. As doctors and others began to deal with the sometimes severely traumatized survivors of the war, the efficacy of Freud's psychoanalytic techniques—especially dream analysis and "free association"—were increasingly accepted by the medical community.

Freud had opened a medical practice in Vienna in 1886, specializing in emotional disorders. Just a year earlier, he had gone to Paris to study with neurologist Jean-Martin Charcot, and in his new practice, Freud began using Charcot's techniques—the use of hypnosis, massage, and cranial pressure to help patients recognize mental conditions related to their symptoms. This would later develop into a practice he called free association, in which patients were asked to say whatever crossed their minds. In 1895, in collaboration with another Viennese physician, Josef Breuer, he published *Studies in Hysteria*. But even then he was changing his techniques. Free association allowed him to abandon hypnosis. Freud had observed that when patients spoke spontaneously about themselves, they tended to relate their particular neurotic symptoms to earlier, usually childhood, experiences.

But Freud understood that free association required interpretation, and increasingly, he began to focus on the obscure language of the unconscious. By 1897, he had formulated a theory of infantile sexuality based on the proposition that sexual drives and energy already exist in infants. Childhood was no longer "innocent." One of the

keys to understanding the imprint of early sexual feeling upon adult neurotic behavior was the interpretation of dreams. Freud was convinced that their apparently irrational content could be explained rationally and scientifically. He concluded that dreams allow unconscious wishes, desires, and drives censored by the conscious mind to exercise themselves. "The dream," he wrote in his 1900 *The Interpretation of Dreams*, "is the (disguised) fulfillment of a (suppressed, repressed) wish." And the wish, by extension, is generally based in the sexual.

Freud theorized, as a result, that most neurotic behavior was the result of sexual trauma stemming from the subconscious attachment of the child to his or her parent of the opposite sex and the child's jealousy of the parent of the same sex. (Freud called this the Oedipus [ED-ih-pus] complex, after the Greek legend in which Oedipus, king of Thebes, unwittingly kills his father and marries his mother. In girls, the complex is called the Electra complex.) Since, as he argued, human behavior was governed by the libido, or sex drive, the guilt that resulted from the repression of the trauma associated with the child's sexual feelings and jealousy leads to powerful inner tensions that manifest themselves as psychic disorders.

During the war itself, Freud continued work at the University of Vienna, speaking in 1916 on the psychological roots of sadism, homosexuality, fetishism, and voyeurism in a lecture called "The Sexual Life of Human Beings." These subjects were still largely taboo, as Freud acknowledged at the lecture's outset: "First and foremost," he began, "what is sexual is something improper, something one ought not to talk about." He then proceeded to shock his audience by talking in detail about sexual behaviors that he knew his audience found to be, in his words, "crazy, eccentric and horrible." Though his conclusions are disputable—predating later research linking homosexuality to biological rather than psychological causes, for example—Freud opened the subject of human sexuality to public discussion, altering attitudes toward sexuality permanently and irrevocably.

Freud's *Civilization and Its Discontents*

But World War I provided Freud with evidence of another, perhaps even more troubling source of human psychological dysfunction—society itself. In 1920, in *Beyond the Pleasure Principle*, he speculated that human beings had death drives (Thanatos) that were in conflict with sex drives (Eros). Their opposition, he believed, helped to explain the fundamental forces that shape both individuals and societies; their conflict might also explain self-destructive and outwardly aggressive behavior. To this picture he added, in the 1923 work, *The Ego and the Id*, a model for the human mind that would have a lasting impact on all subsequent psychological writings, at least in their terminology. According to Freud, human personality is organized by the competing drives of the id, the ego, and the superego. The **id** is the seat of all instinctive, physical desire—from the need for nourishment to sexual gratification. Its goal is

The most famous sequence in *The Battleship Potemkin* is the massacre on the Odessa Steps. Odessa's citizens have responded to the mutiny on the Potemkin by providing the sailors with food and good company. Without warning, tsarist soldiers carrying rifles appear at the top of the flight of marble steps leading to the harbor. They fire on the crowd, many of whom fall on the steps. Eisenstein's cuts become more and more frenetic in the chaos that ensues.

Eisenstein utilized 155 separate shots in 4 minutes and 20 seconds of film in the sequence, an astonishing rate of 1.6 seconds per shot. He contrasts long shots of the entire scene and close-ups of individual faces, switches back and forth between shots from below and from above (essentially the citizens' view up the steps and the soldiers' looking down), and he changes the pace from frenzied retreat at the start of the sequence to an almost frozen lack of action when the mother approaches the troops carrying her murdered son, to frantic movement again as the baby carriage rolls down the steps. Some shots last longer than others. He alternates between traveling shots and fixed shots.

From the "Odessa Steps Sequence," of Sergei Eisenstein's *The Battleship Potemkin*. 1925. Goskino. Courtesy of the Kobal Collection. A mother picks up her murdered child and confronts the troops marching down the steps. At the point where she stands, soldiers in front of her, she is framed by the diagonal lines of the steps and the bodies strewn on each side of her. The soldiers continue to advance.

Eisenstein also understood that sound and image could be treated independently in montage, or used together in support of one another. A phrase of music might heighten the emotional impact of a key shot. Or the rhythm of the music might heighten the tension of a sequence by juxtaposing itself to a different rhythm in his montage of shots, as when the soldiers' feet march to an altogether different rhythm in the editing. Eisenstein called this *rhythmic montage*, as he explains:

> In this the rhythmic drum of the soldiers' feet as they descend the steps violates all metrical demands. Unsynchronized with the beat of the cutting, this drumming comes in off-beat each time, and the shot itself is entirely different in its solution with each of

these appearances. The final pull of tension is supplied by the transfer from the rhythm of the descending feet to another rhythm—a new kind of downward movement—the next intensity level of the same activity—the baby-carriage rolling down the steps.

This attention to the rhythm of his film allows Eisenstein to abandon strict temporality. At the start of the baby carriage scene, for instance, the rhythm of the music slows dramatically and the pace of "real time" is elongated in a series of slow shots. The mother clutches herself. The carriage teeters on the brink. The mother swoons. The carriage inches forward. The mother falls, in agony. This is, as has often been said, "reel time," not "real time."

From the "Odessa Steps Sequence," of Sergei Eisenstein's *The Battleship Potemkin*. 1925. Goskino. Courtesy of the Kobal Collection. The falling body of another mother, shot by the soldiers, falls across her baby's carriage, causing it to roll out of control down the steps. Note the way the diagonals on the steps in the last image at the right echo those of the mother looking up the steps holding her dead child in the earlier scene.

There was, in fact, no tsarist massacre on the Odessa Steps, though innocent civilians were killed elsewhere in the city. Eisenstein's cinematic re-creation is a metaphor for those murders, a cinematic condensation of events that captures the spirit of events so convincingly that many viewers took it to be actual newsreel footage.

From the "Odessa Steps Sequence," of Sergei Eisenstein's *The Battleship Potemkin*. 1925. Goskino. Courtesy of the Kobal Collection. At the end of the sequence, an old woman wearing pince-nez glasses who has looked on horrified as the baby stroller careens down the stairs is attacked and slashed by a saber-bearing Cossack.

Something to Think About . . .

How would you compare Eisenstein's montage to Picasso's collage?

SEE MORE For a Closer Look at Sergei Eisenstein's *The Battleship Potemkin,* go to **www.myartslab.com**

immediate gratification, and acts in accord with the pleasure principle. The **ego** manages the id. It mediates between the id's potentially destructive impulses and the requirements of social life, seeking to satisfy the needs of the id in socially acceptable ways. Freud used the word *sublimation* to describe the redirection of the id's primal impulses into constructive social behavior. So, for example, an artist or a writer might express unacceptable impulses in work or art rather than acting them out.

For Freud, civilization itself is the product of the ego's endless effort to control and modify the id. But Freud's recognition of yet a third element in the psyche—the **superego**—is crucial. The superego is the seat of what we commonly call conscience, the psyche's moral base. The conscience comes from the psyche's consideration of criticism or disapproval leveled at it by the family, where family can be understood broadly as parents, clan, and culture. The superego is always close to the id and can act as its representative to the ego. But, since it does not distinguish between thinking a deed and doing it, it can also instill in the id enormous subconscious guilt.

Freud's thinking culminated in 1930 in *Civilization and Its Discontents* (see **Reading 35.11**, page 1170). In that book, Freud wrote that the greatest impediment to human happiness was aggression, what he called the "original, self-subsisting instinctual disposition in man." Aggression was the basic instinctual drive that civilization was organized to control, and yet, on every count, civilization had failed miserably at its job. "The fateful question for the human species," Freud argued, in terms that would ring truer and truer as the twentieth century wore on,

> seems to me to be whether and to what extent their cultural development will succeed in mastering the disturbance in their communal life by the human instinct of aggression and self-destruction. It may be that in this respect precisely the present time deserves a special interest. Men have gained control over the forces of nature to such an extent that with their help they would have no difficulty in exterminating one another to the last man.

The Jungian Archetype

Almost as influential as Freud was his colleague, the Swiss physician Carl Jung [yung] (1875–1961). Jung believed that the unconscious life of the individual was founded on a deeper, more universal layer of the psyche, which he called the **collective unconscious**, the innate, inherited contents of the human mind. It manifests itself in the form of **archetypes** [AR-kuh-types], those patterns of thought that recur throughout history and across cultures, in the form of dreams, myths, and fairy tales. The "mother archetype," for instance, recurs throughout ancient myth in symbols associated with fertility, such as the garden, the lotus, the fountain, the

cave, and so on. It manifests itself positively in Christianity as the Virgin Mary, and negatively as the witch in fairy tales and legends. Other archetypes include the father figure, the hero (who is essentially the ego), the child (often the child-hero), the maiden, the wise old man, the trickster, and so on. Such archetypal figures are prominent in popular culture—consider Darth Vader, Luke Skywalker, Princess Leia, and Obi-Wan Kenobi in George Lucas's *Star Wars*.

The Dreamwork of Surrealism

In his 1924 *Surrealist Manifesto*, the French writer, poet, and theorist André Breton [bruh-TOHN] (1896–1966) credited Freud with encouraging his own creative endeavors: "It would appear that it is by sheer chance that an aspect of intellectual life—and by far the most important in my opinion—about which no one was supposed to be concerned any longer has, recently, been brought back to light. Credit for this must go to Freud. On the evidence of his discoveries a current of opinion is at last developing which will enable the explorer of the human mind to extend his investigations, since he will be empowered to deal with more than merely summary realities." Breton continued (**Reading 35.12**):

READING 35.12

from André Breton, *Surrealist Manifesto* (1924)

It was only fitting that Freud should appear with his critique on the dream. In fact, it is incredible that this important part of psychic activity has still attracted so little attention. . . . I have always been astounded by the extreme disproportion in the importance and seriousness assigned to events of the waking moments and to those of sleep by the ordinary observer. Man, when he ceases to sleep, is above all at the mercy of his memory, and the memory normally delights in feebly retracing the circumstance of the dream for him, depriving it of all actual consequence and obliterating the only determinant from the point at which he thinks he abandoned this constant hope, this anxiety, a few hours earlier. He has the illusion of continuing something worthwhile. The dream finds itself relegated to a parenthesis, like the night. And in general it gives no more counsel than the night.

In order to restore the dream to its proper authority, Breton adopted the term *surrealism*, previously used by the poet Guillaume Apollinaire, and defined it as follows:

> SURREALISM, noun, masc., Pure psychic automatism by which it is intended to express, either verbally or in writing, the true function of thought. Thought dictated in the absence of all control exerted by reason, and outside all aesthetic or moral preoccupations.

ENCYCL. Philos. Surrealism is based on the belief in the superior reality of certain forms of association heretofore neglected, in the omnipotence of the dream, and in the disinterested play of thought. It leads to the permanent destruction of all other psychic mechanisms and to its substitution for them in the solution of the principal problems of life.

Breton had trained as a doctor and had used Freud's technique of free association when treating shell-shock victims in World War I. As his definition indicates, he had initially conceived of Surrealism as a literary movement, with Breton himself at its center. All of the Surrealists had been active Dadaists, but as opposed to Dada's "anti-art" spirit, their new "surrealist" movement believed in the possibility of a "new art." Nevertheless, the Surrealists retained much of Dada's spirit of revolt. They were committed to verbal *automatism*, a kind of writing in which the author relinquishes conscious control of the production of the text. In addition, the authors wrote dream accounts, and Breton's colleague Louis Aragon [ah-rah-GOHN] (1897–1982), especially, emphasized the importance of chance operations: "There are relations other than reality that the mind may grasp and that come first, such as chance, illusion, the fantastic, the dream," Aragon wrote. "These various species are reunited and reconciled in a genus, which is surreality."

They found precedent for their point of view not only in Freud, but in the painting of Giorgio de Chirico and the Dadaist Max Ernst (1891–1976). When Breton saw *The Child's Brain* (see Fig. 33.22) in the window of Paul Guillaume's [ghee-YOHMZ] gallery in March 1922, he jumped off a bus in order to look at it. He bought the canvas and immediately published a reproduction in his magazine *Littérature*. Breton would later look back at Ernst's 1921 exhibition of small collage-paintings like the aptly titled *The Master's Bedroom* (Fig. 35.11) as the first Surrealist work in the visual arts. This painting consists of two pages from a small pamphlet of clip art, on the left depicting assorted animals and on the right various pieces of furniture. Ernst painted over most of the spread to create his perspectival view, leaving unpainted the whale, fish, and snake at the bottom left, the bear and sheep at the top, and the bed, table, and bureau at the right. This juxtaposition of diverse elements, which would normally never occupy the same space—except perhaps in the dream work—is one of the fundamental stylistic devices of Surrealist art.

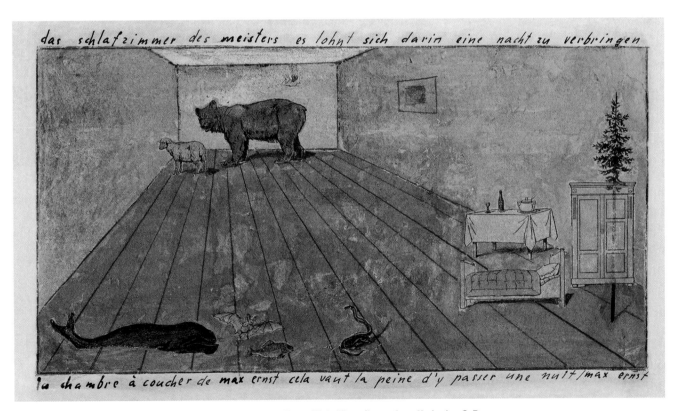

Fig. 35.11 Max Ernst, *The Master's Bedroom, It's Worth Spending a Night There* (Letter from Katherine S. Dreyer to Max Ernst, May 25, 1920). Collage, gouache, and pencil on paper, 6 3/8″ × 8 5/8″. Yale Collection of American Literature, Beinecke Rare Book and Manuscript Library. Translation from German by John W. Gabriel. From "Max Ernst, Life and Work" by Werner Spies, published by Thames & Hudson, page 67. © 2008 Artists Rights Society (ARS), New York. Prior to World War I, Ernst studied philosophy and abnormal psychology at the University of Bonn. He was well acquainted with the writings of Freud.

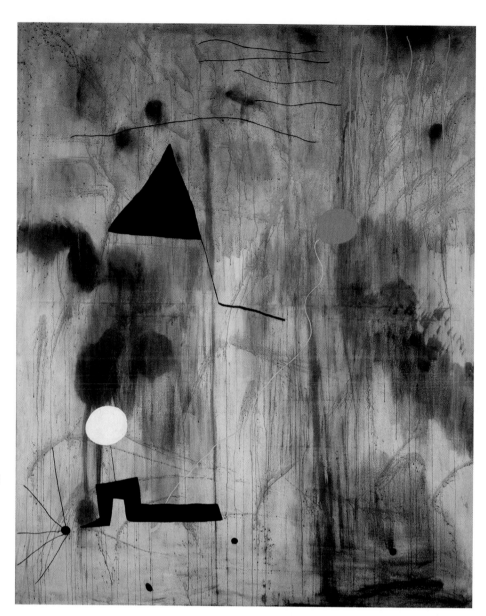

Fig. 35.12 Joan Miró, *The Birth of the World*. 1925. Oil on canvas, 8′ 2 ³/₄″ × 6′ 6 ³/₄″. Museum of Modern Art, New York. Acquired through an Anonymous Fund, the Mr. and Mrs. Joseph Slifka and Armand G. Erpf Funds, and by gift of the Artist. (262.1972). Digital Image © The Museum of Modern Art/Licensed by SCALA/Art Resource, New York. © Artists Rights Society (ARS), New York. André Breton would come to call this painting "the *Demoiselles d'Avignon* of the '*informel*'"—in other words, the founding painting of the European free gesture painting in the 1950s, l'art informel.

Picasso and Miró   Breton argued that Picasso led the way to Surrealist art in his *Les Demoiselles d'Avignon* (see Fig. 34.3), which jettisoned art's dependence on external reality. The great founder of Cubism, Breton said, possessed "the facility to give materiality to what had hitherto remained in the domain of pure fantasy." Picasso was attracted to the Surrealist point of view because it offered him new directions and possibilities, particularly in the example of his fellow Spanish artist, Joan Miró [mee-ROH] (1893–1983), whose work Breton was avidly collecting. Miró's first Paris exhibition was mounted expressly as a Surrealist show, highlighted by a private midnight opening for all the Surrealist crowd. It was followed quickly by an astonishing array of paintings, including *The Birth of the World* (Fig. **35.12**). "Rather than setting out to paint something," Miró explained, "I begin painting and as I paint, the picture begins to assert itself. . . . The first stage is free, unconscious." But, he added, "The second stage is carefully calculated." He equated the first stage with Breton's

"psychic automatism." Like the universe itself, the painting began with the "void"—the blank canvas. This was followed by "chaos," randomly distributed stains and dots. Then, Miró explained, "One large portion of black in the upper left seemed to need to become bigger. I enlarged it and went over it with opaque black paint. It became a triangle to which I added a tail. It might be a bird." He later identified the red circle with the yellow tail as a shooting star, and, at the bottom left, a "personage," with a white head whose foot almost touches a spiderlike black star.

Picasso's Surrealism would assert itself most fully in the late 1920s and early 1930s, especially in a series of monstrous bonelike figures that alternated with sensuous portraits of his mistress Marie-Thérèse Walter (1909–1977), whom he had met when she was only 17 in January 1927. For eight years, until 1935, he led a double life, married to Olga Koklova [koh-KLOH-vah] (1891–1955) while conducting a secret affair with Marie-Thérèse. Since Marie-Thérèse is so readily identifiable in her portraits, it is tempting to see the more monstrous figures as portraits of Olga.

Picasso was indeed obsessed in these years with the duality of experience, the same opposition between Thanatos (the death drive) and Eros (the sex drive) that Freud had outlined in *Beyond the Pleasure Principle*. His 1932 double portrait of Marie-Thérèse, *Girl before a Mirror* (Fig. **35.13**), expresses this—she is the moon, or night, at the right, and the sun, or light, on the left, where her own face appears in both profile and three-quarter view. Her protruding belly on the left suggests her fertility (indeed, she gave birth to their child, Maya, in 1935, soon after Picasso finally separated from Olga), though in the mirror, in typical Picasso fashion, we see not her stomach but her buttocks, her raw sexuality. She is the conscious self on the left, her subconscious self revealing itself in the mirror. Picasso's

work addresses Surrealism's most basic theme—the self in all its complexity. And he adds one important theme—the self in relation to the Other, for Picasso is present himself in the picture, not just as its painter, but in his symbol, the harlequin design of the wallpaper. But the painting also suggests that the self, in the dynamic interplay between the conscious and unconscious selves, might actually be the Other to itself.

Salvador Dalí's *Lugubrious Game* This sense of self-alienation is central to the work of Spanish artist Salvador Dalí [dah-LEE] (1904–1989), who in 1928, at age 24, was introduced to the Surrealists by Joan Miró. Already eccentric and flamboyant, Dalí had been expelled from the San Fernando Academy of Fine Arts two years earlier for refusing to take his final examination, claiming

Fig. 35.13 Pablo Picasso, *Girl Before a Mirror*. 1932. Oil on canvas, 64″ × 51 ¼″. Gift of Mrs. Simon Guggenheim. (2.1938). Digital Image © The Museum of Modern Art/Licensed by SCALA/Art Resource, New York. © Artists Rights Society (ARS), New York. The long oval mirror into which Marie-Thérèse gazes, supported on both sides by posts, is known as a *psyche*. Hence Picasso paints her psyche both literally and figuratively.

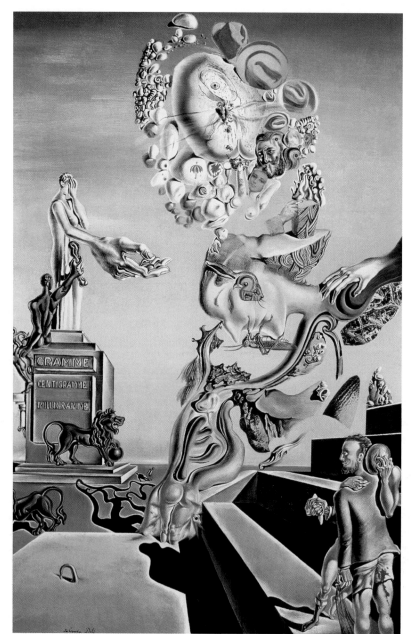

Fig. 35.14 Salvador Dalí, *The Lugubrious Game*. 1929. Oil and collage on card, 17 ½″ × 12″. Private Collection, Paris, France, © DACS. The Bridgeman Art Library. © 2008 Artists Rights Society (ARS), New York. Grasshoppers terrified Dalí—hence its nightmarish presence beneath his nose.

Dalí, in other words, did not hesitate to confront the "lugubrious"—or mournful and gloomy side—of sexuality. He followed, he said, a "paranoiac critical method," a brand of self-hypnosis that he claimed allowed him to hallucinate freely. "I believe the moment is at hand," he wrote in a description of his method, "when, by a paranoiac and active advance of the mind, it will be possible (simultaneously with automatism . . .) to systematize confusion and thus to help to discredit the world of reality." He called his images "new and menacing," and works such as the famous 1931 *Persistence of Memory* (Fig. **35.15**) are precisely that. Again, this is a self-portrait of the sleeping Dalí, who lies sluglike in the middle of the painting, draped beneath the coverlet of time. Ants, which are a symbol of death, crawl over a watchcase on the left. A fly alights on the watch dripping over the ledge, and another limp watch hangs from a dead tree that gestures toward the sleeping Dalí in a manner reminiscent of the statue in *The Lugubrious Game*.

By the mid-1930s, Breton and the Surrealists parted ways with Dalí over his early admiration for Adolf Hitler and his reluctance to support the Republic in the Spanish Civil War. To this could be added Dalí's love of money, for which he earned the name Avida Dollars (Greedy Dollars), an anagram of his name created by Breton. In 1938, he was formally expelled from the Surrealist movement.

that he knew more than the professor who was to examine him. He brought this same daring self-confidence to the Surrealist movement. Among the first paintings executed under the influence of the Surrealists is *The Lugubrious Game* (Fig. 35.14). At the lower right, a man wears a suit jacket but no pants, only his soiled underwear. He holds up one hand that clutches a bloodstained cloth, signifying his castration. He stares at the vision in front of him: a cluster of men's hats at the top (probably signifying the father), metamorphosing into egglike forms. Below it is Dalí's own profile, his eye closed in sleep or dream, with a grasshopper perched on his mouth. Below his mouth stretches a bowel-like form culminating at the bottom of the stairs in a woman's buttocks seen from the rear. The statue of the male figure on the left reaches out an enlarged hand toward Dalí even as it covers its eyes in disgust.

Surrealist Sculpture The work that caused the Surrealists to take serious interest in the possibilities of a Surrealist sculptural project was *Suspended Ball* (Fig. **35.16**), by the Swiss sculptor Alberto Giacometti [jah-koh-MET-tee] (1901–1966) in 1930 to 1931. The work is composed of a crescent-shaped wedge above which hangs a ball with a slotted groove in its underside, the pair contained in an open three-dimensional frame. It invites touch, for the ball is meant to swing in a pendulum fashion across the crescent wedge. Breton and Dalí were both ecstatic with the object. Many years later, in his *History of Surrealism*, Maurice Nadeau recalled the sculpture's impact: "Everyone who saw it experienced a strong but indefinable sexual emotion relating to unconscious desires. The emotion was . . . one of disturbance, like that imparted by the irritating awareness of failure."

For the most part, women were allowed to participate in the movement only as the object of their male companions' dreams and fantasies, but the German-born Meret Oppenheim [OH-pen-hime] (1901–1985) made a significant contribution in her own right, by creating strikingly original objects that captivated the Surrealists' imagination. Oppenheim's sense of humor, which consists largely in the unexpected transformations that she works upon her objects, is at its most obvious in her *Object (Le Déjeuner en fourrure)* [leh day-zhun-AY ahn foo-RURE] (Fig. **35.17**), literally her "luncheon in fur." One day,

Fig. 35.16 Alberto Giacometti, *Suspended Ball*. 1930–1931. Wood and metal, $24" \times 14\frac{1}{2}" \times 14"$. Inv. AM 1996-205. Photo: Georges Meguerditchian. Musée National d'Art Moderne. Centre National d'Art et de Culture. Georges Pompidou. CNAC/MNAM/Dist. Réunion des Musées Nationaux/Art Resource, New York. © 2008 Artists Rights Society (ARS), New York. A plaster version of this sculpture, from which this version was cast, exists in the Kunstmuseum, Basel, Switzerland.

Fig. 35.17 Meret Oppenheim, *Object (Le Déjeuner en fourrure)*. 1931. Fur-covered cup, saucer, and spoon; cup $4\frac{3}{4}"$ diameter; saucer $9\frac{3}{8}"$ diameter; spoon $8"$ long; overall height $2\frac{3}{8}"$. Purchase. The Museum of Modern Art/Licensed by SCALA/Art Resource, New York. © 2008 Artists Rights Society (ARS), New York. This work was given its title by Breton in 1938, when it was included in the new Museum of Modern Art's exhibition "Fantastic Art, Dada, Surrealism."

while Oppenheim and Picasso were at a café, Picasso noticed a bracelet she was wearing of her own design lined with ocelot [OSS-uh-lot] fur. He remarked that one could cover anything in fur, and Oppenheim agreed. Then, her tea having gotten cold, she asked the waiter for "a little more fur." The Freudian slip suggested the work. Its title is a reference to Manet's *Le Déjeuner sur l'herbe* (see Fig. 30.6), in which a naked model blithely sits between two dressed gentlemen in the Bois de Bologne. The sexual frankness of Manet's painting is transformed here into a suggestion of oral eroticism, the potential user of this tea set becoming a kind of animal licking its own fur or cleaning the fur of its children. But what sets Oppenheim's work apart is the good-natured humor that she brings to Surrealism's "lugubrious" game.

EXPERIMENTATION AND THE LITERARY LIFE: THE STREAM-OF-CONSCIOUSNESS NOVEL

Where Hemingway sought to pare down his writing style to the most basic and direct description, perhaps the most important literary innovation of the era was the **stream-of-consciousness** novel. The idea had arisen in the late nineteenth century, in the writings of both William James (1842–1910), the novelist Henry James's older brother, and the French philosopher Henri Bergson (1859–1941). For Bergson, human consciousness is composed of two somewhat contradictory powers: intellect, which sorts and categorizes experience in logical, even mathematical terms; and intuition, which understands experience as a perpetual stream of sensations, a duration or flow of perpetual becoming. Chapter XI of James's 1892 *Psychology* is actually entitled "The Stream of Consciousness." "Now we are seeing," James writes, "now hearing; now reasoning, now willing; now recollecting, now expecting, now loving, now hating; and in a hundred other ways we know our minds to be alternately engaged . . . . Consciousness . . . is nothing jointed; it flows. A 'river' or a 'stream' are the metaphors by which it is most naturally described. *In talking of it hereafter, let us call it the stream of thought, of consciousness, or of subjective life.*"

The rise of the stream-of-consciousness novel in the twentieth century can be attributed to two related factors. On the one hand, it provided authors a means of portraying directly the psychological makeup of their protagonists, as their minds leap from one thing to the next, from memory to self-reflection to observation to fantasy. In this it resembles the free association method of Freudian psychoanalysis. But equally important, it enabled writers to emphasize the subjectivity of their characters' points of view. What a character claims might not necessarily be true. Characters might have motives for lying, even to themselves. And certainly no character in a "fiction" need be a reliable narrator of events. Nothing need prevent characters from creating their own fiction within the author's larger fictional work. Thus, in the stream-of-consciousness novel, the reader is forced to become an active participant in the fiction, sorting out "fact" from "fantasy," distinguishing between the actual events of a story and the characters' "memory" of them.

Joyce, *Ulysses*, and Sylvia Beach

No writer was more influential in introducing the stream-of-consciousness narrative than James Joyce (1882–1941), the Irish writer who left Ireland in 1905 to live, chiefly, in Paris, and no novel better demonstrates its powers than his *Ulysses*.

Early chapters of *Ulysses* had originally been serialized in the American *Little Review*, but postal authorities in both Britain and the United States had banned it for obscenity. Joyce's cause was taken up by Sylvia Beach, owner of an English-language-only bookstore and lending library on the rue l'Odéon [loh-day-OHN] frequented by almost every American writer in Paris. After meeting Joyce at the bookstore, she agreed to publish *Ulysses* in an edition of 1,000, the first two copies of which were delivered on the eve of Joyce's fortieth birthday, February 2, 1922 (Fig. **35.18**).

The novel takes place on one day, June 16, 1904, in 18 episodes spread about an hour apart and ending in the early hours of June 17. It loosely follows the episodes of Ulysses from the *Odyssey* of Homer, with Stephen Dedalus figuring as the new Telemachus, Leopold Bloom as Ulysses,

CONTINUITY & CHANGE
Odyssey, **p. 106**

and Molly Bloom as Penelope. Like Penelope in the *Odyssey*, Molly has a suitor, the debonair Blazes Boylan. To win back her affection, Bloom must endure 12 trials—his Odyssey—in the streets, brothels, pubs, and offices of Dublin. Each character is presented through his or her own stream-of-consciousness narration—we read only what is experienced in the character's mind from moment to moment, following his or her thought process through the

Fig. 35.18 Sylvia Beach and James Joyce reading reviews of Ulysses. **1922.** Princeton University Library, Princeton, NJ. Sylvia Beach Collection. Joyce suffered from glaucoma, and endured a number of operations. In order to support Joyce, Beach went into debt herself to advance him money, printing 11 small editions of the novel over the next decade.

interior monologue. Molly Bloom's final soliloquy, the last episode of the book, underscores the experimental vitality of Joyce's prose. It opens with Molly contemplating her husband's request to be served breakfast in bed in the morning. A full-blown stream-of-consciousness monologue in which the half-asleep Molly mulls over her entire sexual life, it concludes with her rapturous remembrance of giving herself to Bloom on Howth Head, the northern enclosure of Dublin Bay, 16 years earlier.

In its near-total lack of punctuation—there are eight sentences in the entire episode, the first of which is 2,500 words long—as well as its uncensored exploration of a woman's sexuality, Joyce's final episode remains revolutionary, as does the novel as a whole.

Virginia Woolf: In the Mind of Mrs. Dalloway

As soon as episodes from *Ulysses* began to appear in the *Little Review*, Joyce's experiments caught the attention of other writers. Although the English novelist Virginia Woolf (1882–1941) disapproved of Joyce's book—it ultimately seemed to her the product of a "working man," and, she added, "we all know how distressing they are, how egotistic, insistent, raw, striking, & ultimately nauseating"—she was fascinated by Joyce's style. In August 1922, just as she was beginning her novel *Mrs. Dalloway*, a work published in 1925 about a higher social class of people than those of Joyce's *Ulysses*, she wrote that after reading the first 200 pages of Joyce's novel she was "amused, stimulated, charmed[,] interested." So she determined to examine for herself "an ordinary day" of a decidedly different character.

Woolf was at the center of a circle of London intellectuals known as the Bloomsbury Group, named for the London neighborhood in which they lived. Although women in England had gained the right to vote in 1918, Woolf argued that women could realize their full potential only if they achieved both financial and psychological independence from men. In her important 1929 essay "A Room of One's Own," she argues that in order to realize their full creative capacities, women must find the means to possess rooms of their own—spaces freed of male constraints (see **Reading 35.14**, page 1171). By the mid-1920s, Woolf had largely eliminated external action from her prose, concentrating instead on trying to capture the ebb and flow of her characters'—particularly her women characters'—consciousness. It was their psychological makeup, and by extension her own, that most interested her.

Mrs. Dalloway takes place on a single day in post–World War I London as Clarissa Dalloway prepares for a party, and Woolf follows her heroine's stream of consciousness, her memories and feelings, as well as the streams of consciousness of other characters who encounter her as they go through the day. Chief among these other characters is Septimus Warren Smith, a shell-shocked war veteran whose depression in many ways mirrors Woolf's own. These are the novel's opening paragraphs (**Reading 35.15**):

READING 35.15

from Virginia Woolf, *Mrs. Dalloway* (1925)

Mrs. Dalloway said she would buy the flowers herself.

For Lucy had her work cut out for her. The doors would be taken off their hinges; Rumpelmayer's men were coming. And then, thought Clarissa Dalloway, what a morning—fresh as if issued to children on a beach.

What a lark! What a plunge! For so it had always seemed to her, when, with a little squeak of the hinges, which she could hear now, she had burst open the French windows and plunged at Bourton into the open air. How fresh, how calm, stiller than this of course, the air was in the early morning; like the flap of a wave; the kiss of a wave; chill and sharp and yet (for a girl of eighteen as she then was) solemn, feeling as she did, standing there at the open window, that something awful was about to happen; looking at the flowers, at the trees with the smoke winding off them and the rooks rising, falling; standing and looking until Peter Walsh said, "Musing among the vegetables?"—was that it?—"I prefer men to cauliflowers"—was that it? He must have said it at breakfast one morning when she had gone out on to the terrace—Peter Walsh. He would be back from India one of these days, June or July, she forgot which, for his letters were awfully dull; it was his sayings one remembered; his eyes, his pocket-knife, his smile, his grumpiness and, when millions of things had utterly vanished—how strange it was!—a few sayings like this about cabbages.

She stiffened a little on the kerb, waiting for Durtnall's van to pass. A charming woman, Scrope Purvis thought her (knowing her as one does know people who live next door to one in Westminster); a touch of the bird about her, of the jay, blue green, light, vivacious, though she was over fifty, and grown very white since her illness. There she perched, never seeing him, waiting to cross, very upright.

For having lived in Westminster—how many years now? over twenty,—one feels even in the midst of the traffic, or waking at night, Clarissa was positive, a particular hush, or solemnity; an indescribable pause; a suspense (but that might be her heart, affected, they said, by influenza) before Big Ben strikes. There! Out it boomed.

As the 52-year-old Clarissa leaves her house to buy flowers for her party, she recalls standing at the open window of her father's estate when she was 18, chatting with Peter Walsh, and feeling "something awful was about to happen." Clarissa's neighbor, Scrope Purvis, notices her from his window, and we are briefly in his mind. Then we return to Clarissa. As past and present mingle, and points of view shift from character to character, we enter into the private worlds of them all, all ironically frustrated in their attempts to communicate with one another.

Woolf's next novel, the 1927 *To the Lighthouse*, opens with a long stream-of-consciousness account of a day in the life of Mr. and Mrs. Ramsay and their guests vacationing on the Isle of Skye, followed by a shorter poetic description of the passing of 10 years' time, and concluding with another stream-of-consciousness narrative in which the actions of 10 years earlier are finally resolved. The contrast in the passing of time—two days' events narrated at length, 10 years' in a matter of pages—underscores Woolf's sense of the malleability of time. But at the heart of the narrative is the realization that it is the consciousness of Mrs. Ramsay that determines the events of the final day, even though in the intervening years she has died.

Marcel Proust and the Novel of Memory

If Joyce was the first to use stream of consciousness as a narrative device, it was Marcel Proust [proost] (1871–1922) who first imagined the novel as a mental space. Proust grew up in Paris near the Champs-Elysées, spending holidays with relatives in the country towns of Auteuil [oh-TOY] and Illiers [eel-ee-AY]. These two villages inspired Proust's fictional village, Combray [kohm-BRAY], site of the narrator's childhood memories in his monumental seven-volume novel *À la recherche du temps perdu* (literally *In Search of Lost Time*, but known in the English-speaking world for decades as *Remembrance of Things Past*, a title invented by the novel's translator from Shakespeare's Sonnet XXX: "When to the sessions of sweet silent thought/I summon up remembrance of things past"). After a bout of depression that followed the deaths of his father in 1903 and his mother in 1905, Proust gave up his social life almost entirely, retreating to his quiet, cork-lined apartment on the boulevard Haussmann and devoting almost all his waking hours to the composition of his novel.

Calling the novel "psychology in space and time," his plan was to explore the deepest recesses of the unconscious and bring them to conscious life. Thus the famous moment that concludes the "Overture" to *Swann's Way*, the first volume of *À la recherche*, published in 1913, when the narrator, Marcel, tastes a madeleine, "one of those short, plump little cakes . . . which look as though they have been moulded in the fluted scallop of a pilgrim's shell" (**Reading 35.16**):

READING 35.16

from Marcel Proust, *Swann's Way* (1913)

I raised to my lips a spoonful of the tea in which I had soaked a morsel of the cake. No sooner had the warm liquid, and the crumbs with it, touched my palate than a shudder ran through my whole body, and I stopped, intent upon the extraordinary changes that were taking place. An exquisite pleasure had invaded my senses, but individual, detached, with no suggestion of its origin. And at once the vicissitudes of life had become indifferent to me, its disasters innocuous, its brevity illusory—this new sensation having had on me the effect which love has of filling me with a precious essence; or rather this essence was not in me, it was myself. I had ceased now to feel mediocre, accidental, mortal. Whence could it have come to me, this all-powerful joy? I was conscious that it was connected with the taste of tea and cake, but that it infinitely transcended those savours, could not, indeed, be of the same nature as theirs. Whence did it come? What did it signify? How could I seize upon and define it?

What Marcel comes to understand is that, in a process of free association, the taste of the madeleine had evoked his experience of tasting the same little cake, given him by his aunt Léonine [lay-oh-NEEN] on Sunday mornings at Combray, and thus the entire landscape of Combray itself. The past, in other words, comes alive in the present, freeing Marcel from the constraints of time and opening to him the recesses of his subconscious.

The philosopher Henri Bergson, whom Proust considered "the first great metaphysician" of the modern era, had argued that past, present, and future were part of an organic whole, in which the past is a "continuous progress . . . which gnaws into the future and which swells it as it advances." The role of art, he argued, was to capture "certain rhythms of life and breath" which invite us to "join in a dance. Thus," he wrote, "they compel us to set in motion, in the depth of our own being, some secret chord which was only waiting to thrill." Just as the madeleine struck this same secret chord in Marcel, Proust hoped his fiction would strike it in his reader. In the last volume of *À la recherche*, *Time Regained*, not published until 1927, he wrote:

> I thought more modestly of my book and it would be inaccurate even to say that I thought of those who would read it as "my" readers. For, it seemed to me that they would not be "my" readers but the readers of their own selves, my book being merely a sort of magnifying glass like those which the optician at Combray used to offer his customers—it would be my book but with its help I would furnish them with the means of reading what lay inside themselves.

It is the book and the acts of memory that it restores to the present—and hence the future—that time, in all its flux, is finally "regained."

Harlem and the Great Migration

In February 1924, a young African-American student named Langston Hughes (1902–1967), restless, determined to see the world, and equally determined to become a poet, arrived in Paris. He had graduated from Central High School in Cleveland, Ohio, in 1920. After dropping out of Columbia University in 1922, he made three transatlantic voyages working as a seaman on a freighter that took him to Senegal, Nigeria, the Cameroons, the Belgian Congo, Angola, and Guinea in Africa, and later to Italy and France, Russia, and Spain. Paris did not much impress him. In the second week of March, he wrote his friend, Countee Cullen (1903–1946):

Fig. 35.19 Jacob Lawrence, *The Migration of the Negro*, Panel no. 60: *And the migrants kept coming.* 1940–41. Casein tempera on hardboard panel, 18" × 12". Gift of Ms. David M. Levy. (28.1942.30). Digital Image © The Museum of Modern Art/Licensed by SCALA/Art Resource, New York. © Artists Rights Society (ARS), New York.

But about France! Kid, stay in Harlem! The French are the most franc-loving, sou-clutching, hard-faced, hard-worked, cold and half-starved set of people I've ever seen in my life. Heat unknown. Hot water, what is it? You even pay for a smile here. Nothing, absolutely nothing is given away. You even pay for water in a restaurant or the use of the toilette. And do they like Americans of any color? They do not!! Paris, old and ugly and dirty. Style? Class? You see more well-dressed people in a New York subway station in five seconds than I've seen all my three weeks in Paris. Little old New York for me! But the colored people here are fine, there are lots of us.

Over the course of the First World War, Hughes's Harlem—and New York City itself—had changed dramatically. In 1914, nearly 90 percent of all African Americans lived in the South, three-quarters of them in the rural South. But as millions of men in the North went to fight in Europe, a huge demand for labor followed. Lured by plentiful jobs, Southern blacks began to move north—between 200,000 and 350,000 in the years 1915 through 1918 alone. This Great Migration, as it was called, was later celebrated in a series of 60 paintings by the African-American artist Jacob Lawrence (1917–2000) (Fig. **35.19**), who moved to

Harlem in 1924 at the age of seven, into a cultural community so robust, and so new, that the era has come to be known as the Harlem Renaissance. Lawrence was trained as a painter at the Harlem Art Workshop, and in his teens he was introduced to Hughes. "Without the black community in Harlem, I wouldn't have become an artist," he later said. Lawrence painted his *Migration* series when he was just 23 years old. It won him immediate fame. In 1942, the Museum of Modern Art in New York and the Phillips Collection in Washington, D.C. each bought 30 panels. That same year, Lawrence became the first black artist represented by a prestigious New York gallery—the Downtown Gallery. In 1949, he would team up with Hughes to illustrate Hughes's own book of poems about the Great Migration, *One Way Ticket*. "I pick up my life," the title poem begins:

And take it with me,
And I put it down in
Chicago, Detroit,
Buffalo, Scranton,
Any place that is
North and East,
And not Dixie. ∎

What were the effects of trench warfare on the European imagination?

The realities of trench warfare along the Western Front in northeast France and northwest Germany had an immense impact on the Western imagination. The almost unbounded optimism that preceded the war was replaced by a sense of the absurdity of modern life, the fragmentation of experience, and the futility of even daring to hope. How does Wilfred Owens's "The Pity of War" reflect these feelings? What about William Butler Yeats's poetry? Among the most powerful realizations of this condition is T. S. Eliot's poem *The Waste Land*. How does it depict modern love?

What is Dada?

Many found the war incomprehensible, and they reacted by creating an art movement based on negation and meaninglessness: Dada. What beliefs did Dada's sound poetry reflect? What role did chance operations play in their work? One of their most influential spokesmen, Marcel Duchamp, turned found objects into works of art, including the urinal *Fountain*, which he called ready-mades. What are ready-mades? How did the Dadaists use the technique of photomontage? Dada, finally, was an art of provocation, but in its very energy, it posited that the forces of creativity might survive.

How did the arts respond to the Russian Revolution?

In Russia, political upheaval offered the promise of a new and better life. Led by Vladimir Lenin, the Bolshevik party envisioned an ideal utopian state in which society does away with government and life is lived upon the principle "From each according to his ability: to each according to his needs." In the arts, Kasimir Malevich pursued an art he called Suprematism. What is Suprematism? How are its principles reflected in his *Black Square*? Soon Malevich sought to apply these principles in more practical ways that might serve a social purpose—Constructivism, he called it. In film, Sergei Eisenstein's new montage techniques were created to attract a largely illiterate audience through fast-paced editing and composition. What is montage?

How does Freudian psychology manifest itself in the Surrealist art movement?

The era after the war was especially influenced by the work of Sigmund Freud, whose psychoanalytic techniques, especially that of free association, were employed to treat victims of shell shock. What is free association and what theories did Freud develop based on it? After the war, in *Beyond the Pleasure Principle*, he added to his theories the idea that humans might be equally driven by a death drive that begins to explain self-destructive and aggressive human behaviors, including war. Almost as influential as Freud was his colleague Carl Jung, who believed that the unconscious life of the individual was founded on a deeper, more universal layer of the psyche, which he called the collective unconscious. How does the collective unconscious manifest itself?

In the arts, the discoveries of Freud and Jung manifested themselves in the Surrealist projects of André Breton and his colleagues. How did Breton define Surrealism? Breton reproduced the work of Max Ernst in the journals that he published. He recruited Picasso to the movement, as well as Picasso's Spanish colleague Joan Miró. Miró in turn introduced Salvador Dalí to the movement. All of these artists, including sculptors like Alberto Giacometti and Meret Oppenheim, openly pursued the undercurrent of Freudian sexual desire that they believed lay at the root of their creative activity.

What is the stream-of-consciousness style of writing?

After the war, writers struggled to find a way to express themselves authentically in a language that the war had seemed to have left impoverished. The life of the unconscious was the subject of the stream-of-consciousness novel that rose to prominence in the same era, including James Joyce's *Ulysses*, Virginia Woolf's *Mrs. Dalloway*, and Marcel Proust's *À la recherche du temps perdu*. What are the attractions of the stream-of-consciousness style?

PRACTICE MORE Get flashcards for images and terms and review chapter material with quizzes at **www.myartslab.com**

GLOSSARY

archetype In Jung's view, a pattern of thought that recurs throughout history, and across cultures, in the form of dreams, myths, and fairy tales.

collective unconscious The innate, inherited contents of the human mind.

ego In Freudian psychology, the part of the human mind that manages the id, mediating between the id's potentially destructive impulses and the requirements of social life.

id In Freudian psychology, the part of the human mind that is the seat of all instinctive, physical desire; the principal mechanism of the subconscious.

montage An image (whether photographic or cinematographic) made by combining several different images.

photomontage A collage work containing photographic clippings.

stream-of-consciousness A type of narration in which the reader reads only what is experienced in the character's mind from moment to moment, following his or her thought process through the interior monologue.

sublimation The act of modifying and redirecting the id's primal impulses into constructive social behavior.

superego In Freudian psychology, the seat of what is commonly called "conscience," the psyche's moral base.

READINGS

READING 35.6

from T. S. Eliot, *The Waste Land, Part III*, "The Fire Sermon" (1921)

The following selection from Eliot's long poem occurs at the very center of the poem. Eliot describes the sexual encounter between a typist and her "young man carbuncular"—that is, covered with boils—as overseen by the figure of Tiresias. In a note, Eliot describes Tiresias as "the most important personage in the poem," despite the fact that he is a "mere spectator." In his Metamorphoses *(see Chapter 6), Ovid describes how Tiresias spent seven years as a woman. Later, he was asked to settle a quarrel between Zeus and Hera over who enjoyed sex more, men or women. When Tiresias agreed with Zeus that women enjoyed it more, Hera blinded him, but Zeus compensated him by giving him the gift of prophesy. Tiresias, here, blind yet able to see with complete clarity, embodies the modern condition, a doomed individual who can neither hope nor act, but only sit and watch.*

At the violet hour, when the eyes and back
Turn upward from the desk, when the human engine waits
Like a taxi throbbing waiting,
I Tiresias, though blind, throbbing between two lives,
Old man with wrinkled female breasts, can see
At the violet hour, the evening hour that strives
Homeward, and brings the sailor home from sea,
The typist home at teatime, clears her breakfast, lights
Her stove, and lays out food in tins.
Out of the window perilously spread   10
Her drying combinations[1] touched by the sun's last rays,
On the divan are piled (at her night bed)
Stockings, slippers, camisoles, and stays.
I Tiresias, old man with wrinkled dugs
Perceived the scene, and foretold the rest—
I too awaited the expected guest.
He, the young man carbuncular, arrives,
A small house agent's clerk, with one bold stare,
One of the low on whom assurance sits
As a silk hat on a Bradford millionaire.[2]   20
The time is now propitious, as he guesses,
The meal is ended, she is bored and tired,
Endeavours to engage her in caresses
Which are still unreproved, if undesired.
Flushed and decided, he assaults at once;

Exploring hands encounter no defense;
His vanity requires no response,
And makes a welcome of indifference.
(And I Tiresias have foresuffered all
Enacted on this same divan or bed;   30
I who have sat by Thebes below the wall
And walked among the lowest of the dead.)[3]
Bestows one final patronising kiss,
And gropes his way, finding the stairs unlit . . .

She turns and looks a moment in the glass,
Hardly aware of her departed lover;
Her brain allows one half-formed thought to pass:
"Well now that's done: and I'm glad it's over."
When lovely woman stoops to folly and
Paces about her room again, alone,   40
She smoothes her hair with automatic hand,
And puts a record on the gramophone.

READING CRITICALLY

In his notes to *The Waste Land,* Eliot writes: "What Tiresias sees, in fact, is the substance of the poem." How would you summarize that "substance"?

---

[1]**combinations** one-piece underwear.
[2]**Bradford millionaire** The industrial town of Bradford thrived on war contracts during World War I, and thus the gentleman described is, for Eliot, the image of a war profiteer.

[3]**Thebes . . . lowest of the dead** Tiresias was originally from the Greek city of Thebes, but prophesied from Hades.

from Sigmund Freud, *Civilization and Its Discontents* (1930)

Civilization and Its Discontents is among Freud's most philosophical works. In it he traces the effects of archaic instinctual impulses, once necessary for survival, on modern society. In the following passage, he surveys the role that aggression plays in impeding man's ability to live in peace and harmony. Later in this same argument, he will argue that civilization often forces us to turn our aggression inward, to the Self, causing the psychological phenomenon of depression and despair.

Men are not gentle creatures, who want to be loved, who at the most can defend themselves if they are attacked; they are, on the contrary, creatures among whose instinctual endowments is to be reckoned a powerful share of aggressiveness. As a result, their neighbor is for them not only a potential helper or sexual object, but also someone who tempts them to satisfy their aggressiveness on him, to exploit his capacity for work without compensation, to use him sexually without his consent, to seize his possessions, to humiliate him, to cause him pain, to torture and to kill him. *Homo homini lupus* [man is wolf to man]. Who 10 in the face of all his experience of life and of history, will have the courage to dispute this assertion? As a rule this cruel aggressiveness waits for some provocation or puts itself at the service of some other purpose, whose goal might also have been reached by milder measures. In circumstances that are favorable to it, when the mental counter-forces which ordinarily inhibit it are out of action, it also manifests itself spontaneously and reveals man as a savage beast to whom consideration towards his own kind is something alien. Anyone who calls to mind the atrocities committed during the racial migrations or 20 the invasions of the Huns, or by the people known as Mongols under Jenghiz Khan and Tamerlane, or at the capture of Jerusalem by the pious Crusaders, or even, indeed, the horrors of the recent World War—anyone who calls these things to mind will have to bow humbly before the truth of this view.

The existence of this inclination to aggression, which we can detect in ourselves and justly assume to be present in others, is the factor which disturbs our relations with our neighbor and which forces civilization into such a high expenditure [of energy]. In consequence of this primary mutual hostility of human 30 beings, civilized society is perpetually threatened with disintegration. The interest of work in common would not hold it together; instinctual passions are stronger than reasonable interests. Civilization has to use its utmost efforts in order to set limits to man's aggressive instincts and to hold the manifestations of them in check by psychical reaction-formations. . . .

The communists believe they have found the path to deliverance from our evils. According to them, man is wholly good and as well-disposed to his neighbor; but the institution of private property has corrupted his nature. The ownership of private 40 wealth gives the individual power, and waited the temptation to ill-treat his neighbor; while the man who is excluded from possession is bound to rebel in hostility against his oppressor. If private property were abolished, all wealth held in common, and everyone allowed to share in the enjoyment of it, ill-will and hostility would disappear among men. Since everyone's needs would be satisfied, no one would have any reason to regard another as his enemy; all would willingly undertake the work that was necessary. I have no concern with any economic criticisms of the communist system; I cannot inquire into whether the abo- 50 lition of private property is expedient or advantageous. But I am able to recognize that the psychological premises on which the systems based are an untenable illusion. In abolishing private property we deprive the human love of aggression of one of its instruments, certainly a strong one, though certainly not the strongest; but we have in no way altered the differences in power and influence which are misused by aggressiveness, nor have we altered anything in its nature. Aggressiveness was not created by property. It reigned almost before property had given 60 up its primal, anal form; it forms the basis of every relation of affection and love among people (with the single exception, perhaps, of the mother's relation to her male child). If we do away with personal rights over material wealth, there still remains prerogative in the field of sexual relationships, which is bound to become the source of the strongest dislike in the most violent hostility among men who in other respects are on an equal footing. If we were to remove this factor, too, by allowing complete freedom of sexual life and thus abolishing the family, the germcell of civilization, we cannot, it is true, easily foresee what new paths the development of civilization could take; but one thing 70 we can expect, and that is that this indestructible feature of human nature will follow it there.

It is clearly not easy for man to give up the satisfaction of this inclination to aggression. They do not feel comfortable without it. The advantage which a comparatively small cultural group offers of allowing this instinct an outlet in the form of hostility against intruders is not to be despised. It is always possible to bind together a considerable number of people in love, so long as there are other people left over to receive the manifestations of their aggressiveness. . . . In this respect the Jew- 80 ish people, scattered everywhere, have rendered most useful services to the civilizations of the countries that have been their hosts; but unfortunately all the massacres of the Jews in the Middle Ages did not suffice to make that period more peaceful and secure for their Christian fellows. When once the Apostle Paul had posited universal love between men as the foundation of his Christian community, extreme intolerance, part of Christendom towards those who remained outside it became the inevitable consequence. To the Romans, who had not founded their communal life as a State upon love, religious intolerance 90 was something foreign, although with them religion was a concern of the State and the State was permeated by religion. Neither was it an unaccountable chance that the dream of a Germanic world-dominion called for anti-Semitism as its complement; and it is intelligible that the attempts to establish a new, communist civilization in Russia should find its psychological support in the persecution of the bourgeois. One only wonders, with concern, what the Soviets will do after they have wiped out their bourgeois.

READING CRITICALLY

How and why does Freud disagree with Lenin's basic premise as stated in *The State and Revolution*?

from Virginia Woolf, "A Room of One's Own" (1929)

Woolf's long essay, which originated as a series of lectures given at two women's colleges at Cambridge University in October 1928, is a response to a remark by an English clergyman that no woman could ever have approached the genius of William Shakespeare. In the section excerpted here, Woolf imagines what it might have been like to be Shakespeare's sister—a sibling as gifted as her brother but trapped in her time.

Be that as it may, I could not help thinking, as I looked at the works of Shakespeare on the shelf, that the bishop was right at least in this; it would have been impossible, completely and entirely, for any woman to have written the plays of Shakespeare in the age of Shakespeare. Let me imagine, since facts are so hard to come by, what would have happened had Shakespeare had a wonderfully gifted sister, called Judith, let us say. Shakespeare himself went, very probably,—his mother was an heiress—to the grammar school, where he may have learnt Latin—Ovid, Virgil and Horace—and the elements of grammar and logic. He was, it is well known, a wild boy who poached rabbits, perhaps shot a deer, and had, rather sooner than he should have done, to marry a woman in the neighbourhood, who bore him a child rather quicker than was right. That escapade sent him to seek his fortune in London. He had, it seemed, a taste for the theatre; he began by holding horses at the stage door. Very soon he got work in the theatre, became a successful actor, and lived at the hub of the universe, meeting everybody, knowing everybody, practising his art on the boards, exercising his wits in the streets, and even getting access to the palace of the queen. Meanwhile his extraordinarily gifted sister, let us suppose, remained at home. She was as adventurous, as imaginative, as agog to see the world as he was. But she was not sent to school. She had no chance of learning grammar and logic, let alone of reading Horace and Virgil. She picked up a book now and then, one of her brother's perhaps, and read a few pages. But then her parents came in and told her to mend the stockings or mind the stew and not moon about with books and papers. They would have spoken sharply but kindly, for they were substantial people who knew the conditions of life for a woman and loved their daughter—indeed, more likely than not she was the apple of her father's eye. Perhaps she scribbled some pages up in an apple loft on the sly but was careful to hide them or set fire to them. Soon, however, before she was out of her teens, she was to be betrothed to the son of a neighbouring woolstapler. She cried out that marriage was hateful to her, and for that she was severely beaten by her father. Then he ceased to scold her. He begged her instead not to hurt him, not to shame him in this matter of her marriage. He would give her a chain of beads or a fine petticoat, he said; and there were tears in his eyes. How could she disobey him? How could she break his heart? The force of her own gift alone drove her to it. She made up a small parcel of her belongings, let herself down by a rope one summer's night and took the road to London. She was not seventeen. The birds that sang in the hedge were not more musical than she was. She had the quickest fancy, a gift like her brother's, for the tune of words. Like him, she had a taste for the theatre. She stood at the stage door; she wanted to act, she said. Men laughed in her face. The manager—a fat, looselipped man—guffawed. He bellowed something about poodles dancing and women acting—no woman, he said, could possibly be an actress. He hinted—you can imagine what. She could get no training in her craft. Could she even seek her dinner in a tavern or roam the streets at midnight? Yet her genius was for fiction and lusted to feed abundantly upon the lives of men and women and the study of their ways. At last—for she was very young, oddly like Shakespeare the poet in her face, with the same grey eyes and rounded brows—at last Nick Greene the actormanager took pity on her; she found herself with child by that gentleman and so—who shall measure the heat and violence of the poet's heart when caught and tangled in a woman's body?—killed herself one winter's night and lies buried at some cross-roads where the omnibuses now stop outside the Elephant and Castle.

That, more or less, is how the story would run, I think, if a woman in Shakespeare's day had had Shakespeare's genius . . . . [S]o it seemed to me, reviewing the story of Shakespeare's sister as I had made it, is that any woman born with a great gift in the sixteenth century would certainly have gone crazed, shot herself, or ended her days in some lonely cottage outside the village, half witch, half wizard, feared and mocked at. For it needs little skill in psychology to be sure that a highly gifted girl who had tried to use her gift for poetry would have been so thwarted and hindered by other people, so tortured and pulled asunder by her own contrary instincts, that she must have lost her health and sanity to a certainty . . . . To have lived a free life in London in the sixteenth century would have meant for a woman who was poet and playwright a nervous stress and dilemma which might well have killed her. Had she survived, whatever she had written would have been twisted and deformed, issuing from a strained and morbid imagination. And undoubtedly, I thought, looking at the shelf where there are no plays by women, her work would have gone unsigned.

READING CRITICALLY

Although Woolf is imagining what it might have been like to be a talented woman in the sixteenth century, she clearly identifies with her character Judith—her own father had kept her at home while sending her brothers to school. What does this suggest about Woolf's own genius?

36 New York, Skyscraper Culture, and the Jazz Age
Making It New

THINKING AHEAD

What was the Harlem Renaissance?

What is the International Style in architecture?

What is suggested by the adage "make it new"?

What characterizes the "golden age" of silent film?

By the mid-1920s, both white and black Americans understood that New York's Harlem neighborhood was alive with a new, vibrant sense of cultural possibility. This new cultural climate, which came to be known as the Harlem Renaissance, had been inaugurated by the mass migration of blacks out of the South into the North after the outbreak of World War I (see Fig. 35.19). In 1914, nearly 90 percent of all African Americans lived in the South, three-quarters of them in the rural South. But lured by a huge demand for labor in the North once the war began, and impoverished after a boll weevil infestation ruined the cotton crop, blacks flooded into the North. In the course of a mere 90 days early in the 1920s, 12,000 African Americans left Mississippi alone. An average of 200 left Memphis every night. Many met with great hardship, but there was wealth to be had as well, and anything seemed better than life under Jim Crow in the South. They hoped to find a new life in the urban North, the promise of which African-American artist Aaron Douglas (1898–1979) captures in his painting *Aspiration* (Fig. **36.1**). A native of Topeka, Kansas, with a Bachelor of Fine Arts degree from the University of Nebraska, where he had been the only black student in his class, Douglas arrived in Harlem in 1925.

"My first impression of Harlem," he would later write, "was that of an enormous stage swarming with humanity.... Here one found a kaleidoscope of rapidly changing colors, sounds, movements—rising, falling, swelling, contracting, now hurrying, now dragging along without end and often without apparent purpose. And yet beneath the surface of this chaotic incoherent activity one sensed an inner harmony, one felt the presence of a mysterious hand fitting all these disparate elements into a whole."

In fact, what was happening in Harlem was happening in New York City as a whole. From Wall Street to Midtown, construction boomed, and the rapid pace of building mirrored the frenetic pace of New York City itself. Like the pre–World War I years, movement and speed defined the era. Until the stock market crash of 1929, New York was the center of world commerce. Uptown, in Harlem, nightlife thrived—in the clubs and cabarets, life seemed to continue 24 hours a day. Despite Prohibition, which had outlawed the production, transportation, and sale of alcoholic beverages in 1920, liquor was plentiful, and white socialites from downtown filled the jazz clubs, dancing the night away to the bands that catered to their sense of freedom—and the "outlaw" status that their willful disregard for Prohibition underscored.

◀ **Fig. 36.1 Detail of Aaron Douglas, *Aspiration*. 1936.** © Estate of Aaron Douglas, Courtesy Fine Arts Museum of San Francisco. Douglas's painting is composed as a series of stars within stars, all pointing toward the future and the promise he believed it held for African Americans.

HEAR MORE Listen to an audio file of your chapter at **www.myartslab.com**

It was, as one prominent writer of the era recognized, a Jazz Age—a world moving to its own beat, improvising as it went along, discovering new and unheard-of chords with which life might resonate. The stock market boomed, money flowed, and American industry thrived. And everywhere one looked, new buildings, new products, new creations, and new works of art competed for the public's attention. Across the country in Hollywood, the film industry advanced the new, machine-created art that seemed to capture the spirit of the day. "Make it new" was the catchphrase of the era.

THE HARLEM RENAISSANCE

If the social roots of the Harlem Renaissance can be traced back to the Great Migration during the First World War, the philosophical roots reach back to the turn of the century and the work of black historian and sociologist W. E. B. Du Bois (1868–1963), whose *The Philadelphia Negro* (1899) was the first sociological text on a black community published in the United States. In 1903, in his book *The Souls of Black Folk*, Du Bois had proposed that the identity of African Americans was fraught with ambiguity (**Reading 36.1**):

READING 36.1

from W. E. B. Du Bois, *The Souls of Black Folk* (1903)

[America] yields him no true self-consciousness . . . . It is a peculiar sensation, this double-consciousness, this sense of always looking at one's self through the eyes of others, of measuring one's soul by the tape of a world that looks on in an amused contempt and pity. One ever feels his two-ness,—an American, a Negro; two souls, two thoughts, two unreconciled strivings; two warring ideals in one dark body, whose dogged strength alone keeps it from being torn asunder.

The history of the American Negro is the history of this strife—this longing to attain self-conscious manhood, to merge his double self into a better and truer self. In this merging he wishes neither of the older selves to be lost. He would not Africanize America, for America has too much to teach the world and Africa. He would not bleach his Negro soul in a flood of white Americanism, for he knows that Negro blood has a message for the world. He simply wishes to make it possible for a man to be both a Negro and an American, without being cursed and spit upon by his fellows, without having the doors of Opportunity closed roughly in his face.

When in 1909 the National Association for the Advancement of Colored People (NAACP) was founded to advance the rights of blacks, Du Bois became editor of its magazine,

The Crisis. His sense of the double-consciousness informing African-American experience (a double-consciousness that informs the very term "African American") was often expressed in the magazine's pages.

This double-consciousness is especially apparent in the work of Claude McKay (1889–1948), a poet who generally published in white avant-garde magazines and only occasionally in magazines like *The Crisis.* His poem "If We Must Die" was inspired by the race riots that exploded in the summer and fall of 1919 in a number of cities in both the North and South. The three most violent episodes of what came to be known as the "Red Summer" occurred in Chicago, Washington, D.C., and Elaine, Arkansas, all started by whites, who were stunned when blacks fought back. A "Southern black woman," as she identified herself, wrote a letter to *The Crisis,* praising blacks for fighting back: "The Washington riot gave me a thrill that comes once in a life time . . . at last our men had stood up like men . . . . I stood up alone in my room . . . and exclaimed aloud, 'Oh I thank God, thank God.' The pent up horror, grief and humiliation of a life time—half a century—was being stripped from me." McKay's poem expresses the same militant anger (**Reading 36.2**):

READING 36.2

Claude McKay, "If We Must Die" (1919)

If we must die—let it not be like hogs
Hunted and penned in an inglorious spot,
While round us bark the mad and hungry dogs,
Making their mock at our accursed lot.

If we must die—oh, let us nobly die,
So that our precious blood may not be shed
In vain; then even the monsters we defy
Shall be constrained to honor us though dead!

Oh, Kinsmen! We must meet the common foe;
Though far outnumbered, let us show us brave,
And for their thousand blows deal one deathblow!
What though before us lies the open grave?

Like men we'll face the murderous, cowardly pack,
Pressed to the wall, dying, but fighting back!

Ironically, years later, during World War II, British Prime Minister Winston Churchill would use the poem, without acknowledging its source—probably without even knowing it—to rally British and American troops fighting in Europe. That Churchill could so transform the poem's meaning is indicative of its very doubleness. Written in sonnet form, it harks back to the genteel heroism of Alfred, Lord Tennyson's "Charge of the Light Brigade" (see page 1145), and yet it was, in its original context, a call to arms.

McKay's book of poems, *Harlem Shadows,* is one of the first works by a black writer to be published by a mainstream, national publisher (Harcourt, Brace and

Company). Together with the novel *Cane* (1923) by Jean Toomer (1894–1967), an experimental work that combined poetry and prose in documenting the life of American blacks in the rural South and urban North, it helped to launch the burst of creative energy that was the Harlem Renaissance.

"The New Negro"

Perhaps the first self-conscious expression of the Harlem Renaissance took place at a dinner party, on March 21, 1924, hosted by Charles S. Johnson (1893–1956) of the National Urban League. The League was dedicated to promoting civil rights and helping black Americans address the economic and social problems they encountered as they resettled in the urban North. At Johnson's dinner, young writers from Harlem were introduced to New York's white literary establishment. A year later, the *Survey Graphic*, a national magazine dedicated to sociology, social work, and social analysis, produced an issue dedicated exclusively to Harlem. The issue, subtitled *Harlem: Mecca of the New Negro*, was edited by Alain Leroy Locke (1886–1954), an African-American professor of philosophy at Howard University in Washington, D.C. He was convinced that a new era was dawning for black Americans, and wrote a powerful introduction to a new anthology. In his essay, sometimes referred to as the manifesto of the New Negro Movement, Locke argued that Harlem was the center of this new arena of creative expression (**Reading 36.3**):

READING 36.3

Alain Locke, *The New Negro* (1925)

[There arises a] consciousness of acting as the advance-guard of the African peoples in their contact with Twentieth Century civilization . . . [and] the sense of a mission of rehabilitating the race in world esteem from that loss of prestige for which the fate and conditions of slavery have so largely been responsible. Harlem, as we shall see, is the center of both these movements . . . . The pulse of the Negro world has begun to beat in Harlem . . . . The New Negro . . . now becomes a conscious contributor and lays aside the status of beneficiary and ward for that of a collaborator and participant in American civilization. The great social gain in this is the releasing of our talented group from the arid fields of controversy and debate to the productive fields of creative expression . . . . And certainly, if in our lifetime the Negro should not be able to celebrate his full initiation into American democracy, he can at least, on the warrant of these things, celebrate the attainment of a significant and satisfying new phase of group development, and with it a spiritual Coming of Age.

In Locke's view, each ethnic group in America had its own identity, which it was entitled to protect and promote, and

this claim to cultural identity need not conflict with the claim to American citizenship. Locke further emphasized that the spirit of the young writers who were a part of this anthology would drive this new Harlem-based movement by focusing on the African roots of black art and music, but they would, in turn, contribute mightily to a new, more inclusive American culture.

Among the many poems and stories published in the *Survey Graphic* and *The New Negro* is "Heritage" by Countee Cullen (1903–1946) (Fig. **36.2**). Cullen was the adopted son of Frederick Cullen, pastor of the Salem Methodist Episcopal church in Harlem, and his wife, Carolyn, both of whom had strong ties to the NAACP and the National Urban League. Cullen later described his life in their household as a constant attempt at "reconciling a Christian upbringing with a pagan inclination." "Heritage" investigates that tension (see **Reading 36.4**, pages 1207–1208, for the complete poem):

Fig. 36.2 Carl Van Vechten, *Portrait of Countee Cullen in Central Park*. 1941. Gelatin silver photographic print. Library of Congress Prints and Photographs Division, Washington, D.C. The photographer, Carl Van Vechten (1880–1964), was a white journalist and novelist who actively promoted black artists and writers in the 1920s. His popular 1926 novel *Nigger Heaven*, named after the top tier of seats reserved for blacks in a segregated theater, was white America's introduction to Harlem culture, although the black intelligentsia almost unanimously condemned it for its depiction of Harlem as an amoral playground.

Lamb of God, although I speak
With my mouth thus, in my heart
Do I play a double part.
Ever at Thy glowing altar
Must my heart grow sick and falter,
Wishing He I served were black . . .

Although the poem has been criticized for its romantic depiction of Africa, it remains a powerful statement of Du Bois's sense of African-American double-consciousness. As cultural historian Houston Baker, Jr., has described it in *Afro-American Poetics: Revisions of Harlem and the Black Aesthetic*, "The entire poem is placed in a confessional framework as the narrator tries to define his relationship to some white . . . being and finds that a black impulse ceaselessly draws him back."

This theme of "doubleness" was underscored when the poem appeared in *Survey Graphic*. There it was illustrated by photographs of African statues and masks, reproduced from the collection of the Barnes Foundation in Philadelphia. Albert C. Barnes, who had made his fortune from the development of an antiseptic drug, was particularly noted not only for his collection of modern art, including Matisse's *Bonheur de vivre* (see Fig. 34.5), but also for his early and vigorous collecting of African art. In an article for the *Survey Graphic*, entitled "Negro Art and America," Barnes wrote:

> The renascence [sic] of Negro art is one of the events of our age which no seeker for beauty can afford to overlook. It is as characteristically Negro as are the primitive African sculptures. As art forms, each bears comparison with the great art expressions of any race or civilization. In both ancient and modern Negro art we find a faithful expression of a people and of an epoch in the world's evolution.

This kind of support from the white establishment was central to the cultural resurgence of Harlem. Many of New York's whites also supported the uptown neighborhood's thriving nightlife scene. Prohibition, and the speakeasies it spawned, had created in Harlem a culture of alcohol, nightlife, and dancing, and with them, the loose morality of the party life, indulged in particularly by the white clientele to whom the clubs catered.

Langston Hughes and the Poetry of Jazz

As the young poet Langston Hughes (1902–1967) later put it, "Negro was in vogue." Hughes was among the new young poets that Locke published in *The New Negro*, and the establishment publishing house, Knopf, would publish his book of poems, *Weary Blues*, in 1926. Twenty-two years of age in 1924, Hughes had gone to Paris seeking a freedom he could not find at home (see *Continuity & Change*, Chapter 35). He was soon writing poems inspired by the jazz rhythms he was hearing played by the African-American bands in the clubs where he worked as a busboy and dishwasher. The music's syncopated rhythms can be heard in poems such as "Jazz Band in a Parisian Cabaret" (**Reading 36.5a**):

African Americans like Hughes had been drawn to Paris by reports of black soldiers who had served in World War I, in the so-called Negro divisions, the 92nd and 93rd Infantries. Something approaching jazz was introduced to the French by Lieutenant James Reese Europe, whose 815th Pioneer Infantry band played in city after city across the country. They played a combination of standard band music, dance music, and tunes subjected to some degree of "ragging." In fact, he was the principal composer for the white society dancers Vernon and Irene Castle, and his music helped propel the foxtrot into great popularity. But most important, the band experienced something they never had in the United States—total acceptance by people with white skin. But Harlem, largely because of the efforts of Du Bois, Johnson, and Locke, soon replaced Paris in the African-American imagination.

In Harlem, Hughes quickly became one of the most powerful voices. His poems (see **Reading 36.5**, pages 1208–1209, for a selection) narrate the lives of his people, capturing the inflections and cadences of their speech. In fact, the poems celebrate, most of all, the inventiveness of African-American culture, especially the openness and ingenuity of its music and language. Hughes had come to understand that his cultural identity rested not in the grammar and philosophy of white culture, but in the vernacular expression of the American black, which he could hear in its music (the blues and jazz especially) and its speech.

Zora Neale Hurston and the Voices of Folklore

The writer and folklorist Zora Neale Hurston (1891–1960) felt the same way. Slightly younger than many of her other Harlem Renaissance colleagues, while still an undergraduate at Howard University she attracted the attention of Hughes when she published a short story, "Spunk," in the black journal *Opportunity*. She transferred to Columbia, where she finished her degree under the great anthropologist Franz Boas, undertaking field research from 1927 to 1932 to collect folklore in the South. Her novel, *Their Eyes Were Watching God* (1937), takes place in a town very much like her native Eatonville, Florida, where she was raised. Its narrator, Janie Crawford, has returned home after being away for a very long time. The townsfolk, particularly the women, are petty, unwelcoming, and gossipy.

The Quilts of Gee's Bend

From the outset, Hurston's writing concerned itself primarily with the question of African-American identity—an identity she located in the vernacular speech of her native rural South and in the stories of the people who lived there. Hurston's mastery of the dialect and the nuances of African-American speech is unsurpassed. She recognized in this vernacular language something distinctly modern.

In fact, in the isolated community of Gee's Bend, Alabama, an indigenous grassroots approach to textile design had been flourishing since perhaps the late nineteenth century, although it would remain completely unknown until William Arnett, a collector and scholar of African-American art, rediscovered the community and its continuing quilt-making tradition in the late 1990s. Surrounded on three sides by the Alabama River, and open to the world on the other by an often impassable road, Gee's Bend was almost completely isolated, and over the years, its quilters had developed a distinct aesthetic sensibility that they had passed on from one generation to the next. In 2006, the Museum of Fine Arts, Houston, organized an exhibit of quilts made by four generations of Gee's Bend women that rivaled in every way the inventiveness and freedom of modern abstract art. In *Gee's Bend: The Architecture of the Quilt*, Arnett describes the quilts in terms that evoke jazz, that other vernacular form of African-American expression that rose to prominence in the Harlem Renaissance (and which will be discussed in a moment). The quilts are distinguished, he writes, by their preference for "asymmetry, strong contrast, and affective color changes, syncopation and pattern breaks, and an improvisational flair." They take on, especially, the shapes and rhythms of the improvisational rural architecture of Gee's Bend itself, in which, in the case of Jessie T. Pettway's *Bars and String-Pieced Columns* (Fig. 36.3), random scraps of odd-shaped wooden slats might be nailed across a frame of two-by-fours. As the Houston exhibit has traveled around the United States since 2006, it has become clear that a new and unique vernacular modernism has developed independently of the mainstream art world.

All That Jazz

By the time of the Great Migration, jazz had established itself as the music of African Americans. So much did the music seem to define all things American that the novelist F. Scott Fitzgerald (1896–1940) entitled a collection of

Fig. 36.3 Jessie T. Pettway, *Bars and String-Pieced Columns*, 1950s. Cotton, 95″ × 76″. Provided by the Tinwood Alliance (http://www.tinwoodmeida.com) Photo: Steve Pitking / Pitking Studios © 2003. Collection, Atlanta. The loose structure of Pettway's quilt creates an almost giddy sense of imbalance.

short stories published in 1922 *Tales of the Jazz Age*, and the name stuck. By the end of the 1920s, jazz was *the* American music, and it was almost as popular in Paris and Berlin as it was in New York, Chicago, and New Orleans. As we saw in Chapter 32, it originated in New Orleans in the 1890s, probably the most racially diverse city in America, particularly in the ragtime piano music of Scott Joplin and others. But it had deep roots as well in the blues.

The Blues and Their "Empress," Bessie Smith If syncopated rhythm is one of the primary characteristics of jazz, another is the **blue note**. Blue notes are slightly lower or flatter than conventional pitches. In jazz, blues instrumentalists or singers commonly "bend" or "scoop" a blue note—usually the third, fifth, or seventh notes of a given scale—to achieve heightened emotional effects. Such effects were first established in the blues proper, a form of song that originated among enslaved black Americans and their descendants.

The **blues** are by definition laments bemoaning loss of love, poverty, or social injustice, and they contributed importantly to the development of jazz. The standard blues form consists of three sections of four bars each. Each of these sections corresponds to the single line of a three-line stanza, the first two lines of which are the same. In his 1925 poem "Weary Blues," Langston Hughes describes listening

HEAR MORE Listen to Voices about the Harlem Renaissance at **www.myartslab.com**

to a blues singer in a Harlem club (see Reading 36.5, pages 1208–1209 for the entire poem):

> Droning a drowsy syncopated tune,
> Rocking back and forth to a mellow croon,
> I heard a Negro play.
> Down on Lenox Avenue the other night
> By the pale dull pallor of an old gas light
> He did a lazy sway . . .
> He did a lazy sway . . .
> . . . . . .
> Thump, thump, thump, went his foot on the floor.
> He played a few chords then he sang some more—
> "I got the Weary Blues
> And I can't be satisfied.
> I got the Weary Blues
> And I can't be satisfied.
> I ain't happy no mo'
> And I wish that I had died."

The last lines are the standard blues form (expanded by Hughes to six instead of three lines for the sake of his own poetic meter).

Early blues artists whose performances are preserved on record include Ma Rainey (1886–1939) and Robert Johnson (1911–1938). But perhaps the greatest of the 1920s blues singers was Bessie Smith (1892–1937), who grew up in Tennessee singing on street corners to support her family (Fig. **36.4**). In 1923, when she was 29 years old, she made her first recording, and audiences were stunned by the feeling that she brought to her performances. She was noted particularly for the way she added a chromatic note before the last note of a line, so that, in her *Florida-Bound Blues* (track **36.1**), for instance,

becomes

The additional note might be delivered quickly, or it might be stretched out, adding an extended sense of dissonance and anguished tension to the blues form. When, by the early 1930s, audiences began to prefer a smoother approach to the blues, Smith's popularity waned. Nor did she fit the more acceptable image of the light-skinned, white-featured black entertainer. Traveling from one-night stand to one-night stand in honky-tonks across the Deep South, she died in an automobile accident in 1937.

Dixieland and Louis Armstrong in Chicago The bands that played around 1910 to 1920 in the red-light district of New Orleans, the legendary Storeyville, quickly established a standard practice. A "front line," consisting of trumpet (or cornet), clarinet, and trombone, was accompanied by banjo

Fig. 36.4 Carl Van Vechten, Bessie Smith. n.d. Black-and-white negative, 4″ × 5″. Yale Collection of American Literature, Beinecke Rare Book and Manuscript Library. Van Vechten's collection of photographs and other documents pertaining to the Harlem Renaissance remains one of the era's most important documentary records.

(later guitar), piano, bass, and drums. In **Dixieland jazz**, as it came to be known, the trumpet carried the main melody and the clarinet played off against it with a higher counter-melody, while the trombone played a simpler, lower tune. The most popular forms of Dixieland were the standard 12-bar blues and a 32-bar AABA form. The latter consists of four 8-measure sections. Generally speaking, the trumpet plays the basic tune for the first 32 measures of the piece, then the band plays variations on the tune in a series of solo or collective improvisations keeping to the 32-bar format. Each 32-bar section is called a "chorus."

When Storeyville was shut down in 1917 (on orders from the U.S. Navy, whose sailors' discipline they believed was threatened by its presence), many of the bands that had played in the district joined the Great Migration and headed north. Among them was trumpeter Louis Armstrong (1901–1971), who arrived in Chicago in 1922 to play for Joe Oliver's Creole Jazz Band. The pianist and composer Lil Hardin (1898–1971) was the pianist and arranger for Oliver's band, and she and Armstrong were married in 1924. Soon, Armstrong left Oliver's band to play on his own. He formed two studio bands composed of former New Orleans colleagues, the Hot Five and the Hot Seven, with whom he made a series of groundbreaking HEAR MORE at recordings. One, *Hotter Than That* (track **36.2**), www.myartslab.com

((•● HEAR MORE at
www.myartslab.com

written by Hardin and recorded in 1927, is based on a 32-bar form over which the performers improvise. In the third chorus, Armstrong sings in nonsense syllables, a method known as **scat**. This is followed by another standard form of jazz band performance, a **call-and-response** chorus between Armstrong and guitarist Lonnie Johnson, the two imitating one another as closely as possible on their two different instruments.

Swing: Duke Ellington at the Cotton Club The same year that Armstrong recorded *Hotter Than That*, Duke Ellington, born Edward Kennedy Ellington in Washington, D.C. (1899–1974), began a five-year engagement at Harlem's Cotton Club (Fig. **36.5**). The Cotton Club itself was owned by a gangster who used it as an outlet for his "Madden's #1 Beer," which, like all alcoholic beverages, was banned after National Prohibition was introduced in 1920. The Club's name was meant to evoke leisurely plantation life for its "white only" audience who came to listen to its predominantly black entertainers.

Ellington had formed his first band in New York in 1923. HEAR MORE at www.myartslab.com His 1932 *It Don't Mean a Thing (If It Ain't Got That Swing)* (track **36.3**) introduced the term **swing** to jazz culture. (A particularly clear example of a "blue note" can be heard, incidentally, on the first "ain't" of the first chorus of *It Don't Mean a Thing*.) Swing is characterized by big bands—as many as 15 to 20 musicians, including up to five saxophones (two altos, two tenors, and a baritone)—resulting in a much bigger sound. Its rhythm depends on subtle avoidance of downbeats with the solo instrument attacking the beat either just before or just after it.

By the time Ellington began his engagement at the Cotton Club, commercial radio was seven years old, and many thousands of American homes had a radio. Live radio broadcasts from the Cotton Club brought Ellington national fame, and he was widely imitated throughout the 1930s by bands who toured the country. These included bands led by clarinetist Benny Goodman, soon known as "the King of Swing"; trumpeter Harry James; trombonist Glenn Miller; trombonist Tommy Dorsey; pianist Count Basie; and clarinetist Artie Shaw. These bands also featured vocalists, and they introduced the country to Frank Sinatra, Bing Crosby, Perry Como, Sarah Vaughan, Billie Holiday, Peggy Lee, Doris Day, Rosemary Clooney, and Ella Fitzgerald.

Jazz influenced almost every form of music after 1920. Debussy imitated rag in his 1908 *Golliwog's Cakewalk*. Stravinsky composed a *Ragtime for Eleven Instruments* in 1917. The American composer George Gershwin incorporated jazz rhythms into his 1924 piano and orchestra composition, *Rhapsody in Blue*, and his 1935 opera *Porgy and Bess* incorporated jazz, blues, and spiritual in a way that revived musical theater and paved the way for the great musicals of the 1940s and 1950s. In fact, *Porgy and Bess* has been staged and recorded both by jazz greats—Louis Armstrong and Ella

Fig. 36.5 The Cotton Club, Lenox Avenue and 143rd Street. Early 1930s. Corbis-Bettmann Photo Archive. In 1927, Duke Ellington's orchestra was hired to play at the club, and soon Cab Calloway's band alternated with Ellington. It was also at the Cotton Club that Lena Horne began her career in 1933, at age 16.

Fitzgerald—and by professional opera companies, bridging the gap between popular art and high culture as few works before it ever had.

The Visual Arts in Harlem

The leading visual artist in Harlem in the 1920s was Aaron Douglas (see Fig. 36.1). When he arrived in Harlem in 1925, his first major work was as illustrator of a book of verse sermons by the Harlem Renaissance poet and executive secretary of the NAACP James Weldon Johnson (1871–1938), *God's Trombones: Seven Sermons in Verse*. Like his friend and colleague Zora Neale Hurston, Johnson was interested in preserving the voices of folklore, specifically folk sermons. "I remember," Johnson writes in the preface to *God's Trombones*, "hearing in my boyhood sermons that . . . passed with only slight modifications from preacher to preacher and from locality to locality." One of these was the story of "The Prodigal Son," updated to reflect life in the streets of 1920s Harlem (**Reading 36.6**):

READING 36.6

from James Weldon Johnson, "The Prodigal Son" (1927)

And the city was bright in the night-time like day,
The streets all crowded with people,
Brass bands and string bands a-playing,
And ev'rywhere the young man turned
There was singing and laughing and dancing.
And he stopped a passer-by and he said:
Tell me what city is this?

And the passer-by laughed and said: Don't you know?
This is Babylon, Babylon,
That great city of Babylon.
Come on, my friend, and go along with me.
And the young man joined the crowd . . . .

And the young man went with his new-found friend,
And bought himself some brand new clothes,
And he spent his days in the drinking dens,
Swallowing the fires of hell.
And he spent his nights in the gambling dens,
Throwing dice with the devil for his soul.
And he met up with the women of Babylon.
Oh, the women of Babylon!
Dressed in yellow and purple and scarlet,
Loaded with rings and earrings and bracelets,
Their lips like a honeycomb dripping with honey,
Perfumed and sweet-smelling like a jasmine flower;
And the jasmine smell of the Babylon women
Got in his nostrils and went to his head,
And he wasted his substance in riotous living,
In the evening, in the black and dark of night,
With the sweet-sinning women of Babylon.
And they stripped him of his money,
And they stripped him of his clothes,
And they left him broke and ragged
In the streets of Babylon . . . .

Fig. 36.6 Aaron Douglas, Illustration for "The Prodigal Son," in James Weldon Johnson, *God's Trombones: Seven Sermons in Verse*. 1927. University of North Carolina Library. Douglas's inclusion of the fragment of a dollar, the tax stamp from a package of cigarettes (at the bottom right), a playing card, and the fragment of the word "gin" all reflect his awareness of French Cubism.

Douglas's illustration (Fig. **36.6**) makes the timeliness of Johnson's poem abundantly clear. His two-dimensional silhouetted figures would become the signature style of Harlem Renaissance art, in which a sense of rhythmic movement and sound is created by abrupt shifts in the direction of line and mass.

His influence is evident in the later work of Jacob Lawrence (1917–2000) (see Fig. 35.18), who met Douglas soon after arriving in Harlem in the mid-1930s. The angularity and rhythmic repetition of forms that Douglas introduced is evident in many of Lawrence's paintings for the *Great Migration* series of 1939 to 1941, particularly in his illustration of three girls writing on a chalkboard at school (Fig. **36.7**). Here the intellectual growth of the girls, as each reaches higher on the board, is presented as a musical crescendo in a syncopated, four-beat, rhythmic form where the first beat, as it were, is silent and unplayed. But above all, what the art of both Douglas and Lawrence makes clear is the connectedness of literature, music, and visual image in African-American experience. Such connections would continue to inform African-American culture for the rest of the century.

Fig. 36.7 Jacob Lawrence, *In the North the Negro had better educational facilities*, panel 58 from *The Migration of the Negro*. 1940–41. Casein tempera on hardboard, 12″ × 18″. Gift of Mrs. David M. Levy. The Museum of Modern Art/Licensed by SCALA/Art Resource, New York. © 2007 Artists Rights Society (ARS), New York. Note that Lawrence dresses the girls in the primary colors of red, yellow, and blue, thus emphasizing the fundamental nature of primary education.

SKYSCRAPER AND MACHINE: ARCHITECTURE IN NEW YORK

After the First World War, New York experienced a building boom outstripped only by the growth of its population. The skyscraper, a distinctly American invention, was first developed in Chicago, where Louis Sullivan took the lead (see Fig. 32.25), but it found its ultimate expression in New York. There, skyscrapers were usually commissioned by corporations as their national and international headquarters (Map **36.1**). The skyscraper was above all a grand advertisement, a symbol of corporate power and prestige that changed the skyline of New York and became a symbol for the city around the world. The Singer Building of 1902 was followed by the Metropolitan Life Tower (1909), the Woolworth Building (1913), the Shelton Towers (1924), the Chrysler Building (1930) (Fig. **36.8**), the Empire State

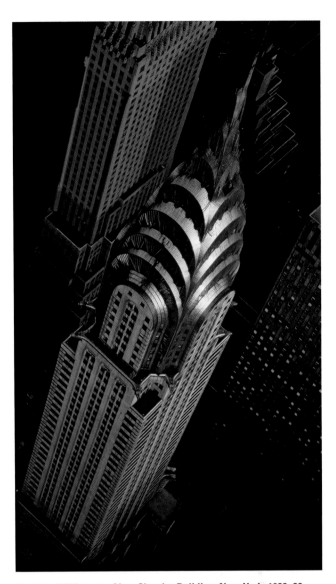

Fig. 36.8 William van Alen, Chrysler Building, New York. 1928–30.
The building's steel crown, shown in this detail, was understood to be an emblem of the new technological ascendancy of not just the Chrysler Corporation, but America itself.

SEE MORE For a Closer Look at William van Alen's Chrysler Building, go to **www.myartslab.com**

Building (1931), and the RCA Building (1933). Each strove to be the world's highest, and briefly was, until it was succeeded, often within a matter of months, by the next.

Walter Chrysler's Chrysler Building was, for instance, pure advertisement. The site was opposite Grand Central Station on 42nd Street and Lexington Avenue, at the very heart of Manhattan. Chrysler informed William van Alen, his architect, that he expected the building to be the tallest building in the world, "higher than the Eiffel Tower." Van Alen's former partner, H. Craig Severance, had already broken ground for the Bank of Manhattan Trust Building at 40 Wall Street (today the Trump Building), and the two entered into a fierce competition. When Severance's building was completed, just months before van Alen's, it was, at

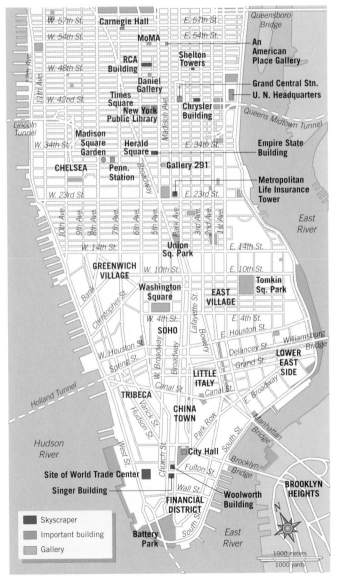

Map. 36.1 New York City skyscrapers.

LEARN MORE Gain insight from an architectural simulation of sckyscrapers at **www.myartslab.com**

71 stories and 927 feet tall, the tallest structure in the world. Then van Alen surprised everyone. He had secretly constructed a 185-foot spire inside his building. At the last minute, he hoisted it up through the roof and bolted it in place. The Chrysler Building was now a staggering 77 stories and 1,046 feet tall.

The first six floors of the crowning spire were reserved for Walter Chrysler's private use. They included an observation deck and a lounge displaying his personal tool box, consisting of forged and tempered steel tools that Chrysler made by hand when he was 17 years of age and that he referred to as the "tools that money couldn't buy." The exterior of the spire was crowned with a stainless steel crest, punctuated by triangular windows in radiating semicircles (designed to evoke Chrysler hubcaps). At night, the windows were lit, adding a new graceful, arcing form to the increasingly rectilinear horizon of the New York cityscape.

Within a year, the Empire State Building became the world's tallest building, at 102 stories and 1,250 feet high. But aside from its sheer size, the Chrysler Building's decoration was what set it apart. It was self-consciously Art Deco, a term coined in the 1960s after the 1925 Arts Décoratifs exhibition in Paris to describe a style that was known at the

Fig. 36.10 Alfred Stieglitz, _The Steerage_. 1907. Photogravure, 13 $^3/_{16}$″ × 10 $^3/_8$″. Courtesy George Eastman House. © 2008 Artists Rights Society (ARS), NY. Stieglitz first published this photograph in _Camera Work_ in 1911.

time as Art Moderne, noted for its highly stylized forms and exotic materials. And among the most exotic of these materials in the late 1920s was stainless steel, first patented in the United States in 1915. The spire's crown was clad in the material and from the sixty-first floor of the Chrysler Building, giant Art Deco stainless steel eagles, replicas of Chrysler's hood ornaments, pointed their beaks outward like gargoyles (Fig. 36.9)

The Machine Aesthetic

Perhaps more than anything else, the Chrysler Building is a monument to the technology and the spirit of the new that technology inspired. Around the thirty-first floor, Chrysler hubcaps were placed in brickwork shaped like tires. It was part and parcel of a machine aesthetic that dominated the day, most fully articulated by Alfred H. Barr, Jr. (1902–1981), director of the new Museum of Modern Art in New York, and his young curator of architecture, Philip Johnson (1906–2005), in an exhibition entitled _Machine Art_. The subject of enormous press coverage when it opened in 1934, the exhibit featured springs, propellers, ball bearings, kitchen appliances, laboratory glass and porcelain (including boiling flasks made from Pyrex, a new durable material that would transform modern kitchenware), and machine parts displayed on pedestals. Crowds thronged to the museum to see the 402 items Barr and Johnson had chosen. All of these objects were defined by

Fig. 36.9 Margaret Bourke-White, _Chrysler Building: Gargoyle outside Margaret Bourke-White's Studio_. 1930. Gelatin silver print, 12 $^{15}/_{16}$″ × 9 $^1/_4$″. Courtesy George Eastman House, Rochester, NY. One of the most important photographers of the day, Bourke-White would become one of _Life_ magazine's most important contributors (the magazine's first cover was shot by her in 1936). This shot was taken from her studio in the Chrysler Building.

their simple geometric forms, symmetry, balance, and proportion—in short a new, machine-inspired classicism.

Earlier in the century, Alfred Stieglitz [STEE-glitz] (1864–1946) had proposed that modern art—and his own photography in particular—should concern itself with revealing the underlying geometries of the world. At a small New York gallery, named simply 291, after its address at 291 Fifth Avenue, Stieglitz had hosted Matisse's first one-person show outside of France. He mounted two more shows of Matisse's work in 1910 and 1912. Stieglitz had also been the first in the United States to exhibit Picasso, showing more than 80 of his works on paper in 1911.

Stieglitz valued both artists for the attention they paid to formal composition over and above any slavish dependence on visual appearance. He valued, in other words, the conceptual qualities of their work as opposed to their imagery. This is perhaps surprising for a photographer, but describing the inspiration of his own 1906 photograph *The Steerage* (Fig. **36.10**), he would later recall:

There were men, women and children on the lower level of the steerage [the lower class deck of a steamship] . . . . The scene fascinated me: A round straw hat; the funnel leaning left, the stairway leaning right; the white drawbridge, its railings made of chain; white suspenders crossed on the back of a man below; circular iron machinery; a mast that cut into the sky, completing a triangle. I stood spellbound for a while. I saw shapes related to one another—a picture of shapes, and underlying it, a new vision that held me . . . .

The photographers and painters Stieglitz championed—including Georgia O'Keeffe (1887–1986), whom he would later marry—were all dedicated to revealing these same geometries in the world. In *Camera Work*, the photography magazine he published from 1903 to 1916, Stieglitz reproduced modern paintings and similarly modern photographs like *Abstraction, Porch Shadows* by Paul Strand (1890–1976) (Fig. **36.11**). Strand's image is an unmanipulated

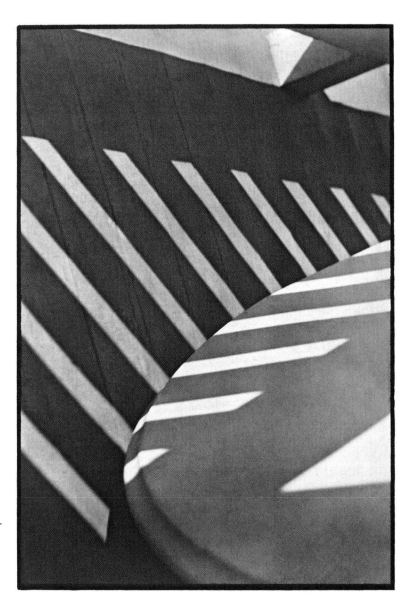

Fig. 36.11 Paul Strand, *Abstraction, Porch Shadows*. 1916. Silver-platinum print, 12$^{15}/_{16}$″ × 9$^{5}/_{8}$″. Inv. Pho1981-35-10. Repro-Photo: Rene-Gabriel Ojeda. Musée d'Orsay, Paris, France. Réunion des Musées Nationaux/Art Resource, New York. When Stieglitz published this photograph in the last issue of *Camera Work*, June 1917, he called it "the direct expression of today."

Fig. 36.12 Alfred Stieglitz, *Looking Northwest from the Shelton, New York*. 1932. Gelatin silver print, 9$\frac{1}{2}$″ × 7$\frac{9}{16}$″. The Metropolitan Museum of Art, New York. Ford Motor Company Collection, Gift of Ford Motor Company and John C. Waddell, 1987 (1987.1100.11). Image © The Metropolitan Museum of Art/Art Resource, New York. © 2008 Artists Rights Society (ARS), New York. The Shelton Towers, on Lexington Avenue between 48th and 49th Streets, was built in 1924. At 36 stories, it was the tallest building in the world, a record soon surpassed as this photograph, taken from Stieglitz's suite on the thirtieth floor, suggests.

photograph (that is, not altered during the development process) of the shadows of a railing cast across a porch and onto a white patio table turned on its side. Its debt to Picasso and Braque's Cubism was not lost on the magazine's audience.

In 1925, Stieglitz moved into an apartment on the thirtieth floor of the 36-story Shelton Towers (see Map 36.1), and from his window, he began to photograph the city rising around him—the grids of buildings under construction, the rhythmic repetition of window and curtain wall, the blocks of form delineated by the intense contrast of black and white in the photographic print (Fig. **36.12**). In the skyscraper, he believed he had discovered the underlying geometry of modernity itself.

The International Style

Stieglitz lived in the Shelton Towers for 12 years, and from his window, he witnessed a building boom like none other in the history of architecture. In the second half of the 1920s, the city's available office space increased by 92 percent. By the early 1930s, after buildings begun before 1929 were completed, the available space increased by another

56 percent. The building frenzy took place in an atmosphere of intense debate among architects themselves. On one side were the traditionalists whose decorative style was epitomized by the Woolworth Building (Fig. **36.13**).

Fig. 36.13 Cass Gilbert, *Woolworth Building, New York City, sketch elevation*. December 31, 1910. Graphite on paper. Library of Congress, Prints and Photographs Division. Gilbert's sketch captures the building's Gothic spirituality even better than actual photographs of the finished building, which was completed in 1913.

Fig. 36.14 Frank Lloyd Wright, Robie House, South Woodlawn, Chicago, Illinois. 1909. Wright derived from Louis Sullivan the belief that good architecture must be rooted in its relation to the natural world.

Writing about its neo-Gothic facade, architect Cass Gilbert (1859–1934) described it as follows: "A skyscraper, by its height . . . a monument whose masses must become more and more inspired the higher it rises . . . . The Gothic style gave us the possibility of expressing the greatest degree of aspiration . . . the ultimate note of the mass gradually gaining in spirituality the higher it mounts." From the modernist point of view, Gilbert's building represented the height of absurdity, and "Woolworth Gothic" became synonymous with bad taste, but building after building continued to emulate the Woolworth's emphasis on decorative styling.

On the other side of the debate were those who advocated an austere, clean modernism that revealed its plain geometries. This new architecture would come to be known as the International Style, after Alfred H. Barr, Jr., and Philip Johnson curated another show, in 1932, two years before the *Machine Art* exhibition, called the *International Exhibition of Modern Architecture* with an accompanying catalogue titled *The International Style: Architecture since 1922*. From the curators' point of view, a new "controlling" architectural style had emerged in Europe after the war without regard to national tastes or individual concerns (its European manifestations are discussed in Chapter 37). The principles of this new International Style were related to the machines they also admired: pure forms ("architecture as volume rather than mass") without "arbitrary applied ornament" (a slap at Louis Sullivan's Chicago School of architecture), and with severe, flat surfaces in its place. The American chosen to represent the style was Frank Lloyd Wright (1867–1959).

It was Barr who insisted that Wright be included in the exhibition. His colleague Philip Johnson regarded Wright

as old-fashioned, of no serious worth, and stylistically inconsistent with the International Style. Wright, in turn, despised both the International Style and Johnson. But he was included because he was a former student of Louis Sullivan and because Europeans considered him the leader of modern architecture. What Wright had done, they understood, was open up the interior of the building, to destroy the boxlike features that traditionally defined a room.

In his early architecture, like the Robie House (Figs. **36.14** and **36.15**), Wright had employed many of the same principles that guided architects of the

Fig. 36.15 Plan of the Robie House.

International Style—open interior spaces, steel-frame construction, concrete cantilevers that extended over porches to connect exterior and interior space, a raised first floor to provide for privacy, and walls consisting entirely of windows. But his inspiration was nature—his sense of place—not the machine. He called houses such as the Robie House "Prairie Houses," because in their openness and horizontality they reflected the Great Plains. The materials he employed were local—brick from local clays, oak woodwork, and so on.

Furthermore, Wright believed that each house should reflect not just its region but also its owner's individuality.

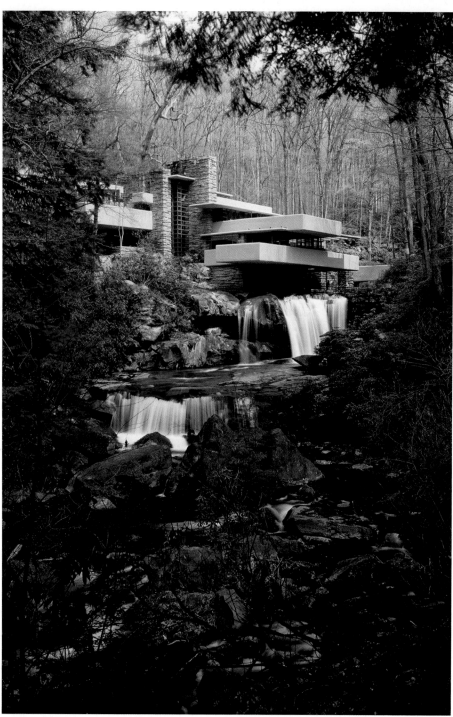

He abhorred the uniformity that the International Style promoted. This is especially evident at Fallingwater, the house at Bear Run in Pennsylvania which he designed in 1935 for Pittsburgh entrepreneur Edgar Kaufmann, owner of the largest men's clothing store in the country (Fig. **36.16**). Wright thought of Fallingwater as consistent with his earlier Prairie Houses because it was wedded to its site. But this site was distinguished by the cascades of Bear Run, falling down over a series of cliffs. Wright opened a quarry on the site to extract local stone and built a three-level house literally over the stream, its enormous cantilevered decks echoing the surrounding cliffs.

Fallingwater, finally, for Wright had to be in harmony with its site, not some white industrial construction plopped into the landscape. "I came to see a building," Wright wrote in 1936, "primarily . . . as a broad shelter in the open, related to vista; vista without and vista within. You may see in these various feelings, all taking the same direction, that I was born an American, child of the ground and of space." Wright's stunning and original design suggests a distinctly American sensitivity to place.

Fig. 36.16 Frank Lloyd Wright, Fallingwater (Kaufmann House), Bear Run, Pennsylvania. 1935–36. The first drawings for Fallingwater were done in a matter of hours after Wright had thought about the project for months.

MAKING IT NEW: THE ART OF PLACE

In the fall of 1929, Stieglitz opened a new gallery called An American Place on the seventeenth floor of a building on Madison Avenue at 53rd Street in New York (see Map 36.1). The name was primarily intended to reflect the gallery's emphasis on American art, but it also defined that art as possessing, as indeed Frank Lloyd Wright's architecture did, a distinct sense of place. The Harlem Renaissance had played an enormous role in creating this sense of an distinct American identity. Its music, especially, was widely understood as one of the first truly "authentic" expressions of American experience, unfettered by European influence or tradition. The blues, jazz, and swing constituted a "new," distinctly American music, to which writer F. Scott Fitzgerald had responded by coining the phrase "Jazz Age."

The New American Novel and Its Tragic Sense of Place

If the music of the era seemed to grow out of the American experience with the ring of certain truth; the Jazz Age itself, as Fitzgerald portrayed it, seemed to rise out of its opposite, the crassly and tragically materialistic culture of the day (the same world of easy money, fast women, and alcohol that swirls around Douglas's illustration of Johnson's "Prodigal Son"), out of the tragedy of war—not only World War I but also the still lingering effects of the American Civil War—which was, in the eyes of many, a direct result of this culture.

Fitzgerald and ***The Great Gatsby*** "That's the whole burden of this novel," Fitzgerald wrote of his novel *The Great Gatsby* in 1924, the year before it was published, "the loss of those illusions that give such color to the world that you don't care whether things are true or false as long as they partake of the magical glory." Set in New York City and on Long Island in the 1920s, the novel tells the story of Jay Gatsby, born Jimmy Gatz, who, as a boy of 17, "his heart . . . in a constant turbulent riot," had imagined for himself "a universe of ineffable gaudiness," and by the time he was 32, realized it. His neighbor, Nick Carraway, the novel's narrator, relates the weekend scene at Gatsby's West Egg home (**Reading 36.7a**):

READING 36.7a

from F. Scott Fitzgerald, *The Great Gatsby* (1925)

In his blue gardens men and girls came and went like moths among the whisperings and the champagne and the stars. At high tide in the afternoon I watched his guests diving from the tower of his raft, or taking the sun on the hot sand of his beach while his two motor-boats slit the waters of the Sound, drawing aquaplanes over the cataracts of foam . . . . And on Mondays eight servants, including an extra gardener, toiled all day with

---

mops and scrubbing-brushes and hammers and garden-shears, repairing the ravages of the night before.

Every Friday, five crates of lemons and oranges arrived from a fruiterer in New York—every Monday these same lemons and oranges left his backdoor in a pyramid of pulpless halves. There was a machine in the kitchen that could extract the juice of two hundred oranges in half an hour if a little button was pressed two hundred times by a butler's thumb.

At least once a fortnight a crop of caterers came down with several hundred feet of canvas and enough colored lights to make a Christmas tree of Gatsby's enormous garden. On buffet tables, garnished with glistening hors-d'oeuvre, spiced baked hams crowded against salads of harlequin designs and pastry pigs and turkeys bewitched to a dark gold. In the main hall, a bar with a real brass rail was set up, and stocked with gins and liquors and with cordials . . . .

By seven o'clock the orchestra has arrived, no thin five-piece affair, but a whole pitful of oboes and trombones and saxophones and viols and cornets and piccolos and high and low drums . . . . The bar is in full swing, and floating rounds of cocktails permeate the garden outside, until the air is alive with chatter and laughter, and casual innuendo and introductions forgotten on the spot, and enthusiastic meetings between women who never knew each other's names.

It is all a great show, a charade conceived by Gatsby to win the heart of Daisy Buchanan, who lives with her husband Tom across the bay in more fashionable East Egg, the green light on her dock forever in his view. Gatsby is "an unbroken series of successful gestures," a fabric of deceit built on an empty morality of wealth as an end itself that inevitably collapses. Nick Carraway goes so far as to say that listening to Gatsby talk "was like skimming hastily through a dozen magazines," the American Dream in all its shallowness.

And yet, Nick recognizes, there is something about Gatsby that is indeed "great." At the novel's end, Gatsby dead, Nick stretches out on Gatsby's beach and recalls the spirit of discovery and wonder that the original settlers of America must have felt (**Reading 36.7b**):

READING 36.7b

from F. Scott Fitzgerald, *The Great Gatsby* (1925)

I gradually became aware of the old island here that flowered once for Dutch sailors' eyes—a fresh, green breast of the new world. Its vanished trees, the trees that had made way for Gatsby's house, had once pandered in whispers to the last and greatest of all human dreams; for a transitory enchanted moment man must have held his breath in the presence of this continent,

---

compelled into an aesthetic contemplation he neither understood nor desired, face to face for the last time in history with something commensurate to his capacity for wonder.

And as I sat there brooding on the old, unknown world, I thought of Gatsby's wonder when he first picked out the green light at the end of Daisy's dock. He had come a long way to his blue lawn, and his dream must have seemed so close that he could hardly fail to grasp it. He did not know that it was already behind him, somewhere back in the vast obscurity beyond the city, where the dark fields of the republic rolled on under the night.

Gatsby believed in the green light, the orgiastic future that year by year recedes before us. It eluded us then, but that's no matter—tomorrow we will run faster, stretch out our arms farther . . . . and one fine morning—

So we beat on, boats against the current, borne back ceaselessly into the past.

As corrupted by the crass materialism of the day as Gatsby's dream is, it remains the quintessential American dream, the dream of a new world in which the imagination is free to create itself anew as well. From Fitzgerald's point of view, Gatsby had simply been born too late for his dream to have been realized—that is both his tragedy and his greatness.

Hemingway's Michigan In 1925, Fitzgerald introduced Ernest Hemingway (1899–1961) to his editor at Scribner's, and a year later Scribner's published Hemingway's first novel, *The Sun Also Rises*. The novel takes for its epigraph Gertrude Stein's famous phrase, "You are all a lost generation," and its cast of hard-drinking, fast-living, essentially aimless American expatriates seemed to capture the spirit of the age. It was an immediate success. As the American critic Malcolm Cowley put it in his 1934 memoir, *Exile's Return*: "Young men tried to get as imperturbably drunk as the hero, young women of fairly good family cultivated the heroine's nymphomania, and the name 'the lost generation' was fixed. It was a boast at first, like telling what a hangover one had after a party to which someone else wasn't invited." The hero, Jake Barnes, an American journalist, has suffered an injury in World War I, which makes it impossible for him to consummate his relationship with the novel's heroine, Lady Brett Ashley. About halfway through the novel, a character named Jeff Gorton mockingly describes to Jake just who he has become: "You're an expatriate. You've lost touch with the soil. You get precious. Fake European standards have ruined you. You drink yourself to death. You become obsessed by sex. You spend all your time talking, not working. You are an expatriate, see? You hang around cafés." It is safe to say that the only thing separating Hemingway from his character—aside from

his own sexual self-esteem—was that Hemingway worked, and worked hard, on his writing.

Hemingway had first come to Europe when the United States entered the war in 1917. He tried to enlist but was judged unfit for service because of his poor eyesight. "I can't let a show like this go on without getting into it," he wrote to his family, and so he volunteered to serve as an ambulance driver for the American Red Cross. He was stationed on the Italian Front where he was almost immediately wounded in the legs from mortar fire. Recuperating in Milan, he fell in love with Agnes von Kurowsky, who nursed him back to health and won immortality as the inspiration for Catherine in Hemingway's 1929 novel, *A Farewell to Arms*. "Abstract words, such as glory, honor, courage, or hallow," Hemingway wrote in that novel, in what amounts to a manifesto of his rhetorical style, "were obscene beside the concrete names of villages, the numbers of roads, the names of rivers, the numbers of regiments and dates." For Hemingway the use of a stripped-down, concrete language became a means of survival. In the concrete he could not be betrayed, either by his own emotions or by his belief in the sincerity of someone else's.

But if in 1925 Fitzgerald's American place was to be discovered in the Gatsby's "blue gardens"—and if the expatriate world of Jake Barnes reflected many of the same problematic values—Hemingway preferred the wilder settings of untamed nature, particularly the lakes and rivers of upper Michigan. In his story "Big Two-Hearted River," published in London in the collection *In Our Time* in 1925, just before Hemingway's lifelong relationship with Scribner's was established, Hemingway's hero, Nick Adams, back from the war and suffering from what is apparently post-traumatic stress syndrome, goes fishing by himself in northern Michigan: "He felt he had left everything behind, the need for thinking, the need to write, other needs. It was all back of him." The story is only ostensibly about fishing. It is more about healing, about doing concrete things—making camp, cooking, smoking, feeding out a line into a stream—that in their very simplicity convince us that we are alive (**Reading 36.8**):

READING 36.8

from Ernest Hemingway, "Big Two-Hearted River" (1925)

In the morning the sun was up and the tent was starting to get hot. Nick crawled out under the mosquito netting stretched across the mouth of the tent, to look at the morning. The grass was wet on his hands as he came out. The sun was just up over the hill. There was the meadow, the river and the swamp. There were birch trees in the green of the swamp on the other side of the river.

The river was clear and smoothly fast in the early morning. Down about two hundred yards were three logs all the way across the stream. They made the water smooth and deep above them. As Nick watched, a mink crossed the river on the logs and went into the swamp. Nick was excited. He was excited by the early morning and the river. He was really too hurried to eat breakfast, but he knew he must. He built a little fire and put on the coffee pot.

The meticulous, careful observations and actions of Nick Adams in "Big Two-Hearted River" are, in essence, means to hold at bay and at the same time allude to the emotional depth and complexities embodied by "the swamp" that Nick does not yet feel he is ready to fish even as he knows he someday must. As Hemingway put it, "I was trying to write then, and I found the greatest difficulty . . . was to put down what really happened in action; what the actual things were which produced the emotion that you experienced." He wanted to write, he said, "one true sentence" that would accurately reflect what he "had seen or had heard someone say." Like Flaubert searching out *le mot juste* (see Chapter 28), Hemingway was striving for something as immediately real as the feeling of wet grass on his hands, something to hold onto in the inauthentic world that had led to a Great War that still seemed unresolved.

William Faulkner and the Southern Novel "I discovered," the native Mississippian William Faulkner (1897–1962) wrote, "that my own little postage stamp of native soil was worth writing about and that I would never live long enough to exhaust it . . . . I opened up a gold mine of other people, so I created a cosmos of my own." This cosmos is the imaginary Mississippi county of Yoknapatawpha, with Jefferson its county seat. *As I Lay Dying* (1930), which Faulkner wrote while working the night shift in the University of Mississippi boiler room, tells the story of the Bundren family's efforts to fulfill their deceased mother's wishes to bury her in Jefferson. Deeply experimental, the story unfolds through the alternating interior monologues of 15 different characters, whose motives and perspectives are sometimes wildly at odds. Also experimental is its use of the stream-of-consciousness technique (see Chapter 35) pioneered by Irish writer James Joyce and English writer Virginia Woolf, and its use of chapters of widely varying length.

Even more experimental is the 1929 novel *The Sound and the Fury*, which tells the story of the Compson family from four perspectives: those of the three Compson brothers, Benjy, Quentin, and Jason, and their maid, Dilsey. In this novel is probably the most daring use of stream of consciousness in modern fiction: Faulkner's representation of the mental workings of the intellectually and developmentally disabled Benjy Compson. It is Benjy's interior monologue that opens the novel (**Reading 36.9**):

READING 36.9

from William Faulkner, *The Sound and the Fury* (1929)

Through the fence, between the curling flower spaces, I could see them hitting. They were coming toward where the flag was and I went along the fence. Luster was hunting in the grass by the flower tree. They took the flag out, and they were hitting. Then they put the flag back and they went to the table, and he hit and the other hit. Then they went on, and I went along the fence. Luster came away from the flower tree and we went along the fence and they stopped and we stopped and I looked through the fence while Luster was hunting in the grass.

"Here, caddie." He hit. They went away across the pasture. I held to the fence and watched them going away.

"Listen at you, now." Luster said. "Aint you something, thirty-three years old, going on that way. After I done went all the way to town to buy you that cake. Hush up that moaning. Aint you going to help me find that quarter so I can go to the show tonight."

This scene takes place in the present, on April 7, 1928, as Benjy accompanies the black servant Luster, who is assigned to take care of him, as he hunts for a quarter beside the golf course. Benjy confuses the golfer's call for his "caddie" with the name of his sister Caddy, who has treated him with more respect than any other member of the family. It is when he thinks of her that he begins to moan and holler.

Benjy's mind moves fluidly by free association across time. In the opening pages of the novel, we are carried back to Christmas Day 1900, when he and Caddy deliver a letter to Mrs. Patterson, then back to the present ("What you moanin' about," Luster says), then back to December 23, 1900, back to the present once more ("Can't you shut up that moaning"), then to a trip to the cemetery shortly after Mr. Compson's funeral in 1912, then back to the present ("Cry baby"), then to Christmas Day 1900 when Benjy delivers the letter ("Mrs. Patterson was chopping flowers"), and finally into the present again ("There ain't nothing over yonder but houses"). Faulkner asks his readers to abandon the traditional literary categories of space, time, and causality, but in compensation he teaches them the humility required of compassion and empathy. In all his novels, Faulkner celebrates the many strengths of his fellow Southerners, while exposing with almost pitiless precision the price their history of racism, denial, and guilt has extracted from them. His work would inspire the next generation of Southern fiction writers— Eudora Welty, Flannery O'Connor, William Styron, and Walker Percy.

The New American Poetry and the Machine Aesthetic

In 1928, Ezra Pound (see Chapter 34) had invoked the necessity of newness when he translated from the Chinese the *Ta Hsio*, or *Great Digest*, a Confucian text dating from the fifth to second century BCE:

As the sun makes it new
Day by day make it new
Yet again make it new

The saying "make it new," Pound well knew, had originated in the eighteenth century BCE, when the Emperor Tang, founder of the Shang dynasty (see Chapter 7), had written the phrase on his bathtub. Pound is obviously not invoking the phrase in the interest of leaving tradition behind. In fact, he invokes tradition—centuries of Chinese tradition—in order to underscore the necessity of continual cultural renewal. Like the poets and artists of the Harlem Renaissance, his short poem is driven by the rhythmic repetition not only of the phrase ("make it new") but "day by day," the diurnal cycle. Even more to the point, it underscores the labor of making the repetitive, often tedious rhythm of writing and rewriting, each successive line a revision of what has come before. And it is, perhaps above all, a "translation," an act of renewal as Pound transforms the original Chinese into English. The lesson is, for Pound, a simple one: In each new context, each new place, tradition is itself renewed.

CONTINUITY & CHANGE
Shang Dynasty, *p. 215*

Pound would publish a collection of essays in 1934 titled *Make It New*, and his "make it new" mantra soon became something of a rallying cry for the new American poetry. It especially influenced his friends, the poets William Carlos Williams (1883–1963), E. E. Cummings (1894–1962), and Hart Crane (1899–1932). Williams met Pound when they were both students at the University of Pennsylvania in 1902. Cummings had been a volunteer ambulance driver for the Red Cross in France, and in 1921 returned to Paris, where he met Pound. They were also attracted to the Imagist principle of verbal simplicity: "Use absolutely no word that does not contribute to the presentation," as F. S. Flint put it in the March 1913 issue of *Poetry* magazine (see Chapter 34). Their language should reflect, in Williams's words, "the American idiom," just as the Harlem Renaissance writers sought to capture black American vernacular in their work.

William Carlos Williams and the Poetry of the Everyday
Williams was a physician in Rutherford, New Jersey, across the Hudson River from New York City. He was immediately attracted to Imagism when Pound defined it in the pages of *Poetry* magazine. He praised it for "ridding the field of verbiage." His own work has been labeled "Radical Imagism," for concentrating on the stark presentation of commonplace objects to the exclusion of inner realities. His famous poem, "The Red Wheelbarrow," is an example (**Reading 36.10**):

READING 36.10

William Carlos Williams, "The Red Wheelbarrow," from *Spring and All* (1923)

so much depends
upon

a red wheel
barrow

glazed with rain
water

beside the white
chickens

The first line of each stanza of Williams's poem raises expectations which the second line debunks in two syllables. Thus a mere preposition, "upon," follows the urgency of "so much depends." A "red wheel" conjures images of Futurist speed, only to fall flat with the static "barrow." "Rain/water" approaches redundancy. Our expectations still whetted by the poem's first line, the word "white" suggests purity, only to modify the wholly uninspiring image, "chickens." Williams's aesthetic depends upon elevating the commonplace and the everyday into the realm of poetry, thus transforming them, making them new.

E. E. Cummings and the Pleasures of Typography
In 1920, when Williams wrote a poem describing a fire engine racing down a Manhattan street in the dark of night (see *Closer Look*, pages 1192–1193), the motorized fire engine was not even a decade old. Williams's poem celebrates the same machine culture, a culture of the "new," to which Alfred Barr, Jr., and Philip Johnson would later pay homage in their *Machine Art* exhibition. As Williams would later put it, in the introduction to a book of poems published in 1944 called *The Wedge*:

To make two bald statements: There's nothing sentimental about a machine, and: A poem is a small (or large) machine made of words. When I say there's nothing sentimental about a poem I mean that there can be no part, as in any other machine, that is redundant.

The newness of this same machine aesthetic is celebrated by E. E. Cummings in his poem "she being Brand" (his name is commonly spelled entirely in lowercase letters, a practice initiated by his publishers to which Cummings objected) (**Reading 36.11**):

E. E. Cummings, "she being Brand" (1926)

she being Brand

-new;and you
know consequently a
little stiff i was
careful of her and(having
thoroughly oiled the universal
joint tested my gas felt of
her radiator made sure her springs were O.

K.)i went right to it flooded-the-carburetor cranked her

up,slipped the
clutch(and then somehow got into reverse she
kicked what
the hell)next
minute i was back in neutral tried and

again slo-wly;bare,ly nudg. ing(my

lev-er Right-
oh and her gears being in
A 1 shape passed
from low through
second-in-to-high like
greasedlightning)just as we turned the corner of Divinity

avenue i touched the accelerator and give
her the juice,good

                              (it

was the first ride and believe i we was
happy to see how nice she acted right up to
the last minute coming back down by the Public
Gardens i slammed on

the

internalexpanding

&

externalcontracting
brakes Bothatonce and

brought allofher tremB
-ling
to a:dead.

stand-
;Still)

Cummings's poem is laden with sexual innuendo, describing his first ride in his new car as if he were making love to the machine, and linking, in a fashion already long exploited by the automobile industry in the 1920s, his own sexual prowess with freedom and mastery of the road. But one of the most notable aspects of this poem is its dependence on the visual characteristics of capitalization, punctuation, and line endings to surprise the reader—effects evident in the first two lines: "Brand / -new." The poem, like Williams's work, is addressed both to the eye and the ear.

Hart Crane and *The Bridge* Although a poet of very different temperament than either Williams or Cummings, both of whom he knew well, Hart Crane (1899–1932) believed like both of them that the modern poet must, in his words, "absorb the machine." For Crane, the symbol of the machine aesthetic was the Brooklyn Bridge, and from 1926 until 1930, he worked on a long, epic poem that attempted to encapsulate, for modernity, the America that Walt Whitman had celebrated in the last half of the nineteenth century. The first great suspension bridge in the United States, the bridge was built in 1883 and was anything but new, yet it was precisely Crane's intention to "make it new" in the poem, to reinvent it as the gateway to modernity itself (**Reading 36.12**):

**from Hart Crane, "To Brooklyn Bridge,"
The Bridge (1930)**

How many dawns, chill from his rippling rest
The seagull's wings shall dip and pivot him,
Shedding white rings of tumult, building high
Over the chained bay waters Liberty—

Then, with inviolate curve, forsake our eyes
As apparitional as sails that cross
Some page of figures to be filed away;
—Till elevators drop us from our day . . .

I think of cinemas, panoramic sleights
With multitudes bent toward some flashing scene
Never disclosed, but hastened to again,
Foretold to other eyes on the same screen;

And Thee, across the harbor, silver-paced
As though the sun took step of thee, yet left
Some motion ever unspent in thy stride—
Implicitly thy freedom staying thee! . . .

O harp and altar, of the fury fused,
(How could mere toil align thy choiring strings!)
Terrific threshold of the prophet's pledge,
Prayer of pariah, and the lover's cry,—

Again the traffic lights that skim thy swift
Unfractioned idiom, immaculate sigh of stars,
Beading thy path—condense eternity:
And we have seen night lifted in thine arms . . . .

O Sleepless as the river under thee,
Vaulting the sea, the prairies' dreaming sod,
Unto us lowliest sometime sweep, descend
And of the curveship lend a myth to God.

As Crane was preparing *The Bridge* for publication, a friend showed Crane a short essay by painter Joseph Stella (1877–1946), who had painted the Brooklyn Bridge as part of a large five-panel painting, *The Voice of the City of New York*

William Carlos Williams often wrote poems on the spur of the moment—on prescription pads, for instance—and as a result, his work has a certain sense of immediacy, even urgency. His poem "The Great Figure" is a case in point. In his *Autobiography*, Williams recalls writing the poem one day after leaving his post-graduate clinic in Manhattan on his way to visit the painter Marsden Hartley (1877–1943) for a drink: "As I approached his number I heard a great clatter of bells and the roar of a fire engine passing the end of the street down Ninth Avenue. I turned just in time to see a golden figure 5 on a red background flash by. The impression was so sudden and forceful that I took a piece of paper out of my pocket and wrote a short poem about it."

Their friend, the painter Charles Demuth (1883–1935), later celebrated the poem in what he called a "poster-portrait."

The focus of the poem, and later the painting, is "the figure 5." It serves to organize the chaotic urban landscape that confronts the artist's vision just as the poem itself organizes the passing engine's cacophony of sirens, clangs, and howls into a formal poetic arrangement. The poem's central image embodies tension, speed, and change, a fact that Williams underscores by placing the lines "moving/tense" at the poem's heart. The figure 5 contradicts this tension. The poet sees the number with a clarity that is very different from the blurry refracted light of the night's rain. As Demuth's painting makes clear, the figure 5 is a kind of ordering design, its curvilinear form echoed in the street lights and light posts, its strong horizontal top echoed in the red engine and its horizontal axle all racing down the street into the geometric one-point perspective of the skyscraper canyon.

"The Great Figure"

from *Sour Grapes* (1921)

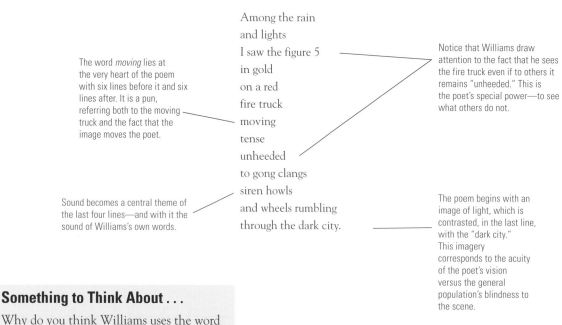

Among the rain
and lights
I saw the figure 5
in gold
on a red
fire truck
moving
tense
unheeded
to gong clangs
siren howls
and wheels rumbling
through the dark city.

The word *moving* lies at the very heart of the poem with six lines before it and six lines after. It is a pun, referring both to the moving truck and the fact that the image moves the poet.

Sound becomes a central theme of the last four lines—and with it the sound of Williams's own words.

Notice that Williams draw attention to the fact that he sees the fire truck even if to others it remains "unheeded." This is the poet's special power—to see what others do not.

The poem begins with an image of light, which is contrasted, in the last line, with the "dark city." This imagery corresponds to the acuity of the poet's vision versus the general population's blindness to the scene.

Something to Think About . . .

Why do you think Williams uses the word "great" to describe the "figure 5" in the title to his poem?

What might be a "billboard" is actually Williams's first name—"Bill."

Williams's middle name, Carlos, lights a marquee on a building down the street.

The curved frame in the corner suggests that it is the inside edge of yet another, even larger "figure 5."

The steep perspective of the street is indicated by the cornices on the buildings, both right and left. As opposed to Duchamp's Nude *Descending a Staircase* (see Fig. 35.4), which Demuth knew well, which indicates movement horizontally from left to right, Demuth indicates movement as a recession into space, one of the most innovative aspects of the painting.

The lamppost is shaped like the base of Demuth's "figure 5," creating yet another rhythmic repetition in the painting.

Although the legible lettering on the window reads "ART Co," there seems to be another letter in front of the "A"—perhaps a "T" or an "F"—in either case a relatively crude joke and perfectly consistent with Demuth's sense of humor.

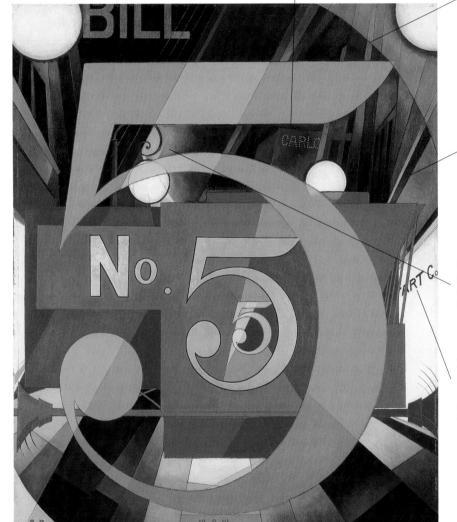

At the bottom of the painting, Demuth has placed both his own and Williams's initials.

Charles Demuth, *The Figure 5 in Gold*. 1928. Oil on cardboard, 35$^1/_2$" × 30". Metropolitan Museum of Art, New York. Alfred Stieglitz Collection, 1949 (49.59.1). Image © The Metropolitan Museum of Art/Art Resource, New York. Demuth's painting was called by his friend William Carlos Williams "the most distinguished American painting that I have seen in years."

Interpreted in 1920–22 (Fig. **36.17**). Stella's essay, "The Brooklyn Bridge (A Page of My Life)," which appeared in the little magazine *Transition* in 1929, captured Crane's attention:

> Many nights I stood on the bridge – and in the middle alone – lost – a defenseless prey to the surrounding swarming darkness – crushed by the mountainous black impenetrability of the skyscrapers – here and there lights resembling suspended falls of astral bodies or fantastic splendors of remote rites – shaken by the underground tumult of the trains in perpetual motion, like the blood in the arteries – at times, ringing as alarm in a tempest, the shrill sulphurous voice of the trolley wires – now and then strange moanings of appeal from tug boats, guessed more than seen, through the infernal recesses below – I felt deeply moved, as if on the threshold of a new religion or in the presence of a new DIVINITY.

Stella's painting is, in fact, a kind of altarpiece to the machine age, and for a while, Stella considered using the painting as the frontispiece to his poem. But he finally settled for three photographs of the bridge by his neighbor, the photographer Walker Evans, whose work is discussed in Chapter 37.

The New American Painting: "That, Madam . . . is paint."

Both Stella's view of the Brooklyn Bridge and Demuth's celebration of Williams's "figure 5" indicated the new direction of American painting. Even its focal point changed. During the early 1900s, Alfred Stieglitz's Gallery 291 had been the place to exhibit. By the late 1920s, his new space in midtown Manhattan, An American Place, and the Daniel Gallery, a few blocks away, at 2 West 47th Street (see Map 36.1), were the places artists and writers gathered routinely to discuss new directions in American art and literature. In his *Autobiography*, Williams recalls a story that, he said, "marks the exact point in the transition that took place, in the world at that time," to the conception of the modern in American art. Alanson Hartpence was employed at the Daniel Gallery (**Reading 36.13**):

Fig. 36.17 Joseph Stella, *The Voice of the City of New York Interpreted: The Brooklyn Bridge (The Bridge)*. 1920–22. Oil and tempera on canvas, 88 1/2″ × 54″. Collection of the Newark Museum, New Jersey. This is one of five panels, each over 7 feet high, celebrating New York. The others are *The Battery (The Port)*, *The Great White Way Leaving the Subway (White Way I)*, *The Prow (The Skyscrapers)*, and *Broadway (White Way II)*.

from William Carlos Williams, *The Autobiography of William Carlos Williams* (1948)

One day, the proprietor being out, Hartpence was in charge. In walked one of their most important customers, a woman in her fifties who was much interested in some picture whose identity I may at one time have known. She liked it, and seemed about to make the purchase, walked away from it, approached it and said, finally, "But Mr. Hartpence, what is all that down in this left hand lower corner?"

Hartpence came up close and carefully inspected the area mentioned. Then, after further consideration, "That, Madam," said he, "is paint."

The object lesson was plain and simple. Painting was not about copying reality, not about "merely reflecting something already there, inertly," in Williams's words, but to make it new, in the new twentieth-century American landscape. It did so, he explained, by recognizing that a picture was "a matter of pigments upon a piece of cloth stretched on a frame . . . It is in the taking of that step over from feeling to the imaginative object, on the cloth, on the page, that defined the term, the modern term—a work of art."

Charles Demuth, Charles Sheeler, and the Industrial Scene

Charles Demuth and Williams met as students at the University of Pennsylvania, and they remained close friends. It was Demuth's wit that most attracted Williams to the painter, and his clear-eyed view of what constituted the new American landscape. He would, for instance, paint a picture of two grain elevators and call it *My Egypt*, ironically suggesting their equivalence to the pyramids on the Nile. Or he would paint a chimney rising in the sky beside a silo and name it *Aucassin and Nicolette*, after the medieval fable of the love affair between a French nobleman and a Saracen slave girl. Without its title, *Incense of a New Church* (Fig. **36.18**) is as depressing an image as any painted in America in the 1920s, its factory chimneys belching forth an almost suffocating flume of soot and smoke. But with the title, the painting becomes a deeply ironic—and funny—commentary on the American worship of machine and manufacture.

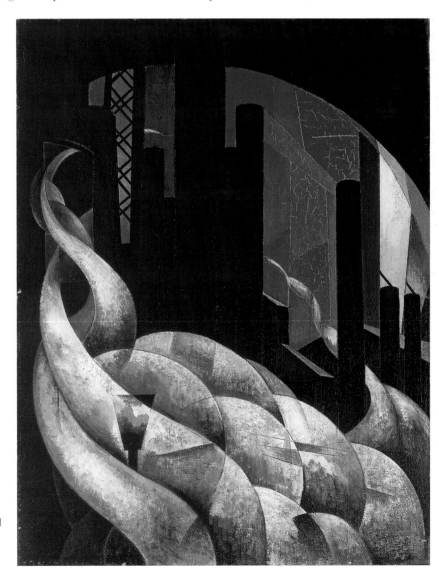

Fig. 36.18 Charles Demuth (American 1883–1935), *Incense of a New Church.* **1921.** Oil on canvas, 26$\frac{1}{4}$" × 20". Columbus Museum of Art, Ohio. Gift of Ferdinand Howald 1931.135; Courtesy Demuth Museum, Lancaster PA. William Carlos Williams owned a painting similar to this—of factories billowing smoke—entitled *End of the Parade—Coatsville, Pa.* He purchased it at the Daniel Gallery in 1920.

Charles Sheeler (1883–1965) was equally gifted as a painter and a photographer, and his painting clearly evidences the impact of photography. In 1927, he was commissioned to photograph the Ford Motor Company's new River Rouge Plant near Detroit, the world's largest industrial complex employing more than 75,000 workers to produce the new Model A, successor to the Model T. The subject, he said, was "incomparably the most thrilling I have had to work with," and he soon translated it into paint. *Classic Landscape* (Fig. **36.19**) depicts an area of the plant where cement was made from by-products of the manufacturing process. The silos in the middle distance stored the cement until it could be shipped for sale. For Sheeler, they evoke the classic architecture of ancient Greece and Rome— which inspired the painting's title, *Classic Landscape.*

Marsden Hartley and the Influence of Cézanne Of all the

CONTINUITY&CHANGE
Mont Sainte-Victoire, **p. 1097**

American modernists, Marsden Hartley was most influenced by the example of Paul Cézanne, especially Cézanne's paintings of Mont Sainte-Victoire (see Fig. 33.16). Stieglitz had exhibited watercolors by Cézanne at 291 in 1913, and by the 1920s, a number of significant Cézannes had entered American collections.

Hartley was particularly drawn to the American Southwest, visiting Santa Fe and Taos in both 1918 and 1919. Like Mont Sainte-Victoire for Cézanne, the mountains there became a motif for Hartley to which he returned again and again. In a June 1918 letter to Stieglitz, he describes them as "Chocolate mountains . . . those great isolated, altarlike forms that stand alone in a great mesa with the immensities of blue around and above them and that strange Indian red earth making such almost unearthly foregrounds."

Although Hartley's painterly and curvilinear forms seem far removed from the machine-age art of Demuth and Sheeler, Hartley's work was as formally balanced and orderly as any classical composition. For example, compare the formal symmetry of Hartley's *New Mexico Landscape* (Fig. **36.20**) to Joseph Stella's *The Bridge* (see Fig. 36.16). Hartley's is a completely natural landscape, rising to a central mountain balanced by two smaller mountains on each side. Stella's is a man-made architectural environment, and yet both are reminiscent of church altarpieces, each placing the viewer before his chosen subject—landscape and bridge—in a

CONTINUITY&CHANGE
Trinity, **p. 470**

composition not far removed from Masaccio's 1425 *Trinity* at Santa Maria Novella in Florence.

Fig. 36.19 Charles Sheeler, *Classic Landscape.* 1931. Oil on canvas, 25″ × 32¹/₄″. Collection of Barney A. Ebsworth. Image © 2009 Board of Trustees, National Gallery of Art, Washington, D.C. The strong perspectival lines created by the railroad tracks underscore the geometric classicism of the scene.

Fig. 36.20 Marsden Hartley, *New Mexico Landscape.* **1920–22.** Oil on canvas, 30″ × 36″. The Alfred Stieglitz Collection, 1949. Philadelphia Museum of Art, Philadelphia Art Resource, New York. Hartley would visit Aix-en-Provence in 1928, where he undertook a series of landscapes with Mont Sainte-Victoire as their theme.

Georgia O'Keeffe and the Question of Gender Of all the American artists who came into their own in the 1920s and 1930s, Georgia O'Keeffe (1887–1986) would become the most famous. But, from her first exhibit on, her work was burdened by its identification with her gender. Alfred Stieglitz showed a group of her abstract charcoal drawings at his Gallery 291 in 1916, calling them an example of "feminine intuition," and for the rest of her career, O'Keeffe's work was described solely in terms of its "female" imagery.

Marsden Hartley wrote an article in 1920 describing her work in Freudian terms as examples of "feminine perceptions and feminine powers of expression." By then she had married Stieglitz, who viewed O'Keeffe's art in the same way, so Hartley's review carried some authority. O'Keeffe's

flower paintings—large-scale close-ups of petals, stamens, and pistols—were especially susceptible to Freudian interpretation. Many viewers found them erotically charged; between 1918 and 1932, she made over 200 of them. O'Keeffe complained that no one read flower paintings by male artists in this way—Demuth and Hartley both did many floral still lifes—and she addressed one critic directly: "Well— I made you take time to look at what I saw and when you took time to really notice my flower you hung all your own associations with flowers on my flower and you write about my flower as if I think and see what you think and see of the flower—and I don't."

O'Keeffe's struggle for recognition of her painting on its own terms was intensified by her closeness to Stieglitz. "His

Fig. 36.21 Georgia O'Keeffe, *Red Hills and Bones*. 1941. Oil on canvas, 29 3/4″ × 40″. The Alfred Stieglitz Collection, 1949. Philadelphia Museum of Art, Philadelphia. © 2008 Artists Rights Society (ARS), New York. In 1940, O'Keeffe bought a house, Rancho de los Burros, a few miles from Ghost Ranch, an isolated dude ranch near the small town of Abiquiu.

power to destroy," she later acknowledged, "was as destructive as his power to build—the extremes went together. I have experienced both and survived, but I think I only crossed him when I had to—to survive." After 1929, one of her major modes of survival was to retreat to New Mexico, to which she returned for part of every year until 1949, three years after Stieglitz's death, when she moved there permanently. *Red Hills and Bones* (Fig. **36.21**) is an example of the many paintings of the New Mexican landscape that so moved her. Its surprising juxtaposition of hills and bones animates the hills, lending them a sort of body, like skin stretched over a hidden skeletal structure. Though, in her words, "the red hill is a piece of the badlands where even the grass is gone," it is anything but dead. In the same breath, she would call it "our waste land . . . our most beautiful country," reminding the viewer that the red hill was made "of apparently the same sort of earth that you mix

with oil to make paint." And explaining her attraction to bones, she wrote: "When I found the beautiful white bones on the desert I picked them up and took them home too . . . . I have used these things to say what is to me the wideness and wonder of the world as I live in it."

O'Keeffe's career would span almost the entire twentieth century. She would, in 1946, become the first woman to have a one-person retrospective of her work at the Museum of Modern Art. In 1970, when she was 83, the Whitney Museum of American Art staged the largest retrospective of her work to date, introducing it to a new generation of admirers just at the moment that the feminist movement in the United States was taking hold. Finally, in July 1997, 11 years after her death, the Georgia O'Keeffe Museum opened its doors in Santa Fe, New Mexico, with a permanent collection of more than 130 O'Keeffe paintings, drawings, and sculptures.

The American Stage: Eugene O'Neill

If many American artists sought to portray the everyday reality of American life, just as poets of the era sought to reflect everyday speech in their poems, it was on the stage that both the visual texture of American life and the language of modern America were best experienced. Eugene O'Neill (1888–1953) took up the challenge. The son of an Irish actor and raised in a Broadway hotel room in New York's theater district, O'Neill was sensitive both to the subtleties of the American scene and to the rhythms and vocabulary of American speech.

Toward the end of 1912, while hospitalized for tuberculosis in a Connecticut sanitarium, O'Neill read Ibsen (see Chapter 33) and the Greek tragedies. Their effect was so powerful that he decided to become a playwright. By 1920, he had won the Pulitzer Prize, the first of four, for his first full-length play, *Beyond the Horizon*, and he had begun to experiment freely with theatrical conventions in another play, *The Emperor Jones*.

The subject of the play was unheard-of. It narrates the life of one Brutus Jones, an African American who kills a man and goes to prison before escaping to a Caribbean island where he declares himself emperor. His story is told, against an incessant beat of drums, almost entirely in monologue, as a series of flashbacks as he flees through a forest chased by his rebellious former subjects. *The Emperor Jones* was soon followed by *The Hairy Ape* (1922), the story of a powerful, hulking engine stoker on an ocean liner, who is called a "filthy beast" by a socialite onboard ship. Unable to understand what she means, he leaves the ship and wanders through Manhattan, seeking someplace to fit in. Finally, dehumanized by his experiences, he enters the gorilla cage at the New York's City Zoo and dies, himself a "hairy ape," in the animal's embrace.

Both of these plays—and O'Neill's many great later plays, including *Desire Under the Elms* (1924), *Strange Interlude* (1928), *The Iceman Cometh* (1946), and the posthumously produced *Long Day's Journey into Night* (1953)—stress the isolation and alienation of modern life. Even in dialogue, his characters seem to talk past one another, not to one another, as this stage direction, from *Strange Interlude*, suggests: "They stare straight ahead and remain motionless. They speak, ostensibly one to the other, but showing by their tone it is a thinking aloud to oneself, and neither appears to hear what the other has said."

THE GOLDEN AGE OF SILENT FILM

It is a bit of an exaggeration to claim that New York invented Hollywood, but in many ways it did. In 1903, Hollywood (Fig. 36.22) was a scattered community in the foothills of the Santa Monica mountains boasting about 700 residents. Twenty years later, it was the center of a "colony" of movie people, almost none of them native Californians, and a large majority of them second-generation American Jews newly arrived from points east. Many had gravitated to the movie business—first as exhibitors, then

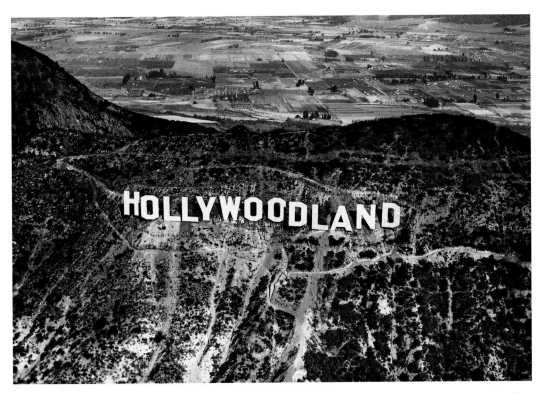

Fig. 36.22 The "Hollywoodland" sign. 1923. The famous sign, rebuilt in 1978 after years of abuse and wear and shortened then to just "Hollywood," was originally constructed to advertise a real-estate development in the foothills above Hollywood.

Fig. 36.23 William Cameron Menzies, sets for *The Thief of Bagdad*, starring Douglas Fairbanks. 1924. Menzies was one of the greatest set designers and art directors of the day. He would design the sets for David O. Selznick's *Gone with the Wind* (see Fig. 37.25), working for roughly two years on the epic motion picture.

distributors, and then producers—from the garment industry in New York City, where they had learned to appraise popular taste and react to it with swift inventiveness. And, indeed, they were so successful in understanding their audience's desires that by 1939, arguably the greatest year in the history of the medium, between 52 and 55 million Americans went to the movies they made each week. There were 15,115 movie theaters, and box office receipts were $673 million.

The Americanization of a Medium

Why Hollywood came to be the center of the movie industry—and not New York, or Chicago, or, for that matter, just about anyplace else—is a complex question. Weather played a role—350 days a year of temperate sunshine, perfect for the slow film speeds of the day. So did the city's remoteness from the East, where the so-called "Trust"—the Motion Picture Patents Company, run by Thomas Edison, which controlled the rights to virtually all the relevant technology—sought to monopolize the industry. There was an abundance of relatively cheap available property on which to build giant "lots" and construct elaborate sets (Fig. **36.23**). It is also true that after the first companies arrived in the early 1900s—producers Jesse Lasky and Sam Goldfish (later Goldwyn) hired Cecil B. DeMille to make the first feature-length American movie, *The Squaw Man*, in a rented barn at Vine and Selma in Hollywood in 1914, and William Fox (born Wilhelm Fuchs in Hungary) set up his studios at the corner of Sunset

and Western in 1916—other Jewish immigrant independent filmmakers followed, sensing the creation of a real community.

But for whatever reason the movie industry was drawn to Hollywood, it is certain that once there, it made Hollywood the center of cinema as a medium. Filmmaking went on all over the city of Los Angeles, not just in Hollywood—in Culver City, in the west, toward the ocean, and Universal City, an incorporated town over the Santa Monica mountains in the San Fernando Valley owned by Universal Pictures. But they were all "Hollywood." Despite the fact that not a single technological innovation in the medium was made anywhere near the city, despite the fact that it depended almost entirely upon New York City institutions for financing, it became the place where dreams came true, where fame and wealth were there for the taking, and where anything seemed possible.

It was the studio system that set Hollywood filmmaking apart from filmmaking anywhere else in the world, an organizational structure of production, distribution, and exhibition within the same company. In this system, studio magnates owned and controlled a "stable" of actors, writers, and directors who contracted to work exclusively for the studio. These companies produced predictable product—westerns, horror pictures, romances, and so forth—featuring stars whom the public adored. By the end of the 1920s, there were five major American studios—Fox, MGM, Paramount, RKO, and Warner—and three smaller ones—Universal, Columbia, and United Artists. These companies all had agents in Europe. Metro-Goldwyn-Mayer and Paramount, for instance, loaned money to help the German film production company UFA establish itself after the war, and in return, UFA distributed their films in Germany. UFA executives soon recognized that it was more profitable to import American movies than to produce their own. The pattern was repeated across Europe, so that during the 1920s and 1930s, somewhere between 75 percent and 90 percent of the films screened in most countries were made in Hollywood. Europeans, who had long imposed their cultures on the world, now found American culture imposing itself on them.

The Studios and the Star System

As early as 1920, Hollywood was making 750 feature films a year and focusing its promotional efforts on the appeal of its stars. Among the most important of the early stars was Mary Pickford. She had risen to fame starring in D. W. Griffith's early one-reelers, specializing in the role of the adolescent girl. By 1917, when "America's Sweetheart," as Pickford soon became known, starred in feature films such as *The Poor Little Rich Girl* and *Rebecca of Sunnybrook Farm*, she was making $10,000 a week, working for Adolph Zukor's Famous Players-Lasky Corporation. Paramount, the Famous Players distributor, soon began block-booking its entire yearly output of 50 to 100 feature films, so that if theaters wanted to show the enormously popular Pickford films, they were forced to show films featuring less-well-known stars as well. When theaters resisted this arrangement, Zukor borrowed $10 million from the Wall Street investment banking firm of Kuhn Loeb and bought them, thus gaining control of the entire process of moviemaking, from production to distribution to exhibition. Other studios followed suit—Metro-Goldwyn-Mayer, Fox, and Universal all soon mirrored Zukor's operations.

It didn't take the stars long to recognize that the studios' successes depended on them. Some negotiated better contracts, but in 1919, three of the biggest stars—Pickford, Douglas Fairbanks, and Charlie Chaplin—and its most famous director, D. W. Griffith, bucked the studio system and formed their own finance and distribution company, United Artists. Chaplin was film's leading comedian, his trademark Little Tramp known worldwide. At his studio in Hollywood, in 1925, he made what many consider his greatest film, *The Gold Rush*. To open the film, Chaplin brought in thousands of extras, many of them hoboes, to the location in northern California near Truckee for a shot of prospectors making their way up the snow-covered Chilkoot Pass in the Alaskan gold rush of 1897 (Fig. **36.24**). Thematically, the gold rush is a vehicle that allows Chaplin to play the pathos of poverty off against the dream of wealth. In one of its most memorable scenes, at once funny and poignant, the starving tramp eats his own boot with the relish of a New York sophisticate, twisting his shoelaces around his fork like spaghetti and sucking on its nails as if they were the most succulent of morsels.

Fairbanks and Pickford married and formed their own studio. Pickford, now over 30, continued to cast herself as an adolescent girl, but Fairbanks began making a series of

Fig. 36.24 Charlie Chaplin in *The Gold Rush*. 1925. Chaplin modeled this opening scene on photographs he had seen of prospectors headed for the Klondike gold fields in 1897.

humorous adventure films, often drawing on stories written for boys. Increasingly elaborate sets were created for these films on the Santa Monica Boulevard lot, culminating with *The Thief of Bagdad*'s, one of the largest sets ever built in Hollywood. Special effects included flying carpets, winged horses, fearsome beasts, and an invisibility cloak, but neither the sets nor the effects could match the audience's attraction to Fairbanks's winning smile (Fig. **36.25**).

Fig. 36.25 Douglas Fairbanks in *The Thief of Bagdad*. 1924. Museum of Modern Art, Film Stills Archive. Almost 40 years old, Fairbanks appeared bare-chested throughout most of the movie, to the delight of his female fans.

Audience and Expectation: Hollywood's Genres

In addition to the appeal of its stars, Hollywood also depended on its audience's attraction to certain **genres** of film. A genre is a standard type, a sort of conceptual template or form readily recognizable by its audience. By the early 1920s, most of the genres that characterized Hollywood production through the 1950s had come into existence—comedy; fantasy; adventure; the crime or gangster film; the coming-of-age film (a Pickford specialty); the so-called woman's film, combining romance and family life; romantic drama; the horror film; war films; and the western chief among them—all, that is, except the musical, which awaited the advent of sound.

From the earliest days of cinema, producers had been well aware that their stars' sex appeal was fundamental to their popularity, and romantic drama was the main genre in which a star's sex appeal could be exploited. Female audience members worshiped Rudolph Valentino, whose soft sensuality infuriated many American males, even as he seduced on-screen actress after actress through the 1920s. The Swedish actress Greta Garbo, who arrived in the United States in 1925 to work at MGM, was appealing on a different level. From the moment of her first American film, the 1926 *Flesh and the Devil*, she exuded a combination of mature, adult sexuality and melancholy sadness. A sex siren like none before her, she was perfectly cast as the adulteress, playing Tolstoy's Anna Karenina in her next picture, *Love* (1927), and *A Woman of Affairs* (1928) in her next. Nearly all of Garbo's Hollywood films were shot in a rich, romantic lighting style that became synonymous in film with romance itself.

Male fans, who of course adored Garbo, also gravitated to Lon Chaney, whose most famous roles were *The Hunchback of Notre Dame* and *The Phantom of the Opera*, 1923 and 1924 respectively. Traditionally, the monster in horror films stands for that which society rejects or is uncomfortable with. Chaney specialized in characters who were disfigured, mutilated, or otherwise physically grotesque, and he single-handedly defined the horror genre in the 1920s. What appealed to his largely male audience was apparently the very horror of his appearance, the romantic agony of his characters' inability to fit comfortably into society, his audience's sense of their own alienation.

The Western was introduced with Edwin S. Porter's 1903 film *The Great Train Robbery*, with its famous final shot of a sheriff shooting his six-gun straight at the camera (and the audience). William S. Hart was the first big Western star, generally playing the part of an outlaw reformed by the love of a good woman. The most popular of the Western stars in the 1920s was Tom Mix (Fig. **36.26**), who had been a working cowboy. Decked out in his huge white hat, Mix performed his own stunts in movies filled with galloping horses, fistfights, and chases. Many of his films were shot on location in spectacular Western landscapes like the Grand Canyon, adding to their appeal.

Fig. 36.26 Tom Mix in *The Great K & A Train Robbery*. 1926. Poster, 11″ × 17″. The film is laden with Mix stunts, opening with Mix sliding down a long cable to the bottom of a gorge. He also, as shown here, jumps off his horse onto a train so that he might fight the villains. This would become a staple of the Western genre—riding on the roof of the moving train.

Cinema in Europe

At the same time Hollywood dominated the American film industry, a distinctly European cinema thrived. Many of Europe's greatest filmmakers and stars were hired by American companies and brought to the United States to work. (Remember that before the talkies, language was not a barrier in the film industry.) Moreover, it seems clear that many of the more experimental and avant-garde contributions to the cinema originated in Europe. (See the *Closer Look* on Sergei Eisenstein in Chapter 35.) Europeans tended to regard cinema, at least potentially, as a high art, not necessarily as the crassly commercial product aimed at a low-brow popular audience that characterized most American movies.

German Expressionism Influenced directly by the Expressionist painting of Ernst Kirchner, Wassily Kandinsky, and Franz Marc (see Figs. 34.12, 34.13, and 34.15), soon after the war, some German filmmakers began to search for ways to express themselves similarly in film. Their films were

Fig. 36.27 The City, in Fritz Lang and Thea von Harbou's *Metropolis*. 1926. The cinematographer for *Metropolis*, responsible for creating the film's towering and sweeping visual effects, was Karl Freund, who later became director of photography for Desilu, supervising over 400 episodes of *I Love Lucy*, where he revolutionized television lighting and production.

deeply affected by the violence of the war and the madness they perceived the war to embody.

Chief among these was Robert Wiene, whose *Cabinet of Dr. Caligari* appeared soon after the war. An inmate at an insane asylum narrates the action, the story of a mysterious doctor, Caligari, who makes a living exhibiting a sleepwalker named Cesare at sideshows. At night, Cesare obligingly murders the doctor's enemies. All the action takes place in a deliberately exotic and weirdly distorted landscape of tilting houses, misshapen furniture, and shadowy atmospherics. As it turns out, the doctor is the head of the mental ward where the sleepwalker is his patient, and the entire story is perhaps a figment of the storyteller's insane imagination.

The word *Stimmung*—an emphasis on mood or feeling, particularly melancholy—is often used to describe German cinema throughout the silent era. A film's entire *mise-en-scène*—a French phrase for the totality of a film's visual style, from decor to lighting, camera movement, and costume—was often constructed to convey this sense of melancholy and resignation. Fritz Lang and his wife Thea von Harbou created one of the most oppressive and disquieting *mise-en-scènes* of all for their 1926 vision of a world in

which humanity is at the edge of extinction, *Metropolis* (Fig. **36.27**). In a city in which workers are virtually cogs in a giant machine, barely human, a scientist by the name of Rotwang has succeeded in constructing a robot, which proves, he says, that "now we have no further use for living workers." But the Master of Metropolis orders Rotwang to recreate the robot in the likeness of Maria, an idealistic young woman who has been preaching to the workers in order to help them free themselves from oppression. Instead, the robot preaches violence and leads them to self-destruction. In retrospect, the film seems ominously prescient, as if Lang and von Harbou have at least subconsciously exposed what influential film historian Siegfried Krakauer (1889–1966) has called "the deep layers of collective mentality" that would soon manifest themselves in the rise of the fascist state. Krakauer's history of German cinema, *From Caligari to Hitler*, revealingly subtitled A *Psychological History of German Film*, was written in the United States after he had fled Germany in 1933. It remains one of the seminal arguments concerning the mass appeal of commercial film and what that appeal reveals about its audience and society as a whole.

Surrealist Film Throughout the late 1910s and 1920s, while moviemakers were striving to make their narratives coherent and understandable to a wide audience, the Surrealists had an entirely different agenda. They saw film's potential to fragment rather than create sense. Through skillful editing of startling images and effects, film became a new tool for exploring the unconscious. Among the first films associated with Surrealism is René Clair's 1924 *Entr'acte*. An entr'acte is the intermission between parts of a stage production. Clair's film, which runs approximately 22 minutes, was conceived to run between the two acts of the ballet *Relâche*, written by Francis Picabia with music by Eric Satie (*relâche* means "closed"). The film is full of visual tricks—views of Paris seen from upside down on a roller coaster, a chase after a coffin filmed alternately at high speed and slow motion, actors disappearing before our eyes, and so on. Marcel Duchamp makes an appearance playing chess on the roof of a Paris building.

The two Spanish Surrealists, Salvador Dalí and Luis Buñuel, collaborated in 1929 on the 17-minute film *Un Chien andalou* (*An Andalusian Dog*) (Fig. **36.28**). Buñuel was a huge fan of Eisenstein and montage, and he used the technique to create a dream logic of fades—from a hairy armpit to a sea urchin, for instance. The film's famous opening sequence, a close-up of a girl's eye being sliced open by a razor (a cow's eye from the local butcher shop was actually used), is probably best understood as a metaphor for giving up dependence on reality and acceptance of Surrealism's inner vision. A year later, this time on his own, Buñuel made *L'Age d'or* (*The Golden Age*), one of the first French sound films. One scene, in which a religious reliquary was placed on the ground in front of an elegant lady getting out of her car, resulted in a riot that led Parisian authorities to destroy all prints of the film (in fact a few copies survived).

But despite the spirit of innovation in Europe, films made in "Hollywood"—which soon simply meant in the general vicinity of Los Angeles—dominated the world market and defined the medium, initiating the exportation of American culture that, for better or worse, would result in the gradual "Americanization" of global culture as a whole.

Fig. 36.28 Scene from Salvador Dalí and Luis Buñuel's *Un Chien andalou* (*An Andalusian Dog*). 1929. Museum of Modern Art, Film Stills Archive. Though it is never easy to say with any conviction just what a Surrealist image might "mean," it seems likely that the two pianos with dead donkeys laid across them, being dragged across the room, suggest the weight of tradition.

The Rise of Fascism

The experimental fervor of the avant-garde did not go forward without meeting resistance. In the Soviet Union, abstract art was banned as the product of "bourgeois decadence," and artists were called upon to create "a true, historically concrete portrayal of reality in its revolutionary development." In other words, artists were expected to create propaganda in support of the Soviet state. In Germany, a similar edict was issued by Hitler, this time motivated by racism. He began a 1934 speech by declaring, "All the artistic and cultural blather of Cubists, Futurists, Dadaists, and the like is neither sound in racial terms nor tolerable in national terms. It . . . freely admits that the dissolution of all existing ideas, all nations and races, their mixing and adulteration, is the loftiest goal."

A year earlier, Nazi Minister for Popular Enlightenment and Propaganda, Joseph Goebbels, had inaugurated a program to "synchronize culture"—that is, align German culture with Nazi ideals. To that end, he enlisted German university students to lead the way, and on April 6, 1933, the German Student Association proclaimed a nationwide "Action against the Un-German Spirit." They demanded, in 12 "theses" (a direct reference to Martin Luther's revolutionary theses), the establishment of a "pure" national culture as opposed to the spread of what they called "Jewish intellectualism."

Then, on the night of May 10, in most university towns, the students staged a national march "Against the Un-German Spirit," culminating in the burning of more than 25,000 volumes of "un-German" books, including works by Thomas Mann, Erich Maria Remarque, Albert Einstein, Jack London, Upton Sinclair, H. G. Wells, Sigmund Freud, Ernest Hemingway, and Helen Keller. The events were broadcast live on radio to the nation. Addressing the crowd in front of the Opera House in Berlin's Opernplatz (Fig. **36.29**), Goebbels proclaimed:

> German students: We have directed our dealings against the un-German spirit; consign everything un-German to the fire, against class conflict and materialism, for people, community, and idealistic living standards . . . .
>
> Against decadence and moral decay! For discipline and propriety in family and state! I hand over to the fire the writings of Heinrich Mann . . . .
>
> Against literary betrayal of the soldiers of the world war, for education of the people in the spirit of truthfulness! I hand over the writings of Erich Maria Remarque to the fire.

Authors whose works were spared felt insulted. Bertolt Brecht, author of *The Threepenny Opera* and *Mother Courage*, wrote an angry poem, *Die Bücherverbrennung* (*The Book Burning*), demanding that the regime burn him, since it had not burned his writings. Soon art criticism was required to be purely descriptive, German Expressionist painting was described as "Nature as seen by sick minds," and the market in modern art was explained as a conspiracy of Jewish dealers to dupe the German public. Conflict extending far beyond the art world soon seemed inevitable. ■

Fig. 36.29 **Burning books on the Opernplatz, Berlin, May 10, 1933.**

What was the Harlem Renaissance?

Originating in the writings of W. E. B. Du Bois, the Harlem Renaissance explored the double-consciousness defining African-American identity. Poet Claude McKay, Charles S. Johnson of the National Urban League, and philosopher Alain Locke all saw Harlem as the center of an avant-garde destined to rehabilitate African Americans from a position of spiritual and financial impoverishment for which, in Locke's words, "the fate and conditions of slavery have so largely been responsible." To this end, first in the Harlem issue of the sociology journal the *Survey Graphic*, and then in his anthology *The New Negro*, both published in 1925, Locke emphasized the spirit of the young writers, artists, and musicians of Harlem. What elements of Harlem culture were they especially interested in capturing in their work? Harlem was, after all, the center of the blues and jazz. The greatest of the blues singers in the 1920s was Bessie Smith. What new kind of phrasing did Smith bring to her work? In jazz, Louis Armstrong's Dixieland jazz originated out of New Orleans and made its way north to Chicago. What are the characteristics of Dixieland? In 1927, Duke Ellington began a five-year engagement at Harlem's Cotton Club. What distinguishes his brand of jazz?

What is the International Style in architecture?

The 1920s represent a period of unprecedented growth in New York City, as downtown skyscraper after skyscraper rose to ever greater heights, and the promise of the machine became a driving force in culture. What did artists and photographers see in both the skyscraper and the machine? The New York building boom of the 1920s, dominated by the highly ornamented and decorative architecture epitomized by Cass Gilbert's neo-Gothic Woolworth Building and William van Alen's Art Deco Chrysler Building, was countered by the International Style. How does the International Style differ from Gilbert's and van Alen's work?

What is suggested by the adage "make it new"?

American novelists of the era responded to the sense of the country's new and unique identity—embodied perhaps most of all in its "jazz"—by concentrating on the special characteristics of the American scene. How would you distinguish between F. Scott Fitzgerald's sense of place and Ernest Hemingway's? What distinguishes William Faulkner's Yoknapatawpha County?

The "new" sound of jazz also embodied the modernist imperative, first expressed by Ezra Pound, to "make it new." In poetry, this imperative was realized in the work of William Carlos Williams, E. E. Cummings, and Hart Crane. The work of all three celebrates the new machine culture of the era even as it attempts to capture the vernacular voice of everyday Americans. These interests are reflected as well in the painting of Joseph Stella, Charles Demuth, Marsden Hartley, and Georgia O'Keeffe. How is the idea of a new "machine-inspired classicism" expressed in American verse and painting of the 1920s? Like the poets of the era, the experimental plays of Eugene O'Neill captured, as perhaps never before in the theater, the vernacular voices of the American character even as they stressed the isolation and alienation of modern experience.

What characterizes the "golden age" of silent film?

During the early 1900s, large numbers of immigrants, particularly second-generation American Jews, migrated out of New York, where many had worked in the garment industry, to California, where they founded the motion picture industry in and around Hollywood. The studio system they developed dominated filmmaking worldwide. What are the features of the studio system? By the end of the 1920s, there were five major American studios—Fox, MGM, Paramount, RKO, and Warner—and three smaller ones—Universal, Columbia, and United Artists. They focused their promotional efforts on the appeal of their stars, including Mary Pickford, Charlie Chaplin, and Douglas Fairbanks. They also depended on their audience's attraction to certain genres. What are some of the chief genres that they developed? Experimental film flourished in Europe—in German Expressionist cinema and Surrealist film—but the American studios dominated the industry, producing between 75 percent and 90 percent of all films in the 1920s.

PRACTICE MORE Get flashcards for images and terms and review chapter material with quizzes at **www.myartslab.com**

GLOSSARY

blue note A musical note that is slightly lower or flatter than a conventional pitch.

blues A musical *genre* consisting of laments bemoaning loss of love, poverty, or social injustice; the standard blues form consists of three sections of four bars each.

call-and-response A technique in which two musicians imitate each other as closely as possible on their different instruments.

Dixieland jazz A musical *genre* in which the trumpet carries the main melody, the clarinet plays off it with a higher countermelody, and the trombone plays a simpler, lower tune.

genre A standard type of musical number that is usually readily recognizable by its audience.

scat A technique in which the performer sings an instrumental-like solo in nonsense syllables.

swing A musical *genre* characterized by big bands that produced a powerful sound and whose rhythm depends on subtle avoidance of downbeats.

READINGS

READING 36.4

Countee Cullen, "Heritage" (1925)

The poem Heritage *is both typical and something of an anomaly in Countee Cullen's work. Cullen longed to write poetry that succeeded not by force of his race but by virtue of its place in the tradition of English verse. In its form, the poem is completely traditional: rhymed couplets and iambic tetrameter (the first foot in each line is truncated—that is, the short syllable of the iambic foot has been dropped, leaving only the long syllable). But in its subject matter—Cullen's sense of his own uncivilized Africanness—its concerns are entirely racial.*

What is Africa to me:
Copper sun or scarlet sea,
Jungle star or jungle track,
Strong bronzed men, or regal black
Women from whose loins I sprang
When the birds of Eden sang?
One three centuries removed
From the scenes his fathers loved,
Spicy grove, cinnamon tree,
What is Africa to me?   10

So I lie, who all day long
Want no sound except the song
Sung by wild barbaric birds
Goading massive jungle herds,
Juggernauts of flesh that pass
Trampling tall defiant grass
Where young forest lovers lie,
Plighting troth beneath the sky.
So I lie, who always hear,
Though I cram against my ear   20
Both my thumbs, and keep them there,
Great drums throbbing through the air.
So I lie, whose fount of pride,
Dear distress, and joy allied,
Is my somber flesh and skin,
With the dark blood dammed within
Like great pulsing tides of wine
That, I fear, must burst the fine
Channels of the chafing net
Where they surge and foam and fret.   30

Africa? A book one thumbs
Listlessly, till slumber comes.
Unremembered are her bats
Circling through the night, her cats
Crouching in the river reeds,
Stalking gentle flesh that feeds
By the river brink; no more
Does the bugle-throated roar
Cry that monarch claws have leapt

From the scabbards where they slept.   40
Silver snakes that once a year
Doff the lovely coats you wear,
Seek no covert in your fear
Lest a mortal eye should see;
What's your nakedness to me?
Here no leprous flowers rear
Fierce corollas in the air;
Here no bodies sleek and wet,
Dripping mingled rain and sweat,
Tread the savage measures of   50
Jungle boys and girls in love.
What is last year's snow to me,
Last year's anything? The tree
Budding yearly must forget
How its past arose or set—
Bough and blossom, flower, fruit,
Even what shy bird with mute
Wonder at her travail there,
Meekly labored in its hair.
One three centuries removed   60
From the scenes his fathers loved,
Spicy grove, cinnamon tree,
What is Africa to me?

So I lie, who find no peace
Night or day, no slight release
From the unremittent beat
Made by cruel padded feet
Walking through my body's street.
Up and down they go, and back,
Treading out a jungle track.   70
So I lie, who never quite
Safely sleep from rain at night—
I can never rest at all
When the rain begins to fall;
Like a soul gone mad with pain
I must match its weird refrain;
Ever must I twist and squirm,
Writhing like a baited worm,

While its primal measures drip
Through my body, crying, "Strip!   80
Doff this new exuberance.
Come and dance the Lover's Dance!"
In an old remembered way
Rain works on me night and day.
Quaint, outlandish heathen gods
Black men fashion out of rods,
Clay, and brittle bits of stone,
In a likeness like their own,
My conversion came high-priced;   90
I belong to Jesus Christ,
Preacher of humility;
Heathen gods are naught to me.

Father, Son, and Holy Ghost,
So I make an idle boast;
Jesus of the twice-turned cheek,
Lamb of God, although I speak
With my mouth thus, in my heart
Do I play a double part.
Ever at Thy glowing altar   100
Must my heart grow sick and falter,
Wishing He I served were black,
Thinking then it would not lack
Precedent of pain to guide it,
Let who would or might deride it;
Surely then this flesh would know

Yours had borne a kindred woe.
Lord, I fashion dark gods, too,
Daring even to give You
Dark despairing features where,   110
Crowned with dark rebellious hair,
Patience wavers just so much as
Mortal grief compels, while touches
Quick and hot, of anger, rise
To smitten cheek and weary eyes.
Lord, forgive me if my need
Sometimes shapes a human creed.
All day long and all night through,
One thing only must I do:
Quench my pride and cool my blood,   120
Lest I perish in the flood.
Lest a hidden ember set
Timber that I thought was wet
Burning like the dryest flax,
Melting like the merest wax,
Lest the grave restore its dead.
Not yet has my heart or head
In the least way realized
They and I are civilized.

READING CRITICALLY

How are the sentiments Cullen expresses in the last three lines reflected in the rest of the poem?

READING 36.5

Langston Hughes, Selected Poems

Hughes began writing poems almost directly out of high school, and by the mid-1920s, his was considered the strongest voice in the Harlem Renaissance. The Weary Blues, *below, reflects Hughes's lifelong interest in the spoken or sung qualities of African-American vernacular language and its roots in musical idiom. The other two poems, from later in Hughes's career, reflect the challenges faced by African-American society, their simultaneous hope and despair in relation to American culture as a whole.*

THE WEARY BLUES (1923)

Droning a drowsy syncopated tune,
Rocking back and forth to a mellow croon,
    I heard a Negro play.
Down on Lenox Avenue the other night
By the pale dull pallor of an old gas light
    He did a lazy sway . . .
    He did a lazy sway . . .
To the tune o' those Weary Blues.
With his ebony hands on each ivory key
He made that poor piano moan with melody.   10
    O Blues!
Swaying to and fro on his rickety stool
He played that sad raggy tune like a musical fool.
    Sweet Blues!
Coming from a black man's soul.
    O Blues!
In a deep song voice with a melancholy tone
I heard that Negro sing, that old piano moan—

"Ain't got nobody in all this world,
Ain't got nobody but ma self.   20
I's gwine to quit ma frownin'
And put ma troubles on the shelf."

Thump, thump, thump, went his foot on the floor.
He played a few chords then he sang some more—
    "I got the Weary Blues
    And I can't be satisfied.
    Got the Weary Blues
    And can't be satisfied—
    I ain't happy no mo'
    And I wish that I had died."   30
And far into the night he crooned that tune.
The stars went out and so did the moon.
The singer stopped playing and went to bed
While the Weary Blues echoed through his head.
He slept like a rock or a man that's dead.

HARLEM (1951)

What happens to a dream deferred?

Does it dry up
like a raisin in the sun?
Or fester like a sore—
And then run?
Does it stink like rotten meat?
Or crust and sugar over—
like a syrupy sweet?

Maybe it just sags
like a heavy load.   10

Or does it explode?

THEME FOR ENGLISH B (1951)

The instructor said,

*Go home and write
a page tonight.
And let that page come out of you—
Then, it will be true.*

I wonder if it's that simple?
I am twenty-two, colored, born in Winston-Salem.
I went to school there, then Durham, then here
to this college on the hill above Harlem.
I am the only colored student in my class.
The steps from the hill lead down into Harlem,
through a park, then I cross St. Nicholas,
Eighth Avenue, Seventh, and I come to the Y,
the Harlem Branch Y, where I take the elevator
up to my room, sit down, and write this page: 10

It's not easy to know what is true for you or me
at twenty-two, my age. But I guess I'm what
I feel and see and hear, Harlem, I hear you:
hear you, hear me—we two—you, me, talk on this page.
(I hear New York, too.) Me—who?   20
Well, I like to eat, sleep, drink, and be in love.
I like to work, read, learn, and understand life.
I like a pipe for a Christmas present,
or records—Bessie, bop, or Bach.
I guess being colored doesn't make me *not* like
the same things other folks like who are other races.
So will my page be colored that I write?
Being me, it will not be white.
But it will be
a part of you, instructor.   30
You are white—
yet a part of me, as I am a part of you.
That's American.
Sometimes perhaps you don't want to be a part of me.
Nor do I often want to be a part of you.
But we are, that's true!
As I learn from you,
I guess you learn from me—
although you're older—and white—
and somewhat more free.   40

This is my page for English B.

READING CRITICALLY

Although Hughes's voice is distinctly African-American, his poetry also reflects his clear understanding of modernist principles. What does it share with the writing of poets like Ezra Pound or William Carlos Williams?

37

The Age of Anxiety
Fascism and Depression, Holocaust and Bomb

THINKING AHEAD

What was Berlin like in the 1920s?

What is fascism?

What is the Mexican mural movement?

What was the WPA?

How did sound and color change the motion-picture industry?

What was the Holocaust?

In the 1920s, Berlin, the capital of Germany, rivaled and may even have surpassed New York and Paris as a center of the arts. Its Philharmonic Orchestra was without equal, its political theater and cabaret were daring and innovative, its architecture was the most advanced and modern in Europe, and its art was challenging, nonconformist, and politically committed. It is no wonder that Dada thrived in Berlin (see Chapter 35).

Not everyone was mesmerized by Berlin's cultural glitter. The Austrian writer Stefan Zweig [tsvike (long "i," as in "eye")] (1881–1942), who arrived in the city in the early 1920s, described the place in disapproving terms:

> I have a pretty thorough knowledge of history, but never, to my recollection, has it produced such madness in such gigantic proportions. All values were changed, and not only material ones, the laws of the State were flouted, no tradition, no moral code, was respected, Berlin was transformed into the Babylon of the world. Bars, amusement parks, honky-tonks sprang up like mushrooms. . . . Along the entire Kurfürstendamm [ker-fer-shten-dahm] powdered and rouged young men sauntered . . . and in the dimly lit bars one might see

government officials and men of the world courting drunken sailors without shame. . . . In the collapse of all values a kind of madness gained hold.

This is the libertine world of homosexuals and prostitutes that the National Socialist (Nazi) party of Adolf Hitler (1889–1945) would condemn in its massive public demonstrations (Fig. 37.1). Hitler blamed intellectuals for his country's moral demise—specifically Jewish intellectuals. And he assumed without question that they were, in one way or another, associated with communism, which he saw as a threat to the economic health of Germany, due to the association of communists with labor unions. Hitler's success at controlling German public opinion brought the Nazi party to power in 1933 and led to the imposition of a fascistic (totalitarian and nationalistic) regime known as the Third Reich on that formerly republican state. Similar regimes arose across Europe as well.

This chapter surveys the rise of fascism and its consequences for art and culture in the two decades after World War I in Germany, Italy, Spain, and the Soviet Union. It also surveys the struggle for freedom in Mexico and the work of the artists who supported the Mexican Revolution

◀ **Fig. 37.1 Nazi Rally, Berlin. 1936.** Faced with the chaos resulting from World War I and the revolution in Russia, much of Europe looked to the uniformity and stability promised by totalitarianism to relieve the anxiety they saw reflected in the arts. In Germany, massive demonstrations, like the one depicted here, were organized in support of Hitler's National Socialist (Nazi) Party.

HEAR MORE Listen to an audio file of your chapter at **www.myartslab.com**

and the effects of the Great Depression in the United States. Over all of these developments, the specter of fascism hung like a dark cloud as, throughout the 1930s, another world war seemed increasingly inevitable.

Ever since the nineteenth century, when Japan, China, India, and Africa experienced social dislocation and upheaval as a result of confrontation with the West (see Chapter 33), and as the West colonized large parts of the globe, the impact of political events and social issues had become increasingly global in impact. World War I had taken place along a fairly compact front in northeastern France and northwestern Germany. By contrast, World War II was a truly worldwide conflict. No other event of the first half of the twentieth century so greatly increased the growing decenteredness of culture. In Germany, in what has come to be called the **Holocaust**, somewhere around 6 million Jews were killed in Hitler's concentration camps along with 5 million others whom the Nazis considered racially inferior or otherwise culturally problematic—particularly Gypsies, Slavs, the handicapped, and homosexuals. In the Pacific, the United States ended the war by dropping atomic bombs on the cities of Hiroshima and Nagasaki. Between them, the concentration camps and the bomb exposed an unprecedented capacity for hatred and genocide at the center of Western culture.

THE GLITTER AND ANGST OF BERLIN

At the end of World War I, the Weimar Republic became successor to the German Empire, with Berlin remaining as its capital (Map **37.1**). Two years later, in 1920, the Greater Berlin Act united numerous suburbs, villages, and estates around Berlin into a greatly expanded city with Berlin as its administrative center. The population of the expanded city was around 4 million. As a result, Berlin was Germany's largest city. It was the center not only of German cultural and intellectual life but also that of Eastern Europe, a city to

Map 37.1 Weimar Germany, 1919–33.

which artists and writers were drawn by the very liberalism and collapse of traditional values that Stefan Zweig bemoaned. The poet and playwright Carl Zuckmeyer [TSOOK-my-er] (1896–1977) described the decadent glitter of the city's brothels and nightclubs in sexually frank terms:

> People discussed Berlin . . . as if Berlin were a highly desirable woman, whose coldness and capriciousness were widely known; the less chance anyone had to win her, the more they decried her. We called her proud, snobbish, nouveau riche, uncultured, crude. But secretly everyone looked upon her as the goal of their desires. Some saw her as hefty, full-breasted, in lace underwear, others as a mere wisp of a thing, with boyish legs in black silk stockings. The daring saw both aspects, and her very capacity for cruelty made them the more aggressive. All wanted to have her, she enticed all.

Here was a city of pleasures that one could not resist, yet its attractions were informed by a deeply political conscience. German communists shuttled back and forth between Moscow and Berlin, bringing with them Lenin's views on culture (see Chapter 35). They scoffed at the politics of the Weimar Republic, which seemed farcical to them. (In the 15 years of its life, there were 17 different governments as the economy plunged into chaos.) Political street fights were common. In Berlin, artists and intellectuals, workers and businessmen wandered through a maze of competing political possibilities—all of them more or less strident.

The painter Georg Grosz [grohs] (1893–1959) would parody this world in his 1926 *The Pillars of Society* (Fig. **37.2**). The title refers to three major divisions of society: the military, the clergy, and above all, the middle class. All varieties of German politics are Grosz's target. Standing at the bar, sword in one hand, beer in the other, is a middle-class National Socialist (identifiable by the swastika on his tie), a warhorse rising out of his open skull. Behind him, the German flag in his hand, is a Social Democrat, his skull likewise open, displaying his party's slogan—"Socialism is work"—as he stands idly at the bar. Beside him is a journalist, chamberpot on his head, quill and pencil in hand, apparently ready to demonstrate to the National Socialist that the pen is mightier than the sword. A clergyman, his eyes closed, turns as if in praise of the fiery streets visible out the door even as soldiers commit violence behind his back. Grosz's vision is of a society at the edge of chaos and doom, led by brainless politicians, incompetent journalists, an angry middle class, a blind clergy, and a vindictive military. Such a vision, shared by many, created a certain feeling of *angst* in Berlin and elsewhere in Germany, a feeling of nervous anxiety and dread that would manifest itself in fiction, the theater, and the arts.

Kafka's Nightmare Worlds

One of the many Eastern Europeans drawn to Berlin—perhaps for its angst as well as its glitter—was the Jewish Czech-born author Franz Kafka [KAHF-kuh] (1883–1924), who wrote in German. He came to Berlin in 1923 only to

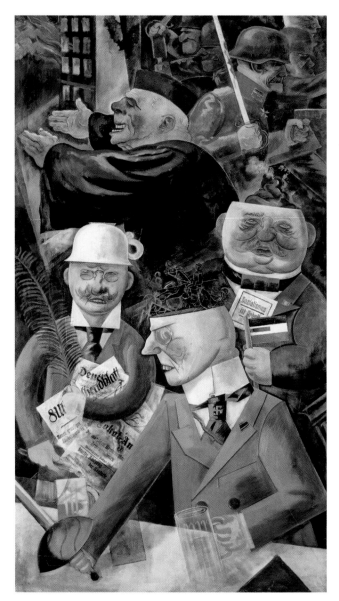

Fig. 37.2 Georg Grosz (1893–1959), *Stuetzen der Gesellschaft* (*The Pillars of Society*). 1926. Oil on canvas, 78 ³⁄₄″ × 42 ¹⁄₂″ (200.0 × 108.0 cm). Inv.: NG 4/58. Photo: Joerg P. Anders. Nationalgalerie, Staatliche Museen zu Berlin, Berlin, Germany. Art © Estate George Grosz/Licensed by VAGA, New York, New York. Grosz's biting wit was not tolerated by Hitler's fascist regime, and in the 1930s he fled Germany to the United States.

leave a year later, just before dying from complications of tuberculosis. His fellow Prague native and friend Max Brod (1884–1968) made sure that Kafka's unpublished works found their way to press in Germany.

Kafka was something of a tortured soul, and the characters in his works of fiction typically find themselves caught in inexplicable circumstances that bear all the markings of their own neuroses. Berliners identified with these characters immediately. His novel *The Trial*, left unfinished but published in Berlin in 1925, opens with this sentence: "Someone must have been telling lies about Josef K., he knew he had done nothing wrong but, one morning, he was arrested." The story is at once an indictment of modern bureaucracy and a classic study in paranoia. Never informed of what he has been

accused, Josef K. can only address the empty court with a virtually paranoid sense of his own impotence (**Reading 37.1**):

READING 37.1
_____

from Franz Kafka, *The Trial* (1925)

There can be no doubt that behind all the actions of this court of justice, that is to say in my case, behind my arrest and today's interrogation, there is a great organization at work. An organization which not only employs corrupt warders, oafish Inspectors, and Examining Magistrates of whom the best that can be said is that they recognize their own limitations, but also has at its disposal a judicial hierarchy of high, indeed of the highest rank, with an indispensable and numerous retinue of servants, clerks, police, and other assistants, perhaps even hangmen, I do not shrink from that word. And the significance of this great organization, gentlemen? It consists in this, that innocent persons are accused of guilt, and senseless proceedings are put in motion against them.

Embodied in this excerpt and in the entire novel is the clash between state politics and individual liberty that fueled Berlin life.

In Kafka's novella *The Metamorphosis*, first published in 1915, Gregor Samsa [SAHM-sah] similarly awakes to a stunning predicament: Overnight he has been transformed into a gigantic insect. (See **Reading 37.2**, pages 1246–1247, for the story's opening paragraphs.) Gregor's predicament is not unlike that of a person suffering from a severe disability, but it also suggests the deep-seated sense of alienation of the modern consciousness. For Gregor's metamorphosis is inexplicable and unexplained. It is simply his condition: dreadful, doomed, and oddly funny—a condition with which many in Berlin identified.

Brecht and the Berlin Stage

In 1924, Bertolt Brecht [brehkt](1898–1954), a young playwright from Munich, arrived in Berlin. He had already achieved a certain level of fame among intellectuals of his own generation for his deeply cynical and nihilistic play *Drums in the Night* (1918). It is the story of a young woman, Anna Balicke, who believes her love, Andreas, has died in the war and who is about to marry a wealthy war materials manufacturer when Andreas returns. It encapsulates the feelings of a generation of soldiers who felt that they had fought for nothing while a greedy older generation profited from their sacrifice.

Drums in the Night is set against the backdrop of the communist-inspired Spartikusbund (Spartacus League) uprising of January 1919 in Germany. (The *bund* took its name from Spartacus, leader of the largest slave rebellion in the Roman Republic.) It was the last act of a postwar revolution that had begun the previous November when sailors in the German navy refused to sacrifice themselves in a pointless final battle with the British Royal Navy. Quickly supported by workers across Germany, the league protested in the streets under the slogan, "Frieden" und "Brot" [FREE-den oond brot] ("Peace and Bread"). So massive was the protest that it forced Kaiser Wilhelm II to abdicate in favor of the Social Democratic Party (SPD) under the leadership of Friedrich Ebert [AY-bert] (1871–1925). But when 500,000 people surged into the streets of Berlin on January 7, 1919, occupying buildings, Ebert ordered the anti-Republican paramilitary organization known as the Freikorps [FRY-kor], which had kept its weapons and equipment after the war, to attack the workers. The Freikorps quickly retook the city, killing many workers and innocent civilians even as they tried to surrender.

These events inspired Brecht to turn to Marxism, which he began to study intensely. The first major hit to result from this study was a collaboration with composer Kurt Weill [vile] (1900–1950) on the "scenic cantata" *Mahagonny-Songspiel*, which premiered in Baden Baden in 1927. Consisting of a series of songs, taking earlier Brecht poems for their lyrics, the success of the 40-minute musical paved the way for a much larger production the next year in Berlin of *The Threepenny Opera*, an updating of John Gay's eighteenth-century play *The Beggar's Opera* (see Chapter 25). When it premiered at Berlin's Schiffbauerdamm [SHIF-bau-er-dahm] Theater in 1928, *The Threepenny Opera* was a huge success. It is not, in fact, an opera but a work of musical theater focusing on the working class of Victorian London, who are as organized and well-connected in their shady businesses as any bourgeois banker or corporation president. Its hero, Macheath, or Mackie Messer (Mack the Knife), is a criminal sentenced to hang at the instigation of his lover Polly's father, Mr. Peachum, an entrepreneur of the crassest kind. Mr. Peachum is boss of London's beggars, whom he equips and trains in return for a cut of whatever they can beg. At the last moment Macheath is unexpectedly saved by a royal pardon and is granted a castle and a pension as an unjust reward for his life of crime.

The play is Brecht's socialist critique of capitalism, but aside from its political message, it embodies a revolutionary approach to theater based on alienation. It rejects the traditional relationship between play and audience, in which the viewer is invited to identify with the plight of the main character and imaginatively enter the world of the play's illusion. Brecht wanted his audience to maintain a detached relationship with the characters in the play and to view them critically. He believed they should always be aware that they were watching a play, not real life. Brecht called his new approach to the stage **epic theater**, which he later explained as follows (**Reading 37.3**):

READING 37.3

from Bertolt Brecht, "Theater for Pleasure or Theater for Imagination" (ca. 1935)

The spectator was no longer in any way allowed to submit to an experience uncritically (and without practical consequences) by means of simple empathy with the characters in a play. The production took the subject matter and the incidents shown and put them through a process of alienation: the alienation that is necessary to all understanding. When something seems "the most obvious thing in the world" it means that any attempt to understand the world has been given up.

What is "natural" must have the force of what is startling. This is the only way to expose the laws of cause and effect. People's activity must simultaneously be so and be capable of being different.

It was all a great change.

The dramatic theater's spectator says: Yes, I have felt like that too—Just like me—It's only natural—It'll never change—The sufferings of this man appall me, because they are inescapable—That's great art; it all seems the most obvious thing in the world— I weep when they weep, I laugh when they laugh.

The epic theater's spectator says: I'd never have thought it—That's not the way—That's extraordinary, hardly believable—It's got to stop—The sufferings of this man appall me, because they are unnecessary— That's great art; nothing obvious in it—I laugh when they weep, I weep when they laugh.

Brecht realizes this alienation effect, as he called it, in many ways. First, the scenes do not flow continuously one to the next; rather, the narrative jumps around. Second, actors make it clear that they are, indeed, acting. Third, there is no curtain; stage sets are visible from the moment the audience enters the theater, and stage machinery is entirely visible. Fourth, although the play's opening song, "Mack the Knife" (track **37.1**), immediately HEAR MORE at www.myartslab.com follows the overture in a highly traditional manner, the other songs are purposefully designed to interrupt, not further, the action.

"Mack the Knife," like the rest of the score, is strongly influenced by what the Germans of the day conceived of as jazz, music largely based on the foxtrot and other popular dance music, with some parodies of "classical" genres. In fact, the original production specified a 15-piece jazz combo. The play opens, then, with a cabaret number, introduced in the original score by a harmonium, that celebrates the dark underworld of murder and mayhem that lies beneath the surface of London life, jarring its audience out of complacency.

Kollwitz and the Expressionist Print

One of the most powerful voices of protest in Berlin during the 1920s was artist Käthe Kollwitz [KOLL-vits] (1867–1945). She trained at art schools in Berlin and Munich but married a doctor whose practice concentrated on tending the poor of the city. As a result, she was in constant contact with workers and their plight. As she explained:

> The motifs I was able to select from this milieu (the workers' lives) offered me, in a simple and forthright way, what I discovered to be beautiful. . . . People from

the bourgeois sphere were altogether without appeal or interest. All middle-class life seemed pedantic to me. On the other hand, I felt the proletariat had guts. . . . [W]hen I got to know the women who would come to my husband for help, and incidentally also to me . . . I was powerfully moved by the fate of the proletariat and everything connected with its way of life.

Kollwitz's work before World War I consisted of highly naturalist portrayals of the German poor, including a series of prints depicting the Peasants' War during the Reformation in 1525 (see Chapter 17). They are profoundly moving images of grief, suffering, and doom. The loss of her son Peter in October 1914, just months into World War I, permanently changed Kollwitz's art, politicizing it, as she became increasingly attracted to communism. The death also radicalized her work stylistically. Before the war, she had concentrated on etching—the rich, densely linear medium of her German forebear Albrecht Dürer (see Chapters 16 and 17). But now she turned to the more dramatic, Expressionist media of woodblock and lithograph favored by members of Die Brücke and Der Blaue Reiter (see Chapter 34). On the block, she could gouge out the areas of white with violent ferocity. In lithographs, which she used particularly to make broadly distributed political posters with messages such as *Never Again War!* (1924) (Fig. **37.3**), she was able to achieve a gestural freedom as powerful and strident as her woodblocks.

THE RISE OF FASCISM

In response to the exciting but disturbing freedom so evident in Berlin's urban art world and nightlife, European conservatives longed to return to a premodern, essentially rural past. In Germany, bourgeois youth thronged to the Wandervogel [VAHN-der-foh-gul] (literally, "freebirds" or "hikers") movement, joining together around campfires in the mountains to play the guitar and sing in an effort to reinvent a lost German romantic ideal. They longed for the sense of order and cultural preeminence that had been destroyed by Germany's defeat in World War I. They longed to be "whole" again, a longing that to many was geographical as well as psychological because the country had been stripped of the territories of Alsace-Lorraine [AHL-sahss-lor-REN] to the west and Silesia [sy-LEE-zhuh] to the east.

Modernity itself, which after all had brought them the war, was their enemy. It was in the city of Weimar [VY-mar], where the nineteenth-century Romantics Goethe and Schiller had lived, that the National Assembly convened to draft a new constitution at the end of World War I, lending the new republic its name even as Berlin remained the German capital (see Map 37.1). But the politics of the Weimar Republic were anything but comfortable. As historian Peter Gay has put it, "The hunger for wholeness was awash with hate: the political, and sometimes the private, world of its chief spokesmen was a paranoid world, filled with enemies: the dehumanizing machine, capitalist materialism, godless rationalism, rootless society, cosmopolitan Jews, and that great all-devouring monster, the city." Out of this hate, the authoritarian political ideology known as fascism was born. Fascism arose across Europe after World War I. It was the manifestation of mass

Fig. 37.3 Käthe Kollwitz, *Never Again War*. 1924. Lithograph, 37″ × 27 ½″. Kollwitz shunned the painting medium, choosing to work in prints, which could be circulated to a wide audience that included the working class.

movements that subordinated individual interests to the needs of the state as they sought to forge a sense of national unity based on ethnic, cultural, and, usually, racial identity. The German fascists led the way.

Hitler in Germany

Late in 1923, Adolf Hitler, the son of an Austrian customs official, staged an unsuccessful *putsch* [pooch], or revolt, at a Munich beer hall. In his youth, Hitler had wanted to be an artist and had served in the German army in World War I, where he was awarded the Iron Cross for bravery but rose only to the rank of private. He was strongly affected by the German defeat to join the National Socialist (Nazi) party. He was accompanied in his revolt by fellow "storm troopers," the private soldiers of the Nazi party noted for their brown shirts and vigilante tactics. Local authorities killed 16 Nazis and arrested Hitler. He used his trial to attract national attention, condemning the Versailles Treaty, Jews, and the national economy, which was suffering from astronomical inflation as paper money became essentially worthless. Convicted and sentenced to five years in jail, he spent the few months that he actually served writing the racist tract *Mein Kampf* [mine kahmpf] (*My Struggle*), published in 1925. In it he argued for the superiority of the German race, which he wrongly described as

"Aryan" in the belief Western languages and civilizations could be traced back to the same Aryan nomads who invaded India in 1500 BCE (see Chapter 7) and that these nomads were themselves descendents of pure, white Nordic stock. In his mind, the Aryan race was distinct, especially, from Semitic peoples (**Reading 37.4**):

READING 37.4

from Adolf Hitler, *Mein Kampf* (1925)

Every manifestation of human culture, every product of art, science and technical skill, which we see before our eyes today, is almost exclusively the product of Aryan creative power. . . . On this planet of ours human culture and civilization are indissolubly bound up with the presence of the Aryan. If he should be exterminated or subjugated, then the dark shroud of a new barbarian era would enfold the earth.

Fig. 37.4 John Heartfield, *Der Sinn des Hitlergrusses: Kleiner Mann bittet um große Gaben.* **Motto:** *Millonen Stehen Hinter Mir!* **(The Meaning of the Hitler Salute: Little Man Asks for Big Gifts. Motto: Millions Stand Behind Me!). 1932.** Photo-mechanical reproduction. The Metropolitan Museum of Art, New York (1987.1125.8). Image © The Metropolitan Museum of Art/Art Resource, New York. After the National Socialists took power in 1933, Heartfield fled to Czechoslovakia, where he continued to create photomontages for *Arbeiter-Illustrierte Zeitung*. He did not return to Germany until after World War II.

Anti-Semitism Hitler felt that the forces of modernity, specifically under the leadership of Jewish intellectuals, were determined to exterminate the Aryan race. Fearmongering was the rhetorical bread and butter he used to drive others to his view:

> [A] Jewish youth lies in wait for hours on end satanically glaring at and spying on the unconscious girl whom he plans to seduce, adulterating her blood with the ultimate idea of bastardizing the white race which they hate and thus lowering its cultural and political level so that the Jew might dominate.

The collapse of world economies in the Great Depression, a direct result of the crash of the New York stock market on October 29, 1929, fueled middle-class fears. As far as Hitler was concerned, Jewish economic interests were responsible for the crash. By 1932, more than 6 million Germans were unemployed, and thousands of them joined the Nazi storm troopers. Their ranks rose from 100,000 in 1930 to over 1 million in 1933.

Artists and intellectuals responded to this anti-Semitic challenge. Some of the most extraordinary examples are the posters of John Heartfield (1891–1968). Heartfield had anglicized his name from Helmut Herzfeld to antagonize Germans who, as a result of World War I, almost reveled in Anglophobia. He had satirized the Weimar Republic from the outset, but he savagely attacked Hitler in political photomontages—collages composed of multiple photographs—many published in the *Arbeiter- Illustrierte Zeitung* [AR-by-tuh-ill-oos-TREER-tuh TSY-toong], a widely distributed workers' newspaper that had 500,000 readers in 1931. Heartfield clearly understood the ability of photomontage to bring together images of a vastly different scale in a single work with an immense impact. In *Der Sinn des Hitlergrusses: Kleiner Mann bittet um große Gaben*. Motto: *Millonen Stehen Hinter Mir!* (The Meaning of the Hitler Salute: Little Man Asks for Big Gifts. Motto: Millions Stand Behind Me!) Heartfield exposes Hitler's reliance on fat, wealthy German industrialists—whom the readers of *Arbeiter-Illustrierte Zeitung* despised— suggesting that the famous Nazi salute is, in reality, a plea for money (Fig. **37.4**).

Many workers were sympathetic to communism. But if they were initially leery of Hitler, enough of them had been won over by the end of January 1933 to elect him chancellor (prime minister) of Germany. This election ended the Weimar Republic and inaugurated the Third Reich [ryek] (1933–1945), Hitler's name for the totalitarian and nationalistic dictatorship he led. When, on February 27, 1933, a mentally ill Dutch communist set fire to the Reichstag, seat of the German government in Berlin, Hitler invoked an act that had been written into the original Weimar Constitution allowing the president to rule by decree in an emergency. (He convinced the president to sign the decree.) By the next day, he had arrested 4,000 members of the Communist Party. Communism was, after all, the creation of yet another German Jew, Karl Marx. So, from Hitler's paranoid point of view, the destruction of the German state was part and parcel of communism's international conspiracy.

The Nazis urged German citizens to boycott Jewish businesses, and they expelled Jews from the civil service. Finally, in September 1935, with the passage of the so-called Nuremberg Laws, anti-Semitism became official German policy. A Jew was defined as anyone with at least one Jewish grandparent, and his or her German citizenship was revoked. Intermarriage and extramarital relationships between Jews and non-Jews were forbidden. Jews were prohibited from writing, publishing, making art, giving concerts, acting on stage or screen, teaching, working in a bank or hospital, and selling books. In this atmosphere of hatred, it is little wonder that, in November 1938, Herschel Grynszpan, a Jewish boy of 17, would take it upon himself to kill the secretary of the German embassy in Paris, driven mad by the persecution of his parents in Germany. And it is even less wonder that mobs throughout Germany and parts of Austria, egged on by the Nazis, responded, on what has become known as the Kristallnacht [kri-SHTAHL-nahkt] (Night of Broken Glass), by burning and looting Jewish shops and synagogues, invading Jews' homes, beating them, and stealing their possessions.

The Bauhaus and the Rise of the International Style The impact on the arts of Hitler's rise to power is nowhere more clearly demonstrated than in the history of the Bauhaus (from the German verb *bauen* [BOW-en (as in "now")], "to build"), the art school created by architect Walter Gropius [GROH-pee-us] (1883–1969) in Weimar in 1919. Its aim, Gropius wrote in the Bauhaus manifesto, was to

> conceive and create the new building of the future, which will combine everything—architecture and sculpture and painting—in a single form which will one day rise towards the heavens from the hand of a million workers as the crystalline symbol of a new and coming faith.

To this end, Gropius recruited the most outstanding faculty he could find. Among them were the Expressionist painters Wassily Kandinsky (see Chapter 34) and Paul Klee [klay] (1879–1940), the designer and architect Marcel Breuer [BROY-ur] (1902–1981), the painter and color theorist Josef Albers [AL-berz] (1888–1976), the graphic designer Herbert Bayer [BY-ur] (1900–1985), and later the architect Ludwig Mies van der Rohe [meez van-der ROH] (1886–1969).

The Bauhaus aesthetic drew on developments from across Europe—the Cubism of Picasso and Braque (see Chapter 34), the geometric simplicity of Kasimir Malevich and the Russian Constructivists (see Chapter 35), and especially the Dutch Modernist movement known as De Stijl, literally "the style." The De Stijl movement was led by the painter Piet Mondrian (1872–1944) and the architect, painter, and theorist Theo van Doesburg (1883–1931), who sought to create a new, "purely plastic work of art" of total abstraction. It completely rejected literal reality as experienced by the senses. Instead it reduced creative terms to the

Fig. 37.5
Piet Mondrian (1872–1944), *Composition with Blue, Yellow, Red and Black*, 1922.
Oil on canvas, 16 $^1/_2$″ ×19 $^1/_4$″ (41.9 ×48.9 cm). Minneapolis Institute
of Arts. © 2010 Mondrian/Holtzman Trust c/o HCR International, VA. USA.
For Mondrian, "each thing represents the whole on a smaller scale; the structure
of the microcosm resembles that of the macrocosm." This painting suggests the
structure of what Mondrian called the "Great Whole."

Fig. 37.6 Gerrit Rietveld, Schröder House, Utrecht, The Netherlands.
1924. Artists Rights Society (ARS), New York/Beeldrecht, Amsterdam.

Fig. 37.7 Gerrit Rietveld, Interior, Schröder House, with "Red-Blue"
Chair, Utrecht, The Netherlands. 1924. Photo: Jannes Linders Photography.
© 2008 Artists Rights Society (ARS), NY. Rietveld explained the openness of
the top floor, seen above: "It was of course extremely difficult to achieve all
this in spite of the building regulations and that's why the interior of the
downstairs part of the house is somewhat traditional, I mean with fixed walls.
But upstairs we simply called it an 'attic' and that's where we actually made
the house we wanted." Note the famous Red-Blue Chair, designed by Rietveld
in 1918, when he was still working as a cabinetmaker.

bare minimum: the straight line, the right angle, the three
primary colors (red, yellow, and blue), and the three basic
noncolors (black, gray, and white). Mondrian believed that
the grid, a network of regularly spaced lines that cross one
another at right angles, represented a cosmic interaction
between the masculine and spiritual (vertical) and the feminine and material (horizontal). By the early 1920s, he had
extended this belief to include a color/noncolor interaction.
More important, he eliminated the traditional figure/ground
relation of representational painting, where the blank white
canvas is considered the painting's "ground." In his
Composition with Blue, Red, Yellow, and Black of 1922, the
white square set off-center in the middle of the painting
appears to be on exactly the same plane as the colored
planes that surround it (Fig. **37.5**).

Like the Bauhaus theorists and despite his own interest in
painting, Mondrian claimed that the culmination of art rested
in architecture. The principles of De Stijl, he wrote, govern
"the interior as well as the exterior of the building." Gerrit
Rietveld's Schröder House, built in Utrecht, Holland, in
1924 to 1925, has been called "a cardboard Mondrian" (Fig.
37.6). To a certain extent this is true, but in other ways
it is the exact opposite of his dogmatically flat canvasses,
as if Mondrian's surface has been stretched out into three-
dimensional space. The house is a cubelike form interrupted by the planar projections of its interior walls. All of the
walls of the upper floor could be removed, sliding back into recesses and transforming a series of small rooms into a single
space (Fig. **37.7**). In other words, the space is fluid and open,

LEARN MORE Gain insight from a primary source document from Piet Mondrian at **www.myartslab.com**

Fig. 37.8 Le Corbusier, Domino House. 1914. The plan's name derives from the six pillars positioned on the floor like the six dots on a domino.

Fig. 37.9 Le Corbusier, Villa Savoye, Poissy-sur-Seine, France. 1928–30. Anthony Scibilia/Art Resource, New York. © 2008 Artists Rights Society (ARS), New York/ADAGP, Paris/FLC. Le Corbusier wrote: "The columns set back from the facades, inside the house. The floor continues cantilevered. The facades are no longer anything but light skins of insulating walls or windows. The facade is free."

waiting to be composed by its inhabitants. Built-in and movable furniture of Rietveld's design is geometric and abstract in concept. The predominant colors are white and gray, highlighted by selective use of primary colors and black lines. According to van Doesburg, it demonstrated that "the work of art is a metaphor of the universe obtained with artistic means."

Equally influential was the architecture of Frenchman Charles-Édouard Jeanneret (1887–1965), known as Le Corbusier [kor-booz-YAY], who founded the magazine and movement known as *L'Esprit Nouveau* (The New Spirit) after World War I. Le Corbusier's importance rested on his belief in the possibility of creating low-cost, easily replicable, but essentially superior housing for everyone. In order to cope with the massive destruction of property in the war, Le Corbusier proposed what he called the "domino" system of architecture, a basic building prototype for mass production (Fig. **37.8**). The structural frame of this building was of reinforced concrete supported by steel pillars. The lack of supporting walls turned the interior into an open, free-flowing, and highly adaptable space that could serve as a dwelling for a single family or be replicated again and again to form apartment units or industrial and office space. In a 1923 article called "Five Points of a New Architecture," Le Corbusier insisted that (1) the house should be raised on columns to provide for privacy, with only an entrance on the ground level; (2) it should have a flat roof, to be used as a roof garden; (3) it should have an open floor plan; (4) the exterior curtain walls should be freely composed; and (5) the windows should be horizontal ribbons of glass.

Calling his homes "machines for living in," Le Corbusier employed those five principles to design the Villa Savoye in Poissy-sur-Seine, France, west of Paris (Fig. **37.9**). The entry is set back, beneath the main living space on the second floor, which is supported by steel columns. Rounded windbreaks shelter a roof garden. The combination of

rectangle, square, and circle creates a sense of geometric simplicity. As Le Corbusier had put it in his 1925 *Towards a New Architecture*: "Primary forms are beautiful forms because they can be clearly appreciated."

This is the new architecture Alfred H. Barr, Jr., and Philip Johnson labeled the International Style in the same 1932 exhibition at the Museum of Modern Art in New York in which they had included the work of Frank Lloyd Wright (see Chapter 36). The show also featured the work of Le Corbusier and two Bauhaus architects, Gropius and Mies van der Rohe.

Nazi pressure had forced the Bauhaus out of Weimar in 1925, when the community withdrew its financial support due to the school's perceived leftist bent. The school moved to Dessau, closer to Berlin, where Gropius designed a new building (Fig. **37.10**). Although its look is familiar enough today—an indication of just how influential it would become—the building was revolutionary at the time. It was

Fig. 37.10 Walter Gropius, Bauhaus Building, Dessau, Germany. 1925–26. Photograph courtesy Bauhaus Dessau Foundation, Dessau, Germany. Gropius described his building as a "clear, organic [form] whose inner logic [is] radiant, naked, unencumbered by lying facades and trickeries."

essentially a skeleton of reinforced concrete with a skin of transparent glass. As Gropius himself explained:

> One of the outstanding achievements of the new constructional technique has been the abolition of the separating function of the wall. Instead of making the walls the element of support, as in a brick-built house, our new space-saving construction transfers the whole load of the structure to a steel or concrete framework. Thus the role of the walls becomes restricted to that of mere screens stretched between the upright columns of this framework to keep out rain, cold, and noise. . . . This, in turn, naturally leads to a progressively bolder (i.e. wider) opening up of the wall surfaces, which allows rooms to be much better lit. It is, therefore, only logical that the old type of window—a hole that had to be hollowed out of the full thickness of a supporting wall—should be giving place more and more to the continuous horizontal casement, subdivided by thin steel mullions, characteristic of the New Architecture.

Gropius stepped down as director in 1928. He was replaced by Hannes Meyer [MY-er], a communist architect who saw nothing wrong with teaching Marxist doctrine in the classroom and who deemphasized fine art in favor of functional goods to benefit the working class. Meyer's communist politics made the Bauhaus an easy target for the Nazis. Even after Mies van der Rohe replaced Meyer in 1930, the Nazis proposed demolishing Gropius's "decadently modern" building. Although the plan was rejected, the school in Dessau was closed in October 1932 and then reopened by Mies in Berlin as a private institution. Finally, on April 11, 1933, Gestapo (secret state police) trucks appeared at the door. They padlocked the school, and it never reopened.

The Degenerate Art Exhibition   To the Nazis, the Bauhaus represented everything that was wrong with modernism— its inspiration by foreigners (especially Russians like Kandinsky), its rejection of traditional values, and its willingness to "taint" art with (leftist) politics. Between the Bauhaus's closing and 1937, virtually all avant-garde artists in Germany were removed from teaching positions and their works confiscated by the state. On July 19, 1937, many of these same works were among the over 600 displayed in the exhibition of Degenerate Art in Munich, organized at Hitler's insistence to demonstrate the mental and moral degeneracy of modernist art. Over 2 million people—nearly 20,000 a day—visited the show before it closed in November.

In the first room, religious art was chosen that, according to the catalogue, illustrated the "insolent mockery of the Divine" that had been championed by the Weimar Republic. It featured a nine-painting cycle by Emile Nolde (see Chapter 34), who was, ironically, a member of the Nazi party and so believed himself to be immune from persecution. In the second gallery, Jewish art was pilloried. In the third gallery, Dada and abstract painting were attacked, and Expressionist nudes were labeled "An insult to German womanhood." In another gallery, Expressionist still lifes were introduced as "Nature as seen by sick minds." After the exhibition, the Commission for the Disposal of Products of Degenerate Art arranged for those pieces with the highest value in the international art market to be sold at auction in Lucerne [loo-SERN], Switzerland. However, most of the confiscated works—1,004 oil paintings and 3,825 works on paper—were burned in the yard of the Berlin Fire Brigade on March 20, 1939.

The Art of Propaganda   The Degenerate Art show was carefully calculated to create public outrage. It coincided with the first of eight Great German Art exhibitions, which opened the day before, on July 18, 1937. Hitler spoke for an hour and a half on the nature and function of art. A pageant with more than 6,000 participants depicting 2,000 years of German culture followed the speech. It was all part of a concentrated effort by the Nazis to control culture by controlling what people saw and heard.

Radio played an enormous role. The Nazis understood that radio was replacing the newspaper as the primary means of mass communication. Since they controlled all German radio stations, they could make effective use of it. Addressing a group of German broadcasters, Joseph Goebbels [GOHB-uls] (1897–1945), Hitler's Minister for Public Enlightenment and Propaganda, emphasized the medium's importance:

> I consider radio to be the most modern and the most crucial instrument that exists for influencing the masses. I also believe—one should not say that out loud—that radio will in the end replace the press. . . . First principle: At all costs avoid being boring. I put that before everything. . . . The correct attitudes must be conveyed but that does not mean they must be boring. . . . By means of this instrument you are the creators of public opinion. If you carry this out well we shall win over the people and if you do it badly in the end the people will once more desert us.

Hitler's extraordinary oratorical skills were perfectly suited to the radio. Loudspeakers were set up throughout the nation so that everyone might hear his broadcasts. "Without the loudspeaker," Hitler wrote in 1938, "we would never have conquered Germany."

Film was likewise understood to be an important propaganda tool. In 1933, Hitler invited the talented director Leni Riefenstahl [REEF-en-shtahl] (1902–2003) to make a film of the 1934 Nazi rally in Nuremberg, providing her with a staff of more than 100 people, 30 cameras, special elevators, ramps, and tracks. The result was *Triumph of the Will*, a film that does not so much politicize art as aestheticize politics. Riefenstahl portrays Hitler as at once hero and father figure, lending him and his Nazi party a sense of grandeur and magnificence. March music dominates the score. The regularity of its beat mirrors the regularity and order of Hitler's storm troopers and suggests military strength and the order and stability that the Nazi regime promised to bring to the German people.

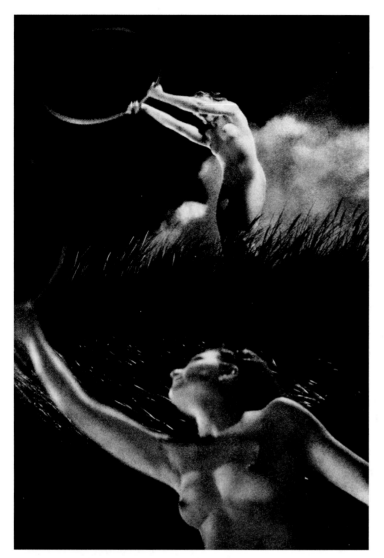

Fig. 37.11 Leni Riefenstahl, still from *Olympia*. 1936. The Museum of Modern Art, New York. Film Stills Archive. Riefenstahl herself appeared briefly nude in the film among a group of nude dancers on a beach on the Baltic Sea.

With Hitler's approval, Riefenstahl was appointed by the International Olympic Committee to film the 1936 Olympic Games in Berlin. Her two-part film, *Olympia*, was less political than *Triumph of the Will* and emphasized the beauty of the human body—albeit, decidedly white and "Aryan" human bodies. For the Games, Hitler inaugurated the tradition of runners carrying the Olympic torch from Athens to the Olympic venue, suggesting that Hitler's Germany was the modern successor to Classical Greece, and Riefenstahl's film begins with a 20-minute prelude filmed at the Parthenon and featuring Greek sculptures of original Olympic athletes which she then transforms, through montage, into live bodies both male and female—all of them nearly nude (Fig. **37.11**). The film was designed to demonstrate that Germans were, first and foremost, a beautiful people, but also fair and friendly competitors capable of cheering even the black American runner, Jesse Owens. Hitler, of course, hoped that German athletes would win many prizes, thus demonstrating Aryan superiority.

Stalin in Russia

Nazism was not the only totalitarian ideology to achieve political power in the aftermath of World War I. The consolidation of the Bolshevik revolution in Russia after World War I produced the longest-lasting totalitarian government. In the power vacuum that followed Lenin's death in 1924, two factions emerged in the Communist Party. Leon Trotsky [TROT-skee] (1879–1940) led one of them and Joseph Stalin [STAH-lin] (1878–1953) headed the other. Their rivalry took the form of a debate over the speed of industrialization of the Russian economy. Trotsky's faction favored rapid industrialization through the collectivization of agriculture; Stalin's faction pressed for relatively slow industrialization and the continuation of Lenin's tolerance of a modest degree of free enterprise in which peasant farmers were allowed to sell their produce for profit. Stalin was a master at manipulating the party bureaucracy, and by 1927, he had succeeded in expelling Trotsky from the party and sending him into exile, first to Siberia and then later to Mexico. He was murdered in Mexico in 1940, probably by one of Stalin's agents.

The Collectivization of Agriculture Once Stalin took power, he behaved very much the way Trotsky had advocated. In 1928, he decided to collectivize agriculture, consolidating individual land holdings into cooperative farms under the control of the government. This alleviated food shortages in the cities, produced enough for export, and freed the peasant labor force for work in the factories. At the same time, he inaugurated a series of five-year plans for the rapid industrialization of the economy. Finally, he accepted Trotsky's position that terror was a necessity of revolution. Stalin blamed the few prosperous peasant farmers, or **kulaks** [KOO-lahks], for the economic ills of the country.

The kulaks represented less than 5 percent of the rural population, but they did not want to collectivize and were unhappy that there were so few goods to purchase with their cash. In protest, they withheld grain from the market. "Now," Stalin proclaimed, "we are able to carry on a determined offensive against the kulaks, to break their resistance, to eliminate them as a class." Before long, anyone who opposed Stalin was considered a kulak, and between 1929 and 1933, his regime killed as many as 10 million peasants and sent millions of others to forced labor on collective farms and **gulags** [GOO-lahgs], labor camps. The peasants retaliated by killing over 100 million horses and cattle, causing a severe meat shortage. But Stalin persevered, not least of all because his plan for rapid industrialization was working. Soviet industrial production rose 400 percent between 1928 and 1940, by far the fastest-growing economy in the world at the time.

The Rise of Social Realism in Art and Music Stalin's five-year economic plans were supported by a series of propaganda posters that appeared across the country, such as *The Development of Transportation, The Five-Year Plan* by Gustav Klucis [kloo-cis] (1895–1944) (Fig. **37.12**). Klucis's poster is an example of social realism, the style of Russian art that followed Constructivism in the early 1920s (see Chapter 35). Klucis was himself a Constructivist, but like his fellow Constructivists, he was drawn to the necessity of communicating clearly with the largely illiterate peasant class. So he, like they, turned to graphic design and photomontage, a technique that seemed at once modern and Realist in the tradition of the great Russian realists of the nineteenth century, especially the revered Travelers (see Chapter 31). In doing so, he sacrificed abstraction in favor of an unwavering political commitment.

As early as 1921, the Soviet government had urged Russian artists to give up their avant-garde experiments on the grounds that abstraction was unintelligible to the masses. Other groups argued that it was necessary to concentrate on themes such as the daily life of the workers and the peasants. By 1934, the First All-Union Congress of Soviet Writers officially proclaimed all expressions of "modernism" decadent and called upon Soviet artists to create "a true, historically concrete portrayal of reality in its revolutionary development." Social realism was from that time on the official state style, and in literature, music, and the visual arts, all other styles were banned.

The Soviet authorities brought all musical activities under their control by a decree in 1932 and attacked Russian avant-garde composers in the same way they had attacked artists. They accused Sergei Prokofiev [pro-KOF-ee-ev] (1891–1953) and Dimitri Shostakovich [shoh-stuh-KOV-ich] (1906–1975) of writing music that was "too formalistic" and "too technically complicated"—and thus "alien to the Soviet people." The party Central Committee pressured both men to apologize publicly for the error of their ways. Prokofiev's very accessible symphonic fairy tale of 1936, *Peter and the Wolf*, is most likely an attempt to appease the Soviet authorities. Two years earlier, in 1934, the Soviet press had hailed Shostakovich's four-act opera *Lady Macbeth of the Mtsensk District* as a model of social realism. The opera was meant to be the first part of a trilogy dealing with Russian womanhood. It featured not only modernist dissonance but also themes of adultery, murder, and suicide. Two years later, in 1936, after Stalin had seen it himself and decided that the themes did not live up to the standards of official Soviet art, the newspaper *Pravda* [PRAHV-dah] condemned it as "Chaos, Not Music," and the opera was dropped from the repertory. Shostakovich repented by composing his 1937 Symphony No. 5, subtitled "A Soviet Artist's Response to Just Criticism."

In its relative lack of dissonance, Symphony No. 5 appeared to conform more closely to the ideals of social realism, but the piece is actually a monument to musical irony. Everything about it is a repudiation of Stalin and the Soviet authorities. The first movement opens with a cry of despair that, after a fairly long development, gives way to a march that is meant to evoke Stalinist authority. The party Central Committee was able to hear this passage as a sign of Shostakovich's capitulation, but Shostakovich hoped that his audience would understand the goose-stepping march as hopelessly shallow. The third movement is a profound work of mourning. If the Central Committee took it as an apology, Shostakovich meant it as a memorial to those lost in the gulags. The final, fourth movement, overtly a celebration of Soviet triumph, is instead a parody of celebration (track **37.2**). In his memoirs, smuggled out of Russia after his death, Shostakovich explained what he had in mind:

HEAR MORE at www.myartslab.com

> What exultation could there be? I think it is clear to everyone what happens in the Fifth. The rejoicing is forced, created under threat. . . . It's as if someone were beating you with a stick and saying "Your business is rejoicing, your business is rejoicing," and you rise, shaky, and go marching off, muttering, "Our business is rejoicing, our business is rejoicing." What kind of apotheosis is that? You have to be a complete oaf not to hear that.

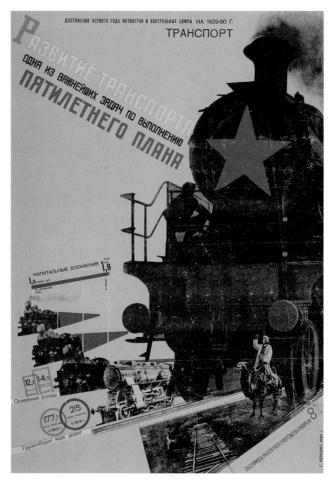

Fig. 37.12 Gustav Klucis, *The Development of Transportation, The Five-Year Plan*. 1929. Gravure, 28 $^7/_8$" × 19 $^7/_8$". Purchase fund, Jan Tschichold Collection. (146.1968). Digital Image © The Museum of Modern Art/Licensed by SCALA/Art Resource, New York. While incorporating realist imagery through photomontage, Klucis retains the dynamic interplay of geometric forms that mark earlier, more abstract Russian Constructivist design (see Chapter 35).

Some music historians doubt the authenticity of this autobiography, but, in truth, the fourth movement is brassy and bombastic, its chords continually rising into an almost shrill hysteria. About seven minutes into the movement, the percussion beats out the rhythms of a militaristic march, asserting a kind of totalitarian control over the symphony. At the end, the percussion seems almost threatening as it insists on its controlling authority.

Mussolini in Italy

One of the most important differences between Stalin's totalitarian state and the totalitarian regimes in the rest of Europe is that the latter all arose out of a vigorously anti-Marxist point of view and fear of the Soviet state. By 1920, the Communist Party in Russia had made it clear that it intended to spread its doctrines across Europe. "The Communist International has declared," it announced, "a decisive war against the entire bourgeois world." Such pronouncements nourished a climate of fear among middle-class small-business owners, property owners, and small farmers, which opportunistic leaders could easily exploit.

Italy's Benito Mussolini [moo-soh-LEE-nee] (1883–1945) was one of these. After World War I, Italy was in disarray. Peasants seized uncultivated land, workers went on strike and occupied factories, and many felt that a Communist revolution was imminent. In the face of inaction by the government of King Victor Emmanuel III, Mussolini and his followers formed local terrorist squads, called Black Shirts because they always dressed in shirts of that color. These squads beat up and even murdered Socialist and Communist leaders, attacked strikers and farm workers, and systematically intimidated the political left.

By 1921, Mussolini's Fascist Party had hundreds of thousands of supporters, and when in October 1922 they marched on Rome, Victor Emmanuel III appointed Mussolini prime minister in order to appease them. In November, the king and Parliament granted Mussolini dictatorial powers for one year in order to produce order in the country. By 1926, Mussolini had managed to outlaw all opposition political parties, deny all labor unions the right to strike, and organize major industries into 22 corporations that encompassed the entire economy.

Although the king remained nominal ruler, Mussolini had established a single-party totalitarian state, declaring himself Il Duce [DOO-cheh], "the leader."

Of all the Fascist leaders of Europe, Mussolini was the most supportive of modernist architecture. "In five years' time," Mussolini proclaimed in 1925, echoing the popes in the fifteenth century (see Chapter 15), "Rome must astonish the peoples of the world. It must appear vast, orderly and powerful as it was in the days of Augustus." It took another ten years for Mussolini's vision to begin to take shape. In 1936, Mussolini won the right to host the next World Exhibition in Rome, scheduled for 1941, but delayed until 1942 in order to celebrate the twentieth anniversary of Mussolini's rule. The plan was to build a vast fairground outside the city walls above the Tiber on the road to Rome's port at Ostia. The architect Marcello Piacentini [pee-ah-chin-TEEN-ee] (1881–1960) was asked to coordinate the development of the site, which was envisioned as becoming a permanent new quarter of the city. Piacentini's plan emphasized the monumental aspects of the new quarter, which came to be known as EUR, the acronym of Esposizione Universale Roma, the World Exposition in Rome. Among the first buildings finished was the Palazzo degli Uffici, the Building of Offices, the administrative headquarters for the fair (Fig. 37.13)—most of the other buildings proposed by Piacentini would not be completed until after World War II. But Piacentini's sense of what a Fascist architecture might be is readily apparent. The EUR district was laid out according to the urban-planning techniques of the Roman republic (see Fig. 6.2), and that sense of order and geometric regularity is repeated in the facade of the Palazzo degli Uffici. The facade itself is travertine, a white limestone chosen to imitate the marble of ancient Rome. The scale is enormous, suggesting the imperial power of the Fascist state.

Fig. 37.13 Marcello Piacentini, Palazzo degli Uffici, Expositione Universale Europa (EUR). 1937–39. The Art Archive. This building is full of mosaics and reliefs, some of which recall the scenes of Roman soldiers sacking the Temple of Jerusalem on the Arch of Titus (see Fig. 6.21).

Franco in Spain

The Fascist ideologies that dominated Germany and Italy spread to Spain by the mid-1930s. Spain was in political turmoil. A free election in 1931 had resulted in a victory for republican democrats and the declaration of the Second Republic of Spain. Support for the monarchy collapsed, and King Alfonso XIII, who had called for the elections hoping to establish a constitutional monarchy, left the country without abdicating. This gave conservatives the hope that the monarchy might one day be restored. A strong anarchist movement soon developed, however, resulting in major uprisings, strikes, and full jails. In February 1936, the Spanish Popular Front, a coalition of republicans, communists, and anarchists that promised amnesty to all those previously imprisoned, was elected to office. This dismayed the Falange [fah-LAHN-hay] ("Phalanx"), a right-wing fascist organization with a private army much like Hitler's and that had the sympathy of the Spanish army stationed in Morocco. In July, the Falange retaliated, the army in Morocco rebelled, and General Francisco Franco [FRAHN-koh] (1892–1975) led it into Spain from Morocco in a coup d'état against the Popular Front government.

In the civil war that ensued, Germany and Italy supported Franco's right-wing Nationals, while the Soviet Union and Mexico sent equipment and advisors to the leftist Republicans. The United States remained neutral, but liberals from across Europe and America, including Ernest Hemingway, joined the republican side, fighting side by side with the Spanish.

Hitler conceived of the conflict as a dress rehearsal for the larger European conflict he was already preparing. He was especially interested in testing the Luftwaffe [LOOFT-vah-fuh], his air force. Planes were soon sent on forays across the country in what the German military called "total war," a war not just between armies but between whole peoples. This allowed for the bombing of civilians, as in the famous incident of Guernica, in the Basque region of Spain, which inspired Spanish-born artist Pablo Picasso to produce a painterly act of searing rage from his base in Paris (see *Closer Look*, pages 1226–1227).

The Spanish Civil War extended from 1936 to 1939 and tore the country apart (Map 37.2). With the help of the Falangists, Franco was able to overcome the Republicans, first capturing Madrid in March 1939 and then, a few weeks later, Barcelona. He ruled Spain in a totalitarian manner until 1975.

REVOLUTION IN MEXICO

Armed conflict had begun in Mexico in 1910, when Francisco I. Madero [mah-DHAY-roh] (1873–1913), a respectable upper-class politician, led the overthrow of Mexican dictator Porfirio Díaz [DEE-ahs] (1830–1915). In trying to modernize Mexico, Díaz had turned over large landholdings to foreign investors for the United States and Britain to the dismay of many, including Madero. But Madero quickly lost control of events, and Díaz's supporters soon deposed and executed him. This inaugurated a period of intense bloodshed during which some 900,000 Mexicans (of a population of about 15 million) lost their lives.

Guerrilla groups led in southern Mexico by Emiliano Zapata [zah-PAH-tah] (1879–1919) and in northern Mexico by Doroteo Arango Arámbula [ah-RAHM-boo-lah] (1878–1923), better known as Pancho Villa [VEE-yah], demanded "land, liberty, and justice" for Mexico's peasant population. Their primary purpose was to give back to the people land that the Díaz government had deeded to foreign investors. Technically, the Mexican Revolution ended in 1921 with the formation of the reformist government of Álvaro Obregón [oh-rbay-GOHN] (1880–1928), but bloodshed continued through the 1920s. Zapata and Villa were assassinated, as was Obregón himself. Peace was not finally restored until the administration of Lázaro Cárdenas [KAR-day-nahs] (1895–1970) in 1934, when the reforms of the 1917 Constitution of Mexico were finally implemented.

The Mexican Mural Movement

The Mexican Revolution fueled a wave of intense nationalism to which artists responded by creating art that, from their point of view, was true to the aspirations of the people of Mexico. When the government initiated a massive building campaign, a new school of muralists arose to decorate these buildings. It was led by Diego Rivera [ree-VAIR-ah] (1886–1957), David Siqueiros [see-KAIR-ohs] (1896–1974), and José Clemente Orozco [oh-ROH-skoh] (1883–1949).

Rivera had lived in Europe from 1907 to 1921, mostly in Paris, where he had developed a Picasso-inspired Cubist technique. But responding to the revolution—and the need to address the Mexican people in clear and concise terms—he transformed his style by using a much more realist and accessible imagery focused on Mexican political and social life. He shared the style with the other muralists as well. The large fresco *Sugar Cane* depicts the plight of the Mexican worker before the revolution (Fig. **37.14**). Armed

Map 37.2 The Spanish Civil War on March 30, 1937.

Fig. 37.14 Diego Rivera, *Sugar Cane*. 1931. Fresco, 57 ⅛″ × 94 ⅛″. Philadelphia Museum of Art. Gift of Mr. and Mrs. Herbert Cameron Morris. 1943-46-2. © Banco de Mexico Diego Rivera & Frida Kahlo Museums Trust. Av. Cinco de Mayo No. 2, Col. Centro, Del. Cuauhtemoc 06059, Mexico, D.F. Reproduction authorized by the Instituto Nacional de Bellas Artes y Literatura. This is one of eight portable murals that Rivera created for a special exhibition at the Museum of Modern Art in New York in 1931. It replicates a stationary mural at the Palace of Cortez in Cuernavaca, Mexico, painted in 1929.

overseers hired by foreign landowners, including one lounging on a hammock in the shade with his dogs, force the peasants to work. But in the foreground, Rivera celebrates the dignity of the Mexican peasants, as they collect coconuts from a palm. Their rounded forms echo one another to create a feeling of balance and harmony.

From 1930 to 1934, Rivera received a series of commissions in the United States. They included one from Edsel B. Ford and the Detroit Institute of Arts to create a series of frescoes for the museum's Garden Court on the subject of *Detroit Industry*, and another from the Rockefellers to create a lobby fresco entitled *Man at the Crossroads Looking with Hope and High Vision to a New and Better Future* for the RCA Building in Rockefeller Center in New York. When Rivera included a portrait of Communist leader Lenin in the lobby painting, Nelson A. Rockefeller insisted that he remove it. Rivera refused, and Rockefeller, after paying Rivera his commission, had the painting destroyed.

Rivera reproduced the fresco soon after in Mexico City and called it *Man, Controller of the Universe* (Fig. **37.15**). At the center, Man stands below a telescope with a microscope in his hand. Two ellipses of light emanate from him, one depicting the cosmos, the other the microscopic world. Beneath him is the earth, with plants growing in abundance, the products of scientific advancements in agriculture. To the right, between healthy microbes and a starry cosmos, is Lenin, holding the hands of workers of different cultures. On the left, between microscopic renderings of syphilis and other diseases and a warring cosmos, is New York society, including Nelson Rockefeller enjoying a cocktail. At the top left, armed figures wearing gas masks and marching in military formation evoke World War I, while at the upper right, workers wearing Communist red scarves raise their voices in solidarity. Man must steer his course between the evils of capitalism and the virtues of communism, Rivera appears to be saying.

Fig. 37.15 Diego Rivera, *Man, Controller of the Universe*. 1934. Fresco, main panel 15′11″ × 37′6″. Palacio de Bellas Artes, Mexico City, D.F. Mexico. © 2003 Banco de Mexico Diego Rivera & Frida Kahlo Museums Trust. Av. Cinco de Mayo No. 2, Col. Centro, Del. Cuauhtemoc 06059, Mexico, D.F. Reproduction authorized by the Instituto Nacional de Bellas Artes y Literatura. Photo Credit: Schalkwijk/Art Resource, New York. Rivera's mural is a plea for social and economic reform through industrial progress.

On April 26, 1937, a German air-force squadron led by Wolfram von Richthofen, cousin of the famous Red Baron of World War I, bombed the Basque town of Guernica, in Spain, during the Spanish Civil War. The attack was a blitzkrieg, the sudden, coordinated air assault that the Germans would later use to great effect against England in World War II. It lasted for three and a quarter hours. The stated target was a bridge used by retreating Republican forces at the northern edge of the town, but the entire central part of Guernica—about 15 square blocks—was leveled, and 721 dwellings (nearly three-quarters of the town's homes) were completely destroyed and a large number of people killed. In Paris, Picasso heard the news a day later. Complete stories did not appear in the press until Thursday, April 29, and photographs of the scene appeared on Friday and Saturday, April 30 and May 1. That Saturday, Picasso began a series of sketches for a mural that he had already been commissioned to contribute to the Spanish Pavilion at the 1937 Exposition Universelle in Paris. Only 24 days remained until the Fair was scheduled to open.

In the final painting, Picasso links the tragedy of Guernica to the ritualized bullfight, born in Spain, in which the preordained death of the bull symbolizes the ever-present nature of death. The work portrays a scene of violence, helpless suffering, and death. Picasso's choice of black-and-white instead of color evokes the urgency and excitement of a newspaper photograph. When the exposition closed, the painting was sent on tour and was used to raise funds for the Republican cause. *Guernica* would become the international symbol of the horrors of war and the fight against totalitarianism. Below is a history of the painting's life.

A *Guernica* Chronology

January 8, 1937 – Picasso accepts commission from Republican Spain for a painting for the Spanish Pavilion at the 1937 Exposition Universelle in Paris.

April 26 – Guernica bombed.

April 28 – Guernica occupied by Franco's troops; French Press coverage begins.

May 1 – Picasso draws six initial studies for *Guernica*.

May 11 – First photograph of the *Guernica* canvas.

May 28 – Picasso is paid 150,000 francs for *Guernica*, which he completes on June 4.

July 12 – Inauguration of the Spanish Pavilion at the Paris Exposition.

November 25 – Exposition closes, having received 33 million visitors.

Spring 1938 – *Guernica* exhibited in Stockholm and Copenhagen.

October 1938 to January 1939 – *Guernica* exhibited in London.

May 1, 1939 – *Guernica* arrives in New York, where it begins a fundraising tour to Los Angeles, San Francisco, and Chicago, concluding at the Museum of Modern Art, New York, November 15 to January 7, 1940, as part of the exhibition *Picasso: Forty Years of His Art*. After the outbreak of war in Europe, Picasso asks the Museum of Modern Art to accept *Guernica* for safekeeping.

1940–41 – The Picasso retrospective tours America with *Guernica*, traveling to Chicago, Saint Louis, Boston, San Francisco, Cincinnati, Cleveland, New Orleans, Minneapolis, and Pittsburgh.

1942 – *Guernica* exhibited at Fogg Art Museum, Cambridge, Massachusetts; thereafter, on continuing display at the Museum of Modern Art.

1950s – *Guernica* travels worldwide, until given to the Museum of Modern Art "on extended loan" in 1958. Picasso expresses the wish that the museum return the painting to Spain when and if civil liberties are restored in his native land.

November 20, 1975 – Franco dies in Madrid; two days later, Juan Carlos is crowned constitutional monarch.

June 15 – First general elections in Spain since the Civil War.

February 1981 – Picasso's lawyer approves returning *Guernica* to Spain.

October 24, 1981 – *Guernica* exhibited in Madrid and put on permanent display at Museo Nacional Centro de Arte Reina Sofia.

SEE MORE For a Closer Look at the history of Pablo Picasso's *Guernica*, go to **www.myartslab.com**

Picasso's *Guernica*

The bull is a symbol of the Spanish character and a reference to the legendary Minotaur of classical myth. For the Surrealists, the bull represented the irrational forces of the human psyche.

A spear penetrates the flank of the horse, whose scream echoes that of the mother at the left holding her dead child in her arms.

A woman screams to the sky, her house in flames.

The figure lying face up is both a dead soldier and a slain picador (the chief antagonist of the bull and the one who torments him on horseback with a lance).

Pablo Picasso, *Guernica*, **1937.** Oil on canvas, 11′5 $^1/_2$″ × 25′5 $^1/_4$″. Museo Nacional Centro de Arte Reina Sofia, Madrid, Spain. John Bigelow Taylor/Art Resource, New York. © 2007 Estate of Pablo Picasso/Artists Rights Society (ARS), New York.

Ruins of Guernica, Spain. April 1937.

Something to Think About...

Why do you think *Guernica* became the seminal antiwar painting of the twentieth century?

The Private World of Frida Kahlo

Rivera's wife, Frida Kahlo [KAH-loh] (1907–1954), was also an artist. Although she was as political as her husband, her paintings document her personal tragedy. Already crippled by a bout of polio in childhood, she was injured severely in 1925 at the age of 18 when a tram hit the bus in which she was riding home from school. A metal handrail pierced her body through, her spine and pelvis were broken, and so were her right leg and foot. Her long recuperation was not completely successful, requiring some 30 operations and eventually the amputation of her right leg. In the hospital, she began painting, using a small lap easel, and somewhat miraculously regained the ability to walk.

A close friend introduced Kahlo to Diego Rivera, and in 1929, they were married. In addition to leftist political views, they shared a love for Mexican culture—Frida [FREE-dah] often dressed in traditional Mexican costume—and a passion for art. But they were also a study in contrasts, Kahlo small and slender, barely five feet tall, Rivera much taller, of considerable girth, and 20 years her senior. Frida's father remarked, "It was like the marriage between an elephant and a dove." Their stormy relationship survived infi-

Fig. 37.16 Frida Kahlo, *The Broken Column.* 1944. Oil on canvas. 15 ¹¹⁄₁₆″ × 12″. Collection Museo Dolores Olmedo Patiño, Mexico City. © 2008 Banco de Mexico Diego Rivera & Frida Kahlo Museums Trust. Av. Cinco de Mayo No. 2, Col. Centro, Del. Cuauhtemoc 06059, Mexico, D.F. Reproduction authorized by the Instituto Nacional de Bellas Artes y Literatura. The fractured and barren landscape behind Kahlo may symbolize her inability to bear children—another result of her injuries.

delities, the pressures of Rivera's career—she was clearly second fiddle to his murals—a divorce and remarriage, and Kahlo's poor health.

Kahlo's paintings—mostly self-portraits—bear witness to the trials of her health and marriage. "I have suffered two grave accidents in my life," she once said, "one in which a street car ran me over; the other accident is Diego." Many of the self-portraits are violent, showing, for instance, in *The Broken Column* (Fig. 37.16), her body pierced with nails and ripped open from neck to navel to expose her spine as a broken stone column. Her work not only evokes her intense personal struggle, but also sets that struggle in an almost mythic or heroic universal struggle for survival.

Kahlo and Rivera traveled to the United States and France, where Kahlo met luminaries from the worlds of art and politics. Surrealist André Breton [bruh-TOHN] was especially attracted to her work. Although grateful for Breton's attention, she was quick to emphasize that she was by no means a Surrealist herself. "I never painted my dreams," she said. "I painted my own reality."

THE GREAT DEPRESSION IN AMERICA

After World War I, American money had flowed into Europe, mostly in the form of short-term loans, but by 1928, most of it was withdrawn and placed in the booming New York stock market, jeopardizing European economies. Investors borrowed freely from banks and overinvested in stocks. When the market crashed on October 29, 1929, investors lost huge amounts of money and could not repay their loans. Across the country, one bank after another closed its doors, savings were lost, businesses failed, and unemployment grew. Nearly 16 million men were out of work by the early 1930s, about one-third of the national workforce. Franklin Roosevelt's election as president in 1932 was understood as a mandate for the federal government to bring its resources to bear against what became known as the Great Depression.

The Road to Recovery: The New Deal

Roosevelt quickly implemented a host of measures that came to be known as the **New Deal**. To safeguard bank deposits, he created the Federal Deposit Insurance Corporation. The National Recovery Act regulated industrial competition and ensured the right of workers to organize and bargain. The 1935 Social Security Act provided for unemployment insurance and old-age pensions. New-home construction was encouraged by the Home Owners' Loan Corporation. The 1933 Civil Works Administration created 4 million make-work jobs on public projects for persons on relief in an effort to help them contribute to economic recovery by increasing their purchasing power. The program continued when it was replaced by the Work Projects Administration (WPA) two years later.

The WPA peaked at about 3.5 million people employed, but over its lifespan, it helped about 8.5 million people get back to work. The WPA's work force constructed 116,000

Fig. 37.17 Thomas Hart Benton, Missouri Mural (detail). 1936. Oil on canvas. Missouri State Capitol, Jefferson City, Missouri. © T. H. Benton and R. P. Benton Testamentary Trusts/UMB Bank Trustee. Art © Licensed by VAGA, NY. Reading from left to right, the traditional ways of Missouri agriculture are threatened by the specters of industry and litigation.

buildings, 78,000 bridges, and 651,000 miles of road, and improved 800 airports. But its most important contributions to American culture were the Federal Art Project, the Federal Writers' Project, the Federal Theatre Project, and the Federal Music Project. Through the WPA, artists produced nearly 10,000 drawings, paintings, and sculptures and decorated many public buildings (especially post offices) with murals. Theater performances under the project averaged 4,000 a month. Writers were employed to create a series of state and regional guidebooks, and musicians found work in newly created orchestras.

The Mural Movement The WPA mural project was led in large part by the example of Thomas Hart Benton (1889–1975), who between 1930 and 1936 created four enormous murals that required about 7,000 square feet of canvas and included more than 1,000 figures. They are *America Today* (for the New School of Social Research in New York, 1930), *The Arts of Life in America* (for the Whitney Studio Club in New York, 1932), *A Social History of Indiana* (for the Indiana pavilion at the 1933 Chicago World's Fair), and *A Social History of the State of Missouri*

(for the House Lounge in the Missouri State Capitol Building, Jefferson City, 1935/36). For the last of these, he was paid $16,000 over two years—a handsome sum at the time—and offered a position at the Kansas City Art Institute. The north wall of the Capitol lounge depicts Missouri's "Pioneer Days" and is highlighted by a depiction of Huckleberry Finn and Jim over the doorway. The east wall, the right half of which is illustrated here, is dedicated to "Politics, Farming, and Law in Missouri" (Fig. **37.17**). The south wall celebrates the state's two great cities, "St. Louis and Kansas City," including the lover's quarrel of the 1880s immortalized in the popular song "Frankie and Johnny." Benton worked in egg tempera, a medium seldom used in such a large scale since the Renaissance. He liked the medium's bright, clear colors and the fact that the paint dried quickly.

The WPA created special programs focused on three centuries of African-American cultural accomplishments. In 1935, it hired Aaron Douglas to paint a four-panel series, called *Aspects of Negro Life*, for the 135th Street branch of the New York Public Library in Harlem (today the Schomburg [SHOM-berg] Center for Research in Black Culture). It traces

African-American history from freedom in Africa to enslavement in the United States and from liberation after the Civil War to life in the modern city in a style very much like that of his painting *Aspiration* (see Fig. 36.1).

The Music Project: Aaron Copland's American Music The Depression had an enormous impact on the music industry. Thousands of musicians lost their jobs as orchestras and opera companies closed their doors, hotels and restaurants eliminated orchestras, and music education disappeared from school and university budgets. Even worse, the introduction of sound to motion pictures, discussed later in this chapter, meant that movie theater after movie theater dismissed the orchestras that had accompanied silent films. By 1933, two-thirds of the national membership of the American Federation of Musicians was unemployed. The WPA's Federal Music Project addressed this situation, organizing orchestras around the country.

When the project first began, there were only 11 recognized symphony orchestras in the United States. At the peak of the WPA, 34 more new orchestras had been created, and thousands of Americans were attending concerts. From October 1935 to May 1, 1937, almost 60 million people listened to 81,000 separate performances of WPA musical events. And through the Composers' Forum Laboratory, new music was created and performed.

One of the beneficiaries of this support was composer Aaron Copland [KOPE-lund] (1900–1990). Copland had begun his career deeply influenced by European modernism, particularly the work of Arnold Schoenberg (see Chapter 34), but he became increasingly interested in folk music. This interest began in the fall of 1926, when he met Mexican composer Carlos Chávez [SHAH-vays] (1899–1978), who was rooming with Mexican artist Rufino Tamayo [tah-MAH-yoh] (1899–1991) in a tenement on Fourteenth Street in New York and who introduced him as well to Diego Rivera. Writing about Chávez in 1928, Copland declared that the composer's "use of folk material in its relation to nationalism" constituted a major strain of modern music, one that he himself would soon begin to pursue.

In the early 1930s, Copland composed *El Salón México* [el sah-LOHN MAY-hee-koh], based on Mexican folk music he had heard when visiting Chávez in Mexico. Soon after this, he began to use purely American themes and material, including New England hymns, folk songs, and jazz, particularly in his work for the ballet: *Billy the Kid* (1938), *Rodeo* (1942), and *Appalachian Spring* (1944).

Copland composed *Appalachian Spring* for dancer and choreographer Martha Graham (1894–1991). Copland simply called it "Ballet for Martha," but Graham renamed it when she decided to set the ballet in the Pennsylvania hill country early in the nineteenth century. In Graham's dance, a young woman and her fiancé both express their excitement and joy at the prospect of their upcoming marriage and their sober apprehension of the responsibilities that their new life demands. While an older neighbor conveys a mood of confidence and satisfaction, a religious revivalist reminds the new bride and groom of their tenuous place in God's cosmos. At the end, the couple have evidently grown into their new life as they come to live in their new house. Copland's score for this concluding section is built around a single Shaker hymn, "Simple Gifts," which serves as the basis for a stirring set of variations that occur just before the final slow coda (track **37.3**). The orchestral version of *Appalachian Spring*, actually a suite, was extremely popular and demonstrated that Copland had found a truly American style.

HEAR MORE at www.myartslab.com

The Dust Bowl in Film and Literature Copland was not the only American composer moved by the Depression to pursue distinctly American themes. Virgil Thomson (1895–1989), who like Copland had studied in Paris, was hired in 1936 by the Resettlement Administration to score two documentary films directed by Pare Lorentz (1905–1992) in order to raise awareness about the New Deal. *The Plow That Broke the Plains* is about the devastation of the almost-ten-year drought that struck the American Midwest, particularly the southern Great Plains, and turned the region into a virtual dust bowl. *The River* celebrates the accomplishments of the Tennessee Valley Authority to harness water for electrical energy.

Thomson's score for *The Plow That Broke the Plains* consists of six movements that follow the transition from fertile plain to Dust Bowl: *Prelude*, *Pastorale* (*Grass*) (track **37.4**), *Cattle*, *Blues* (*Speculation*), *Drought*, and *Devastation*. Thomson spent considerable time researching the rural music of the Great Plains. He also incorporated military marches, gunfire, and the sound of rolling tanks into the score to accompany a film sequence of farmers plowing the land. In doing so he addressed musically a theme ignored in the narration: the contribution of agriculture to the war effort.

HEAR MORE at www.myartslab.com

Lorentz shot *The Plow That Broke the Plains* in Montana, Wyoming, Colorado, Kansas, and Texas, and was able to capture extraordinary dust-storm sequences and the pathos of those caught in their wake. The film's public premier was at the Mayflower Hotel in New York on May 10, 1936, at an evening sponsored by the Museum of Modern Art. The event also featured several foreign documentaries, including portions of Leni Riefenstahl's *Triumph of the Will*. Although *Plow* was critically acclaimed, none of the Hollywood studios would agree to distribute it commercially because, they claimed, it was strictly government propaganda. But the movie was shown at independent theaters with great success, and its popularity soon changed the distributors' minds. When *The River* was released in 1937, Paramount jumped to distribute it. The script was nominated for the Pulitzer Prize in Poetry in 1938.

The great novel of the Dust Bowl years was *The Grapes of Wrath* by John Steinbeck [STINE-bek] (1902–1968). Published in 1939, its interplay between panoramic interludes and close-up accounts of a family's cross-country journey was inspired by Lorentz's films. Steinbeck even worked briefly with Lorentz on the documentary *The Fight for Life*, about a maternity ward in Chicago, the year after *The Grapes of Wrath* was published. The title of Steinbeck's novel comes from "The Battle Hymn of the Republic":

> Mine eyes have seen the glory of the coming
>   of the Lord
> He is trampling out the vintage where
>   the grapes of wrath are stored,
> He has loosed the fateful lightning
>   of His terrible swift sword
> His truth is marching on.

This mention of "grapes of wrath," as Steinbeck knew, was a reference back to the Bible: "And the angel thrust his sickle into the earth, and gathered the vine of the earth, and cast it into the great winepress of the wrath of God" (Rev. 14:19).

In a style so realistically detailed that it might be called cinematic, Steinbeck tells the story of the Oklahoma Joads, who lose their tenant farm and join thousands of others traveling to California on Route 66, the main migrant road. Their motivation is summarized in a handbill that they find on the road: "PEA PICKERS WANTED IN CALIFORNIA. GOOD WAGES ALL SEASON. 800 PICKERS WANTED." Things in California do not turn out as planned—thousands of workers turn up for the few available jobs, and food is scarce: "In the souls of the people," Steinbeck writes, "the grapes of wrath are filling and growing heavy, growing heavy for the vintage." Steinbeck's Joads are stoically heroic (especially Ma Joad) but also deeply perceptive about the social injustices that pervade the America they encounter in their journey. The novel is an outcry against the injustice encountered by all migrant workers in the Great Depression.

Photography and the American Scene
One of the important cultural contributions of the New Deal was the photographic documentation of the plight of poor farmers and migrant workers during the Dust Bowl and Great Depression under the auspices of the Farm Security Administration (FSA). The head of the FSA's photographic project, Roy Stryker, found in the work his team of 15 photographers created the same stoic heroism that

Steinbeck had portrayed in the Joad family: "You could look at the people and see fear and sadness and desperation," Stryker wrote. "But you saw something else, too. A determination that not even the Depression could kill. The photographers saw it—documented it."

This is certainly the quality that Dorothea Lange (1895–1965) captures in *Migrant Mother*, a portrait of Native American Florence Owens Thompson and three of her children in a pea-pickers' camp (Fig. **37.18**). Stryker said of this image: "When Dorothea took that picture, that was the ultimate. She never surpassed it. To me it was the picture of Farm Security. She has all the suffering of mankind in her, but all the perseverance too. A restraint and a strange courage." In the 1940s, Lange's documentary work included photo essays of the Japanese internment camps as well as a series focusing on World War II factory workers. She later was the first

Fig. 37.18 Dorothea Lange, *Migrant Mother, Nipomo, California*. 1936. Gelatin silver print, 37 1/8″ × 40 5/8″. Library of Congress, Washington, D.C. The original caption for this photograph, taken for the Farm Security Administration, was: "Destitute pea pickers in California. Mother of seven children."

woman awarded a Guggenheim fellowship and spent nearly ten years making photo essays for *Life* and other magazines.

Of all the FSA photographs, the most well-known today are those of Walker Evans (1903–1975) first published in *Let Us Now Praise Famous Men*, a book produced in 1941 with writer James Agee [AY-jee] (1909–1955). The book's title is ironic, for Agee's subject is the least famous, the poorest of the poor: sharecroppers, the men, women, and children of Depression-ridden central Alabama in the summer of 1936 when he and Evans lived among them. But again, it is the simple life and inherent nobility of these poor people that form Evans and Agee's theme. This theme is captured in the rich textures and clean lines of Evans's photograph of a sharecropper's humble dwelling (Fig. **37.19**). The photo is a revelation of the stark beauty in the middle of sheer poverty.

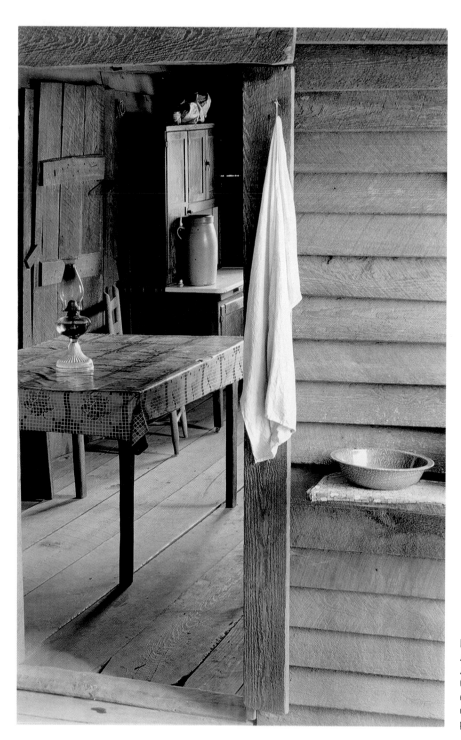

Fig. 37.19 Walker Evans, *Washroom and Dining Area of Floyd Burroughs's Home, Hale County, Alabama*. 1936. 35mm photograph, Library of Congress, Washington, D.C. During its eight-year existence, the Farm Security Administration created over 77,000 black-and-white documentary photographs.

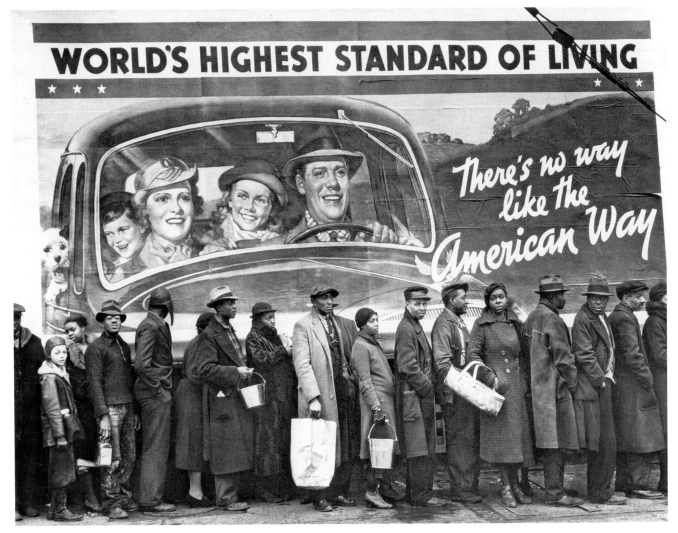

Fig. 37.20 Margaret Bourke-White, *At the Time of the Louisville Flood*. 1937. Gelatin silver print, $9\frac{3}{4}'' \times 13\frac{1}{2}''$. The Hallmark Photographic Collection, Hallmark Cards, Inc., Kansas City, Missouri. Bourke-White later covered World War II and the Korean War for *Life*. She was the first woman photographer attached to the U.S. armed forces, and the only American photographer to cover the siege of Moscow in 1941.

Not all of the important photographers with social consciences worked for the FSA. Margaret Bourke-White (1904–1971) was one of the first four photographers hired by publisher Henry Luce for the new picture magazine *Life*, founded in 1936. That same year, she traveled the American South with writer Erskine Caldwell, documenting the living conditions of poor tenant farmers, a project that resulted in the 1937 book *You Have Seen Their Faces*. That same year, *Life* published one of her most famous photographs, *At the Time of the Louisville Flood* (Fig. **37.20**). Over 900 people had died when the Ohio River inundated Louisville, Kentucky, in January 1937. Bourke-White's photo stunningly indicts the American dream by juxtaposing desperately poor folk who have lost their homes (reality) with a government billboard touting well-being (propaganda).

CINEMA: THE TALKIES AND COLOR

Throughout the Great Depression, going to the movies was America's favorite leisure activity. The movies took people's minds off the harsh realities of the era, and although ticket prices were relatively expensive, ranging between 25 cents and 55 cents (between $4 and $9 in terms of today's buying power), people still found the means to flock to the movies. By the late 1930s, some 50 million viewers were drawn into American theaters each week.

Prior to the Depression, two forces were transforming motion pictures simultaneously—the introduction of sound and the advent of color film. Technicolor, the brainchild of Herbert Kalmus (1881–1963), was the first widely successful color-film process in which two film strips were dyed and pasted together to create a single positive print containing all the colors that the audience would see. Douglas Fairbanks's 1926 film *The Black Pirate* was the first feature film in full color. By the mid-1930s, a three-color Technicolor process had been perfected, and motion-picture companies gradually began to work it into their productions.

What slowed the introduction of color in the industry was sound, the development of which consumed the attention of the industry. Before the advent of motion-picture sound, movies were by no means "silent." Every theater had a piano or organ to provide musical accompaniment to the films it projected. This made cinema a multimedia event, a live musician or orchestra reacting to and participating in the presentation of the film, mediating between audience and image. In this sense, films, before sound, were literally local events. But the introduction of sound radically changed the motion-picture industry. For one thing, theaters everywhere had to be wired, a process that took several years to accomplish. For another, incorporating sound into the film itself changed the culture of film viewing. In the 1920s, the cinema was the world's largest employer of musicians. Then, as noted earlier, just as the Great Depression hit, thousands of cinema musicians found themselves out of work.

Sound and Language

Sound also changed the nature of acting in the cinema. Before sound, communication with the audience depended on facial expression and physical gesture, often exaggerated. Now actors had to rely on speech to communicate, and many silent-era stars simply lacked a compelling voice. Foreign actors were especially affected—Greta Garbo, with her deeply sonorous and melancholy voice ("I vhant to be alone"), was one of the few foreign stars to make the transition successfully, except for English actors. Dialogue writing had never been important before, but now playwrights became an instrumental force in movie production. Most important, sound brought foreign languages into the theaters—English into European theaters, various European languages into each other's and American theaters. At first, some producers tried to produce their films in several languages, but this proved too expensive.

In Europe, English-language films were commonly produced using **dubbing** (shorthand for "vocal doubling"), with native speakers synchronizing new dialogue to the lip movements of the actor. In the United States, where a large part of the audience for foreign films were immigrants who spoke the foreign language, English-language text was more commonly scrolled across the bottom of the screen as subtitles. Interestingly, subtitles tend to announce the "foreignness" of the film, while dubbing suppresses it, so dubbing played a major role in the "Americanization" of world cultures.

***The Jazz Singer*: The First Feature-Length Talkie** Sound came to the feature-length motion picture on October 6, 1927, when Warner Bros. Studio premiered *The Jazz Singer*,

Fig. 37.21 Opening night crowd gathering to see Al Jolson in *The Jazz Singer*, Warner's Theatre, Times Square, New York, October 6, 1927. The film convinced producers and audiences that sound could be more than a novelty.

starring Al Jolson [JOL-sun] (1886–1950) (Fig. **37.21**). The first words of synchronous [SING-kruh-nus] speech were Jolson's prophetic statement, "Wait a minute. Wait a minute. You ain't heard nothing yet." *The Jazz Singer* is the story of a cantor's son, Jakie Rabinowitz [ruh-BIN-oh-vits], who longs to play jazz (calling himself Jack Robin) rather than follow his family's footsteps into the synagogue. Jakie/Jack falls in love with a woman outside his own faith, performs in minstrel-style blackface makeup, and otherwise challenges every notion of ethnic identity. The film contained only two dialogue scenes (in other respects it was a silent-era feature), but its success lay as much in this story line as in its introduction of sound. Audiences everywhere recognized it as an "American"—as opposed to an ethnic—tale.

The Blue Angel One of the most interesting early experiments with sound was the two-language production *Der blaue Engel* [der BLAU-uh EN-gul]/*The Blue Angel*, directed by Josef von Sternberg [SHTERN-berg] (1894–1969). Sternberg had emigrated from Germany to the United States at the turn of the century, and through the 1920s, he had gradually worked his way up the directorial ladder in Hollywood. In 1930, Paramount hired him to go to Germany to direct a co-production in both German and English with UFA (Universum Film Aktiengesellschaft), one of the largest studios in Europe. Marlene Dietrich (1901–1992) starred in the film as the nightclub performer Lola Lola opposite Emil Jannings as Professor Rath, a sexually repressed instructor at a boys' school whom Lola Lola seduces by exploiting his self-loathing (Fig. 37.22). Dietrich's portrayal of a temptress secured her fame. Sternberg would bring her back to Hollywood, where he would feature her in the role of the vamp who sexually humiliates her masochistic male counterpart in six more films over the next five years. The films demonstrate how thoroughly Freudian psychology had taken hold of the popular imagination.

Fig. 37.22 Marlene Dietrich in _Der blaue Engel/The Blue Angel_. 1930. UFA (Germany). Not unjustifiably, Sternberg was accused of putting Dietrich on display to exploit her sexuality.

Disney's Color Animation

Between 1928 and 1937, Disney studios, headed by Walt Disney (1901–1966), created over 100 animated cartoons, most starring Mickey Mouse but depending, for variety and development, on Mickey's entourage of sidekicks, particularly Pluto, Goofy, and Donald Duck. At least as important technically, however, were Disney's so-called Silly Symphonies, with scores that are masterpieces of parody, subjecting classical music—from opera to the piano concerto—to the good-natured fun of the cartoon medium. In essence, Disney's animation gave rise to the art of **postsynchronization**, in which sound is added as a separate step after the creation of the visual film. Actors became increasingly adept at speaking lines mouthed by cartoon characters, and musical scores could be adapted to fit the action.

Disney studios began work on its first feature-length Technicolor animation, _Snow White and the Seven Dwarfs_, in 1934. Over 300 animators, designers, and background artists worked on the film, with Disney hiring animators away from other studios and training many other artists who had never worked at animation before. The film took three years to finish and premiered in December 1937. It was an instant success, and Disney immediately set his team to work on three more features: _Bambi_, _Pinocchio_, and _Fantasia_ [fan-TAY-zhuh]. The last of these animated classical music in order to introduce young people to the various classical forms. The didactic nature of _Fantasia_ is unique in the annals of cartoon animation.

1939: The Great Year

As the nation recovered from its economic downturn, and audiences were able to afford to go the movies more often,

Hollywood responded by making more and better films. In 1939, Hollywood created more film classics than at any time before or since. Among these are _Stagecoach_, _Mr. Smith Goes to Washington_, _Drums Along the Mohawk_, _Wuthering Heights_, _Of Mice and Men_, _Gone with the Wind_, and _The Wizard of Oz_, to name just a few.

The Wizard of Oz _The Wizard of Oz_ was the most expensive film MGM made in 1939. It was in fact MGM's most expensive film of the decade—costing $2.77 million to produce (Fig. **37.23**). It starred Judy Garland (1922–1969), by then well known by movie audiences for her work with Mickey Rooney (1920–) in his string of box-office hits in the role of "Andy Hardy." The film begins in the black-and-white "reality" of Kansas. It switches to color when Dorothy and her dog Toto arrive in Oz after being transported there by a tornado. The sudden intrusion of color announced to the audience that Oz was the stuff of fantasy. Despite grossing over $3 million, _The Wizard of Oz_ lost nearly $1 million, owing to higher-than-usual marketing costs.

Although the film launched Garland into stardom, virtually guaranteeing future income from her performances, it also taught the studio an important corporate lesson. Having paired Garland with Rooney once again in a series of remakes of Broadway musicals, beginning with _Babes in Arms_, the studio reaped similar or larger grosses with much less expenditure. The formula for studio success was clear: the economical production of star-driven vehicles with recyclable narrative traits. In this rested both Hollywood's financial success and its artistic limitations.

Gone with the Wind The most ambitious project of 1939 was _Gone with the Wind_, produced by David O. Selznick [SELZ-nik] (1902–1965) and based on the Civil War novel by Margaret Mitchell (1900–1949). Arguably the first true "blockbuster," its running time was 3 hours 42 minutes, plus an intermission, keeping audiences in theaters for over 4 hours. They came to see English actress Vivien Leigh in

Fig. 37.23 Judy Garland, as Dorothy, sees the Yellow Brick Road in _The Wizard of Oz_. 1939. © 1939 The Kobal Collection/ MGM. Warner Brothers Motion Picture Titles. Until this film, audiences associated color almost exclusively with cartoons.

the role of Southern belle Scarlett O'Hara, for Selznick had made sure everyone knew that America's biggest stars had all auditioned for the part, including Katharine Hepburn, Susan Hayward, Barbara Stanwyck, Joan Crawford, Lana Turner, Mae West, Tallulah Bankhead, and Lucille Ball. Errol Flynn, Ronald Colman, and Gary Cooper were also considered for Clark Gable's role as the Southern gunrunner Rhett Butler. Selznick spent an unheard-of $4 million to produce the film, but he was rewarded when it became the highest-grossing film ever—$400 million in lifetime box-office gross receipts. Finally, audiences were stunned by its sweeping Technicolor, a technology to which producer Selznick was more fully committed than any other Hollywood producer.

Fig. 37.24 The burning of Atlanta from *Gone with the Wind*. 1939. Selznick and Menzies shot the burning-of-Atlanta sequence first so that the studio lot could be cleared for other sets.

The film was not easy to make. Selznick went through three directors during production, with Victor Fleming, who was responsible for about half the film and had just finished directing *The Wizard of Oz*, finally getting credit. As usual in Hollywood, a number of writers had a hand in the script. There were over 50 speaking roles and 2,400 extras. The subject matter was controversial—the fate of *Birth of a Nation* weighed on Selznick's mind—and the film was carefully scripted to avoid racial caricature. Indeed, Hattie McDaniel, who played the house servant Mammy in the film, would become the first African American to win an Academy Award (as Best Supporting Actress).

Much of the film's success can be attributed to art director William Cameron Menzies [MEN-zeez], whose reputation had been established years before when he designed the sets for *The Thief of Bagdad* (see Fig. 36.22). Menzies worked on visualizing the film for two years before production began, creating storyboards to indicate camera locations for the sets. This allowed the determination of camera angles, locations, lighting, and even the editing sequence well in advance of actual shooting. His panoramic overviews, for which the camera had to pull back above a huge railway platform full of wounded Confederate soldiers, required the building of a crane, and they became famous as a technical accomplishment. For the film's burning-of-Atlanta scene, Menzies's storyboard shows seven shots, beginning and ending with a panoramic overview, with cuts to close-ups of both Rhett Butler and Scarlett O'Hara fully indicated (Figs. **37.24** and **37.25**).

The Rules of the Game Not made in Hollywood but France, perhaps the greatest film of 1939 was *La Règle du jeu* (*The Rules of the Game*), directed by Jean Renoir (son of Impressionist painter Auguste Renoir). With *The Battleship Potemkin*, it is the only film always on the list of the top ten films ever made in the poll conducted every decade since 1952 by the European magazine *Sight and Sound*. At the most basic level, the film is a love farce with a double upstairs/downstairs plot that takes place one weekend at the country chateau of the Marquis de la Chesnaye. Upstairs are the rich: the Marquis, Robert; his wife, Christine; his mistress, Genevieve; and a famous aviation hero named André Jurieux, who is desperately in love with Christine. Downstairs among the hired help are Lisette, private maid to Christine; Schumacher, her

Fig. 37.25 William Cameron Menzies, storyboard for the burning-of-Atlanta scene from *Gone with the Wind*. 1939. Photofest. Such storyboards reflect the detailed level of planning necessary before filming could begin.

groundskeeper husband; and the newly hired valet, Marceau, whom the Marquis is intent on assisting in his efforts to seduce Christine. But Renoir's film is much more than a tale of his lovers' intrigues. It is a scathing indictment of French society at the brink of World War II, of a society intent on maintaining the status quo as each person pursues his or her own individual desires at the expense of social responsibility and engagement.

As a result, the movie was greeted by hisses and boos when first screened in 1939 and banned as demoralizing by the French government after the outbreak of war. Renoir himself called it a "war film" with "no reference to the war." War, in fact, seems imminent in the film as, in the forest surrounding the chateau, the random gunfire of "hunters" periodically startles the weekend party. Yet—and this is the point—it is a sound they choose to ignore.

Orson Welles and *Citizen Kane*

One of the most cinematographically inventive films of the postwar era was the 1940 *Citizen Kane*, directed by Orson Welles (1915–1985). The story is presented in a series of flashbacks as told to a journalist who is seeking to unravel the mystery of why media baron Charles Foster Kane (generally understood as a character based on actual newspaper mogul William Randolph Hearst) spoke the single word "Rosebud" on his deathbed. So the story is nonlinear, fragmented into different voices and different points of view, and its various perspectives carry over into the film's unorthodox construction.

Welles had made history—and a large reputation—in 1938 when his Halloween radio dramatization of H. G. Wells's novel *The War of the Worlds* convinced many listeners that Martians had actually invaded New Jersey. RKO gave him unprecedented freedom to make *Citizen Kane* in any manner he chose. Working as writer, director, producer, and actor simultaneously—and collaborating with cinematographer Gregg Toland on almost every shot—Welles produced a film unprecedented in its fresh look. In fact, he insisted that Toland experiment with almost every shot. Toland employed a special deep-focus lens that maintains focus from foreground to background in the deep space of the sets, in order to highlight multiple planes of action in the same shot (Fig. **37.26**). These shots were often lit with **chiaroscuro lighting**, a term borrowed from Renaissance painting to describe pools of light illuminating parts of an otherwise dark set. Toland also had the sets constructed in such a way that he could shoot from well above or well below the action.

Citizen Kane marked the end of the great era of the American motion picture. By 1945, with World War II in full swing, Hollywood production had fallen by more than 40 percent. Great films would continue to be made—the 1943 war film *Casablanca*, starring Humphrey Bogart [BOH-gart] and Swedish star Ingrid Bergman, was everyone's favorite wartime movie. After the war, the population began to shift to the suburbs, increasingly engaging in outdoor leisure activities, and television began to replace film as the primary delivery system of the moving image. As a result, motion-picture attendance began a slow decline.

Fig. 37.26 Orson Welles as Kane campaigning for governor in *Citizen Kane*. 1941. CITIZEN KANE © 1941 The Kobal Collection/RKO. Warner Brothers Motion Picture Titles. This shot is a subtle reference to film editing, simultaneously both a medium shot of Kane and a close-up in the poster behind him.

WORLD WAR II

As the motion picture industry was enjoying its greatest year, the war in Europe that Jean Renoir's *Rules of the Game* predicted broke out. The immediate causes of World War II can be traced to the meeting in Munich, on September 29 to 30, 1938, of Adolf Hitler and Benito Mussolini with the leaders of Britain and France. In an effort to appease the German dictator, the English and French granted him control of the Sudetenland [soo-DAY-tuhn-lahnd], an area of Czechoslovakia near the German border and home to 3.5 million Germans. In return, Hitler promised to spare the rest of Czechoslovakia and make no further territorial demands in Europe. Neville Chamberlain (1869–1940), the British prime minister, returned from Munich announcing he had secured "peace in our time." Statesman Winston Churchill (1874–1965) predicted a different outcome in Parliament: "All is over," he said. "Silent, mournful, abandoned, broken, Czechoslovakia recedes into the darkness." Six months later, his prediction proved true. On March 15, 1939, Hitler occupied Prague, and Czechoslovakia was no more. Poland would be next. On September 1, 1939, Hitler invaded that country, employing the blitzkrieg [BLITZ-kreeg] tactics he had practiced in Spain. Two days later, Britain and France declared war on Germany. As the United States attempted to maintain its neutrality, the following spring, Hitler invaded Norway and Denmark, then

Belgium, the Netherlands, and Luxembourg. The fighting lasted only two days in the Netherlands, two weeks in Belgium. Hitler quickly marched on Paris. By mid-June 1940, France fell, and the Nazis installed the Vichy [VEE-shee] government of Marshall Pétain [pay-TEHN], with which they pursued a policy of collaboration.

From this point, the struggle continued on many fronts (Map 37.3). The Luftwaffe [LOOFT-wah-fuh], the German air force, attacked Britain. At first it targeted Britain's air bases, but then it bombed London itself nearly every night throughout September and October. The raids only steeled British resolve to resist. To the east, Hitler turned his sights on Russia and the Ukraine, which he planned to invade in May 1941, a blitzkrieg assault that he hoped would be complete by the onset of winter. But meanwhile Mussolini attacked the British in Egypt and invaded Greece, meeting with little success. This caused Hitler to send General Erwin Rommel into North Africa and considerable forces into the Balkans. As a result, the Russian campaign was delayed six weeks, which together with several tactical errors on Hitler's part resulted in the loss of the entirety of his eastern forces at the Battle of Stalingrad in the summer of 1942.

The Holocaust

Meanwhile Hitler had instigated a plan to rid Europe of what he considered its undesirable populations, particularly Jews. To this end, he constructed a series of concentration and extermination camps, the largest of which was Auschwitz-Birkenau [AUSH-vits-BER-ken-ow], located near the provincial Polish town of Oswiecim [osh-FYEN-cheem], from which it took its Germanized name. The first camp on that site, known as Auschwitz I, was reserved for political prisoners, mainly Poles and Germans, but in October 1941, Birkenau (so named because birch trees surrounded the site) supplemented it. Here a subdivision of Adolf Hitler's protection units known as the SS developed a gigantic extermination complex. It included "Bathing Arrangements," lethal gas jets disguised as showerheads. Upon their arrival in cattle cars at the Hell's Gate (Fig. 37.27), Jewish prisoners

Fig. 37.27 Philippe Giraud, *Entrance, Auschwitz-Birkenau Death Camp*. Photographed 2003. Known as "Hell's Gate," this is the main entrance to Birkenau viewed from the unloading ramp where prisoners arrived by railroad. Nearly one-third of the 6 million Jews killed by the Nazis in World War II died here.

underwent a "Selection." Those deemed able-bodied were selected to work in the forced-labor camp, while the others—the old and the weak, as well as young children and their mothers—were exterminated in the "Bathing Arrangements." Every newcomer, except those selected for extermination, was given a number, which was tattooed on the arm. Altogether 444,000 numbers were officially issued, but the total number of Jews killed at Auschwitz-Birkenau can never be known with certainty because so many arrivals were exterminated and never registered. Estimates range from 1 to 2.5 million.

Auschwitz-Birkenau was one of six extermination camps. The others—Belzec [BEL-zek], Chelmno [KELM-no], Majdanek [my-DAH-nek], Sobibor [SO-bih-bore], and Treblinka [treb-LING-kah]—were also in Poland, off German soil and in a country that Hitler had invaded. All were equally dedicated to making Europe *Judenrein* [yoo-den-RINE], "free of Jews." There were many other concentration camps scattered across Germany and German-occupied territories (Map **37.4**). One of the largest on German soil was Buchenwald [BOO-ken-vahld], situated on the northern slope of Ettersberg [ETT-urz-berg], a mountain five miles north of Weimar. In February 1945, just before the American troops reached the camp, it housed over 85,000 prisoners. Of these, more than 25,500 people, severely weakened by their experience,

died as the Germans tried to evacuate the camp in order to hide their crimes before the Americans arrived.

The Buchenwald dead (Fig. 37.28) were photographed by Lee Miller (1907–1977), an American photographer and

Fig. 37.28 Lee Miller, *Buchenwald, Germany*. April 30, 1945. © Lee Miller Archives, England 208. All rights reserved. www.leemiller.co.uk. Miller's pictures of Buchenwald and Dachau (liberated a few days earlier) appeared in British *Vogue* magazine in June under the headline "Believe It."

Map 37.4 German concentration camps in Europe. 1942–45.

former model who had worked with the Surrealists in Paris. The only woman combat photojournalist to cover the war in Europe, she had arrived on the Continent a mere 20 days after American forces assaulted the beaches of Normandy on D-Day. She witnessed the liberation of Paris and then followed American soldiers into Germany. The horror of her photograph is not just its depiction of the dead, but also its evidence of their starvation and suffering before dying.

The War in the Pacific

Meanwhile, in the Pacific, Japan was emboldened by the war in Europe to step up its imperial policy of controlling Asia. It had initiated this policy as early as 1931 with an invasion of Manchuria [man-CHOOR-ee-uh], followed by the conquest of Shanghai [SHANG-high] in 1932 and the invasion of the rest of China in 1937. By 1941, Japan had occupied Indochina, and when the United States in response froze Japanese assets in the United States and cut off oil supplies, Japan responded by attacking Pearl Harbor, Hawaii, the chief American naval base in the Pacific, on December 7, 1941. The surprise attack destroyed 188 aircraft, five battleships, one minelayer, and three destroyers, and left 2,333 dead and 1,139 wounded. The next day, the United States declared war on Japan, and Germany and Italy, with whom Japan had joined in an alliance known as the Axis, declared war on the United States. During the war, the American government interred thousands of Japanese and Japanese Americans (many of whom were U.S. citizens) living in California, Oregon, and Washington on the theory that they might be dangerous. (In 1988, President Ronald Reagan signed legislation that officially apologized for this act of racism.) Racism and consciousness of ethnic identity flourished in the American armed forces as well.

Six months later, the U.S. Navy began to recover from the Pearl Harbor air strike and moved on the Japanese, who had meanwhile captured Guam [gwahm], Wake Island, and the Philippines [fill-ih-PEENZ] (Map **37.5**). A decisive naval battle in the Coral Sea, in which the Americans sank many Japanese ships, was followed by a victory at Midway Island and the landing of American Marines at Guadalcanal [gwah-dul-kuh-NAL] and the Solomon Islands. This turned the tide and enabled the United States to concentrate more fully on Europe.

The Allied Victory

Even as Russian forces were pushing westward, driving the Germans back through the Ukraine, Hungary, and Poland, Allied forces—largely troops from the United States and Great Britain—attacked the Germans on the Normandy coast on June 6, 1944, known as D-Day. Two months later, the Allies landed in southern France and advanced northward with little resistance. By the beginning of September, they had pushed back the Germans to their own border and had liberated France.

In December 1944, an increasingly desperate Hitler, his oil refineries decimated by Allied air strikes, launched a counterattack on Antwerp, the Allies' port of supply, through the Ardennes Forest of Belgium. Surprise and weather almost won him the day, as the Germans pushed forward into the Allied lines—hence the name, the Battle of the Bulge—but he was turned back. By March, the Allies had crossed the Rhine, and the Russians, the eastern arm of the Allied offensive, had approached the outskirts of Berlin. On May 1, 1945, Hitler and his intimates, recognizing that the war was lost, committed suicide in an underground bunker in Berlin. On May 8, the war in Europe came to an official end.

Meanwhile, in the Pacific, American troops had advanced as far north as Iwo Jima [ee-woh JEE-muh] and the southern Japanese island of Okinawa [oh-kih-NAH-wah], but the Japanese steadfastly refused to surrender. Faced with the possibility that an invasion of Japan itself might cost 1 million American lives, the Americans made the decision to drop the newly developed atomic bomb on the city of Hiroshima on August 6, 1945. Two days later, the Soviet Union declared war on Japan and invaded Manchuria. The next day, the United States dropped an atomic bomb on Nagasaki. The power of the atomic bomb, which devastated Hiroshima and Nagasaki, convinced Japan to surrender on August 14, 1945.

Decolonization and Liberation

The war was felt far beyond the Pacific and European theaters, in the many nations subject to colonial rule. The war had drawn the military forces of the colonial powers back to Europe, and in their absence, indigenous nationalist movements arose in Africa, Asia, and the Middle East. The American president Franklin D. Roosevelt felt especially strongly that it was hypocritical to fight tyranny in Europe and then tolerate colonial dominance in the rest of the world. His moral position was strengthened by the realization that American economic interests were far more likely to thrive in a decolonized world. Furthermore, the founding of the United Nations in 1945 guaranteed that the argument against colonization would find a public forum.

In Southeast Asia, the French had occupied Indochina (Laos [laus (rhymes with "mouse")], Cambodia, and Vietnam) since the late nineteenth century. But as early as 1930, Ho Chi Minh [ho chee min] (1892–1969) had transformed a nationalist movement resisting French rule into the Indochina Communist Party. During World War II, Ho Chi Minh led the military campaign against the invading Japanese and the pro-Vichy colonial French government allied with the Japanese. He established himself as the major anticolonial player in the region. When, in 1945, he declared Vietnam an independent state, civil war erupted. It ended with the artificial division of Vietnam at the seventeenth parallel of northern latitude, with Ho Chi Minh in control north of that line and centered in Hanoi, and the French in charge south of that line and centered in Saigon (Map **37.5**).

Meanwhile, France had to deal with growing unrest in North Africa. It had maintained a strong base in Algeria

Area under Japanese domination, August 1942
→ U.S. – Australian joint drive

Map 37.5 Asian and Pacific theaters in World War II, 1941–45.

since the early nineteenth century, and during World War II, the antifascist government of Free France had headquartered there (see Map 37.3). But at the end of the war, violence broke out between French and European settlers, comprising about 1 million people, and a much larger population of Algerian Muslim nationalists who quickly demanded independence. The postwar French Republic, however, declared Algeria an integral part of France. Guerrilla resistance to the French began in 1954, led by the National Liberation Front (FLN), and lasted until 1962, during which time hundreds of thousands of Muslim and European Algerians were killed. Finally, in 1962, French president Charles de Gaulle [deh gohl] (1890–1970) called for a referendum in Algeria on independence. It passed overwhelmingly. Algeria became independent on July 3, 1962.

Mohandas Gandhi [moh-HAHN-dus GAHN-dee] (1869–1948) led the anticolonial movement in India (Fig. **37.29**). While studying law in England, he had learned the concept of **passive resistance** from reading American writer Henry David Thoreau (see Chapter 27). Gandhi had worked for 20 years as an advocate for Indian immigrants in South Africa, and after returning to India in 1915, he began a long campaign against the British government. He was repeatedly arrested, and during his imprisonments, he engaged in long hunger strikes, bringing himself to the brink of death on more than one occasion. Gandhi's campaign of nonviolence finally convinced the British to leave India, which they did in 1947, partitioning the country into two parts, India and

Pakistan. This partition acknowledged the desire of the Muslim population within India to form their own distinctly Muslim state.

Almost simultaneously, Burma and Sri Lanka became independent, the Dutch were forced out of Indonesia, and the British packed up and left Palestine, which they had occupied since the end of the Ottoman Empire in 1918. The British left behind a murderous conflict

Fig. 37.29 Margaret Bourke-White, *Gandhi.* **1946.** Gelatin silver print, 14″ × 11″. © Time, Inc. Bourke-White's photojournalistic work for *Life* magazine (see Fig. 37.20) led her to photograph Gandhi many times. He is shown here reading in a photograph that emphasizes his ascetic lifestyle. The spinning wheel in the foreground is the symbol of Indian independence, signifying, for Gandhi, tradition, patience, self-sufficiency, and peace.

between Arab nationalists and Jews whom they had helped to install in the new country of Israel. In the following decade, the British withdrew from Ghana, Nigeria, Cyprus, Kenya, and Aden (now part of Yemen), sometimes at their own choosing, sometimes under pressure from militant nationalists. The British never resisted decolonization militarily, but this was not the case with France.

Bearing Witness: Reactions to the War

The human cost of World War II was enormous. Somewhere in the vicinity of 17 million soldiers had died, and at least that many civilians had been caught up in the fighting. Hitler had exterminated 6 million Jews, and millions of other people had died of disease, hunger, and other causes. The final toll approached 40 million dead.

It was what Hitler had done to the Jews that most troubled Western consciousness and a large body of literature and film grew out of the events as survivors began to tell their stories to the world. Italian chemist Primo Levi's memoir, *If This Is a Man* (also known as *Survival at Auschwitz*), is the wrenching story of a man attempting to fathom why he survived the death camp. Levi would go on to write stories and novels for the rest of his life that he himself described as "accounts of atrocities." American cartoonist Art Spiegelman's graphic novel *Maus: A Survivor's Tale*, in which Jews are depicted as mice, Germans as cats, and Americans as dogs, recounts his parents' experiences as Jews in Poland before and at Auschwitz during the war. Paris-based documentary filmmaker Claude Lanzmann's 9 1/2-hour *Shoah* (a Hebrew word meaning "catastrophe") is a series of deeply moving testimonies about the Holocaust drawn from survivors, those who stood by without doing anything, and the perpetrators themselves.

Wiesel's *Night* One of the most important memoirs to come out of the Holocaust is *Night* by Elie Wiesel [vee-ZELL] (1928–). "Auschwitz," wrote Wiesel, "represents the negation and failure of human progress: it negates the human design and casts doubts on its validity."

Wiesel was 16 years old in 1944 when he and his family were taken to Auschwitz, where he and his father were separated from his mother and younger sister. He never saw them again and learned later that they had died in the gas chambers. During the following year, Wiesel was moved to the concentration camps at Buna, Gleiwitz [GLY-vits], and finally Buchenwald, where his father died from dysentery, starvation, exposure, and exhaustion, like the many whom Lee Miller had photographed when the camp was liberated in April 1945 (see Fig. 37.28). The author of 36 works dealing with Judaism, the Holocaust, and the moral responsibility of all people to fight hatred, racism, and genocide, Wiesel's powerful prose and commitment won him the Nobel Peace Prize in 1986. He recounts his first day at Auschwitz (**Reading 37.5**):

READING 37.5

from Elie Wiesel, *Night* (1958)

Never shall I forget that night, the first night in camp, which has turned my life into one long night, seven times cursed and seven times sealed. Never shall I forget that smoke. Never shall I forget the little faces of the children, whose bodies I saw turned into wreaths of smoke beneath a silent blue sky.

Never shall I forget those flames which consumed my faith forever.

Never shall I forget that nocturnal silence which deprived me, for all eternity, of the desire to live. Never shall I forget those moments which murdered my God and my soul and turned my dreams to dust. Never shall I forget these things, even if I am condemned to live as long as God Himself. Never.

Wiesel subsequently led the way to the creation of the United States Holocaust Memorial Museum in Washington, D.C.

Resnais's *Night and Fog* In 1955, the young French filmmaker Alain Resnais [ray-NAY] (1922–) startled the world with a 32-minute documentary about the Holocaust called *Night and Fog*. Combining contemporary footage of the eerily abandoned Auschwitz landscape with archival documentary footage recorded during the liberation, Resnais posed the question that desperately needed to be addressed: Who was responsible? The question stands for many more specific ones. Why did so many ordinary Germans passively stand by as Jews were hauled off to the camps? Why did the Soviets, as they moved into Poland, not halt it? Why had the Allies—and the United States in particular—not responded to the situation more quickly? And why had the Jews themselves not organized more active resistance in the camps? Resnais's narrator, Michel Bouquet [boo-KAY], himself a camp survivor, concludes with a dire warning. As the events of the Holocaust retreat into the past, it seems possible, he says, to hope again. It seems possible to believe that what happened in the camps was a one-time occurrence that will never be repeated. But, he insists, the Holocaust is symptomatic of humanity's very indifference to suffering and pain. Its truth always surrounds us.

The Japanese Response Japan was haunted for generations by the bombing of Hiroshima and Nagasaki. Both cities were civilian sites that contributed almost nothing to the Japanese military effort, and President Truman's motives for bombing them were unclear—to many Americans as well as the Japanese. Some argued that the bombings spared both the United States and the Japanese from a painful and devastating invasion and saved the lives of thousands of American soldiers if the war had continued. Others argued that the bombings were a means of forcing the question of the emperor's fate, a major sticking point in

Fig. 37.30 Shomei Tomatsu, *Man with Keloidal Scars*. 1962. From the series *11:02—Nagasaki*. 1966. Gelatin silver print, 16 1/8″ × 10 7/8″. Gift of the photographer. (700.1978). Digital Image © The Museum of Modern Art/Licensed by SCALA/Art Resource, New York. As horrified as they were by images such as this, the Japanese, who were near starvation by war's end, were equally attracted to the obvious wealth and plenty of the occupying American forces.

peace negotiations before the bombs were dropped. Still others felt that the bombings were a just retribution for devastation at Pearl Harbor. Truman's archives suggest that the president wanted to demonstrate U.S. military might to the Soviets, whom he recognized would be a threat to world stability after the war. There is probably some truth in all of these points, but none justified the bombings in the eyes of the Japanese.

One of the most powerful responses to the events is a series of photographs entitled *11:02—Nagasaki* by Shomei Tomatsu [toh-mah-tsoo] (1930–). The series is dedicated to the enduring human tragedy wrought by the atomic bomb, not merely to depicting keloidal burns and physical deformities that radiation from the explosion wreaked upon its survivors (Fig. 37.30). The images are metaphors for the process of Americanization that Japan underwent at the war's conclusion. "If I were to characterize postwar Japan in one word," Tomatsu would write in an essay entitled "Japan Under Occupation," "I would answer without hesitation: 'Americanization.'" His photographs of survivors propose that to become "Americanized" is not necessarily a good thing. It is to become scarred, mutilated, deformed.

One of the more interesting ways in which the Japanese came to deal with the atomic bomb and its aftermath is the creation, in 1954, of the movie monster known in this country as *Godzilla*, but in Japan as *Gojira* [go-jee-rah], a hybrid name which joins the Western word *gorilla*—in honor of the 1933 film *King Kong*—with the

Japanese *kujira* [koo-jee-rah], meaning "whale." The radiation-breathing monster, born from the sea after an American test of an atomic bomb in the Pacific, was a creation of Toho Studios in Tokyo. This, the first of many Godzilla films, was directed by Ishiro Honda (1911–1993). It was inspired by the success of the 1953 U.S. film *The Beast from 20,000 Fathoms*, in which Rhedosaurus, a giant dinosaur, is awakened from eons of dormancy after an atomic bomb test in the northern polar ice cap. The dinosaur wreaks havoc on New York City, culminating in a showdown with military marksmen at Coney Island amusement park.

Godzilla became for the Japanese a vehicle through which they could confront the otherwise unspeakable significance of the atomic bomb. At the same time they could also shift blame for World War II from themselves to the Americans. Scenes of Tokyo devastated by the radiation-breathing monster leave little doubt as to the symbolic intent of the film (Fig. 37.31). In its original form, it remains a powerful indictment of the bomb, but that was not the version available in the United States until 2004. *Gojira* was acquired by U.S. distributors in 1956. They renamed it *Godzilla: King of the Monsters* and completely reedited it. Leaving only its monster scenes, they excised most of the human story, replacing it with scenes featuring a U.S. reporter (played by Raymond Burr, television's Perry Mason) who has come to Tokyo to chronicle the devastation caused by "a force which until a few days ago was entirely beyond the scope of man's imagination." But, of course, the film represents not the unknown but a force completely within the scope of human imagination—the bomb—a fact that today American audiences can finally appreciate.

Fig. 37.31 Godzilla destroys Tokyo, in Ishiro Honda's *Gojira* (*Godzilla*). 1954. The Japanese have made at least 27 other Godzilla films.

The Bauhaus in America

After the Bauhaus closed in April 1933, many of its teachers left Germany for the United States. By the early 1950s, they dominated American architecture and arts education. Walter Gropius and Marcel Breuer moved to Cambridge, Massachusetts, to teach at the Harvard Graduate School of Design. Gropius would go on to design the Harvard Graduate Center (1949–1950) and Breuer the Whitney Museum of American Art (1966) in New York. Joseph Albers would become head of the design department at Yale University in New Haven, Connecticut. Ludwig Mies van der Rohe was appointed head of the architecture school at Chicago's Armour Institute of Technology (later the Illinois Institute of Technology), where he was commissioned to design the new buildings for the campus.

These Bauhaus artists came into their own in America after World War II, when the nation's economy was once again on the rebound. Their influence was nowhere more dramatically felt than in Mies van der Rohe's Seagram Building in New York, completed in 1958 on Park Avenue between 52nd and 53rd streets (Fig. **37.32**). Just ten blocks from the Chrysler Building, it set a new standard for skyscraper architecture. Mies van der Rohe had begun to experiment with designs for glass towers in the early 1920s, and by the time he joined with Philip Johnson on the Seagram Building, he had cultivated an aesthetic of refined austerity summed up by the phrase "less is more."

The siting of the building, separated from the street by a 90-foot-wide plaza and bordered on either side by reflecting pools and ledges, used open space in a manner unprecedented in urban architecture, where every vertical foot above ground spells additional rent revenue. A curtain wall of dark, amber-tinted glass wraps the building and is interrupted by bronze-coated I-beams and by spandrels and mullions (the horizontal and vertical bands between the glass). Depending on the light, the reflective qualities of the glass make the skin appear bronze from one angle and almost-pitch-black from another. At night, the building is entirely lit, creating a golden grid framed in black.

The Seagram Building gives the impression of a giant monolith set on a granite plinth—a sort of sacred homage to the modernist spirit. As one critic rhapsodized, "The commercial office building in this instance has been endowed with a monumentality without equal in the civic and religious architecture of our time." ■

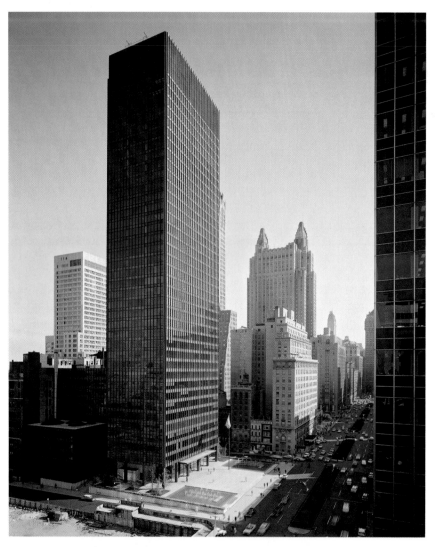

Fig. 37.32 Ludwig Mies van der Rohe and Philip Johnson, Seagram Building, New York City. 1954–58. The entry is set back beneath the columns on the first floor, just as it is at the Villa Savoye (see Fig. 37.9).

THINKING BACK

What was Berlin like in the 1920s?

In the 1920s, Berlin was a thriving center of the arts, rivaling New York and Paris in its innovation. It was notable especially for the libertine atmosphere of its cafés and cabarets, the deep political commitment of its artists. What characterizes the other side of Berlin life, as evidenced in the writing of Franz Kafka, the theater of Bertolt Brecht, and the Expressionist prints of Käthe Kollwitz?

What is fascism?

European conservatives were horrified at the Berlin lifestyle and yearned for a return to a lost past that they idealized as orderly and harmonious. In Germany, Adolf Hitler harnessed this interest. Who did he blame for the country's economic and social problems? How did Leni Riefenstahl's filmmaking support Hitler's cause? Hitler's Nazi party forced the Bauhaus, the leading exponent of modernist art and architecture in Germany inspired by the Dutch De Stijl movement, to close down. What characterizes De Stijl? How are its values reflected in the work of the Bauhaus?

In Russia, Stalin likewise attacked modernist art, which he proposed to replace with social realism, an art designed to be totally intelligible to the masses. And in Italy, Benito Mussolini's Fascist government came to power. What characterizes the Fascist architecture he promoted? Finally, in Spain, with Hitler's aid, Francisco Franco instigated a civil war. The blitzkrieg attack of the German air force on the Basque city of Guernica would be memorialized by Pablo Picasso in his painting *Guernica*.

What is the Mexican mural movement?

In 1910, guerrilla groups in Mexico had initiated a civil war to overthrow the government and restore to the peasants land that had been confiscated and turned over to foreign companies. The war inspired the nationalist feelings of many artists, including a number of painters, chief among them Diego Rivera. What characterizes Rivera's art? Rivera's wife, Frida Kahlo, long crippled by a debilitating childhood accident, developed an intensely personal and autobiographic painting style.

What was the WPA?

The collapse of the stock market in 1929 led to severe economic depression in the United States which President Franklin D. Roosevelt sought to remedy, in part, by the Work Projects Administration. The WPA funded painting projects (especially murals in public buildings, a project inspired by the example of muralist Thomas Hart Benton) and performances by musicians and theater companies, and employed writers to create a series of state and regional guidebooks. The effects of the Depression were heightened by drought in the Great Plains. In what ways can the creative works produced under the WPA and other New Deal agencies be viewed as propaganda? How does it differ from Hitler's propaganda?

How did sound and color change the motion-picture industry?

In the 1930s, the motion picture changed dramatically and became the most popular American art medium. Al Jolson's 1927 *The Jazz Singer* introduced sound into feature films. Producers were forced to perfect sound technology on the set and in theaters. Walt Disney introduced color film, but in 1939, perhaps the greatest year in the history of cinema, color became a real force. *The Wizard of Oz* led the way, soon followed by *Gone with the Wind*. To what ends did *The Wizard of Oz* use color? To what can we attribute the great success of *Gone with the Wind*? The most technically innovative film of the era was Orson Welles's *Citizen Kane* of 1940.

What was the Holocaust?

No event underscores the growing globalization of twentieth-century culture more than World War II. The fighting occurred across the Pacific region, in Southeast Asia, in North Africa and the Middle East, and in Europe, from France to Russia. As colonial powers withdrew their troops from occupied territories to fight in the war, nationalist movements arose in India, Palestine, Algeria, Indonesia, and across Africa, making the war's impact truly global. The human destruction was staggering—some 40 million dead—but even more devastating was the human capacity for genocide and murder revealed by the Holocaust in Germany and the American bombing of Hiroshima and Nagasaki in Japan. How did Elie Wiesel and Alain Resnais respond to the Holocaust? How did photographer Shomei Tomatsu respond to the atomic bomb? How do the *Godzilla* films of director Ishiro Honda reflect Japan's reaction to the bomb?

PRACTICE MORE Get flashcards for images and terms and review chapter material with quizzes at **www.myartslab.com**

GLOSSARY

chiaroscuro lighting In cinema, a term borrowed from Renaissance painting to describe pools of light illuminating parts of an otherwise dark set.

dubbing In cinema, shorthand for "vocal doubling," in which native speakers synchronize new dialogue to the lip movements of the actor.

epic theater A brand of theater created by Bertolt Brecht in which the audience is purposefully alienated so that it might approach the performance with a critical eye.

gulags Labor camps in Stalinist Russia.

Holocaust The systematic extermination of 6 million Jews and 5 million others—particularly Gypsies, Slavs, the handicapped, and homosexuals.

kulaks Prosperous peasant farmers in Russia blamed by Stalin for the country's economic ills.

New Deal President Franklin D. Roosevelt's economic recovery program.

passive resistance The method of protest used by Gandhi in his nonviolent campaign against the British in India, resulting in his repeated arrest.

postsynchronization The term that refers to the addition of sound as a separate step after the creation of a visual film.

READINGS

READING 37.2

from Franz Kafka, *The Metamorphosis* (1915)

Franz Kafka's novella The Metamorphosis *is one of the few works he published during his lifetime. Dreamlike in its central premise—it begins with its main character, Gregor Samsa, waking from "uneasy dreams" transformed into a "gigantic insect"—it is narrated in a direct, matter-of-fact style that seems at odds with its fantastic plot. While Kafka never questions the fact of Samsa's transformation, which leads inevitably to his death, we as readers understand that the story is something of a parable for the modern individual's alienation from his or her own humanity as well as from society.*

THE METAMORPHOSIS

I

As GREGOR SAMSA awoke one morning from uneasy dreams he found himself transformed in his bed into a gigantic insect. He was lying on his hard, as it were armor-plated, back and when he lifted his head a little he could see his domelike brown belly divided into stiff arched segments on top of which the bed quilt could hardly keep in position and was about to slide off completely. His numerous legs, which were pitifully thin compared to the rest of his bulk, waved helplessly before his eyes.

What has happened to me? he thought. It was no dream. His room, a regular human bedroom, only rather too small, lay quiet between the four familiar walls. Above the table on which a collection of cloth samples was unpacked and spread out—Samsa was a commercial traveler—hung the picture which he had recently cut out of an illustrated magazine and put into a pretty gilt frame. It showed a lady, with a fur cap on and a fur stole, sitting upright and holding out to the spectator a huge fur muff into which the whole of her forearm had vanished!

Gregor's eyes turned next to the window, and the overcast sky—one could hear raindrops beating on the window gutter—made him quite melancholy. What about sleeping a little longer and forgetting all this nonsense, he thought, but it could not be done, for he was accustomed to sleep on his right side and in his present condition he could not turn himself over. However

violently he forced himself toward his right side he always rolled onto his back again. He tried it at least a hundred times, shutting his eyes to keep from seeing his struggling legs, and only desisted when he began to feel on his side a faint dull ache he had never experienced before.

Oh God, he thought, what an exhausting job I've picked on! Traveling about day in, day out. It's much more irritating work than doing the actual business in the office, and on top of that there's the trouble of constant traveling, of worrying about train connections, the bed and irregular meals, casual acquaintances that are always new and never become intimate friends. The devil take it all! He felt a slight itching up on his belly; slowly pushed himself on his back nearer to the top of the bed so that he could lift his head more easily; identified the itching place which was surrounded by many small white spots the nature of which he could not understand and made to touch it with a leg, but drew the leg back immediately, for the contact made a cold shiver run through him.

He slid down again into his former position. This getting up early, he thought, makes one quite stupid. A man needs his sleep. Other commercials live like harem women. For instance, when I come back to the hotel of a morning to write up the orders I've got, these others are only sitting down to breakfast. Let me just try that with my chief; I'd be sacked on the spot. Anyhow, that might be quite a good thing for me, who can tell? If I didn't have to hold my hand because of my parents I'd have given notice long ago, I'd have gone to the chief and told him exactly what I think of him. That would knock him endways from his desk! It's a queer way of doing, too, this sitting on high at a desk and talking down to employees, especially when they have to come quite near because the chief is hard of hearing. Well, there's still hope; once I've saved enough money to pay back my parents' debts to him—that should take another five or six years—I'll do it without fail. I'll cut myself completely loose then. For the moment, though, I'd better get up, since my train goes at five.

He looked at the alarm clock ticking on the chest. Heavenly Father! he thought. It was half-past six o'clock and the hands were quietly moving on, it was even past the half-hour, it was getting on toward a quarter to seven. Had the alarm clock not gone off? From the bed one could see that it had been properly set for four o'clock; of course it must have gone off. Yes, but was it possible to sleep quietly through that ear-splitting noise? Well, he had not slept quietly, yet apparently all the more soundly for that. But what was he to do now? The next train went at seven o'clock; to catch that he would need to hurry like mad and his samples weren't even packed up, and he himself wasn't feeling particularly fresh and active. And even if he did catch the train he wouldn't avoid a row with the chief, since the firm's porter would have been waiting for the five o'clock train and would have long since reported his failure to turn up. The porter was a creature of the chief's, spineless and stupid. Well, supposing he were to say he was sick? But that would be most unpleasant and would look suspicious, since during his five years' employment he had not been ill once. The chief himself would be sure to come with the sick-insurance doctor, would reproach his parents with their son's laziness, and would cut all excuses short by referring to the insurance doctor, who of course regarded all mankind as perfectly healthy malingerers. And would he be so far wrong on this occasion? Gregor really felt quite well, apart from a drowsiness that was utterly superfluous after such a long sleep, and he was even unusually hungry.

As all this was running through his mind at top speed without his being able to decide to leave his bed—the alarm clock had just struck a quarter to seven—there came a cautious tap at the door behind the head of his bed. 'Gregor,' said a voice—it was his mother's—'it's a quarter to seven. Hadn't you a train to catch?' That gentle voice! Gregor had a shock as he heard his own voice answering hers, unmistakably his own voice, it was true, but with a persistent horrible twittering squeak behind it like an undertone, which left the words in their clear shape only for the first moment and then rose up reverberating around them to destroy their sense, so that one could not be sure one had heard them rightly. Gregor wanted to answer at length and explain everything, but in the circumstances he confined himself to saying: 'Yes, yes, thank you, Mother, I'm getting up now.' The wooden door between them must have kept the change in his voice from being noticeable outside, for his mother contented herself with this statement and shuffled away. Yet this brief exchange of words had made the other members of the family aware that Gregor was still in the house, as they had not expected, and at one of the side doors his father was already knocking, gently, yet with his fist, 'Gregor, Gregor,' he called, 'what's the matter with you?' And after a little while he called again in a deeper voice: 'Gregor! Gregor!' At the other side door his sister was saying in a low, plaintive tone: 'Gregor? Aren't you well? Are you needing anything?' He answered them both at once: 'I'm just ready,' and did his best to make his voice sound as normal as possible by enunciating the words very clearly and leaving long pauses between them. So his father went back to his breakfast, but his sister whispered: 'Gregor, open the door, do,' However, he was not thinking of opening the door, and felt thankful for the prudent habit he had acquired in traveling of locking all doors during the night, even at home.

READING CRITICALLY

Not long after Kafka's death, the term *Kafkaesque* began to be widely employed to describe the vision of modern life that his writing embodies. How would you define the Kafkaesque?

After the War

Existential Doubt, Artistic Triumph, and the Culture of Consumption

THINKING AHEAD

What is existentialism?

What is Abstract Expressionism?

Who are the Beats?

What is Pop Art?

What is Minimalism in art?

The Holocaust and the nuclear bombings of Hiroshima and Nagasaki compounded the pessimism that had gripped intellectual Europeans ever since the turn of the century. How could anyone pretend that the human race was governed by reason, that advances in technology and science were for the greater good, when human beings were not only capable of genocide, but also possessed the ability to annihilate themselves? For French philosopher Jean-Paul Sartre [SAR-tr] (1905–1980), the only certainty in the world was death. But he would go on to articulate a philosophy in which each person is capable of defining his or her existence for himself or herself—for good or evil.

In America, the 1950s were years of unprecedented prosperity, a fact reflected in the proliferation of new goods and products—literally hundreds of the kinds of things that Duane Hanson's *Supermarket Shopper* has loaded into her shopping cart in his hyperrealistic sculpture of 1970 (Fig. **38.1**): CorningWare, Sugar Pops, and Kraft Minute Rice (1950); sugarless chewing gum and the first 33-rpm long-playing records, introduced by Deutsche Grammophon (1951); Kellogg's Sugar Frosted Flakes, the Sony pocket-sized transistor radio, fiberglass and nylon (1952); Sugar Smacks cereal and Schweppes bottled tonic water (1953); Crest toothpaste and roll-on deodorant (1955); Comet cleanser, Raid insecticide, Imperial margarine, and

Midas mufflers (1956); the Wham-O toy company's Frisbee (1957) and Hula Hoop (1958); Sweet'n Low, Green Giant canned beans, and Teflon frying pans (1958). Tupperware, which had been introduced in 1945, could be found in every kitchen after its push-down seal was patented in 1949. In July 1955, Walt Disney opened Disneyland in Anaheim, California, the first large-scale theme park in America. That same year, two of the first fast-food chains opened their doors—Colonel Sanders's Kentucky Fried Chicken (KFC) and McDonald's. In 1953, the first issue of *Playboy* magazine appeared, featuring Marilyn Monroe as its first nude centerfold, and by 1956, its circulation had reached 600,000. Sales of household appliances exploded, and women, still largely relegated to the domestic scene, suddenly found themselves with leisure time. Diner's Club and American Express introduced the charge card in 1951 and 1958 respectively. Both cards required payment in full each month, but they paved the way for the BankAmericard, introduced in 1958 (eventually evolving into the Visa card), which allowed for individual borrowing—and purchasing—at an unprecedented level.

Television played a key role in marketing these products and services since advertisers underwrote entertainment and news programming by buying time slots for commercials. In television commercials, people could see

◀ **Fig. 38.1 Duane Hanson,** *Supermarket Shopper.* **1970.** Fiberglass, height 65″. Neue Galerie – Sammlung Ludwig, Aachen, Germany. Hanson's sculptures are so lifelike that museum visitors often speak to them.

HEAR MORE Listen to an audio file of your chapter at **www.myartslab.com**

products firsthand. Although television programming had been broadcast before World War II, it was suspended during the war and did not resume until 1948. By 1950, four networks were broadcasting to 3.1 million television sets. By the end of the decade, that number had swelled to 67 million. Even the food industry responded to the medium. Swanson, which had introduced frozen potpies in 1951, began selling complete frozen "TV dinners" in 1953. The first, in its sealed aluminum tray, featured turkey, cornbread dressing and gravy, buttered peas, and sweet potatoes. It cost 98 cents, and Swanson sold 10 million units that year. Consumer culture was at full throttle.

Against this backdrop of prosperity and plenty, more troubling events were occurring. After the war, the territories controlled by the Nazis had been partitioned, and the Soviets had gained control of Eastern Europe, which they continued to occupy. Berlin, fully enclosed by Soviet-controlled East Germany, was a divided city, and it quickly became a focal point of tension when the Soviets blockaded land and river access to the city in 1948. President Truman responded by airlifting vital supplies to the 2 million citizens of West Berlin, but the crisis would continue, culminating in the construction of the Berlin Wall in 1961.

Events in Asia were equally troubling. In China, the communists, led by Mao Zedong [mauw (rhymes with "cow") dzu-doong] (1893–1976), drove the pro-Western nationalists, led by Chiang Kaishek [kigh-shek] (1887–1975), off the mainland to the island of Taiwan and established the pro-Soviet People's Republic of China on October 1, 1949. Korea was likewise partitioned into a U.S.-backed southern sector and a Soviet-backed northern sector, culminating in the 1950 invasion of the South by the North and the Korean War (1950–1953), which involved American and Chinese soldiers, the latter supported by Russian advisors and pilots, in another military conflict. As the tension between the Soviet Bloc and the West escalated throughout the 1950s, nuclear confrontation seemed inevitable.

This chapter traces the arc of these years in both Europe and America. On the one hand, in America, the realities of the Cold War and what many perceived as the country's crass materialism muted the sense of well-being that accompanied the rapid economic expansion. Artists and writers responded by creating a rebellious, individualistic art that, on the one hand, seemed to affirm American creativity and genius even as, on the other, it critiqued the inauthenticity and emptiness of American life. In Europe, the horrors of World War II provoked a profound philosophical uneasiness revolving around the idea of mankind's existential quest.

EUROPE AFTER THE WAR: THE EXISTENTIAL QUEST

If, after World War II, the urban landscape of Europe was in no small part destroyed—from Dresden to London, whole cities were flattened—the European psyche was even more devastated. In the face of countless deaths, pessimism reigned, and ideological conflict between the Western powers and the Eastern bloc exacerbated a growing sense of meaninglessness, alienation, and anxiety. And yet, even in the face of a future some felt was devoid of hope, existentialism, arguably the most important philosophical movement of the twentieth century, offered a path in which every individual might find at least some sense of meaning in life.

Christian Existentialism: Kierkegaard, Niebuhr, and Tillich

Christianity found itself in crisis as well. In the face of World War II's horrors, Christians had to question God's benevolence, if not his very existence. Their faith was put to a test that had been first articulated by the nineteenth-century Danish philosopher Søren Kierkegaard [keer-keh-GAHRD] (1813–1855). Kierkegaard had argued that Christians must live in a state of anguish caused by their own freedom of choice. They must first confront the fundamental Christian paradox, the assertion that the eternal, infinite, transcendent God became incarnated as a temporal, finite, human being (Jesus). To believe in this requires a "leap of faith" because its very absurdity means that all reason be suspended. So Christians must choose to live with objective uncertainty and doubt, a situation that leaves them in a state of "fear and trembling." But if the individual Christian can never really "know" God, he or she can and must choose to act responsibly and morally. What humans can define, in other words, are the conditions of their own existence. This is their existential obligation.

After World War II, Protestant theologians Reinhold Niebuhr [KNEE-bor] (1892–1971) and Paul Tillich [TILL-ick] (1886–1965) further articulated this position of **Christian existentialism** in America. When Tillich was forced to leave Germany in 1933 following Hitler's rise to power, Niebuhr arranged for Tillich to join him on the faculty of the Union Theological Seminary in New York City. There Tillich lectured on modern alienation and the role that religion could play as a "unifying center" for existence. Religion, he believed, provides the self with the courage *to be*. Niebuhr shared Tillich's dedication to reconciling religion and modern experience. "Without the ultrarational hopes and passions of religion," he wrote, "no society will ever have the courage to conquer despair."

The Philosophy of Sartre: Atheistic Existentialism

During and after World War II, the French philosopher Jean-Paul Sartre (1905–1980) rejected the religious existentialism of Kierkegaard, Niebuhr, and Tillich and argued for what he termed **atheistic existentialism**. "Existentialism isn't so atheistic," Sartre would write, "that it wears itself out showing that God doesn't exist. Rather, it declares that even if God did exist, that would change nothing. . . . His existence is not the issue." Living in a universe without God, and thus without revealed morality, individuals unable to make Kierkegaard's "leap of faith" must nevertheless choose to act ethically. "Existence precedes essence" was Sartre's basic premise; that is, humans must define their own essence (who they are) through their existential being (what they do, their acts). "In a word," Sartre explained, "man must create his own essence; it is in throwing himself into the world, in suffering it, in struggling with it, that—little by little—he defines himself." Life is defined neither by subconscious drives, as Freud had held, nor by socioeconomic circumstances, as Marx had argued: "Man is nothing else but what he makes of himself. Such is the first principle of existentialism."

For Sartre there is no meaning to existence, no eternal truth for us to discover. The only certainty is death. Sartre's major philosophical work, the 1943 *Being and Nothingness*, outlines the nature of this condition, but his argument is more accessible in his play *Huis Clos* [hwee kloh] (*No Exit*). As the play opens, a Valet greets Monsieur Garcin [gahr-SEN] as he enters the room that will be his eternal hell (**Reading 38.1**):

READING 38.1

from Jean-Paul Sartre, *No Exit* (1944)

GARCIN (enters, accompanied by the VALET, and glances around him):

So here we are?

VALET Yes, Mr. Garcin.

GARCIN And this is what it looks like?

VALET Yes.

GARCIN Second Empire furniture, I observe . . . Well, well, I dare say one gets used to it in time.

VALET Some do, some don't.

GARCIN Are all the rooms like this one?

VALET How could they be? We cater for all sorts: Chinamen and Indians, for instance. What use would they have for a Second Empire chair?

GARCIN And what use do you suppose I have for one? Do you know who I was? . . . Oh, well, it's no great matter. And, to tell the truth, I had quite a habit of living among furniture that I didn't relish, and in false positions. I'd even come to like it. A false position in a Louis-Philippe dining room—you know the style?—well, that had its points, you know. Bogus in bogus, so to speak.

VALET And you'll find that living in a Second Empire drawing-room has its points.

GARCIN Really? . . . Yes, yes, I dare say . . . Still I certainly didn't expect—this! You know what they tell us down there?

VALET What about?

GARCIN About . . . this—er—residence.

VALET Really, sir, how could you believe such cock-and-bull stories? Told by people who'd never set foot here. For, of course, if they had—

GARCIN Quite so. But I say, where are the instruments of torture?

VALET The what?

GARCIN The racks and red-hot pincers and all the other paraphernalia?

VALET Ah, you must have your little joke, sir.

GARCIN My little joke? Oh, I see. No, I wasn't joking. No mirrors, I notice. No windows. Only to be expected. And nothing breakable. But damn it all, they might have left me my toothbrush!

VALET That's good! So you haven't yet got over your—what-do-you-call-it?—sense of human dignity? Excuse my smiling.

The play was first performed in May 1944, just before the liberation of Paris. If existence in existential terms is the power to create one's future, Garcin and the two women who will soon occupy the room with him are in hell precisely because they are powerless to do so. Garcin's "bad faith" consists in his insistence that his self is the creation of others. His sense of himself derives from how others perceive him. Thus, in the most famous line of the play, he says, "*l'enfer, c'est les autres*" [lehn-fair, say layz-ohtr]—"Hell is other people." In the drawing room, there need be no torturer because each character tortures the other two.

De Beauvoir and Existential Feminism

Sartre's existential call to self-creation resonated powerfully with Simone de Beauvoir [deh boh-VWAHR] (1908–1986), who argued that women had passively allowed men to define them rather than creating themselves. Sartre and de Beauvoir lived independent lives, but they maintained an intimate relationship that intentionally challenged bourgeois notions of decency. The open and free nature of their liaison, described and defended by de Beauvoir in four volumes of memoirs, became part of the mystique of French existentialism.

In her classic feminist text *The Second Sex*, which first appeared in 1949, de Beauvoir debunked what she called "the myth of femininity." She was well aware, as she said, that woman "is very often very well pleased with her role as *Other*"—that is, her secondary status beside men, what de Beauvoir describes as "the inessential which never becomes the essential." The reason for this, she writes, is women's unwillingness to give up the advantages men confer upon them (**Reading 38.2**):

READING 38.2

from Simone de Beauvoir, *The Second Sex* (1949)

Now, woman has always been man's dependent, if not his slave; the two sexes have never shared the world in equality. . . . To decline to be the Other, to refuse to be a party to the deal—this would be for women to renounce all the advantages conferred upon them by their alliance

---

with the superior caste. Man-the-sovereign will provide woman-the-liege with material protection and will undertake the moral justification of her existence; thus she can evade at once both economic risk and the metaphysical risk of a liberty in which ends and aims must be contrived without assistance. Indeed, along with the ethical urge of each individual to affirm his subjective existence, there is also the temptation to forgo liberty and become a thing. This is an inauspicious road. . . . But it is an easy road; on it one avoids the strain involved in undertaking an authentic existence.

The need to create an authentic existence motivates de Beauvoir's feminism. How much she personally succeeded in realizing her own existence, given her lifelong dedication to Sartre, remains a matter of some debate. What is indisputable, however, is the centrality of *The Second Sex* in defining the boundaries of the ever-growing feminist movement.

The Literature of Existentialism

Apart from Simone de Beauvoir, Sartre's closest companions were the novelists Albert Camus [kah-MOO] (1913–1960), Jean Genet [zhuh-NAY] (1910–1986), Boris Vian [vee-YAHN] (1920–1959), and fellow philosopher Maurice Merleau-Ponty [mare-loh-pon-TEE] (1908–1961), editor-in-chief of *Les Temps Modernes* [lay tahm moh-DAIRN], the journal founded by Sartre in 1945 to give "an account of the present, as complete and faithful as possible." Merleau-Ponty was a particular champion of Camus, whose novels he believed embodied the existential condition. The main protagonist of Camus's 1942 novel *The Stranger* is a young Algerian, Meursault [mer-SOH], who is more an antihero than a hero, since he lacks the personal characteristics that we normally associate with heroes. Meursault becomes tangled up with a local pimp whom he somewhat inexplicably kills. He is imprisoned and brought to trial. His prosecutors' case is absurdly beside the point—they demonstrate, for instance, that he both was unmoved by his mother's death and, worse, attended a comic movie on the eve of her funeral. Despite the irrelevance of the prosecutors' evidence, the jury convicts Meursault. Camus explained why in a preface written for a 1955 reissue of the novel (**Reading 38.3**):

READING 38.3

from Albert Camus, Preface to *The Stranger* (1955)

I summarized *The Stranger* a long time ago, with a remark I admit was highly paradoxical: "In our society any man who does not weep at his mother's funeral runs the risk of being sentenced to death." I only meant that the hero of my book is condemned because he does not play the game. In this respect, he is foreign to the society in which he lives; he wanders, on the fringe, in the suburbs of private, solitary, sensual life. And this is why some readers have been tempted to look upon him as a piece of social wreckage. A much more accurate idea of the character, or, at least one much closer to the author's intentions, will emerge if one asks just how Meursault doesn't play the game. The reply is a simple one; he refuses to lie. To lie is not only to say what isn't true. It is also and above all, to say more than is true, and, as far as the human heart is concerned, to express more than one feels. This is what we all do, every day, to simplify life. He says what he is, he refuses to hide his feelings, and immediately society feels threatened. He is asked, for example, to say that he regrets his crime, in the approved manner. He replies that what he feels is annoyance rather than real regret. And this shade of meaning condemns him. For me, therefore, Meursault is not a piece of social wreckage, but a poor and naked man enamored of a sun that leaves no shadows. Far from being bereft of all feeling, he is animated by a passion that is deep because it is stubborn, a passion for the absolute and for truth.

The absurdity of Meursault's position found its fullest expression in what critic Martin Esslin in the 1960s termed the **Theater of the Absurd**, a theater in which the meaninglessness of existence is the central thematic concern. Sartre's own *No Exit* was the first example, but many other plays of a similar character followed, authored by Samuel Beckett (1906–1989), an Irishman who lived in Paris throughout the 1950s, the Romanian Eugène Ionesco [ee-oh-ness-KOH] (1909–1994), the Frenchman Jean Genet, the British Harold Pinter (1930–), the American Edward Albee (1928–), and the Czech-born Englishman Tom Stoppard (1937–). All of these playwrights share a common existential sense of the absurd plus, ironically, a sense that language is a barrier to communication, that speech is almost futile, and that we are condemned to isolation and alienation.

The most popular of the absurdist plays is Samuel Beckett's *Waiting for Godot* [goh-DOH], first performed in French in 1953 and subtitled *A Tragicomedy in Two Acts*. The play introduced audiences to a new set of stage conventions, from its essentially barren set (only a leafless tree decorates the stage), to its two clownlike characters, Vladimir and Estragon, whose language is incapable of affecting or even coming to grips with their situation. The play demands that its audience, like its central characters, try to make sense of an incomprehensible world in which nothing occurs. In fact, the play's first line announces, as Estragon tries without success to remove his boot, "Nothing to be done." In Act I, Vladimir and Estragon await the arrival of a person referred to as Godot (**Reading 38.4a**):

That is exactly what the audience must do as well—wait. Yet nothing happens. Godot does not arrive. In despair, Vladimir and Estragon contemplate hanging themselves but are unable to. Then they decide to leave but do not move. Act II takes place the next day (for the opening of the second act, see **Reading 38.4**, pages 1278–1279). But nothing changes—Vladimir and Estragon again wait for Godot, who does not arrive, and again contemplate suicide. There is no development, no change of circumstance, no crisis, no resolution. The play's conclusion, which repeats the futile decision to move on that ended Act I, demonstrates this (**Reading 38.4b**):

The promise of action and the realization of none—that is the Theater of the Absurd.

The Art of Existentialism

Faced with the lack of life's meaning that Sartre's existentialism proposed, painters and sculptors sought to explore the truth of this condition in their own terms. The Swiss-born Paris resident Alberto Giacometti took up sculpture while exiled from France in Switzerland during World War II, abandoning his earlier Surrealist mode (see Fig. 35.16). The existential position of his new figurative sculpture was clear to Jean-Paul Sartre, whose essay "The Search for the Absolute" appeared in the catalogue for the 1948 exhibition of Giacometti's sculpture at the Pierre Matisse Gallery in Paris. It was Giacometti's first exhibition in ten years, and Sartre tells the story of the artist beginning with life-size plaster sculptures and working at them obsessively until, in Sartre's words, "these moving outlines, always halfway between nothingness and being, always modified, bettered, destroyed and begun once more" were reduced to the size of matchsticks.

What impressed Sartre most was Giacometti's commitment to a search for the absolute, admittedly doomed to failure, but important for that very reason. The figures on the giant metal field in *City Square* are all uniformly striding men, each heading in a different direction to seek fulfillment (Fig. **38.2**). These figures, which do not interact, do not merely embody the alienation of the human condition. In their very frailty, they also embody the will to survive, which Giacometti guaranteed by finally casting his plaster sculptures in bronze.

Fig. 38.2 Alberto Giacometti, *City Square* (*La Place*). 1948. Bronze, 8 ½" × 25 ⅜" × 17 ¼". Digital Image © The Museum of Modern Art/Licensed by SCALA/Art Resource, New York. © Artists Rights Society (ARS), New York. Purchase. In 1958, Giacometti proposed transforming this small piece into a monumental composition for the plaza in front of the Chase Manhattan Bank in New York, with these figures towering over pedestrians. The project was never realized.

One of the most important ideas contributing to post-war artists' understanding of what an existential art might be was the notion writer Georges Bataille [bah-TIGH] (1897–1962) first articulated in 1929, that beneath all matter lies a condition of formlessness that requires the artist to "un-form" all categories of making. This notion led the French artist Jean Dubuffet [doo-boo-FAY] (1901–1985) to collect examples of what he called *art brut*, "raw art," from psychotics, children, and folk artists—anyone unaffected by or untrained in cultural convention. His own work ranged from scribbling gesture and cut-up canvases reconstructed as collages to paintings employing sand and paste. In a series of nudes created during 1950 and 1951, he expanded the human body to fill the whole canvas (Fig. **38.3**). He described the result in the following terms:

disorder of images, of beginnings of images, of fading images, where they cross and mingle, in a turmoil, tatters borrowed from memories of the outside world, and facts purely cerebral and internal—visceral perhaps.

The existential basis of Dubuffet's art resides both in its acceptance of the formlessness of experience and its quest for what he called an "authentic" expression, divorced from convention and tradition.

AMERICA AFTER THE WAR: TRIUMPH AND DOUBT

Only in Europe, where economic recovery lagged far behind the United States because its industries had been devastated by the war, did the magnitude of American

Fig. 38.3 Jean Dubuffet, *Corps de Dame.* **June–December, 1950.** Pen, reed pen, and ink, 10 ⅝″ × 8 ⅜″. The Museum of Modern Art/Licensed by SCALA/Art Resource, New York. The Joan and Lester Avnet Collection. Photograph © 2000 The Museum of Modern Art/Licensed by SCALA/Art Resource, New York. © 2005 Artists Rights Society (ARS), New York/ADAGP, Paris. Although one might interpret this work as having been done by someone who hates women, it is certainly an attack on tradition by targeting academic figure painting.

Fig. 38.4 Jackson Pollock, *Guardians of the Secret*. 1943. Oil on canvas, 4′ 3/8″ × 6′ 3 3/8″. San Francisco Museum of Modern Art. Albert M. Bender Collection. Albert M. Bender Bequest Fund Purchase. © Pollock-Krasner Foundation/Artists Rights Society (ARS), New York. SFMOMA Internal Number: 45.1308. The rooster (top center) had deep psychological and autobiographical meaning to Pollock because, as a boy, a friend accidentally chopped off the top of Pollock's right middle finger with an ax, and a rooster ran up and stole it.

consumption seem obvious. It was in Europe, specifically London, that the first artistic critiques of consumer culture were produced by a group of artists known as the Independents (see *Closer Look*, pages 1256–1257). But, at the same time, the U.S. Department of State toured mammoth exhibitions of paintings and sculpture by contemporary American artists across Europe—and in Paris, especially—in order to demonstrate the spirit of freedom and innovation in American art (and, by extension, American culture as a whole). The individualistic spirit of these artists, whose work was branded **Abstract Expressionism**, was seen as the very antithesis of communism, and their work was meant to convey the message that America had not only triumphed in the war, but in art and culture as well. New York, not Paris, was now the center of the art world.

The Triumph of American Art: Abstract Expressionism

These artists included immigrants like Arshile Gorky [GOR-kee] (1904–1948), Hans Hoffmann (1880–1966), Milton Resnick (1917–2004), and Willem de Kooning [KOO-ning] (1904–1997), as well as slightly younger American-born artists like Franz Kline (1910–1962) and Jackson Pollock (1912–1956). All freely acknowledged

their debts to Cubism's assault on traditional representation, German Expressionism's turn inward from the world, Kandinsky's near-total abstraction, and Surrealism's emphasis on chance operations and psychic automatism. Together the Abstract Expressionists saw themselves as standing at the edge of the unknown, ready to define themselves through a Sartrian struggle with the blank canvas, through the physical act of applying paint and the energy that each painted gesture reveals.

Action Painting: Pollock and de Kooning In 1956, Willem de Kooning commented that "every so often, a painter has to destroy painting. Cézanne did it. Picasso did it with Cubism. Then Pollock did it. He busted our idea of a picture all to hell. Then there could be new paintings again." Around 1940, Pollock underwent psychoanalysis in order to explore Surrealist psychic automatism and to reveal, on canvas, the deepest areas of the unconscious. His 1943 *Guardians of the Secret* is an expression of that effort (Fig. **38.4**). Locked in the central chest are indecipherable "secrets," watched over by a dog (perhaps the Id) and two figures at each side (perhaps the Ego and the Superego). Rising from the trunk are a mask, a rooster, and perhaps even a fetus.

In the mid-1950s in London, a group of artists seeking to express contemporary culture in art formed the Independents. Headed by Richard Hamilton (1922–) and critic Lawrence Alloway (1926–1990), they were fascinated with the goods and products advertised in the American magazines that poured into an England still recovering from World War II. The third leader of the group, Edouardo Paolozzi [pow-LOH-tzee] (1924–2005), avidly collected these ads. The group soon began to describe their work as "Pop Art." It was meant to evoke the tension between popular culture and highbrow art.

In August and September 1956, the group staged an exhibition at the Whitechapel Gallery in London called "This Is Tomorrow." The show consisted of individual pavilions, each designed by a team of artists working in three different media. Hamilton and his two collaborators built a sort of funhouse just inside the gallery's front door. It included a working jukebox, a live microphone so that visitors might participate, films, and a 14-foot-high cutout of the poster for the 1956 film *The Forbidden Planet* showing Robby the Robot carrying off a pinup model. Beneath her knees, they stenciled in the famous photograph of Marilyn Monroe standing over an air vent in the 1955 film *The Seven Year Itch*, her skirt blowing up to reveal her legs.

Hamilton's collage *Just What Is It That Makes Today's Homes So Different, So Appealing?* was used as a catalog illustration to the exhibition and reproduced as a poster for the show. Its title came from a magazine, as did its imagery. In a later commentary, Hamilton listed the following as the subject of the work: "Journalism, Cinema, Advertising, Television, Styling, Sex symbolism, Randomization, Audience participation, Photographic image, Multiple image, Mechanical conversion of the imagery, Diagram, Coding, Technical drawing." In 1957, he created a second list, this one defining the Independents' art in general: "Popular (designed for a mass audience); Transient (short-term solution); Expendable (easily forgotten); Low Cost; Mass Produced; Young (aimed at Youth); Witty; Sexy; Gimmicky; Glamorous; and Big Business." Hamilton and his fellow British artists recognized the power of advertising to manipulate human desire for commercial ends, but at the same time, they celebrated that power.

Richard Hamilton, John McHale, and John Voelcker, pavilion for the "This Is Tomorrow" exhibition at the Whitechapel Gallery, London. 1956.

Something to Think About . . .

How does this English example of Pop Art compare to the later American versions, as seen in the work of Tom Wesselmann, Andy Warhol, and Roy Lichtenstein discussed later in the chapter?

Richard Hamilton, *Just What Is It That Makes Today's Homes So Different, So Appealing?* 1956. Collage on paper, 10 $\frac{1}{4}$″ × 9 $\frac{3}{4}$″. Kunsthalle Tübingen. Sammlung Zundel, Germany. © 2007 Artists Rights Society (ARS), New York/DACS, London.

SEE MORE For a Closer Look at Richard Hamilton's *Just What Is It That Makes Today's Homes So Different, So Appealing?*, go to **www.myartslab.com**

Outside the false window, the movie marquee advertises the first "talkie," Al Jolson's *The Jazz Singer* (see Fig. 37.21).

This advertisement for a Hoover vacuum cleaner reads "Ordinary cleaners reach only this far."

The *Romance* magazine cover on the back wall is at once an ironic comment on the relationship between the body builder and the stripper on the couch and a reference to such traditional depictions of relationships as Jan van Eyck's *Giovanni Arnolfini and His Wife Giovanna Cenami* (see Fig. 16.7).

A telescopic rendering of the surface of the moon serves as the room's ceiling, a reference to the theme of space and *The Forbidden Planet* in the "This Is Tomorrow" exhibition.

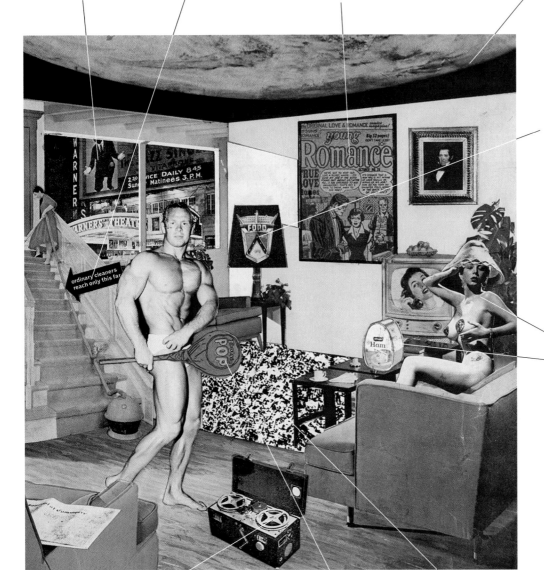

The Ford Motor Company logo decorates a lampshade that casts a strangely geometric white light on the wall behind it.

The canned ham on the table and the nearly nude stripper sitting on the sofa are "meat," consumable flesh, as is the body builder in the center of the room.

The reel-to-reel tape recorder, introduced in the early 1950s, symbolizes, like the television set and the newspaper on the chair in the foreground, the impact of the media on modern life.

The Tootsie Roll Pop, reproduced in giant scale, is a direct reference to *popular* culture.

The carpet is a blowup of the photograph of a beach by Weegee, the pseudonym of Arthur Felig (1899–1968), who became famous in 1945 with the publication of his first book of black-and-white photographs, *The Naked City*. That title resonates with Hamilton's composition.

Fig. 38.5 Jackson Pollock, *Number 27.* **1950.** Oil on canvas, 4'1" × 8'10". Collection, Whitney Museum of American Art, NY. Purchase. © 2008 ARS Artists Rights Society, NY. The year *Number 27* was painted, *Life* magazine ran a long, profusely illustrated story on Pollock asking, "Is he the greatest living painter in the United States?" It stimulated an astonishing 532 letters to the editor, most of them answering the question with a definitive "No!"

Fig. 38.6 Willem de Kooning, *Seated Woman.* **ca. 1940.** Oil on charcoal on masonite, 54 ¹/₄" × 36". The Albert M. Greenfield and Elizabeth M. Greenfield Collection, 1974. Philadelphia Museum of Art, Philadelphia, Pennsylvania. U.S.A. Art Resource, New York. © Artists Rights Society (ARS), New York. The remarkable color contrasts reveal de Kooning's stunning sense of color.

Fig. 38.7 Willem de Kooning, *Pink Angels.* **1945.** Oil on canvas, 52" × 40". Frederick Weisman Company, Los Angeles. The female anatomy here seems to have been disassembled, stretched, pushed, and pulled, and then rearranged in a sort of collage.

This depiction of a mental landscape would soon develop into large-scale **"action paintings,"** as described by the critic Harold Rosenberg in 1942 (Fig. **38.5**). The canvas had become, he said, "an arena in which to act." It was no longer "a picture but an event." Pollock would drip, pour, and splash oil paint, house and boat paint, and enamel over the surface of the canvas, determining the top and bottom of the piece only after the process was complete. The result was a galactic sense of space, what Rosenberg called "all-over" space, in which the viewer can almost trace Pollock's rhythmic gestural dance around the painting's perimeter.

De Kooning was 12 years Pollock's senior and had begun in the late 1930s and early 1940s in a more figurative vein.

CONTINUITY&CHANGE

Girl Before a Mirror, **p. 1161**

His 1940 *Seated Woman* shows the influence of Picasso's Cubist portraits of the 1930s (see *Girl Before a Mirror*, Fig. 35.13), even as it allows various anatomical parts to float free of the body or almost dissolve into fluid form (Fig. **38.6**). By the mid-1940s, in works like *Pink Angels*, the free-floating forms seem to refer to human anatomy even as they remain free from it (Fig. **38.7**). An eye here, a seated figure there, an extended arm, a breast, all set free of any logical skeletal relationships, begin to create the same allover space that distinguishes Pollock's work. The difference is that de Kooning's space is composed of shapes and forms rather than the woven linear skein of Pollock's compositions.

By 1950, the surface of de Kooning's paintings seemed densely packed with free-floating, vaguely anatomical parts set in a landscape of crumpled refuse, earthmoving equipment, concrete blocks, and I-beams. None of these elements is definitively visible, just merely suggested. *Excavation* is a complex organization of open and closed cream-colored forms that lead from one to the other, their black outlines overlapping, merging, disappearing across the surface (Fig. **38.8**). Small areas of brightly colored brushwork interrupt the surface.

When, in 1951, *Excavation* was featured in an exhibition of abstract painting and sculpture at the Museum of Modern Art in New York, de Kooning lectured on the subject "What Abstract Art Means to Me." His description of his relationship to his environment is a fair explanation of what we see in the painting: "Everything that passes me I can see only a little of, but I'm always looking. And I see an awful lot sometimes."

Fig. 38.8 Willem de Kooning (American 1904–1997 b. Netherlands), *Excavation.* **1950.** Oil on canvas, 205.7 × 254.6 cm (81″ × 100 ¼″). Unframed. Mr. and Mrs. Frank G. Logan Purchase Prize Fund; restricted gifts of Edgar J. Kaufmann, Jr., and Mr. and Mrs. Noah Goldowsky, Jr., 1952.1 Reproduction, The Art Institute of Chicago. All rights reserved. © 2009 Artists Rights Society (ARS), New York. This is one of de Kooning's largest paintings. "My paintings are too complicated," he explained. "I don't use the large-size canvas because it's too difficult for me to get out of it."

De Kooning's abstraction differs from Pollock's largely in this. As opposed to plumbing the depths of the psyche, he represents the psyche's encounter with the world. Even in such early figurative works such as *Seated Woman*, where the curvilinear features of his sitter contrast with the geometric features of the room, de Kooning's primary concern is the relation of the individual to his or her environment. The tension between the two is the focus of his works.

Women Abstract Expressionists In many ways, women Abstract Expressionist artists held a position in the movement as a whole that is comparable to the women associated with the Surrealists in Europe. From the point of view of the men—and the critics who wrote about the men—they were spouses or lovers and, when noticed at all as artists, part of a "second generation" following on the heels of the great male innovators of the first generation. In 1948, for instance, the male Abstract Expressionists organized a group known as The Club, a social gathering that met regularly in a rented loft on East 8th Street in New York City. According to Pat Passlof, herself a painter and married to fellow Abstract Expressionist Milton Resnick, The Club's charter explicitly excluded communists, homosexuals, and women because, she was told, "those are the three groups that take over." In fact, women did attend meetings, though they were excluded from board meetings or policy discussions.

Although excluded from the inner circle, a number of the women associated with Abstract Expressionism were painters of exceptional ability. Elaine de Kooning (1918–1989), who married Willem in 1943, was known for her highly sexualized portraits of men. Lee Krasner [KRAZ-ner] (1908–1984), who married Jackson Pollock in 1945, developed her own distinctive allover style of thickly applied paint consisting of calligraphic lines. Though these lines sometimes enclose symbol-like forms, in *White Squares* their architecture possesses some of the energy of automatic writing—a kind of visual equivalent to "noise poetry" (Fig. **38.9**). Krasner later defined her relationship to the Abstract Expressionists and Pollock in particular:

> I was put together with the wives. They worked, they supported their husbands, they taught school and kept their mouths absolutely closed tight. I don't know if they were instructed never to speak publicly, I don't know if they had a thought. Jackson always treated me as an artist but his ego was so colossal, I didn't threaten him in any way. So he was aware of what I was doing, I was working, and that was that. That was our relationship.

One of the major tensions in Abstract Expressionism is the dynamic relationship between figuration and abstraction. As de Kooning once said, "Even abstract shapes must have a likeness." In *River Bathers* by Grace Hartigan [HAR-tih-gan] (1922–), the broad, gestural abstract washes of color have a powerful emotional and visual presence (Fig. **38.10**). She would later say, "My art was always about something," which in this case is five or six figures standing at a river's edge. For

Fig. 38.9 Lee Krasner (1908–1984), *White Squares*. ca. 1948. Oil on canvas, 24″ × 30″ (61 × 76.2 cm). Gift of Mr. and Mrs. B. H. Friedman. 75.1. Collection of the Whitney Museum of American Art, New York. The painting creates a tension between the geometric regularity of the grid and the gestural freedom of Krasner's line.

Fig. 38.10 Grace Hartigan, *River Bathers*. 1953. Oil on canvas, 5'9 3/8" × 7'4 3/4". Given anonymously. (11.1954). Digital Image. The Museum of Modern Art/Licensed by SCALA/Art Resource, New York. The most obvious bather is at the top right. Another seems to be splashing in the water in the middle section of the painting. Two others are behind her and another appears to be standing at the left.

Hartigan the painting is not realistic, but it captures real feelings experienced in a specific place and time.

Inspired by de Kooning, Joan Mitchell (1926–1992) began painting in New York in the early 1950s, but after 1955, she divided her time between Paris and New York, moving to Paris on a more permanent basis in 1959. Ten years later, she moved down the Seine to Vétheuil [vay-TOY], living in the house that Monet had occupied from 1878 to 1881. Although she denied the influence of Monet, her paintings possess something of the scale of Monet's water lily paintings, and her brushwork realizes in large what Monet rendered in

CONTINUITY&CHANGE

Water Lilies, **p. 1101**

detail. Like Monet, she was obsessed with water, specifically Lake Michigan, which as a child she had constantly viewed from her family's Chicago apartment. "I paint from remembered landscapes that I carry with me—and remembered feelings of them, which of course become transformed." As in most of her works, the unpainted white ground of *Piano mécanique* takes on the character of atmosphere or water, an almost touchable and semitransparent space that reflects the incidents of weather, time, and light (Fig. **38.11**).

Fig. 38.11 Joan Mitchell, *Piano mécanique*. 1958. Oil on canvas, 78" × 128". Gift of Addie and Sidney Yates. Image © 2009 Board of Trustees, National Gallery of Art, Washington, D.C. Alberto Giacometti and Samuel Beckett were among Mitchell's closest friends after she moved to Paris in 1959.

Fig. 38.12 Mark Rothko (American 1903–1970), *Green on Blue*. 1956. Oil on canvas, 89 $^{3}/_{4}$" × 63 $^{1}/_{4}$" (228.0 × 161.0 cm). Collection of the University of Arizona Museum of Art, Tucson, Gift of E. Gallagher, Jr. Acc. 64.1.1. The religious sensibility of Rothko's painting brought him, in 1964, a commission for a set of murals for a Catholic chapel in Houston, Texas.

The Color-Field Painting of Rothko and Frankenthaler A second variety of Abstract Expressionism offered viewers a more meditative and quiet painting based on large expanses of relatively undifferentiated color. Mark Rothko (1903–1970) began painting in the early 1940s by placing archetypal figures in front of large monochromatic bands of hazy, semitransparent color. By the early 1950s, he had eliminated the figures, leaving only the background color field.

The scale of these paintings is intentionally large. *Green on Blue*, for instance, is over 7 feet tall (Fig. **38.12**). "The reason I paint [large pictures]," he stated in 1951,

> is precisely because I want to be very intimate and human. To paint a small picture is to place yourself outside your experience, to look upon an experience as a stereopticon view or reducing glass. However you paint the larger picture, you are in it. It isn't something you command.

Viewers find themselves enveloped in Rothko's sometimes extremely somber color fields. These expanses of color become, in this sense, stage sets for the human drama that transpires before them. As Rothko further explains:

> I am interested only in expressing the basic human emotions—tragedy, ecstasy, doom, and so on—and the fact that lots of people break down and cry when confronted with my pictures shows that I communicate with those basic human emotions. The people who weep before my pictures are having the same religious experience I had when I painted them.

The emotional toll of such painting finally cost Rothko his life. His vision became darker and darker throughout the 1960s, and in 1970, he hanged himself in his studio.

In 1952, directly inspired by Pollock's drip paintings, 24-year-old Helen Frankenthaler (1928–) diluted paint almost to the consistency of watercolor and began pouring it onto unprimed cotton canvas to achieve giant stains of color that suggest landscape (Fig. **38.13**).

Fig. 38.13 Helen Frankenthaler, *The Bay*. 1963. Acrylic on canvas, 6′ 8 ³/₄″ × 6′ 9 ¹/₂″. The Detroit Institute of Arts, Founders Society Purchase, Dr. & Mrs. Hilbert H. DeLawter Fund/The Bridgeman Art Library. This is one of the first paintings in which Frankenthaler used acrylic rather than oil paint, resulting in a much stabler surface.

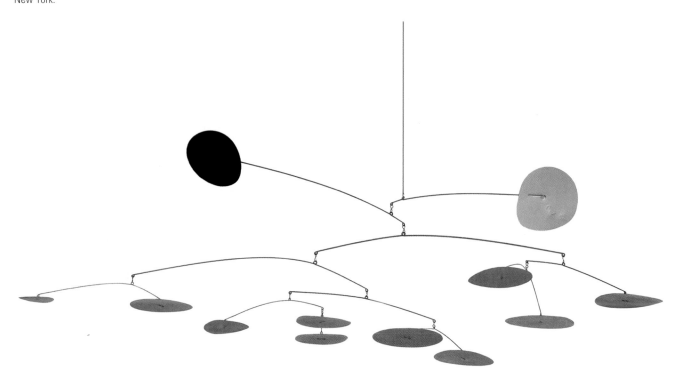

The risk she assumed in controlling her flooding hues, and the monumentality of her compositions, immediately inspired a large number of other artists.

The Dynamic Sculpture of Calder and Smith Sculpture, too, could partake of the same gestural freedom and psychological abstraction as Abstract Expressionist painting. It could become a field of action, like Pollock's and de Kooning's paintings, in which the sculptor confronts the most elemental forms of being.

When the American sculptor Alexander Calder (1898–1976) arrived in Paris in 1926, his studio was a favorite haunt of the Surrealists, who came to witness performances of Cirque Calder (1926-31), a miniature arena in which he manipulated diminutive figures built of wire and wood, including bareback riders, acrobats, sword swallowers, and the like. So time and chance—the happenstance of live performance—were built into his work. By the early 1930s he began to make what Marcel Duchamp labeled **mobiles**, which in French refer not only to things that move but "motives" as well, the causes or incentives for action (Fig. **38.14**). The movement of Calder's mobile comes from accidental and often unpredictable currents of air that hit the suspended sculpture—a breeze, a sudden

gust from the air-conditioning system, a wave of air from a passing bus. The mobile's appearance changes as continuously and as arbitrarily as a cumulus cloud on a summer's day, suggesting familiar shapes—fish, lily pads, birds—in the manner of a cloud. As the mobile turns in space, it defines a virtual volume like that defined by the linear tracery of a handheld light swung in an arc and photographed with a long exposure time. In other words, its path is like a dancer's over the space of a stage, a choreography of graceful forms. In a 1946 catalog for an exhibition of Calder mobiles, Jean-Paul Sartre summed up the mobile's appeal as stemming from "the beauty of its pure and changing forms, at once so free and so disciplined."

The sculpture of David Smith (1906–1965) offers the same sense of change but in a more stable form. Here it is not the sculpture that moves, but the viewer who must. For instance, when one views *Blackburn: Song of an Irish Blacksmith* from the front, the sculpture seems totally open and airy, consisting of negative spaces defined by linear elements, whereas from the side it becomes a complex network of densely packed forms (Fig. **38.15**). There is really no way for the viewer to intuit all of the sculpture's aspects without walking around it. From any single view it remains unpredictable. And the surprises that the sculpture presents

Fig. 38.15 David Smith, _Blackburn: Song of an Irish Blacksmith_, frontal and profile views. 1949–50. Steel and bronze, 46 $\frac{1}{4}$″ × 49 $\frac{3}{4}$″ × 24″. Wilhelm Lehmbruck Museum, Duisburg, Germany. Art © Estate of David Smith/Licensed by VAGA, NY. Smith was the descendant of a pioneer blacksmith in Indiana. The piece resonates with that autobiographical reference.

extend to its materials. It is constructed out of found objects from the industrial world—bent steel rods, cotter pins, and what appears to be the metal seat of a farm tractor—all transformed, in a consciously Surrealist manner, into something new, unique, and marvelous.

What most distinguishes Smith's work is the requirement of active participation from the viewer to experience it fully. So the responsibility for the creation of meaning in art begins to shift from artist to audience, as it does in Abstract Expressionism generally if less clearly. This shift will profoundly alter the direction of art in the last half of the twentieth century, when a work of art will increasingly have as many meanings as the viewers it attracts.

THE BEAT GENERATION

The participation of the audience and the multiple perspectives that the work of both Calder and Smith embodies became the central focus of the group of American poets, writers, and artists that we have come to call Beats or hipsters. _Beat_ was originally a slang term meaning "down and out," or "poor and exhausted," but it came to designate the purposefully disenfranchised artists of the American 1950s who turned their backs on what they saw as the duplicity of their country's values. The **Beat generation** sought a heightened and, they believed, more authentic style of life, defined by alienation, nonconformity, sexual liberation, drugs, and alcohol.

Robert Frank and Jack Kerouac

The Beats' material lay all around them, in the world, as they sought to expose the tensions that lay under the presumed well-being of their society. One of their contemporary heroes was the Swiss photographer Robert Frank (1924–), who with the aid of a Guggenheim fellowship had traveled across America for two years, publishing 83 of the resulting 2,800 photographs as _The Americans_ in 1958. The book outraged a public used to photographic compilations like the 1955 exhibition *The Family of Man*, which drew 3,000 visitors daily to the Museum of Modern Art in celebration of its message of universal hope and unity. Frank's photographs offered something different. They capture everyday, mundane things that might otherwise go by unseen, with a sense of spontaneity and directness that was admired, especially, by writer Jack Kerouac (1922–1969), who had chronicled his own odysseys across America in the 1957 *On the Road*.

On the Road describes Kerouac's real-life adventures with his friend Neal Cassady (1926–1968), who appears in what Kerouac called his "true-story novel" as Dean Moriarty. Cassady advocated a brand of writing that amounted to, as he put it in a letter to Kerouac, "a continuous chain of undisciplined thought." In fact, Kerouac wrote the novel in about three weeks on a single, long scroll of paper, improvising, he felt, like a jazz musician, only with words and narrative. But like a jazz musician, Kerouac was a skilled craftsman, and if the novel seems a spontaneous outburst, it reflects the same sensibility as Robert Frank's *The Americans*. Frank, after all, had taken over 2,800 photographs, but he had published only 83 of them. One senses, in reading Kerouac's rambling adventure, something of the same editorial control.

Ginsberg and "Howl"

The work that best characterizes the Beat generation is "Howl," a poem by Allen Ginsberg (1926–1997). This lengthy poem in three parts and a footnote has a memorable opening (**Reading 38.5**):

READING 38.5

from Allen Ginsberg, "Howl" (1956)

I saw the best minds of my generation destroyed by
    madness, starving hysterical naked,
dragging themselves through the negro streets at dawn
    looking for an angry fix,
angelheaded hipsters burning for the ancient heavenly
    connection to the starry dynamo in the machinery of
    night,
who poverty and tatters and hollow-eyed and
    high sat up smoking in the supernatural darkness of
    cold-water flats floating across the tops of cities
    contemplating jazz
who bared their brains to Heaven under the El and saw
    Mohammedan angels staggering on tenement roofs
    illuminated,
who passed through universities with radiant cool eyes
    hallucinating Arkansas and Blake-light tragedy among
    the scholars of war,
who were expelled from the academies for crazy & pub-
    lishing obscene odes on the windows of the skull,
who cowered in unshaven rooms in underwear, burning
    their money in wastebaskets and listening to the Ter-
    ror through the wall . . .

Fig. 38.16 Robert Rauschenberg (1925–), *Bed*. 1955. Combine painting: oil and pencil on pillow, quilt, and sheet on wood supports, 6'3 $^1/_4$" × 31 $^1/_2$" × 8". Gift of Leo Castelli in honor of Alfred H. Barr, Jr. (79.1989). Digital Image © The Museum of Modern Art/Licensed by SCALA/Art Resource, New York. © Art Robert Rauschenberg Foundation/VAGA, Visual Artists & Galleries Association, NY. The mattress, pillow, quilt, and sheets are believed to be Rauschenberg's own and so may be thought of as embodying his famous dictum: "Painting relates to both art and life. . . . (I try to act in that gap between the two.)"

Ginsberg's spirit of inclusiveness admitted into art not only drugs and alcohol but also graphic sexual language, to say nothing of his frank homosexuality. Soon after "Howl" was published in 1956 by Lawrence Ferlinghetti's City Lights bookstore in San Francisco, federal authorities charged Ferlinghetti with obscenity. He was eventually acquitted. Whatever the public thought of it, the poem's power was hardly lost on the other Beats. The poet Michael McClure (1932–) was present the night Ginsberg first read it at San Francisco's Six Gallery in 1955:

> Allen began in a small and intensely lucid voice. At some point Jack Kerouac began shouting "GO" in cadence as Allen read it. In all of our memories no one had been so outspoken in poetry before—we had gone beyond a point of no return—and we were ready for it, for a point of no return. None of us wanted to go back to the gray, chill, militaristic silence, to the intellective void—to the land without poetry—to the spiritual drabness. We wanted to make it new and we wanted to invent it and the process of it as we went into it. We wanted voice and we wanted vision. . . .
>
> Ginsberg read on to the end of the poem, which left us standing in wonder, or cheering and wondering, but knowing at the deepest level that a barrier had been broken, that a human voice and body had been hurled against the harsh wall of America and its supporting armies and navies and academies and institutions and ownership systems and power-support bases.

Here, in fact, in the mid-1950s were the first expressions of the forces of rebellion that would sweep the United States and the world in the following decade.

Cage and the Aesthetics of Chance

Ginsberg showed that anything and everything could be admitted into the domain of art. This notion also informs the music of composer John Cage (1912–1992), who by the mid-1950s was proposing that it was time to "give up the desire to control sound . . . and set about discovering means to let sounds be themselves." Cage's notorious *4' 33"* (*4 minutes 33 seconds*) is a case in point. First performed in Woodstock, New York, by pianist David Tudor on August 29, 1952, it consists of three silent movements, each of a different length, but when added together totaling four minutes and thirty-three seconds. The composition was anything but silent, however, admitting into the space framed by its duration all manner of ambient sound—whispers, coughs, passing cars, the wind. Whatever sounds happened during its performance were purely a matter of chance, never predictable. Like Frank's, Cage's is an art of inclusiveness.

That summer, Cage organized a multimedia event at Black Mountain College in North Carolina, where he occasionally taught. One of the participants was 27-year-old artist Robert Rauschenberg [RAUW-shen-berg]

(1925–2008). By the mid-1950s, Rauschenberg had begun to make what he called **combine paintings**, works in which all manner of materials—postcards, advertisements, tin cans, pinups—are combined to create the work. If Rauschenberg's work does not literally depend upon matters of chance in its construction, it does incorporate such a diverse range of material that it creates the aura of representing Rauschenberg's chance encounters with the world around him. And it does, above all, reflect Cage's sense of all-inclusiveness. *Bed* literally consists of a sheet, pillow, and quilt raised to the vertical and then dripped not only with paint but also with toothpaste and fingernail polish in what amounts to a parody of Abstract Expressionist introspection (Fig. **38.16**). Even as it juxtaposes highbrow art-making with the vernacular quilt, abstraction with realism, *Bed* is a wryly perceptive transformation of what Max Ernst in the early days of Surrealism had called "The Master's Bedroom" (see Fig. 35.11).

The Art of Collaboration Rauschenberg had known Cage since the summer of 1952 when, not long before the premiere of *4' 33"* in New York state, Cage had organized an event, later known as *Theater Piece #1*, in the dining hall of Black Mountain College near Asheville, North Carolina. Although almost everyone who participated remembers the event somewhat differently, it seems certain that the poets M. C. Richards (1916–1999) and Charles Olson (1910–1970) read poetry from ladders, Robert Rauschenberg played Edith Piaf [pee-AHF] records on an old windup phonograph with his almost totally "White Paintings" hanging around the room, Merce Cunningham (1919–2009) danced through the audience, a dog at his heels, while Cage himself sat on a stepladder, sometimes reading a lecture on Zen Buddhism, sometimes just listening. "Music," Cage declared at some point in the event, "is not listening to Mozart but sounds such as a street car or a screaming baby."

The event inaugurated a collaboration between Cunningham (dance), Cage (music), and Rauschenberg (decor and costume) that would span many years. Their collaboration is unique in the arts because of its insistence on the *independence*, not interdependence, of each part of the dance's presentation. Cunningham explains:

> In most conventional dances there is a central idea to which everything adheres. The dance has been made to the piece of music, the music supports the dance, and the decor frames it. The central idea is emphasized by each of the several arts. What we have done in our work is to bring together three separate elements in time and space, the music, the dance and the decor, allowing each one to remain independent.

So Cunningham created his choreography independently of Cage's scores, and Rauschenberg based his decors on only minimal information offered him by Cunningham and

Fig. 38.17 Merce Cunningham, *Summerspace*. 1958. Set and costumes by Robert Rauschenberg. Photo by Jack Mitchell. Courtesy of Cunningham Dance Foundation, Inc. © Estate of Robert Rauschenberg/VAGA, NY. *Summerspace*, Cunningham said, was "about space. I was trying to think about ways to work in space. . . . When I spoke to Bob Rauschenberg—for the decor— I said, 'One thing I can tell you about this dance is it has no center. . . .' So he made a pointillist backdrop and costumes."

Cage (Fig. **38.17**). The resulting dance was, by definition, a matter of music, choreography, and decor coming together (or not) as a chance operation.

The music Cage composed for Cunningham was also often dependent on chance operations. For instance, in 1959, Cage recorded an 89-minute piece entitled *Indeterminancy* (track **38.1**). It consisted of Cage narrating short, humorous stories while, in another room, out of earshot, pianist David Tudor performed selections from Cage's 1958 *Concert for Piano and Orchestra* as well as pre-recorded tape from another 1958 composition, *Fontina Mix*. For a 1965 collaboration with Cunningham, *Variations V*, Cage's score consisted of sounds randomly triggered by sensors reacting to the movements of Cunningham's dancers. This results in what Gordon Mumma, a member of Cunningham's troupe, called "a superbly poly: -chromatic, -genic, -phonic, -morphic, -pagic, -technic, -valent, multi-ringed circus."

Johns and the Obvious Image   Whereas the main point for Cunningham, Cage, and Rauschenberg was the idea of composition without a central focus, Rauschenberg's close friend and fellow painter Jasper Johns (1930–) took the opposite tack. Throughout the 1950s, he focused on the most common, seemingly obvious subject matter—numbers, targets, maps, and flags—in a manner that in no way suggests the multiplicity of meaning in his colleagues' work. Johns's painting *Three Flags* is nevertheless

capable of evoking in its viewers emotions ranging from patriotic respect to equally patriotic outrage, from anger to laughter (Fig. **38.18**). But Johns means the imagery to be so obvious that viewers turn their attention to the wax-based paint itself, to its almost sinuous application to the canvas surface. In this sense, the work—despite being totally recognizable—is as abstract as any Abstract Expressionist painting, but without Abstract Expressionism's assertion of the primacy of subjective experience.

Fig. 38.18 Jasper Johns (b. 1930), *Three Flags*. 1958. Encaustic on canvas, 30 $^7/_8$ × 45 $^1/_2$ × 5 in. (78.4 × 115.6 × 12.7 cm). 50th Anniversary Gift of the Gilman Foundation, Inc., The Lauder Foundation, A. Alfred Taubman, an anonymous donor, and purchase. 80.32. Collection of Whitney Museum of American Art, New York. Photo by Geoffrey Clements. Art © Jasper Johns/Licensed by VAGA, NY. Each of the three flags diminishes in scale by about 25 percent from the one behind. Because the flags project outward, getting smaller each time, they reject pictorial perspective's illusion of depth and draw attention to the surface of the painting itself.

Allan Kaprow and the Happening Cage's aesthetic of diversity and inclusiveness also informs the inventive multimedia pieces of Alan Kaprow (1927–2006). In an essay called "The Legacy of Jackson Pollock," written just two years after Pollock's death in an automobile accident in 1956, Kaprow described Pollock's art, with its willingness to bury nails, sand, wire, screen mesh, even coins in its whirls of paint, as pointing toward new possibilities for the subsequent generation of artists (**Reading 38.6**):

READING 38.6

from Allan Kaprow, "The Legacy of Jackson Pollock" (1958)

Pollock, as I see him, left us at the point where we must become preoccupied with and even dazzled by the space and objects of our everyday life, either our bodies, clothes, rooms, or, if need be, the vastness of Forty-second Street. Not satisfied with the suggestion through paint of our other senses, we shall utilize the specific substances of sight, sound, movements, people, odors, touch. Objects of every sort are materials for the new art: paint, chairs, food, electric and neon lights, smoke, water, old socks, a dog, movies, a thousand other things that will be discovered by the present generation of artists. Not only will these bold new creators show us, as if for the first time, the world we have always had about us but ignored, but they will disclose entirely unheard-of happenings and events, found in garbage cans, police files, hotel lobbies; seen in store windows and on the streets; and sensed in dreams and horrible accidents. An odor of crushed strawberries, a letter from a friend, or a billboard selling Drano; three taps on the front door, a scratch, a sigh, or a voice lecturing endlessly, a blinding staccato flash, a bowler hat—all will become materials for this new concrete art.

Young artists of today need no longer say, "I am a painter" or "a poet" or "a dancer." They are simply "artists." All of life will be open to them.

It is hardly surprising that it was Kaprow who founded the **Happening**, a new multimedia event in which artists and audience participated as equal partners. Kaprow's *18 Happenings in 6 Parts* took place over the course of six evenings in October 1959 at the Reuben Gallery in New York. It was inspired by *Theater Piece #1*. In order to add sound to his environment, Kaprow enrolled in Cage's music composition course at the New School for Social Research in New York. Included in the environment were record players, tape recorders, bells, a toy ukulele, a flute, a kazoo, and a violin. Kaprow scored the directions for playing them in precisely timed outbursts that approximated the cacophony of the urban environment. He divided the gallery into three rooms, created by plastic sheets and movable walls, between which audience members were invited to move in unison. Performers played instruments and records, painted, squeezed orange juice, spoke in sentence fragments—all determined by chance operations. The audience, although directed to move according to Kaprow's instructions, was also invited to participate in the work, and Kaprow would increasingly include the audience as a participant in his later Happenings.

Architecture in the 1950s

If the Beat generation was antiestablishment in its sensibilities, the architecture of the 1950s embodied the very opposite. The International Style aesthetic that Mies van der Rohe brought to his 1954 to 1956 Seagram Building (1954–1956; see Fig. 37.32) could also be applied to the private residence, as he made clear with the 1950 Farnsworth House (Fig. **38.19**). A more direct homage to Le Corbusier's

Fig. 38.19 Ludwig Mies van der Rohe, Farnsworth House, Fox River, Plano, Illinois. 1950. © 2008 Artists Rights Society (ARS), New York/VG Bild-Kunst, Bonn. The house was commissioned as a weekend retreat. Its bathroom and storage areas are behind non-load-bearing partitions that divide the interior space.

Fig. 38.20 Frank Lloyd Wright, The Solomon R. Guggenheim Museum, New York, 1957–59. Photo: David Heald/Courtesy of the Solomon R. Guggenheim Museum. FL W#7. © 2008 Artists Rights Society (ARS), New York. The tower behind Wright's original building was designed much later by Gwathmey Siegel and Associates. It contains 51,000 square feet of new and renovated gallery space, 15,000 square feet of new office space, a restored theater, new restaurant, and retrofitted support and storage spaces. Wright had originally proposed such an annex to house artists' studios and offices, but the plan was dropped for financial reasons.

Villa Savoye (see Fig. 37.9), though more severe in its insistence on the vertical and the horizontal, it is virtually transparent, opening out to the surrounding countryside, with views of the Fox River, and also inviting the countryside in.

Frank Lloyd Wright's design for the Solomon R. Guggenheim [GOO-ghen-hime] Museum in New York is a conscious counterstatement to Mies van der Rohe's severe rationalist geometry, which, in fact, Wright despised (Fig. **38.20**). Situated on Fifth Avenue directly across from Central Park, the museum's organic forms echo the natural world. The plan is an inverted spiral ziggurat, or stepped tower, that dispenses with the right-angle geometries of standard urban architecture and the conventional approach to museum design, which led visitors through a series of interconnected rooms. Instead, Wright whisked museumgoers to the top of the building via elevator, allowing them to proceed downward on a continuous spiral ramp from which, across the open rotunda in the middle, they can review what they have already seen and anticipate what is to come. The ramp is cantilevered to such an extent that several contractors were frightened off by Wright's plans. The plans were complete in 1943, but construction did not begin until 1956

because of a prohibition of new building during World War II and permit delays stemming from the radical nature of the design. It was still not complete at the time of Wright's death in 1959. In many ways, Wright's Guggenheim Museum represents the spirit of architectural innovation that still pervades the practice of architecture to this day.

POP ART

In the early 1960s, especially in New York, a number of artists created a "realist" art that represented reality in terms of the media—advertising, television, comic strips—the imagery of mass culture. The famous paintings of Campbell's Soup cans created by Andy Warhol (1928–1987) were among the first of these to find their way into the gallery scene (Fig. **38.21**). In the fall of 1962, he exhibited 32 uniform 20″ × 16″ canvases, at the Ferus Gallery in Los Angeles. Each depicted one of the 32 different Campbell's Soup "flavors." Even as the paintings debunked the idea of originality—are they Campbell's or Warhol's?—their literalness redefined the American landscape as the visual equivalent of the supermarket aisle. The works were

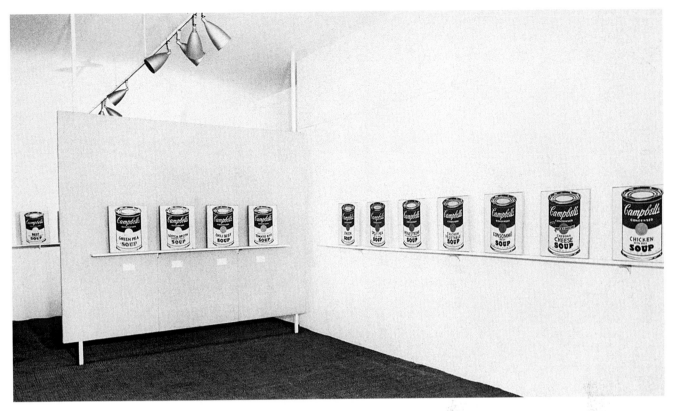

Fig. 38.21 Andy Warhol, Installation view of *Campbell's Soup Cans,* installation at Ferus Gallery. 1962. Founding Collection, The Andy Warhol Museum, Pittsburgh. In order to evoke the way we encounter Campbell's Soup on the grocery shelf, Warhol placed the cans on narrow shelves on the gallery walls.

deliberately opposed to the self-conscious subjectivity of the Abstract Expressionists. It was, in fact, as if the painter had no personality at all. As Warhol himself put it, "If you want to know all about Andy Warhol, just look at the surface of my paintings and films and me, and there I am. There's nothing behind it."

The term Pop Art quickly became attached to work such as Warhol's. Coined in England in the 1950s (see *Closer Look,* pages 1256–1257), it soon came to refer to any art whose theme was essentially the commodification of culture—that is, the marketplace as the dominant force in the creation of "culture." Thus, *Still Life #20* (Fig. **38.22**) by Tom Wesselmann (1931–2004) is contemporaneous with Warhol's *Soup Cans,* though neither was aware of the other until late in 1962, and both are equally "pop." Inside the cabinet with the star stenciled on it—which can be either opened or closed—are actual household items, including a package of SOS scouring pads and a can of Ajax cleanser. Above the blue table on the right, covered with two-dimensional representations (cut out of magazines) of various popular varieties of food and drink, is a reproduction of a highly formalist painting by the Dutch artist Piet Mondrian (see Fig. 37.5). The implication, of course, is that art—once so far removed from everyday life, not even, in this case, referring to the world—has itself become a commodity, not so very different from Coke or a loaf of Lite Diet bread. In fact, the structure and color of Wesselmann's collage subtly reflect the structure and color of

Mondrian's painting, as if the two are simply two different instances of "the same."

By late 1962, Warhol had stopped making his paintings by hand, using a photo-silkscreen process to create the

Fig. 38.22 Tom Wesselmann, *Still Life #20.* 1962. Mixed media, 48″ × 48″ × 5 ¹/₂″ (104.14 × 121.92 × 13.97 cm). Albright-Knox Art Gallery, Buffalo, New York. Gift of Seymour H. Knox, Jr. Art © 2008 Estate of Tom Wesselmann/VAGA, NY. An actual sink faucet and soap dish are incorporated into the composition. Its fluorescent light can be turned on or off.

Fig. 38.23 Andy Warhol, *Marilyn Diptych.* 1962. Oil, acrylic, and silkscreen on enamel on canvas, 6' 8 $^7/_8$" × 4'9". Tate Gallery, London. Art Resource, New York. © 2003 The Andy Warhol Foundation for the Visual Arts/Artists Rights Society (ARS), New York. ™ 2002 Marilyn Monroe LLC under license authorized by CMG Worldwide Inc., Indianapolis, IN 46256 www.MarilynMonroe.com. Warhol was obsessed with Hollywood, especially with the false fabric of fame that it created.

SEE MORE For a Closer Look at Andy Warhol's *Marilyn Diptych*, go to **www.myartslab.com**

images mechanically and employing others to do the work for him in his studio, The Factory. One of the first of these is the *Marilyn Diptych* (Fig. **38.23**). Marilyn Monroe had died, by suicide, in August of that year, and the painting is at once a memorial to her and a commentary on the circumstances that had brought her to despair. She is not so much a person, as Warhol depicts her, but a personality, the creation of a Hollywood studio system whose publicity shot Warhol repeats over and over again here to the point of erasure.

The enlarged comic strip paintings of Roy Lichtenstein [LIK-ten-stine] (1923–1997) are replete with heavy outlines and Ben Day dots, the process created by Benjamin Day at the turn of the century to produce shading effects in mechanical printing. Widely used in comic strips, the dots are, for Lichtenstein, a conscious parody of Seurat's pointillism (see Chapter 33). But they also reveal the

extent to which "feeling" in popular culture is as "canned" as Campbell's Soup. In *Oh, Jeff* . . . (Fig. **38.24**), "love" is emptied of real meaning as the real weight of the message is carried by the final "But. . ." Even the feelings inherent in Abstract Expressionist brushwork came under Lichtenstein's attack (Fig. **38.25**). In fact, Lichtenstein had taught painting to college students, and he discovered that the "authentic" gesture of Abstract Expressionism could easily be taught and replicated without any emotion whatsoever—as a completely academic enterprise.

One of the most inventive of the Pop artists was Claes Oldenburg (1929–), born in Sweden but raised from age seven in Chicago. Inspired by Allan Kaprow's essay "The Legacy of Jackson Pollock," in 1961, he rented a storefront on New York's Lower East Side, and in time for Christmas, opened *The Store*, filled with life-size and

EXPLORE MORE View a studio technique video about silkscreen at **www.myartslab.com**

Fig. 38.24 Roy Lichtenstein, *Oh, Jeff . . . I Love You, Too . . . But. . . .* 1964. Oil on magma on canvas, 4′ × 4′. © Estate of Roy Lichtenstein. The large size of these paintings mirrors the scale of the Hollywood screen and the texture of the common billboard.

Fig. 38.25 Roy Lichtenstein (1923–1997), *Little Big Painting*. 1965. Oil on synthetic polymer on canvas, 70″ × 82″ × 2 ¼″ (177.8 × 208.3 × 5.7 cm). Purchase, with funds from the Friends of the Whitney Museum of America Art. 66.2. Collection of the Whitney Museum of American Art, New York. This "detail" of an imaginary larger painting is nonetheless a giant in its own right.

over-life-size enameled plaster sculptures of everything from pie à la mode, to hamburgers, hats, caps, 7-Up bottles, shirt-and-tie combinations, and slices of cake. "I am for an art," he wrote in a statement accompanying the exhibition,

> that is political-erotica-mystical, that does something other than sit on its ass in a museum.
>
> I am for an art that grows up not knowing it is art at all, an art given the chance of having a starting point of zero.
>
> I am for an art that embroils itself with the everyday crap & still comes out on top. I am for an art that imitates the human, that is comic, if necessary, or violent, or whatever is necessary.
>
> I am for an art that takes its form from the lines of life itself, that twists and extends and accumulates and spits and drips, and is heavy and coarse and blunt and sweet and stupid as life itself.

Admiring the way that cars filled the space of auto showrooms, Oldenburg soon enlarged his objects to the size of cars and started making them out of vinyl stuffed (or not) with foam rubber. These objects toy not only with our sense of scale—a giant lightplug, for instance—but with the tension inherent in making soft something meant to be hard (Fig. **38.26**). They play, further, in almost Surrealist fashion, with notions of sexuality as well—the analogy between inserting a lightplug into its socket and sexual intercourse was hardly lost on Oldenburg, who delighted even more at the image of cultural impotence that his "soft" lightplug implied.

Fig. 38.26 Claes Oldenburg, Swedish, (b. 1929), *Soft Toilet*. 1966. Vinyl, Kapok, Liquitex, Wood, 52 × 32 × 30. Collection of Whitney Museum of American Art, NY. Oldenburg's art is epitomized by his slightly but intentionally vulgar sense of humor.

Fig. 38.27 Frank Stella (American, b. Malden, MA 1936), *Pagosa Springs.* **1960.** Copper metallic (enamel?) and pencil on canvas, 99 ³/₈″ × 99 ¹/₄″ (252.3 × 252.1 cm). Hirshhorn Museum and Sculpture Garden, Smithsonian Institution, Gift of Joseph H. Hirshhorn, 1972. © 2009 Artists Rights Society (ARS), New York. The shaped canvas draws attention to one of the fundamental properties of painting—the support.

LEARN MORE Gain insight from a primary source document from Frank Stella at **www.myartslab.com**

MINIMALISM IN ART

At first it seems that nothing could be further in character from Pop Art than *Pagosa Springs* (Fig. **38.27**), a 1960 painting by Frank Stella (1936–). Stella's work is contemporaneous with Pop, but it seems, in its almost total formality and abstraction—its overtly unsymbolic and minimal means—to turn its back almost entirely on popular culture. It is composed, simply, of copper metallic parallel lines painted carefully between visible pencil marks on an I-shaped canvas. But in its austere geometry and lack of expressive technique, it represents a revolt against the same commodity culture targeted by the Pop artists. In fact, nothing could be further from the onslaught of mass-media images in the culture of consumption than Minimal Art's almost pure and classical geometries. Cool and severe where Pop is brash and sardonic, Minimal Art is nevertheless equally concerned with challenging the presumption that art's meaning originates in the "genius" of the individual artist. If Warhol could say, "just look at the surface of my paintings and . . . and there I am. There's nothing behind it," so Stella would say of paintings such as *Pagosa Springs*: "What you see is what you see. Painting to me is a brush in a bucket and you put it on a surface. There is no other reality for me than that."

Like Warhol producing series of silkscreen works at the Factory, Minimalist artists were also intrigued with utilizing

Fig. 38.28 Carl Andre, 10 × 10 *Altstadt Copper Square.* **1967.** Copper, 100 units, ³/₁₆″ × 19 ¹¹/₁₆″ × 19 ¹¹/₁₆″ each; ³/₁₆″ × 197″ × 197″ overall. Solomon R. Guggenheim Museum, Panza Collection. 91.3673. Space is defined by both the work and the spectator who is free to walk across it.

Fig. 38.29 Sol LeWitt, *Wall Drawing #146A: All two-part combinations of arcs from corners and sides, and straight, not straight, and broken lines within a 36-inch (90 cm) grid*. June 2000. White crayon on blue wall. LeWitt Collection, Chester, Connecticut. Mass MoCA, North Adams, MA. LeWitt conceived of the exhibition at Mass MoCA, of which this drawing is a small part, in 2004, but did not live to see it installed.

the processes of mass production, the use of ready-made materials, the employment of modular units. A sculptural piece by Carl Andre (1935–), *10 × 10 Altstadt Copper Square* (Fig. **38.28**), is composed of 100 identical copper tiles. In form, it closely parallels Warhol's 32 *Soup Cans* or the 50 Marilyns that make up the *Marilyn Diptych*, except that it has no imagery.

The ultimate question Minimalist Art asks is "What, minimally, makes a work of art?" This was not a new question. Marcel Duchamp had posed it with his "ready-mades" (see Fig. 35.5), and so had Kasimir Malevich with his Suprematist paintings (see Fig. 35.9). In many ways, Pop itself was asking the same question: What, after all, made a picture of a soup can or a comic strip "art"? But Minimalist artists stressed the aesthetic quality of their works; they were confident that they were producing works of (timeless) beauty and eloquence. Perhaps most of all, Minimalism invites the viewer to contemplate its sometimes seductively simple beauty. It invites, in other words, the active engagement of the viewer in experiencing it.

This is precisely the point of a room installation at the Massachusetts Museum of Contemporary Art (Mass MoCA) by Sol LeWitt (1928–2007), one of 105 wall drawings installed at the museum in 2008 as part of a survey exhibition of LeWitt's work that will be on display until 2033 (Fig. **38.29**). The piece literally surrounds the viewer, covering every wall of a 26-by-46-foot room. Like the other wall drawings in the exhibition, which cover over one acre of interior walls in a 27,000-square-foot, three-story historic old mill building situated at the heart

of Mass MoCA's campus, the drawing began as a set of instructions to be followed by workers who execute the work independently of the artist. "The idea," LeWitt says, in one of his most famous statements, "becomes the machine that makes the art." The instructions are comparable to a composer's musical score—notations designed to guide those executing the piece as if it were a performance. For *Wall Drawing #146A*, LeWitt proposed a "vocabulary" of 20 different kinds of lines to be combined in pairs of two in order to realize 192 different pairs. His inspiration was the work of photographer Eadweard Muybridge, who in the late nineteenth century created photographic sequences of animals and humans in motion (see Fig. 34.17). "I've long had a strong affinity toward Muybridge," LeWitt has said. "A lot of his ideas appear in my work." In this case, LeWitt captures the sense of a logical, serial movement through space.

Nevertheless, the "art" in works such as Andre's and LeWitt's is extremely matter-of-fact—unmediated, that is, by concerns outside itself. One hardly needs to know of LeWitt's interest in Muybridge to find oneself totally immersed in and engaged by the work. The wall drawing is about the simple beauty of its form, insisting specifically that we pay attention to its order and arrangement. But the order reflected in Andre's and LeWitt's work does not represent belief in a transcendent, universal order, as the work of Mondrian did (see Fig. 37.5). Andre's copper squares and LeWitt's white chalk lines are simply conscious arrangements of parts, without reference to anything outside themselves. To paraphrase Frank Stella: What they are is what they are.

The Civil Rights Movement

Soon after Reconstruction, the period immediately following the Civil War, Southern states passed a group of laws that effectively established a racial caste system that relegated black Americans to second-class status and institutionalized segregation. In the South, the system was known as Jim Crow, but discrimination against blacks was entrenched in the North as well. At the outset of World War II, A. Philip Randolph (1889–1979) had organized a march on Washington "for jobs in national defense and equal integration in the fighting forces." Ten thousand blacks were scheduled to march on July 1, 1941, when President Roosevelt issued Executive Order 8802 on June 25, banning discriminatory hiring practices in the defense industry and the federal government.

But it was not until 1954 that the U.S. Supreme Court ruled that racially segregated schools violated the Constitution. In *Brown v. Board of Education*, the Court found that it was not good enough for states to provide "separate but equal" schools. "Separate educational facilities are inherently unequal," the Court declared, and were in violation of the Fourteenth Amendment to the Constitution's guarantee of equal protection. The Justices called on states with segregated schools to desegregate "with all deliberate speed."

Within a week, the state of Arkansas announced that it would seek to comply with the court's ruling. The state had already desegregated its state university and its law school. Now it was time to desegregate elementary and secondary schools. The plan was for Little Rock Central High School to open its doors to African-American students in the fall of 1957. But on September 2, the night before school was to start, Governor Orval Faubus ordered the state's National Guard to surround the high school and prevent any black students from entering. Faubus claimed he was trying to prevent violence. The nine black students who were planning to attend classes that day decided to arrive together on September 4. Unaware of the plan, Elizabeth Eckford arrived alone (Fig. **38.30**). The others followed, but were all turned away by the Guard. Nearly three weeks later, after a federal injunction ordered Faubus to remove the Guard, the nine finally entered Central High School. Little Rock citizens then launched a campaign of verbal abuse and intimidation to prevent the black students from remaining in school. Finally, President Eisenhower ordered 1,000 paratroopers and 10,000 National Guardsmen to Little Rock, and on September 25, Central High School was officially desegregated. Nevertheless, chaperoned throughout the year by the National Guard, the nine black students were spit at and reviled every day, and none of them returned to school the following year.

The momentum of the civil rights movement really began soon after, on December 1, 1955, when Rosa Parks (1913–2005) was arrested in Montgomery, Alabama, for refusing to move to the Negro section of a bus. Dr. Martin Luther King, then pastor of the Dexter Avenue Baptist Church in Montgomery, called for a boycott of the municipal bus system in protest. The boycott lasted over a year. In November 1956, the U.S. Supreme Court declared that the segregation of buses violated the Fourteenth Amendment. A federal injunction forced Montgomery officials to desegregate their buses, and Dr. King and a white minister rode side by side in the front seat of a city bus, setting the stage for a decade of liberation and change that reached across American society. ■

Fig. 38.30 One of the "Little Rock Nine," Elizabeth Eckford, braves a jeering crowd, September 4, 1957. Alone, as school opened in 1957, Elizabeth Eckford faced the taunts of the crowd defying the Supreme Court order to integrate Central High School in Little Rock, Arkansas. The image captures perfectly the hatred—and the determination—that the civil rights movement inspired.

THINKING BACK

What is existentialism?

After the war, Europe was gripped by a profound pessimism. The existential philosophy of Jean-Paul Sartre was a direct response. What did Sartre mean by the phrase "Existence precedes essence"? He agreed that the human condition is defined by alienation, anxiety, lack of authenticity, and a sense of nothingness, but he said that this did not abrogate the responsibility to act and create meaning. How did Sartre's lifelong companion, Simone de Beauvoir, extend Sartre's argument in *The Second Sex*? Others in Sartre's circle contributed to the existential movement. What existential virtue does Albert Camus's anti-hero Meursault, in *The Stranger*, possess? Sartre's own play *No Exit* and Samuel Beckett's *Waiting for Godot* are examples of the Theater of the Absurd. What are the characteristics of this brand of theater? In art, Alberto Giacometti's emaciated figures seemed to capture the human condition as trapped halfway between being and nothingness. Jean Dubuffet's *art brut*, "raw art," projected a condition of formlessness that reflected the disorder and chaos of the age.

What is Abstract Expressionism?

The unprecedented prosperity of the United States after the war included the introduction of new products and services and the mass adoption of television as the primary form of entertainment. A counternote of sincerity was struck by the Abstract Expressionists. How did they apply Sartre's theories to the act of painting? Jackson Pollock and Willem de Kooning inspired a generation of artists, including their own wives, to abandon representation in favor of directly expressing their emotions on the canvas in totally abstract terms. Color-field painters Mark Rothko and Helen Frankenthaler created more meditative spaces based on large expanses of undifferentiated color. The sculptors Alexander Calder and David Smith created dynamic works that, in the first instance, literally moved, and in the second, required the viewer to move around them.

Who are the Beats?

At the same time, the Beat generation, a younger, more rebellious generation of writers and artists, began to critique American culture. Swiss photographer Robert Frank's *The Americans* revealed a side of American life that outraged a public used to seeing the country through the lens of a happy optimism. Allen Ginsberg lashed out in his poem "Howl" with a forthright and uncensored frankness that seemed to many an affront to decency. What was the nature of the collaboration between composer John Cage, dancer Merce Cunningham, and artist Robert Rauschenberg? What characterizes Rauschenberg's combine paintings? What defines Cage's *4′33″* as music? What are the characteristics of Allan Kaprow's Happenings? In what ways do the American Beats reflect the existentialism of Jean-Paul Sartre?

In architecture, Mies van der Rohe, transplanted from the Bauhaus to Chicago, brought the International Style to America. Frank Lloyd Wright's Solomon R. Guggenheim Museum, however, is a conscious counterstatement to Mies van der Rohe's rationalist geometry, its organic forms echoing the natural world. To the Beats, the architecture of both represented all that was wrong with America. How would you explain their thinking?

What is Pop Art?

Pop Art reflected the commodification of culture and the marketplace as a dominant cultural force. In what terms did Andy Warhol compare Marilyn Monroe to Campbell's soup? How did Tom Wesselmann suggest that painting itself was a commodity? How did Roy Lichtenstein parody Abstract Expressionist painting? Claes Oldenburg created witty reproductions of American goods. How did he change them?

What is Minimalism in art?

Minimalism reduces art to almost total formality and abstraction in terms that at first seem diametrically opposed to Pop Art. But, in fact, Pop Art and Minimalist art have much in common. What values do they share? What differentiates them?

PRACTICE MORE Get flashcards for images and terms and review chapter material with quizzes at **www.myartslab.com**

GLOSSARY

Abstract Expressionism A style of painting practiced by American artists working during and after World War II.

action painting A term coined by critic Harold Rosenberg to reflect his understanding that the Abstract Expressionist canvas was "no longer a picture, but an event."

art brut Literally "raw art," any work unaffected by cultural convention.

atheistic existentialism A philosophy that argues that individuals must define the conditions of their own existence and choose to act ethically even in a world without God.

Beat generation The American poets, writers, and artists of the 1950s who sought a heightened and, they believed, more authentic style of life, defined by alienation, nonconformity, sexual liberation, drugs, and alcohol.

Christian existentialism A philosophy that argues that individuals must define the conditions of their own existence and that religion can provide a "unifying center" for that existence.

combine painting Work created by Robert Rauschenberg beginning in the mid-1950s that combines all manner of materials.

Happening A type of multimedia event in which artists and audience participate as equal partners.

mobile Alexander Calder's suspended sculpture, the movement of which is subject to the unpredictable currents of air.

Theater of the Absurd A theater in which the meaninglessness of existence is the central thematic concern.

READING

READING 38.4

from Samuel Beckett, *Waiting for Godot* (1953)

Beckett wrote Waiting for Godot *between early October 1948 and late January 1949. It was first produced in French in 1953 and in English in 1955. In many respects, the play radically changed theater because, as the following selection suggests, its stage directions are for all practical purposes as important as the actual dialogue. Thus, as Vladimir and Estragon wait for Godot in this scene from the beginning of Act II, contradictions of their interchange with one another are matched by the wide range of feelings Beckett demands of them in his stage directions.*

Enter Vladimir agitatedly. He halts and looks long at the tree, then suddenly begins to move feverishly about the stage. He halts before the boots, picks one up, examines it, sniffs it, manifests disgust, puts it back carefully. Comes and goes. Halts extreme right and gazes into distance off, shading his eyes with his hand. Comes and goes. Halts extreme left, as before. Comes and goes. Halts suddenly and begins to sing loudly.

VLADIMIR: A dog came in—
    Having begun too high he stops, clears his throat, resumes:
    A dog came in the kitchen   10
    And stole a crust of bread.
    Then cook up with a ladle
    And beat him till he was dead.

    Then all the dogs came running
    And dug the dog a tomb—
    He stops, broods, resumes:
    Then all the dogs came running
    And dug the dog a tomb
    And wrote upon the tombstone   20
    For the eyes of dogs to come:

    A dog came in the kitchen
    And stole a crust of bread.
    Then cook up with a ladle
    And beat him till he was dead.

    Then all the dogs came running
    And dug the dog a tomb—
    He stops, broods, resumes:
    Then all the dogs came running
    And dug the dog a tomb—   30
    He stops, broods. Softly.
    And dug the dog a tomb . . .

He remains a moment silent and motionless, then begins to move feverishly about the stage. He halts before the tree, comes and goes, before the boots, comes and goes, halts extreme right, gazes into distance, extreme left, gazes into distance. Enter Estragon right, barefoot, head bowed. He slowly crosses the stage. Vladimir turns and sees him.

VLADIMIR: You again! (*Estragon halts but does not raise his head. Vladimir goes towards him.*) Come here till I embrace you.

ESTRAGON: Don't touch me!   40

Vladimir holds back, pained.

VLADIMIR: Do you want me to go away? (*Pause.*) Gogo! (*Pause. Vladimir observes him attentively.*) Did they beat you? (*Pause.*) Gogo! (*Estragon remains silent, head bowed.*) Where did you spend the night?

ESTRAGON: Don't touch me! Don't question me! Don't speak to me! Stay with me!

VLADIMIR: Did I ever leave you?

ESTRAGON: You let me go.

VLADIMIR: Look at me. (*Estragon does not raise his head. Violently.*) Will you look at me!   50

Estragon raises his head. They look long at each other, then suddenly embrace, clapping each other on the back. End of the embrace. Estragon, no longer supported, almost falls.

ESTRAGON: What a day!

VLADIMIR: Who beat you? Tell me.

ESTRAGON: Another day done with.

VLADIMIR: Not yet.

ESTRAGON: For me it's over and done with, no matter what happens. (*Silence.*) I heard you singing.   60

VLADIMIR: That's right, I remember.

ESTRAGON: That finished me. I said to myself, He's all alone, he thinks I'm gone for ever, and he sings.

VLADIMIR: One is not master of one's moods. All day I've felt in great form. (*Pause.*) I didn't get up in the night, not once!

ESTRAGON: (*sadly*). You see, you piss better when I'm not there.

VLADIMIR: I missed you . . . and at the same time I was happy. Isn't that a strange thing?

ESTRAGON: (*shocked*). Happy?

VLADIMIR: Perhaps it's not quite the right word.   70

ESTRAGON: And now?

VLADIMIR: Now? . . . (*Joyous.*) There you are again . . . (*Indifferent.*) There we are again. . . (*Gloomy.*) There I am again.

ESTRAGON: You see, you feel worse when I'm with you. I feel better alone too.

VLADIMIR: (*Vexed*). Then why do you always come crawling back?

ESTRAGON: I don't know.

VLADIMIR: No, but I do. It's because you don't know how to defend yourself. I wouldn't have let them beat you.   80

ESTRAGON: You couldn't have stopped them.

VLADIMIR: Why not?

ESTRAGON: There was ten of them.

VLADIMIR: No, I mean before they beat you. I would have stopped you from doing whatever it was you were doing.

ESTRAGON: I wasn't doing anything.

VLADIMIR: Then why did they beat you?

ESTRAGON: I don't know.

VLADIMIR: Ah no, Gogo, the truth is there are things that escape you that don't escape me, you must feel it yourself.   90

ESTRAGON: I tell you I wasn't doing anything.

VLADIMIR: Perhaps you weren't. But it's the way of doing it that counts, the way of doing it, if you want to go on living.

ESTRAGON: I wasn't doing anything.

VLADIMIR: You must be happy too, deep down, if you only knew it.

ESTRAGON: Happy about what?

VLADIMIR: To be back with me again.

ESTRAGON: Would you say so?

VLADIMIR: Say you are, even if it's not true.   100

ESTRAGON: What am I to say?

VLADIMIR: Say, I am happy.

ESTRAGON: I am happy.

VLADIMIR: So am I.

ESTRAGON: So am I.

VLADIMIR: We are happy.

ESTRAGON: We are happy. (*Silence.*) What do we do now, now that we are happy?

VLADIMIR: Wait for Godot. (*Estragon groans. Silence.*) Things have changed here since yesterday.   110

ESTRAGON: And if he doesn't come?

VLADIMIR: (*after a moment of bewilderment*). We'll see when the time comes.

READING CRITICALLY

How does Beckett convey a sense of the absurd through his treatment of happiness in this passage?

Multiplicity and Diversity

Cultures of Liberation and Identity in the 1960s and 1970s

THINKING AHEAD

What factors contributed to changes in African-American self-definition in the 1960s?

How did artists respond to the Vietnam War?

How did "high" culture and "popular" culture coexist in the musical world?

How did the feminist movement find expression in the arts?

How did male self-definition come into question?

By April 1963, the focus of the civil rights movement that had begun with Rosa Parks and the Little Rock Nine had shifted to Birmingham, Alabama (Map **39.1**). In protest over desegregation orders, the city had closed its parks and public golf courses. In retaliation, the black community called for a boycott of Birmingham stores. The city responded by halting the distribution of food normally given to the city's needy families. In this progressively more heated atmosphere, the Southern Christian Leadership Conference (SCLC), led by the Reverend Martin Luther King, Jr. (1929–1968), decided Birmingham would be their battlefield. Just a few months later, King would deliver his famous "I Have a Dream" speech to a crowd of more than 200,000 people from the steps of the Lincoln Memorial in Washington, D.C. (Fig. **39.1**). But in the spring of 1963, King led groups of protesters, gathering first at local churches, who descended on the city's downtown both to picket businesses that continued to maintain "separate but equal" practices, such as different fitting rooms for blacks and whites in clothing stores, and to take seats at

Map 39.1 The city of Birmingham, Alabama.

◀ Fig. 39.1 August 28, 1963: American minister and civil rights leader Dr. Martin Luther King, Jr., waves to the crowd of more than 200,000 people gathered on the Mall during the March on Washington after delivering his "I Have a Dream" speech, Washington, D.C. Photo by Hulton Archive/Getty Images.

HEAR MORE Listen to an audio file of your chapter at **www.myartslab.com**

"whites-only" lunch counters. The city's police chief, Bull Connor, responded by threatening to arrest anyone marching on the downtown area. On April 6, 50 marchers were arrested. The next day, 600 marchers gathered, and police confronted them with clubs, attack dogs, and the fire department's new water hoses, which, they bragged, could rip the bark off a tree. But day after day, the marchers kept coming, their ranks swelling. A local judge issued an injunction banning the marches, but on April 12, King led a march of 50 people in defiance of the injunction. Crowds gathered in anticipation of King's arrest, and, in fact, he was quickly taken into custody and placed in solitary confinement in the Birmingham jail.

From jail, King dispatched a letter to a group of local white clergy who had publicly criticized him for willfully breaking the law and promoting demonstrations. Published in June 1963 in *The Christian Century*, what came to be known as the "Letter from Birmingham Jail" became the key text in the civil rights movement, providing the philosophical framework for the massive civil disobedience that King believed was required (**Reading 39.1**):

READING 39.1

from Martin Luther King, "Letter from Birmingham Jail" (1963)

You express a great deal of anxiety over our willingness to break laws . . . [but] there are two types of laws. There are just laws and there are unjust laws. One has not only a legal but a moral responsibility to obey just laws. Conversely, one has a moral responsibility to disobey unjust laws. . . . We can never forget that everything Hitler did in Germany was "legal" and everything the Hungarian freedom fighters did in Hungary was "illegal." It was "illegal" to aid and comfort a Jew in Hitler's Germany.

In the days between King's incarceration and the letter's publication, the situation in Birmingham had worsened. A local disc jockey urged the city's African-American youth to attend a "big party" at Kelly Ingram Park, across from the 16th Street Baptist Church (see Map 39.1). It was no secret that the "party" was to be a mass demonstration. At least 1,000 youth gathered, most of them teenagers but some as young as seven or eight years old. As the chant of "Freedom, freedom *now!*" rose from the crowd, the Birmingham police closed in with their dogs, ordering them to attack those who did not flee.

Police wagons and squad cars were quickly filled with arrested juveniles, and as the arrests continued, the police used school buses to transport over 600 children and teenagers to jail. By the next day, the entire nation—in fact, the entire world—had come to know Birmingham Police Chief Bull Connor, as televised images documented

his dogs attacking children and his fire hoses literally washing them down the streets.

The youth returned, with reinforcements, over the next few days. By May 6, over 2,000 demonstrators were in jail, and police patrol cars were pummeled with rocks and bottles whenever they entered black neighborhoods. As the crisis mounted, secret negotiations between the city and the protestors resulted in change: Within 90 days, all lunch counters, restrooms, department-store fitting rooms, and drinking fountains would be open to all, black and white alike. The 2,000 people under arrest would be released.

It was a victory, but Birmingham remained uneasy. On Sunday, September 15, a dynamite bomb exploded in the basement of the 16th Street Baptist Church, a center for many civil rights rallies and meetings, killing four girls— one 11-year-old and three 14-year-olds. As news of the tragedy spread, riots and fires broke out throughout the city and two more teenagers were killed.

The tragedy drew many moderate whites into the civil rights movement. Popular culture had put them at the ready. In June 1963, the folk-rock trio Peter, Paul, and Mary released "Blowin' in the Wind," their version of the song that Bob Dylan (1941–) had written in April 1962. The Peter, Paul, and Mary record sold 300,000 copies in two weeks. The song famously ends:

How many years can some people exist,
Before they're allowed to be free?
How many times can a man turn his head,
Pretending he just doesn't see?
The answer, my friend, is blowin' in the wind,
The answer is blowin' in the wind.

At the March on Washington later that summer—an event organized by the same A. Philip Randolph who had conceived of a similar event over 20 years earlier, this time to promote passage of the Civil Rights Act—Peter, Paul, and Mary performed the song live before 250,000 people, the largest gathering of its kind to that point in the history of the United States. Not many minutes later, Martin Luther King delivered his famous "I Have a Dream" speech to the same crowd. The trio's album, *In the Wind*, released in October, quickly rose to number one on the charts. The winds of change were blowing across the country.

The civil rights movement that was ignited in Birmingham was just one manifestation of a growing dissatisfaction in America—and abroad—with the status quo, especially among a younger generation that had not experienced the hardships of the Great Depression and the horrors of the Second World War. African-American artist Faith Ringgold (1934–) captures something of the dynamics of this dissatisfaction in her 1964 painting *God Bless America* (Fig. **39.2**). The blue-eyed white woman portrayed in the painting, hand over her heart as she hears the same Irving Berlin song that a generation earlier Woody Guthrie had found jingoistic and elitist (see Chapter 37), embodies the status quo of blind patriotism. But this same woman, the image implies, is also a racist, as on

Fig. 39.4 Jeff Wall, *After* Invisible Man *by Ralph Ellison, "The Preface," Edition of 2*. 1999–2000. Cibachrome transparency, aluminum light box, fluorescent bulbs, 75 ¼" × 106 ¼" × 10 ¼". Marian Goodman Gallery, New York. In his photographic re-creation of the setting of Ellison's novel, Wall emphasizes, as does the novel, the 1,269 light bulbs in the room, all illegally connected to the electricity grid. "I love light," Ellison writes, "perhaps you'll think it strange that an invisible man should need light, desire light, love light. But it is precisely because I am invisible. Light confirms my reality, gives birth to my form." Wall recognizes in these words a definition of photography as well.

loudspeaker blaring a languid blues. I stopped. Was this all that would be recorded? Was this the only true history of the times, a mood blared by trumpets, trombones, saxophones and drums, a song with turgid, inadequate words?

The blues is not enough. His new self-appointed task is to take the responsibility to find words adequate to the history of the times. Up to this point, his own people have been as invisible to him as he to them. He has opened his own eyes as he must now open others'. At the novel's end, he is determined to come out of his "hole." "I'm shaking off the old skin," he says, "and I'll leave it here in the hole. I'm coming out, no less invisible without it, but coming out nevertheless. And I suppose it's damn well time. . . . Perhaps that's my greatest social crime, I've overstayed my hibernation, since there's a possibility that even an invisible man has a socially responsible role to play."

Asserting Blackness in Art and Literature One of Ellison's narrator's most vital realizations is that he must, above all else, assert his blackness instead of hiding from it. He must not allow himself to be absorbed into white society. "Must I strive toward colorlessness?" he asks.

But seriously, and without snobbery, think of what the world would lose if that should happen. America is woven of many strands; I would recognize them and let it so remain. . . . Our fate is to become one, and yet many—This is not prophecy, but description.

There could be no better description of the collages of Romare Bearden (1911–1988), who had worked for two decades in an almost entirely abstract vein, but who in the early 1960s began to tear images out of *Ebony*, *Look*, and *Life* magazines and assemble them into depictions of

Fig. 39.5 Romare Bearden (1914–1988), *The Dove.* **1964.** Cut-and-pasted photoreproductions and papers, gouache, pencil and colored pencil on cardboard, 13 ⅜″ × 18 ¾″. Blanchette Rockefeller Fund. (377.1971). The Museum of Modern Art/Licensed by SCALA/Art Resource, New York. Art © Estate of Romare Bearden/Licensed by VAGA, NY. The white dog at the lower left appears to be stalking the black cat at the foot of the steps in the middle, in counterpoint to the dove above the door.

LEARN MORE Gain insight from a primary source document from Romare Bearden at **www.myartslab.com**

black experience. *The Dove* (Fig. **39.5**)—named for the white dove that is perched over the central door, a symbol of peace and harmony—combines forms of shifting scale and different orders of fragmentation. For example, a giant cigarette extends from the hand of the dandy, sporting a cap, at the right, and the giant fingers of a woman's hand reach over the windowsill at the top left. The resulting effect is almost kaleidoscopic, an urban panorama of a conservatively dressed older generation and hipper, younger people gathered into a scene nearly bursting with energy—the "one, and yet many." As Ellison wrote of Bearden's art in 1968:

> Bearden's meaning is identical with his method. His combination of technique is in itself eloquent of the sharp breaks, leaps of consciousness, distortions, paradoxes, reversals, telescoping of time and surreal blending of styles, values, hopes, and dreams which characterize much of [African] American history.

The sense of a single black American identity, one containing the diversity of black culture within it that

Bearden's work embodies, is also found in the work of poet and playwright Amiri Baraka [buh-RAH-kuh] (1934–). Baraka changed his name from Leroi Jones in 1968 after the assassination of the radical black Muslim minister Malcolm X in 1965. Malcolm X believed that blacks should separate themselves from whites in every conceivable way, that they should give up integration as a goal and create their own black nation. As opposed to Martin Luther King, who advocated nonviolent protest, Malcolm advocated violent action if necessary: "How are you going to be nonviolent in Mississippi," he asked a Detroit audience in 1963, "as violent as you were in Korea? How can you justify being nonviolent in Mississippi and Alabama, when your churches are being bombed, and your little girls are being murdered? . . . If violence is wrong in America, violence is wrong abroad."

Baraka's chosen Muslim name, Imamu Amiri Baraka, refers to the divine blessing associated with Muslim holy men that can be transferred from a material object to a person, so that a pilgrim returning from Mecca is a carrier of *baraka*. Baraka's 1969 poem, "Ka'Ba" [KAH-buh], seeks to imbue *baraka* upon the people of Newark, New Jersey, where Baraka lived (**Reading 39.3**):

READING 39.3

Amiri Baraka, "Ka'Ba" (1969)

A closed window looks down
on a dirty courtyard, and Black people
call across or scream across or walk across
defying physics in the stream of their will.

Our world is full of sound
Our world is more lovely than anyone's
tho we suffer, and kill each other
and sometimes fail to walk the air.

We are beautiful people
With African imaginations
full of masks and dances and swelling chants
with African eyes, and noses, and arms
tho we sprawl in gray chains in a place
full of winters, when what we want is sun.

We have been captured,
and we labor to make our getaway, into
the ancient image; into a new

Correspondence with ourselves
and our Black family. We need magic
now we need the spells, to raise up
return, destroy, and create. What will be

the sacred word?

The sacred word, the poem's title suggests, is indeed "Ka'Ba." But, despite the spiritual tone of this poem, Baraka became increasingly militant during the 1960s. In 1967, he produced two of his own plays protesting police brutality. A year later, in his play *Home on the Range*, his protagonist Criminal breaks into a white family's home only to find them so immersed in television that he cannot communicate with them. The play was performed as a benefit for the leaders of the Black Panther party, a black revolutionary political party founded in 1966 by Huey P. Newton (1942–1989) and Bobby Seale (1936–) and dedicated to organizing support for a socialist revolution.

Other events, too, reflected the growing militancy of the African-American community. In August 1965, violent riots in the Watts district of South Central Los Angeles lasted for six days, leaving 34 dead, over 1,000 people injured, nearly 4,000 arrested, and hundreds of buildings destroyed. In July 1967, rioting broke out in both Newark and Detroit. In Newark, six days of rioting left 23 dead, over 700 injured, and close to 1,500 people arrested. In Detroit, five days of rioting resulted in 43 people dead, 1,189 injured, over 7,000 people arrested, and 2,509 stores looted or burned. Finally, it seemed to many that Martin Luther King's pacifism had come back to haunt him when he was assassinated on April 4, 1968.

It was directly out of this climate that the popular poetry/music/performance/dance phenomenon known as rap, or hip-hop, came into being. Shortly after the death of Martin Luther King, on Malcolm X's birthday, May 19, 1968, David Nelson, Gylan Kain, and Abiodun Oyewole founded the group the Last Poets, named after a poem by South African poet Willie Kgositsile (1938–) in which he had claimed that it would soon be necessary to put poetry aside and take up guns in the looming revolution. "Therefore we are the last poets of the world," Kgositsile concluded. In performance, the Last Poets were deeply influenced by the musical phrasings of Amiri Baraka's poetry. They improvised individually, trading words and phrases back and forth like jazz musicians improvising on each other's melodies, until their voices would come together in a rhythmic chant and the number would end. Most of all, they were political, attacking white racism, black bourgeois complacency, the government and the police, whoever seemed to stand in the way of significant progress for African Americans. As Abiodun Oyewole put it, "We were angry, and we had something to say."

Equally influential was performer Gil Scott-Heron, whose recorded poem "The Revolution Will Not Be Televised" appeared on his 1970 album *Small Talk at 125th and Lenox* (**Reading 39.4**):

READING 39.4

from Gil Scott-Heron, "The Revolution Will Not Be Televised" (1970)

You will not be able to stay home, brother.
You will not be able to plug in, turn on and cop out.[1]
You will not be able to lose yourself on skag[2] and
skip out for beer during commercials because
The revolution will not be televised.

The revolution will not be televised.
The revolution will not be brought to you by Xerox
    in 4 parts without commercial interruptions. . . .
There will be no highlights on the Eleven O'clock News
and no pictures of hairy armed women liberationists
and Jackie Onassis blowing her nose.
The theme song will not be written by Jim Webb or
    Francis Scott Key,
nor sung by Glen Campbell, Tom Jones, Johnny Cash,
Englebert Humperdink, or Rare Earth.
The revolution will not be televised.

[1]**turn on and cop out:** A play on the motto of Timothy Leary (1920–1996), advocate and popularizer of the psychedelic drug LSD, who in the 1960s urged people to "turn on, tune in, drop out."
[2]**skag:** Slang for heroin.

The revolution will not be right back after a message
    about a white tornado, white lightning or white people.
You will not have to worry about a dove in your
    bedroom,
a tiger in your tank, or the giant in your toilet bowl.
The revolution will not go better with coke.
The revolution will not fight the germs that may cause
    bad breath.
The revolution *will* put you in the driver's seat.
The revolution will not be televised,
will not be televised,
  not be televised,
    be televised.
The revolution will be no re-run, brothers;
The revolution will be LIVE.

As the next section of this chapter underscores, as angry as Scott-Heron's poem is, the poet's attitude toward American popular culture, which he strongly condemns, is closely aligned with that of Pop artists of the 1960s as well (see Chapter 38).

THE VIETNAM WAR: REBELLION AND THE ARTS

Even as the civil rights movement took hold, the Cold War tensions with the Soviet Union were increasingly exacerbated by the United States' involvement in the war in Vietnam. By the mid-1960s, fighting between the North Vietnamese Communists led by Ho Chi Minh and the pro-Western and former French colony of South Vietnam (see Chapter 37) had led to a massive troop buildup of American forces in the region, fueled by a military draft that alienated many American youth, the population of 15- to 24-year-olds that over the course of the 1960s increased from 24.5 million to 36 million.

Across the country, the spirit of rebellion that fueled the civil rights movement took hold on college campuses and in the burgeoning antiwar community. Events at the University of California at Berkeley served to link, in the minds of many, the antiwar movement and the fight for civil rights. In 1964, the university administration tried to stop students from recruiting and raising funds on campus for two groups dedicated to ending racial discrimination. Protesting the administration's restrictions, a group of students organized the Free Speech Movement, which initiated a series of rallies, sit-ins, and student strikes at Berkeley. The administration backed down, and the Berkeley students' tactics were quickly adapted by groups in the antiwar movement, which focused on removing the Reserve Officers' Training Corps from college campuses and helped to organize antiwar marches, teach-ins, and rallies across the country. By 1969, feelings reached a fever pitch, as over a half million protesters, adopting the tactics of the civil rights movement in 1963, marched on Washington.

Kurt Vonnegut's *Slaughterhouse-Five*

Antiwar sentiment was reflected in the arts in works primarily about earlier wars, World War II and Korea, as if it were impossible to deal directly with events in Southeast Asia, which could be seen each night on the evening news. Joseph Heller's novel *Catch-22* was widely read, and the Robert Altman (1925–2006) film *M*A*S*H*, a smash-hit satiric comedy about the 4077th Mobile Army Surgical Hospital in Korea, opened in 1970 and spawned an 11-year-long television series that premiered in 1972. But perhaps the most acclaimed antiwar work was the 1969 novel *Slaughterhouse-Five* by Kurt Vonnegut [VON-uh-gut] (1922–2007). It is the oddly narrated story of ex–World War II GI Billy Pilgrim, a survivor, like Vonnegut himself, of the Allied fire-bombing of Dresden [DREZ-den] (where 135,000 German civilians were killed, more than at Hiroshima and Nagasaki combined). Pilgrim claims to have been abducted by extraterrestrial aliens from the planet of Trafalmadore. At the beginning of the book, the narrator (more or less, Vonnegut himself) is talking with a friend about the war novel he is about to write (*Slaughterhouse-Five*), when the friend's wife interrupts (**Reading 39.5**):

READING 39.5

from Kurt Vonnegut, *Slaughterhouse-Five* (1969)

"You'll pretend that you were men instead of babies, and you'll be played in the movies by . . . John Wayne. . . . And war will look just wonderful, so we'll have a lot more of them. And they'll be fought by babies. . . ." She didn't want her babies or anyone else's babies killed in wars. And she thought wars were partly encouraged by books and movies.

In response, Vonnegut creates, in Pilgrim, the most innocent of heroes, and subtitles his novel: *The Children's Crusade: A Duty-Dance with Death*. Pilgrim's reaction to the death he sees everywhere—"So it goes"—became a mantra for the generation that came of age in the late 1960s. The novel's fatalism mirrored the sense of pointlessness and arbitrariness that so many felt in the face of the Vietnam War.

Artists Against the War

In the minds of many, the Vietnam War was symptomatic of a more general cultural malaise for which the culture of consumption, the growing dominance of mass media, and the military-industrial complex were all responsible. Among many others, Pop artist James Rosenquist explicitly

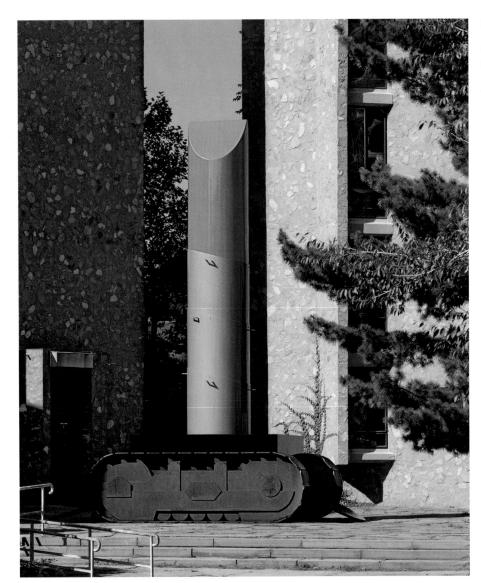

Fig. 39.6 Claes Oldenburg, *Lipstick (Ascending) on Caterpillar Tracks.* 1969. Cor-Ten steel, steel, aluminum; coated with resin and painted with polyurethane enamel. 23' 6" × 24' 11" × 10' 11" (7.16 × 7.58 × 3.33 m). Collection Yale University Art Gallery, Gift of Colossal Keepsake Corporation. Photo by Attilio Maranzano. © 2008 Oldenburg Van Bruggen Foundation, NY. Initially made of a soft material that would slowly deflate until someone wishing to speak from the sculpture's platform pumped it up with air to attract attention, the lipstick was constructed of more permanent materials when the piece was reinstalled in 1974.

tied the American military to American consumer culture (see *Closer Look*, pages 1290–1291).

The establishment itself, especially as embodied by university administrations and their boards of trustees, was often the target of protests. Just such a work was Pop artist Claes Oldenburg's *Lipstick (Ascending) on Caterpillar Tracks* (Fig. **39.6**). The work was pulled into a central square at Yale University, Oldenburg's alma mater, in the fall of 1969 to stand in front of a World War I monument inscribed with the words "In Memory of the Men of Yale who True to her Traditions Gave their Lives that Freedom Might not Perish from the Earth." In Oldenburg's typically audacious way, the piece consists of a three-story-high inflatable lipstick tube mounted on tank-like caterpillar treads. At once a missile-shaped phallic symbol and a wry commentary on the fact that Yale had admitted women to the university for the first time that fall, it was commissioned by the university's architecture graduate students as an antiwar demonstration. Yale authorities were not amused, and had the

piece removed before convocation (though it was subsequently reinstalled on campus in 1974).

By the fall of 1969, many other artists had organized in opposition to the war. In a speech at an opening hearing that led to the creation of the antiwar Art Workers' Coalition, art critic and editor Gregory Battcock outlined how the art world was complicit in the war effort:

> The trustees of the museums direct NBC and CBS, The New York Times, and the Associated Press, and that greatest cultural travesty of modern times—the Lincoln Center. They own AT&T, Ford, General Motors, the great multi-billion dollar foundations, Columbia University, Alcoa, Minnesota Mining, United Fruit, and AMK, besides sitting on the boards of each other's museums. The implications of these facts are enormous. Do you realize that it is those art-loving, culturally committed trustees of the Metropolitan and the Modern museums who are waging the war in Vietnam?

For Pop artist James Rosenquist (1933–) the society of the spectacle is above all a society of billboards, which, in fact, he once painted for a living. "Painting," he says, "is probably much more exciting than advertising, so why shouldn't it be done with that power and gusto, with that impact?" The mammoth *F-111* possesses precisely the impact Rosenquist was seeking.

The painting was specifically designed as a wraparound work, like Monet's *Water Lilies* murals (see Chapter 33), for Rosenquist's first solo exhibition at the Leo Castelli Gallery in New York, where it filled all four walls of the space. It depicts an F-111 fighter bomber at actual scale, "flying," in

Rosenquist's words, "through the flack of an economy." In 1964, when Rosenquist was at work on the piece, the F-111, although still in its planning stages, was understood to be obsolete. Nevertheless, production continued on it, by and large to keep those working on it employed and General Dynamics, the company responsible for it, afloat. In his farewell address to the nation in January 1961, President Dwight David Eisenhower (1890–1969) had warned: "This conjunction of an immense military establishment and a large arms industry is new in the American experience. The total influence—economic, political, even spiritual—is felt in every city, every statehouse, every office

SEE MORE For a Closer Look at James Rosenquist's *F-111*, go to **www.myartslab.com**

James Rosenquist (b. 1933), *F-111.* **1964–65.** Oil on canvas with aluminum, 10′ × 86′ overall. Purchase Gift of Mr. and Mrs. Alex L. Hillman and Lillie P. Bliss Bequest (both by exchange). (00473.96.a-w). Digital Image © The Museum of Modern Art/Licensed by SCALA/Art Resource, NY. © Art James Rosenquist/VAGA Visual Artists Galleries & Association, NY.

The aluminum panels on this end of the painting would have met up with the strip of aluminum panels at the other end of the painting when installed around the four walls of a gallery. They not only evoke industry, but their reflective quality incorporates viewers into the painting's space, implicating them in the artist's critique of American culture. The scale of the painting makes it impossible to take it all in at once; viewers are always aware that there is more work in their peripheral vision. "I'm interested in contemporary vision," Rosenquist has explained, "the flick of chrome, reflections, rapid associations, quick flashes of light. Bing-bang! Bing-bang!"

The Italian flowered wallpaper, according to Rosenquist, "had to do with atomic fallout."

A runner's hurdle is meant to evoke the arms race.

The Firestone tire, according to Rosenquist, resembles a "crown," becoming a symbol of the supremacy and power of corporate America, the military-industrial complex that Eisenhower warned against. By emphasizing the tire's tread, Rosenquist focuses our attention on the sense of safety that corporate America claimed to provide consumers.

The angel food cake is decorated, stadiumlike, with little pennants listing food additives such as riboflavin and Vitamin D. One even boasts "Food Energy." The chemical manipulation of food is Rosenquist's target here, together with the lack of any real food value in sugar-laden "angel" food.

The three light bulbs can probably best be explained by a comment Rosenquist made in an interview in the *Partisan Review* in 1965: "All the ideas in the whole picture are very divergent, but I think they all seem to go toward some basic meaning . . . [toward] some blinding light, like a bug hitting a light bulb." They also evoke consumer culture and corporations like General Electric or Westinghouse that were also major defense contractors.

James Rosenquist (b. 1933), *F-111,* 1964–65. Oil on canvas with aluminum, twenty-three sections, 10′ × 86′ (304.8 × 2621.3 cm). Gift of Mr. and Mrs. Alex L. Hillman and Lillie P. Bliss Bequest (both by exchange). (473.1996.a-w) The Museum of Modern Art, New York. Digital Image. The Museum of Modern Art/Licensed by SCALA/Art Resource, New York. Art © Estate of James Rosenquist/VAGA, NY. For its MoMA exhibition in 2000, the painting turned one corner to fill two walls, but did not wrap around the viewer on four walls as originally exhibited.

of the federal government. . . . In the councils of government, we must guard against the acquisition of unwarranted influence, whether sought or unsought, by the military-industrial complex. The potential for the disastrous rise of misplaced power exists and will persist." It is precisely this military-industrial complex and its pervasiveness throughout American consumer culture that Rosenquist's painting addresses. As the Vietnam War escalated, and the painting traveled to eight museums in Europe, the painting became more generally associated with the antiwar movement. It returned to the United States in 1968, and remains on display at New York's Museum of Modern Art.

The bars of the Air Force logo, on each side of the hairdryer, function like equal signs in the picture.

"The little girl," Rosenquist says, "was the pilot under a hairdryer." She is also a figure, he says, for "a generation removed, the post-Beat young people. They're not afraid of atomic war and think that sort of attitude is passé, that it won't occur." Thus she smiles happily, her face turned away from the mushroom cloud behind her. She also represents consumer economy, the idea of female beauty, and female passivity in general—the opposite of the phallic jet fighter.

The umbrella, like the Italian flowered wallpaper, is meant to suggest both the defense umbrella of national security and atomic fallout, from which it offers no real protection.

"The swimmer gulping air," Rosenquist explains, "was like searching for air during an atomic holocaust." Visually it echoes the atomic mushroom cloud to its left.

A plate of Franco-American canned spaghetti lies behind the nose of the plane like a pile of entrails. "Franco-American" also suggests French and American involvement in the Vietnam War.

Something to Think About . . .

Rosenquist's enormous painting also makes reference, in its technique as well as its size, to the highway billboard. What makes this appropriate?

Fig. 39.7 Ron Haeberle, Peter Brandt, and the Art Workers' Coalition, *Q. And Babies? A. And Babies.* 1970. Offset lithograph, 24″ × 38″. The Museum of Modern Art, New York. Gift of the Benefit for the Attica Defense Fund. Brandt was the poster's designer.

In other words, the museums embodied, in the minds of many, the establishment politics that had led to the war in the first place. On October 15, 1969, the first Vietnam Moratorium Day, artists managed to close the Museum of Modern Art, the Whitney Museum, and the Jewish Museum, but the Metropolitan and the Guggenheim refused to close.

The Art Workers' Coalition also quickly reacted to reports that American soldiers, the men of Charlie Company, had slaughtered men, women, and children in the Vietnam village of My Lai on March 16, 1968. Over a year later, in November 1969, as the army was investigating Charlie's Company's platoon leader, First Lieutenant William L. Calley, Jr., photographs taken at My Lai by army photographer Ron Haeberle appeared in the *Cleveland Plain Dealer.* Four days later, in an interview by Mike Wallace on CBS-TV, Paul Meadlo, who had been at My Lai, reported that Lt. Calley had rounded up 40 or 45 villagers and ordered them shot. "Men, women, and children?" Wallace asked. "Men, women, and children," Meadlo answered. "And babies?" "And babies." The transcript of the interview was published the next day in the *New York Times,* accompanied by the photograph. Quickly, the Art Workers' Coalition added Wallace's question and Meadlo's response to the image (Fig. **39.7**), printed a poster, and distributed it around the world.

Conceptual Art

Rather than attacking the museums directly, another strategy designed to undermine the art establishment emerged—making art that was objectless, art that was conceived as either uncollectible or unbuyable, either intangible, temporary, or existing beyond the reach of the museum and gallery system that artists in the antiwar movement believed was, at least in a de facto way, supporting the war. The strategies for creating this objectless art had already been developed by a number of artists who, reacting to the culture of consumption, had chosen to stop making works of art that could easily enter the marketplace. In the catalogue for an exhibition entitled "January 5–31, 1969," a show consisting, in fact, of its catalog but no objects, artist Douglas Huebler (1924–1997) wrote: "The world is full of objects, more or less interesting: I do not wish to add any more." In this way, he sidestepped both the museum and the individual collector. His *Duration Piece #13,* for instance, consists of one hundred $1 bills listed by serial number and put into circulation throughout the world, the serial numbers to be reprinted 25 years later in an art magazine. Each person holding one of the bills would receive a $1,000 reward.

In light of such works, critics began to speak of "the dematerialization of art" and "the death of painting," even as California artist John Baldessari (1931–) destroyed 13 years worth of his paintings, cremating them at a mortuary. The following year, he created a lithograph with the single phrase "I will not make any more boring art" written over and over again across its surface.

Land Art

Closely related to both the conceptualists and the minimalists (see Chapter 38) are those artists who, in the 1960s, began to make site-specific art. (Such art defines itself in relation to the particular place for which it was conceived.) Many of these were earthworks, conceived as enormous mounds and excavations made in the remote regions of the American West. One of the primary motivations for making them was to escape the gallery system. In an essay published in 1972, Robert Smithson (1938–1973) put it this way: "A work of art when placed in a gallery loses its charge, and becomes a portable object or surface disengaged from the outside world. . . . Works of art seen in such spaces . . . are looked upon as so many inanimate invalids, waiting for critics to declare them curable or incurable. The function of the warden-curator is to separate art from society. Next comes integration. Once the work of art is totally neutralized, ineffective, abstracted, safe, and politically lobotomized it is ready to be consumed by society."

Robert Smithson's *Spiral Jetty* One of the most famous of works designed specifically to escape the gallery system is Smithson's *Spiral Jetty* (Fig. **39.8**), created in 1970. Using dump trucks to haul rocks and dirt, Smithson created a simple spiral form in the Great Salt Lake. The work is intentionally outside the gallery system, in the landscape—and a relatively inaccessible and inhospitable portion of the Utah landscape at that. Smithson chose the site, on the shores of the Great Salt Lake about 100 miles north of Salt Lake City and 15 miles south of the Golden Spike National Historic Monument, where the Eastern and Western railroads met in 1869, connecting both sides of the American continent by rail, because, in his mind, it was the very image of *entropy*, the condition of decreasing organization or deteriorating order. For Smithson, the condition of entropy is not only the hallmark of the modern, but the eventual fate of all things—"an ironic joke of nature," as one historian has described the lake, "water that is itself more desert than a desert."

Smithson's work on the jetty in fact coincided with the rise of ecology as a wider public issue. On April 22, 1970, the first Earth Day inaugurated the environmental movement, which could trace its roots back to the publication, in 1953, of Eugene P. Odum's textbook *The Fundamentals of Ecology* but, more importantly, in terms of its wide popularity,

to the 1962 publication of a book by Rachel Carson (1907–1964), *Silent Spring*, first serialized in three issues of *The New Yorker* magazine. Carson was a marine biologist who had previously published a series of meditative books on the sea that serve as models of nature writing to this day. But *Silent Spring* was far more polemical, arguing that the introduction of synthetic pesticides, particularly DDT, into the environment threatened human life itself.

Smithson's jetty was, as a result, widely understood as a work of environmental art. Humans had already degraded the site: Jetties had once stretched out into the lake to serve now-abandoned oil derricks. As Smithson wrote not long after completing the *Spiral Jetty*, "Across the country there are many mining areas, disused quarries, and polluted lakes and rivers. One practical solution for the utilization of such devastated places would be land and water re-cycling in terms of 'Earth Art.'"

As he was constructing the jetty, Smithson made a film of the event. The typical camera angle is aerial, looking straight down at the surface of the lake from above, so that the spiral seems to lie flat, like a two-dimensional design. The image reinforces the spiral's status as one of the most widespread of all ornamental and symbolic designs on Earth, suggesting, too, the motion of the cosmos. The spiral is also found in three main natural forms: expanding like a nebula, contracting like a whirlpool, or ossified as in a snail's shell. Smithson's work suggests the ways in which these contradictory forces are simultaneously at work in the universe.

At the end of the film, a helicopter follows Smithson as he runs out the length of the spiral in a dizzying swirl of cinematography that leaves the viewer unsure which direction is which. When Smithson arrives at the center of the

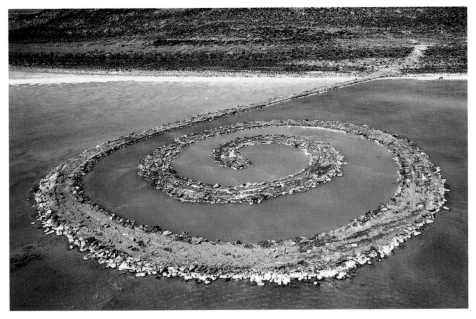

Fig. 39.8 Robert Smithson, *Spiral Jetty*, Great Salt Lake, Utah. April 1970. Black rock , salt crystals, earth, red water (algae). 3 $^1/_2$' × 15' × 1500'. Art © Estate of Robert Smithson/Licensed by VAGA, New York. Courtesy James Cohan Gallery, New York. Collection: DIA Center for the Arts, New York. Photo: Gianfranco Goroni. Smithson's film of the *Jetty*'s construction mirrors the earthwork not only by imaging it, but, as a spiral loop of 16mm film, by formally mirroring its structure.

spiral, he pauses, breathless, then turns to walk back, a purposefully deflated image of purposelessness, the very image of the tensions between motion and stasis, entropy and creation, expansion and contraction, even life and death, that inform Smithson's work.

Michael Heizer's New Sublime One of Smithson's good friends, Michael Heizer (1944–), preferred working in the desert landscapes of Nevada. In the summer of 1968, accompanied by Smithson, he made a 520-mile-long series of loops, troughs, and other intrusions into the desert landscape, connecting nine separate dry lake beds on government-owned land along the California–Nevada border. In 1969, however, he conceived of a much more ambitious project. On property purchased by Virginia Dwan, whose gallery was the first to support earthworks created precisely to avoid the gallery space, Heizer carved two notches out of the side of the Virgin River Mesa about 80 miles northeast of Las Vegas, Nevada. The two notches face each other across a broad escarpment. They were excavated with dynamite and bulldozers, which pushed the soil and rock from the troughs into the chasm below. Originally 42 feet deep and 30 feet wide, Heizer expanded them the following year, making them 50 feet deep and thus extending the length of the work from the top of one trough, down and across the escarpment and up the other side to 1,500 feet. He called the work *Double Negative*—literally, two minus signs on each side of the escarpment, but also, grammatically, two negatives that cancel each other out to produce an affirmative (Fig. **39.9**).

To this day, in fact, many see this work as a desecration of the landscape. But if originally the work's perpendicular walls and rigid geometry underscored the impact of human intervention on the environment in a negative sense, today, some 40 years after the fact, as the walls have given way to the vicissitudes of weather and time and crumbled to floors of the troughs, it is quite clear that at least one of Heizer's goals was to draw attention to the difference between the relative brevity of human time and the vastness of geological time. For the impact of *Double Negative* on the environment is actually minimal beside the deep cut that the Virgin River has, over the millennia, gorged out of the Nevada desert. In fact, it is quite clear that *Double Negative* will one day disappear, absorbed by the erosion of the mesa's escarpment. To come to such an understanding is to confront the sublime. As John Beardsley, one of the major historians of land art, has put it: "*Double Negative*, in fact, provides the experience of awe inspiring vastness, solitude, and silence that has long been associated with the sublime. . . . [It] is thus somewhat paradoxical: executed in a contemporary geometric idiom, meant to refute the artistic conventions and escape the economic fate of traditional sculpture, it nevertheless evoked some very familiar metaphors of American landscape."

Temporary Intrusions: Christo and Jeanne-Claude If Heizer's works evoke the vastness of time, the works of Christo (1935–) and Jeanne-Claude (1935–2009) seem to evoke, instead, time's very passing and the fragility of human experience. Christo and Jeanne-Claude's works are literally here today and gone tomorrow, leaving no lasting footprint on the landscape and impacting the environment minimally if at all—considering the enormous scale at which they work, an extraordinary feat. *Running Fence*, which took nearly five years to realize, from 1972 to 1976, is a case in point (Fig. **39.10**). Eighteen feet high and running

Fig. 39.9 Michael Heizer, *Double Negative*. 1969–70. 240,000-ton displacement of rhyolite and sandstone, 1500' × 50' × 30'. The Museum of Contemporary Art, Los Angeles. Gift of Virginia Dwan. 85.105. Location: Mormon Mesa, Overton, Nevada. The work was owned by Dwan and Heizer until 1985, when it was donated to the Museum of Contemporary Art in Los Angeles.

Fig. 39.10 Christo and Jeanne-Claude, *Running Fence*, Sonoma and Marin Counties, California. 1972–76. Photo: Jeanne-Claude. © 1976 Christo. Perhaps the most compelling aspect of *Running Fence* is the way its line defines the contour of the landscape, making it visible as if for the first time.

for 24.5 miles through Sonoma and Marin Counties in Northern California, it extended from US Route 101 across 14 other roadways and the rolling hills of 59 private ranches until descending into the Pacific Ocean at Bodega Bay. It required more than 2.2 million square feet of white nylon fabric, hung from a steel cable stretched between 2,050 steel poles. It stood in place for 14 days, from September 10 to September 24, 1976. All expenses for the temporary work of art were paid by Christo and Jeanne-Claude through the sale of studies, preparatory drawings and collages, scale models, and original lithographs. On the occasion of the 2010 exhibition at the Smithsonian American Art Museum, "Christo and Jeanne-Claude: Remembering the *Running Fence*," Christo explained the thinking behind both the site-specificity of the work and its temporary qualities: "This project is entirely designed for that specific landscape and nothing can be transported. Nobody can buy the work, nobody can own the work, and nobody can charge tickets for the work. We do not own the projects, they are beyond the ownership of the artists because freedom is the enemy of possession, that's why these projects do not stay. They are absolutely related to artistic and aesthetic freedom."

One of the primary features of *Running Fence*—and all of Christo and Jeanne-Claude's work—is the public debate and buy-in that was required to execute it, including the ranchers' participation, 18 public hearings, three sessions at the Superior Courts of California, and the drafting of a 450-page Environmental Impact Report. The debate about the work's merits as art, the spirit of collaboration that resulted, and, perhaps above all, the stories and memories that the piece subsequently evoked (including Albert and David Maysles's extraordinary documentary film of the project, released in 1978), are all equally part and parcel of the work itself. But the tranquility and beauty of the *Running Fence*—to say nothing of the sense of community and cooperation it embodied—could, finally, be taken as a counterstatement to the political climate in which it was realized. In fact, the poles used to construct the fence were Vietnam surplus, used in the construction of military airports in Vietnam, and Christo and Jeanne-Claude were able to purchase them from the Army for $42 each. Then, after the *Fence* was dismantled, the local ranchers used them for their own fences and to build cattle guards. *Running Fence* thus literally transformed war materials into artistic and peaceable use.

The Music of Youth and Rebellion

Given the involvement of American youth in the antiwar movement, it was natural that their music—rock and roll—helped to fuel the fires of their increasingly passionate expressions of dismay at American foreign policy. Rock-and-roll music had, after all, originated in an atmosphere of youthful rebellion. Beginning at the end of the 1940s, it gained increasing popularity in the 1950s when the gyrating hips and low-slung guitar of one of its earliest stars, Elvis Presley (1935–1977), made the music's innuendo of youthful sexual rebellion explicit. In the 1960s, led by the Beatles, British rock bands (including Led Zeppelin and the Rolling Stones) transformed rock into the musical idiom of a youthful counterculture that embraced sex, drugs, and rock 'n' roll.

Fig. 39.11 Bonnie MacLean, *Six Days of Sound*. December 26–31, 1967. Poster. © Bill Graham Archives, LLC. All rights reserved. The lineup of artists includes the Doors, Freedom Highway, Chuck Berry, Salvation, Big Brother & the Holding Company, Quicksilver Messenger Service, and Jefferson Airplane.

Audiences at most concerts openly smoked marijuana, and hallucinogenic mushrooms and LSD, a semisynthetic psychedelic drug which was not made illegal in the United States until 1967, were regularly used by rock groups such as the Beatles, the Doors, Pink Floyd, the Grateful Dead, and Jefferson Airplane. The Airplane's "White Rabbit," which appeared on their 1967 album *Surrealistic Pillow*, draws clear analogies between the experiences of Alice in Lewis Carroll's *Alice's Adventures in Wonderland* and the hallucinatory effects of taking LSD. And in their self-titled debut album of 1967, the Velvet Underground describes in dark, almost sardonic terms, which would deeply influence the later punk movement, the heroin addiction of its leader, Lou Reed (1942–).

One of the great promoters of rock in the 1960s was Bill Graham (1931–1991), a refugee from Nazi Germany who was raised by foster parents in New York City. Graham operated two rock venues in San Francisco, the Fillmore West and Winterland, and another in New York, the Fillmore East. Almost every major rock group of the era performed in these halls, and the posters Graham commissioned for these concerts became the emblems of the era.

Bonnie MacLean, a recent graduate of Penn State, was one of the founders of the Fillmore poster "look." Her poster for *Six Days of Sound* (Fig. 39.11), a Christmas-to-New-Year's celebration in 1967, captures the mood of the era. Deeply indebted to Art Nouveau posters by artists such as Jan Toorop (see Fig. 33.5), many of the posters convey the same sexual energy as Art Nouveau, but combined with a spirit of political protest. In her right hand, the long-haired lady of MacLean's poster carries mistletoe; in her left, the peace sign, large and colored red and green, a Christmas ornament that she is about to hang from the branches of a Christmas tree.

The presence of the peace sign in the Fillmore poster is not only appropriate to the season—"Peace on earth, goodwill to men"—but signals the intimate association between rock music and the antiwar movement. As in the civil rights March on Washington in 1963, which was highlighted by Peter, Paul, and Mary's rendition of Bob Dylan's "Blowin' in the Wind" in front of the Lincoln Memorial, most peace marches concluded in large public spaces where speakers and bands alternately shared the stage. The peace march in San Francisco on the nationwide Vietnam Moratorium Day, November 15, 1969, concluded at Golden Gate Park, where, among others, Crosby, Stills, Nash, & Young performed. A quarter of a million people attended. That same day, a half million people marched in Washington, D.C. (and in Columbus, Ohio, Dave Thomas opened the first Wendy's restaurant).

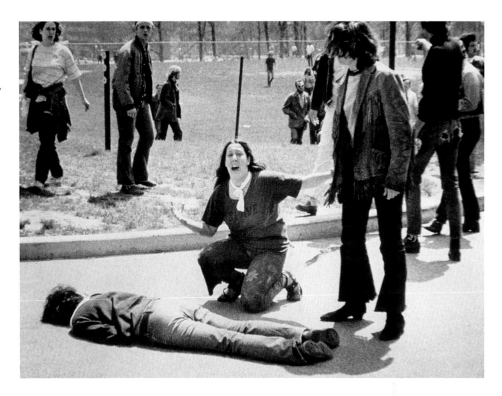

Fig. 39.12 John Paul Filo, *Kent State—Girl Screaming over Dead Body.* **May 4, 1970.** Collection of John Paul Filo. Filo's photograph appeared on the cover of *Newsweek* on May 18, 1970, beside the headline "Nixon's Home Front." Filo was awarded the Pulitzer Prize in photography for his work at Kent State.

The quartet of David Crosby (1941–), Stephen Stills (1945–), Graham Nash (1942–), and Neil Young (1945–) had come together just months before. Their first performance together was at the Fillmore East in July, their second at Woodstock in August.

The Woodstock Festival, held on a 600-acre dairy farm outside Woodstock, New York, from August 15 to August 18, 1969, known soon after, by the subtitle of the film documenting it, as "3 Days of Peace and Music," has, for an entire generation, become legendary. Approximately 500,000 people attended—and thousands more claim to have been there. On both Saturday, August 16, and Sunday, August 17, bands played all night. Crosby, Stills, Nash, & Young began their 16-song set at 3 AM on Sunday, a marathon evening that concluded on Monday morning with guitarist Jimi Hendrix playing his notorious version of "The Star-Spangled Banner" on a wailing, weeping, whining electric guitar that to conservative ears seemed a direct assault on American tradition.

Perhaps as important as the event itself was the release, in March 1970, of the documentary film of the event, with Crosby, Stills, Nash, & Young performing "Woodstock," written by Joni Mitchell (1943–), over the closing credits. The last verse makes the politics of the event concrete (**Reading 39.6**):

READING 39.6

from Joni Mitchell, "Woodstock" (1970)

By the time we got to Woodstock
We were half a million strong
And everywhere there was song and celebration

And I dreamed I saw the bombers
Riding shotgun in the sky
And they were turning into butterflies
Above our nation
We are stardust
Billion year old carbon
We are golden
Caught in the devil's bargain
And we've got to get ourselves
Back to the garden

The utopian dream of "Woodstock," the desire to return to "the garden," was quickly shattered. Just days before the national Moratorium Day March, reporter Seymour Hersh (1937–) broke the story of the My Lai massacre in the *New York Times* (see Fig. 39.7). A few months later, on April 30, 1970, President Nixon announced that American troops had invaded Cambodia five days earlier. Protests erupted on college campuses across the United States. At Kent State University near Akron, Ohio, the governor of Ohio called out the Ohio National Guard, who arrived on campus as students burned down an old ROTC building (already boarded up and scheduled for demolition). On Monday, May 4, some 2,000 students gathered on the school commons. The National Guard ordered them to disperse. They refused. A group of 77 guardsmen advanced on the students, and for reasons that have never been fully explained, opened fire. Four students were killed, nine wounded. Photojournalism student John Paul Filo's photograph of 14-year-old runaway Mary Ann Vecchio kneeling over the dead body of 20-year-old Jeffery Miller became an instant icon of the antiwar movement (Fig. **39.12**).

Neil Young quickly penned what would become Crosby, Stills, Nash, & Young's most famous protest song, "Ohio," commemorating the four who died. The song quickly rose to number two on the charts.

American involvement in Vietnam would not end until January 1973, when a ceasefire was agreed upon in Paris and American troops were finally withdrawn. Two years later, on April 30, 1975, the Viet Cong and North Vietnamese army took control of Saigon, renaming it Ho Chi Minh City, and Vietnam was reunited as a country for the first time since the French defeat in 1954.

HIGH AND LOW: THE EXAMPLE OF MUSIC

Rock and roll's ascendancy as the favorite music of American popular culture in the 1950s and 1960s underscores a shift in cultural values in which the line between "high" and "low" art became more and more difficult to define. Composers from the time of Dufay and Josquin had based their work on secular melodies, but the phenomenon really began to take shape in the nineteenth century, as nationalist composers like Giuseppe Verdi in Italy and Peter Ilyich Tchaikovsky in Russia began to draw on traditional folk songs for their otherwise classical compositions. Over the course of the nineteenth century, classical music was increasingly considered the provenance of elite and intellectual audiences while lighter fare was understood to appeal to wider, more populist tastes. By the jazz era, everyone from the American George Gershwin to the Russian Igor Stravinsky incorporated jazz idioms into their work, and Aaron Copland, as we have seen, looked to the regional traditions of the Appalachian hills and the American West for inspiration. The Boston Pops Orchestra was founded as early as 1885 to present "concerts of a lighter kind of music." Its conductor of over 50 years, Arthur Fiedler (1894–1979), was followed by academy-award winner John Williams (1932–), composer of the soundtracks to the films *Star Wars* and *Indiana Jones and the Raiders of the Lost Ark*. Of all of them, twentieth-century composer Leonard Bernstein (1918–1990) was probably most at home in both classical and popular idioms. High and low were distinctions that, in his own work, he tried to ignore. He could write Broadway hit musicals such as *Candide* (1956) and *West Side Story* (1957), as well as profoundly moving symphonies such as his 1963 Third Symphony, *Kaddish*, a musical interpretation of the Jewish prayer for the dead, written for an orchestra, a chorus, a soloist, a children's choir, and a narrator.

György Ligeti and Minimalist Music

Minimalist music was inspired by advances in new media—particularly electronic recording and production innovations—but their sound was so different that both popular and classical audiences were often put off. Like Minimalist artists, minimalist composers emphasized the use of consciously limited means, but rather than creating Minimalist Art's simple geometric compositions, minimalist

musicians transformed the simple elements with which they began into dense, rich compositions.

Interest in electronic music was stimulated, in New York, by the Radio Corporation of America's development of the electronic synthesizer in 1955. But Europeans were equally committed to its development, among them Hungarian composer György Ligeti [lih-get-tee] (1923–2006). After World War II, the USSR controlled all of Eastern Europe, and when Hungary tried to break away in 1956, the Soviets sent their tanks into Budapest. Ligeti, then 32 years of age, ignored the gunfire and shellbursts that had sent most of his fellow citizens into basement shelters so that he could continue to listen to a West German radio broadcast of a piece by German composer Karlheinz Stockhausen [SHTOK-howzun] (1928–2007). Stockhausen had composed the first piece of music using synthesized tones in 1953, *Studie I*. Its instrumentation consisted of three tape recorders, a sine wave generator, and a "natural echo chamber." Stockhausen felt he was returning to the very basis of sound, which, in his words, rises from "pure vibration, which can be produced electrically and which is called a sine wave. Every existing sound, every noise, is a mixture of such sine waves—a spectrum." For the first time, the musical composition existed entirely on tape and required no performer to produce it.

When Ligeti escaped Hungary late in 1956, he joined Stockhausen at the Studio for Electronic Music in West Germany. Stockhausen was editing tapes of electronically generated sounds—as well as music generated by traditional instruments and voices—in the same way that a filmmaker edits film. And he was experimenting with the ways in which sound was heard by an audience as well. In what is probably the hallmark electronic composition of the era, Stockhausen's *Gesang der Jünglinge* [geh-SAHNG der YOONG-ling-uh] (*Song of the Children*), composed in 1956, was one of the first works to include spatialization as a compositional element, inaugurating the "stereo" and "surround sound" era. Combining taped voices in combination with taped electronic sounds, the original version utilized five loudspeakers, positioned to surround the audience. Stockhausen's plan was to play the work at the Cologne Cathedral, but the archbishop didn't think loudspeakers belonged in church. As Stockhausen describes it: "The direction and movement of the sounds in space is shaped by the musician, opening up a new dimension in musical experience"—and, he thought, spiritual experience as well.

Meanwhile, throughout the 1960s, Ligeti was moving in a very different direction. Rather than exploring the vast diversity of sound, as Stockhausen did, he developed a rich, but much more minimal, brand of polyphony—which he called "micropolyphony"—dense, constantly changing clusters of sound that blur the boundaries between melody, harmony, and rhythm. This effect can be heard in Ligeti's 1966 *Lux Aeterna* [luks ee-TER-nuh] (track **39.1**), the parts of which seem to blend together in a sort of shimmering

HEAR MORE at
www.myartslab.com

atmosphere of overall sound. The piece is actually a canon, an arrangement of theme and variations, except that the entrances are neither contrapuntal nor harmonic, but rather densely compacted and atonal. In 1968, the composition reached a mass audience when American director Stanley Kubrick (1928–1999) used it in the soundtrack of his film *2001: A Space Odyssey*.

Ligeti gradually became aware of the young American "minimalist" composers Terry Riley (1935–), Steve Reich (1936–), and Philip Glass (1937–). Like the Minimalist artists, their work relied on repetition of units that differ only slightly or that vary only gradually over extended periods of time. In his ground-breaking *In C* of 1964, Riley created 53 brief thematic fragments, to be played in any combination by any group of instruments. Though each musician plays these fragments in the same sequence, they are free to repeat any fragment as many times as they like. The one constant, providing a foundation for the texture of interweaving fragments in the piece, is a C octave played in a high range of the piano throughout the piece, repeating as many as ten or fifteen thousand times in any given performance (the length of performance will vary depending upon how many times each musician repeats each fragment). Steve Reich's 1965 *It's Gonna Rain* consists of the repetition of a single phrase of text (the title), taken from a tape recording of a street preacher by the name of Brother Walker sermonizing on the subject of Noah and the Flood. Reich spliced together two copies of the same tape played at slightly different speeds, so that they gradually shift, in his words, "out of phase," and the monotony of the repetition is transformed as the original sound of the phrase gradually comes to sound entirely different.

John Adams (1947–) echoed Reich's practice in *It's Gonna Rain* to create a composition for the Shaker religion, *Shaker Loops*. But in this piece, Adams added a profoundly emotional, almost Romantic dynamic to its minimalist repetition. In 1987, Adams wrote an opera, *Nixon in China*, based on the February 1972 meeting between American president Richard Nixon (1913–1994) and Chinese communist leader Mao Zedong. Adams created what he describes as "the first opera ever to use a staged 'media event' as the basis for its dramatic structure." Nixon and Mao were both adept manipulators of public opinion, and in his opera, Adams sought to reveal "how dictatorships on the right and on the left throughout the century had carefully managed public opinion through a form of public theater and the cultivation of 'persona' in the political arena." Nixon made much of his visit, the first by an American president to Communist-controlled China, and the driving propulsion of Adams's repetitive score captures perfectly Nixon's excitement, his passionate desire to leave an indelible mark on history.

The Theatrical and the New *Gesamtkunstwerk*

The ambition and scope of Adams's opera reflects a renewed interest in reinventing what, in the nineteenth century, the German composer Richard Wagner had called the *Gesamtkunstwerk*, or "total work of art," merging visual art, music, opera, dance, and so on, into a single integrated whole (see Chapter 30). Decades later, Bertolt Brecht, the German playwright, warned in response:

> So long as the expression "Gesamtkunstwerk" means that the integration is a muddle, so long as the arts are supposed to be "fused" together, the various elements will all be equally degraded, and each will act as a mere "feed" to the rest. The process of fusion extends to the spectator who gets thrown into the melting pot too and becomes a passive (suffering) part of the total work of art. . . . Words, music, and setting must become more independent of one another.

It was this aesthetic philosophy that guided Merce Cunningham, John Cage, and Robert Rauschenberg in their collaborations that combined independent compositions (see Chapter 38). In its intentional heterogeneity, the Cunningham, Cage, and Rauschenberg "events" created a clear precedent for postmodern theatrical practice, which sought not to "fuse" the arts but underscored their *difference* within the same stage space.

Robert Wilson and Postmodern Opera Describing his 1976 postmodern opera *Einstein on the Beach*, innovative director and producer Robert Wilson (1941–) explained:

> In making *Einstein*, I thought about gestures or movements as something separate. And I thought about light . . . the decor, the environments, the painted drops, the furniture, and they're all separate. And then you have all of these screens of visual images that are layered against one another and sometimes they don't align, and then sometimes they do. If you take a baroque candelabra and you put it on a baroque table, that's one thing. But if you take a baroque candelabra and you place it on a rock, that's something else. . . .

The music for Wilson's opera is also its own "separate" entity. Created by minimalist composer Philip Glass, *Einstein on the Beach* has a score that brims with slowly developing variations that accompany recurring patterns. As Glass himself says, "The difficulty is not that it keeps repeating, but that it almost never repeats." It is thus a fabric composed not of sameness but *difference*. The five-hour opera unfolds, subtly, as in John Ashbery's expression, like "A whispered phrase passed around the room" (track **39.2**).

HEAR MORE at www.myartslab.com

Glass was chiefly inspired by the music of Indian sitarist and composer Ravi Shankar [SHAN-kar] (1920–), whose raga improvisations he had transcribed into Western notation for a soundtrack to the 1966 counterculture film *Chappaqua*. He was fascinated by the structure of Indian ragas, which he perceived to be made up of small units of notes built up into chains of larger rhythmic patterns. The compositions Glass subsequently created based on this understanding had little in common with Indian music, but they did incorporate the hypnotic, almost mystical, cyclic repetitive patterns that he equated with meditative aural space.

In *Einstein on the Beach*, Wilson sets Glass's music to dance sequences choreographed by Lucinda Childs (1940–) to create contrasting elements (Fig. **39.13**). "I thought of the dances as landscapes, as fields," Wilson said, "And so the space is the biggest. They break apart the space." In much of the opera, the visual backdrops create a shallow visual field, but the dances occur in a space that is lighted as if receding into the infinite. Each dance sequence occurs twice, the second time to music so distinctly different from the first instance that it is virtually unrecognizable the second time around. This doubling—at once the same and not the same—is another facet of postmodern experience.

Laurie Anderson and Rock Postmodern While Robert Wilson's *Einstein* remained a relatively "high art" phenomenon, the possibility of creating a work of "total art" that spoke more directly to a popular culture, rock-'n'-roll aesthetic, remained an attractive alternative, one addressed first by the rock band The Who when they created the "rock opera" *Tommy* in 1969. However, it was Laurie Anderson, who most fully realized the *Gesamtkunstwerk* ideal, with her four-part, four-night, eight-hour multimedia *United States*, which premiered at the Brooklyn Academy of

Music's "New Wave Festival" in 1983 a year before Wilson's *Einstein on the Beach* was revived there.

Anderson's work was categorized as a "rock" phenomenon, and drew the kind of criticism that rock music has often attracted, especially after a song from *United States, Part II*, "O Superman," became a pop hit in 1981, selling over 1 million records. "O Superman's" eight-minute video version even helped inaugurate MTV, being broadcast during that channel's first year of existence. The song was an indictment of the American dream—"So hold me, Mom, in your long arms, in your petrochemical arms, your military arms, in your arms"—as a mother's arms and the country's armaments combine to form a distinctly chilly postmodern embrace. But despite the song's antiestablishment attitude, Anderson's success was, to many in the avant-garde art scene, a sure sign that she had "sold out," just as many other artists in New York seemed to have submitted to the attractions of postmodern consumer culture. After she reached a lucrative agreement with Warner Brothers records and then made a feature-length performance film, *Home of the Brave*, in 1985, their suspicions seemed confirmed.

But Anderson remains one of the most distinctive innovators in the postmodern scene. Early on, in her role as a musician, she began creating new electronic instruments, including a series of electronic violins, called "tape-bow violins," on which a tape playback head has been mounted on

Fig. 39.13 Robert Wilson, *Einstein on the Beach*, Dance, Field. 1976. Performers, Lucinda Childs Company. The dance is almost devoid of the visual resources that dominate the rest of the production, a fact that draws attention to the "openness" of the space in which it occurs, itself a metaphor for the openness of interpretation itself.

Fig. 39.14 Laurie Anderson performing "O Superman," from *United States, II.* 1983. Anderson's imagery is almost always ambiguous. Here the projection of a hand evokes both the authoritative pointing finger of the mother and a gun—the primary themes of "O Superman."

the body of the instrument and a strip of recorded audiotape on the bow. She transforms her voice, in the narratives that compose what she calls her "talking operas," by means of a harmonizer that drops it a full octave and gives it a deep male resonance, which she describes as "the Voice of Authority," an attempt to create a corporate voice. She has attached microphones to her body, transforming it into a percussion instrument. And the projected imagery and lighting that provide the backdrop for her performances (Fig. **39.14**) are a combination of pop imagery and cultural critique, which unite the local and the global in an image that underscores the not always positive results of the "American dream."

THE BIRTH OF THE FEMINIST ERA

At the same time that the antiwar and civil rights movements galvanized political consciousness among both men and women, "the Pill" was introduced in the early 1960s.

As women gained control over their own reproductive functions, they began to express the sexual freedom that men had always taken for granted. The struggle for gender equality in the United States found greater and greater expression throughout the 1960s until, by the early 1970s, a full-blown feminist era emerged.

The Theoretical Framework: Betty Friedan and NOW

In 1963, a freelance journalist and mother of three, Betty Friedan (1921–2006), published *The Feminine Mystique*. In many ways, hers was an argument with Freud, or at least with the way Freud had been understood, or misunderstood. While she admits that "Freudian psychology, with its emphasis on freedom from a repressive morality to achieve sexual fulfillment, was part of the ideology of women's emancipation," she is aware that some of Freud's writings had been misused as a tool for the suppression of women (**Reading 39.7**):

READING 39.7

from Betty Friedan, *The Feminine Mystique* (1963)

The concept "penis envy," which Freud coined to describe a phenomenon he observed in women—that is, in the middle-class women who were his patients in Vienna in the Victorian era—was seized in this country in the 1940s as the literal explanation of all that was wrong with American women. Many who preached the doctrine of endangered femininity . . . seized on it—not the few psychoanalysts, but the many popularisers, sociologists, educators, ad-agency manipulators, magazine writers, child experts, marriage counsellors, ministers, cocktail-party authorities—could not have known what Freud himself meant by penis envy. . . . What was he really reporting? If one interprets "penis envy" as other Freudian concepts have been reinterpreted, in the light of our new knowledge that what Freud believed to be biological was often a cultural reaction, one sees simply that Victorian culture gave women many reasons to envy men: the same conditions, in fact, that the feminists fought against. If a woman who was denied the freedom, the status, and the pleasures that men enjoyed wished secretly that she could have these things, in the shorthand of the dream, she might wish herself a man and see herself with that one thing which made men unequivocally different—the penis. She would, of course, have to learn to keep her envy, her anger, hidden: to play the child, the doll, the toy, for her destiny depended on charming man. But underneath, it might still fester, sickening her for love. If she secretly despised herself, and envied man for all she was not, she might go through the motions of love, or even feel a slavish adoration, but would she be capable of free and joyous love? You cannot explain away woman's envy of man, or her contempt for herself, as mere refusal to accept her sexual deformity, unless you think that a woman, by nature, is a being inferior to man. Then, of course, her wish to be equal is neurotic.

Latent in Friedan's analysis, but central to the feminist movement, is her understanding that in Freud, as in Western discourse as a whole, the term *woman* is tied, in terms of its construction as a word, to man (its medieval root is "*wifman*," or "wife [of] man"). It is thus a contested term that does not refer to the biological female but to the sum total of all the patriarchal society expects of the female, including behavior, dress, attitude, and demeanor. *Woman*, said the feminists, is a cultural construct, not a biological one. In *The Feminine Mystique*, Friedan rejects modern American society's cultural construction of women. But she could not, in the end, reject the word *woman* itself. Friedan would go on to become one of the founders of the National Organization for Women (NOW), the primary

purpose of which was to advance women's rights and gender equity in the workplace. In this, she dedicated herself to changing, in American culture, her society's understanding of what "woman" means.

Feminist Poetry

The difficulties that women faced in determining an identity outside the patriarchal construction of "woman" became, in the 1960s, one of the chief subjects of poetry by women, particularly in the work of the poets Anne Sexton (1928–1974) and Sylvia Plath (1932–1963). Both investigate what it means *to be*, in an existential sense, "woman."

Plath had famously examined the psychology of being in her poem "Lady Lazarus" (see **Reading 39.8**, page 1311, for the full text). The title alludes to T. S. Eliot's "Love Song of J. Alfred Prufrock," specifically to Eliot's lines: "I am Lazarus, come from the dead, / Come back to tell you all, I shall tell you all." Like Lazarus, Lady Lazarus is reborn in the poem in order to attack the male ego, specifically that of her husband, the poet Ted Hughes (1930–1998). The poem concludes:

Out of the ash
I rise with my red hair
And I eat men like air.

Sexton's marriage was probably more problematic than Plath's. An affluent housewife and mother, she lived in a house with a sunken living room and a backyard swimming pool in the Boston suburb of Weston, Massachusetts. But she was personally at odds with her life, and as her husband saw his formerly dependent wife become a celebrity, their marriage dissolved into a fabric of ill will, discord, and physical abuse. The poem with which she opened most readings, the ecstatically witty "Her Kind," published in 1960 in her first book of poems, *To Bedlam and Part Way Back*, captures the sense of independence that defined her from the beginning (**Reading 39.9**):

READING 39.9

Anne Sexton, "Her Kind" (1960)

I have gone out, a possessed witch
haunting the black air, braver at night;
dreaming evil, I have done my hitch
over the plain houses, light by light:
lonely thing, twelve-fingered, out of mind.
A woman like that is not a woman, quite.
I have been her kind.

I have found the warm caves in the woods,
filled them with skillets, carvings, shelves,
closets, silks, innumerable goods;
fixed the suppers for the worms and the elves:
whining, rearranging the disaligned.

A woman like that is misunderstood.
I have been her kind.

I have ridden in your cart, driver,
waved my nude arms at villages going by,
learning the last bright routes, survivor
where your flames still bite my thigh
and my ribs crack where your wheels wind.
A woman like that is not ashamed to die.
I have been her kind.

Another important poet of the era is Adrienne Rich (1929–), whose poem "Diving into the Wreck" was published in 1973. The poem delves into a metaphoric wreck created by a patriarchal culture that inherently devalues anything female or feminine, a wreck that would include the lives of both Plath and Sexton. Rich's project is to dissolve myth, discover truth, and recover the treasures left by her feminist forebearers (**Reading 39.10**):

READING 39.10

from Adrienne Rich, "Diving into the Wreck" (1973)

I came to explore the wreck.
The words are purposes.
The words are maps.
I came to see the damage that was done
and the treasures that prevail.
I stroke the beam of my lamp
slowly along the flank
of something more permanent
than fish or weed

the thing I came for:
the wreck and not the story of the wreck
the thing itself and not the myth
the drowned face always staring
toward the sun
the evidence of damage
worn by salt and sway into this threadbare beauty
the ribs of the disaster
curving their assertion
among the tentative haunters.

This is the place.
And I am here, the mermaid whose dark hair
streams black, the merman in his armored body
We circle silently
about the wreck
we dive into the hold.
I am she: I am he

The first-person "I" of her poem is androgynous, a figure who has given up the sexual stereotyping that constitutes the battered hulk of the wreck. And what Rich discovers in her explorations there is the will to survive.

Feminist Art

In the 1960s and 1970s—in fact well into the 1990s—the art world was dominated by male artists. Although in 1976 approximately 50 percent of the professional artists in the United States were women, only 15 in 100 one-person shows in New York's prestigious galleries were devoted to work by women. Eight years later, in 1984, the Museum of Modern Art reopened its enlarged facilities with a show entitled *An International Survey of Painting and Sculpture*. Of the 168 artists represented, only 13 were women.

As a result, many women artists were insistent that their work be approached in formal, not feminine terms—that is, in the same terms that the work of men was addressed. Eva Hesse [HESS-uh] (1936–1970), for instance, when asked if works such as *Ringaround Arosie* (Fig. **39.15**) contained

Fig. 39.15 Eva Hesse, *Ringaround Arosie.* **March 1965.** Varnish, graphite, ink, enamel, cloth-covered wire, papier-mâché, unknown modeling compound, Masonite, wood, 26 ⁵/₈ × 16 ³/₄ × 4 ¹/₂ (67.5 × 42.5 × 11.4 cm). Museum of Modern Art, New York, fractional and promised gift of Kathy and Richard S. Fuld, Jr., 2005. © The Estate of Eva Hesse, Hauser & Wirth Zurich, London. Photo: Abby Robinson/Barbora Gerny, New York. "A woman is sidetracked by all her feminine roles," Hesse wrote in 1965. "She also lacks the conviction that she has the 'right' to achievement."

female sexual connotations, quickly shot back: "No! I don't see that at all." Of the work's circular forms, she later said, "I think the circle is very abstract. . . . I think it was a form, a vehicle. I don't think I had a sexual, anthropomorphic, or geometric meaning. It wasn't a breast and it wasn't a circle representing life and eternity."

Even when an artist like Judy Chicago (1939–) would try to invest her work with feminist content, the public refused to recognize it. Her series of 15 *Pasadena Lifesavers* (Fig. **39.16**) exhibited in 1970 at Cal State Fullerton, expressed, she felt, "the range of my own sexuality and identity, as symbolized through form and color." Their feminist content was affirmed by a statement on the gallery wall directly across from the entrance, which read:

> Judy Gerowitz hereby divests herself of all names imposed upon her through male social dominance and freely chooses her own name Judy Chicago.

But male reviewers ignored the statement. As Chicago says in her 1975 autobiography, *Through the Flower: My Struggle as a Woman Artist*: "[They] refused to accept that my work was intimately connected to my femaleness." But, in part, their misapprehension was her own doing. As she explains in *Through the Flower*, "I had come out of a formalist

Fig. 39.16 Judy Chicago, *Pasadena Lifesavers, Yellow No. 4*. 1969–70. Sprayed acrylic on Plexiglas (series of 15) 59″ × 59″. Whereabouts unknown. © 2008 Artists Rights Society (ARS), New York. Photo © Donald Woodman. To many viewers, the geometry of Chicago's forms completely masked their sexual meaning.

Fig. 39.17 Judy Chicago, *The Dinner Party.* 1979. Mixed media, 48′ × 48′ × 48′ installed. Collection of the Brooklyn Museum of Art, Gift of the Elizabeth A. Sackler Foundation. Photograph © Donald Woodman. © 2005 Judy Chicago/Artists Rights Society (ARS), New York. The names of 999 additional women are inscribed in ceramic tiles along the table's base.

background and had learned to neutralize my subject matter. In order to be considered a 'serious' artist, I had had to suppress my femaleness. . . . I was still working in a frame of reference that people had learned to perceive in a particular, non-content-oriented way."

Chicago's great collaborative work of the 1970s, *The Dinner Party* (Fig. **39.17**), changed all that. In its bold assertion of woman's place in social history, the piece announced the growing power of the women's movement itself. More than 300 women worked together over a period of five years to create the work, which consists of a triangle-shaped table, set with 39 places, 13 on a side, each celebrating a woman who has made an important contribution to world history. The first plate is dedicated to the Great Goddess, and the third to the Cretan Snake Goddess (see Fig. 4.4). Around the table the likes of Eleanor of Aquitaine (see Chapter 10), Artemisia Gentileschi (see Fig. 21.17), novelist Virginia Woolf (see Chapter 35), and Georgia O'Keeffe (see Fig. 36.20) are celebrated. Where the *Pasadena Lifesavers* had sheltered their sexual content under the cover of

their symbolic abstraction, in *The Dinner Party*, the natural forms of the female anatomy were fully expressed in the ceramic work, needlepoint, and drawing. But, as Chicago is quick to point out, "the real point of the vaginal imagery in *The Dinner Party* was to say that these women are not known because they have vaginas. That is all they had in common, actually. They were from different periods, classes, ethnicities, geographies, experiences, but what kept them within the same historical space was the fact that they had vaginas."

One of the woman artists who has most consistently explored the construction of female identity in contemporary American society is Eleanor Antin (1935–). Beginning in the early 1970s, Antin began assuming a series of personae designed to allow her to explore dimensions of her own self that might otherwise have remained hidden if she had not adopted these other identities. One of the earliest of these personae was the King—a medieval knight errant, decked out in a false beard, a velvet cape, lacy blouse, and leather boots, who would wander the streets of "his" kingdom, the small town of Solana Beach, just north of San Diego,

California, conversing with his "subjects" (Fig. **39.18**). "The usual aids to self-definition," Antin wrote the same year as this performance piece, "sex, age, talent, time, and space—are merely tyrannical limitations upon my freedom of choice." Here she explores the possibilities of being not merely male, but a powerful male—something wholly at odds with her diminutive physical presence. "I took on the King," Antin further explained, "who was my male self. As a young feminist I was interested in what would be my male self . . . he became my political self." Beginning in 1979, Antin adopted another persona, this time a black ballerina by the name of Eleanora Antinova who had once danced with Diaghilev's Ballets Russes (see Chapter 34). In this guise, which she performed in black face (actually more of an artificial tan), she explored the dimensions of racism in America by imagining the fate of a black ballerina in the "white machine" that is classical ballet.

Antin's King was designed to reveal that gender is constructed—her sex remained constant even as her gender changed—and, by extension, that our social "being" is equally constructed. This too would become the project of Cindy Sherman (1954–) who in 1977 began casting herself in a variety of roles, all vaguely recognizable as stereotypical female characters in Hollywood and foreign movies, television shows, and advertising. These *Untitled Film Stills*, as the original series of black-and-white photographs are known, do more, however, than simply assert that "woman" is a construction of consumer society. They address, in particular, the question of the *gaze*. In *Untitled Film Still # 35* (Fig. **39.19**), Sherman turns to

Fig. 39.19 Cindy Sherman, *Untitled Film Still #35.* **1979.** Photograph mounted on board, 10″ × 8″. Courtesy of the artist and Metro Pictures, New York. The entire series of *Film Stills* consists of 69 photographs shot between 1977 and 1980.

LEARN MORE Gain insight from a primary source document from Cindy Sherman at **www.myartslab.com**

Fig. 39.20 Richard Prince, *Untitled (Cowboy)*. 1989. Ektacolor photograph, edition of two, 50″ × 70″. © Richard Prince. One of the underlying themes of this image is that the Marlboro cowboy, apparently riding free on the range, is actually galloping headlong toward his death.

face someone—perhaps another figure in the room, perhaps the camera, perhaps the audience—but she is clearly the object of someone's gaze. The image purposefully evokes the 1975 essay by film critic Laura Mulvey (1941–), "Visual Pleasure and Narrative Cinema." For Mulvey, women in cinema reflect a "traditional exhibitionist role" in which they are "simultaneously looked at and displayed, with their appearance coded for strong visual and erotic impact." This, she says, is "the magic of the Hollywood style," which "arose, not exclusively, but in one important aspect, from its skilled and satisfying manipulation of visual pleasure. Unchallenged, mainstream film coded the erotic into the language of the dominant patriarchal order." Mulvey's project, in writing her essay, was to subvert this pleasure and the patriarchal order it sustained by exposing it. Sherman's project is the same. She is, after all, both subject and object of her own gaze, literally exposing in her photographs the vocabulary of the patriarchal order. In essence, she returns our gaze with the same sense of condescension and superiority as Manet's Olympia (see *Closer Look*, Chapter 30).

QUESTIONS OF MALE IDENTITY

It stands to reason that if female identity is not essential but socially constructed, the same should hold true for men. One of the first artists to address this theme was Richard Prince, who during the late 1970s had lived with Sherman in New York. By 1980—the year that horse-riding Hollywood hero Ronald Reagan was elected president—Prince had taken to photographing advertisements of cowboys, specifically the Marlboro Man, a practice that has continued down to the present day (Fig. **39.20**). Prince recognized that Philip Morris Co. was not so much selling cigarettes as it was an image—the smoker as the independent, rough-and-tumble hero. Thus in rephotographing the original ads, Prince underscored the inauthenticity of the ad campaign itself. As he well understood, in identifying with the image, the American male was mistaking dependence for independence.

If Prince's cowboys represent the macho side of American male identity, the gay rights movement would play a dramatic role in challenging such American attitudes about the nature of masculinity. In the early hours of Saturday morning, on

Fig. 39.21 Andy Warhol, *Lance Loud,* from *America.* 1985. Black-and white photograph. In the late 1970s and early 1980s, Warhol was rarely seen without his Polaroid camera. In 2007, the Andy Warhol Foundation gave away about 28,000 photographs by Warhol to 185 museums nationwide.

June 28, 1969, police officers entered a gay nightclub in New York's Greenwich Village called the Stonewall Inn, more or less expecting to close the establishment down for lack of a liquor license. But the Inn's patrons reacted violently, throwing garbage cans, bricks, beer cans, and bottles at the windows and what a reporter for the *Village Voice* called "a rain of coins" at the police. Very soon after, the Inn was on fire. Rioting continued until about 4 AM, and nightly for several days thereafter. A year later, the first ever gay pride parade was staged to celebrate the events of June 1969.

The gay struggle for equal rights continues, of course, to this day. Even 16 years after Stonewall, in 1985, Andy Warhol conceived of his book *America*, a collection of his Polaroid photographs, at least in part as a means to "out" America, to show it its own gay side. At the very heart of the book is a "Physique Pictorial," showing male bodybuilders. Early on he includes a portrait of himself in drag, just one of many he shot in the early 1980s . There's an image of a gay pride parade. And then there are the portraits of gay celebrities, such as Liberace (with punk star John Sex), Keith Haring, and Robert Rauschenberg.

Warhol also includes a portrait of Lance Loud (Fig. **39.21**). Loud was the first reality TV star. Born in 1951, he grew up in Eugene, Oregon, before moving to Santa Barbara for his teenage years He discovered Warhol in his early teens, became his pen pal, and then, as a young man, moved to New York. When he was 22, in 1973, PBS featured the William C. Loud family—Mom and Dad, Bill and Pat (who incidentally separated and divorced on the show) and their five children, Delilah, Kevin, Grant, Michele, and Lance—in a 12-hour documentary series entitled *An American Family*. It chronicled the day-to-day lives of the family for seven months, and it attracted 10 million viewers. As a *Newsweek* cover story proclaimed in March 1973, the show torpedoed the fantasy of the American family embodied in shows like *The Brady Bunch*. Lance's openly gay lifestyle spurred a national controversy, especially after he appeared on the Dick Cavett Show and other talk shows, and as it became apparent that he was inspiring countless other gay and lesbian Americans to acknowledge their own sexuality. By 1978, Lance had started the band The Mumps, a rock band that played weekly at CBGBs and Max's in New York; Warhol's photograph is of Lance Loud, the rock star. American attitudes about masculinity and male identity were in a state of transition. If nothing else, sexual stereotypes were being challenged as never before.

The Global Village

On the morning of October 9, 1991—a morning that began 16 hours earlier in Japan than in California—along a stretch of interstate highway in the Tehachapi [ti-HACH-uh-pee] Mountains north of Los Angeles, 1,760 yellow umbrellas, each 19 feet 8 inches tall, and 28 feet 5 inches wide, weighing 448 pounds, appeared. Each one was slowly opened across the parched gold hills and valleys (Fig. **39.22**). Meanwhile, in the prefecture of Ibaraki [ee-buh-RAHK-eh], Japan, north of Tokyo, in the fertile, green Sato River valley, with its small villages, farms, gardens, and fields, 1,340 blue umbrellas had opened as well (Fig. **39.23**). Built at a cost of $26 million, which the artists Christo and Jeanne-Claude (see Fig. 39.10) had raised entirely through the sale of their proprietary work, *The Umbrellas*, blue on one side of the Pacific, yellow on the other, symbolized both the differences underlying global culture and its interdependency. California and Japan were, after all, the two places from which the electronic revolution of the 1970s and 1980s had sprung, California's Silicon Valley providing the innovation and invention and Japan providing the practical application in its massive industrial complex south of Tokyo. Together they changed the world, but their differences were as striking as their interdependence, and Christo and Jeanne-Claude's work underscored this. The landscapes in which the *Umbrellas* rose differed dramatically. In Japan, where less space is available (steep volcanic mountains make most of the land unusable), 124 million people live on only 8 percent of the land. Christo and Jeanne-Claude responded by densely positioning the *Umbrellas*, sometimes following the geometry of the rice fields. In California, in the vast grazing lands of the Tehachapis, the *Umbrellas* seemed to stretch in every direction, along the ridges, down hills, with great spaces between them. Still, in both cultures, the umbrella is an image of shelter and protection, from both rain and sun, and therefore a symbol of community life. If visitors could never experience the work as a whole, they were always aware that the work continued, in a way, on the other side of the world, that in some sense the umbrellas sheltered a global village.

The term "global village" was coined in 1962 by Marshall McLuhan (1911–1980) to describe the way that electronic mass media fundamentally altered human communication, enabling people to exchange information instantaneously, across the globe. In the nearly half century since then, of course, the introduction of personal computers,

Fig. 39.22 Christo and Jeanne-Claude, *The Umbrellas, Japan – USA*. 1984–91. © 1991 Christo. Each umbrella could be cranked open in about 45 seconds. Over 4,000 workers opened them in about four hours. They remained on view for 18 days.

Fig. 39.23 Christo and Jeanne-Claude. *The Umbrellas, Japan – USA*. 1984–91. © Christo. As opposed to California, where Christo and Jeanne-Claude had to negotiate with 26 landowners, in Japan, they worked with 452 different landowners.

cell phones, and pagers has empowered individuals to expand this communication further on an almost unimaginable scale. McLuhan idealistically viewed media as the means of creating a united, global community bridging the gap between the world's haves and have-nots. But because much of the electronic mass media has been controlled by the West, many critics saw it as a new means of asserting commercial and political control over the rest of the world—a new kind of imperialism. But in fact, the globalization of mass media has resulted in a crisis of identity for most world cultures as local values and customs have come into conflict or been assimilated by those of the West.

Global media—whether it be motion pictures, cable television channels such as CNN, or Internet sites like Google and Wikipedia—have also transmitted many elements of popular foreign culture to the West. Asian and Mideastern cuisines, Japanese comic books and video games, and a vast array of foreign films, fashions, and fads have become popular in the West, aided by the "unlimited bandwidth" of modern telecommunications that offers individuals massive quantities of whatever information or entertainment they desire. International art exhibits, music and film festivals, and book fairs attract visitors and collectors from around the world in search of the latest trends and directions in contemporary art.

In the late twentieth and early twenty-first centuries, artists increasingly find themselves in a double bind—how, they ask, can they remain true to their native or ethnic identities and still participate in the larger world market? What happens to their work when it enters a context where it is received with little or no understanding of its origins? How, indeed, does the global threaten the local? Is the very idea of the "self" threatened by technology and technological innovation?

THINKING BACK

What factors contributed to changes in African-American self-definition in the 1960s?

By 1963, the Southern Christian Leadership Conference (SCLC), led by the Reverend Martin Luther King, Jr., had decided that Birmingham, Alabama, would be the focal point of the burgeoning civil rights movement. What message to the movement did King provide in his 1963 "Letter from Birmingham Jail"? In the summer of 1963, 250,000 people marching in Washington, D.C. heard Martin Luther King deliver his famous "I Have a Dream" speech, shortly after the folk-rock trio Peter, Paul, and Mary sang Bob Dylan's "Blowin' in the Wind."

One of the most important factors contributing to the success of the civil rights movement was the growing sense of ethnic identity among the African-American population. How did French existentialist philosopher Jean-Paul Sartre contribute to this newfound sense of self? How did it find expression in Ralph Ellison's novel *Invisible Man*? How did Romare Bearden celebrate the diversity of black experience? What contributed to the growing militancy of the civil rights movement, as reflected, for instance, in the poetry and drama of Amiri Baraka?

How did artists respond to the Vietnam War?

As American involvement in the war in Vietnam escalated throughout the 1960s, artists and writers responded in a number of ways. What tack did Kurt Vonnegut take in his 1969 novel *Slaughterhouse-Five*? Artworks like Claes Oldenburg's *Lipstick (Ascending) on Caterpillar Tracks* were conceived as antiwar protests, but more direct protests were taken up by the Art Workers' Coalition. What steps did they take? How did the artists' relationship with museums and galleries motivate both Conceptual Art and Land Art? But it was rock music that most reflected the spirit of rebellion and protest that characterized the antiwar movement. Musicians called for peace at festivals such as Woodstock and wrote songs reflecting the events of the day.

How did "high" culture and "popular" culture coexist in the musical world?

The ascendancy of rock and roll in popular culture underscores the ongoing intrusion of "low" or popular forms into the world of "high" culture that had begun with nationalist music movements in the nineteenth century. But minimalist musicians such as Karlheinz Stockhausen and György Ligeti put off both classical and popular audiences. What characterizes Ligeti's music? On what techniques did American minimalist composers like Terry Riley, Steve Reich, and Philip Glass rely? How does Glass's *Gesamtkunstwerk*, *Einstein on the Beach*, differ from Wagner's conception of the form? How does Laurie Anderson's *United States* transform the *Gesamtkunstwerk* in a popular idiom?

How did the feminist movement find expression in the arts?

In 1963, in her book *The Feminine Mystique*, Betty Friedan attacked the patriarchal construction of the idea of "woman." What was the primary object of her attack? Women artists and writers were equally engaged in asserting their place in an art world from which their work was, if not completely excluded, then demeaned as second rate. Poets Sylvia Plath, Anne Sexton, and Adrienne Rich wrote overtly feminist tracts directed against the social institutions that relegated women to second-place status in American society. Painters Eva Hesse and Judy Chicago fought to find a place in an art world that almost totally excluded women from exhibition and even gallery representation. However, the primary focus of artists like Eleanor Antin and Cindy Sherman was the social construction of female identity. How did each approach the issue?

How did male self-definition come into question?

Following the lead of feminists, artists like Richard Prince explored the ways in which male identity is socially constructed. What in particular did Prince focus on? How did the growing gay rights movement challenge male stereotypes?

PRACTICE MORE Get flashcards for images and terms and review chapter material with quizzes at **www.myartslab.com**

READINGS

Sylvia Plath, "Lady Lazarus" (1962)

Most of Sylvia Plath's best poetry was published posthumously. The major tension of the poem lies in its flippant tone compared with the seriousness of its subject—repeated suicide attempts. Plath wrote the poem and several other of her greatest works in the last month of her life, after her separation from her husband, the poet Ted Hughes, and just before her suicide in London. It establishes her poetic voice as a kind of performance, making light of her desire to die and her failure to succeed in accomplishing the deed. She is, thus, a deeply ironic Lazarus, returned from the dead, resurrected, but not in joy.

I have done it again.
One year in every ten
I manage it—

A sort of walking miracle, my skin
Bright as a Nazi lampshade,
My right foot

A paperweight,
My face featureless, fine
Jew linen.

Peel off the napkin   10
O my enemy.
Do I terrify?—

The nose, the eye pits, the full set of teeth?
The sour breath
Will vanish in a day.

Soon, soon the flesh
The grave cave ate will be
At home on me

And I a smiling woman.
I am only thirty.   20
And like the cat I have nine times to die.

This is Number Three.
What a trash
To annihilate each decade.

What a million filaments.
The peanut-crunching crowd
Shoves in to see

Them unwrap me hand and foot—
The big strip tease.
Gentlemen, ladies   30

These are my hands
My knees.
I may be skin and bone,

Nevertheless, I am the same, identical woman.
The first time it happened I was ten.
It was an accident.

The second time I meant
To last it out and not come back at all.
I rocked shut

As a seashell.   40
They had to call and call
And pick the worms off me like sticky pearls.

Dying
Is an art, like everything else.
I do it exceptionally well.

I do it so it feels like hell.
I do it so it feels real.
I guess you could say I've a call.

It's easy enough to do it in a cell.
It's easy enough to do it and stay put.   50
It's the theatrical

Comeback in broad day
To the same place, the same face, the same brute
Amused shout:

'A miracle!'
That knocks me out.
There is a charge

For the eyeing of my scars, there is a charge
For the hearing of my heart—
It really goes.   60

And there is a charge, a very large charge
For a word or a touch
Or a bit of blood

Or a piece of my hair or my clothes.
So, so, Herr Doktor.
So, Herr Enemy.

I am your opus,
I am your valuable,
The pure gold baby

That melts to a shriek.   70
I turn and burn.
Do not think I underestimate your great concern.

Ash, ash—
You poke and stir.
Flesh, bone, there is nothing there—

A cake of soap,
A wedding ring,
A gold filling.

Herr god, Herr Lucifer
Beware   80
Beware.

Out of the ash
I rise with my red hair
And I eat men like air.

READING CRITICALLY

Why does Plath evoke the Holocaust in this poem? What does she see as analogous to her own situation?

40 Without Boundaries
Multiple Meanings in a Postmodern World

THINKING AHEAD

What characterizes postmodern architecture?

How does postmodern theory reflect pluralist thought?

How are pluralism and diversity reflected in art and literature?

It is difficult to pinpoint exactly when "modernism" ended and "postmodernism" began, but the turning point came in the 1970s and 1980s. Architects began to reject the pure, almost hygienic uniformity of the Bauhaus and International styles, represented by the work of Mies van der Rohe (see Figs. 37.32 and 38.19), favoring more eclectic architectural styles that were anything but pure. A single building might incorporate a classical colonnade and a roof line inspired by a piece of Chippendale furniture. Or it might look like the Rasin Building in Prague (Fig. **40.1**). Built on the site of a Renaissance structure destroyed in World War II, the building's teetering sense of collapse evokes the postwar cityscape of twisted I-beams, blown-out facades with rooms standing open to the sky, and sunken foundations, all standing next to a building totally unaffected by the bombing. But that said, the building is also a playful, almost whimsical celebration, among other things, of the marvels of modern engineering—a building made to look as if it is at the brink of catastrophe, even as it is completely structurally sound. So lighthearted is the building that it was called the "Dancing House," or, more specifically, "Ginger and Fred," after the American film stars Ginger Rogers and Fred Astaire. The more solid tower on the corner seems to be leading the transparent tower—Ginger—by the waist, as the two spin around the corner.

The building was the idea of Czech architect Vlado Milunic [MILL-un-itch] (1941–), and he enlisted American architect Frank Gehry [GHEH-ree] (1929–) to collaborate on the project. To many eyes in Prague, a city renowned for its classical architecture, it seemed an absolutely alien American element dropped into the city. But Milunic conceived of the building as addressing modern Prague even as it engaged the city's past. He wanted the building to consists of two parts: "Like a society that forgot its totalitarian past—a static part—and a society that forgot its totalitarian past but was moving into a world full of changes. That was the main idea. Two different parts in dialogue, in tension, like plus and minus, like Yang and Yin, like man and woman." It was Gehry who nicknamed it "Ginger and Fred."

The use of many different, even contradictory elements of design is the hallmark of **postmodern** architecture. The English critic Peter Fuller explained the task of the postmodern architect this way:

> The west front of Wells Cathedral, the Parthenon pediment, the plastic and neon signs on Caesar's Palace in Las Vegas, even the hidden intricacies of a Mies curtain wall, are all equally "interesting." Thus the Post-Modern designer must offer a shifting pattern of changing strategies

◀ Fig. 40.1 Frank Gehry and Vlado Milunic, the Rasin Building, also known as the Dancing House or "Ginger and Fred," Prague, Czech Republic. 1992–96. The building was championed by Václav Havel (1936–), the Czech playwright who served as president of first Czechoslovakia and then the Czech Republic from the fall of the Soviet Union in 1989 until 2003. Havel had lived next door since childhood.

HEAR MORE Listen to an audio file of your chapter at **www.myartslab.com**

Fig. 40.2 Las Vegas, Nevada, Superstock, Inc. Especially at night, Las Vegas attacks the senses with a profusion of signs and lights. Known as the "Strip," it represents the overload of sensory input that has created the postmodern condition. The neon cowboy on the left is known as "Vegas Vic." In 1981, Vegas Vickie rose across the street above Glitter Gulch, which took its name from what locals were already calling the four-block length of Fremont Street. This photograph dates from about 1985.

and substitute a shuffling of codes and devices, varying ceaselessly according to audience, and/or building type, and/or environmental circumstance.

But perhaps the clearest and most seminal statement of the postmodern aesthetic is that of architect Robert Venturi (1925–), whose 1966 "Gentle Manifesto" described criteria for a new eclectic approach to architecture that abandoned the clean and simple geometries of the International Style (see Chapters 36 and 37). For Mies van der Rohe, "less is more" had become a mantra which he used to describe the refined austerity of his designs. Venturi argued for the opposite:

> An architecture of complexity and contradiction has a special obligation toward the whole: its truth must be in its totality or its implications of totality. It must embody the difficult unity of inclusion rather than the easy unity of exclusion. More is not less.

The model for this new architecture became, for Venturi, Las Vegas (Fig. 40.2). In *Learning from Las Vegas*, written in

1972 with his wife Denise Scott Brown (1931–) and fellow architect Steven Izenour (1940–2001), Venturi describes Las Vegas as a "new urban form":

> Although its buildings suggest a number of historical styles, its urban spaces owe nothing to historical space. Las Vegas space is neither contained and enclosed like medieval space nor classically balanced and proportioned like Renaissance space nor swept up in a rhythmically ordered movement like Baroque space, nor does it flow like Modern space around freestanding urban space makers.
>
> It is something else again. But what? Not chaos, but a new spatial order. . . . Las Vegas space is so different from the docile spaces for which our analytical and conceptual tools were evolved that we need new concepts and theories to handle it.

In what the authors describes as "the seemingly chaotic juxtaposition of honky-tonk elements," they also discovered an "intriguing kind of vitality and validity." Thus, for

Venturi and his colleagues, faced with the multiplicitous visual stimuli of Las Vegas, the postmodern architect has no choice but to design with various, even contradictory elements in order to communicate not a homogenous sense of unity, but rather "a difficult whole."

Living in this "difficult whole" constitutes the postmodern condition. The postmodern art and architecture examined in this chapter cannot be understood as a product of a single style, purpose, or aesthetic. It is defined by multiple meanings and its openness to interpretation. "Meaning" itself becomes contingent and open-ended. Indeed, postmodern media art introduces situations in which sight, sound, and text each challenge the "undivided" attention of the audience, sometimes creating a sensory overload in which meaning is buried beneath layers of contradictory and ambiguous information. Confronting the postmodern object, the postmodern mind must ask itself, "How do I sort this out?" And this is a question that, as people living in the postmodern age, we are increasingly adept at answering.

POSTMODERN ARCHITECTURE: COMPLEXITY, CONTRADICTION, AND GLOBALIZATION

Architects and builders exemplify the affluent nomads of the new postmodern society. They, like the people for whom they design and build, inhabit the "world metropolis," a vast, interconnected fabric of places resembling Las Vegas in large measure, where people do business, and between which they travel, work, and seek meaning. Travel, in fact, accounts for nearly 10 percent of world trade and global employment. As nearly 700 million people travel internationally each year, a half million hotel rooms are built annually across the globe to house them.

Today's architect works in the culture first introduced by the Sony Walkman and carried forward by the iPod and iPhone. These are technologies "designed for movement," as cultural historian Paul du Gay describes their function, "for mobility, for people who are always out and about, for traveling light . . . part of the required equipment of the modern 'nomad.'" And architects also are also responsible for helping to provide the most elusive of qualities in the postmodern world—a sense of meaning and a sense of place.

Architecture in this culture is largely a question of creating distinctive buildings, markers of difference like Frank Gehry's Ginger and Fred building in Prague that stand out in the vast sameness of the "world metropolis," so that travelers feel they have arrived at someplace unique, someplace identifiable. In this climate, contemporary architecture is highly competitive. Most major commissions are competitions, and most cities compete for the best, most distinctive architects.

Gehry first distinguished himself with the design of his own home in Los Angeles (Fig. 40.3). On the surface, it is a collision or eruption of parts. In the mid-1970s, still a young and relatively unknown architect, Gehry and his wife moved into a Santa Monica house that fulfilled their

Fig. 40.3 Frank Gehry, residence, Santa Monica, California, and axonometric drawing. 1977–78. Photograph by Tim Street-Porter. Gehry's neighbors were not at all pleased with his new house, but Gehry claims that he was trying to use "materials that were consistent with the neighborhood." He explains: "When I built that house, that neighborhood was full of trailer trucks in the back yards, and often on the lawn. A lot of old, aging Cadillacs and big cars on blocks on the front lawn, people fixing their cars. A lot of chain link fences, corrugated metal; I know they didn't use it like I did, and that's the difference."

Fig. 40.4 Frank Gehry, Guggenheim Museum, Bilbao. 1997. Photo: David Heald. © The Solomon R. Guggenheim Foundation, New York. The official description of the building begins: "The building itself is an extraordinary combination of interconnecting shapes. Orthogonal blocks in limestone contrast with curved and bent forms covered in titanium. Glass curtain walls provide the building with the light and transparency it needs." Even in its materials, it embodies complexity and contradiction.

main criterion—it was affordable. "I looked at the old house that my wife found for us," Gehry recalls, "and I thought it was kind of a dinky little cutesy-pie house. We had to do something to it. I couldn't live in it. . . . Armed with very little money, I decided to build a new house around the old house and try to maintain a tension between the two." The new house surrounding the old one is deliberately unfinished, almost industrial. A corrugated metal wall, chain-link fencing, plywood walls, and concrete block surround the original pink frame house with its asbestos shingles. The surrounding wall, with randomly slanted lines and angled protrusions, thus separates not only the "outside" house from the house within, but the entire structure from its environment. The tension established by Gehry between industrial and traditional materials, between the old house and the almost fortresslike shell of his home's new skin, intentionally creates a sense of unease in viewers (one certainly shared by Gehry's neighbors). The sense that they are confronting the "difficult whole" Venturi speaks about defines, for Gehry, the very project of architecture. If Gehry's architecture is disturbingly unharmonious with its surroundings, it cannot be ignored or taken for granted. It draws attention to itself *as* architecture.

Gehry's use of sculptural frames to surround his house—note the steel and wire fencing that extends over the roof behind the front door, which would be "decorative" or "ornamental" were it not so mundane—has continued throughout his career, culminating in his design for the Guggenheim Museum in Bilbao [bill-BOW ("bow" as in

"now")], Spain (Fig. **40.4**). Working on the models with the Catia computer program originally developed for the French aerospace industry, Gehry notes, "You forget about it as architecture, because you're focused on this sculpting process." The museum itself is enormous—260,000 square feet, including 19 gallery spaces connected by ramps and metal bridges—and covered in titanium, its undulating forms evoking sails as it sits majestically along the river's edge in the Basque port city. But it is the sense of the museum's discontinuity with the old town and the surrounding countryside (Fig. **40.5**) that most defines its postmodern spirit. It makes Bilbao, as a city, a more "difficult whole," but a more interesting one, too.

Gehry's design for the Guggenheim in Bilbao was stunningly successful, drawing critical raves, massive numbers of visitors, and even reservations that the architecture was so noteworthy that it overshadowed the art within the structure. One of the key elements of this success was Gehry's ability to ensure that the "organization of the artist" prevailed, as he put it, "so that the end product is as close as possible to the object of desire that both the client and architect have come to agree on." So postmodern architectural design and theory were not necessarily incompatible with the efficient completion of large, complex, and innovative structures like the Guggenheim in Bilbao (or the Experience Music Project museum in Seattle, another large-scale Gehry structure). And it turns out that the digital design models produced by the Catia program were not only useful for envisioning the shapes of "sculpted" buildings.

The data produced by such computerized designs was critical in estimating construction costs and budgets.

Besides Gehry, one of the most successful architects in these international competitions where contemporary architects make their reputations has been Spaniard Santiago Calatrava [kah-lah-TRAH-vah] (1951–), who has degrees in both engineering and architecture. Known especially for the dynamic curves of his buildings and bridges, his designs include the Athens Olympics Sports Complex (2001–2004), the Tenerife Opera House in the Canary Islands (2003), and the Turning Torso residential tower in Malmø, Sweden (2005). Based on the model of a twisting body, the 54-story Malmo tower consists of nine cubes, twisting 90 degrees from bottom to top, and rising to a rooftop observation deck with vistas across the Øresund [UR-uh-sun] strait to Copenhagen. Calatrava also won the

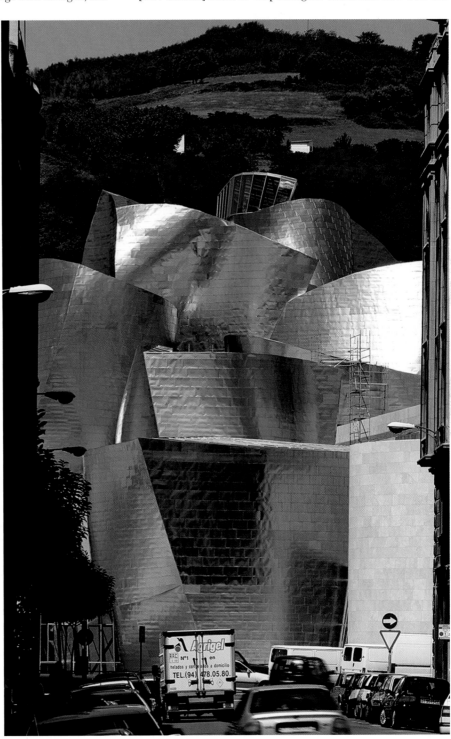

Fig. 40.5 Frank Gehry, Guggenheim Museum, Bilbao. 1997. Photo: David Heald. © The Solomon R. Guggenheim Foundation, New York. This view of the building looks through the streets of the old town to the hills beyond.

design competition for the Port Authority Trans Hudson (PATH) train station at the site of the former World Trade Center in New York (Fig. **40.6**). Scheduled for completion in 2014, it is based on a sketch Calatrava drew of a child's hands releasing a bird into the air. Calatrava said that the goal of his design was to "use light as a construction material." At ground level, the station's steel, concrete, and glass canopy functions as a skylight that allows daylight to penetrate 60 feet to the tracks below. On nice days, the canopy's roof retracts to create a dome of sky above the station.

One of the newest approaches to contemporary architecture takes into consideration the compatibility of the building with its environment. Increasingly, a building's viability—even beauty—is measured by its environmental self-sufficiency. Rather than relying on unsustainable energy sources, architects strive to design using sustainable building materials—eliminating steel, for instance, since it is a nonrenewable resource. The other important factor in modern architecture is adapting new buildings to the climate and culture in which they are built. These are the principles of what has come to be known as "green architecture."

One of the more intriguing new buildings to arise in the South Pacific region is the Jean-Marie Tjibaou [jee-bah-OO] Cultural Center in Nouméa, New Caledonia, an island northeast of Australia. It illustrates green architecture at work (Fig. **40.7**). The architect is Renzo Piano (1937–), an Italian, but the principles guiding his design are indigenous to New Caledonia. Named after a leader of the island's indigenous people, the Kanak, the center is dedicated to preserving and transmitting indigenous culture as well as incorporating sustainable environmental principles. The buildings are constructed of wood and bamboo, easily renewable resources, and each of the center's ten pavilions represents a typical Kanak dwelling. Piano left the dwelling forms unfinished, as if under construction, but they serve a function as wind scoops, catching breezes from the nearby ocean and directing them to cool the inner rooms. As in a Kanak village house, the pavilions are linked with a covered walkway. Piano describes the project as "an expression of the harmonious relationship with the environment that is typical of the local culture. They are curved structures resembling huts, built out of wood joists and ribs; they are containers of

Fig. 40.6 Santiago Calatrava, Design for Port Authority Trans Hudson (PATH) station, World Trade Center Site. 2004. Courtesy Santiago Calatrava/Port Authority of New York. The memorial to those who lost their lives at the World Trade Center lies directly behind the station.

Fig. 40.7 Renzo Piano, Jean-Marie Tjibaou Cultural Center in Nouméa, New Caledonia. 1991–98. The center's namesake, Jean-Marie Tjibaou, was assassinated in 1989 while trying to forge an agreement to free his country of French colonial rule. New Caledonia remains under French control today.

an archaic appearance, whose interiors are equipped with all the possibilities offered by modern technology."

The principles of environmentally sensitive architecture are, of course, harder to implement in densely populated urban environments. But when the city of Fukuoka, Japan, realized that the only space available for a much-needed government office building was a large two-block park that also happened to be the last remaining green space in the city center, Argentine-American architect Emilio Ambasz presented a plan that successfully maintained, even improved upon, the green space (Fig. **40.8**). A heavily planted and pedestrian-friendly stepped terrace descends down the entire park side of the building. Reflecting pools on each level are connected by upwardly spraying jets of water, to create a ladderlike climbing waterfall, which also serves to mask the noise of the city streets beyond. Under the building's 14 terraces lie more than 1 million square feet of space, including a 2,000-seat theater, all cooled by the gardens on the outside. The building is not entirely green—it is constructed of steel-framed reinforced concrete—and its interior spaces are defined by an unremarkable and bland white that might be

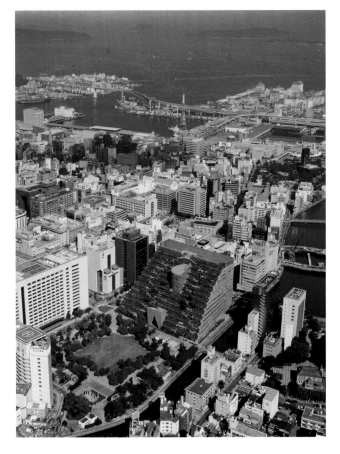

Fig. 40.8 Emilio Ambasz, ACROS Building (Fukuoka Prefecturial International Hall), Fukuoka, Japan. 1989–95. © Emilio Ambasz & Associates. On the street side of the building facing away from this view, the building looks like any other modern office building.

found in any modern high-rise office building. Still, the building suggests many new possibilities for reconceptualizing the urban environment in more environmentally friendly terms.

In planning for the 2008 Olympic Games in Beijing, the Chinese government invested in expensive energy-efficient heating and transportation systems and water-saving technologies that were designed to improve greatly the environmental quality of the city—one of the world's most populated. For the Olympic Stadium (Fig. **40.9**), the Chinese hired the Swiss design firm of Herzog and de Meuron, who conceived of a double structure, dubbed the "Bird's Nest": a red concrete seating bowl and, 50 feet outside the bowl, the outer steel frame, which structurally resembles the twigs of a bird's nest. The stadium floor provides enough space for the underground pipes of a geothermal heat pump (GHP) system, which in winter absorbs the heat from the soil and helps heat the stadium, while in summer the soil cools the stadium. A rainwater-collection system, on the stadium roof and the surrounding areas, purifies water and recycles it for use in the venue. The translucent roof provides essential sunlight for the grass below, and a natural, passive ventilation system.

PLURALISM AND POSTMODERN THEORY

During the Beijing Olympic Games in 2008, a painting by Chinese artist Zhang Hongtu [jang hong-too] (1943–), *Bird's Nest, in the Style of Cubism* (Fig. **40.10**), was seized by Chinese officials when it arrived at customs for exhibition at the German embassy. They were holding it, they said, pending "clarification of its meaning." As it turned out, officially, the painting's muted palette was deemed inappropriate for the celebratory nature of the Olympic games, and the government demanded that the painting be removed from China. But more than the painting's Cubist idiom, the government was provoked by the inclusion of the word "Tibet" just above "Human Right," both of which directly refer to China's 50-year occupation of that country (or province, from China's point of view). Also prominently displayed in the picture are the Chinese characters for the French supermarket chain Carrefour, which has stores all over China and whose purported support of the Dalai Lama (the Buddhist head of the Tibetan government in exile) resulted in protests across the country in the spring of 2008. The number "8" is repeated 23 times: the Chinese had decided to open the Olympics at 8 PM on August 8,

Fig. 40.9 Herzog & de Meuron, the Bird's Nest—Beijing National Stadium. 2004–08.
Corbis. The stadium was designed to be supplied with Beijing's first wind power plant.

Fig. 40.10 Zhang Hongtu, *Bird's Nest, in the Style of Cubism*. 2008. Oil on canvas, 36″ × 48″. © 2009 Zhang Hongtu Studio. "I'm a Chinese Muslim," Zhang Hongtu told the *New York Times* in 2008. "I don't care about anything pure—pure Chinese culture, or pure European culture. I don't think there's anything pure. I just want to mix, and from the mixture to make something new."

2008, and Zhang Hongtu was mocking what he called China's "stupid" numerological superstitions. At the bottom right is the letter *J* beside four horizontal lines, a reference to June 4, the date of the Tiananmen Square massacre in Beijing in 1989. Finally, the motto for the 2008 Olympics appears in Chinese characters: "One World, One Dream." If nothing else, these words clearly mean different things to Zhang Hongtu and Chinese government officials.

Zhang Hongtu's *Bird's Nest, in the Style of Cubism* is a clear-cut demonstration of one of the primary theoretical principles of postmodern thought: the growing conviction that meaning resides not in the work itself but in its audience, together with the understanding that the audience is itself diverse and various. Such thinking in turn gives rise to the belief that meaning is itself always plural in nature. There is no meaning, only a plurality of *meanings*.

Structuralism

The roots of this idea lie in French structuralism, which argues that meaning occurs not through identification but through difference. For instance, the words *woman* and *lady*

both refer to the human female, and yet their meanings are determined by cultural markers or codes of enormous difference. Structuralism also forms the basis for semiotics, the study of signs. A sign consists of the relation between the signifier and the signified—that is, the relation between the word *tree*, for instance, and all the possible trees to which that word might refer. Semiotic theory thus posits the following formula as fundamental to the study of signs:

$$\text{Sign} = \frac{\text{S [signifier]}}{...s1...s2...s3...s4...}$$
[possible signifieds]

The string of signifieds is potentially infinite. That is, the word *tree* technically refers to every possible tree, and we understand its reference only in context. For instance, we add other words to "tree" to differentiate it from other trees—"pine tree" or "willow tree"—to delimit the plurality of its potential meanings, or still more words, "the tallest pine tree in the park." This construction of difference is fundamental to understanding, but it is important to understand that the word *tree* in and of itself is infinitely plural in its potential meanings.

Some signs carry with them larger cultural meanings. The French philosopher Roland Barthes [BART] (1915–1980) described these as "mythologies." Anything can take on the characteristics of myth. For example, two-story pillars supporting the portico of a house are a mythic signifier of wealth and elegance, and Barthes's great self-appointed task as a philosopher was to expose the mythologies—instances of what he calls the "falsely obvious"—that inform contemporary understanding. Zhang Hongtu's *Bird's Nest, in the Style of Cubism* could usefully be approached as an example of just such a reading of the Beijing Olympic Games. The act of reading cultural "texts"—and "texts" need not be thought of here as actual sentences strung together, but as any system of signs, including painting, performance, advertising, film, and so forth—becomes an act of decoding and revealing the mythologies at work in the text. We have come to call this process *deconstruction*.

Deconstruction and Poststructuralism

The chief practitioner of deconstruction was the French philosopher Jacques Derrida (1930–2004). Deconstruction is not synonymous with "destruction," as is commonly thought, but rather it suggests that the "text" be analyzed and taken apart in order to show what has been left out or overlooked. Why does this matter? Because it indicates that there is always more to be said, that meaning is never complete. Deconstruction poses meaning as an arena of endless and open possibility.

Derrida is considered a poststructuralist (as is Barthes in his later writing) because one of the "texts" that poststructuralists most thoroughly submit to deconstruction is structuralism itself. Because it is founded on the principle of difference, structuralism tends to focus on the binary opposition as fundamental to the structure of thought. In his most famous work, *Of Grammatology* (published in France in 1967 and in English translation in 1976), Derrida points out that binary oppositions are algebraic (a = not-b), and thus the two terms in binary pairs (good/evil; conscious/unconscious; masculine/feminine; light/dark; presence/absence) can't exist without reference to the other. That is, light (as presence) is defined as the absence of darkness, goodness as the absence of evil, and so on. *Of Grammatology* looks particularly at the opposition speech/writing. In Western philosophy, speech has always been privileged over writing because in the act of speech the self is fully present in its being; on the other hand, writing, in its dissemination across time and space to an audience necessarily removed from the originary moment of meaning, is always experienced as an absence, as second-hand speech. Metaphoric speech is a particularly potent example of this. A metaphor is a form of substitution, at one remove from its meaning. It is but a *trace* (Derrida's word) of what is already absent. In the end, what Derrida reveals in his deconstruction of the speech/writing binary in Western culture is that the emphasis on that fullness of being realized in the act of speech is actually a cultural nostalgia for a wholeness that has long since—perhaps always—been lost.

Chaos Theory

Derrida is by no means easy to understand, but it should be clear that his thinking is not unrelated to Robert Venturi's idea of the "difficult whole." It is also akin to developments taking place in the natural sciences first introduced to a wider public in James Gleik's 1987 *Chaos: Making a New Science*. To many, in fact, the new chaos theory offered a way to go beyond deconstruction, which seemed doomed to subvert endlessly the binary structures that structuralists construct. Chaos theorists posited that biological and mathematical patterns that appear random, unstable, and disorderly are actually parts of larger, more "difficult wholes." The fractal geometry of Benoit Mandelbrot (1924–2010) is a prime example. Mandlebrot disdained traditional Euclidean geometry because it was incapable of describing such forms as clouds, mountains, and coastlines, all of which, like most things in nature, exhibit a different order of complexity than the traditional building blocks of geometry—the sphere, the cylinder, and the cone, for instance. Mandlebrot was convinced that such irregular shapes as coastlines and mountains display previously unrecognized orders. When certain basic forms, he argues, are repeated again and again at different scales of length, structures emerge that are quite different from the basic forms of which they are composed. One of Mandlebrot's favorite examples is the so-called Koch snowflake in which the structure of an equilateral triangle is repeated again and again to create remarkably intricate curvilinear and twisted shapes. Equipped with mathematical models he developed to describe these shapes, Mandlebrot was able to generate dynamic, unpredictable, and seemingly living organisms on the computer screen from basic rectilinear or triangular forms.

The computer has, in fact, made it possible to visualize this complexity. If each pixel on a computer screen is assigned a numerical value and then submitted to what is known in mathematics as iterative equations, a series of increasingly and infinitely complex patterns emerge that have come to be known as the Mandelbrot set (Fig. **40.11**). If the result of these iterative equations is stable, the pixel is colored black. If the equation moves off toward infinity, the pixel is assigned a color, depending on its rate of acceleration—blue, for instance, for slow rates, red for faster ones. Acceleration occurs at the boundaries of the set, and it is possible, in these areas, to bring out finer and finer detail by zooming in to smaller and smaller areas of the edge. The haunting beauty of these designs has attracted artists and scientists alike.

Of at least equal importance to chaos theory is the work of meteorologist Edward Lorenz (1917–2008). In 1961, he was working on the problem of weather prediction. His computer was equipped with a set of 12 equations to model what the weather might be. One day, he wanted to see a

Fig. 40.11 The Mandelbrot set. From Hans-Otto Peitgen and Peter H. Richter, *The Beauty of Fractals* (Berlin: Springer-Verlag, 1986). Since an infinite number of points exist between any two given points, by zooming in to a small area of the set, the infinite complexity of the set reveals itself. The detail of the Mandelbrot set is infinite. By focusing in on the area between the left-hand circle and the largest black form, an area known as the "seahorse valley," with its spiraling tails, reveals itself.

particular sequence again, and to save time, he started in the middle of the sequence, instead of at the beginning. When he came back an hour later, he discovered that instead of the same pattern as before, a wildly different one had emerged. He eventually discovered what caused the difference. In the original sequence, the beginning number had been 0.506127, but to save paper, in the second instance, he had only typed the first three digits, 0.506. This result came to be known as the *butterfly effect*. The amount of difference in the starting points of the two curves is so small that it is comparable to a butterfly flapping its wings, thus producing a minute change in the state of the atmosphere, but one of profound consequence—producing, in a monthtime, perhaps a hurricane in the Atlantic, or, as the case may be, averting one that was otherwise bound to happen.

The Human Genome

Today, chaos theory is being usefully applied to everything from project management to population dynamics, to the descriptions of the spread of disease, and to DNA and genome research. In fact, in 2003, the federally sponsored Human Genome Project, initiated in 1990, succeeded in identifying all of the approximately 20,000 to 25,000 genes in human DNA and determining the structural sequences of the approximately 3 billion chemical base pairs that make up human DNA that regulate the human cellular system in its operations and functions. There are four similar chemicals that make up DNA, paired in the human genome and repeated 3 billion times; their order determines

how we look, how we eat and fight disease, and even, sometimes, how we behave. Through their understanding of this order, scientists are increasingly able to diagnose and predict hereditary disease and, perhaps the most exciting application of DNA research, use gene therapy to repair and regenerate tissue. Among the more recent outcomes of this revolutionary new medical practice are a treatment for a type of inherited blindness, the use of reengineered immune cells to attack cancer cells in patients with advanced metastatic melanoma (the most deadly form of skin cancer), the cure of deafness in guinea pigs, and the eradication of sickle cell anemia in mice—these last two, treatments that scientists hope to apply to human subjects one day.

PLURALISM AND DIVERSITY IN THE ARTS

Our understanding of the complexities of experience as realized in the practice of deconstruction, chaos theory, and the opportunities opened to science by the mapping of the human genome, has found expression in the arts as well. Despite the apparent plurality of its many "-isms," modern art, from the moment that Braque and Picasso affirmed the primacy of the conceptual over the optical, systematically replaced the representation of the world with the representation of an "idea." This was a process that led to ever greater abstraction, culminating in many ways in the art of Minimalism. Pop Art offered a different model—works that aimed at inclusion, not exclusion, and the promise that anything might be permissible. A photograph by Louise Lawler

Fig. 40.12 Louise Lawler, *Pollock and Tureen*. 1984. Cibachrome, 28″ × 39″. Courtesy Metro Pictures, New York. The formal parallel of linear rhythm and color harmonies in both the painting and the tureen contradicts their obvious differences.

(1947–), *Pollock and Tureen* (Fig. **40.12**), summarizes this sense of diversity and multiplicity. Lawler's work attempts to demonstrate how context, from museums to exhibition catalogues to private homes, determines the ways in which images are received and understood. Thus, the Pollock painting in this photograph is transformed into a decorative or ornamental object, much like the tureen centered on the side table in front of it. Lawler both underscores the fact that the painting is, like the tureen, a marketable object and suggests that the expressive qualities of the original work—its reflection of Pollock's Abstract Expressionist feelings—have been emptied, or at least nearly so, when looked at in this context.

A Plurality of Styles in Painting

By the end of the 1960s, artists felt free to engage in a wide spectrum of experimental approaches to painting, ranging from the stylized imagery introduced by Pop artists to the street style of graffiti writers (see the *Closer Look* on Jean-Michel Basquiat, pages 1326–1327), and from full-blown abstraction to startlingly naturalistic realism. Indeed, the exchange of ideas between proponents of realism and those of abstraction during the post–World War II era had far-reaching effects. Rather than an either/or proposition, there is abundant cross-fertilization between the approaches. We can see this in the work of the contemporary German artist Gerhard Richter [RIKH-ter] (1930–), who moves freely between the two—sometimes repainting

photographs, black-and-white and color—and sometimes creating large-scale abstract works. Richter uses photographs, including amateur snapshots and media images, because, he says, they are "free of all the conventional criteria I had always associated with art . . . no style, no composition, no judgment." To him, they are "pure" pictures, unadulterated by the intervention of conscious aesthetic criteria. *Meadowland* (Fig. **40.13**), an oil painting on canvas, might as well have been taken from the window of a passing car. The questions it raises are quite simple: Why did he select this photograph to translate into a painting? How and when does the eye sense the difference between a painting and the photographic surface?

In comparing *Meadowland* to the artist's abstractions, which he concentrated on throughout the 1980s and 1990s, we can begin to answer these questions. Works such as *Ice (2)* (Fig. **40.14**) are obviously paintings. One senses that Richter begins with a realistic image, and before the ground completely dries, he drags another layer of paint through it with a squeegee or palette knife. The result is like viewing an object close up while passing it at high speed. But the resulting work is above all a painterly surface, not a photographic one. Nevertheless, in Richter's words:

> abstract paintings . . . visualize a reality which we can neither see nor describe but which we may nevertheless conclude exists. We attach negative names to this reality; the unknown, the ungraspable, the infinite, and for

thousands of years we have depicted it in terms of substitute images like heaven and hell, gods and devils. With abstract painting we create a better means of approaching what can be neither seen nor understood because abstract painting illustrates with the greatest clarity, that is to say with all the means at the disposal of art, "nothing." . . . [Looking at abstract paintings] we allow ourselves to see the un-seeable, that which has never before been seen and indeed is not visible.

Given this artistic strategy, Richter's photograph-based works are paintings of the graspable and visible. Why did he select the photograph upon which *Meadowland* is based? Precisely because it is so mundane, a prospect we have so often seen before. How and when do we recognize *Meadowland* as a painting and not a photograph? When we accept photographic clarity—or photographic blurring, for that matter—as one of the infinite methods of painting. Richter's photographic paintings are thus the very antithesis of his abstractions, except that both styles are equal statements of the artist's vision. Together, in them, Richter explores not only the conditions of seeing but the possibilities of painting. Richter might be the ultimate postmodernist: "I pursue no objects, no system, no tendency," he writes. "I have no program, no style, no direction. . . . I steer clear of definitions. I don't know what I want. I am inconsistent, non-committal, passive; I like the indefinite, the boundless; I like continued uncertainty."

Charles the First by Jean-Michel Basquiat [bah-skee-AH] (1960–1988) is an homage to the great jazz saxophonist Charlie Parker, one of a number of black cultural heroes celebrated by the graffiti-inspired Basquiat. Son of a middle-class Brooklyn family (his father was a Haitian-born accountant, his mother a black Puerto Rican), Basquiat left school in 1977 at age 17 and lived on the streets of New York for several years, during which time he developed the "tag"—or graffiti pen-name—SAMO, a combination of "Sambo" and "same ol' shit." SAMO was most closely associated with a three-pointed crown (as self-anointed "king" of the graffiti artists) and the word "TAR," evoking racism (as in "tar baby"), violence ("tar and feathers," which he would entitle a painting in 1982), and, through the anagram, the "art" world as well. A number of his paintings exhibited in the 1981 New York/New Wave exhibit at an alternative art gallery across the 59th Street Bridge from Manhattan attracted the attention of several art dealers, and his career exploded.

Central to his personal iconography is the crown, which is a symbol of not only his personal success but also the other African-American heroes that are the subject of many of his works—jazz artists, as is the case here, and "famous Negro athletes," as he calls them, such as boxer Sugar Ray Leonard and baseball's Hank Aaron.

The price of a halo at 59¢ suggests that martyrdom is "for sale" in Basquiat's world.

Beneath the crown that Basquiat had introduced in his SAMO years is a reference to Thor, the Norse god; below it, the Superman logo; and above it, a reference to the Marvel comic X-Men heroes. Thor is, in fact, another X-Man hero. Marvel describes the X-Men as follows: "Born with strange powers, the mutants known as the X-Men use their awesome abilities to protect a world that hates and fears them." Basquiat clearly means to draw an analogy between the X-Men and his African-American heroes.

The X in Basquiat's work is never entirely negative. In Henry Dreyfuss's Symbol Sourcebook: An Authoritative Guide to International Graphic Symbols, Basquiat discovered a section on "Hobo Signs," marks left, graffiti-like, by hobos to inform their brethren about the lay of the local land. In this graphic language, an X means "O.K.; All right."

This phrase is a reference to the other "Charles the First"—King Charles I of England, beheaded by Protestants in the English Civil War in 1649 (see Chapter 23). But it also suggests, especially considering the crossed-out word young, Basquiat's sense of his own martyrdom. In fact, four months before his twenty-eighth birthday, in 1978, he would become the victim, according to the medical examiner's report, of "acute mixed drug intoxication (opiates–cocaine)."

The S, especially crossed out, also suggests dollars, $.

Something to Think About . . .

Many viewers are at least initially put off by the apparent sloppiness of Basquiat's distinctive style. But Basquiat has adopted this style for a purpose. What do you imagine his purpose might be?

SEE MORE For a Closer Look at Jean-Michel Basquiat's Charles the First, go to **www.myartslab.com**

Beneath the word *Opera*, and apparently on a par with the most aristocratic of musical genres, is the title of one of Parker's greatest tunes, "Cherokee," topped by four feathers in honor of Parker's nickname, *Bird*. The feathers and song also evoke the Cherokee Indians' forced removal from Georgia to Oklahoma in 1838 (see Chapter 32).

The hand probably represents the powerful hand of the musician, and equally the painter.

The copyright sign, ©, which also appears spelled out at the top of the middle panel, is repeated again and again in Basquiat's work and suggests not just ownership but the exercise of property rights and control in American society, which Basquiat sees as the root cause of the institution of slavery (to say nothing of the removal of the Cherokee nation to Oklahoma).

Jean-Michel Basquiat, *Charles the First*. **1982.** Acrylic and oil paintstick on canvas, three panels, 78″ × 62$^1/_4$″ overall. © The Estate of Jean-Michel Basquiat/© 2009 Artists Rights Society (ARS), New York.

Another approach to the question of the relation between abstraction and representation is seen in the works of Pat Steir [steer] (1940–). In 1989, she adapted Pollock's drip technique to her own ends, allowing paint to flow by force of gravity down the length of her enormous canvases to form recognizable waterfalls. *Yellow and Blue One-Stroke Waterfall* (Fig. **40.15**) is 14 feet high, its format reminiscent of Chinese scroll paintings of waterfalls. Steir explained the rationale behind her series of waterfall paintings in a 1992 interview:

> I don't think of these paintings as abstract. . . . These are not only drips of paint. They're paintings of drips which form waterfall images: pictures. . . . [Nor are] they realistic . . . I haven't sat outdoors with a little brush, trying to create the illusion of a waterfall. The paint itself makes the picture. . . . Gravity make the image. . . .
>
> These paintings are, in a sense a comment on the New York School [i.e., the first generation of Abstract Expressionists, including Pollock and de Kooning], a dialogue and a wink. They [her waterfall paintings] say, "You didn't go far enough. You stopped when you saw abstraction." . . . I've taken the drip and tried to do something with it that the Modernists denied.

Multiplicity in Postmodern Literature

The pursuit of meaning lies at the heart of postmodern literature, but because meaning is always plural and fleeting, attempting to find any permanent or stable meaning in the postmodern world can only lead to frustration. The postmodern hero seeks meaning, but accepts the fact that the search is never-ending. At the beginning of his study of the Western experience of order, entitled *The Order of Things* (in English translation), French historian Michel Foucault [foo-KOH] (1926–1984) describes the origins of his study (**Reading 40.1**):

Fig. 40.15 Pat Steir, *Yellow and Blue One-Stroke Waterfall*. 1992. Oil on canvas, 14'6 $\frac{1}{4}$" × 7'6 $\frac{3}{4}$". The Solomon R. Guggenheim Museum, New York. Gift, John Eric Cheim, 1999. 99.5288. Steir's work is deeply informed by her interest in Tibetan and Chinese religious lore, and she is interested in creating something of their meditative space.

READING 40.1

from Michel Foucault, *The Order of Things* (1966)

This book first arose out of a passage in Borges, out of the laughter that shattered, as I read the passage, all the familiar landmarks of my thought—our thought, the thought that bears the stamp of our age and our geography—breaking up all the ordered surfaces and all the planes with which we are accustomed to tame the wild profusion of existing things. . . . This passage quotes a "certain Chinese encyclopedia" in which it is written that "animals are divided into: (a) belonging to the Emperor, (b) embalmed, (c) tame, (d) suckling pigs, (e) sirens, (f) fabulous, (g) stray dogs, (h) included in the present classification, (i) frenzied, (j) innumerable, (k) drawn with a very fine camelhair brush, (l) et cetera, (m) having just broken the water pitcher, (n) that from a long way off look like flies." In the wonderment of this taxonomy, the thing we apprehend in one great leap, the thing that . . . is demonstrated as the exotic charm of another system of thought, is the limitation of our own, the stark impossibility of thinking that.

The impossibility of Borges's encyclopedia is based on how impossible it is for contemporary thought to recognize difference with no relation to opposition or relation to a common ground—each element in Borges's taxonomy requires a complete shift in point of view, requiring readers to reposition their viewpoint. There is, as Foucault points out, "no *common locus*" beneath this taxonomy, no *center* around which to organize its elements. But it is precisely this possibility of "thinking *that*" that is the goal of postmodern literature. To this point in this survey of the Western humanities, we have referred to a historical series of shifting geographic centers, each one providing a common cultural locus for thought. Postmodern thought alters the situation. The postmodern world consists of multiple centers of thought, each existing simultaneously and independently of one another.

Jorge Luis Borges's [BOR-hays] (1899–1986) short essay entitled "Borges and I" (see **Reading 40.2**, page 1345) may be the first postmodern exploration of this state of affairs. Borges describes himself as a bodily self divided from his persona as a writer. In the postmodern world, meaning shifts according to place and time and, Borges teaches us, point of view—not only the writer's but our own. Meaning might well be determined by a myriad of semantic accidents or misunderstandings, or by a reader whose mood, gender, or particular cultural context defines, for the moment, how and what he or she understands. Postmodern writing produces texts that willingly place themselves in such an open field of interpretation, subject to uncertainty.

Postmodern Fiction A working definition of postmodern fiction thus might include any form of writing that defeats the readers' expectations of coherence, that dwells on the uncertainty and ambiguity of experience, and that requires readers who can adjust to that situation. Among its most notable practitioners are Paul Auster (1947–), William Gass (1924–), Don DeLillo (1936–), Donald Barthelme (1931–1989), John Barth (1930–), John Hawkes (1925–1998), Italo Calvino (1923–1985), Umberto Eco (1932–), and Thomas Pynchon (1937–).

Pynchon's 1963 novel V. is a good example. Set in the mid-1950s, it takes its title from the ongoing quest of one of its two protagonists, Herbert Stencil, for a woman mentioned in his late father's journals. The journal entry is cryptic: "Florence, April, 1899 . . . There is more behind and inside V. than any of us had suspected. Not who, but what: what is she." She is connected, Stencil understands, "with one of those grand conspiracies or foretastes of Armageddon which seemed to have captivated all diplomatic sensibilities in the years preceding the Great War. V. and a conspiracy." Stencil is convinced that "she" still exists, that she is something of an explanation for World War II, for the bomb, for apartheid in South Africa, for all evil. And, as it turns out, "she" is everywhere. She is Venus, the Virgin, the Vatican, Victoria Wren (who had seduced Stencil's father in Florence in the late nineteenth century), Veronica Manganese (Victoria Wren's reinvention of herself in World War I Malta), and Vera Meroving (her next incarnation in Southwest Africa). Ultimately she is transformed from the animate human being to an inanimate "force" behind Germany's V-1 missiles, which devastated London in World War II. Perhaps most of all, V. is the *vanishing point*, the place on the horizon where two parallel lines appear to converge, but is never reachable. Pynchon's novel ends as a conventional murder mystery, in which the criminal does not turn out to be a person so much as a metaphysical force.

In another metaphysical detective story, *City of Glass* (1985), Paul Auster finds himself a character in his own story, suddenly confronting another of his characters, a mystery writer named Daniel Quinn who writes under the pseudonym William Wilson. Quinn has come to Auster's door (**Reading 40.3a**):

READING 40.3a

from Paul Auster, *City of Glass* (1985)

It was a man who opened the apartment door. He was a tall dark fellow in his mid-thirties, with rumpled clothes and a two-day beard. In his right hand, fixed between his thumb and first two fingers, he held an uncapped fountain pen, still poised in a writing position. The man seemed surprised to find a stranger standing before him.

"Yes?" he asked tentatively.

Quinn spoke in the politest tone he could muster. "Were you expecting someone else?"

"My wife, as a matter of fact. That's why I rang the buzzer without asking who it was."

"I'm sorry to disturb you," Quinn apologized. "but I'm looking for Paul Auster."

"I'm Paul Auster," said the man.

The elimination of any distance between the author and his work draws attention to the act of writing, a typical strategy of postmodern fiction. In blurring the boundaries between life and art, reality and fiction, Auster's fictional work becomes *real* in some sense. We can thus gain a clue to Auster's motivation by his character Quinn's explanation early in the novel, about why he writes detective stories (**Reading 40.3b**):

READING 40.3b

from Paul Auster, *City of Glass* (1985)

What he liked about these books was their sense of plenitude and economy. In the good mystery there is nothing wasted, no sentence, no word that is not significant. And even if it is not significant, it has the potential to be so—which amounts to the same thing. The world of the book comes to life, seething with possibilities, with secrets and contradictions. Since everything seen or said, even the slightest, most trivial thing, can bear connection to the outcome of the story, nothing must be overlooked. Everything becomes essence; the center of the book shifts with each event that propels it forward. The center, then, is everywhere, and no circumference can be drawn until the book has come to its end.

The detective is one who looks, who listens, who moves through this morass of objects and events in search of the thought, the idea that will pull all these things together and make sense of them. In effect, the writer and the detective are interchangeable. The reader

---

sees the world through the detective's eyes, experiencing the proliferation of its detail as if for the first time. He has become awake to the things around him, as if, because of the attentiveness he now brings to them, they might begin to carry a meaning other than the simple fact of their existence.

By abolishing distinction between detective, writer, and reader, Auster not only highlights the act of writing, but the act of reading as well, with the reader becoming implicated in the novel's intrigues. Literally caught up in his own fiction, Auster's fictional self spins into a life "seething with possibilities, with secrets and contradictions."

Postmodern Poetry

Because the postmodern self is plural, postmodern literature—including poetry—encompasses a plurality of meanings. Indeed, one of the principal strategies of postmodern poetry is to take advantage of the indeterminacy of certain words—particularly "it," and so-called "pointers," such as "this" and "that"—which, without clear antecedent, might designate anything and everything. This short poem, by David Antin (1932–), is a clear example (**Reading 40.4a**):

READING 40.4a

David Antin, "If We Get It" (1987–1988)

IF WE GET IT   TOGETHER
CAN THEY   TAKE IT   APART
OR   ONLY IF WE LET THEM

To make the point even more indeterminate (and evanescent), Antin's poem was traced out by skywriters in the skies above Santa Monica beach, one line at a time, each line disappearing as the planes circled back to start the next, on Memorial Day, May 23, 1987. Over a year later, on Labor Day weekend, 1988, skywriters wrote the second stanza of Antin's poem over a beach in La Jolla, north of San Diego (**Reading 40.4b**):

READING 40.4b

David Antin, "If We Make It" (1987–1988)

IF WE MAKE IT   TOGETHER OR
FIND IT   WILL THEY BREAK   IN
OR OUT OF IT   OR LEAVE   IT
AS THEY FIND IT   STRICTLY ALONE

The "it" here is completely imprecise and open to interpretation, but the opacity of its reference was exacerbated by the fact that each line of the poem disappeared from sight before the next was written even as the second stanza followed the first by 15 months. Always in the process of its own dissolution and revision, the poem is never "wholly" present to its audience, its meaning always disappearing.

The abolition of meaning is the express subject of many of the poems of one of America's most prominent—and eclectic—poets, John Ashbery (1927–). As Ashbery relates in "On the Towpath," every time we arrive at meaning, we realize, "No, / We aren't meaning that any more." The poem opens as narrative, but the promise of a story almost immediately recedes (**Reading 40.5**):

READING 40.5

from John Ashbery, "On the Towpath" (1977)

At the sign "Fred Muffin's Antiques" they turned off the road into a narrow lane lined with shabby houses.

If the thirst would subside just for awhile
It would be a little bit, enough.
This has happened.
The insipid chiming of the seconds
Has given way to an arc of silence
So old it had never ceased to exist
On the roofs of buildings, in the sky.

The ground is tentative.
The pygmies and jacaranda that were here yesterday
Are back today, only less so.
It is a barrier of fact
Shielding the sky from the earth.

When Ashbery writes, "This has happened," the reader asks, *what* has happened? Ashbery's "This" is entirely ambiguous. What is "tentative" ground? Muddy? Slippery? Along the "towpath" it might well be, but it is also possible for "the ground" to mean "meaning" itself. Isn't "meaning" frequently tentative and slippery? Similarly, when Ashbery writes "It is a barrier of fact," to what does his "it" refer? Later in the poem, he writes,

The sun fades like the spreading
Of a peacock's tail, as though twilight
Might be read as a warning to those desperate
For easy solutions.

Ashbery's sense of play and experimentalism, along with his subversive humor, deliberately frustrates those who desire closure, or meaning. "No," he writes at the end of the poem:

We aren't meaning that any more.
The question has been asked
As though an immense natural bridge had been
Strung across the landscape to any point you wanted.
The ellipse is as aimless as that,
Stretching invisibly into the future so as to reappear
In our present. Its flexing is its account,
Return to the point of no return.

The pun here involves the elliptical arch of Ashbery's imaginary bridge: "The ellipse is" is also "the ellipsis," literally omitting from a sentence a word or phrase that would complete or clarify its meaning. The poem, finally, returns to the point where we recognize we must go on, "into the future," with however little "meaning" there is. For Ashbery, there are only questions, uncertainties, and tentative ground—a concise statement of the postmodern condition.

A Diversity of Cultures:
The Cross-Fertilization of the Present

"Language is a virus," declared American author William S. Burroughs (1914–1997), referring, at least in part, to the fact that American English has become the international language of business, politics, the media, and culture—a plague upon indigenous languages that threatened their extinction. In this context, the collision of global cultures could hardly be ignored. In Asia and Africa, in the Latino, Hispanic, and American Indian worlds, and in Islam, artists have responded by acknowledging that life in a global world increasingly demands that they accept multiple identities. They increasingly find themselves in a double bind—how, they ask, can they remain true to their native or ethnic identities and still participate in the larger world

market? What happens to their work when it enters a context where it is received with little or no understanding of its origins? How, indeed, does the global threaten the local? Is the very idea of the "self" threatened by technology and technological innovation?

The Asian Worldview Although the Japanese have traditionally considered their culture as literally "insular," and largely isolated from outside influence, by the late 1980s, artists like Yasumasa Morimura [mor-ih-moo-rah] (1951–) directly engaged the West. In *Portrait (Twins)* (Fig. 40.16), the artist poses as both Manet's *Olympia* (see the *Closer Look*, Chapter 30) and her maid, manipulating the photograph with a computer in the studio, while subverting the idea of

Olympia, p. 1001

Japanese isolationism even more pointedly. On the one hand, he copies the icons of Western culture, but at the same time he undermines them, drawing attention to the fact that the courtesan and her maid share the same identity—they are "twins"—slaves to the dominant (male) forces of Western society. He places Japanese culture as a whole—and in particular the Japanese male—in the same position, as prostitute and slave to the West.

Fig. 40.16 Yasumasa Morimura, *Portrait (Futago)*. 1988. Color photograph, clear medium, 82 $^3/_4$" × 118" inches. Courtesy of the artist and Luhring Augustine, New York. By cross-dressing—and in this image, un-cross-dressing, Morimura challenges Japanese male gender identity as well.

Fig. 40.17 Zhang Huan, *To Raise the Water Level in a Fish Pond*. August 15, 1997. Performance documentation (middle distance detail), Nanmofang Fishpond, Beijing, China. C-Print on Fuji archival, 60″ × 90″. Courtesy Max Protetch Gallery. Though the performance was a political act, Zhang Huan acknowledged that raising the water in the pond one meter higher was "an action of no avail."

In Morimura's photograph, transcultural exchange is also a transgendered performance. All boundaries, between East and West, male and female, seem to disintegrate, as does the distinction between humans and machines. Morimura's work is a parable of the real possibility of the loss of the self—imagined as the loss of the body—in the technological space of the global future. In China, where, after the rise to power of Mao Zedong in 1949, the government tightened its control over individual expression, the loss of the self has been taken for granted, and the arts have focused on exposing the mechanisms of repression and overthrowing them. For many, like Zhang Hongtu, this has meant leaving China, and his painting, *Bird's Nest, in the Style of Cubism* (see Fig. 40.10), is firmly entrenched in the protest tradition. Despite the fate of that painting, however, in post-Mao China, Chinese artists have been somewhat freer to state their opposition to the government's oppression. In 1997, for instance, performance artist Zhang Huan [hwahn] (1965–) invited 40 peasants who had recently emigrated to Beijing looking for work to stand with him in a pond (Fig. **40.17**). In this way, the city's class of new poor raised the level of the water one meter, an act that Zhang Huan considered a metaphor for raising the government's consciousness. The performance was, Zhang Huan says, "an action of no avail," and yet as an image of people working together in all their vulnerability, the performance is an image of hope.

The African Experience in Art The controversial painting *The Holy Virgin Mary* by Chris Ofili (1968–) (Fig. **40.18**), British-born Nigerian painter, is a case in point. Ofili portrays the Virgin as a black woman, and surrounding her are *putti* (winged cherubs) with bare bottoms and genitalia cut out of pornographic magazines. Two balls of elephant dung, acquired from the London Zoo, support the painting, inscribed with the words "Virgin" and "Mary," a third clump

defining one of her breasts. The son of black African Catholic parents, both of whom were born in Lagos [LAY-goss], Nigeria, and whose first language was Yoruba, Ofili has used this West African culture as a source of inspiration for his art.

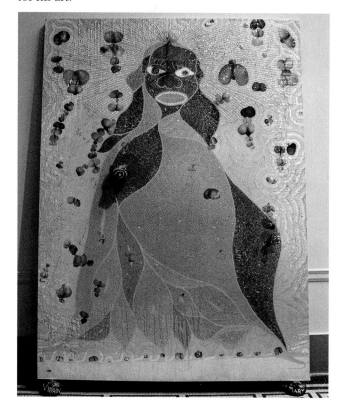

Fig. 40.18 Chris Ofili, *The Holy Virgin Mary*. 1996. Paper collage, oil paint, glitter, polyester resin, map pins, and elephant dung on linen, 8′ × 6′. The Saatchi Gallery, London. Photo: Diane Bondareff/AP World Wide Photos. While on display in Brooklyn, the painting was smeared with white paint by an angry 72-year-old spectator.

Fig. 40.19 Yinka Shonibare, *Victorian Couple*. 1999. Wax-printed cotton textile L: 153 × 92 × 92 cm (60″ × 36″ × 36″). R: 153 × 61 × 61 cm (60″ × 24″ × 24″). Courtesy of the artist, Stephen Friedman Gallery, London, and James Coehn Gallery, New York. Part of the power of these pieces is that they possess no identity—no heads, no hands.

The display of sexual organs, especially in representations of female divinities, is common in Yoruba culture, and Ofili's putti are meant to represent modern examples of this indigenous tradition, symbolizing the fertility of the Virgin Mary. As for elephant dung, in 1992, during a trip to Zimbabwe [zim-bah-bway], Ofili was struck by its beauty after it was dried and varnished. He also came to understand it was worshiped as a symbol of fertility in Zimbabwe, and he began to mount his paintings on clumps of dung as a way, he said, "of raising the paintings up from the ground and giving them a feeling that they've come from the earth rather than simply being hung on a wall."

The Holy Virgin Mary artwork thus reflects Ofili's African heritage. But he understood that the African association of genitalia and dung with fertility and female divinities would be lost on his Western audience. Indeed it was. When the painting was exhibited at the Brooklyn Museum in late 1999, it provoked a stormy reaction. The Catholic Cardinal in New York called it a blasphemous attack on religion, and the Catholic League called for demonstrations at the Museum. New York's Mayor Rudolph W.

Giuliani threatened to cut off the museum's funding as well as evict it from the city-owned building it leased. (He was forced to back down by the courts.) For Ofili, the conflict his painting generated was itself emblematic of the collision of cultures that define his own identity. At the same time, it can be said that the controversy helped make Ofili even more prominent and did nothing to diminish the "marketability" of his art. In 2003, he was chosen to represent Great Britain at the Venice Biennale, perhaps the most prominent contemporary global art exhibition.

Like Chris Ofili, Yinka Shonibare (1962–) was born in England to Nigerian parents, but unlike Ofili, he was raised in Nigeria before returning to art school in London. In the mid-1990s, he began creating artworks from the colorful printed fabrics that are worn throughout West Africa, all of which are created by English and Dutch designers, manufactured in Europe, then exported to Africa. At that point, they are remarketed in the West as authentic African design (Fig. **40.19**). "By making hybrid clothes," Shonibare explains, "I collapse the idea of a European dichotomy against an African one. There is no way you can work out where the opposites are. There is no way you can work out the precise nationality of my dresses, because they do not have one. And there is no way you can work out the precise economic status of the people who would've worn those dresses because the economic status and the class status are confused in these objects." Sometimes, even the time period of these costumes is drawn into question. They are identified as "Victorian," and indeed the bustle on the woman is a Victorian fashion, but the man's dress seems startlingly hip.

The Latino and Hispanic Presence in the United States A cross-fertilization of traditions has traditionally infused the art of Latino and Hispanic culture in North America. From the beginning of the sixteenth century, the Hispanization of Indian culture and the Indianization of Hispanic culture in Latin and South America created a unique cultural pluralism (see Chapter 23). By the last half of the twentieth century, Latino culture became increasingly Americanized, and an influx of Hispanic immigrants helped Latinize American culture. The situation has been summed up by Puerto Rico–born poet Aurora Levins Morales [moh-RAH-lays] (1954–), in "Child of the Americas" (**Reading 40.6**):

READING 40.6

Aurora Levins Morales, "Child of the Americas" (1986)

I am a child of the Americas,
a light-skinned mestiza of the Caribbean,
a child of many diaspora, born into this continent at
    a crossroads.
I am a U.S. Puerto Rican Jew,
a product of the ghettos of New York I have never
    known.

An immigrant and the daughter and granddaughter
  of immigrants.
I speak English with passion: it's the tongue of my
  consciousness,
a flashing knife blade of crystal, my tool, my craft.
I am Caribeña, island grown. Spanish is my flesh,
Ripples from my tongue, lodges in my hips:
the language of garlic and mangoes,
the singing of poetry, the flying gestures of my hands.
I am of Latinoamerica, rooted in the history of my
  continent:
I speak from that body.

I am not African. Africa is in me, but I cannot return.
I am not taína. Taíno[1] is in me, but there is no way back.
I am not European. Europe lives in me, but I have no
  home there.

I am new. History made me. My first language was
  spanglish.
I was born at the crossroads
and I am whole.

[1] **Taino:** The first Native American population encountered by Christopher Columbus.

Just such a "difficult whole" is also captured by Chicana muralist Judith F. Baca (1946–) in a 1990 project created for the town of Guadalupe [GWAHD-ul-oop], California (Fig. **40.20**), in an area whose economy is almost entirely dependent on enormous farms that employ 80 percent of the population of Mexican heritage. The project offers a thought-provoking glimpse of the new "Mexican towns" that have become more commonplace in rural California.

Reflecting the community's pride in its heritage, the mural refers directly to César Chávez's [SHAH-vez] (1927–1993) successful efforts to unionize farm workers through the creation of the National Farm Workers Association in 1962 (today known as the United Farm Workers). One of the union's most effective actions was the boycott of table grapes from 1966 to 1970. Beginning with local strikes, marches, and demonstrations, the movement spread across the state and then nationwide. Chávez and a coalition of Hispanic and Filipino farm workers effectively challenged the substandard wages and working conditions imposed by large vineyards. Political and labor activism had cultural consequences, as a vital theatrical tradition developed alongside Chávez's new union.

Luis Valdez (1940–) was a playwright before joining Chávez to help organize farm workers in Delano, California. There he founded El Teatro Campesino [el tay-AH-troh kahm-pay-SEE-noh] (The Farmworkers Theater) to raise funds for "La Causa" (the cause), the simple but effective term that helped transform a local strike into a broad, instantly identifiable global movement. Combining Italian commedia dell'arte [koh-MEH-dee-ah dell-AR-teh] (improvisational comedy) and Mexican vaudeville, by 1968, the Farmworkers Theater had redefined itself as a "teatro chicano" and moved out of the fields and into Los Angeles in an effort to portray a wider range of Chicano experience.

Valdez's national success came in 1978, when he produced *Zoot Suit*, a play that exposed the police brutality and injustices faced by the Chicano community during the "Zoot Suit Riots" and the "Sleep Lagoon" trial of the 1940s. The main character in the play, Henry Reyna, is the leader of the 38th Street Gang. Heading to a party that had been terrorized by rival gang members just moments before, Henry and his friends were mistaken for members of the rival gang and attacked. After a man from the party was killed, the entire gang was indicted on charges

Fig. 40.20 Judith F. Baca, *Farmworkers at Guadalupe*. 1990. One of four murals, 8′ × 7′. Guadalupe, California. © 1997 Judith F. Baca. Courtesy of the artist. To make the murals, Baca hired five local teenagers to construct a town chronology, collected family photos and stories, and called town meetings to discuss her imagery.

of murder. Their identity, both cultural and criminal, was tied to "zoot suits," two-piece suits consisting of a long jacket and pegged pants, accompanied by a long keychain that looped almost to the ankle. The importance of the apparel is expressed by the character El Pachuco [pah-CHOO-koh]—part Aztec god, part quintessential 1940s Zoot Suiter, and part Greek chorus—when he sings the following *corrido* [kor-REE-doh], or traditional Mexican narrative ballad (**Reading 40.7**):

READING 40.7

from Luis Valdez, *Zoot Suit* (1978)

Trucha, ese loco, vamos al rorlo
Wear that carlango, tramos y tando
Dance with your huisa
Dance to the boogie tonight!
'Cause the zoot suit is the style in California
También en Colorado y Arizona
They're wearing that tacuche en El Paso
Y en todos los salones de Chicago
You better get hep tonight
And put on that zoot suit!

Valdez's use of "Spanglish" is like that of Aurora Levins Morales in "Child of the Americas," and both exemplify the confluence of cultures that the Latino experience in the United States represents—a plural language for a plural self.

Recovering Tradition: Contemporary Native American Art

Native North Americans have been among the most isolated and marginalized of all the world's indigenous peoples. Diverse but sequestered on arid reservations, enmeshed in poverty and unemployment, their traditions and languages on the brink of extinction, Native Americans seemed the consummate "Other." However, in 1968, in Minneapolis, Minnesota, a gathering of local Native Americans, led by Dennis Banks, George Mitchell, and Clyde Bellecourt, decided to address these problems through collective action, and founded the American Indian Movement (AIM). Almost a quarter-century later, Banks recalled what motivated them:

> Because of the slum housing conditions; the highest unemployment rate in the whole of this country; police brutality against our elders, women, and children, Native Warriors came together from the streets, prisons, jails and the urban ghettos of Minneapolis to form the American Indian Movement. They were tired of begging for welfare, tired of being scapegoats in America and decided to start building on the strengths of our own people; decided to build our own schools; our own job training programs; and our own destiny. That was our motivation to begin. That beginning is now being called "the Era of Indian Power."

AIM was, from the outset, a militant organization. On Thanksgiving Day 1970, AIM members boarded the *Mayflower II* at its dock in Plymouth harbor as a countercelebration of the three hundred and fiftieth anniversary of the Pilgrims' landing at Plymouth Rock. A year later, they occupied Mount Rushmore National Monument. In AIM's point of view, the site, which was sacred to their culture, had been desecrated by the carving of the American presidents Washington, Jefferson, Roosevelt, and Lincoln into the mountain. The occupation was designed to draw attention to the 1868 Treaty of Fort Laramie, which had deeded the Black Hills, including Mount Rushmore, to the Lakota Sioux. The U.S. military had ignored the treaty, forcing the Lakota onto the Pine Ridge reservation on the plains south of the Black Hills. There, on December 29, 1890, with the Battle of Wounded Knee, conflict erupted (see Chapter 32). In 1973, AIM militants took control of Wounded Knee and were quickly surrounded by federal marshals. For over two months, they exchanged gunfire, until the AIM militants surrendered. Of course, not everyone agreed with AIM's tactics, but the group did help to revitalize Native American cultures throughout the hemisphere and furthered an interest in traditional art forms.

A member of AIM's Central Council, who served as representative to the United Nations, Cherokee-born Jimmie Durham (1940–) makes what he calls "fake Indian artifacts," in which non-Indian materials, such as the bright red, chrome automobile bumper, is transformed into something that looks completely Indian (Fig. 40.21). As he explains: "We took glass beads, horses, wool blankets, wheat flour for frybread, etc., very early, and immediately made them identifiably 'Indian' things. We are able to do that because of our cultural integrity and because our societies are dynamic and able to take in new ideas." But the cultural forces at work here are highly complex. As much as Indian culture has the ability to absorb Western materials and make them its own, anything an Indian makes, Durham knows, is always seen by the dominant Anglo-American culture as an "artifact,"

Fig. 40.21 Jimmie Durham, *Headlights*. 1983. Car parts, antler, shell, etc. Private collection. Courtesy of the artist. The presence of the antler on the bumper suggests that the Native American reaction to European contact was comparable to that of "a deer caught in the headlights."

Fig. 40.22 David P. Bradley (White Earth Ojibwe and Mdewakaton Dakota), *Indian Country Today.* 1996–97. Acrylic on canvas, 70″ × 60″. Museum Purchase through the Mr. and Mrs. James Krebs Fund. Photograph courtesy Peabody Essex Museum. In the foreground is the Rio Grande River, teeming with fish, the lifeblood of region.

In the center of the pueblo, Bradley depicts a traditional kachina [kah-CHEE-nuh] dance taking place in the pueblo. Performed by male dancers who impersonate kachinas, the spirits who inhabit the clouds, the rain, crops, animals, and even ideas such as growth and fertility (see Chapter 1), the dances are sacred and, although tourists are allowed to view them, photography is strictly prohibited. The actual masks worn in ceremonies are not considered art objects by the Pueblo. Rather, they are thought of as active agents in the transfer of power and knowledge between the gods and the men who wear them in dance. Kachina figurines are made for sale to tourists, but they are considered empty of any ritual power or significance. This commercialization of native tradition is the real subject of Bradley's painting. The native peoples' ability to withstand this onslaught is suggested by the giant mesa, endowed with kachina-like eyes and mouth, that overlooks the entire scene, suggesting that the spirits still oversee and protect their people.

a surviving fragment of a "lost" people that does not quite qualify as "art" proper. His "fake" artifacts expose this assumption.

Contemporary life in the Southwestern pueblos is the subject of *Indian Country Today* (Fig. **40.22**) painted by David P. Bradley (1954–), a Native American of Ojibwe [oh-JIB-way] descent who has lived for the last 30 years in Santa Fe, New Mexico. Behind the pueblo, to the left, the parking lot of an Indian-run casino is filled with tourist buses. Behind it, in the distance, is the city of Santa Fe. The train passing behind the pueblo is the Santa Fe Railroad's "Chief"—the very image of Anglo-American culture's appropriation of Native traditions. To the right of the central mesa is the Four Corners Power Plant in northwestern New Mexico, one of the largest coal-fired generating stations in the United States and one of the greatest polluters. (Note the smoke reemerging on the far side of the mesa.) Behind the plant is an open-pit strip mine. Fighter jets rise over the landscape, reminders of the nearby Los Alamos National Laboratory, where classified work on the design of nuclear weapons is performed.

Imaging Islam The tension between political reality, cultural identity, and personal identity is especially evident in the work of Middle Eastern women artists who have moved between their homelands and the West. Shirin Neshat (1957–) grew up in Iran in an upper-middle-class family, but after graduating from high school, she moved to the United States to study art. When the Islamic Revolution overtook her homeland in 1979, 22-year-old Neshat found herself living in exile. When she returned home 11 years later, Iran had completely changed. She recalls:

> During the Shah's regime, we had a very open, free environment. There was a kind of dilution between West and East—the way we looked and the way we lived. When I went back everything seemed changed. There seemed to be very little color. Everyone was black or white. All the women wearing the black chadors. It was immediately shocking. Street names had changed from old Persian names to Arabic and Muslim names. . . .

This whole shift of the Persian identity toward a more Islamic one created a kind of crisis. I think to this day there's a great sense of grief that goes with that.

In Neshat's series of photographs, *Women of Allah*, of which *Rebellious Silence* (Fig. **40.23**) is characteristic, many of the women hold guns, subverting the stereotype of women as submissive. At the same time, they bury their individuality beneath the black *chador*, and their bodies are inscribed in Farsi calligraphy with poetry by Tahereh Saffarzadeh, whose verses express the deep belief of many Iranian women in Islam. Only within the context of Islam, they believe, are women truly equal to men, and they claim that the *chador* [CHAH-dor], by concealing a woman's sexuality, prevents her from becoming a sexual object. The *chador* also expresses the women's solidarity with men in the rejection of Western culture. Yet, even as she portrays the militant point of view, Neshat does not blindly accept the Islamic fundamentalist understanding of the *chador*. It is clear that the *Women of Allah* photographs underscore the Islamic world's inability to separate beliefs that focus on religion and spirituality from those that concern politics and violence.

The Pakistani painter Shahzia Sikander (1969–) addresses her heterogeneous background in works such as *Pleasure Pillars* (Fig. **40.24**) by reinventing the traditional genre of miniature painting in a hybrid of styles. Combining her training as a miniature artist in her native Pakistan with her focus on contemporary art during her studies at the Rhode Island School of Design, Sikander explores the tensions inherent in Islam's encounter with the Western world, Christianity as well as the neighboring South Asian tradition of Hinduism. In the center of *Pleasure Pillars*, Sikander portrays herself with the spiraling horns of a powerful male ram. Below her head are two bodies, one a Western Venus (see Fig. 5.20), the other Devi, the Hindu goddess of fertility, rain, health, and nature, who is said to hold the entire universe in her womb (see Chapter 7). Between them, two hearts pump blood, a reference to her dual sources of inspiration, East and West. Eastern and Western images of

Fig. 40.23 Shirin Neshat, *Rebellious Silence*, from the series *Women of Allah*. 1994. Gelatin silver print and ink. Photo: Cynthia Preston. © Shirin Neshat, courtesy Gladstone Gallery, New York. "The main question I ask," Neshat has said, "is, what is the experience of being a woman in Islam? I then put my trust in those women's words who have lived and experienced the life of a woman behind the *chador*."

power also inform the image as a lion kills a deer at the bottom left, a direct artistic quote from an Iranian miniature of the Safavid [sah-FAH-weed] dynasty (1499–1736), and at the top, a modern fighter jet roars past.

Fig. 40.24 Shahzia Sikander, *Pleasure Pillars*. 2001. Watercolor, dry pigment, vegetable color, tea, and ink on wasli paper, 12″ × 10″. Courtesy Sikkema Jenkins & Co., New York. As part of her ongoing investigation of identity, Sikander has taken to wearing the veil in public, something she never did before moving to America, in what she labels "performances" of her Pakistani heritage.

Fig. 40.25 Eleanor Antin, _Minetta Lane—A Ghost Story_. 1994–95. Filmic installation. View [one, two, three] of three. Installation view (left), two stills from video projections (below and right). Below: Through the Lover's Window. Right: Through the Artist's Window. Copyright Eleanor Antin Courtesy Ronald Feldman Fine Arts, New York. Each of the installation's three films is about ten minutes long.

A Multiplicity of Media: New Technologies

Just as the electronic media have revolutionized modern culture, dating from Thomas Edison's first audio recording to the motion picture, radio, television, and digital technologies, from the Internet to the iPod, so too have the arts been revolutionized by these media. This transformation was most fundamentally realized in the visual arts through the medium of video

Eleanor Antin, for instance, came to video art through performance. She understood that her race- and gender-blurring performances—as the invented personae the King of Solana Beach (see Fig. 39.18) and Eleanora Antinova, the black ballerina of Diaghilev's Ballets Russes—could be documented by video camera. But she also realized that she could project multiple versions of herself and others simultaneously in installation settings.

An example is _Minetta Lane—A Ghost Story_ (Fig. **40.25**), first exhibited in New York City in 1995. It consists of a re-creation of three buildings on a Greenwich Village (New York) street that runs for two blocks. In the 1940s and 1950s, it was the site of a low-rent artists' community, and

Antin's installation recreates the bohemian character of that lost world. The installation itself consists of three narrative films, transferred to video disc, and back-projected onto the tenement windows of the reconstructed lane. The viewer, passing through the scene, thus voyeuristically peers into each window and views what transpires inside. In one window, two lovers play in a kitchen tub. In a second, an Abstract Expressionist painter is at work. And in a third, an old man tucks in his family of caged birds for the night. Ghosts of a past time, these characters are trapped on celluloid, but their world is inhabited by another, unseen ghost. A little girl, who is apparently invisible to those in the scene but clearly visible to us, paints a giant "X" across the artist's canvas and destroys the relationship of the lovers in the tub. She represents a destructive force that, in Antin's view, is present in all of us—and, in fact, present in the very nature of her electronic medium. For the artist, the lovers and the old man represent the parts of us that we have lost—our youth. They represent ideas about art, sexuality, and life that, despite our nostalgia for them, are no longer relevant.

Contemporary video art is, in fact, haunted by ghosts. In a catalogue essay that she wrote for another installation of _Minetta Lane_, Antin mused, "What I'm after is some image in my mind that I want to make visible, knowable, perceivable. Make the immaterial material, so that someone else can turn it back into some other immaterial image that I hope is not too alien from my own." Antin's films produce images that are imprinted on our minds, where they become immaterial again, summoned by an act of memory. The filmic image is the trace—or what remains—of a lost past. It is, of its nature, inherently "ghostly."

As the "ghost" metaphor suggests, temporal media like video art are often concerned with the passing of time itself, the life cycle from birth to death. Video artist Bill Viola [vye-OH-la] (1951–) has been fascinated, throughout his career, by the passage of time. His principal metaphor for this passage is water, which not only flows, like time, but because it can be seen, seems to make both time and space tangible and palpable. His video installation piece _Five Angels for the Millennium_ (Fig. **40.26**) is composed of five individual video sequences that show a clothed man plunging into a pool of water. The duration of each video is different, with long sequences of peaceful aqueous landscape suddenly interrupted by the explosive sound of the body's dive into the water. He describes the process of making the piece:

> _Five Angels_ came out of a three-day shoot in Long Beach that I had undertaken for several other projects. All I knew was that I wanted to film a man plunging into water, sinking down, below, out of frame—drowning. A year or so later, going through this old footage, I came across five shots of this figure and started working with them—intuitively and without a conscious plan. I became completely absorbed by this man sinking in water, and by the sonic and physical environment I had in mind for the piece.

Fig. 40.26 Bill Viola, *Five Angels for the Millennium.* **2001.** Video/sound installation, five channels of color video projection on walls in a large, dark room (room dimensions variable); stereo sound for each projection; project image size 7'10 $\frac{1}{2}$" × 10' × 6" each. Edition of three. Photo: Mike Bruce, courtesy Anthony d'Offay, London.

When I showed the finished work to Kira [Perov], my partner, she pointed out something I had not realized until that moment: this was not a film of a drowning man. Somehow, I had unconsciously run time backwards in the five films, so all but one of the figures rush upwards and out of the water. I had inadvertently created images of ascension, from death to birth.

Because the videos are continuously looped and projected onto the gallery walls, their different durations make it impossible to predict which wall will suddenly become animated by the dive—the one behind you, the one in front of you, the one at your side. The experience is something like being immersed in both water and time simultaneously, in the flow of the moment. For Viola, video differs from film in exactly this sense. The most fundamental aspect of video's origin as a medium is the *live* camera. Video is in the moment. And Viola's installation literally spatializes time, even as time becomes as palpable as the watery surfaces that Viola depicts.

Today, of course, video art *per se* no longer exists—the medium has become entirely digital, and, in fact, although it is far more expensive, artists working with time-based media have preferred, given the higher quality of the image, to work with film. One of the seminal time-based works of the late twentieth century, *The Way Things Go*, was shot on film by Swiss artists Peter Fischli (1952–) and David Weiss (1946–) (Fig. **40.27**). It was first screened in 1987 at Documenta, the international art fair that takes place every five years in Kassel, Germany. There it caused an immediate sensation, and since then it has been screened in museums around the world. It consists of a kinetic sculptural installation inside a 100-foot warehouse that begins when a black plastic bag (full of who knows quite what), suspended from the ceiling,

Fig. 40.27 Peter Fischi and David Weiss, two stills from *Der Lauf der Dinge (The Way Things Go).* **1987.** 16mm color film, 30 min. © Peter Fischli, David Weiss, Courtesy of Matthew Marks Gallery, New York. Fischli and Weiss's film is widely available on DVD (released by First Run/Icarus Films).

spins downward until it hits a tire on top of a slightly inclined orange-colored board and nudges it over a small strip of wood down the shallow slope. This initiates a series of physical and chemical, cause-and-effect chain reactions in which ordinary household objects slide, crash, spew liquids onto, and ignite one another in a linear 30-minute sequence of self-destructing interactions. In part a metaphor for the history of Western culture, in part an hilarious slapstick comedy of errors, for many viewers *The Way Things Go* captures the spirit of modern life.

The 21-minute film *Flooded McDonald's*, by the Danish collaborative group Superflex, consisting of Jakob Fenger (1968–), Rasmus Nielsen (1969–), and Bjørnstjerne Reuter Christiansen (1969–), reenacts a similar scenario (Fig. **40.28**). The film was shot in a hangar outside Bangkok, Thailand, where they built an exact replica of a McDonald's restaurant on a scale of 1:1 at the bottom of a swimming pool, which they then proceeded to flood. The restaurant is empty as water begins to seep in under the doors and then slowly fills the entire establishment, eventually rising to a

level where French fries, burgers, and soft drink containers float off the tables and counters, and then submerging even their cameras which shoot the floating detritus like some parody of a Jacques Cousteau underwater adventure. "McDonald's," the group has explained, "is a global living-room," and to flood it is to raise the apocalyptic specter of

Fig. 40.28 **Superflex, two stills from *Flooded McDonald's*. 2008.** Film (color, sound), 21 min. Produced by Propeller Group (Ho Chi Minh City) in association with Matching Studio (Bangkok) and co-commissioned by the South London Gallery, the Louisiana Museum of Modern Art (Denmark) and Oriel Mostyn Gallery (Wales) with generous support from the Danish Film Institute. Production: Director: Tuan Andrew Nguyen and Superflex. Cinematography: Ha Thuc Phu Nam. Sound Design: Alan Hayslip. Editing: The Propeller Group. Louisiana Museum of Modern Art. Acquired with the support of a private donor. As the credits make clear, the work is itself an example of international artistic collaboration.

Fig. 40.29 **Pipilotti Rist, three stills from *I'm Not a Girl Who Misses Much*. 1986.** Single-track video (color, sound), 5 min. As much as Rist's video is a parody of music videos in general, it also evokes the horror of John Lennon's assassination in 1980 and the terrible irony that would come to inform the lyrics of *Happiness is a Warm Gun*.

global warming at the same time that it seems to take comedic revenge on global merchandising, putting the filmmakers in the absurdist role of God bringing down the deluge upon the world.

One of the more innovative artists exploring the technological possibilities of time-based media is the Swiss-born Pipilotti Rist (1962–), who began working with video in 1986 with a single-track video, *I'm Not the Girl Who Misses Much* (Fig. **40.29**), a sort of parody of the videos that had begun to air on television with the advent of MTV in 1983. The video transforms the lyrics to John Lennon's song *Happiness Is a Warm Gun* (1968) from "She's not a girl," to "I'm not the girl." Rist, who would play percussion, bass, and flute in the all-girl rock band Les Reines Prochaines (The Next Queens) from 1988 to 1994, bounces up and down as she dances, manipulating her voice by speeding it up to a frenetic pace and slowing it down to the pace of a funereal march, her image sliding in and out of focus. Her

blatant dismissal of high production values is equally a dismissal of the social values of MTV itself, where women had quickly been diminished to mere sexual objects.

In an installation first screened at the Venice Biennale in 1997, *Ever Is Over All* (Fig. **40.30**), a woman is seen walking down a street, dressed in a conservative blue dress and bright red shoes à la Dorothy in *The Wizard of Oz*. She is carrying a large red flower—in fact, a flower known as a red-hot poker, images of which are simultaneously projected around the corner of the room. A soft, even soothing "la, la, la" of a song accompanies her. With a broad smile on her face, she lifts the long-stemmed flower in her hand and smashes it into the passenger window of a parked car. Glass shatters. She moves on, smashing more car windows. Up from behind her comes a uniformed woman police officer, who passes her by with a smiling salute. Her stroll down the boulevard plays in a continuous loop in the gallery. This is the new Oz, the Emerald City that we discover "somewhere

Fig. 40.30 Pipilotti Rist, ***Ever Is Over All.*** **1997.** Video installation, National Museum of Foreign Art, Sofia, Bulgaria, 1999; sound with Anders Guggisbert; two overlapping video projections, audio system. Collection, The Museum of Modern Art, New York. The person playing the part of the hit woman is Swiss journalist and documentary filmmaker Silvana Ceschi.

Fig. 40.31 Janine Antoni, _Touch._ 2002. Color video, sound (projection), 9:36 min. loop. The Art Institute of Chicago. Gift of Donna and Howard Stone, 2007.43. A short segment of _Touch_, narrated by Antoni, is available for viewing at www.pbs.org/art21/artists/antoni/index.html#.

over the rainbow," where the tensions between nature and civilization, violence and pleasure, the legal and the criminal, impotence and power—all seem to have dissolved.

Artist Janine Antoni (1964–) works in a variety of media, including performance and video, often making art out of everyday activities such as eating, bathing, and sleeping. The tension between the mundane qualities of her activities and the technical sophistication of their recording results in a sense of almost magical transformation comparable to that of the Surrealists (see Chapter 35). In the video, _Touch_ (Fig. **40.31**), Antoni appears to walk along the horizon, an illusion created by her walking on tightrope stretched between two backhoes on the beach directly in front of her childhood home on Grand Bahama Island. She had learned to tightrope walk, practicing about an hour a day, as an exercise in bodily control and meditation. As she practiced, she realized, she says, that "it wasn't

that I was getting more balanced, but that I was getting more comfortable with being out of balance." This she took as a basic lesson in life. In _Touch_, this sense of teetering balance is heightened by the fact that she appears to be walking on an horizon line that we know can never be reached as it continually moves away from us as we approach it. We know, in other words, that we are in an impossible place, and yet it is a place that we have long contemplated and desired as a culture—the same horizon that Romantic painters such as Caspar David Friedrich looked out upon in paintings like _Monk by the Sea_ (see Fig. 27.9). When, in the course of the full-length video, both Antoni and the rope disappear, we are left, as viewers, contemplating this illusory line and what it means. And we come to understand that the horizon represents what is always in front of us. "It's a very hopeful image," Antoni says, "it's about the future, about the imagination."

The Environment and the Humanist Tradition

What is the role of art today? What does the museum offer us? What about literature, the book, the poem? Is the museum merely a repository of cultural artifacts? Is the poem a tired and self-indulgent form of intellectual narcissism? Can opera move us even more meaningfully than popular music? How can the arts help us to understand not only our past, but our present and our future? These are questions that artists, writers, and musicians are continually asking themselves, and questions that a student of the humanities, coming to the end of a book such as this one, might well ask themselves as well.

Consider an installation by Danish artist Olafur Eliason (1967–), *The Weather Project* (Fig. **40.32**). When he installed it in the mammoth Turbine Hall of the Tate Modern, London, in the winter of 2003, it was roundly criticized as "mere" entertainment, in no small part because it attracted over 2 million visitors. At the end of the 500-foot hall hung a giant yellow orb, 90 feet above the floor. The ceiling itself was covered with mirrors, thus doubling the size of the space. The "sun" was actually a semicircle of some 200 yellow sodium streetlights, which, when reflected in the ceiling mirrors, formed a circle. Artificial mist machines filled the hall with a dull, wintry fog. What was the attraction?

In no small part, it seemed to reside in the very artificiality of the environment. Visitors to the top floor of the gallery could easily see the trussing supporting the mirrored ceiling as well as the construction of the sun shape. The extraordinary visual effects of Eliason's installation were, in the end, created by rather ordinary means. But this ordinariness, in turn, suggested profound and somewhat disturbing truths about our world and our environment. If Eliason could create this almost postapocalyptic environment—with its dead, heatless sun, perpetual fog, and cold stone ground—with such minimal means, what might we, as a world, create with the advanced technologies so readily at our disposal? In other words, as viewers laid on the floor of the museum, and

Fig. 40.32 Olafur Eliason, *The Weather Project*, installation view at the Tate Modern, London. 2003. Monofrequency lights, projection foil, haze machine, mirror oil, aluminum, and scaffolding. Courtesy of the artist, Tanya Bonakdar Gallery, New York, and neugerriemschneider, Berlin.

saw themselves reflected on the ceiling above, were they viewing themselves in the present, or seeing themselves in the future? What hath humanity wrought?

The Weather Project was, then, something of a chilling experience, both literally and figuratively. "I regard . . . museums," Eliason has said, "as spaces where one steps even deeper into society, from where one can scrutinize society." It is perhaps relevant for you to consider this book as such a space. To conclude, what is it about your world that you have come to understand and appreciate more deeply and fully? ■

THINKING BACK

What characterizes postmodern architecture?

The 1972 book *Learning from Las Vegas* argued that the visual complexity of Las Vegas, with its competing sign systems, created a condition of contradiction that was inclusive, not exclusive. How does the new spatial order epitomized by Las Vegas reflect the postmodern condition? How would you describe Robert Venturi's "difficult whole"? Among the most itinerant artists of our increasingly nomadic postmodern era are its architects. Responding to competitions that will lend individual sites in the "world metropolis" a sense of being unique, they design monuments to national and corporate identity. How have architects responded to environmental concerns in their work? One useful way to define the "postmodern" is to create a list of words—like "uncertainty"—that define it. What other words help you to define the postmodern?

How does postmodern theory reflect pluralist thought?

The roots of postmodern theory rest in the linguistic model of meaning established in French structuralism. How would you describe that linguistic model? How does the poststructuralist thought of Jacques Derrida build on and differ from Saussure's example? How would you describe deconstruction as a philosophical methodology? Chaos theorists posit that biological and mathematical patterns that appear random, unstable, and disorderly, are actually parts of larger, more "difficult wholes." How does the fractal geometry of Benoit Mandelbrot counter traditional Euclidean geometry? What is the butterfly effect? How has chaos theory helped us to understand the human body and begin to cure disease?

How are pluralism and diversity reflected in art and literature?

The postmodern sense of inclusiveness authorized a wide variety of experimentation in painting, often mediating between the competing and contradictory demands of realism and abstraction. How do artists like Gerhard Richter and Pat Steir approach this problem?

Postmodern literature pursues meaning where meaning is always plural, multiplicitous, and fleeting—frustrating any kind of significant final answer. Multiple, contradictory centers of thought exist simultaneously and independently of one another. In fiction, a novel like Thomas Pynchon's *V.* creates a world of uncertainty and ambiguity, similar to Paul Auster's *City of Glass*, in which the line between fiction and reality totally collapses. How do poets like David Antin and John Ashbery approach the problem of meaning in their work?

The mobility of modern artists has led many to feel they have multiple identities. How do artists like Chris Ofili and Yinka Shonibare mediate between their British training and their Nigerian roots? How does the work of Yasumasa Morimura collapse the boundaries between East and West, male and female? In the United States, the encounters of Hispanic with North American society, especially in California, led to political murals and theater. How does "Spanglish" reflect this encounter? In the late 1960s, the American Indian Movement (AIM) sought to restore power to Native American peoples, the plurality of whose cultures was itself enormous. How do artists like Jimmie Durham and David P. Bradley address the confrontation between native and Anglo cultures? Finally, how do Islamic artists like Shirin Neshat and Shahzia Sikander negotiate the boundaries between Islam and the West?

Artists have also used new electronic media in creating new artistic spaces. Artists like Eleanor Antin make installations designed to be viewed for a specific length of time and then be dismantled. Bill Viola creates video installations that take advantage of the medium's ability to evoke the world of dreams, memories, and reflections, and Viola's especially immerses the viewer in the flow of time, the cycle of life and death. How do films like Peter Fischli and David Weiss's *The Way Things Go* and Superflex's *Flooded McDonald's* address the contemporary historical moment? How do Pipilotti Rist's videos address popular culture?

PRACTICE MORE Get flashcards for images and terms and review chapter material with quizzes at **www.myartslab.com**

from Jorge Luis Borges, "Borges and I" (1967)

Although Jorge Luis Borges published widely in almost every imaginable form, his reputation as one of the leaders of modern Latin-American literature rests almost entirely on a series of some 40 short stories, tales, and sketches—"fictions," as he called them—the bulk of them published between 1937 and 1955. Many of these sometimes very brief fictions take on a quality of dreamlike mystery. The short fiction, reprinted here in its entirety, "Borges and I," is a late example of the form.

BORGES AND I

The other one, the one called Borges, is the one things happen to. I walk through the streets of Buenos Aires and stop for a moment, perhaps mechanically now, to look at the arch of an entrance hall and the grillwork on the gate; I know of Borges from the mail and see his name on a list of professors or in a biographical dictionary. I like hourglasses, maps, eighteenth-century typography, the taste of coffee and the prose of Stevenson; he shares these preferences, but in a vain way that turns them into the attributes of an actor. It would be an exaggeration to say that ours is a hostile relationship; I live, let 10 myself go on living, so that Borges may contrive his literature, and this literature justifies me. It is no effort for me to confess that he has achieved some valid pages, but those pages cannot save me, perhaps because what is good belongs to no one, not even to him, but rather to the language and to tradition. Besides, I am destined to perish, definitively, and only some instant of myself can survive in him. Little by little, I am giving over everything to him, though I am quite aware of his perverse custom of falsifying and magnifying things. Spinoza knew that 20 all things long to persist in their being; the stone eternally wants to be a stone and the tiger a tiger. I shall remain in Borges, not in myself (if it is true that I am someone), but I recognize myself less in his books than in many others or in the laborious strumming of a guitar. Years ago I tried to free myself from him and went from the mythologies of the suburbs to the games with time and infinity, but those games belong to Borges now and I shall have to imagine other things. Thus my life a flight and I lose everything and everything belongs to oblivion, or to him.

I do not know which of us has written this page.

Translated by J. E. I.

READING CRITICALLY

In this short parable, the "I" accuses "Borges" of "falsification and exaggerating." Whom are we to trust, or are we to trust anyone, and how would you say that defines the postmodern condition?

INDEX

PHOTO CREDITS

Chapter 21

PO Erich Lessing / Art Resource, NY; **21-1** © Tibor Bognar / Alamy; **21-2** © Eddie Gerald / Alamy; **21-4** Scala / Art Resource, NY; **21-5** Erich Lessing / Art Resource, NY; **21-6** Canali Photobank, Milan, Italy; **21-7** Scala / Art Resource, NY; **21-8** © Achim Bednorz, Koln; **21-9** Scala / Art Resource, NY; **21-10** Electra/Art Resource, NY; **21-12** Alinari / Art Resource, NY; **21-13** Canali Photobank, Milan, Italy; **21-14** Canali Photobank, Milan, Italy; **21-15** The Art Archive / Galleria degli Uffizi Florence / Alfredo Dagli Orti; **21-16** Elisabetta Sirani (Italian, 1638-1665), "Virgin and Child". 1663 Oil on canvas, 34 × 27 1/2 in. National Museum of Women in the Arts, Washington, D.C. Gift of Wallace and Wilhelmina Holladay. Conservation funds generously provided by the Southern California State Committee of the National Museum of Women in the Arts.; **21-17** Atemisia Gentileschi, "Judith and Maidservant with the Head of Holofernes". 1625. The Detroit Institute of Arts. Gift of Leslie H. Green. 52.253. Photo ©1984 Detroit Institute of Arts/The Bridgeman Art Library, NY; **21-18** Cameraphoto Arte, Venice / Art Resource, NY; **21-19** Music Room (fresco), Guarana, Jacopo (1720-1808)/Santa Maria dei Derelitti, Venice, Italy/The Bridgeman Art Library; **21-20** Bernini, Gian Lorenzo (1598-1680). First project for the Louvre, elevation for the main facade, Rec1folio4. Photo: Michele Bellot. Musee du Louvre/RMN Reunion des Musees Nationaux, France. SCALA/Art Resource, NY; **21-21** © Achim Bednorz, Koln; page 685 (top), Scala / Art Resource, NY; page 685 (bottom), The Art Archive / Gianni Dagli Orti; pages 686-687, Scala / Art Resource, NY.

Chapter 22

22-1 Jan Vermeer, "The Geographer". 1668-69. Oil on Canvas. 20 1/8" × 18 1/4". Stadelsches Kunstinstitut, Frankfurt. Courtesy Blauel/Gramm—ARTHOTEK, Peissenberg. The Granger Collection, New York; **22-2** Amsterdams Historisch Museum; **22-3** Special Collections, Wageningen UR Library; **22-4** Peter Janswz (1597-1665), "Interior of the Choir of St. Bavo's Church at Haarlem". 1660. Oil on Panel. Worcester Art Museum, Massachusetts, USA. The Bridgeman Art Library, NY; **22-5** Hals, Frans (1580-1666), "Portrait of Rene Descartes". Musee du Louvre/RMN Reunion des Musees Nationaux, France. Erich Lessing/Art Resource, NY; **22-6** Courtesy of the Bancroft Library, University of California, Berkeley; **22-7** HIP / Art Resource, NY; **22-8** HIP / Art Resource, NY; **22-9** Johannes Goedaert, "Flowers in a Wan-li Vase with Blue-Tit". c. 1660. Medium. Photo: Charles Roelofsz/RKD Images. Bob P. Haboldt & Co., Art Gallery, N.Y.; **22-10** The Royal Cabinet of Paintings / Mauritshuis; **22-11** Jan Steen, "The Dancing Couple". 1663. Oil on Canvas, 1.025 × 1.425 cm (40 3/8" × 56 1/8"); framed: 1.314 × 1.718 (51 3/4" × 67 5/8"). Widener Collection. Photograph © 2007 Board of Trustees, National Gallery of Art, Washington, D.C.; **22-12** Leyster, Judith (c.1600-1660), "The Proposition (or The Rejected Offer)". 1631. Oil on panel, 309 × 242 mm. Mauritshuis, The Hague, The Netherlands. SCALA/Art Resource, NY; **22-13** Vermeer (van Delft), Jan (1632-1675), "Young Woman with a Pearl Necklace". Ca. 1662-1665. Oil on canvas, 55 × 45 cm. Post-restoration. Inv.: 912 B. Photo: Joerg P. Anders. Gemaeldegalerie, Staatliche Museen zu Berlin, Berlin, Germany. Bildarchiv Preussischer Kulturbesitz/Art Resource, NY; **22-14** Alinari / Art Resource, NY; **22-15** Frans Hals Museum, Harlem; **22-16** Rembrandt van Rijn, "Captain Frans Banning Cocq Mustering His Company (The Night Watch)". 1642. Oil on Canvas. 11'11" × 14'4" (3.63 × 4.37 m). Rijksmuseum, Amsterdam; **22-17** Giraudon / The Bridgeman Art Library; **22-18** Rembrandt Harmensz van Rijn (1606-1669), "The Slaughtered Ox". 1655. Musee du Louvre/RMN Reunion des Musees Nationaux, France. Erich Lessing/Art Resource, NY; **22-19** Rembrandt Harmensz. van Rijn (1606-1669) Dutch, "Self-Portrait". 1658. Oil on Canvas (lined) 52 5/8" × 40 7/8" (133.7 × 103.8 cm). Signed and dated on the arm of the chair at right: Rembrandt/f.1658.Purchased in 1906. Acc #"06.1.97. The Frick Collection, NY; **22-20** The Royal Collection © 2006, Her Majesty Queen Elizabeth II; **22-21** Rijksmuseum; **22-22** Rembrandt Harmensz van Rijn (1606-1669), "Descent from the Cross". 1634. Alte Pinakothek, Munich, Germany. SCALA/Art Resource, NY; **22-23** Rubens, Peter Paul (1577-1640), "Descent from the Cross". Center panel from triptych. Cathedral, Antwerp, Belgium. SCALA/Art Resource, NY; page 721, Rembrandt van Rijn, "The Anatomy Lesson of Dr. Nicolaas Tulp". 1632. Oil on Canvas. 5'3 3/4" × 7' 1 1/4" (169.5 × 216.5 cm). Royal Cabinet of Paintings Mauritshuis Foundation, The Hague, Netherlands.

Chapter 23

23-1 Rigaud, Hyacinthe (1659-1743). "Louis XIV, king of France (1638-1715)". 1701. Oil on Canvas. 277 × 194 cm. Musee du Louvre/RMN Reunion des Musees Nationaux, France. Herve Lewandowski/Art Resource, NY; **23-2** Mickael David/Robert Harding; **23-3** Artedia/Leemage.com; **23-4** © The Gallery Collection / Alamy; **23-5** © nobleIMAGES / Alamy; **23-6** Rubens, Peter Paul (1577-1640). "The Disembarkation of Marie de' Medici at the Port of Marseilles on November 3, 1600". Oil on Canvas. 394 × 395 cm. Musee du Louvre/RMN Reunion des Musees Nationaux, France. Erich Lessing/Art Resource, NY; **23-7** Rubens, Peter Paul (1577-1640), "La Kermesse". Musee du Louvre/RMN Reunion des Musees Nationaux, France. Erich Lessing/Art Resource, NY; **23-8** Poussin, Nicolas (1594-1665), "The Shepherds of Arcadia (Et in Arcadia Ego)". Oil on canvas. 85 × 121 cm. INV7300. Photo: René-Gabriel Ojéda. Musee du Louvre/RMN Reunion des Musees Nationaux, France. Art Resource, NY; **23-9** King Louis XIV of France in the costume of the Sun King in the ballet 'La Nuit', 1653 (b/w photo), French School, (17th century)/Bibliotheque Nationale, Paris, France, /The Bridgeman Art Library; **23-10** Interior of the Comedie Francaise Theatre in 1791, after an original watercolour (colour litho), French School, (19th century) / Bibliotheque Nationale, Paris, France, Archives Charmet / The Bridgeman Art Library; **23-11** Anthony van Dyck, "Portrait of Charles I Hunting". c. 1653. Oil on Canvas. 8'11" × 6'11" (2.7 × 2.1 m). Inv 1236. Musee du Louvre/RMN Reunion des Musees Nationaux, France. SCALA/Art Resource, NY; **23-12** Purchased with assistance from the Art Fund and the Pilgrim Trust 1974; **23-13** RICHARD MATHER (1596-1669). American Congregational cleric. Woodcut, c1670, attributed to John Foster (1648-1681): the earliest portrait engraving known to have been made in America. Credit: The Granger Collection; **23-14** John Closterman. Daniel Parke II, 1706. Virginia Historical Society (1985.35); **23-15** John Freake, c.1671-74 (oil on canvas) (see 183406 for pair), American School, (17th century)/Worcester Art Museum, Massachusetts, USA /The Bridgeman Art Library; **23-16** Mrs Elizabeth Freake and Baby Mary, c.1671-74 (oil on canvas) (see 183405 for pair), American School, (17th century)/Worcester Art Museum, Massachusetts, USA/The Bridgeman Art Library; **23-17** Velazquez, Diego Rodriguez (1599-1660), "Triumph of Bacchus (Los Borrachos)". 1628. Oil on canvas, 165 × 225 cm. Location: Museo del Prado, Madrid, Spain. SCALA/Art Resource, NY; **23-18** © Rodrigo Balaguer/LATINPHOTO.org; **23-19** Luis Nino (Bolivian), "Our Lady of the Victory of Malaga. 1740. Gift of John C. Freyer for the Frank Barrows Freyer Collection. Denver Art Museum, CO; **23-20** Paul Franklin © Dorling Kindersley, Courtesy of the Catedral Metropolitana; **23-21** © Michael Freeman / CORBIS All Rights Reserved; **23-22** © A. T. Willett / Alamy; **23-23** Laguna Pueblo, New Mexico, United States. San Jose Mission church, interior with historically significant retablo. PR © Julien McRoberts / DanitaDelimont.com; **23-24** Testelin, Henri (1616-95), "Jean-Baptiste Colbert (1619-1683) Presenting the Members of the Royal Academy of Science to Louis XIV (1638-1715)". c.1667. Oil on Canvas. Chateau de Versailles, France, Lauros. Giraudon/The Bridgeman Art Library; page 738, © The Gallery Collection/Corbis; page 748, The Art Archive / Galleria degli Uffizi Florence / Alfredo Dagli Orti; page 751, Derechos reservados © Museo Nacional Del Prado–Madrid.

Chapter 24

24-1 Goodwood Trustees/The Goodwood Estate Company Limited; **24-2** ©Topham / The Image Works; **24-3** HIP / Art Resource, NY; **24-4** Hogarth, William (1697-1764). "Gin Lane". Published in London, 1751. Engraving. British Museum, London, Great Britain. © British Museum/Art Resource, NY; **24-5** © Erich Lessing/National Gallery, London / Art Resource, NY; **24-6** © National Gallery, London/Art Resource, NY; **24-7** Image by courtesy of the Wedgwood Museum Trust Limited, Barlaston, Staffordshire, England.; **24-8** © Adams Picture Library t/a apl / Alamy; **24-9** Special Collections and University Archives, Rutgers University Libraries; **24-10** National Portrait Gallery, London; **24-11** By permission of The British Library; **24-12** © James L. Amos/CORBIS All Rights Reserved; **24-13** Bis Pole. Mid 20th century. New Guinea, Irian Jaya, Faretsj River, Omadesep village, Asmat people. Wood, paint, fiber, H. 216 in (548.6 cm). The Michael C. Rockefeller Memorial Collection, Bequest of Nelson A. Rockefeller, 1979 (1979.206.1611). Image copyright © The Metropolitan Museum of Art / Art Resource, NY; **24-14** E. Brandl/Courtesy of AIATSIS Pictorial Collection; **24-15** © The Trustees of the British Museum; **24-16** Wisconsin Historical Society, Image ID: 23966; **24-17** Johann Zoffany, "Dido Elizabeth Belle Lindsay and Lady Elizabeth Murray". Oil on Canvas. 35 1/2" × 28 1/4". From the Collection of the Earl of Mansfield, Scone Palace, Scotland; page 791, Image courtesy of John Vernor-Miles, Executor for A.F. Kersting.

Chapter 25

25-1 Boffrand, Germain (1667-1754), "Salon de la Princesse de Soubise (Salon ovale)". Photo: Bulloz. Hotel de Soubise, Paris, France. Reunion des Musees Nationaux/Art Resource, NY; **25-2** Charles Joseph (1700-77), "Psyche and Cupid". Ceiling panel from the Salon de la Princesse, Natoire. Hotel de Soubise, Paris, France. Peter Willi/The Bridgeman Art Library; **25-3** Erich Lessing / Art Resource, NY; **25-4** Erich Lessing / Art Resource, NY; **25-5** Boucher, Francois (1703-70), "Madame de Pompadour". Alte Pinakothek, Munich, Germany. The Bridgeman Art Library; **25-6** Wallace Collection, Lodon/AKG-Images; **25-7** Erich Lessing/Art Resource, NY; **25-8** © Achim Bednorz, Koln; **25-9** Stiftung Preussische Schlosser und Garten Berlin-Brandenburg/Bildarchiv; **25-10** Stiftung Preussische Schlosser und Garten Berlin-Brandenburg/Bildarchiv; **25-11** Nick Meers/The National Trust Photo Library; **25-12** Claude Lorrain (Claude Gellee) (1600-82), "The Rest on the Flight into Egypt". Oil on Canvas. Hermitage, St. Petersburg, Russia. The Bridgeman Art Library; **25-13** A Plan of the Gardens of the Most Noble Marquis of Buckingham at Stowe, from the Visitor's Guide Book, published in 1797. Lithograph. English School, (18th century). Private Collection. The Bridgeman Art Library; **25-14** Hervé Lewandowski/Musee du Louvre/RMN Reunion des Musees Nationaux, France. SCALA/Art Resource, NY; **25-15** © Mary Evans Picture Library/The Image Works; **25-16** D. Arnaudet. Chateaux de Malmaison et Bois-Preau, Rueil-Malmaison, France. RMN Reunion des Musees Nationaux/Art Resource, NY; **25-17** SCALA/Art Resource, NY; **25-18** From Jay D. Zorn and June August, Listening to Music, 5th edition, © 2007 Pearson Education, Inc.; **25-19** From Jay D. Zorn and June August, Listening to Music, 5th edition, © 2007 Pearson Education, Inc.; **25-20** From Jay D. Zorn and June August, Listening to Music, 5th edition, © 2007 Pearson Education, Inc.; **25-21** From Jeremy Yudkin, "Understanding Music", 6th ed. © 2008, Pearson Education, Inc.; **25-22** Scala / Art Resource, NY; **25-23** Jean-Etienne Liotard, "Still Life: Tea Set". The J. Paul Getty Museum, Los Angeles; **25-24** V & A Images/Victoria and Albert Museum/Art Resource, NY; **25-25** Francois Boucher, "Le Chinois Galant". Oil on Canvas. 41" × 57". The David Collection, inv.B275. Photo: Pernille Klemp; **25-26** Jean Denis Attiret, "The Presentation of Uigur Captives". From Battle Scenes of the Quelling of Rebellions in the Western Regions, with Imperial Poems. c. 1765-1774; poem dated 1760. Etching, mounted in album form, 16 leaves plus two additional leaves of inscriptions; 51 × 87 cm. © The Cleveland Museum of Art, John L. Severance Fund. 1998.103.14; **25-27** V & A Images/Victoria and Albert Museum; **25-28** Color print from woodblock. 1734. 42 3/4" × 22" (108 × 56 cm). Ohsha'joh Museum of Art, Hiroshima, Japan; **25-29** Wang Hui, "A Thousand Peaks and Myriad Ravines". Qing Dynasty. 1693. Hanging Scroll. Ink on Paper. 8'2 1/2" × 3' 4 1/2" (2.54 × 1.03 m). Collection of The Palace Museum, Beijing; **25-30** Yu the Great Taming the Waters. Qing Dynasty. Jade Carving 7' 1/4" × 3' 1 3/4". Collection of The Palace Museum, Beijing; **25-31** Elisabeth-Louise Vigee, "Marie Antoinette en Chemise". 1973. Oil on Canvas. 33 1/2" × 28 1/4". Hessische Hausstiftung (Hessian House Foundation) Museum Schloss Fasanerie; **23-32** SCALA/Art Resource, NY; pages 804-805, Erich Lessing / Art Resource, NY; page 805 (bottom), Scala / Art Resource, NY; page 807, © 1996 Harry N. Abrams, Inc.; page 818, Scala / Art Resource, NY.

Chapter 26

26-1 The Bloody Massacre on 5th March 1770, 1770 (coloured engraving), Revere, Paul (1735-1818). © Massachusetts Historical Society, Boston, MA, USA. The Bridgeman Art Library; **26-2** Yale University Art Gallery/Art Resource, NY; **26-3** Gérard Blot. Location: Chateaux de Versailles et de Trianon, Versailles. RMN Reunion des Musees Nationaux/Art Resource, NY; **26-4** Giraudon / Art Resource, NY; **26-5** Musee National du Chateau de Versailles. Art Resource/Reunion des Musees Nationaux; **26-6** Cussac/Musees Royaux des Beaux-Arts de Belgique; **26-7** © eye35.com / Alamy; **26-8** Robert Adam (1728-92), "Line Interior of the Marble Hall" (photo). Kedleston Hall, Derbyshire, UK, John Bethell. The Bridgeman Art Library; **26-9** Ceramics-Pottery. English, Wedgwood. 18th century, ca. 1780-1800. Flower pot, vase, and box w/cover. Metropolitan Museum of Art, Rogers Fund, 1909, (09.194.7-9). Art Resource, NY; **26-10** Courtesy of the Library of Congress; **26-11** C. Lautman/C. Lautman/Monticello/Thomas Jefferson Foundation, Inc.; **26-12** Courtesy of The Maryland Historical Society; **26-13** Archivo Iconografico, SA/Corbis; **26-14** Courtesy of the Library of Congress; **26-15** Sir Joshua Reynolds, "Benjamin Henry Latrobe, Tobacco Leaf Capital for the United States Capitol, Washington, D.C.". c. 1815. Courtesy of the Architect of the Capitol, Washington, D.C.; **26-16** Courtesy of The Library of Virginia; **26-17** Musee du Louvre, Paris. RMN Reunion des Musees Nationaux/Art Resource, NY; **26-18** Angelica Kauffmann (born Swiss,

1741-1807), "Cornelia Pointing to her Children as her Treasures," ca. 1785. Oil on canvas, 40 in. H × 50 in. W (101.6 × 127.0 cm). Signed on base of column at right: Angelica Kauffmann pinxt. Virginia Museum of Fine Arts, Richmond. The Adolph D. and Wilkins C. Williams Fund. Photo: Ann Hutchison. © Virginia Museum of Fine Arts. 75.22/50669.2; **26-19** Musee National du Chateau de la Malmaison, Rueil-Malmaison. RMN Reunion des Musees Nationaux/Art Resource, NY; **26-20** © Erich Lessing/Art Resource, NY; **26-21** © Lebrecht Music and Arts Photo Library / Alamy; **26-22** © V&A Images / Alamy; **26-23** Scala/Ministero per i Beni e le Attività culturali / Art Resource, NY; **26-24** Snark / Art Resource, NY; **26-25** A Negro hung alive by the Ribs to a Gallows, from 'Narrative of a Five Years' Expedition against the Revolted Negroes of Surinam, in Guiana, on the Wild Coast of South America, from the year 1772, to 1777', engraved by William Blake (1757-1827), published, Stedman, John Gabriel (1744-97) (after)/Private Collection, Archives Charmet/The Bridgeman Art Library; **26-26** This item is reproduced by permission of The Huntington Library, San Marino, California; **26-27** Image by courtesy of the Wedgwood Museum Trustees, Barlaston, Staffordshire, (England); **26-28** John Singleton Copley (American, 1738-1815), "Watson and the Shark". 1778. Oil on Canvas. 1.821 × 2.297 (71 3/4 × 90 1/2); Framed: 2.413 × 2.642 × .101 (95 × 104 × 4). Ferdinand Lammot Belin Fund. Photograph © 2006 Board of Trustees, National Gallery of Art, Washington, D.C.; **26-29** Thomas Coram (American, 1756-1811), "View of Mulberry House and Street". ca.1800. Oil on Paper. Gibbes Museum of Art/Carolina Art Association, 1968. 1968.18.01; **26-30** Musee du Louvre/RMN Reunion des Musees Nationaux, France. Erich Lessing/Art Resource, NY; page 848 (left) Araldo de Luca Archives/Index Ricerca Iconografica; page 848 (right) Pedicini/Index Ricerca Iconografica; page 852, John Decopoulos; page 856, G. Blot/C. Jean. Musee du Louvre/RMN Reunion des Musees Nationaux, France. Art Resource, NY; page 857, G. Blot/C. Jean. Musee du Louvre/RMN Reunion des Musees Nationaux, France. Art Resource, NY.

Chapter 27

PO Eugene Delacroix (1798-1863), "Liberty Leading the People". July 28, 1830. Painted 1830. Oil on canvas, 260 × 325 cm. Photo: Hervé Lewandowski. Musee du Louvre/RMN Reunion des Musees Nationaux, France. SCALA/Art Resource, NY; **27-1** Joseph Mallord William Turner (1775-1851), "Transept of Tintern Abbey". Exhibited 1794. Watercolor. 12-5/8 × 9-7/8" (32.2 × 25.1 cm). Victoria and Albert Museum/Art Resource, NY; **27-2** John Constable (1776-1837), "Landscape and Double Rainbow". 1812. Inv.: 328-1888. Victoria and Albert Museum, London/Art Resource, NY; **27-3** John Constable (English - 1776-1837), "Stour Valley and Dedham Church". 1815. Oil on Canvas, 55.6 × 77.8 cm (21 7/8" × 30 5/8"). William Wilkins Warren Fund, 48.266 Photograph © 2008 Museum of Fine Arts, Boston; **27-4** Courtauld Institute of Art Gallery, London; **27-5** The Hay Wain, 1821 (oil on canvas), Constable, John (1776-1837) / National Gallery, London, UK / The Bridgeman Art Library International; **27-6** Joseph Mallord William Turner (1775-1851), "Upper Falls of the Reichenbach". (w/c on paper). Yale Center for British Art, Paul Mellon Collection, USA. The Bridgeman Art Library; **27-7** Joseph Mallord William Turner (1775-1851), "The Fall of an Avalanche in the Grisons". Exhibited 1810. Clore Collection, Tate Gallery, London/Art Resource, NY; **27-8** Joseph Mallord William Turner (1775-1851) "Snow Storm - Steam-Boat off a Harbour's Mouth". Exhibited 1842. Oil on canvas, 91.4 × 121.9 cm. Clore Collection/Tate Gallery, London/Art Resource, NY; **27-9** Nationalgalerie, Staatliche Museen zu Berlin, Berlin, Germany. Joerg P. Anders/Bildarchiv Preussischer Kulturbesitz/Art resource, NY; **27-10** Caspar David Friedrich (1774-1840), "Wanderer Above a Sea of Fog". Ca. 1817. Oil on canvas, 94,8 × 74,8 cm. Inv.: 5161. On permanent loan from the Foundation for the Promotion of the Hamburg Art Collections. Photo: Elke Walford. Hamburger Kunsthalle, Hamburg, Germany. Bildarchiv Preussischer Kulturbesitz/Art Resource, NY; **27-11** Thomas Cole (American 180-1848), "View from Mount Holyoke, Northampton, Massachusetts, after a Thunderstorm - The Oxbow". 1936. Oil on Canvas. 51 1/2" × 76" (1.30.8 × 1.93 m). The Metropolitan Museum of Art, NY. Gift of Mrs. Russell Sage, 1908 (08.228). Photograph © 1995 The Metropolitan Museum of Art; **27-12** Frederic Edwin Church (1826-1900), "Twilight in the Wilderness". Oil on canvas. Cleveland Museum of Art, OH, USA/The Bridgeman Art Library; **27-13** © CORBIS All Rights Reserved; **27-14** Antoin-Jean Gros, "Napoleon in the Pesthouse at Jaffa, 11 March 1799". 1804. Oil on Canvas. 17'5 1/2" × 23' 7 1/2" (5.32 × 7.2 m). Musee du Louvre, Paris. RMN Reunion des Musees Nationaux/Art Resource, NY; **27-15** Thomas Phillips (1770-1845), "Portrait of George Gordon (1788-1824) 6th Baron Byron of Rochdale in Albanian Dress". 1835. Oil on Canvas. National Portrait Gallery, London, UK. The Bridgeman Art Library; **27-16** Theodor M. von Holst (1810-44). "Illustration from 'Frankenstein' by Mary Shelley (1797-1851)". 1831. Engraving. Private Collection. The Bridgeman Art Library; **27-17** Tischbein, Johann Heinrich the Elder (1722-1789), "Goethe in the Roman Campagna". 1787. Location: Staedelsches Kunstinstitut, Frankfurt am Main, Germany. Kavaler/Art Resource, NY; **27-18** Eugene (Ferdinand Victor) Delacroix (1798-1863), "First Meeting between Faust and Mephistopheles: `Why all this Noise?'". From Goethe's Faust. 1828. Illustration, Lithograph. The Stapleton Collection. The Bridgeman Art Library; **27-19** Francisco de Goya y Lucientes (1746-1828), "The Sleep of Reason Produces Monsters (El sueno de la razon produce monstruos). Plate 43 of 'The Caprices (Los Caprichos)', first edition; etching, aquatint, drypoint and burin; 8-7/16 × 5-7/8 in (21.5 × 15 cm). The Metropolitan Museum of Art, Gift of Knoedler & Co., 1918 (18.64). Photograph © 1994 The Metropolitan Museum of Art; **27-20** Francisco de Goya, (Spanish, 1746-1828). "The Third of May, 1808". 1814-1815. Oil on canvas, approx. 8'8" × 11'3". Derechos reservados © Museo Nacional Del Prado - Madrid. Photo Oronoz; **27-21** Goya y Lucientes, Francisco Jose de (1746-1828). "A heroic feat! With dead men!, plate 39 of 'The Disasters of War', 1810-14, pub. 1863" Etching. Private Collection, Index. The Bridgeman Art Library; **27-22** Francisco de Goya y Lucientes (1746-1828), "Saturn Devouring One of His Sons", Mural transferred to Canvas (146 × 83 cm). Derechos reservados © Museo Nacional Del Prado – Madrid; **27-23** Joseph Mallord William Turner (English 1775-1851), "The Whale Ship". ca. 1845. Oil on Canvas, 36 1/8" × 48 1/4" (91.8 × 122.6 cm). The Metropolitan Museum of Art, Catherine Lorillard Wolfe Collection, Wolfe Fund, 1896 (96.29). Image copyright © The Metropolitan Museum of Art. Art Resource, NY; **27-24** Carl Schuetz (1745-1800), "Neuer Markt (New Market) Vienna". 18th c. Mozart and Haydn lived nearby. Wien Museum Karlsplatz, Vienna, Austria. Erich Lessing, Art Resource, NY; **27-25** Stieler, Joseph Carl (1781-1858). "Ludwig van Beethoven (1770-1827) Composing his 'Missa Solemnis'". 1819-1820. Oil on Canvas. Beethoven Haus, Bonn, Germany. The Bridgeman Art Library; **27-26** Andreas Geiger (1765-1856). "A Concert of Hector Berlioz (1803-69) in 1846". Engraving. Musee de l'Opera, Paris, France. The Bridgeman Art Library; **27-27** © Lebrecht Music & Arts; **27-28** Gericault, Theodore (1791-1824), "Kleptomania: Portrait of a Kleptomaniac". c.1819/22. Museum voor Schone Kunsten, Ghent, Belgium. The Bridgeman Art Library; page 888, Roy Rainford/Robert Harding; page 889, Hubert Robert, French (1733-1808). Pyramids, ca. 1760. Oil on wood panel, 24 × 28 1/2 in.; 60.96 × 72.39 cm. Smith College Museum of Art, Northampton, Massachusetts. Purchased.

Chapter 28

28-1 Anonymous, "Old Hetton Colliery, Newcastle". Beamish, North of England Open Air Museum, Durham, UK. The Bridgeman Art Library; **28-2** The New York Public Library, New York, NY USA/Art Resource, NY; **28-3** Courtesy of The Culture Archive; **28-4** © Stewart Mcknight Q / Alamy; **28-5** Joseph Mallord William Turner (1775-1851), "Rain, Steam, and Speed". Oil on canvas. 90.8 × 121.9 cm. National Gallery, London, Great Britain. Erich Lessing/Art Resource, NY; **28-6** Credit: Renty, a slave taken from the Congo to the USA, 1850 (b/w photo) by American Photographer (19th century)Private Collection/ Peter Newark American Pictures/ The Bridgeman Art Library; **28-7** National Portrait Gallery, Smithsonian Institution/Art Resource, NY; **28-8** Sojourner

Truth (c.1797-1883) (b/w photo), American Photographer, (19th century). Private Collection, Peter Newark American Pictures. The Bridgeman Art Library; **28-9** Robert Scott Duncanson (1821-72), "Uncle Tom and Little Eva". 1853. Oil on canvas. ÊThe Detroit Institute of Arts, USA.ÊThe Bridgeman Art Library; **28-10** Theodore Gericault (1791-1824). "The Raft of the Medusa". First oil sketch. Oil on Canvas. 37 × 46 cm. Louvre, Paris. Photo: Herve Lewandowski. Inv.: RF 2229. © Reunion des Musees Nationaux/Art Resource, NY; **28-11** Eugene Delacroix (1798-1863). "Scene from the Massacre at Chios: Greek families awaiting death or slavery". 1824. Oil on canvas. 419 × 354 cm. Louvre, Paris, France. Photo: Le Mage. © Reunion des Musees Nationaux/Art Resource, NY; **28-12** Jean Auguste Dominique Ingres (1780-1867), "The Vow of Louis XIII (1601-43)". 1824. Oil on Canvas. Montauban Cathedral, France, Lauros. Giraudon/The Bridgeman Art Library; **28-13** Ingres, Jean Auguste Dominique (1780-1867). The Great Odalisque. Oil on canvas, 91 × 162 cm. Inv.: RF 1158. Musee du Louvre/RMN Reunion des Musees Nationaux, France. Herve Lewandowski/Art Resource, NY; **28-14** Ferdinand Victor Eugene Delacroix(1798-1863, "Odalisque". 1825. Oil on Canvas. © Fitzwilliam Museum, University of Cambridge, UK/The Bridgeman Art Library; **28-15** Eugene Delacroix (1798-1863), "Liberty Leading the People". July 28, 1830. Painted 1830. Oil on canvas, 260 × 325 cm. Photo: Hervé Lewandowski. Musee du Louvre/RMN Reunion des Musees Nationaux, France. SCALA/Art Resource, NY; **28-16** Honore Daumier (French 1809-1879), "Gargantua" 1831. Lithograph. Fine Arts Museums of San Francisco, Museum purchase, Herman Michels Collection, Vera Michels Bequest Fund, 1993.48.1; **28-17** Honore Daumier (1808-1879). "Rue Transnonain, 15 Avril 1834. A murdered family". 28.5 × 44.1 cm. Inv. A 1970-67. Kupferstichkabinett, Staatliche Kunstsammlungen, Dresden, Germany Erich Lessing/ Art Resource, NY; **28-18** Daumier, Honore (1808-1879). "The Third-Class Carriage". ca. 1862-64. Oil on canvas; 25 3/4 × 35 1/2 in. (65.4 × 90.2 cm). The Metropolitan Museum of Art, H. O. Havemeyer Collection, Bequest of Mrs. H. O. Havemeyer, 1929 (29.100.129). The Metropolitan Museum of Art, New York, NY, U.S.A. Image © The Metropolitan Museum of Art / Art Resource, NY; **28-19** Jean-Francois Millet (French, 1814Đ 1875), "The Sower". 1850. Oil on Canvas, 101.6 × 82.6 cm (40" × 32 1/2"). Gift of Quincy Adams Shaw through Quincy Adams Shaw, Jr. and Mrs. Marian Shaw Haughton, 17.1485. Photograph © 2008 Museum of Fine Arts, Boston; **28-20** Gustave Courbet (1819-1877), "The Stone Breakers". 1849. Oil on canvas. (destroyed in 1945). Galerie Neue Meister, Dresden, Germany, © Staatliche Kunstsammlungen Dresden. The Bridgeman Art Library; **28-21** Gustave Courbet(1819-1877), "Burial at Ornans". 1849-1850. Oil on canvas, 311.5 × 668.0 cm. Hervé Lewandowski/Musee d'Orsay, Paris, France. RMN Reunion des Musees Nationaux/Art Resource, NY; **28-22** William Henry Fox Talbot (English 1800-1877),, "Wrack". 1839. Photogenic drawing (salted paper print), 22 × 17.5 cm (8 11/16" × 6 7/8") (36.37.20) The Metropolitan Museum of Art, Harris Brisbane Dick Fund, 1936 (36.37.20). Image copyright © The Metropolitan Museum of Art. Art Resource, NY; **28-23** Louis-Jacques-Mande Daguerre, "Le Boulevard du Temple", 1839, Daguerreotype. Bayerisches Nationalmuseum Munchen; **28-24** Charles Richard Meade (Daguerreotypist) American 1826-1858, "Portrait of Louis-Jacques-Mande Daguerre". 1848. 22.1 × 17.8 cm (8 11/16" × 7"). The J. Paul Getty Museum, Los Angeles; **28-25** J. Paul Getty Museum, Los Angeles/Getty Images, Inc.; **28-26** Adoc-photos / Art Resource, NY; **28-27** Scenes of the 'Beagle' being repaired, on the distant cordillera of the Andes, and laid ashore on the Santa Cruz River, engraved by Thomas Landseer (1795-1880) (engraving) (b/w photo), Martens, Conrad (1801-78) (after), Private Collection. The Bridgeman Art Library; page 940, Jean Auguste Dominique Ingres (1780-1867), "Bathing Woman (Baigneuse de Valpincon)", 1808. Oil on canvas, 146 × 97.5 cm. Louvre, Paris. Erich Lessing/Art Resource, NY; page 941, Jean Auguste Dominique Ingres, Turkish Bath (Bagno Turco), Louvre, Paris, France. Scala/Art Resource, NY.

Chapter 29

29-1 Ernest Meissonier (1815-1891), "The Barricade, rue de la Mortellerie (Souvenir of the Civil War)." June 1848. Oil on canvas, 29 × 22 cm. Inv. RF1942-31. Location: Louvre, Paris, France. Musee du Louvre/RMN Reunion des Musees Nationaux, France. SCALA/Art Resource, NY; **29-2** Barricades in Rue Saint-Maur-Popincourt after the Attack by the troops of General Lamoriciere, 26th June 1848 (daguerreotype) by Thibault (1830-1927). Private Collection/ Archives Charmet/ The Bridgeman Art Library; **29-3** Alfred G. Stevens (1823-1906), "Those Whom They Call the Vagabonds (The Hunters of Vincennes)". 1855. Oil on canvas, 130 × 165 cm. Musee d'Orsay, Paris, France. Photo: Herve Hewandowski/Reunion des Musees Nationaux. Art Resource, NY; **29-4** © Roger Viollet; **29-5** J. Eastman Johnson (1824-1906), "Old Kentucky Home Life in the South". 1859. Oil on Canvas. © Collection of the New-York Historical Society, USA/The Bridgeman Art Library; **29-6** J. Eastman Johnson, (1824-1906), "A Ride for Liberty, or The Fugitive Slaves". c. 1862. Oil on board. © Brooklyn Museum of Art, New York, USA/The Bridgeman Art Library Nationality/copyright status: American/out of copyright; **29-7** Winslow Homer (1836-1910), "The Army of the Potomac— A Sharp Shooter on Picket Duty". 1862. Wood Engraving on paper, 9 1/8 × 13 13/16 in. (23.2 × 35 cm). Gift of International Machines Corp. Location: Smithsonian American Art Museum, Washington, DC. Art Resource, NY; **29-8** Timothy O'Sullivan (1840-1882), "A Harvest of Death, Gettysburg, Pennsylvania". Location: The New York Public Library, New York, NY/Art Resource, NY; **29-9** Winslow Homer (American 1836-1910), "The Veteran in a New Field". 1965. Oil on canvas, 24 1/8" × 38 1/8" (61.3 × 96.8). The Metropolitan Museum of Art, New YorkBequest of Miss Adelaide Milton de Groot (1876-1967), 1967 (67.187.131). Image copyright © The Metropolitan Museum of Art. Art Resource, NY; **29-10** Photograph courtesy Peabody Essex Museum; **29-11** The Art Archive / Eileen Tweedy; **29-12** Shekh Muhammad Amir, "A Horse and Groom". 1830-1850, Calcutta, India. Pencil and Opaque Watercolor with touches of white and bum Arabic. 11" × 17 1/2". Arthur M. Sackler Gallery, Smithsonian Institution, Washington, DC. Purchasse, S1999.121; **29-13** The Art Archive / Chateau de Compiegne / Gianni Dagli Orti; **29-14** © Asian Art & Archaeology, Inc. / CORBIS All Rights Reserved; **29-15** Suzuki Harunobu (Japanese, 1725-1770), "Two Courtesans, Inside and Outside the Display Window". Japanese, Edo period, about 1768-69 (Meiwa 5-6) Woodblock print (nishiki-e); ink and color on paper Hashira-e; 67 × 12.8 cm (26 3/8 × 5 1/16 in.). Museum of Fine Arts, Boston Denman Waldo Ross Collection, 06.1248. Photograph © 2010 Museum of Fine Arts, Boston; **29-16** Suzuki Harunobu (Japanese, 1725-1770), "Visiting (Kayoi)", from the series Seven Komachi in Fashionable Disguise (Furyu yatsushi nana Komachi) Japanese, Edo period, about 1766-67 (Meiwa 3-4). Woodblock print (nishiki-e); ink and color on paper Hosoban; 30.7 × 13.5 cm (12 1/16 × 5 5/16 in.). Museum of Fine Arts, Boston William Sturgis Bigelow Collection, 11.16497 Photograph © 2010 Museum of Fine Arts, Boston; **29-17** Kitagawa Utamaro (Japanese, 1754-1806), "How the Famous Brocade Prints of Edo are Produced," (Edo Meibutsu Nishiki-e Kosaku). Ink and color on paper, 38.3 × 74.3 cm. Clarence Buckingham Collection, 1939.2141. © The Art Institute of Chicago, All Rights Reserved; **28-18** Kitagawa Utamaro (1753-1806), "The Fickle Type Uwaki no so = 'The fancy-free type'" from the series "Ten Physiognomies of Women," c. 1793. Color woodcut, 14 × 9 7/8 in. (36.4 × 24.5 cm). Print Collection. Miriam and Ira D. Wallach Division. The New York Public Library/Art Resource, NY; **28-19** Historical Picture Archive/CORBIS; **29-20** Vincent van Gogh, "Japonaiserie: The Courtesan" (after Kesai Eisen), 1887. Oil on canvas, 41 3/8 × 24 in. (105.5 × 60.5 cm.). Amsterdam, Van Gogh Museum (Vincent van Gogh Foundation); **29-21** "Le Japon," cover of Paris "Illustre," May 1886. © Amsterdam, Van Gogh Museum (Vincent van Gogh Foundation); page 972, A Visit from the Old Mistress. 1876. Oil on canvas, 18 × 24 1/8 in. (45.7 × 61.3 cm), Winslow Homer (1836-1910). Smithsonian American Art Museum, Washington, DC, U.S.A. Smithsonian American Art Museum, Washington, DC / Art Resource, NY; page 973, A Visit from the Old Mistress. 1876. Oil on canvas, 18 × 24 1/8 in. (45.7 × 61.3 cm), Winslow Homer (1836-1910). Smithsonian

American Art Museum, Washington, DC, U.S.A. Smithsonian American Art Museum, Washington, DC / Art Resource, NY.

Chapter 30

30-1 Erich Lessing / Art Resource, NY; 30-2 Gustave Caillebotte (French 1848-1894), "Paris Street: Rainy Day". 1877. Oil on Canvas. 83 1/2" × 108 3/4" (212.2 × 276.2 cm). Charles H. and Mary F.S. Worcester Collection, 1964.336. Photograph © 2006, The Art Institute of Chicago. All Rights Reserved; 30-3 Réunion des Musées Nationaux / Art Resource, NY; 30-4 Réunion des Musées Nationaux / Art Resource, NY; 30-5 Edouard Manet (1832-1883), "Jeanne Duval (Baudelaire's mistress) reclining". 1862. Location: Museum of Fine Arts (Szepmuveszeti Muzeum), Budapest, Hungary. Giraudon/Art Resource, NY. © 2009 ARS Artists Rights Society, NY; 30-6 Edouard Manet, "Luncheon on the Grass (Le Dejeuner sur l'Herbe)". 1863. Oil on Canvas. 7' × 8'10" (2.13 × 2.6 m). Musee d'Orsay, Paris. RMN Reunion des Musees Natioaux/Art Resource, NY; 30-7 Marcantonio Raimondi (1480-1527/34), "The Judgement of Paris". Inv. 4167LR. Rothschild Collection. Musee du Louvre/RMN Reunion des Musees Nationaux, France. SCALA/Art Resource, NY; 30-8 Edouard Manet (1832-1883), "Portrait of Emile Zola". Ca. 1868. Oil on canvas, 146.5 × 114 cm. RF2205. Musee d'Orsay, Paris, France. Photo: Hervé Lewandowski. Reunion des Musees Nationaux/Art Resource, NY. © 2009 ARS Artists Rights Society, NY; 30-9 The Paris Opera House, Ille de France, France, Europe. Image courtesy of Robert Harding Picture Library Ltd.; 30-10 Edouard Detaille (1848-1912), "Inauguration of the Paris Opera House, January 5, 1875: Arrival of Lord Mair (with entourage) from London, Greeted by Charles Garnier". Gouache on paper. Photo: Gerard Blot. Chateaux de Versailles et de Trianon, Versailles, France. Reunion des Musees Nationaux/Art Resource, NY; 30-11 © Corbis; 30-13 © 2003 Yale University Press/Spotts, BAYREUTH: A History of the Wagner Festival (1994), image p. 9. Courtesy George C. Izenour Archive, New Haven, CT; 30-14 Credit: Poster advertising 'La Vie Parisienne', an operetta by Jacques Offenbach (1819-90) 1886 (litho), Cheret, Jules (1836-1932) / Bibliotheque de l'Opera Garnier, Paris / Archives Charmet / The Bridgeman Art Library International; 30-15 Edouard Manet, "The Railway". 1873. Oil on Canvas, .933 × 1.115 (36 3/4" × 45 1/8"). Framed: 1.130 × 1.327 × .054 cm (44 1/2" × 52 1/4" × 2 1/8"). Gift of Horace Havemeyer in memory of his mother, Louisine W. Havemeyer. 1956.10.1. Image © 2007. Board of Trustees, National Gallery of Art, Washington, D.C.; page 1000, Scala/Ministero per i Beni e le Attività culturali /Art Resource, NY; page 1001 (top) Edouard Manet(1832-1883), "Olympia". 1863. Oil on canvas, 130.5 × 190.0 cm. Inv. RF 2772. Hervé Lewandowski/Musée d'Orsay, Paris, France. RMN Reunion des Musees Nationaux/Art Resource, NY. © 2008 Edouard Manet/Artists Rights Society (ARS), New York; page 1001 (bottom) Alexandre Cabanel (1824-1889), "Birth of Venus". 1863. Oil on canvas, 130 × 225 cm. P. Selert/Musee d'Orsay, Paris, France. Reunion des Musees Nationaux/Art Resource, NY.

Chapter 31

30-1 "The Barricades"", 1871. Edouard Manet. Szepmüvészeti Muzeum/ akg-images; 31-2 Edouard Manet (1832-1883), "The Execution of Emperor Maximilian of Mexico, June 19, 1867". Oil on canvas. Location: Staedtische Kunsthalle, Mannheim, Germany. Art Resource, NY; 31-3 Studio at Batignolles: Otto Schoelderer, Manet, Renoir, Zacharie Astruc, Zola, Edmond Maitre, Bazille and Monet. 1870. Henri Fantin Latour. Hervé Lewandowski/Réunion des Musées Nationaux / Art Resource, NY; 31-4 Claude Monet (1840-1926), "Regatta at Argenteuil". c.1872. Musee d'Orsay, Paris, France. Erich Lessing/Art Resource, NY; 31-5 Claude Monet (1840-1926), "Carnival on the Boulevard des Capucines in Paris". 1873. Location: Pushkin Museum of Fine Arts, Moscow, Russia. Scala/Art Resource, NY; 31-7 Claude Monet (French, 1840-1926), "Grainstack (Snow Effect)". 1891. Oil on Canvas, 65.4 × 92.4 cm (25 3/4" × 36 3/8"). Gift of Miss Aimee and Miss Rosamond Lamb in memory of Mr. and Mrs. Horatio Appleton Lamb, 1970.253. Photograph © 2008 Museum of Fine Arts, Boston; 31-8 Berthe Morisot (1841-1895), "Summer's Day". Oil on Canvas. 45.7 × 75.2 cm © National Gallery, London; 31-9 Camille Pissarro (1830-1903), "Red Roofs, a Village Corner, Winter". 1877. Oil on canvas. 54.5 × 65.6 cm. Musee d'Orsay, Paris, France. Erich Lessing/Art Resource, NY; 31-10 Auguste Renoir. Oarsmen at Chatou. 1879. Oil on canvas, 31 15/16? × 39 7/16?. National Gallery of Art, Washington, DC. Gift of Sam A. Lewisohn. 1951.5.2; 31-11 Hilaire-Germain-Edgar Degas (French 1834-1917), "The Dance Class". 1874. Oil on canvas, 32 7/8" × 30 3/8" (83.5 × 77.2 cm). The Metropolitan Museum of Art Bequest of Mrs. Harry Payne Bingham, 1986 (1987.47.1). Image copyright © The Metropolitan Museum of Art. Art Resource, NY; 31-12 The Floor Scrapers [Raboteurs de parquet]. 1875.Gustave Caillebotte. Herve Lewandowski/Réunion des Musées Nationaux / Art Resource, NY; 31-13 Edgar Degas(1834-1917), "Cafe Concert aux Ambassadeurs". Pastel. Musee des Beaux-Arts, Lyon, France. Erich Lessing/Art REsource, NY;31-14 Edouard Manet, "A Bar at the Folies-Bergere", 1881-82. The Samuel Courtauld Trust, The Courtauld Gallery, London; 31-15 Mention obligatoire Les Arts Decoratifs, Paris (Inv. 7972); Musee de la Publicite (Inv. 10531); Photo: Laurent Sully Jaulmes. Tous droits reserves; 31-16 Ilya Repin(1844-1930), "Tolstoy Ploughing in the Field". 1882. Photo: Roman Beniaminson. Tretyakov Gallery, Moscow, Russia. Bildarchiv Preussischer Kulturbesitz/Art Resource, NY; 31-17 © 2009 State Russian Museum, St. Petersburg; 31-18 Guildhall Library, Corporation of London, UK/The Bridgeman Art Library; 31-19 © Historical Picture Archive/CORBIS; 31-20 Morris and Company, "The Woodpecker", 1885. Wool tapestry designed by Morris. William Morris Gallery, Walthamstow, England; 31-21 Aberdeen Art Gallery & Museums Collections; 31-22 The Granger Collection, New York; 31-23 May Morris (1862-1938), Bed Hangings (Two Curtains), 1917 or earlier. Embroidered wool on linen, each panel 76 3/4 × 27 in. Collection of Cranbrook Art Museum, Bloomfield Hills, Michigan. Gift of George Gough Booth and Ellen Scripps Booth. Photo: R. H. Hensleigh. (CAM 1955.402.); 31-24 Kitagawa Utamaro (Japan 1753-1806), "Shaving a Boy's Head". 1801 (Edo Period, 18th Century). Color woodblock print. 14 15/16 × 9 13/16 in. (38 × 25 cm) (image) 15 3/8 × 10 1/4 in. (39 × 26 cm) (sheet). Signed Utamaro hitsu. Bequest of Richard P. Gale. The Minneapolis Institute of Arts; 31-25 Mary Cassatt (American 1844 - 1926), "The Bath". c. 1891. Drypoint and soft-ground etching in yellow, blue, black and sanguine, (mathews and Shapiro 1989 5.xvi/xvii), Plate: .389 × .249 (12 9/16" × 9 13/16"); Sheet: .367 × .275 (14 7/16" × 10 13/16"). Rosenwald Collection. Photograph © Board of Trustees, National Gallery of Art, Washington, D.C. Photo: Dean Beasom; pages 1028-1029, Pierre Auguste Renoir, "Luncheon on the Boating Party". 1880-81. Oil on Canvas. 51 1/4" × 69 1/8" (130.18 × 175.58 cm). Acquired 1923. The Phillips Collection., Washington, D.C.; page 1040 Scala / Art Resource, NY.

Chapter 32

32-1 Albert Bierstadt (American 1830-1902), "The Rocky Mountains, Lander's Peak". 1863. Oil on canvas, 73 1/2" × 120 3/4" (186.7 × 306.7 cm). The Metropolitan Museum of Art, Rogers Fund, 1907 (07.123). Image copyright © The Metropolitan Museum of Art. Art Resource, NY; 32-2 Emanuel Gottlieb Leutz (1816-1868), "Westward the Course of Empire Takes Its Way (Mural Study, U.S. Capitol)", 1861. Oil on canvas, 33 1/4" × 43 3/8" (84.5 × 110.1 cm). Smithsonian American Art Museum, Washington, DC / Art Resource, NY; 32-3 John Vanderlyn (American, 1775-1852), "The Murder of Jane McCrea". 1803-1804. 32 × 26 1/2". Courtesy Wadsworth Atheneum Museum of Art, Hartford, Connecticut. Purchased by subscription; 32-4 George Catlin (1796-1872), "The Last Race, Mandan O-kee-pa Ceremony". 1832. Smithsonian American Art Museum, Washington, DC/Art Resource, NY; 32-7 Catalogue No. 77-13301, Smithsonian Institution; 32-8 Navajo (Southwestern United States), "Blanket". 1875-1890. Wool, cotton and Dye, 613/4" × 40 3/4". Collection of the Lowe Art Museum, University of Miami. Gift of Alfred I. Bardon, 57.152.000; 32-9

Arizona State Museum, The University of Arizona. Photo: Jannelle Weakly. (26496-x-2); 32-10 © The Field Museum, #A113021c; 32-11 Portrait of Walt Whitman, July 1854. Engraving, 15.5 × 11 cm, after daguerreotype by Gabriel Harrison. Frontispiece to Leaves of Grass, 1855. Samuel Hollyer (1826-1919)Rare Books Division. The New York Public Library / Art Resource, NY; 32-12 Childe Hassam, "The Manhattan Club." Ca. 1891. Oil on canvas, 18 1/4" × 22 1/8". Santa Barbara Museum of Art, Gift of Mrs. Sterling Morton to the Preston Morton Collection. 1960.62; 32-13 16.4, George Bellows, "Cliff Dwellers". 1913. Oil on Canvas, 40 3/16" × 42 1/16" (102.07 × 106.82 cm). Los Angeles County Museum of Art. Los Angeles County Fund. Photograph © 2008 Museum Associates/LACMA. Art Resource, NY; 32-14 Robert Koehler(1850-1917), "The Strike". 1886. Oil on canvas. Deutsches Historisches Museum, Berlin, Germany/The Bridgeman Art Library, NY; 32-15 Thomas Wilmer Dewing (1851-1938), "A Reading". 1897. Oil on canvas, 20 1/4" × 30 1/4" (51.3 × 76.8 cm.). Bequest of Henry Ward Ranger through the National Academy of Design. Smithsonian American Art Museum, Washington, DC / Art Resource, NY; 32-16 Winslow Homer (1836-1910), "The Life Line". 1884. Oil on canvas, 28 5/8" × 44 3/4" (72.7 × 113.7 cm). The Philadelphia Museum of Art, The George W. Elkins Collection, 1924. The Philadelphia Museum of Art/Art Resource, NY; 32-17 © Philip F. Gura 2000. All Rights Reserved; 32-17 Philip F. Gura; 32-18 Frank Driggs Collection/Getty Images, Inc.; 32-19 James Abbott McNeil Whistler, "Nocturne in Black and Gold: The Falling Rocket". c. 1874. Oil on Panel. 23 3/4" × 18 3/8" (60.2 × 46.8 cm). Detroit Institute of Arts. Gift of Dexter M. Ferry, Jr. 46.309. The Bridgeman Art Library Inc.; 32-20 John Singer Sargent (American, 1856Ð 1925), "The Daughters of Edward Darley Boit". 1882. Oil on Canvas, 221.93 × 222.57 cm (87 3/8" × 87 5/8"). Gift of Mary Louisa Boit, Julia Overing Boit, Jane Hubbard Boit, and Florence D. Boit in memory of their father, Edward Darley Boit, 19.124 Photograph © 2008 Museum of Fine Arts, Boston; 32-21 Mary Stevenson Cassatt , American, 1844-1926, "In the Loge," 1878. Oil on canvas, 81.28 × 66.04 cm. (32 × 26 in.). Museum of Fine Arts, Boston. The Hayden Collection - Charles Henry Hayden Fund, 10.35. Photograph © Museum of Fine Arts, Boston; 32-22 Mary Cassatt, "Modern Woman". Mural, 13' × 58'. Reproduced in Harper's New Monthly Magazine, Vol. 86, May 1893, p. 837. Courtesy of Chicago History Museum; 32-23 Mary Stevenson Cassatt (American, 1844Ð 1926), "Gathering Fruit". about 1893. Drypoint, softground etching, and aquatint printed in color from three plates Catalogue Raisonne_: Breeskin 157, ninth state (only known impression of this state, not in Breeskin; cf Mathews and Shapiro cat.15) Platemark: 42.2 × 29.8 cm (16 5/8" × 11 3/4"); Sheet: 50.5 × 39 cm (19 7/8" × 15 3/8"). Gift of William Emerson and The Hayden CollectionñCharles Henry Hayden Fund, 41.813. Photograph © 2008 Museum of Fine Arts, Boston; 32-24 The Granger Collection, New York. COLUMBIAN EXPOSITION, 1893. Women's Building, World's Columbian Exposition, Chicago, 1893: water color, 1893, by Charles Graham; 32-25 Vanni / Art Resource, NY; 32-26 John Bachman, "Line Central Park, Summer, Looking South". 1865. Colour Litho. (fl.1850-77). © Museum of the City of New York, USA/The Bridgeman Art Library; 32-27 National Park Service, Frederick Law Olmsted National Historic Site; 32-28 John Cast, "American Progress". 1872. Oil on Canvas. (fl.1872). Private Collection. Photo © Christie's Images/The Bridgeman Art Library; page 1064, Thomas Cowperthwait Eakins (1844-1916). "The Gross Clinic". 1875. Oil on Canvas. Jefferson College, Philadelphia, PA, USA/The Bridgeman Art Library; page 1065, Courtesy of The University of Pennsylvania.

Chapter 33

33-1 L' Exposition de Paris (1900), c. 1900. Smithsonian Institution Libraries; 33-2 Courtesy of the Library of Congress, LC-USZ62-106562; 33-3 Mention obligatoire Les Arts Decoratifs, Paris (Inv. 7972); Musee de la Publicite (Inv. 10531); Photo: Laurent Sully Jaulmes. Tous droits reserves; 33-4 SOFAM, Brussels/Ch. Bastin & J. Evrard; 33-5 Jan Toorop, "Delftsche Slaolie". Dutch advertisement poster. Scala/Art Resource, NY; 33-6 The Kiss, 1888-98 (marble), Rodin, Auguste (1840-1917)/Musee Rodin, Paris, France, Philippe Galard/The Bridgeman Art Library; 33-7 Vanni / Art Resource, NY; 33-8 Auguste Rodin, "Dancing Figure". 1905. Graphite and watercolor, .326 × .250 cm (12 7/8" × 9 7/8"). Gift of Mrs. John W. Simpson. 1942.5.36. Image © 2007 Board of Trustees, National Gallery of Art, Washington, D.C.; 33-9 Henri de Toulouse-Lautrec, "Miss Loie Fuller". 1893. color lithograph. 1947.7.185 Rosenwald Collection. Image © 2007 Board of Trustees, National Gallery of Art, Washington, D.C.; 33-10 Henri Marie Raymond de Toulouse-Lautrec (1864-1901 French), "At the Moulin Rouge". 1892-95. Oil on Canvas. 123 × 141 cm. Helen Birch Bartlett Memorial Collection, 1928.610. Photograph © 2006, The Art Institute of Chicago. All Rights Reserved; 33-11 Georges Seurat (French 1859-1891). "A Sunday on La Grande Jatte - 1884". 1884-86. Oil on Canvas. 81 3/4" × 121 1/4" (207.5 × 306.1 cm). Helen Birch Bartlett Memorial Collection, 1926.224. Photograph © 2006, The Art Institute of Chicago. All Rights Reserved; 33-12 Georges Seurat (French 1859-1891), "Models". 1886-1888. Oil on Canvas. 78 3/4" × 98 3/8". The Barnes Foundation, Merion, Pennsylvania; 33-13 Vincent van Gogh (1853-1890), "Night Cafe (Le Cafe de nuit)". 1888. Oil on canvas, 28 1/2 × 36 1/4 in. 1961.18.34. Yale University Art Gallery, New Haven, Connecticut/Art Resource, NY; 33-14 Vincent van Gogh(1853-1890), "The Starry Night". 1889. Oil on Canvas. 29 × 36 1/4". Acquired through the Lillie P. Bliss Bequest. (472.1941). Digital Image © The Museum of Modern Art/Licensed by Scala-Art Resource, NY; 33-15 Paul Cezanne (French 1839-1906), "The Bay of Marseilles, Sean from L'Estaque". c. 1885. Oil on canvas, 80.2 × 100.6 cm. Mr. and Mrs. Martin A. Ryerson Collection. 1933.1116. Reproduction, The Art Institute of Chicago. All Rights Reserved; 33-16 Paul Cezanne, "Mont Sainte-Victoire". 1902-4. Oil on Canvas, 28 3/4" × 36 3/16" (73 × 91.9 cm). Photo Graydon wood. Philadelphia Museum of Art: The George W. Elkins Collection, 1936. E1936-1-1; 33-17 Paul Gauguin, Mahana no atua (Day of the God)". 1894. Oil on canvas. 27 3/8" × 35 5/8" (69.5 × 90.5 cm). The Art Institute of Chicago. Helen Birch Bartlett Collection (1926.198) Photograph © 2007, The Art Institute of Chicago. All Rights Reserved; 33-18 Claude Monet(1840-1926), "Waterlilies - Sunset". Oil on canvas. Musee de l'Orangerie, Paris, France. Erich Lessing/Art Resource, NY; 33-19 Claude Monet (1840-1926), "Room 1 of the Waterlilies (Nympheas)". Photo: Gérard Blot/Hervé Lewandowski. Musee de l'Orangerie, Paris, France. Reunion des Musees Nationaux/Art Resource, NY; 33-20 Edvard Munch, "Skrik (The Scream). 1893. Tempera and wax crayon on cardboard. 91.00 × 73.50 cm. Nasjonalgalleriet, Oslo. Photo: J. Lathion © Nasjonalgalleriet 02. © 2010 Artists Rights Society (ARS), New York/ADAGP, Paris; 33-21 Erich Lessing / Art Resource, NY; 33-22 Giorgio de Chirico, "The Child's Brain". 1914. Oil on Canvas. 31 1/8" × 25 5/8". Moderna Museet, Stockholm; page 1098, Paul Cezanne (1836-1906), "The Peppermint Bottle", 1893/1895, oil on canvas, .659 × .821 (26 × 32-3/8); framed: 1.057 × .908 (41-5/8 × 35-3/4). Image © 2007 Board of Trustees, National Gallery of Art, Washington. Chester Dale Collection; page 1099, The Samuel Courtauld Trust, Courtauld Institute of Art Gallery, London; page 1105, Atemisia Gentileschi, "Judith and Maidservant with the Head of Holofernes". 1625. The Detroit Institute of Arts. Gift of Leslie G. Green. 52.253. Photo ©1984 Detroit Institute of Arts/The Bridgeman Art Library, NY.

Chapter 34

PO Diego Rivera (1866-1957). "Man Controller of the Universe or Man in the Time Machine (El hombre controlador del universo o El hombre en la maquina del tiempo). 1934. Fresco. 485 × 1145 cm. Palacio de Bellas Artes, Mexico City, D.F. Mexico. © 2009 Banco de Mexico Diego Rivera & Frida Kahlo Museums Trust/ARS Artists Rights Society, NY. Av. Cinco de Mayo No. 2, Col. Centro, Del. Cuauhtemoc 06059, Mexico, D.F. Reproduction authorized by the Instituto Nacional de Bellas Artes y Literatura. Photo Credit: Schalkwijk / Art Resource, NY; 34-1 Robert Delaunay, L'Equipe de Cardiff (The Cardiff Team), 1913. Collection Van Abbemuseum © L & M Service B.V. The Hague 20100903; 34-2 Pablo Picasso (1881-1973), "Gertrude Stein". 1906. Oil on canvas, H.

39-3/8, W. 32 in. (100 × 81.3 cm). Bequest of Gertrude Stein, 1946 (47.106). The Metropolitan Museum of Art, New York, NY, U.S.A. Image copyright © The Metropolitan Museum of Art / Art Resource, NY. © ARS Art Rights Society, NY; **34-3** Pablo Picasso, "Les Demoiselles d'Avignon". 1907. Oil on Canvas. 8' × 7'8" (2.44 × 2.34 m). Acquired through the Lillie P. Bliss Bequest. Digital Image © The Museum of Modern Art/Licensed by Scala-Art Resource, NY. © 2008 ARS Artists Rights Society, NY; **34-4** Maurice Radiguez, "Le Bouillon de Tête," L'Assiette au beurre, 11 March 1905. Courtesy of Special Collections, Morris Library, University of Delaware; **34-5** Henri Matisse, "Joy of Life". 1905-1906. Oil on Canvas. 69 1/8 × 94 7/8 in. Photo: © 1995 The Barnes Foundation. 2008 Succession H. Matisse/Artists Rights Society (ARS), New York; **34-6** Henri Matisse, "Dance". Oil on Canvas. 260 × 391 cm. Inv. No. 9673. The State Hermitage Museum, St. Petersburg, Russia. © 2008 Succession H. Matisse/Artists Rights Society (ARS), New York; **34-7** Georges Braque (1882-1963), "Houses at L'Estaque", 1908, oil on canvas. Rupf Foundation, Bern, Switzerland / Bridgeman Art Library. Giraudon / Bridgeman Art Library. © 2004 Artists Rights Society (ARS), New York / ADAGP, Paris; **34-8** Pablo Picasso (1881-1973), "Horta de Ebro - Houses on a Hill". 1909. Oil on canvas. 65.09 × 81.28 cm. Jens Ziehe/Nationalgalerie, Museum Berggruen, Staatliche Museen zu Berlin, Berlin, Germany. Bildarchiv Preussischer Kulturbesitz/Art Resource, NY. © ARS Artists Rights Society, NY; **34-9** George Braque (1882-1963, French), "Violin and Palette". 1909. Oil on Canvas. 36 1/2" × 16 1/4". Solomon Guggenheim Museum. 54.1412. George Braque © 2008 Artists Rights Rights (ARS), NY/ADAGP, Paris; **34-10** Carlo Carra(1881-1966), "Interventionist Manifesto, or Paintings-Words in Liberty". 1914. Collage on cardboard, 38.5 × 30 cm. Coll. Mattioli, Milan, Italy. Scala/Art Resource, NY. © 2008 ARS Artists Rights Society, NY; **34-11** The Museum of Modern Art/Boccioni, Umberto (1882-1916), "Unique Forms of Continuity in Space". 1913. Bronze. 43 7/8 × 34 7/8 × 15 3/4". Acquired through the Lillie P. Bliss Bequest. (231.1948). Digital Image © The Museum of Modern Art/Licensed by SCALA/Art Resource, NY; **34-12** Ernst Ludwig Kirchner (1880-1938), "Self-portrait with Model". 1910, reworked 1926. Oil on canvas, 150.4 × 100 cm. Inv. 2940. Photo: Elke Walford. Hamburger Kunsthalle, Hamburg, Germany. Bildarchiv Preussischer Kulturbeisitz/Art Resource, NY; **34-13** Franz Marc, "The Large Blue Horses". 1911. Oil on Canvas. 3'5 3/8" × 5'11 1/4" (1.05 × 1.81 m). Walker Art Center, Minneapolis, Gift of T. B. Walker Collection, Gilbert M. Walter Fund, 1942; **34-14** Maurice Radiguez, "Le Bouillon de Tête," L'Assiette au beurre, 11 March 1905. Courtesy of Special Collections, Morris Library, University of Delaware; **34-15** Erich Lessing / Art Resource, NY; **34-16** "It's Raining" by Guillaume Apollinaire. Anvil Press Poetry; **34-17** Eadweard Muybridge (English 1830-1904)," "Annie G. Cantering, Saddled," 1887. Collotype print, Size: sheet: 19 in. × 24 in., image: 7 1/2 in. × 16 1/4 in. Philadelphia Museum of Art: City of Philadelphia, Trade & Convention Center, Dept. of Commerce (Commercial Museum); **34-18** Mary Evans Picture Library/Everett Collection; **34-19** D.W. Griffith, battle scene from "The Birth of a Nation", 1915. The Museum of Modern Art / Film Stills Archive. Courtesy of the Library of Congress; **34-20** Pablo Picasso, "Glass and Bottle of Suz (Le Bouteille de Suze)" 1912. Pasted papers, gouache, and charcoal on paper. 25 2/5 × 19 2/3" (64.5 50 cm). Mildred Lane Kemper Art Museum, Washington University in St. Louis. University purchase, Kende Sale Fund, 1946. © Succession Picasso/DACS 1998. © 2008 Estate of Pablo Picasso / Artists Rights Society (ARS), New York; page 1122 (left top), Edouard Manet(1832-1883), "Olympia". 1863. Oil on canvas, 130.5 × 190.0 cm. Inv. RF 2772. Hervé Lewandowski/Musee d'Orsay, Paris, France. RMN Reunion des Musees Nationaux/Art Resource, NY. © 2008 Edouard Manet/Artists Rights Society (ARS), New York; page 1122 (left middle) Ingres, Jean Auguste Dominique (1780-1867). The Great Odalisque. Oil on canvas, 91 × 162 cm. Inv.: RF 1158. Musee du Louvre/RMN Reunion des Musees Nationaux, France. Herve Lewandowski/Art Resource, NY; page 1122 (left bottom), The Samuel Courtauld Trust, Courtauld Institute of Art Gallery, London; page 1122 (right), Paul Gauiguin, Mahana no atua (Day of the God). 1894. Oil on canvas. 27 3/8" × 35 5/8" (69.5 × 90.5 cm). The Art Institute of Chicago. Helen Birch Bartlett Memorial Collection (1926.198) Photograph © 2007, The Art Institute of Chicago. All Rights Reserved; page 1126, Pablo Picasso (1881-1973), "Violin". 1912. Charcoal and papier colles on paper. Musee National d'Art Moderne, Centre Georges Pompidou, Paris, France. Musee National d'Art Moderne. Centre National d'Art et de Culture. Georges Pompidou. CNAC/MNAM/Reunion des Musees Nationaux/Art Resource, NY. © 2008 Estate of Pablo Picasso / Artists Rights Society (ARS), New York; page 1127 (left), Henry M. Sayre; page 1127 (right), Pablo Picasso, "Guitar, Sheet Music, and Wine Glass". 1912. Charcoal, gouache, and papier colle, 18 7/8" × 14 3/8". The McNay Art Museum, San Antonio, Texas. Bequest of Marion Koogler McNay. © 2008 Estate of Pablo Picasso/Artists Rights Society (ARS), New York; page 1128, Réunion des Musées Nationaux / Art Resource, NY.

Chapter 35

35-1 Ernst Ludwig Kirchner, "Self Portrait as Soldier". 1915. Oil on Canvas, 27 1/4" × 24". The Allen Memorial Art Museum, Oberlin College, Oberlin, OH. Charles F. Olney Fund, 1950. 1950.29; **35-2** John Singer Sargent (1856-1925), "Gassed, an Oil Study". 1918-19 Oil on Canvas. Private Collection. Imperial War Museum, Negative Number Q1460; **35-3** Haags Gemeentemuseum, The Hague, Netherlands/ The Bridgeman Art Library; **35-4** Marcel Duchamp, "Nude Decending a Staircase No. 2". 1912. 58" × 35". Oil on Canvas. Philadelphia Museum of Art: The Louise and Walter Arensberg Collection. Photo: Graydon Wood, 1994. © 2008 ARS Artists Rights Society, NY; **35-5** Marcel Duchamp(1887-1968), "Fountain 1917". Replica 1964. Porcelain, unconfirmed: 360 × 480 × 610 mm. Purchased with assistance from the Friends of the Tate Gallery 1999. Tate Gallery, London, Great Britain. © 2008 ARS Artists Rights Society, NY; **35-6** Marcel Duchamp (American, b. France 1887-1968), "Replica of L.H.O.O.Q." from "Boite-en Valise". The Louise and Walter Arensberg Collection. Lynn Rosenthal, 1998/Philadelphia Museum of Art. ©2006 ARS Artists Rights Society, NY; **35-7** Raoul Hausmann (1886-1971) , "The Art Critic", 1919-20. Lithograph and photographic collage on paper, 31.8 × 25.4 cm. Tate Gallery, London, Great Britain/Art Resource. ©2010 Artists Rights Society (ARS), New York; **35-8** Painterly Realism. Boy with Knapsack-Color Masses in the Fourth Dimension. 1915. Oil on canvas, 28 × 17 1/2 in. Acquisition confirmed in 1999 by agreement with the Estate of Kazimir Malevich and made possible with funds from the Mrs. John Hay Whitney Bequest (by exchange). Photo Credit : Digital Image © The Museum of Modern Art/Licensed by SCALA / Art Resource, NY; **35-9** © Achim Bednorz, Koln; **35-10** El Lissitzky, "Beat the Whites with the Red Wedge", 1919. Lithograph. Collection Stedelijk Van Abbemuseum, Eindhoven, Holland. © 2007 Artists Rights Society (ARS), New York/VG Bild-Kunst, Bonn; **35-11** Letter from Katherine S. Dreyer to Max Ernst, May 25, 1920. Yale Collection of American Literature, Beinecke Rare Book and Manuscript Library. Translation from German by John W. Gabriel. From "Max Ernst, Life and Work" by Werner Spies, published by Thames & Hudson, Page 67. © 2008 Artists Rights Society (ARS), NY; **35-12** Joan Miro (1893-1983) "The Birth of the World". Montroig, late summer-fall 1925. Oil on canvas, 8' 2 3/4" × 6' 6 3/4". Acquired through an anonymous fund, the Mr. and Mrs. Joseph Slifka and Armand G. Erpf Funds, and by gift of the artist. (262.1972). Digital Image © The Museum of Modern Art/Licensed by SCALA / Art Resource, NY. © ARS Artists Rights Society, NY; **35-13** Pablo Picasso (1881-1973) "Girl Before a Mirror". Boisgeloup, March 1932. Oil on canvas, 64 × 51 1/4". Gift of Mrs. Simon Guggenheim. (2.1938). Digital Image © The Museum of Modern Art/Licensed by SCALA / Art Resource, NY. ©ARS Artists Rights Society, NY; **35-14** Salvador Dali (1904-89). "The Lugubrious Game". 1929 Oil & collage on cardboard. Private Collection, Paris, France, / DACS. The Bridgeman Art Library. © 2008 ARS Artists Rights Society, NY; **35-15** Salvador Dali "The Persistence of Memory" 1931, oil on canvas, 9 1/2 × 13 in. (24.1 × 33 cm). The Museum of Modern Art/Licensed by Scala-Art Resource, NY. © Salvador Demart Pro Arte (R), Geneva/Artists Rights Society (ARS), New York; **35-16** Alberto Giacometti (1901-1966), "Suspended Ball", 1930-31. Wood, iron and cord, 60.4 × 36.5 × 34.0 cm. Inv. AM 1996-205. Photo: Georges Meguerditchian. Musee National d'Art Moderne. Centre National d'Art et de Culture. Georges Pompidou. CNAC/MNAM/Dist. Reunion des Musees Nationaux/Art Resource, NY. © 2008 ARS Artists Rights Society, NY; **35-17** Merel Oppenheim, "Object". 1936. Fur-Covered Teacup, Saucer and Spoon. D: Cup 4 3/4" (12.1 cm); D: Saucer 9 3/8" (23.8 cm); L: Spoon 8" (20.3 cm). Purchase. The Museum of Modern Art/Licensed by Scala-Art Resource, NY. © 2008 ARS Artists Rights Society, NY; **35-18** © Bettmann/CORBIS; **35-19** Jacob Lawrence (1917-2000), "The Trains were Packed Continually with Migrants". 1940-41. Panel 60 from The Migration Series. Tempera on gesso on composition board, 12 × 18". Gift of Ms. David M. Levy. (28.1942.30). Digital Image © The Museum of Modern Art/Licensed by SCALA / Art Resource, NY. © ARS Artists Rights Society, NY; page 1144, Scala / Art Resource, NY; page 1156 (top), Goskino/The Kobal Collection; page 1156 (bottom left), © Everett Collection; page 1156 (bottom right), Goskino/The Kobal Collection; page 1157, ©Everett Collection; Goskino/The Kobal Collection; Henry M. Sayre; © Everett Collection; Goskino/The Kobal Collection; Henry M. Sayre; Goskino/The Kobal Collection.

Chapter 36

36-1 Aaron Douglas, American, 1899-1979, "Aspiration," 1936. Oil on canvas. 60 × 60" (152.4 × 152.4 cm). Fine Arts Museums of San Francisco. Museum purchase, the estate of Thurlow E. Tibbs Jr., The Museum Auxiliary, American Art Trust Fund, Unrestricted Art Trust Fund, partial gift of Dr. Ernest A Bates, Sharon Bell, Jo-Ann Beverely, Barbara Carleton, Dr. & Mrs. Arthur H. Coleman, Dr. & Mrs. Coyness Ennix, Jr, Nicole Y. Ennix, Mr & Mrs. Gary Francois, Dennis L. Franklin, Mr. & Mrs. Maxwell C. Gillette, Zuretti L. Goosby, Mr. & Mrs. Richard Goodyear, Marion E Greene, Mrs. Vivian S W Hambrick, Laurie Gibbs Harris, Arlene Hollis, Louis A & Letha Jeanpierre, Daniel & Jackie Johnson, Jr, Stephen L Johnson, Mr. & Mrs. Arthur Lathan, Mr. & Mrs. Gary Love, Lewis & Ribbs Mortuary Garden Chapel, Glenn R Nance, Mr. & Mrs. Harry S. Parker III, Mr. & Mrs. Carr T. Preston, etc.; **36-2** Courtesy of the Library of Congress; **36-4** Courtesy of the Library of Congress/Carl Van Vechten (1880-1964), LC=USZ62-84619 DLC; **36-5** © Culver Pictures, Inc. / SuperStock; **36-6** Used with Permission of Documenting the American South, The University of North Carolina at Chapel Hill Libraries. Penguin Publishing, Inc.; **36-7** Lawrence, Jacob (1917-2000), "In the North the African American had more educational opportunities". Panel 58 from The Migration Series. (1940-41; text and titled revised by the artist, 1993) Tempera on gesso on composition board, 12 × 18" (30.5 × 45.7 cm). Gift of Mrs. David M. Levy. The Museum of Modern Art/Licensed by Scala-Art Resource, NY. © 2007 ARS Artists Rights Society, NY; **36-8** Nathan Benn/Woodfin Camp & Associates, Inc.; **36-9** Time & Life Pictures/Getty Images; **36-10** Alfred Stieglitz, "The Steerage", 1907. Courtesy George Eastman House. © 2008 ARS Artists Rights Society, NY; **36-11** Paul Strand (1890-1976) © Aperture Foundation. "Camera Work". June 1917: Abstraction, Porch Shadows. 24 × 16.5 cm. Inv. Pho1981-35-10. Musee d'Orsay, Paris, France. Reunion des Musees Nationaux/Art Resource, NY; **36-12** Alfred Stieglitz (1864-1946) "Looking Northwest from the Shelton, New York". 1932. Gelatin silver print, 24.2 × 19.2 cm (9 1/2 × 7 9/16 in.). Ford Motor Company Collection, Gift of Ford Motor Company and John C. Waddell, 1987 (1987.1100.11). The Metropolitan Museum of Art / Art Resource, NY, U.S.A. Image copyright © The Metropolitan Museum of Art / Art Resource, NY. © 2008 ARS Artists Rights Society, NY; **36-13** Courtesy of the Library of Congress; **36-15** Frank Lloyd Wright, Frederick C. Robie House. Hedrich-Blessing Architectural Collec, Chicago History Museum; **36-16** Scott Frances/Esto/Arcaid; **36-17** Joseph Stella(1879-1946), "The Voice of the City of New York Interpreted: The Bridge". 1920-1922. Oil & tempera on canvas, 88 1/2" × 54". Collection of The Newark Museum, 37.288e. Art Resource, NY; **36-18** Charles Demuth (American 1883-1935), "Incense of a New Church". 1921. Oil on Canvas, 26 1/4" × 20". Columbus Museum of Art, Ohio: Gift f Ferdinand Howald 1931.135; Courtesy Demuth Museum, Lancaster PA; **36-19** Charles Sheeler, "Classic Landscape". 1931. Oil on Canvas, .635 × .819 (25" × 32 1/4"). Collection of Barney A. Ebsworth. Image ©2009 Board of Trustees, National Gallery of Art, Washington, D.C.; **36-20** Marsden Hartley (1877-1943), "New Mexico Landscape". 1919. Oil on canvas, 30 × 36 inches (76.2 × 91.4 cm). The Alfred Stieglitz Collection, 1949. Philadelphia Museum of Art, Philadelphia, Pennsylvania, U.S.A. Art Resource, NY; **36-21** Georgia O'Keeffe (1887-1986), "Red Hills and Bones". 1941. Oil on canvas, 29 3/4 × 40 inches (75.6 × 101.6 cm). The Alfred Stieglitz Collection, 1949. Philadelphia Museum of Art, Philadelphia, Pennsylvania, U.S.A. © 2008 ARS Artists Rights Society, NY; **36-22** Bison Archives; **36-23** Bison Archives; **36-24** United Artists/The Kobal Collection; **36-25** United Artists/The Kobal Collection; **36-26** Fox Film Corp./Photofest; **36-27** UFA/The Kobal Collection; **36-28** Bunuel-Dali/The Kobal Collection; **36-29** © Bettmann/CORBIS All Rights Reserved; page 1193, Charles Demuth (American, 1883-1935), "The Figure 5 in Gold". 1928. Oil on cardboard, 35 1/2" × 30" (90.2 × 76.2 cm). The Metropolitan Museum of Art, New York, NY, 1949 (49.59.1). Image © The Metropolitan Museum of Art / Art Resource, NY; page 1196 (left), Paul Cezanne, "Mont Sainte-Victoire". 1902-4. Oil on Canvas, 28 3/4" × 36 3/16" (73 × 91.9 cm). Photo Graydon wood. Philadelphia Museum of Art: The George W. Elkins Collection, 1936. E1936-1-1; page 1196 (right), Canali Photobank, Milan, Italy.

Chapter 37

37-1 ©AP Images; **37-2** George Grosz (1893-1959), "Stuetzen der Gesellschaft (Pillars of Society)". 1926. Oil on canvas, 200.0 × 108.0 cm. Inv.: NG 4/58. Photo: Joerg P. Anders. Nationalgalerie, Staatliche Museen zu Berlin, Berlin, Germany. Art © Estate George Grosz/Licensed by VAGA, New York, New York; **37-3** Kaethe Kollwitz (1867-1945) "Never Again War! [Nie Wieder Krieg!]. "Poster for the Central German Youth Convention in Leipzig, August 2-4, 1924. Photo: DietmarKatz/Bildarchiv Preussischer Kulturbesitz / Art Resource, NY. © Artists Rights Society, NY; **37-4** John Heartfield (German 1891-1968), "Der Sinn Des Hitlergrusses: Kleiner Mann bittet um grosse Gaben. Motto: Millonen Stephen Hinter Mir! (The Meaning of the Hitler Salute: Little man asks for big gifts. Motto: Millions Stand Behind Me!)". 1932. Photomechanical reproduction (Montage on cover of Arbeiter Illustrierte Zeitung, vol. 11, no. 42 16 October 1932). The Metropolitan Museum of Art, New York, NY (1987.1125.8). Image © The Metropolitan Museum of Art / Art Resource, NY; **37-5** Piet Mondrian (1872-1944), "Composition with Blue, Yellow, Red and Black", 1922. Oil on canvas, 16 1/2" × 19 1/4" (41.9 × 48.9 cm). Minneapolis Institute of Arts. © 2008 Mondrian/Holtzman Trust c/o HCR International, Warrenton, VA, USA; **37-6** Florian Monheim/Artur Architekturbilder Agentur GmbH, Cologne, Germany; **37-7** Gerrit Rietveld. Interior, Schroder House, with "Red-Blue" Chair. Photo: Jannes Linders Photography. © 2008 ARS Artists Rights Society, NY; **37-8** Courtesy of the French Embassy; **37-9** Le Corbusier. Exterior. Villa Savoye, Poissy, France. Anthony Scibilia/Art Resource, NY. © 2008 Artists Rights Society (ARS), New York/ADAGP, Paris/FLC; **37-10** Vanni / Art Resource, NY; **37-12** Gustav Klucis (1895-1940), "The Development of Transportation, The Five-Year Plan". 1929. Gravure, 28 7/8 × 19 7/8" (73.3 × 50.5 cm). Purchase Fund, Jan Tschichold Collection. (146.1968). Digital Image © The Museum of Modern Art/Licensed by SCALA / Art Resource, NY; **37-13** Picture Desk, Inc./Kobal Collection; **37-14** Jose Diego Maria Rivera, "Sugar Cane". 1931. Fresco. 57 1/8 × 94 1/8 in. (145.1 × 239.1 cm). Philadelphia Museum of Art/Art Resource, NY. Gift of Mr. and Mrs. Herbert Cameron Morris. 1943-46-2. © Banco de Mexico Diego Rivera & Frida Kahlo Museums Trust/Artists Rights Society (ARS), NY. Av. Cinco de Mayo No. 2, Col. Centro, Del. Cuauhtemoc 06059, Mexico, D.F. Reproduction authorized by the Instituto Nacional de Bellas Artes y Literatura; **37-15** Diego Rivera (1866-1957). "Man Controller of the Universe or Man in the Time Machine (El hombre controlador del universo o El hombre en la maquina del tiempo). 1934. Fresco. 485 × 1145 cm. Palacio de Bellas Artes, Mexico City, D.F. Mexico. © 2009 Banco de Mexico Diego Rivera & Frida Kahlo Museums Trust/ARS Artists Rights Society, NY. Av. Cinco de Mayo No. 2, Col. Centro, Del. Cuauhtemoc 06059, Mexico, D.F. Reproduction authorized by the Instituto Nacional de Bellas Artes y Literatura. Photo Credit: Schalkwijk / Art Resource,

Peter Fischli & David Weiss, "Still from Der Lauf der Dinge (The Way Things Go)". 1987. © Peter Fischli David Weiss, Courtesy of Matthew Marks Gallery, New York; page 1327, Jean-Michel Basquiat, "Charles the First". 1982. Acrylic and Oilstick on Canvas. Triptych. 6'6" × 5'2 1/4" (1.98 × 1.58 m). © The Estate of Jean-Michel Basquiat/© 2009 Artists Rights Society

(ARS), NY; page 1331, Edouard Manet(1832-1883), "Olympia". 1863. Oil on canvas, 130.5 × 190.0 cm. Inv. RF 2772. Hervé Lewandowski/Musee d'Orsay, Paris, France. RMN Reunion des Musees nationaux/Art Resource, NY. © 2008 Edouard Manet/Artists Rights Society (ARS), New York; page 1337, P. Zigrossi/Vatican Museums, Rome, Italy.

TEXT CREDITS

Chapter 21

Reading 21.1, page 680: Teresa of Avila, "Visions" from THE COMPLETE WORKS OF SAINT TERESA OF JESUS, Vol 1. trans. and ed. by E. Allison Peers. New York: Sheed and Ward, 1946. Reprinted by permission of Rowman & Littlefield Publishers, Inc. **Reading 21.2a,** page 684: Ignatius Loyola, from THE SPIRITUAL EXERCISES OF ST. IGNATIUS: A NEW TRANSLATION by Louis J. Puhl (Newman Press 1953, 1951; Loyola Press 1968).

Chapter 23

Reading 23.1a, page 741: Molière, excerpts from TARTUFFE by Moliere. English translation copyright © 1963, 1962, 1961 and renewed 1991, 1990 and 1989 by Richard Wilbur, reprinted by permission of Harcourt, Inc. **Reading 23.4,** page 754: Sor Juana Inés de la Cruz, "To Her Self-Portrait" trans. by Willis Barnstone, first published in SIX MASTERS OF THE SPANISH SONNET: ESSAYS AND TRANSLATIONS by Willis Barnstone. Copyright © 1993 by the Board of Trustees, Southern Illinois University. **Reading 23.1,** pages 761-763: Molière, excerpts from TARTUFFE by Moliere. English translation copyright © 1963, 1962, 1961 and renewed 1991, 1990 and 1989 by Richard Wilbur, reprinted by permission of Harcourt, Inc.

Chapter 24

Reading 24.5a, page 772: John Milton, from PARADISE LOST: A NORTON CRITICAL EDITION 2/e by John Milton, ed. by Scott Elledge. Copyright © 1993, 1975 by W.W. Norton & Company, Inc. Used by permission of W.W. Norton & Company Inc. **Reading 24.5b,** page 772: John Milton, from PARADISE LOST: A NORTON CRITICAL EDITION 2/e by John Milton, ed. by Scott Elledge. Copyright © 1993, 1975 by W.W. Norton & Company, Inc. Used by permission of W.W. Norton & Company Inc. **Reading 24.5,** page 796-797: John Milton, from PARADISE LOST: A NORTON CRITICAL EDITION 2/e by John Milton, ed. by Scott Elledge. Copyright © 1993, 1975 by W.W. Norton & Company, Inc. Used by permission of W.W. Norton & Company Inc.

Chapter 25

Reading 25.3, page 815: Jean-Jacques Rousseau, from THE SOCIAL CONTRACT AND DISCOURSES by Jean-Jacques Rousseau, translation by G.D.H. Cole revised by J.H. Brumfitt and John C. Hall. Originally published by J.M. Dent in 1973. Reprinted by permission of Everyman's Library, an imprint of Alfred A. Knopf (UK). **Reading 25.5,** pages 834-835: Voltaire, From CANDIDE by Voltaire, translation by Tobias Smollett edited by William F. Fleming. Originally published by J.M. Dent in 1937. Reprinted by permission of Everyman's Library, an imprint of Alfred A. Knopf (UK).

Chapter 26

Reading 26.3, page 846: Olympe de Gouges, from "Declaration of the Rights of Woman and the Female Citizen" by Olympe de Gouges, from WOMEN IN REVOLUTIONARY PARIS, 1789-1795: SELECTED DOCUMENTS, translators Darline Gay Levy, Harriet Branson Applewhite, and Mary Durham Johnson. Urbana, Ill.: University of Illinois Press, 1979.

Chapter 27

Reading 27.19a, page 900: Johann Wolfgang von Goethe, from FAUST: AN ABRIDGED VERSION, trans. by MacNeice (1951), lines from p. 19-20, copyright © 1951, 1954 by Frederick Louis MacNeice; 1979 by Hedi MacNeice. By permission of Oxford University Press, Inc. and David Higham Associates Ltd. **Reading 27.19b,** page 900: Johann Wolfgang von Goethe, from FAUST: AN ABRIDGED VERSION, trans. by MacNeice (1951), ines from p. 54, 63-64, copyright © 1951, 1954 by Frederick Louis MacNeice; 1979 by Hedi MacNeice. By permission of Oxford University Press, Inc. and David Higham Associates, Inc. **Reading 27.19c,** page 901: Johann Wolfgang von Goethe, Faust, from FAUST: AN ABRIDGED VERSION, trans. by MacNeice (1951), lines from p. 303, copyright © 1951, 1954 by Frederick Louis MacNeice; 1979 by Hedi MacNeice. By permission of Oxford University Press, Inc. and David Higham Associates, Inc. **Reading 27.21,** pages 907-908: Ludwig van Beethoven, from THAYER'S LIFE OF BEETHOVEN by Elliott Forbes. © 1964 Princeton University Press, copyright renewed 1992. Reprinted by permission of Princeton University Press.

Chapter 28

Reading 28.9, pages 933-934: Harriet Beecher Stowe, Letter from Harriet Beecher Stowe to Mrs. E[liza] L[ee] Follen, Dec. 16, 1852 is reproduced by permission of the Trustees of Dr. Williams's Library, London.

Chapter 30

Reading 30.4, page 996: Charles Baudelaire, "Carrion" from LES FLEURS DU MAL by Charles Baudelaire, trans. from the French by Richard Howard. Reprinted by permission of David R. Godine, Publisher, Inc. Translation copyright © 1982 by Richard Howard. **Reading 30.5,** page 996: Charles Baudelaire, "The Head of Hair" from LES FLEURS DU MAL by Charles Baudelaire, trans. from the French by Richard Howard. Reprinted by permission of David R. Godine, Publisher, Inc. Translation copyright © 1982 by Richard Howard. **Reading 30.10a,** page 1003: Émile Zola, from GERMINAL by Emile Zola, translated by Paul Brians, from READING ABOUT THE WORLD, ed. Paul Brians et al., vol 2, 3rd edition. Harcourt Custom Publishing, 1999. Reprinted by permission of Paul Brians. **Reading 30.10,** pages 1013-1015: Émile Zola, from GERMINAL by Emile Zola, translated by Paul Brians, from READING ABOUT THE WORLD, ed. Paul Brians et al., vol 2, 3rd edition. Harcourt Custom Publishing, 1999. Reprinted by permission of Paul Brians.

Chapter 32

Reading 32.4a, page 1067: Emily Dickinson, Poem #249 is reprinted by permission of the publishers and the Trustees of Amherst College from THE POEMS OF EMILY DICKINSON, Thomas H. Johnson, ed., Cambridge, Mass.: The Belknap Press of Harvard University Press, Copyright © 1951, 1955,

1979, 1983 by the President and Fellows of Harvard College. **Reading 32.4,** pages 1080-1081: Emily Dickinson, Poems # 465, #712, #754 are reprinted by permission of the publishers and the Trustees of Amherst College from THE POEMS OF EMILY DICKINSON, Thomas H. Johnson, ed., Cambridge, Mass.: The Belknap Press of Harvard University Press, Copyright © 1951, 1955, 1979, 1983 by the President and Fellows of Harvard College.

Chapter 33

Reading 33.1, page 1087: Henrik Ibsen, from "A Doll's House" translated by Eva Le Gallienne, copyright © 1957 by Eva Le Gallienne, from SIX PLAYS BY HENRIK IBSEN by Henrik Ibsen, trans. by Eva Le Gallienne. Used by permission of Modern Library, a division of Random House, Inc. and International Creative Management, Inc. **Reading 33.2,** pages 1091-1092: Stephane Mallarme, from "The Afternoon of a Faun" by Stephane Mallarme, trans. by Roger Fry, from POEMS, copyright © 1951 by New Directions. Reprinted by permission of New Directions Publishing Corp. **Reading 33.4,** pages 1111-1112: Friedrich Nietzsche, from THE GAY SCIENCE by Friedrich Nietzsche, trans. by Walter Kaufmann, copyright © 1974 by Random House, Inc. Used by permission of Random House, Inc. From BEYOND GOOD AND EVIL by Friedrich Nietzsche, trans. by Walter Kaufmann, copyright © 1966 by Random House, Inc. Used by permission of Random House, Inc. and the Walter Kaufmann Copyright Trust

Chapter 34

Reading 34.3, page 1134: Guillaume Apollinaire, "Lundi, rue Christine" by Guillaume Apollinaire from APOLLINAIRE: SELECTED POEMS trans. by Oliver Bernard. New edition published by Anvil Press Poetry in 2004. Reprinted by permission of the publisher. **Reading 34.4,** page 1134: Guillaume Apollinaire, "Il Pleut" by Guillaume Apollinaire from APOLLINAIRE: SELECTED POEMS trans. by Oliver Bernard. New edition published by Anvil Press Poetry in 2004. Reprinted by permission of the publisher. **Reading 34.5,** page 1135: Ezra Pound, "In a Station of the Metro" from PERSONAE, copyright 1926 by Ezra Pound. Reprinted by permission of New Directions Publishing Corp. and Faber & Faber Ltd. Electronic rights by permission of New Directions Publishing Corp. **Reading 34.6,** page 1135: Ezra Pound, "A Pact" from PERSONAE, copyright 1926 by Ezra Pound. Reprinted by permission of New Directions Publishing Corp. and Faber & Faber Ltd. Electronic rights by permission of New Directions Publishing Corp. **Reading 34.2,** page 1141: Filippo Marinetti, from MARINETTI: SELECTED WRITINGS by FT. Marinetti, edited by R.W. Flint, translated by R.W. Flint and Arthur A. Coppotelli. Translation copyright © 1972 by Farrar, Straus & Giroux, Inc. Reprinted by permission of Farrar, Straus and Giroux, LLC

Chapter 35

Reading 35.6a, page 1148: T. S. Eliot, from "The Waste Land" from COLLECTED POEMS 1909-1962 by T.S. Eliot. Reprinted by permission of the publisher, Faber & Faber Ltd. Copyright © the Estate of T.S. Eliot. **Reading 35.15,** page 1165: Virginia Woolf, excerpt from MRS. DALLOWAY by Virginia Woolf, copyright 1925 by Harcourt, Inc. and renewed 1953 by Leonard Woolf, reprinted by permission of the publisher and The Society of Authors as the Literary Representative of the Estate of Virginia Woolf. **Page 1167:** Langston Hughes, lines from "One Way Ticket" by Langston Hughes from THE COLLECTED POEMS OF LANGSTON HUGHES, ed. by Arnold Rampersad with David Roessel, Associate Editor, copyright © 1994 by the Estate of Langston Hughes. Used by permission of Alfred A. Knopf, a division of Random House, Inc. and Harold Ober Associates, Inc. Electronic rights administered by Harold Ober Associates, Inc. **Reading 35.6,** page 1169: T.E. Eliot, from "The Waste Land" from COLLECTED POEMS 1909-1962 by T.S. Eliot. Reprinted by permission of the publisher, Faber & Faber Ltd. Copyright © the Estate of T.S. Eliot. **Reading 35.11,** page 1170: Sigmund Freud, from CIVILIZATION AND ITS DISCONTENTS by Sigmund Freud, trans. by James Strachey. Copyright © 1961 by James Strachey, renewed 1989 by Alix Strachey. Used by permission of W.W. Norton & Company, Inc. and The Random House Group Ltd. Published in Great Britain in THE STANDARD EDITION OF THE PSYCHOLOGICAL WORKS OF SIGMUND FREUD, trans. and ed. by James Strachey (Hogarth Press). Electronic rights by permission of Paterson Marsh Ltd. on behalf of Sigmund Freud copyrights. **Reading 35.14,** page 1171: Virginia Woolf, from A ROOM OF ONE'S OWN by Virginia Woolf, copyright © 1929 by Harcourt, Inc. and renewed 1957 by Leonard Woolf, reprinted by permission of Houghton Mifflin Harcourt Publishing Company and The Society of Authors as the Literary Representative of the Estate of Virginia Woolf.

Chapter 36

Reading 36.2, page 1174: Claude McKay, "If We Must Die" courtesy of the Literary Representative for the Works of Claude McKay, Schomburg Center for Research in Black Culture, The New York Public Library, Astor, Lenox and Tilden Foundations. **Reading 36.3,** page 1175: Alain Locke, reprinted with the permission of Scribner, a division of Simon & Schuster, Inc. from THE NEW NEGRO: VOICES OF THE HARLEM RENAISSANCE by Alain Locke. Copyright © 1925 by Albert & Charles Boni, Inc. All rights reserved. **Reading 36.5a,** page 1176: Langston Hughes, lines from "Jazz Band in a Parisian Cabaret" from THE COLLECTED POEMS OF LANGSTON HUGHES, ed. by Arnold Rampersad with David Roessel, Associate Editor, copyright © 1994 by the Estate of Langston Hughes. Used by permission of Alfred A. Knopf, a division of Random House, Inc. and Harold Ober Associates, Inc. Electronic rights administered by Harold Ober Associates, Inc. **Reading 36.6,** pages 1179-1180: James Weldon Johnson from "The Prodigal Son" from GOD'S TROMBONES by James Weldon Johnson, copyright © 1927 The Viking Press, Inc., renewed © 1955 by Grace Nail Johnson. Used by permission of Viking Penguin, a division of Penguin Group (USA) Inc. **Reading 36.7a,** page 1187: F. Scott Fitzgerald, Reprinted with the permission of Scribner, a Division of Simon & Schuster, Inc. and Harold Ober Associates from THE GREAT GATSBY by F. Scott Fitzgerald. Copyright © 1925 by Charles Scribner's Sons. Copyright renewed © 1953 by Frances Scott Fitzgerald Lanahan. All rights reserved. **Reading 36.7b,** page 1187-1188: F. Scott Fitzgerald, Reprinted with the permission of Scribner, a Division of Simon & Schuster, Inc. and Harold Ober Associates from THE GREAT GATSBY by F. Scott Fitzgerald. Copyright © 1925 by Charles Scribner's Sons. Copyright renewed © 1953 by Frances Scott Fitzgerald Lanahan. All rights reserved.